Contemporary
Literary Criticism

Guide to Gale Literary Criticism Series

For criticism on	Consult these Gale series
Authors now living or who died after December 31, 1959	*CONTEMPORARY LITERARY CRITICISM (CLC)*
Authors who died between 1900 and 1959	*TWENTIETH-CENTURY LITERARY CRITICISM (TCLC)*
Authors who died between 1800 and 1899	*NINETEENTH-CENTURY LITERATURE CRITICISM (NCLC)*
Authors who died between 1400 and 1799	*LITERATURE CRITICISM FROM 1400 TO 1800 (LC)* *SHAKESPEAREAN CRITICISM (SC)*
Authors who died before 1400	*CLASSICAL AND MEDIEVAL LITERATURE CRITICISM (CMLC)*
Black writers of the past two hundred years	*BLACK LITERATURE CRITICISM (BLC)*
Authors of books for children and young adults	*CHILDREN'S LITERATURE REVIEW (CLR)*
Dramatists	*DRAMA CRITICISM (DC)*
Hispanic writers of the late nineteenth and twentieth centuries	*HISPANIC LITERATURE CRITICISM (HLC)*
Native North American writers and orators of the eighteenth, nineteenth, and twentieth centuries	*NATIVE NORTH AMERICAN LITERATURE (NNAL)*
Poets	*POETRY CRITICISM (PC)*
Short story writers	*SHORT STORY CRITICISM (SSC)*
Major authors from the Renaissance to the present	*WORLD LITERATURE CRITICISM, 1500 TO THE PRESENT (WLC)*
Major authors and works from the Bible to the present	*WORLD LITERATURE CRITICISM SUPPLEMENT (WLCS)*

ISSN 0091-3421

Volume 107

Contemporary Literary Criticism

Excerpts from Criticism of the Works
of Today's Novelists, Poets, Playwrights,
Short Story Writers, Scriptwriters, and
Other Creative Writers

Deborah A. Schmitt
EDITOR

Jeffrey W. Hunter
Timothy J. White
CLC COORDINATORS

Tim Akers
Pamela S. Dear
Daniel Jones
John D. Jorgenson
Jerry Moore
Polly Vedder
Thomas Wiloch
Kathleen Wilson
ASSOCIATE EDITORS

GALE

DETROIT • NEW YORK • LONDON

STAFF

Deborah A. Schmitt, *Editor*

Jeffrey W. Hunter, Timothy J. White, *Coordinators*

Tim Akers, Pamela S. Dear, Daniel Jones, John D. Jorgenson, Jerry Moore,
Polly Vedder, Thomas Wiloch, and Kathleen Wilson, *Associate Editors*

Tracy Arnold-Chapman, Nancy Dziedzic, Josh Lauer,
Linda Quigley, Paul Serralheiro, and Fred Wheeler, *Contributing Editors*

Susan Trosky, *Permissions Manager*
Kimberly F. Smilay, *Permissions Specialist*
Sarah Chesney, Steve Cusack, and Kelly Quin, *Permissions Associates*

Victoria B. Cariappa, *Research Manager*
Julia C. Daniel, Tamara C. Nott, Michele P. Pica, Tracie A. Richardson,
Norma Sawaya, and Cheryl L. Warnock, *Research Associates*
Laura C. Bissey, Alfred A. Gardner I, and Sean R. Smith, *Research Assistants*

Mary Beth Trimper, *Production Director*
Deborah L. Milliken, *Production Assistant*

Barbara J. Yarrow, *Graphic Services Manager*
Sherrell Hobbs, *Macintosh Artist*
Randy Bassett, *Image Database Supervisor*
Robert Duncan and Mikal Ansari, *Scanner Operators*
Pamela Reed, *Imaging Coordinator*

Library of Congress Catalog Card Number 76-46132
ISBN 0-7876-2030-0
ISSN 0091-3421

Printed in the United States of America
10 9 8 7 6 5 4 3 2 1

Contents

Preface vii

Acknowledgments xi

Preface

A Comprehensive Information Source on Contemporary Literature

Named "one of the twenty-five most distinguished reference titles published during the past twenty-five years" by *Reference Quarterly,* the *Contemporary Literary Criticism (CLC)* series provides readers with critical commentary and general information on more than 2,000 authors now living or who died after December 31, 1959. Previous to the publication of the first volume of *CLC* in 1973, there was no ongoing digest monitoring scholarly and popular sources of critical opinion and explication of modern literature. *CLC,* therefore, has fulfilled an essential need, particularly since the complexity and variety of contemporary literature makes the function of criticism especially important to today's reader.

Scope of the Series

CLC presents significant passages from published criticism of works by creative writers. Since many of the authors covered by *CLC* inspire continual critical commentary, writers are often represented in more than one volume. There is, of course, no duplication of reprinted criticism.

Authors are selected for inclusion for a variety of reasons, among them the publication or dramatic production of a critically acclaimed new work, the reception of a major literary award, revival of interest in past writings, or the adaptation of a literary work to film or television.

Attention is also given to several other groups of writers-authors of considerable public interest—about whose work criticism is often difficult to locate. These include mystery and science fiction writers, literary and social critics, foreign writers, and authors who represent particular ethnic groups within the United States.

Format of the Book

Each *CLC* volume contains about 500 individual excerpts taken from hundreds of book review periodicals, general magazines, scholarly journals, monographs, and books. Entries include critical evaluations spanning from the beginning of an author's career to the most current commentary. Interviews, feature articles, and other published writings that offer insight into the author's works are also presented. Students, teachers, librarians, and researchers will find that the generous excerpts and supplementary material in *CLC* provide them with vital information required to write a term paper, analyze a poem, or lead a book discussion group. In addition, complete bibliographical citations note the original source and all of the information necessary for a term paper footnote or bibliography.

Features

A *CLC* author entry consists of the following elements:

- The **Author Heading** cites the author's name in the form under which the author has most commonly published, followed by birth date, and death date when applicable. Uncertainty as to a birth or death date is indicated by a question mark.

- A **Portrait** of the author is included when available.

- A brief **Biographical and Critical Introduction** to the author and his or her work precedes the excerpted criticism. The first line of the introduction provides the author's full name, pseudonyms (if applicable), nationality, and a listing of genres in which the author has written. To provide users with easier access to information, the biographical and critical essay included in each author entry is divided into four categories: "Introduction," "Biographical Information," "Major Works," and "Critical Reception." The introductions to single-work entries—entries that focus on well known and frequently studied books, short stories, and poems—are similarly organized to quickly provide readers with information on the plot and major characters of the work being discussed, its major themes, and its critical reception. Previous volumes of *CLC* in which the author has been featured are also listed in the introduction.

- A list of **Principal Works** notes the most important writings by the author. When foreign-language works have been translated into English, the English-language version of the title follows in brackets.

- The **Excerpted Criticism** represents various kinds of critical writing, ranging in form from the brief review to the scholarly exegesis. Essays are selected by the editors to reflect the spectrum of opinion about a specific work or about an author's literary career in general. The excerpts are presented chronologically, adding a useful perspective to the entry. All titles by the author featured in the entry are printed in boldface type, which enables the reader to easily identify the works being discussed. Publication information (such as publisher names and book prices) and parenthetical numerical references (such as footnotes or page and line references to specific editions of a work) have been deleted at the editor's discretion to provide smoother reading of the text.

- Critical essays are prefaced by **Explanatory Notes** as an additional aid to readers. These notes may provide several types of valuable information, including: the reputation of the critic, the importance of the work of criticism, the commentator's approach to the author's work, the purpose of the criticism, and changes in critical trends regarding the author.

- A complete **Bibliographical Citation** designed to help the user find the original essay or book precedes each excerpt.

- Whenever possible, a recent, previously unpublished **Author Interview** accompanies each entry.

- A concise **Further Reading** section appears at the end of entries on authors for whom a significant amount of criticism exists in addition to the pieces reprinted in *CLC*. Each citation in this section is accompanied by a descriptive annotation describing the content of that article. Materials included in this section are grouped under various headings (e.g., Biography, Bibliography, Criticism, and Interviews) to aid users in their search for additional information. Cross-references to other useful sources published by Gale Research in which the author has appeared are also included: *Authors in the News, Black Writers, Children's Literature Review, Contemporary Authors, Dictionary of Literary Biography, DISCovering Authors, Drama Criticism, Hispanic Literature Criticism, Hispanic Writers, Native North American Literature, Poetry Criticism, Something about the Author, Short Story Criticism, Contemporary Authors Autobiography Series,* and *Something about the Author Autobiography Series.*

Other Features

CLC also includes the following features:

- An **Acknowledgments** section lists the copyright holders who have granted permission to reprint material in this volume of *CLC*. It does not, however, list every book or periodical reprinted or consulted during the preparation of the volume.

- Each new volume of *CLC* includes a **Cumulative Topic Index,** which lists all literary topics treated in *CLC, NCLC, TCLC,* and *LC 1400-1800.*

- A **Cumulative Author Index** lists all the authors who have appeared in the various literary criticism series published by Gale Research, with cross-references to Gale's biographical and autobiographical series. A full listing of the series referenced there appears on the first page of the indexes of this volume. Readers will welcome this cumulated author index as a useful tool for locating an author within the various series. The index, which lists birth and death dates when available, will be particularly valuable for those authors who are identified with a certain period but whose death dates cause them to be placed in another, or for those authors whose careers span two periods. For example, Ernest Hemingway is found in *CLC,* yet F. Scott Fitzgerald, a writer often associated with him, is found in *Twentieth-Century Literary Criticism.*

- A **Cumulative Nationality Index** alphabetically lists all authors featured in *CLC* by nationality, followed by numbers corresponding to the volumes in which the authors appear.

- An alphabetical **Title Index** accompanies each volume of *CLC.* Listings are followed by the author's name and the corresponding page numbers where the titles are discussed. English translations of foreign titles and variations of titles are cross-referenced to the title under which a work was originally published. Titles of novels, novellas, dramas, films, record albums, and poetry, short story, and essay collections are printed in italics, while all individual poems, short stories, essays, and songs are printed in roman type within quotation marks; when published separately (e.g., T. S. Eliot's poem *The Waste Land),* the titles of long poems are printed in italics.

- In response to numerous suggestions from librarians, Gale has also produced a **Special Paperbound Edition** of the *CLC* title index. This annual cumulation, which alphabetically lists all titles reviewed in the series, is available to all customers and is typically published with every fifth volume of *CLC.* Additional copies of the index are available upon request. Librarians and patrons will welcome this separate index: it saves shelf space, is easy to use, and is recyclable upon receipt of the next edition.

Citing *Contemporary Literary Criticism*

When writing papers, students who quote directly from any volume in the Literary Criticism Series may use the following general forms to footnote reprinted criticism. The first example pertains to material drawn from periodicals, the second to material reprinted in books:

[1]Alfred Cismaru, "Making the Best of It," *The New Republic,* 207, No. 24, (December 7, 1992), 30, 32; excerpted and reprinted in *Contemporary Literary Criticism,* Vol. 85, ed. Christopher Giroux (Detroit: Gale Research, 1995), pp. 73-4.

[2]Yvor Winters, *The Post-Symbolist Methods* (Allen Swallow, 1967); excerpted and reprinted in *Contemporary Literary Criticism,* Vol. 85, ed. Christopher Giroux (Detroit: Gale Research, 1995), pp. 223-26.

Suggestions Are Welcome

The editors hope that readers will find *CLC* a useful reference tool and welcome comments about the work. Send comments and suggestions to: Editors, *Contemporary Literary Criticism,* Gale Research, Penobscot Building, Detroit, MI 48226-4094.

Acknowledgments

The editors wish to thank the copyright holders of the excerpted criticism included in this volume and the permissions managers of many book and magazine publishing companies for assisting us in securing reproduction rights. We are also grateful to the staffs of the Detroit Public Library, the Library of Congress, the University of Detroit Mercy Library, Wayne State University Purdy/Kresge Library Complex, and the University of Michigan Libraries for making their resources available to us. Following is a list of the copyright holders who have granted us permission to reproduce material in this volume of CLC. Every effort has been made to trace copyright, but if omissions have been made, please let us know.

COPYRIGHTED EXCERPTS IN *CLC*, VOLUME 107, WERE REPRODUCED FROM THE FOLLOWING PERIODICALS:

The American Book Review, v. 10, Jan/Feb, 1989. Copyright © 1989 by The American Book Review. Reproduced by permission.—*Ariel: A Review of International English Literature*, v. 25, October, 1994 for "Gay Sebastian and Cheerful Charles: Homoeroticism in Waugh's 'Brideshead Revisited'" by David Leon Higdon. Copyright © 1994 The Board of Governors, The University of Calgary. Reproduced by permission of the publisher and the author.—*The Armchair Detective*, v. 27, Summer, 1994. Copyright © 1994 by The Armchair Detective. Reproduced by permission.—*The Atlantic*, v. 230, October, 1972 for "The Floating World" by Melvin Maddocks. Reproduced by permission of the author.— *Book World--The Washington Post*, November 21, 1993; July 21, 1996. © 1993,1996 Washington Post Book World Service/Washington Post Writers Group. Both reproduced by permission.—*Books in Canada*, v. 12, March 26, 1983 for a review of "House of Beauties" by Paul Stuewe; v. XIX, August, 1990 for "Economy of the Moment" by Larry Scanlan; v. XXII, March, 1993 for "Mistress of Tart Remarks" by Elisabeth Harvor; 1995 for "Looking for Betrayal" by Lynne Van Luven. All reproduced by permission of the respective authors.—*boundary 2*, v. 3, 1975. Copyright © boundary 2, 1975. Reproduced by permission.—*The Canadian Fiction Magazine*, 1982 for "Journies to the Interior: The African Stories of Audrey Thomas" by Wayne Grady. Copyright © 1982 by The Canadian Fiction Magazine. Reproduced by permission of the author.—*Canadian Forum*, v. LXIX, February, 1991 for "Tales of Gender" by Kathryn Barnwell; July-August, 1993 for "Imaging the Writer" by Gwendolyn Guth. Both reproduced by permission of the respective authors.—*Canadian Literature*, Autumn, 1968 for "Mini-Novel Excellence" by Donald Stephen; n. 55, Winter, 1973 for "Writer and Subject" by Herbert Rosengarten; n. 100, Spring, 1984 for "Basmati Rice: An Essay about Words" by Audrey Thomas; n. 102, Autumn, 1984 for "Thomas and Her Rag-Bag" by Pauline Butling; Winter, 1993 for "Word Work" by Laurie Ricou. All reproduced by permission of the respective authors.—*Chicago Review*, v. 25, Summer, 1973. Copyright © 1973 by Chicago Review. Reproduced by permission.—*Chicago Tribune*, Section 14, December 20, 1992 for "Betrothals and Beheadings" by Connolly Cole. Copyright © 1992 Chicago Tribune Company. All rights reserved. Reproduced by permission.—*Chicago Tribune--Books*, October 7, 1990 for "Vast Roman Saga: Colleen McCullough Tackles Marius and Sulla" by James Idema. © copyrighted 1990, Chicago Tribune Company. All rights reserved. Reproduced by permission of the author.—*The Christian Science Monitor*, June 7, 1989. Copyright © 1989 The Christian Science Publishing Society. All rights reserved. Reproduced by permission from The Christian Science Monitor.—*The Classical*

McCullough" by Kay Cassill. Both reproduced by permission of the author.

COPYRIGHTED EXCERPTS IN *CLC*, VOLUME 107, WERE REPRODUCED FROM THE FOLLOWING BOOKS:

Andriano, Josephine. From *Our Ladies of Darkness: Feminine Daemonology in Male Gothic Fiction*. The Pennsylvania State University Press, 1993. Copyright © 1993 Joseph Andriano. All rights reserved. Reproduced by permission.—Blayac, Alain. From "Evelyn Waugh and Humour" in *Evelyn Waugh: New Directions*. Edited by Alain Blayac. Macmillan, 1992. St. Martin's Press, 1992. © Alain Blayac 1992. © Macmillan Academic and Professional Ltd. 1992. All rights reserved. Reproduced by permission of Macmillan, London and Basingstoke. In North America by St. Martin's Press., Inc.—Bosky, Bernadette. From "Stephen King and Peter Straub: Fear and Friendship" in *Discovering Stephen King*. Edited by Darrell Schweitzer. Starmont House, Inc., 1985. Copyright © 1985 by Darrell Schweitzer. All rights reserved. Reproduced by permission of the editor.—Bosky, Bernadette Lynn. From "Mirror and Labyrinth: The Fiction of Peter Straub" in *A Dark Night's Dreaming: Contemporary American Horror Fiction*. Edited by Tony Magistrale and Michael A. Morrison. University of South Carolina Press, 1996. © 1996 by the University of South Carolina. Reproduced by permission.—Bridgwood, Christine. From "Family Romances: The Contemporary Popular Family Saga" in *The Progress of Romance: The Politics of Popular Fiction*. Edited by Jean Radford. Routledge & Kegan Paul, 1986. © Routledge & Kegan Paul 1986. Reproduced by permission.—DeMarr, Mary Jean. From *Colleen McCullough: A Critical Companion*. Greenwood Press, 1996. Copyright © 1996 by Mary Jean DeMarr. All rights reserved. Reproduced by permission of Greenwood Publishing Group, Inc., Westport, CT.—Dorscht,Susan Rudy. From "Blown Figures and Blood: Toward a Feminist/ Post-Structuralist Reading of Audrey Thomas' Writing" in *Future Indicative: Literary Theory and Canadian Literature*. Edited by John Moss. University of Ottawa Press, 1987. © University of Ottawa Press, 1987. Reproduced by permission.—Ferraro, Thomas J. From *Ethnic Passages: Literary Immigrants in Twentieth-Century America*. The University of Chicago Press, 1993. Copyright © 1993 by The University of Chicago. All rights reserved. Reproduced by permission of the publisher and the author.—Gardaphé, Fred L. From *Italian Signs, American Streets: The Evolution of Italian American Narrative*. Duke University Press, 1996. © 1996 by Duke University Press, Durham, NC. Reproduced by permission.—Green, Rose Basile. From *The Italian-American Novel: A Document of the Interaction of Two Cultures*. Fairleigh Dickinson University Press, 1974. © 1974 by Associated University Presses, Inc. Reproduced by permission.—Kaplan, Cora. From "The Thorn Birds: Fiction, Fantasy, Femininity" in *Formations of Fantasy*. Victor Burgin, James Donald and Cora Kaplan, eds. Methuen, 1986. © 1986 Victor Burgin, James Donald and Cora Kaplan. All rights reserved. Reproduced by permission of the publisher and the author.—O'Connell, Nicholas and Jean M. Auel. From an interview in *At The Field's End: Interviews with Twenty Pacific Northwest Writers*. Madrona Publishers, 1987. Copyright © 1987 Nicholas O'Connell. All rights reserved. Reproduced by permission of Nicholas O'Connell.—Pérez-Torres, Rafael. From "The Ambiguous Outlaw: John Rechy and Complicitous Homotextuality" in *Fictions of Masculinity: Crossing Cultures, Crossing Sexualities*. Edited by Peter F. Murphy. New York University Press, 1994. Copyright © 1994 by New York University. All rights reserved. Reproduced by permission.—Ringnalda, Don. From *Fighting and Writing the Vietnam War*. University Press of

Mississippi, 1994. Copyright © 1994 by the University Press of Mississippi. All rights reserved. Reproduced by permission.—Sutherland, John. From *Bestsellers: Popular Fiction of the 1970s*. Routledge & Kegan Paul, 1981. © John Sutherland 1981. Reproduced by permission.—Tiger, Virginia. For "The I As Sight and Site: Memory and Space in Audrey Thomas's Fiction" in *Canadian Women Writing Fiction*. Edited by Mickey Pearlman. University Press of Mississippi, 1993. Copyright © 1993 by the University Press of Mississippi. All rights reserved. Reproduced by permission.—Tsuruta, Kinya. From *Explorations*. Edited by Makoto Ueda. University Press of America, 1986. Copyright © 1986 University Press of America, Inc. All rights reserved. Reproduced by permission.—Ulanov, Barry. From "The Ordeal of Evelyn Waugh" in *The Vision Obscured: Perceptions of Some Twentieth-Century Catholic Novelists*. Edited by Melvin J. Friedman. Fordham University Press, 1970. © Copyright Fordham University Press 1970. Reproduced by permission.

PHOTOGRAPHS AND ILLUSTRATIONS APPEARING IN *CLC*, VOLUME 107, WERE RECEIVED FROM THE FOLLOWING SOURCES:

Auel, Jean, photograph by S. Wassen. Archive Photos, Inc. Copyright © S. Wassen/SAGA 1991. All rights reserved. Reproduced by permission.—Fraser, Antonia, photograph. Archive Photos, Inc. Reproduced by permission.—Kawabata, Yasunari, photograph. AP/Wide World Photos, Inc.. Reproduced by permission.—McCullough, Colleen, photograph. AP/Wide World Photos, Inc. Reproduced by permission.—Puzo, Mario, 1971, photograph by Bernard Gotfryd. Archive Photos, Inc. Reproduced by permission.— Rechy, John, 1995, photograph by Christopher Felver. Archive Photos, Inc. Reproduced by permission.—Straub, Peter, photograph by Frank Capri. Archive Photos, Inc. Copyright © Frank Capri/SAGA. All rights reserved. Reproduced by permission.—Thomas, Audrey, photograph by John Reeves. Reproduced by permission.—Waugh, Evelyn (sitting at desk, checked jacket), photograph. The Library of Congress.

Jean M. Auel
1936-

American novelist and poet.

The following entry presents an overview of Auel's career through 1994. For further information on her life and works, see *CLC,* Volume 31.

INTRODUCTION

Jean Auel has enjoyed uncommon commercial success since the very beginning of her literary career. The publication of her first novel, *The Clan of the Cave Bear* (1980), created a stir in the publishing world when Auel was given a $130,000 advance, at the time a record-setting amount for a first novel. *The Valley of Horses* (1982) followed *The Clan of the Cave Bear,* and the third novel, *The Mammoth Hunters* (1985), had an initial publication run of one million books and went to number one on the best-seller lists in the first week of sales. Readers waited five years for *The Plains of Passage,* published in 1990. Auel states that from the beginning she had intended *Clan* to be the first of a six-part series entitled "Earth's Children"; accordingly, readers expect two more "Earth's Children" novels in coming years. Each of the books is set in the last Ice Age, when the Neanderthal and Cro-Magnon sub-species co-existed. Auel demonstrates this co-existence in her novels with Ayla, a Cro-Magnon orphan girl adopted by a tribe of Neanderthals. Although meticulously researched, gaps in scientific knowledge require that Auel fill in much of the details of Paleolithic life with her own speculation. Consequently, although praised by many members of the scientific world, there is debate about the probabilities of her suppositions.

Biographical Information

Jean Auel was born February 18, 1936, in Chicago, Illinois. She was the second of five children born to Neil S. Untinen and Martha (Wirtanen) Untinen. She graduated from Jones Commercial High School in Chicago, and in 1954, at age eighteen, married her childhood sweetheart, Ray B. Auel. They lived for a few years in New Mexico, where their first child was born, then moved to Oregon, where they continue to live. By 1961, the Auels had four more children. She went back to school, hoping to become a physicist, but decided that pursuing that goal by taking one or two classes a semester was impractical; instead, she transferred into a special M.B.A. program at the University of Portland in 1964. While attending school Auel worked at Tektronix, an electronics firm in Beaverton, Oregon. She worked her way to the position of credit manager, and completed her M.B.A.

in 1976. Around that time, according to several interviews with the author, she found herself wondering what she really wanted to do with her life. One evening in 1977, she was struck with an idea for a short story about an orphan girl living with a group of people more primitive than herself. Auel began to write the story, but soon realized that she did not know enough about primitive cultures and began a period of extensive research. She was surprised by the "humanity" of the paleolithic cultures, the many ways in which archaeologists had discovered them to be similar to modern humankind, and decided this was the central theme of the story she wanted to tell. Auel supplemented her literary research with more "hands-on" experience, taking courses in wilderness survival and plant identification, learning how to snare animals and make clothing out of buckskin. When she completed the bulk of her research, Auel began writing, twelve or more hours a day, seven days a week. Six months later she completed a first draft, but she found the manuscript lacked the sense of enthusiasm she felt about the people of whom she was writing. Auel embarked on a second round of research, this time about the techniques of writing. As she worked her manuscript through several more drafts, she came to realize that she had more than one book. She decided to break the story into six novels, each one a self-contained story, but each also a part of the life story of Ayla, her Cro-Magnon heroine. After finishing the first novel, Auel met Jean Naggar, a literary agent, at a Portland writer's workshop. Naggar took on the novel and sold it to Crown Publications for a record advance of $130,000.

Major Works

In Auel's first novel, *The Clan of the Cave Bear,* she begins the story of Ayla, a Cro-Magnon girl orphaned in her early teens. She is taken in by a tribe of Neanderthals, although they regard her with suspicion because of her fair appearance and different type of intelligence. In Auel's tale, the intellectual differences of the two sub-species are of type rather than quantity. The Neanderthals possess racial memory, containing the sum of experience of their race. When confronted with a problem he has not personally encountered before, the Neanderthal man can "remember" the experiences of his ancestors. While not sharing this instinct, the Cro-Magnons are better at cognitive adaptation and problem-solving. As the Ice Age recedes and the physical world begins to change, the evolutionary adaptation of the Neanderthals, a sort of human instinct, has ceased to be advantageous. They do not possess the necessary racial memories to deal with their changing environment. Another twist to the racial memory theme is that the memories are gender-specific: the men have a set of memories different from the ones possessed by the women. Men, for example, have no "memory" of how to cook, while women do not know how to hunt. This results in rigid sexual role definitions within the tribe, a central metaphor for the series. The Cro-Magnon become the surviving species because they have the ability to adapt to, among other things, new and less rigidly defined gender roles. Because of this plot element, many critics and readers have regarded the stories as a feminist manifesto. Auel, in several interviews, mentioned being profoundly affected by reading Betty Freidan's 1963 book, *The Feminine Mystique.* It is the violation of role-related taboos that results in Ayla's expulsion from the Clan at the end of the book. In the second novel of the series, *The Valley of Horses,* Ayla wanders alone for several years. During that time she is able to domesticate a wild horse and a cave lion. As a result of traveling with these animals, she is held in awe by the tribes she encounters. In alternating chapters Auel tells the story of Jondolar, the central male protagonist and Ayla's eventual love interest. Together they set out to find Jondolar's tribe, the Zelandonii. In *The Mammoth Hunters,* Ayla and Jondolar become involved with the Mamutoi, a tribe of mammoth hunters. This is the first Cro-Magnon tribe Ayla has encountered, but again she is not fully accepted. Although they have high regard for her knowledge and skill, they are suspicious of her because she was raised by the Neanderthals, whom they liken to animals. Ayla's defense of the humanity of the Clan further alienates her from the Mamutoi and from Jondolar, who fears that his tribe will not accept her. When another member of the tribe seeks Ayla's affection, she finds herself romantically torn between the two men. Finally Jondolar reasserts his love for her. In *The Plains of Passage* Ayla and Jondolar once again set out to find the Zelandonii. They journey across Europe, from the Crimea to what is now central France. Riding horses and accompanied by a domesticated wolf, the pair are met with suspicion by the peoples they encounter. However, Ayla's skills as a healer win her the admiration and appreciation of many.

Critical Reception

Critics have approached Auel's work from several perspectives. In addition to evaluating the literary merits of her work, the novels are discussed in terms of their archeological accuracy and also in terms of their value as feminist literature. From all of these perspectives, the reviews have been mixed. The style of her dialogue has been criticized by some for an inappropriate use of modern vernacular and colloquialism. Other critics feel this is an appropriate choice for Auel's underlying message that these prehistoric people are not so different from modern humans. Many reviewers classify Ayla's story as a romance. Gene Lyons, in a favorable review of *The Mammoth Hunters,* finds Auel's work "a shrewdly diverting mix of hard-researched fact about our prehistoric ancestors and the sheerest of romantic fantasies— a late-Pleistocene Harold Robbins epic, if you will. Early Robbins, that is, before the master became an industry and his plots grew formulaic." But Diane S. Wood asserts that Ayla's story is a classic adventure. She states: "The woman protagonist in Auel's novels faces the challenge of the wilderness and survives, conforming to the pattern expected of the male hero in adventure tales. Love remains secondary to heroic action. Ayla is not a heroine of romance, but, rather, a true hero." Later in her essay, Wood observes that Jondolar's story is the romance: "One might even say that the man's tale is the romance, since . . . his preoccupation is with finding the ideal woman whereas Ayla struggles to survive and passes tests of bravery typical of the adventure story." Through this role reversal of the "classic" adventure formula of the superhero and the damsel in distress, Wood says, "The novels question narrow definitions of masculinity and femininity to arrive at new answers which have implications for today's society." In a similar comment about the implications of Auel's story, Clyde Wilcox says, "Auel seems to suggest that the Neanderthals died out because they were unable to adapt to the end of the Ice Age, because their brains were wired to remember the past and not to plan for the future. Creb and Ayla see that the Cro-Magnon will triumph because of their greater flexibility and adaptability. Auel may be making a more general point that any society that uses past behavior as an invariable guide to present decisions will fail. Auel's novel implies that any society that rejects the innovations of its most creative citizens because of their gender, race or other characteristics, will ultimately perish." But other critics see the depiction of the cavemen as an unintended implication that there are inherent sexual roles. Lindsay Van Gelder says, "The margins of my books are marked with dozens of similar examples of modern sexual and domestic assumptions which, when transplanted wholesale into the Ice Age, take on the nature of eternal human verities." She goes on to suggest that the defense of the Neanderthal's humanity is in fact condescending: "The equation is rigged so that we automatically identify with the Others [Cro-Magnons] (who, we also know, are the ultimate evolutionary winners). The message that emerges is a kind of post-colonialist chauvinist liberalism: people 'like us' can be secure enough in our historic destiny to tolerate 'less evolved' cultures. But Van Gelder does credit Auel for a strong female character and a wealth of technical detail; the depth of Auel's research is favorably received by several critics. Many reviewers note that Auel has been a guest speaker for organizations such as the National Geographic Society and the Museum of Natural History. Grover Sales observes, "Even readers turned off by the gimmicky form this novel assumes may find fascination in the technique of human survival in the late Pleistocene Epoch: weapon-making, horse-taming, the invention of bow and arrow, the early science of herbal medicine, boat building, and much conjecture on primitive religion, clan structure, spirit worship, totem and taboo." Roy Bongartz says, "The verisimilitude in her writing of the details of everyday life among ancient peoples has won Auel admiration from the scientific community." Even the speculative aspects of the story are favorably received. Margot Hornblower notes, "Auel gets passing grades from archaeologists on how she interprets the facts. 'We can tell you how the paintings were made, but not why,' says American archaeologist Roy Larick. 'Jean does as good a job at speculating as anyone else.'"

PRINCIPAL WORKS

The Clan of the Cave Bear (novel) 1980
The Valley of Horses (novel) 1982
The Mammoth Hunters (novel) 1985
The Plains of Passage (novel) 1990

CRITICISM

Grover Sales (review date 12 September 1982)

SOURCE: "Primordial Passions of the Pleistocene Times: The Flesh Is Willing, But the Diction Is Weak," in *Los Angeles Times Book Review*, September 12, 1982, p. 3.

[*In the following review, Sales finds the plot weak and the dialogue anachronistic in* The Valley of Horses.]

The Valley of Horses, Jean M. Auel's sequel to her blockbuster novel *The Clan of the Cave Bear,* set in ice age Ukraine, 30,000 BC, is a well-researched children's story fleshed out with steamy primordial sex, women's lib, soap opera plots and "Me, Tarzan, you, Jane," dialogue.

One must admire the painstaking anthropological research Auel has poured into her proposed trilogy. Even readers turned off by the gimmicky form this novel assumes may find fascination in the technique of human survival in the late Pleistocene Epoch: weapon-making, horse-taming, the invention of bow and arrow, the early science of herbal medicine, boat building, and much conjecture on primitive religion, clan structure, spirit worship, totem and taboo.

Ayla, the ice age heroine outlawed by her clan for violating the taboo against women hunting, is several cuts above her tribe, something of a primordial genius: medicine-woman, animal tamer, gourmet cook, craftsperson and ravishing beauty. Her story is entwined with the wanderings of Jondolar, 6-foot-6 superstud making the long trek down the Danube to the Black Sea. Early on, the author telegraphs their cataclysmic coupling, and readers who have stuck it out this far are rewarded with epic copulations.

> **One must admire the painstaking anthropological research Auel has poured into her proposed trilogy. Even readers turned off by the gimmicky form this novel assumes may find fascination in the technique of human survival in the late Pleistocene Epoch.**
> **—Grover Sales**

There may be the sound idea of a novel in all this, but Auel's odd notions of primitive speech are a continual nuisance, as in the following exchange between two brothers:

> "There isn't an unmated woman in all the Caves . . . who wouldn't jump at the chance to tie the knot with Jondolar of the Zelandonii, brother of Joharran, leader of the Ninth Cave, not to mention brother of Thonolan, dashing and courageous adventurer."
>
> "You forget son of Marthona, former leader of the Ninth Cave of the Zelandonii, and brother of Folara, beautiful daughter of Marthona, or she will be when she grows up. . . ."

And if this weren't enough, Auel's narrative style seems

weirdly at variance with the era she's describing. When Ayla finds she can start fire with flint, "That was the serendipity." Again, when Ayla's cave becomes fetid with the stink of rotting corpses, "She wanted a breath of air untainted by malodorous emanations." This goes on for 500 pages; the pages are large and the type small.

Gene Lyons (review date 18 November 1985)

SOURCE: "Sweet Savage Love," in *Newsweek,* November 18, 1985, pp. 100-101.

[*Below, Lyons provides a favorable review and plot summaries of Auel's first three novels.*]

Long ago and far away. Once upon a time. For centuries, storytellers enchanted audiences with the promise of exotic imaginary worlds in which gods, goddesses, heroes, heroines, demigods and mythical beasties shared robust adventures. But such is the tyranny of facts in our own degraded time that all but supermarket tabloid customers need excuses better than mere curiosity and wonder for reading about adventure and romance. At 20 bucks a throw, novels must improve as well as divert us. Hence the immense commercial success of Jean M. Auel's "Earth's Children" series, of which *The Mammoth Hunters* is the third of six projected novels.

The Mammoth Hunters continues the saga of Auel's estimable heroine Ayla, the stunning blond Cro-Magnon woman orphaned by an earthquake at an early age and raised by a Neanderthal clan on the Eurasian steppes just north of the Black Sea about 25,000 years ago. The novel has a hardcover printing of a cool million copies. (James Michener's previous record-holder, *Texas,* had a first printing of only 750,000 or so.) Very likely it will sell every copy. Like its predecessors, *The Clan of the Cave Bear* (1980) and *The Valley of Horses* (1982), Auel's latest is a shrewdly diverting mix of hard-researched fact about our prehistoric ancestors and the sheerest of romantic fantasies—a late-Pleistocene Harold Robbins epic, if you will. Early Robbins, that is, before the master became an industry and his plots grew formulaic.

For readers who came in late, *The Clan of the Cave Bear,* which to date has sold 320,000 hardback and 3,575,000 paperback copies, gave us Ayla's early years among a fully imagined tribe of hunter-gatherers kind enough to take the poor, deformed little girl in and teach them their ways. Born to the "Others," she's as ugly as she can be—too tall, with long, unfashionably straight legs, shiny blond hair, startling blue eyes and a chin, of all things. What self-respecting cave dweller would wish even to "relieve his needs," much less

to mate for life, with a female so deformed as to resemble—ugh—Darryl Hannah (who plays Ayla in the movie, due out in January)? Under the tutelage of her beloved stepmother, Iza, and Creb, the crippled but immensely wise "mog-ur" (shaman), Ayla becomes a medicine woman. But she's a protofeminist as well, increasingly resentful of the total submission required of Clan women. ("It's his right," she's told. "He's a man. He can beat you anytime he wants, as hard as he wants.") Eventually she incurs the leader's wrath and is condemned to exile.

The Valley of Horses (with 620,000 hard cover, 2,945,000 paperbacks sold) teaches our putative Ugly Duckling to survive on her own in the immense fecundity of her "cold, ancient Eden." Necessity demands that she violate Clan taboo by hunting with a sling (fortunately, Ayla's got a throwing arm like Ozzie Smith). Among a number of human firsts, Ayla invents horseback riding, raises a Cave Lion cub and pines for love. In alternating chapters, Prince Charming, in the person of one Jondalar of the Zelandonii, wends his lonely way in her direction through many adventures. Jondalar is an Other, too, and a devotee of the "Great Earth Mother." Regal in his bearing, the impossibly handsome young man is wonderfully endowed, in every way, for the "Rites of First Pleasure." "You are *not* big and ugly," he tells her. "You are the most beautiful woman I've ever seen."

But first Ayla must learn to speak in words, rather than the grunts and gestures of the Clan; he, in turn, must conquer his disgust over her having lived with "a pack of flatheads." When at long last they're aroused—Auel's plots have the predictable majesty of the glaciers against which they're set—Ayla's passions prove copious enough for Jondalar. Indeed they've proved a bit too much for a few prudish librarians around the country.

> **Summarizing the plots of Auel's books fails to capture their offbeat but genuine appeal—a charm shared by their likable and energetic author.**
> **—Gene Lyons**

Now, in *The Mammoth Hunters,* Ayla is introduced to society. Will she be accepted by the tribe of mammoth hunters known as the Mamutoi? Complications ensue when an artist named Ranec invites her to his hearth to examine his ivory carvings of the Great Mother. An adopted member of the tribe, Ranec hails from south of the Great Sea. He is what Chuck Berry called a "brown-eyed handsome man." Given her background, the poor girl quite literally can't say no. ("If any man of the Clan gave the signal to any woman, she was expected to render the service . . .") Lying in his own furs listening, Jondalar is consumed with a jealousy all the more painful because it's considered ignoble. He begins to act badly. Which lover will she choose—dusky or fair?

Summarizing the plots of Auel's books fails to capture their offbeat but genuine appeal—a charm shared by their likable and energetic author. As she tells it, her decision to write fiction at all, much less prehistoric romances, was a bit fortuitous. Always an avid reader, the Chicago native married her husband, Ray, at 18 and had five children in the next six years. "Believe me, it was accidental," she laughs. "When the pill came, I was one of the first women on it."

When she was 28, Auel's feminist eyes were opened by Betty Friedan's *The Feminine Mystique,* and she began to take night classes at nearby Portland (Ore.) State. Her intention was to become a physicist. Meanwhile, Auel took a competitive exam and exchanged her secretarial job for a much better-paying one designing circuit boards for electronic equipment. Realizing at length that "you don't get to be a physicist by taking one or two night courses a semester," Auel eventually switched her major to business and earned an M.B.A. in 1976, on the same day her husband got his.

By then, with three daughters in college and two boys in high school, the 40-year-old Auel was making a good salary as a credit manager for a large Oregon company, but she found the work unsatisfying and quit. A self-described "closet poet—isn't everybody?", she began to tinker one winter day in 1977 with a short story about a young girl adopted by cave dwellers. Then she realized she didn't know the first thing about them. She went to the Portland library, emerged with an armload of books and soon found herself utterly immersed in prehistory.

> Auel's real passion, she says, is to rescue our distant ancestors from the condescending stereotype that their lives were, in Hobbes's words, "nasty, brutish and short."
> —*Gene Lyons*

The results are evident on every page of her "Earth's Children" series. Ever had a hankering to hunt woolly mammoth, bison or reindeer with flint-tipped spears? To master such Stone Age technologies as ax making, basket weaving, skinning and curing hides? Learn the burial rites of Neanderthal men? Play hymns to the Great Earth Mother on bone instruments of your own devising? Then "Earth's Children" is the series for you. If something is known to anthropologists, Auel has incorporated it into her story—and in very readable form.

But Auel's real passion, she says, is to rescue our distant ancestors from the condescending stereotype that their lives were, in Hobbes's words, "nasty, brutish and short." All evidence, she insists, indicates a "rich, deep emotional life. If I have gotten any criticism from the scientific community, it's that I didn't make them advanced enough." Certain of Auel's notions—that the structure of Neanderthal man's brain gave him a "racial memory" and an ability to communicate almost telepathically, for example—are admittedly sheer speculation, if not fantasy. But nothing in the series, she insists, violates what *is* known about the prehistoric past.

But a million copies? "I'm still overwhelmed and a bit scared by it," Auel, now 49 and a grandmother, says from the oceanside home she shares with her business-manager husband in Arch Cape, Ore. "I wrote the story I wanted to read. I didn't write it for critics or for a mass audience. To me it's very serious fiction: it's about adventure, love, danger, fear, loneliness, jealousy and belonging. I like stories that pick me up and put me down somewhere else. 'What if'— that's the great thing fiction writers work with."

Jean Auel with Roy Bongartz (interview date 29 November 1985)

SOURCE: "Jean Auel," in *Publisher's Weekly,* Vol. 228, November 29, 1985, pp. 50-51.

[*In the following interview, Bongartz provides biographical information about Auel and describes the development of her "Earth's Children" series.*]

Jean Auel, the nonstop neophyte author of the fast-selling Earth's Children fictional saga—*The Valley of Horses, The Clan of the Cave Bear* and, just out from Crown, *The Mammoth Hunters* (Fiction Forecasts, Nov. 1), with three more novels to follow—began her writing career after reaching 40, having engaged in several others, including housewifery and the raising of five children, in Portland, Ore. Auel, a plump, cheerful woman with blue eyes and blonde hair, had, with her husband Ray, also earned a college degree by attending night classes for 12 years.

In 1977, with the children growing up and the studies completed, she was just about to raise her sights and go into the banking profession when one night at bedtime, an inspiration came to write a story. Suddenly alive, unbidden, in her head, was a tale concerning a young woman in some undetermined prehistoric era who, having attained a higher level of mental and physical development, was shunned by the other members of her society. To this day Auel has no inkling of how the idea arose, but she was determined to write it down. At first she thought she would simply be passing the time until she found the right job. "I didn't know I had just found it," she says now. But it is characteristic of Auel that she did not wait until morning to begin writing.

She did not get very far into the story before running into a snag: "It was great fun, but I didn't know what I was writing about. I didn't know whether these people had the use of fire or not, or what part of the world they were living in." With typical directness, she went to the *Encyclopaedia Britannica* and next morning to the Portland library. "I just started digging through the anthropology and archeology texts," she recalls. "Within a short period I had taken out about 50 books. I had no background for this. All I had to start with was a story—and I thought it was going to be a short story!"

Auel remembers her state of mind at the time. "I was looking for something to do. I had had five kids before I was 25, and then I started going to college when I was 28. By the time I was 40 I had a master's degree in business administration, three daughters in college and two boys in high school. I had been spending practically every minute of my life raising my family, working [as a computer programmer and credit manager] and going to school, and now suddenly I had my degree. My kids were grown up. I had quit my job with the idea of getting to a higher level, so I was in this free-floating state . . . ."

The research for the story took her "into a world I did not know existed. As I read about prehistoric people, the story kept growing in my mind, and before long I knew I had a novel. So I simply tried to tell the whole story to myself on the typewriter. For six months I did nothing else. I was literally obsessed. I worked at it 16 hours a day, seven days a week—you could not have dragged me away. I ended up with a rough draft for a novel in six parts.

On rereading her work, however, Auel discovered "it was just awful!" Hardly deterred, she returned to the library and checked out books on how to write. "Every writer goes through a period when you play it safe," she says. "You don't tell anyone you're writing—in case you fail at it. But there has to come a point when you say to yourself, 'I'm serious, I'm going to give this every bit of effort I have.' That time finally came for me, even though I still thought that writing was a way to fill time until a wonderful job came along. During this period I replied to an ad for a credit analyst in the Portland branch of a large California bank. After an interview, they called to offer me, not the job I'd applied for, but a position as manager of the bank's credit department. I negotiated a higher salary than their original offer and then found myself saying: 'Wait a minute, I must tell you I'm considering an alternative—one with a much higher risk factor.' I said I needed a week to consider it.

"My husband and I went hiking in the Columbia Gorge, and I kept thinking that this was the kind of job I had wanted. I knew Ray wanted me to take it; we had three kids in college. But I was half-way through this first big chunk of material in my story, and the thought of giving up and not finishing it brought tears to my eyes. I had to make a choice." Her husband said he would be supportive whatever her decision. When she called the bank to decline the position, they offered "anything anybody else is paying—just tell us how much you want."

Auel frequently gives herself warnings and advice, and at this point she told herself: "Okay, if you are going to give up *this* for writing, you had better be serious about the writing!" She also vowed that she would persevere until she got published, no matter how long it took. Then, of course, she turned to the Portland library for help and pored through books on how to go about it.

The book she found most helpful was *Techniques of Fiction Writing* by Leon Surmelian. "I bet I've read it three times," she says. "I knew that to make my story believable I would have to get in some depth of description. Anyway, I hate a book that just says, 'They went out and got food and ate it.' How did they get it? Where did they get it? How did they cook it? I want to know."

She also determined, from Surmelian, how to find her writer's viewpoint. "I came out with the 'omniscient author.' I had to be able to think for each of my characters, but I also had to be able to step back into the author's voice to give description and information the characters could not provide. Sometimes I get into a tone that is like nonfiction." She likes this tone, she admits in a pleased, conspiratorial whisper, "because people believe it!"

Auel's original story holds the germ for the whole of the six novels she is embarked on. After completing her research and starting a rewrite, she was only halfway through the first of the six sections of the story when she had written 100,000 words, and the realization the whole thing would take a million and a half words before it was finished brought the project to a brief halt. "That was the point where I realized I didn't have one book—I had six books," she recalls. "Now when people ask me how I know I have six books to write, I tell them it is because all six of them are contained in that rough draft. That is the outline for the entire Earth's Children series."

She devised a separate story for each of the six novels, which are nevertheless all linked. "I am striving hard to write them as individual books," she declares. "I want each book to be complete; I don't believe in leaving loose ends." The woman Ayla is the central figure in all the books and serves to unify the series, and other characters reappear as well. "I want you to care enough about those characters that you want to go on to the next book."

Auel has not only read a good deal about the Neanderthal people, but also has learned at first-hand some of their ways of living. She knows how they might have survived in winter in a snow cave, because she went with a group to Mt. Hood and spent the night in one. She learned how to trap animals, to build a fire—without matches—from sticks found by digging down through 20 feet of snow. She enrolled in classes in wild plant and wild food identification, learned flint knapping at a wilderness area field station, took part in an aboriginal life skills course in which she made her own buckskin clothing.

She has come to have a deep love and respect for the characters in her books and is a champion of their human, caring qualities. "I wanted to make it clear that we are talking about people no different from ourselves," she says. "I tried to show that these young brothers [Jondalar and Thonolan] are thoroughly modern in their emotional responses, their intelligence, their psychological reactions. Anything we allow ourselves, we have to allow them."

From a book on an archeological excavation in Iran titled *Shanidar*, by Ralph R. Soleckl, Auel read of the discovery of the skeleton of an old man in the Shanidar caves. His arm had been amputated; he was lame and blind. "The question is," Auel says, "who took care of him when he was a crippled boy? Who took care of an old man who obviously could not hunt mammoths? I began to get this sense of *why* they took care of him." Auel believes that the weak and wounded were protected in prehistoric society. "Suddenly I was seeing a real humanity in these people, and that became my obsession—what I really wanted to tell."

> **The verisimilitude in her writing of the details of everyday life among ancient peoples has won Auel admiration from the scientific community. She found herself treated as a celebrity at a symposium on prehistoric people at the Museum of Natural History in New York not long ago, and she lectured a group of specialists at the Smithsonian Institution in Washington on the subject, "The Novelist's View of Paleoanthropology."**
> **—Roy Bongartz**

In Auel's first novel, her heroine Ayla takes care of an old man with a crippled arm. "When I read about him in *Shanidar*, I said, 'There's my man! He really existed!'" She is convinced that "these ancient ancestors of ours were very

human. We call them *homo sapiens*—they are not a different species. This idea that we were savages is wrong! We cannot try to prove that we are violent by nature and therefore warlike. We are by nature cooperative, compassionate."

The verisimilitude in her writing of the details of everyday life among ancient peoples has won Auel admiration from the scientific community. She found herself treated as a celebrity at a symposium on prehistoric people at the Museum of Natural History in New York not long ago, and she lectured a group of specialists at the Smithsonian Institution in Washington on the subject, "The Novelist's View of Paleoanthropology." She explains, "I told them that I start from a base of *their* work, but I can extrapolate on a human level." When she read about the discovery of ancient musical instruments made of mammoth bones, she wanted details for use in her new book; to get the information, she made a five-week research trip to Kiev, where the objects are displayed. Finding that the only book on the subject was published in Russian, she commissioned an English translation. From the excavations of a Czech archeologist, Auel has determined the exact floor plans of dwellings of people 25 millennia in the past.

Scientists disagree on how much speech prehistoric people had developed, but Auel sees them as talkative and uses a modern idiom. She explains, "In fiction you can't cite one expert who says these prehistoric people could talk and another authority who say they couldn't; here they all either talk or they don't, and whatever you do you are going to upset some part of the academic community. Because there may have been some limit to their articulation, I decided to limit the names of characters to certain letters, with all the male names starting and ending in a consonant, and all the female names starting and ending in a vowel."

When Auel had rewritten enough of ***The Clan of the Cave Bear*** to show a publisher, she went about finding one in her usual straightforward way by reading every issue of *PW* and such books as *Maybe You Should Write a Book* and *How to Get Happily Published*. After query letters and sample chapters got no response, Auel met literary agent Jean Naggar, who spoke to a Portland writers' group. Naggar suggested she write a letter describing the project. "I wrote her the best sales letter I could manage—it must have taken me two weeks. I had no writing background; I had no background in anthropology or archeology. But I tried, in one page, to get her interested in my book. And it did!"

Not only did Naggar agree to represent Auel, she decided, in a rare move, to put up for auction this first novel by an unknown writer. There were offers from two publishers, both with an advance of $130,000. Auel recalls Naggar told her to sit down before relaying this news on the phone. "We decided to go with Crown," Auel says, "and I am very pleased.

They treat people like individuals, and they know how to get behind a book." That first novel went through eight printings and stayed on bestseller lists for more than a year; Bantam's 3,473,000 paperback printing did almost as well; there is a movie in the works. The second volume's sales were comparable; the third, *The Mammoth Hunters,* greets the world with a hardcover print order of one million plus and hit the national bestseller charts at #1 in its first week on sale.

The Auels now live in a bright new multi-level modern seaside mansion with many windows and decks overlooking the Pacific surf. Ray Auel has quit his job as a computer-plant executive to become his wife's business manager. Jean Auel likes to say, "We raised five kids in a one-bathroom house, and now we've got no kids in a five-bathroom house." It is here within the sound of the sea that Auel has her writing studio in a top-story room. She writes from right after dinner, at about eight, straight through the night to five or six in the morning.

"I like the night for working," she says. "It's the way my daily cycle goes." She tries to put in 10 hours a day, but cannot predict how many pages she may write. "I may have Ayla out hunting ermine, and she had better really know how you hunt this animal. So I may have to read five books to find out everything I can about weasels and ermines before I can go on. I work seven days a week, straight through." Explaining her unflagging enthusiasm, Auel says: "I was over 40 before I learned what I wanted to do when I grew up!"

Andrea Chambers and Dirk Matheson (review date 16 December 1985)

SOURCE: "A Mammoth First Printing Makes Jean Auel's New Epic an Instant Best Seller," in *People,* Vol. 24, No. 25, December 16, 1985, pp. 113-15.

[*In the following review, Chambers and Matheson provide biographical information on Auel and a favorable assessment of* The Mammoth Hunters.]

High on a cliff above the rocky Oregon coast sits a dramatic modern house, built, its owner might say, by Neanderthals. This is the abode that Portland author Jean Auel, 49, constructed with some of the proceeds from her 1980 best-seller, *The Clan of the Cave Bear* and its 1982 sequel, *The Valley of Horses.* Both are doorstop-size sagas about the slings, flings and fortunes of hotblooded cavemen. Appropriately, Auel's living room is adorned with a collection of ancient flint arrowheads, aboriginal spears and a five-by-seven-foot painting of a prehistoric horse copied from a cave drawing. In the midst of this minimuseum is a display case filled with

some 15 translations of Auel's works, including the Finnish, Israeli and Japanese editions.

With the release last month of her third Ice Age opus, *The Mammoth Hunters,* Auel (pronounced "owl") and her husband, Ray, 50, a retired operations manager for an electronics firm, may need a new wing on the house to accommodate all the editions and accompanying artifacts. Advance orders were so huge that the publisher rushed more than one million copies into the stores—a record hardcover first printing that topped the million for James Michener's *Texas.* The book shot to No. 1 on the best-seller lists *before* its official publication date.

Readers are apparently clamoring for the further adventures of Ayla, the leggy blond Cro-Magnon who was rejected by the Neanderthals and now goes hunting for mammoth (an extinct elephant) with a new tribe, the Mamutoi. Her faithful lover, Jondalar, a big blond hunk who seems to lack Ayla's Pleistocene pizzazz and ingenuity, gets some competition from a more intellectual newcomer, Ranec . . . and so the Ice Age world continues to turn.

Just as slower readers are getting to the end of Auel's 645-page opus, moviegoers will get their chance to see Daryl (*Splash*) Hannah bedecked in skins as Ayla. *Clan of the Cave Bear* will be released early next year, and the author is none too pleased. Last spring she filed a lawsuit against the production company, claiming that they owe her $42,155 for the movie rights, and that the filmmakers did not honor her prerogative to approve the final product. Insisting that certain inaccuracies will sully her reputation for thorough research, Auel is asking more than $14 million in damages. (Neither she nor the movie company will elaborate while the suit is pending.)

> **Auel has become a jack of all Ice Age trades. She can make flint arrowheads and trap animals almost as well as Ayla. She has happily spent the night in a snow shelter and once headed off into the Oregon woods for a week with nothing more than a blanket and a knife.**
> **—Andrea Chambers and Dirk Matheson**

A little steep, perhaps, but not to a commercial novelist who has suddenly become a recognized authority on early man—a reputation she relishes. Auel has received an honorary doctorate of letters from the University of Portland and has been invited to speak at the Smithsonian and other prestigious institutions. In September she was a guest lecturer at the Center for Early Man Studies at the University of Maine. "I want people to understand that our ancestors were not a bunch of savage, groping animals," she explains. "I'm trying to show the diversity and complexity of Ice Age man. These men aren't that different from your sons or your college room-mates."

Obsessed with her discovery, Auel has become a jack of all Ice Age trades. She can make flint arrowheads and trap ani-mals almost as well as Ayla. She has happily spent the night in a snow shelter and once headed off into the Oregon woods for a week with nothing more than a blanket and a knife. Three years ago Auel took a six-week tour of Cro-Magnon caves through three European countries and the Soviet Union. The most memorable were in Niaux, France, where she waded hip-deep in dank water through darkness. "About an hour and a half into the cave," she recalls, "we looked up and saw these two beautiful shaggy horses painted on the wall. I thought, 'Someone had to come all this way with a torch just to paint these.' I felt an overwhelming sense of magic.'"

The same response got Auel, daughter of a Chicago housepainter, into this strange new world in the first place. In 1977, when Ayla first came into her life and mind, she had just quit her job as a credit manager for an electronics firm. The five children she had with husband Ray, her child-hood sweetheart, were all grown. Though she had worked her way up from a keypunch operator, Auel had felt little professional satisfaction. Then, one night around 11, she got an idea for a story about a prehistoric girl. "I quickly fig-ured out that I didn't know a thing about my subject, not even when man first used fire," she says. So Auel visited her county library and eventually read hundreds of books on her subject. A chance meeting with a New York agent at an Oregon writers' conference led to the submission of her manuscript to Crown, which anted up a $130,000 advance—then considered a record for a first novel.

The rest is prehistory. Auel has become a weary veteran of the book tour. (In preparation for the current two-month, 18-city blitz she has lost weight and spruced up her wardrobe). Her publishing proceeds have gone not only to her dream house, but also to her collection of primitive art and plane tickets for her kids. Husband Ray even left his job three years ago to become her full-time business manager.

He may have to work overtime in the years to come; Auel plans three more books about Ayla and notes that after that she has "about 259" ideas in her file. "When you start as far back as I did," she says, "there's a whole world to go."

Lindsay Van Gelder (review date March 1986)

SOURCE: "Speculative Fiction," in *Ms.,* Vol. XIV, No. 9, March, 1986, pp. 64, 70.

[*While praising Auel's creation of a strong female protago-nist in the review below, Van Gelder faults the author for creating social interactions which are too similar to "mod-ern" society.*]

I began hearing about them several years ago, always from feminist friends who said things like "You absolutely *have to* read these books." Jean M. Auel's "Earth's Children" nov-els—*The Clan of the Cave Bear, The Valley of Horses,* and *The Mammoth Hunters*—have since gone from feminist word-of-mouth classics to a major mainstream phenomenon. *Hunters* hit the number-one spot on the best-seller list last winter even before its official publication date, and a movie version of *Cave Bear* (starring Daryl Hannah, with a screen-play by John Sayles) has recently been released. In the era of "Rambo," Auel has given us a resourceful, *female* super-hero.

She is Ayla, a prehistoric Cro-Magnon woman who is or-phaned as a small child by an earthquake. Ayla, wandering alone, gets mauled by a cave lion before she is rescued by the Clan—a group of Neanderthals who also inhabited Eu-rope during the Ice Age more than 25,000 years ago. The Cro-Magnons are the precursors of modern Europeans, and Ayla is tall, blue-eyed, and blond. The Neanderthals are short and swarthy, with no chins, ridges over their eyebrows, and flat heads; they accept Ayla—one of the group they call the Others—only with difficulty. In their eyes, she is ugly.

Clan of the Cave Bear portrays Ayla's life in the Clan, which is rigid and harsh for a girl of her spirit. Women are forbid-den to hunt (although Ayla learns in secret and becomes an expert); they are taught to be submissive and required to do anything any man tells them, including putting out sexually, anytime and anywhere. (When Ayla refuses Broud, one of the Clan men, she is raped.) People of the Clan produce no art, have no spoken language (although they do communi-cate in sign language and have ritual storytelling and move-ments not unlike dance), and are physically unable to laugh or weep; they can't even learn anything new, unless their an-cestors have already done it, since their brains are based not on adaptation but on racial memory (Auel's fictional theory of why the Neanderthals died out). When people need to know something about a plant or animal, they don't learn, they "remember" what their ancestors knew—and over time, male and female brains have become so differentiated that men, for example, genuinely can't "remember" how to cook. Religion is also restricted to males (and in one scene, the men ritually eat the brains of a slain Clan hero). While there are some loving (and beautifully drawn) individuals in the Clan, Ayla never entirely learns to fit in. Eventually, as a teenager, she is cast out and cursed—for the sin of talking back to the male leader, the man who raped her, and by whom she consequently has a child from whom her exile separates her.

Valley of the Horses tells the story of how Ayla survives alone for several years (during which time she tames a wild horse and a cave lion, and together they become a kind of family unit), but she ultimately encounters a man of the Others, Jondalar (also tall, blue-eyed, and blond). Through him she meets others of her own kind. *The Mammoth Hunters* is about one such tribe Jondalar and Ayla attach themselves to for a time. The Others worship the Great Earth Mother, regard rape as a sacrilege, and allow women to hunt. (Jondalar even knows how to cook, although he doesn't do it very often; he also knows how to give Ayla sexual pleasure for the first time in her life—although the 20th century feminist reader might observe that her clitoris only figures in "fore-play.") Ayla, meanwhile, seems to excel at virtually everything—hunting, healing, practical science (she invents the flint fire-lighter, the stitching of wounds, the threaded needle, and a special double-stone slingshot, among other things), spirituality, languages, toolmaking, sewing, cooking. She also discovers that the Others find her uncommonly beautiful. Her only problem in her dealings with Jondalar and the Others is their horror when they realize that she was raised by "flatheads"—in their view, subhuman animals. But Ayla refuses to renounce the people who saved her life.

> **Despite all that's positive and riveting and informative about [Auel's] books, I found them problematic. Like Scarlett O'Hara and the women in Ayn Rand's novels, Ayla is, alas, a great female character who comes with some cumbersome baggage.**
> **—Lindsay Van Gelder**

Beyond giving us a strong female character, Auel's books are rich in technical details. We learn about the plants that an Ice Age medicine woman might use to cure different ills, how to build an earthlodge out of mammoth bones and skins, how to knap flint, how to use mashed animal brains and stale human urine to process soft, white leather, and much, much more. Auel is famous as a researcher, and she gleaned some of her survival lore firsthand on field trips into the wilds of her native Pacific North-west, where she slept in an ice cave, hunted, made arrowheads, and learned to start a fire without matches. (The author—who had five children before she was 25, went from clerical work to earning an M.B.A., and wrote her first novel when she was over 40—is something of a superwoman herself.)

And yet despite all that's positive and riveting and informative about the books, I found them problematic. Like Scarlett O'Hara and the women in Ayn Rand's novels, Ayla is, alas, a great female character who comes with some cumbersome baggage.

First of all, Auel's research into the artifacts and the ecology of the Ice Age is so first-rate that it's easy to lose sight of the fact that the rest of the story—the human relationships—is speculative fiction. At the root of what's troublesome, I suspect, is Auel's decision to make the Others as much "like us" as possible, in everything from their speech patterns to their humor to their family lives. "These men aren't that much different from your sons or your college roommates," Auel told *People*. According to another interview in *Publishers Weekly*, "I tried to show that [Jondalar and his brother Thonolan] are thoroughly modern in their emotional responses, their intelligence, their psychological reactions. Anything we allow ourselves, we have to allow them." In fact, Jondalar and his brother sit around the cave talking what we would call thoroughly modern locker-room talk. (*"Markeno is right," Carlono said. "Never take [the river] for granted. This river can find some unpleasant ways to remind you to pay attention to her." [Thonolan replies:] "I know some women like that, don't you, Jondalar?"*).

The margins of my books are marked with dozens of similar examples of modern sexual and domestic assumptions which, when transplanted wholesale into the Ice Age, take on the nature of eternal human verities. Although nobody knows how babies are made (and although the tribe as a whole is the key survival unit), most characters pair off Noah's Ark style and form nuclear families. (A boy whose mother is single "needs a man around"—although, in fact, there are lots of men a few feet away at the next hearth.) In every tribe of the Others, women have one kind of name (say, a name ending with an *a*) and men have another. Among Jondalar's people, even though girls and women are allowed to hunt if they wish, only boys become men after their first kill; girls become women after they lose their virginity. Among all the tribes, Jondalar explains to Ayla, people believe that if a man of the Others rapes a Clan woman it's "not approved, but overlooked. [But] for a woman to 'share pleasures' with a flathead male is unforgivable . . . [an] abomination." (Sound familiar?)

My objection isn't necessarily that such things couldn't possibly have been true, but that there's no evidence that they were, and they often seem particularly illogical in the woman-centered cultures Auel has created. Thus, whenever Auel falls into sex-roles-as-usual, she's exercising a *choice*— and it's no more imaginative than the guys who put 1950s' suburbanites in a cave and invented the Flintstones. Her Others really tell us more about ourselves than about Cro-Magnon people; indeed, Ayla is in many ways a projection of the 1980s' female ideal—a woman who brings home the bison and fries it.

The fact that the Others are so much "like us" also informs and complicates another problem—the books' subtle racism. I say "subtle" here to distinguish a different point from the more obvious Aryan blond superiority bias, although it should also be noted in fairness that a dark-skinned half-African Cro-Magnon character figures prominently in the newest book. (Unfortunately, he's cut off from African culture, having been adopted by the Others at an early age, and his blackness is merely something that looks nice next to white fox fur clothing—or Ayla's white skin.)

But more subtly, if Auel had made the Others less familiar we might have seen their conflicts with the Clan from a genuine historical perspective. As it is, although we know that the Others are wrong—that the members of the Clan *aren't* subhuman—the equation is rigged so that we automatically identify with the Others (who, we also know, are the ultimate evolutionary winners). The message that emerges is a kind of post-colonialist chauvinist liberalism: people "like us" can be secure enough in our historic destiny to tolerate "less evolved" cultures. In the new book, the character who is the only representative of the Clan is a sickly, doomed half-Clan child who reminds Ayla of the son she has lost and who needs her protection against discrimination. The character is sympathetic, but I think his sickliness is rigged. As a white North American I feel I'm already programmed to view "primitives" not as true equals, but as the inevitable "victims of progress." This character does not challenge such liberal smugness in any way.

I certainly wouldn't want Auel to provide us with Ice Age black militants or politically correct Cro-Magnon men who do exactly half the cavework, but I do wish she'd allow us some ancestors who *aren't* like our college roommates, for better or worse. In fact, I thought Auel was at her best with the Clan and with other "exotic" characters whom she perhaps doesn't expect her average reader to "relate" to. In *Horses* we meet the Shamud, a Cro-Magnon healer and religious leader who is so androgynous that Jondalar honestly can't determine his/her gender. We later learn that people like the Shamud are always channeled into the tribe's priesthood, where they suffer a certain loneliness, but are compensated by respect and knowledge. "It is not easy to be different," the Shamud explains. "But it doesn't matter—the destiny is yours. There is no other place for one who carries the essence of both man and woman in one body." This isn't exactly the stuff of liberation, but what's wonderful and convincing about Shamud is that s/he doesn't resemble any gay man, lesbian, or transsexual you've ever met; s/he is instead a logical product of a particular culture, familiar enough to be human but magically alien in a way that the singlesbarsy heterosexual characters aren't.

Auel has promised three more novels in the series. I hope that in them she'll perhaps be able to balance our present-day need for strong female characters with the genuine mysteries and complexities of the past.

Diane S. Wood (essay date Spring 1986)

SOURCE: "Female Heroism in the Ice Age: Jean Auel's Earth Children," in *Extrapolation,* Vol. 27, No. 1, Spring 1986, pp. 33-38.

[*In the essay below, Wood examines the psychological development of Auel's protagonist in the author's first two novels. She also suggests that, in spite of the strong romantic overtones of the plots, the story is a classic adventure.*]

By its very nature, speculative fiction has great potential to explore variations in patterns of human interaction. Jean M. Auel, in *The Clan of the Cave Bear* (1980) and its sequel *The Valley of Horses,* demonstrates how such fiction can delve into basic human problems. Set in the Ice Age near the Black Sea, the novels trace the growth and perseverance through adversity of its adolescent female protagonist. The author gives careful attention to detail and thus creates a believable portrait of the distant past. Nonetheless, the remote settings do not obscure the fact that the main character is a young woman, Ayla, caught in an essentially male-oriented world, striving for independence and self-respect. The novels question narrow definitions of masculinity and femininity to arrive at new answers which have implications for today's society.

> **The woman protagonist in Auel's novels faces the challenge of the wilderness and survives, conforming to the pattern expected of the male hero in adventure tales. Love remains secondary to heroic action. Ayla is not a heroine of romance, but, rather, a true hero.**
> **—Diane S. Wood**

Auel's main character represents a relatively new type of protagonist for the adventure story, the female hero. The main character of the adventure genre is traditionally male. John G. Cawelti contrasts this kind of formulaic literature with its masculine main characters to the romance which features female characters:

The central fantasy of the adventure story is that of the hero overcoming obstacles and dangers and accomplishing some important moral mission. . . .The feminine equivalent of the adventure story is the romance. . . .The crucial defining characteristic of romance is not that it stars a female but that its organizing action is the development of a love relationship. . . .Because this is the central line of development, the romance differs from the adventure story. Adventure stories, more often than not, contain a love interest, but one distinctly subsidiary to the hero's triumph over dangers and obstacles.

The woman protagonist in Auel's novels faces the challenge of the wilderness and survives, conforming to the pattern expected of the male hero in adventure tales. Love remains secondary to heroic action. Ayla is not a heroine of romance, but, rather, a true hero. In her study of heroines in English novels, Rachel M. Brownstein suggests that being a heroine necessitates a plot which ends in marriage:

> The marriage plot most novels depend on is about finding validation of one's uniqueness and importance by being singled out among all other women by a man. The man's love is proof of the girl's value, and payment for it. Her search for perfect love through an incoherent, hostile wilderness of days is the plot that endows the aimless (life) with aim. Her quest is to be recognized in *all* her significance, to have her worth made real by being approved. When, at the end, this is done, she is transformed: her outward shape reflects her inner self, she is a bride, the very image of a heroine.

Ayla does not seek external validation by men but instead actively initiates the direction of the narrative without waiting for a man to take charge. She acts courageously without regard for her own safety. She not only protects children (an acceptable role for a woman), but in several instances she saves the lives of men. The creation of a female hero thus necessitates allowing the woman to assume the active, dominant role of rescuer expected in adventure fiction.

In addition to her heroic actions, Ayla possesses inherent skills which are generally associated with men. She is not passing through a "tomboy" stage, but has talents and inclinations of the opposite sex which create tension with the rest of the social order. Ayla is a *Homo sapien* adopted into a Neanderthal clan. The dexterity of her species makes her a natural hunter, an activity taboo to women of her adopted clan. Hunting is proscribed to women although it is actively encouraged for males as behavior extremely important to the survival of the group. The designation by the Neanderthals of certain behaviors as appropriate only to men runs contrary to Ayla's talents. Expression of her "masculine" nature and skill is repressed by society, resulting in a sense of personal alienation and eventually provoking rebellion. According to Auel's fictional account. Neanderthal women are expressly forbidden to touch weapons. Nonetheless, Ayla teaches herself to use a sling and even invents the technique of firing two rocks in rapid succession. The challenge of the hunt beckons irresistibly despite the fact that she can show no one her kill. While outwardly seeming to conduct herself as a passive female, she secretly violates the norm of the clan. Single-minded adherence to pursuing an activity

unacceptable to her sex characterizes this protagonist, and the reader is expected to perceive her tenacity as a positive trait. While she conforms in public, she does not allow others to decide what she must do in private and eventually breaks out of the rigidly narrow sex role assigned to her.

The development of these masculine pursuits results in an increase not only in Ayla's physical strength but also in her self-esteem. When Ayla masters hunting with a sling, her whole demeanor changes without her realizing it: "She didn't know there was freedom in her step, an unconscious carryover from roaming the forests and fields: pride in her bearing, from learning a difficult skill and doing it better than someone else; and a growing self-confidence in her mien." The transformation sets her apart from members of her own sex and causes her to be described in masculine terms: "As her hunting skill grew, she developed an assurance and sinewy grace unknown to Clan women. She had the silent walk of the experienced hunter, a tight muscular control of her young body, a confidence in her own reflexes and a far-seeing look in her eye . . ." (*Clan,* p. 210). This muscular tone and development is alien to the traditional romantic heroine who never needs a muscle of her own. It is possible to see in Ayla's athletic body the new feminine ideal of the 1980s with its emphasis on participation in sports and even bodybuilding.

Male characters in the clan perceive this "masculine" female as a threat and react savagely. Auel explains how tradition calls for Neanderthal women to accept the sexual advances of any adult male of the group. Broud, a sadistic Neanderthal man who delights in repeatedly raping Ayla in the most brutal manner, embodies the resentments of the men. Dominance over the young woman forms an essential ingredient in their relationship: "Broud reveled in his newfound dominance over Ayla and used her often. . . . After a time, it was no longer painful, but Ayla detested it. And it was her hatred that Broud enjoyed. He had put her in her place, gained superiority over her, and finally found a way to make her react to him. It didn't matter that her response was negative, he preferred it. He wanted to see her cower, to see her fear, to see her force herself to submit" (*Clan,* p. 316). The anger directed by men toward her does not result in eliminating the offensive masculine inclinations or talents. Rather, it actually brings about the opposite effect, and instead of being broken into submission and passivity, Ayla is strengthened by this cruel treatment and becomes even more masculine. She undergoes stages in the life of the typical male hero, including an initiation trial similar to a male puberty rite. When Ayla uses a sling in front of clan members to save a child from a predator, she reacts instinctively without regard for possible consequences to her. The wise clan leader resolves the dilemma of an appropriate punishment for her heroic but unpardonable behavior by reducing the customary sentence to a month-long "death curse." She survives this test despite a harrowing experience in a blizzard. As a result, the clan accepts her into the ranks of hunters and her totem is symbolically marked on her thigh as would be the case with a young man at puberty. After the ceremony, the clan celebrates with the customary feast. Lest she forget her proper place, the men of the clan are careful to point out that hunting is the only male prerogative which Ayla may pursue. The leader states: "Ayla, you have made your first kill; you must now assume the responsibilities of an adult. But you are a woman, not a man, and you will be a woman always, in all ways but one. You may use only a sling, Ayla, but you are now the Woman Who Hunts" (*Clan*, p. 303). Through her courageous persistence, she earns the right to assume a male persona and enjoys increased opportunities.

The ending of *The Clan of the Cave Bear* clearly delineates Ayla's "masculine" courage and defiance as contrasted with Broud's "feminine" impulsiveness. His leadership ability and judgment are questioned. One of Broud's first acts as leader is to banish Ayla forever with a permanent "death curse," but instead of ignoring her after the curse is performed, he raises his fist in fury to her, an act of acknowledgment. Even his father realizes Broud's lack of character and gives the ultimate insult, that Ayla is more of a man than Broud is: "You still don't understand, do you? You acknowledged her, Broud, she has beaten you. She's dead, and still she won. She was a woman, and she had more courage than you, Broud, more determination, more self-control. She was more man than you are. Ayla should have been the son of my mate" (*Clan*, p. 495). There could be no harsher reproach in a society with such rigid sex-role expectations than for a man to be unfavorably compared to a woman.

The social organization of the clan fails to provide flexibility for exceptional members. Neanderthal groups, according to Auel's narrative, function because of proscribed roles maintained through racial memory. Despite inherent differences in the species, Ayla adjusts to clan life and lives happily as long as the clan has a tolerant leader. Her very nature as a *Homo sapien* arouses intense hatred in Broud and, when he finally receives power in the closing pages of the novel, she is unjustly expelled from the group. Ayla wanders northward alone, seeking others of her kind. *The Clan of the Cave Bear* ends with her being cursed and forced to leave the clan. The sequel begins with her arduous and lonely search for a new life. The plot thus advances from conflicts within society to survival alone in a hostile wilderness. Ayla's great physical stamina, her tenacity, and her basic intelligence make her story credible and her survival possible.

In *The Valley of Horses* Ayla's relationships with animals prove more satisfying than with people. She lives happily for four years with a mare and a cave lion which she raises from orphans and tames to the point where they accompany her on the hunt and allow her to ride them. This relation-

ship between the protagonist and a horse has an erotic edge. Although she is not ignorant of the basic mechanics of sexuality, she has never felt profound yearnings. The rut of Ayla's mare provokes strange feelings in the woman which she does not understand, since sexuality among the Neanderthals is limited to the male's "relieving his needs" with the female. Ayla is distressed when her mare follows her sexual urges and freely joins a wild stallion, but since the horse, like the cave lion, is not her possession, she realizes that the mare is free to depart at will to join her own kind. In fact, Ayla envies the horse's good fortune. While the animals do not remain constantly with the young woman, they prove good companions in an otherwise lonely environment.

Whereas Ayla has certain characteristics of a male hero, she remains profoundly female. For instance, her great strength does not change her basic biological makeup. Monthly cycles still occur, and leather straps fulfill sanitary needs during menstruation. Ayla excels in traditional feminine handiwork, spending her spare time making exquisite baskets and learning how to sew. She clearly sees herself as the female in potential sexual situations with men. This heterosexual orientation remains constant throughout the novel regardless of her experiences with male brutality. She wants to find a mate/husband and raise children, but the difference between her and the typical romantic heroine is that Ayla simultaneously can accept both masculine and feminine aspects of her androgynous being. The fact that she can become a mother, for instance, does not preclude her from riding horses or hunting.

Ayla's isolation is a necessary step in allowing her to develop a more balanced sense of herself which eventually leads to her successful reintegration into a less repressive society. The changes in attitudes and experiences brought about by her separation from the group in which she was raised produce a new outlook for Ayla. The injustice she suffered as a sex object does not, however, cause her to reject all men. Indeed, the novels are *bildungsromans* exploring Ayla's nascent sexuality and her search for a meaningful relationship with a sympathetic man. She does not become sexually awakened until finding a compatible human partner in *The Valley of Horses*. She finally encounters a man who takes for granted that women hunt and make tools and that men help with food gathering and preserving. Mutual respect and admiration sparks affection between the two characters. The novel ends with the meeting of a human group, a signal of Ayla's entry into a new social order. She manages to have it all—independence and companionship—the fantasy of the modern American woman.

While Auel creates in these novels an active and heroic female figure grappling with tensions between her basic nature and her society, she also presents the difficulties males have adjusting socially. *The Valley of Horses* introduces a male protagonist, Jondolar, whose story is followed in chapters alternating with Ayla's adventures until the two finally meet and Ayla saves his life. Naturally, they fall in love. One might even say that the man's tale is the romance, since following Cawelti's definition, his preoccupation is with finding the ideal woman whereas Ayla struggles to survive and passes tests of bravery typical of the adventure story. Jondalar accompanies his brother on a journey. He would have preferred to stay at home. He serves as a companion rather than initiating action on his own as does Ayla. While he is proficient in the act of love, he does not know how to risk loving until he finds Ayla. One woman who loves him points out that he may be destined for an especially strong woman: "Maybe you haven't found the right woman. Maybe the Mother has someone special for you. She doesn't make many like you. You are really more than most women could bear. If all your love were concentrated on one, it could overwhelm her, if she wasn't one to whom the Mother gave equal gifts. Even if you did love me I'm not sure I could live with it. If you loved a woman as much as you love your brother, she would have to be very strong." In the Ice Age world Auel creates, neither men nor women are exempt from difficulties. The author rejects the idea of dominance by either of the sexes in favor of freedom of all people.

These popular novels reflect the author's optimism regarding the resolution of the difficult problems of individual choice which plague contemporary society. Just as Ayla is isolated, present day women all too often find themselves with no role models and no positive support from society as they attempt to function in today's world. While the situation of the Ice Age is different from our own, the solutions worked out in speculative fiction mirror those that must be worked out in lives of twentieth-century women. The success of these two books as popular fiction stems from the appeal of the strength of the female hero and the positive ending to her story.

The difficulty of integrating personal and professional life can be especially challenging in a complex society. William S. Barnbridge suggests a possible effect on present society of Sword-and-Sorcery novels which applies just as well to other novels of speculative fiction such as Auel's: "While Sword-and-Sorcery imagines fantastic worlds, the analysis of alternate ascribed roles and family structures it offers may contribute indirectly to create innovation in our own society." Speculative fiction leads the way for new patterns of human interaction. In this manner, literature posits and tests creative approaches to human dilemmas, working out theoretical cases to be either accepted or rejected by the evolving social order.

Nicholas O'Connell (interview date 1987)

SOURCE: An interview with Jean Auel, in *At the Field's End*, Maronda Publishers, 1987, pp. 208-19.

[*In the following interview, Auel discusses the research and development behind her series.*]

Jean M. Auel is the author of some of the most popular books in the world today. Her titles **The Clan of the Cave Bear** (*1980*), **The Valley of Horses** (*1982*) *and* **The Mammoth Hunters** (*1985*) *have set publishing records and won acclaim from critics for their accurate and imaginative portrayals of the lives of prehistoric peoples. Despite her phenomenal success, Auel did not begin writing with the intention of becoming a best-selling author. She first sat down at the typewriter because she had a story to tell, a story that she felt the world needed to hear.*

The story concerned a young woman living in prehistoric times with people who were different from her. Auel wasn't sure who these other people might be, but subsequent research revealed that during the last Ice Age the earth was populated with two different kinds of human beings, Cro-Magnons, who were the first modern humans, and Neanderthals, who were also Homo sapiens and quite advanced, but different from Cro-Magnons. In Auel's story, Ayla, the young woman, a Cro-Magnon, was growing up among Neanderthals and was caught between the two cultures and two ways of thinking.

Extensive research enriched and enlarged the story; the original novel entitled Earth's Children became an outline for a series of six books. The first book in the series, **The Clan of the Cave Bear,** *was followed by* **The Valley of Horses** *and* **The Mammoth Hunters.** *Auel plans to continue the saga of Ayla in three forthcoming volumes.*

Auel is a longtime resident of Oregon, a firmly rooted transplant from Chicago, where she was born in 1936. She attended Portland State University, and received an M.B.A. from the University of Portland in 1976. She is married to Ray Auel, and they have five children and nine grandchildren.

The interview with Auel, a bright and engaging woman, took place over the telephone in the spring of 1986.

[*O'Connell*] *When you started writing the Earth's Children series, did you have any idea how popular it would become?*

[Auel] No. I hoped what every writer hopes: that the first book would find a market and an audience, and maybe the second one would do a little better. That certainly has happened; it just started at a much higher level. The first printing of *The Clan of the Cave Bear* was 75,000 books. And the first printing in hardcover for *The Mammoth Hunters* was a million books. It broke the record. Somebody figured out that that would be a stack of books twenty-nine miles high.

Did you have any model in mind when you wrote these books?

No. I was just trying to write these stories. I'm still writing for myself. I'm writing the story I always wanted to read. As it turns out a whole lot of others want to read it, too. I'm not writing for critics, or to please a teacher or to please the public, or anyone else; I'm writing stories to please myself.

The first rough draft has become an outline for the *Earth's Children* series. That's why I know I'm going to have six books. People think, "She wrote **The Clan of the Cave Bear** and since it was successful, she decided to do a sequel."

But this series is not like *Clan II,* and *Rocky III* and *Jaws IV*. It is a continuation, not a repetition. I won't be telling the same story over and over again. I really did know, before I finished **The Clan of the Cave Bear,** that I had six books in the series.

Do the other books go further into Ayla's life?

All of the books feature Ayla. They are the story of her life. It's not a generational saga, one of those things where you start with the first generation and you end up with the great-grandchildren. I'm trying to show the diversity, complexity and sophistication of the various cultures during the Pleistocene. Ayla's story is the thread that ties them together.

Did you base the cave dwelling described in **The Clan of the Cave Bear** *on a particular archeological site?*

Not expressly. It's more like a typical site. It was based in many ways on the cave at Shanidar in Iraq on the southern side of the Black Sea, but the setting is in the Crimea on the northern shore of the Black Sea, because there were Neanderthal caves all through that area. It typifies a Neanderthal setting.

How did you become interested in prehistoric people?

[Laughs] I wish I had a wonderful answer for that. Everyone asks, and I don't have an answer. I started out with an idea for a story. I thought it would be a short story. That was in January, 1977. I had quit my job as a credit manager. I had received an M.B.A. in 1976, so I wasn't going to school, and my kids were almost grown. I was in between, not sure what I wanted to do, in a floating state, which I hadn't been in before. I had had a very busy life.

It was eleven o'clock at night. My husband said, "C'mon, let's go to bed." I said, "Wait a minute. I want to see if I can do something."

An idea had been buzzing through my head of a girl or young

woman who was living with people who were different. I was thinking prehistory, but I don't know why. I was thinking, "These people were different, but they think she's different." They were viewing her with suspicion, but she was taking care of an old man with a crippled arm, so they let her stay. This was the beginning. That night I started to write the story. I had never written fiction before. It got to be the wee hours of the morning, I was about ten or twelve pages into it and I decided, "This is kind of fun." Characters, theme and story were starting.

But I was also frustrated because I didn't know what I was writing about. I'd want to describe something and I wouldn't know how or where they lived or what they looked like, what they wore, or what they ate, or if they had fire. I didn't have any sense of the place or the setting. So I thought, "I'll do a little research."

I started out with the Encyclopedia Britannica, and that led to books at the library. I came home with two armloads, and started reading them. I learned that the people we call Cro-Magnon were modern humans. The stereotype of Neanderthal is of a knuckle-dragging ape, but they were Homo sapiens also, quite advanced human beings.

I felt as though I'd made a discovery. "Why don't we know this? Why aren't people writing about our ancestors the way these books are depicting them?" That became the story I wanted to tell: the scientifically valid, updated version.

So you wanted to clear up this misunderstanding?

Also tell a story. It's always been the story first. I discovered that I love being a storyteller. I wanted to write a good story, but also to characterize these people in a way that is much more acceptable currently by the anthropological and archeological community.

Was it difficult to turn this archeological material into a story?

Well, any kind of writing is difficult. Basically, as I was reading those first fifty books, I began to take notes of what might be useful to the story. Then I put together a page, or page-and-a-half outline for a novel. I sat down at my typewriter, and started to tell the story to myself.

Now, if I were to compile a bibliography of my reading for the series, it would approach a thousand entries. I've also traveled to Europe, and taken classes in wilderness survival and native life ways. In terms of the research, I probably read about ten or 100 times more than I needed, until I got so comfortable with the material that I could move my characters around in the story with ease.

I wasn't thinking of getting it published. I was just thinking of the story. As I started to write it, the story started to grow and develop, and the ideas I had picked up in the research were finding their way into it.

How long did it take you to write the rough draft?

It didn't take any more than six or seven months, from the time of the first idea to the time I finished a huge six-part manuscript that became the outline for the series. I had free time then. I didn't have any other demands on my time, except just to live and say hello and goodbye to my husband once in a while. He was really quite supportive. I became totally obsessed and involved and excited. I found myself putting in every waking moment. I'd get up and I'd almost resent taking a shower before sitting down at the typewriter. I was putting in twelve, fourteen, sixteen hours a day, seven days a week.

What happened to the rough draft?

I went back and started to read it, and it was awful. I was telling the story to myself but it wasn't coming through on the page. I thought, "My feeling and my passion are not there." So then I went back to the library to get books on how to write fiction.

After doing a lot of self-study, I started to rewrite this big mass of words. I thought I was going to cut it down. About halfway through the first of these six parts I discovered I had 100,000 words. In adding scene and dialogue and description and everything necessary to write a novel, the thing was growing. I thought, "I'm doing something wrong. At this rate I'm going to end up with a million-and-a-half words." Talk about a writer's block.

I went back and really looked at the six different parts, and realized that I had too much to cram into one novel. What I had was six different books. I can still remember telling my husband, "I've got six books," He said, "You've never written a short story, and now you're going to write six books?"

Earth's Children became the series title, and the first book became *The Clan of the Cave Bear.*

The series seems to have a very modern sensibility. Is it as much about people today as it is about prehistoric people?

It's about the struggles of human society. My characters are fully human; they have as much facility with their language as we do, which is why I started to write it in perfectly normal English, even though it would have pleased some critics if I had invented some kind of a phony construct of a language.

I think it's more accurate to show them speaking with ease. So I said, "I'm going to write this as though I am translating it from whatever language they spoke into our language." And good translators don't translate word for word, they translate idiom. There were some words I was careful with. For example, you can say, "Just a moment," but you can't say, "Just a minute."

What made these people's lives different from our own?

The world they lived in. There are a lot of things that we take for granted that hadn't been invented yet. But when Ayla in *The Clan of the Cave Bear* is five years old, she could have been anyone's five-year-old daughter today.

Because we're talking about people like ourselves, it allows me to look at ourselves from a different perspective, through a long-distance lens. I try to see what makes us human. What is basic to being human?

For example, if you plunk somebody down in a hunting-and-gathering society rather than a society where you go into your supermarket and get your meat out of a nice clean plastic package, what will be different and what will be the same? And is one society more or less violent? In most hunting-gathering societies, people feel a great deal of reverence for the animals they hunt. And we who get our packaged, sterilized meat that doesn't even bleed any more really have very little sensitivity to animals.

So there are some definite changes. But there certainly had to be some things that we suffer from, that they also suffered from.

Did you find that you admired these people?

Well, I felt that they were as human as we are, and I admired them, the same way I admire us. Unlike some people, I don't think the world is necessarily going to hell in a handbasket. I think that the human race is a very young race, and I am hoping that we will have the sense to keep ourselves from the destruction that we are potentially capable of dealing to ourselves. For all the stereotype about the brutal savagery of our ancestors, you find almost no evidence of it in the research, not among the Neanderthals and not among the Cro-Magnon.

One of the skeletons found at that Shanidar cave was of an old man. If you read about an old man with one arm amputated at the elbow and one eye that was blind, then you'd have to start asking, "How did he live to be an old man?" Paleopathologists believe that he had probably been paralyzed from an early age, because there was extensive bone atrophy and he was lame on that side. The paralysis may have been the reason his arm was amputated. So he was probably a paralyzed boy and at some time in his life became blind in one eye.

How does that fit in with survival of the fittest? These were Neanderthals taking care of a crippled boy and a blind and crippled old man. Evidence indicates he died in a rock fall as an old man. When I read about him I said, "Oh, my God, there's my old man with the crippled arm. There's the character in my story." That made me feel I was heading in the right direction. He became Creb.

And as you researched this book, did you find that your story grew in a lot of ways?

Exactly. And it was so much more interesting and fun to write within the modern scientific interpretation. I thought, "There's so much to write about, and I'm going to be the one to write it."

Did you do research in fields other than archeology?

Oh, yes. Many others. I would wonder, "How did they carry water? What kinds of things will carry water?" And by reading the reports of field anthropologists into more modern societies—the aborigines, the Bushmen, or the American Indians—you find out that watertight baskets will carry water, or carved wooden bowls, or water-tight stomachs.

I drew from all over the world. If it was appropriate and came together, then that's what I would use. I tried to give the sensitivity, the feeling of the hunting-gathering society.

For example, the idea of ancestor worship: when I was reading about the Australian aborigines, I learned that at one time they didn't really have a full understanding of procreation, particularly the male role in procreation. They knew a woman gave birth, but they weren't sure how she got pregnant. That led to speculation for my story. I thought, "What if this was a time so long ago, that the male role wasn't understood by most people. What would be the result?" Well, the only parent they would know for certain would be their mother, and her mother before that, and the mother before that, and maybe somebody would think, "Who was the first mother?"

You could see how a whole mythology based on the miracle of birth could evolve. Then I remembered about all these little figurines dating back to the early Cro-Magnon period, these round, motherly women carvings. I thought, "I wonder if they aren't meant to represent a great mother sense." That's how I derived some of the culture ideas.

> People say, "You're writing fiction. What do you do research for? Why don't you just make it up?" Well, in a work of fiction, even if it's a modern novel set in Washington, D.C., if you're going to mention the address of the White House, you'd better have that address right. Because if all the basic facts that you put down are as accurate as you can get them, it aids readers in suspending their sense of disbelief. As a novelist you want to have readers believe, at least while they're reading the story, that all this could be true.
>
> *—Jean M. Auel*

When you were telling a story, did you have to pick and choose among the evidence to decide what pieces to use?

Of course. For instance, did Neanderthals talk? There are two schools of thought on that. Professor Lieberman at Brown University is the proponent of the idea that there probably was some limitation in Neanderthals' ability to communicate, to talk, verbalize, and Lewis Binford finds little in the archeological record to show that they were able to make the necessary abstractions for full speech. But their cranial capacity, the size of their brains, was, on the average, larger than ours. And other scientists say that the evidence of their culture suggests that they were able to understand some abstractions. They were the first people to bury their dead with ritual and purpose. Somebody must have been thinking, "Where are we coming from and where are we going?" That gives us a clue that the way they thought might not be so different from the way we think, or at least feel. Emotions such as compassion, love and caring come through most strongly.

So they must have had, if not language, at least. . . .

At least a very strong ability to communicate, which is why I came up with the sign language idea. I said, "Okay, I'll take both of these ideas and combine them. I will say, 'Yes, there was a limitation in their language, but not in their ability to communicate.'" Sign languages are very complex. I did some research into that.

So if there's a gap between pieces of evidence, you can bridge the gap with your imagination?

Yes. And sometimes I can push things out. I can go a little farther than a scientist can go, because I am writing a novel. I might stretch the barrier, but I don't want to break through it. I don't want to write anything that would do a disservice to the latest findings of science. I want the background to be as accurate as I can make it. If the basis is factual, then I have something for my imagination to build on.

The character of Jondalar is based on an actual skeleton found at the site called Cro-Magnon, the site that gives the name to the early race. They found five skeletons at this particular site. One of them was of a man who was 6 feet, 5 3/4 inches tall. As soon as I read that, I said, "That's got to be Ayla's man."

Does this attention to detail make the story more believable?

People say, "You're writing fiction. What do you do research for? Why don't you just make it up?" Well, in a work of fiction, even if it's a modern novel set in Washington, D.C., if you're going to mention the address of the White House, you'd better have that address right. Because if all the basic facts that you put down are as accurate as you can get them, it aids readers in suspending their sense of disbelief. As a novelist you want to have readers believe, at least while they're reading the story, that all this could be true.

Where did the information about the herbs and medicines that the people used come from?

I have a research library now of books I've purchased, and I got some of the information from public libraries. We know that they were hunting-gathering people and we know that modern hunter-gatherers are very, very familiar with their environment. Some groups can name 350 plants, know all of their stages and all of their uses. While we don't know precisely what plants Neanderthals or Cro-Magnons used, from pollen analysis and from the way we're able to tell climate, we know what plants were probably growing there because the same plants are around today. Except domestic plants were in their wild form.

Did it give the people any advantage to be closely tied to the natural world?

It would give them the advantage of being able to live in their world. They needed it to survive. That is survival in the natural world. There's also survival in New York City. If you were to take an aborigine, or a Cro-Magnon moved up in time and set him in the middle of the modern world, and if he were an adult, how would he make a living? He wouldn't have grown up in our society, or gone to school. He might have all kinds of knowledge and background but it would not be useful to him any more, and would not have the same value.

That happened in this country to native cultures when the white Europeans invaded and began to settle. For example, the Northwest Coast Indian society was a very rich culture

and they built houses out of cedar planks. It is very difficult to split a log and make it into planks by hand with wedges and mauls; it takes knowledge, skill and effort, so each one of those planks had a high value.

Now, if a white settler puts in a sawmill, and suddenly they're whipping out planks at many many times the number per day than a person can do by hand, the plank no longer has the same value; it has lost its meaning within Indian society. Culturally and economically the Native American people were deprived. And that's part of the problem today, the displacement that many of them feel.

What our early ancestors knew enabled them to live and survive in their world. We wouldn't know how to follow the tracks of an animal or when they migrate, but we have to know airline schedules and how to cross a street without getting hit by a car.

Do you use elements of the Northwest landscape in your work?

Oh, absolutely. It was really kind of fun when I discovered, particularly in *The Clan of the Cave Bear,* that there's a little mountain range at the south end of the Crimea, which is a peninsula in the Black Sea, and a strip of coastland which is Russia's Riviera today. During the Ice Age that was a temperate climate. There were cold steppes to the north, but the mountain range protected the southern end. This small coastal area was a well-watered, temperate, mountainous region subject to maritime influences, not so different from the Northwest. I even discovered that azaleas grow wild there, as they do here.

Did setting the story in that particular kind of landscape create certain constraints?

Well, you can't have a story, you can't have anything, if you don't have limits, boundaries. You can't have one setting that is arctic and equatorial all at the same time. So yes, it puts limits, constraints, but those are usually fairly welcome limits. It gives you a frame to write within.

Was there an abundance of food during that period?

Most scientists and most researchers think that the last Ice Age period was probably richer than it was later during more temperate times. The glaciers caused a certain kind of environment that made for open steppes, or grasslands. Those vast grasslands fed grazing animals in hundreds of thousands of millions. It was also rich in terms of the produce that was available, so there were both animal and vegetable resources.

As the glaciers retreated, the forest started to move in, and forests aren't as rich. They don't support great herds of animals. Instead, animals stay either in small family groups or alone. The deer that run through the forest don't congregate in huge herds like the bison on the plains, and they're also harder to hunt because the animals can find trees and brush to hide among. It's much easier to hunt an animal on an open plain than when it's hidden in the woods.

In forests, there's more tree-growth, but not necessarily as much variety of plant-growth. So when the glacier melted, it reduced the abundance and variety of plant species. In the late Pleistocene, after the Ice Age, evidence of much more use of fishing and shell food was found. Such climatic changes may have caused pressures toward agriculture. The great variety and abundance was gone. Some way had to be found to feed the population.

Do you get a lot of mail back from your readers?

I do get a lot of letters from readers, and I'm very grateful for them. People become quite ardent; there are readers who feel very, very strongly about these books. It's a surprise to me. I'm delighted, but I'm a little overwhelmed. I don't really know what I'm doing right.

I get letters from men and women of all ages, twelve to ninety-two, and all walks of life—engineers, scientists, marines, lawyers, teachers, and people who barely can put together a grammatical sentence.

I even get letters from prisoners in jail. The one that I didn't know quite know how to handle was a letter from a man who said he was on death row, and would I hurry up and finish *The Mammoth Hunters* so he could read it before he died? I didn't know what to say.

What do you plan to write in the future?

I intend to write all six books in the series. That's an internal pressure. I have to finish telling Ayla's story. She won't let me alone.

And after that?

I may do anything. I may write about other prehistoric people. I may change to a different part of the world. I may write about later prehistoric periods. I may write something historical. I may write something modern. I might write science fiction. I might write a horror story, or a mystery. Who knows? I've got many things that I'd like to try. What I do know now is that I want to keep on writing, but I was forty before I knew what I wanted to do when I grew up.

Why was that?

I don't know. I suspect part of it is that I couldn't have done it any earlier. There are many young people who are fine writers, but I could not have been one. I needed to live some life and gain some experiences. I couldn't have written what I did without having gone through having a family, raising children, accepting responsibility, being out there in the world, working, coming across many different kinds of people and learning how to live with them.

Judy Bass (review date 14 October 1990)

SOURCE: "Interfacing in the Ice Age," in *Los Angeles Times Book Review*, October 14, 1990, pp. 2, 15.

[*In the review below, Bass compares* The Plains of Passage *to another recent novel set in the Ice Age. Though the novels differ in theme and execution, Bass has praise for both.*]

"Judge the goodness of a book by the energy of the punches it has given you," wrote Gustave Flaubert, author of "Madame Bovary." According to him, "the greatest characteristic of genius is, above all, force."

Two new novels about prehistoric hunter-gatherers—*The Plains of Passage* by Jean M. Auel and Elizabeth Marshall Thomas' *The Animal Wife*—both exemplify the kind of narrative power that Flaubert equated with virtuosity. Nevertheless, these are vastly different renditions of broadly similar themes.

Auel, a superlative raconteur, has crafted a consistently engaging adventure story with a solid historical underpinning. Set in Ice Age Europe, it also incorporates numerous touches commonly found in commercial fiction: lusty, protracted sex scenes (the heroine's sweetly ingenuous euphemism for intercourse is "pleasures"); natural and man-made adversity; and a suspenseful "Perils of Pauline" atmosphere in which the protagonists must grapple with unanticipated, potentially lethal hazards ranging from mammoths to mudslides.

Anthropologist Elizabeth Marshal Thomas approaches her material in a more detached, meditative manner than does Auel. Somber verisimilitude supersedes dramatic embellishment in *The Animal Wife*, which concerns the daily exigencies of survival in Siberia 20,000 years ago.

Simply put, what Thomas actually presents is a nearly 300-page "snapshot" of Paleolithic life. Filled with evocative descriptions of an environment that offers sustenance as well as daunting hardships, this tale features the interrelated members of several hunting groups. As narrated by an earnest, unworldly young man named Kori, we see these people gamely struggling to retain their fragile unity even while friction between the sexes jeopardizes it.

The last book in Jean Auel's multivolume "Earth's Children" series was *The Mammoth Hunters* (1985). In *The Plains of Passage,* she brings back Jondalar and Ayla, itinerant lovers who now attempt to traverse a continent in order to join Jondalar's kin, the Zelandonii. Three personal qualities help them to withstand this seemingly interminable trek: ingenuity, fortitude and mutual devotion.

Once again, Ayla is depicted as possessing "knowledge beyond the ken of ordinary people." This dazzlingly innovative 18-year-old outshines everyone around her, including the able Jondalar. Clearly blessed with a more sophisticated intelligence than her peers, versatile Ayla can sew, cook delectable meals, utilize the medicinal properties of certain vegetation, aid the sick and instantly start a fire merely by rubbing iron pyrite with a piece of flint.

However, Ayla's most wondrous feat involves two horses and a wolf. While her Ice-Age contemporaries slaughter such animals for their hides or to be consumed as food, she chooses to tame the beasts, transforming them into benign companions. Strangers whom Ayla and Jondalar meet along the way are inevitably transfixed—and highly alarmed—at the bizarre sight of humans astride horses, accompanied by an obedient wolf.

Ayla's eagerness to demonstrate to these people that they can trust creatures whom they customarily dislike illustrates a pivotal message conveyed by *The Plains of Passage*—that good will, open-mindedness, toleration and patience are almost always preferable to unthinking hostility. Consequently, those with selfish, belligerent attitudes who display no respect for the rights of others or the sanctity of life are the villains of this novel, villains whom Jondalar and Ayla jointly vanquish.

A corollary subplot of the book concerns the callous mistreatment of women by men, a theme dealt with far more extensively in *The Animal Wife.* As Auel shows, females make vulnerable targets for the unchecked lust and violence of aggressors. In her view, though, even victims of barbarism can be physically and spiritually reinvigorated via salutary doses of love.

Misogyny surfaces repeatedly in *The Animal Wife,* which Elizabeth Marshall Thomas calls "a companion piece" to her 1987 novel, *Reindeer Moon.* The narrator, Kori, declares, "My story is the story of women." With electrifying clarity, Thomas soon reveals that the abuse of women will figure prominently in his saga.

The characters in *The Animal Wife* confront the same conditions that Jondalar and Ayla face. They require food and shelter, cope with harsh weather and constantly need to outwit predators. Since these tasks are better accomplished through collective action than individual effort, Kori's relatives all try to cooperate. Regrettably, genuine harmony isn't sustainable due to the men's overt chauvinism and their conception of women as chattel.

"Marry as many as you can," Kori's father, Swift the shaman, cavalierly instructs his son. Virile and authoritative, Swift—like other men—puts high value upon wedding often, as well as advantageously. His latest bride, Pinesinger, is a seductive young woman whose past contains an eyebrow-raising entanglement. Unbeknownst to Swift, she and Kori have had a sexual liaison, and Kori's now forbidden yearning for Pinesinger hasn't abated.

With all the fiery bravado of youth, he sets out to claim the emblems of swaggering manhood: a wife, prowess as a hunter and true camaraderie with adults. Pinesinger is beyond his grasp, so Kori devises alternative ways to flaunt his maturity. During one unforgettably graphic episode, he, Swift and Swift's brothers kill a bison, then gulp down its blood in a grotesque ritual of male solidarity.

"When my turn came," Kori rhapsodizes, "a rush of strength and heat from the fresh blood filled my body."

> Auel's book consists of pure entertainment at its sublime, wholly exhilarating, best. Brimming with thrills, emotionally charged confrontations and moments of high passion, the novel resembles a fairy tale in that every impending catastrophe is averted, thus allowing the saintly hero and heroine to flourish. Such contrivances in *The Plains of Passage* are forgivable, for Jondalar and Ayla enchant us so completely that we revel in their charmed destinies.
>
> —*Judy Bass*

Eventually, Kori notices a strange new woman whom he decides to nab. Assisted by his uncle, Andriki, he punches her, hoists her inert body over one shoulder and transports her to his people's lodge. Like an ecstatic child with a delightful plaything, Kori proudly names this acquisition Muskrat, and thrusts her amongst his startled folk. They immediately bristle, fearing that she might have relatives who will retrieve her by force.

In addition, Muskrat suffers ostracism because she is different. Her language sounds peculiar; she has lice, and out of ignorance, she eats without sharing, a trait that affronts others. Kori, thinking mainly of amorous gratification and not of Muskrat's feelings, does little to integrate her with the group.

She and Pinesinger finally stalk out of the camp together, livid about the numerous humiliations they have received from their mates. When tragedy occurs as a direct result of their departure, it seems virtually preordained. "Everyone was unhappy, but it was to be," Kori fatalistically concludes.

Both Auel and Thomas excel at portraying complex social interactions, along with the richly dynamic milieu of a long-ago epoch. Beyond some obvious similarities in content, however, *The Plains of Passage* and *The Animal Wife* have little in common.

Auel's book consists of pure entertainment at its sublime, wholly exhilarating, best. Brimming with thrills, emotionally charged confrontations and moments of high passion, the novel resembles a fairy tale in that every impending catastrophe is averted, thus allowing the saintly hero and heroine to flourish. Such contrivances in *The Plains of Passage* are forgivable, for Jondalar and Ayla enchant us so completely that we revel in their charmed destinies. By coaxing, readers to suspend disbelief, Auel beckons them into her comforting fantasy world of ideal resolutions and triumphant valor.

The Animal Wife relies upon hard-edged authenticity for its impact. The wanton misconduct of various characters is eerily modern and thoroughly repugnant, yet Thomas refrains from tossing in any lighthearted frills to make it more palatable. Instead, she focuses on the grave reverberations of certain acts, such as shunning a hapless outsider and blithely degrading women.

This novel imparts no gleeful reassurances about decency inevitably prevailing over injustice. Only one chilling message emanates from Elizabeth Marshall Thomas' sleek prose. Human nature has improved very little over thousands of years.

Margot Hornblower (review date 22 October 1990)

SOURCE: "Queen of the Ice Age Romance," in *Time*, Vol. 136, No. 17, October 22, 1990, p. 88.

[*In the following review, Hornblower comments favorably on the "Earth's Children" series, but finds some elements of the most recent novel,* The Plains of Passage, *to be implausible.*]

In the musty chill of the Dordogne, 30 ft. below ground, gi-

ant bulls, painted in red and black, gallop across undulating walls. Nearby, a cavalcade of horses, ibex, tiny deer and cave lions dances along the curves of rough limestone. Are these soaring images sacred or profane? A large bespectacled woman closes her eyes and sighs in wonder. She imagines a time, perhaps 20,000 years ago, when rituals were performed in this same hidden cave in the flickering light of animal-fat lamps. Slowly, tears stream down her cheeks. "It's like a church," she whispers. "You feel you can understand the people who painted this."

Few have tried harder than Jean Auel, the Oregon chronicler of Ice Age romance, to fathom the mysteries of Cro-Magnon life. From her 1980 best seller, *The Clan of the Cave Bear,* through three popular sequels, including the just-published *The Plains of Passage,* Auel has fleshed out the stone-and-bone discoveries of archaeology to create a fully realized world for her prehistoric heroine, Ayla. In the latest 757-page volume, Ayla sets forth from her home among the Mammoth Hunters of the Eurasian steppes and, braving blizzards, a locust swarm and a fall into a glacier crevasse, reaches what is now the Dordogne, in southwest France. The region harbors a rich trove of Upper Paleolithic remains, including the mystically painted caverns. The Lascaux cave "overwhelms me," Auel says. "These weren't dumb savages."

Prehistory is not only Auel's passion: it has proved improbably profitable. A former credit manager at a Portland electronics firm, the mother of five, then 40, had never written a word of fiction when the idea for an Ice Age epic popped into her head in 1977. From an outline scribbled at the kitchen table grew a publishing phenomenon. The first three books have sold more than 20 million copies worldwide and have been translated into 18 languages. *The Plains of Passage,* Auel's first book since 1985, has a 1.4 million-copy advance sale. Crown Publishers has reportedly paid Auel about $25 million for *Plains* and two yet-to-be-written volumes completing the saga.

The further escapades of Ayla and her blond boyfriend, Jondalar the toolmaker, are set in the Dordogne, where Auel has been exploring caves and sifting dirt on an archaeological dig. "I found some pieces of flint and a reindeer milk tooth," she says proudly, as she huffs up a path to an Ice Age rock shelter. Far below, a narrow valley is bathed in mist. On a forested bluff, a medieval fortress glows in pale yellow light. "The vegetation was different then," she says. "But I need to know the lay of the land, where the ridges are, where the high points are, so I can move my characters through here."

A few days later, a French archaeologist guides Auel through Laugerie Haute, a vast excavation site under a cliff. She asks for details about how hearths were spaced, seeking hints on how families may have guarded their privacy. "This will be Jondalar's apartment building," she says. At Font-de-Gaume, a grotto of magnificent prehistoric artwork, she examines a painting of a wolf: "I have a feeling this will be Ayla's cave." It fits, since the adventurer travels with a wolf, albeit one she has trained to behave uncannily like a golden retriever.

Auel gets passing grades from archaeologists on how she interprets the facts. "We can tell you how the paintings were made, but not why," says American archaeologist Roy Larick. "Jean does as good a job at speculating as anyone else." Where knowledge falls short, ideology takes over. An ardent feminist, Auel makes a case for a matriarchal Cro-Magnon society, basing her theory on Upper Paleolithic female fertility figures known as Venuses. These statuettes with exaggerated breasts and buttocks have been found by the hundreds, whereas no male sexual symbols have been uncovered. "I'm trying to psych out an entire culture when all we have are bits and pieces to go on," she says. But of one thing she's sure: "It's wrong to think of our ancestors bopping women over the head and dragging them by the hair. Anthropologists have found that most hunter-gatherer societies are very equal."

Nonetheless, Ayla is a stereotyped wonderwoman: she stops a cave lion's attack with the wave of her hand, learns languages in minutes and uses birth control before anyone else even knows how babies are conceived. In *The Clan of the Cave Bear,* fact and fiction were plausibly balanced. But *Plains* verges on the ludicrous as Ayla expounds on clitoral vs. vaginal orgasm and rescues Jondalar from manhating Amazons. And much of *Plains* reads like a textbook: page after page listing animals and plants. The archaeology may be accurate, but stilted dialogue and "his-loins-ached-with-need" sex scenes are alternately hilarious and pathetic.

By and large, Auel has succeeded in popularizing a misperceived period. Nonetheless, even she may sense that her prehistoric cash cow may be overmilked. "Ayla's good company, but after a while you want to write about something else," she says. Then Auel is likely to make an important discovery of her own: whether her fans will remain loyal once the glaciers recede.

Clyde Wilcox (essay date Winter 1994)

SOURCE: "The Not-so-Failed Feminism of Jean Auel," in *Journal of Popular Culture,* Vol. 28, No. 3, Winter, 1994, pp. 63-70.

[*In the following essay, Wilcox argues that Auel's works can be considered feminist.*]

The Clan of the Cave Bear and the three other novels in Jean Auel's Earth's Children series are surprising bestsellers. They blend carefully researched and detailed accounts of the making of flint tools, the construction of lodges from mammoth bones, and the flora and fauna of Europe during the last Ice Age with an almost soap-opera account of the life of a blond, blue-eyed woman named Ayla. Orphaned by an earthquake at an early age, Ayla was raised by a clan of Neanderthals, who teach her to be a healer. When Ayla continues to violate clan taboos, she is exiled, where she meets another Cro-Magnon man and begins a long journey to what is now Eastern Europe to visit his home.

Recently, Bernard Gallagher has argued that *The Clan of the Cave Bear* constitutes a failed feminist novel. He reports that he initially regarded the novel as a real triumph but is now disappointed in the book. He graciously notes that he is "not suggesting, now, that Auel rewrite the ending to her novel" that sold millions of copies, inspired a rather awful film, and has led to the publication of additional books in the series. But he does suggest that the book reflects the view that relations between the sexes are "a matter of either/or. Either men are dominant or women are dominant." He sees the book primarily as a tale of the conflict between an independent and talented woman and a patriarchal culture that reviles her, yet he argues that the book contains certain elements that prevent it from fitting a feminist category.

I think that Gallagher is too hard on this novel, and that perhaps a reconsideration will enable him to again think of Auel's work as truly feminist. I will suggest that Auel's work must be considered in a wider context—that of the types of humans of which she writes, and that of the other novels in the series. Within that broader context, Auel's work can be considered feminist. Of course, there are a wide variety of feminist theories and approaches (Pateman and Gross). Auel's feminism might be described as one that entails equality of access to political power and occupations, and a blending of gender roles.

Gallagher is correct that Auel depicts women of the Neanderthal clan as quite subservient to men. Indeed, a woman of the Clan must kneel before a man and wait for a signal before she speaks, and must allow any man who wishes, to "relieve his needs" with her. Yet it is not the sexism of the Neanderthals that troubles Gallagher, for he finds Auel's account of the sexism embedded in Clan customs and language to be a truly feminist critique. Rather he makes three arguments. First, in the battle between the sexes, Ayla is given a weak and unworthy opponent. Second, Ayla is described as a classic blond-haired beauty. Finally, the novel ends with the banishment of Ayla for violating tribal taboos.

Let us consider the ending of *The Clan of the Cave Bear,* in which Ayla is banished by the new leader of the Clan.

Throughout the novel, Ayla is unable to always behave in the subservient way that Neanderthal men expect. Although only Neanderthal men are allowed to hunt, Ayla teaches herself to hunt, and invents a method of using a sling that is better than that of any man. When she gives birth to a half-Neanderthal, half-Cro-Magnon child, she refuses to obey an order by the Clan leader to let it die (for it appears initially deformed because of the mixed traits of the two human species). Each of these acts leads to some sort of penalty, including a temporary banishment. Finally, she violates the order of the Clan leader and rushes to the aid of a dying man, and this leads to her final banishment and a declaration that she is "dead."

Gallagher correctly notes that Ayla's independence has led her to banishment, and to her separation from her son. He concludes that "the novel seems to suggest that male-female relationships, by their nature, involve a struggle for power that never ends, a struggle in which someone must be the slave and someone must be the master." And the message seems to be that women who seek to become the master are ultimately cut off from society.

Yet Gallagher misses one important point—this is also a clash between Cro-Magnons and Neanderthals. Gallagher notes that Auel paints a physical picture of Neanderthals that is a bit more primitive than many current anthropologists would support. Yet he ignores one other fictional characteristic of the Neanderthals—the one that is most clearly an invention of Auel. Auel exaggerates the differences between Neanderthal and Cro-Magnon skulls, where the Neanderthal had a smaller frontal but an enlarged rear portion of the brain. From this, she posits the existence of a racial memory that almost dictates the actions of Neanderthals. Early in the novel, she notes that this memory had served the Neanderthals well as the ice advanced and retreated, for they could recall from an earlier period whether new vegetation was poisonous or good to eat. When confronted with a seemingly new situation that an ancestor had encountered before, a Neanderthal would simply remember the course of action that had worked in the past. Most surprising is that these memories are sex specific. Auel writes that Memories in Clan people were sex differentiated. Women had no more need of hunting lore than men had of more than rudimentary knowledge of plants. The difference in the brains of men and women was imposed by nature, and only cemented by culture. It was another of nature's attempts to limit the size of their brains in an effort to prolong the race.

These racial memories were associated with an inability to rapidly adjust to new developments. Ayla presented the clan with a challenge, for they could not understand a woman who would hunt. Women of the clan had no interest in, and no facility for, hunting because they lacked the memories. Men were similarly incapable of cooking. Although the notion of

a racial memory has no basis in scientific research, the Neanderthals inhabited Europe for 100,000 years but showed no evidence of cultural accumulation—their stone tools did not become more subtle, they persisted in the use of heavy spears for thrusting instead of lighter ones for throwing, and in no Neanderthal site has there been any figurative art.

> They were slow to adapt. Inventions were accidental and often not utilized. . . .Change was accomplished only with great effort. . . .But a race with no room for learning, no room for growth, was no longer equipped for an inherently changing environment.

The Neanderthals are shown as mentally limited. When Creb, the Neanderthal spiritual leader, tries to teach Ayla a few "counting words," he is astonished that she is immediately able to grasp abstract mathematical concepts that are beyond his ability. In another passage, Creb and Ayla explore their common past and different future in a drug-induced journey. Creb sees that his people will become extinct, while Ayla's will go on to inherit the earth. Although Creb is portrayed as the most intelligent Neanderthal, Ayla is more mentally agile.

In this light, the unwillingness of the Neanderthals to accommodate Ayla's feminism is a bit more understandable. They are unable to change, and like Topol in *Fiddler on the Roof*, they bend and bend and finally break. Broud, the young leader who ultimately expels Ayla is a twisted, jealous man who had raped her to gain power over her, but the other Neanderthals who go along with the banishment are often portrayed as caring, decent individuals. They also are unable to accept or understand her behavior, for it is beyond their limited cognitive abilities. What we see in this book is not an inevitable war between the sexes, but a war between competing species of humans. Gallagher's first problem with the novel, that Broud was an inadequate foil for Ayla, misses the point. The book is not about Ayla vs. Broud, although this occupies a portion of the novel, but rather about how Neanderthals and Cro-Magnon humans would deal with an entirely new and challenging situation.

The extinction of the Neanderthals remains one of the most interesting mysteries of prehistory. Some have argued that Cro-Magnon humans killed the Neanderthals, others that the superior hunting tools enabled them to kill off some of the game on which the Neanderthals relied. Still other anthropologists have suggested that the Neanderthals and Cro-Magnon peoples interbred, although at least one anthropologist suggests that they would have been unable to produce offspring. Auel seems to suggest that the Neanderthals died out because they were unable to adapt to the end of the Ice Age, because their brains were wired to remember the past and not to plan for the future. Creb and Ayla see that the Cro-Magnon will triumph because of their greater flexibility and adaptability. Auel may be making a more general point that any society that uses past behavior as an invariable guide to present decisions will fail. Auel's novel implies that any society that rejects the innovations of its most creative citizens because of their gender, race or other characteristics, will ultimately perish.

The ending of the book remains a problem, however. Clearly Ayla's banishment is an unhappy event. In a later book she notes that she would have gladly stayed with the Clan as second woman to the jealous leader to be near her son. Is the message of the book that feminism ultimately leads to a loss of family? The last line in *The Clan of the Cave Bear* is a plaintive call of "Maamaaa!" from Ayla's son. No mother or father can read the ending of this book without a pang of sorrow.

To put this in a broader perspective, it is useful to examine the three additional books in the series that have appeared to date. In *The Valley of the Horses,* Ayla lives alone in a valley for three years. During this time, she learns to hunt with a spear, and she domesticates a horse and a cave lion and rides each in the hunt. When her future husband Jondalar suffers a deep thigh gash from her cave lion, she examines the stitching in his garments (Neanderthals did not sew) and threads together his flesh. She learns to speak (Auel depicts Neanderthals as speaking primarily in sign language—a point of some controversy today among anthropologists,) and learns to throw a spear more accurately than Jondalar. Jondalar is described as in a manner much like Ayla—tall, blond-haired, blue-eyed and very attractive. Thus Gallagher's second concern, that Ayla is described as a physical beauty, can be seen in a different light. That Ayla and Jondalar must be Aryan beauties is perhaps a concession to the soap-opera part of Auel's market, but it is not a mark of sexism. Presumably Auel believes it is necessary to have attractive characters to help fuel her somewhat predictable sex scenes in the later novels.

More importantly, Ayla meets many other Cro-Magnon people—who act and think like she does. Thus although Ayla has lost her half-Neanderthal son, she has found people like herself. Jondalar is a feminist ideal man, interested in cooking, anxious to have Ayla help with the hunt, and truly in awe of her abilities. He displays a troubling racism (or speciesism) about the Neanderthals, but he gradually comes to terms with this and accepts the Neanderthals as fully human. Ayla mourns the loss of her son throughout the next two books, although by the end of the fourth novel, she is pregnant again. It appears that the novels in this series are building to a confrontation between her fully Cro-Magnon child and her half-Neanderthal son in the final book of the series. The banishment of Ayla can be interpreted as a rejection by a society unable to change, but it ultimately leads

Ayla into a broader Cro-Magnon society of people who think and act like she does.

Consider Auel's view of gender politics among the Cro-Magnon. In the third novel *The Mammoth Hunters* the pair stay for a time on the plains with a group of Cro-Magnon hunters. This group is part of the Matutoi people, who hunt mammoths. The tribe is ruled by a headman and headwoman, who share equal power and responsibility. Decision-making is by consensus, with everyone taking a chance to speak by holding the speaking stick, and women taking an active role. The larger Matutoi people are governed by a Council of Sisters (made up of the headwomen of the tribes) and a Council of Brothers (made up of the headmen), but the women make the final decision because they are closer to the "Great Mother." All of the Cro-Magnon people encountered in these novels appear to believe in a female deity, and the Danube river is referred to as the Great Mother River.

In the fourth novel, *The Plains of Passage,* Ayla and Jondalar leave the Matutoi and journey toward Jondalar's home. They visit first the Samudoi. Women of the Samudoi take part in tribal decision-making, and men help with the cooking while women help with the hunting.

In this novel, however, is the best evidence for anti-feminism in Auel's writings, for Auel depicts a very disfunctional society ruled by women. Jondalar is captured by the S'Armunai, a tribe in which the headwoman has penned up the men of the tribe in a prison structure. The woman who heads the tribe is mad, and dislocates the legs of young boys as they pass through puberty. She challenges Jondalar to mate with her, and tries to kill him. Yet Ayla rescues him with a perfectly thrown spear. Her domesticated wolf finally kills the demented leader, and the men and women of the tribe cautiously reunite and begin to patch up a relationship.

In some ways, this section reads like a Phyllis Schlafly nightmare. Before Ayla intervenes, the women who rule this tribe torment the men, and all are starving because the entire burden of gathering food has fallen to the women. It is possible to read this story as suggesting the ultimate failure of a society in which women control government power. A more narrow reading might suggest that if angry feminists ever gained power, men would suffer from discrimination, families would be broken, and society would suffer.

Yet there is evidence within this story to suggest that Auel does not intend it as an anti-feminist parable, or at least that she does not mean to imply that a society in which women make the crucial decisions will be disfunctional. Auel does not imply in this section that women are unable to rule, for Jondalar's mother once ruled his tribe, and the Council of Sisters rule the mammoth hunters. Rather, she appears to hold that, like the Neanderthal, the S'Armunai are unable to fully function as a people without the close cooperation of men and women. Jondalar initially is stunned to learn that the tribe would prevent half of its population from helping with the hunting and gathering. Note that Jondalar is unable to free himself, and only Ayla is able to depose the mad ruler, so relief comes from a strong woman, not from a man. Interestingly, the mad woman ruler had been seriously abused by a half-Neanderthal mate, which appears to have caused her mental problems. Auel may intend this section to show that men and women must work together, regardless of previous discrimination, if society is to prosper.

Of course, there are some parts of these four novels that do not strike a consistent feminist theme. We learn that Jondalar's mother voluntarily relinquished her rule of her tribe to her son. Ayla chooses a man to rule the S'Armunai after the death of the mad woman ruler. Ayla follows Jondalar to his home, despite her preference to stay with some of the peoples they visit along the way. These are not utopian novels, and Auel writes for several seemingly distinct audiences. Yet overall, there are obvious elements of an egalitarian feminism in Auel's work.

Throughout these four novels, we see Ayla as a resourceful woman who generally does what she wants. She hunts and heals, combining the traditional masculine with the feminine. Her hunting skills astonish everyone, as do her abilities in medicine. The shamen of the tribes she visits constantly marvel at her spiritual gifts, and she appears to have genuine visions of the future. She is tough but compassionate. She domesticates a horse, a lion and a wolf. She invents surgical stitching, and many other things too numerous to mention. That she is also a beautiful blue-eyed blond does not detract from her feminist credentials.

[Auel's] novels may not portray a prehistoric feminist utopia, but taken in context they have a strongly feminist message. She depicts a pre-history that is perhaps even more egalitarian than our present society, in which men and women must share evenly the burdens and opportunities in order for both to survive.
—*Clyde Wilcox*

In the later novels, she frequently confronts adversity from strength. In *The Mammoth Hunters* many Mamutoi at a large gathering of the tribes muttered among themselves about Ayla's previous ties with the Neanderthals. Indeed, Ayla faces up to this apparently deep-seated speciesism among the Cro-Magnon at every occasion. In this novel, a half-Neanderthal child adopted by the tribe she was visiting came to the meeting, and Ayla let it be known that she had given birth to such a child. When some of the more speciesist members of the Mamutoi want to expel her, the tribe with which she stayed claims her as a member. Yet it is with a show of power that Ayla wins the battle, for she rescues a girl who appears in danger from a cave lion—the one she had domesticated. The muttering is halted when Ayla mounts and rides a lion that is as large as modern horse.

In *The Plains of Passage,* Ayla rescues Jondalar by throwing a spear that cuts the ropes that bind him—an accuracy that is almost impossible. She liberates the people of this tribe when her tame wolf kills the woman who ruled. This is a confrontation between two strong women, and Ayla wins by a real show of strength. Where Ayla left the Neanderthals in defeat, among the Cro-Magnon her drive and skills are amply rewarded. After her victory through the tough use of force, she uses her skills as a healer to begin to rebuild the tribe.

Moreover, Cro-Magnon peoples are shown as generally egalitarian in the sex roles. Jondalar is as interested in cooking as Ayla is in hunting. Women are consistently shown in real decision-making authority. In contrast, the now-extinct Neanderthals are shown as sexist and unable to accept women as equals. Those who are unable to move beyond rigid sex roles are now extinct, while the more flexible Cro-Magnon are our direct ancestors. Overall, this seems a strongly feminist message.

Gallagher can resume his respect for Auel's feminism. Her novels may not portray a prehistoric feminist utopia, but taken in context they have a strongly feminist message. She depicts a pre-history that is perhaps even more egalitarian than our present society, in which men and women must share evenly the burdens and opportunities in order for both to survive.

FURTHER READING

Criticism

Auel, Jean M. "'Commercial vs. Literary'—The Artificial Debate." *The Writer* 100, No. 10, (October 1987): 9-12, 46.
In this essay, Auel gives her perspective on the proposition that works must be either commercial or literary, and cannot be both.

Crichton, Jean. "The Marketing of 'The Plains of Passage': A Lot of Anticipation." *Publishers Weekly* 237, No. 35, (31 August 1990): 44-45.
Examines the world-wide marketing campaign surrounding the book.

Additional coverage of Auel's life and career is contained in the following sources published by Gale: *Authors and Artists for Young Adults,* Vol. 7; *Bestsellers,* 1990, Vol. 4; *Contemporary Authors,* Vol. 103; *Contemporary Authors New Revision Series,* Vol. 21; *DISCovering Authors Modules: Popular Fiction* and *Genre Authors;* and *Something about the Author,* Vol. 91.

Lady Antonia Fraser
1932-

English biographer, historian, and novelist.

The following entry presents an overview of Fraser's career through 1996. For further information on her life and work, see *CLC*, Volume 32.

INTRODUCTION

Lady Antonia Fraser has produced works that are both popular with general readers and acclaimed by academics. Some reviewers attribute her success to an ability to tell a good story combined with an attention to detail. "She writes fluently, spins yarns with verve, and knows the secret of the significant fact," Reed Browning affirmed. Fraser's taste for history and writing is deep-rooted. Her father, mother, daughter, and brother are all writers; collectively her family is known as the "Literary Longfords." Fraser's talents as a historian found their first expression with books on dolls and toys, then developed with projects on figures of British history, beginning with *Mary Queen of Scots* (1969) and continuing most recently in her exploration of the evidence surrounding the 1605 case of Robert Catesby and Guy Fawkes in *Faith and Treason: The Story of the Gunpowder Plot* (1996). In addition to her wide interests and achievements, Fraser is particularly accomplished in her investigation of women in history. She has also launched into crime fiction, creating the detective Jemima Shore.

Biographical Information

Born August 27, 1932, the eldest of eight children, Antonia Fraser is the daughter of Francis Aungier Pakenham, a politician and writer, and the 7th Earl of Longford (a title he acquired in 1960 after his brother's death) and Elizabeth Pakenham, Countess of Longford and biographer of such figures as Queen Victoria, the Duke of Wellington, and Lord Byron. As a child, Fraser attended a convent school (which served as the setting for her first mystery novel) and developed an early interest in Mary Queen of Scots and other figures from English history. She earned a B.A. and an M.A in History at Oxford, where her classmates included novelist V. S. Naipaul. After graduating, she worked as General Editor of the Kings and Queens of England series for the London publishers Weidenfeld and Nicholson, and herself published books of history for children on King Arthur and Robin Hood, a book on dolls, and her *History of Toys* (1966). During this time Fraser had six children with her husband Hugh Fraser, a Conservative Member of Parliament and war hero whom she married in 1956. Her first big success

in publishing came when, at her mother's suggestion, Fraser undertook a biography of Mary Queen of Scots, which led to the publication of her first important book *Mary Queen of Scots.* Subsequently she published *Cromwell Our Chief of Men* (1973), *King James: VI of Scotland, I of England* (1974), *King Charles II* (1979), *The Weaker Vessel* (1984), *Boadicea's Chariot: The Warrior Queens* (1988) and *The Wives of Henry VIII* (1992). In the mid-1970s she began writing mysteries featuring private investigator Jemima Shore, who first appeared in *Quiet as a Nun* (1977). With this and subsequent Jemima Shore novels, and as her novels were turned into TV adaptations as a series entitled *Jemima Shore, Investigator,* Fraser acquired a new readership and became a prominent media figure, appearing on popular television shows such as "My Word!" Around this time her marriage dissolved, and in 1980 she married playwright Harold Pinter. In addition to her writing, Fraser has also played an important social role as the chair of the Prison Committee and president of the international writers' organization known as PEN (Poets, Essayists, Novelists). In 1986 she also served as president of the Crime Writers' Association, and is a past chair of the Society of Authors (1974-

75). In her work and public image, Fraser is considered by some to be an important role model. As Mel Gussow pointed out in a profile of the writer, "because she synthesises beauty, intelligence and artistic talent, she is a kind of heroine to other women."

Major Works

Fraser's first major work, and to many her finest, is *Mary Queen of Scots* (1969), in which the legendary Queen emerges as a powerful, influential woman who defies stereotypes. In the biography Fraser pursued a long-standing interest in the subject, and it marked the direction her work was to take: the genre of historical biography and the themes of politics and gender. Her method was also set in this work: breathing life into stories about the past by telling them with passion. For this she has acquired an enthusiastic readership and garnered many laudatory reviews. While she explored male figures in *Cromwell, King James: VI of Scotland, I of England* and *King Charles II,* her attention has turned more often and with more popular and critical success to the history of women. *The Weaker Vessel,* subtitled *Woman's Lot in Seventeenth-Century England,* looks at the social conditions of women in the 17th century. *Boadicea's Chariot: The Warrior Queens*—later published in America as *The Warrior Queens* (1989)—examines women in warfare from Boadicea to Margaret Thatcher. In a more recent study of historical women, *The Wives of Henry VIII* (1992), the usual focus of the dominant, eccentric patriarch at the center of the historical facts is set aside in favor of the women in the story. In the genre of crime fiction, Fraser has fashioned a strong feminine protagonist in Jemima Shore, who made her first appearance in *Quiet as a Nun.* In a review of Fraser's book by mystery writer P. D. James, Shore's character is described as "a contemporary heroine, a successful television investigator, liberated, prosperous, unencumbered with husband or child, and with all the fashionable accoutrements of success." Fraser's crime writing is considered as artistically successful as her history. Anne Tolstoi Wallach, reviewing *The Cavalier Case* (1990), points out that Fraser writes mysteries as she writes her biographies, "with zest and verve," and that "her primary interest is people."

Critical Reception

Fraser is lauded for her attention to detail while recreating a version of the past that has the spark of life. *Mary Queen of Scots* was received with comments such as those made by J. P. Kenyon, who announced that Fraser had produced "a first-rate historical biography" distinguished by a "tense, muscular narrative." Historian Lawrence Stone, reviewing *The Weaker Vessel,* praised Fraser for thorough and careful research, high-quality writing, and "good judgment and a subtle appreciation of human psychology." Blair Worden, reviewing *The Six Wives of Henry VIII,* offered the follow-

ing: "Fraser's scholarship, albeit unambitious, is always diligent, clear-headed, responsible." He went on to compare Fraser to Victorian writer Agnes Strickland, a writer of popular history who also came from a literary family and who also wrote about Mary Queen of Scots and the lives of the queens of England, but points out that while Strickland was guilty of "errors of scholarship and judgement," Fraser is not. However, unlike Strickland, who "was able to carve out fresh historical territory," Worden maintained that Fraser is limited in her research to the learned articles upon which bases her work. Ives suggested that in Fraser readers find "above all imaginative sympathy." Her risk-taking in the interests of a passionate story are generally admired, although her method does draw some criticism in the area of accuracy. Her perspective is also an area of concern for some reviewers. In *The Weaker Vessel,* Stone objected to Fraser's focus on nobility and complained that Fraser lacks a "profound immersion in all aspects of seventeenth-century English history." He added that she "attempts little in the way of interpretation. She selects a striking story, tells it extremely well, and then moves quickly on to the next." Most critics acknowledge that Fraser's passion for women's history is expressed through a reliable and effective method. Kenyon, in his estimation of *Mary Queen of Scots,* noted with relief that the work did not display the undesirable quality that "afflicts female historians writing about women," namely, "a special kind of martyred sentimentality."

PRINCIPAL WORKS

A History of Toys (history) 1966
Mary Queen of Scots (biography) 1969
Cromwell: Our Chief of Men (biography) 1973
King James: VI of Scotland, I of England (biography) 1974
The Lives of the Kings and Queens of England [editor] (nonfiction) 1975
Quiet as a Nun (novel) 1977
King Charles II (biography) 1979
The Weaker Vessel (history) 1984
*Boadicea's Chariot: The Warrior Queens (history) 1988
The Cavalier Case (novel) 1990
†The Six Wives of Henry VIII (history) 1992
Jemima Shore at the Sunny Grave and Other Stories (shorts stories) 1993
Faith and Treason: The Story of the Gunpowder Plot (history) 1996

*Published in the U.S. as *The Warrior Queens.*
†Published in the U.S. as *The Wives of Henry VIII.*

CRITICISM

J. P. Kenyon (review date 6 November 1969)

SOURCE: "A Discordant Queen," in *New York Review of Books,* November 6, 1969, pp. 40-42.

[*In the following review, Kenyon presents an informed account of the history of Mary Queen of Scots and the political environment of the time, while commenting on Fraser's* Mary Queen of Scots *and comparing it to the work of other historians.*]

Lady Antonia Fraser is young, beautiful, and rich, an earl's daughter married to a busy and successful politician, the mother of a large family; yet she has surmounted all these handicaps to authorship to produce a first-rate historical biography. I do not mean to sound sarcastic or patronizing. Only a practicing historian knows the hours of boring and backbreaking labor that go into a book like this; and in a well-trampled field like the life of Mary Stuart the burden of such labor is not lightened by the hope of some exciting find.

> [*Mary Queen of Scots*] is a beautifully written book, thoroughly but unostentatiously researched. Lady Antonia avoids the temptation to romanticize an inherently romantic and tragic story, and her tense, muscular narrative generates a flow which carries the reader on unwearying to the end.
> —*J. P. Kenyon*

It is the defect of most "amateur" historians that they evade this drudgery, or abandon it halfway through. They pad out their bibliographies and cut back their footnotes (blandly announcing that this is to humor their illiterate readers, the poor dears), they hopefully cram their prefaces with acknowledgments to Professor X and Doctor Y, and in the last resort they pretend that a book to which they have devoted years of effort, of one kind or another, is only an interim report. It is easy for any biographer, trained or otherwise, to put the emotional stress in the wrong place, and to forget in the agonies of her heroine the agonies she created, and there is always the temptation to "stretch" sources which are always inadequate and often ambiguous. From conjecturing that Queen Mary *may* have thought such-and-such it is a short step to saying that she *thought* it. (The final step, of making her *say* it, is one that some authors do not shrink from.) Finally, there is a special kind of martyred sentimentality that afflicts female historians writing about women, paralleled by the jovial locker-room camaraderie which infects many male historians writing about men.

I approached Lady Antonia's book [*Mary Queen of Scots*] expecting to find some, if not all of these faults, and my con-fidence was not bolstered by the fact that most of the reviewers who greeted it so rapturously in England were also women, and women innocent hitherto of any historical knowledge or expertise. To my relief it is a beautifully written book, thoroughly but unostentatiously researched. Lady Antonia avoids the temptation to romanticize an inherently romantic and tragic story, and her tense, muscular narrative generates a flow which carries the reader on unwearying to the end. It is as definitive a life as we shall get of a woman whom her cousin Elizabeth called "the daughter of debate that eke discord doth sow," who has sown discord among historians to this day.

The first task is to strip away the layers of varnish plastered on Queen Mary's portrait, and here the Scots are the sinners, not the English. It was the English who imprisoned her for the last nineteen years of her life, but it was the Scots who gave them the excuse, it was the Scots who denounced her as the murderer of her husband, and even turned her own son decisively against her.

Mary was to all intents and purposes a Frenchwoman. Born of a French mother, she never knew her father, and she was sent to Paris at the age of five, and remained there until she was nineteen. In the interval she married Francis, eldest son of Henry II of France, and on Henry's premature death in 1559 she was even raised to the French throne. A future spread before her in which she would rule Scotland jointly with her husband, and no doubt through deputies, making only occasional visits to a country she can scarcely have remembered with any clarity. Beyond that lay the throne of England, for Elizabeth, who succeeded her sister Mary in 1558, was the last of the Tudors in the direct line and was still officially illegitimate in the eyes of the Roman Church.

But King Francis's death in December 1560 left Mary a widow at the age of eighteen. All her life she would be a daughter of France, but, most unexpectedly, her future now lay in Scotland. Moreover, that year Scotland had risen in revolt against popery and the French connection. With timely assistance from Elizabeth the rebels forced on the government the Treaty of Edinburgh, which recognized the reformed kirk and barred Mary from the English throne. The English succession always had the most powerful hold on Mary's imagination, so much so that in 1558 she had quartered the arms of England with her own, and laid claim to the throne itself, not just the succession. Her obstinate refusal to withdraw this claim, or ratify the Treaty of Edinburgh, prejudiced her relations with Elizabeth from the outset.

Mary left for Edinburgh in 1561, but it is not surprising that she regarded her stay there as "a wearisome interlude between the France of her memories and the England of her dreams." It was not just the weather which gave sixteenth-century Scotland the reputation of being "the arse of the world." It was a poor country, thinly populated; its natural resources meager and inefficiently exploited. It is questionable whether it could even support a monarchy as monarchy was then understood in western Europe. Its kings were feudal overlords, still living mainly on the income from their estates, their power based on their ability to control a nobility which existed in a state of fractiousness and indiscipline not seen in England or France for nearly a hundred years, and then only as a temporary phenomenon. A middle class was only just emerging, and the Scottish Universities, despite their antiquity and comparative abundance, had failed to train that bureaucracy which was taken for granted in most European countries. Maitland of Lethington, Mary's Secretary of State, was the only servant she had who could possibly have taken a similar post in England, France, or Spain.

For the rest, the aristocracy was as irresponsible as it was contentious, and the Reformation had given it yet another bone of contention. Only the fact that no nobleman could trust another for more than six weeks prevented the country from falling completely to pieces. Much of the sheer inanity of Scottish politics is summed up in the name and fact of the "Chaseabout Raid" in 1565, in which Mary's wisest councillor, her half-brother, James Stewart, Earl of Moray, made a sickening reversion to type. Fearing loss of influence at court, he could think of no more sensible way of settling the matter than a demonstration rebellion, which ended with his flight to England, having accomplished nothing. Yet the position of chief minister was a dangerous one, as the assassination of Cardinal Beaton (1546), the Earl of Moray (1569), and the Earl of Morton (1580) showed.

In such conditions there could be no tradition of administration or even government. Analyzing Queen Elizabeth's first Privy Council, a recent historian notes that the Marquess of Winchester should be classified as a bureaucrat rather than as a great magnate, since he was still engaged in a major program of administrative reform at the Treasury which extended back into the previous reign. The whole concept behind this casual remark is so alien to contemporary Scottish conditions that it might well refer to events in another universe. Scots government was at about the same stage of development as English government under Edward the Confessor.

Mary's initial success in these conditions is astonishing, and even Lady Antonia does not give it its full value. This finely bred girl survived for four years virtually unscathed. She not only survived, in some ways she flourished. For a brief period she imposed law and order on the jungle of Scottish politics. Moreover, she insisted on choosing her own husband, in Henry, Lord Darnley, and beat down considerable opposition to it; and since Darnley, like her, had a claim to the throne of England as well as Scotland, dynastically it was

an astute move. (Time was to show that it was perhaps too astute, but no matter.) Above all, her willingness to accept the fact of the Scottish Reformation, and her refusal to make her own sincere Catholic beliefs a matter of state or to build up a Catholic party among the nobility—in fact, one of her most decisive and successful acts was the suppression of the Earl of Huntly, a powerful and troublesome co-religionist— won her a degree of general acceptance which no one had expected.

Lady Antonia seems surprised at this; Catholic historians are more accustomed to explaining away the intolerance and bigotry of their heroes. But Gordon Donaldson has recently shown that the Scottish Reformation was far from being the swift, conclusive, and total event which its leader John Knox tried to pretend. Reversal was unthinkable, of course, but there was plenty of room for compromise or maneuver within an accepted Protestant framework. Moreover, the European Reformation was far from complete, and the lines between Protestant and Catholic were not yet firmly drawn. In the early 1560s the Council of Trent was still deliberating and Queen Elizabeth was invited to send representatives. Two generations later the dream entertained by Mary's son James, of reuniting Christendom by a Council under the joint chairmanship of himself and the Pope, was not quite the visionary nonsense it appears to be. With the exception of Phillip II of Spain most contemporary monarchs were willing to trim their religious sails according to political or personal expediency, and it is ironic that the true age of bigotry, when monarchs like James II and Louis XIV sanctimoniously persisted in their religious beliefs to their grave disadvantage, immediately preceded the Age of Reason.

In the sixteenth century, on the other hand, many French and German Protestant leaders were suspected, with good reason, of adopting the new religion for political ends, and the greatest of them, Henry IV, thought Paris well worth a mass, a decision unthinkable a century later. Soon after her arrival in England Mary Queen of Scots showed a disposition to flirt with Anglicanism which Lady Antonia cannot credit; but it was perfectly natural. William the Silent began life as a Roman Catholic; Elizabeth's personal beliefs are unfathomable, but almost certainly they did not coincide with the state Anglicanism she sponsored; and so on. In this context it is not strange that Mary found no difficulty in accommodating herself to her Scottish subjects, and John Knox's diatribes, though eminently quotable, are not typical of public opinion. His hatred for Mary was largely motivated by fear, which is significant in itself.

Yet Mary's effective reign ended in a bloody melodrama which not only besmirched her reputation as a woman but decisively undermined her position as a ruler. Donaldson, the leading Marian scholar, has paid tribute to her achievements in Scotland, but he is almost alone. General opinion is summed up in the words of another professor, who dismisses her as "a vain, artful, bewitching creature," ("bewitching" clearly used pejoratively), who "played at being queen as she played at nearly everything"—in other words, an oversexed, irresponsible scatterbrain, who got no worse than she deserved.

True, she was betrayed by sexual passion. But this is surprising in itself. Contrary to general belief, very few rulers have ever been seriously inconvenienced by the scandal of their private lives, let alone ruined by it. In Mary's case, no breath of scandal touched her in France, and it is extremely doubtful whether her marriage with the sickly Francis II was ever consummated. In Scotland, though she was surrounded by men of voracious appetites, their sexual lives in scandalous disorder, and though she was subject to the unwearying scrutiny of many ill-wishers, for nearly four years she remained completely unscathed.

Then came the eruption. Maddened by Elizabeth's attempts to block any negotiations for marriage except with her own cast-off lover, the Earl of Leicester (an insulting and ludicrous proposal), she hit upon young Darnley. It was a slap in the face to Elizabeth, personal as well as political, and her subsequent pregnancy secured her position further. She was carrying the undoubted heir to the throne of England as well as of Scotland; as it proved. Unfortunately she fell in love with Darnley, and as a king, or even a consort, he proved worthless. He objected to the favor enjoyed by her hunchback Italian secretary, Riccio, in terms which put another indelible slur on her reputation, and had him dragged from her dinner table one evening and brutally murdered in the next room. Her revulsion against her husband was as passionate as her previous love for him, and when a group of bloodthirsty Scots noblemen, in an orgy of violence, blew up his house and strangled him in the garden afterwards, it was in circumstances which deeply implicated her.

On the whole, historians have agreed that Mary had no direct responsibility for this tragedy of Kirk O'Fields, but contemporaries were less kind. Even Lady Antonia likens her role to that of Henry II in the assassination of Becket. Paralyzed by shock (to be kind), she made no effort to pursue the murderers, though they were well-enough known, and when she married their leader, James Hepburn, Earl of Bothwell, only a few months later there was only one conclusion to be drawn. Her general popularity in Scotland, which had been her only weapon, disappeared overnight. With the quite unaccustomed support of public opinion, a gang of nobles led by her brother Moray deposed her, replaced her by her infant son, then drove her across the Border into England, in 1568.

The new government of Scotland, led by Moray as Regent, affirmed its solemn belief in Mary's guilt, and to prove it produced the famous Casket Letters, purporting to be written by her and Bothwell. As Lady Antonia points out, contemporaries did not treat these letters with much seriousness; they were forgeries, and perhaps recognized as such at the time. The commissioners who viewed them on Elizabeth's behalf delivered no verdict. But Mary remained a prisoner in England, and the young James VI, as he grew to manhood, was schooled to regard his mother as a murderess and a whore.

> **Lady Antonia pursues the course of a sympathetic but responsible biographer. She explains what she can and deplores what she cannot.**
>
> **—J. P. Kenyon**

Lady Antonia pursues the course of a sympathetic but responsible biographer. She explains what she can and deplores what she cannot. The most bitter pill for any admirer of Mary is her marriage to this undistinguished thug, Bothwell. Lady Antonia disposes, I think, of any idea that she was pregnant by him before marriage—an idea still current in most austere circles—but this only makes the marriage less, not more, explicable. She suggests that he raped her, making marriage imperative, but surely this is not so, since the rape was never publicized (and raping the queen was a prominent though little invoked element in the law of treason). Did she like being forced? Certainly all the evidence put before us here suggests a normally frigid woman; even Darnley was unable to engage her physical passions for more than a few months, perhaps only a few weeks, which is why he feared that he had been supplanted by Riccio. During her long periods of self-denial she showed no apparent strain.

All this is speculation. Mary is one of those characters who encourages prurient speculation, and this may be why she is unloved by prudent and sober historians. Her death was tragic, and her influence upon England, France, and Scotland was negligible; she was dam to a dynasty of kings whose name is a byword for failure.

When the over-busy Dean Stanley opened her vault in Westminster Abbey in 1867 it was found that she shared her resting place with more than thirty princes and princesses of the Stuart line. Lady Antonia finds an appropriate text in the Marian motto, *In my end is my beginning.* But who were these princes and princesses? The ten children of James II, dead in infancy, eighteen children of Queen Anne dead at birth, plus Rupert of the Rhine, the most spectacular failure of them all, and two princes whose premature death had closed off whole chapters of English history; Henry, Prince of Wales, James I's eldest son, who would have displaced

Charles I if he had lived, and William, Duke of Gloucester, who stood between England and the Hanoverians, and died in 1700 at the age of eleven. Her company in death expresses the futility of Mary Stuart's life.

Edwin M. Yoder (review date 23 May 1975)

SOURCE: "James Made Even Stronger," in *National Review*, May 23, 1975, pp. 571-72.

[*In the following review, Yoder comments on Fraser's portrayal of her subject in* King James: VI of Scotland, I of England.]

Having bracketed the fascinating figure of James I in previous biographies of his mother, the Queen of Scots, and of Cromwell, the nemesis and executioner of his son, Antonia Fraser seemed destined to write about him. And this she has done [in *King James: VI of Scotland, I of England*]—but strangely. She finds James an abler king than is commonly portrayed—Trevelyan, who is typical, calls him "comic." But she has written a cameo, a sketch, which in its elegant way features the unusual and has the perverse effect of rendering James a stranger figure than he was. And he was quite strange.

James, while in some ways sympathetic, lacked qualities usually deemed essential to a prince. He was a coward, a physical wreck, and a man of unorthodox sexual predilections. At the age of 13 he fell madly in love with a male French cousin, Esmé Stuart, sent to his court as emissary of the Guise family. Years later, by now Queen Elizabeth's successor on the English throne, his unseemly mooning over the royal favorite, Buckingham, stirred the ridicule of the court. But he could always explain—he had a penchant for explanations: "Jesus Christ," he told the Privy Council one day in 1617, "did the same and therefore I cannot be blamed. Christ had his John and I have my George." Lady Antonia believes, in fact, that James's aberrations stemmed, like those of his descendant George III, from porphyria. But contemporary glimpses were not so sympathetic. According to one, written by Anthony Weldon, his tongue was too big for his mouth; his skin "as soft as taffeta sarsnet"; he never washed his hands, and he walked only with the support of others, "his fingers ever in that walk fiddling about his codpiece."

James's eldest son, the doomed Prince Henry, found him professorial. And indeed, crammed with learning from childhood, he took an eager (but often self-defeating) scholarly interest in almost everything, from the nature of kingship to tobacco and witchcraft (which he resoundingly denounced in royal pamphlets). For a king, he had a strange sense of humor. Told that the English people would like to see more of him, he blurted: "God's wounds, I will pull down my breeches and they shall also see my arse."

The circumstances of his birth (hard) and youth (harrowing) make him seem, all told, a specimen barely snatched from oblivion. Scotland was a nest of feudal intrigue when he was born there in June 1566. By the time of his baptism, his father, the doomed intriguer Lord Darnley, had vanished. And since his mother insisted on the Catholic rite, Queen-Elizabeth, though she was the royal godmother, bade her representative "lurk . . . outside the chapel . . . like a bad fairy to signify the firm protestantism of her mistress."

Scotland's extreme instability was perhaps the result of generations of child-kings and child-queens. There had been no adult successor to the Scottish throne since the fourteenth century. Mary had become queen when six days old; James himself was only 14 months of age when turbulent courtiers forced Mary's abdication in his favor. And with the high assassination rate, the kingdom ran through regents like tissue. James "grew to manhood wearing a padded doublet against the steel of assassination" and "his neurotic fears concerning his safety were the talking point of his generation." The start was not auspicious.

Yet if English monarchs were measured by the state of literature in their reigns—and under the eye of eternity perhaps there is no better measure—this curious cripple would surpass all others. Every schoolboy knows that "the most high and mighty Prince James" after succeeding Elizabeth in 1603 presided over the richest burst of genius in our literature—not only the translation of the great King James Bible, which he encouraged, but the great tragedies and later comedies of Shakespeare (*Macbeth*, Lady Antonia suggests, was a nod at James's fascination with witches, while *The Tempest* was partly a *pièce d'occasion* for the marriage of his daughter, Elizabeth). And there was the sublime prose and poetry of Dr. John Donne, James's favorite preacher, whom he made royal chaplain and then dean of St. Paul's.

Lady Antonia also tries to make the case, however, that James I was a reasonably good administrator. If so, Scotland, where order was a thin crust indeed and where contention over church governance was murderous, was no school for monarchs. It was Robert Cecil who decided that James would be king of England, although his claim was not "incontrovertible." Had the crown not fallen to him, was it in his character to fight or intrigue for it? One doubts it. Yet his theoretical views on monarchy were extreme. His advocacy of divine right was of a piece with his dogmatism on religion (at once Calvinist and Arminian, an odd combination). A king was God's anointed; and if he were a bad king? "Even a bad king, he argued, had his inalienable rights over the people, on the grounds that he had been sent by God to punish the people. . ."

Given that James, like all the Stuarts, was a free spender this was not congenial doctrine to lay before an English Parliament increasingly Puritan, self-assertive, and affected by Coke's queer notion that kings—even kings—were under common law. These political tensions, as we know, were to reach a snapping point only after James's death. But James, pedantic and doctrinaire, brought to England the fatal virus of princely prerogative that was to be his second son's undoing. Its psychological sources, in the misty realm of feudal Scotland, seem obvious: where government is strong and settled there is far less theorizing from first principles about right than where it is shaky. And in Scotland it was very shaky.

Conceivably, a larger and more leisurely portrait of James VI and I would also be a soberer one. Lady Antonia, his new-found friend, focuses not only on the warts but on all the tics, infirmities, complaints, and neuroses—her narrative constantly threatening to ignore all else for what is bizarre, arresting, diverting, and faintly scandalous. Had such a profile appeared in the press of James's day—had such a press, indeed, existed—it would qualify as yellow journalism. Since it is obvious that James I stirs the author's sympathy, she must plan to redeem him with a longer, more considered biography. Otherwise, it would be a mercy to leave James to his familiar enemies, the old Whig historians.

Roger Fulford (review date 11 August 1975)

SOURCE: "Chronicles of the Monarchy," in *Times Literary Supplement*, August 11, 1975, p. 893.

[*In the following review, Fulford outlines the contents of* The Lives of the Kings and Queens of England, *a work edited by Fraser.*]

[*The Lives of the Kings and Queens of England*] is a businesslike and readable account of our kings and queens from William I to Elizabeth II. The authors are not, as the Victorians used to say, "viewy", and they spare their readers too much of those personal stories by which kings and queens are particularly afflicted. Antonia Fraser opens with a spirited defence of royal biography which, she trenchantly argues, gives us a theory of history. Certainly no one would dispute her emphasis on the popularity of royal biography, and she even calls in aid that industrious spinster Agnes Strickland, who seems to be the first serious royal biographer to cause offence at Windsor. Her life of Queen Victoria in 1840 was fiercely annotated by the Queen.

Whether everyone would agree that the lives of our monarchs provide us with a theory of history is perhaps open to question, but they certainly give us a sensible boundary to the past within which an individual can deviate according to fancy. While it may not always have been by positive action, what our monarchs did or did not do has affected our lives for nearly a thousand years. Would cabinet government have progressed as it has if George I had the beautiful command of English enjoyed by his mother? This is borne out by John Clarke's excellent chapter on the Hanoverians, though King George's remark about hating pots and painters suggests some command of English and the capacity to express himself with unexpected originality and force.

It is certainly true that through studying the lives of our sovereigns we are able to catch some glimpse of the inner feelings of the nation. Lord Salisbury, in a public tribute to Queen Victoria, said that she had an extraordinary power of divining what the middle classes would think, and that was the moment when middle-class opinion was becoming all-powerful.

The difficulties of King Edward VIII reveal the strength of that opinion before it began to decline. Going back in history we can see that Henry II was largely absorbed by the struggles of family politics. The feelings of the English people were probably neither with Angevin or Capet but were much more concerned with the emergence of administrative government, about which public opinion probably felt far more strongly than about all the battles in the Dordogne. The experiences of James II clearly show the strength and almost morbid feelings of English people against Roman Catholicism. Maurice Ashley, in his chapter on the Stuarts, does well to remind us of the affinity with Europe which marked that unlucky dynasty—at least until the reign of its last member.

There is an especially good chapter on Edward II by Peter Earle, who says what may be said for that unhappy man, but rounds off his comment by saying that Edward II is a standing indictment of hereditary monarchy. Lord Eldon, emphasizing the prerogative of birth, observed that a king of England is always king. "King in the helplessness of infancy, king in the decrepitude of age." Though protected by regency, sovereignty belongs to primogeniture sanctioned by time and by popular opinion. Indeed we might argue that when primogeniture threw up a weakling—Edward II, Henry VI or possibly Charles I—the horrible convulsions of the time were to lead to valuable shifts of power.

The Lives of the Kings and Queens of England is well written and terse, and a particular word of gratitude and commendation is due for the illustrations and explanations of the various arms of the sovereigns supplied by J. P. Brooke-Little, the Richmond Herald of Arms.

P. D. James (review date 27 May 1977)

SOURCE: "Nunnery Whodunnery," in *Times Literary Supplement,* May 27, 1977, p. 644.

[*In the following review of* Quiet as a Nun, *James comments on Fraser's handling of the elements of crime fiction.*]

Antonia Fraser is the latest recruit to the ranks of established writers who have turned their hands to crime fiction. "And when are you going to write a serious work?" crime novelists are always being asked; it would be nice to think that the question may now be reversed. Lady Antonia has chosen to describe *Quiet as a Nun,* a judicious mixture of puzzle, excitement and terror, as a thriller, and the setting has, indeed, all the Gothic horrors reminiscent of much earlier excursions in the genre: Catherine Morland would have relished it.

> **Lady Antonia's detective, Jemima Shore, is, as her name suggests, a contemporary heroine, a successful television investigator, liberated, prosperous, unencumbered with husband or child, and with all the fashionable accoutrements of success including a married lover.**
>
> **—*P. D. James***

"And is it horrid, are you sure that it is horrid?" Yes, indeed, very satisfyingly horrid, but with a modern heroine well equipped to cope, with its perils, rational if not spiritual, both above and under ground. Every detective writer knows the advantage of a closed community for the convenient containment of victim, villain and suspects—and what more closed than a convent? Lady Antonia is not the first crime writer to make use of it as a setting—Gladys Mitchell, in particular, has done so twice with conspicuous success—but she moves with confidence in what to most of us is an alien and vaguely disquieting world. Her nuns may all look like black crows, but their characters are nicely differentiated: the formidable Mother Ancilla who apparently believes that God is chiefly preoccupied with preserving the lineage of ancient Catholic families; Sister Elizabeth who thanks Our Blessed Lord on her knees for making Wordsworth write *The Prelude* at such length.

Lady Antonia's detective, Jemima Shore, is, as her name suggests, a contemporary heroine, a successful television investigator, liberated, prosperous, unencumbered with husband or child, and with all the fashionable accoutrements of success including a married lover. It is when his activities as an MP cause the postponement of the holiday they had planned to take together that she decides to respond to a call

for help from Mother Ancilla Curtis, Superior of Blessed Eleanor's Convent in Sussex where Jemima was a pupil during the war. One of the nuns, Sister Miriam, has been found dead in a tower on the edge of the convent grounds. The coroner has been critical; the country folk are suspicious; antipopery is raising its head. Sister Miriam (then the very rich Rosabelle Powerstock) was at school with Jemima and thought of her as a friend. But Mother Ancilla has a particular reason, apart from this briefly shared girlhood, for calling in Jemima, vaguely Protestant unbeliever though she is. And as her investigation into Sister Miriam's death proceeds, Jemima realizes that the old convent world of her schooldays and the new brash world of Megalith Television are dangerously linked.

The crime writer with a nonprofessional investigator must circumvent that awkward moment when the reader is liable to ask why the police were not called in. There was one such moment in *Quiet as a Nun*—but I may be partisanly overoptimistic about the ability of the Sussex Constabulary to stand up to Mother Ancilla. *Quiet as a Nun* is written with humour and sympathy and has a heroine of whom happily it is promised that we shall know more.

Mel Gussow (essay date 9 September 1984)

SOURCE: "Antonia Fraser: The Lady as a Writer," in *New York Times Magazine,* September 9, 1984, pp. 60-62, 75-78.

[*The following essay provides a portrait of Fraser's personal life as background to her work.*]

Antonia Fraser lives on a quiet, tree-shaded square in the Kensington section of London in a large, airy house that she shares with her second husband, the playwright Harold Pinter. With them live the four youngest of her six children by her first marriage, to the late Sir Hugh Fraser. Sitting in her garden on a recent afternoon, Lady Antonia looked softly feminine, a portrait of gentility. A large white picture hat shielded her face from the sun. A wasp buzzed her ear, and she seemed unperturbed. "I prefer to believe that nature's on my side," she said, "but Harold gets worried," and she indicated, high overhead, his response to nature's sting—an electric bug catcher.

Lady Antonia is a serious gardener, growing amaryllis from bulbs and bringing them indoors in winter. Her fig tree was soon to be joined by an olive tree, a gift from her husband for her coming 52d birthday. But Lady Antonia at home—as wife, mother and gardener—represents only one aspect of a woman who seems to lead a dozen lives. She is a best-selling historian and biographer, as the author of *Mary*

Queen of Scots, Cromwell, Royal Charles and her 14th book, *The Weaker Vessel,* published in America this month, a pioneering study of the suppression of women in 17th-century England. In recent years she has also become a writer of popular mystery novels (the Jemima Shore series, beginning with *Quiet as a Nun*), which have been adapted to television. In England, her television and radio appearances have added to her celebrity.

> **Because she synthesizes beauty, intelligence and artistic talent, she is a kind of heroine to other women, provoking simultaneous feelings of admiration and envy. As one friend says, "She's a formidable woman. She has a rather regal quality. Sometimes I think she's really the Queen, and the present Queen is the usurper. London would be a very much duller place without her."**
> —*Mel Gussow*

Because she synthesizes beauty, intelligence and artistic talent, she is a kind of heroine to other women, provoking simultaneous feelings of admiration and envy. As one friend says, "She's a formidable woman. She has a rather regal quality. Sometimes I think she's really the Queen, and the present Queen is the usurper. London would be a very much duller place without her."

One might say that Lady Antonia is not so much prolific as generative—in her personal as well as in her professional life. She is devoted to her family and to her friends, and they return the devotion. As Lady Antonia suggests, were she to throw a stone from her garden she might strike any of three brothers, two sisters and several friends of 30 years' standing, all of whom live in the neighborhood.

Of course, she is not about to throw stones, even at those academics who criticize her books as popularizations. One London book critic says that she has a genuinely ambiguous literary reputation. Her work receives respectful reviews—for her impressive research and readability. Her primary strength is her sense of narrative. At the same time some professional historians consider her approach a storybook view of history. She is at her best when dealing with subjects with which she has the greatest personal commitment, such as in *Mary Queen of Scots* and her current *The Weaker Vessel.*

Though she is not a theoretician with opinions about the changing tides of world economics and politics—and does not pretend to be—she is zealous about her need to know as much as can be known about her chosen area and ada-

mant about accuracy. "If I write that it was a cold day," she says, "you can be sure I know it was a cold day because Pepys told us." In America, reviewers have been more willing to meet her on her own terms, as a writer, she says, of "historical reconstruction."

Lady Antonia may be, at the moment, the most famous member of her family, popularly known in England as the "literary Longfords." In the Longford tradition, writing comes as naturally as good manners. The Longfords and their relatives have written more books and filled more shelves than the Churchills and the Mitfords combined—and there is no cessation in productivity. Lady Antonia's mother, Elizabeth Longford, 78, has written more than a dozen books, including *Victoria: Born to Succeed,* as well as biographies of Wellington, Byron and Queen Elizabeth II. Her father, Lord Longford, also 78 (Frank Pakenham before he received his hereditary title), has written some 15 volumes, including several memoirs. Her sister Rachel Billington has written eight novels, and another sister, Judith Kazantzis, is a feminist poet. Thomas Pakenham, the eldest Longford son, is an historian. When asked how many books he has written, he answers sheepishly, "Only three," although one is his massive study, The Boer War. Keeping the family torch aloft are Lady Antonia's eldest daughters: Rebecca Fraser is writing about the Brontes, and Flora Powell-Jones, who has already published a romance novel, is writing about Lady Hamilton.

Visit the reading room in the British Museum and one is almost guaranteed to find a Longford or a Fraser working diligently on research, or both a mother and a daughter, in some combination. As Rachel Billington says, "My mother and Antonia look so happy when they go off to the library."

Looking at the family tree, one finds other literary branches. Anthony Powell, the esteemed English novelist, is married to Lady Antonia's aunt Violet, and another artistic presence was Lord Dunsany, Lady Antonia's great-uncle, famous as an Irish playwright and man of letters. In this enormous family there are also successful barristers, bankers and foreign-service officers, and it was in politics that they made their first impression on their countrymen. But it is literature that is the family's primary mark of distinction, and it is largely literature produced by women.

Though each has roamed freely in choice of subjects, a chief concern of Lady Antonia and her mother has been with heroines. In Lady Antonia's case, "heroine" is an especially appropriate word, not only to describe Mary Queen of Scots, but also the untitled, un-dowried sisters of the 17th century, who were forced to make their way as courtesans, midwives, warriors in men's clothing and actresses. These stalwart characters throng the pages of *The Weaker Vessel,* underscoring the intended irony of the title. Among the legion is Betty Mordaunt, who saved the life of her husband when he was condemned to death for conspiring against Oliver Cromwell. She did it by seducing the man who had the power to pardon her husband. For her selfless deed, she was remembered on her husband's tombstone as "lectissima Heroina," or "most excellent heroine." Lady Antonia savored the compliment and used it in her dedication to describe her mother, "lectissima Heroina Elizabeth Longford."

It is her mother who has been Lady Antonia's principal inspiration—as mentor in her childhood, as role model in her apprenticeship and as colleague and critic in her maturity. From the vantage point of a third generation, Rebecca Fraser says her mother and grandmother have "wills of iron," which they use "in harmony." Each continues as the other's first and most painstaking reader.

In the 1940's, when the Pakenham children were growing up, the family was upper-middle class and academic. As Frank Pakenham, Antonia's father was an Oxford don. It was not until 1960, when his older brother died, that Pakenham became the Earl of Longford, his wife became a Countess and his daughters, Ladies. The family lived in a large house that seemed to shrink as more children were, born. First came Antonia on Aug. 27, 1932, followed within a year by her brother Thomas, and then by three other brothers and three sisters.

In common with her husband, Lady Longford was educated at Oxford. As Anthony Powell wrote in his memoirs, she "had been a celebrated belle of the undergraduate generation following my own." Despite her incipient literary talent, she put aside art and devoted herself to bringing up her family. Among other things, she read to "groups" of her children, beginning with the two oldest. Antonia was an early, quick reader and was soon sneaking downstairs to finish a book by Dickens or Sir Walter Scott (still her favorites) that her mother had begun. To this day, she remains a speed reader, finishing a novel in an afternoon and astounding strangers on planes or trains who cannot believe that such swift page turning actually constitutes reading.

The importance of education was instilled in the children: As a young girl, Antonia was already fascinated by history, creating genealogical charts, including one that began with Mary Queen of Scots and ended, naturally, with Antonia Pakenham. "All the children turned out clever," says Lady Longford, "but Antonia was the most precocious of them all." Looking back, Lady Longford suggests that her children picked up writing "as a kind of virus." In trying to explain the family's collective literary impulse, the "hothouse" atmosphere of his youth, Thomas Pakenham wrote: "We are talkers disguised as writers. Ten talkers in one family and no listeners; it was inevitable that half at best—the weaker half, perhaps—should be driven to take refuge in authorship in order to try to find an audience."

Next door to the family house in Oxford was a boy's school, ominously named the Dragon School, which admitted a limited number of girls, all siblings of enrolled boys. Both Antonia and Thomas attended. From this mostly male environment, she went to the cloistered all-female world of a convent school, St. Mary's, Ascot, many years later the setting of her first Jemima Shore mystery. Just as she was a minority at the boy's school, here she was a Protestant among Catholics. While at St. Mary's, following her parents' lead, she' converted to Catholicism.

Here it must be noted that Antonia's father underwent two significant conversions, both of which had dramatic effects on his family. A Conservative, he switched to socialism and joined the Labor Party. He ran unsuccessfully for the House of Commons, as did his wife, twice. Later he occupied several high positions in the cabinet of Prime Minister Harold Wilson. Born a Protestant, he converted to Catholicism. The combination of socialism and Catholicism made him a kind of born again crusader, leading him to take public positions against pornography (he became known as "Lord Porn") and for prison reform, his major concern in recent years. He has led a campaign to improve the lot of such condemned killers as the infamous Moors murderers. He is a minister without portfolio to, in his words, "the outcasts" in his society. His daughter thinks of him as "a philanthropist." Were a pornographer also a murderer, undoubtedly he would strike up a correspondence and visit him in prison.

During World War II, with, as Thomas Pakenham recalls, their "Old Mother Hubbard house bursting with children," he and his sister were packed off on holidays to visit their legendary great-uncle Lord Dunsany in Ireland. "It was in all respects a memorable experience," says Thomas Pakenham. "He lived in a medieval castle, filled with trophies—lions, tigers and bison. He was like a Renaissance prince, a big game hunter buffoon, eccentric, playwright and poet. He had a long white beard and wrote with a quill pen. Every day he would read us a new poem. There he was with a rifle in one hand and a quill pen in the other. Suddenly he would say, 'Throw up that window.' Rather frightened, you would lift the sash, and, bang, he'd fire a bullet straight under one's arm and shoot a rabbit out in the park. He was an extraordinary person; it was like staying with Yeats. If you wanted to infect somebody with the idea of writing as a dramatic theatrical profession, there was the man."

Antonia was very much the big sister, larger physically than her brother, and, when she had a mind to, able to dominate a situation. "When I was 14," she says, "I decided I was going to do whatever I wanted to do, whatever that happened to be."

Family tradition led her to Oxford, followed by her brother, and she was swept up by popularity. As V.S. Naipaul, a classmate at Oxford and later a good friend, observed, if he were "submerged" at Oxford, Antonia was "emerged." Too late she made a run for a "first" or honors and missed.

Her sister Rachel, then 10, remembers her at 20 in London as "a beautiful goddess figure, very glamorous and existing outside of the family. I would be allowed to dress her, to try on her earrings. She was a wonderful creature who went out and brought back dashing boyfriends."

Lady Antonia started work at George Weldenfeld's publishing house as an all-purpose assistant. Her first assignment was to extract the expletives from Saul Bellow's *The Adventures of Augie March,* censored for British publication. Lord Weidenfeld, a family friend, soon became not only her employer but also her publisher (beginning with children's books and histories of toys and dolls). He still is, and he performs the same role for Lady Longford. With her children grown or growing up, Lady Longford, in her 50's, shifted her attention from her family to the Royal Family and wrote her biography of Queen Victoria, which solidly established her reputation.

At 23, Lady Antonia married Sir Hugh Fraser. He was 15 years older, a handsome and charming Scottish nobleman, a war hero along with his famous brother, Lord Lovat. As her mother had done before her, she subordinated her own creative instincts and became a wife and mother, while also taking time to campaign for her husband for Parliament. The family lived in London and spent summers at the Fraser retreat on an island in Inverness-shire in Scotland, later used as a setting in Lady Antonia's mystery, *The Wild Island.*

When it was suggested to Lady Longford that she write a book about Mary Queen of Scots, Lady Antonia claimed the queen as her subject. After all, she had studied and admired her since she was a young girl. With her siblings as her court, Antonia had acted out scenes from Mary's life and death— and in emulation of her had even worn a heart-shape tiara on her own wedding day. With the fifth of her six children on the way, Lady Antonia walked into her study and began working. As she says, "I can remember literally rocking a pram as I wrote." *Mary Queen of Scots* won the James Tait Black Prize for Biography and was a major best seller.

Says her mother about *Mary:* "It had one of the best beginnings of any biography. I always remember Mary's birth on a savage night, and Antonia's choice of that adjective." Lady Longford moved on to the Duke of Wellington, and between them mother and daughter split up English history, Lady Antonia assuming rights to the 17th century, Lady Longford choosing the 19th. When their books on Mary and Wellington came out, as Lady Antonia remembers, "we were constantly bracketed as an amazing phenomenon." "I asked her—I don't know why—what meant more to her, her own

success or mine? She said, Darling, *nothing* I've ever done has given me more pleasure than your success with *Mary Queen of Scots.* I believed her: she's very, very truthful. I was rather surprised, but I must say when my own children had grown up, and when they had successes, I felt the same way."

In bringing up her children, she followed her mother's prescription, offering guidance along with encouragement. On her own, she had kept a diary since childhood and suggested that her children do the same, especially on vacations. The inducement was "heavy cash prizes." She paid, she said, a pound a page (her children remember a smaller sum, a pound a diary), and she would read and grade the results as if they were term papers. Eventually, diaries became habitual. When her daughter Flora went to Venice on her honeymoon, she told her husband that she had to keep her diary. Amazed, he informed her, "You don't *have* to now. You're married!"

While achieving international celebrity for her books, Lady Antonia continued to play a supportive role in her husband's life. In their house in London, she became known as a gracious hostess, giving elegant dinner parties for politicians, writers and others of their circle. Naipaul remembers most of all her "generosity." He once told her that, as a guest he liked to feel "cherished," which he did at her house. In response, Lady Antonia wrote an article entitled **"Cherishing the Guest."** As he said recently, "I'm devoted to Antonia and to those years."

At some point (approaching 40?), Antonia Fraser began making drastic changes in her life. Her romances became the staple of gossip columns. Nine years ago, while still married to Sir Hugh, she began living with Harold Pinter, whose own equally long marriage to the actress Vivien Merchant was ending. The romance between the Lady and the playwright brought the paparazzi and the moralists out of the woodwork. Lady Antonia said, "When I left my first husband and went off with Harold, people said, 'How could you do such a thing?' and I said, 'I've done it!'" She has steadfastly refused to offer further comment on the breakup of her marriage. Trying to explain it, one friend says that both Sir Hugh and Harold Pinter were the right people for her at the right—but different—time, and that it was Pinter who was insistent about making it a permanent relationship.

When the Pinters were married in a civil ceremony in 1980, the registrar had to record the profession of each party on the marriage form. Pinter, of course, was listed as a playwright, but in the space for his wife's profession, the word "lady" was accidentally entered. She was dismayed, and the registrar responded by placing a comma after "lady" and inserting the word "writer." In her marriage certificate, Antonia Fraser is therefore immortalized as "lady writer," which one could consider as a progressive and apt description.

The marriage is an amalgam of opposites. Lady Antonia herself characterizes the couple as Jack Sprat and his wife, a comparison that has a validity in creative as well as personal terms. She is a warm, giving person. In her elegant Jean Muir clothes, she radiates femininity and has a kind of intuitive glamour. Her expansiveness is reflected in her books, which are abundant with flavorful detail. In contrast, Pinter is reserved, some would say, cool, an intensely private individual who can seem intimidating. In conversation he can be terse to the point of curtness, and his plays mirror his manner, distilling life to essences, separated by Pinter pauses. At the same time, he can be quite outgoing with friends and genuinely amusing.

When she is asked what makes her angry, Lady Antonia says, "All forms of racism." What about small things, such as burnt toast? She laughs. "That's the carve-up of our marriage. Harold has the burnt-toast slot."

You have world prejudice, he has burnt toast?

"Not quite," she corrects herself. "He has burnt toast and world prejudice. When we first lived together, Harold was accustomed to starting the day very silently, and I was accustomed to starting the day with the newspaper sorting out Zimbabwe. Over nine years, he's become very concerned about Zimbabwe, so it's surprising the country is not in better shape."

One key to the apparent richness of their relationship is that they allow each other breathing space. They each have a study (his is in a mews house adjoining their garden) a secretary, a telephone and a car. Each respects the other's time and work. When she said about Naipaul, "To have known him is to have known at least one genius," I asked her if she knew any other geniuses. She responded, "I married the second." There is a great closeness about the couple and about the entire extended family. This summer the combined Pinter-Fraser-Longford clan went on holiday together to Portugal—Lady Antonia, Pinter, two daughters (one with a husband, one with a friend) one son (with two friends) and Lady Longford.

Lady Antonia has many friends of longstanding, including some, such as the novelist Emma Tennant, the designer Diana Phipps and the foundation director Marigold Johnson, who go back with her several decades. Many of her current friends, however, came with the marriage. There is a definite theatrical cast to the Pinter-Fraser circle, including at least three playwrights, Simon Gray, Ronald Harwood and Tom Stoppard, all of whom are members of Pinter's cricket team, which meets for an annual all-day match.

Whenever the Pinters are in Paris, they see Samuel Beckett. Lady Antonia recalled the most recent meeting: "Harold was

talking about nuclear disarmament, about which he feels very strongly. He stopped and said, 'Sam, I'm sorry to sound so gloomy.' Sam said, 'My dear Harold, you couldn't be gloomier than I am. I thought this was the most wonderful bit of dialogue between Pinter and Beckett. It's exactly what people think they say to each other."

While continuing to write histories, Lady Antonia created a diversion for herself by writing mysteries. For her protagonist she invented the character of Jemima Shore, a television investigative reporter, who becomes involved in solving crimes. For the author, as for her readers, the free-spirited Jemima is a kind of fantasy figure.

The Jemima Shore books gave birth to a television series and what her creator calls a "cultette" of enthusiasts. The fifth Jemima Shore will take her to Lady Antonia's childhood home, Oxford. Among her many activities, the author is now vice chairman of both the Crime Writers Association and the British PEN. Analyzing her reasons for taking up the mystery sideline, she says, "It would be very strange if I said it had nothing to do with my going to live with Harold. If you have a great change in your life at the age of 42, it's not surprising that a new form emerges."

She writes her books in her small, neat study upstairs in their home—the former Fraser family house. The room is lined with books, including a complete collection about Mary Queen of Scots. Mary is on the wall, along with Cromwell and Charles II. In a bookcase next to her desk are notebooks cataloging her histories. They are uniform clothbound volumes, the kind of dainty diarylike journals that might have been kept by an Edwardian lady. The volumes are densely packed with notes quotes and cross-references. In the room there is also a Jemima Shore file. She types her histories on an electric portable but writes her mysteries in longhand; the bulk of the history work is done at home, but mysteries are often written in hotel rooms and on vacation. "When I'm writing history," she says, "I've got to be in my shell." Wearing her dressing gown, she writes from 9 to 12:30 and then dresses for lunch. In contrast, her husband writes very late at night.

Twelve years ago, when she was researching *Cromwell,* she came across stories about women of the 17th century. In preparation for writing *The Weaker Vessel,* she read every diary and autobiography by women of the period, which, she says were not abundant. When she finished the book, it was read by her husband, her mother and Emma Tennant, among others.

As Miss Tennant remembers: "I have to admit to a sinking heart when she arrived with three and a half carrier bags of manuscript. I thought, a friend's a friend, but oh Christ. My books are very short. She finishes reading them in 10 minutes. It's like the tortoise and the hare. But I could not put her book down. I thought it was absolutely brilliant. It had such a strong feeling of what this alien, distant culture was like."

In common with her mother, Lady Antonia loves reading long books as well as writing them. After talking to Lady Longford, I noticed on the coffee table a copy of *The Perspective of the World,* the third volume of *Civilization and Capitalism, 15th-16th Century,* by the eminent French historian Fernand Braudel a mighty tome if there ever was one. I remarked that her daughter was reading the same tome and had told me how difficult (and stimulating) it was "Has she gotten as far as I have?" asked Lady Longford inquisitively and with a fair sense of competition. Then she explained that she was reading the history in order to review it. In contrast, her daughter was reading it for pleasure.

Recently, Lady Antonia taped a television show in which celebrities select "My Favorite Things." Her choices—being in a box for the opera at Covent Garden; working in her garden; visiting a favorite hotel, such as the Carlyle in New York or the Grand Hotel in Eastbourne in England, and looking through her photograph albums. The director of the show concluded, about her, choices that she was "always trying to have a series of little homes."

One afternoon over tea, we shared a favorite thing. She took down a few of her several dozen albums and we browsed through them. They were filled with photographs, newspaper clippings and mentos, with occasional comments in the margin. Under a picture of her 50th birthday celebration there was a caption that read, "The prime of life."

In an album from her youth, we saw Pakenhams galore. Almost every photograph seemed crowded with smiling people. Are all happy family photographs alike? She admitted that the pictures were somewhat misleading. There were, for example, pictures of her youngest sister, Catherine, but no mention that she had been killed in an automobile accident in 1969 at the age of 23. That death is a lingering family tragedy, and every year on the anniversary, Lady Antonia ritualistically calls her mother.

One day we had lunch at her favorite restaurant, a festive French bistro. At one point I left the table and suggested that she might want to say something privately into the tape recorder. In my absence, she said into the recorder, "I never wrote a word of my own books. I'll tell you who wrote them." Pause, and then the repeated words, "It was. . . It was. . . It was. . . It was. . ." The playful message was a variation on the scene from the movie of Graham Greene's *Brighton Rock,* in which the hero leaves a message denying his love. But the record is cracked, and what she hears is,

"You think I'm going to say I love you, I love you, I love you."

Lady Antonia's cleverness was further in evidence that evening at a taping of "My Word," a BBC radio show that has had a life almost as long as the play *The Mousetrap.* For six years, Lady Antonia has been a regular panelist on this lexiconic equivalent of America's "Information Please," with four pundits taking turns and winning points by defining obscure words and tracing quotations to their source. Lady Antonia fielded her questions with philological finesse. Her first word was "nugatory." Without a pause, she said, "'My Word' is not nugatory," and the moderator immediately gave her full marks. Nugatory, she explained, means worthless. She was just as speedy with "stithy" and "baker's dozen," and carefully culled Keats from Shelley and Shakespeare from Marlowe.

After the broadcast, we all met backstage for a drink, and Pinter arrived to escort his Lady to dinner. She had informed me that he was composing a brief statement about her and suggested that I telephone him the next day.

When I called, he said, "She's terrific." Pause. I said, "That's it?" Even for him, the comment was cryptic. "She's terrific in every way," he elaborated and added, with finality, "I'm very happy where I am without having to tell the world."

With his natural expansiveness, Tom Stoppard had more to say. He described the scene at their annual cricket day. As usual, Pinter invited his team and wives and children to their house for lunch before the match. During the match, there were few spectators, and fewer still as the day lengthened. By the end, Stoppard said, "Antonia was the only faithful supporter left and served a conciliatory drink to those who did not score. She has a loyalty about Harold's weekend interest." And, he said, "They're a super couple." He added, "She's a person without malice."

As Emma Tennant says: "The point of Antonia is that she has always enjoyed herself without neglecting any duty as a child or parent. She's incapable of taking offense—the least touchy person I know. This has enabled her to give out this very constant affection to all the people she's fond of, and particularly the children. She was somebody who refused to be miserable at a time when a Jean Rhys atmosphere was building up among women, when practically everybody felt they had something to complain about. When she's angry, she rises above it and passes on to something more constructive. Her family is so important to her. She's sort of like an African woman with her neck hung around by huge pots and pans—buried up to here with all her attachments and devotions."

The portrait that one receives from talking to Lady Antonia, her family and friends is of a person totally in command of herself. She appears to have it all, doing exactly what she wants and exuding contentment without ever suggesting complacency. Naturally one starts to look for chinks in the armor. One friend mentions that she is absolutely unable to cook. Another comments on her "frou-frou" taste in decorating—minor issues. There is of course, the major matter of her romantic life—leaving a husband of 20 years, the father of their six children.

One story can serve as an illustration of how this remarkable woman manages the balancing act of her full life. Before she and Pinter were married, they went off to Paris together for a holiday. They were in their room at l'Hôtel when they heard a voice in the courtyard below, shouting, "Hello, Mummy." Emma Tennant analyzes the incident, "It's sort of the opposite of the scarlet woman who's gone off with her lover and her children don't know where she is. She's given her address to every one of them." Pinter says it is the story of her life—there is always someone shouting "Hello, Mummy."

Naturally her life is not without emotional scars. She suffers from migraines and knows that they are stress-related. A "small one" she can think away—mind over migraine—as long as no one "asks after it," but a major headache fills her with pain and sends her into depression. Such was the case last February when her first husband was dying of cancer. She visited him frequently in the hospital, visits, she said, that "were punctuated by migraines."

She said, however, that she never gets a migraine when she is working. "Work is the opposite of stress. When I'm depressed, it cheers me up. I consider my work the greatest piece of good fortune," she said. "When Jemima Shore gets blocked, I can do historical research, and it always unblocks me." Asked if she considered herself a positive person, she said, "I think I'm quite pleasure-loving. Someone once asked Elizabeth Taylor, a person who interests me, how she stayed so lovely, and she said, 'I take a sensual pleasure in eating and drinking,' and I thought, 'That's my girl. How sensible.'"

> In several senses, *The Weaker Vessel* is a breakthrough for her. It is her first collective biography, the first time she has dealt foursquare with feminist issues and the first time that she has felt a kind of missionary zeal.
> —*Mel Gussow*

At one point in her new book she lists what were considered to be the feminine virtues—fidelity, modesty, meekness, patience and humility. I wondered how she would measure up in her own eyes. "Not too well." she said. "Well, maybe I would give myself a point for patience. I think all writers are a bit arrogant and should be. They must think that no one else can do it as they do. I would have thought that modesty was more of a danger." Then, relating her feeling to that of the 17th century, she said that there was "a gap between what was expected of a woman and what she actually was." The most admirable women were not "modest, meek and humble."

She agreed that she would have had a difficult time if she lived in that century. "And that bit of me that is strongly nonconformist—I'm going to do what I'm going to do—would have assured that I would have done very badly. The people who did well intuitively understood the system and made their way around it. Hence, they were courtesans. I don't think I would have had the patience to be a courtesan, though I might have enjoyed my work." About her favorite century, she said, "This is not the fashionable view, but I think the 17th is the century. It has our revolution in it. In 1688 our course was set. I found the people, particularly the women, easier to relate to than the more languid ladies of the 18th and 19th centuries. I love the 17th, but I don't want to be in it. I like to come home at the end of the day in my time capsule."

In several senses, *The Weaker Vessel* is a breakthrough for her. It is her first collective biography, the first time she has dealt foursquare with feminist issues and the first time that she has felt a kind of missionary zeal. She pointed to two chapters, one about childbirth, the other about midwives, as being essential parts of the book. "The suffering in childbirth!" she said. "What would strike a time traveler is that everyone between 15 and 50 would be permanently pregnant. There was no birth control as we understand it, and there was such high infant mortality. Women would regularly have 19 pregnancies and end up with four or five children."

When it was pointed out that she was herself the mother of six and the sister of seven, she said "Women's expectations have risen. I'm sure it won't go on in the next generation." Her motherhood, she said, gave her a "built-in interest in gynecology," and she read a great number of books on the subject and then wrote about it in graphic detail. "When I read my first draft, there was a small part that was perhaps a bit strong. My secretary, a married woman with two children, said when she typed it she nearly fainted. I said, 'Nonsense.' Then Harold read it and gasped. I thought, 'Really' Then my mother said, 'I must say, I cried a bit.' And she had eight children! So I toned it down. You may think of it as rather mealy-mouthed."

The book dutifully holds to its century, but in an epilogue she plants a message, quietly and forcefully, as if it were an amaryllis in her garden. After talking about the rise and dip of the "status of the so-called weaker vessel," she places a parenthesis and inside these words appear:

> This cyclical pattern, whatever the special favors which brought it about in the 17th century, is perhaps worth bearing in mind, as with all forms of liberation, of which the liberation of women is only one example, it is easy to suppose in a time of freedom that the darker days of repression can never come again.

Antonia Fraser, lady, writer, remains on her guard.

Maureen Quilligan (review date 22 September 1984)

SOURCE: "Women at Large," *The Nation,* Volume 239, No. 8, September 22, 1984, pp. 244-46.

[*In the following review, Quilligan contemplates the ideas on women and society that arise from Fraser's* Weaker Vessel.]

The Weaker Vessel, Lady Antonia Fraser's study of women in seventeenth-century England, opens with a personal anecdote. Fraser described the topic of her new book to a distinguished (male) friend; before vanishing into his club, he turned and asked, *"Were there any women in seventeenth-century England?" The Weaker Vessel* is her attempt "in part at least" to answer that question. The answer, more than 500 pages long, is armed with a host of anecdotes as telling as the one about the jesting clubman. As any modern historian might have told the fellow, it requires a significant degree of perversity to persist in thinking that history has been a masculine enterprise. Obviously there were women in seventeenth-century England. The question for us, heirs and heiresses of that pivotal moment in early modern England, is: What kinds, and what were they doing?

Fraser's unofficial subtitle gives us a preview of her findings and approach: "Women in 17th-century England—heiresses and dairymaids, holy women and prostitutes, criminals and educators, widows and witches, midwives and mothers, heroines, courtesans, prophetesses, businesswomen, ladies of the court, and that new breed, the actress." That generous list illustrates the book's virtue—its teeming fullness and diversity—and its vice, if such profligacy can be termed a vice—its crowded particularity. Reading *The Weaker Vessel* is rather like looking at Brueghel's "Children's Games," where each inch of canvas is crammed with life: some groups

of figures salacious, some edifying, some enigmatic. Insofar as Fraser gives this picture a unifying theme, it is the powerful impediment posed by the definition of woman as "the weaker vessel." Supported by theological, social, legal and political edicts and backed up by the nearly perpetual pregnancy that seventeenth-century women endured (with fifteen to twenty a not unusual number), this definition shaped a woman's life.

The most obvious counter to this description of seventeenth-century women can be found in the behavior of a great many women during England's civil war, nine years of martial mayhem that preoccupied and disrupted much of the population during the middle years of the century. Fraser tells us that she was first attracted to her topic by the numerous stories she encountered of valiant women who fought in that war. They are the "heroines" of Fraser's subtitle, and include such notable viragos as Mary Lady Bankes, intransigent defender of (royalist) Corfe Castle, who during a siege took command of the castle's upper ward and, aided by her daughters, her women servants and five soldiers, defeated the enemy by heaving stones and hot embers over the walls onto their scaling ladders. By way of contrast, Fraser recounts the tactics of a more "modest" heroine, Brilliana Lady Harley, whose defense of Brampton Bryan Castle relied on manipulations of the attacking (royalist) army's chivalrous reluctance to assault a "weaker vessel." The castle surrendered only after Lady Harley had died and its defenders could no longer rely on the protection due her "sex and honour."

These generally highborn Boadiceas provide the most predictable stories Fraser tells. Far more compelling are the anecdotes that reveal the extensive range of female activity in less traumatic, if no less political, contexts during the revolutionary century between the death of Queen Elizabeth and the accession of Queen Anne. We meet, for example, Mrs. Constance Pley, an indefatigable and successful businesswoman who ran her family's marine supply company, boldly dunning her King for payments constantly in arrears. We meet Cromwell's eccentric granddaughter, Bridget Bendish, at work all day beside male laborers in the salt mines she inherited from her husband and, in the evenings, a brilliant presence splendidly dressed for social occasions. We meet Joan Dant, who began as a penniless widow and died at the age of 84 worth more than £9,000, with business connections in Paris and Brussels.

Fraser's guess as to why seventeenth-century women were permitted to engage in business activities when female authorship, for instance, was a serious social transgression is an example of the acute commentary that accompanies her stories: "After all, business practice in a woman could be seen as an extension of her role as the mainstay of her household, whereas learning and authorship were dangerously unfeminine pursuits." (Just now, when the politics surrounding

Geraldine Ferraro have made domestic expertise in its largest sense a qualification for high office, such reasoning seems quite apt.) Fraser is always aware of how the grid that overlay women's opportunities decreed the form of whatever achievements were made. But she does not pause to suggest that the businesswoman may also have been an acceptable and honored figure because no one realized (or would admit) that business was in great part what the civil war had been about: the revolution and the subsequent Restoration had an economic impact as profound as, and more pervasive than, the political and theological upheavals. As for the prejudice against women authors, I suggest that it descended from Renaissance Humanism, which made knowledge of the classical languages, especially Latin, a prerequisite for membership in the ruling elite. It was worth censuring female authorship because it seemed close to laying claim to such membership, just as it was worth omitting classical training from female education (a lack Fraser passionately laments). Very much later, when literature had dwindled into social ornament, divorced from the real business of society—business itself—petticoat authors were allowed more freedom, and petticoat entrepreneurs far less.

This is not to suggest that all radical developments in the seventeenth century were unconscious—although a midcentury confusion over what privileges property ownership conferred allowed a temporary accident of local female suffrage, a freedom soon squelched. In the personal history of Elizabeth Lilburne, wife to the famous Leveller John Lilburne, Fraser analyzes the transformation of the "petitioning women" of the 1640s—women who claimed for themselves a "proportionate share in the freedom of this Commonwealth"—into the "despairing—but still soliciting—wife of the 1650s."

One of the most absorbing sets of stories Fraser tells concerns women from the independent religious sects that arose during the period Christopher Hill described as the moment "the world turned upside down." While these women did not float to the top on the breath of sacred inspiration, they could make political claims for themselves that had not been possible before, and Fraser traces the effects of religious experimentation on their lives.

The extraordinary travels and travails of some Quaker women, preaching both in England and New England, do indeed "compel one's awe." One Elizabeth Hooton, although she had petitioned and won from King Charles a certificate empowering her to settle in New England, was hounded wherever she went. She was tied to a Cambridge, Massachusetts, whipping post and "lashed ten times with a three-stringed whip, three knots in each string." Subsequently, "at Watertown, willow-rods were used; at Dedham . . . she received ten lashes at the cart-tail." Beaten and torn, she refused to give up, persisting in her ministry for five years in

Massachusetts before returning to England. Mary Fisher went even further: having suffered her share of flogging in New England, she was later received hospitably by the Sultan and Vizier of Turkey: "There was a certain irony in the fact that the low position of women in the Moslem world enabled the Turks . . . to appreciate . . . how remarkable an individual Mary Fisher must be."

Fraser traces a general arc of opportunity for English women that rises to its high point with "The Petition of Women" (for government reforms and the release of imprisoned Levellers) in 1649 and moves toward its nadir as the century draws to a close and the monarchy returns. It is regrettable that there is no considered discussion here of the impact of the Restoration on women's position. Doubtless Fraser's attention to such analysis was diverted by her interest in an intriguing creation of the Restoration: the actress, spectacular star of the new and wittily decadent stage. No women had, of course, played on English stages before Charles II brought back with him a continental taste for seeing pretty women perform—and a concomitant taste for pretty women as mistresses. One of the intriguing bits of information Fraser lavishly dispenses is that the forms of address "Mrs." and "Miss" did not distinguish women in terms of their marital status but in terms of *moral* categories: "Mrs." was used for respectable women and "Miss" for the other kind. Many of the "Mrs. Johnsons" and "Mrs. Uphills" listed in Restoration dramatis personae bore honorifics which granted respectability where few expected—and many wanted—to find it. "Mrs." was pronounced "Mistress"—which with these actresses was often (and often royally) the case.

In a sense, Fraser can't help but portray the age as a reflection of its monarch or, in the case of Cromwell, its Protector. It is almost as if the undeniably attractive and charming personality of Charles II (a personality Fraser has chronicled in her engaging *Royal Charles*) was the pivot that turned his glittering world. (Perhaps the character of the King does have an impact equal to the muter political forces of the economy at large.) Oliver Cromwell, another of Fraser's earlier subjects, was not without gallantry himself, and in one of the stranger developments described in *The Weaker Vessel,* the Protector's own weakness for pleading ladies led to long lines of royalist women asking for mercy (and certificates of sequestration) at the hands of the Committee for Compounding after the civil war. As the imprisoned Thomas Knyvett wrote to his wife in 1644, "Women solicitors are observed to have better Audience than masculine malignants."

Fraser has written lengthy and masterful biographies of three English rulers, James I, Charles II and Cromwell, and is, of course, the author of the immensely and deservedly popular *Mary Queen of Scots.* That she has chosen not to devote an entire book to any one of the intriguing commoners in her latest work does not mean that for this biographer it takes the lives of innumerable ordinary women to equal in historical importance the life of a single ruler. Her interests here differ, and thus her procedures begin to move her from the study of personality to demographics and social history. For the need to chronicle so specifically the deeds of so many stretches the biographer's art—almost to the breaking point. Because Fraser wishes to exemplify different arguments, she often breaks up an individual woman's story into widely separated chapters. This necessitates many references backward and forward in the book, which impedes her narrative and blurs the impact of any single figure. If she has felt compelled to sacrifice pace and analysis to inclusiveness, she has done so in order to persuade us that the real experience of seventeenth-century women was in the heterogeneous lives of individuals. Other historians and theoreticians may choose to neaten her picture by other kinds of analysis or feel the need to make her points more precise and explanatory. But it will be hard for anyone to paint a fuller, more vivid or more abundantly detailed portrait of women in seventeenth-century England.

Lawrence Stone (review date 11 April 1985)

SOURCE: "Only Women," in *The New York Review of Books*, Vol. XXXII, No. 6, April 11, 1985, pp. 21-22.

[*In the following review, historian Stone objects to several features of Fraser's* Weaker Vessel *and praises others.*]

Before beginning a discussion of the books under review, I must first set out the ten commandments which should, in my opinion, govern the writing of women's history at any time and in any place:

1. Thou shalt not write about women except in relation to men and children. Women are not a distinct caste, and their history is a story of complex interactions;

2. Thou shalt strive not to distort the evidence and the conclusions to support modern feminist ideology: social change is by no means always the product of an activist minority, and all change is relative not absolute;

3. Thou shalt not forget that in the past nearly all women paid at least lip service to the idea that they were in all respects inferior to men, as ordained by God. The only area in which they were thought to be clearly stronger was in their sexual voracity, their capacity to have multiple orgasms, but this was more a source of shame and temptation than of pride;

4. Thou shalt not confuse prescriptive norms with social reality;

5. Thou shalt exercise subtlety in recognizing diversity, ambivalence, and ambiguity concerning the relative strength of love, sex, money, birth, parental authority, and brute force in determining the choice of a spouse;

6. Thou shalt not assume the ubiquity in the past of modern emotional patterns—neither premarital love, nor conjugal affection, nor maternal devotion to infants. Circumstances and culture are often stronger than natural instincts;

7. Thou shalt not exaggerate the importance in the past of gender over that of power, status, and wealth, even if all women experienced the same biological destiny;

8. Thou shalt not use the biographies of a handful of exceptional (usually upper-class) ladies to describe the experience of the majority of (necessarily lower-class) women;

9. Thou shalt be clear about what constitutes real change in the experience and treatment of women;

10. Thou shalt not omit to analyze with care the structural constraints on women created by values, religion, customs, laws, and the nature of the economy.

Antonia Fraser has already carved out for herself a distinguished place as the author of four royal, or quasi-royal (i.e., Cromwell), biographies in sixteenth- and seventeenth-century England, which have achieved the unusual feat of earning both popular acclaim and the respect of professional historians. Her work has been thorough and carefully researched, using all the available printed documents. It is also very well written and shows good judgment and a subtle appreciation of human psychology. Her high reputation as a biographer is well deserved.

[With *The Weaker Vessel*] she has now embarked on a social history of the lives of women in seventeenth-century England—"a study of woman's lot." This is a subject that demands a different methodology, not biography but close analysis, and a different subject matter, not elite, like queens, but ordinary women. But Antonia Fraser has made no such radical adjustments to her usual methods of work. Noting that her book is not intended as a "dictionary of female biography" and that she has "selected those characters who interested me," she has produced a long and fascinating series of biographical vignettes of a number of exceptional, or exceptionally well-documented, women, almost all of them upper class and most of them aristocratic. Her subject matter is largely the tiny world of the court and its gossip mongers, and her approach is to tell a lot of potted biographies, ranging from two to ten pages each.

Her book therefore raises in an acute form questions about the value of, and appropriate methodology for, the newly developing genre of microhistory. The intensive exploration of individual case studies—a practice borrowed by historians from anthropology—has already produced a few works of exceptional power, each of which has thrown a brilliant search-light on a narrow sector of the generally dark and foggy landscape of the past. When handled by historians who are deeply immersed in the cultural, religious, social, political, and economic background of the time and place, the results can be stunning. Notable examples are Jonathan Spence's *The Death of Woman Wang,* set in seventeenth-century China, Carlo Ginzburg's *The Cheese and the Worms,* set in early sixteenth-century northern Italy, and Natalie Zemon Davis's *The Return of Martin Guerre,* set in mid-sixteenth-century France.

But the extraordinary power of these case studies derives only partly from the intrinsic interest of the stories themselves or the rhetorical skill with which they are told, although both are important. The critical ingredient is the accumulated scholarly experience of the authors, which enables them to evaluate their material, set it in context, and tell us what it means. Antonia Fraser lacks this profound immersion in all aspects of seventeenth-century English history, and she attempts little in the way of interpretation. She selects a striking story, tells it extremely well, and then moves quickly on to the next.

The result makes absorbing but disjointed and episodic reading. Of my ten commandments, she has faithfully followed the first six, but almost entirely violated the last four. Antonia Fraser's technique for examining women's lot is to offer the reader twenty-two short chapters, each devoted to what some, mostly upper-class, women achieved or suffered in various roles: as rich young girls, the mercenary arranged marriages; as wives, the pains and perils of repeated childbirth; as rich widows, the pursuit by rapacious fortune-hunters; as poor old women, the accusations of witchcraft; as young girls, the denial of the scholarly education given to their brothers; as spinsters, a life almost outside the social system—Antonia Fraser thinks that life as a Catholic nun was probably preferable to that of a Protestant spinster.

The topics, all illuminated by a series of striking anecdotes of unusually fortunate or unfortunate women, take us up to 1640 and the outbreak of the revolution. There follow exciting chapters about heroic aristocratic ladies leading the defense of castles; women serving in the army as nurses or as transvestite male soldiers; rich ladies negotiating with the revolutionary government on behalf of their husbands; London women arranging political protests; and sectarian women preaching. For the period from 1660 to 1700, Antonia Fraser tells us about forced marriage for money; divorce; and education; then about female authors, high-class courtesans, ac-

tresses as sex objects, and midwives. The one chapter on women in business tells stories about peculiar upper-class women, like the Countess of Bristol, who received a royal license to import and sell wine; or Mrs. Pley, who supplied the Navy with canvas; or Cromwell's granddaughter, Bridget Bendish, who operated a profitable saltworks—hardly typical of the lives of working women.

> It has to be said, with regret, that despite her great descriptive talents, and despite her remarkable knowledge of the printed sources, Antonia Fraser has written a lively and very readable but fundamentally unsatisfactory book, distorted and intellectually rather shallow.
> —*Lawrence Stone*

In the epilogue Antonia Fraser tells us sadly that in 1700 a woman's lot was still very much what it was in 1600—"always the same." Many of these vignettes are very revealing, especially of the way women took charge of troops and business affairs while their husbands were away at the wars. They performed—as usual—with great efficiency, only to retire once more to the drawing room and the bedroom when the men came home again.

But it has to be said, with regret, that despite her great descriptive talents, and despite her remarkable knowledge of the printed sources, Antonia Fraser has written a lively and very readable but fundamentally unsatisfactory book, distorted and intellectually rather shallow. In the first place, Lady Antonia's preoccupation with the elite leads her to omit almost entirely the lives of the great majority of women who did not belong to the top 1 percent. She virtually ignores the lives of the middle class and the poor, and their deep involvement in productive labor for the family economy, although we already know that getting a living was their dominant preoccupation. As Joan Thirsk points out in her foreword to *Women in English Society,* in the country they were deeply involved in spinning, lace making, and other by-industries, as well as looking after the poultry, milking the cows, making and marketing butter and cheese, in addition to running the household. In towns, they served in the shop while their husbands were collecting their stock in trade, and they helped to supervise the apprentices as an extension of their household duties. They also, like their husbands, spent long hours in the alehouse, where there is no sign of sexual segregation in seventeenth-century England. This social mixing of the sexes shows up in English legal cases, even if for visual evidence we have to look at Dutch genre paintings of the period.

The daily round of hard work and exuberant relaxation of

the average woman leaves hardly a trace on the pages of Antonia Fraser's book. Even more troubling is her lack of interest in the structural constraints upon women. It is only at page 291 that the ignorant reader discovers that full divorce with remarriage was legally forbidden in England, alone among all Protestant countries, and even then he is not told why. What occurred, however, which Lady Antonia does not examine except in passing, was a huge number of desertions or private separations among the poor. These were followed by the formation of new households, either by the adoption of a mistress posing as a wife, or by a bigamous second marriage which was almost certain to pass undetected.

Another feature altogether peculiar to English life was the persistence of the medieval law by which a verbal marriage contract in the present tense before witnesses was legally binding, and enforceable in the courts. This greatly facilitated the abduction of heiresses and also the seduction of women on the basis of promises of marriage which, for lack of hard proof or unambiguous wording, turned out to be unenforceable. Antonia Fraser pays only passing attention to the loss of legal economic independence by most women upon marriage, so that years after separation their earnings and furniture were still the legal property of their husbands. In practice things did not usually work out as badly as this suggests, but if a marriage turned sour, the wife's economic dependence upon her husband could be catastrophic. These are aspects of middle-class and low life which Antonia Fraser hardly mentions, absorbed as she is in dramatic stories of the abduction of heiresses and the pragmatic negotiations between greedy aristocratic parents over the financial details of a marriage settlement. Even there, she never clearly explains exactly what was a portion and what a jointure, or why the ratio between the two altered over time and with what consequences.

Finally, there is the question whether the book's dismal conclusion—"always the same"—is really true. The answer is yes and no. Obviously nothing fundamental could change in women's biological experience before the development of contraceptives, antibiotics, and anesthetics, and nothing in their power relations with men before a radical change in patriarchal values and laws. But to answer this question at a more sophisticated level we first have to break down the female population into at least three socio-economic categories, the elite of the rich and wellborn, the middling sort, and the mass of the poor, who still made up at least two-thirds of the population.

For the first group, things undoubtedly improved in some important ways. By 1700, unlike 1600, the brutality and ruthlessness with which parents disposed of daughters in marriage, in the exclusive interest of kin solidarity and aggrandizement, were no longer the norm. The Court of

Wards, which had sold female orphans to the highest bidder had been abolished. Antonia Fraser tells the story of Sir Edward Coke, who was said to have tied his daughter to a bedpost and whipped her into agreeing to marry an insane brother of the all-powerful Duke of Buckingham. Such episodes, however, had become a shocking rarity by 1700. Most wealthy parents by then had conceded the right of veto to their children, inspired by Protestant ideology about "holy matrimony" and the need for marital affection. The same ideology had penetrated the middling sort at least as early and possibly earlier, and freedom of choice based on affection and married love were being vigorously propounded by influential propagandists like Daniel Defoe in the 1690s. In the lower, propertyless, classes, young women had always been free to choose their own spouses. But the growing sexual freedom following the decline of Puritan morality not only led to a sharp rise in prenuptial pregnancies, but also to a rise of bastardy, with tragic consequences for the many abandoned mothers. Without contraception, sexual liberation was a positive disaster for some women.

Upper-class women were no longer encouraged to study the classics, and the learned lady became a figure of fun. To that extent there was perhaps a loss. But the level of articulate literacy continued to grow among upper-class women, as displayed in their spelling, grammar, and

Reed Browning (review date Spring 1985)

SOURCE: "The Name of Frailty," in *The Kenyon Review,* Vol. VII, No. 2, Spring, 1985, pp. 130-33.

[*In the following review, Browning scrutinizes* The Weaker Vessel *and comments on its strengths and failings.*]

[*The Weaker Vessel*] teems with entertaining stories: Ann Fanshaw braves the turbulent seas; Joan Flower dons the identity of a witch; Mary Ward fights for educational reform; Lady Eleanor Davies scans the future; Jane Whorwood plots to spring Charles I; Joan Dant becomes the queen of pedlars. Whatever else may be said of these women, they were not weak. And that is the burden of Lady Antonia Fraser's examination of the lot of English womankind from the final years of Elizabeth I to the reign of Queen Anne: despite the attention given to Saint Peter's dictum about women being "the weaker vessel," women were in fact strong—in spirit, in resourcefulness, in resolve, in devotion, in enterprise, and even at times in physical prowess.

The work falls into three broad sections: in the first, Lady Antonia treats the enduring matrimonial matrix which, above all other factors, determined a woman's status during the course of the entire seventeenth century. Through a series of vignettes, she canvasses attitudes toward affection and spinsterhood, addresses the realities of pregnancy and widowhood, and reminds us that in the hierarchical world of the Stuarts women held an unmistakably subordinate position. It was man's right to command, woman's duty to obey. The second section focuses on the tumultuous years from 1640 to 1660, the only period during the century when voices spoke out against the verities of subordination and dependence. The dislocations of war and the convulsions of ideological disputations opened avenues for women or forced novel opportunities on them. Some preached, some pleaded, some plundered, and Lady Antonia chronicles their exploits. The final section deals with the recrudescence of custom in the decades after 1660. Lady Antonia discerns a few signs that not all of the achievements of the years of revolution perished, but she argues that in general Charles II's accession marked the beginning of the ebbing phase of a dreary cycle. Her examples do not invariably bear out this pessimistic reading of the latter part of the century, but neither do they give grounds for truly challenging it. After this sprawling and elaborate tapestry of engaging tales, the conclusion of the work is brief and anticlimactic. "Where the status of the so-called weaker vessel was concerned," she declares, "the seventeenth century saw very little improvement in real terms" (p. 464).

Drawing from the richness of the self-revelatory writings of the seventeenth century and especially on the diaries and epistles of literate and usually well-born women, Lady Antonia has culled her collection of edifying and illuminating tales. She has sorted these tales into their fitting topical slots. She has piled account on account, displaying that sheer joy in gossip that, to bare a secret, energizes so many historians. What has emerged is an excursion into collective biography: lives are set forth for the reader's moral instruction. Considered as a whole, her achievement brings to mind Lord Bolingbroke's famous definition of history—that it is philosophy, teaching by examples. Lady Antonia is, of course, no novice to the art of biography. With well-received lives of Oliver Cromwell and Charles II to her credit, she has shown that she understands the demands of the narrative, the importance of pacing, and the uses to which the arresting event can be put. Though this is her first venture into multiple biography, she is tilling ground which, beneath other plows, has often proved fertile. But for collective biography to succeed—for it to serve as a model of inductive social science—the examples must be exemplary. Lady Antonia's are not. And on that discrepancy hangs the first of several problems.

Consider, for example, the age at which women married. Lady Antonia begins her study with the apt reminder that young heiresses were coveted for their wealth. She proceeds with the striking datum that the age of consent for a female was 12. She presents extended examples of three girls who

were married for their money, all 14 or younger. Then, relying on Peter Laslett (*The World We Have Lost,* p. 83) to point up a contrast, she states that women below the propertied classes—that is, essentially the poorer women of England—married "really quite late" (p. 39), at an average age in excess of 23. All of this suggests, I believe, that females from the gentry or the aristocracy were often married by their mid-teens. But in fact, as the same table from Laslett would show, gentry brides were (on average) close to 22 when first married, and aristocratic brides were 19 in the first quarter of the century and over 20 by the second quarter. Child brides were clearly the exception, not the rule.

Consider next the survival rate for children. Lady Antonia tells of Sir William and Elizabeth Brownlow, who endured the loss of thirteen of their nineteen offspring. The percentage that survived, she generalizes (citing Lawrence Stone), "was something like the average survival rate for upper-and middle-class families of the time" (p. 74). That is an astonishing assertion. Lady Antonia characterizes six of nineteen as one-third, though it is of course an even smaller proportion. Stone's own graph (*The Family, Sex and Marriage in England 1500-1800*, p. 69) shows a survival rate (through age 15) that never dips below 60 percent in the seventeenth century and occasionally rises above 70 percent. Thus the unfortunate Brownlows, rather than being representative, suffered losses at almost twice the national rate. Even a minimal degree of statistical sophistication is sufficient to understand how cavalierly Lady Antonia produces her demographic generalizations.

To this carelessness about figures must be added a peculiar confidence in interpreting seventeenth-century documents. On several occasions Lady Antonia treats the formulaic as revelatory, when, precisely because it is formulaic, it could as easily be a mask as a mirror, as easily a sign of inattention as of thoughtfulness. Viscountess Mordaunt's prayer for being delivered of a male child (p. 119) is an example of the former; Lady Russell's reminder (p. 398) that life is hard, of the latter. At one point Lady Antonia infers from the frequent reiteration of the need for choosing wet nurses who have milk that they were often dry. Perhaps. But it seems equally likely that because the advice comes from handbooks, it is precisely the kind of crystallization of the obvious that passes for wisdom in written guides. All these points are uncertain. But it is one of the responsibilities of the historian to respect uncertainty.

Historiographical innocence produces flaws of a different order. Though her bibliography fairly bursts with studies old and new, certain salient issues are strangely neglected. Lady Antonia begins the book by referring to her long-standing interest in the condition of women during the Civil War; the middle section of the book is presumably the most tangible fruit of that interest. It is odd then that she ignores the relevant contribution of Christopher Hill, the doyen of Stuart scholars in our day, whose chapter on women's campaign for sexual liberation during the Civil War (*The World Turned Upside Down*, pp. 247-60) touches several themes central to her own study. She seems similarly unaware of the efforts by recent historians to plot the changing structure of the family. By Lawrence Stone's account, the seventeenth century stands at the epicenter of a tectonic shift in the nature of familial relations. Older notions, grounded in commitments to lineage and honor and devoid of concerns with affection, were passing through a powerfully patriarchal stage toward the modern sensibility that elevates personal autonomy, privatism, romantic love, and sexual expression. Each of the stages of Stone's tripartite model was presumptively present in the seventeenth century. And yet Lady Antonia writes of families as if size alone, or the attitude of the husband, differentiated them. Despite her considerable learning, she thus makes no deliberate contribution to this lively scholarly issue.

Works on the history of women have proliferated in recent years, and the author notes that she shares an interest that many scholars are professionally committed to. But *The Weaker Vessel* stands apart from the dominant trends of feminist historiography. Lady Antonia is not interested in minimizing gender differences. She thinks, for example, that women are instinctively maternal, obeying a natural prompting foreign to the male experience. Yet neither is she interested in celebrating, except tangentially, the domestic virtues often ascribed to women. The book is, among other things, a brief for recognizing that women are as capable as men of displaying the courage that convention treated as the preserve of the male sex. Lady Antonia writes with a firm grounding in the older ways. Her subject matter may be new, but her assumptions are traditional.

Fortunately for Lady Antonia, Clio's house has many mansions. Because she writes fluently, spins her yarns with verve, and knows the secret of the significant fact, there is an honorable niche for this book. But *The Weaker Vessel* displays the flaws of—the word cannot be avoided—the dilettante. Anecdotes are chosen not for their representativeness but for their entertainment value. The world of conceptualization is ignored. Text is divorced from context. The result is a book that passes more readily as a diversion than as an analysis. It is difficult to believe that *The Weaker Vessel* advances our understanding of the seventeenth century.

Susanne Woods (review date June 1985)

SOURCE: "The Bad Old Days," in *Women's Review of Books*, Vol. II, No. 9, June, 1985, pp. 17-18.

[*In the following review, Woods compares* The Weaker Vessel *with another work on the cultural history of women.*]

Anyone who investigates the social of cultural history of women is painfully aware of how little of our past is accessible, even the relatively well-documented past of the English speaking culture. Some things are retrievable, including the expressed attitudes of men toward women and the legal and social restrictions imposed by men or women; less well understood are the motives and conditions of men's writing about the nature and position of women, and the actual lives of women themselves. For the England of the Renaissance and seventeenth century, two new complementary studies shed welcome light.

Linda Woodbridge, a literary scholar, uses literary and historical evidence to analyze the sense of threat that men in the Renaissance apparently experienced from women—especially from aggressive and vocal women, from female dominance in love and marriage, and from female, friendships—and investigates the cultural expression of and reaction to men's fears, particularly through a study of the stock literary figure of the "woman-hater." [In *The Weaker Vessel*] Antonia Fraser, biographer and historian, depicts the general condition of women in seventeenth-century England through an account of the economics of marriage, the role of love (negligible for the most part), the wifely virtues (chastity, silence and obedience), widowhood, attitudes to the old and ugly (always in danger of charges of witchcraft), and women's education.

Fraser finds one moment, during the Civil War of the mid-seventeenth century, when women's institutionalized inferiority briefly diminished. During the Civil War women were often less restricted: the Puritan women of Lyme, for example, joined the men in attacking the Royalist forces, and destroyed their complex fortifications. Several women, both Puritan and Royalist, commanded castles and withstood sieges while their husbands were away. Wives of dissidents, such as Leveller John Lilburne's Elizabeth, heroically held together homes while their husbands were imprisoned, and spent years in the complex (male) legal world, petitioning for the release of their husbands and relief of family financial distress.

But like the short-lived intellectual liberalism of the Jacobean stage, the freedom and authority of Civil War women faded quickly; with the Restoration in 1660 all the brave women, the "Rosie the Riveters" of their day, gave back their independence in the name of stability and right order. From then through the reign of Queen Anne with which her book concludes, Fraser describes a situation that grew, if anything, to be more confining than it had been in 1600.

Both Woodbridge and Fraser hunt for examples of self-directed women in the chokingly repressive atmosphere of the period. Neither lingers long at the accommodationist fountain of Maybe It Wasn't So Bad, though Fraser looks harder than Woodbridge for mitigating attitudes and personal heroisms. What both authors inevitably encounter are the undeniable longings of women for full (meaning, in this period, largely manlike) dignity in the face of institutionalized and internalized oppression. Their work serves to underscore the extent of that oppression even as it searches for the challenges.

By the seventeenth century, as both writers make clear, the arguments for or against woman's character were already cliches. Aristotle had called her an imperfect man; Tertullian and Jerome had blasted her as the cause of the fall and therefore of Christ's terrible suffering and death; her representatives were traitorous Delilah, destructive Helen of Troy, murderous Medea, and (under an assortment of names) the shrewish scolding wife and the lustful widow out to capture yet another unsuspecting husband to dominate and cuckold.

Women's self-appointed champions were not much more helpful. They argued that woman was God's last and therefore best creation, made from the flesh of Adam's rib rather than the baser earth of which Adam himself was made, and given as a helpmate to Adam so that man would not be alone. The mutual virtues of man and woman are what make civilization possible. In the first important handbook of Renaissance humanist education, Thomas Elyot's *Book Named the Governor* (1531), the virtues women contribute are fairly typically outlined: "The good nature of woman is to be mild, timorous, tractable, of sure remembrance, and shamefast." In his 1540 *Defence of Good Women* Elyot again assumes conventional virtues and relationships between men and women:

> To men nature hath given puissance in members, braveness hard and consolidate, the skin thick, and perchance more bones . . . to sustain outward labours. . . . To women she hath given the contrary . . . that her debility should make her more circumspect, in the keeping at home such things as her husband, by his puissance, hath gotten.

What do comments like these and the many others that Woodbridge cites from the "woman controversy" of the age have to do with life as it was lived? Woodbridge rightly claims that in *The Defence of Good Women* Elyot is offering a "piece of literature, written out of a long literary tradition which it modifies but whose conventions it nonetheless observes," and she emphasizes the need for great care in reading any reference to actual historical incidents or people into such literary exercises. The Renaissance was a bookish age, and the display of wit through the use of conventional materials was indeed a common entertainment. But

Woodbridge is in fact wrong to disconnect Elyot's book from historical events. Elyot dedicated it to Queen Anne of Cleves, the fourth wife of Henry VIII, on the occasion of her wedding. For whatever intellectual enjoyment *The Defence of Good Women* was intended, it was also a politic wedding gift from one of the king's resident humanists. It is hardly far-fetched to suggest that its conventional praise of obedience to one's husband was well-meant advice to the new wife of a king who had already divorced one queen and buried two more.

Woodbridge does agree that literature inevitably bears a relation to life (the dichotomy itself is a tricky one), though that relation may be complex. Seldom are correspondences between book and event so simple, or readily identifiable as Elyot's gift to Anne. More often, as Woodbridge stresses, such treatises and their fictive counterparts in romance, poetry, and drama are motivated by society's fears about the groups to whom they are directly or indirectly addressed. Their admonitions and instructions have a discernible, if unspecific, impact on human attitudes and behavior.

One of Woodbridge's most effective analyses reveals the relation of misogynistic humor to female oppression. Noting that most of the attacks on women seem mainly to be opportunities for misogynist jesting, and that it was (ironically) the defenses of women, built as they were on a continuing assumption of male supremacy, that were in fact more dangerous, Woodbridge nonetheless argues that "literary jest has not been without its effect on real women." Jokes about women's shrewishness, weakness or timidity allow men to dismiss women's legitimate complaints or potential:

> The spirit of . . . genial misogyny hovers over everything a woman says and does: a woman cannot debate an issue without fearing criticism of female illogically, cannot take a moral stand without suspecting that her auditors consider her a scold, cannot hold a simple conversation without wondering whether she is talking too much. Women have internalized all the old jokes: was that the jokes' purpose all along? Beginning by paying her the insidious compliment that she is magnanimous enough to laugh at herself, the jester ends by inducing in a woman through his jokes the same contempt for herself that he feels for her. (pp. 31-32)

And she adds wryly that, "An anthology of antimasculist humor would be among the world's shortest books."

This sort of deft reading, analysis and observation is the strongest element of Woodbridge's book. Her treatment of the wider historical context is less convincing: for example, she notes the decline of the jest tradition in the first two decades of the seventeenth century, and suggests that "one might ascribe Jacobean suspicion of jest to the humorlessness of advancing Puritanism or the gloom of impending civil war." Puritanism in this period was by no means always humorless, and it is doubtful if anyone felt an impending civil war in the Jacobean period. James died in 1625; hostilities did not break out until 1642.

Or again, in explaining Jacobean distress at women who dressed in fashionable imitation of men (broad-brimmed hats with feathers, French doublets, bobbed hair, and swords), Woodbridge probably errs in attributing James I's own documented irritation to his open homosexuality and fear that women in man's clothing touched too closely on his and his male courtiers' effeminacy. James' misogyny was no worse than the norm for his day, and effeminacy was by no means associated with homosexuality in this period. Woodbridge herself cites Sidney's *Arcadia,* where Pyrocles dresses as an Amazon to be near his adored Philoclea and is admonished by his friend Musidorus: "This effeminate love of a woman doth so womanish a man that, if you yield to it, it will not only make you a famous Amazon, but a launder, a distaff spinner." Effeminacy was associated with being too much under the sway of women, not too little.

> **Fraser does remind us of the historical conditions which militated against any kind of feminist action. Not only were women bound by the cultural and literary conventions that condemned them to second-class status; most adult women were physically bound down for much of the time by pregnancy.**
> **—*Susanne Woods***

Woodbridge's point, however, is that art is more liberal than life; her astute reading of subversions inherent in the literature is put to good advantage. Strong women appear commonly in English plays of 1610-20, "exactly contemporary with the height of the controversy over women in male attire." Unlike James and the preachers who railed against such women, literature in the same period "rejoices in assertive women."

Fraser is unsurprisingly stronger than Woodbridge in historical matters, though more credulous in interpreting literary materials and even a shade conciliatory about the misogyny inherent in the entrenched doctrines of masculine superiority. Her lack of literary sophistication leads her to treat, or at least appear to treat, conventional literary materials as historically literal, precisely the pitfall Woodbridge so carefully avoids. Fraser takes as a useful biographical source John Batchiler's *The Virgin's Pattern* (1661), for example, though it is actually a Protestant hagiography romanticizing the story of Susanna Perwick, who died at 24 without ever having married. It is likely that Batchiler's book has not much more to do with the real Susanna Perwick than John Donne's *Anniversaries* have to do with the real Elizabeth Drury (which is to say, some, but related as didactic treatise to exemplar, not as biography to subject).

Fraser does remind us of the historical conditions which militated against any kind of feminist action. Not only were women bound by the cultural and literary conventions that condemned them to second-class status; most adult women were physically bound down for much of the time by pregnancy:

> If we try to envisage the appearance of the women of the seventeenth century in relation to our own, we should allow of course for the evil effects of diseases now vanished such as smallpox, or dental decay before competent dentistry. Both of these depredations, taken for granted at the time, might come as a shock to the curious time-traveller. But the fact that most of the leading female characters of the seventeenth century were in a state of virtually perpetual pregnancy would probably come as a far greater surprise. (p.59)

Those who endured this common aspect of woman's lot ranged from Charles I's Queen Henrietta Maria ("pregnant almost without intermission from the autumn of 1628 until January 1639") and Barbara, Duchess of Cleveland (who "produced five children in as many years during the very height of her ascendancy" over Charles II) to those whom Fraser calls the "humbler sisters" of these eminent ladies.

Fraser vividly illustrates much of what we vaguely know, and some of what we may never have considered, about the actual situation of women of that age. While Woodbridge delineates the image of women in theory and literature, Fraser focuses firmly on the rules of the culture, and on how specific women lived with them or transgressed them. Her survey of such professions or extramarital activities as writing, religion, courtesanship and the theatre illustrates what we would expect: clever, beautiful or determined women did find ways, though not easily or always happily, to survive or even transcend oppression and dependency.

Fraser and Woodbridge not only offer the differing skills of historian and literary analyst; they are also on somewhat different theoretical wavelengths. Fraser, while clearly the champion of strong women and women's rights, remains what we tend to think of as male-identified. Her women, even the bravest, are often described in relation to their men. Men's occupations, especially war, are taken to be essential for defining women's strength, and much emphasis is placed on the perils and pitfalls of romantic love. One could argue that these were the concerns and values of the seventeenth century itself, but I would have preferred a more critical twentieth-century eye to be cast on the assumption that women are defined in relation to men and male activities.

Woodbridge, on the other hand, is explicitly a feminist looking for evidence of some nascent feminism in the controversies of the Renaissance. To the credit of her fair and careful reading, she finds very little; what she does find is interesting and mostly persuasive. But she also tends to demand that Renaissance writers ask analytical questions they could scarcely have thought of. If, as Suzanne Langer among others has argued, a culture is defined by the questions it asks rather than by the answers it gives, Woodbridge's drawing attention to the questions not asked may be a legitimate modernist critique of Renaissance culture. Sometimes, though, it simply feels anachronistic:

> The very effort in deciding whether talkativeness is good or bad, as well as the rhetorical habit that reduced all questions to good versus bad, prevented analytic examination. For example: are women really more talkative than men, or do their speeches loom larger because men assume that women have nothing worthwhile to say? If it is true that women talk more than men, why is it true? Does a woman inundate her husband with words when he comes home simply because she has had no adult company all day? (pp. 131-132)

This last question may be appropriate for the housewife in the nuclear family of the present day, but it is unlikely to have much relevance to the very unsolitary life of her Renaissance counterpart.

Certain topics escape the notice of Fraser and Woodbridge alike. The situation of lower-class women remains hazy at best, no doubt in part because of the lack of evidence. If information on aristocratic and gentle women is scarce, it is much the more so for the working and lower classes. Unmarried women, too, appear only briefly, though Fraser makes a particular attempt to consider them. The possibility of lesbian relationships is completely ignored, even though both Woodbridge and Fraser write at length about "martial" women and women dressing as men, and the sainted Susanna Perwick, as Fraser observes, "was buried in the Hackney church, in the same grave as. . . Anne Carew, a school-friend."

Yet there is far more to enjoy than criticize in these two books. However sophisticated feminist theory becomes, it will not be informed and effective unless we slog through the foggy and uneven trenches of the past. Woodbridge and Fraser have done some of that slogging for us, and we should be abundantly grateful both for the information and for the wit and clarity that infuse both books.

Lady Antonia Fraser with Rosemary Herbert (interview date 19 June 1987)

SOURCE: "Lady Antonia Fraser," in *Publisher's Weekly,* Vol. 231, No. 24, pp. 104-105.

[*In the following interview, Fraser discusses her writing life and her crime fiction.*]

During an early spring evening in London, when the daffodils in the square across the way are just beginning to blossom, Lady Antonia Fraser opens the door of her Kensington home to *PW.* On the occasion of the U.S. publication of her short story anthology, **Jemima Shore's First Case** . . . and of her new Jemima Shore novel **Your Royal Hostage** in England, the author talks about her varied writing career, as well as her life as wife, daughter and mother in a celebrated literary family.

While pouring tea from a silver service in her graciously furnished sitting room, Fraser tells us that writing came naturally to the eldest daughter in the family known fondly in Britain as "the literary Longfords." Her father, Lord Longford, was an Oxford don and a prolific writer (later a politician), and her mother, Elizabeth Longford, is the biographer of queens Victoria and Elizabeth II, as well as Byron, Wellington and others. Fraser's siblings, too, include writers: her sister Rachel Billington is a successful novelist; another sister, Judith Kanzantzis, is a poet; her brother Thomas Pakenham is a historian. Asked when she first began to write, Fraser replies modestly, "I just *always* wrote. And if I didn't write I wouldn't be able to do anything else. I'm not full of amazing talents."

Although writing was clearly "in the atmosphere" during Fraser's childhood, she doesn't recall it as being the chief preoccupation of her household. Politics were discussed more frequently by her "family of talkers." Her father changed from Conservative to Labour politics and then thrust another conversion upon family life by becoming a Catholic. At 14, Fraser chose to follow his lead and converted to Catholicism.

While today Fraser radiates upper-class graciousness, she is absolutely unpretentious. Perhaps this is largely due to the fact that she did not perceive herself, in growing up, as being a member of the upper class. Born Antonia Pakenham in 1932, she was "brought up as the daughter of a don— even if he *was* Lord Longford." She attended the famous Dragon School in Oxford where girls were admitted only if they were the siblings of enrolled boys, and then went on, initially as a Protestant, to an upper-crust convent school. She later used the convent's setting and gothic atmosphere to advantage in her first mystery novel, *Quiet as a Nun,* featuring her sleuth Jemima Shore.

When she did begin writing in earnest, [Fraser's] literary family proved invaluable to her. Her mother was a significant critic for her five historical volumes, which was a "tremendous advantage," Fraser says. As Fraser's children reached adulthood, and some— predictably—became writers, they too provided appreciated critiques, particularly regarding Fraser's fiction.
—*Rosemary Herbert*

After completing her education at Oxford, Fraser took an entry-level position at Weidenfeld publishers. They later published her first books, which were histories of dolls and toys, as well as her highly successful biography of Mary, Queen of Scots and those that followed. At 23, she married Sir Hugh Fraser, a dashing war hero. Like her mother, who delayed her writing career to bring up a large family, Fraser put off literary pursuits in favor of raising her six children and supporting her husband's political career.

When she did begin writing in earnest, her literary family proved invaluable to her. Her mother was a significant critic for her five historical volumes, which was a "tremendous advantage," Fraser says. As Fraser's children reached adulthood, and some—predictably—became writers, they too provided appreciated critiques, particularly regarding Fraser's fiction. "My oldest daughter, Rebecca, who has a biography of Charlotte Brontë coming out in the fall, has a very good eye, and it works well for me because she is *absolutely* frank. There's something about being frank to your mother that she enjoys," Fraser adds with a smile. (Fraser's second daughter, Flora, has just published a biography of Emma, Lady Hamilton.)

Fraser's second husband, the eminent playwright Harold Pinter, whom she married in 1980, is also "a terrific help" in making small, key suggestions, she says. Although their work is quite different, the Pinters are a congenial literary couple who entertain a wide circle of literary friends. They customarily work in separate studies but are capable of writing in the same room when the occasion demands. "Once we worked in the same room when we had a hotel suite by the sea," Fraser recalls. "I was very surprised. Harold never seemed to do anything at all. He'd read the *Guardian,* the cricket scores. He'd walk about, silently. He'd light a black

Sobranie. And at the end of it, he'd written a play! I'd been typing away *furiously,* and at the end of it, I'd written half a chapter!"

Not only does Fraser find it easy to work in the company or at least the vicinity of another writer, she is able to keep her own two disparate areas of writing, "history and mystery, as I think of them," comfortably unmuddled. "I'm not particularly tidy outside of my mind. I live in a great, happy clutter, and I like it. But I think I have a very, very, tidy mind. I practically don't need a filing cabinet."

With or without the benefit of a filing cabinet, Fraser's historical work, which put her career on the map, has been acclaimed for its grounding in extensive and accurate research. She is credited with bringing a lively personal voice to the previously dry and donnish field of historical writing. This has made her books, however long, appeal to an audience stretching far beyond the usual academic sphere. Fraser humanizes her subjects by bringing in personal detail and character development. She is also a crusader for those who might otherwise be lost in history, particularly women. Her latest historical volume, *The Weaker Vessel,* celebrates the courage of women in 17th century England. She depicts a panoply of women from all classes facing life and death issues in childbirth, as well as crises in political, social and personal life.

Despite the fact that she was able to bring a personal style to the writing of history, in the mid-'70s Fraser "felt that there was something in myself that history didn't express." She gave in to the impulse to write fiction and created the TV commentator/sleuth Jemima Shore, a stylish, liberated woman who shares some of the author's characteristics. "I gave her all of my private tastes, such as white wine and flowers and Jean Muir clothes and [a] love of cats. On the other hand, she is in some ways very much unlike me. She drives fast cars, for instance, while I am a *tortoise.*"

Fraser's crime novels are written in the tradition of Dorothy L. Sayers, Wilkie Collins and P. D. James, writers she admires enormously. She didn't consciously set out to update the traditional detective novel with a sleek, sophisticated female sleuth but she was concerned to "put a female presenter [commentator] in the television screen when no such woman existed in England. I go a lot to the States, and I had noticed the power of Barbara Walters and how everybody recognized her. I thought that having a sleuth in such a position would make it possible for people in all sorts of trouble to confide in her," Fraser comments.

Fraser "turned to crime" during a time of crisis in her own life. "I've asked myself why I did start writing crime at that time. I always used to parry this question because I didn't want to talk about my personal life. But now, looking back on it, I think to have a marriage of 20 years break up and begin a whole new life, and to start writing fiction for the first time—well, if I were an historian I would say 'These things *have* to be connected.' And I think perhaps I'd always wanted to write amusingly; perhaps there was that in me that could never be freed in my historical work." Indeed, Fraser's mysteries, several of which have been made into TV episodes, have been consistently hailed as entertaining. "I wrote *Oxford Blood* at a time when I was extremely depressed, for good reason. My former husband, the father of my children, had just died, young and painfully, so if *ever* I had a bad time. . . . And yet here comes a novel that everybody kindly describes as being very jolly."

Like many other crime writers, Fraser finds power over life and death within the murder mystery appealing. She adds, "I think crime writing is my link with trying to preserve a sort of order. I'm very interested in good and evil and the moral natures of my people. People in my books tend to get their just deserts, even if not at the hands of the police."

With *Your Royal Hostage,* to be published here in January 1988, Fraser makes her departure from Norton, the publisher which has published all of her crime fiction here to date. She has found Norton to be a very agreeable publisher but feels that a change to a house with a definite mystery list might help Jemima Shore reach a larger audience. "Atheneum and Scribners look to have a very exciting mystery list," she says of her future U.S. publisher, "and I wanted to be a part of it."

Fraser has always published her history here with Knopf, believing in the advice of her agent, Michael Shaw, of Curtis Brown, who counseled her to publish history and fiction with different publishers in the States. The arrangement has worked out well, and, unlike some British authors whose English houses strongly advise them where to "farm out" their work to American publishers, Fraser has always made her own decisions in this matter.

In both history and fiction, Fraser makes no particular changes in her writing for the American audience, relying on American editors to clarify necessary points for us. She strongly believes that American editing is superior to the English. "English publishers say that the Americans nit-pick, but I like that. I say, 'Better for the publisher to nit-pick than the reviewer.' There's a nun, you know, in *Quiet as a Nun,* who is always quoting Wordsworth. The American editor checked all the Wordsworth quotations and came up with some *howlers.* And you know, I thought I knew my Wordsworth."

For some time Fraser has taken an active and leading role in writers' organizations, campaigning for authors' rights and helping to win the successful battle for the Public Lending Right, which now brings money to authors based on the frequency with which their books are used in libraries. She is also determined that writers should have approval rights on jacket design, that they should receive a greater percentage of paperback earnings, and that they have the right to be informed of the print run on their books. "Here, if you know the print run, it's because your editor weakened or got drunk," she jokes. Presently, she devotes her efforts to another kind of authors' rights, civil liberties, as chairman of the English PEN Writers in Prison Committee. "That is my major concern: writers who are in prison *for* writing," she says.

Fraser has also recently begun reviewing crime fiction in a monthly column for the London *Daily News.* She believes crime writing attracts some of the best talent in writing today. Why? "Possibly, the novel became too experimental; but I think just as when Bjorn Borg from nowhere in Sweden became a tennis star, and everybody in Sweden took up tennis, in the same way, the success of P.D. James and Ruth Rendell attracts more writers of quality to crime fiction." Perhaps Fraser's success will inspire new writers too.

Mary Beard (review date 11-17 November 1988)

SOURCE: "Manifestations of a Myth," in *Times Literary Supplement,* No.4467, November 11-17, 1988, p. 1248.

[*In the following review of* Boadicea's Chariot: The Warrior Queens, *Beard assesses Fraser's version of Boadicea's story in relation to several other available accounts.*]

Boadicea is myth. She was already a part of mythology for the Romans who first wrote about her and about her hopelessly doomed rebellion against the forces of occupation in Britain. At the time her story, retold and embellished, evoked both admiration and fear. For some Romans she was the noble savage, who at least for a few days jolted the complacency of an imperial power, effete and corrupt at its centre. For others she was the mad witch, who made real those dread male fantasies of female control. In Britain, at the margins of the civilized world, the Romans escaped from her only by the skin of their teeth. It was a useful reminder of woman's potential for destruction—and Roman writers made the most of it.

From the time of Boadicea's rediscovery in (significantly) Elizabethan England, she has been invented and re-invented as a symbol for a variety of quite incompatible causes. Feminism, not surprisingly, is one of these causes. She was a guest among the galaxy of female stars at Judy Chicago's installation "Dinner Party". And—no doubt with rather greater popular appeal—she has been heralded as a firm favourite of the feminist pop-star and actress Toyah Wilcox. "Boadicea is a character I greatly admire", she is reputed to have said, so following in the footsteps of Cicely Hamilton, who gave the queen a leading role in her *Pageant of Great Women* (1909). This *Pageant* optimistically enacted the defeat of (male) Prejudice, in the face of female talent and strength. The final scene showed the cowardly departure of Prejudice from the stage, sloping away at the mere sight of a posse of female warriors, led by Boadicea.

Those of us familiar with the Roman stories of Boadicea's habits in war (cutting off the breasts of her female enemies and then sewing the severed parts into their mouths, for example) cannot help but feel curious at what particular aspects of the royal character Toyah and Hamilton found so admirable. But even so, their enthusiasm is less unsettling than the outright misogyny of the seventeenth-century treatment of the story. Fletcher's play *Bonduca* turns Boadicea into a junior partner of the real hero Caratach (Caratacus), whose energy is devoted to keeping his unruly female allies in their place. His loyalty to his fellow men, rather than his fellow Britons, emerges clearly when he prevents Boadicea's daughters from harming the Roman soldiers who had raped them. "Ye should have kept your legs closed then" is his argument—almost enough by itself to justify the women's status as feminist heroines.

At first sight Thorneycroft's famous statue of Boadicea in her chariot (on the Embankment near Westminster) seems to evoke this same liberated woman. But the careful observer sees a surprisingly neatly groomed queen—despite her daringly eccentric, "no hands" control of her horses. And underneath the group run the lines of Cowper: "Regions Caesar never knew/Thy Posterity shall sway". This is the Boadicea of imperialism, not of feminism. It is the visual counterpart of Marie Trevelyan's biography of the queen, *Britain's Greatness Foretold*. Writing in the final years of Victoria's reign, Trevelyan found in Boadicea the well-springs of British power and patriotism, the ancient counterpart of Victoria herself. Of course, it is a paradox that a rebel against Roman imperial power should have become such a winning symbol of the British empire. But it is very much characteristic of myth that it can incorporate, and even parade, such paradoxes.

[In *Boadicea's Chariot: The Warrior Queens*] Antonia Fraser guides the reader deftly through the changing patterns of the myth of Boadicea, ending with the Boadicean image of Margaret Thatcher. By far the most successful parts of the book are those in which she analyses the mad passions of later ages for the British queen—smiling indulgently at the seventeenth-century antiquarians who claimed that Boadicea was buried under Stonehenge, and at the modern Americans who have speculated on her lesbianism. Surprisingly, though, Lady Antonia seems less aware of her own

role in the myth-making process. For she offers us an eminently twentieth-century "historical" Boudicca, and an analysis which presents her (both in reality and legend) as representative of a whole class of warrior queens. In pursuit of this "history", she constructs four chapters on the "facts" of the Boudiccan story (where the more cautious historian might have restricted them to a few pages). And she offers a series of mini-biographies of the other warrior queens—Zenobia of Palmyra, Matilda, Maud, Tamara of Georgia and the rest. Their stories involve the reader in detailed accounts of the social and political background of regions as far apart as third-century Palmyra and the nineteenth-century Raj. And there is, predictably in the stories of warrior queens, a burden of military accounts that the more faint-hearted academic historian would have consigned to the footnotes.

Naomi Bliven (review date 24 April 1989)

SOURCE: "Women at Arms," in *The New Yorker*, April 24, 1989, pp. 108-111.

[*In the following review, Bliven examines the characteristics of the historical figures outlined by Fraser in* The Warrior Queens *and comments on their significance.*]

Antonia Fraser's *The Warrior Queens* is an intelligent and artful study of women rulers who commanded in battle. The book begins in prehistory—practically every pagan pantheon featured a warrior goddess—and comes down to the present; its heroines lived in Europe, Asia, and Africa. (The New World has produced no warrior queens known to history.) The author's ground rules exclude the West's most famous woman warrior, Joan of Arc, because she did not wield political power, but Ms. Fraser finds a place for Margaret Thatcher, who, living at a time when a nation's political chief is no longer expected to appear on the battlefield, made the decision that sent British soldiers to fight for the Falkland Islands.

The book—inevitably, I think—leads to feminist conclusions, but it is not a feminist tract. I would call it an exploration, and what it explores is a repeated pattern that a woman biographer and historian cannot help noticing. Women have ordinarily been denied public authority, and women who have become rulers (in the past, usually through the workings of mortality in hereditary systems), and particularly women rulers who have been called upon to make war, have elicited either extravagant admiration or even more extravagant odium. Mother of her country and/or savage slut—both responses echo down the centuries. In juxtaposing the myths about women with the careers of some extraordinary women, Ms. Fraser at once clarifies history and suggests the many ways that myths betray history.

One way is that the myths are always the same, while the warrior queens demonstrated considerable individuality. The empire builders—for examples, Queen Tamara, who ruled Georgia from 1184 to 1212 and greatly enlarged her Caucasian Kingdom; and Isabella of Castile, who, with her husband, Ferdinand of Aragon, completed the reconquest of Spain in 1492—justified their aggressions very differently. They do not resemble each other or the numerous queens who became warriors by responding to aggression with arms instead of tears. In a common scenario, an aggressive male attacks a woman ruler because he assumes she is weak. Ms. Fraser recalls Tomyris, the Queen of the Massagetae, who, in Book I of Herodotus' "The Persian Wars," adjures the Persian Emperor Cyrus, "Rule your own people, and try to bear the sight of me ruling mine": Cyrus ignored her advice, invaded her kingdom, and was killed in battle.

The Celtic warrior queen Boadicea was less fortunate. She was a king's widow who ruled the Iceni, a rich tribe of East Anglia, as regent for her two daughters. Her husband had been a friend of Rome, and there is no suggestion that she planned to alter his policy. Nonetheless, the Roman financial officer in Britain, the procurator Catus Decianus, sent a force that invaded her kingdom, flogged the queen, raped her daughters, confiscated the royal treasure, and expropriated the fortunes of the Icenian nobility. Ms. Fraser remarks that, like Cesare Borgia's rape of Caterina Sforza after he captured her fortress of Ravaldino, in 1500, the rape of the Icenian princesses was a humiliation inflicted to demonstrate women's helplessness. In the case of Boadicea's daughters, the gesture was expensive: the revolt she led in 60-61 destroyed Colchester, London, and St. Albans. Sometimes history tells us just what we want to hear—for example, that bullies are cowards: when the Celtic tribes rebelled, the procurator fled Britain. However, the Roman governor, Suetonius Paulinus, who had no part in the wretched procurator's banditry, wiped out Boadicea's army. It is thought that she committed suicide after her defeat.

> **Throughout history Ms. Fraser finds an obsessional interest in the sex lives of warrior queens, who must conform to one of two stereotypes: icily chaste or blazingly lascivious.**
> —*Naomi Bliven*

Boadicea reigns over this volume; Ms. Fraser not only recounts her career but follows her legend through some startling transformations. In the sixth century, the monk Gildas thought Boadicea a wicked rebel, but the sixteenth century saw her as a forerunner of Elizabeth I. Purcell's Boadicea is positively genteel, while Cowper's is a British imperialist: "Regions Caesar never knew Thy posterity shall sway," he wrote, justifying Great Britain's war to retain her North American colonies. Presently, Boadicea became an Eminent Victorian, and then, in the twentieth century, her memory was invoked in the cause of woman suffrage, although it is doubtful whether the original Boadicea would have given *any* commoner a vote.

Throughout history Ms. Fraser finds an obsessional interest in the sex lives of warrior queens, who must conform to one of two stereotypes: icily chaste or blazingly lascivious. One sentence tells all we really know about Sammu-ramat: she was the widow of an Assyrian king who died in 811 B.C., and she reigned for five years as regent for their son. Yet Ms. Fraser cites work after work concocted about lustful Semiramis. Among the chaste there is (maybe) Zenobia of Palmyra. In the two hundred-sixties, she tried to carve an empire for herself out of Rome's Middle Eastern provinces. Although no chronicler can tell us the names and ages of her sons, all assure us that she allowed her husband's embraces only for the purpose of conception. Historians' and biographers' mania about the sexuality of women rulers causes them to misunderstand the women *as* rulers; Ms. Fraser observes that historians fascinated by Cleopatra's love life often overlook sources that show her devotion to power politics.

Some commentaries that Ms. Fraser records seem remote or archaic, but, surprisingly, many of the concerns of antiquity survive. Ms. Fraser notes that historians have always taken care to tell us whether the voice of a woman commander was harsh, and points out that whenever Mrs. Thatcher raises her voice in Parliament the Opposition calls her a fishwife. The author also remarks that, while Mrs. Thatcher's toughness is considered unfeminine by her opponents, when Geraldine Ferraro ran for the Vice-Presidency she was challenged to prove herself sufficiently unfeminine—tough enough—for the job. Ms. Fraser finds a single universal agreement about women and conflict: everyone, at all times, has believed that it is natural, normal, and feminine for women to fight for their children.

Ms. Fraser has thought about all the ramifications of women commanders, and she writes so easily that her inclusiveness never feels merely dutiful. She holds our attention and she misses nothing. For example, in her discussion of Queen Louise of Prussia, who goaded and nagged her husband, Frederick William, and their intermittent ally, Czar Alexander I, into resisting Napoleon, Ms. Fraser cites Napoleon's insistence that women must be subordinate. He expressed this opinion so often, so forcefully, and so gratuitously that one suspects it was his way of coping with his powerful mother. In her last chapter Ms. Fraser cites feminist thinkers who suspect that many men resent female authority because it reduces them to children. In their eyes, whatever costume a woman wears—even a general's uniform—trails Mommy's apron strings.

Though women warriors may not be important in the history of war, they are important in the history of women. Ms. Fraser recalls that, in her girlhood, reading about Boadicea helped her feel equal to her brothers. Here, I think, the author touches all her women readers.
—Naomi Blivens

Ms. Fraser does not claim that any of her warrior queens ranks among the great commanders. Of all the battles in her book, I find only one among the twenty decisive battles of the world in Joseph Mitchell's 1964 revision of the Creasy classic: the defeat of the Spanish Armada, in 1588. Ms. Fraser recalls Queen Elizabeth's famous speech to her troops awaiting the Spanish invasion at Tilbury but considers the armor she wore on that occasion a sort of masquerade, and agrees with other historians and biographers that Elizabeth was almost neurotically peace-loving. On the other hand, it does not look as if the wars or battles that women lost would have been won by male commanders. No British chieftain of Boadicea's era could have enforced the discipline that her unruly host needed to defeat the Romans.

Though women warriors may not be important in the history of war, they are important in the history of women. Ms. Fraser recalls that, in her girlhood, reading about Boadicea helped her feel equal to her brothers. Here, I think, the author touches all her women readers. In my girlhood, I was taught that American women were the freest in the world, but the only heroine offered for my admiration was Betsy Ross, the patriotic seamstress. In a sense, Ms. Fraser's real subject is the childhood quest for heroes and heroines, which repeats itself in every generation. In recalling this quest, she raises a momentous and perplexing matter: shaping the imagination of the young. In the past, that activity has been allotted to unspectacular women, a contribution to history that is unmeasured but very likely measureless. It may be that humanity would be better off if both boys and girls learned to admire pacific, domestic attainments. It may also be that until we appreciate the dramatic achievements of a few women the humble talents of many women will be undervalued.

S. J. Tirrell (review date 7 June 1989)

SOURCE: "A History of Women at the Helm," in *The Christian Science Monitor,* June 7, 1989, p.12.

[*In the following review of* The Warrior Queens, *Tirrell objects to some of the methods and assumptions in Fraser's study.*]

Within a pride of lions, it has always been the female of the species that hunted and killed. By contract humankind has traditionally relegated women to the home and family circle, often in an inferior status, and certainly far from the amphitheaters of battle.

Still, throughout history there have been women who have defied convention and risen to meet the exigencies of war, often leading their peoples to victory. This idea is the subject of Lady Antonia Fraser's newest work, *The Warrior Queens,* published earlier in Great Britain as *Boadicea's Chariot.*

Though it begins with a discussion of warrior queens from antiquity, such as Semiramis and Cleopatra, Part One of Fraser's book focuses on Boudica (as her name is spelled in early references). The author tries to unravel the twisted strand of fact and fiction that has become the legend of Boadicea.

Boudica, queen of the Celtic tribe Iceni, in AD 60 led a revolt against the occupying Romans. Under her leadership, the Celts sacked and burned Colchester, London, and St. Albans, until they were stopped and brutally slain by the Roman troops under the leadership of the then governor of Britain, Suetonius Paulinus.

Legend has not left Boudica where it found her. It has transmogrified her name into Boadicea and endowed her with, among other things, a chariot with knives attached to the wheels, and a cult status as defender of the British against alien invaders.

But this discussion of Boudica quickly degenerates into quasi-psychological babble as Fraser attempts to grapple with the few known facts of Boudica's life, and the mythical underpinnings of this warrior queen. In trying, the author fails to get a grip on either. She digresses constantly, and her text is littered with parenthetical asides.

The text is sprinkled with inaccuracies. She speaks of the samurai warriors of Japan and the warriors of Homer as ancient chivalric orders. (The samurai culture dates to the 10th century AD, and flourished well into the 18th century. As such, it can hardly be classified as ancient.)

Nor does Fraser ever question Tacitus, her main source of information on Boudica. It never seems to occur to her that, like Sir Thomas More and his famous blackening of Richard III—an ingenious means of whitewashing the reputation of his patrons, the Tudors—so Tacitus must have been at pains to paint the past in grim colors so that it might contrast favorably with the reign of his patron.

Part Two of *The Warrior Queens* deals with famous historical female leaders in the light of the revelations gleaned in Part One. Among the women Fraser investigates are Elizabeth I of England, Catherine the Great of Russia, Queen Louise of Prussia, and Prime Minister Thatcher of Britain. The chapter on Elizabeth I does indeed offer a great deal of insight into that queen's subtle and effective use of femininity and masculine strength. But, like Part One, the whole of Part Two is riddled with attempts to judge the people and events of the past by late 20th-century standards of behavior. Fraser seems not to know that life was cheap; that rape was considered an acceptable way for a man to gain a rich wife—the only shame was if the man failed to impregnate the lady.

Instead, Fraser concentrates on analyzing the various women as victims of the "Appendage Syndrome," by which she means women who come to power through their relationship to a man either as wife, daughter, or mother; the "Voracity Syndrome"; or the "Chastity Syndrome." And it is just this sort of quasi-historical feminist jargon that gives women such a dubious intellectual reputation.

One day, a thorough and unbiased assessment of these prodigious women will be written. When it is, I'd like to read it.

Bonnie Angelo (essay date 15 January 1990)

SOURCE: "Not Quite Your Usual Historian," in *Time*, Vol. 135, No. 3, January 15, 1990, pp. 66, 68.

[*In the following essay Angelo presents details of Fraser's life and records comments on Fraser's crime fiction and historical work.*]

She is the kind of woman Maureen O'Hara used to play in big-budget costume movies: Lady Antonia Fraser, beautiful, hot-blooded, titled daughter of a noble line, turreted castles in her background and the whiff of scandal in her past. But the portrait of a romance-novel heroine slips out of focus with a closer look, for that same Lady Antonia is an internationally established historian, the author of best-selling biographies and a social activist. She is mother of six, protective wife of renowned playwright Harold Pinter, and also dashes off detective stories, wafts along the British TV celeb circuit, and displays an admirable tennis serve.

But forget Goody Two-Shoes. This paragon wades into controversy with brio. She has publicly criticized Prime Minister Margaret Thatcher's policies and rallied British writers

to think more politically. She marches for Soviet Jewry. She organizes petitions and badgers officials to help free dissident writers in jails across Europe and Africa. One of these has made history: playwright Vaclav Havel, the new Czech President. For years, from his prison cell, he exchanged letters with Pinter. The couple will visit Havel to share his triumph in February.

She speaks her mind. And Fleet Street's columnists speak theirs, making the high-profile Lady Antonia a high-priority target. A succinct explanation for this targeting is offered by the London *Daily Mail's* senior feature writer, Geoffrey Levy: "She's an aristocrat. She's beautiful. She's a celebrity. And she is a successful writer. She is an irresistible target." Her father, the seventh Earl of Longford, sums up Fleet Street's anti-Antoniasm in a word: "Jealousy!"

At home in London's fashionable Kensington, Antonia Pakenham Fraser Pinter is a composition by Gainsborough. Her English skin would make peaches weep in their cream. Blue eyes seem to savor a secret, shared but not revealed. She is tall, not willowy but womanly, and at 57 she is, by any standard, beautiful.

Harold Pinter looks in for a bit of householdish chat on his way to his studio in an adjacent mews house. Such an easy, conventional moment, but achieved, some ten years ago, at such a personal price.

Lady Antonia—"the title has cachet," notes her agent Michael Shaw—is dismissive of the personal attacks. "My father brought me up not to mind criticism or ridicule," she says. Lord Longford, a former Labour Cabinet minister, has endured both in his crusades against pornography and for prisoners' rights. The disparagement, in his family's view, stems from the fact that he, a nobleman who turned socialist, violated Britain's class order.

Antonia much admires this man with the courage of his convictions, the progenitor of Britain's fabled Literary Longfords, a family unmatched—possibly in history—for its eight esteemed writers in three generations publishing contemporaneously. They are prizewinning and prodigious: at last count their output topped 80 volumes, most of them digging deep into British and Irish history. Scholarly research is the family hallmark.

The brightest star in the family firmament is Antonia. Her mother recalls that this precocious firstborn "always wrote, even before she could write—poems, little stories. She could read before she had any idea of the meaning of the words. Frank and I called her the wonder child." Which is not to say she was candy-coated. Young Antonia was fiercely competitive, on the tennis courts with her brother Thomas and on the football team at a boys school that admitted a handful of girls on equal footing. The genesis, perhaps, of her view of woman-as-equal.

As a student at Oxford, Antonia Pakenham (the family name) was the centerpiece of an oh, so uppah-crusty circle. "She was already a bit of a star at Oxford," says her father. But even as swains queued eagerly for her attention, "all of the time there was a more profound, intellectual side."

At 22 she published her first book, on the mythical King Arthur. Her typewriter never cooled down, even after she married Hugh Fraser, a Conservative Member of Parliament, and produced three sons and three daughters. The result: 23 volumes.

All the while she was ubiquitous on the TV-radio "chat show" circuit, bright and quippy for *Call My Bluff,* articulate and opinionated on the weighty *Question Time.* Last month Americans tuned to a highbrow quiz program on National Public Radio could hear Lady Antonia deftly identify an arcane quotation: "It's Milton—*Lycidas.*"

She gained her place as a major historian and writer in 1969 with her definitive biography of Mary, Queen of Scots, a best seller in eight languages. Then came Puritan ruler Oliver Cromwell and Charles II, the Restoration King.

Each famous subject, perhaps not coincidentally, had a personal tie to her family. Cromwell granted her Anglo-Irish forebears land in West Meath in the heart of Ireland. (The Longfords, originally Protestant, converted to Catholicism one by one in the 1940s, in individual decisions.) The family is directly descended from Charles II. "Most people in England are," she chuckles, "and I'm no exception." All, of course, from "the wrong side of the blanket." She likes the fact that her line stems from the classy Duchess of Cleveland rather than the King's more ordinary mistress, actress Nell Gwyn.

Some of the royal genes crop out now and then. Author Michael Holroyd, clearly a partisan, portrays Antonia entering a crowded room: "There's a stateliness about her. It's almost like a member of the royal family; people feel they should make a little bow. Some people are dazzled, some feel overawed. She can intimidate some and charm others. It's chemistry—and possibly height. But as soon as she laughs, the formality is completely dissolved." Adds playwright Arthur Miller, a frequent guest of the Pinters: "She has great elegance as a writer and as a person." Marigold Johnson, a devoted friend since Oxford days who is married to the sharply conservative writer and historian Paul Johnson, muses, "Men like her better than women."

For a change of pace and a piece of change, the prolific Antonia takes breaks between works of history, which eat

up three to four years, to write mystery stories featuring female detective Jemima Shore, who has made the leap to TV. But when she first joined the Crime Writers' Association, she was snubbed. "This glittering butterfly was too much for them," says an observer. Eventually, her seriousness won them over and—what else?—she became chairman.

Beguiled by power, she writes of kings and queens. "And," she interjects, "the other side of the picture, the powerless. The powerful have such an extraordinary effect on the lives of people around them." This led to the work she found most demanding, *The Weaker Vessel,* her prize-winning tapestry of the harsh lot dealt to 17th century women. Her current project is the suggestion of old friend Robert Gottlieb, editor of the *New Yorker:* the six wives of Henry VIII, combining her three specialties, royalty, power and women.

Her fascination with women of power resulted in *The Warrior Queens,* her last book, an analysis of women rulers who led their people into battle, from British Queen Boadicea in 60 A.D. to Israel's Golda Meir, India's Indira Gandhi and Prime Minister Thatcher, triumphant in the Falklands. Fraser identified history's typecasting of women leaders: the appendages, those who gain power by virtue of being wives, widows or daughters of a male ruler; the honorary male who rejects her femininity; and the female chieftain who is either "supernaturally chaste or preternaturally lustful." Fraser observes that when a woman holds power, "her sexuality is always relevant. That fascinates me."

Assessing Thatcher, Fraser compares her to Queen Elizabeth I. "She's like a 16th century queen—not a modern one, powerless, gracious, noncontentious. Her handling of her femininity is astonishingly similar to that of Elizabeth I. She says, 'I'm feminine, don't you forget it. I'll dress as a woman, but at the same time, I'm as good as a man.' She's like Elizabeth: 'I've got the heart and stomach of a king!' She's old style, with courtiers and endless speculation about her favorites. Look at that photograph of her with her Cabinet—it says it all: she *is* the queen, among her dinner-jacketed knights. I think the fact that she has no woman in the Cabinet is extremely significant. Another woman would spoil the picture!"

As a strong feminist, she voted for Thatcher in her first election, but now is deeply troubled about the Prime Minister and "the socially divisive effects of her policies that make it increasingly difficult for the really poor, who are very often hopeless." When Fraser expressed these concerns, she sparked charges that she was a "chateau-bottled socialist" who has prospered under the Thatcherism she deplores. In rebuttal, championing the independence of writers, Antonia snaps, "In France they would have given me a medal." She readily acknowledges that personal attacks sting. "Yes. Absolutely. Fair criticism is hurtful; unfair criticism is doubly hurtful." But Lady Antonia is past her Perfect Woman stage. That ended in 1975, when Antonia Fraser and Harold Pinter discovered each other. Then came the gossip, the headlines, the charges in divorce court. Five turbulent years later they were married. (Both former spouses have since died.)

Through it all, her staunchly Catholic family stood by her. Says Lady Longford: "From the word go, Antonia wanted a literary life. Her first husband was a Conservative M.P. I could see that wasn't really the kind of life she was meant for. What she is doing now with Harold and on her own perfectly fits in with everything."

The gilded young aristocrat at Oxford and the Jewish lad from London's East End would never have intersected. "But it was our great good luck," Antonia says, "that by the time we met, we were both recognized." Opposites, fully formed, attracted.

How do two famous talents under the same roof manage the egos, the stresses? She replies with a laugh, "A lot of our sentences begin, 'I completely understand that you, too, are having a rotten time, but. . .' We read each other's things. We talk about them." A London critic comments that "living with Pinter has been a terrific influence for the better on her writing."

"He wins on some things. I win on some things, too," she says. She wins on opera, he on cricket. But Antonia casts herself as the junior talent. "I don't criticize Harold's work. I influence Harold, I contribute to his work by living with him, by talking to him." She contributes in another way repeatedly cited by friends: Pinter's manner is as angular and abrupt as his characters, but, observes a friend, "Antonia smooths over the offenses before the evening is out. She is quite good as stage manager."

Marigold Johnson pinpoints Pinter's greatest effect on Antonia: "She has become a lot more involved in public issues, a much more public figure." And she is planted distinctly to the left of her days as wife of a Tory M.P.

Activist Antonia is deeply committed to writers imprisoned for their written words. "I feel passionately about this," she declares, and she leads the cause for English PEN. Holroyd, former PEN president, sings her praises: "She knows when to press and when not to; she can let loose the dogs on them, or she can charm them. Pinter tends to blow his top; she's got a great deal of common sense." Arthur Miller, longtime advocate for imprisoned writers, concurs: "She is very effective."

She regularly writes to the prisoners: "We may never hear from them but we keep writing, for years." She rejoices that now for the first time Russian writers are in PEN and Czech

writers are back in the fold. "It's a labor of Sisyphus," she sighs. "Just as they are let out in Russia, they've increased in Turkey and Kenya."

The kaleidoscopic Lady Antonia, a dishy blue-blood intellectual, seems tailor-made as the heroine of a romantic novel. Pity that Fraser the writer shuns that pop genre—it would make a lively autobiography.

Anne Tolstoi Wallach (review date 6 January 1991)

SOURCE: "All the Best Houses Have Ghosts," in *New York Times Book Review,* January 6, 1991, p.18.

[*In the following review of* The Cavalier Case, *Wallach considers Fraser's contribution to crime fiction.*]

It's hard to fathom, but there *are* authors who relax from writing books by writing different books. Larry McMurtry took six weeks off from *Lonesome Dove* to write *Desert Rose,* one of his best novels. Agatha Christie, in among 60 full-length mysteries, 19 short-story collections and 14 plays, wrote romance novels as Mary Westmacott. William Buckley seems to relax, if at all, by writing thrillers; Anne Rice writes erotic novels as A. N. Roqueture. And we all know the Rev. Charles Dodgson, who relaxed from mathematical treatises by writing the best children's books of all as Lewis Carroll.

Lady Antonia Fraser is a star member of this industrious group. Her vast biographies of Mary, Queen of Scots and Oliver Cromwell are works of scholarship; no library would be a library without them. She has produced careful and fascinating histories of dolls and toys. Her recent nonfiction book, *The Warrior Queens,* was acclaimed both left and right of the Atlantic. Still, she has found time to invent Jemima Shore, who in just eight books has become a memorable heroine of the mystery genre.

Jemima is not as lovably eccentric as Peter Wimsey, Jane Marple, Hercule Poirot or the great Sherlock Holmes, but she's prettier, sexier and far more in tune with today's London. Thoroughly modern Jemima was at Cambridge, is a television news personality and, though much pursued, disdains the men who want her to marry and settle down. (She thinks settling down is a dreary expression, let alone an idea.) Her mind is good enough to appreciate the details of a Van Dyck portrait, while her legs are long enough to dazzle in a doubles match at a fashionable tennis club. What's more, Jemima's character and good looks bloom from book to book.

In this one, *The Cavalier Case,* Jemima is assigned by the brilliant but batty chairman of her network to produce a television series on historic houses with ghosts and their chic modern owners. It's "a new form of who's in, who's out, if you like," he tells her. She's to begin at Lackland Court, home of a 17th-century Cavalier poet known to every British school-child, whose body disappeared before burial and whose ghost is seen only by children and those about to die. Jemima gets to Lackland Court and finds its handsome new owner planning to turn the place into a tennis club. So she's faced with both historical and modern problems. Jemima handles them with pluck and good humor, taking a few swipes at modern London society along the way. They're the sort Americans can enjoy, on such subjects as the rooms at the National Portrait Gallery, sound-and-light pageants and Englishwomen whose tennis costumes include the family pearls.

The Cavalier Case is the seventh full-length Jemima Shore novel. (There are short stories as well, and Jemima Shore has been the heroine of two major television series, an honor usually kept for fictional detectives with far more cases to their credit.) Antonia Fraser is never so relaxed from scholarship that she doesn't write with intelligence or tell us interesting things. We learn, for example, that the name Jemima is a form of James, and that what we used to call the National Trust is now English Heritage. She parodies the Cavalier poets to perfection, involving us in literary questions like the possible corruption of "I fain would be thy swan" to "I fain would be thy swain."

The mix is great fun, and explains the enormous popularity of the Jemima Shore books. It also explains the popularity of Lady Antonia's biographies, all international best sellers. She writes both history and mystery with zest and verve, and her primary interest is people—foolish queens, military commanders, former wives, rival siblings or stepdaughters desperate for attention. Antonia Fraser is a wonder, and so is *The Cavalier Case*. Her time out is our good fortune.

Blair Worden (review date 29 August 1992)

SOURCE: "Return of the Monarch," in *The Spectator*, Vol. 269, No. 8564, August 29, 1992, pp. 25-26.

[*In the following review, Worden comments on Fraser's previous work and examines the style and content of* The Six Wives of Henry VIII.]

It is a surprise to realise that Antonia Fraser has not written about Henry VIII's wives already. She has written so many books on monarchs and women. There are her long biographies of Mary Queen of Scots and Oliver Cromwell and Charles II. There is *The Weaker Vessel,* a long study of 17th-century women. There is *The Warrior Queens,* an account of women leaders from Boadicea to Margaret Thatcher which, exceptionally among her history books, she kept below 400 pages. There is a novel about a royal wedding. Then there is Weidenfeld's *Kings and Queens of England* series, which she edited and to which she contributed a life of James I. Yet, she tells us, it took a friend to suggest the subject of Henry VIII's consorts, with the words, 'This may not sound like a good idea, but. . .'

It could be a good idea. Kings and queens are back in historical business, after the decades when they seemed to have been mere puppets of social and economic forces, and when interest in them seemed a frivolous distraction from serious issues of class and ideology. So long as the civil wars of the mid-17th century appeared to have been caused by the rise of the gentry or of the bourgeoisie, the shortcomings of Charles I seemed to have been at most the trigger of the conflict. Now that social and economic explanations of the wars have collapsed, Charles's character looks once more to have been at the heart of the problem.

The same pattern is observable in accounts of the break with Rome. So long as the Reformation was regarded as an explosion of popular and progressive sentiment, Henry VIII's matrimonial problems seemed merely to have affected its timetable. Now that we know how deeply entrenched was the old religion and how little support there was for the new, we remember that the Reformation was an act of state, and realise that England might well have remained a Catholic country but for Henry's roving eye and his need for a male heir.

The return to a Court-centred history is something more than a rediscovery of the effects of Cleopatra's nose, or of Anne Boleyn's black eyes. Historians, increasingly drawn to the relationship between political power and visual or literary statements, have seen that the rituals and entertainments of the Renaissance Court, its elaborate masques and chivalric displays, can help us to reconstruct not merely the power struggles of Tudor England but its political and social values.

If these and other historiographical developments have largely passed Fraser by, it is hard to blame her. Specialist historians write for each other. I say 'specialist' rather than 'professional', for the term 'professional historian' has come, by a sleight of hand convenient to those who recognise themselves in the term, to conflate two qualities: the quality of having scholarly standards, and the quality of earning a salary.

Fraser's scholarship, albeit unambitious, is always diligent, clear-headed, responsible. Even so, salaried history has made her kind hard to write. Fraser is the 20th century's equivalent to the popular Victorian writer Agnes Strickland. Like

Fraser, Strickland came from a versatile literary family; like Fraser, she was devoted to Mary Queen of Scots; and like her she wrote lives of the queens of England. Strickland, with few predecessors to guide her and few salaried historians to look over her shoulder, made errors of scholarship and judgement which Fraser would not commit. Yet, for the same reason, she was able to carve out fresh historical territory. Fraser can travel only where learned articles have been before her.

She has a high respect for Henry's long-suffering wives, most of them women of intellect and strength of character. She wants to banish the clichés: 'The Betrayed Wife' (Catherine of Aragon), 'The Temptress' (Anne Boleyn), 'The Good Woman' (Jane Seymour), 'The Ugly Sister' (Anne or Anna or Cleves), 'The Bad Girl' (Katherine Howard), and 'The Mother Figure' (Catherine Parr). All her characterisations are shrewd and sympathetic and, as far as they go, persuasive. But none of them is three-dimensional

---

Perhaps Fraser's prose would be sprightlier if her grasp of historical context were stronger. In *Mary Queen of Scots,* much the best of her books, it was strong. Here she is unable to bring alive the political and religious conflicts to which the fate of Henry's queens belonged, and which would give the book a spine. Without that context the reader's interest is unlikely to be sustained, unless by pity for blighted lives or by interest in the clothes or the jewels or the sex.
                                    —*Blair Worden*

There are two problems, one of style, one of content. Fraser's books evidently sell in large numbers, and if those who buy them read them, and thus learn about a past that would otherwise remain closed to them, she is performing a valuable service. But do they read them? Can they really get through so many pages of nerveless prose? 'On the Welsh borders that spring, the weather was notably cold and wet, as a result of which sickness of various kinds was rife.' It is one thing to pen a sentence like that in a tired moment, another not to tear it up next day.

Solecisms jostle with limp constructions. Of Henry's final parting with Catherine of Aragon we learn that 'Unlike his behaviour towards Wolsey, he did not bid her an affable—if false—farewell.' At Anne Boleyn's coronation 'the celebrations of the City were not an unalloyed success at the grass roots level such things were supposed to reach.' Catherine Parr, nursing Henry, 'moved into a small bedroom next to his, out of her queenly apartments, emphasising the

fact that a man on his sixth wife must be assumed to stand in need of a nurse and for this role the widowed Lady Latimer'—Catherine herself—'was well equipped.'

Perhaps Fraser's prose would be sprightlier if her grasp of historical context were stronger. In *Mary Queen of Scots,* much the best of her books, it was strong. Here she is unable to bring alive the political and religious conflicts to which the fate of Henry's queens belonged, and which would give the book a spine. Without that context the reader's interest is unlikely to be sustained, unless by pity for blighted lives or by interest in the clothes or the jewels or the sex.

The result, far beneath Fraser's honorable aim, is a sort of slow-moving Tudor *Dallas.* Henry VIII is 'lithe and golden-haired' in his youth, when 'a vast love of life in all its forms exuded from him'. In time he is captured by the 'tempestuous, challenging Anne Boleyn'. Anne's outfit for her coronation is 'a mixture of the virginal and the resplendent'. For her execution she favours 'a mantle of ermine over a loose gown of dark grey damask, trimmed with fur, and a crimson petticoat'. In Catherine Parr, who 'comes across as someone who enjoyed the small pleasures of life', 'shoes were a real passion'.

The divorcees, Catherine of Aragon and Anne of Cleves, linger at the ranch. Anne of Cleves takes to drink. There are beauties and fast women. Lady Margaret Douglas is 'the best-looking Tudor girl of her generation'. The 'Bad Girl', Katherine Howard, proves to be merely a Good Time Girl, but, being 'the sort of girl who lost her head easily over a man', she commits infidelities which 'tick away like a time-bomb'.

In a shorter, tauter book the limits of Fraser's vision would matter less. *The Six Wives of Henry VIII* is dedicated to Harold Pinter, whose plays reduce experience to the smallest number of words in which it can be communicated. Fraser seems to work on an opposite principle. She needs a word-limit.

Lady Antonia Fraser with Polly Samson (interview date November 1992)

SOURCE: "My Fair Lady," in *Harper's,* No. 3371, November, 1992, pp. 58, 60.

[*In the following interview, Samson and Fraser discuss* The Wives of Henry VIII.]

When her friend and erstwhile *New Yorker* editor Bob Gottlieb suggested she write her next book on the wives of Henry VIII, Lady Antonia Fraser remembers thinking that it was the book she was born to write. "I felt like rushing around the streets of New York, accosting people and telling them what I was going to do," she says.

The idea was a natural for a writer who had long since earned her place as a major historian. At 27, Lady Antonia wrote the definitive biography *Mary, Queen of Scots,* which was a best seller in eight languages. It was followed by equally acclaimed volumes on Oliver Cromwell and Charles II. Then she moved on to *The Weaker Vessel,* about women's sufferings in the 17th century, and *The Warrior Queens,* which she wrote afterward "because I felt so depressed that I had to cheer myself up."

Yet for all her renown as an established biographer, Lady Antonia resists pigeonholing. Between her more serious works, she writes crime novels featuring the female detective Jemima Shore and is a fixture—along with her husband, the playwright Harold Pinter—on London's fashionable literary circuit. (She inherited her title from her father, the Earl of Longford, and uses it on feminist grounds—insisting that Lady, like Ms., is a form of address all women should adopt.) During her tenure as president of English PEN, the international writers' association, Lady Antonia has also proved to be a formidable ambassador for freedom of expression, most notably in her tireless dealings with the British Foreign Office over controversial novelist Salman Rushdie and then-visiting dissident Vaclav Havel.

On the day of our interview, Lady Antonia was in the midst of doing publicity for *The Wives of Henry VIII,* which had just been published in England. . . . One morning newspaper praised her "Gioconda smile," while another commented that her skin "would make peaches weep in their cream." She dismisses the gushing references to her beauty: "I suppose one's vanity is pleased by it, but if I could be born again with more beauty or more brains, I'd take the brains," she says.

In any case, having recently turned 60, Lady Antonia has found that the label has become a burden. "Once you are called a beauty, then you are either an ex-beauty, a fading beauty, or 'still surprisingly beautiful.' But at least one gets more shortsighted, so when you remove your spectacles to put on makeup, the image in the mirror is pleasingly blurred," she says, laughing.

The author credits her success as a historian to her "ordinary eye." "When I'm reading a diary or looking at a document," she says, "I pick out the things that will interest other readers. I don't do it on purpose, I just see things the way most people do, which is very useful." In *The Wives of Henry VIII,* she divulges the sort of details one longs to know about royal marriages. Details of court life emerge in a way hitherto ignored by historians: the sleeping arrange-ments, the hazardous business of sexual intercourse in the public rooms of Hampton Court Palace, and the methods of contraception. She writes of the filthy passageway between Henry's and Catherine of Aragon's rooms and of Anne Boleyn's assessment of Henry's performance as a lover, which lacked both "vertu" (skill) and "puissance" (staying power).

Lady Antonia's obvious enjoyment of research is what brings the book to life. She worked each morning for six years in the British Library, keeping Mediterranean hours, often breaking for lunch with a friend at a nearby Greek restaurant. She also visited the scenes of the crimes: At the Tower of London, she felt the ghosts of Anne Boleyn and Catherine Howard as she studied the block where they both lay down their necks. "Unless you can imagine the feel of the ax on your own neck, you shouldn't be writing this book," she says.

Lady Antonia has dealt with the wives as individuals, rather than as the "Divorced, Beheaded, Died, Divorced, Beheaded, Survived" cardboard classifications by which they've previously been categorized. Each of the women is a colorful, headstrong character rather than merely a victim. Lady Antonia admits that, had she been around at the time, she, too, might have fallen for Henry's charms. "When he was young, he was terribly attractive. He wasn't born with a 54-inch waistline and a face like a potato marked with little eyes. When he came to the throne, he was 18, tall, with a slim waist and hips, broad shoulders, golden hair, very athletic, loved music. I think anybody might have fancied him. He sounds marvelous."

And would she have survived? "I think I would have been like Anne Boleyn and needed too much independence," she says. "But I would have produced sons, as I've had three." Lady Antonia doesn't identify with any of the six wives in particular, but says she likes Anne Boleyn for her spirit and Catherine of Aragon for her intelligence: "People tend to think of Catherine as a bigoted old Spanish boot, but she was probably the cleverest queen consort England ever had."

Given the current state of the British royal family, one cannot help but speculate on how Fergie and Diana might have fared at the hands of Henry. The Duchess of York, it's agreed, would have lost her head. "She has no common sense. I think that is the kindest comment to make," Lady Antonia says. The Princess of Wales, however, would have survived. "Royalty had privacy then. It's tragic what's happening. As long as heirs were produced, we, the people, wouldn't have known about the rest of it."

And what would a biographer make of Lady Antonia's own life? "Oh, I don't think writers make very interesting subjects," she says, a touch disingenuously. "Well," she adds, after a moment's reflection, "it was Hilary Belloc who said,

'[Her] sins were scarlet, but [her] books were read.' I think that says it all."

Connolly Cole (review date 20 December 1992)

SOURCE: "Betrothals and Beheadings," in *Chicago Tribune,* December 20, 1992, p.7.

[*In the following review of* The Wives of Henry VIII, *Cole examines the intricate individual stories that make up the work.*]

In this new study of King Henry VIII and his wives [entitled *The Wives of Henry VIII*], Antonia Fraser sets out to dispel the historical perception that stereotypes those six women—Catherine of Aragon as the Abandoned Wife, Anne Boleyn as the Temptress, Jane Seymour as the Good Woman, Anna of Cleves as the Flanders Mule, Katherine Howard as the Bad Girl and Catherine Parr as the Mother Figure. Fraser points out that those images, while true in some measure, will not bear the hard scrutiny of history.

Anne Boleyn was certainly more than the King's goggle-eyed whore and Anna of Cleves more dignified than the cruel sobriquet that attaches to her name. Catherine of Aragon was a woman of character who bravely resisted banishment, fighting to the end for the legitimacy of her daughter, Mary. But to a greater or lesser extent, all six of Henry's wives were created or destroyed by what Fraser describes as their biological destiny—their capacity, in an age of grim infant mortality, to fructify the sovereign's bed with royal progeny, especially male offspring, and thus to perpetuate a dynasty insecure from its inception in 1485, when Henry of Lancaster killed Richard III on Bosworth Field and proclaimed himself Henry VII, the first of the Tudor kings.

It was an accession won at the point of a sword, and there were others with superior dynastic claims to the throne. Throughout his long reign, Henry VIII was constantly aware and wary of those deciduous loyalties lurking about his court. One cannot understand his marital career without taking into account this obsession to have male heirs, for the royal Tudors proved not to be highly philoprogenitive as a family. If Henry could not father a male successor, God, it would seem, could not establish His seed upon the throne of England.

The giant personality of Henry VIII has long over-shadowed the six women who shared his kingdom. With a firm grasp of her material, Fraser chronicles their lives at court triumphs as well as disasters, and admirably catches the lusty flavor of the period in this well produced and handsomely illustrated book.

Of the six women brave or foolish enough to marry Henry, only Jane Seymour retained his lasting affection, and she died giving birth to his son. Catherine of Aragon and Anna of Cleves were first courted and then cast aside for political purposes, while Anne Boleyn and Katherine Howard, both young and wayward, were caught in the caprice of infidelity and beheaded to assuage the King's anger.

Kingship in England reached a pinnacle of power and authority in the 16th Century. Henry was more than an absolute head of state, he also was the supreme head of the church, the spiritual as well as temporal ruler. Immortalized by the painter Hans Holbein as a Renaissance prince ruling in the image of God, Henry not only dominated the royal court, with its palaces at Greenwich, Windsor and Hampton, its tournaments and hunting lodges, but also the upheavals of the Reformation and the statesmen and princes—Cardinal Wolsey, Thomas Cromwell and Thomas Cranmer, the Emperor Charles V and Pope Clement VII—who used the King's wives as pawns in the powerful game of politics.

If Henry was a born ruler, he was not born to be king. He might never have reigned except that his older brother, Arthur Prince of Wales, died young. Henry was 12 when he became heir apparent, succeeding to the throne six years later on the death of his father, Henry VII. He conducted affairs of state much as he approached matrimony—with an axe.

His first wife, Catherine of Aragon, the daughter of Queen Isabella and King Ferdinand of Spain, actually had been his dead brother's wife for about six months. Catherine was betrothed to Arthur to consolidate an alliance of England and Spain against the common enemy, France.

Six years older than Henry, Catherine was a plain, pious woman. A man of appetite and ambition, Henry, at age 19, did not feel compelled to marry her. But he was weary of a variety of mistresses culled from the ladies at court, the imperatives of power underlined the importance of the Spanish alliance and there was the need to produce a son. They were married for almost 20 years, but Catherine, having given birth to Mary Tudor, failed to bring to life a male heir, and the marriage evaporated in serial miscarriages, still-born infants or others who were short-lived.

The marriage might have endured, however, had Anne Boleyn been a harlot. Instead, having bewitched the King, she demanded marriage and the throne. It is said that the length of the siege is a woman's glory, and Anne Boleyn resisted the rampant war-lord until he made her queen. Young and attractive, she had grown up in France and was wise in the ways of the coquette. In the end, there was no divorce. Henry's marriage to Catherine was simply annulled, she was pensioned off as the Dowager Princess of Wales, wife of the late lamented Arthur, and England acquired a new queen. The first child was a girl, christened Elizabeth; the second was still-born, and the whole tragic litany of conjugal miscarriages began again. Naturally flirtatious, Queen Anne had many admirers at court and many enemies who envied her position. Quick to become jealous and suspicious, the King began to believe the pervasive whispers about the Queen's capacity for dalliance circulating throughout the court. Arrested and put on trial, she went to the scaffold, in the words of one witness, looking "as gay as if she was not going to die."

Henry, who liked to combine betrothals with beheadings, secretly married Jane Seymour, a lady-in-waiting at court, two days after Anne's execution. The Seymours were landed gentry with sound aristocratic connections, but what appealed to Henry was that they were a prolific family. The new Queen died giving birth to Edward, Henry's first legitimate male heir to survive, (Edward would die at age 16, of tuberculosis.)

Henry, now an aging, corpulent man, was once more without a wife. New political alliances were explored without much success. Mary of Guise and Christina of Denmark spurned the King's overtures, and eventually, on assurance of his advisers, Henry decided on Anna of Cleves, a petty princess from the lower Rhineland. The marriage would provide England with the support of the North Germans, from Scheldt to the Zuider Zee. The Low Countries would be his, and beyond the North Sea, Henry would possess a people who, like himself, had cast off the Pope and who would also prove invaluable to trade.

Anna was 34, prudent, unprepossessing and bored. Marriage to the English King would be an escape. Amid considerable pomp and ceremony, she arrived in England. But she was no beauty, and Henry recoiled. (Fraser cites Anna's "slightly bulbous nose" as "one explanation of the King's disappointment.") In vain he tried to rescind the contract but was finally persuaded to go through with the ceremony.

Henry found Anna dismal and could not bring himself to consummate the marriage. Instead, he sought distractions among the ladies of the court, among whom was 18-year-old Katherine Howard, who bore a faint resemblance to her cousin, the ill-fated Anne Boleyn.

At age 50, King Henry had not lost his taste for a pretty face and flashing eyes. Queen Anna was informed that the King was divorcing her because their marriage had taken place under constraint. He assured her of his affection and hoped for her compliance. Tired of virginal matrimony, the Queen readily agreed, with certain conditions—she would remain in England and be provided with a suitable residence and income. The King was generous, and the Lords, the Com-

mons and the clergy, bidden to obedience by their royal master, quickly pronounced the divorce.

Henry neither wished for nor expected a child from Katherine. She was like a child to him, and he rejoiced in her youthful radiance. But in less than two years, the serenity of the aging satyr was savaged by ugly innuendoes concerning the Queen's chastity. When she was 15, a music master had tried to seduce her, and, in the words of Katherine's confession, she "suffered him at sundry times to handle and touch the secret parts of my body." There were rumors of other, later amatory audacities. Arrested, put on trial, Queen Katherine was decapitated as a lesson to ladies of loose morals who trifle with kings.

An ogre of obesity, ulcerous, spent in spirit and slipping into melancholy, Henry now contemplated his sixth marriage. Catherine Parr, a consolable widow of excellent breeding, was in her 30s and less than good-looking. Sensible and intelligent, she had already outlived two husbands and was adept at caring for and pleasing elderly men. She was not enamoured of the King but resigned herself to becoming queen.

While his nights may have been prosaic, Henry was at last at peace in the companionship of a woman. He died after a series of strokes, having reigned for almost 40 years. Two weeks after the funeral, Catherine quietly married a handsome man of minor nobility, Thomas Seymour.

The final historical irony would be that, out of the wreckage of all Henry's marriages, the female child at whose birth he had winced would take the scepter, meant for the sons he lacked, and, as Queen Elizabeth I, become the greatest Tudor monarch of them all.

Angeline Goreau (review date 20 December 1992)

SOURCE: A review of *The Wives of Henry VIII,* in *The New York Times Book Review,* December 20, 1992, p.11.

[*In the following review, Goreau considers Fraser's perspective on Henry VIII and his wives.*]

"Who does not tremble when he considers how to deal with a wife?" asked Henry VIII in 1521.

That the King was writing on behalf of marriage, emphasizing the precious and sacred charge involved in such a union, must surely be one of the odder ironies of history. Odder still, given subsequent events, was that his motive in writing "The Defence of the Seven Sacraments" was to refute Martin Luther's heretical challenge to Pope and church.

For Henry's efforts, the Pope granted to him and his successors the title Defender of the Faith.

> **To keep track of the dizzying list of royal mates, Lady Antonia Fraser tells us in the introduction to her latest work of popular history, people took to counting them off in a little refrain: "Divorced, beheaded, died; divorced, beheaded, survived." The six women in question, Lady Antonia observes, have come to be "defined in a popular sense not so much by their lives as by the way these lives ended." She proposes, in *The Wives of Henry VIII*, to rescue them from this historical injustice.**
> **—*Angeline Goreau***

Just six years later, Henry initiated the divorce that ultimately propelled England into the maw of schism. The divorce (never, of course, recognized by the Holy See) took another six years to orchestrate, but, once accomplished, ushered in a period of marital chaos whose extremes have rarely been equaled—even in our own era of rampant family dysfunction. Renaissance Europe watched aghast as the King of England ordered his second wife, Anne Boleyn, beheaded on trumped-up charges of treason after only three and a half years of marriage, then registered with disbelief the coronation of four more Queens of England in the space of little more than a decade. When apprised of the news that Henry had repudiated his fourth wife, whom he had married just six months before, to place on the throne an adolescent named Katherine Howard, the King of France shook his head in wonderment and asked: "The Queen that now is?"

To keep track of the dizzying list of royal mates, Lady Antonia Fraser tells us in the introduction to her latest work of popular history, people took to counting them off in a little refrain: "Divorced, beheaded, died; divorced, beheaded, survived." The six women in question, Lady Antonia observes, have come to be "defined in a popular sense not so much by their lives as by the way these lives ended." She proposes, in *The Wives of Henry VIII,* to rescue them from this historical injustice.

One might object in passing that to be remembered for the manner of one's demise, provided it was spectacular enough, is not an uncommon fate. But a much stronger objection to Lady Antonia's point is that divorce, as modern experience has proved, need not be the end of one's life. Indeed, the popular refrain that Lady Antonia cites reveals a more important point, for it fixes the moment—and means—at which these women ceased to be regarded by the King as his wife (with the exception, naturally, of his widow, Catherine Parr).

One of the most interesting aspects of Lady Antonia's book, in fact, is its exploration of the manner in which the two divorced wives, Catherine of Aragon and Anne of Cleves, dealt with the limbo in which they were cast by divorce.

There have been many fine individual biographies of Henry VIII's queens, but until the publication earlier this year of Alison Weir's lively study *The Six Wives of Henry VIII.* there were few responsible collective treatments, probably because the very idea of uniting these six biographies in one volume requires that their subjects be defined, first and foremost, as wives. Putting these life stories together, however, turns out to have an unexpected advantage: it throws into relief the ways in which six women of very different character and background learned—or failed to learn—to cope with a prodigiously difficult man. Conversely, looking at the story as a whole allows us to see how grappling with Catherine of Aragon and Anne Boleyn, two very powerful and (each in her own way) defiant women, fundamentally influenced not only Henry's next choice of a wife, the relatively docile Jane Seymour, but also determined the way he would behave toward wives who followed. After Henry's experience with the fiery, intelligent, plotting Mistress Anne, Lady Antonia notes, "the King would specifically order his future wives to avoid argument." If they failed to keep this caveat in mind, he would darkly remind them of their predecessor's fate.

Not surprisingly, the King's favorite wife was his third, Jane Seymour, who took as her motto "Bound to obey and serve." Of all his wives, she alone produced a male heir, and she did him the favor of dying before he could tire of her. For it was Henry's own peculiar destiny to be attracted to women of spirit and discover afterward that spirit in a wife was an irritation he could not suffer gladly.

Another strength of *The Wives of Henry VIII* is its author's determination to retell the story as though she did not know what its end might be. "Although we know Henry VIII will marry six times," Lady Antonia writes in her introduction, "we must always remember that he did not." Unfolding the story from its relatively innocent beginning, she takes us step by step through the process of moral compromise through which the Renaissance's splendid, golden boy king was transmogrified into a repulsive old tyrant whose monstrous proportions perfectly mirrored his ego. Like that of Oscar Wilde's Dorian Gray, Henry VIII's character coarsened by degree with each violation.

Yet, despite her obvious disgust with Henry, Lady Antonia is determined to be fair. She puts events carefully in context, supplying the political and social underpinnings of what looks to 20th-century eyes suspiciously like one long royal nervous breakdown. She reminds us, for example, that by 16th-century standards Henry was a fairly good husband to his first wife for nearly 20 years until, deeply distraught over

Catherine's repeated miscarriages and the realization that no more children would come from the marriage, he finally turned to divorce as a means of freeing himself to produce a male heir. Lady Antonia points out, furthermore, that Henry's desperation over the succession had its roots in the fact that his father had won his crown at the battle of Bosworth Field. Henry VIII, the usurper, passed on to his son what might be called an intense throne anxiety. Without an indisputable—that is to say, male—heir, Henry feared that England might well fall once again into civil war.

Lady Antonia also disentangles the highly complicated strategies by which the King justified his actions, always managing to preserve "the tender conscience on which he prided himself." The same man who did not shrunk from letting his minister's invent the charges on which Anne Boleyn was tried was nevertheless reluctant to tell an outright lie himself. "Taxed many years later with having had an affair with *three* Boleyns, two daughters and a mother," Lady Antonia writes, "the best he could do was to reply shamefacedly: 'Never with the mother.'"

The Wives of Henry VIII does, as it promises, admirably succeed in bringing to life, with economy of detail, the six women who married England's ruler. But, despite Lady Antonia's assertion that "this is not his story," the biography's focus keeps wandering inevitably back to "the gigantic Maypole . . . round which these women had to dance." This may be, however, an unavoidable consequence of the fact that what these six women had in common was coming to terms with Henry. Finally, the book's greatest interest lies in its deeply engaging portrait of a marriage—in serial.

Eric Ives (review date November 1994)

SOURCE: "A Good Crumb," in *History Today,* Vol. 44, No. 11, November, 1994, p. 60.

[*In the following review, Ives assesses the strengths and failings of Fraser's approach to writing history as evidenced in* The Wives of Henry VIII.]

That Antonia Fraser's *Six Wives of Henry VIII* is available in paperback as well as on library shelves should guarantee circulation to the only current account of Henry VIII's wives and by far the best of its kind. It has all the Fraser virtues: liveliness, enough but not too much detail, a grasp of up-to-date scholarship and an eye for the memorable—I shall treasure St Bernadino of Siena's remark that the mother who fails to tell her daughter what to expect on her wedding night 'sends her to sea with no biscuit'. Above all imaginative sympathy; the past *lives* as is too rarely the case in academic history today. After half-a-century Eileen Power's quip still

remains true: 'Once upon a time there was a historian who was so dull that all the *other* historians began to notice'.

The dullness of academics is partly fear of being wrong, and it is the case that the Fraser method does take risks. Points are sometimes missed. The evidence suggests that Henry divorced Anne Boleyn not on grounds of precontract to the Earl of Northumberland but on grounds of his own previous intercourse with Anne's sister (macabre consistency). Feel for a good story sometimes overcomes proper scepticism. The tax collector whom the Lincolnshire rebels in 1536 sewed in a cowskin to be eaten by dogs is a fiction. Occasionally connections are jumped at too readily; William Herbert's advancement antedated his sister-in-law's becoming queen in 1543.

There are also errors. For example, the ambassador to France in 1542 was not John Paget but William; Thomas Seymour was not Lord Admiral in 1544; the illegality in torturing Anne Ascue was not that she was a gentlewoman but that she had already been condemned; the misprint on p.372 of 'progress' entirely distorts the sense. So, too, with the illustrations. These are plentiful, well-chosen and varied but 'Thomas Boleyn' is probably 'James Butler' Anne's intended husband; the Horenbout miniature captioned 'Anne Boleyn' is improbable, so too the Holbein drawing at Windsor; the sixteenth-century view of the Tower is a Victorian redrawing; the Wyngaerde of Richmond Palace is actually of Hampton Court.

But such matters are rarely more than venal. The importance is the overall interpretation. Here, of course, any writer has a problem of balance. Katherine of Aragon—and quite clearly that was how Tudor Englishmen spelt the name—was involved with Henry for thirty-four years and Anne Boleyn for ten, but the next three wives for under two years each and the last for less than four.

The temptation to skimp after Anne Boleyn's death is strong, especially as political considerations suggest that it was the first two wives who mattered and that the only significant thing about the others was that Jane had a son and the rest remained childless. Antonia Fraser, however, resists this, treating each woman at a decent length. In consequence, although there are full-scale scholarly biographies to set alongside her accounts of Katherine of Aragon and Anne Boleyn, her treatment in depth of the last four wives gives the book a unique value.

Lady Antonia claims that she has no favourites but she certainly tries to redress some balances. One example is Jane Seymour, portrayed as a serene and submissive creature, not the schemer I made her. Not that I am persuaded—nobody who had been around a Tudor court for as long as Jane could possibly have been so unaware. The Fraser rehabilitation of

Anne of Cleves is, by contrast, very convincing. Anne is shown to have been by no means ill-favoured—the 'Flanders Mare' sneer dates from the eighteenth century—and once settled in England as an independent and wealthy woman she enjoyed life (particularly alcohol) and some popularity.

I am not, however, like Antonia Fraser, 'mystified' at Henry's disappointment with her. Anglicised, Anne was one thing, Anne arriving in England for the first time was another. Completely naïve, wholly unsupplied with the 'biscuit' of the facts of life, she understood no English and was totally ignorant of courtly etiquette and courtly devices. It is no wonder that she effectively ignored the complete stranger who burst in to give her presents and became totally bewildered when he changed costume and appeared as king. Henry had expected a sophisticated woman only to have his chivalric gallantries fall flat before this repressed provincial *hausfrau*. Had he been available, a few lessons with Professor Higgins might have done the trick, but the forty-nine year old Henry had been made to look a fool and sulked at how badly he had been treated.

Antonia Fraser's interpretations are worth listening to, whether one agrees or not. I would, for example, certainly want to question the notion that during the long years of waiting Anne Boleyn and Henry practised *coitus interruptus*. I agree that Katherine Howard probably did know the technique but it requires some male co-operation and while I can accept that in emergency she might be ready to force away a lover, I cannot imagine Henry VIII tolerating such treatment. Habsburg enemies called Anne 'the Concubine' but her determination to be more than a mistress and Henry's obsession to beget a son in wedlock must together have limited the intimacies they allowed themselves. It is the twentieth-century reading history backwards to assume that chastity was not the preferred contraceptive option of past generations.

In one respect, however, the book disappoints. It points out the links between the wives but deals only indirectly with what really united them—Henry VIII himself. What did he look for in them? Sophistication we have seen. Maturity? Apart from the least satisfactory of his wives, the nineteen-year-old and knowledgeable Katherine Howard, the remainder were well past youth, three in the later twenties and two over thirty. Was this because Henry wanted someone to manage, even mother him? There are certainly hints of this with both the Katherines and with Anne Boleyn. It is here that our knowledge of Henry's youth is so disabling. His mother died when he was eleven, but his even more formidable grandmother, Margaret Beaufort, survived to see him crowned and has been credited with the dominant role in the transition from father to son. Whether this was the case is, not, unfortunately, clear from the latest biography of her by M.K. Jones and M.G. Underwood.

In *The King's Mother, Lady Margaret Beaufort,* the authors make a valiant attempt to demonstrate that Margaret played an important political role from 1485, but data to enable a firm decision one way or the other is simply not available. One would like to believe in the Tudor matriarch who stood behind both son and grandson and there are some indications of this, but she comes out far more strongly as a tough-minded Tudor widow, concerned with family, status and property but with a genuine concern for charity and above all her Cambridge colleges. It is nicely ironic that of all her grandson's wives it was Anne Boleyn who shared this enthusiasm!

Mel Gussow (review date 4 December 1996)

SOURCE: "Playing Modern Detective In the Gunpowder Plot," in *The New York Times,* December 4, 1996, pp. C3, C7.

[*In the following review, Gussow investigates Fraser's ideas on the research she conducted for* Faith and Treason: The Story of the Gunpowder Plot.]

While writers as diverse as John le Carré and V. S. Naipaul journey to exotic places in search of material, Antonia Fraser habitually goes to the reading room of the British Museum, where she is surrounded by her research (and sometimes by her mother, daughter or other members of her family of writers, the literary Longfords). For Lady Antonia there is also a sense of adventure, despite the quietude and the archival aspect of her creativity.

In her books she has looked deeply into the lives of major figures in English history, searching for facts behind myths. For her new work, *Faith and Treason: The Story of the Gunpowder Plot,* there is also a mystery. In 1605, Robert Catesby, Guy Fawkes and other Roman Catholic dissidents threatened to blow up Parliament and assassinate King James I of England as a protest against religious persecution.

As she says in her book, the problem was to draw conclusions from "imperfect records and testimonies taken under torture." As a result, some historians have raised doubts that the plot ever took place, suggesting that the Government may have imagined it in order to blame the Catholics. Over tea during a recent visit to New York (with her husband, Harold Pinter), Lady Antonia said: "You have to assess the evidence, read the primary sources and make up your own mind. I happen to think there was a plot, and that the Government penetrated it 10 days before it happened." To reach that conclusion, she consulted all available documents, historical papers as well as the pamphlet on torture that is sold to tourists in the Tower of London. She also gathered atmosphere through field work, what she calls "optical research." For example, she explored closets and crannies where priests were hidden.

As with her other books like *Mary Queen of Scots* and *The Wives of Henry VIII, Faith and Treason* peripherally serves as a guidebook. Book in hand, readers go to castles, National Trust houses and dungeons described in the text. "Forget the Blue Guide," Lady Antonia said. "I am the Guide."

In England, the tourists are already on Guy Fawkes's trail. Even more will be if the book becomes a film. The movie rights have been sold, and the novelist William Boyd is writing the screenplay.

It would be the first of Lady Antonia's histories to reach the screen, although dramatizations of her mystery-novels about Jemima Shore, a television reporter and amateur sleuth, have been presented on public television. In a sense, *Faith and Treason* is a bridge between those mysteries and the author's biographies. Because she uses detective tools in investigating the complex case, she was especially pleased when one reviewer compared the book to the work of Mr. le Carré.

Speaking about the plotters, she wondered how they "could have chucked everything away, not only for themselves but for their wives and children," all, of course, for the sake of a cause. The central figure was not Fawkes but Catesby. Fawkes became the one most remembered because he was found with gunpowder in the basement of Parliament.

Subsequently England celebrated the exposure of the plot as Guy Fawkes Day. Each year on Nov. 5, bonfires are lighted and Fawkes is burned in effigy, sometimes along with the Pope. In a turnabout, there is some sympathy for Fawkes in Britain. To illustrate, Lady Antonia repeated a joke about the country's natural antipathy to politicians: "Guy Fawkes is the only man who got into Parliament with the right intentions."

Her own allegiance is neither with James I nor the plotters but with the priests and courageous women who gave them shelter, at risk to their own lives. Priests were arrested, tortured and executed, but most of the women avoided arrest by playing on the idea that they were "weak" and therefore incapable of action. Echoing Lady Antonia's earlier book, *The Weaker Vessel, Faith and Treason* depicts strong women behind the scenes.

It is dedicated to her son-in-law and daughters-in-law, to "Edward, who would have defended them; Lucy, who would have hidden them; Paloma, who would have succored them in exile." What would Lady Antonia, a Catholic, have done if confronted with a recusant seeking shelter? "I hope I would have been like Magdalen Montague, a great Catho-

lic lady who never compromised, and all the time she was hiding people."

Faith and Treason is detailed in its descriptions of life and culture in the period. For example, people drank beer and not water, because water was so contaminated that it became "a lethal substance."

There are frequent references to Shakespeare, who was contemporaneous with James I. Lady Antonia said that in writing *Macbeth,* with its theme of regicide, Shakespeare was influenced by the Gunpowder Plot. *Hamlet* and *King Lear* came later, and therefore were Jacobean rather than Elizabethan plays. Because Ben Jonson and others were writing at the time, she said, the period was artistically a "kind of cusp." In her biography *Royal Charles,* the author reminds readers that several years after the Gunpowder Plot, others seeking religious freedom sailed from England on the Mayflower. Since she has visited the 17th century in this and other books, it is clearly her favorite age.

"It is the century," she said, adding quickly: "But I'm actually quite happy in my own time. I don't have a sentimental feeling about the past. I want to recreate it, but I don't want to drag about in those clothes." She would not mind time-traveling, she said, "if I could wander about and be invisible."

She said biographers and historians should establish an order of values and not be submerged in trivialities. In this area, she defers to the English historian E. H. Carr, who said that everything that happens every day is not history, no matter how famous a person may be. "By the next day it's the past, but it's not necessarily history," Lady Antonia said.

Through footnotes and textual references, she parallels the Gunpowder Plot with recent events in Northern Ireland and the Middle East, but in characteristic fashion does not underscore the relevance. The work is not intended as a polemic.

For her next book, a biography of Marie Antoinette, Lady Antonia will leave the British Museum. In a change of place, with pen and author poised, she will take up new research residence at the Bibliothèque Nationale in Paris.

FURTHER READING

Criticism

Review of *Mary Queen of Scots,* by Antonia Fraser. *Times Literary Supplement* No. 3514 (July 3, 1969): 729-30.
    Juxtaposes details and perspectives on Mary from other sources with Fraser's biographical portrait.

Additional coverage of Fraser's life and career is contained in the following sources published by Gale: *Contemporary Authors,* Vol. 85-88; *Contemporary Authors New Revision Series,* Vol. 44; *Major Twentieth-Century Writers;* and *Something about the Author,* Vol. 32.

Yasunari Kawabata
1899-1972

Japanese short story writer, novelist, and critic.

The following entry presents an overview of Kawabata's career. For further information on his life and works, see *CLC*, Volumes 2, 5, 9, and 18.

INTRODUCTION

During his career, critics had difficulty classifying Kawabata because he developed a unique style combining elements of traditional and modern literature. International audiences, including the Nobel Prize Committee, thought of Kawabata as representing traditional Japanese literature. This view often confused Japanese audiences, who considered Kawabata a modernist. He was involved in the development of new literary styles and movements in Japan, but tradition did play a role in his style and themes.

Biographical Information

Kawabata was born in Osaka in 1899. His early life was filled with loss. His father died when he was two years old, his mother when he was three, his sister when he was nine, and his grandfather when he was 16. He spent most of his childhood living in school dormitories. Family life is very important in Japanese culture, and the loneliness and alienation that characterized his youth infused his later fiction. Kawabata attended the elite First Higher School from 1917 to 1920 and received a degree from the English Literature Department of Tokyo Imperial University in 1920; in 1924 he received a degree from the Japanese Literature Department. As a young writer in 1924, Kawabata worked with other writers to create the *Bungei jidai,* or Literary Era, in opposition to the proletarian literature popular at the time. They were known as "Neoperceptionists," and they were concerned with the aesthetics of literature. Their work focused on diction, lyricism, and rhythm. While involved in this literary movement, Kawabata was better known as a critic than as a writer himself. In 1926 he gained attention for his fiction with the publication of his short story "The Izu Dancer" in a literary monthly. He went on to write short stories and several novels which earned him an international reputation. He became a member of the Art Academy of Japan in 1953, and in 1957 was appointed chairman of the P.E.N. Club of Japan. Kawabata received the Goethe Medal in 1959 in Frankfurt and in 1961 was awarded Japan's highest recognition for a man of letters, the Order of Culture. He went on to win the Nobel Prize for Literature in 1968.

He committed suicide in April of 1972, leaving no note or explanation.

Major Works

Kawabata's fiction combines elements of modern and traditional literature. In addition to remaining true to traditional forms, Kawabata often focused on retaining traditional culture in the face of the modern world as the subject of his fiction. He presented and defended such traditional Japanese forms as the tea ceremony in *Sembazuru* (*Thousand Cranes;* 1952), the game of Go in *Go sei-gen kidan* (*The Master of Go;* 1954), and folk art in *Koto* (*The Old Capital;* 1962). Kawabata wrote in a style similar to traditional Japanese haiku poetry, known as *renga,* or linked poetry. His work is filled with imagery and symbolism. Kawabata never wrote about political turmoil, but instead focused on personal and spiritual crises. His major themes included loneliness, alienation, the meaninglessness and fleeting nature of human passion, aging, and death. *The Master of Go* is an example of Kawabata's theme of tradition versus modernization, using the traditional Japanese game of Go. The Master represents tradition and views Go as an art form. The young challenger Otaké represents the modern rational approach to Go. In the end the Master is overcome by modern rationalism. *Nemureru bijo* (*House of the Sleeping Beauties and Other Stories;* 1953) is a collection of short stories depicting the changing effects of eroticism on the aging male. *Yama no oto* (*Sound of the Mountain;* 1954) looks at the Japanese extended family and Japanese business. The novel's main theme is the effects of aging on the protagonist, who believes he hears the mountains signalling his imminent death. *The Old Capital* traces the struggle of Kyoto, Japan's ancient capital, as the city attempts to retain its identity in the face of industrialization. Twin sisters who have been separated at birth represent the dichotomy of tradition vs. modernization, city vs. country, and folk art vs. mass production. Typical of Japanese literature, there are no clear-cut good or evil forces in Kawabata's fiction. He leaves matters unresolved, and his endings are ambiguous. Kawabata's fiction relies on his readers and their imagination to decide the fate of his characters.

Critical Reception

Some reviewers have pointed out the difference in characterization found in Japanese literature as opposed to Western literature. They assert that Kawabata's characterization is not fully fleshed out and sometimes falls into symbolism. Many critics also assert that there is a vagueness to Kawabata's writing style. In discussing Kawabata's lyricism and appeal, Marlene A. Pilarcik states his works "are noted for their delicate, wistful beauty and haunting lyricism. They express the essence of the Japanese soul, but also draw on the universality of human experience." Critics often comment on the complicated relationship between Kawabata's writing style, modernism, and traditional Japanese poetry. James T. Araki states, "The general reader in Japan has probably regarded Kawabata as a modernist rather than a traditionalist, for his stories are often difficult to apprehend fully, owing to the rich, allusive imagery, a suggestive quality that requires a matured sensibility of the reader, an elliptical sentence style, and a mode of story progression that often relies on linking through imagery rather than through contextual or sentence logic—a technique of the traditional *renga* or 'linked verse.'" Beyond the style question, one of the most widely discussed issues relating to Kawabata's work was his relationship to the traditional and modern worlds. Sidney DeVere Brown explained it this way: "The modern world provides merely a dim, mostly unseen context in his novels for the admirable people and culture rooted in Old Japan."

PRINCIPAL WORKS

Izu no odoriko [*The Izu Dancer and Other Stories*] (short stories) 1926

Tenohira no shosetsu [*Palm-of-the-Hand Stories*] (short stories) 1926
Asakusa kurenaidan [*The Red Gang of Asakusa*] (novel) 1930
Kinju [*Of Birds and Beasts*] (short stories) 1935
Yukiguni [*Snow Country*] (novel) 1937
Aishu [*Sorrow*] (short stories and essays) 1949
Sembazuru [*Thousand Cranes*] (novel) 1952
Nemureru bijo [*House of the Sleeping Beauties and Other Stories*] (short stories) 1953
Suigetsu ["The Moon on the Water"] (short story) 1953
Go sei-gen kidan [*The Master of Go*] (novel) 1954
Yama no oto [*The Sound of the Mountain*] (novel) 1954
Mizuumi [*The Lake*] (novel) 1955
Koto [*The Old Capital*] (novel) 1962
The Izu Dancer and Others (short stories) 1964
Kata-ude [*One Arm*] (novel) 1965
Utsukushisa to kanashimi to [*Beauty and Sadness*] (novel) 1965

CRITICISM

Earl Miner (essay date Summer 1957)

SOURCE: "Traditions and Individual Talents in Recent Japanese Fiction," in *The Hudson Review,* Vol. X, No. 2, Summer, 1957, pp. 302-8.

[*In the following excerpt, Miner discusses how Tanizaki Junichiro and Kawabata use different aspects of traditional Japanese literature, and how their work differs from the literature of the West.*]

There is little of the West in the mature art of the two greatest contemporary Japanese novelists, Tanizaki Junichiro and Kawabata Yasunari.... After periods of experimentation, they have modelled their styles on the two most important Japanese fictional traditions—Tanizaki on the classical *monogatari* style represented at its greatest in Murasaki's *Tale of Genji* (c. 1000), and Kawabata on the highly imagistic and compressed style of Ihara Saikaku (1642-1693). These two traditions differ from each other considerably but have common qualities which distinguish them from Western fiction....

Tanizaki is a novelist of states of mind and attitude which are developed bit by bit in plots where time seems to float by. As in reading *The Tale of Genji,* we must constantly add and subtract—this person's thought to that character's action, this woman's attitude from that man's conversation. Like Joyce's manicuring God, the author has retired and sits Buddha-fashion with tucked-up legs in unperturbed reflection. What is truth? or what has really happened? we ask.

For a reply, we must look at the *presentation,* at Tanizaki's "The Mother of Captain Shigemoto," for example. Narration is laden with "as though," "but," "however," "as if," "it is not clear," "were probably," and hosts of conditionals and subjunctives—Mr. Seidensticker's skillful equivalents of the elusive aspects and moods of Japanese verbs. Whether Tanizaki's characters are macabre like Captain Shigemoto's father, sensual like Kaname in *Some Prefer Nettles,* or commonplace like the sisters in *A Dust of Snow,* we feel less what they do or say, than what they are or seem. We can see the very essence of this art in a few sentences from "The Firefly Hunt."

> The events of the evening passed through Sachiko's mind in no particular order. She opened her eyes— she might have been dreaming, she thought. Above her, in the light of the tiny bulb, she could see a framed kakemono that she had noticed earlier in the day: the words "Pavilion of Timelessness," written in large characters and signed by one Keido. Sachiko looked at the words without knowing who Keido might be. A flicker of light moved across the next room.

To say that the meaning of this event is only the lustre of the commonplace in a seeming timelessness is to mistake Tanizaki's art for preciosity; the world is also a pavilion of splendor lovingly created in his rich details of experience, the past, and art. When Knopf issues his *Dust of Snow* (*Sasame-Yuki*), we shall appreciate more fully both his style, formed over the years on Poe, Baudelaire, and the *Genji,* and his great if often complexly Japanese humanism.

If Tanizaki persists in a fluid extension, Kawabata enters his characters so completely that he seems to disappear in a dramatic intensiveness reminiscent at times of Dostoevsky; but he remains completely impersonal, as even Saikaku does not. In **"The Mole,"** for example, the drama is that of a woman whose life and relations with her family and husband have been shaped and changed by her habit of fingering a mole on her right shoulder. Her words are couched as a sort of diary meant for her husband's eyes and tell the history of the mole and what it has meant in her life. This is an incredible basis for a short story which conveys a woman's life and essential femininity with complete conviction, but it is just this quality of consuming immediacy without intimacy which Kawabata achieves so unsurpassedly.

Snow Country is far greater in sweep, technique, and style, however. **"The Mole"** has much of the intensity, but little else, of this novel and of the Saikaku tradition from which Kawabata derives his most fully realized art. One of Saikaku's chief subjects was human passion, and his technique an almost unbelievably imagistic style. Kawabata has the same *haiku*-like style of reduction to image become sym-bol which makes each detail verge upon the emblematic. There are three main characters to the story—Shimamura the sensualist, so precious that he is finally overwhelmed by his senses, Komako the geisha who lives by wasting her love on him, and the friend and rival, Yoko, who is a soft echo of Komako. The novel ends with Shimamura overcome by life: he is shocked into unconsciousness when Komako rushes from a burning building with Yoko's all but lifeless body in her arms.

Snow Country was written at different periods between 1934 and 1947, and its surpassing beauty grows out of this unhurried, considered art. The novel is divided into two parts, corresponding with Shimamura's two depicted visits to the snow country. At the beginning of the second part, Kawabata places Shimamura in Tokyo, shows the solicitude of his wife—thereby stressing by implication his culpability for infidelity—gets him back to the resort in the snow country, and suggests the time of year in two short sentences:

> It was the egg-laying season for moths, Shimamura's wife told him as he left Tokyo, and he was not to leave his clothes hanging in the open. There were indeed moths at the inn.

This polished style glows in a perfected structural setting. The novel opens and closes with similar scenes. It begins with Shimamura on the train observing Yoko as she attends to the sick Yukio and savoring her with a vague pruriency which amounts to wondering who she is and whether he will possess her. The novel ends with him overcome by the sight of her mangled body and still unsure of her identity or of his relation to her. Part One begins and ends with Shimamura's impressions on a train journey. Part Two begins with the image of a moth, "a spot of pale green . . . oddly like the color of death," an anticipation of Yoko's dying state at the end of the novel—which is in turn parallel to the death of Yukio at the end of part one; and their deaths represent Shimamura's gradual spiritual dissolution in the course of the story. These are merely the most obvious of the many structural motifs in the novel, so that the question is rather one of its meaning than of its formal beauty.

Mr. Seidensticker writes in his Introduction that the theme of the novel is the impossibility of love in an earthly paradise, but I find this reduction unsatisfying. The novel is surely founded upon a contrast between Shimamura's precious sterility and Komako's immediate vitality. While on the train to visit the snow country, he bends and straightens the forefinger of his left hand, that part of him (symbolically?) which so sweetly, achingly remembers Komako. She is repeatedly bathing and tidying, is described in terms of images of light and red, and is shown in sudden impulses of action. What she represents is best revealed in the symbolism of the Milky Way at the end of the novel. Kawabata alludes to a *haiku* by Basho—

> *High above the raging sea*
> *In an arch afar to Sado Island*
> *Streams the Milky Way—*

where the Sea of Japan is the same sea near the snow country. What the Milky Way symbolizes here and throughout is clear from four passages which I quote somewhat out of order. Shimamura sees the Milky Way come down

> . . . just over there, to wrap the night earth in its naked embrace. There was a terrible voluptuousness about it. Shimamura fancied that his own small shadow was being cast up against it from the earth.

> The Milky Way spread its skirts to be broken by the waves of the mountain, and, fanning out again in all its brilliant vastness higher in the sky, it left the mountain in a deeper darkness.

> [Komako] seemed to have her long skirts in her hands, and as her arms waved the skirts rose and fell a little. He could feel the red over the starlit snow.

> As he caught his footing [in stumbling toward the fire scene], his head fell back, and the Milky Way flowed down inside him with a roar.

The last sentence ends the novel. Komako and the Milky Way are one; both represent the superior life and beauty which overcome the sterility of Shimamura: some sensualists "by aromatic splinters die," but he drowns in an excess of life. Komako tragically wastes her vitality on him, but tragic waste is also tragic exaltation in fullness of being. She has lived. Like Tanizaki, Kawabata affirms life, but life as passionate vitality rather than Tanizaki's patterns of tradition and subtle shades. These two great writers in the two important Japanese fictional traditions complement each other perfectly. . . .

To begin with, it is extraordinary that these novels can affirm, even in translation, the importance of style— . . . *Snow Country* by a texture as rich as poetry. Second, these novels declare the function of taste in the Japanese tradition as a mode of apprehending and shaping experience. By taste I mean the ability to evaluate "the object as in itself it really is," but without Arnold's emphatic moral sense. But if taste may be opposed to moral preoccupation, there is indeed a moral passivity about these novels—and most Japanese art—which has troubled a Ruskin in the past and will continue to upset Westerners who desire authors to suggest moral judgments or create characters more completely good or bad.

The best and most characteristic Japanese fiction tends to accept, recreate, and esteem the esthetic particular and to avoid such issues of abstraction as conflicts between Good and Evil or Body and Soul (as opposed to good or evil protagonists). This leads to the third conclusion, that the Japanese go from the quasi-formal and particular realm of taste to what may be called metaphysical ultimates in ways different from ours. Our literature tends to alter or affirm life by making decisions in the way of poetic justice, but Japanese taste functions selectively and affirms by appreciation. The relation between this selective taste and metaphysical ultimates is established, I believe, in three ways which can only be named here: by a monistic treatment of materials, in which artistic judgment is exercised over a whole including man and nature, thought and action—poles for us but almost a single entity to a culture with a Buddhist heritage; second, by a narrative point of view which is at once closer to the materials and less omniscient—the air of "this is what things seem to have been"; and by a different concept of time which I can describe in brief only imagistically as the sensation for the reader of observing a traveler on a river-boat who observes now himself, now the shore, and now the river of flowing time—a merging of patterns of motion and stasis relative to each other. However, these random conclusions put an awkward intellectual superstructure upon many examples of fiction which often defy generalization and which certainly can be appreciated with far less self-consciousness. These stories are, after all, less the products of a foreign tradition than individual works of art which promise to give pleasure for many a reader and many a reading.

William F. Sibley (review date Winter 1969-70)

SOURCE: A review of *House of the Sleeping Beauties,* in *Pacific Affairs,* Vol. XLII, No. 4, Winter, 1969-70, p. 573.

[*In the following review, Sibley asserts that the title story of Kawabata's* House of the Sleeping Beauties *is "one of the finest works of Kawabata's late career."*]

There would seem to be a special place in modern Japanese literature for works set "in the autumn of the flesh," as Tanizaki Jun'ichiro once put it, by writers past the prime of life—swan songs (often deliberately premature) steeped in waning sensuality. The title story of this collection is an excellent specimen of the type and one of the finest works of Kawabata's late career. On the recommendation of a friend, "old Eguchi" pays several visits to an establishment where young women lie drugged into oblivion, solely for the discret delectation of a senile clientele. Though proud of his continuing potency, he resists the temptation to break the strict house rules against full possession of the sleeping beauties.

In the course of the five lonely nights that Eguchi passes beside the warm yet less than wholly alive bodies, he drifts from a state of heightened awareness of all the senses in a deep sleep filled with disquieting dreams of women he has known. With the death of his companion on the last night from an overdose of drugs, the illusory air of satiation which the house has so far succeeded in creating is dispelled. All that remains is an impression of inhumanity and impotence. But, up to the final page, illusion is the stuff of which this story is made, both in substance and style. Kawabata's prose, which is translated by Edward Seidensticker with something surpassing mere faithfulness, speaks in sighs and whispers throughout.

While **"Of Birds and Beasts"** belongs to a much earlier period in Kawabata's career, its central figure is analogously an aging and lonely man. A detailed description of the cold, detached pleasure he has derived from a succession of pet birds and dogs is masterfully interwoven with a fragmentary, and almost equally detached, review of an affair begun some ten years ago. The third selection, **"One Arm,"** is a brief, lyrical excursion into fetishistic fantasy. Unavoidably, it appears rather inconsequential between the two small masterpieces that make up the bulk of this volume.

Melvin Maddocks (essay date October 1972)

SOURCE: "The Floating World," in *The Atlantic*, Vol. 230, No. 4, October, 1972, pp. 126-29.

[*In the following essay, Maddocks discusses Kawabata's* The Master of Go, *Yukio Mishima's* Spring Snow, *and the tradition of Japanese literature.*]

There is a fascinatingly mysterious print by Hiroshige called *The Cave at Enoshima*. At the left, three figures are shown entering the island's grotto, a famous shrine. Dwarfs frozen in awe, they are blind to the enormous white-capped wave that seems to be reaching in after them like a dragon's tongue. A gnarled tree worthy of Samuel Beckett stands watch above the mouth of the cave like a crippled sentry. But the background is a bland denial of the foreground motif. A flat blue sea stretches off vaguely into the distance, and three motionless white sails add a touch of postcard lyricism. It is as if two different artists were at work here: a complacent copier of pretty conventions and a recorder of demoniac nightmares.

The paradox of Hiroshige's cave runs through Japanese art, through Japanese life. There are ultimates of disclosure and ultimates of concealment. One hides the body beneath kimonos and parasols; one hides the face under ritualistic smiles. Then one gives the body away in the grotesque (and

often comic) exaggerations of Japanese erotica; one gives the face away in the Kabuki actor's grimacing caricature of jealousy or vengeance. Nature is suppressed by the absolute control of a Japanese garden or revised into an artifact: a toylike bird arranged on a branch of idealized plum blossoms. But then one takes a look at those stones in that garden—petrified force, as sobering as the monoliths of Stonehenge. And one turns one's beguiled eyes from those flawlessly dainty finches to, say, the Tokoyuni print, *Revenge at Mount Fuji*, with the peak—aloof, icy, as white as Moby Dick—looking down upon the Soga brothers' massacre.

What accounts for these profound self-contradictions? The amateur Japanese-watcher—and all Westerners are amateurs—will have to take the long way around to the mystery of Hiroshige's cave. For he must deal first with the general inclination to explain the phenomenon of "Enoshima double-image" historically. The premise goes like this: Japan, due to the accident of its brief, intense modernity, still contains within itself irreconcilable elements of pure medievalism and late-twentieth-century supercivilization. The "black ships" of Commodore Perry steamed their dotted course like a moral dividing line across the Japanese cosmos; and as a consequence, the great-grandsons of samurai warriors are destined, as it were, to wear double-knit suits and ride their Hondas to jobs in public relations. When a Japanese intellectual sorts out his confusions, his impulse—his temptation—is to label them "Westernization."

> In *Thousand Cranes*, Kawabata virtually set the tea ceremony to plot, like an Oriental Henry James manipulating a four-hundred-year-old teabowl as his elegiac symbol.
> —*Melvin Maddocks*

In the case of a number of Japanese writers, like the 1968 Nobel Prizewinner Yasunari Kawabata, this historical theory has also become an artist's theme. Shortly after World War II, the supreme disaster in Japan's Westernization, Kawabata announced that he would write only "elegies." *Thousand Cranes, The Sound of the Mountain,* and now *The Master of Go,* written in 1954 but just published in the United States, fulfill their author's prophecy. In this last novel—really novella—Kawabata has composed a kind of parable which could be read as an extension of the Japanese poem:

> If only the world
> Would always remain this way,
> Some fishermen
> Drawing a little rowboat
> Up the river bank.

What can compare in persistent subtlety with a Japanese love song to the Old Ways—to the moment of perfect taste arrested forever? In *Thousand Cranes,* Kawabata virtually set the tea ceremony to plot, like an Oriental Henry James manipulating a four-hundred-year-old teabowl as his elegiac symbol. In *The Master of Go,* the ritual is the ancient game of black and white stones, loosely described as the Japanese equivalent of chess. Requiring infinitely patient turns of strategy—there are 361 intersections on a board—Go must appear to the Westerner as a nice metaphor of the Japanese soul.

The Master is Honnimbo Shusai. The novella, based on a Go match Kawabata covered for Tokyo and Osaka newspapers in 1938, details the Master's defeat, an event which with Old Japan leisureliness takes nearly six months to consummate. Kawabata carefully loads his contest. Otaké, the challenger, is a perfectly likeable young man but fretty. At thirty, he is a bit of a hypochondriac. He carries with him a small clinic's supply of medicines, yet continually fusses from eye and throat ailments as well as from apparently chronic indigestion. In addition, he suffers from a kidney weakness, which, combined with his compulsive tea-drinking, forces him to gather up his kimono and rush from the Go board at annoyingly frequent intervals.

By contrast, the Master bears his grave illness—a heart condition—with stoic equanimity. Weighing less than seventy pounds, only five feet tall, a frail old man with tufted eyebrows, the Master is the epitome of tradition. Otaké, on the other hand, stands for "modern rationalism," for "science and regulation," for "this new equality" that simply is tone-deaf to the Old Ways. Otaké is the technologist of Go who plays to win. The Master, redolent with "grace and elegance," is the artist who plays toward that mystical moment when the conscious intent of style is imposed upon the unconscious intent of life. At the critical instant, Otaké makes the ruthless, slightly treacherous move that wins him the match while at the same time spoiling it—in the Master's words, "smearing ink over the picture we had painted."

At first, the Western reader may find *The Master of Go* charming: that fatal adjective by which the Occident simultaneously praises and dismisses Japanese art. But behind the charm of Kawabata—as behind the charm of Hiroshige and behind all that quaintness described as "*Japonaise*"—lies a hidden darkness. Kawabata refers to the Master's "addiction," his "obsession." Day and night he "gave himself" to games—Mah-Jongg, billiards, and chess as well as Go—as if, Kawabata writes, he were giving himself to "devils." Do those Go stones he holds so authoritatively in his hands end up possessing him?

In his introduction to *The Master of Go,* the translator, Edward G. Seidensticker, writes: "One was puzzled to know why the flamboyant Mishima and the quiet, austere Kawabata should have felt so close to each other." Yet for all his spokesman-for-the-new-generation swagger, Yukio Mishima turned out to be a traditionalist, indeed a fanatical traditionalist. *Spring Snow,* the first novel of a posthumous tetralogy entitled *The Sea of Fertility,* reveals a Mishima who is more of a Japanese purist than Kawabata.

Spring Snow is a historical novel, set in 1912, about a very rich, very precious seventeen-year-old named Kiyoaki, an all-too-beautiful, all-too-sensitive young man, born jaded. He devotes himself rather languidly to "the cultivation of his anxiety." Perhaps Kiyoaki can best be defined as the sort of adolescent who keeps a diary of his *dreams.*

Only "the beauty of the unattainable" can excite Kiyoaki, and so he falls in love with Satoko, once she is made properly unattainable by her engagement to the third son of an imperial prince. At least it is stipulated that Kiyoaki has fallen in love. He is, in fact, so narcissistic that Satoko's first kiss leaves him "gazing over her head at the cherry trees"—the pink "made him think of an undertaker's cosmetics."

As a doomed love story, *Spring Snow* might qualify as Far East Erich Segal. But Mishima intended—and achieved—far more. Kiyoaki is his symbol of "a plant without roots," a samurai descendant with the instincts for heroism but no model to follow. The novel is finally about fathers who fail. Kiyoaki's father, the Marquis, represents "the new ascendancy of money." In his Western-style house the oak paneling is English, the marble is Italian, the steam heating is from Chicago. At parties in the Marquis' set, an air of "'English' absentmindedness" is cultivated, along with gold-tipped Westminster cigarettes. European phonograph records are played, and the *pièce de résistance* is likely to be a British silent-film version of Dickens. At this point, the Far East Erich Segal turns into something like a Japanese Proust. With what mocking pleasure Mishima satirizes his bourgeois sons of samurai. With what sentimental reverence he treats Kiyoaki's old-fashioned grandmother.

"Purely Japanese literature died out completely around the year 1897," the late novelist Kafu Nogai observed a little bitterly. "The literature written after then is not Japanese literature. It is Western literature written in the Japanese language." With a young novelist like Kenzaburo Oë citing *Huckleberry Finn* as his favorite work, and even Kawabata acknowledging the influence of Flaubert, European and American readers have felt free to criticize Japanese novels as failed Western fiction. The "faults" (by Western standards) in both Kawabata and Mishima are obvious:

Everything tends to turn into a symbol. Mishima in particular goes in heavily for snapping turtles, black dogs, and the like. Worse, everybody tends to turn into a symbol, too. Few

Japanese novelists have a gift for what Western readers think of as "character"; their characters fuzz at the edges into representative myths, leaving passions without their proper focus. Even the most aroused passages of love or hate or lyricism seem to float like clouds above the novel, self-contained if not detached exercises. The words go on and on—elegant diffusions of haze, "interminable sentences" (in Donald Keene's comment) "left incomplete, at the end of the twentieth or fortieth subtle turn of phrase."

But these "faults" may finally suggest a failure on the part of the reader. The Western reader, insisting upon his much admired conciseness, his crisp narrative rhythms, his sharp definition of person, is positing the book he is used to reading rather than the one he is given. He is camouflaging under criticisms of style a criticism—or rather a puzzlement—in the face of Japanese attitudes. For whatever the Japanese novel becomes in the future, *The Master of Go* and *Spring Snow* indicate that the Westernization of Japanese literature has been overestimated.

To understand the Japanese novel—that is, to understand what one does not understand—the Western reader must return to Hiroshige at Enoshima. The Hiroshige print, like *The Master of Go* and *Spring Snow*, gives off to the Westerner unmistakable intimations of damnation. But just when the poor Western moralist, confronted by the specter of death if not apocalypse, prepares his climatic shudder, the Japanese artist drifts off into anticlimactic frivolity: white sails off Enoshima.

Perhaps the Japanese word *ukiyo* provides the clue. In its origins it was roughly the Buddhist equivalent of Christian "vanity." Meaning "this fleeting, floating world," *ukiyo* marked off all that was transient and illusory in mortal life: not worth a serious man's attention. But by a kind of linguistic, if not moral, detour, *ukiyo* came to take on hedonistic connotations: this pleasant, delightful "floating world," full of what Mishima once called absolutely "useless beauty."

A brilliant short story by Ryunosuke Akutagawa (better known for *Rashomon*) postulates a painting, a masterpiece, that two connoisseurs devote a considerable portion of their lives and their hopes to discovering and verifying. Each sees it once, but upon comparing impressions they begin to wonder if they have seen the same painting, or if the painting even exists. By a Westerner's values, this should be a moment of agony, when faith disintegrates into doubt, meaning into meaninglessness. Instead, at curious exhilaration enters Akutagawa's story: a total joy at the point of total indifference, what a Japanese poet called "the bliss of nothingness." One masterpiece-lover turns to the other and concludes: "Even if it never existed, there is not really much cause for regret."

Here is "floating" for a fact. This sudden cool at the temperature of hellfire—a phenomenon in almost every Japanese novel—can attract a Westerner or it can frighten him. He may find it unspeakably cruel or an admirable case of poise. No matter. At that moment he has taken one step too many into Hiroshige's cave. Charmed or terrorized, aghast or envious, he is, above all, *lost*. Like the Master of Go, he is cut off from "the better part of reality," or at least his kind of reality, and that is his peculiar pleasure. That is his nightmare.

Alan Friedman (review date 22 October 1972)

SOURCE: A review of *The Master of Go,* in *The New York Times Book Review,* October 22, 1972, pp. 4, 24.

[*In the following review, Friedman asserts that Kawabata's "The Master of Go may not be a novel, but it is a journalism recollected in tranquility."*]

The Chess Match of the Century is over. Bobby Fischer's chair and Boris Spassky's pride have been pulled to pieces and reassembled. But what if *The Times,* say, had presumed upon Vladimir Nabokov's well-known passion for chess and had managed to persuade our most illustrious novelist to travel to Reykjavik to cover the match? And what if Nabokov had then given us a book, not only analyzing chess strategies, but dissecting with all the tender mercy of *his* art the two players themselves, together with their families, friends, managers, judges, lesser chess masters and lesser reporters, while everywhere viewing the event as a scene in the play of art and history?

The Master of Go is the improbable Oriental equivalent, *mutatis mutandis,* of that improbable book. Yasunari Kawabata, who received the Nobel Prize for Literature in 1968, was considered until his recent death the Master of Japanese letters. A novelist of a peculiarly penetrating subtlety, he was also a lover of the game of Go. In 1938 the Tokyo Nichinichi Shimbun asked him to attend the Go Match of the Century as a newspaper reporter. It was a classic match, a contest between two men and at the same time two cultures, between the Old Japan and a New one, between conservative tradition and dynamic ambition, between a polite, ailing Master and a young Challenger, neurotic, fussy, complaining and unpredictable.

The game took months, and to help the reader follow it, *The Master of Go* is well furnished with diagrams of the board, notes at the back of the book, and frequent analyses by Kawabata of the tides of battle. Since I used to play Go myself—however ineptly—I was fascinated. But no doubt a good number of readers will skim over such data as: "a space removed on the 'S' line from Black 87." Similar details of play are given in abundance, for this is a log of the match—or is it? Edward G. Seidensticker, whose translation flows elegantly, calls the work a "chronicle-novel" but "rather more chronicle than novel." A tad less particular, the dust jacket labels it simply "a novel." Well, there is an honorable blur between fiction and nonfiction, nowadays and earlier, but my point here is that the reader who opens this book expecting a novel may be in for a surprise. Kawabata, loving Go as Nabokov loves chess, keeps one eye on the board. If the reader expects a chronicle of the match, however, he will be amazed.

For Kawabata has two eyes, and everywhere his vision of the board makes him see more. The progress toward death, the unity of adversaries, the veils of pride and the shadows of enlightenment are never far from the foreground of the match. "It was a wholly unexpected play. I felt a tensing of my muscles, as if the diabolic side of the Master had suddenly been revealed." Or again: "The waves that passed through his shoulders were quite regular. They were to me like a concentration of violence, or the doings of some mysterious power that had taken possession of the Master. . . . I wondered if I was witness to the workings of the Master's soul as, all unconsciously, it received its inspiration, was host to the afflatus. Or was I watching a passage to enlightenment as the soul threw off all sense of identity and the fires of combat were quenched?" Reading passages like these, one thinks of other Masters, those of Hesse, Mann, Bulgakov, even James, and of other contests in the soul, and of the differences that illuminate.

In his Nobel Prize acceptance speech, Kawabata spoke feelingly of the underlying spirit of Zen in Japanese poetry. That spirit—the emptiness that enlightens—rises to the surface here in Go. "I was presently able to feel not only interest in the match but a sense of Go as an art, and that was because I reduced myself to nothing as I gazed at the Master." Still, one of the most gratifying things about Kawabata's work elsewhere is his genius for empty spaces. As one reads between his lines, the spaces he deliberately leaves there seem to widen. Here is a brief passage from the novel, *Thousand Cranes:*

> Fumiko had no way of knowing her mother as a woman.
>
> To forgive or to be forgiven was for Kikuji a matter of being rocked in that wave, the dreaminess of the woman's body.
>
> It seemed that the dreaminess was here too in the pair of Raku bowls.
>
> Fumiko did not know her mother thus.

In *The Master of Go* this delicate directness gives way to plain explicitness. Kawabata intended, I think, to treat the ritual of Go and the death of the Master here as he treated the tea ceremony in *Thousand Cranes* and as Junichiro Tanizaki treated the Bunraku puppets in *Some Prefer Nettles:* to convey in single human beings, and therefore at the deepest levels, an entire culture slipping away. In *The Master of Go* such matters are apt to be stated quite badly, not subtly: "the end of an age and the bridge to a new age." And yet, since this work lies somewhere between reportage and fiction, one hesitates to carp. "The Master had put the match together as a work of art." *The Master of Go* may not be a novel, but it is journalism recollected in tranquility.

Marian Ury (review date 22 October 1972)

SOURCE: "A Man and the Idea of a Woman," in *The New York Times Book Review,* October 22, 1972, p. 11.

[*In the following review, Ury praises the stories in Kawabata's* Palm-of-the-Hand Stories.]

A woman, breaking with her married lover, gives him a pair of canaries as a memento of their affair. The birds, which initially had been placed in the same cage by the bird seller through chance and are now unable to survive without each other, come to symbolize for the lover his relationship with his wife, who had cared for the birds and averted her eyes from his affair. Now that she is dead, the husband writes to his former mistress asking her permission to kill the birds and bury them with his wife. In another story, a man who has taken an aversion to his wife and left her, sends a series of letters from ever more distant post offices enjoining her and their daughter to make no sound. Mother and daughter cease "eternally to make even the faintest sound. In other words," Yasunari Kawabata says, they die. "And strangely enough, the woman's husband lay down beside them and died, too."

In yet another of Kawabata's "palm-of-the-hand stories," a little girl carrying a branch of crimson berries with green leaves gives it to a woman in a new silk kimono who is seated on the veranda of a shabby inn. The girl's father is a charcoal burner, and he is sick; the woman has been receiving unstamped love letters from her postman. The season is autumn. This is less a story in the usual sense than a mode of storytelling, where sounds, textures, tastes, colors, trajectories and intimations are gathered, ready to expand over an invisible canvas. Inevitably, the stories, like Kawabata's longer fiction, are compared with haiku; but another comparison might be with the work of Virginia Woolf, especially the autobiographical fragments of "Moments of Being" and "Mrs. Dalloway," with its deceptive appearance of fragmented time and movement, its moments of illumination and its flashes of an immanent, inexplicable reality. Insistently Japanese, Kawabata was also well acquainted with European modernist literature.

Kawabata's stories are difficult to summarize; many of the finest elude even the attempt. In one of my favorites, **"The Wife of the Autumn Wind"** (the translation of the title seems not quite right; "The Wife in the Autumn Wind" might be better, or perhaps "The Autumn-Wind Wife"), the event narrated is the shadowy encounter between the protagonist and the devoted wife of a dying man, his neighbors at a hotel—or rather, between the protagonist and the idea of the woman, for what we are made to see is his discovery of some strands of her hair after she has left the hotel on a brief errand. What the story is about is sweetness, drabness (and its sensuous appeal), cold, the nearness of death, the coming of an autumn typhoon, the varieties of love and tenderness and the unbridgeable gap between the protagonist and the woman. It is just over two pages. There is not a word in it that could be dispensed with.

The longest of these palm-of-the-hand stories are perhaps a half-dozen pages; the shortest are less than a page. There are 70 in this volume, about half of an output that spanned their author's writing career. He is said to have considered these very short stories his finest work.

Yasunari Kawabata was born in 1899. He received the Nobel Prize in Literature in 1968—the only Japanese writer thus honored so far and a somewhat controversial choice, since not every Japanese critic likes him. He died in a gas-filled room in 1972, a probable suicide. He is well known in the West for *The Master of Go,* a minimalist novelization of a newspaper account of a competition at go, a distant cousin of chess, in which an aging master was defeated, and for *Snow Country,* an enigmatic novel of unreciprocated love set in what is, for Kawabata, a region of voluptuous white and cold. As a child, he was repeatedly orphaned. His father died when he was 2 years old, his mother when he was 3, his only sister when he was 9 and his grandfather—his last surviving close relative—when he was 16. According to the instructive chapter on Kawabata in Donald Keene's history of modern Japanese literature, *Dawn to the West,* the boy came to be known as a "master of funerals" from his authoritative demeanor at funeral services.

Kawabata's characters, incapable of ordinary human intimacy, dream of the merging and dissolution of the self.
                                                            —Marian Ury

---

Intense sorrow often brings with it a heightened esthetic per-

ception to the sufferer, shabby tenements seem to glow with color, and past and present time to collapse into one and become almost tangible. Not only death but deafness and blindness appear repeatedly in these stories—the latter depicted as a special, ecstatic kind of seeing. Death itself is a metamorphosis, one of many kinds in these stories. An older sister gives herself to the lover of her younger sister who is ill, and imagines herself also marrying the sister's husband after the sister's death. A woman recognizes the face of her mother in her daughter. A meek young woman, loving her husband to distraction, cuts her hair, wears thick spectacles and tries to grow a mustache and join the army so as to be exactly like him; ultimately, God transforms her into a lily. Kawabata's characters, incapable of ordinary human intimacy, dream of the merging and dissolution of the self.

The translators, Lane Dunlop and J. Martin Holman, have dealt respectfully with their texts, but just because they have done such a careful job over all, the occasional rough spots are noticeable. Each of the translators has contributed a prefatory note. For Mr. Dunlop especially, the translating seems to have been something of a personal journey.

The Times Literary Supplement (review date 23 August 1974)

SOURCE: "Sweet Dreams," in *The Times Literary Supplement,* No. 3781, August 23, 1974, p. 911.

[*In the following review, the critic asserts that the stories in Kawabata's* House of the Sleeping Beauties *are "linked . . . by the theme of a lonely subject and his peculiar eroticism, and by the interplay of reality and fancy within a lonely mind."*]

Of the three stories in this volume, [*House of the Sleeping Beauties*], **"Of Birds and Beasts"** was written in the early 1930s, while **"One Arm"** and the longer, **"House of the Sleeping Beauties"** are among Kawabata's later works. But there is a firm continuity between the stories, linked as they are by the theme of a lonely subject and his peculiar eroticism, and by the interplay of reality and fancy within a lonely mind.

"Of Birds and Beasts" is perhaps the least skilful; the transition from the reality of the middle-aged man's strange attachment to his bird and animal pets to the memories of an affair with a dancer is without the facility of the later writing. **"One Arm"** is a bizarre dialogue between a man and a young girl's right arm which has been left with him for the night and is eventually exchanged for his own. Here Kawabata exploits his lyricism and its capacity to explore private and deeply hidden moods with exquisite minuteness.

There is the same strangling tightness which Mishima (Kawabata's protégé) senses in **"House of the Sleeping Beauties"** and there is in both pieces a tactful use of the traditional poetic technique of an allusive hint at the season of the year: "the pressing dampness invaded my ears to give a wet sound like the wriggling of myriads of distant earthworms".

"House of the Sleeping Beauties" describes the visits of an old man to a strange establishment where the girls, always drugged in sleep before the clients' arrival, evoke memories of earlier affairs. Deprived of the use of dialogue or character description, Kawabata manages to evoke a vivid sense of individual life by his accounts of the sleeping girls. With each of the unconscious figures, Eguchi, the old man, wants to see the eyes, to hear the voice, to talk. One of them overflows "with a sensuousness that made it possible for her body to converse in silence". The transitions are smoothly effected, on the same intuitive and emotional level and often with the same techniques of sound, scent and colour "echo" that enabled three poets to link verses in the traditional poetry. Mishima rates this story as a masterpiece of Kawabata's esoteric style. It recalls some aspects of the spirit of the erotic and the grotesque of the Japan of half a century ago.

Wolfgang Freese and Angela B. Moorjani (essay date 1980)

SOURCE: "The Esoteric and the Trivial: Chess and Go in the Novels of Beckett and Kawabata," in *Perspectives on Contemporary Literature,* Vol. 6, 1980, pp. 37-48.

[*In the following excerpt, Freese and Moorjani analyze the symbolism of the Go match in Kawabata's* The Master of Go, *and assert that the story is a movement toward the Master's death.*]

Yasunari Kawabata's *The Master of Go,* written and rewritten from 1938 until 1954, when it first appeared in book form, is not a novel in the strict sense of narrative fiction. The Japanese form of *shosetsu* is known to be more flexible than the Western form of the novel. In this case it mixes a chronicle, based on sixty-six newspaper installments Kawabata wrote about an actual Go match in 1938 for the Osaka and Tokyo *Mainichi,* with structural and stylistic elements of fiction.

Kawabata's novel begins with a note on the Master's death: "Shusai, Master of Go, twenty-first in the Honnimbo succession, died in Atami, at the Urokoya Inn, on the morning of January 18, 1940. He was sixty-seven years old by the Oriental count." It is clear from the very outset that the

Master's illness is a critical aspect of the novel, and that his death, anticipated in this very beginning, will overshadow the match. Seen from this angle the novel is analytical like most of Kawabata's writings. If the known result is death, each of the 41 chapters, and each of the 237 moves of the game (illustrated in 12 diagrams throughout the novel) leads closer to it. The novel, and, as the real and symbolic heart of it, the game, become more than a report or a chronicle: they are the *anamnesis* in both its historical and medical/psychiatric meaning, of a development leading to death.

> **Kawabata's art accomplishes more than the reflection of social or historical change, the agony of the old and the triumphant rise of the new. Like all conservative authors, he lets us know the price which has to be paid for the challenger's victory.**
> —*Wolfgang Freese and Angela B. Moorjani*

It is quite clear in the novel that this movement toward death transcends the two individuals involved in the match. Their function of representing an older order and a newer trend in Japanese history is far too obvious to necessitate "detection" by skillful literary analysis. Nor does the narrator, focusing again beyond the players to changes in the organization of the game itself, leave us in the dark about his partisanship:

> It may be said the Master was plagued in his last match by modern rationalism, to which fussy rules were everything, from which all the grace and elegance of Go as art had disappeared, which quite dispensed with respect for elders and attached no importance to mutual respect as human beings. From the way of Go the beauty of Japan and the Orient had fled. Everything had become science and regulation. The road to advancement in rank, which controlled the life of a player, had become a meticulous point system. One conducted the battle only to win, and there was no margin for remembering the dignity and the fragrance of Go as an art. The modern way was to insist upon doing battle under conditions of abstract justice, even when challenging the Master himself. The fault was not Otaké's. Perhaps what happened was but natural, Go being a contest and show of strength.

The last sentence leads us to consider the narrator's perspective. Kawabata is usually counted among the conservative Japanese writers, and this may explain the elegiac reading given most of his novels. If there is a Nietzschean element in his interpretation of the contest, however, it is certainly not a very active force in Kawabata's thinking. Nevertheless, Otaké is treated throughout the novel as an instrument of history. On one occasion in the novel—and here the context would have to be examined very carefully, since the author/narrator tries to convince Otaké not to forfeit the game—the narrator steps forward as protagonist, showing for the first time great self-assurance: "I spoke boldly. I said that as challenger in this the Master's last game he was fighting in single combat, and he was also fighting a larger battle. He was the representative of a new day. He was being carried on by the currents of history." A little later the narrator continues: ". . . the retirement match meant the end of an age and the bridge to a new age. There would be vitality in the world of Go. To forfeit the game would be to interrupt the flow of history. The responsibility was a heavy one. Was Otaké really to let personal feelings and circumstances prevail?"

But Kawabata's art accomplishes more than the reflection of social or historical change, the agony of the old and the triumphant rise of the new. Like all conservative authors, he lets us know the price which has to be paid for the challenger's victory. His loving portrait of the Master, his affection for the Master's grace and frailty, his deep understanding of the Master's nature, skill and strength have certainly to do with his acceptance of the Master's social function and with the institution he represents, the title of Master of Go. This title and this institution, with all their hierarchical symbolism can only be compared to the emperor's sovereign and supreme rule, its total and irrational autocracy. In the world of Go the decline of these attributes was anticipated (in 1938) before the Japanese public became aware of it with the Tenno Hirohito's radio-message in 1945. This parallel is of an ultimate character, and needs to be explained.

Of the Master we hear that he showed occasionally "quite astonishing autocratic tendencies," albeit mostly pertaining to entirely trivial matters, it seems. The Master of the old order had the right to determine the time and place, the special circumstances and conditions of a match. In Shusai's case, his long lasting tenure of the title had led to the idea that he was invincible, in fact his title had become that of the "invincible master." It seemed, therefore, justified for him to protect the title as an institution almost remote from his own personal ambitions and feelings. Even after he broke a promise, none of the managers of the match were prepared to act as umpire or hand down an order. This indeed seems like a relic from the past to younger players, to whom the title of "Master" is about to become but a "mark of strength and no more." Whereas the narrator stresses that in former times "the holder of the title, fearful of doing injury to it, seems to have avoided real competition even in practice matches," this is unthinkable in the future, so that Shusai, playing at age sixty-four in a title-match, "would seem in a variety of meanings, to have stood at the boundary between

the old and the new. He had at the same time the lofty position of the old master and the material benefits of the new," i.e., he would receive the prize-money from a sponsoring newspaper, the common economic way of financing modern sports.

If these quarrelsome trivialities and dubious privileges cannot possibly explain the grandeur of the old order, where then can we find its real merits and beauty, its legitimacy and truth?

Some of these questions are answered by the manner in which the match proceeds, and how it reflects in a very refined and sometimes esoteric manner, not only broad cultural phenomena of an era of transition but also the psychological structure of characters made possible by the old or the new order. A brief description of how both players are portrayed may serve as a starting point.

In various suggestive ways the contrast between old and new, which happens to be also the contrast between old and young, is expressed by trivialities as well as highly esoteric modes of behavior. The Master, although obviously moribund, is quiet; his manners are dignified throughout the match. He will frequently sink into meditation, show outward signs of indifference, and there are occasions when, in a sudden epiphany, the Master's retreating figure seems to become unreal, moving the narrator and observer to tears: "I was profoundly moved, for reasons I do not myself understand. In that figure walking absently from the game there was still sadness of another world. The Master seemed like a relic left behind by Meiji."

Otaké, the young challenger, is restless both physically and mentally. He drinks enormous amounts of tea, suffers from nervous enuresis, and leaves the board frequently, excusing himself with his condition. He is talkative, tries to joke, turns the Master's stones right side up so that the inner stripeless side of the clamshell shows, and he would, like most younger players, "indulge all manner of odd quirks."

Otaké's fidgeting, however, is not reflected in the game in a direct way, that is, Otaké's style of playing is not erratic but concentrated and powerful. He releases all the tension in his behavior, whereas the Master, following and inheriting venerable traditions, seems to be in total control of his emotions. This cannot be interpreted as an advantage in the match itself, as it might have been when self-control was the equivalent of superiority in various disciplines, including Go. Since the Master is obviously not concerned with winning, his tension does not show. Throughout his more than thirty years as a titleholder, winning has become, one might say, an attribute of the title. The Master was instrumental in assuring the purity of this record, he derived his own strength from it. His victories, it seems, were almost assured. He had only played with the white stones during these years, making his task even more difficult, and yet, during his lifetime "no one among his juniors advanced as far as the Eighth Rank. All through the epoch that was his own he kept the opposition under control. . . ."

The modern, post-Meiji way of Go is characterized by rules and laws laid down by associations to guarantee its democratic organization. And it is in this context that Kawabata deplores the loss of Go as an art: "When a law is made, the cunning that finds loopholes goes to work. One cannot deny that there is a certain slyness among young players, a slyness which, when rules are written to prevent slyness, makes use of these rules themselves." Consequently, Otaké's psychology of winning creates disagreements, since he refuses to give an inch in questions concerning a relocation of living quarters or playing-room, or a delay of a day or two during the match, which lasted after all from June 26 (Tokyo) until December 4 (Ito) of 1938, for a total of 14 sessions. Otaké's manner suggests to the narrator "an inability to understand the courtesies due to an elder, a want of sympathy for a sick man, and a rationalism that somehow missed the point." What Otaké fails to grasp is the situation in which the Master and the game of Go find themselves. Since this match is officially known as the Master's last, it attains the level of a ritual. As in a particular Japanese tradition of suicide, where for reasons often totally unknown to outsiders, a person has chosen the "right" moment to end his life, which in an esthetic sense can also mean the "most beautiful" moment, the match has been composed by the Master as a piece of art going back to its ritual origins. From the challenger's manner and from the general physical condition of the Master, it becomes clear, however, that Otaké is assigned the role not only of playing partner, adversary, and representative of the new era, but also of executor and executioner. Unaware of the historical as well as of the esthetic dimensions of the match, Otaké is unable to conceal or suppress the aggressiveness reflected both in his gestures ("Otaké's way of sitting down and getting up again was as if readying himself for battle") and his playing style, and this attitude, which may have its functional value on the more trivial level of mere historical transition, cannot possibly do justice to the pursuit of beauty and Go as an art that is on the Master's mind. For this we have to take a closer look at the game.

Having the advantage of playing Black, Otaké takes the initiative from the opening and keeps it, so it seems, far into the middle-game. His "impatience" results in early gains. He has developed a wall on the side, and a strong center influence; he has a large upper right corner, a smaller upper left corner, has created potential for the lower left corner, and positioned a "spy" on the lower side. This "spy," move Black 63, is perhaps the most visible sign of Black's unconcern for what would be called esthetically the "flow" of the game. It is played against the spirit of give and take in Go, mak-

ing a very early and somewhat speculative invasion into the Master's sphere of influence. And here we can see from a little dialogue between the players the two different levels of concern, the esthetic and esoteric of the Master's and Otaké's more trivial consciousness. The Master deliberated for twenty minutes after Black's last move: "Apparently Black 63 struck him as a trifle unorthodox. At the outset of the game, Otaké had been careful to warn the Master that he would frequently ask to be excused; but his departures from the board had been so frequent during the proceeding session that the Master had thought them a little odd. 'Is something wrong?' he asked. 'Kidneys. Nerves, really. When I have to think I have to go,'" is Otaké's answer. The Master's concerned question, however, goes beyond his opponent's physical and nervous condition; it pertains to his sense of collaborating on a work of art.

In following the Master's reactions to several ruthless moves by Otaké, the reader becomes aware that even Otaké's strength has been entered into the Master's artful design. Black's constant aggressiveness has not resulted in an insurmountable lead: "Black had made gains, and yet it seemed that White, casting away the dressings from his wounds, had emerged with greater lightness and freedom of action."

The crisis will arrive and eventually lead to catastrophe with Black 121. With this sealed play, the game loses its character as a piece of art. The move was expected with great excitement as perhaps "the climax of the game," but when it was revealed, nobody seemed at first able to locate it on the board. It was far from where the present action was localized, and a "wave of revulsion" came over the narrator when he finally saw it. One twenty-one was a thoroughly trivial move. A few moves later the Master makes a fatal mistake that loses the game. In this move, White 130, there was "something that spoke less of a will to fight than of angry disdain," as the narrator sees it. At lunch with the narrator the Master says in "a low but intense voice: 'The match is over. Mr. Otaké ruined it with that sealed play. It was like smearing ink over the picture we had painted. The minute I saw it I felt like forfeiting the match.'"

Only now does it become clear to spectators, narrator, and reader that the Master "had put the match together as a work of art," and in this context Kawabata identifies himself with this definition of Go as an art: "That play of black upon white, white upon black, has the intent and takes the forms of creative art. It has in it a flow of the spirit and a harmony as of music. Everything is lost when suddenly a false note is struck, or one party in a duet suddenly launches forth on an eccentric flight of his own. A masterpiece of a game can be ruined by insensitivity to the feelings of an adversary." The trivial, so it seems, has defeated the esoteric beauty of art, has not allowed the old order to die in a beautiful manner and at the "right" moment, has denied it the honor and superiority of designing its own death.

If we could consider this a "message" of Kawabata's novel, we might find ourselves in danger of trivializing it in spite of all the seemingly esoteric details revealed, because—and that is the meaning of the problematized perspective—from the standpoint of the overall narrative strategy of the *shosetsu,* we cannot speak of a total identification with the Master's feelings about the match. Not only does a realistic principle prevail (since the novel is part chronicle), leaving even the Master and the old order open to criticism despite the narrator's warm veneration, but also an element of esthetic justice is at work integrating historical and social forces into a piece of art reflecting the end of all art, a theme struck first around the turn of the 19th century and hotly debated in the 1960's and 70's. . . .

. . . By basing his novel, published in 1954, largely on his own 1938 newspaper articles, which chronicled an actual Go match of the same year, Kawabata provides both a 1938 perspective and multiple retrospective points of view.

Joseph H. Bourke (essay date 1982)

SOURCE: "Tragic Vision in Kawabata's *The Master of Go,*" in *Rocky Mountain Review of Language and Literature,* Vol. 36, No. 2, 1982, pp. 83-94.

[*In the following essay, Bourque analyzes Kawabata's* The Master of Go *as a modern tragedy.*]

At first glance the application of the thoroughly Western dramatic concept of tragedy to an Oriental novel may seem to be critical madness. Both the genres and the traditions are jarringly incongruous: the process may seem a bit like trying to examine a flower with a sword. Yet, unlike most Japanese novels, *The Master of Go* seems to invite examination from the perspective of Western concepts. At its most accessible symbolic level the novel presents the Go match between the old Master, Shusai, and the young challenger, Otaké, as the objectification of a conflict between tradition and change in Japanese culture, a change intimately associated with Western ideas. Beyond that, the most fundamental level of that conflict is the confrontation of two completely different ways of understanding the nature of human existence at the moment when one is giving way to the other and while both are still vital enough to sustain the conflict's intensity: on the one hand, the traditional Japanese culture's organic view of human beings as emotional and subjective participants in the integrative process of experiencing a complex universe of which they are a functioning element; on the other hand, a systematic view of human be-

ings as objective observers of the universe, categorizing, systematizing, and controlling their experience of a world from which they try to stand apart.

The most obvious precedent for such a confrontation is to be found in the classical Greece of the sixth and fifth centuries B.C., where the same kind of conflict took place between an organic, mythological view of humanity as part of the great cosmic cycle and the systematic view of humanity attempting rational control of its own destiny with the beginnings of theoretical science and the reflexive humanism of the Sophists. There, too, a transition occurred from the organic to the systematic at a moment when the conflict was still vital; the human anguish produced by that conflict is expressed in tragedy. The tragic flaw that brings about the hero's downfall is the assumption that he can control his own destiny through the exercise of logic and will, the attributes of rationality. From that limited perspective, the only real tragedy is Greek classical tragedy. Modern Western tragedy is not possible because the confrontation is no longer vital: we have become predominately rationalistic, and the memory of an organic conception of humanity is too dim to provoke a genuine conflict. Humanity still feels anguish, but it is the anxiety of the alienated hero. Yet, if the conflict can be found in its dynamic state once again, as it seems to be in *The Master of Go,* perhaps we can find there a modern literary equivalent to the Greek classical tragic vision.

There can be little doubt that the implications of the Go match in Kawabata's novel are meant to extend to Japanese culture in general. The contestants are isolated, but their activities are being reported in the newspapers as events of national importance. The game itself is frequently referred to as an art form, and relationships are continually established with music, poetry, history, and the Japanese landscape. It is inextricably entwined with the cultural tradition, the spirit, and the mentality of the Japanese people when Uragami, Kawabata's persona and narrator, plays a game of Go with an American on the train:

> One did not of course wish to take a game too seriously, and yet it was quite clear that playing Go with a foreigner was very different from playing Go with a Japanese. I wondered whether the point might be that foreigners were not meant for Go. . . . One is of course rash to generalize from the single example of an American beginner, but perhaps the conclusion might be valid all the same that Western Go is wanting in spirit. The Oriental game has gone beyond game and test of strength and become a way of art. It has about it a certain Oriental mystery and nobility. The "Honnimbo" of Honnimbo Shusai is the name of a cell at the Jakkoji Temple in Kyoto, and Shusai the Master had himself taken holy orders. On the three hundredth anniversary of the

death of the first Honnimbo, Sansa, whose clerical name was Nikkai, he had taken the clerical name Nichion. I thought, as I played Go with the American, that there was no tradition of Go in his country.

In addition, the Master's priesthood contributes to his near-mythical status in a unique and pervasive tradition:

> It was his good fortune to be born in the early flush of Meiji. Probably never again will it be possible for anyone—for, say, Wu Ch'ing-yüan of our own day—knowing nothing of the vale of tears in which the Master spent his student years, to encompass in his individual person a whole panorama of history. It will not be possible even though the man be more of a genius at Go than the Master was. He was the symbol of Go itself, he and his record shining through Meiji, Taisho, and Showa, and his achievement in having brought the game to its modern flowering.

But the changes taking place in the game of Go and in Japanese culture are not simply the changes of taste and attitude that are always typical of the difference between one generation and another. They represent the cataclysmic rupture of a centuries-old tradition for the sake of a new one. No subtle transition here, no gradual shading off into other forms and other perspectives. The break is violent and abrupt because it represents a conflict between two incompatible views of humanity. Uragami, the narrator, leaves no doubt about the end of the tradition. He has played chess with the Master a few days before the old man's death, and he remarks: "Those were his last games of the chess of which he was so fond. I did the newspaper accounts of his last championship match at Go, I was his last adversary at chess, and I was the last to take his picture." The word "last" is significantly repeated, and since the Master has been set up in the novel as the last and only exemplar of the old tradition, it dies with him.

The death of that tradition is sometimes blamed on the encroachment of Western influences, especially American ones. We have already encountered the American on the train, and there is a significant passage in which the Master, fallen ill, is taken to St. Luke's, an American hospital: "I went to see him at St. Luke's Hospital during the three-month recess in his retirement match. The furnishings were huge, to fit the American physique. There was something precarious about the Master's small figure perched on the lofty bed." And probably the ultimate irony centers on one of the fussy rules that have become the new way of Go: the practice of isolating the players to prevent outside interference with the match. The process is called "sealing in a tin can." The tin can is the most prominent symbol of the American occupa-

tion of Japan after World War II. Cigarette lighters, the first products of the birth of the modern Japanese industrial giant, were made with the metal salvaged from American beer cans.

But it is not the source of the change (if, indeed, that source is ever clearly determined), but rather the nature of the change that really concerns Kawabata:

> It may be said that the Master was plagued in his last match by modern rationalism, to which fussy rules were everything, from which all the grace and elegance of Go as art had disappeared, which quite dispensed with respect for elders and attached no importance to mutual respect as human beings. From the way of Go the beauty of Japan and the Orient had fled. Everything had become science and regulation. The road to advancement in rank, which controlled the life of a player, had become a meticulous point system. One conducted the battle only to win, and there was no margin for remembering the dignity and fragrance of Go as an art. The modern way was to insist upon doing battle under conditions of abstract justice, even when challenging the Master himself. The fault was not Otaké's. Perhaps what had happened was but natural, Go being a contest and a show of strength.

To put it as simply as possible, in the Master's tradition the process itself is the substance, but, in the new way, the goal is the substance. Of course Go is definitely an exercise in rationality. It is a game of tactics and strategy, complete with military terms of attack and defense. But in the Master's tradition the process also involves aesthetic, cultural, and philosophical components: there is an appreciation of the board and stones in terms of color, texture, and design; the game adheres to certain time-honored forms and procedures; it is also an expression of an attitude toward existence and a mode of behavior. For Otaké and the new way, there are only three variations of a single concern; to win, to collect the prize money, to become the new Master. Only rational goals and values are worth considering.

The changes are traceable to Western influences: scientific systematization, goal-oriented competition, theoretical abstraction, iconoclastic individualism—all under the pervasive shadow of rationalism. But Kawabata does not waste his time exploring the historical, or philosophical, or economic sources of these changes nor their implications. Rather, he records the effects of the conflicts among them on a people represented in microcosm by Shusai, Otaké, and, of course, Uragami. To that extent, Kawabata's novel achieves the scope of Greek tragedy in that both, using different metaphors as vehicles, constitute a fictionalized record of the culture's development from an organic to a systematic self-conception. Aeschylus's *Oresteia* provides a good parallel. In that trilogy, the dramatic theme revolves around Orestes's dilemma in the face of conflicting demands posed by the blood-vengeance tradition: he must avenge his father, but he must not kill his mother, an act that constitutes the only acceptable form of vengeance. He is finally vindicated in a court of law especially formed for the purpose by Athena, the goddess of wisdom, and the trilogy becomes a symbolic re-creation of the Greek culture's historical process of transition from the old mythological beliefs to the more rational systems of civil law. Orestes is the objectification, the symbolic embodiment of that transition. In the same way the Go match in Kawabata's novel is the metaphor for the Japanese culture's transition from the old tradition to the more rational systems of the modern world. In fact, it is to a considerable degree the same tradition in both cultures. Not that the Japanese tradition can be characterized as pre-analytical in the same sense as the Homeric tradition which describes warriors as generations of leaves, but both traditions express a remarkably similar view of what humanity becomes when rationality begins to dominate culture and overshadows whatever organic tradition existed before it. And that vision of humanity is an important element in tragedy.

Within the context of that cultural record, the Master can easily be envisioned as a tragic hero, contingent upon the nature of his death. In the meantime, he has all of the aristocratic background and demeanor of that office. He is a man of high stature, noble sentiments, and strength. For a man his age he demonstrates remarkable discipline in his posture and bearing at the Go board. He inspires confidence in his mastery of self; he is calm where others are perturbed, he is energetic where others are lethargic, he displays refined tastes in poetry, music, and art. In short, he is a highly complex individual who assumes heroic proportions in comparison with the people around him.

> **If Western humanity has gained its freedom and individuality, it has lost the sense of stability and cohesion. If it has gained mobility and a greater potential for improving its condition, it has also acquired a fear of the unknown future.**
> **—*Joseph H. Bourke***

Uragami, for instance, takes on the aspect of the Greek chorus, commenting on the proceedings as the representative of ordinary people whose fate is encompassed by the heroic conflict they can only observe. Like the chorus, he is often confused about what is actually happening, about the motives of the participants, about the implications of the actions he is reporting. Further, he is often ambivalent about

which values are the more legitimate. And, in the final analysis, like the Greek chorus, he is left to report the ending of the tragic hero—this time with a camera.

But if Shusai is a tragic hero and Uragami is the chorus, what function does Otaké fulfill? It is there that Kawabata expands his tragic vision to bridge the gap between past and present. For Otaké bears all the marks of the alienated hero. And, after all, that is not so surprising, since the alienated hero is no more than the literary culmination of Western culture's logical development into the rational, analytical phase begun with the Greeks. Where humanity's assumption of control over its own destiny can be seen as a positive step from the point of view of the *Oresteia*—Orestes's acquittal marks the end of the bloodletting—it can be seen pessimistically from the present since the analytical approach has failed to produce a comprehensive world view. If Western humanity has gained its freedom and individuality, it has lost the sense of stability and cohesion. If it has gained mobility and a greater potential for improving its condition, it has also acquired a fear of the unknown future. This is not the place to debate the issue in cultural terms, but it seems evident that modern literature has emphasized the negative elements of that dichotomy and coalesced them in the figure of the anti-hero who is always as distantly removed from any sense of tradition as we are from the ancient Greeks. But Kawabata had one advantage over the Greek tragedians. With Western culture as a precedent and Western literature as a guide, he could foresee the direction his own culture would take, and display, in one startling contrast: both the inception of the new world view in a tragic vision and its logical culmination in the alienated hero.

Otaké is so completely different from the Master that we are shocked by the comparison. They do indeed seem centuries apart in their attitudes and habits. A few examples merely suggest the extent and depth of the contrast. Otaké has absolutely none of the majesty and dignity that attend the Master. Uragami notes:

> Otaké's trouble was more extreme. He was unique among competitors at the grand spring and autumn tournaments. He would drink enormously from the large pot he kept at his side. Wu of the Sixth Rank, who was at the time one of his more interesting adversaries, also suffered at the Go board from nervous enuresis. I have seen him get up ten times and more in the course of four or five hours of play. Though he did not have Otaké's addiction to tea, there would all the same (and one marveled at the fact) come sounds from the urinal each time he left the board. With Otaké the difficulty did not stop at enuresis. One noted with curiosity that he would leave his overskirt behind him in the hallway and his obi as well.

What could be more antiheroic than a winner with a weak bladder and diarrhea? But the Master is very different: "Seated at the board, the Master and Otaké presented a complete contrast, quiet against constant motion, nervelessness against nervous tension. Once he had sunk himself into a session, the Master did not leave the board." Uragami notes, however, that Otaké's nervousness does not detract from the power of his game. Later, when the Master falls ill, suffering from pain in his chest, his face swollen:

> Seated at the board, the Master quietly took up a tea bowl in both hands and sipped at the strong brew. Then he folded his hands lightly on his knees and brought himself upright. The expression on his face was like that of a child about to weep. The tightly closed lips were thrust forward, there was a dropsical swelling in the cheeks, and the eyelids too were swollen.

In extreme pain, the Master sits straight and suffers silently, with dignity. Otaké is another type altogether: "Otaké reported that he too was indisposed. His digestion was troubling him. He was taking three stomach medicines and a medicine to prevent fainting as well. He had been known to faint during a match." His weakness, as we discover, is not a sign of failing health. Rather, it is a sign that he is playing badly and running out of time. The Master is a man of many talents and interests; Otaké is a Go player and nothing else. The Master appreciates the process of the game as an art; Otaké emphasizes the outcome of the game as a test of power. The contrasts could be extended indefinitely, but the results are the same: the Master is, above all, master of himself, while Otaké cannot even control his bodily functions. The Master is a many-faceted, nearly legendary figure who seems to carry over from the distant past; his world view has a well-integrated complexity. Otaké is a single-minded rationalist of the immediate present; he is a specialist.

But it is the tragic vision that concerns us here, and the special character of the tragic hero is that he attempts to bridge the gap between two world views. While he is firmly rooted in the traditional past, he is also the hope of the future, predicated upon the action of the present. And, in that respect, there are some remarkable correspondences between Shusai the Master and Oedipus the King. For instance, both seem to achieve, if only briefly, that delicate balance between the two worlds in question. Indeed, that is one of the principal qualities among those that make them heroic. In Sophocles's tragedy the Priest petitions Oedipus, in the name of the people, with these words:

> You are not one of the immortal gods, we know;
> Yet we have come to you to make our prayer
> As to the man surest in mortal ways
> And wisest in the ways of God.

The dramatic action is a demonstration of that balance. Oedipus is firmly committed to the spiritual values of his heritage. When the oracle indicates the cause of the plague and its cure, Oedipus dedicates himself totally to fulfilling its terms. Within the context of that spiritual heritage, he exercises his rational powers, which are definitely superior to those of ordinary people, in a detective-style search for the culprit. To that extent Oedipus is entirely heroic: his balanced approach certainly succeeds in discovering the guilty party, and, in Oedipus, the culture seems to have achieved its finest flowering—even if it is an imperfect blossom and lasts but a moment. With Oedipus humanity has learned that it can act effectively, with the guidance of spiritual authority, to achieve a measure of control over its own destiny: after all, the Thebans are rescued by Oedipus's action. It is only Oedipus himself who is destroyed, and his destruction is certainly not due to the thoroughly honorable action we see him take in the play as rational human investigator of a divine orderliness. It is the result of actions that have occurred prior to the present time of the play. And what is the nature of those actions? Excessive reliance on human logic. When the first oracle predicted Oedipus's fate, he simply fled, basing his flight on the logical assumption that Polybus was his father—obviously a false assumption. Relying on his own logic, he tried to change destiny. But, since the way of divine authority is not to justify itself but to maintain order, the oracle had foreseen the excessive reliance on logic, the excessive confidence in self that comes from an imbalance toward the side of rationality. That is the hubris of Oedipus. And the ever-increasing reliance on human logic in developing Western culture's attempt to control destiny becomes an iconoclastic individualism, already hinted at by the Greek tragedians, that eventually produces the alienated hero without roots, without tradition, and without a cohesive world view; the individualism produces only theoretical and rational systems that constantly break down.

The Master, like Oedipus, is firmly committed to the values of his heritage, and, like Oedipus, he is the best that his culture can produce. He possesses the ability to achieve the fine balance between two world views. On the one hand, he is himself a priest, and he has the sensibility that transforms a mere game into an artistic and spiritual achievement. On the other hand, Go is the supreme exercise in rationality, and Shusai is indeed the Master. But what is it that makes the last game so different? As in the ancient tragedy, we know the outcome from the very start. We are shown the images of the dead man, and we are told: "One may say that in the end the match took the Master's life." The remainder of the novel is the working out of that inevitable fate. The dramatic strength of the action lies not in the suspense over the outcome of the match—that would require a focus on Otaké and his values—but in the anguish generated by the vision of a great man working toward his own destruction. And since the Master himself does not know the outcome, as we do, the novel produces the same kind of dramatic irony that we find in the tragedy of Oedipus.

Moreover, like Oedipus, the Master has brought his own fate upon himself by extending the rational elements of the game beyond the boundaries of the traditional, thereby destroying the delicate balance. The fatal error in this case is his conceding to, rather than resisting, all of those very things that Uragami told us were the result of modern rationalism, not the least of which is the profit motive. Uragami tells us: "It may in fact be said that the Master sold his last match to a newspaper at a price without precedent. He did not so much go forth into combat as allow himself to be lured into combat by the newspaper." With his acceptance of that sponsorship come all the "fussy rules" such as the sealed play and the extended time limit that eventually conspire to destroy the Master's commitment to the match. By giving in to modern rationalism, Shusai has made what seems to be the logical choice, but it is a logic that is not informed by the spiritual nature of his art.

There comes a moment, of course, when the Master realizes his fatal error and the destiny that awaits him, but that moment does not occur when the wrong play has been made, the play that decides the logical outcome of the game. Rather, the Master's enlightenment occurs when Otaké has made a wholly unexpected play that is not, however, decisive. After that day's session the Master says to Uragami:

> The match is over. Mr. Otaké ruined it with that sealed play. It was like smearing ink over the picture we had painted. The minute I saw it I felt like forfeiting the match. Like telling them it was the last straw. I really thought I should forfeit. But I hesitated, and that was that.

Of course, there is never any real possibility of forfeiture for a man like the Master; that is only a passing temptation. He may be tempted to stop the inevitable workings of fate. He could simply disengage, as Oedipus could do, when he begins to realize what his destiny will be; but he must continue. And he, too, is betrayed by anger and his own commitment. Though he maintains his composure, the rapidity of his next move betrays his attitude:

> I had not been aware, at the moment of play, that the Master was so angry and so disappointed as to consider forfeiting the match. There was no sign of emotion on his face or in his manner as he sat at the board. No one among us sensed his distress. We had been watching Yawata, of course, as he was having his troubles with the chart and the sealed play, and we had not looked at the Master. Yet the Master had played White 122 in literally no time, less than a minute.

His response does not conform to the situation. Black 121, the opponent's smearing tactic, has been so unusual that it should require considerable thought and adjustment on the Master's part, especially since the Master has not yet spent even half of the time allotted him for the match. Yet the Master plays without any thought whatsoever. And by the end of that day's session he has made the fatal play, White 130, that ensures his defeat. Once again, we are reminded of Oedipus who has first betrayed his spiritual nature by fleeing from the oracle and then betrays his rational nature by giving in to a fit of anger on the road to Thebes. Likewise, the Master has betrayed the spirit of his art by agreeing to the conditions of his match and then betrays his rational nature by reacting emotionally in a burst of anger. In this case, his anger is directed at himself as well as at Otaké, because he realizes that it is his own concession that has made possible the system in which Otaké makes the sealed play that so angers him.

And there is little doubt that the Master finally makes the only response possible to that realization. In a move somewhat less dramatic than Oedipus's blinding, the Master makes the only choice left to him under the circumstances. A victory for him in this match would mean that he has become what his opponent is already: dedicated only to winning without regard for the spiritual value of the process. After Black 121, he could still win, logically; but now that the match has lost its artistic and spiritual value, it can have no meaning in the Master's tradition. He must lose in order to assert the validity of humanity's attempt to find the balance even as he fails himself. And so he deliberately and knowingly makes the move, White 130, that destroys him. Uragami asks: "Another puzzle: why did the Master play White 130 and so ensure his own defeat?" Just as the chorus in *Oedipus Rex* asks: "What god was it drove you to rake black / Night across your eyes?" But we know. And just as the Master has made the fatal move, the sound of a flute comes drifting into the room. The next morning he has begun the final ritual: "I do not know when he had called a barber, but this morning he resembled a shaven-headed priest."

Yasunari Kawabata has written a tragedy of the modern era, using the only context in which tragedy is still possible: a fundamental shift of emphasis from one world view to another, with humanity, in the person of the tragic hero, attempting to maintain a delicate balance between the two.
—Joseph H. Bourke

The world goes on, of course, just as it does in Sophocles's play, though not in the same way. The people of Thebes are rescued from their plague by Oedipus's action, while the people of Japan seem condemned to the insecurity of modern rationalism in Kawabata's novel. Otaké is fundamentally a good man, and he deservedly reaps the rewards of his victory: he lives well, and he can afford to keep disciples, along with his family, in a large home. But his real fate is expressed in one of Uragami's typical observations:

> The fact that today, a decade after the Master's death, no method has been devised for determining the succession to the title Master of Go probably has to do with the towering presence of Honnimbo Shusai. Probably he was the last of the true masters revered in the tradition of Go as a way of life and art.

But while Sophocles seems to revert to tradition and Kawabata plunges us into rationalism, the difference in prospects for the future is not surprising, nor is it crucial. It is the tipping of the balance in either direction by a human being's willful action that produces the tragic destruction. Oedipus's reliance on logic reveals the inadequacy of logic alone. Antigone's total commitment to tradition precipitates her destruction. Creon's excessive attention to political expediency is equally destructive. Haimon, who cannot find the balance between the two, is crushed. Phaedra's excessive passion destroys her, while Hippolytus, with his excessive self control, is ground up in a complex of fates and curses. Only Aeschylus's Orestes seems to live on, precisely because Athena has chosen to provide him with what seems to be the ideal balance: the rational human institution of law and justice under the guidance and protection of the gods. Significantly, Orestes is not the typical tragic hero. For Kawabata, who had the precedent of Western tradition to observe, the balance must tip in the direction of rationalism. In his tragic vision excessive rationality provides both the loss of equilibrium that leads to a tragic fate and the projection of its effects on humanity. And that excessive rationality takes the metaphoric guise of Western rationalism's most pervasive characteristic: analytical systematization.

Yasunari Kawabata has written a tragedy of the modern era, using the only context in which tragedy is still possible: a fundamental shift of emphasis from one world view to another, with humanity, in the person of the tragic hero, attempting to maintain a delicate balance between the two. Such a balance is impossible, of course, and one in which the hero can finally choose only to assert his humanity with his destruction. Kawabata's tragic vision is vitally alive, and it is faithful to the Greek conception, not because it attempts to imitate the earlier form, but because it is based on a similar cultural crisis. Tragedy has interested Westerners since its inception; they have always felt a fundamental dichotomy between the demands of the soul and those of the intellect,

and tragedy has objectified that dichotomy. But perhaps the most vital tragedy can only be written when the vehicle, the living metaphor, is derived from a culture that is itself on the balance midway between the two. In that sense, tragedy transcends the limitations of genre and of time.

Paul Stuewe (review date 26 March 1983)

SOURCE: A review of *House of the Sleeping Beauties,* in *Books in Canada,* Vol. 12, No. 3, March 26, 1983, p. 26.

[*In the following excerpt, Stuewe asserts that in* House of the Sleeping Beauties, *"Kawabata's writing . . . confronts the most basic contradictions of human life with poise and serenity, and makes high art out of the existential ebb and flow that will ultimately lay us low."*]

Bodily decline, and in the case of the story **"One Arm,"** dismemberment, play prominent roles in Yasunari Kawabata's **House of the Sleeping Beauties and Other Stories** translated into English in 1969 and now available in an attractive paperback edition. . . . The title novella relates an elderly man's fascination with an unusual kind of brothel, where those who can no longer make love to women pay to watch them sleep. This may sound like an unpromising or even precious conceit, but Kawabata develops it beautifully. Evocative memories of love affairs past are delicately compared to the subtler attractions of voyeurism, and the starker contrast between old age and youth is muted by expressing it in terms of the corresponding varieties of sleep: turbulent but refreshing for the young, fitful and imminently permanent for the aged. Life must end in death, but in **"House of the Sleeping Beauties"** a life is temporarily revived by the contemplation of youth in temporary repose, and the manifold nuances of this charged situation are stunningly rendered.

The book also includes two short stories of similar excellence. The narrator of **"One Arm"** first borrows and then exchanges his own arm for that of a young girl, as what initially seems an amusingly surreal experiment gradually becomes a very serious exploration of the boundaries of individual identities. In **"Of Birds and Beasts"** the protagonist, who can no longer tolerate human companionship, seeks solace in the observation of his pets. But this too proves dissatisfying, and as the story ends he is becoming fascinated with the diary of a girl who died at an early age: the implicit conclusion is that life is attractive when fixed at a beautiful moment, and death may be negated by artful preservation. This could also serve as a motto for Kawabata's writing, which confronts the most basic contradictions of human life with poise and serenity, and makes high art out of the existential ebb and flow that will ultimately lay us low.

Kinya Tsuruta (essay date 1986)

SOURCE: "The Twilight Years, East and West: Hemingway's *The Old Man and the Sea* and Kawabata's *The Sound of the Mountain*," in *Explorations,* edited by Makoto Ueda, University Press of America, 1986, pp. 87-99.

[*In the following essay, Tsuruta compares and contrasts the journeys undertaken by the aging main characters of Ernest Hemingway's* The Old Man and the Sea *and Kawabata's* The Sound of the Mountain.]

If anyone were to think of comparing Hemingway with a Japanese writer, the first name to come to mind would most likely be that of Mishima Yukio. The two writers share a wide area of common ground: an intense concern with masculinity, an obsession with violence and death, a strong, colorful personality which often overshadowed their literary work, and finally the fact that both ended their lives in violent suicide. On the other hand, Kawabata Yasunari, who tried to assuage loneliness with the beauty of art, women and nature, seems to offer little basis for comparison with the American novelist. Nevertheless, I have chosen Mishima's mentor here with the hope that this very contrast will shed some light on the workings of one modern Eastern mind against one Western mind in the face of a similar crisis.

Although it has no direct bearing on the actual comparison of these authors' works, it is intriguing to note that both Hemingway and Kawabata were born in 1899, both were the sons of doctors, both were awarded the Nobel Prize, and both committed suicide. Literary parallels exist also: both writers are known as superb stylists who abhorred abstraction, though their styles are quite different in texture; both writers' works explore the meanings of man's isolation; and finally, more than any other writer in their respective countries, each represents the sensitivities of his own cultural tradition at its deepest. When we compare *The Old Man and the Sea* and *The Sound of the Mountain,* we also realize that, even though the two writers were so different in temperament, they dealt with a surprisingly similar theme in their last important novels. Both works present a hero at the penultimate stage of his life struggling to live out his final days in the fullest way he knows. Both novels, considered by many critics to be the best works of their respective authors, have a deceptively simple style which hides a web of complex meanings.

Hemingway's novel starts: "He was an old man who fished alone in a skiff in the Gulf Stream." The reader is not told the exact age of the Cuban fisherman but that he is "thin and gaunt with deep wrinkles in the back of his neck." After eighty-four unlucky fishless days, Santiago rows far out into the Gulf Stream to hook a giant marlin of over fifteen hundred pounds, but sharks reduce the big fish to a skeleton by the time Santiago returns to shore. During the ordeal, Hemingway's hero displays an impressive mastery of skill and an almost superhuman energy and endurance. Kawabata's hero, on the other hand, is hardly that heroic. Shingo, a sixty-one-year-old businessman, thinks one night that he has heard the mountain in back of his house mysteriously make a sound. He vaguely interprets this occurrence as the beckoning knell of his death. During the fifteen months that follow, Shingo resorts to several ingenious devices to reverse time's flow. However he gradually comes to accept that he cannot be eternal; indeed, he is a part of that nature which keeps on living through a cycle of birth and death.

The purpose of this paper is to analyze the way these two old heroes confront death by examining their responses to primarily two major factors in life: space and time. *The Old Main and the Sea* operates very much like **The Sound of the Mountain** in three distinct spaces: the sea, the land (that is, Cuba) and Africa. The sea is obviously the novel's main stage where a battle between man and nature is waged. A man is alone here on the vast ocean and must prove his worth against his adversary. Here also diurnal time ticks away, and a minimum of time-stopping fantasy is tolerated. The overall effect is that a man becomes a sharply outlined individual and seeks an infinite expansion of his ego.

> When we compare *The Old Man and the Sea* and *The Sound of the Mountain,* we also realize that, even though the two writers were so different in temperament, they dealt with a surprisingly similar theme in their last important novels. Both works present a hero at the penultimate stage of his life struggling to live out his final days in the fullest way he knows.
> —*Kinya Tsuruta*

The land is where Santiago is with people. He is with Martin, the owner of the restaurant—significantly named the Terrace—who gives the old man food; Perico, who looks after his skiff; and above all, his youthful admirer Manolin, who fetches him food and drink, listens to his stories and puts him to bed. It is on the land that the old man allows himself to rest, to sleep and to dream about Africa, a place he visited in his youth. The land locale appears only twice: at the beginning and at the end quite briefly, but it undoubtedly provides a contrast to the sea. Africa is not an actual space in this novel but reveals itself nearly every time the old man dreams. When he was Manolin's age, he was on a ship that sailed to Africa; while there, he saw lions on the beach. And in his dreams every evening he sees those same African lions. If the sea represents the present where time definitely flows, Africa suggests the past, where the old man's time has been frozen. In his dream, Africa does not change; it is constant. It is always there unchanged when the old man goes to sleep. Africa represents his eternal youth. The land, however, is somewhere in between the present and the past. It is a half-awake reality as opposed to the stark naked reality of the sea where every second counts. The old man is well cared for here and is a part of the locale. Not as frightening or as beautiful as the sea, the village is a place for inactivity.

Space in *The Sound of the Mountain* is similarly divided into three distinct places: Tokyo, where Shingo works, Kamakura where he lives, and finally Shinshu where he lived in his youth and about which he dreams. Tokyo is equivalent to Santiago's sea in that it is the place of his livelihood and in that it represents the harshest reality. This is where his old classmates are dying one by one, reminding him that time is running out. Tokyo is where Kikuko, his graceful daughter-in-law, and her friend have abortions and where Shingo takes it upon himself to counsel his son's girlfriend, Kinu, to have an abortion.

If Tokyo represents life-struggle and responsibility, Kamakura imparts more of a sense of harmony. Kamakura affords a glimpse of an unattended natural order, provides contact with various aesthetic objects and is where Kikuko, who functions somewhat like Manolin in *The Old Man and the Sea*, is. In Kamakura Shingo exerts himself at self-rejuvenation, but it is not the Garden of Paradise. It has its share of failed responsibilities and of disappointments for Shingo. At best, Kamakura is a half-way place. The real paradise for Shingo is Shinshu, except that it is a lost one. Shingo apparently grew up there and fell in love with his wife's beautiful sister, who later died. In Shingo's mind, the image of the sister is frozen with the background of u. He constantly reminisces about u and the sister, and once in his dream, he goes back there to see her.

As with Santiago's three spatial locales, each with its corresponding period of time, Shingo's Tokyo represents the present, u the past, and Kamakura a mixture of the present and the past. One of the differences between the two heroes in terms of space is that while for Santiago the main stage is the sea, which represents the present, for Shingo the main stage is not Tokyo but Kamakura, the half-way place between the present and the past. The significance of this difference will be clear when we analyze the two heroes' attitudes toward and actual dealings with time.

We must stress that both men face a crisis of old age which may be somewhat different in appearance though essentially the same in nature. Both realize that they are in the penultimate stage of life and that, mentally as well as physically, their strength is waning. At the outset of the novel, Santiago is referred to as *salao,* which is in Spanish the worst form of unlucky, because the old man has not caught a fish for eighty-four days straight. Shingo's power of memory is weakening; he forgets things easily, and so on. Then one night he hears the ominous sound of the mountain and realizes that he may not have much time left in life. Santiago's crisis takes a much more dramatic form: an eighteen-foot marlin whose conquest demands great skill, enormous energy and an iron will bordering on the superhuman. Shingo's crisis is more internal but just as real; to cope with it he must reach down very deep inside to tap his inner resources.

During the four days of his fight with the giant fish and with the sharks afterwards, Santiago does everything to restore his youthful energy—not just to stay alive but also to triumph over the fish. He uses for this purpose the young boy Manolin, nature, his baseball hero Joe DiMaggio, his fishing skills, his memory of the glorious past, his capacity for psychological self-splitting, and finally the dream of Africa. Surprisingly, the Japanese hero so different in occupation, temperament, social position and cultural reflexes, employs almost exactly the same methods to reverse his time flow. Following are item-by-item comparisons of the two old men's struggles against their eventual extinction.

Manolin means several things to Santiago. First of all, the boy understands and appreciates the old man in a way nobody else does. While no one else believes in Santiago, Manolin knows he is the best fisherman. Between them is what appears to be a private ritual: the old man tells the boy that he has a pot of yellow rice with fish and also a cast net. He knows that the boy in fact knows Santiago does not have these things, but the boy respects and goes along with the old man's fiction. The ritual confirms their bond. The old man can rely on the boy without losing his pride. Manolin is not only the food-bearer and the keeper of the old man, but he also represents the old fisherman's future: the boy, always eager to learn fishing skills from his senior, is Santiago's successor. Manolin will carry on where the old man leaves off. Thus on one level Manolin is the youthful double of Santiago, a future extension of him. But Manolin also reminds Santiago of his past. "When I was your age I was before the mast on a square-rigged ship that ran to Africa," Santiago says. Thus when the old man, struggling with the big fish, says aloud to himself, "I wish I had the boy" or "I wish the boy was here," he is invoking a youthful energy through an overlay of himself, both in past and future form, with the young boy.

Kikuko, the delicate daughter-in-law in *The Sound of the*

Mountain, functions very much the way Manolin does. She is the water-bearer to Shingo and also the one who looks after him. Shingo dislikes meals and tea not prepared by Kikuko. Special areas exist which only Shingo and his daughter-in-law can understand and communicate, such as nature, art and death. She is an important link to his past, for she conjures up the vision of his wife's beautiful sister. At the same time, in Shingo's mind Kikuko also represents the future in that she may hopefully give birth to a child who is a reincarnation of the beautiful sister. This double function in regard to both the past and the future tends to diminish Kikuko's role in the present. Thus she remains, except towards the end of the novel, not a fleshed-out woman to whom one can relate but essentially a medium for Shingo's secret desires. Kikuko stirs the smouldering sexual emotions in Shingo but ultimately does not direct them to herself. Rather, she serves as a vehicle that carries him back to the beautiful sister of his fantasies and dreams.

Nature plays a vital part in both heroes' struggles to ride out their respective crises. Younger fishermen speak of the sea as *el mar,* which is masculine—thinking of it as a contestant or an enemy—but the old man calls it *la mar.* To him, the sea is a woman who gives and withholds great favors. If she does wicked things, it is because she cannot help it. The old man knows the sea thoroughly: its currents, winds, birds and fish. Nothing about the sea can surprise him. He can tell a hurricane is coming days ahead of time. The sea with its tuna, flying fish and shrimps nourishes and rejuvenates him, and with its salt water heals the wounds on his hands.

The old man has something of the sea about him. We are told at the outset, "Everything about him was old except his eyes and they were the same color as the sea and were cheerful and undefeated." Perhaps because of this rapport with the sea, the old fisherman begins to identify himself with the giant marlin he has hooked. The fish undergoes several stages of metamorphosis in Santiago's mind. It starts out as something of an adversary, then turns into something that demands a great deal of the old man's respect. A little later Santiago begins to address the fish as "brother." After he sees the fish jump out of the water, it becomes "beautiful" and "noble." But it is the shark attack that firmly establishes Santiago's identity with the fish. "When the fish had been hit, it was as though he himself were hit." This process becomes finalized when the old man eats a piece of the flesh of the great marlin. When sharks strip the big fish to the skeleton, Santiago is also being reduced to the bone. But he knew all along that he had gone too far out, that the sharks would come and that this would happen. Nature gives and also takes. There is no surprise in nature for Santiago for he is part of it.

Nature is full of surprises for the aged Japanese hero: the mountain sounds the knell of death, an old ginkgo tree puts forth young shoots in autumn, cherry trees bloom in the middle of winter, and a two-thousand year-old lotus seed comes into flower. To Shingo, in the beginning, nature is a mysterious entity which hides far more than it reveals. Shingo does not act upon nature but merely observes it. Yet through a keen power of observation he looks for and finds in nature phenomena which seem to defy the flow of time. Frightened by his approaching death, Shingo initially looks to nature for the assurance of a miracle that would show that time can be reversed. Thus the old gingko tree putting forth young leaves out of season seems to tell Shingo what he would like to hear. His observation of nature, however, gradually leads him away from his search for miracles, and to the discovery that things in nature flourish and decay but come back again in a renewed form. It dawns on him that although this year's kite that circles over his house may not be the same as last year's, it may in fact be last year's offspring. In the end, Shingo compares himself, without bitterness but not without a ring of sadness, with a descending trout, as mentioned in a haiku. He is aware now that the trout has laid its eggs upstream.

Joe DiMaggio is the old fisherman's hero not only because he is the best ballplayer but also because he performs perfectly, even with the pain of the bone spur in his heel. The old man feels that he himself must become worthy of the great DiMaggio; he wonders if DiMaggio could endure his—the old man's—pain. Thus by directly comparing himself with his hero, Santiago whips up his own courage to continue the fight.

In one of his weakest moments, Shingo resorts to a similar method, though somewhat more obliquely. He discovers through a dream that he secretly harbors a sexual fantasy in regard to his daughter-in-law. Feeling depressed, Shingo remembers having seen a picture of a lone crow enduring a rainstorm at dawn, by the celebrated Edo artist Watanabe Kazan. Shingo saw the picture at a friend's house and was told that the friend looked at the crow in the picture during the War and thereby tried to endure the hard times. The suggestion here is that Shingo derives some strength by linking himself with the artist Kazan, who underwent personal ordeals, and also with the crow patiently awaiting daybreak.

The old hero of Hemingway's last novel is a skillful, experienced fisherman. The fisherman says, "It is better to be lucky. But I would rather be exact. Then when luck comes you are ready." To be skillful and to be exact with fishing is what helps him to survive and eventually hook the big fish. Skill means one's control of time. With skill, the old man is able to anticipate events which will occur. On the eighty-fifth day, he looks at the current and predicts that the day will be good for fishing. Later he knows that if the marlin turns east with the current, it is tiring; he can also foretell when the fish will jump clear of the water by looking at the slant of the line. Again, the old fisherman can sense when the fish is going to circle the boat. He knows that sharks will be after him and when that happens, "God pity him and me." Skill comes also from repeated experiences and affords a man control over flowing and otherwise capricious time by equipping him with the power of prediction. Hence time under the control of skill is cyclic, like the hands of a clock. Manolin the boy says to the old man, "You are my alarm clock." To this statement the old man replies, "Age is my alarm clock." When the old man himself is the alarm clock, there is very little harm for him in the sequence of things that are to happen.

If the Cuban fisherman has a cyclic clock inside him and seems to go along with the flow of time without protest, the Japanese hero is terrified at the prospect of reaching the terminal point of linear time. One of the ways he tries to arrest the flow of this time is through art. An artist can scoop up human feelings out of the swiftly moving river of time and crystallize them into a time-defying form like a painting or a poem. Shingo is surrounded by many forms of art. As Santiago is a practitioner of skill, Shingo is an observer. The Japanese hero appreciates art deeply and tends to move from life towards art: Eiko reminds him of an erotic print by Harunobu, and a stumbling puppy calls to mind a painting by Sotatsu. Shingo's effort to stop time through art comes to its climax when he overlays on Kikuko's face a *jido* mask, an unmistakable symbol of eternity. This act turns into a critical moment when Shingo comes to the threshold of having a glimpse of eternity. But toward the end, his faith in art is slowly undermined: he finds that the calligraphy by Ryokan is a fake. He also discovers that a famous tanka of Yosano Akiko carved in a stone monument contains an error. A Buson haiku comes to mind when Shingo tries to brush away the dark thoughts about Kikuko revealed in one of his dreams. The haiku goes: "I try to forget this senile love: a chilly autumn shower." In this case, art, instead of reversing time, nudges Shingo toward the stream of time and makes him realize the hopelessness of love. Thus art in Shingo begins as a time-arresting device, but it gradually disintegrates and finally ends up being a reminder of flowing time.

One of Santiago's extremely effective ways of gathering up courage to face his crises is to recall his younger days when he was physically much stronger. The old fisherman remembers how he once played the hand game with the strongest negro on the block. He recalls how they played one day and one night until blood oozed from under the fingernails of his hand, and until he finally won the game. The old man remembers that everyone called him the Champion. The memories of his glorious past renews Santiago's confidence.

The memories of the past are equally important in Shingo's rejuvenation process. While he easily forgets things of a few

days ago, his memory of Yasuko's beautiful sister from about four decades ago is unbelievably vivid. Whenever life is felt to be too hard, Shingo evokes the sister's memory. Again, towards the end of the novel Shingo resorts less and less to memories of the past, until at the very end his memories are not so much about the sister the person but about u the place, and about haiku which she taught him. One such haiku reads: "A trout in the autumn, abandoning itself to the water." The haiku shows that Shingo has not only embraced his old age but also that he, having stopped fighting against the flow of time, goes down the stream like an old trout. Again, like the other time-stopping devices, his remembrance of the past gradually loses its effectiveness in the end, leading the hero to come to terms with himself.

Fighting the gigantic marlin, Santiago must mobilize every part of his body if he is to win. Suddenly his left hand becomes cramped. The old man resorts to a fascinating technique to regain the use of his left hand. He first distances himself from his hand and talks to it as if it were an independent entity completely separate from him. He curses, sweet-talks, encourages and commands the cramped hand. Finally, he is able to regain the use of it. But at another crucial time when the fisherman must sink his harpoon into the marlin's heart, his head goes numb. Thereupon he disassociates himself from his own head and treats it as if it did not belong to him. He says, "Clear up, head." In a crisis, then, Santiago psychologically dismembers a malfunctioning part of his body and tells it to shape up. Apparently this self-splitting method works for him.

Shingo does not go that far, but characteristically only fantasizes self-splitting. As he is looking at gigantic sunflowers one day, his beautiful daughter-in-law comes along and joins him. Shingo is reminded by the flowers of a virile male symbol, but he chooses to talk to her about a man's head instead:

> My head hasn't been very clear these last few days. I suppose that's why sunflowers made me think of heads. I wish mine could be a clean as they are. I was thinking on the train—if only there were some way to get your head cleaned and refinished. Just chop it off—well, maybe that would be a little violent. Just detach it and hand it over to some university hospital as if you were handing over a bundle of laundry. "Do this up for me, please," you'd say. And the rest of you would be quietly asleep for three or four days or a week while the hospital was busy cleaning your head and getting rid of the garbage. No tossing and no dreaming.

It is in dreaming that Shingo gets his wish—not having his head cleaned, but his secret wish underneath his sunflower/ man's head talk: rejuvenation of his male virility. In the seventh dream, he is a young army officer who, carrying three pistols and an heirloom sword, goes to u to meet the object of his passion, his wife's sister.

Dreams have been thoroughly exploited for various literary purposes by a good number of novelists in the past. In the two novels under consideration, dreams are accorded a vital role. The reader is told that every night Santiago dreams about the golden beach of Africa where lions come out and play. After hooking the giant marlin, the old fisherman keeps up with the fish for two days without any sleep and knows that he must get some sleep soon if he is to win the fight. Santiago manages to doze off for a while and dreams. His dream is really a series of three short dreams: he sees a school of porpoises in their mating time leaping high into the air, then himself at the village on his bed, and finally the lions on the African beach. It is interesting to note that what he has dreamed will all come true. The big fish will jump out of the water, and with it Santiago's identity with it will be intensified. Then later he will be back in his village on his bed, dreaming of the lions. The dream function seems to be two-fold for Santiago: besides predicting events that will occur, it energizes the old man by taking him back to his boyhood and putting him in contact with the king of beasts.

The dreams in *The Sound of the Mountain* are probably the most important method by which Shingo achieves what he achieved at the end. His dreams, eight in all, are definitely designed so that he will undergo, dream by dream, a complete reversal of time until, toward the end, he is the young army officer with the heirloom sword going back to u to see the beautiful sister. Shingo uses his dreams as a time-tunnel leading into the past and fulfilling his fantasy, which can in no way be realized in actuality. It is precisely because Shingo has been able to visit his Garden of Paradise in his dreams that he is prepared to relieve Kikuko of her role as medium and also to embrace the circular concept of time as found in the four seasons of nature. The Garden of Paradise, Shingo discovers in his dream, is also the netherland and the terminal point in the linear time of which he has been so afraid. Thus in Shingo's case, dreams are given the function of ending his unfulfilled love affair with the dead woman by putting him in touch with her through their time-tunnel. With the very cause of his unhappiness dislodged in his past, he can now liberate himself from the clutch of linear time and gladly identify himself with a descending trout.

Santiago is Hemingway's idealized hero, a fearless fighter endowed with the wisdom of an old man, the unbounded energy of a youth and a characteristic capacity to endure pain. He is conscious of death neither in the beginning nor in the end. Every drop of his energy is concentrated on the present moment at sea, and his objective is to win the fight. He catches the fish only to lose it to the sharks, but little has

changed inside this hero, or so it seems at least. He goes back to the same dream and may be out again to sea the next day, looking for another big fish to match the size of his ego. Santiago's identification with nature is highly selective. The sea is, after all, a woman; and a Hemingway man would not be caught dead completely merging with her. Santiago's object of self-identification is a giant fish with a spear the size of a baseball bat. If he hides his fear of death in his fierce battle against the fish, we cannot detect the fear. If we could, he would not fare well as a good Hemingway hero.

If there is an idealization in the character of Shingo, it is certainly not to the point in using a parable-like style as in *The Old Man and the Sea*. Shingo comes through as very human with his fears and failures, with which we can identify. He is not alone on the vast ocean pursuing his prize, but in the midst of a tangled web of human relationships, both past and present. His fish is not somewhere in the harsh present reality of Tokyo, but in u, a place lost to the past. Nevertheless, Shingo somehow catches the fish. It is only a trout, tiny, old, descending and female. It has no spear, but then again, no sharks can take it away from him.

Marlene A. Pilarcik (essay date Fall 1986)

SOURCE: "Dialectics and Change in Kawabata's *The Master of Go*," in *Modern Language Studies*, Vol. XVI, No. 4, Fall, 1986, pp. 9-21.

[*In the following essay, Pilarcik asserts that Kawabata's "The Master of Go . . . captures the poignantly beautiful fading of an era as Japan enters the modern age."*]

The works of the Nobel Prize winning author, Yasunari Kawabata, are noted for their delicate, wistful beauty and haunting lyricism. They express the essence of the Japanese soul, but also draw on the universality of human experience. *The Master of Go,* one of Kawabata's most elegiac novels, captures the poignantly beautiful fading of an era as Japan enters the modern age. The narrative is based on the 1938 championship Go match between the aging Master Shusai and his youthful challenger, Kitani Minoru, known as Otaké in the novel. With the defeat and death of the aristocratic Master, the past gives way to the progressive, competitive, and time-obsessed forces of the new age; the grace of an elegant tradition succumbs to an unchivalrous modernity; Eastern sensibility feels the thrust of Western scientific rationalism; and ending verges on beginning in a fluid, continually changing universe. The pervasive sense of transition and flowing movement in the novel emanates from the dynamic tension of opposition inherent in the Go game, in the players, and in the very nature of the work as a blend of reportage and a lyrical point of view. This study focuses on the dialectics of the novel as the source of its subtle power and evocative beauty.

The Japanese game of Go has a profundity and spiritual depth which are often little understood in the West. For the Japanese, Go has traditionally been more than a contest of skill or endurance—it is a discipline and a creative art that originated in ancient China but developed and flowered in Japan. According to Kawabata, the Japanese "elevated" and "deepened" the game and cultivated its mysteries. The game itself consists of a board with 19 vertical and 19 horizontal lines and two sets of stones, one black and one white. The stones are placed on the 361 intersections with the intent of defining an area or territory. Symbolically, the first stone placed on the empty board is a first definition in space, and a limitation in time. The next stone stands in opposition as a reaction to it and begins a process animated by the fundamental principle of dialectical interaction and change. A dynamic tension is thereby established reminiscent of the interplay of yin and yang, opposing forces within a universal unity. The players respond to each other like the two primal forces, pushing and yielding, not with the intent of destroying each other, but in order to create together in harmony. As Kajiki in his introduction to the game says, the visual image of black and white stones represents the universe as a duality in harmonious unity: "If both players of distinguished skill do their best till the end of a game, the board will be covered with black and white stones in perfect harmony. Such a game is equal to an excellent work of art beyond the result of victory or defeat."

The works of the Nobel Prize winning author, Yasunari Kawabata, are noted for their delicate, wistful beauty and haunting lyricism. They express the essence of the Japanese soul, but also draw on the universality of human experience.
—*Marlene A. Pilarcik*

Kawabata illustrates a game which lacks this harmony when the narrator Uragami is drawn into play with an American who has taken lessons at the Go Association. He claims to be "fascinated" with this "great invention" and is very conscious of his level of skill: "I am Grade thirteen, he said with careful precision as if doing a sum." His playing reveals that he has mastered the external forms and rules of the game but he remains detached and offers no inner resistance to his opponent. Uragami senses an "utter foreignness" that has less to do with skill than with a lack of spirit: ". . . he had a way of playing thoughtlessly, without really putting himself in the game. Losing did not bother him in the least. He went happily through game after game, as if to say that it was silly to take a mere game seriously. . . . Indeed this quickness to

lose left me wondering uncomfortably if I might not have something innately evil concealed within me . . . The spirit of Go was missing." The game between the American and Uragami acquires an unpleasant one-sidedness which prohibits the realization of harmonious interaction, thus degenerating into something quite trivial, meaningless, and spiritless.

When Shusai confronts his opponent Otaké over the Go board, however, Uragami has the "sense of Go as an art." He is also aware of profound forces at work which transcend the fates of the individual players and even the outcome of this particular match. Their interaction mirrors the universal dialectic and the placement of stones on the board speaks of universal mysteries.

Shusai represents for Kawabata the grace and nobility of Japan's cultural heritage because his life and his approach to the game are firmly rooted in the traditions and sensibility of the past. At the very beginning of the novel he is identified as twenty-first in the Honnimbo succession of Go masters founded in the seventeenth century by the Zen Buddhist monk, Sansa. Shusai is the last to bear the title of Honnimbo in this continuous line. In addition, his life, which spans the years from 1874 to 1940, forms a bridge from the Meiji Era to the modern age. Kawabata says that in his person he embodies a "whole panorama of history . . . He was the symbol of Go itself. . . ."

Shusai is the Master, a *meijin* who, according to Uragami, is "the last of the true masters revered in the tradition of Go as a way of life and art." Traditionally, the title, *meijin*, has meant more than an expert in a particular art. As D. T. Suzuki explains,

> He is one who has gone beyond the highest degree of proficiency in his art. He is a creative genius . . . one becomes a *meijin* only after experiencing infinitely painstaking discipline, for only such a series of experiences leads to the intuition of the secret depths of art, that is, to the lifespring.

Meijin Shusai has dedicated his life to the pursuit of Go and the disciplining of the spirit. His playing emanates from the meditative consciousness of Zen, where, immersed totally in the game, he loses all sense of self and time. In his Nobel Prize acceptance speech Kawabata describes this state of mind which is achieved by Zen disciples:

> . . . he enters a state of impassivity, free from all ideas and all thoughts. He departs from the self and enters the realm of nothingness. This is not the nothingness or emptiness of the West. It is rather, a universe of the spirit in which everything

communicates freely with everything, transcending bounds, limitless.

For the Master, therefore, Go transcends the bounds of mere game and becomes a mystical art or the means for a spiritual experience of "void."

The Master attributes his style of playing and his success in the game to having "no nerves" or "a vague absent sort." The term "vagueness" (*bonyari*) can have different connotations. In Osaka it implies absence, lack of definition, or unobtrusiveness as one would find in a Japanese painting; in Tokyo it refers to a slowness of apprehension or stupidity. The term suggests a certain ambiguity about the Master. On one hand, he draws on the emptiness of mind as the source of his creativity in playing, and this heightened spirituality evokes a sense of absence or other-worldliness about him. Uragami says he suggests "some rarefied spirit floating over a void." On the other hand, he appears to have a rather tenuous and detached hold on every-day life. People, scenery, and events pass before him unnoticed: "He sat in silence, as if not aware of the view before him. He did not look at the other guests." Even physically he gives the appearance of lacking substance—his body is like that of an under-nourished child, and his temperature remains at a cool 96-97 degrees. Looking at a picture of the dead man's face, Uragami sees "the ultimate in tragedy, of a man so disciplined in an art that he had lost the better part of reality."

When seated at the Go board, however, the Master commands a powerful and distinctive position. He is a "grand figure"—the invincible Master towering over the board in an unself-conscious ease. Lost in meditation, he experiences the game, his opponent, and his own self as one; thus the game flows spontaneously, effortlessly from him, as though it were unfolding of its own accord: "It perhaps told of his age and experience, the fact that like the flow of water or the drifting of clouds a White formation quietly took shape over the lower reaches of the board in response to careful and steady pressure from Black. . . ." The impression of power and strength that emanates from his spiritual involvement in the game stands in marked contrast to the frailty of his ailing body.

There is also an extremeness about the Master which manifests itself as coldness and insensitivity. He is not inclined to express emotions, warmth or gratitude even to his most ardent disciples and supporters. His wife assumes the responsibility for social niceties and acts as his spokesman. Swann interprets this as an understandable "narrowness" arising from a total immersion in his art. The insatiable hunger he exhibits for games, however, borders on obsession. When he is not at the Go board, he constantly looks for other games in which he can lose himself. Uragami describes him as a "starving urchin" and indicates the presence of inner con-

flict: "Even after the August 10 session he had to have games to divert him. To me it was as if he were suffering the torments of hell." This raises some doubt about the purity of the Master's spiritual desire. Is he seeking escape from the exigencies of ordinary reality in the mystical state of "void?" Or is it, as Iwamoto and Wagenaar suggest, an indication that he is finding it increasingly difficult to achieve the mystical state?

Uragami also questions whether the Master has betrayed his ideal by his very participation in this match at the age of sixty-four and in failing health. Because he accepted the challenge for a "price without precedent" from the sponsoring newspaper, the possibility exists that he did not "go forth in combat" but rather allowed himself "to be lured" in by the newspaper. In former times the title of *meijin* was more than a sign of skill for competition purposes, and the holder of the title would often deliberately avoid real competition in order not to do injury to it. In the new age, however, emphasis shifts to a more competitive involvement in title matches with monetary rewards. Thus, Shusai stands "at the boundary between the old and the new," an anachronism whose art no longer fits in with the spirit of the times.

The new age finds its representative in the challenger Otaké. Despite an inconsistent record, Otaké defeated several opponents, including his own teachers, in the contest sponsored by the Go Association to determine who would oppose the Master in this historic match. The contrast he presents with the Master is striking. Instead of the cold, severe dignity of a sublime spirituality, he manifests the warm amiability of a world-oriented personality. This is apparent even in the fact that he is physically sturdier, weighing nearly twice as much as the Master. He exudes a sense of virility, and robust earthiness, maintains a lively household with several students, and demonstrates a light-hearted humor, and social ease. Although he is clearly dedicated to Go, he has not sacrificed life for it, nor has he been "bled" by it. His approach to the game has a distinctly professional and competitive focus. Unlike the Master who loses himself in the spiritual void beyond the concerns of winning or losing, Otaké desires success. The tension thus generated by the pressures of the match provoke numerous stress-related disorders such as enuresis, diarrhea, fainting, restlessness, fidgeting, and absent-mindedness. Kawabata describes the two players seated at the board as a contrast of "quiet against constant motion, nervelessness against nervous tension."

Otaké's playing relies on deliberate effort, careful planning, and even scheming to attain his end because he cannot abandon himself to the harmony of spontaneous play. Despite his nervousness, however, he has a powerful concentration and resolve that are manifested as an aggressive driving force. The Master's playing is compared to the flowing of water or drifting of clouds, but Otaké's style is almost brutally determined. Uragami feels that he "would avert defeat even if in the process he must chew the stones to bits." Iwamoto and Wagenaar describe it as an "egoistic will to power" quite different from the "Oriental ideal of self-negation." This creates the atmosphere of darkness and oppression in his game:

> There was something oppressive about it, something that seemed to push up from deep within, like a strangled cry. Concentrated power was on a collision course, one looked in vain for a free and natural flow. The opening moves had been heavy and a sort of inexorable gnawing had followed.

Uragami frequently focuses on the gap in the amount of playing time used by the players to reveal their fundamental spiritual incompatibility. The Master's playing has the characteristic speed and spontaneity of intuitive non-intellectualization. He says, "I'm not much of a thinker." On the other hand, Otaké indicates, "I start thinking and there's no end to it." Otaké's total time spent in play equals nearly twice that of the Master precisely because of his tendency to engage in endless mental debate. In fact, he habitually runs out of time and almost exhausts the allowed limits set for the match. For the Master external time is not a conscious factor because while playing he is centered in the experience of *now*. In keeping with the spirit of Zen, he makes his moves in an unself-conscious, noncontrived manner as though they evolved of their own accord at the right moment. Otaké's method of evaluating, weighing, planning, and analyzing can consume as much time as is available and only result in mental frenzy and indecision. Instead of a nowcenteredness, Otaké finds himself in constant conflict with the ticking clock.

Both players have restrictions of time placed on them by the establishment of time allotments set at forty hours per person. The Master had determined the number, believing that by setting the total deliberately high he had in effect eliminated the temporal limitation. Since he had been trained in a period when such rules did not exist, the time allotments have little meaning for him and exert no influence on his playing. Otaké, however, is subject to fainting when running out of time. His internal time sense is obscured by the demands of linear temporality. Instead of losing himself to the natural flow and movement of the game, he succumbs to the turmoil of a time-obsessed consciousness. Because time is such a conscious element in his playing, he turns his attention to ways by which he can circumvent it. The time allotments and sealed play become for him a potential means for new tactics and strategy.

Traditionally, Go has relied on very few formal rules in order to allow as much creative freedom as possible to the players. For this match, however, special restrictions are imposed in order to insure equality and fair play. In the past,

elitism and unspoken social customs of courtesy, respect, and deference could have easily worked to the advantage of the higher-ranked player, but the incorporation of the time allotments and sealed play deny the Master any special status due to his rank and force him to curb his whims. According to Uragami, it made no difference that the Master's art was forged by the arbitrariness of spontaneity: "he could not stand outside the rules of equality." Thus, courtesy gives way to justice, and the game undergoes a shift in emphasis from the finesse and mysterious elegance of Go as art to the regulation and objectivity of Go as competitive sport:

> It may be said that the Master was plagued in his last match by modern rationalism, to which fussy rules were everything, from which all the grace and elegance of Go as art had disappeared . . . One conducted the battle only to win, and there was no margin for remembering the dignity and fragrance of Go as an art.

It is evident from the outset that Otaké is approaching the game on a different level from that of the Master, and that he is less concerned with art than with his personal victory. Throughout the game he is adamant about adherence to the rules and fights to maintain the letter of the law on technical matters even when the request is made to shorten the four-day recesses to two days because of the Master's worsening health. He feels that any concession made to the Master could threaten the imposed structure of the game and work to his disadvantage. And yet he does not hesitate to use any legal strategy to advance himself even if it is ruthless and unorthodox.

There is a saying in the *Tao Te Ching:*

> The more prohibitions there are, . . .
> The more benighted will the whole land grow.
> The more cunning craftsmen there are,
> The more pernicious contrivances will be invented.

In similar fashion, Uragami notes: "When a law is made, the cunning that finds loopholes goes to work. One cannot deny that there is a certain slyness among young players, a slyness which, when rules are written to prevent slyness, makes use of these rules themselves."

Otaké's disregard for the aesthetics of the game becomes evident fairly early. For example, the positioning of Black 63 as a "spy" in the white formation is an aggressive invasion not in keeping with the natural flow of the game. It strikes the Master as "a trifle unorthodox." The subsequent playing of Black 69, however, reveals the use of cunning and deceit. Otaké had obviously sealed an irrelevant move and used the long recess to deliberate his plan of attack. Then he attempted to conceal this fact by pretending to deliberate for nearly 20 minutes before placing his stone on the board. His Black 69 cuts boldly into the Master's formation and is described as a "violent attack," "a diabolic stroke," and is even likened to "the flash of a dagger." Uragami says, "A little unkind of you?" The Master feels that this is a ruthless violation of the sanctity of the game—"a sealed play that seemed to take advantage of the fact that it was a sealed play." Although on the verge of forfeiting, the Master responds with White 70—a move that makes the spectators "speechless with admiration." He did not attempt a counterattack, meeting force with force, but instead, had yielded to the attack, sacrificed his stones, and allowed the aggression of his opponent to turn against itself: "Black had made gains, and yet it seemed that White, casting away the dressings from his wounds, had emerged with greater lightness and freedom of action." The Master thus incorporates Otaké's aggression into the harmony and art of the game.

The final smear on the art of Go and the decisive conflict that determines the outcome of the match are again initiated by Otaké's clever manipulation of the regulations to gain a personal advantage. The moves from Black 121 to White 130 reduce the game to the level of a personal battle in which the Master suffers an unchivalrous death-blow. Black 121 is Otaké's sealed play and should have been fairly predictable given the situation on the board. However, when Yamata opens the envelope, he has difficulty locating it because it is quite removed from the tense conflict brewing in the center of the board. Attention is thus diverted from the crucial battle while the Master responds to the new threat against his stones. It is an abrupt and unexpected jolt from the natural course of the game and an obvious tactical attempt to gain more time. The Master perceives this as a trick, an offense against the game, and a violation of the harmonious creation of art. Although outwardly composed, this move brings the Master to the breaking point. The physical ailments, the rules that rob him of any special status and courtesy, the strains of prolonged playing, and the ignoble techniques of his opponent all contribute to the rupture that comes with the unexpectedness of Black 121. He says in an intense voice, "'The match is over. Mr. Otaké ruined it with that sealed play. It was like smearing ink over the picture we had painted. . . .'" Pushed to the limit, the Master lashes out against Otaké on a personal and vengeful level by using White 130 to strike a strong retaliatory counter-attack against the Black position in the lower right. Uragami reacts in the following manner:

> I was startled. It was a wholly unexpected play. I felt a tensing of my muscles, as if the diabolic side of the Master had suddenly been revealed. Detecting a flaw in the plans suggested by Black 129, so much in Otaké's own characteristic style, had the Master dodged away and turned to infighting by way of counter-attack? Or was he asking for a slash

so that he might slash back, wounding himself to down his adversary?

With White 130 his disappointment and "angry disdain" are vented but the short-lived moment of revenge reduces the game to a personal clash that ultimately costs him the match. Otaké forces him back to the defensive and he becomes powerless to turn back "the crushing wave" that follows. The Master is defeated—but not with honor, not with dignity.

As the Master plays White 130, the sound of a virtuoso flute drifts into the room and seems "to quiet somewhat the storm on the board." The flute signals a reassertion of equilibrium after the disruption and conflict between the two players. Afterwards, the game resumes a natural flow, but the course of the match has produced noticeable changes in the Master and even in Otaké. After his return from St. Luke's Hospital, the Master no longer clips his hair short in the Buddhist fashion, but leaves it long and dyed black. He also becomes significantly time-conscious. For the first time he comments on the amount of time consumed by Otaké: "'He does take his time,' . . . 'More than an hour already?'" On the morning of the crucial battle, the Master makes an uncharacteristic observation: "'The Condor flew in last night at ten thirty.' . . . 'Can you imagine such speed?'" In addition, Uragami notes that he continually looks at his watch! He also shows signs of impatience, irritability and indecisiveness as is evidenced by his rapping on the rim of the brazier and muttering to himself. Towards the end of the match he begins to reminisce about the past and expresses a new sense of amiability, inviting the observers to come closer to the board in order to get a better view.

> **Kawabata in the persona of his narrator, Uragami, has clearly created more than an objective report of this Go match. Not only does he personally interact with the players, even interceding when necessary to reconcile tensions, but he also responds subjectively and intimately to what he observes.**
>
> **—*Marlene A. Pilarcik***

Otaké, on the other hand, is no longer subject to the same sort of anxieties and tensions once his success is assured. His pace in the game accelerates and he slips into an internally generated momentum unaffected by the time allotments. At one point, he even appears to lose himself so completely in the game that he experiences the sort of mystical surrender that had previously characterized the Master. Uragami is struck by his appearance: "The round full face had the completeness and harmony of a Buddha head. It was an indescribably marvelous face—perhaps he had entered a realm of artistic exaltation. He seemed to have forgotten his digestive troubles." At the end of the match, Otaké sits quietly with head bowed, then retreats to the garden where he sinks into deep meditation. The Master, however, shows considerable interest in the amount of time he used in playing.

For the Master this match marks the end of a long career, the dissipation of his life energies, and the death of his art. A year later during a brief visit, Uragami experiences this unsettling death. He sees it in the way the Master places his stones on the Go board during two practice matches with his disciples—they no longer make the distinct clicking sound. He sees it in the human and personal loneliness now emanating from the frail figure which is quite different from the lonely isolation of the artist who is removed from the mundane affairs of ordinary life. The Master has become very human, "a sweet old gentleman" desiring company and a good talk. Distressed by this change in the Master, Uragami hurries away declining the Master's entreaties to stay for dinner. As he explains to his wife, "I don't like having people die."

Kawabata in the persona of his narrator, Uragami, has clearly created more than an objective report of this Go match. Not only does he personally interact with the players, even interceding when necessary to reconcile tensions, but he also responds subjectively and intimately to what he observes. His accurate and detailed record of the proceedings is combined with a sensitive and personal point of view which shapes the tone and structure of the novel. In his perceiving consciousness the intuitive and subjective are counter-balanced with the rational and objective. One result is the frequent juxtaposing of a subjective response with a rational explanation. For example, the Master appears to grow larger at the Go board which Uragami feels is the result of the power of his art and long years of discipline and training, but he also includes the explanation that he has a disproportionately long trunk. In another instance, Uragami observes the Master's quickened breathing and responds to it on different levels:

> Yet the heaving of those thin, hunched shoulders was what struck me most forcefully. I felt as if I were the uninvited witness to the secret advent of inspiration, painless, calm, unknown to the Master and not perceived by others.

> But afterwards it seemed to me that I had rather outdone myself. Perhaps the Master had but felt a twinge of pain in his chest. His heart condition was worse as the match progressed, and perhaps he had felt the first spasm at that moment.

This dual vision can be likened to the defective camera with which he takes pictures of the dead Master. Because of the defective shutter, Uragami must adjust the shutter speed manually. Thus the technical precision of the camera is coupled with his own subjective judgment about the quantity of light that strikes the film. The Master once said of Uragami that he had a "remarkable eye for details." Equally significant is the manner in which the details strike the perceiving consciousness. When Uragami first sees the photographs of the dead Master, he feels there are major discrepancies between the reality that he photographed and the images that appear on the film. The face that he photographed has a softness, richness, and intensity of feeling that were not evident in the actual face of the dead man nor in the nature of the man while living. In life the Master seemed remote, apart from reality, vague, absent; but in death his image possesses a life-likeness that blurs the separation of life and death. Like the novel itself, they capture a mood, a power, and a sadness that are inexplicable and yet "true." The truth derives from the harmonious tension of inner and outer reality. Kawabata is not concerned with revealing an inner landscape or penetrating the multiple facets of an individual personality at the expense of external reality. In fact, the perceiving consciousness of the narrator, rather than dominating the narrative, often becomes transparent or mirror-like as it receives stimuli from the external world.

The entire novel is filled with camera-like snapshots of brief thoughts, impressions, and observations. Uragami catches these instants and positions them in such a way that they evoke a hidden meaning. The lack of explanations and logical connectives creates a silence or emptiness against which the images strike. In the following passage as image follows image directly and without causal connectives, all senses are brought into play to create an impression of simultaneity:

> When play began, however, the sky was lightly clouded over once more. There was a strong enough breeze that the flowers in the alcove swayed gently. Aside from the waterfall in the garden and the river beyond, the silence was broken only by the distant sound of a rock cutter's chisel. A scent of red lilies wafted in from the garden. In the almost too complete silence a bird soared grandly beyond the eaves. There were sixteen plays in the course of the afternoon. . . .

In this suspended moment, the distant sounds intensify the silence, and the subtle movements of a swaying branch and soaring bird give an internal dynamism to the stillness. The last sentence abruptly ends the moment, jolting us with the realization that considerable time has passed.

The juxtapositioning of images also prevents the work from becoming sentimental or maudlin. When emotions become too deep, Uragami resorts to silence or dissolves them into an impersonal atmosphere. For example, during a recess he focuses on the aristocratic, frail figure of the Master as he takes a walk up a short slope. His delicately veined hands are clasped behind his back:

> He was carrying a folded fan. His body, bent forward from the hips, was perfectly straight, making his legs seem all the more unreliable. From below the thicket of dwarf bamboo, along the main road, came a sound of water down a narrow ditch.

The Master appears like an exquisite blossom on the point of fading, evoking a sense of poignant nostalgia or what the Japanese refer to as *mono no aware*—the sad awareness of beauty in a fleeting moment. The connection between the Master and sound of water is aesthetic and intuitive, not logical, and it affects a profound reaction in Uragami:

> Nothing more—and yet the retreating figure of the Master somehow brought tears to my eyes. I was profoundly moved, for reasons I do not myself understand.

Shattering this moment before it becomes sentimentalized are the Master's words: "A swallow, a swallow." Suddenly, as if given a subtle shock, our attention shifts away from the Master up to the sky, then in the next sentence down again: "Beyond him was a stone informing us that the Meiji Emperor had deigned to stay at the inn." In this brief passage, present, past, man and nature are held in an impersonal, timeless instant.

In his *Shosetsu no Kenkyu* (*Studies of the Novel*) Kawabata wrote that a well-ordered plot is inconsistent with the laws of nature and that in his writing he attempts to follow nature as it is. His work reflects a spontaneous, organic process rather than an intellectually conceived one, and it produces the effect of flow but not progression.
—Marlene A. Pilarcik

Intuitive, associative leaps also affect the pace and structure of the novel creating a tension between the chronological progression of events and the flow of memory. On one hand, Uragami has noted precise times and dates for the events of the match. Like Otaké, he indicates a careful consciousness of clock-time that divides reality into objective segments. The narrative, however, does not follow a linear progression. He relies on the intuitive associations of memory to fragment the chronology and juxtapose various points to create the sense of an unfolding of what already is. In the first four

chapters, for example, the movement threads chronologically backwards from the Master's death to his final days, then to the last play of the match at precisely 2:42 on the afternoon of December 4th. It then reverses direction moving ahead to the day after the match, skips ahead a few more days, and ends a few years after the match. The game begins in Chapter Four. In subsequent chapters he weaves together various points along the linear continuum, disregarding sequential order, and concludes with the Master's death and the shipment of his body to Tokyo. The careful recording of dates and time expenditures establishes a chronological framework which is then reshuffled, obscuring our sense of causality and forming a time-shape that is more fluid and subjective. In his *Shosetsu no Kenkyu* (*Studies of the Novel*) Kawabata wrote that a well-ordered plot is inconsistent with the laws of nature and that in his writing he attempts to follow nature as it is. His work reflects a spontaneous, organic process rather than an intellectually conceived one, and it produces the effect of flow but not progression. The movement can be compared to the unfolding of a picture scroll in which the sequence is not causal or linear but simultaneously part of a whole.

Despite the spontaneous associations and leaps in time, there is an underlying pattern that unifies and shapes the work. It begins and ends with the Master's death, thus creating one large circle embracing the entire narrative. In the middle of the novel is another circle that is created by the Master's own premonition of his death and the repetition of a conversation between Uragami and the Master. Chapter Eighteen begins:

> Once shortly after play was resumed at Ito I asked the Master whether he meant to return to St. Luke's Hospital when the match was over, or winter as usual in Atami.

> "The question is whether I last that long," he said as if taking me into his confidence.

And Chapter Thirty One ends:

> I asked whether at the end of the match he meant to winter in Atami or Ito or return to St. Luke's.

> He replied, as if taking me into his confidence: "The question is whether I last that long."

After this internal loop there is a noticeable change in the temporal progression. Events are depicted in a more chronological and linear fashion than previously. This change in form reflects the change occurring in the Master after his return from St. Luke's, i.e. his increased concern with clock-time. The over-all effect is of a unified whole, animated by its own internal rhythm.

In form and in content, Kawabata interweaves various external and internal time experiences. Besides the associative flow of memory and the precise time references, he creates a cyclical rhythm that is enhanced by his pervasive use of nature imagery and references to changing seasonal and weather patterns. Human actions and natural occurrences continually interact or merge in a kind of animated unity. In the following passage, for example, the tensing and easing of the mood surrounding the Go game is reflected in the cyclical rhythms of the natural world:

> The sky was dark with the squall Otaké had called a tempest, and the lights were on. The white stones, reflected on the mirror-like face of the board, became one with the figure of the Master, and the violence of the wind and rain in the garden seemed to intensify the stillness of the room.
>
> The squall soon passed. A mist trailed over the mountain, and the sky brightened from the direction of Odawara, down the river. The sun struck the rise beyond the valley, locusts shrilled, the glass doors at the veranda were opened again. Four puppies were sporting on the lawn as Otaké played Black 73. Once more the sky was lightly clouded over.

The nature images also reinforce the sense that the times are in a state of upheaval and conflict. On the day that Black 121 is played, the weather is unseasonably warm and red dragonflies lie dead on the ground. Other indications of disorder are the uncharacteristic weather patterns, with frequent rains and floods, and the appearance of an azalea with two unseasonal blooms. As the Master plays the decisive White 130, however, he recalls the words from a piece of music learned in his childhood: "From high in the hills, see the valley below. Melons in blossom, all in a row." These words from the past evoke a natural scene of order and calm, suggesting that a balance will ultimately be regained in nature as well as in human affairs. The changes and disruptions are part of the cyclic unity of the universe. In fact, Uragami provides the suggestion that the hollow and superficial times into which the way of Go has fallen will not be permanent: "Examples must be legion of wisdom and knowledge that shone forth in the past and faded toward the present, that have been obscured through all the ages into the present but will shine forth in the future."

Despite this subtle indication of eventual resurgence, the main focus in the novel is the evanescent moment of ending and death. Like the eleventh century Heian writers, Murasaki and Sei Shonagon, Kawabata depicts a time when "ripeness" is "moving into decay" and "one feels the sadness at the end of glory." He laments the fading sensibilities and elegance of the past but on a level that transcends the characters personally. As he says of Otaké, "The modern way was to insist upon doing battle under conditions of abstract justice, even when challenging the Master himself. The fault was not Otaké's." And he says of the Master, "The Master himself could not have measured the tides of destiny within him, or the mischief from those passing wraiths." Their lives have led them to this particular moment of transition from the past to the modern age, and they are but part of vaster forces at work in the flux of time. The fall of the grand Master, the corruption of his art, the decline of the old sensibilities and traditions of Japan are inescapable realities. On the wall behind the board is a framed inscription: "My life, a fragment of a landscape." All things are but a minute part of a greater whole, a brief instant in eternity.

Like the eternal fluctuation of yin and yang, the conflicts and dialectical tensions that arise from the Go game and the players generate the dynamism inherent in change within a simultaneous unity. Kawabata's novel draws its subtle, provocative strength from the tension of dialectics, its beauty from a poignant sensitivity to the ephemerality of life, and its sense of harmony from an acceptance of man's place in the eternal scheme of things.

Leza Lowitz (review date Spring 1988)

SOURCE: "Oriental Angst," in *The San Francisco Review of Books,* Vol. XII, No. 4, Spring, 1988, p. 19.

[*In the following review, Lowitz discusses the opposing forces of tradition and modernity in Kawabata's* The Old Capital.]

Though Yasunari Kawabata, the only Japanese novelist to receive the Nobel Prize, is best known for the novels *Snow Country* and *Thousand Cranes,* readers will find *The Old Capital* a welcome addition to the English-language works of Japan's great elegiac writer. Written in 1961, *The Old Capital* was one of the three novels cited by the Nobel Committee, but has only now been translated into English by a doctoral student, J. Martin Holman, at Berkeley. The respectable translation embues the story with a stillness that allows the beauty of the language to surface while the mysteries of the character's lives open and close like a succession of folding screens.

The Old Capital takes place in Kyoto, Japan's ancient capital which struggles to keep its identity while incorporating influences from the West. The difficulties of such an adjustment are a cause for spiritual *angst* in the characters of the story, as they watch the familiar fabric of their kimonos turn into synthetic material and see their ancient summer festival become a crowded tourist's spectacle.

Chieko Sada is the novel's beautiful twenty-year-old protagonist who discovers that the people she has called her parents for twenty years are not her real parents, and that (like Kawabata himself) she is an orphan. This discovery is compounded by the chance meeting of her twin, Naeko, whom she never knew existed. Naeko lives in a forest village nearby, and has come to Kyoto to seek out her sister. The two become mirrors for each other and what each represents: country and city, tradition and change. Everything in the book has a counterpart and soon the dichotomy of opposing forces stretches into art vs. imitation, family-run business vs. industry, man-made forests vs. natural growth, all of which reverberate the concerns of modern Japan.

Chieko's father is a kimono merchant who struggles to keep the old way but soon the influence of Western artists like Paul Klee, Henri Matisse, and Marc Chagall find their way into his designs. His daughter is courted by two men, one a designer who handlooms *obi* (the thick sash worn around the kimono) and the other a son of a wealthy textile wholesaler.

Since every character has an alter ego, the central conflict in the novel becomes not how the twain shall meet, but whether a meeting is ever possible. Chieko looks at two violets and asks "Do the upper and lower violets ever meet? Do they know each other? . . . What could it mean that the violets 'meet' or 'know' one another?"

> **There are writers who see the similarities in the world, writers who see the differences. Kawabata sees them both at the same moment and draws into focus the tension between the two.**
> —*Leza Lowitz*

Kawabata's affinity for nature permeates the text and provides an odd sense of balance, as if somehow the Seasons are the only predictable, comfortable element of change. A lightning storm accentuates Chieko and Naeko's meeting: violets grow side by side as they do, close yet distant; and snow falls when they meet for the last time.

Kawabata once wished to be a painter, and his impressionistic writing often casts *chiaroscuro* patterns to play out the contrast of the characters. There are writers who see the similarities in the world, writers who see the differences. Kawabata sees them both at the same moment and draws into focus the tension between the two.

In each of Kawabata's novels there is a symbol which provides a metaphor for the character's plight. In *Thousand Cranes,* the tea bowl is used to symbolize the containment of dark histories. In *Snow Country* it is the *Noh* mask which

serves to illustrate the denial of emotions and the paradoxical mask which makes expression possible. In *The Old Capital* it is the *obi* sash which symbolizes the transcendent moment when the worlds of past and present, East and West, young and old, are tied together. This sash becomes the landscape of synthesis, which Kawabata artfully ties only to finally untie, leaving the reader to make his own connections.

Sidney DeVere Brown (essay date Summer 1988)

SOURCE: "Yasunari Kawabata (1899-1972): Tradition versus Modernity," in *World Literature Today,* Vol. 62, No. 3, Summer, 1988, pp. 375-79.

[*In the following essay, DeVere Brown discusses how Kawabata focused on traditional culture in his major works.*]

Yasunari Kawabata is Japan's only Nobel laureate in literature. The prize, once monopolized by Western writers, was given to a Japanese for the first time in 1968. Japan had arrived as a modern nation in the economic and political sense, and it had staged the Tokyo Olympics in 1964 superbly. Perhaps the time had come to recognize a great Japanese writer, a hundred years after Japan's entry into the modern world with the Meiji Restoration of 1868. The paradox is that Kawabata, who seems to have been recognized for Japan's modernity, focused on traditional culture and gave little attention to things modern and Western, even though he wrote in a Japan undergoing modernization and all his novels had a contemporary setting.

It is a truism that novels provide some of the best primary sources for writing social history, as the popularity of such works tells us what people think is important about themselves. One would expect that Japan's one writer to achieve worldwide celebrity as a Nobel laureate would provide a deep well of materials on class and family, on work and leisure. Such is not the case. The historian would do better to look to Kawabata's contemporaries such as Jun'ichiro Tanizaki, who wrote the classic novel of the Japanese family *The Makioka Sisters,* or even Yukio Mishima, who recreated both the world of the Taisho elites (in *Spring Snow*) and that of the right-wing patriots of the early Showa era (in *Runaway Horses*). Instead, it is a private world of beauty and culture that engages Kawabata, who belonged to the so-called lyric school of Japanese writing. He consciously rejected the "proletarian school," which was in vogue during his university days in the 1920s; and he eschewed commentary on social and political problems, at least in his literary works, throughout his career.

Still, the historian must put Kawabata in the context of his times and reconstruct those times as best he can from the fragments about the world around the writers and artists, the dilettantes and lovely traditional Japanese women who inhabit his stories. This most eminent writer lived and worked through turbulent times: the Taisho democracy, Showa militarism, the Pacific War, the American Occupation, and at the end the Economic Miracle—or at least its beginnings.

As with most Japanese writers, Kawabata's work tends to be autobiographical. Edward Seidensticker has asserted that Kawabata was much like the men he wrote about, in contrast to Tanizaki, who created protagonists very different from himself. The young student depicted in **"The Izu Dancer"** who goes down the Izu peninsula on vacation and carries on a tentative romance with the little dancer from the traveling troupe is undoubtedly the adolescent Kawabata. The Tokyo dilettante Shimamura who is the protagonist of *Snow Country,* with his half-baked learning about the European ballet, is ostensibly the kind of person Kawabata disdained, yet he has the same tastes in women and an identical love of traditional crafts such as the making of *chijimi* cloth by peasants working in the snows of the North. The old men who have memory lapses or face death or are romantically linked with much younger women in the later works are undoubtedly alter egos of the author. Kawabata was a man of his times, one who emphasized certain themes at the expense of others and was more concerned about the decline of an old culture than about the emergence of a new society or economy.

The two greatest translators and critics of Japanese literature in the West, Edward Seidensticker and Donald Keene, have both written about Kawabata. It was Seidensticker who translated the two finest Kawabata works, *Snow Country* and *Thousand Cranes,* into English—thereby enhancing his prospects for the Nobel—and who accompanied him to Stockholm for acceptance of the prize, in the role of interpreter. Together the two critics/translators have nurtured the reputation in the West of this most Japanese of contemporary writers. As Keene notes, "Kawabata was unquestionably a modern man, and his works dealt exclusively with the lives of contemporaries, but the Nobel Prize Committee honored him because of the special affinities his works revealed with Japanese traditions."

Kawabata was born in the mercantile city of Osaka in 1899, orphaned at the age of two, and deprived even of his grandfather in 1914, living a lonely life in school dormitories until he graduated from the English Literature Department of Tokyo Imperial University in 1920. A degree from the Japanese Literature Department of the same university followed in 1924. The great editor (and novelist) Kan Kikuchi, founder of the literary monthly *Bungei Shunju,* launched Kawabata's career with the publication of **"The Izu Dancer"** in 1926. By the time of the appearance of his masterpiece, *Snow Country,* in 1935, he was a presence in the world of Japanese letters. A look at his six major novels will help us discern his point of view toward this modern world into which he was propelled.

Snow Country, in its first published form, appeared during the era of Showa militarism, yet the reader will learn nothing of the national crisis or of governmental efforts at national spiritual mobilization from it. The 1957 movie version of the novel, starring Keiko Kishi, was fleshed out with contemptuous remarks about the young officers who murdered a senior bureaucratic general in Tokyo and with considerable asperity regarding corrupt provincial politicians, but there is no such preaching in the novel which has come down to us.

Modernity meets the reader in the very first sentence, however, a sentence denominated the most famous in all Japanese literature: "When the train emerged from the long tunnel at the provincial boundary, they were in the snow country." Shortly afterward, "The train stopped at the signalling station." Snowplows are waiting at another point, and we learn that an electric avalanche system has been installed at the entrances to the tunnel. Kawabata may have implicitly accepted the steam train as part and parcel of traditional Japan, not separate from it. Here he treats it poetically: "The train moved off in the distance, its echo fading into a sound of the night wind" as it returned to Tokyo. A famous image, the Light in the Window, utilizes the fogged-over window of the passenger car to intersect the light in the distance with the beautiful young Yoko's eye in reflection. Modern transportation facilitates traditional esthetic expression; there is no conflict between the two.

The railway has recently reached the hot-springs resort, which seems to be modeled on Tazawa in Akita prefecture. The telegraph is also available in this remote place, and Shimamura once hurries off to the post office to wire a request for money before it closes. Radios bring news of a disastrous snow avalanche (but not of tense Tokyo politics, so far as we know). A statement on the impact of the West on Japanese health appears indirectly through the tale of the music teacher's son, who has returned home from Tokyo suffering from "intestinal tuberculosis." This disease from the West in its deadly form was the scourge of Japan before antibiotics. Komako, the country geisha, goes to work at her profession to pay the young man's medical bills—out of love or out of some kind of obligation to his mother. The reason is unclear.

People in the back country include a White Russian refugee woman, here a peddler. Japanese rustic types in the background include small shopkeepers and even farmers at the rice harvest. The sway of the farm girl's hips as she throws the rice bundles up to a man for placement on the drying racks commands the attention of this connoisseur of women as much as the harvest itself.

Beauty, not modernity, is Kawabata's theme in *Snow Country,* the ambience of the hot-springs resort, a place of special pleasure to the Japanese. The snow-covered mountains and the village streets piled high with snow up to the second story of buildings form another dimension of Japan the beautiful; but it is the Japanese woman who occupies stage center here, specifically Komako, who plays the samisen and sings the traditional "Dark Hair." She has drawn Shimamura away from Tokyo. Her younger friend and possible rival in love, Yoko, possesses "a clear voice, so beautiful it was almost sad." The Light in the Window illuminates Yoko's eye, just as the Mirror in the Morning reflects the beauty of Komako's rouged face framed by the reflection of falling snowflakes.

The Master of Go is a celebration of a different aspect of Japanese tradition, unique to Japan as it has evolved and one favored by feudal warriors because of its simulation of the battlefield. This work is Kawabata's nonfiction novel, for essentially it is the story of a 1938 championship match which he covered as a newspaper reporter. Shusai, the Master, defends his title "at the advanced age of sixty-four," using the deliberate, traditional style of play against an aggressive young competitor half his age who wins by rapid, disconcerting moves near the end of the match. Death for the Master, and perhaps the demise of a tradition, follows the loss. The match occurred in 1938, at the height of Showa militarism; publication of the novel began during the Pacific War in 1942, but the definitive final version did not appear until 1954, after the American Occupation was over. Nothing of militarism or war attends the match as retold in the novel, even though Go was the game of early-day samurai militarists. The book is as divorced from political or social concerns as any work of literature could be. Seidensticker has described it as an elegy for a great tradition which had fallen just as had Japan in war, a work confined to the game, the psychology of the contestants, and the superbly beautiful settings in which play was conducted, most often at inns in hot-springs resorts.

The Naraya in Miyanoshita is an ideal setting for contemplation of the next move by Go competitors. The inn is quiet as well as scenic, unlike the inn by the waterfall which triggered the Master's insomnia, and it commands a view of the nearby mist-covered mountains. Testimonials to the inn's excellence come in the form of a memorial stone to the Emperor Meiji, who once stayed there, and a framed inscription by the early nineteenth-century historian Sanyo Rai, a revolutionary nationalist. (I have seen another framed inscription at the Naraya by the Meiji statesman Takayoshi Kido, who stayed there in 1876; it was shown to me by the elderly proprietress whose family has owned the inn for more than a century. Kido called the Naraya the best inn in Miyanoshita. An American vice-president who wanted to stay at a traditional inn was slated to come there, said the proud proprietress, but a rail strike prevented it; Spiro Agnew sent an autographed photograph instead. Secretary of the Treasury Robert Anderson, who did stay there, told her that he would like to take the scenic landscape back to America with him.) Writing during the war era, Kawabata chose to describe not battle deaths in China or political crises in Tokyo, but only the national cultural treasure, a game of Go, played out quietly in the rustic simplicity of a hot-springs inn.

Thousand Cranes is a product of the American Occupation period. The tea ceremony is the element of tradition and beauty featured in this moving novel, one of the three masterworks cited by the Nobel Prize Committee. In point of fact, the work is a lament for the decline of the ceremony into vulgarization and commercialism. Anyone might drop in on Chikako Kurimoto's weekly public demonstrations. "The other day I even had some Americans," she admits. The title was inspired by the kerchief with the thousand-cranes pattern carried to a tea ceremony by a Miss Inamura, who has been proposed as a bride for Kikuji Mitani, the protagonist. Chikako, a mistress to his father, regards the meeting as a *miai*. No marriage occurs, but the tangled personal relationships of his late father, the latter's mistress, and the son unfold. The war was still a fresh and unpleasant memory when this book was written, and Fumiko, daughter of one of the mistresses, was considered courageous because she "went to the country for rice, even during the raids."

The tea vessels are described in loving detail by Kawabata in *Thousand Cranes* and take on personalities of their own, especially the four-hundred-year-old Shino Bowl which seems to have a trace of the lipstick of the late Mrs. Ota. One American reviewer, in fact, believed the main character of the novel *was* that tea bowl. It is possessed with a curse, and only when Fumiko breaks the vessel is she freed from the curse and from the Mitani family. At a time when Japanese civilization itself seemed threatened under the American Occupation, Kawabata made his statement on behalf of the Way of Tea and the proper tea vessels, preserving in literature that indispensable part of Japan's past.

The Sound of the Mountain, also from the period of the American Occupation, celebrates the artistic mask of the No theater which old Shingo has begun to study with such enthusiasm as death nears. "Clouding" means dropping the mask to indicate sadness; "shining" means raising it to indicate joy, for example. The beauty of the mask in use is so great it makes him cry. It is the prospect of death which turns his attention to the beautiful aspects of Japan. Shingo's preoccupation with death began during the war, and he believes that the sound of the mountain is a forewarning. "I heard the mountain rumbling," he once remarks as he opens the shutters. If Shingo is Kawabata's alter ego, then the author may have meant to face up to the prospect of personal physical death here as well as the death of a civilization. One classmate of Shingo has gone to his death, ridiculed by others because he was tormented continually by his wife; another has died in the arms of his young mistress at a hot-springs resort. As the visages of those deceased friends appear in his dreams, Shingo regrets that he will never climb Mount Fuji as death beckons, and also that he has never seen Matsushima, one of the Three Great Sights of Japan, though he dreams of those pine covered islets.

Shingo is very attached to his young daughter-in-law Kikuko, whose husband has taken up with a mistress in the Hongo section of Tokyo. *The Sound of the Mountain* is a fuller, more complete story than Kawabata's earlier works, and we are treated to an exposition of the tangled relationships of the three generations of Shingo's family. The novel does for the postwar family what Tanizaki's *Makioka Sisters* did for the traditional prewar extended family, but inevitably in sparer detail. Shingo and his son Shuichi are commuters, riding the train in daily to their Tokyo office from North Kamakura, the seaside resort which is for them a remote suburb of the Tokyo metropolis. The American Occupation is a part of their lives but is barely hinted at. At the fishmonger's Shingo observes some "prostitutes of the new sort," their "bare backs, cloth shoes, and good figures" revealing that they cater to American military men.

The Old Capital provides a shift of locale to Kyoto, the home of artistic craft goods. The story of twin girls separated at birth and later reunited as young women seems incidental to the main task of presenting to the reader the old capital in all its traditional glory. Kyoto was the one great Japanese urban center untouched by the American air raids of the Pacific War. The Kiyomizu Temple at sunset, Mount Daimonji in bloom with colorful flowers, and the Heian Shrine at festival time are all described in loving detail. At the shrine's small pool, "cherry blossoms and pines seemed to tremble in the pond as goldfish surfaced." As Seidensticker has noted, Kawabata wanted to set down the beauty of the old city, Japan's capital from 794 to 1868, before it disappeared forever.

The cedars of Kitayama, north of the city, where the more rustic of the twins lives, provided wood of uniform size for teahouses in Tokyo and Kyushu. The cedars in their straight rows conjure up "the elegant air of the tea ceremony," but it is the silk-weaving business in small shops which trained apprentices that is important, and threatened. The obi, the kimono sash, should be designed to reflect the personality of the individual wearer. Industrialization has threatened all that. A portent of things to come is the Western-style, four-story factory, newly opened and capable of turning out five hundred obi per day. "Some home businesses like mine with hand looms will probably disappear within twenty or thirty years," a shopkeeper laments. Kawabata wrote at the beginning of the Economic Miracle. Doubtless small home workshops, facing pressure from a government committed to economic modernization, were phased out much sooner than the shopkeeper anticipated.

The Americans have come to Kyoto, and the city is the worse for their presence. "These are the kind of customers who buy portable radios," notes a boy who needs extra work as his family's silk-cloth business declines, leading him to hire out as a guide. "They're American women staying at the Miyako Hotel." Another replies, "Portable radios or silks—a dollar is a dollar." Kawabata's feelings are obviously the opposite, that the city should be uncontaminated with Americans and their lack of taste. European judges may have elevated this work to a higher level than deserved in making it one of the three books on which the Nobel selection was based, believes Keene, but seemingly did so out of pleasure at Kawabata's re-creation of the Old Japan "unaffected by the blight of Americanization," which had its critics in Europe at the same time.

Beauty and Sadness likewise glorifies Kyoto in the early days of the Economic Miracle. Toshio Oki, a novelist who posts his daily installment to the newspaper at North Kamakura Station, has gone to Kyoto to hear the tolling of the New Year's bells at the Chionin Temple, 108 strokes at midnight. Previously he had only listened to this Buddhist ceremony on the radio. It is in fact a woman, Otoko Ueno, his mistress of two decades earlier, who has drawn him to the city. He last saw her in Tokyo, where an abortion was performed in a sleazy, remote suburb. Taken to Kyoto to live by her mother, Otoko has now become an accomplished artist in the traditional fashion. Her devious, vengeful, but beautiful young female protégée is sent to receive Oki and later makes contact with him back in Kamakura, bringing along her own avant-garde paintings of the Shizuoka tea fields; these tea fields represent a bad memory to her teacher Otoko, who had observed them as she fled Tokyo in disgrace. The book is a vehicle for Kawabata's comments on painting, both traditional Japanese and European, but it is also another tour of Kyoto and its classic sights: the Ryoanji, a garden which was "almost too famous, though it may be said to embody the very essence of Zen aesthetics," and the Moss Garden, another dry landscape which the priest Muso had laid out in 1939. The stone lanterns put in place by the abbot seem to have always been there.

There was by now the familiar complaint about the Americans and modernity. Those annoying Americans occupy a marginal position in *Beauty and Sadness*. The novelist-protagonist watches them photograph Mount Fuji from the train to Kyoto when the sacred mountain is still barely visible and then lose interest by the time the train nears the mountain in all its glory. The Americans' luggage includes a large leopard-skin handbag which is the epitome of bad taste, and American children chatter in a foreign language in the hallways of the novelist's Kyoto hotel, making life miserable.

Still, Kyoto is beautiful in spite of the disagreeable American presence: "Compared with Tokyo, Kyoto was such a small intimate city that the Western Hills are close at hand. As the writer gazed a translucent pale gold cloud above the hills turned a chilly ashen color, and it was evening." Kawabata's fascination with trains continues: "From somewhere off in the Western Hills came a plaintive, lingering whistle of a train entering . . . a tunnel"; as the novelist's train makes its way back to Tokyo, "the rails glinted crimson far into the distance in the rays of the setting sun." Trains were a part of Kawabata's old-fashioned world. Typewriters were not; neither were printing presses. *The Tale of Genji* makes an entirely different impression on Oki when he reads it in "handsome old block-printed" characters rather than in the mechanically printed version; and he has taken to reading Saikaku, the writer of stories about bawdy merchants, in contemporary "seventeenth-century facsimiles."

> **Businessmen and politicians dominated the emerging Japanese superstate, but their world held little interest for Kawabata. The modern world provides merely a dim, mostly unseen context in his novels for the admirable people and culture rooted in Old Japan.**
> —*Sidney DeVere Brown*

The old ways were better, Kawabata seems to say here and in the earlier novels. He was a cultural nationalist who sought to preserve the world of tradition in novels before those traditions vanished forever. It is doubtful that he was a true ultranationalist in the political sense during the Pacific War. He was "esteemed by the militarists, even though he had done nothing to ingratiate himself," notes Donald Keene. He did such things as visit the Kamikaze pilots of the Special Attack Force in Kagoshima and stayed a month, but he did not lament the lost war much. Defeat "actually brought freedom of the spirit and the sense of what it means to live in peace," he said.

Between defeat in 1945 and his death in 1972 Kawabata wrote to preserve the world of tradition. It was the world of hot-springs resorts and old-fashioned compliant Japanese beauties who played the samisen and sang "Dark Hair," of the tea ceremony and its ancient artistic vessels, of No masks and all that they symbolized, of the game of Go and its traditions, and above all of the old capital of Kyoto, whose

temples and gardens had emerged from the war intact. Kawabata wrote about small shopkeepers, craftsmen, and silk traders in the export business. He seemed only remotely aware of the big bankers and large industrialists, and of the Liberal-Democratic Party politicians who were the movers and shakers of the New Japan (in his novels at least, though he supported one of them for governor of Tokyo in 1972). The Americans, important though they may have been to the remaking of Japan, inhabit only the fringe of his novels, at most tourists with debased tastes or low-class soldiers in pursuit of Japanese prostitutes. Businessmen and politicians dominated the emerging Japanese superstate, but their world held little interest for Kawabata. The modern world provides merely a dim, mostly unseen context in his novels for the admirable people and culture rooted in Old Japan.

Frederick Smock (review date January/February 1989)

SOURCE: "Small Lanterns," in *American Book Review,* Vol. 10, No. 6, January/February, 1989, p. 15.

[*In the following review, Smock calls Kawabata's* Palm-of-the-Hand Stories *one of "those dozen or so volumes necessary to life."*]

Somewhere in my future is a small, simple apartment, maybe a couple of rooms near the sea somewhere, with high windows and a fireplace. On the mantel over the fireplace is a small stack of books, the only books in the place, those dozen or so volumes necessary to life. One of those books is Yasunari Kawabata's *Palm-of-the-Hand Stories.*

These very short stories, which span his writing life, are the distillation of a beautiful talent. Kawabata won the Nobel Prize for Literature in 1968 for his novels, *The Izu Dancer, Thousand Cranes, Snow Country,* and the others, which were so important to Japan's modern literature. But Kawabata believed that the very short story—the story that fits into the palm of one's hand—holds the essence of the writing art. It is to fiction what the haiku is to poetry. (His last work was a miniaturized version of *Snow Country,* shortly before he committed suicide in 1972.)

The grand themes are all here—love, loneliness, our capacity for disillusionment, the tensions between old and new— under the lens of Kawabata's microscope. The short form is suited to his love of detail, his preference for the finite gesture whose meaning reverberates through time.

In **"A Sunny Place,"** the oldest story in the collection, a young man meets a woman at a seaside inn—it is the beginning of love—but the woman is painfully disconcerted by his habit of staring, and turns her head away. Embarrassed, he averts his own gaze, to a sunny spot on the beach, and thus discovers the origin of his bad habit. "After my parents died," he tells us, "I had lived alone with my grandfather for almost ten years in a house in the country. My grandfather was blind. For years he sat in the same room, in the same spot, facing the east with a long charcoal brazier in front of him. Occasionally he would turn his head toward the south, but he never faced the north. . . . Sometimes I would sit for a long time in front of my grandfather staring into his face, wondering if he would turn to the north. . . . I wondered if the south felt ever so slightly lighter even to a blind person." As a happy result, this memory heightens the intimacy the young man feels toward the woman.

A further testament to the power of Kawabata's economical stories: a movie was once made of **"Thank You,"** a four-page story whose dialogue consists chiefly of *thank-yous.* It tells of a bus driver who takes a mother and daughter from their harbor town to the city, where the daughter is to be sold into a wealthy man's harem; but the driver's politeness to the cartmen they pass on the way so touches the daughter that her mother implores him to allow her one night of genuine affection before her enslavement.

I have returned many times to this story, looking for the source of its power—their (ambiguous) night together, the enigmatic figure of the bus driver, the journey's dreaded end? And I cannot be sure that I have located it. But I have felt it.

His better stories work this way. Swiftly. Mysteriously.

Kawabata wrote nearly 150 "palm" stories, of which 70 are published here, including **"Gleanings from Snow Country,"** his last. The translators have rendered the stories in faultlessly simple language, as befits them.

For these stories are like small lanterns whose colored lights can be seen from very far away—little truths, nestled in a valley, the valley of the palm.

James T. Araki (essay date Spring 1989)

SOURCE: "Kawabata: Achievements of the Nobel Laureate [1969]," in *World Literature Today,* Vol. 63, No. 2, Spring, 1989, pp. 209-12.

[*In the following essay, Araki traces Kawabata's changing style and notes "a steady progression in the refinement of his technical mastery and a development of the ability to enter deeply into his characters."*]

Although Yasunari Kawabata has for years been considered the most distinguished member of the Japanese world of letters, the news of the selection of the sixty-nine-year-old author as the recipient of the 1968 Nobel Prize in Literature—a surprise to readers throughout much of the world—was initially received with a sense of disbelief by his countrymen. The insight revealed in the citation by the Novel Committee, which praised the author for "his narrative mastership, which with great sensibility expressed the essence of the Japanese mind," seemed to mystify all but the most sensitive readers and critics, to whom the judgment seemed incredibly astute.

The typical Japanese reader tends, like readers elsewhere, to favor a well-paced narrative designed to quicken his interest in the story. He has been content to accept the high evaluation of Kawabata by professional critics and, rather than read his stories, has been inclined to enjoy them through the modified medium of the cinema. Indeed, Japanese moviemakers since the early fifties have produced some twenty film versions of his novels. The general reader in Japan has probably regarded Kawabata as a modernist rather than a traditionalist, for his stories are often difficult to apprehend fully, owing to the rich, allusive imagery, a suggestive quality that requires a matured sensibility of the reader, an elliptical sentence style, and a mode of story progression that often relies on linking through imagery rather than through contextual or sentence logic—a technique of the traditional *renga* or "linked verse." Many native readers are now avidly reading Kawabata novels to discover for themselves the traditional Japanese qualities that foreign readers were able to perceive through the reading of translations.

Snow Country (Yukiguni), Thousand Cranes (Semazuru) and *The Old Capital (Koto)* are the novels by which the Nobel Committee judged Kawabata's worth as a writer of fiction. These are novels in which the author's bent for the traditional is particularly evident, in depiction of outward forms of traditional culture (the tea ceremony, folk art, Shinto festivals, Buddhist temples) and the use of nature imagery for their cumulative, traditional lyrical implications, yet they do not fully represent the vast range of the author's creative capacity. . . . Translations of several of Kawabata's short stories have appeared in anthologies or magazines—among them, **"The Izu Dancer"** ("*Izu no odoriko*"), **"The Mole"** ("*Hokuro no tegami*") **"Reencounter"** ("*Saikai*"), and **"Moon on the Water"** ("*Suigetsu*").

In Japan, in the twentieth century, new literary trends were frequently set by coteries of writers who cooperated in the publication of literary journals. A particularly memorable year was 1924, when, in June, "Literary Battle Line" (*Bungei Sensen*) was founded as a monthly for Marxist writers and, in October, the publication of "Literary Era" (*Bungei Jidai*) was inaugurated by a group of young authors who were concerned primarily with the esthetics of literature. Yokomitsu Toshikazu (1898-1947) and Kawabata were the prime movers of the latter group, who were promptly labeled the "neoperceptionists" by the critic Kameo Chiba. In an essay, "The Birth of the Neoperceptionists" (in *Seiki*, November 1924), Chiba stated, "There is no doubt whatever that these writers, whom we might call the 'Literary Era' coterie, are sensually alert to diction, lyricism, and rhythm that are far fresher than anything ever before expressed by any of our sensitive artists." The expressive style of the neoperceptionists, literary historians tell us, was influenced considerably by the many startling examples of figurative language those young writers discovered in Paul Morand's *Ouvert la nuit,* which had appeared in Japanese translation that year.

> Because Kawabata avoids the explicit, his stories often seem veiled by vagueness, a quality that the native reader finds attractive. Because his writings contain so many diverse elements, they are at once subtle and complex, and they can be enjoyed for their sheer tonal and textural beauty.
> —*James T. Araki*

Kawabata, by his own admission, has probably participated in the setting of more new trends than any other living writer. More important, however, has been his ability to experiment with new approaches and techniques and to adopt them into a larger embodiment which can be identified as a style uniquely his own; and his many years of experience, starting in his twenties, as a practicing critic have without doubt contributed much to the development of his own literary sensibility.

Although imprints of literary expressionism and psychological realism are rather clearly evident in Kawabata's stories, traditional Japanese themes have been more subtly infused into his writings. We may note coursing through all his major novels a sense of sorrow and loneliness, a recognition of an emotional and spiritual vacuity in man, and the recurring theme of the evanescence and meaninglessness of passion, even of temporal existence. The general tenor of the author's outlook has much in common with that of the *Tale of Genji* and diaries of the Late Classical Era (10th-12th century), with much of the prose of the Medieval Era (12th-16th century), and with traditional poetry. Because Kawabata avoids the explicit, his stories often seem veiled by vagueness, a quality that the native reader finds attractive. Because his writings contain so many diverse elements, they are at once subtle and complex, and they can be enjoyed for their sheer tonal and textural beauty.

Reading Kawabata's major works in chronological sequence, one may note a steady progression in the refinement of his technical mastery and a development of the ability to enter deeply into his characters. **"The Izu Dancer,"** best known among his earliest writings, is a lyric description of a journey made by a high-school student, from the vicinity of Mount Fuji to the lower tip of Izu Peninsula, in the company of a troupe of traveling entertainers. Narrated in the first person and in a confessional vein, the short tale depicts a love that stirs the heart of the youth, whose eyes filter out the unsightly and create an idealized image of a lovely dancer who is about to blossom into womanhood. The inevitable parting and the lonely aftertaste remind him of the sorrow of having grown up an orphan, yet the memory of the fleeting encounter becomes a pleasurable one even while he continues to shed tears of regret. In composing this attractive tale, the author employed none of the techniques that were to characterize his later writings.

Kawabata's first full-length novel, *The Crimson Gang of Asakusa (Asakusa kurenaidan)*, published in 1930, is considered the only noteworthy product of a short-lived movement for modernity and artistry that was launched by a loosely organized group of writers intent on stemming the tide of proletarian literature. This novel is in many respects antithetical to **"The Izu Dancer."** The Crimson Gang is a band of delinquents whose members are caught in a web of sex and violence. The setting is Asakusa, the colorful, raucous and sinful center of urban entertainment for the middle and lower classes of Tokyo. The author presents a panorama which unfolds in a series of rapidly changing scenes sketching various aspects of life in Asakusa. The ugly and evil are depicted along with the innocent and beautiful. Descriptions of the activities of the gang are woven into the panorama so that some semblance of unity is achieved. The author is a keenly sensitive observer, uninvolved in the story.

Snow Country, which was written sporadically between 1934 and 1937 and expanded into its present form after the war, is the first novel in which we find all the artistic elements, both modern and traditional, that have since characterized the distinctive style of Kawabata. Rich in imagery and symbolism, suggestive by association, the novel can be reexplored through repeated readings to new discoveries of meaning. The opening passage is arresting: "When the train came out of the long tunnel separating the provinces, it was in the snow country. The bottomless depth of the night was imbued with whiteness." Typical of the author's style is the delicacy of expression that verbalizes the profundity of a common winter scene, the subtle contrast between black sky and night-darkened snow.

The hero, Shimamura, studies the face of a girl reflected in the train window. The mirror filters out the ugly and the unpleasant; what remains for Shimamura to observe is only the beautiful, detached from those associations of sadness and pain that are evident in the totality of the image. As Shimamura concentrates on the reflected face, his time track shifts from the external to the "concrete" or internal psychological time; we are presented with a flashback, and then a flashback within a flashback, as the image evokes one recollection and then another in his mind.

Even though the point of view of *Snow Country* is essentially that of Shimamura, the author does not enter deeply into him. The novel can hardly be considered autobiographical. Shimamura is the observer of two women—the innocent Yoko, whose reflected image has fascinated him, and the sensual geisha Komako. Through his characterization of these two, the author describes the eternal sorrow of the Japanese woman as well as his admiration for her quality of forlornness and passivity. The vacuity in Shimamura's heart, however, may well be the vacuity in the heart of the author, or of an archetype of the modern Japanese male. The concluding paragraph presents the reader with an example of the author's elliptical sentence style: "The voice that shouted the half-crazed Komako Shimamura tried to get nearer to. . . ." This English approximates the syntactic and idiomatic level of the original. A Japanese would reread and ponder it before he could grasp the intended meaning: "The voice that shouted was Komako's; Shimamura recognized it and tried to get nearer to the half-crazed Komako. . . ." The concluding sentence, "The River of Heaven (the Milky Way) seemed to flow down with a roar into Shimamura," seems to be an expressionistic attempt to objectify an inexpressibly complex state of mind.

Thousand Cranes is a novel that exhibits many of the qualities of *Snow Country*, but we note a bolder approach to the topic of eroticism. The mode of fiction is that of imaginative storytelling, the author being nowhere evident. The relationship depicted is at best an unhealthy one—that between a young man and the women who had been mistresses to his late father. The motif is similar to that in Maupassant's "Hautot and His Son," but the eroticism in *Thousand Cranes* is more explicit, and is pervaded by a sense of sin and guilt which is absent from the French story. Kawabata adds to the complexity of incestuous relationship by involving the young hero in carnal association with the daughter of his father's former mistress. Here, as in *Snow Country*, we are afforded glimpses of traditional esthetic forms—graphic patterns, the tea ceremony, ceramics—often invested with symbolic suggestion. The instant transitions and fantastic leaps in time are techniques that anticipated those used many years later in films—recently in *The Graduate*, for instance.

Kawabata's finest novel in his unique modernist-traditionalist mode of fiction is *Sound of the Mountain* (*Yama no oto*), published in 1954. Because the novel sheds much light on the immemorial Japanese household—an extended family—and on the often fast-and-loose world of Japanese business, we may say that it resembles the "novel of manners," which Japanese literary critics tend to regard with disdain. *Sound of the Mountain,* however, is essentially a psychological novel in which the process and effects of aging are drawn with remarkable sensitivity.

The narrative point of view is that of the sixty-year-old Ogata, who might be a fictional extension of the youthful "I" of **"The Izu Dancer"** and Shimamura of *Snow Country.* Like the shadowy hero of *Snow Country,* the gentle, aging Ogata is constantly observing and listening, absorbing all that happens about him, but, unlike Shimamura, he is keenly aware of his own reactions and gropes to identify the motives for his own thoughts and actions. His married son is involved in a sordid extramarital liaison with a war widow. Kikuko, the son's neglected wife, has a beauty that symbolizes purity and innocence—womanly qualities attractive to Ogata—and a mutual bond of sympathy and understanding draws the two close together. Kikuko shares Ogata's sensibilities, which his wife does not. The Western reader might be amused to note the corresponding levels of perceptivity assigned to Ogata, his daughter-in-law, and Mrs. Ogata, and to Mr. Bennet, Elizabeth, and Mrs. Bennet in *Pride and Prejudice.* The fading but persistent yearning for youthful femininity in Ogata's unconscious is revealed to him occasionally in erotic dreams. In a moment of stupefying realization, Ogata identifies the faceless woman he has often embraced in dreams with his own daughter-in-law. The eroticism, however, is presented subtly, and the texture of *Sound of the Mountain* is softened considerably by frequent references to traditional esthetics.

Although, having completed *Sound of the Mountain,* Kawabata could have rested on his laurels, he was busily at work in 1954 writing *The Lake* (*Mizuumi*), a novel of stark psychological realism, infused with a dark lyricism which places it a fictional world apart from *Sound of the Mountain* and marks the beginning of yet another phase in the author's creative career. It is remarkable for its absence of references to traditional beauty. Instead, its emphasis is on symbolism, the bold use of interior monologue, the constantly shifting time track, and particularly the characterization of the hero: Gimpei's overpowering desire for beautiful women will never be fulfilled because of the ugliness of his feet—feet which he himself can regard only with morbid fascination, if not with abhorrence.

Another novel in a similar vein, *House of the Sleeping Beauties* (*Nemureru bijo*), depicting the behavioral and psychological manifestations of eroticism in the aging male, was published in 1961 and was immediately acclaimed as Kawabata's major work by a number of critics and authors. The novelist Yukio Mishima, among others, expressed regret that the Nobel Committee could not have read *Sleep-*

ing Beauties to learn how the passing years had served to hone, rather than to dull, Kawabata's perceptivity and to enrich his creative and expressive capacities.

In *The Old Capital* (*Koto*), published in 1962, Kawabata reverted abruptly to the beauty and sadness he sees in youth and innocence. As in *The Crimson Gang of Asakusa,* the story itself is less important than the traditional beauty of Kyoto, which is woven into a soft brocade, attractive for its sheer textural elegance.

Thanks to the Nobel Committee, readers of English should soon be given access by our commercial publishers to translations of Kawabata novels which have won praise for their literary quality but have seldom been published in large editions in Japan. The reader might be forewarned, however, of one peculiarity of Kawabata's stories that is distinctly Japanese. Almost all of his stories represent a non-dramatic mode of fiction and remain unresolved. There is no explicit statement of what the tomorrow will bring to Shimamura, Ogata, Gimpei, "old" Eguchi of *Sleeping Beauties,* or the many women in his stories. Most Japanese readers enjoy the pathos born of such vagueness. We too might learn to enjoy pondering the eventual fates of characters in novels. Their lives are no less real than our own. No one, after all, lives quite happily or unhappily ever after.

Paul Anderer (review date November 1989)

SOURCE: A review of *Palm-of-the-Hand Stories,* in *The Journal of Asian Studies,* Vol. 48, No. 4, November 1989, pp. 865-66.

[*In the following review, Anderer discusses the style and themes of Kawabata's* Palm-of-the-Hand Stories.]

Palm-of-the-Hand Stories gives us an opportunity to redirect attention and critical inquiry toward the beginnings of what we have come to know—chiefly on the evidence of longer and later *shosetsu*—as Kawabata's style. In this collection of 70 *tanagokoro no shosetsu,* Lane Dunlop and J. Martin Holman, working independently, have made available not just some fine Kawabata writing but much of his earliest work. Forty-three of these stories were published between 1924 and 1929. Since literary historians generally agree that Kawabata wrote 146 such stories throughout his career, and that 85 of these had been written by 1929, this abridged collection reflects the distribution of this work over the course of Kawabata's writing life. In every decade through to his final publication (**"Gleanings from Snow Country"**), Kawabata wrote *tanagokoro no shosetsu,* although it is apparent that he most intensively cultivated such writing in his youth.

The opening editorial note acknowledges the especially close link between *tanagokoro no shosetsu* and youth, quoting Kawabata's own retrospective remark in evidence: "the poetic spirit of my young days lives on in them." In the same context, Kawabata observes that "many writers, in their youth, write poetry: I, instead of poetry, wrote the palm-of-the-hand stories." It is also the case that in his youth, Kawabata was better known for his criticism and reviews than for his fiction, and for his advocacy of a modernist movement—the *Shinkankaku-ha*—of which he was an active and crucial participant.

I mention this not to deflect from the pleasures of Kawabata's text, which Dunlop and Holman have rendered in uniformly good English prose (there are differences: Dunlop seems more concerned with getting the diction right, Holman more with sentence rhythm), but to suggest that many of these stories possess a sharp experimental intention and edge that is dulled if we search too deeply for traces of a *renga* tradition or are mesmerized by an image of Kawabata as a master traditionalist. At its best Japanese modernism of the 1920s, as pursued by the young Kawabata and Yokomitsu Riichi, represented a challenge to normative literary perception and response and cultivated a willful idiosyncrasy, even eccentricity, of style. This could invite a less conventional treatment in English than many of the stories receive here. A more concentrated, experimental translation might have produced interesting results (when Kawabata published his *Yukigunisho* in the *Sand Mainichi,* typographically it appeared in verse form).

There is a sense of warmth and fragility in the earliest stories, conveyed in their very titles—**"A Sunny Place," "The Weaker Vessel," "The Girl Who Approached the Fire"**—which offsets the cool formalism of Kawabata's spare and rigorous method. We encounter here an abstract "world without sound" whose contours are powerfully determined by memory and dream. Yet this world seems close to experience, to the feeling of some actual loss or betrayal, and so issues of a personal or a generational history are as pressing as the aesthetic method that distills beauty from them. Again, many of the stories appear childlike in their innocence of realism or of sociopolitical incident (**"Glass"** and **"Water"** are notable exceptions to this). But they often take bizarre, less-than-innocent turns. And so "a perfect snowy morning scene" is broken as sparrow heads poke through the breast holes of a dying girl's discarded corset (**"The Younger Sister's Clothes"**) leading the narrator to say, as readers might, to describe the effect of many such stories: "It was like a painful fairy tale."

Indeed very basic elements generate Kawabata's condensed, almost implosive short fiction: sun and snow, light and darkness, desire and deprivation. Over time this style, increasingly refined and abstracted from experience, drifts more toward a cold isolation: "the snowy landscape was all there was" ("Snow").

At the very end, red cheeks, detached from a woman's face, "float[ed] amid the snow" ("**Gleanings from Snow Country**") Preoccupied as he had been for so long with the snow country of his art, it is no wonder that in his last *tanagokoro no shosetsu*, Kawabata distilled and crystallized his favorite landscape, his own otherworldly and deeply modernist home.

Sidney DeVere Brown (review date Winter 1990)

SOURCE: A review of *Palm-of-the-Hand Stories*, in *World Literature Today*, Vol. 64, No. 1, Winter, 1990, p. 197.

[*In the following review, DeVere Brown praises the spare style of Kawabata's* Palm-of-the-Hand Stories.]

Kawabata's masterpiece, the novel **Snow Country**, is written in a spare, elliptical style. It seems as abbreviated as a work of literature can possibly be—until one reads the author's "palm-of-the-hand stories," which often tell a story or evoke an image in less than a page. "**Gleanings from Snow Country**," indeed, presents the highlights of the novel in a series of haiku-like images in five pages. That is much longer than the usual story, however.

Most of the selections juxtapose two images in less than a page and reveal a story by indirection. If Japanese literature requires much of its readers because it relies on suggestion rather than graphic detail and because resolution of the plot is incomplete, then the palm-of-the-hand stories require an incredible effort, but an enjoyable one. The orphaned girl of "**A Sunny Place**" stares at her blind grandfather as he turns toward the sun; at the same time she remembers being at a sunny place on the beach with him earlier. In "**Hair**" an exhausted hairdresser who is called upon to do the hair of all the village girls because soldiers are billeted in town passes word to her hairdresser friend in the next village that she would do well if she followed soldiers around; the second woman's husband, a miner, is not amused and slaps her around just as a trumpet sounds. "**Hometown**" centers on a village festival to which everyone is invited back to partake of dumplings in bean soup. Men are few in wartime, and the sister-in-law who has a letter from the front has grown plump.

What do the stories mean? Each reader will craft his own plot from the fragmentary evidence, which often is even less revealing than in the three examples cited above. Kawabata wrote palm-of-the-hand stories throughout his career, from 1923 to 1972, and they evidently had a market value in the

periodicals of his time. Certain themes recur. Kawabata was a cultural traditionalist who wrote of hot springs, girls in the bath at an inn, or beautiful black hair in several contexts; but he also wrote of a taxi dancer in Asakusa (1932), of the water shortage in wartime Manchuria (1944), and of a woman who fled to London to recover from a failed marriage (1962). Prewar pride in culture, wartime privation, and postwar affluence and cosmopolitan life-style all come through in the works of this most Japanese of modern writers. The translators have performed the exacting task of transferring the obscure thoughts and misty images of his palm-of-the-hand stories into English successfully.

Nobuko Miyama Ochner (review date Spring 1991)

SOURCE: A review of *The Old Capital*, in *Southern Humanities Review*, Vol. XXV, No. 2, Spring, 1991, pp. 197-203.

[*In the following review, Miyama Ochner analyzes the problems involved in translating Kawabata's work and asserts that J. Martin Holman's translation of Kawabata's* The Old Capital *"emerges as a generally faithful and competent work."*]

There have been many English translations of novels and essays by Yasunari Kawabata (1899-1972), Japan's only recipient of the Nobel Prize for Literature (1968) to date. Seven titles (***The Izu Dancer and Other Stories; Snow Country; Master of Go; Thousand Cranes; The Sound of the Mountain; Japan, the Beautiful, and Myself;*** and ***House of Sleeping Beauties***) have been translated by Edward G. Seidensticker, who, since he has also translated other short stories by Kawabata, is the person most responsible for introducing Kawabata's works to the West. Other book-length English translations of Kawabata's works, all of which appeared after his Nobel Prize award, include ***The Lake*** by Reiko Tsukimura, ***Beauty and Sadness*** by Howard S. Hibbett, ***The Existence and Discovery of Beauty*** by V. H. Viglielmo, and ***Palm-of-Hand Stories*** by Lane Dunlop and J. Martin Holman. Therefore, ***The Old Capital*** is Holman's second translation of Kawabata's fiction.

Together with **Snow Country** and **Thousand Cranes**, this novel was cited by the Nobel Prize Committee as grounds for selection. The committee had available several European-language translations, including one in German by Walter Donat entitled *Kyoto*. The prominent Japanologist Donald Keene states in his history of modern Japanese literature, *Dawn to the West*, that ***The Old Capital*** "by no means deserved" such distinction. Now, nearly two decades after Kawabata received the Nobel Prize, English-speaking readers have access to the novel that generated such apparently divergent assessments.

To know certain aspects of Kawabata's life that appear to have influenced his development as a writer would be a helpful preface to a discussion of the novel. Born to a physician's family near Osaka, Kawabata was orphaned early in his life; between the ages of two and fifteen, he lost, one after another, his father, mother, grandmother, older sister, and grandfather. He called himself "an expert at funerals," and the sense of loneliness, of not belonging to a family (an extremely important social unit in Japanese society), pervades the spiritual life of many a protagonist in his works. After going through the elite course of the First Higher School (1917-1920) and the Imperial University of Tokyo (1920-1924), where he majored first in English then in Japanese literature, he and several friends began an avant-garde literary magazine, *Bungei jidai* (Literary Age, 1924-1930), and published stories, poems, and criticism heavily influenced by European modernism (e.g., Dadaism, Surrealism, et cetera). Calling themselves *Shinkankakuha*, which may be rendered as Neo-Perceptionist (or Neosensualist, or New Sensationalist) School, the group advocated the creation of a new style to express new perceptions: they favored startling images, unusual metaphors, and abrupt transitions. Although the modernist movement of the *Shinkankakuha* was short-lived, it had a lasting influence on many modern writers, perhaps because it struck a sympathetic chord with traditional poetic practice, in which associational leaps and linking between images or juxtapositions of seemingly unrelated images were frequent features. Kawabata's fiction is often explained as having the quality of haiku or *renga* (linked poetry). Extremely short paragraphs, often consisting of single sentences, also give a poetic rhythm to his narrative. His diction, too, is artfully simple yet subtle and evocative.

From the youthful lyricism of **"The Izu Dancer"** to the old man's fantasy and reverie in *The House of Sleeping Beauties,* Kawabata pursued his preoccupations with beauty, loneliness, transience, decay, death, and eroticism. He was already an established writer in the 1930s and 1940s with the publication of *Snow Country,* among others. His works usually contained both topicality and timelessness. Changing human events were often contrasted with nature in its recurrent cycle of seasons and renewal.

Kawabata was detached from the jingoism of the World War II years; he showed his independent spirit during the postwar era, when it was popular to denounce the old Japan and cater to the prevalent waves of Westernization, by declaring that henceforth he would write only elegies for the beauty of old Japan. Traditional arts and crafts, such as those represented by the ceramic tea bowls (*Thousand Cranes*) and the No masks (*The Sound of the Mountain*), are described in loving detail to emphasize their sensuousness and virtual timelessness, which are the expressions of the love and care that went into the creating and preserving of those artifacts. The same admiration for artistic excellence and the craftsman's devotion to his work are portrayed in *The Old Capital* as well.

Kawabata was active during the postwar era, serving as president of the Japan P. E. N. Club (1948-1965) and hosting its International Congress in Tokyo in 1957. In 1961 he was awarded the Order of Culture, Japan's highest recognition of achievement for a man of letters. His award of the Nobel Prize for Literature in 1968 signified the international recognition of Japanese culture, a century after the Meiji Restoration of 1868. Kawabata's sudden suicide in 1972, therefore, surprised the world.

The Old Capital was serialized in the *Asahi Shinbun,* one of the three leading Japanese newspapers with national circulation, between October 1961 and January 1962. Newspaper serialization is a commonly used means of publication in Japan, and distinguished novelists such as Soseki Natsume (1867-1916) have published their novels in newspapers. Serialization has left its mark on *The Old Capital* in some repetitions or overlaps that were necessary to remind the reader of what had occurred earlier in the story. Kawabata revised the novel extensively prior to its publication in book form. Another curious fact about this novel, according to Kawabata's own afterword to the Japanese edition, is his heavy use of sleeping medicine during its writing; after the novel was completed he stopped the medication, and consequently had to be hospitalized because of severe withdrawal symptoms. It is noteworthy that hardly any hint of such an abnormal state of mind can be observed in the novel (with the possible exceptions of the heroine's father's *obi* [sash] design, which suggests his spiritual desolation, and of the heroine's nightmares).

The story is set in contemporary Japan, in the traditional city of Kyoto, the capital of Japan from AD 794 to 1868. The central character is a beautiful young woman named Chieko, a foundling adopted and cherished by the childless couple named Takichiro and Shige, who own an established but declining wholesale dry goods business. Takichiro is an artist by temperament and ill-suited to business. His gentle nature and lack of business acumen are taken advantage of by his employees. The story of a foundling who grows up to become a beautiful woman has its classic precedent in *The Tale of the Bamboo Cutter,* a late-ninth- to early-tenth-century tale of Kaguyahime, the "shining" princess of the moon, who is temporarily banished to the earthly realm and, after rejecting all suitors, returns to the moon. Kawabata refers to this tale in *The Old Capital.* The tale of the beautiful unearthly princess Kaguyahime had deeply impressed the young

Kawabata, as he explained in his 1969 lecture titled *The Existence and Discovery of Beauty.*

The events in *The Old Capital* take place between spring and winter, and in nine chapters they encompass seasonal observances and famous festivals of Kyoto, such as the Hollyhock Festival in May, the Bamboo Cutting Ceremony of Kurama Temple in June, the Gion Festival in July, the Daimonji bonfires in August, and the Festival of Ages in October. Running through the parade of festivals, reminiscent of picture scrolls in traditional art, is the plot line involving beautiful identical twin sisters, Chieko and Naeko, who have been separated since infancy. Chieko had been abandoned by her poor parents. The sisters meet by chance during the Gion Festival, but they are destined to live apart because of their different stations in life. Chieko and Naeko are typical Kawabata heroines—beautiful, pure, virginal, and good. Such young women represent the essence of beauty and pure love in Kawabata's aesthetic. The critic Makoto Ueda points out in *Modern Japanese Writers and the Nature of Literature* that Kawabata's concept of pure love relies on its unattainability and that young maidens are the ones most capable of it. The emphasis on purity and beauty connects aptly with the religious element of the novel: Chieko is a parishioner of the Yasaka Shrine; in Shinto belief, the purification ritual is of central importance, since it is believed that one can become blessed only in a state of purity.

Revolving around the twins are Chieko's devoted parents and her three admirers. Chieko's beauty attracts her childhood friend Shin'ichi, his brother Ryusuke, and a young *obi* weaver named Hideo. One of the characteristics of *The Old Capital* is the absence of a "villain" among major characters: everyone is basically kind and considerate. The conflict, or tension, in the novel is therefore much more internalized within each character than in some other novels by Kawabata, such as *Thousand Cranes,* in which the tea master Chikako assumes the role of the villain. This internal conflict in *The Old Capital* is usually between duty and sentiment, a recurrent theme in the Kabuki and puppet theater of the Edo Period (1600-1868). For instance, Chieko does not feel free to choose her own marriage partner despite her affection for Shin'ichi, because her choice will directly affect her father's business and her parents' future security. She feels that she must honor their wishes. This constraint is largely self-imposed, as that of a dutiful and loyal daughter, to repay the kindness of her parents by doing what is right. Her parents, on the other hand, do not really wish to impose their will on her. The orphaned Naeko, a country girl of the working class, feels strongly that her presence should not jeopardize the happiness of her sister, the heiress to a comparatively affluent merchant household. Therefore, she restrains her natural desire to see her sister more often. Naeko is depicted as the more resolute of the two sisters: by refusing to benefit from her family connection to Chieko, she demonstrates her sense of honor and independence. Hideo, an expert weaver of the Nishijin district, is in love with Chieko, but he knows that he cannot presume to propose to her because of his family's poverty. The only expression of his feelings for her he allows is the *obi* he weaves for her, into which he pours his heart and soul. When he discovers that Chieko has a twin sister, he asks Naeko to marry him. However, it is strongly suggested that Naeko will refuse his proposal, because she does not wish to become a substitute for her sister. In the meantime, Shin'ichi's older brother, who is the more forceful of the two, becomes enamored of Chieko and hopes eventually to marry her. Caught in the network of human relationships, Chieko at the end of the novel looks into the falling snow, as her twin sister departs after spending a night at Chieko's home for the first and the last time. With a typically Kawabatan sense of open-endedness, there is no clear resolution of plot.

The self-restraint of the characters is remarkable, in contrast to such typically Kawabatan self-indulgent male characters as Shimamura in *Snow Country* or Kikuji in *Thousand Cranes.* One might say that the characters in *The Old Capital* are idealized and somewhat lacking in complexity, at least on the narrative surface. Sensuality, a quality prominent in many of Kawabata's works, is suppressed in this novel, with no description of sexual encounters between men and women.

The beauty of nature provides the backdrop to the human drama. From the cherry-blossom viewing in spring to the appreciation of the austere beauty of the cedars (actually cryptomerias) at Kitayama in winter, the characters derive pleasure and solace from flowers and trees in season. White bush clovers attract Takichiro, while camphor trees calm the spirit of Hideo's father. The backdrop of nature is a constant reminder of the brevity of human life, and possibly of its duality, i.e., its inconsequentiality and preciousness. Another aspect of nature in Japan that is discussed in this novel is its *bonsai*-like quality: it is not wild nature but nature cultivated by man. Kitayama cedars are the prime example, being shaped and grown to a uniform size to produce fine timber.

One of the major impulses that caused Kawabata to write this novel is his apparent wish to preserve in writing some of the traditional beauty of Kyoto. The period from the late 1950s to the early 1960s was marked by the Japanese national resolve to achieve economic advancement, symbolized by Premier Hayato Ikeda's call to double the income of all Japanese. Such an "economic miracle" was often achieved at the expense of aesthetic and cultural considerations. Thus, in virtually all episodes Kawabata contrasts the old and the new, and what is new seems almost invariably negative in its impact. For instance, the great wave of tourism caught the old capital in the postwar economic recovery, causing Zen temples to "sell" mass-produced and hurriedly served tea ceremonies or to have monks give loud speeches to large numbers of tourists, in the interest of efficient processing. Even the traditional craft of silk weaving was being replaced gradually by mechanized looms that could produce five hundred *obis* in a day; hand weavers like Hideo were no match in productivity. These changes are viewed with regret by the characters in *The Old Capital;* however, their emotions are more resignation and acceptance than revolt or rejection. Thus the author's attitude toward social change parallels the protagonist's attitude toward her lot in life.

The emotional timbre of the novel is strongly Japanese, in the pervasive mood of sadness and acceptance of one's circumstances. However, it is not a defeat but a choice on the part of the characters. Choosing self-sacrifice for the sake of others instead of seeking self-fulfillment without regard to others signifies inner strength and stoic fortitude. For this reason, a part of Chieko's and Naeko's, character is reminiscent of the Japanese self-discipline described so eloquently by Lafcadio Hearn in his essay "The Japanese Smile" nearly a century ago.

Despite its emphasis on the traditional culture of Japan, *The Old Capital* also contains topical non-Japanese references, such as those to the surrealistic paintings of Marc Chagall (1887-1985) and the abstract paintings of Paul Klee (1879-1940), which appear to have been fashionable in Japan in the early 1960s. For example, Chieko gives her father a volume of photographic reproductions of paintings by Klee, Chagall, and other modern painters. The novel refers several times to the fact that the postwar occupation of Japan by the Allied (American) Forces had officially ended in 1952 and the American housing in the Kyoto Botanical Garden was vacated. The atmosphere thus created, and reinforced by such events as the discontinuation of streetcar service, is one of transition and mutability. It is a time of nostalgic retrospection of the old capital in its various seasonal moods. For this reason, the critic Kenkichi Yamamoto regards the city of Kyoto as the true protagonist of the novel, with the story of the twin sisters only subsidiary in importance. Nevertheless, the depiction of subtle emotions and thought sequences, much of which clearly reflect Japanese modes of human relationship, makes the novel a valuable "case study" of self versus other in traditional Japanese society. Consideration for others always comes before fulfillment of self. Such a manner of life is beautiful but also can be painful, as evidenced in the frequent pauses and silences of the characters. Keene notes in *Nihon bungaku o yomu* that what is Japanese about Kawabata is more the suggestiveness (*yojo*), i.e., the unstated but implied meaning, of his prose than any direct material indebtedness to classical Japanese literature.

Holman's translation is generally accurate, but it contains a number of problems, including omissions, misunderstandings of idioms, changing of nuances, misleading English equivalents, and errors of fact. Kawabata's use of the Kyoto dialect undoubtedly caused more than the usual level of difficulty for the translator, since Kawabata's dialogues are often cryptic and suggestive, never loquacious. This point is underscored, for instance, by Seidensticker, who states in his essay "Translation: What Good Does It Do?" in the collection *Literary Relations East and West: Selected Essays,* that he prefers to translate Kawabata's works, because they are more ambiguous and elusive, hence more challenging, than the works by Tanizaki (1886-1965) or Mishima (1925-1970). Since it is impractical to discuss all the problems in this translation of *The Old Capital,* only a few examples will be treated below.

Omissions are presumably the conscious choice of the translator and they are justified in passages containing too many specific details that add little to the substance of the work or puzzle those unfamiliar with the language and culture of Japan. A case in point is the list of eighteen terms for types of fabrics and styles of kimono. Omissions may be problematic when they affect the substance of the novel. For instance, Chieko's adoptive mother, Shige, tells her, "If you wanted to seek out your real parents [and leave us], I couldn't stop you, but I would probably die." The bracketed words are omitted. Since Shige's concern is not about Chieko's desire to find her real parents but about her leaving, the omission seems to alter Shige's characterization. At several points in the novel whole sentences, generally descriptions, are omitted; these do not detract substantially from the effect of the novel.

Misunderstanding of idioms occurs occasionally, and sometimes it creates an odd situation. For instance, in conversation with her friend, Chieko is described as being curt: "Chieko cut her off shortly." But the passage actually means that "Chieko paused for a moment." At another juncture, Naeko cries out in surprise, "although she was alone"; however, this phrase "*hitoride ni*" should be rendered as "spontaneously" or "automatically." In two passages the expression "*aratamatta*" or its variant "*aratamatte,*" meaning "formal" or "formally," is confused with "*aratamete,*" which means "again" or "anew."

Changes of nuances and uses of misleading English equivalents occur sporadically. The most frequent case (about ten times) is the consistent rendition of "*shibaraku*" (for a while) as "for a moment." Even though it is not too far off the mark, the translation speeds up the action, thus altering the emotional tone of the novel. If the action in an Ozu film, such as *Tokyo Story,* is faster, with fewer silences and pauses, the audience will receive a different impression of it. Similarly, the genteel people of Kyoto would speak and act more slowly and deliberately than average Westerners. Another example of change of nuance occurs when Kawabata's characteristic ambiguity is removed by rendering passages containing such terms as "*yo da*" (seem to) or "*rashii*" (appear to) as definite statements of fact. For instance, "Chieko seemed to envy Masako's freedom," is rendered as "Chieko envied Masako's freedom." The choice concerns a shift in point of view, whether the narration at that point is external or internal to Chieko's mind. Generally, Kawabata carefully controls his narrative point of view, as seen in such masterpieces as *Snow Country, Thousand Cranes,* and *The Sound of the Mountain.* In the case of *The Old Capital,* the perspective shifts among Chieko, Takichiro, and a few other characters, showing the characters sometimes internally and at other times externally.

Misleading English equivalents include the following: a "storage shed" should be a "storehouse," which is more like a strongroom and much more substantial than the term "shed" implies. Another example of this sort is Chieko being described as wearing "galoshes over her shoes": Japanese rubber rain boots are not worn over any shoes, since there is no need for indoor footwear. A number of such misleading English equivalents suggest that this is a cultural problem; either the translator was unfamiliar with certain aspects of Japanese life or he was unable to convince the editor who was.

A few examples of errors of fact are as follows: for "two or three hundred houses" read "a hundred twenty or thirty houses"; "one hundred candles" should be large candles weighing "one hundred *momme* [unit of weight]"; for "their kimonos looked so shabby" read "I felt sorry for their fine kimonos [because their dance was so unskillful]." Errors of fact also occur when an action is attributed to a wrong person, a situation possible in translating from the Japanese language in which the subject of a sentence is omitted when the context makes it clear. For instance, in the recollected scene when Takichiro found the abandoned baby in front of his shop, he tells Shige, "I'm in a daze now"; however, the remark actually means "Why do you look so dazed?" Another example occurs when Shin'ichi and Ryusuke are visiting Chieko. Shin'ichi tells his brother that Chieko had said that since some years earlier she had regarded the two violets growing separately in the trunk of an old maple tree as adorable sweethearts and that they were close to each other but they would never be able to come together. To this, Chieko replies, "Stop it. Aren't you ashamed?"; however, the actual remark is "Stop it. You are embarrassing me."

Incidentally, the same passage paraphrased above is rendered in the translation as "Some years *ago,* Chieko said that the two violets are like two lovers. Though they are close to one another, *they've never met.*" The parts emphasized by this reviewer have the wrong tense (or aspect, according to some linguists). The rendition of this passage raises interesting in-

terpretative differences concerning the symbolism of the violets. The Japanese version suggests at least two possibilities for the "two lovers," namely Chieko and Shin'ichi for one and Chieko and Naeko for another. The English translation, on the other hand, by specifying that "they've never met," seems to limit the possibility to one couple, Chieko and Naeko, who had longed for each other but had not met; the use of the term "lovers," however, is problematic.

The above are but samples of problems in translation that this reviewer noted. However, it should be reiterated that, given the inherent ambiguities of Kawabata's evocative style and the use of dialect in all his dialogue, the translation emerges as a generally faithful and competent work. Most importantly, *The Old Capital* offers readers without direct access to the Japanese original a chance to read another acclaimed novel by Kawabata and to judge for themselves how it fits into the totality of the writer's aesthetic and novelistic vision. To that end the translator's efforts should be welcomed and appreciated.

Martin Lebowitz (essay date Autumn 1991)

SOURCE: "The Mysterious East," in *The Virginia Quarterly Review,* Vol. 67, No. 4, Autumn, 1991, pp. 778-79.

[*In the following essay, Lebowitz discusses the prevalent themes in Kawabata's* The Palm-of-the-Hand Stories, *and how their compactness "reflects elements at once of primitivism and sophistication."*]

If, as historians have noted, giantism is an aspect of decadence, miniaturization—emblematic of love, tenacity, and control—expresses the mystique or teleology of a humane society. These stories [in *Palm-of-the-Hand Stories*] are rarely more than four pages in length. The particularity and concreteness of the Japanese mentality reflect a sort of primitive vitalism or vitality. Still, it is correct to say of all liberal, humane, and progressive societies that they embody, along with pristine elements of energy, formal prototypes that are civilizing in their implications and effect. So far as miniaturization partakes of the primeval energy of things, it reflects elements at once of primitivism and sophistication. One is tempted to say that the combination of these two factors defines civilization, as opposed, for one thing, to decadence.

In one of these stories, a character remarks that the girl he loves is remembered well, but only by his finger (!). Human association—"love"—particularly in our time, contains something so casual that it is nothing as much as physical or material contact. It is not simply violence or sex that accounts for such events but the random character of modern experience in which the immanence and imminence of disorder impart a physical ascendancy to romanticism itself. Romantic materialism as an aspect of modernity is a notable subject, quite relevant here.

> **Death for the Japanese mentality, as mystical as it is rationalistic, becomes a sort obsession for Kawabata, in respect to the tone of his writings and its pervasive overtones. Its overtones becomes a subject matter, and death is a controlling theme.**
> —*Martin Lebowitz*

In the same story, snow is symbolic of repression. The woman in this story has "cold hair," and the hero is psychologically cold. This "coldness" reflects something essential to an advanced or cultivated association—the creative dialectic of passion and repression—plus that formal principle essential to functional progress. The elusive question is what here to define as primitive.

Kawabata died in April 1972, a suicide. A Nobel laureate (1968), his controlling themes are loneliness, love, time as something concrete both for the mystic and the rationalist, and perhaps above all death. Death for the Japanese mentality, as mystical as it is rationalistic, becomes a sort obsession for Kawabata, in respect to the tone of his writings and its pervasive overtones. Its overtones becomes a subject matter, and death is a controlling theme.

The publisher prints one of the stories on the dust jacket, called **"Love Suicides."** The protagonist takes a dislike to his wife and deserts her. Two years later, a letter comes from a distant land, saying, "Don't let the child bounce a rubber ball. It strikes at my heart." The wife complies. More and more letters come making similar requests. The wife continues to comply. Finally a letter from a different land insists, "don't make any sound at all, the two of you, not even the ticking of a clock!" Thus they cease eternally to make even the faintest sound. The husband lies down, curiously, beside them and dies, too.

On a prosaic level the theme is that husband and wife never parted, overcome rather by a fatal disenchantment or spell. The true theme is that the incongruity or ambivalence of so-called interpersonal relations is itself a type of suicide.

An old lady planning to sell her daughter to a strange man, possibly brutal and oppressive, confronts the bus driver who is to take them to their destination. The bus driver is the incarnation of courtesy and graciousness, and the lady remarks, "So it's your turn today . . . If she has you to take her there, Mr. Thankyou, she is likely to meet with good fortune. It's

a sign that something good will happen." Is the view expressed here based on psychology, metaphysics, superstition, or mysticism? Or is it based on naturalism? Naturalism, too, is an effort to integrate moral and existential considerations. It is the philosophy of the Orient, particularly Japan and China, that suggests that the cultivated personality has it all over intellectualism as such.

The culture of the Orient, based on formalism, repression, and teleology, is highly cultivated but not lacking in primitive overtones. This is a combination of attributes that may define the quality of humanistic society in any age. Yet again, it is not easy to define what, if anything, in this context is truly primitive.

Primitivism is a static relation to the past, an incarceration in the past. Primitivism may be defined as the opposite of moral development, which may be synonymous with development itself. Thus the question whether the culture of Japan is primitive or not—or in what degree—is not that easy. One might note that the alterations introduced by science are existential rather than moral, although they sometimes have more effects.

No doubt the cultures of Japan and China defy the conventional categories of primitive or retrograde as against progressive and enlightened. The essence of Japanese culture is sufficiently "advanced" without being decidedly humane to be better than much in the West. Without being truly liberal or "forward-looking," some cultures may be superior to others that are.

Masaki Mori (essay date May 1994)

SOURCE: "Decoding the Beard: A Dream-Interpretation of Kawabata's *The Sound of the Mountain*," in *The Comparatist*, Vol. XVIII, May, 1994, pp. 129-49.

[*In the following essay, Mori uses dream-interpretation to analyze the dreams of the main character of Kawabata's* The Sound of the Mountain. *He concludes that the analysis "shows at once Kawabata's great interest in Freudian concepts and his adroit use of psychoanalytic motifs in one of his major novels."*]

Apart from the Japanese sensibility and literary tradition woven into many of his works, Kawabata Yasunari eagerly absorbed new ideas and techniques from the West during the early stage of his career as a writer. For instance, it is well known that, together with his friend Yokomitsu Riichi, Kawabata was involved with the activities of *Shin Kankakuha* (Neosensualism or Neoperceptionism), a literary movement that tried to incorporate such avant-garde trends as cubism, dadaism, futurism, symbolism and expressionism into Japanese literature in 1920s. Kawabata was also greatly interested in surrealism and stream of consciousness. Psychoanalysis is not an exception. Although Jungian psychology has been well accepted in Japan, it is Freudian psychoanalysis which has made remarkable impacts, direct or indirect, on Japanese artists including Kawabata.

Suisho Genso [*Crystal Fantasy*], for example, has often been noted for its experimental use of the stream of consciousness to express the contour of the distressed mind of a childless married woman. In this early novella, Kawabata already shows his unmistakable interest in Freud by having his female protagonist mention the Austrian scholar's name twice along with such terms as "psychology," "psychologist" and "the death instinct." Nor is this an isolated instance of an interest in Freud. According to Kim Chae-Soo, through his early tentative use of Freudianism and the stream of consciousness, Kawabata established a mode of "internal narration" in which the author describes things through the "limited viewpoint" of only one character, and most of Kawabata's critically acclaimed novels such as *Yukiguni* [*Snow Country*], *Senbazuru* [*Thousand Cranes*] and *Nemureru Bijo* [*The House of the Sleeping Beauties*] are written in this way. Moreover, twenty years after *Crystal Fantasy,* the writer seems to have found a long-awaited opportunity to make extensive use of the psychoanalytical approach in *Yama no Oto* [*The Sound of the Mountain*].

In the case of *The Sound of the Mountain,* the story is almost entirely narrated from the viewpoint of the protagonist Ogata Shingo. While still retaining an active role as the head of a family at Kamakura and as an executive of a Tokyo company, this man over sixty has two fundamental problems which are related to each other—anxiety about his weakened sexuality and fear of impending death. He is keenly aware of the latter problem when his old friends die one after another a few years after World War II. The former problem is often repressed by his moral consciousness, because the object of his sexual interest is his daughter-in-law Kikuko who lives with his three-generational family.

Throughout the novel, Shingo has a number of dreams, most of which readily yield to Freudian dream-interpretation, suggesting a disguised, repressed incestuous desire. However, at least one of his dreams seems totally irrelevant to the psychological scheme which underlies the work: this is the dream of a man with an elaborate beard which conforms to American ethnic patterns. Always regarded as "naïve, uncomplicated," according to the text, this dream, unlike the other ones, has not attracted serious critical attention. At the same time, four of Shingo's dreams appear in two pairs on separate occasions. One pair of successive dreams in the second chapter is about Shingo's encounter with two of his dead acquaintances. The other pair of dreams, which includes the

one about the extraordinary beard, happens much later at a moment of moral crisis. Apart from what each of these dreams might indicate, the significance of coupling itself has been little explored. When correlated with the overall meaning of the work, however, the nonsensical dream about the beard and the coupling of dreams also acquire a certain psychological significance.

Freudian psychoanalysis as presented in *Introductory Lectures on Psycho-Analysis* (1916-17) and Freud's other works are helpful here, because the protagonist makes good use of this popular approach in his attempts to understand the hidden messages of his dreams. Thus, our study is doubly comparative, first in exploring Kawabata's use of Freudianism in his novel, and subsequently in applying Freudian psychoanalysis to reveal the meanings of some of Shingo's dreams.

In order to develop the full implications of a Freudian interpretation of Shingo's dream about the beard, the protagonist's preoccupations with a death fear and sexual dysfunction will first be situated in relation to the arts, nature, and other people. Then, his dreams will be explored in order to extract the possible meanings of the double dreams and the dream of the beard. In dealing with the dream of the beard, the social background of occupied Japan and the role played by the United States will be examined, since the American presence at that time penetrated many aspects of people's lives, both real and fictional. In the end, these dreams will hopefully enhance our sense of the organic coherence of this novel, in spite of its loose sequence of chapters, which has created the misleading impression that its components are "assembled but unconnected," as Miyoshi Masao puts it, and are like "the stringing together of little vignettes with no great regard for over-all form," as Edward Seidensticker has argued.

The Sound of the Mountain is fraught with psychological symbolism. The title itself derives from an undefinable sound which Shingo hears on a quiet summer night at the beginning of the story:

> He thought he could detect a dripping of dew from leaf to leaf.
>
> Then he heard the sound of the mountain. . . .
>
> It was like wind, far away, but with a depth like a rumbling of the earth. . . . He wanted to question himself, calmly and deliberately, to ask whether it had been the sound of the wind, the sound of the sea, or a sound in his ears. But he had heard no such sound, he was sure. He had heard the mountain.

Somehow convinced of the reality of the eerie phenomenon, Shingo immediately associates the sound with his fear of death, since he feels with a chill "as if he had been notified that death was approaching." Remarkable here is the description suggestive of the unconscious from which a dream emerges, for there is "a vast depth to the moonlit night, stretching far on either side." While the primary sense is auditory with tense quietude intoning the sound of the mountain, the visual sense, which dominates our dream, introduces Kikuko with the unreality of her moonlit dress "hanging outside, unpleasantly gray," like an obtrusive, insubstantial dream image. This unpleasantness around Kikuko's first appearance should be regarded as a result of the unconscious, instantaneous negation of what Shingo might otherwise feel sexually attracted to. A moment later, he imagines this piece of clothing "sweat-soaked," thereby divulging his latent interest.

This entire nocturnal scene resembles a bad joke, which is characteristic of anxiety-dreams as Freud defined them. Moreover, Shingo remembers the discarded suicide plan he heard ten days earlier from a geisha. She intended to die with her lover, but, not sure of the effect of the potassium cyanide he brought, she changed her mind at the last moment. The sudden recollection of the planned love suicide, which also looks like a spoiled game, is reminiscent of dream formation, because this "strange memory" is taken at random from an everyday, unimportant occurrence and is forcibly associated, through the notion of death, with an unrelated, significant element. Although not an actual dream, this nocturnal scene distinguishes itself from a working of the conscious mind by its temporary, hallucinatory nature. Moriyasu Masafumi calls this scene "a reality transformed into another reality by a dream," and Takahashi Hideo considers it "a dream sphere." In this initial stage, we already notice the effect of Shingo's two obsessions, death and sexuality, in a Freudian framework.

A few days later, the sound of the mountain is traced back to the remote past in a conversation with Kikuko and his wife Yasuko. As Shingo tells them of his uncanny experience, Kikuko recalls that, according to her mother-in-law, Yasuko's beautiful sister had a similar experience just before her death in her twenties. This precedent, however, which took place a few decades before, had not come to Shingo's mind until his daughter-in-law mentioned it. Shingo as a young man loved Yasuko's elder sister. With his desire unfulfilled, he married Yasuko, hoping in vain that his offspring would inherit his sister-in-law's beauty through his wife. He is attracted to Kikuko partly because her "delicate figure made him think of Yasuko's sister." His attachment to his daughter-in-law is so perceptibly strong as to invite some criticism from the other family members.

Although Shingo is used to his own frequent forgetfulness of recent events, his failure to associate the two occurrences of the same phenomenon shocks him. In this case, we should

rather suspect that the two instances of the sound, which originates in the death of someone dear to him, were unconsciously kept from being associated with each other in memory by his fear of death. The sound of the mountain as a foreboding of death is thus related to sexual desire still lingering from Shingo's younger days, and the sound turns out to be the psychological undertone of the novel, although he hears it only once.

The death knell actually sounds inside and around Shingo in far more tangible ways. His fitful senile amnesia, one typical instance of which opens the novel, is ironically a constant reminder of "a life . . . being lost," and makes him feel "a twinge of something like fear." Later in the last chapter, Shingo temporarily forgets how to tie a necktie, "a process he had repeated every morning through the forty years of his office career," and he fears that he might be facing "a collapse, a loss of self." As Jaime Fernández argues, his loss of memory is equated with the loss of life. And, one year before hearing the sound of the mountain, Shingo spits blood, presumably from his lungs. Although there has been no other symptom indicative of tuberculosis since then, "to spit blood at his age gave him the darkest forebodings." When he is shaken with emotion, he feels "the fatigue of his years" come "flooding over him."

At the same time, like the recurring tones of a reminding bell, Shingo hears of the deaths of friends from his university days. All of these reported deaths take place in autumn, which seems to be a corresponding metaphor for the age of Shingo and his generation. They are all far advanced in the penultimate season of life, and there is no turning back in time as they experience daily the steady approach of death. Moreover, a devastating storm called war has made the autumn of Shingo's generation far worse than usual:

> His schoolmates were now in their sixties. Among
> them were considerable numbers whose luck, from
> the middle of the war on into the defeat, had not
> been good. Since they were already then in their late
> fifties, the fall was cruel and the recovery difficult.
> And they were of an age to lose sons in the war.

The "scar" left by the war, from which the title of the twelfth chapter is derived according to Ochi Haruo, often extends far into the psyche. Kitamoto, who was one of Shingo's friends from his school days and who died during the air raids, lost three sons and went insane when, having proven useless in his wartime company, he was forced to stay home. According to a friend who tells Shingo of Kitamoto's last years, he sat all day in front of a mirror, pulling out his white hairs in an effort to strive "against the years." Once his obsession "to be young again" had resulted in complete baldness, his resistance against time seemed to bring about "a miracle," for a "fine crop of black hair came out on his naked head." But he died shortly thereafter, since he apparently "used up all his energy growing that crop of dark hair."

In Shingo's case, although he does not lose his son in the war, he loses his virility and can not regain it. He knows that he is "not very old," but "[w]hat had been killed by the war had not come to life again" and "that was how it was with him." Lying down beside Yasuko at night, he no longer reaches out to touch his wife except when he tries to stop her snoring, which he takes as an "infinitely saddening" fact. Even when he has a chance with a young geisha in Tokyo, he does "nothing out of the ordinary" and resignedly accepts the idea that "in sex, too, there were riches and poverty, good luck and bad." Obviously, World War II profoundly affected the inner life of Shingo's generation in terms of both sexuality and a fear of death.

Shingo's existence is shaken because of "a fundamental sense of debility" in Ookubo Takaki's words, or of "the most inner aging" which enfeebles "the energy of life," as Iwata Mitsuko puts it. In this situation, although not as single-mindedly as the deranged Kitamoto, Shingo nevertheless feels an irresistible attraction to things which seem to resist, freeze, or reverse the flow of time—specifically, to certain works of arts and to certain objects in nature.

Shingo's fascination with the arts is easily understandable, for the arts freeze time within their creations and give us a sense of pseudoeternity, a motif Keats celebrated in "Ode on a Grecian Urn." The list of artifacts which interest Shingo includes Noh masks, a Buddha statue, a filmed Kabuki play, a framed scroll of calligraphy, paintings by ancient masters, *haiku* and *tanka* poems, and a few lines from a Noh play. The most important object is a Noh mask called *jido*. Having been handed down from one generation to another for about four hundred years, and representing the seductive beauty of the opposite gender for Shingo, this mask of an early teenage male symbolizes "eternal youth." Shingo has one of the closest, emotional contacts with his daughter-in-law when she utters, through the mask which she has placed in front of her face, her hope of staying with him after her probable divorce. Putting it away in a closet on the day of purchase, Shingo avoids the sight of the *jido* mask that inadvertently discloses his latent desire for restored youth and sexuality.

Wild vegetation also tends to be endowed with symbolism peculiar to the workings of Shingo's mind. A large gingko tree behind Shingo's house, stripped bare of its leaves by a typhoon, sprouts new leaves in the fall. Partly because of his position at the dinner table, Shingo, not the observant Kikuko, first takes notice of this unseasonable phenomenon. The dialogue between the two on this occasion is telling:

"I've been thinking the ones that live long are dif-

ferent from the others. It must take a great deal of strength for an old tree like that to put out leaves in the fall."

"But there's something sad about them."

"I've been wondering whether they'd be as big as the leaves that came out in the spring, but they refuse to grow."

Besides being small, the leaves were scattered, too few to hide the branches. They seemed thin, and they were a pale yellowish color, insufficiently green.

It was as if the autumn sun fell on a gingko that was, after all, naked.

With their short promise of life, these new leaves anticipate the anecdote of Kitamoto's renewed black hair, and Shingo's close observation of the change in the gingko tree betrays his latent wish for rejuvenation. Shingo is also impressed by the strength of "a broken thistle," the stem of which still stands "fresh green," in the midst of winter (December the 29th).

His latent wish to get away from death by stopping time, and to have his life reinvigorated and renewed, manifests itself most clearly when he talks about staying buried in the ground "without dying" only to "wake up after fifty thousand years and find all your own problems . . . and the problems of the world" solved, which, he says, would put him "in paradise." This fantasy is induced by a newspaper article on the excavated lotus seeds that came to life with shoots and flowers after having stayed dormant for as long as fifty thousand years, or in Shingo's words, for "[a]lmost an eternity, when you compare it with a human life."

In some cases, plants are shown to have explicit sexual connotations. One afternoon during the same summer when he hears the sound of the mountain, Shingo finds himself with Kikuko gazing up at blooming sunflowers in front of a neighbor's house. Each of these plants has a flower "larger in circumference than a human head," and he is particularly impressed by "the strength of the great, heavy, flowering heads" and by the orderly arrangement of the stamens. According to Kobayashi Ichiro, Shingo's interest in these specific aspects of the sunflowers is analogically generated by his wish for a brain of "systematic reason or intelligence," including clear memory, which he feels he is losing with "futile searchings" in his old age. On this occasion, Shingo, who is confessedly "tired," tells Kikuko that his head "hasn't been very clear these last few days," and he wishes that his head "could be as clean as they [the sunflowers] are."

These sunflowers are highly suggestive of Freud's phallic symbolism. Not surprisingly, Shingo looks upon the flowers as a symbol of male sexuality, although the yellow petals around the stamens look feminine:

> He felt the regularity and order with which they were put together. The petals were like crowns, and the greater part of the central discs was taken up by stamens, clusters of them, which seemed to thrust their way up by main strength. There was no suggestion that they were fighting one another, however. They were quietly systematic, and strength seemed to flow from them. . . .

> The power of nature within them made him think of a giant symbol of masculinity. He did not know whether they [stamens] were male or not, but somehow he thought them so.

Shingo rightly suspects that "it was Kikuko's coming that had set him to thinking strange thoughts." The admired sunflowers stand for what he is now losing, that is, clearheadedness and, more importantly, his sexual vigor. The fate of the sunflowers is highly suggestive of this psychic correlation, for all of them are later struck down in a typhoon:

> Blossoms had lain in the street, broken off with six inches or so of stem. They had been there for several days, like severed human heads.

> First the petals withered, and then the stems dried and turned dirty and gray.

The remaining, standing stems are left leafless by the gate. Shingo walks over the fallen flowers every day on his way to and from work. By trying to avoid the sight of the decaying plants, Shingo unconsciously identifies with the fate of the once vigorous sunflowers in terms both of his waning masculinity and his approaching death.

The question is how Shingo tries to cope with "something flickering inside" (my translation), "a flicker of youth," or "a flicker of something youthful" in himself, which he unconsciously has kept unquenched from his young days only to find its potential fulfillment in his daughter-in-law. He is vaguely aware that what he seeks in his daughter-in-law goes far beyond mere kindness. However, his moral consciousness cannot admit the full emergence of such a latent sentiment, because that would suggest incest. Even if he admitted to that sentiment and followed up on it, he would still have to face his weakened potency. On the other hand, he cannot do without this suppressed feeling, which now functions for him as an indispensable means of resisting eroding time and the fear of death. As Ochi and Kim argue, sex stands for life here. To deal with this dilemma, we as well as the protago-

nist have to understand his dreams through Freudian psychoanalysis.

In Shingo's dreams, his two major concerns of death and sexuality appear time and again in distorted forms. Before we begin our dream-interpretation, however, two points ought to be noted. First, according to Freud, the problem which discloses itself in a dream is fundamentally based on an unsolved problem in the dreamer's childhood. In *The Sound of the Mountain,* Shingo's problem of unfulfilled love stems, if not from childhood, then from a quite early stage in his life. In fact, Kawasaki Toshihiko infers from the fact that Shingo calls the house where he is finally reunited with Yasuko's sister-in-law in the seventh dream "his home" (my translation) that "Shingo was probably brought up as an orphan boy in the house of Yasuko and her sister (or at least in its vicinity)." Perceiving a projection of the orphan Kawabata in Shingo, Isogai Hideo assumes that Shingo did not have a home of his birth after all. Second, when he has physical contact with a woman in some of his dreams, which usually does not happen in Freud's examples, we should consider Shingo's age and experience. As a man over sixty, Shingo has a sense of morality which, while it does not restrict his dreams of direct sexual contact, is strong enough to prohibit him from enjoying unrestrained sexual fantasies involving his daughter-in-law.

Shingo is aware that he has many dreams in his old age, in spite of his basic hope to have a sound sleep of "no dreaming." The novel reports eight of his dreams and one of Yasuko's (excluding the one at the end of the sixth chapter ["The Cherry in the Winter"], in which Shingo only hears Yasuko's sister call his name). All of Shingo's dreams have some sexual connotation, and he has physical contact with young girls in three of them. In his waking consciousness, he cannot remember who those girls were. In his old age, Shingo seldom has obscene dreams, which makes him all the more curious about the identity of the dreamed girls.

In the first dream, for instance, which takes place at dawn on the same day he looks up at the impressive sunflowers, he finds himself in the house of a cabinetmaker whom he had occasionally employed but who has been dead for three years. The cabinetmaker has six daughters, whose faces Shingo does not remember. Still, it seems to Shingo that he slept with one of them in the dream and that he knew who she was when he momentarily woke up before resuming sleep. Yet, in the evening, he vainly tries to recall her identity, and is not even sure whether she was one of the cabinetmaker's daughters:

> He remembered clearly having touched someone, but he had no notion who she might have been. He could remember nothing that even gave him a hint.

All that remains is a dull sensation with the awareness that she was a virgin, "a mere girl":

> Not, of course, that it had been a sharp enough sensation to wake him.
>
> Here, too, nothing definite of the dream remained. The figure had gone, and he could not bring it back; all that remained was a sense of physical disparity, a failure of physical contact.

This "certain sensual disappointment," which "reduced the sexual excitement almost to insipidity" (my translation), betrays his concern about the dwindling vigor of his life and sexuality. Most probably, the dream-work intervened to disguise the object of his latent desire. In fact, Shingo asks himself if it would not be "true to the laws of dreams" for him to have been "awakened at the shock of contact with the girl," although "the clearest image in his mind" upon waking up was "the noodles" offered by the cabinetmaker. He also wonders whether, "from feelings of guilt, he had managed to forget" who that girl was.

In a second dream, which follows immediately on the same night, he sees someone else who had died less than a year before. This time, it is Aida who had been a director of Shingo's company until about ten years before. In the dream, he visits Shingo at home. Although he did not drink alcohol in real life, Aida appears to have "drunk a good bit already" to the extent that the "pores on his red face were agape." Instead of "a medicine bottle" which he always used to carry around, he brings "a half-gallon bottle of sake in his hand." He is not emaciated, as he was near his death, but fat.

There are two points to be noted about this dream in relation to the preceding one. First, Shingo's strong concern with death is evident, in that both Aida and the cabinetmaker are dead. Shingo thinks, with half joking superstition, that these two men might have come to take him to their world. These two men, however, appear in the dreams "as living people." Moreover, Aida is endowed with perfect health, which he never had in reality. Second, a certain object has symbolical importance in each dream. Tsuruta Kinya thinks that the noodles of the first dream, which were "laid on bamboo, in a frame lacquered black on the outside and red on the inside," might stand for the female sexual organ, while the large bottle of sake in the second dream could symbolize the penis ("Jikan to Kukan"; "Yume no Kaishaku"). Moriyasu shares this view, in support of which Siegfried Scharschmidt finds a parallel between "the dreaming Shingo—the noodles—the young girl" and "Shingo in reality—meals—Kikuko." We may suspect again the strong intervention of the dream-work in substituting these symbols for sexual organs.

When two seemingly unrelated dreams occur successively, we as dream interpreters are supposed to provide the missing semantic conjunction, understanding that the mode of expression in dreams is regressive. In Freud's words, because "in the course of the dream-work all the relations between the dream-thoughts drop out" and result in the "picture-language" of manifest dreams, "it is the task of the interpretation to re-insert the omitted relations," such as "'because,' 'therefore,' however,' etc." In this case, the noodles, details of which he remembers most vividly at the very moment of awakening, pose a hard challenge to the dreaming Shingo. As a symbol of the female genitalia, they represent an object of desire which he has no confidence to deal with after his failed contact with the unidentified girl in the dream. To enjoy her, he has to regain his vitality, just as a patient recuperates from a very serious illness and gains exuberant health, or even as a dead person comes back to life. Therefore, the link to be semantically supplied between the two dreams is "because," and the hidden message can be summed up as follows: "because" he lacks the virility to handle the object of his desire, he has to be sexually invigorated beyond any probability. The large bottle, which Aida brings Shingo, thus represents what he ultimately wishes to obtain.

The motifs of an unidentified girl and a lack of sexual excitement persist in the next two dreams. In the third dream, a few months later in early winter, Shingo finds himself holding a girl in his arms on the grass under the pine trees of an island (hence the title of the fifth chapter, "A Dream of Islands"). He is not sure about his own age in the dream. Here we may observe a synthesis of contraries (youth and old age), which is one of the operations characteristic of dream formation:

> He did not seem to feel a difference in their ages as he held her in his arms. He embraced her as a young man would. Yet he did not think of himself as rejuvenated, nor did it seem to be a dream of long ago. It was as if, at sixty-two, he were still in his twenties. In that fact lay the strangeness.

Yet, far from enjoying this adventure, he feels frightened and tries to hide himself. This is an instance of an anxiety-dream, in which the pleasure expected of a fulfilled, but forbidden wish is transmuted into distressful non-pleasure. And, once more, Shingo remembers "neither face nor figure" of the girl, although he does not forget that the woman was "very young, a mere girl." Even the sense of touch eludes him.

The situation remains largely the same in Shingo's fourth dream during the early spring of the following year, a dream about a girl in her mid-teens who "has become a holy child forever" after an abortion:

> The girl must have had a name, and he must have

seen her face, but only her size, or more properly her smallness, remained vaguely in his mind. She seemed to have been in Japanese dress.

Shingo thinks that it is not "a vision of Yasuko's beautiful sister." The evening before, he was shocked by a newspaper article reporting on the unexpectedly high rate of pregnancy of high school girls, which Shingo believes is the "source of the dream." The recurrent physical immaturity of the dreamed girls seems to be just another indication of Kawabata's partiality for young female virgins, as best exemplified by the student-protagonist who feels greatly relieved to find out that the girl he likes is "a mere child" in *Izu no Odoriko* [*The Izu Dancer*]. In *The Sound of the Mountain,* however, Shingo is often found to be attentively observing the smallest change of Kikuko's maturing body, in spite of a lack of conscious lasciviousness. By transforming the original shock of repugnance into "something beautiful," the dreaming self probably carried out the paradoxical wish of rendering the sexually initiated Kikuko virginally pure. Tachibana argues that this fleeting balance of virginity and sexuality poses the most desirable femininity for Kawabata. This is another instance of coalesced opposites, which is only possible in dreams. In any case, Shingo was "completely the onlooker" in this dream, without any direct sexual involvement. This distance removes all of his anxiety, in contrast to the foregoing dream where a decisive action uncharacteristic of the dreamer brings about a fear of punishment.

Another few months later, one night in the pre-summer rainy season, Shingo has two dreams again, the first of which is the dream about the unique beard:

> It took place in America, where Shingo had never been. . . .

> In his dream, there were states in which the English were most numerous, and states in which the Spanish prevailed. Accordingly, each state had its own characteristic whiskers. He could not clearly remember, after he awoke, how the color and shape of the beards had differed, but in his dream he had clearly recognized differences in color, which is to say in racial origins, from state to state. In one state, the name of which he could not remember, there appeared a man who had gathered in his one person the special characteristics of all the states and origins. It was not that all the various whiskers were mixed in together on his chin. It was rather that the French variety would be set off from an Indian beard, each in its proper place. Varied tufts of whiskers, each for a different state and racial origin, hung in sprays from his chin.

> The American government designated the beard a national monument; and so he could not of his own free will cut or dress it.

Sometime before Shingo's dream, Kikuko returned to Kamakura after a few days spent at her parents' house in Tokyo in order to hide her embarrassment about her secret abortion, bringing a gift for every family member in Shingo's house. The present for her husband was "an American comb" while Shingo got "an electric razor of Japanese make." On the subsequent mornings, Shingo enjoys shaving "his own face clean" with the small device which was a rarity in those days. Waking up first from the dream of the long American beard that rainy night, he naturally ascribes the dream content to the new electric razor and comb, and considers the dream just "naïve, uncomplicated."

And then, falling asleep again, he has another dream which appears to have nothing to do with the foregoing one. This is the last of the three dreams in which Shingo makes physical contact with a girl. The lack of sexual excitement, which haunted his dubious encounter with the dreamed girls in the previous cases, defines the entire nature of this dream:

> His hands were against drooping, vaguely pointed breasts. They remained soft, refusing to rise. The woman was refusing to respond. All very stupid.

At first, the image is no more than "two breasts floating in space," and then, it takes the shape of a woman. Characteristically, the dreamer is unable to recognize her. More precisely, it is "not so much that he did not know as that he did not seek to find out." But when Shingo asks himself in the dream who she is, he sees her assume the identity of the younger sister of a friend of his son. The recognition neither excites him nor vexes him with a sense of guilt. He considers her to have no experience with childbirth, and he is surprised to see "traces of her purity on his finger." Still, he does not feel particularly guilty, and he wakes up.

Interestingly, Shingo himself develops a highly Freudian psycho-analysis of this dream upon awakening. At first, he ascribes the insipid nature of the dream to his strong moral disapproval of adultery. Then, he remembers that, contrary to the dream, this specific girl has full breasts in reality. The fact that he dreamed about such a girl who has little to do with him appears to be perplexingly inexplicable. But, suddenly, he finds the relevance of the dream when he also remembers that, before Shuichi got married to Kikuko, there was some talk of arranging his marriage to this girl. The two young people kept company for a while. He now suspects that his superego intervened in the dream and replaced his daughter-in-law by the other girl to disguise his latent incestuous desire:

Had not moral considerations after all had their way even in his dream, had he not borrowed the figure of the girl as a substitute for Kikuko? And, to coat over the unpleasantness, to obscure the guilt, had he not made her a less attractive girl than she was?

. . .

Even in the dream, had he sought to hide it, to deceive himself? . . . [T]hat he had given her an elusive, uncertain form—was it not because he feared in the extreme having the woman be Kikuko?

This reflection exhibits distinctly Freudian concepts, such as repression and displacement. Because of the intervention of the superego which does not permit any aberration from the dreamer's moral standard, the "subconscious wish" for a sexual relationship with Kikuko is "[s]uppressed and twisted" in the dream. The pleasure which might arise from the intercourse is denied in the dream. The woman with whom he unconsciously desires physical contact is replaced by a totally different individual with some "unlovable" disfigurement. Furthermore, the seemingly innocent words "All very stupid," which Shingo mutters in the dream, are indirectly related to Shingo's other psychological problem, death, because he remembers that they were the last words of a famous novelist (Mori Ogai) on his deathbed.

The relevance of this self-interpretation to the past dreams is evident. It explains the dull sensation devoid of sexual excitement, typically felt in the first dream. Shingo suspects that he latently wishes he could redesign his life and love "the virgin Kikuko, before she was married to Shuichi." This accounts for the persistent virginity of the dreamed girls, including the curiously mixed case of the fourth dream in which an abortion is turned into a purifying act of eternally preserving virginity. This analysis also accounts for the ambivalence of his age in the third dream, where the dreaming self is felt to be specifically "still in his twenties," that is, of his son's age. Shingo unconsciously wishes to embrace Kikuko by taking the place of Shuichi, at once without losing his self-identity as a man in his early sixties and without being troubled with his age-plagued sexuality. In the end, he realizes once and for all that his inability to identify the girl upon awakening and the obscurity of the dream's plot might have been caused because "at the moment of awakening, a certain cunning went adroitly to work at erasing the dream."

Upon discovering his naked desire for his daughter-in-law, Shingo immediately attempts to get over this moral crisis by having recourse to a conventional measure, that is, by rejecting this "evil dream" (my translation) as a fleeting vision that is meaningless, unreliable, and not founded on any fact. In order to reassure himself, he thinks of the dream about the beard, which he had experienced earlier that night, as a good example of a mere, senseless dream. He even tries to deny what he has found out with analytical reasoning, telling himself that he does not believe in "dream-interpretation" (my translation). However, in light of the uninterrupted continuation of the two dreams and the poignant complexity of the second dream, we should not dismiss the first dream about the monumental beard as just naïve and simple as Shingo tries to.

The image of America, to which the beard is inseparably linked, has to be examined before we can fully understand what the dream stands for. In spite of the scarcity of direct references to political situations, Kawabata was not totally indifferent to, nor unaffected by, social upheaval. Far from "completely precluding the air fraught with keen, strong, violent motion and tension" of "people's rough life," as Sugiura Akihira has argued, Kawabata rendered in some of his works the social and political situations around him as something more than "vaguely atmospheric" indexes of "intense reality." In *The Sound of the Mountain,* with the story set in the early years of post-WWII Japan when the loss of national sovereignty was a reality, there are several short but unmistakable references to the occupying forces and to their formidable weapons. For example, foreign military airplanes roar over Shingo's house in otherwise peaceful Kamakura, reminding the protagonist of his war-time experience of air raids:

> Two American military planes flew low overhead. Startled by the noise, the baby [Kuniko, one of Shingo's granddaughters by his daughter Fusako] looked up at the mountain. . . .
>
> Shingo was touched by the gleam of surprise in the innocent eyes. . . .
>
> "I wish I had a picture of her eyes just now. With the shadow of the airplanes in it. And the next picture. . . ."
>
> Of a dead baby, shot from an airplane, he was about to say; . . .
>
> In fact, there were numberless babies like Kuniko as he had seen her in the two pictures.

A few pages earlier, when he hears astoundedly from Shuichi about Kikuko's abortion, Shingo does not forget family privacy and, though on a train, he makes sure that the fellow passengers seated in front of them are indeed "two American soldiers" who probably do not understand their conversation in Japanese. As these instances demonstrate, Americans represented conspicuously the main forces of occupation in those days. With its overwhelming military presence, America stood for power in occupied Japan.

In *The Sound of the Mountain,* American power connotes more than sheer military might. The United States appeared to the war-devastated Japanese as a nation of affluence. The American luxuries include the "German pointer" which an American family takes for a walk in a park in central Tokyo and the latest fashion for which Shuichi's mistress, who is a dressmaker, reads "all sorts of American magazines." It is also the technologically advanced country to which the excavated ancient lotus seeds are sent to measure their age with "[c]arbon radiation tests." And wonderful things can happen there. A newspaper article, for example, reports that, thanks to the doctor's immediate grafting treatment, an accident-torn ear was successfully "stuck . . . back on" the original body in Buffalo, New York. Especially important are the two episodes of the lotus seeds and the torn ear, for they imply Shingo's concerns with the brevity and potential resuscitative power of human life. In a word, the United States is viewed as a place of economic, intellectual and miraculous power, not merely as an immense military warehouse. People's interest in such a land is also indicated by other passing references. Another newspaper article, which Shingo mentions to his new secretary, tells of a questionnaire distributed to one thousand secretaries, which "some sociologists at Harvard University and Boston University" had designed in order to learn what pleases them most. When Fusako utters Popeye's name in an emotion-fraught dinner at the beginning of chapter eleven ("A Garden in the Capital"), even her old mother perfectly understands this popular American symbol of diet-empowered masculinity.

On the other hand, the military aspect of American power is often tinged with sexual vigor. Shingo perceives this mixed symbolism in a foreign soldier whom he finds sitting in front of him one day on a train. The soldier appears to be about Shingo's age, but he possesses an energetic body which is far bigger than the meager counterpart of the ordinary Japanese. He has "a fierce countenance," a thick neck, and heavy arms which remind Shingo of "a shaggy red bear." Above all, he is accompanied by a Japanese boy who is apparently a male prostitute. Except for the hint of homosexuality, this kind of sight which betrays the powerful sexuality of the occupying troops constitutes a part of Shingo's everyday experience. In the first chapter ("The Sound of the Mountain"), he furtively observes two female prostitutes with "good figures" in a fish shop. One of these girls considers lobsters for her foreign customer, whom she calls her "boy friend." In the park of central Tokyo, Shingo notices not only the American couple with a German pointer but also a "white soldier" (my translation) who is "joking with a prostitute."

Similar instances are not too difficult to find in Kawabata's other novels written around the Occupation. In *Hamachidori* [*Beach Plovers*], which is an unfinished sequence to *Thousand Cranes,* the newly married protagonist watches together with his bride, from their honeymoon hotel, several American warships "loaded with the thirst of sexual desires" (my translation), coming to a town of hot springs for one night of pleasure. This makes an ironical contrast to the new husband who, with his mind disturbed by previous affairs, cannot consummate his marriage. Later at night, he watches the warships exhibit their deadly force in naval firing practice off the shore. In this case, the symbolism of male sexuality is obvious because of the thundering cannons. On the other hand, the General Headquarters offer the important background of a secret date that opens the story *Maihime* [*The Dancer*]. The austere GHQ building, at the top of which the U.S. and U.N. flags are visible in the daytime, and red lights flicker in the evening, seems to be another instance of the same symbolism. In *Kawa no Aru Shitamachi no Hanashi* [*A Story of a Town with a River*], the militarism of masculinity takes the form of direct action. A beautiful, timid girl, who has become a waitress at a night club near an American base, is half jokingly abducted by a few GIs on her way back home, and her young admirer, who barely rescues her, receives a fatal wound during the incident.

What counts here is that, in Shingo's mind as well as Kawabata's, American military power connotes sexual vitality; this throws light on the hidden nature of the dream about the beard. Given the common psychoanalytic reading of a head with a full-grown beard as a phallic symbol, it follows that this monumental beard is a symbol of male sexuality. Important here is the shifted attribution of American nationality from the son's comb to the dream content, the emergence of which Shingo unreflectively ascribes to his newly acquired Japanese electric razor. Of course, the more absurd and unrealistic the dream, the better are the chances of censorship and disfigurement of the latent desire; this is probably one reason why a foreign land far away, picked at random from recent experience, is chosen as the location of the dream. However, there seem to be other, subtle workings of the mind which explain the transference of American nationality from the comb.

Perhaps in Shingo's unconscious, his pains of aging overlap with those of his contemporary, war-traumatized Japan, and he wishes to get away from them. In the park where Shingo has a date-like walk with Kikuko, the "vast green expanse" fashioned with a Western "vista" makes him feel "free" as if they were "getting out of Japan." According to Hyodo Masanosuke, in his own life Kawabata was heavily despondent over the defeat of Japan until the writing of *The Sound of the Mountain.* As Kawasaki points out, Shuichi's extramarital affair, which causes Shingo nothing but distress, is "a part of the 'national' desolation." At the same time, as a Japanese of the old moralistic school, he is at a loss with this new "freedom of feelings" which "inevitably leads to sexual association," in Catherine Merken's words. The exotic, Edenic situation, amidst which he unexpectedly finds himself, "did not rest well with him," and he feels it "very odd" to walk with his daughter-in-law among "liberated" young people, including some Americans.

Probably more relevant is the preoccupation with hair, which forms one of the serious concerns of Shingo and his friends in terms of their waning life power, and which is acutely illustrated in Kitamoto's case. Cleaning the electric razor which he calls "a finely tooled product of modern civilization," Shingo finds "only white hairs" falling on his knees to his silent dismay. By extracting an intangible attribute from Shuichi's comb, Shingo's dreaming ego wishes to be as young as his son, as it had once happened in the sexually overt dream of the islands.

At the same time, the extracted American nationality is associated with the beard through the electric razor, because this small device that mechanically removes the beard is functionally similar to the American militarism that eliminates its enemy with such machines as bombers and men-of-war. By contrast, in its unproductive, "peaceful" use, the comb more fittingly stands for Japan that had little industrial capability immediately after World War II and proclaimed in its new constitution the abandonment of war as a means of solving international disputes. What takes place covertly in Shingo's dream is thus a shift from metonymy to metaphor, that is, from nationality linked to original places of production to a nationality of qualitative attributes.

Furthermore, the dislocated nationality has a more immediate political implication in the dream. The bearded man cannot "of his own free will" change his beard, since it is now designated a national monument by the American government. Tsuruta stresses the significance of the governmental authority in this prohibition. But why does the government in the dream have to be American? In fact, this kind of forcibly imposed restriction was commonplace in occupied Japan. For instance, on January 31, 1947, an impending general strike was miscarried not because of the opposition of the Japanese government but through an order from the GHQ. The dream-work cunningly puts it so that the man must let the beard grow with the authority of none other than the American government.

Significantly, Kikuko, who provided the day's residues of the comb and the electric razor, is completely deleted from the manifest dream, a fact that makes us suspect her as the real cause of this dream in Shingo's latent desire. In this sense, the beard in the dream stands for the wished-for vitality of a man's exuberant life.

Earlier in the novel, Shingo was similarly impressed by another phallic symbol, i.e., the huge sunflower heads with their stamens systematically arranged. In his persistent, but stifled desire for revitalization, the beard of the dream is associated with this botanic image in four ways. First, they are both symbols of male sexuality in a Freudian sense. Second, in terms of head imagery, the sunflowers, which made Shingo think of "heads of famous people," at least partially have given rise to the dream of a celebrated head with a monumental beard. Third, the massive, but calm "strength" that Shingo felt in the flowers is analogous to several kinds of power, especially sexual and miraculous ones, statically inherent in the very American nationality of the cumbersome beard. Fourth, the repeated orderliness of "quietly systematic" stamens and various whiskers "each in its proper place" reveals Shingo's incessant longing for a brain of unclouded intellect. This last point is compatible with his notion of a technologically advanced America. In addition, as if to reinforce the symbolic connection between beard and plants, the quiet manner he brushes away his "very short white hairs" cut off with the electric razor reminds us of how he did not like to see the fallen sunflowers.

In this dream, Shingo seeks the vitality of life—especially sexual life, which he always feels is being lost—in the shape of a wonderful but impossible beard. This is verified at the end of the dream, when "[l]ooking at the wondrous assortment of colors in the beard, Shingo half felt that it was his own;" and further, "[s]omehow he felt the man's pride and confusion as his own." It follows that the dream about the beard is a reversal of the fear of death his old age brings about. Only after he regains confidence in his sexual power in this dream, is his dreaming ego directed to the unconsciously desired physical relationship with his daughter-in-law in the next dream as a possible antidote to that fear.

With the pictorial, regressive nature of dreams in mind, the missing conjunction between two successive dreams ought to be supplemented again. In the earlier set of two dreams, the hidden conjunction was "because," since the fact of Shingo's crippled sexuality was first exposed and then he wished for a revitalized self. In the present case, the erased conjunction is "if," for something improbable first happens before the dreaming ego turns to the real object of its desire. "If" he became rejuvenated and acquired the sexual vigor symbolically inherent in the foreign beard, "if" such impossibilities came true, then, he would be able to enjoy the love of his daughter-in-law with secure confidence. But, because of the intervening superego, the second dream undergoes great changes and is made extremely insipid and unpleasant. Unlike the earlier cases in which he felt "a flicker of youth," he considers it to be "too dreary that no flicker of lust had come over him" this time, and he calls it the "ugliness of old age." His failure in the unconscious attempt at a revitalized life is obvious.

Having interpreted the second dream in a disturbing way, Shingo momentarily resists his own moral conscience:

What was wrong with loving Kikuko in a dream?

What was there to fear, to be ashamed of, in a dream? And indeed what would be wrong with secretly loving her in his waking hours? He tried this new way of thinking.

But a *haiku* by Buson came into his mind: "I try to forget this senile love; a chilly autumn shower." The gloom only grew denser.

Admittedly, he still keeps his emotional attachment to Kikuko after this night of two dreams, and his last two subsequent dreams contain some sexual elements. But it is only after this full recognition of his latent desire that Shingo comes out of the "filthy slough" of his psyche. Now that this libidinal problem is undisguisedly detected, he understands what it is and where it lies. With this realization, it is impossible for his moral conscience to let his smoldering, incestuous impulse run its course. He not only tries to detach himself from his daughter-in-law, but also makes more serious attempts to resolve family problems, especially the marriage troubles involving Kikuko, Shuichi, and his mistress.

Towards the end of the novel, when Shingo suggests that she live with Shuichi away from him and Yasuko, he feels "a certain danger" in Kikuko's wish rather to look after him if she gets divorced. Her words sound to him "like a first expression of ardor." Still, unlike upon the previous occasion when Kikuko made a similar confession from behind the Noh mask, he can consciously resist the undoubtedly imagined seduction and tell her, in Shuichi's words, that she should be "freer" from him. In the seventh dream, as Tsuruta notices, Shingo appears as a young army officer with a number of phallic symbols (a sword and three pistols) ("Jikan to Kukan"; "Yume no Kaishaku"). This time, it is not Kikuko but Yasuko's sister whom he visits after a perilous trip through the mountains. According to Tsuruta's interpretation, one of the two eggs, from which a small snake is hatched in the eighth dream, might stand for the procreative result of his intercourse with his disfigured daughter-in-law in the "evil dream" ("Jikan to Kukan"; "Yume no Kaishaku"). At the same time, however, this last dream no longer shows even implicitly a desire for sexual contact itself, a fact that suggests his mixed sentiments of lingering affection and growing restraint.

Thus, the pair of dreams on that rainy night force Shingo to directly face what has been covertly kept from conceptualization. As Hatori Tetsuya points out, once he is confronted with the real desire of his unconscious, he can no longer have dreams of the same sexual implications. This new self-awareness eventually makes him prepared to reject the terminative linearity of time, since his artificial means of resisting time have collapsed. He accepts instead, as Tsuruta argues, the unending cyclicity of time which includes death as a natural solution ("Jikan to Kukan"; *"Yama no Oto*

to Ishi no Tenshi"). In the last chapter, talking about the seasonal *topoi* in *haiku,* Shingo compares himself to an autumn trout. "Worn out, completely exhausted," these creatures descend to the sea after they "have laid their eggs" for the next cycle of life. Shingo thus reaches a final, relatively peaceful state of mind. The dream of the beard is particularly significant in the sense that, with its implicit symbolism, it provides the requisite condition for the liminal wish-fulfillment of Shingo's latent desire. And, through the ultimate failure of this desire, this dream helps him bring about his self-realization as a man of full maturity and responsibility.

Along with the coupling of the dreams, the dream of the extraordinary, foreign beard shows the protagonist's grave concern with life and death. It is also closely related to the reality of occupied Japan where the American military presence penetrated all the strata of society, even the psyche of an aging man. Far from being absurd or irrelevant, the dream of the beard thus proves to be an integral part of the novel. Originating in dispersed references to the social situation as well as in the protagonist's unsolved psychological problems, this particular dream gives more coherence to a work that critics tend to regard as loosely organized. Its fundamental problem is aging which brings about the fear of death symbolized by the rumbling sound of the mountain. Shingo's dream visions, including the beard and the pairing, are the attempts of his psychic being to resist and escape this fear. The Freudian model proves to be of pivotal importance in this analysis that shows at once Kawabata's great interest in Freudian concepts and his adroit use of psychoanalytic motifs in one of his major novels.

FURTHER READING

Criticism

Baird, James. "Contemporary Japanese Fiction." *Sewanee Review* 67, No. 3 (Summer 1959): 477-96.

> Discusses what Japanese fiction of the 1950s has in common with Western literature focusing on specific authors, including Yasunari Kawabata.

Donahue, Neil H. "Age, Beauty and Apocalypse." *Arcadia* (1993): 291-306.

> Discusses the Japanese dimension of Max Frisch's *Der Mensch erscheint in Holozän* by comparing it to Kawabata's *The Sound of the Mountain.*

Dunlop, Lane. "Three Thumbprint Novels from the Japanese of Yasunari Kawabata." *Prairie Schooner* 53, No. 1 (Spring 1979): 1-10.

> Translates three of Kawabata's short stories including, "The Grasshopper and the Bell Cricket," "The Silverberry Thief," and "The Young Lady of Suruga."

Jones, Richard. "Craters." *The Listener* 82, No. 2107 (14 August 1969): 223.

> Provides a favorable review of Kawabata's *House of the Sleeping Beauties.*

Jordan, Clive. "Sleeping and Waking." *New Statesman* 78, No. 2003 (1 August 1969): 153-54.

> Reviews Kawabata's *House of Sleeping Beauties* and discusses the Western approach to the stories.

Ueda, Makoto. "Kawabata Yasunari." *Modern Japanese*

Writers and the Nature of Literature, Stanford: Stanford University Press, 1976, pp. 173-218.

> Discusses the works of Yasunari Kawabata and his reviews of other novelists.

Watson, S. Harrison. "Ideological Transformation by Translation: *Izu no Odoriko. Comparative Literature Studies* 28, No. 3 (1991): 310-21.

> Analyzes two scenes from Kawabata's *Izu no Odoriko* that are missing from the Edward Seidensticker translation of the novel.

Additional coverage of Kawabata's life and career is contained in the following sources published by Gale Research: *Contemporary Authors,* **Vols. 33-36R, 93-96;** *Dictionary of Literary Biography,* **Vol. 180;** *DISCovering Authors Modules: Multicultural;* **and** *Short Story Criticism,* **Vol. 17.**

Colleen McCullough
1937-

Australian novelist.

The following entry presents an overview of McCullough's career through 1996. For further information on her life and works, see *CLC,* Volume 27.

INTRODUCTION

Colleen McCullough is best known as the author of *The Thorn Birds* (1977), a popular generational saga set in Australia that made publishing history as an international bestseller. Often regarded as an Australian version of Margaret Mitchell's *Gone with the Wind, The Thorn Birds* established McCullough as a celebrated author of mainstream fiction. Though she earned a reputation as a romance writer with this novel and *Tim* (1974), McCullough has produced a diverse body of fiction in several genres, notably the psychological novel *An Indecent Obsession* (1981), the dystopic fantasy *A Creed for the Third Millennium* (1985), and an ambitious series of historical novels set in ancient Rome beginning with *The First Man in Rome* (1990).

Biographical Information

A native Australian born in Wellington, New South Wales, McCullough spent most of her childhood in Sydney, where her family settled after a series of relocations in the Outback. As a child McCullough was an avid reader and took an early interest in literature and history; she also displayed an aptitude for science while in high school. Choosing science over the humanities for practical reasons, McCullough attended Holy Cross College and the University of Sydney intending to enter the medical profession, but an allergy to soap precluded a surgical career. Finding temporary employment as a teacher, librarian, bus driver, and journalist, McCullough eventually settled into work as a neurophysiology researcher in Sydney and London, and finally the Yale University School of Internal Medicine, where she remained from 1967 to 1976. While at Yale, McCullough wrote *Tim* and *The Thorn Birds* in the evening hours after work, both of which she sought to publish as a source of additional income. With the enormous success of *The Thorn Birds,* McCullough abandoned her scientific employment to devote her full attention to writing. She soon left the United States for the quiet isolation of Norfolk Island, an idyllic locale in the remote South Pacific. There she met Ric Robinson, a former house painter; they married in 1984. McCullough's sudden literary fame also prompted the production of a film version of *Tim* in 1981 and the popular miniseries adaptation of *The Thorn*

Birds which aired in 1983. Since McCullough's resettlement to Norfolk Island, she has produced additional best-selling novels, including *An Indecent Obsession, A Creed for the Third Millennium, The Ladies of Missalonghi* (1987), and the first four volumes of her "Masters of Rome" series—*The First Man in Rome, The Grass Crown* (1991), *Fortune's Favorites* (1993), and *Caesar's Women* (1996).

Major Works

McCullough's first novel, *Tim,* describes the romance and marriage of a wealthy, middle-aged woman and a much younger, mentally retarded man endowed with striking classical beauty. Their uncommon attachment blossoms as the woman teaches the man to read and function independently in the world. Through the realistic depiction of their tender relationship, McCullough conveys the profound power of love to bring meaning into solitary lives and to defy social expectations. McCullough also addresses the subject of mental retardation with unusual compassion and understanding. *The Thorn Birds* is a family saga that spans the Australian continent and three generations of Cleary descendants between 1915 and 1969. The central character is Meggie Cleary, whose frustrating lifelong love for a handsome Roman Catholic priest, Ralph de Bricassart, dominates the plot and underscores the theme of female suffering in the novel. Meggie's futile longing for Ralph is suggested by the title, which refers to a legendary bird that impales itself on a thorn and sings stoically as it dies. Meggie subsequently enters into an unhappy marriage to another man with whom she has a daughter, Justine. During a brief adulterous affair, Ralph fathers an illegitimate son with Meggie but remains devoted to his religious calling and resists commitment to her in favor of a promising career in the church hierarchy. The son, Dane, eventually enters the priesthood under the tutelage of Ralph, unaware that his teacher is also his father. The novel culminates with Dane's tragic drowning in Greece shortly after his ordination. In *An Indecent Obsession* McCullough combines themes from both *Tim* and *The Thorn Birds* to portray tension caused by the conflicting obligations of love and duty. The story involves a nurse, Sister Honour Langtry, who cares for a small group of men with physical and psychological ailments in a South Pacific hospital near the end of World War II. While focusing primarily on the psychological motivations of the characters, McCullough introduces elements of mystery with a suspicious suicide and increasingly complicated relationships among the men and Honour. *A Creed for the Third Millennium* is a novel of ideas that addresses contemporary social, political, and environmental issues. Set in the United States in the year 2032, McCullough describes a dystopic future world plagued by an impending ice age, frequent suicide, family size limitations, and the vast bureaucratization of society. The central character is Dr. Joshua Christian, a messianic figure selected by the Department of the Environment to inspire the American people with his message of hope. After leading a triumphant march on Washington, DC, Dr. Christian suffers an emotional breakdown and kills himself. McCullough returned to romance with *The Ladies of Missalonghi*, a modern variation of the Cinderella story involving a poor woman who convinces a mysterious stranger to marry her by feigning a terminal illness. As in earlier novels, McCullough describes love as a transformative force, though adds a more pronounced moral and ethical dimension. With *The First Man in Rome* McCullough initiated an expansive series of epic historical novels set in ancient Rome during the first century B.C. *The First Man in Rome*, along with *The Grass Crown, Fortune's Favorites,* and *Caesar's Women,* are the first four installments of McCullough's projected six-volume "Masters of Rome" series and recount in prodigious detail the political and personal intrigue behind the decline of the Roman Republic and the ascendancy of Julius Caesar. Each of these massive volumes includes a large cast of characters and complex plots supported by meticulous historical research.

Critical Reception

While *The Thorn Birds* remains McCullough's greatest popular achievement, critical assessment of the novel is uneven. Though most critics dismiss the work as piquant escapist literature at best, others examine the significance of underlying attitudes about sexuality and gender roles in the novel, especially patriarchal assumptions and the role of female suffering in terms of either feminist or anti-feminist perspectives. Quietly received upon publication and overshadowed by *The Thorn Birds, Tim* is regarded as a competent early literary effort. As with this novel, McCullough's fiction is typically faulted for its uninspired characterizations and contrived action. Subsequent experimentation with genres other than romance failed to duplicate the success of *The Thorn Birds*. Both *An Indecent Obsession* and *A Creed for the Third Millennium* produced modest sales and mixed reviews. *The Ladies of Missalonghi* is considered among her least effective novels and even opened McCullough to controversial charges of plagiarism. According to her detractors, the story is stolen from Lucy Maud Montgomery's *The Blue Castle,* an allegation that McCullough has denied. Since turning to historical fiction with the "Masters of Rome" series, McCullough has won favorable critical attention at the expense of a mass readership. Criticized by some reviewers for the overbearing detail and abundance of difficult Latin names in these novels, many praise the engrossing narrative and the impressive accuracy of McCullough's Roman history. A novelist with wide-ranging interests and remarkable storytelling ability, McCullough is highly regarded as a leading author of popular contemporary fiction.

PRINCIPAL WORKS

Tim (novel) 1974
The Thorn Birds (novel) 1977
An Indecent Obsession (novel) 1981
A Creed for the Third Millennium (novel) 1985
The Ladies of Missalonghi (novel) 1987
The First Man in Rome (novel) 1990
The Grass Crown (novel) 1991
Fortune's Favorites (novel) 1993
Caesar's Women (novel) 1996

CRITICISM

Walter Clemons (review date 25 April 1977)

SOURCE: "Bed of Thorns," in *Newsweek*, April 25, 1977, pp. 93, 96, 97.

[In the following review, Clemons provides a brief analysis

of The Thorn Birds *and commentary on the novel's popular appeal.*]

It has, as they say, everything: three generations of suffering (from 1915 to 1969); an indomitable cast of dozens, who move from rags to riches (money doesn't bring happiness); scene shifts from a bleak New Zealand farm to a huge sheep ranch in the Australian outback to the inner chambers of the Vatican; sexual frustration and brief-lived bliss (the latter duly paid for in grief); plus fire, flood, drought, myxomatosis and World War II. Since *The Thorn Birds* has already sold to paperback for a record $1.9 million, a reviewer can only make a fool of himself by getting all hot and red in the face and protesting that it's junk. Better get out of its way and, as it rolls by, try to explain its appeal.

The Thorn Birds offers big, simplified emotions, startling coincidences and thumping hammer blows of fate. It is an old-fashioned family saga, featuring decades of tribulation on studded with dire forebodings that more often than not come true. One look at a newborn baby and a mother can predict her future: "I think she's always going to belong to herself." An imperious old woman throws a party on her 72nd birthday, announces she will die that night, does so— and because she is evil, her body decomposes faster than any in the watchers' experience.

> **The Thorn Birds offers big, simplified emotions, startling coincidences and thumping hammer blows of fate. It is an old-fashioned family saga, featuring decades of tribulation on studded with dire forebodings that more often than not come true.**
> —*Walter Clemons*

The lives of the Cleary clan in this book may be tougher than yours or mine, but they are never afflicted with any humdrum waiting around for something awful to happen. The central character, Meggie, loves a breathtakingly handsome priest who is usually ringingly addressed by his full name— as in "You're the most beautiful man I've ever seen, Ralph de Bricassart." Meggie marries an unfeeling brute named Luke, who happens to look like Ralph, and gives birth to a daughter who grows up to become the toast of the London stage. Meggie also has a son by Father Ralph, who drops by to visit her on his way to becoming a cardinal, but her love-child is lost to her when he, in turn, decides to enter the priesthood. On hearing the news, "Meggie sat down. 'I think I've been struck by a retributory bolt of lighting.'"

They all talk like that. Colleen McCullough, a 39-year-old Australian, is described by her publisher as "exuberant but

extraordinarily disciplined." Her little-noticed first novel, *Tim,* we're told, "went through ten drafts in three months before it satisfied her," but *The Thorn Birds* took longer. When she gets up a full head of steam, McCullough can write tirades the likes of which can seldom have been heard on land or sea. Try this tongue-twister, for instance—Meggie on the subject of men: "You're all the same great big hairy moths bashing yourselves to pieces after a silly flame behind a glass so clear your eyes don't see it . . . You're nothing but a romantic, dreaming fool, Ralph de Bricassart! You have no more idea what life is all about than the moth I called you! No wonder you became a priest! You couldn't live with the ordinariness of life if you were an ordinary man any more than ordinary man Luke does!"

McCullough's title refers to her characters' penchant for impaling themselves on self-induced miseries. "Like the old Celtic legend of the bird with the thorn in its breast, singing its heart out and dying," Meggie lays it on the line to Ralph. "Don't you see? We create our own thorns, and never stop to count the cost. All we can do is suffer the pain, and tell ourselves it was well worth it." Company loves misery, and the publishers are probably justified in their gamble that readers by the millions will press *The Thorn Birds* to their bosoms.

Christopher Lehmann-Haupt (review date 2 May 1977)

SOURCE: "The Song Is Familiar," in *The New York Times,* May 2, 1977, p. 31.

[*In the following review, Lehmann-Haupt approves of* The Thorn Birds *as a good example of predictable escapist fiction.*]

Going over the notes I kept while reading *The Thorn Birds*—and there were many pages of them because an awful lot happens in Colleen McCullough's novel about 54 years in the life of an Australian sheep-farming family—I found that one entry I wanted to check read "Dane drowns— P. 485." This was curious, because when I actually turned to the cited page it turned out that Dane had not actually drowned until page 487. And when I consulted several other important events in the three-generation history of the Clearys—mostly these events are deaths, because the Clearys do a great deal of dying—I found the same pattern repeated. The page number 'cited' for the event would almost always precede the actual page on which the event occurred.

Now this apparent carelessness of mine doesn't mean that I was totally indifferent to what happens in *The Thorn Birds*. In fact I often cared considerably. Father Dane O'Neill's drowning in the sea off Crete, for example, is really quite upsetting, because Dane is young and attractive and has just fulfilled his ambition to be ordained a priest in the Roman Catholic Church. What's more, he is the love-child of the novel's heroine and hero, Meggie Cleary O'Neill and Cardinal Ralph Raoul de Bricassart, both appealing, vividly drawn characters whose frustrated love for each other supplies almost as much energy to **The Thorn Birds** as does Scarlett O'Hara's and Rhett Butler's romance to *Gone With the Wind*.

Women's Frustration

Furthermore, Dane's drowning is thematically significant, for it comments ironically on a central frustration of Miss McCullough's passionate women. This is that if their men are truly dedicated to an ideal such as service to the Lord, and they are perfect in their dedication, then they can no longer serve life, and by extension their women. Shortly before he dies, Father Dane asks God to "Plunge Thy spear into my breast, burying it there so deeply I am never able to withdraw it! Make me suffer. . . . For Thee I forsake all others, even my mother and my sister and the Cardinal."

In praying thus, Dane recalls the novel's Epigraph, which tells the legend of the bird that sings only after it has impaled itself upon the longest, sharpest spine of the thorn tree. A little while after his prayer, he goes swimming, feels a sharp pain in his chest and drowns. It is a nice point. And yet I could see it coming from several closely printed pages away. All Miss McCullough had to tell us was that Dane was alone and headed for the seashore, and I stopped to scribble in my notes, "Dane drowns—P. 485."

Is this predictability a defect of **The Thorn Birds?** After all, predictability is inevitable in good old-fashioned story-telling, and **The Thorn Birds,** all 280,000 words of it, is nothing if not good old-fashioned story-telling. It certainly isn't the originality of the prose we savor when the author can write of women who "work their fingers to the bone," parlor rugs that are "beaten within an inch of their lives," and one of Dane O'Neill's ancestors who was "flogged . . . to jellied pulp," to mention but a handful of phrases so clichéd that we began to think that Miss McCullough is up to something.

Nor is it the dialogue we relish, if Miss McCullough's heroine can deliver a set speech that goes as follows: "Just a man. You're all the same, great big hairy moths bashing yourselves to pieces after a silly flame behind a glass so clear your eyes don't see it. And if you do manage to blunder your way inside the glass to fly into the flame, you fall down burned and dead. While all the time out there in the cool night there's food, and love, and baby moths to get. But do you see it, do you want it? No! It's back after the flame

again, beating yourselves senseless until you burn yourselves dead!"

Wanted: Predictability

But we want predictability in our popular escape literature—and **The Thorn Birds** is nothing if not popular escape literature, to judge from the advance publicity it has been receiving, and the record price of almost $2 million it has received for its paperback rights. Well, yes, but there is predictability and predictability. There is the sort of predictability where you know what is going to happen, yet relish the anticipation of it so much that you purposely deny that you know what is going to happen. And there is the sort where you know what is going to happen, and it has happened so many times before that you pay only half your attention to it.

The Thorn Birds, I'm afraid, has happened before. Its theme and its form are familiar. Even its locale, the Outback of Australia's New South Wales, although topically novel is generically familiar. (And incidentally, Miss McCullough, while Australian born and the author of a previous novel, **Tim,** still retains that tiresome English habit of separating her lengthy nature descriptions from the substance of her plot.) That is why we always know what is going to happen in **The Thorn Birds** before it happens. And that is why I couldn't be bothered to wait for it to happen before noting it down.

Steven Kroll (review date 22 July 1977)

SOURCE: A review of *The Thorn Birds*, in *Commonweal*, July 22, 1977, pp. 473-5.

[*In the following review, Kroll commends McCullough's "touching" romantic world view and prose, but criticizes the excessive scope of* The Thorn Birds *and its monotonous passages.*]

By now almost everyone will have heard of **The Thorn Birds.** How Colleen McCullough wrote it at the rate of fifteen thousand words a night, once did thirty thousand in a sitting, finally produced a manuscript of a thousand pages weighing ten pounds. How the decision-makers at Harper & Row—the trade chief, the marketing director, the subsidiary rights director—took the manuscript home for the weekend and realized they had to go all out. How the Literary Guild snapped it up as their June selection and, in an incredible auction among paperback publishers, Avon Books paid a record-setting $1.9 million for the paperback reprint rights.

All of this is enough to send any aspiring writer straight to the typewriter. It's particularly interesting because the author is unknown—she's published one earlier novel, *Tim,* that didn't sell—and because both she and her book are Australian. Up until now, selling fiction about Australia in America has been like trying to sell chocolate cake for breakfast. There have been the Patrick Whites, the Thomas Keneallys, the Sumner Locke Elliotts, but even when they've been appreciated critically, the books have not begun to sell big. Now, with *The Thorn Birds* approaching major bestsellerdom, the worm has turned.

But what of this fat family saga, this tale of tribulation on a huge sheep station in the Australian outback between 1915 and 1969, this giant novel called *The Thorn Birds?* Does it really merit all this attention and money? Does it really measure up? The answer, unfortunately, is no.

Which is not to say that the book is a total failure. It has a romantic view of the world that is often quite touching. The prose has a fullness about it, and a density of detail, that sometimes overwhelms. There is the title metaphor of the thorn birds, of the bird that, from its first breath, searches for a thorn tree, impales itself upon the sharpest spine, and dying, "rises above its own agony to out-carol the lark and the nightingale. One superlative song, existence the price." Best of all there is the feeling for the land, and for the Australian landscape. When the Cleary family arrives from New Zealand, on their way to the sheep station Drogheda, this is what they see: "It was all brown and grey, even the trees! The winter wheat was already turned a fawnish silver by the glaring sun, miles upon miles of it rippling and bending in the wind, broken only by strands of thin, spindling, blue-leafed trees and dusty clumps of tired grey bushes. . . ."

But even the descriptions of the land tend to go on too long too often, and to break down into lists. And at Drogheda the endless Wet and Dry periods (one drought lasts almost ten years) become monotonous in the extreme.

Going on too long too often, becoming monotonous and slack, not creating dramatic peaks or valleys, these are the book's principal failings. When Frank, the eldest son, confronts the father who is not his, when Paddy, that father, dies in a fire on Drogheda, when Father Ralph de Bricassart breaks his vows and finally makes love to Meggie, the only Cleary daughter among many sons, there are only slight ripples in the surface of the narrative. And then there is all the information given, then repeated, then repeated again. Whatever the words may say, the tension is missing from them and from the action.

Perhaps it has something to do with Ms. McCullough's inability to recognize what might have been sharpened and what left out. Her overall structure is sound; it's the scenes within that suffer and produce the yawns. And then there is

the question of the material. Tara, after all, has more built-in drama than a two-story yellow sandhouse surrounded by gardens, dust, and flies. And the Civil War and the burning of Atlanta are going, quite naturally, to be more sensational than years of drought and a fire spreading over acres of bare land.

But not necessarily. Not if the characters are strong enough. In Meggie Cleary and Father Ralph de Bricassart, Colleen McCullough had the chance to create characters of real substance and she did not. Only the shadows of what might been are there.

When Paddy's mean-spirited older sister, Mary Carson, invites him to Drogheda to be her head stockman and eventual heir, Meggie is ten years old, with fascinating gray eyes and red-gold hair. Handsome, young, Father Ralph—in exile for insulting his bishop—is the district priest, and he falls in love with her the moment he sees her. All through Meggie's childhood their love continues to grow. When Mary Carson leaves her fortune and Drogheda to the Church to further Ralph's career and Paddy agrees to stay on as manager instead of owner and Ralph leaves the area to fuel his ambition, the love remains. When Meggie marries a stockman for his gall and moves to North Queensland to work as a household maid while her husband cuts sugar cane, Ralph must seek her out.

Of course the love is thwarted. Ralph will never abandon his ambition, never leave the Church—and will eventually become a cardinal. But at least there is a brief affair on Matlock Island, and Meggie comes away with the only part of Ralph she can ever hope to have: his child.

How extraordinary these two could have been. Ralph could have joined that group of distinguished fictional priests, from Father Zossima in *The Brothers Karamazov* through Father Urban in J. F. Powers' *Morte D'Urban,* but we learn virtually nothing about him beyond his endless frustration and his Norman and Irish ancestry. And Meggie's only real importance seems to lie in her ability to survive.

With all its scope and shifting scenery—from New Zealand and Australia to Rome and London—*The Thorn Birds* lacks any real dimension.

Kay Cassill (interview date March 1980)

SOURCE: "Confessions of a Chain Smoker," in *Writer's Digest,* March, 1980, p. 35.

[In the following interview, McCullough comments on her writing, the creation of The Thorn Birds, *and book critics.]*

She chain smokes Carleton cigarettes as she works at the typewriter, and when Colleen McCullough takes a break from writing—for a smoke—she speaks candidly about the agonies and ecstasies of writing, publishing, fame, fortune, and some precious little critics. Some thoughts from the smoke-filled room:

"I wouldn't let anyone else type my work. For one thing I'm a better typist than anybody I know—much more accurate and meticulous than any professional. Like Truman Capote said, 'When I type it I *know* it's right.' But then you have to deal with copy editors! My grammar and spelling are English, but both are better than a copy editor's. Still, they insist on changing everything. That's why some of the sentences in *Thorn Birds* lost their cadence. I didn't spot the copy editor's changes in time. There's a comma missing in the little introductory paragraph in *Thorn Birds*. That comma is *important.* As for spelling, there were two words I insisted not be changed to the American spelling. *Axe* with an *e* and *grey* with an *e* instead of *a.* I still maintain *grey* with an *e* is greyer. The copy editor changed a word in the scene where Frank is chopping wood. It's in the summer and he's chopping the winter wood. She changed it to winter. I said, 'Come *on,* you don't chop winter wood in the *winter!*'"

"If I were in the middle of a manuscript and lost it in a fire I'd just start over. Of course I'd be sorry but you can't cry over spilt milk. I'd just have to start over, that's all."

"Unfortunately, fiction is out of fashion with the critics at the moment. But it's fiction, not nonfiction, that lasts. It's the novels you give to your daughters and sons to read and they give to their daughters and sons. I don't have any children, so my books had better live forever. You put so much of yourself into a novel, you want everyone to go on reading it long after you're gone. You want a reader to put down the last book you'll ever write because you've died and say: 'Oh, I wish there were another. Oh, Gawd, why did she have to die? I can't *stand* it.'"

"When I was writing *Thorn Birds* I resented bitterly having to go to work at the medical school. I resented leaving the book. I think had I not had to leave it it would have been far better. Going to a job when you're writing means you have to keep shifting gears. I can do it, but I don't like it. I'm not the kind of writer who stops in mid-sentence or mid-paragraph so I can start right on again. I break off at a logical stopping point—a natural pause in the story."

"I tried journalism long ago and didn't like it *at all.* But I get along famously with journalists. Especially male journalists. There's quite a large Colleen McCullough fan club among them around the globe. Still, they make errors all the time. They make me bigger than life. I'm either Amazonian or Junoesque. I gave a speech in which I said that every morning of my life I wake up feeling as though I weighed 300 pounds and was 8 1/2 months pregnant. I was talking about creative energies. Naturally, the press picked it up. *People* magazine reported, 'Millionaire author Colleen McCullough boasts that she is 8 1/2 months pregnant.' They wouldn't apologize either. I'm not pregnant. I'm not a single parent."

"I've been treated well by most critics, but there are always a few bitchy ones. *The New York Times* reviewer didn't like *Thorn Birds,* as I recall. I think he was the one who said it was nice I'd made all this money because maybe I could catch the man I couldn't catch without it. Generally, I find critics rather anemic. I get more angry over what they do to somebody else's book or film than what they say about my own. I know how much time and effort goes into a book. Then this twit comes along and, to make himself look clever—twisting a phrase, punning on this and that—he's willing to tear a book apart. Some critics are just precious little people."

"I learned a lot about the marketing of books during the tours. I talked to everyone, from the printer to the marketing director to the subsidiary rights editor. If I were to advise anyone with a book coming out I'd say, 'Be willing to do publicity and learn how to.' I have a tendency to call a spade a bloody shovel. Audiences like that. And I'm happy. That pleases them, too. The other advice is 'Get an agent and don't begrudge your agent his 10%. It's worth every penny.'"

"I think I'm a born teacher as well as writer. I've always been able to get across to people. You must care enough to make them understand. I watch their faces when I'm talking to them. If there's a blank look they haven't got what you're talking about. You have to go back and repeat it. This is true in writing books. Some writers lose sight of the fact that you can't say something once and forget it. You've got to repeat it. Otherwise it goes in one ear, out the other. You have to keep hammering points home."

"Usually my first drafts are the shortest and the tenth the longest. Every so often I find I haven't explained something adequately. Occasionally I'll cut out some purple prose. On the whole I think over the years I've grown out of the purple prose. *Tim* had more of it than *Thorn Birds.* I think that's one of the reasons I don't like *Tim* as well."

Kay Cassill (essay date March 1980)

SOURCE: "The Thorned Words of Colleen McCullough," in *Writer's Digest,* March, 1980, pp. 32, 34, 36.

[*In the following essay, Cassill offers insight into McCullough's views on writing and the editorial process behind the publication of* The Thorn Birds.]

Even though Colleen McCullough has been writing since she was five, she didn't think about publishing her work until she was 32. "I always wrote to please myself," she says. "I was a little snobby about it—that way I could write entirely as I wished. To write for publication, I thought, was to prostitute myself."

She changed her mind at 32 when, working as a teacher at the Yale Medical School, she decided she'd wind up an old maid in a cold-water walk-up if she didn't change her ways. And changing her ways meant writing for publication—and eventually meant her bestseller, *The Thorn Birds*.

McCullough's scientific training as a neurophysiologist helped her approach commercial writing systematically: "I sat down with six girls who were working for me. They were very dissimilar types, and not especially avid readers. Yet, they were all mad about Eric Segal's *Love Story*. I thought it was bloody awful and couldn't see what girls so basically intelligent could love about it. I asked them what they wanted most out of a book. First, they liked the idea that *Love Story* was about ordinary people. They didn't want to read about what was going on in Hollywood and all that codswallow, and they wanted something with touches of humor. Yet they enjoyed books that made them cry. That was criterion number one. If you didn't cry the book wasn't worth reading. I said to myself, 'Yeah, that's true, that makes a lot of sense.' The first book I ever read as a child is something called *The Green Horse*. I was five and loved it. It made me cry. Think of *East Lynne, Ann of Green Gables, Little Women*. When Beth dies, *awhhhh!* So, I said, 'That's it, mate. No matter what else you do in a book, don't forget the buckets of tears. If you do, readers won't remember it from one day to the next.' So, every book I ever write will have heaps of buckets of tears."

McCullough—41, 5'10", big, smiling, in a flowing silk and linen designer dress that "only cost around a hundred dollars, though, and is a bloody nuisance, always pulling threads"—was born in a small country town in Australia's New South Wales. She grew up in Australia, and worked as a neurophysiologist there and in England before coming to the United States to work at the Yale school of internal medicine. She calls herself "a kitchen-sitter," and over a lunch of cold cuts she launches into five hours of straight-on, diluvial discourse, Irish humor, a wee speck of Australian chauvinism (despite her own disavowal of it), spontaneous throaty laughter, teasing and no-holds-barred expletives.

The effect is anodyne. She's as unencumbered by pretention as she is sure of herself, her many talents and the formula behind best-sellerdom.

Icky Wicket

Instead of tears, a sour February day has dumped buckets of slush on the Connecticut landscape as she talks. She admits she doesn't like either *The Thorn Birds* or her first novel, *Tim*, very much—despite their buckets of tears. Of the two, she likes *Tim* least. "It's an icky book." Still, if someone says she hasn't written great literature, just a bestseller, she laughs at them. "Only time tells. If it lasts, it's good literature. If it dies, it's just another book. Very often the books the critics like today are gone tomorrow."

The Thorn Birds hasn't yet died—and it's hardly just another book. Its original manuscript weighed ten pounds, and it has often been called the Australian *Gone With the Wind*. The book takes place mostly on an enormous sheep ranch in the outback from 1915 to 1969. It tells the woes of the Cleary family and especially those of Meggie Cleary, the heroine, who seems destined to heartbreak at every turn. Her brother she loves most leaves home and ends in prison. Her father and another brother die violent deaths. She loves a handsome priest, Ralph de Bricassart, who loves her but is married to the church. In desperation, Meggie eventually marries a man she doesn't love. She has a daughter, Justine, by him. But her constantly thwarted love for Father Ralph remains the reader's primary concern. Eventually she does manage to conceive the longed-for child—a son, Dane—by the priest. But he just reaches manhood, goes off to Rome to become a priest himself and tragically drowns. "My brother drowned off Crete exactly the way Dane did," McCullough explains. "That's how death with the young happens. You get a phone call and your whole world falls apart."

McCullough has been facing the public and the press almost continually since her second novel hit it big. "Avon Books bought *The Thorn Birds* for 1.9 million in February 1977. From the first of March, 1977 to the end of November, 1978, I've been back and forth all over the globe."

To the Tuna $50,000

She admits that such book tours are important to her phenomenal success, but they've left little time to manage other matters. So she has a business manager. And she's moved in with her friends, Maureen (Mo) and Eamonn Whyte and their two children. At first it was just a casual arrangement, a place to stay on weekends between speaking engagements. But they've hit it off so well she's now building a house for herself and the Whytes on 35 nearby acres. "I'm traveling so much I'd just have to find someone to stay in it anyway. This makes more sense."

McCullough's success can be attributed to tuna. "I'd been going the ethical route, sending the manuscript out unsolicited, unagented, waiting months for a printed rejection slip. The parcel would come back completely untouched. You could tell it hadn't even been unwrapped, let alone read. I decided I'd be an old lady before I published my first book. I knew I had to get an agent but couldn't since I hadn't published anything. I tried phoning to get one but it was no use. OK, I thought, I'll write one a letter. If I'm as good as I think I am—if I'm a *writer*—I should be able to persuade an agent to at least read my manuscript simply by writing one a persuasive letter."

"Still, I didn't know which one to send the letter to. Then, one day I was making a friend something special. She'd been on a diet for two years—eating nothing but tuna fish. It was her birthday and the manuscript had just come back for the third time. I decided to make her a cake. Out of tuna fish, of course. And I *hate* fish. I got a Jello mold in the shape of a fish. I stewed the tuna in white wine and some herbs and things. While it was stewing the smell of fish was *all* through the house. And the list of agents was on the table. I looked down and the name, Frieda Fishbein, popped up.

"I sat right down and wrote the world's most persuasive letter—five or six pages—and sent it off. Frieda wrote back saying, 'If the manuscript is half as entertaining as the letter, I'll read it.' I sent *Tim* to her and she loved it. But she wasn't very encouraging. 'After all, it's set in Australia and its hero is mentally retarded and its heroine is this frustrated old maid.' After one turndown, though, Harper & Row took it. It sold over 10,000 copies in hardcover, which was much better than 99 out of every 100 first novels sell. I made $50,000 from *Tim*. Then, of course, Harper & Row had the option on the next one, which was *The Thorn Birds*.

"I had *The Thorn Birds* written in my head before *Tim*," she says. "But I knew no one would publish such a long book as a first novel. So I wrote *Tim*."

Both books were written while she was still living in a rambling, ordinary apartment in New Haven. In the Whyte's unprepossessing dark brown split-level ranch in the Connecticut woods she has an L-shaped bed-sitting-workroom on the lower level. She may work 16 hours at a stretch, then sleep for a while, depending on how she feels. She keeps an internal schedule of her own now that she no longer must teach for a living. "I can work anywhere, I don't need anything special around me," she says. "Except perhaps my plants, 'Johann,' 'Sebastian' and 'clinging Ernie,' and a little supermarket music."

The 40-Book Work Week

She has numerous typewriters. The electrics for letter writing are named "Prince," "Rex" and "Spot." "Rover," an old manual, is kept just for novels. "He's getting old, so I don't use him for the menial stuff anymore," jokes McCullough. "When his keys stick and he gets balky, I threaten him with a brand new IBM electric and he straightens right up."

She doesn't write every day. "And I don't find writing agonizing. I don't believe the average writer who complains that every word comes out like a drop of blood. If it were that bad he wouldn't be doing it." She believes "if you're a novelist you'll never be a great short story writer because the two disciplines are so different." She attributes her ability to write a "page-turner" to a life of reading: "I used to read 40 books a week. *Four-oh.* I've slacked off lately, though." And to her penchant for sitting around the kitchen table and telling stories: "All the members of my family were highly articulate and great readers. I think there are two kinds of writers: those who write because they can't talk and those who write because they talk so much nobody listens to them. I belong to the second group. And it's super. At Yale when I started to talk they'd all groan, 'Oh, Gawd, there she goes again.'"

McCullough claims her medical background came in handy when she turned to writing novels. "Being a trained scientist, one is used to research. I usually know where I'll find my sources. And I do all my own research. I don't believe in employing staff to do it for me." One useful source is her memory, though she sometimes doesn't tap recent memories. For example, she has to get away from a place for about ten years before she is able to write about it. "Material I've used in the first two books was 20 years old or more," she says.

A careful observer, she claims ideas, characters, images and dialogue have a way of "imprinting themselves" on her brain. "I stash them away and don't even know I've remembered them until suddenly they just pop out when I'm writing. One of my English friends said that I was one of the few people she knew who could build a bridge between my subconscious and my conscious thoughts, just trot across and carry back all sorts of goodies.

"I don't consciously do it. I'm not the sort of person who thinks a lot about myself or why I do things. I have a feeling if you think too much about what you're going to do you're never going to do it. You're either a thinker or a doer. I'm a doer from way back. I just sit down at the typewriter and trot across that bridge."

The bridge was used extensively in creating characterizations—Tim, for example: "I've had patients like him for years. The British old maid? I worked with so many of them! Every ward in every hospital in the British Emm-pah is headed by an old maid like Mary Horton—don't laugh—who takes off all her clothes to go to the bathroom. The people

Tim worked for were like people in the building trade who were my father's colleagues."

An early scene in this first novel—a brief love story set in the working-class of Sydney—describes a disgusting joke the workmen play on the unfortunate Tim. "But they're just the kind of people who'd do such a thing. In fact, that scene about the turd sandwich came straight out of real life. People ask, 'Oh, why did you put *that* in the book?' For one thing, it's a saccharine-sweet book. That's probably the only scene that jars. It was a true and shocking way to show Tim's mentality more effectively than any other. It's close to the beginning of the book because it wouldn't have had any impact later on. Once you have established the character and are comfortable with Tim, it wouldn't have worked. It had to come before he was involved with Mary, with this gentler kind of relationship."

Horror Story

She wasn't afraid the scene might turn readers off. "It *didn't.* But I think one has an instinct or one hasn't, knowing how a scene like that will affect readers. I rely on instinct and my editor is far too smart to gainsay it. Sometimes she tests me. She'll say, 'I don't like so-and-so.' By my reaction she'll know how important that scene is in my thinking about a book. If it's something I'm not going to change or even think twice about, she sees the reaction on my face immediately and she'll back-pedal. If it's something I've had doubts about myself, she'll see that, too, and then she'll push.

"I was so exhausted after writing **The Thorn Birds**. I thought when I finished the second full draft, 'I'm not going to do eight more drafts of this bloody, creepy book just to have my editor say *no*.' I sent it to her in all its horrors, to see if the publishers would be interested. If *yes,* then I'd go ahead with more drafts. It took her five months before she replied, during which time I wrote two more drafts anyway because I'd got over the exhaustion. When she finally broke her silence I talked with her. She had suggestions. A lot of what she said made sense. But it also meant I had to write a lot that I hadn't written before. She talked me into changing the last part of *Thorn Birds*. I didn't like Justine, wasn't interested in her in the least. She said she didn't think in the early draft the character of Justine worked, because Justine was very selfish and hard-boiled. She felt Justine wasn't strong enough to carry the last of the book as much as she had to and suggested I soften her up. I went home and thought about it. If I softened her she'd become a different person. What I wanted was someone who was a complete foil for her brother, Dane, and I wanted three generations of women who were entirely different from each other. The only kind of softening I could conceive was to give her a man. In a way, the man I invented, Reiner Moerling Hartheim, was, perhaps, the man I always wished I'd met but never did. He had to

be a German because he had to be prepared to wait ten years for a woman. The Germans are the only nationality I know with that kind of romanticism and hard-headedness. They are tremendously romantic, very disciplined and patient. After I wrote it I met four different Germans whose life histories were almost like Hartheim's. When I was in Germany the Germans said, 'Who is it? Who is it?' It turned out it could have been Helmut Schmidt, the German chancellor. It could have been Willy Brandt. And a couple of others. I didn't know any of them at the time.

"I put Reiner in and wrote two drafts, then sent it to my editor. She loved it. But still I had contented Justine with a kiss. My editor said, 'Reiner is just great, but the last third of the book needs a damn good love scene.' *That* was hard to do. I find it very difficult to write love scenes anyway. It's one thing to write them red-hot, you know, but another to go back cold-bloodedly with two characters you're fed up with anyway and put them into bed and make it work.

"Love scenes *are* the most difficult part of writing. They drive me batty. Those in most books are so bad. You know, the Harold Robbins 'he stuck it in her' type. They're just untrue. Sex is a monotonous, repetitive, nonverbal activity. There is a problem translating that into words. The interesting thing about sex scenes are the moods. The emotion involved is very hard to duplicate in print. I put a love scene through about 60 drafts. It will take me weeks and weeks to write. It's a mistake to make such scenes physically explicit. If you do, you encounter the reader's sexual preferences. They may not be your own or the character's own. It's wise to steer clear of that—which means you're going to dwell on the emotional content. Still, it has to be highly erotic or you'll lose your reader.

"I have written as many as 30 or more pages of a novel in a night. But, when I come to a love scene, I slow down. All this talk about my writing **Tim** in three months is codswallow. I did the first draft of *Thorn Birds* in 30 days. The first two drafts in under six weeks. But then I did eight more drafts! That's what journalists always fail to mention. They make it sound as if I whiz along and am perfectly satisfied with the first draft and just send it off to the publisher. That's just not the case.

"The first thing out of the typewriter is not perfect by any means. A book as long as *Thorn Birds* takes a lot of revising. It's not that everything that was in the first draft isn't still there. But it's rearranged, mostly expanded."

Mud- and Muck-Raking

McCullough has been criticized for the love affair in *Thorn Birds* between a Catholic priest and the heroine. "Actually, Ralph was supposed to be a minor character. Yet, when I was planning it in my head I was aware I didn't have a dominant male lead. The minute the priest walked into the book I said, 'Ah ha, this is it. This is the male character I've lacked!' But I had to keep him in the story and, logically, he didn't belong in it. The only way I could do it was to involve him emotionally with Meggie, the only woman available. It worked beautifully because again it made more interesting reading to have a love that couldn't be fulfilled. It keeps the reader going. Are they going to get together or aren't they? The reader has to want something to happen. If he doesn't want it badly enough, then you haven't caught him."

McCullough likes to tackle, big, spectacular, dramatic stories. If she were to choose another's work to have written, she thinks it might be T.S. Eliot's *The Waste Land* or William Faulkner's *As I Lay Dying*. "It's great how they drag this poor old woman's body through the mud and muck all those miles just to bury her where she wanted to be buried. Maybe that's it. Women are tremendously attracted to the life-birth-death cycle in literature."

As if summing up her work—and her self—she adds: "I always write books with peculiar themes. I don't like writing about boy meets girl, boy loses girl, boy gets girl." And she means it. "If an editor had seen *Thorn Birds* in manuscript and 'just *loved* it,' but suggested it would make a better book if I cut it to a nice 300-page love story, I'd have simply said, 'Get stuffed, mate.'"

Kirsten Grimstad (review date 25 October 1981)

SOURCE: "A Microuniverse in a Mental Ward," in *Los Angeles Times Book Review*, October 25, 1981, pp. 12-3.

[*In the following review, Grimstad provides a brief plot summary of* An Indecent Obsession *and comments that the novel lacks complexity.*]

In her third novel, the author of the large-canvas epic *The Thorn Birds* trades in her telescope for a microscope, to peer into the self-contained microuniverse of the mental ward of an Australian military hospital, located on an unnamed Pacific island. World War II is just drawing to a close. Patients and staff await their imminent discharge—the rupture of their artificial world—with apprehension.

The ingredients in the Ward X mix include blind Matt, diagnosed as hysteric, obsessed with fear of facing his wife with his disability; Benedict, whose dark broodings hint of psychosis; Nuggett, a hypochondriac fussing over imagined ailments and yearning for his mum to take care of him; Neil, the officer in the group, whose belief that his error had cost

the lives of men under his command precipitated the breakdown from which he is now on the rebound; and Luce, the bad boy of the lot, who gets his kicks out of setting people against each other. Luce is mad because his mother had to take in laundry when he was a boy. The snubs he endured because of this left their mark. Ever since that time, Luce has been out to even the score by sexually humiliating and exploiting victims of both sexes. Naturally, Luce is equipped with the physical endowments to achieve his ends. Where once they scorned him, now they desire him.

The patients of Ward X, all variously diminished or even infantalized by their disorders, share devotion to their dutiful and devoted Nurse Honour Langtry, a veteran of six years of service. Nurse Langtry is the center of their universe, keeping the men in line in her lovingly prim and starchy way. For them she is "beacon, hearth, madonna, rock, succor." For Matt she represents the bond with home; for Benedict, female goodness and purity; for Nugget she substitutes as a caretaker-mum; Neil desires her strength and hopes to have it by marrying her; for Luce she is the object of vindictive desire. In other words a good selection of the trite stereotypes of male-female relations is represented on Ward X.

The story begins in an unsettling calm, soon disrupted by the arrival of a new patient, Michael Wilson; in contrast to the others, he seems emotionally intact. Michael is physically attractive and has the demeanor of a kindly and helpful he-man, a protector of the weak. Suddenly Nurse Langtry's long-dormant passions are ignited, presumably by Michael's Eagle Scout ways. When Nurse Langtry, the archetypal female provider, ever so subtly shifts her role by experiencing her own vulnerability and longing, the others feel abandoned and the neat little world explodes with the force of primitive passion. Sexual jealousy and domination turn to murder and disfigurement.

> **Plot and characters serve as mere vehicles for a stunning profusion of empty platitudes about the conflict between love and duty, the responsibilities borne by those who are strong, woman's role as the nurturer of men, the dimensions of male loyalty and friendship, and so on.**
> —*Kirsten Grimstad*

Poor Nurse Langtry is forced to face that ultimate female choice between love and career, vulnerability and strength. That these seeming opposites might in fact be able to coexist is never considered. She wants to choose Michael ("Keeping your home, having your babies"), but Michael sees it differently: "You are a complete person. You don't need help. And not needing my help, I know you can get along without me." It's just like the cliche says: The woman with strength loses the man. The strong men (Michael and Neil) embrace their responsibility to the weak men (Matt and Benedict) while Nurse Langtry is left to embrace devotion to duty.

Life as it's presented here is devoid of genuine emotional center or grounding. Plot and characters serve as mere vehicles for a stunning profusion of empty platitudes about the conflict between love and duty, the responsibilities borne by those who are strong, woman's role as the nurturer of men, the dimensions of male loyalty and friendship, and so on. No real complexity threatens to complicate this once-over-lightly world. Even in the most dramatic moments, such as when Michael renounces the love of Langtry, the characters are posing, acting out an afternoon soap-opera fantasy of what life is supposed to be like.

I kept hoping for some literary wink of the eye, cluing me in that the deadly earnestness of this novel was really just parody. I never found that satisfaction.

Christopher Lehmann-Haupt (review date 29 October 1981)

SOURCE: "Books of the Times," in *The New York Times,* October 29, 1981, p. C24.

[*In the following review, Lehmann-Haupt views* An Indecent Obsession *as an improvement over* The Thorn Birds *but asserts that the novel lacks depth.*]

Michael is the unknown quantity. Michael seems well enough—altogether sane, in fact. But what is he doing here in Ward X, this isolated part of the hospital, set aside for "troppos," (for tropicals) or soldiers gone round the bend from jungle warfare? According to his medical papers, which Luce and Sister Langtry have read, Michael may be homosexual. What is known, and the reason that Michael is here in Ward X, is that he tried to kill a man in his unit who made some sort of pass at him. Tried to choke him to death and, according to a brief dip we take into Michael's point of view, rather enjoyed it.

So what will happen when Luce, a psychopathic seducer, gets around to pushing Michael beyond the limit of his control? Will Michael go berserk and kill Luce, or will it bring out the "shirt-lifting poofter" that Luce believes Michael to be? How will this affect the other Australian soldiers in Ward X? Will it perhaps cure Matt's hysterical blindness? What will it do to Sister Honour Langtry, Ward X's nurse, who appears to be in love with Michael? Will it reinforce her "indecent obsession," whatever that may be? We turn the pages.

Emotional Steam

I do not mean to make light of Colleen McCullough's already best-selling successor to her gigantically successful *The Thorn Birds*. Michael's little problem happens to be very deftly worked into this drama about a military mental ward on a tropical Indo-Pacific island at the end of World War II. Miss McCullough is a natural storyteller, more than merely clever at getting up a head of emotional steam.

> **If Miss McCullough expects to be taken seriously as a novelist—and, to judge from the improvement of this book over *The Thorn Birds*, there's no reason why she shouldn't be—she's going to have to write just a little less slickly.**
> **—*Christopher Lehmann-Haupt***

Her characters—Michael Wilson, the mysterious new boy; blind Matt Sawyer, hypochondriacal Nugget Jones, satyric Luke Daggett, guilty Benedict Maynard and the ward leader, Neil Parkinson, who is in love with Sister Langtry—are so immediately present in these pages that one can see them played by those wonderful troupes of English actors who appeared in such military films as "Tunes of Glory" and "Bridge on the River Kwai." Some of their scenes, like the one in which Luce Daggett tries to talk Sister Langtry into sleeping with him—"Sweetie, I'm *anything*. Anything you like to name! Young, old, male, female—it's all meat to me." "Try me. I'm the best there is."—leaves one's pulse racing a little faster.

And because Miss McCullough paints in very vivid colors—"A great black thunderhead swimming in bruised light sat down on the tops of the coconut palms, stiffening and gilding them to the panoply of Balinese dancers. The air glittered and moved with a languid drifting of dust motes, so that it seemed a world sunk to the bottom of a sun-struck sea."—no reader can avoid visualizing her tropical island.

But if Miss McCullough expects to be taken seriously as a novelist—and, to judge from the improvement of this book over *The Thorn Birds,* there's no reason why she shouldn't be—she's going to have to write just a little less slickly. Her characters' psychological tics are plausible enough, but somehow her people remain two-dimensional. They remind one of those novelty barometers from which a frowning boy emerges when the forecast is rainy and a smiling girl when the outlook is fair. There's nothing else to them but a wooden frame.

Then, too, one has to wonder why, if the omniscient narrator can arbitrarily jump into any character's thoughts at any given moment, she withholds for so long what Michael remembers about the incident that put him in Ward X, or what actually happened to Luce Daggett down in the bathhouse? The answer, of course, is that if the narrator didn't pick the right moments to feed us this information, there wouldn't be any tension or surprise to the story. But since surprise and tension are the only criteria that guide what the narrator may do, we soon begin to feel manipulated by the story. It's almost as if our tears were being jerked.

Medical Soap Opera

Finally, though Miss McCullough tries to give her title a variety of meanings—indeed, every major character in the book could be said to be indecently obsessed to one degree or another—it is all too predictable that the obsession that will finally prevail is Sister Langtry's particular commitment. As the last paragraph of the novel puts it: "Nurse Langtry began to walk again, briskly and with out any fear, understanding herself at last. And understanding that duty, the most indecent of all obsessions, was only another name for love." Gee.

It's a line like this that makes one want to say that *An Indecent Obsession* is merely a gilded version of what I believe teen-age readers used to refer to as a nurse book. It isn't really. But far too often, its faults reduce it to medical soap opera.

John Sutherland (essay date 1981)

SOURCE: "Women's Fiction I: *The Thorn Birds*," in *Bestsellers: Popular Fiction of the 1970s*, Routledge & Kegan Paul, 1981, pp. 74-81.

[*In the following essay, Sutherland discusses the publishing history of* The Thorn Birds *and the novel's great popular appeal.*]

In the *New York Times Book Review*'s survey of the decade's top ten sellers there are only two works by women. One of the great realizations by the book trade in the 1970s, however, was that the woman reader accounted for much more than a fifth of the market for fiction. In fact, surveys—taken to heart by the book trade—revealed that women consumed around 60 per cent of all novels sold. It was a mark of this realization in 1979 when a work by Judith Krantz earned the highest ever advance sale for paperback rights to a novel ($3.2 m.). If the 1970s demonstrated anything to the publishing industry, it was that women's fiction was not restricted to genre products, but could have its 'blockbusters'. The following two chapters deal with the top-selling novel by a woman (*The Thorn Birds*), the top-selling woman novelist (Erica Jong), and the top-selling line of women's novel ('sweet and savages').

> *The Thorn Birds* has sold more copies than any other novel of the past ten years, and rights have been sold all over the world for more money than publishers have ever paid for a book before.
>
> (Futura blurb)

> The pokiest pig ever sold in the Australian sucker market.
>
> (Max Harris, in *The Australian*)

The Thorn Birds was indisputably 'the number one international bestseller' of 1977-9; according to its publishers it was also 'the publishing legend of the decade.' In fact, well before publication *The Thorn Birds* was legendary. Of the seven who started, Bantam and Avon 'slugged it out like gladiators' for two days at the paperback auction, to acquire rights from Harper & Row. The final price Avon paid, $1.9 m., topped Bantam's $1.85 m. for *Ragtime* in 1975 and stood as a record until the $2.2 m. given for Puzo's *Fools Die* in 1978. British hard and paperback rights were acquired by Futura for $266,000; German rights brought in $220,000; and together with the sale of Australasian rights *The Thorn Birds* drew in some $650,000 in overseas (meaning, here, outside-America) earnings. McCullough's agent held onto the film rights until a little after publication, turning down a *Rich Man, Poor Man* style TV mini-series, parting finally with the novel to Warner Brothers in September 1977 for an undisclosed sum, but one which added considerably to the overnight millionairess's investment fund.

The Thorn Birds was a presold winner. Harper & Row put $100,000 into their launch campaign in April 1977 achieving what they claimed (probably correctly) was 'the biggest publicity promotion blitz of the year.' Among other things, 2,000 advance-reading copies were circulated through the American book trade. Three weeks before official publication day there were 225,000 hardback copies in print and some booksellers were already reporting it top of their list. Such was pre-publication excitement that it reached the #9 position in the official lists a week before anyone in America could legitimately buy the novel and it made the #1 spot on 6 June. By August, 365,500 copies had been printed. As a hardback it remained in the American charts for a year. As a paperback it was, by 1979, well on the way to becoming one of the very few 10 m. sellers of the decade.

As the *Guardian* observed, there was something of a 'publishing mystery' in this landslide success. Before *The Thorn Birds* McCullough was a virtually unknown writer—and an Australian at that—with only one obscure book to her credit. (*Tim*, 'a warm Australian romance,' chronicles the love between a middle aged spinster and a mentally retarded—but physically magnificent—young man.) Why, then, did Harper & Row, Avon and Futura go overboard, so early and so perceptively, for *The Thorn Birds?*

One reason was the new sense of global market which had developed in the American book trade following the abolition of the Traditional Market Agreement in 1976. This had opened the previously protected 'Empire' markets to America—and Australia, with its world's highest *per capita* book consumption—was now very much in the forefront of American publishers' minds. Significantly, on the publication of *The Thorn Birds* McCullough undertook three consecutive promotion tours—in the US, to the UK and to Australia.

> Like *Centennial . . .* and *Roots . . . The Thorn Birds* is a panoramic saga of national emergence, narrated in terms of a series of representative individual lives.
> —*John Sutherland*

For their part, Avon may have been induced to go over the odds by their proven ability to pick winners from the slush pile. They had done so with Rosemary Rogers and Kathleen Woodiwiss—probably the most valuable finds any paperback publisher made in the 1970s. And, by their 'open door policy,' Avon, a paperback house, discovered them first, they did not inherit them from a hardback house. Although McCullough was not entirely unknown, and Harper & Row could claim to have recognized her potential first, Avon had by the mid-1970s a millions-strong, brand-loyal women's readership who trusted the firm to come up with steamy romances. And *The Thorn Birds* with its three heroines was clearly a book which would appeal to the women's market.

One may surmise that Harper & Row were less attracted by any one feature of *The Thorn Birds* manuscript than by its nice mix of selling points, in terms of what was currently dominating the charts. Two of the very biggest novels of the mid-1970s were *Centennial* and *Trinity*. Uris's novel made over seventy appearances on the *Publishers Weekly* list and gave him his first top-spot since *Exodus*. *Centennial* was such a surefire thing that it remained a bestseller even after the hardback publisher hiked the price nearly three dollars to an unprecedented $12.50. Like *Centennial* ('An epic American experience that captures the soul of a country') and *Roots* (an even bigger seller) *The Thorn Birds* is a panoramic saga of national emergence, narrated in terms of a series of representative individual lives. Like Uris's Ireland, McCullough's Australia is interestingly foreign—yet has a shared language and, in large part, a shared cultural tradition with America. And just as Ireland had the historical advantage (for the novelist) of a more recent revolution than

America's, so Australia had the advantage of a more recent pioneer era. Both Australia and Ireland had freed themselves from the status of colonial possession, and the bicentennial had made a mild xenophobia a good selling point. There is, incidentally, an understated but quite audible anti-English sentiment in *The Thorn Birds,* whose main protagonists are all Irish Catholic: 'It is not causeless, you know, the Irish hatred of the English,' one of them observes.

The Thorn Birds has elements of the Michener/Uris/Haley 'birth of a nation' theme as well as these authors' massive spread of narrative. But in other ways it is closer to the family saga or 'dynasty' style of epic. These were also doing excellent business in the period that American publishers were making their expensive decisions about *The Thorn Birds*. John Jakes's 'Kent Family Chronicles' (the American Bicentennial Series) had come from nowhere to sell over 10 m. in two years. And for the specifically female readership there were the English Diane Pearson's *Csardas* (1975, the saga of a Hungarian family from the glittering late nineteenth-century Austro-Hungarian Empire to 'today's totalitarian state') and Susan Howatch's *Cashelmara* (1974), both of which had done extremely well in America. *Cashelmara* is as it happened, particularly close to *The Thorn Birds* in organization and subject matter. Both works offer the saga of a representative Irish family; Howatch's covers the period 1859-90 and is segmented into six narratives, each given to a narrator with a different point of view. McCullough offers seven segments, covering the period 1915-69 and taking as its focus a different member of the Clearly family (or, in two cases, associates by intimate sexual relationship). *Cashelmara, Csardas* and *Thorn Birds* were all insistently promoted as the 'new' *Gone With the Wind,* a label which seems to have irritated McCullough intensely, as well it might since her own authorial professionalism is in stark contrast to Mitchell's small-town amateurism.

The title of McCullough's novel is explained by the italicized 'legend' which prefaces it. Thorn birds spend their lives searching for a thorn tree. Having found one, they impale themselves 'on the longest sharpest spine' and dying sing 'one superlative song, existence the price . . . For the best is only bought at the cost of great pain.'

This prefatory legend (which I assume McCullough has invented) recalls the life-giving mother pelican tearing its breast to feed its selfish young. McCullough's symbolism is—however—more directly genital; and the suggestion of feminine surrender to the victimizing phallus is transparent. Also recalled is the swan-song—conventionally figurative of the artist's tragic sacrifice of life for art.

The opening sections of the novel descend a long way from the poetic prelude. One of the strengths of *The Thorn Birds* for overseas readers (less so for Australians, judging by Max

Harris's home-town hatchet job) is the gritty evocation of rural life in a pioneer era which extended up to the Second World War. McCullough is very convincing in her descriptions of the filthy business of shearing and tending Merinos in the semi-desert of back-country Australia, or the rigours of canecutting in semi-tropical North Queensland. The scene painting of Australian landscape and of the sheep station/ country town settings are (with a few gushy lapses for sunsets and so on) well done. And some of the set-piece scenes come off brilliantly (the lightning-exploded gum tree which immolates the Cleary patriarch, Paddy, stands out as a descriptive *tour de force*).

But the virtue of *The Thorn Birds* is not that it has a single strength or selling quality; rather it has a specific strength for everybody, man, woman, young, old, emancipated, reactionary, American, English, Australian. Its wide-ranging appeal can be conveniently gathered under four main heads, or component parts, each appropriate to a different market sector.

(1) *The Thorn Birds* offers the sweeping panorama of an 'epic moment' in the formation of a nation (historically *The Thorn Birds* covers Australia's progress from minor colony, through dominion to national independence). The organization of the novel intimates that many small lives go to make up a family history and many small family achievements make up a national identity. This aspect of the novel depends on the assumption, legitimate enough in the early sections, that the Clearys are 'ordinary' immigrants. At the beginning of the narrative Paddy Cleary is an itinerant New Zealand sheep shearer who emigrates to the Australian outback to work as head stockman on a sheep station. In the subsequent drama of adaptation, McCullough evokes an anti-pastoral world where hardship is inseparable from the immigrant struggle with the continental spaces of an uncolonized country. The relationship between suffering and creativity, the thorn and the song, is clearest cut in this section of the novel.

(2) Grafted onto this stock is a novel of high life and gracious living, in the *Gone With the Wind* manner. By a most improbable chance, the indigent Clearys are the sole relatives, and eventually heirs (together with the Catholic Church, another odds-against likelihood) to the richest woman in Australia. Thus the vagrant family become masters of Drogheda's 250,000 acres. As the belle of Drogheda (sheep station and plantation interchange easily enough) Meg's life story is dominated by her fifty-years-long love affair with a grandee of the Catholic Church, Ralph de Bricassart ('a magnificent man'). De Bricassart's elevation in the novel is as precipitate as the Clearys'. He rises from priest, to bishop, archbishop and finally cardinal. (While just a bishop he fathers a son on the 26-year-old Meg.) Meg herself is revealed as a Perdita figure, the princess in peasant disguise. Through her mother's family we understand she has

inherited aristocratic blood, 'titian' hair, natural breeding. This finer being is set off by her being the only Cleary girl (the numerous boys all take after the bog-trotting Paddy except, of course, the madcap Frank who is the by-blow of his mother's premarital fling with the brilliant Pakeha).

(3) 'At the heart of the tale,' as the blurb tells us, are the forbidden loves of Fiona and Meg, the first two generations of Cleary women. Both have husbands who are worthy 'working men' and 'cultured, sophisticated, very charming' lovers whom society prohibits their openly acknowledging: Fiona's 'Pakeha' because he is half Maori; Meg's de Bricassart because he is a priest. The 'thorn' in this central situation is the woman's self denial of sexual gratification, denial which is given a final poignancy when the consolatory children of these love affairs are taken prematurely from them (Frank into life imprisonment, Meg's Dane by drowning). This masochistic aspect of *The Thorn Birds* would seem designed to appeal to the mature, married woman reader.

(4) Subordinate to the above is a preoccupation with female emancipation, designed apparently to appeal to a younger group of women. The chronicle of the three generations from Fiona through Meg to Justine Cleary follows, in social terms, an advance from the slavery of frontier womanhood to the liberation of modern woman on near-equal terms in the man's world. Justine (a rather Jacqueline Susannish conception) is a freebooting modern young woman. Her grandmother had half a dozen sons (girls didn't count); her mother two children; Jussy repudiates the whole breeding business with a breezy feminist scorn ('Not bloody likely! Spend *my* life wiping snotty noses and cacky bums?'). In her young womanhood Fee was a bondslave to the domestic economy. Meg has a less drudging time of it, though she is still indentured to the house and, in a larger sense, to Drogheda. Justine, by contrast, has a profession; she is an actress, and this removes her from home into the cosmopolitan world. In the last, climactic scene of the novel Justine is shown (at her mother's prompting) rejecting Drogheda's good earth and the bondage it represents. The thorn is now less sharp, and the modern, emancipated woman less likely to drive it into her bosom.

The Thorn Birds is a highly efficient, broad-appeal product. Few categories of reader can have been disappointed in their purchase. Nonetheless the novel does have weaknesses. The descriptions of Justine's jet-set life do not seem to me to come off. And the extended descriptions of the ecstatic physical consummation that produces Meg and de Bricassart's love-child is an embarrassing failure:

> Did he carry her to the bed, or did they walk? He
> thought he must have carried her, but he could not
> be sure: only that she was on it, he was there upon

it her skin under his hands, his skin under hers. Oh, God! My Meggie, my Meggie! How could they rear me from infancy to think you profanation? Time ceased to tick and began to flow, washed over him until it had no meaning, only a depth of dimension more real than time.

As it happens, McCullough is not entirely to blame for this scene. As she explained to the *Guardian*'s reporter, she produced it only under duress:

My editor told me that the second half of the book needed a damn good love scene, and there is nothing I dislike writing more. Love-making is such a non-verbal thing, I hate that explicit 'he stuck it in her' kind of thing because it is boring. You can only say 'he stuck it in her' so many ways.

Paul Gray (review date 20 May 1985)

SOURCE: "A Creed for the Third Millennium," in *Time*, May 20, 1985, p. 82.

[*In the following review, Gray provides an unfavorable review of* A Creed for the Third Millennium.]

Author Colleen McCullough's fourth novel began selling briskly weeks before its official publication. The easy explanation is that the vast audience that enjoyed ***The Thorn Birds*** (1977) will buy anything McCullough writes. But something else may be fueling this phenomenon. The appearance of perfection in any form is a rare and noteworthy event. News of its arrival is bound to spread, and perhaps, in this case, the world is already out: ***A Creed for the Third Millennium*** could well be the most perfectly awful novel ever published.

The year is 2032, and a new ice age is slowly freezing up the earth. Northern U.S. cities must be largely evacuated every winter and their residents relocated in the Sunbelt. Strict population control is in force, and only a few lucky couples can win the right, in a Government-run lottery, to have a second child. Their chilly, straitened lives have made people understandably glum; the Department of the Environment has been ordered by the President to find some way to cheer them up. Dr. Judith Carriol, a high-ranking official in the department, conducts a massive search and finally finds the person who might be able to inspire the citizenry to go on living: an obscure psychologist in Connecticut named Dr. Joshua Christian.

The hero's surname and initials tip off exactly how the plot

will end, which is just as well. McCullough's claim to inverse greatness in this book does not rest on what she tells but on her miraculous ability to tell it ludicrously. She seems to emulate a process she admiringly ascribes to Dr. Christian: "to ruminate some particularly knotty concept into smooth mental paste." Hence the cascade of cliches, many per page and even paragraph. An adviser tells the President: "It's a hot potato, none hotter. We may be biting off more than we can chew." The "cool lustrous brain" of Judith Carriol manifests itself dimly: "The less people involved, the better," or, "If there is any reason in the world why you are where you are and who you are in this day, the reason is me!"

Carriol thinks Dr. Christian might be a good ersatz messiah because "the man had coined some very quotable quotes." None happens to be included in the novel, but Christian obviously has some way with words: "Too many people are so busy earning salvation in the next life that they only end by screwing this one up." Listening to such remarks, Judith experiences strange sensations indeed: "Her gut was crawling, shivering horrific tides of joy washed higher and higher up the shores of her mind."

Innards are terribly important to all the characters. The President approvingly decides that Dr. Christian has "guts. Scads of guts." Skeptics may argue that such a remark is no funnier than those that appear in many best sellers. They underestimate McCullough's mastery of sublime inanity. What other writer would somberly portray a heroine "feeling her purpose trickle away between her legs like a slow haemorrhage"? Where else could one find a statement both so unconsciously offensive and grammatically inept as "A devout Jew but nonetheless the most Christian of gentlemen, his sins were purely sins of omission and due to thoughtlessness and lack of perception"? No wonder this novel promises to become a blockbuster; readers will be savoring its thousands of gaffes well into the third millennium.

Lisa Mitchell (review date 21 July 1985)

SOURCE: "A Creed for the Third Millennium," in *Los Angeles Times Book Review,* July 21, 1985, p. 6.

[*Below, Mitchell offers an unfavorable review of* A Creed for the Third Millennium.]

We're pushing the fast-forward button here to 2032-33—not quite 50 years from now. But when you think that 50 years ago, Rudolph Valentino had already been dead for almost a decade, you see how fast time flies. So what's good about Colleen McCullough's novel, set in a future where people are freezing to death, is that it's not too *far* in the future.

We don't have a lot of exotic hardware to confound those of us who can barely set a digital watch.

Still, we want explanations for things that are not forthcoming. If, for instance, the Greenhouse Theory—among others—is correct and the Earth is getting warmer, why, in fewer than 50 years, will we be in an ice age? What *happened?* And at one point, the hero mentions—only in passing, mind you—that the average life expectancy is now 40. What *happened* in 50 years to lower it? (We are told that people don't smoke anymore, that "the expectancy of nuclear war disappeared, as did really irresponsible government" as well as "territorial usurpation, even starvation.")

But what really confounds about *A Creed for the Third Millennium* is the blurb on its cover: "A novel by the author of *The Thorn Birds.*" No! *That* writer had an inner ear for graceful prose! *She* would never create the awkward, rambling, clumpy sentences in *Millennium.* *She* wouldn't reverse the basic writing dictum of "show, don't tell" the way this author does—especially about her female protagonist, Dr. Judith Carriol, who is "tall and fashionably elegant," "obsessively tidy and formidably efficient." Would a McCullough novel suffer mortally, as this does, from lack of subtlety and nuance? About our hero, Dr. Joshua Christian's sister-in-law, we read: "snorted Miriam"; "sneered Miriam"; "snarled Miriam"—and that's all on just pages 90 and 91! The author of this futuristic novel is also curiously given to archaic "nays" and "perforces." People are even "wont to enveigh." And all the main characters chew their lips in consternation. What with all this snarling, snorting and chewing, it's small wonder that one of the best things in the book is a little illustration on the nature of cats.

As to the main story, with a hero named Joshua *Christian* (J.C., get it?), who lives with his mother and a band of disciplelike family members called Mary, Martha, James and Andrew and who, we are told over and over, has "charisma" and is "chosen" to save the people, it isn't too hard to guess the ending.

Though much of the first and last sections of the book are embarrassingly bad, there is a treasure in the middle comprised of some of the spiritual message put into Joshua Christian's mouth. In a world gone gray, where everyone is cold and rootless through perpetual "relocations," where population is government controlled, where too much leisure ("Men nowadays are more often paid not to work") has increased national apathy, Christian has some healing words for his people suffering from "millennial neurosis." But anyone in 1985 who is given to blaming the "times" or "circumstances" for not getting on with their lives could underline a few things here. Instead of mooning for the past, make the best of a present that's *not* all you wish it were! Get up in the morning and find some purpose and peace and

love in your life *anyway.* *Make* it happen! This "Christian philosophy" tells us to look to a God of our own understanding: "Don't shut out God from your mind or spirit because you can't take up membership in a church." However, *A Creed for the Third Millennium*'s Christian philosophy is so far from the fundamentalists' that if this novel becomes a TV movie and is run during Easter week, it will be denounced from the pulpits. And that *would* be exactly like *The Thorn Birds.*

Christine Bridgwood (essay date 1986)

SOURCE: "Family Romances: The Contemporary Popular Family Saga," in *The Progress of Romance: The Politics of Popular Fiction*, edited by Jean Radford, Routledge & Kegan Paul, 1986, pp. 167-93.

[*In the following excerpt, Bridgwood explores characteristics of the family saga genre found in* The Thorn Birds. *According to Bridgwood, the presentation of extended historical processes in the novel is problematic because it reinforces the "social and sexual status quo" while offering new possibilities for women within the safety of family and tradition.*]

Realism and Romance

It has often been pointed out that in contemporary popular romantic novels the external world drops away from the text except as a setting, leaving the hero and heroine viewing each other in a one-dimensional universe. If one function of romance is to move woman from her position of heterosexual subordination to one of unified and secure subjectivity, then the romantic relationship is the place where women find their authentic selves and have their identities established, completed and confirmed—in a kind of natural, absolute possession outside of any social, economic, or political context. The narrative leads to resolution through heterosexual union, which closes down the possibility of other desires and other narratives, and relegates women to a position beyond culture and history, firmly placed in the realm of 'nature' and 'eternal truth'.

In the family saga, however, marriage, with its consequent integration into the social order, is never the straightforward means of precipitating the narrative's climax and conclusion that it is in romance. The saga differs from other popular fiction genres in its lack of drive towards narrative closure and in its tendency to begin at the point where romance stops. The romantic fiction is structured into a coherent linear narrative around a few moments of transcendence (the first glimpse of the hero, the first sign of his admiration in the gaze, the kiss), whereas the family saga is, by definition, structured as a long-term process.

This brings me to the relationship of the family saga to realism. Although many of the saga's strategies remain those of classic realism, the form does lack some of the most important conventions of dominant ways of storytelling—the impetus towards the resolution of the plot, the circularity of a narrative that solves all problems it encounters, the successful completion of the individual's quest and, to some extent, the process of identification. Any full identification between reader and character (which has been seen as another of the principal means by which the realist text secures the recognition of its particular representations as 'real,' diverting the reader from what is contradictory in the text to what s/he already 'knows'), tends to be undermined in the saga narrative. Here, three-dimensionality of character is subordinated to the structure of repetition, contrast, variation and antithesis by which the text constructs its cross-generational profile of the *family* in its multiformity. In this sense individual characters in the saga are merely facets of a collective character constructed at a broader narrative level. The conflicts and problems which propel the saga forward tend to be structured in a series of oppositions, and it is the function of many of the characters to carry one or other of the terms of the opposition, as in the antithetical pairs of rebel/conformist, good mother/bad mother, promiscuous/faithful, rightful heir/rival claimant. In discussing the texts I will be considering how far this undermining of any full process of identification and the lack of drive towards narrative closure combine with other features to interrogate such primary ideological agencies as the family, romantic love and nationalism.

Writing and Reading

As a genre, the popular family saga is remarkable for employing a marketing strategy which appears to be attempting to reduce the sense of distance and difference between writers and readers. Most begin with a detailed potted author's biography presenting writer to reader:

'Danielle started working for *Supergirls* . . . when the recession hit, the firm went out of business and Danielle "retired" to write her first book, *Going Home*. She moved to California, seeking "an easier climate, gentler people and a better place to write."'

'Susan Howatch . . . was an only child and her father was killed in the Second World War . . . after working for a year as an articled clerk she was bored with practical law and decided to devote herself to writing. . . .'

'Catherine Gaskin married an American and settled down in New York for ten years. . . .'

Apart from the marked contrast to the anonymity and interchangeability of, say, Mills & Boon authors, what is striking about these doubtless carefully selected biographical details is the implication that the author, despite her glamour, is really not so different from the reader herself—she too has experienced common disasters (the firm went out of business, her father died), dilemmas (she was bored) and delights (she married and settled down). Cosy, intimate, first-name terms are being established.

Furthermore, the process of writing, although documented as being arduous and time-consuming—

'She began *The Thorn Birds,* writing it at night, after her work as head technician in a neurophysiology laboratory had ended. . . .'

'Writing this book has been rather like writing a real-life detective story, with the facts given in old letters, stories and newspaper cuttings forming the framework around which my tale is woven.'

—is still depicted as springing almost spontaneously from the author's own history and experience. Judith Saxton, for example, dedicated *The Pride* (1981) to her grandmother and stresses in her acknowledgements that the idea for the book 'sprang from my grandmother's charmingly written memoirs.' This appeal to the unmediated matrix of (specifically female) experience, memory and writing as spontaneous growth, is of course belied by the complexity of the actual texts, but the ideology of the text as sold to the reader is that of oral history: we have all, as women, got such stories to tell, and, given the necessary effort, perhaps could. Look, for example, at the following extracts from the author biographies prefacing each saga:

'Her northern roots are strongly reflected in her work. She is an author who sets her characters against a backcloth she knows well.'

'The desire to write, she says, has been her one and only lifeline during a tumultuous and changeable life.'

'Her work with "wayward" girls and her own family has increased her interest in the female situation, present and past.'

The implication is that anyone could have a go, as it is too in a *Guardian* interview with Colleen McCullough (15 April 1977) which stresses her rise from ordinary student nurse to world-famous novelist.

In this sense, the marketing of the family saga produces significantly different implications from the escapism generally attributed to romance. The ideology of authorship in saga publicity appears to be directing the reader back into the potentialities of her own experience, into her family history as potential saga, to writing as a 'natural' product of living, achievable through application, strength of will, a harnessing of the general capabilities that women display in their everyday domestic and work situations. This universalisation of the potential power to write such fiction is matched by a universalisation of the fiction's material—despite the variants of geographical, historical and class settings, the saga families' fictionalised lives are nevertheless structured around a number of dilemmas which can be essentially similar for women of entirely different national, social and economic groups.

The construction of the family as a universal form, then, produces a series of crucial mediations between writer and reader, writing and reading, the production of a text and the pre-text of 'experience.' Linked through the shared experience of the family, the writer is merely a reader who has got her act together. Reading can be a rehearsal for your own transition to writing, and experience, through the family's historical dimension, is already on the way to becoming text. Far from being positioned in a simply passive, powerless relation to the text, the reader of the saga, in order for the text's central terms of family and experience to function, is established in a curious space of creative potentiality; poised between her personal experience, which is being valorised as potential 'material,' and a writing which declares itself as the 'material-ised' experience of someone not unlike herself. For sagas to work the reader must be, at least potentially, the next bestseller herself.

The Family

The great subject of the novelist, as Stephen Heath has suggested, has been crucially the family—the family as bridge between the individual and society, the private and the public. It has been posited as the site of the conflict and resolution of these terms in the world apart which it purports to offer: marriage and the family, a firm social unit offering a privileged mode of individuality and a haven of personal happiness. In this sense, the modern family saga explores the same terrain as the realist novel of the nineteenth century: the family and its dynastic considerations such as inheritance, the continuation of the male line, family duty, and alliances with outsiders and rivals. In the nineteenth century novel what is often at stake is the integration of a male pattern of inherited social power. Novels such as *Pride and Prejudice, Middlemarch* and *Daniel Deronda,* which are concerned with the specifically *female* relation to this system of social power, have tended to represent women settling within that system through a struggle towards marriage,

which once again occupies a decisive position in the 'individual and society' organization, proposed as a mediation between the two.

Where the contemporary popular saga differs, as it differs too from popular romance, is in its exploration not of the achievement of that state but of the maintenance of it. Although the saga undoubtedly works, on one level, to reinforce prevailing ideological definitions of the family, in other ways it challenges the concept of the family as definable purely in terms of blood relations and kinship, and moves towards a redefinition of the meanings of the primacy and exclusivity of the family. The 'family' in Catherine Gaskin's *Family Affairs,* for example, consists of an all-female group of two sisters, a woman who was briefly married to their father, her stepdaughter and a friend, all living in a house split into separate flats.

It is partly this redefinition and extension of the family in the saga that allows its representation as a highly sexualised site, a representation which (apart from guaranteeing a good read!) resists western industrial society's conceptualisation of the family as at once legitimating and concealing sexuality. The question of what actually constitutes the family is repeatedly stretched and renegotiated in the saga, activating conflicting discourses which are not easily contained by the text. Ideological contradictions within the family are opened up and then an attempt is made to sidestep them by the imaginary resolution of the redefined, expanded and sexualised family.

The Thorn Birds: Historical Process and Common Sense

An issue which continually resurfaces when thinking about the popular family saga is that of the contradictory effects of the narrative's extended time-span, with its invocation of historical process. Lillian S. Robinson, in her discussion of historical romance, argues that this kind of text obliges the reader to entertain *some* definition of history. By her account, the family saga, in its representation of history and women's lives over time, would necessarily show to some extent the overlapping and contradictory ways in which sexual differences are instituted under different conditions at different historical moments, with the sense of historical process working to interrogate exiting power relations and ideological definitions of sexuality and the social. And yet, as this analysis of *The Thorn Birds* attempts to show, it is precisely this historical materiality and the extended temporal perspective of the family saga which serves to make the social and sexual order appear as the natural state of things.

The Thorn Birds (1977) chronicles three generations of the Cleary family and their relation to the family home, Drogheda, a sheep farm in southern Australia. The narrative follows, in social terms, the advance from the slavery of frontier womanhood to the emancipation of the modern woman on near equal terms in a man's world. The Clearys are a non-dynastic dynastic family, the third generation consisting only of one daughter, Justine. Her grandmother Fee had eight sons (girls didn't count), and her mother two children, but Justine is able to repudiate the whole breeding business—'Not bloody likely! Spend my life wiping snotty noses and cacky bums?' Femininity is placed in the text as a site of social change and it is made clear that the pull of the homeland must be resisted to achieve this change. A critical point occurs at the end of the narrative when Justine has to choose whether to return home to Drogheda or to continue her career in Europe. She is on the point of flying back to Australia ('I want something safe, permanent, enduring, so I'm coming home to Drogheda, which is all those things'), marrying a local boy and retracing her roots after her European flutter, but is stopped in the end by the letter from her mother advising her to stay away for the sake of her career and happiness. Justine in the penultimate climactic scene is shown rejecting Drogheda and the bondage it represents to her.

> The narrative [of *The Thorn Birds*] follows, in social terms, the advance from the slavery of frontier womanhood to the emancipation of the modern woman on near equal terms in a man's world.
> —*Christine Bridgwood*

Superficially, then, the moral trajectory of *The Thorn Birds* is towards the acceptance of a necessary distancing from tradition, the land, the home, one's country (all signified by the property Drogheda) in order to create space for individual growth. The bonds of the family are denied (Drogheda can give Justine nothing), yet at the same time sanctified (it takes her grandmother and mother, blood relations, to know her well enough to realise that Drogheda can give her nothing). What is more, Justine is able to move decisively outside the family circle only by moving into another stable, approved societal unit—that of marriage.

This last point suggests another discourse at work in the text alongside that of women's 'emancipation,' and which undercuts and problematises it. This is the discourse of common sense—'that's life'—the stoic acceptance of fate. The text is threaded through with the lugubrious insights of now enlightened characters—'we can't change what we are . . . we are what we are, that's all . . . what must be, must be . . . it is the way things are . . . it's just common sense.' This discourse produces the idea of a human essence which exists independently of the social, bringing with it the category of an essential femininity.

The appeal in the text to fate, common sense and an essentially masochistic female 'nature' are all synthesised in the legend of the thorn bird which prefaces and completes the text and is invoked at one crucial moment in the narrative. The thorn bird, following 'an immutable law,' spends its life searching for a thorn tree and having found it 'impales itself on the longest, sharpest spine' and dying sings 'one superlative song, existence the price.' The suggestion of feminine masochistic surrender to the victimising phallus is transparent, and is made explicit in Meggie's final-page reverie when, in epitomising her life-long frustrated love for Ralph, she reflects, 'I did it all myself. I have no one else to blame.' The final words of the text reach out to implicate its readers in this masochism:

> The bird with the thorn in its breast . . . is driven by it knows not what to impale itself and die singing. At the very instant the thorn enters there is no awareness in it of the dying to come . . . but we, when we put the thorns in our breasts, we know. We understand. And still we do it. Still we do it.

In Meggie and Ralph's retrospective discussion of their relationship, the legend is invoked by Meggie to exonerate Ralph for his sacrifice of her to his clerical ambitions. For Ralph, the 'thorn' can be that of ambition, the will to power, but for women it is necessarily that of love and sexual experience. Female subjectivity is constructed within sexual categories, and even the shift from this with the third generation makes it clear that the thorn is only slightly less sharp for the autonomous, career-oriented modern woman.

There is then a contradiction in *The Thorn Birds* between the opening out with the third generation to a more independent, self-determining lifestyle for women (albeit within marriage) and the undercutting of any idea of social change by the discourse of fate and cyclical repetition which frames the text and operates powerfully within it—a contradiction which is clearly played out in the final few paragraphs of the text, which consists of an evocation of 'the same endless, unceasing cycle' and yet simultaneously asserts that it is 'time for Drogheda to stop' in order for progress and change to be made possible. This contradiction is common to most popular family sagas and can be explained further by reference to the double temporal structure which they are based on.

The saga is structured upon two parallel temporal axes, the one short, the other extended. The shorter axis produces a dramatic structure of various episodes, incidents and climaxes which revolve around and are supported by concepts of progress, the individual and (given that the text foregrounds female experience) the feminine—in *The Thorn Birds,* the life histories of Fee, Meggie and Justine. The extended axis, however, works to defuse this structure of individual drama, experience and change by overlaying it with a discourse of the 'long view' which speaks in favour of tradition, the family, the heritage, the dynasty. This is the ironic overview at work in *The Thorn Birds'* evocation of destiny, common sense and time as healer. The text itself has an investment in this ironic overview—it is after all on this axis that its key terms of family and saga are situated.

The tensions I have pointed to in *The Thorn Birds* stem not merely from the long-term/short-term antithesis, but also from the contradictions inherent in this ironic position itself. For irony, while declaring itself as an analytical, 'deconstructive' mode, is also classically conservative in its operations. It implies that if a long enough view is taken, all current events and individual dramas are insignificant in the face of the immensity of life ('the rhythmic endless cycle'). But individual histories can be swallowed up and individual experience ironised only because the longer time-span they are being set against is itself subjected to no questioning. The text rests on an unchallenged basis of tradition, history and family continuity, and in the end takes up a position entirely identified with these concepts, although of course some interplay between the two temporal perspectives is necessary for the narrative to function.

This then is the structural contradiction at work in the family saga. What *The Thorn Birds* in particular makes clear is that the ironic, male, long-term overview which is ostensibly in conflict with the specifically female short-term perspective does in fact hold some positive uses for women. The ironic 'life's like that' philosophy becomes a way of validating the suffering and frustration that Fee and Meggie's lives bring them. This is acted out in a great number of small details and incidents throughout the text, particularly in the scenes depicting their later relationship as two ageing women. Meggie as a girl was ignored by Fee precisely because of her femaleness, and the development traced in the narrative of their relationship, culminating in Fee's admission that 'I used to think having a daughter wasn't nearly as important as having sons, but I was wrong . . . a daughter's an equal' constitutes a powerful representation of female bonding. Like Justine's life story, it would seem to gesture towards an ideal of progress, towards social change making personal change possible. Yet this representation is critically undermined by the discourses which I've shown as clustering around the extended, ironic temporal axis; nothing really changes, everything comes full circle, 'history does repeat itself.' Meggie and Fee are constructed as women bound together by the inexorable patterns and cycles of nature, fate, family and love, agreeing, when looking back over their lives, that 'memories are a comfort, once the pain dies down.'

The mother-daughter relationship echoes the rest of the text by interrogating female subject positions in the framework

of short-term drama and incident, while in the same breath recuperating any disturbance by setting it in the safer context of the 'long view.' This is how history in the saga works as a double-edged discourse; it is at once the sharp nudge of awareness of historical process—the 'vision of historical possibility' discussed by Lillian S. Robinson—and the soothing balm of an ideology of stoical acceptance which naturalises the social and sexual status quo, and is ultimately dependent upon essentialist categories of femininity. . . .

I have tried to show how the popular family saga attempts the representation of ideological contradictions in a form which provides their imaginary resolution, and that this takes place through a fiction which entertains and exposes contradiction on one condition, that of final unity and reconciliation. This process is both aided and impeded by the double-edged discourse of the family, tradition, heritage, the 'long-view,' which on the one hand provides a secure foundation from which to interrogate short-term practices, and on the other renders any attempt to follow the reassuring pattern of classical narrative (that of an original settlement disrupted and finally restored) deeply problematic.

The analysis of romance fiction has happily moved beyond that earlier phase in which the genre was righteously denounced for its facile and yet (strangely) coercive ideological effects, an analysis which brought with it the image of women readers as the passive consumers of a discourse which could only further their oppression. The necessary re-reading of romance has produced an understanding of the genre which exposes the crudity of that earlier model and its underlying assumptions about the relationship between texts and women reading. If the implications of this process of re-definition are to be drawn out fully, it needs to extend outside romance to those associated but distinct genres of which the family saga is one important instance. By attempting to situate romance within the broader field of women's reading, we can move towards not only a clearer definition of romance in its relationships of affiliation and difference with other genres, but also an understanding of the range and variety of the interactions between texts and women readers.

Cora Kaplan (essay date 1986)

SOURCE: "*The Thorn Birds:* Fiction, Fantasy, Femininity," in *Formations of Fantasy,* edited by Victor Burgin, James Donald, and Cora Kaplan, Methuen, 1986, pp. 142-66.

[*In the following excerpt, Kaplan identifies elements of fantasy and female sexuality in romance literature through analysis of* The Thorn Birds. *Kaplan draws attention to the novel's incest motif, portrayal of seduction, and treatment of sexual identity in light of Freudian psychoanalysis and feminist theory.*]

The Thorn Birds confirms not a conventional femininity but women's contradictory and ambiguous place within sexual difference. Feminist cultural criticism has initiated a very interesting debate about the meaning of reading, and watching, romance. What follows is a contribution to that discussion which tries to see how, in historical, political and psychoanalytic terms, texts like *Gone with the Wind* and **The Thorn Birds** come to have such a broad appeal for women, centering the female reader in a particular way, and reworking the contradictory elements which make female subjectivity such a vertiginous social and psychic experience.

History

Fiction, fantasy and femininity. Since the rise of the popular novel directed at a female audience, the relationship between these three terms has troubled both progressive and conservative analysts of sexual difference, not least those who were themselves writers of narrative. The terms of the debate about the relationship between 'reading romance' and the construction of femininity have remained surprisingly constant in the two hundred years since Mary Wollstonecraft and Jane Austen first engaged with the issue as a response to the expansion of sensational literature directed at the woman reader.

Both Wollstonecraft and Austen agreed that the 'stale tales' and 'meretricious scenes' of the sentimental and gothic novel triggered and structured female fantasy, stirring up the erotic and romantic at the expense of the rational, moral and maternal. Both thought that such reading could directly influence behaviour—inflamed and disturbed readers might, in Wollstonecraft's evocative phrase 'plump into actual vice.' But Wollstonecraft's main concern was not with junk reading as the route to adultery but as the path to conventional, dependent, degenerate femininity—to the positioning of the female self in the degraded, dependent role as 'objects of desire.' At the time she was writing *A Vindication of the Rights of Woman* Wollstonecraft was defending a relatively conventional sexual morality. Even so, she was much less concerned with the danger to women's sexual virtue which romance reading might breed than with the far-reaching political effects of such indulgence. As the narrative of desire washed over the reader, the thirst for reason was quenched, and the essential bridge to female autonomy and emancipation, a strengthened 'understanding' was washed out. The female psyche could not, it seemed, sustain or combine two mental agendas; for them it must be either reason or passion, pleasure or knowledge. Austen's version of this libidinal economy was perhaps slightly less punitive, but this was only because her ambitions for her heroine/reader were a less

radical and more limited moral autonomy within the dominant convention as wife, mother and lover. Moral and spiritual integrity and, to some extent, independence for women were essential, but an independent life and an independently productive life were not unthinkable within her novels. Both Wollstonecraft and Austen assumed, as most analysts of romance reading do today, that romance narrative works on the reader through rather simple forms of identification. The reader aligns herself with the heroine and suffers her perils, passions and triumphs. The narrative structure of the fiction then 'takes over' everyday life, and gender relations are read through its temptations, seductions and betrayals. Alternatively romance provides an escape from the everyday realities; the pleasure of fantasy numbs the nerve of resistance to oppression.

Wollstonecraft's implicit theory of reading assumed the reader would identify herself with the female heroine. The reading of popular fiction and the fantasy induced by it depend at one level on the identification of reader and heroine, and the subsequent acting-out of a related narrative trajectory. Late-eighteenth-century theories of reading, as they appeared in both aesthetic and political discourses, assumed a fairly direct relationship between reading and action, especially from the naïve reader, i.e. the barely literate, uneducated working-class person—and women. In this period of expanding literacy and political turmoil, the question of the ability to read is at the centre of both progressive platforms of radicalization and transformation of the mass of people, and conservative fears of revolution. A great deal of attention was given to not only the dynamic effects of reading on the unschooled subject but also to the distinction between reading as a social act (a pamphlet read to others in a coffee house or village square, books read at the family hearth) and reading as a private act, unregulated and unsupervised by authority. Both forms of reading could be subversive, but the latter, less open to surveillance and control, more defiantly announcing the mental autonomy of individual subjects whose 'independence' is not acknowledged by the dominant social and political order, offered a particularly insidious form of subversion.

The question of women's reading, as it was understood in the 1790s was situated within these wider anxieties about reading and revolution, literacy and subjectivity. Accordingly both Wollstonecraft and Austen knew women must read to achieve even minimal independent status as subjects and were, in somewhat different ways, concerned with something more intangible and complex than a simple incitement, which sensational novels may produce, to misbehave. Private reading is already, in itself, an act of autonomy; in turn it sets up, or enables, a space for reflective thought. Fiction gives that reflection a narrative shape and sensational fiction produces a sort of general excitement, the 'romantic twist of the mind' that concerned Wollstonecraft. The desire to inhabit that provocative landscape and mentally live its stories rather than those of the supposed social real was as worrying as any specific identification with romantic female protagonists. In fact Wollstonecraft's analysis of the construction of a degraded and dependent femininity in *A Vindication* insists that although female children have no innate sexuality—she bitterly rejected Rousseau's insistence that they did—women come to see themselves narcissistically through the eyes of men. Through the gaze of the male rake, they become 'rakes themselves.' Female subjectivity was characterized in this account by its retrograde tendency to take up other subject positions and identify self as object. It was this already unstable degraded subject (constructed in childhood and early adolescence) that reads romance and fantasizes about it. For Wollstonecraft and Austen popular sensational literature both reinforced and evoked a set of romantic scenarios which the reader will use at once to interpret, act through and escape from ordinary lives. Each part of this reading effect is 'bad,' each involves different elements of projection and displacement and together they constitute the negative effect of fiction and fantasy.

There was very little possibility in late-eighteenth-century progressive or conservative thought for a positive account of fantasy for women, the lower classes or colonial peoples. For all of these lesser subjectivities the exercise of the imagination was problematic, for the untutored, 'primitive' psyche was easily excited and had no strategies of sublimation; a provocative narrative induced imitation and disruptive actions, political or social. When radicals supported the subjective equality of any of these groups, they generally insisted that their reasoning capacity was equal to that of a bourgeois male. The psyche of the educated middle-class male was the balanced psyche of the period: reason and passion in a productive symbiosis. Men of this class were felt to have a more fixed positionality. Radical discourses presented them as the origin of their own identities, as developing independent subjects, the makers and controllers of narrative rather than its enthralled and captive audience. This capacity to produce a master narrative like their rational capacity to take civic, political actions remained latent in them as readers. Men of the ruling class, so went the dominant mythology, read critically, read not to imitate but to engage productively with argument and with narrative. They understood the difference between fiction and fact, between imagination and reason. The normative male reader, unlike his credulous female counterpart, could read a gothic novel for amusement and pleasure. Like the poet whose writing practice used 'emotion recollected in tranquility,' the two modes of reason and passion were ever open to him; in the same way he could inhabit both a public and private sphere and move between them. The enlightenment asked man to subordinate passion to reason. Romanticism argued for a productive interaction between them, assuming optimistically that the rational would act as a check to passion, and that

passion itself would be transformed, sublimated through the imagination.

As literacy spread and reading became one of the crucial practices through which human capacity, integrity, autonomy and psychic balance could be assessed, reading habits and reading response were increasingly used to differentiate readers by class and sex. By the 1790s reading by the masses was being argued *for* as a necessary route to individual and group advancement, as the crucial preparation for social and political revolution, and, at the same time, argued *against* as the significant activity which might stem the revolutionary tide. Thomas Paine pushed the polemic furthest, conflating reading with civil liberty itself—prophesying that censorship would breed its own revenge—that it would become dangerous to tell a whole people that 'they shalt not read.' Reading, both as an activity and as a sign of activities it may engender, became a metonymic reference to forms of good and bad subjectivity, of present and potential social and psychic being. So Wollstonecraft in 1791 ends her diatribe against romance reading on an uncertain note, insisting that it is better that women read novels than not read at all.

Fantasy

In the preceding two sections I have been deliberately using the term fantasy in its contemporary everyday sense: as a conscious construction of an imaginary scene in which, it is invariably assumed, the fantasist places him/herself in an easily identified and constant role in the narrative. This common-sense working definition has been undermined at various points in the discussion of autobiography and history, but it is more or less adequate for a preliminary account of fantasy as 'daydream,' as a conscious, written narrative construction, or as an historical account of the gendered imagination. Yet fantasy used solely or unreflectingly in this way invokes a notion of the relation between dream and fiction, without actually theorizing that connection. Unless we actually do work through that relationship and distinguish between fantasy as an unconscious structure and as forms of social narrative, we are unlikely to break free from the stigmatizing moralism which taints most accounts of romantic fantasy and gender, representing romance as a 'social disease' which affects the weaker constitution of the female psyche.

Psychoanalytic discussions of fantasy are not wholly free of elements of moralization but, as Alison Light has commented in her illuminating discussion of romance fiction, sexuality and class, psychoanalysis at least 'takes the question of pleasure seriously, both in its relation to gender and in its understanding of fiction as fantasies, as the explorations and productions of desires which may be in excess of the socially possible or acceptable.' . . .

Text: The Thorn Birds

In 'Returning to Manderley' Alison Light reclaims Daphne du Maurier's *Rebecca* as a text which provides 'a classic model of romance fiction while at the same time exposing many of its terms.' I would like to adopt a similar critical strategy towards Colleen McCullough's **The Thorn Birds,** a family saga whose events start in 1915 in rural New Zealand and end in 1965 in a London town house. Written by an Australian emigrée living in America in the mid-seventies, the novel subtly appropriates elements of feminist discourse, integrating the language of romance fiction with new languages of sexuality and sexual difference. Fantasy is quite unashamedly mobilized in **The Thorn Birds** both at the level of content—the narrative scenario—and at the level of rhetoric—the various styles which mark out its different registers within the story. Through these means the novel weaves a seeming social realism together with a series of original fantasies so that the text resembles the heterogeneous or hybrid form of fantasy described by psychoanalysis. Although, like a retold dream, the text rationalizes fantasy scenes into a coherent narrative sequence, the plot is in fact full of unlikely incident and coincidence which characters and authorial voice are constantly trying to justify. The implausible elements of the plot and their elaborate rationalization signals the presence of original fantasy in the text. Like many family sagas, **The Thorn Birds** inscribes all of the generic original fantasies, often mapping them over each other and repeating them with variations in the experience of different generations. Laplanche and Pontalis describe these fantasy categories as:

> Fantasies of origins: the primal scene pictures the origin of the individual; fantasies of seduction, the origin and upsurge of sexuality; fantasies of castration, the origin of the difference between the sexes.

Ambiguities about paternity run through the text. Intimations of incest affect almost all the familial and extra-familial relations, as father-daughter, mother-son and brother-sister ties. These fantasy scenes are structured and elaborated from the women's position, which sometimes means only that they offer a mildly eccentric elaboration of the classic fantasy scripts. For example, castration fantasy in the narrative emphasizes both lack and power in women and mothers, on the one hand, and retribution by that eternally absent father, God, on the other. The third-person narration, typical of family saga romance, allows a very free movement between masculine and feminine positions, and different discursive genres and registers. It also permits the narrative as a whole to be contained within a set of determinate political ideologies for which the characters themselves bear little responsibility. Like *Gone with the Wind,* but with significant differences, **The Thorn Birds** pursues an interesting and occasionally radical interrogation of sexual difference inside a reactionary set of myths about history.

At the heart of **The Thorn Birds** lies a scandalous passion between a Catholic priest, Ralph de Bricassart, and Meggie Cleary, whose family are the focus of the novel. Ralph meets Meggie when she is 9 years old, the only and somewhat neglected girl child in a large brood of boys. Ralph himself is a strikingly handsome and ambitious Irish-born priest in his late twenties, sent into temporary exile in this remote bit of rural New South Wales because he has quarrelled with his bishop. Ralph loves the child for her beauty, and for her 'perfect female character, passive yet enormously strong. No rebel, Meggie: on the contrary. All her life she would obey, move within the boundaries of her female fate.'

The whole first half of the novel follows the Clearys' fortunes on Drogheda, the vast Australian sheep station, which belongs first to the widowed millionaire matriarch, Mary Carson, and after her death to the church, with Ralph as its agent. Its narrative moves in a tantalizingly leisurely fashion towards the seduction of the proud, virginal Ralph by Meggie, whose female fate seems to include some fairly fundamental disobedience to church and state. Ralph 'makes' Meggie, as he tells his Vatican superior and confessor later in the text, shaping her education and sensibility from childhood. She, like a dutiful daughter in someone's fantasy, returns his seemingly non-sexual love with a fully libidinized intensity.

The text plays with great skill on the two narratives of prohibition, familial and ecclesiastic, that are bound together in Meggie and Ralph's romance. 'Don't call me Father,' he keeps insisting, while disentangling himself reluctantly from the arms of the teenage girl who assaults him at every opportunity. Ralph is represented as mother, father and lover in relation to Meggie. Somehow it is Ralph, in the confessional, who has to tell the 15-year-old Meggie about menstruation, because mother Fee is too busy with the boys. Somehow it is Ralph, not Meggie's negligent macho husband, who arrives in a distant part of the outback to hold her hand in her first painful experience of childbirth.

The ideal feminine man—he has a way, he tells us, with babies—Ralph is bound to the church by pride and ambition, sure that it will give him a transcendent identity: 'Not a man, never a man; something far greater, something beyond the fate of a mere man.' Losing his virginity at 40 odd, Ralph discovers *in media res* that he is a 'mere man' after all, while Meggie finds out that only symbolic incest and transgression can make a woman of her. Their brief week's consummation takes place on a remote South Sea island. After an Edenic interlude, Ralph leaves for Rome and his rising career in the church. Meggie, gestating his son, returns to the Cleary family base at Drogheda with Justine, her daughter, by her husband Luke. Here, under her mother's benign matriarchy (her biological father, significantly dies before her marriage and adultery), she will raise her children and even enjoy a short second honeymoon when Ralph comes to Drogheda to visit years later.

The novel, 591 pages long, deals with major events in the life of three generations of Clearys as well as Ralph's trajectory from country priest to cardinal via his broken vows. Like *Gone with the Wind* and other family saga romances, part of its pleasure is in the local, historical detail. Most of the energy of the text, however, is reserved for the emotional encounters. Its power to hold the female reader, in the first half anyway, is linked to the inexorable unfolding of Meggie and Ralph's story, the seduction scenario played through the narrative of another durable fantasy—the family romance in which a real-life parent is discarded as an imposter and a more exalted figure substituted.

The incest motif is everywhere in the novel, saturating all the literal familial relations as well as the metaphorical ones. Within the Cleary household all the boys remain unmarried; they are, as Meggie tells Ralph during their island idyll 'terribly shy . . . frightened of the power a woman might have over them . . . quite wrapped up in Mum.' Most wrapped up in Fee Cleary is her eldest son Frank, the illegitimate child of a New Zealand politician, half Maori. Through her affair with him Fee has lost her social position; her upper-class Anglican family marry her off to their shy dairy hand, the Irish Catholic immigrant Paddy Cleary, and then disown her. Frank acts out an Oedipal drama with Paddy who he believes is his real father, until he goads Paddy into revealing his illegitimate status. They quarrel. Frank calls his father 'a stinking old he-goat . . . a ram in rut' for making his mother Fee pregnant yet again. The father, stung, calls the boy 'no better than the shitty old dog who fathered you, whoever he was!' This quarrel takes place in front of the child Meggie and Father Ralph. After it Frank leaves home, eventually commits murder and is given a life sentence. His fate is seen in the text quite specifically as Fee's punishment for her sexual transgression. In the second half of the novel, Meggie too will lose her much loved son by Ralph, first to the church and then by death.

These symmetrical events are reinforced by the deep but sexually innocent attachment of brother-sister pairs in each generation: Frank and his half-sister Meggie; Justine and her half-brother Dane. Within the male Cleary brood there are homosocial attachments too, the twin boys Patsy and Jims are represented as a symbiotic couple. And *The Thorn Birds* extends and elaborates the homosocial, homoerotic themes, though never in a very positive way, through Meggie's husband Luke's preference of his workmate Arne, and, within the church, through Ralph's friendship with his Italian mentor. Male bonding is seen as something of a problem in the

book, a problem certainly for Meggie who, as she says, seems drawn to men who don't have much need of women and fear too much closeness with them.

Meggie (and Ralph) witness two primal scenes—in discursive form to be sure—in watching and hearing the revelations in the argument between Paddy and Frank. They hear a graphic, animalized account of the act between Paddy and Fee, and between Fee and some unknown lover, whom we later discover to be the half-caste politician. (Children often interpret parental coitus as a fight.) Ralph fears that Meggie will be psychologically damaged by witnessing the argument. The text doesn't follow this up with any reflexive comment. At a narrative level, in relation to the sequence of the fantasy scenes involving Meggie which now begin to move inevitably towards the seduction scenario, the fight, as a stage in the destruction of her innocence and perhaps an erosion of her father's authority, is certainly important.

Having sorted out in one part the question of the origin of babies, the next fantasy sequence is the one in which Ralph tells the super-innocent 15-year-old that she is menstruating, not dying of cancer. Meggie is presented as peculiarly ignorant of the facts of life for a girl who lives on a working farm. The author has to insert a long justifying didactic passage which claims, incredibly, that the sexual division of labour on the station, together with the patriarchal Puritanism of Paddy Cleary, has kept her wholly innocent. Even this touching moment of instruction stops short of full knowledge. When Ralph asks Meggie whether she knows how women get pregnant her answer is wholly within the register of fantasy:

'You wish them.'

'Who told you that?'

'No one. I worked it out for myself,' she said.

The next scene in the seduction sequence is the first unintended kiss between Ralph and Meggie, aged 16, which she half initiates. Ralph then leaves Drogheda for some time. In his absence Meggie has a conversation with her father in which it is clear that she believes that Ralph will, when she tells him to, leave the church and marry her. Paddy tries, without much luck, to disabuse her of this illusion:

'Father de Bricassart is a *priest*, Meggie. . . . Once a man is a priest there can be no turning away . . . a man who takes those vows knows beyond any doubt that once taken they can't be broken, ever. Father de Bricassart took them, and he'll never break them. . . . Now you know, Meggie, don't you? From this moment you have no excuse to daydream about Father de Bricassart.'

But Paddy is unconvincing as bearer of the reality principle, either to the reader or to Meggie.

After one more unsuccessful attempt to seduce Ralph in the hours after her father's death, Meggie is temporarily persuaded to give him up. She marries Luke, one of the seasonal sheep shearers, because he reminds her of Ralph physically. The substitution is an abominable failure, although it gives McCullough a rich opportunity to expand on the incompetent sexual style and homosocial tendencies of working-class Aussie males. Luke is like Ralph in that he can do without women, preferring the world of work and men, but he is unlike Ralph in that he has no nurturant qualities whatever. The text records Meggie's painful, incompetent deflowering in graphic and ironic detail which combines the style of a sixties sex manual with a feminist debunking of heterosexuality. Luke sets her to work as a servant for a crippled farmer's wife and goes off with the boys to cut cane.

Although the book's account of their brief marriage is convincingly realistic in its local incident, the extremity of Luke's punitive treatment of Meggie actually extends the fantasy register of the narrative. Ralph's accidental arrival during Meggie's difficult labour is the penultimate scene in the seduction sequence. He takes her through the menarche and childbirth and will, on Matlock Island, answer her wish at last and take her sexually.

Through the novel sexuality is discussed in at least two different languages. Sex which is pleasurable for women is narrated in the generic style of historical romance—steamy, suggestive and vague: 'It had been a body poem, a thing of arms and hands and skin and utter pleasure.' Bad sex is exposed in the new pragmatic realism of post-war prose: 'with a great indrawn breath to keep her courage up she forced the penis in, teeth clenched.' Ralph fucks Meggie in Barbara Cartland's best mode. In the process of losing his virginity he also forgoes his exalted notion of himself as above sexual difference. In sexual pleasure Meggie's femininity is confirmed. Meggie and Ralph conceive a male child, though Ralph's punishment is to be ignorant of this fact until after his son's death, since this is a fantasy from the women's position. Keeping men in ignorance of their paternity can be seen a female prerogative. The question of origins is thus reopened for the next generation in the final seduction, but the question of identity, sexuality and difference is temporarily resolved for Ralph, Meggie and reader.

Narrative rationalization binds the fantasy scenarios together. No amount of tricky discursive justification really explains why Meggie should witness Frank and Paddy's quarrel, need to be told by a priest about menstruation, time her labour for Ralph's visit—and so on. Yet all these events are necessary to construct a complex fantasy, a series of scenarios in which the reader's position *vis-à-vis* Ralph and Meggie is

constantly shifting. Until the sequence reaches its penultimate moment, it is fair to say that the reader oscillates from the woman's position to the man's position—represented as poles of subjectivity rather than fixed, determinate identities. For it is wholly unclear that these subject positions can be actually identified with the gendered characters Ralph and Meggie.

What, in text and context, creates this reading effect which is responsible in great part for the pleasure of the novel? *The Thorn Birds* is directed at a female audience, one that by the late seventies has certainly been affected by debates around feminism, if only in their most populist and watered-down form. Even through media representations of feminist discourse there had developed among women a more inquiring attitude towards traditional masculinity and femininity. The acceptable social content of daytime fantasies had shifted enough to allow the woman to be the sexual initiator, especially if, like Meggie, she is also the model of femininity who only wants marriage and babies, content to stay out of modern, urban public space, down on the farm. Within the terms of the fantasy Meggie is allowed to be both active *and* feminine. With certain fundamental reservations about her social role *The Thorn Birds* offers the female reader a liberated de-repressed version of the seduction fantasy, a written-out, up-front story of 'A daughter seduces a father' in place of that old standard 'A father seduces a daughter.'

Most mass-market romance, as Modleski and others point out, has stuck with the conservative androcentric version, counting on the third-person narrative which looks down on the woman in the text to inscribe the active female as the knowing reader in the narrative 'a man seduces a woman.' Shifts in the public discourses about sexuality, specifically feminist discourse, permit the seduction fantasy to be reinscribed in a more radical way in popular fiction. They allow the narrative itself to express the terms of original fantasy from the place of the woman, while reassuring us through Meggie's character that such a fantasy, however transgressive in social terms, is perfectly feminine. If the text stopped there it would still be disruptive for, if we put the relationship between femininity and transgression another way, the fantasy sequence suggests also that, in order to be perfectly feminine, a woman's desire must be wholly transgressive. But the role reversal of the seduction fantasy is only the first and simplest stage in the transformation of the seduction story.

More unexpected and eccentric is the way in which Ralph as the feminine man and virgin priest is mobilized within the fantasy. Critiques of traditional macho masculinity abound in the popular fictions of the seventies, especially perhaps in Hollywood film. Decentred masculinity can be represented through a figure like Ralph, whose maternal characteristics are balanced by his public power. Ralph's feminine side is also signified, however, by his great personal beauty, to which he himself calls attention in the early scenes, and his prized virginity. As a beautiful and pure object of desire he stands in the text in place of the woman, often obscuring Meggie. As decentred man, Ralph displaces Meggie as the object to be seduced. This blurring of masculine and feminine positions is worked through in all but the last seduction scene.

Meggie's passion is usually straightforwardly expressive; Ralph's is held back by taboo. His desire is accompanied by shame, disgust and horror at his own wayward libido on whose control he so prides himself: 'I can get it up. It's just that I don't choose to.' 'Spider's poison,' 'snakes,' 'ghastly drive' are the phrases used to describe Ralph's illicit desire for Meggie. Yet Ralph is at last moved by his love for her, and his suppressed desire, to consummate the relationship. In the final scenario it is Ralph who pursues and takes action, restoring the initiatives of sexual difference to their right order. The moment of absolute transgression, when Ralph breaks his vows to the church, is later described by him as another kind of 'sacrament.' It is also the moment when the even more transgressive definitions of sexual difference that have been offered the reader are withdrawn. Incest makes real men and women of us all.

It is not simply plot and character that structure the text's unstable inscriptions of sexual difference. The narrative strategy and the language of the novel contribute centrally to this effect. Third-person narration helps a lot. Although the novel starts out with Meggie's early childhood traumas, setting her up as a figure who endures loss and punishment at an early stage, her psyche is always held at one remove. The authorial voice is adult and knowing about her, its tone sympathetic and realistic but never really intimate. Ralph's consciousness, on the other hand, especially where it touches on his feeling for Meggie, is presented consistently in lyrical and philosophical terms. Long paragraphs speculate on Meggie's attraction for the priest:

> Perhaps, had he looked more deeply into himself, he might have seen that what he felt for her was the curious result of time, and place and person . . . she filled an empty space in his life which God could not. . . .

Ralph 'redecorates' a room for Meggie at the presbytery in which she is installed as surrogate daughter. The text 'decorates' Ralph's feelings for her, offering us a running inner narrative on them, while Meggie's growing feeling for Ralph is rarely given such discursive space. The text gives us a 'natural' identification with Meggie because of her initial priority in the story and because she is the woman in the novel, but it also offers us a seductive alternative identifi-

cation with Ralph, as a more complex and expressive subjectivity. The oscillation between the realistic and lyric modes, the disruption of the terms of sexual difference, is both titillating and vertiginous. It makes obvious what is perhaps always true in romance reading for women: that the reader identifies with both terms in the seduction scenario, but most of all with the process of seduction. In *The Thorn Birds* sequence the term in which subjectivity is most profoundly inscribed is the verb: *seduces*. It is both disappointing and a relief when the scenario reverts to a more conventional set of positions:

> Go, *run*! Run, Meggie, get out of here with the scrap of pride he's left you!
>
> Before she could reach the veranda he caught her, the impetus of her flight spinning her round against him.

It is as if the act itself, so long deferred, textually speaking, so long the subject of daydream within the narrative, stabilizes the scandalous encounter in terms of socially normative gendered activity and passivity.

There is a whole further generation of things to say about the rewriting of sexual difference in *The Thorn Birds,* but for the purposes of this argument it is perhaps enough to note that Meggie's 'liberated' 'bitchy' actress daughter makes, in the end, a typically feminine match with a macho German financier into whose hands Ralph delivers the stewardship of the Cleary family estates. The novel ends in the moment of European modernity with the union of Rainer and Justine. Twin 'stars' in public life, they also represent socially acceptable and highly polarized versions of late-twentieth-century masculinity and femininity in which tough public men are privately tender and ambitious, successful women are little girls at heart. There are fantasy elements in the 'European' part of the novel, but they are relatively superficial ones. And the seduction scenario between Rainer and Justine is definitely the right way round: 'A man seduces a woman.' Modernity turns out to be pretty old-fashioned after all.

The most daring interrogation of gendered subjectivity is located in the story of Meggie and Ralph and articulated through original fantasy. The English-speaking sub-continent, New Zealand and Australia, before World War II, and especially its idealized rural locations, Drogheda and Matlock Island, stand in as the 'archaic' and 'primitive' setting for the origins of modern sexuality and difference. They work in this way *historically* for the Australian reader, just as the pre-Civil-War American South does for the American reader, or early nineteenth-century Yorkshire for the British reader. But for the 'foreign' reader—and *The Thorn Birds* is written with an international reading market in mind—the setting is doubly displaced and mythologized through distance and history. It is as if, to paraphrase John Locke's famous colonial metaphor about America, 'In the beginning, all the world was down under.'

> In *The Thorn Birds*, racial and religious taboo serve to express the transgressive and asocial character of original fantasy, just as class, race and symbolic incest do in *Wuthering Heights*.
> —*Cora Kaplan*

Myths of origin need actors as well as settings. *The Thorn Birds* does not revise biblical wisdom in this respect; transgression and sexuality are set in motion by Fee's adulterous, cross-racial affair with the half-Maori Pakeha. And I must admit, dear reader, that I have been an unreliable narrator and have held back a crucial piece of information from the text so that it can round out my argument. When Fee and Meggie confess their transgressions to each other, Fee lets slip an important piece of information.

> I have a trace of Maori blood in me, but Frank's father was half Maori. It showed in Frank because he got it from both of us. Oh, but I loved that man! Perhaps it was the call of our blood. . . . He was everything Paddy wasn't—cultured, sophisticated, very charming, I loved him to the point of madness. . . .

How does this 'trace' of 'Maori blood'—McCullough, like Freud, chooses a racist definition of race—work to explain an heredity of transgression in the text? In the first place the inscription of sexual difference at any historical moment not only requires an 'original' myth of a primal scene, it frequently takes on a third term of social difference and prohibition. This acts as defence, perhaps, against the scandal of the child watching the scene of its own origins or, in castration and seduction fantasy, the scandal of sexual difference itself. In any case, it is interesting that in modern Western myth this social difference frequently takes both a racial and specular form, projecting and displacing sexual taboo and illicit desire into cultural taboo and hierarchy. In *The Thorn Birds*, racial and religious taboo serve to express the transgressive and asocial character of original fantasy, just as class, race and symbolic incest do in *Wuthering Heights*. Although the men in these texts may threaten social coherence by their 'hybrid' nature and their deceptive veneer of civilization, it often turns out to be the 'savage' nature and original taint of the women who love them that are most profoundly disruptive. It is Cathy, not Heathcliff, who stands most absolutely outside the social, knocking at the window in vain. In these texts written by and for women, women nevertheless end up responsible for the scandalous origins of

sexuality and difference. *The Thorn Birds* makes this point quite explicitly, adding Fee's own drop of 'primitivism' as a gratuitous racialist confirmation. These two anarchic women are contained in the narrative by the chosen role as mothers and matriarchs. Kept on the plantation, they are not allowed to affect the modern resolution of sexual difference and invade the public sphere. '. . . where *do* we go wrong?' Meggie asks Mum, 'In being born,' Fee replies.

The second half of the novel disappoints in terms of its normalization of sexual difference, rather like the last section of *Wuthering Heights*. But the really worrying elements of the European portions of the narrative reside in their overt politics. I have said very little about the novel's lengthy and interesting treatment of the Catholic church and the priesthood, a treatment which was in dialogue, no doubt, with elements of the reformist debates within the Catholicism in the seventies. Although the author takes a liberal Catholic line on the chastity of priests, the rest of her views on the church are anything but progressive. Despite acknowledging its economic opportunism and political infighting, the novel is largely uncritical of the church's international influence. Indeed, it openly defends the Vatican's record in relation to fascism and endorses its steadfast opposition to revolution. When Meggie and Ralph's son Dane becomes the perfect priest, he goes on holiday to Greece where his visit is shadowed by a threatening crowd which is 'milling' and 'chanting' in support of 'Pap-an-dreo.'

> Reading *The Thorn Birds* should warn us away from those half-baked notions embedded in certain concepts of 'post-modern' culture and 'post-feminism' which see the disruption of subjectivity and sexual difference as an act which has a radical autonomy of its own and a power to disrupt hierarchies beyond it.
> —*Cora Kaplan*

Although the story contains a rags-to-riches element, the origins and morality of wealth are never questioned. Rainer's rise to fortune and power endow him, in the novel, with wholly admirable and desirable qualities. With Ralph and Dane dead, he becomes the secular inheritor of the power which the church held earlier in the narrative. Fantasies of wealth and power find a lot of scope in family sagas, where they intersect with and support the original fantasies which are represented there. Like *Lace*, *Dallas* or *Dynasty*, *The Thorn Birds* masks the origins of wealth, naturalizing and valorizing it even as it exposes and, up to a certain point, reflects upon the nature of social myth and psychic fantasy about the origins of sexuality and sexual difference. It is this appropriation of fantasy, not fantasy itself, that is implicitly dangerous.

Reading *The Thorn Birds* should warn us away from those half-baked notions embedded in certain concepts of 'post-modern' culture and 'post-feminism' which see the disruption of subjectivity and sexual difference as an act which has a radical autonomy of its own and a power to disrupt hierarchies beyond it. *The Thorn Birds* is a powerful and ultimately reactionary read. In its unashamed right-wing bias the text assumes that its millions of women readers have become progressively reflective about sexuality, but remain conservative, uninterested and unreflective in their thinking about other political and social concerns. Indeed, to return to my initial analysis of the pleasure of reading *Gone with the Wind,* the reactionary political and social setting secure, in some fashion, a privileged space where the most disruptive female fantasy can be 'safely' indulged.

If we ask why women read and watch so much popular romance, the answers seem at one level mundane and banal. Still excluded in major ways from power (if not labour) in the public sphere, where male fantasy takes on myriad discursive forms, romance narrative can constitute one of women's few entries to the public articulation and social exploration of psychic life. It is wrong to imply, as many studies of romance reading seem to, that fantasizing is a female specialty. On the contrary fantasy is, as Freud's work suggests, a crucial part of our constitution as human subjects. It is neither the contents of original fantasies nor even necessarily the position from which we imagine them that can, or ought, to be stigmatized. Rather, it is consciousness of the insistent nature of those fantasies for men and women and the historically specific forms of their elaboration that need to be opened up. Our priority ought be an analysis of the progressive or reactionary politics of the narratives to which they can become bound in popular expression. Those narratives—which of course include issues around sexual difference as well as around race, class and the politics of power generally—can be changed.

Jane Yolen (review date 26 April 1987)

SOURCE: "Vacant Lives in Great Big Australia," in *The New York Times Book Review,* April 26, 1987, p. 15.

[*Below, Yolen offers an unfavorable review of* The Ladies of Missalonghi.]

Colleen McCullough's new novel, *The Ladies of Missalonghi* makes the mistake of confusing the inevitability of fairy-tale logic with predictability, of confusing the accuracy of an account with textbook prose.

The short novel has fairy-tale antecedents—most notably Cinderella—visible in the heroine, Missy Wright, a girl whose real beauty is hidden behind a wardrobe of brown dresses and whose patrimony has been stolen from her by her wicked cousins. There is a handsome rich man, as close to a prince as Australia could produce, who chooses Missy above all the others. And a fairy godmother in the form of a beautiful, glowing woman named Una, who is ultimately revealed as an angel.

The book tries hard to portray Australia and the Australian mind accurately in the years just before World War I with occasional outbursts of leaden prose: "That they acquiesced so tamely to a regimen and a code inflicted upon them by people who had no idea of the loneliness, the bitter suffering of genteel poverty, was no evidence of lack of spirit or lack of courage. Simply, they were born and lived in a time before the great wars completed the industrial revolution, when paid work and its train of comforts were a treason to their concepts of life, of family, of femininity." A perfectly acceptable sentence for a history or sociology text, but hardly the kind of prose that sings in fiction.

In fact, the studied, ornate, empty prose echoes the studied, ornate, empty life that so many of the women of the period suffered through. But it is lucky for the reader that *The Ladies of Missalonghi* is novella length, a quick 189 pages plus several undistinguished line drawings by Peter Chapman, for that prose would wear down even the most ardent readers of romantic fiction or Colleen McCullough's many fans.

In her previous novels, Ms. McCullough showed herself to be a wonderful storyteller, with a gift for breezy characterizations and tales that galloped across the pages of her books. In *Tim* or *The Thorn Birds* one would never come across a sentence like this: "Answering the lure of the valley, she crossed to the far side of Gordon Road and lifted her face to the kindly sky and swelled her nostrils to take in the heady tang of the bush." *Swelled her nostrils?* Yes, *The Ladies of Missalonghi* is meant to be, in part, a gentle, genteel parody of the romantic novels that Missy reads. But fairy tale, textbook, romance, and parody do not sit well side by side. *The Ladies of Missalonghi* is a strange, silly bit of froth that tries to straddle too many genres and ends up simply being annoying.

Sybil Steinberg (essay date 14 September 1990)

SOURCE: "Colleen McCullough: The Indefatigable Author Has Embarked on a Five-Volume Series Set in Ancient Rome," in *Publishers Weekly,* September 14, 1990, pp. 109-10.

[*In the following essay, Steinberg reports on McCullough's*

Roman history series and offers insight into the author's motivations for writing it.]

To meet with Colleen McCullough one generally must take a 13-hour nonstop flight from Los Angeles to New Zealand, then board another plane to Norfolk Island, in the South Pacific Ocean, a three-by-five-mile bit of land that she calls "a remote speck at the end of the world." Small wonder, then, that *PW* sought out the author at the recent ABA in Las Vegas. The reason was not contiguity alone: McCullough's name will be much bandied about this fall, as Morrow issues the first of her five-volume series of historical novels set in the waning days of the Roman Republic. *The First Man in Rome: Marius* would be an achievement on any terms; running 896 pages, with copious notes, a chatty glossary, maps and illustrations all provided by the author, it is yet another departure for the writer who made her name with *The Thorn Birds* and has surprised her readers each time out with a novel quite different from the one before.

As advance readers of *The First Man in Rome* have discovered, it is not frivolous stuff. Exhaustively researched for historical accuracy and humanized through a plethora of small, telling details that bring Roman politics and society vividly to life, this is a complex story that requires respectful attention. Although she pronounces the book "not daunting for your average novel reader," McCullough admits that "a certain kind of *Thorn Bird* fan won't hack it." On the other hand, she crows, "at least I've written something that men won't be ashamed to be caught reading on the subway."

Nor does she feel that readers will be put off by the characters' cumbersome names, with their similar or identical praenomens and strings of cognomens. "Latin is the major root of out English language," McCullough says firmly. "Metullus is easier to pronounce than Raskolnikov." As for such monikers as Quintus Caecilius Metullus Numidicus and Quintus Lutatius Catulus Caesar, two characters prominent in the first book, McCullough is confident that their sharply delineated personalities will make them spring off the page.

McCullough has never been shy of taking chances. Having dreamed about this saga for 30 years and having researched for a decade, she is confident that it will find an audience commensurate with its 300,000 prepublication printing and status as a Book of the Month Club selection. So determined was she to do these books that she left Harper & Row, her longtime publisher, because of its reluctance to guarantee the entire five-book series.

Her fascination with the Roman Republic dates back to her college years in Australia. According to McCullough, she and her five best friends—all boys—had been "brilliant in high school, and when we got to first-year university we were bored dry. We'd all been science-streamed so we decided

we'd embark on a program of culture. Amongst other things, we read the Penguin translations of the Greek and Roman classics. I always wanted to read them again, and after *Thorn Birds* I did. I came to the letters and speeches of Cicero and the Commentaries of Julius Caesar. And I was fascinated." McCullough pronounces the last word portentously, emphasizing each syllable. She lights another of a chain of cigarettes, smooths her hair, pulled back in a no-nonsense bun.

"One glaring fact hit me square between the eyes. For the first and last time in the history of the world until very recently, these were words written by the men who ran the joint. Not some historian scribbling away after the fact. I was awed! Reading Cicero's letters as he wavers between loyalty to Pompey and the temptation to turn to Caesar, and his glancing references to Cleopatra—whom he loathed—I suddenly saw a world that I wanted to enter as a novelist, desperately. At no other time in the history of the world did so many truly intelligent and talented men walk across a political stage at one time. And the Roman Republic gave us our law, our political systems, our engineering—so much! I thought, it's germane, it's relevant to modern living."

Determined to render the era with exactitude, McCullough assembled in her home on Norfolk Island "the best private library on Republican Rome in private hands anywhere in the world." She enlisted the aid of a full-time researcher, Sheelah Hidden, who was fluent in four languages and who interviewed experts in many countries. Hidden also located portrait busts of the characters, so that McCullough, who had decided that she was "fed up with people thinking that Cleopatra looked like Elizabeth Taylor," could draw the novel's illustrations.

"I did all this research and I put two million words on paper and of course, being me, I drafted it. Three drafts. This was all nonfiction preparation for the book—a monograph of each of the major characters. Next, I got continuous computer paper, and I made a chronological list of every single thing that happened. I did all that before I started writing the first volume. And I did it for the lot; it is done!"

To her surprise, however, Harper & Row was less than eager for the enormous project. "Fred [Mason, her agent] and I couldn't get a contract out of them. They dickered. Money was never at the root of it because we weren't asking for a lot of money. This hemming and hawing went on for six months."

McCullough finally wrote out a precis of each of the five books she contemplated: Marius, Sulla, Pompey the Great, Caesar, Augustus—and sent it to Harper along with a monograph on Cleopatra, so that they would see "how important the women in the books were going to be." The upshot was that Harper pressed her to abandon the first two books and start directly with the events involving Pompey. "When they informed me of this I was 55,000 words into Marius. I was crushed," McCullough intones dolefully. Though she is recalling a bad time, she is also indulging the raconteur's gift of spinning out a tale.

Convinced that the series should appear as planned, that "in order to understand what happened to the Roman Republic, one must start with Marius," McCullough recalls her anger at Harper's unwillingness to go along with the plan. "A creative artist can't work in that kind of atmosphere. You can't work for a publisher who doesn't want you. Money has never mattered to me, but by God, my work does!"

It was at this point that Carolyn Reidy, president of Avon, which had published all of McCullough's works in paperback, ventured to Norfolk Island to urge the author not to cut Avon out of reprint rights for the projected saga. McCullough, who had always enjoyed working with Reidy, sensed the time was ripe to jump ship to Morrow, and stipulated that Reidy edit all five books. She now professes herself "hugely pleased" at the arrangement.

Quite a lot about McCullough is outsize: her big, comfortable frame, clothed in a muumuu and absent of feminine adornment; her booming, uninhibited laugh; her open friendliness and large, unrestrained smile; her storytelling, delivered with gusto; her ego. But if she doesn't suffer for undue modesty, she is matter-of-fact about her accomplishments.

Born in Australia's outback, she says that she and her brother, who died 25 years ago, were both gifted children of a mean-spirited father and a mother determined to guarantee her children's education: McCullough attended Holy Cross College and the University of Sydney. Possessing what she calls "amazing mathematic and artistic and scientific gifts," as a child of the Depression McCullough decided to opt for security and "do science." An allergy to soap kept her from being a surgeon ("I couldn't scrub, you see"), so she became a medical scientist. Having earned an appointment at Yale as a research assistant in the department of neurophysiology, she arrived in New Haven on April Fools' Day 1967. She loved her job but was very poor, so she decided to write a novel at night to earn extra money. The result was *Tim,* "my bucket of tears book."

McCullough sent *Tim* to agent Freida Fishbein, then "a very ancient lady of 87, who placed the novel with Harper & Row. Fishbein had died by the time McCullough started *The Thorn Birds,* which was "very loosely based" on her family's history in Australia, so she herself delivered the manuscript to editor Ann Harris at Harper. "It was about four times the length of *Tim,* which had earned me $50,000. I thought, with any luck, maybe it would earn me four times that amount."

McCullough then went off to England, where she was due to start nurse's training at London's ancient St. Bartholomew's Hospital, to get background for the hospital novel she was "desperate" to write. "I didn't tell them I wrote books, of course. I was looking forward to some really hard physical labor because I am a workhorse."

Training was due to start on April 11, 1977. On February 2, *The Thorn Birds* made a record sale in paperback auction, and, McCullough recalls, "I hit the headlines everywhere. My cover was sprung. It was manifestly impossible that I go on to nursing. Can you imagine: a millionairess author carrying a bedpan!"

Other major changes in her lifestyle soon proved necessary. "When I became rich and famous, life became very complicated. It was unsafe for me to live on my own on any major landmass; you become prey to all sorts of nuts and bolts in the community." Hearing about tiny Norfolk Island, with its controlled population, she applied to live there. And, soon after, at the age of 46, married an island native, Ric Robinson, a descendant not only of one of the Bounty mutineers (as are many of the island's residents) but also of a Samoan princess and Isaac Newton.

Robinson, who is some years her junior, is "a colonial aristocrat in every way," according to McCullough a planter of the kentia palm ("it's the very hardy plant you see in all the hotel foyers"), Robinson modeled a reconstructed toga for his wife, providing irrefutable evidence that Romans did not sport underwear when wearing the garment. "It would have been impossible to pee in a toga if you wore anything underneath, you see. There's your left arm, weighted down by an immensity of toga: it's 16' by 9'. You can't possibly lower that hand . . ." McCullough rises from our table in a Las Vegas coffee shop, pantomimes the situation. *PW* is convinced.

On Norfolk Island, McCullough wrote *Indecent Obsession,* which she calls "my whodunit"; *Creed for the Third Millennium,* "my pessimistic novel of the future"; and the novella *Ladies of Missalonghi,* "my fairy tale."

The Roman series is her "bash at the historical novel." Happily embarked on the second volume, she is confident that she will produce the books at the rate of one a year. "The first one's always the hardest, and I got it out in less than a year, from go to whoa. It's not hard to do if you're well organized and well ordered. I'm not short of words. Maybe it's my scientific training, but my feeling is that for a writer, words are tools.

"Nobody expects a neurosurgeon to lay down his tools. I'm good with my tools. I don't mislay them. I'm a fluent writer. I do multiple drafts. Once I start, I'm consumed to finish. I work at a pace a lot of writers couldn't cope with."

McCullough slows her rapid-fire recital. She smiles broadly. "I'm such a nitpicker. I love the little details. If you're going to make it sing, it's the little details that will do it. I found one small detail in Caesar's *Commentaries*. Before a major battle, all the men sit down and make their wills. That's it, you see; that sort of detail makes it a world, and makes the world very real." To McCullough, writing feverishly on her remote island, that world is very real indeed.

James Idema (review date 7 October 1990)

SOURCE: "Vast Roman Saga: Colleen McCullough Tackles Marius and Sulla," in *Chicago Tribune Books,* October 7, 1990, p. 3.

[*In the following review, Idema offers a generally favorable assessment of* The First Man in Rome, *though noting its daunting length and large cast of characters with unfamiliar Latin names.*]

At the beginning of the last century of the Roman Republic, which was already deteriorating under pressures of economic stress and class conflict, two leaders emerged whose friendship helped preserve the republic for a time and whose rivalry hastened its subsequent collapse.

Colleen McCullough's prodigious novel, first in a series, is concerned with the 11 years of friendship, years during which the relentless drive for supreme political power by Gaius Marius, a war hero who had transcended his humble origins, was abetted by his confidant, Lucius Cornelius Sulla, a brilliant and corrupt aristocrat. Although at the close of *The First Man in Rome* the two still seem inseparable, there have been enough hints of unease in the late pages of the novel to suggest, even to the historically naive, the doom of their relationship and what that entails for the republic.

That process—the disintegration of the ancient regime and the establishment of the Roman Empire—is the background of Colleen McCullough's proposed saga. The next novel, she tells us in an author's note, is tentatively titled *The Grass Crown*. How many after that? She doesn't say. How many pages in all? The mind boggles.

Sheer bulk is what inevitably first impresses a reader encountering this book, and one surely can be forgiven for wondering how he or she is ever going to get through it. Nor is one reassured, flipping pages, to note the densely labeled maps and diagrams and the 111-page general glossary and pronunciation guide.

Indeed, *The First Man in Rome* is not an easy book to get

through, unlike *The Thorn Birds,* McCullough's immensely popular novel about Australia. But the story is both entertaining and compelling—persevering readers will want to pursue the next book to discover the fate of Marius, the title character—and the novelist renders the volatile political and social fabric of ancient Rome convincingly. (Politics were even dirtier in 110 B.C. than they are in 1990 A.D., and a lot bloodier.)

Several of the major characters in McCullough's enormous cast—the women in particular—come through as real humans facing real and recognizable problems. Sulla's wife, Julilla, is especially sympathetic. Another attractive character is Publius Rutilius Rufus, a wise old friend of the First Man, whose long letters from Rome to Marius on the battlefields are diverting as well as functional to the plot.

But McCullough bludgeons us with her scholarship. In a somewhat defiant tone, she reports in the author's note that she has "gone to the ancient sources" and done her own research. She has executed all the maps and drawings herself, including the portraits of leading characters, and she directs readers who might be skeptical about historical details to consult the glossary, which she also wrote. Trust her, she implies.

Actually, the glossary is a most worthwhile pursuit in itself. Not only is it full of appealing facts, but it is also written in amusing, accessible prose—a good deal more user-friendly than the main text. Here one will find everything from the composition of the Roman Senate to how the toga is properly draped to what Gaius Julius Caesar's dining room looked like.

But the book as a whole is burdened with excessive information, as though in striving for verisimilitude the author felt compelled to empty her files—and the threads of the story frequently become entangled in needless digressions.

Easily the most troublesome element of the text, however, is the use of proper Latin names. Most often they are triple names, sometimes quadruple, and with an epic cast of characters the effect is at first disconcerting, very soon numbing. To keep track of them requires extreme vigilance, because before long, with their repetitive meter, they begin to register like limericks.

The author explains in a special note why custom dictated this elaborate form of address among citizens of the republic but not why it must be imposed on her readers.

Don G. Campbell (review date 28 October 1990)

SOURCE: "McCullough's Roman à Clef," in *Los Angeles Times Book Review,* October 28, 1990, p. 11.

[*In the following review, Campbell praises* The First Man in Rome *as "an absolutely absorbing story" that is well-researched and well-told.*]

In at least one respect the parallel is discomfiting: a national political leadership in which great wealth is essential to achieve power. But it's not Washington, D.C., 1990, where dug-in incumbents defy political unknowns with lean pocketbooks to unseat them. It is, instead, the city-state of Rome in 110 BC, and the republic that has endured for more than 300 years has become fat, corrupt and inept, and is beginning to unravel faster than a 39-cent pair of socks.

This is the critical juncture that novelist Colleen McCullough—she, primarily, of the enormously popular *The Thorn Birds*—has chosen as the take-off point for her awesome and epic new work, *The First Man in Rome.* And, for her protagonist, she has wisely zeroed in on a most unusual man living in a most unusual time frame: Gaius Marius, tremendously gifted both militarily and organizationally and, alas, doomed in spite of his wealth to second-rate political status.

For it is not enough in this flaccid period of the Republic to have vote-buying and favor-granting wealth, alone. Inbred and obsessed with blood lineage, the path to the senate and, ultimately, to the post of *consul,* also requires an impeccable pedigree. Even though Marius, wealthy through land holdings and mining interests, has attained a seat in the senate through powerful friends, it is pretty well the end of the political line for a man sneeringly dismissed by his enemies as "an Italian hayseed with no Greek."

This is a complex and critical period in Roman history. In the previous century, beginning in about 264 BC, the city-state has become the undisputed military and political leader of the civilized world. But its reach is exceeding its grasp and it is saddled with generals who can't general and a citizen-army (one must be a landholder to serve) that has become disillusioned and burned out. Politicians buy their way to the revolving post of consul only as a stepping stone to a post consul appointment to the post of governor of a province that, at their leisure, they can then ravage and loot without restraint.

Fittingly, McCullough, in referring to Marius as *The First Man in Rome,* is labeling him, also, as Rome's first "New Man"—a new breed rising to prominence in spite of his lineage and, in effect, opening up the era of one-man rule characterizing the Roman Empire that would follow on the heels of the republic. For Marius, though, nothing would have been possible without the intervention of the powerful Gaius Julius Caesar Nepos, father of the Julius Caesar whose name has become synonymous with the Roman Empire, and whose bloodline is flawless.

But flawless bloodline, or not, Caesar is not wealthy enough to assure both of his sons the gold needed to climb the political ladder and, at the same time, provide his two daughters with handsome dowries. It is the vital *quid pro quo* of Marius' life—his wealth to assure Caesar the inheritance he needs, and in exchange, Caesar's 18-year-old daughter, Julia, as Marius' wife. (Never mind that the 48-year-old Marius has a wife of 20 years—divorce in Rome in 110 BC was a simple matter of the husband signing a parchment of divorcement.) It is, perhaps surprisingly, a most harmonious marriage in addition to giving Marius the entree he needs.

Firmly established as the consul, Marius quickly resolves the African revolt headed by Jugurtha, King of Numidia and becomes the instant darling of Rome to the point where he is reelected to the post of *consul in absentia,* which, at the time, was without precedent.

This six-time consul is a remarkable man, surrounded by other remarkable men—many of them venal, cowardly and self-seeking, but others, such as Lucius Cornelius Sulla, Marius' chief aide in both the African and German campaigns, fully as complex and as talented as the consul himself.

Sulla is a brooding and curious man: Although with an untainted blood-line, he was as shut out of Roman political affairs by his poverty as Marius himself had been by his humble birth. Most of his early life has been spent on the low side of the social scale—debauchery and blatant misconduct with members of both sexes for openers. How Sulla resolves *his* shortcoming (the necessary wealth for ascendancy) is vastly different from Marius' solution and up a far darker path. And yet, as different in temperament and morality as they are, these two men, both born leaders, fit together like a hand in a well-oiled glove.

> This is an absolutely absorbing story—not simply of the military and political intrigues that went into the final days of the Republic but also of what it was like to live, love and survive at this pivotal point in our civilization.
> —*Don G. Campbell*

Latin purists may quarrel with some of McCullough's use of phrases that, admittedly, sometimes clang on the ear as anachronisms. We can accept that, in one form or another,

Latin had words literally translating as "a pimp and a pansy"—not to mention any number of bodily functions—for instance, but some of the expletives in particular have more of the ring of the language heard in a 20th-Century truck stop than in a patrician household in Rome in 110 BC.

Let's face it, too: *The First Man in Rome,* is, far and away, the story of the *men* who shaped Rome's destiny in an age where women were chattel (bought, sold, traded, given away in marriage without question); most of the women emerge two-dimensionally. In all fairness, though, McCullough's treatment of the women foremost in both the life of Marius (Julia, Gaius Julius Caesar Nepos' eldest daughter) and of Sulla (Julilla, Julia's younger sister) are fleshed out more richly. Julia is strong-willed; Julilla, knowing full well that there is something drastically wrong in her relationship with her husband, is weak and tragedy-prone—conditions that have no chronological boundaries.

This is an absolutely absorbing story—not simply of the military and political intrigues that went into the final days of the Republic but also of what it was like to live, love and survive at this pivotal point in our civilization. McCullough's research is mind-boggling (the illustrations and maps are by her, too), but this is pretty dry stuff by itself. It takes a master storyteller to weave this sort of tapestry into a 900-plus-page novel that is every bit as hard to put down as it is to pick up.

Much has been made of the mastery of the novelist who can condense an unforgettable story into a few pages (Stephen Crane's *The Red Badge of Courage* takes just 250 pages); too little has been said about the skill that goes into a sprawling story almost four times that length without the reader's interest flagging at any point.

Nothing in life is free, though, and *The First Man in Rome* requires some concentration, and back-tracking, by the thoughtful reader. Geographic names, for instance, are confusing, and while McCullough's plentiful maps are helpful, it is still touchy business; for instance, trying to relate Numidia Occidentis to our 20th-Century understanding of North Africa's coastline.

Readers who delighted, in the late Mary Renault's novels built around ancient Greece will be equally enchanted by *The First Man in Rome,* and by McCullough's promise that it is but one of several she plans on the waning days of the Roman Republic and the birth of the Empire. No less delightful, too, is the author's 123-page glossary with absolutely fascinating trivia in it. The Roman toga measured 15 feet wide and more than 7 feet long and made the wearing of underwear, and certain biological functions, logistic impossibilities.

Carol E. Rinzler (review date 4 November 1990)

SOURCE: "Roman Soap," in *The New York Times Book Review,* November 4, 1990, p. 19.

[*In the following review, Rinzler commends McCullough's research for* The First Man in Rome *but faults the novel for excessive length and slow plot development.*]

When I finally get around to writing the history of 20th-century literature, I plan to devote a chapter to the withering away of the story, the virtual disappearance of the literate page-turner that Wharton, O'Hara, Nabokov and Cheever used to toss off every few years.

The pickings aren't much fatter if you're willing to settle for novels merely zippy enough to see you through a bout with the flu. Judith Krantz and Dominick Dunne are beginning to tire. Scott Turow and Jonathan Kellerman don't write fast enough to fill the shelves that are emptied of new Stouts and Creaseys. Because the historical novel is in a similar state of disarray, flu sufferers and others in need of diversion have eagerly awaited Colleen McCullough's new meganovel. Alas, only accomplished potboiler skimmers are likely to have much fun with *The First Man in Rome.*

Based loosely on historical events, the new novel, unlike *The Thorn Birds,* Ms. McCullough's huge 1977 success, spans only a decade (110 to 100 B.C.); this is sufficient time, however, for the book's mostly upper-crust Romans to undergo sufficient change (love, hate, birth, death, triumph, tragedy and so forth) to hold the reader—at least through the sections that deal with private Romans rather than public Rome.

> **Ms. McCullough is terrific when she's writing about women. All of her female characters quiver with life; a patrician woman who falls in love with a man who spurns her; another who is starved by her brother until she submits to marriage with a man she hates; a third who finds her vocation as that Roman rarity, a working mother.**
> —*Carol E. Rinzler*

The book revolves around its eponymous hero, Gaius Marius—Rome's ablest general, a man destined to be six times a consul—and his wife, Julia, a grave, beautiful and steady aristocrat who makes a love match of a marriage arranged by her father for money. (Julia also turns out to be the aunt of Julius Caesar, who appears as a baby at the end of the novel. Presumably we will see more of him; according to an author's note, this book is only the first in a projected series.)

Ms. McCullough is terrific when she's writing about women. All of her female characters quiver with life; a patrician woman who falls in love with a man who spurns her; another who is starved by her brother until she submits to marriage with a man she hates; a third who finds her vocation as that Roman rarity, a working mother. A handful of Ms. McCullough's legion of men are also successful characters, notably Lucius Cornelius Sulla. When we meet him he is a bisexual, libertine patrician with no money, living off two women in a *ménage à trois*. But the sheer overpopulation of the male cast of characters fogs them with a perplexing sameness, at least if you don't accord commercial fiction the same attention you pay Plutarch. (Let's see, was that Marcus Livius Drusus who threw his political support to Marius 300 pages ago, or was it Marcus Aemilius Scaurus?)

The plot moves along smartly when there's a woman on stage and Ms. McCullough is writing about love, emotion or sex (the last quite tame). What slows the book down are the arid stretches, making up roughly half of its length, that deal with politics and military campaigns. Whenever Marius is with Julia, *The First Man in Rome* is utterly engaging; when he goes off to war or the Forum, cleaning you closets is a more exciting alternative. Sustaining even such momentum as this ambitious novel somehow attains is as difficult for Ms. McCullough as it would be for most. The last hundred-odd pages, trailing off into a weak and confusing ending, suggest that she was simply exhausted.

Adding to the boredom factor is the frequent awkwardness of Ms. McCullough's prose. Forget the constant lapses of grammar and diction. What makes *The First Man in Rome* eminently put-downable is the author's determination to shoehorn in as much of her research as possible, marring the book with bulky, obese passages. To choose just one:

"When Saturninus introduced his second agrarian law, the clause stipulating an oath burst upon the Forum like a clap of thunder; not a bolt of Jovian lightning, rather the cataclysmic rumble of the old gods, the real gods, the faceless gods, the *numina*. Not only was an oath required of every senator, but instead of the customary swearing in the temple of Saturn, Saturninus's law required that the oath be taken under the open sky in the roofless temple of Semo Sancus Dius Fidius on the lower Quirinal, where the faceless god without a mythology had only a statue of Gaia Caecllia—wife of King Tarquinius Priscus of old Rome—to humanize his dwelling." (Bet you didn't get through that on the first try.)

Despite such meanderings, Ms. McCullough requires 95 pages at the conclusion of the novel to display still more of her research in the form of a glossary. I rather enjoyed this lagniappe, as well as the several maps the author provides, although her drawings of the characters, interspersed among the chapters, are amateurish.

Perhaps if Ms. McCullough had written a longer glossary and a shorter novel she might have avoided the odd and unsatisfying alternation of gripping sections with others that make one's eyes glaze over. Could she have lingered so long with the military and political material as a play for a larger male audience than she had with *The Thorn Birds?* Whatever the answer, it would have been a great help if only the novel had been rounded out to an even 900 pages with one more brief appendix: a list of the pages the story was on.

Gwen Morris (essay date Spring 1991)

SOURCE: "An Australian Ingredient in American Soap: *The Thorn Birds* by Colleen McCullough," in *Journal of Popular Culture,* Vol. 24, No. 4, Spring, 1991, pp. 59-69.

[*In the following essay, Morris identifies conventional American literary themes in* The Thorn Birds *and considers McCullough's treatment of social, racial, and gender issues as a source of the novel's popularity in the United States.*]

The Australian cartoonist Horner probably summed up the views of many Australians when he suggested Colleen McCullough be given the Order of Super Suds (O.S.S.) in the New Year's Honors list "for introducing an Australian ingredient into American soap."

While this assessment of *The Thorn Birds,* particularly of the television miniseries, contains more than a grain of truth, the book cannot be dismissed so lightly. It has set records for sales and popularity. Published in 1977, over half a million hardback copies of the book had been sold by 1979. Avon paid $1.9 million for the paperback rights, at that time the highest price ever paid for paperback rights of a book. It was on the top of the American best-seller lists for six months. In 1983 it was made into a very popular television miniseries. By 1985, 10.5 million copies of the book had been sold, 750,000 of them in Australia and New Zealand. An examination of the content of the book, therefore, is highly likely to reveal useful data on American popular culture, as well as something about the Australian ingredient.

The Australian Ingredient

The most obvious Australian ingredient is the setting. There is also a secret Australian ingredient which may not be recognized by Americans.

The story is set first in a rural area of New Zealand, and then in Australia, on a sheep station, Drogheda, in the plains country of New South Wales. There are occasional forays into other parts of the world, such as Britain and Rome, but most of the action takes place in Australia. The plains are described as "all brown and grey, even the trees!" "horrible, fenceless and vast, without a trace of green." The nearest town is "on the very edge of the Back of Beyond, a last outpost in a steadily diminishing rainfall belt; not far away westward began two thousand miles of the Never Never, the desert land where it could not rain."

Although this country is something of a fiction, it would not appear out of place to many Americans. Despite the lack of cactus, the setting evokes images of the sweeping dry plains and desert of the American western. The producer of the television series of *The Thorn Birds* said "We looked into shooting it on authentic Australian locations, but there's nothing in New South Wales that we couldn't match right here [California's Simi Valley, a dry, hilly area north of Los Angeles]."

An American Soap

Colleen McCullough was born in Wellington in western New South Wales, Australia in 1937. Her father was an Ulster Orangman who had immigrated to Australia in the 1920s. She had a link to New Zealand through her mother who was a New Zealander of Irish Catholic and Maori ancestry. In 1967 she went to the United States. She therefore had almost ten years' experience of American life to draw on when she wrote *The Thorn Birds*.

McCullough says that she has no literary pretensions. It pleases her to think that "Joe the Garbage Man" can read her books. When she decided to write *The Thorn Birds* she made a hard-headed decision to appeal to popular taste, particularly American popular taste, because that was where the money lay. She has described how she came to write *The Thorn Birds*:

> And I suppose I was 32 or 33, single, living on my own because I hated—until I met my husband—living with anyone, when I looked at my pay cheque and thought 'you are going to be a 70-year-old spinster in a cold-water, walk-up flat with one 60 watt light bulb.' So I turned professional writer.

> Having already written hundreds of books—I burnt them all except one—I turned professional writer for the money. I didn't set out to be a best-seller because I didn't want to be a best-seller. I just wanted to earn a nice little sum of pocketmoney from writing.

I thought I'd achieved that. *Tim* earned me $50,000 which was lovely. I thought *Thorn Birds* was three times as long so I'd probably earn $150,000 for that. That'll do fine. Of course, it didn't work out that way.

The three principal characters in *The Thorn Birds* are aristocratic. They are commonly encountered in the nineteenth century "sentimental novel," in modern light romances and soap operas. Father Ralph de Bricassart is a direct descendant of a baron in the court of William the Conqueror. Meggie Cleary and her mother, Fiona (Fee) are aristocratic by colonial standards, being descended from one of the first settlers of New Zealand, an escaped Australian convict named Armstrong who fathered "a brood of thirteen handsome half-Polynesian children." Through money and the best boarding schools, a new line of colonial aristocracy was formed.

The marriage of a pioneer to a beautiful Indian "princess" is a common American literary device. For some European Americans, having an Indian female ancestor is a matter of prestige. The marriage of a white woman to an Indian male, however, is not acceptable. By setting the first part of the book in New Zealand McCullough was able not only to draw on her own family history but to include a Maori equivalent of an Indian princess in the story. It is doubtful if a black Australian aboriginal female ancestor would be acceptable to the popular American imagination.

Meggie's father, Paddy, though "a penniless immigrant from the wrong side of the Pale," is a common character type of the American western from the nineteenth century until the present. He is "a small man, all steel and springs in build, legs bowed from a lifetime among horses, arms elongated from years shearing sheep; . . . His eyes were bright blue, crinkled up into a permanent squint like a sailor's from gazing into the far distance . . . His temper was fiery and he had killed a man once." Fee is forced to marry Paddy when her cultured, half-Maori, but married lover, the father of her child, refuses to consider divorce. As breadwinner and father of a large family, Paddy plays an essential supporting role in the book.

The Thorn Birds is long, spanning three generations from 1915 to 1969. The action and the language are often very melodramatic. The actors live a life remote from that of the book's readers. These are some of the ingredients of American soap.

A Sermon of Afflictions

The reason for the title of *The Thorn Birds* is explained in a note at the beginning of the book. The thorn bird spends its life looking for a thorn tree. Having succeeded in its search it impales itself "upon the longest, sharpest spine" and in death sings "One superlative song. Existence the price . . . . For the best is only bought at the cost of great pain." This is almost an ornithological Crucifixion: death is sought willingly by an actor who is without guilt. As the story develops in *The Thorn Birds,* however, some of the actors are very guilty indeed. They gain happiness through sin. Then they (or someone they love) die. For these characters it is more accurate to say that the message of the book is the biblical statement that "the wages of sin is death." Fee pays for Frank, the son of her Maori lover, by his ruin, her husband's death, and finally her own. The death of Ralph's child, Dane is what Meggie receives for her sins. When he learns not only that he has a son (Dane), but that Dane has died, Ralph pays the price of his own death for his love of Meggie.

McCullough is very aware of the American feeling of national guilt:

> I've never understood why Americans belabour themselves with guilt; why a generation that had nothing to do with slavery, and worked so terribly hard to integrate, blames itself so much for the sins of its ancestors.

The Thorn Birds is a modern sermon of afflictions, a Puritan jeremiad. The afflictions of American life are proof that the people have broken their covenant with God. By reciting the sins of the people some of the guilt can be relieved.

The Affliction of Race

Frank, the illegitimate son of Fiona and her half-Maori lover, is described as a dark and unstable force. He has a "vicious streak," there is something "wild and desperate" about him. He has an "alien" face, "black, black eyes" and "a dark heart, a spirit lacking inner light." His Maori "blood" is inescapable. His mother, says,

> I have a trace of Maori blood in me, but Frank's father was half Maori. It showed in Frank because he got it from both of us. Oh, but I loved that man! Perhaps it was the call of our blood, I don't know!

He has some good traits. He helps his mother with the housework and he is the only one who hugs Meggie when she is a child, but he refuses to conform to family expectations. In popular American novels and films miscegenation almost always results in death, either of the alien wife, (rarely the husband) or of the resulting child or both. Frank must pay for Fee's sin. He leaves the family, kills a man, spends many years in jail and returns "a ruined man."

The Afflictions of Gender

McCullough says that she set out in the book to illustrate "the martyr type of woman." The women are slaves to their men, to their children and to housework. The sons are forbidden to help.

The women are capable of doing "men's work"—Meggie is a good stockman, and Fee successfully manages the property after Paddy dies—but they see themselves as weak. Meggie says to her husband: "Oh Luke! I know I'm young and strong, but I'm a woman! I can't take the sort of physical punishment you can." Meggie sums up her attitude to life,

> I'm just an ordinary sort of woman; I'm not ambitious or intelligent, or well educated . . . All I want is a husband, children, my own home. And a bit of love from someone.

Most of the men are also shown as martyrs. They are crippled by their inability to show emotion, by their ambitions to succeed in the world, or by both. McCullough has defended her depiction of males in *The Thorn Birds*—"It's not that the men are weak but they're hamstrung, for some good reason." Meggie's husband, Luke, however, is the archetypal, male, chauvinist pig. He treats her abominably, finally leaving to go cane cutting with his mates. He is possibly based on McCullough's own father who she described as "very, very good-looking . . . who used his good looks . . . He was a bastard. Tight as a fish's bum."

Relations between men and women are seen as a constant battle for power. Women succeed through subterfuge. Both Fee and Meggie consider they had tricked their lovers by having a permanent part of them—their children.

The Afflictions of Nature

The land makes the Cleary family rich, but it exacts a price. It is sometimes an Australian "howling wilderness." Paddy is burnt to death in a bushfire. Stuart, one of Fee's favorite sons, is charged by a wild pig and dies of suffocation when it falls on him. The other Cleary men (there are six sons) never marry. The land has taken away their manhood:

> After all, what could you expect from the men? Stuck out here as shy as kangas, never meeting the girls to boot . . . And besides, the land's demanding in a neutered way. It takes just about all they've got to give, because I don't think they have a great deal. In a physical sense, I mean.

The Afflictions of the City

McCullough uses two other types of description of the land which are common in American literature, that of land as the connection with a time of innocence; and land as farmland tamed to man's agrarian needs. In New Zealand, for example, McCullough describes "an undulating plain as green as the emerald in Fiona Cleary's engagement ring, dotted with thousands of creamy bundles close proximity revealed as sheep." And in Australia,

> Life went on in the rhythmic, endless cycle of the land; the following summer the rains came, not monsoonal but a by-product of them, filling the creek and the tanks, succoring the thirsting grass roots, sponging away the stealthy dust.

The Clearys (especially Meggie) are often portrayed as drawing their strength from this innocent land. When Meggie returns home to the plains from tropical Queensland, she comes,

> Back to brown and silver, back to dust, back to that wonderful purity and spareness North Queensland so lacked. No profligate growth here, no hastening of decay to make room for more; only a slow, wheeling inevitability like the constellations.

The city, however is a decadent place. Frank finds his ruin in the city. Paddy says of city people,

> Down in the city they don't know how the other half lives, and they can afford the luxury of doting on their animals as if they were children. Out here it's different. You'll never see man, woman or child in need of help go ignored out here, yet in the city those same people who dote on their pets will completely ignore a cry of help from a human being. Fee looked up. 'He's right . . . We all have contempt for whatever there's too many of. Out here, it's sheep, but in the city it's people.'

The Afflictions of Comfort

The Clearys are successful in worldly terms but their lives are full of tragedy. Although they are Catholic, they have achieved success through adhering to the values of American Protestantism. They are models of Calvinist Christianity. Their success is achieved through hard work, frugality, education and discipline. They are not fat—"No one carried a pound of superfluous flesh, in spite of the vast quantities of starchy food. They expended every ounce they ate in work and play." They spend large amounts of time reading and although they are poor, have several shelves of books behind the kitchen table. The children are strictly disciplined by their father and are sent to school, despite the cruelty of the teachers. The family goes to church regularly. Fiona gave up the Church of England for Paddy, but misses "the little touches" . . . like grace before meals and prayers before bed, an everyday holiness.

The "calvinistic, stoic upbringing" of the Clearys is contrasted with that of Meggie's schoolfriend, Teresa, whose family is Italian and very indulgent towards the children. Paddy distrusts Teresa's family and when he finds lice in Meg's hair, he horsewhips Teresa's father. After this, Meggie receives for her birthday the willow pattern tea set, like Teresa's, which she had coveted—another use of the "thorn bird" metaphor. She receives a gift at the price of losing a friend. As Ralph says, patting the dashboard of his new Daimler, "Nothing is given without a disadvantage in it." Success brings with it affliction.

Catholics are presented as comfort-loving and worldly, easily-swayed by temptation, and in the case of the nuns at the school attended by the Clearys, as sadistic. They also contrast strongly with the strict Cleary upbringing and system of morals.

McCullough believes in achievement through hard work and appears to discount good fortune as having any influence on success. She says,

> . . . I earned my money and there's nothing in Marx that philosophically negates that . . . I remember one young man saying, 'Oh, all I can afford is one paperback at a time.' And I looked at him and said: 'Well, if you got off your butt'—he was a bright young man—'and did something about it, maybe you could afford to buy books by the carton. [as McCullough does] Because when I was your age I bought paperbacks too.'

Over the Counter Remedies

In ***The Thorn Birds*** McCullough also provides some simple prescriptions for curing the afflictions of the people. The formulae are as follows:

The afflictions of race: People from ethnic groups are inherently bad. They can't help themselves. For their own good, they must be made to conform.

The afflictions of gender: Men and women are a burden to each other. If a man really puts a woman down, she must retaliate by subterfuge.

The afflictions of nature: Whatever the cost, keep fighting nature until it is beaten into submission.

The afflictions of the city: Don't try to improve the city. It is an unnatural excrescence on the land. Retreat to the untouched countryside, if you can find any, as often as possible.

The afflictions of comfort: Everyone can become rich if they work hard. Good fortune has nothing to do with it. God is a very strict and success-oriented being. He watches for those who stray from the straight path of righteousness and become too complacent and happy. To keep people aware of their obligations to Him, He makes sure that every happiness is balanced by a tragedy. There is very little you can do to change this.

These formulae have the virtue of ethical simplicity. They involve no outlay of money and can be easily implemented by anyone. In providing simple answers to complex problems, McCullough is fulfilling a fundamental need of the American people.

Remedies in the Old; Remedies in the New

The remedies for the afflictions of the American people provided in *The Thorn Birds* are exactly like those which have been provided for them in American literature and life since the time of early settlement. Go back to the old is the message.

Another old message which can be found in *The Thorn Birds* is that of seeking salvation in the new. The story ends:

Meggie . . . stared wide-eyed through the window. . . . How beautiful the garden was, how alive. To see its small things grow big, change and wither; and new little things come again in the same endless, unceasing cycle. Time for Drogheda to stop. Yes, more than time. Let the cycle renew itself with unknown people . . .

Seeking salvation in a "New Israel" has preoccupied Americans for a long time. Part of the popularity of *The Thorn Birds* seems to rest on its portrayal of "new" lands in the same innocent state as the United States before it became an urban nation. *The Thorn Birds* shows Australia (and New Zealand) as unspoiled frontiers where Americans can live again their old dreams.

The Secret Australian Ingredient

For many Australians *The Thorn Birds* is an embarrassment as it presents a romantic and unrealistic view of Australian life, even of Australian life in the past. At least part of the story is based on McCullough's family history and many of the descriptions and dialogue ring true. Others are simply fanciful. It is irritating to have American customs and language transposed to the Australian bush. Meggie makes green fir tree cookies, for example, at Christmas time. Although many Americans make fancy cookies at Christmas time, Australians in general follow British customs, such as making Christmas puddings, pies and cakes, crammed full of dried fruit. This certainly would have been so between

the years 1915-1969. In any case, the Australian word for "cookie" is "biscuit."

It is sometimes hard to resist the conclusion that McCullough is indulging in the old Australian pastime of the quiet, devastating joke and the tall story. Of her latest book, *The Ladies of Missalonghi,* she says:

I adored writing it. I've got a whole humorous side which you can't display in even an ordinary size novel because you just can't be irreverent about your characters for too long. The readers gets sated and starts to believe you're being smart—which, of course, you are. So, this was the first time I'd been able to do that.

Although she gets frustrated when she can't include her humorous side in something like *The Thorn Birds,* she says that she puts funny material in anyway. Then at the redrafting stage she takes it out.

The Thorn Birds is very funny at times. Even for an Australian, it is sometimes difficult to decide if there is any truth in some of the assertions in the book. Do shearers really get elongated arms as a result of prolonged shearing? Assuming that you are in the unenviable position of having a wild boar fall on you, how easy it is to die of suffocation as a result? Are there really any places in the deserts of Australia where it *never* rains? Do people in western New South Wales call kangaroos "kangas," or do they usually call them "roos?" Is it correct to call an Australian blue heeler dog a "Queensland blue" or should that name be reserved for a blue-gray skinned pumpkin? Did McCullough leave some of her funny passages in? Two of her favourite fiction writers are the Australian, Patrick Wright and the black American writer, Toni Morrison, both of whom write work which is often surreal. *The Thorn Birds* is sometimes so like a fantasy that it verges on the surreal.

There is an amoral, larrikin quality about the book which should alert an Australian that a good joke or a tall story is in the offing. But when many Americans do not know where Australia is, it is unlikely that they will be aware of the niceties of Australian humor.

In an interview with the Australian band, Men at Work, who made Vegemite an American household word with their song "Down Under," one of the band members said:

We managed to suck those people [Americans] in— a bunch of dags like us. . . . They don't know anything about us either. . . . They have a romantic view of Australia full of cuddly animals and pioneering men—or cuddly men and pioneering animals.

Australians love putting people on. The secret Australian ingredient in *The Thorn Birds* is Australian humor. McCullough presented the American public with a book which is an amalgam of American literary styles—a cross between a jeremiad, a western, a nineteenth century sentimental novel, and a light romance, in short, a classic American soap. She also provided remedies for the afflictions of American society, but these are nothing more than good old American snake oil, and out-of-date snake oil at that. Modern afflictions cannot be cured by a return to old, simplistic values. The old world is no more. Nor can a cure be found in new countries. Australia and New Zealand are not new, nor are they, unfortunately, unspoiled. If the American people swallow these remedies, their afflictions will not be cured, their sins will not go away. Colleen McCullough has fooled the American reading public. In *The Thorn Birds* she is quietly pulling the collective American leg.

Gary Jennings (review date 6 October 1991)

SOURCE: "Roman Scandals," in *The New York Times Book Review,* October 6, 1991, p. 13.

[*Below, Jennings offers an unfavorable review of* The Grass Crown, *finding fault with the novel's slow development and excessive incorporation of historical minutiae.*]

In *The Grass Crown,* Colleen McCullough continues the work she began with *The First Man in Rome,* a history of the Roman Republic and its surrounding world of the first century B.C. There is really no need for this volume's 74-page glossary and other endpaper flauntings of Serious Scholarship. The author, best known for *The Thorn Birds,* all too obviously did voluminous research, because every last fact and detail she unearthed seems to be included here, not a jot or title discarded as superfluous, irrelevant or reader-numbing. Observe:

"Drusus's house was right on the corner of the Germalus of the Palatine where the Clivus Victoriae turned at right angles to run along the length of the Forum Romanum, so it possessed a wonderful view; in earlier days the view had extended to the left into the Velabrum when the vacant space of the *area Flacciana* had existed next door, but now the huge porticus Quintus Lutatius Catulus Caesar had erected on it reared columns skyward, and blocked that old look-out."

If Ms. McCullough's attempts at evoking ancient Rome are only leaden, her evocation of ancient Romans is downright ludicrous. She makes them speak a yuppie jargon of "expertise" and "role-model" and "résumé" and "overreacting" and "off-putting." Also, never once do these ancient Romans *not* misuse the word "hopefully," a solecism very difficult to

commit in Latin. Come to that, I should dearly love to hear the ostensible Latin for such lines as "Either you streamline your operation, Julia, or . . ."

I reckon this remorselessly detailed history is called a novel just because a good deal of the history gets put between quotation marks, purporting to be human conversation. As often as not, in these dialogues the characters regale one another with history they certainly ought already to know:

"'My dear little niece,' said Publius Rutilius Rufus . . . . 'Only consider . . . . Two hundred and forty-four years of the kings, then four hundred and eleven years of the Republic. Rome has been in existence now for six hundred and fifty-five years, growing ever mightier. But how many of the old families are still producing consuls, Aurelia? The Cornelii. The Servilii. The Valerii. The Postumii. The Claudii. The Aemilii. The Sulpicii.'"

There are a few action scenes in the book, notably some nice gory butcheries, but they are far between, separated by great swads of that dreadful dialogue-history and even drearier accounts of back-room political backbiting. To sum it up in blurbspeak, *The Grass Crown* is in the grand tradition of the Congressional Record, masses of gassy morass with a nugget of interest here and there. So I shall perform a public service. To save anyone's having to rummage for the Real Juicy Bits, here is a sample, the climax of the big sex scene:

"Fruit, sweet and sticky—thin bare twigs tangled amid a bluest sky—the jerky pain of hair caught too tight—a tiny bird with stilled wings glued to the tendrils of a webby cloud—a huge lump of packed-down exultation struggling to be born, then suddenly soaring free, free—oh, in such an ecstasy!"

Hopefully, off-putting.

Fred Mench (review date July 1993)

SOURCE: A review of *The First Man in Rome* and *The Grass Crown,* in *Classical World,* Vol. 86, No. 6, July, 1993, pp. 517-8.

[*In the following review, Mench commends McCullough's recreation of Roman history in* The First Man in Rome *and* The Grass Crown, *recommending both novels as supplementary reading for students of ancient Rome.*]

Classicists will dispute some details and some unusual interpretations of the dynamics of the period 110 to 86 BC, but most will regret only that there are no footnotes in these two excellent historical novels. McCullough supplies maps (Rome, Italy, and elsewhere), plans (e.g., Aurelia's insula), authentic-looking drawings of major characters, casts of characters, pronunciation guides for Latin names and terms (*First Man*), a consular list for 99-86 (*Grass Crown*), author's notes and a glorious glossary in each novel (94 pp. in *First Man*; 74 pp. in *Grass Crown*).

The extensive glossaries (with singulars *and* plurals for most Latin words) constitute a lively course in Roman history, though not everything is precisely correct; e.g. Plautus did not, as McCullough says, shift his locales from Greece to Rome. She gives conflicting accounts of Jugurtha's death s.v. Jugurtha and s.v. Oxyntas, and *cursus honorum* would be better translated as "sequence of offices" than "way of honor." But, in 1600 pages of story, based on original sources and secondary analyses, she is essentially correct on verifiable historical details and understands Roman government and plebeian/patrician (as well as nobilis) distinctions.

McCullough depicts historical figures we all feel a proprietary interest in (Marius, Sulla, Drusus) but parts company with many historians in interpreting motives and relationships. For example, most would not see Marius (titular character in *First Man*) and Sulla (who gains the titular grass crown in the sequel) as cooperating so amicably all through the Jugurthan and Cimbric wars and the Saturninus fiasco. *First Man* ends with Sulla's arm affectionately around Marius' shoulder, and, though their relations are "tensely wary" as *Grass Crown* opens, they warm again as both see the danger of Mithridates and support M Livius Drusus in his efforts for the Italian allies. In fact, this accord between Marius and Sulla lasts almost 600 pages (through most of the Social War); according to McCullough, Sulla begins to hate Marius for upstaging him at his procession as new consul to the Senate and resolves to ruin Marius for stealing the affection of the crowd from him. After that we have the Sulpician legislation, Sulla's march on Rome and the Marian proscriptions, ended by Marius' death.

As novels, both read well, though some detail (e.g., troop movements in the Marsic war) may bog readers down. Non-classicists will refer frequently to those casts of characters provided. *First Man* has the big battles (military and political) straight out of history, but also much about less crucial players. For example, from the charming but steel-backboned Aurelia, mother of Julius Caesar and well-developed as a feisty young bride who owns and manages a 9-story Subura insula, we see a lot of daily·life. P Rutilius Rufus, uncle to both Aurelia and Drusus and (contra Plutarch) a close personal and military friend of Marius, writes many of the letters McCullough uses well in both novels to communicate information compactly. Occasionally McCullough's help to the non-classicist reader is intrusive: a tribune of the plebs would never call out, "I declare a contio, a preliminary discussion." But McCullough tells the stories well and creates interesting characters—some witty, brave, warm, some evil

and cruel, some you like and some you hate (and a few you have mixed emotions about, such as Sulla and M Aemilius Scaurus, Princeps Senatus). Classicists will recognize some very young characters who will be important on the historical scene (and McCullough's sequels?) decades later (e.g. Cicero as a talkative 13-year old, or a very young and precocious Julius Caesar).

Unlike the five Roman historical mystery novels I recently reviewed (*CW* 86.1), even in paperback the two McCullough novels may be too long to use as supplementary reading for Roman history classes, though anyone teaching the post-Gracchan period should at least recommend both novels to students who want to look more closely at the events of these 25 years. Much of the material is, of course, fiction, not verifiable history, but it may help that period come alive for students who otherwise find Drusus dull or the Social war unintelligible.

The sequel will be titled *The Rising Sun* (presumably Pompey or Caesar).

Judith Tarr (review date 21 November 1993)

SOURCE: "On the Way to the Forum," in *Washington Post Book World*, November 21, 1993, p. 4.

[*In the following review, Tarr offers a generally favorable assessment of* Fortune's Favorites, *which she finds more fluent and engaging than the previous two novels in McCullough's Roman history series.*]

Colleen McCullough has found her stride. *Fortune's Favorites,* the third massive volume of her saga of ancient Rome, picks up where *The Grass Crown* left off. Sulla, both hero and anti-hero of the previous volume, has come to both the height and the end of his career. The beautiful, deadly creature has grown old and hideous and more powerful than any Roman before him—he demands and receives the office of Dictator of Rome.

The younger generation, meanwhile, is coming into its own, as the middle of the first century B.C. approaches. If *The First Man in Rome* was Marius's story and *The Grass Crown* was Sulla's, *Fortune's Favorites* is that of two powerful personalities, Julius Caesar and Pompey the Great.

The novel follows the two of them through the years of their young manhood. Pompey marshals armies all over the Roman world and lays claim to the consulship of Rome. Caesar escapes from the dreadfully restrictive priesthood (a condition in which he could not touch iron or ride a horse, which effectively kept him, for the moment, from a military career) to which Marius sentenced him in boyhood, to a lively and varied career as soldier, diplomat, politician, and legal advocate.

The protagonists act out their roles amid a huge cast of characters: Sertorius, the rebel general in Spain; Spartacus the gladiator, who led the legendary slave revolt; and King Nicomedes of Bithynia, whom McCullough (perhaps cravenly, perhaps not) chooses to portray not as Caesar's homosexual lover but as a sort of grandfather-figure. Faces familiar from earlier volumes appear as well: Aurelia, the mother of Caesar; Caesar's aunt, Julia; the widow of Marius; and Metellus Pius the Piglet.

The great strength of McCullough's previous volumes was the depth and extent of her research, and their weakness was the resulting tendency to lose the characters in the mass of historical detail. Her avowed purpose, as she affirms in her author's afterword to this volume, is to relate all the major events of the period, apparently without exception. A laudable ambition—but a bit too ambitious. The result is often a loss of focus and a failure of Story in the face of History.

In *Fortune's Favorites,* McCullough still seems wary of getting too deeply into character. She shortcuts and short-circuits moments of powerful emotion: "He broke down, wept, dashed the tears away impatiently," she says of Spartacus in between stiffly impassioned speeches, giving him little time to emote as well as speechify.

Some of her facts are shaky—surprising amid such a plethora of research. She seems convinced here as in previous volumes that Roman horses were not only shod in the time of Caesar, but shod with iron shoes by farriers—a striking anachronism. Characters frequently pull out "a piece of paper," although strictly speaking they would have been making use of wax tablets or sheets of papyrus.

McCullough has developed an annoying stylistic tic, a tendency to repeat phrases several times in a paragraph and even within a sentence, as if the reader might not get the point the first time: "Pompey was not a type who appealed to Sulla physically, and he never liked to touch men or women who didn't appeal to him physically." She does, however, make use of this device to excellent effect in a letter of Pompey to Sulla, in which he never ceases to repeat the phrase, "My men hailed me imperator in the field." Sulla's reply is wonderfully nasty and very funny.

McCullough seems afraid also to let herself invent anything that might cause a pedant to object. After a glorious scene in which Aurelia pleads before Sully on Caesar's behalf, McCullough undercuts the effect with a bit of coyness that falls flat. "No one who participated ever recounted the story

. . . Not from fear of their lives. Mostly because no one thought Rome would ever, ever believe it."

And yet, wobbles and weaknesses aside, McCullough seems at last to have found her stride. At last, she has characters and a story with which she appears comfortable.

The clunking and clanking of style and characterization in the earlier novels have smoothed perceptibly. The dialogue moves more quickly, and the speeches are much less wooden. The characters are still a bit transparent around the edges, but now, more often than not, they seem to come closer to living, breathing humanity.

Readers who found *The First Man in Rome* and *The Grass Crown* to be a bit of a slog should be pleasantly surprised by this latest addition to the saga. *Fortune's Favorites* is by far the best of the three. For all its ponderous mass, it moves lightly. It reads less like an overly conscientious imitation of Livy or Tacitus and more like a novel—and quite an entertaining one at that.

Norma Jean Richey (review date Summer 1994)

SOURCE: A review of *Fortune's Favorites,* in *World Literature Today,* Vol. 68, Summer, 1994, p. 632.

[*In the following review, Richey offers high praise for* Fortune's Favorites.]

Fortune's Favorites is the third novel in Colleen McCullough's projected Roman series, focused on the world of Julius Caesar. Like the first two books, *The First Man in Rome* and *The Grass Crown,* the new work is a joy to read both for its marvelous narrative and for its presentation of truly extraordinary details, including maps and illustrations drawn by the author. Furthermore, McCullough incorporates extensively researched information into her story, such as women's use of cork-soled shoes to keep their feet dry, family relationships through generations of marriages and births, et cetera.

What some readers may not know is that McCullough, whose fame in the past has rested largely on the romantic novel *The Thorn Birds,* is in fact a brilliant researcher who has spent ten years preparing for her Roman series, which is the culmination of her life's work. For three years she paid a researcher $36,000 per year to travel and collect needed information and highly specialized data about her subject: clothing, extant likenesses of projected characters, genealogical data, military costumes, coins, and the like. Added to this is McCullough's ownership of the largest privately held collection of Roman materials in the world and her own first-rate intellect, all organized and planned to depict everything about the world into which Caesar was born, his life, and the influence of that world in history.

Fortune's Favorites forms a picture of Julius Caesar and his world that is better than Plutarch's, whose cameo analysis of characters has offered inimitable glimpses into the personalities behind historical figures. Whereas Plutarch gives readers intriguing snapshots of individuals, McCullough provides full pictures. Her Caesar is definitive, as she shows him to be a product of his world and his own love of that Roman world, always defined by his own *dignitas*.

The novel tells the ending of Sulla's story, so fully captured in *The Grass Crown,* and illustrates the long-range effects of the influence of Gaius Marius, introduced in *The First Man in Rome.* This continuation of the Roman saga covers early incidents of Caesar's career: organizing naval fleets, fledgling military and religious duties, family and political influences, and his public refusal to lessen his own sense of *dignitas* when burying his Aunt Julia—Gaius Marius's widow—by including banned images of her husband and son in the funeral procession. Every step of Caesar's story, which encompasses his family, his contemporaries, and his own devotion to Roman standards and law, is wonderfully clear, showing readers a world so complete that they can absorb everyday life along with events shaping Caesar for his role in Roman and world history.

All readers—scholars and laypersons alike—who love a wonderful, exciting, and eminently readable book will enjoy *Fortune's Favorites.* Colleen McCullough is presenting her life's work in this series, which is the best overview of Rome ever written. By the time Caesar crosses the Rubicon, readers who have followed his story will understand how this step forever altered Caesar's life and the foundation for the Western world, in which personality and power shape reality as change. The only criticism of the series that is not glowingly positive is that McCullough deserves a better editor to catch the sentence fragments that intrude on an otherwise constant reading pleasure.

Mary Jean DeMarr (essay date 1996)

SOURCE: "*The Thorn Birds* (1977)," in *Colleen McCullough: A Critical Companion,* Greenwood Press, 1996, pp. 57-86.

[*In the following excerpt, DeMarr provides a critical overview of* The Thorn Birds, *including analysis of thematic concerns, narrative style, and feminist interpretations of the novel.*]

McCullough's second published, though her first planned, novel is her greatest success. Published in 1977, it propelled her into the ranks of writers with names recognizable and sought out by readers. The success of her later novels probably depended heavily on the public won by this blockbuster book and the immensely popular television miniseries made from it. Many writers with such popular successes continue to write similar works and thus fall into a personal and recognizable formula, so that a Stephen King novel or a Danielle Steele book promises certain characteristics to a devoted and regular following. McCullough, however, refuses to be placed into any neat pigeonhole, and each new book (or group of books) creates its own type and rules. All this seems, perhaps, a bit paradoxical for an author who had carefully done research into what made a novel succeed with a public of ordinary readers and followed up on her results by creating *The Thorn Birds.* In fact, Breslin calls it "fiction by the numbers." Nevertheless, McCullough's professionalism and her desire for financial success as a writer were clearly instrumental in her first great achievement. That success enabled her to direct the later course of her career as she wished. She will not be restricted to any particular set of readers' expectations. And even in *The Thorn Birds,* she breaks new ground by using a Roman Catholic priest as her dynamic romantic hero.

The usual critical observations about *The Thorn Birds* are that it fits in the category of the family saga and that it is an Australian *Gone with the Wind.* As a family saga, it belongs to a genre which follows several generations of a particular family and thus has several protagonists and covers a lengthy span of years. Describing both the genre and this novel, Clemons calls it "an old-fashioned family saga, featuring decades of tribulation studded with dire forebodings that more often than not come true." Reviewers noticed a number of similarities between McCullough's and Margaret Mitchell's books. Both concern the families, especially the daughters, of Irish immigrant fathers who have come to wealth in their new countries. Both depict large rural estates with beautiful and gracious mansions. Both contain strong-willed heroines who love men they cannot have and marry men who are to them poor substitutes. Both heroines create their own disasters through their short-sighted behavior. And both novels seem made to order for lavish dramatization: *Gone with the Wind* in the 1939 film and *The Thorn Birds* in the 1983 television miniseries. Both, it might be added, reached tremendous audiences as novels, and each made the reputation of its author as a storyteller and creator of strong and fascinating women....

Style, Images, and Symbols

McCullough has never been known as a stylist, that is for having a facility with language or for using images in a particularly effective way. *The Thorn Birds* was severely criticized by reviewers, in fact, for a plodding and ungraceful style which included unbelievable dialogue. It is agreed that her talent is that of a storyteller who can make her readers care about her characters and what happens to them, not that of one who creates a narrative with a graceful texture which enhances the telling. *The Thorn Birds* nevertheless contains some useful images which serve particular functions in the presentation of the novel's materials. Several are especially helpful in depicting characters and relationships. The most important one grows from the novel's title, which states its central theme.

One important image is used by Ralph for Mary Carson. Repeatedly he thinks of her as a spider, an image which captures her malice and her conscious weaving a web of evil as well as his emotional rejection of her as a woman, the rejection that ironically increases her desire to punish him. Like a spider, she intentionally ensnares her prey and destroys it. Her will and the accompanying letter challenging Ralph to do the right thing and destroy the will create her cleverest, most destructive web. The repeated use of the spider image, always in Ralph's thoughts, reveals his awareness of her true nature even as it stresses her actual malice and cruelty.

In contrast to Ralph's persistent vision of Mary Carson as a spider is his repeated view of Meggie as "a sacrament." This way of seeing her illustrates his need to define things in religious terms. He cannot admit his love for a completely human person but must translate that loved object into spiritual language. One brief scene, in which Ralph twice thinks of her in this language, will illustrate. Long after their liaison on Matlock Island, they briefly renew their physical relationship at Drogheda. As they kiss, his thoughts are indirectly conveyed. He is aware of "that mouth alive under his, not a dream, so long wanted, so long. A different kind of sacrament, dark like the earth, having nothing to do with the sky." And a few pages later, his thoughts compare her with the actual sacrament of the mass: "Tomorrow morning I'll say Mass," he thinks. "But that's tomorrow morning. . . . There is still the night, and Meggie. . . . She, too, is a sacrament."

In the sacrament of the Mass, the bread and wine become the body and blood of Christ, with whom the worshipper is united in the act of partaking of the elements. Ralph's association of the Mass with Meggie suggests that she symbolizes something spiritual for him, with which he is united in the sexual act. Perhaps he is here attempting to join his physical and spiritual sides, the man and the priest in him. That he is rationalizing about his passion for her is clear, and his making her into an abstraction is a kind of idealization and romanticization which contrasts with her earthy need of him.

More important for the novel as a whole is the image of

roses, especially the "dusky, pale pinkish grey, the color that in those days was called ashes of roses." When the Clearys first arrive at Drogheda, the masses of rosebushes around the homestead help make it seem like the lush, green New Zealand they have left, so unlike dusty, dry New South Wales. Throughout the novel, the roses are repeatedly mentioned, often in association with Meggie. Her first party dress, when she is sixteen, is in the ashes of roses shade, and she is particularly lovely in it. Ralph is torn by conflicting feelings, pride in her beauty and sorrow that she is growing up. Memories of that party and that dress are referred to throughout the novel, so that the moment becomes a special one and is seen as one which changed their relationship from that of a mature man and a child to that between two adults. It is also the color she is wearing when they briefly renew their affair after many years of separation. Meggie becomes Ralph's rose. In a moment of renunciation after Paddy's death, when he thinks he is leaving forever, Ralph urges Fee to help Meggie find some suitable young man to marry. Meggie, saying farewell, gives Ralph a rose, described as "pale, pinkish-gray" and thus similar in shade to "ashes of roses." He presses it in his missal and it becomes his romantic memento of Meggie. Later he tells her about the rose in his missal and calls her his rose, expecting these tender words to bring her joy. Instead, she explodes angrily at him and points out his romanticism, which she considers foolish. She tells him he does not know what love is really about, and she reminds him that roses have thorns, a line which connects this rose imagery to the thorns of the novel's title.

Another association, suggested by Meggie, occurs later. When Dane tells her he wishes to become a priest, she is shocked and horrified. She sees God as winning the battle she has been carrying on against Him all her life. In taking Dane from her, He is taking away her victory over Ralph. Now she connects the name of the color that had meant so much to her to the phrase associated with death and funerals. "Ashes of roses," she gasps and bursts into blasphemy.

> "And I didn't understand. . . . Ashes thou wert, unto
> ashes return. To the Church thou belongest, to the
> Church thou shalt be given. . . . God rot God, I say!
> God the sod! The utmost Enemy of women, that's
> what God is!"

The beautiful flower, associated with her home and with her love as well as her anger, now becomes connected to her great loss. And when Dane is buried, his casket is covered with roses, associating the flowers again with pain and grief.

Roses are a trite symbol for love, but the symbol is inverted in *The Thorn Birds*. In associating roses with Drogheda, McCullough used them rather conventionally. The use of ashes of roses continued that conventional usage, but within the name that color already contains a paradox. To become ashes, the roses must burn. They must go through fire in order to create the beauty of the color. Through suffering and pain, beauty is created. This motif connects obviously with the meaning of the novel's title, and McCullough uses the shifting meaning of roses and ashes of roses to convey her central theme.

The novel's title is explained by an epigraph placed before its opening. It summarizes a Celtic legend of a bird which searches all its life for a thorn on which it may impale itself. That act, which kills it, enables it to sing so beautifully that its song is the loveliest thing in the world. The moral is, we are told, that "the best is only bought at the cost of great pain." The title is referred to only occasionally in the course of the novel. In a moment of acceptance, Meggie explains to Ralph what she has learned:

> "Each of us has something within us which won't be denied, even if it makes us scream aloud to die. . . . Like the old Celtic legend of the bird with the thorn in its breast, singing its heart out and dying. Because it has to, it's driven to. We can know what we do wrong even before we do it, but self-knowledge can't affect or change the outcome, can it? Everyone singing his own little song, convinced it's the most wonderful song the world has ever heard. . . . We create our own thorns, and never stop to count the cost. All we can do is suffer the pain, and tell ourselves it was well worth it."

The novel closes in Meggie's thoughts, when she receives a cable telling her of Justine's marriage to Rainer. She smells the perfume of the roses in the Drogheda garden and thinks of its beauty but also of its ending. The ending of the Clearys and their descendants on Drogheda is now certain, and she sees that as the conclusion of a cycle. She accepts her own responsibility for its happening, but she regrets nothing. Then, in the book's final paragraph, the point of view becomes less clear. Whether Meggie is still meditating on the meaning of her life or whether the author is commenting on the meaning of her story is ambiguous. That final paragraph refers again to the legend of the thorn bird, ecstatic in the beauty of its song but unaware of its dying, and ends by universalizing its message: "But we, when we put the thorns in our breasts, we know. We understand. And still we do it. Still we do it."

Thematic Issues

All fiction, whether intentionally on the part of the author or not, expresses themes or abstract ideas. *The Thorn Birds,* which is not particularly theme driven, relies on characters and story for its interest and its achievement of a sense of deeper meaning through the use of images and symbols.

Among the themes which are particularly obvious are the effects of repressive methods of child-rearing and the difficulties of life for members of the working classes in the early years of this century in New Zealand and Australia. Changes in life on Australian sheep stations over the period from World War I to the late 1960s are illustrated. Irish Catholicism and the hierarchy of the Roman Catholic Church are depicted critically. Most of these themes are inherent in the historical materials used in the novel and relate to the book as an example of the multigenerational family saga. They create a context for the characters and relationships and for the central theme of suffering.

That central notion examined in *The Thorn Birds* is pointed out in the Celtic legend of the title. All the major characters suffer, and for each there is some repayment though frequently not enough. For Fee, the thwarted love for her first lover brings her Frank, who is taken from her, and Paddy, whom she does not realize she loves until it is too late. Meggie's obsession with Ralph brings a few moments of rapture and the gift of Dane, who is also taken from her—first by the Church and then by his untimely death. Meggie and Justine both feel unworthy because of their mothers' inability or refusal to show them any love. For Justine, there is guilt for being unable to love and for, she thinks, causing her brother's death. The men suffer, too. Paddy loves Fee desperately and never knows she cares at all for him. Frank is torn by his rage and his devoted love for the mother he thinks is being abused by her husband. His ultimate suffering, of course, occurs off stage, in the long imprisonment that breaks his spirit. Ralph is torn between his two sides, his love for God and the Church and his passion for Meggie. Only Luke and Dane do not truly suffer: Luke is not sensitive enough, and Dane is too good. Dane, in fact, prays for the suffering that will enable him to become the perfect priest, and his prayers are answered by the brief physical pain he endures at his death.

Related to the theme of suffering is that of love and lust as destructive forces. Love leads to the suffering of Fee and Meggie and causes Ralph to break his vow of chastity. Lust impels Mary Carson to create the cruel choice Ralph must make. By making him decide whether to present the will leaving her fortune to the Church (but in his control), she forces him to choose between his integrity and his love for Meggie, on the one hand, and his ambition to rise in the Church, on the other. Love becomes lust in the lives of these characters when it is not joined by true concern for the one loved. Selfish love repeatedly leads individual characters to behave in ways that damage others. Fee, obsessed with her first lover and with his son, withholds herself from her loving second husband and her children by him. In so doing she deprives herself as well as Paddy and Meggie of joy and support. Meggie, unable to think of anyone except Ralph, marries Luke, who is totally unsuited for her; withholds herself from her daughter, as Fee had withheld herself from Meggie; and separates Ralph and Dane from any possibility of being father and son. Ralph teases Meggie by refusing her and yet by returning repeatedly to her. Only Rainer finally loves unselfishly, considering Justine's needs as much as he considers his own. Thus it is through his wisdom that he and Justine are able to bring closure to the cycle of thwarted love which had followed three generations of Cleary women.

Another aspect of the theme of love is connected to ambition and the idea of the perfect priest. Both Ralph and Dane are referred to as perfect priests, but this reference is always ironic in relationship to Ralph. He seems to be the perfect priest, for he does all the external things well and makes an outwardly ideal impression. He is effective in ministering to others, but his rise in the Church removes him from the priestly functions of caring for and comforting ordinary human souls. His sexual involvement with Meggie is only the most dramatic illustration of the flaws that make him a very imperfect priest in the reality which underlies his appearance. Ralph's perfection is outward. Dane's, on the other hand, is inward and real. Dane is whole hearted and whole souled in a way that Ralph, tormented with internal conflict, can never be. A very new priest, just ordained, he gives his life to save another and, in suffering and dying, proves that he represents the reality of the perfect priest. Ironically, it is in the moment of achieving that perfection, through the suffering which he knew he had lacked, that he must die. Perhaps perfection in priests is no more possible in this imperfect world than is perfection in anything else. Just as the color ashes of roses represents a joining of suffering and beauty, so here perfection joins with death.

A Feminist Reading of The Thorn Birds

Feminist criticism is based on feminism, a social movement related to the struggle of women to achieve complete equality. In actuality, it is probably better to speak of "feminisms," using the plural, for there are many varieties of feminism, stressing various goals and using various methods. Many radical feminists urge the destruction of the present social structure, which gives most power and authority to men; other feminists believe in working for a gradual change within the system. Feminists have undertaken a variety of causes, among which are the adoption of the Equal Rights Amendment (which failed after a long and bitter struggle), the accomplishment of equal pay for equal or equivalent work, the protection of women and their children from abuse by husbands and other men, equal access to education and jobs and professional advancement, and many other goals.

Feminist writers tend to present their ideas in fiction in two basic ways. One is to show what is wrong and the other is exemplify what is more desirable. One who uses the first method might depict women who are traditional in their attitudes (who desire only to marry and have children and live a life of domesticity). Such a writer might then show how those attitudes may lead to disaster (the seemingly perfect marriage ending in divorce or the death of the husband, perhaps), leaving the woman unable to support and care for herself and her children because she has no training or skills. Domesticity may be shown to be a trap, not a "happy ending." A writer who uses the second method might create strong women who succeed despite all the obstacles a patriarchal society (that is, one run by and for men) can put in their way. Independence, rather than reliance on a male, will be shown as desirable. Both writers would have the same goal of helping readers focus on the needs of women and showing them how women can live effective and fulfilled lives. Feminist writers also examine issues and problems facing women, such as poverty, abuse, discrimination based on gender, and so on. They dramatize the lives of female characters facing those issues. They illustrate attitudes toward women of both women and men. Definitions of "femininity" and what the ideal woman should be like may also be discussed.

Feminist critics look at writings by feminist and nonfeminist writers in different ways. They assume that women are as important, talented, and interesting as men and point out that this assumption is not universal. They point out how literature examines the ways in which women have been exploited and suppressed. Such critics point out social conditions, prejudices, inimical legal provisions, and many other ways in which women have not been treated equally with men in literature. Feminist critics also look at the work of women writers, trying to ensure that the work of these writers is treated fairly and not dismissed simply because of their female authorship. These critics point out issues or themes of particular importance to women and study the ways in which female characters are depicted. Feminist approaches sometimes lead critics to examine the presentation of male characters and themes, for these often affect female characters and themes as well.

In reading **The Thorn Birds** as a feminist, one immediately recognizes the emphasis within the plot and characterization of this novel on women as being born to suffer. The parallel experiences of three generations of Cleary women illustrate the pain that comes to women because they love and the guilt and need for atonement that follow obsessive love for men who do not really need them. Fee suffers all her life as a result of her youthful love for a prominent, married politician. She showers all her love on her son by that man and cheats both the husband, who truly does love her, and her other children, especially her daughter. After the death of her husband and one of their sons, she realizes that she deeply loved them both and finds herself unable to love her daughter because her daughter is a reminder of her own errors, someone who will repeat her own mistakes and relive her own suffering. She tries not to think of Meggie as any different from her sons. Meggie repeats Fee's rejection of her, finding herself unable to love Justine as she dotes on her son Dane. The lot of women is to love and suffer—or so it seems until the end of the novel, when Justine finally overcomes her guilt and sense of unworthiness and is able to give herself to Rainer.

The feminist critic might argue that McCullough has stacked the decks. She has presented Fee and Meggie with men who are not available—Fee's lover is already being married, and Meggie's is married to the Church. Justine is more fortunate in finding Rainer, who not only is available but is willing to wait patiently for her to be ready for him. As Fee and Meggie eventually realize, they have caused much of their own suffering, and Meggie comes to believe that her few moments of ecstasy and her motherhood of Dane made the suffering worthwhile. Ironically, when Fee and Meggie finally come to an understanding late in the novel, Fee tells Meggie that she enjoys her because they are equals, though she never enjoyed her sons in that same way. Perhaps their very sharing of the burdens of womanhood is what enables them to empathize with and enjoy each other.

The novel is based on patriarchal assumptions and set in a strongly patriarchal society. Patriarchy, literally "rule by the fathers," is involved whenever men have power over women, whether that power be exercised through the legal system, through the force of custom, or through internalized acceptance by women of their own inferiority. Luke's assumption that Meggie's money will become his personal property when they marry, an assumption that he baldly expresses to her and which she accepts unquestioningly, illustrates the power of patriarchal thinking. Meggie is a very feminine woman in the traditional sense—having her own home and babies is the central goal of her life. Domesticity is what she longs for and can never have with Ralph. Ralph thinks of her ability to bear burdens as being particularly "womanly," one of the things he especially loves in her. All these details underscore the patriarchal nature of the society and reveal the assumptions of the characters that women are lesser beings than men, born to suffer and to support the efforts of their men.

In this patriarchal world, relationships between men become important, and McCullough illustrates male bonding in three different contexts: within the Cleary family, among male laborers, and in the Roman Catholic hierarchy. With the partial exception of the Cleary family, these are three different worlds in which women have no place and from which they are consciously and intentionally excluded. Within the family, there are a number of sons and only one daughter. The carrying on of the Cleary name to the next generation should have been assured, and yet Meggie is the only member of

the second generation of the family to marry or to have children. The sons elect to remain part of the family on the homestead, and they form no meaningful relationships outside the family. They never become involved with women, seemingly unable or uninterested in romantic or sexual connections. Frank leaves home, but the result is his commission of a murder, his long prison sentence, and his return to his family a broken man. The youngest sons, twins, who serve together in World War II, are so close to each other that there is no room for anyone else in their lives. When one is wounded in such a way that his sexual function is destroyed, little is actually lost—the permanent effects of the wound seem more symbolic than practical. The Cleary men are perhaps not very highly sexed. Or perhaps they are so close to each other that they have no need of sex or of women.

Luke is less aware of his male bonding than are Meggie's brothers. He thinks he wants to achieve his own place, but in fact he becomes a part of a male culture which has no need of women and little interest in them (except as sex objects) when he joins the crew of cane cutters. When he enters the story, he is part of a group of sheep shearers who travel about the stations hiring out as needed. That status seems a temporary expedient but turns out to represent the sort of life he demands. With his "mate" (an Australian slang term for "close male friend" but particularly appropriate in this context) and the other cane cutters, he becomes immersed in a culture which values a man by the amount of cane he can cut and which fills his life with the comradeship of those with whom he lives and works. His visits to Meggie taper off as he becomes more and more a part of this male world. He repeatedly postpones leaving the cane fields, always saying they need a particular amount of additional money, but it is clear to Meggie and to the reader that there will never be enough money, that the money is just a pretext. Despite his protestations, he does not really want to leave the backbreaking work because it offers him rewards in male companionship that he does not find with a woman.

The third male society is Ralph's, the Roman Catholic hierarchy which no woman can enter since no woman can be ordained to the priesthood (though the novel does not raise this issue) and which no woman can connect with because priests are vowed to celibacy. The conflict within Ralph between man and priest, of course, is based on that requirement of celibacy, and the novel would not work if the characters were not Roman Catholic. Perhaps as a result of the absence of women (except in tangential ways—as nuns, as housekeepers), the priests create for themselves a society no less male than that of Luke in the cane fields. The scenes among priests, particularly the friendship between Ralph and his mentor, Cardinal Vittorio Scarbanza di Contini-Verchese, illustrate the intimacy which grows up between these men who are denied intimacy with women.

The priests at least regret that part of their humanity must be repressed, and their sensitivity contrasts sharply with the vulgarity of the cane cutters. But their society is no less exclusive, and its exclusion of women is no less indicative of a low status for women.

McCullough does not write as a professed feminist, and in some ways her fiction, including **The Thorn Birds,** can be considered antifeminist since it makes use of patriarchal assumptions without necessarily questioning them. And yet her novel demonstrates the cruel effects of women's exclusion from men's worlds and of the harm done by relegating women to subordinate roles and to suffering.

FURTHER READING

Criticism

Dougherty, Margot. Review of *A Creed for the Third Millennium,* by Colleen McCullough. *People Weekly,* 24 (July 15, 1985): 13.
Generally favorable review of *A Creed for the Third Millennium.*

Review of *Caesar's Women,* by Colleen McCullough. *Publisher's Weekly,* 242, No. 42 (October 16, 1995): 42.
Favorable review of *Caesar's Women.*

Review of *The Grass Crown,* by Colleen McCullough. *Publisher's Weekly,* 238, No. 36 (August 9, 1991): 43.
Favorable review of *The Grass Crown.*

Vespa, Mary. Review of *The Ladies of Missalonghi,* by Colleen McCullough. *People Weekly,* 27 (May 11, 1987): 18.
Generally favorable review of *The Ladies of Missalonghi.*

Mario Puzo

1920-

American novelist, screenwriter, essayist, short story writer, and nonfiction writer.

The following entry presents an overview of Puzo's career through 1996. For further information on his life and works, see *CLC*, Volumes 1, 2, 6, and 36.

INTRODUCTION

Described by critic R. Z. Sheppard as "the godfather of Mafia fiction," Mario Puzo has built an empire of best-selling fictional tales from the world of organized crime. Puzo's best-known work, *The Godfather* (1969), the story of an Italian-American crime family, is purported to be the fastest-selling novel in American history. Its success led Puzo to continue in the same vein with the novels *The Sicilian* and *The Last Don* and the screenplays *The Godfather, The Godfather: Part II*, and *The Godfather: Part III*. Credited with defining the public image of organized crime, *The Godfather* remains popular thirty years later.

Biographical Information

A native of New York City, Puzo was born and raised in an impoverished and predominantly Italian neighborhood known as Hell's Kitchen. His father, an illiterate railroad laborer, abandoned the family when Puzo was twelve, leaving Puzo and his six siblings in the care of their mother, a formidable Italian immigrant who ran the household under strict rules. While developing an affinity for sports and gambling as an adolescent, Puzo also took an early interest in literature, particularly the novels of Fyodor Dostoyevsky, and decided at age sixteen to become a writer. Puzo's opportunity to liberate himself from the economic and social pressures of his upbringing came with the outbreak of the Second World War, upon which he enlisted in the United States Air Force and served in Germany. In 1946 he married Erika Lina Broske (now deceased), with whom he had five children. During the late 1940s and 1950s, Puzo studied literature and writing at Columbia University and the New School for Social Research in New York. His first short story, "The Last Christmas," appeared in *American Vanguard* in 1950. Five years later he published his first novel, *The Dark Arena* (1955). In 1963 Puzo left a civil service position with the Army Reserve for employment with Magazine Management as an editor and contributor to various periodicals of adventure stories, book reviews, and short pieces, some of which are collected in *The Godfather Papers and Other Writings* (1972). Puzo's second novel, *The Fortunate Pilgrim* (1965),

received modest critical praise upon its publication but failed to win fame or fortune for its author. The next year a Putnam editor offered Puzo a sizeable advance for a novel about the Italian underworld, which became the unprecedented best seller *The Godfather*. At last treated to the material rewards of literary success, Puzo continued to write popular novels about the Mafia including *Fools Die* (1978), *The Sicilian* (1984), and *The Last Don* (1996). In the early 1970s he collaborated with Francis Ford Coppola to produce screenplays for the enormously popular film version of *The Godfather* (1972) and the sequel *The Godfather: Part II* (1974), both of which earned Academy Awards for best screenplay. Puzo also coauthored screenplays for other major feature films, including *Earthquake* (1972), *Superman* (1978), and *Superman II* (1981). In the early 1990s Puzo produced a third film with Coppola, *The Godfather: Part III* (1990), and the novel *The Fourth K* (1991). Since recovering from a near fatal heart condition and quadruple-bypass surgery in 1991, Puzo has continued to write screenplays and fiction in semi-retirement.

Major Works

Puzo's depiction of the organized crime subculture is distinguished for its wide popular appeal and compelling insight into power and the dark side of human nature. Puzo's early novels, *The Dark Arena* and *The Fortunate Pilgrim*, exhibit the realistic narrative style typical of his later fiction and are considered minor classics of Italian-American literature. *The Dark Arena* involves an American soldier who returns to occupied Germany after the Second World War. Introducing the theme of violent retribution, Puzo's protagonist murders a black market drug supplier to vent his rage at government bureaucracy, corruption in postwar Europe, and his own failure to secure lifesaving medication for his German girlfriend. In *The Fortunate Pilgrim*, Puzo relates the experiences of an Italian woman who struggles to surmount poverty and crime in Hell's Kitchen. Though extolling her courage, cunning, and traditional values, Puzo's description of petty criminal activity in the poor Italian-American neighborhood offers ironic justification for the life of crime as an alternate means of achieving the American Dream. The themes of criminal legitimacy and revenge are central to *The Godfather,* in which Puzo chronicles the ascent of the Corleone Mafia family under the leadership of Don Vito Corleone, a criminal mastermind, and his sons Sonny, Freddie, and Michael. Drawing parallels to American corporate structure, Don Vito's benevolent authority is founded on supreme organizational control, calculated judgment, and swift retaliation against all enemies of the family, including traitors and the incompetent within the clan as well as members of opposing factions. In *The Godfather* Puzo begins to explore the dubious status of organized crime as a self-sufficient social entity governed by its own hallowed customs and rigid codes of behavior, particularly personal honor and loyalty. With *The Sicilian,* regarded as a sequel to *The Godfather,* Puzo revisits the Corleone family saga and the subject of the Mafia. The plot involves Michael Corleone's orders to locate and recruit Salvatore Giuliano, a notorious Robin Hood figure revered by the Sicilian peasantry for his crimes against the aristocracy. Michael's search for Giuliano allows Puzo to relate the troubled political history of Sicily and the Old World origins of the modern American Mafia. Returning again to the inner sanctum of the Mafia in *The Last Don,* Puzo introduces a new crime family, the Clericuzio, whose aging Don attempts to convert his illegal empire into legitimate businesses. In this novel, more directly than in others, Puzo addresses the conflicting interests of the successful criminal and the American legal system, whose official sanctions jeopardize the hard-won private fortunes of the Mafia family. As in most of Puzo's best-selling fiction, the story is dominated by strong male characters and vivid depictions of treachery, betrayal, and sadistic acts of violence that illustrate the excesses of ambition, wealth, and power beneath the placid surface of mainstream American society. Puzo also penned the best-selling *Fools Die* (1978), set primarily in Las Vegas during the 1950s and 1960s, and *The Fourth K,* a fast-paced thriller set in the near future. In *Fools Die* Puzo examines both the alluring and destructive aspects of power and corruption in the gambling, filmmaking, and publishing industries. He turned to world politics and terrorism in *The Fourth K,* in which the American president, a descendent of John F. Kennedy, works to defend the United States and himself against violent political extremists.

Critical Reception

Puzo received quiet critical praise for *The Dark Arena* and *The Fortunate Pilgrim,* the latter of which is highly regarded for its skillful rendering of Italian immigrant values and city life. However, it is *The Godfather,* along with its book and film sequels, that is by far Puzo's most celebrated literary creation. Though criticized for glamorizing violent crime and reinforcing false ethnic stereotypes of Italian-Americans, the novel's central figure and Puzo's most compelling character, Don Vito Corleone, has become a near mythic figure and a permanent fixture in American popular culture. Interpreted by many as a cynical commentary on the reality of American individualism and the quest for the good life, Puzo's straightforward narrative reveals the indomitable influence of money and the necessity of violence for the survival of the self-made individual. Puzo often relies upon the sensational appeal of sex, drugs, and violence in his best-selling novels. While some critics object to Puzo's unabashed formula for large book sales, others find refreshing honesty and understated artistry in his naturalistic depiction of the Italian-American experience and ironic elevation of the chivalrous gangster.

PRINCIPAL WORKS

The Dark Arena (novel) 1955

The Fortunate Pilgrim (novel) 1965

The Godfather (novel) 1969

The Godfather [with Francis Ford Coppola] (screenplay) 1972

The Godfather Papers and Other Confessions (essays) 1972

Earthquake [with George Fox] (screenplay) 1974

The Godfather: Part II [with Francis Ford Coppola] (screenplay) 1974

Inside Las Vegas (nonfiction) 1977

Fools Die (novel) 1978

Superman [with David Newman, Leslie Newman, and Robert Benton] (screenplay) 1978

Superman II [with David Newman and Leslie Newman] (screenplay) 1981

The Sicilian (novel) 1984

The Godfather: Part III [with Francis Ford Coppola] (screenplay) 1990

The Fourth K (novel) 1991
Christopher Columbus: The Discovery [with John Briley and Cary Bates] (screenplay) 1992
The Last Don (novel) 1996

CRITICISM

David Boroff (review date 31 January 1965)

SOURCE: "Pasta with Gusto," in *The New York Times Book Review,* January 31, 1965, pp. 36-7.

[*In the following review, Boroff offers a favorable assessment of* The Fortunate Pilgrim.]

One of the mysteries of literary life in America is why Italian-Americans have contributed so little to it. A people of enormous vitality, Italians in this country have prospered, moved into the middle class, but have produced relatively few novelists, especially vis à vis the Jews and the Irish. This can be explained in part by the fact that Italian immigrants, largely from the impoverished South, were cut off from their own cultural traditions. It may well be, too, that the very cohesiveness of Italian-American life has militated against creativity. Yet with the erosion of the tight, tumultuous Italian family, the Italian-American novel may at last come into its own.

Certainly, Mario Puzo's *The Fortunate Pilgrim* augurs well for that possibility. The author previously of *The Dark Arena,* Puzo has written a chronicle of Italian immigrant life which is a small classic. An evocative portrait of almost two decades of immigrant travail in the West 30's of New York, the novel is lifted into literature by its highly charged language, its penetrating insights, and its mixture of tenderness and rage. If it doesn't quite attain the poetic intensity of Henry Roth's brilliant Jewish immigrant novel, *Call It Sleep,* it is still a considerable achievement.

The leitmotif is provided at the opening when we see Larry Angeluzzi riding his jet black horse "as straight and arrogantly as any Western cowboy" through a canyon formed by two great walls of tenements. The time is 1928, and Larry is a "dummy boy," who on horseback guides the New York Central trains through the streets of New York. But the real frontiersman in this urban jungle is Lucia Santa, mother of Larry and five others, a twice-widowed matriarch, an indomitable shrew when she has to be, a hard-eyed fanatic bent on family preservation. Her first husband dies in an industrial accident; her second husband, a saturnine, haunted man, loses his mind and is locked up until his death. The family is run, with the cunning of the poor, by Lucia Santa and her

daughter Octavia, a beautiful girl with a wicked tongue, a taste for books—and her mother's passion for survival.

And survive they do. The oldest son is an insatiable amorist but is yoked to family responsibility even after he becomes a small-time gangster. Octavia gives up her dream of college, becomes a forelady in a garment factory and marries a Jew. (This occasions little distress, for her mother takes a dim view of Italians as husbands.) One son, a gentle, passive boy, dies in an ambiguous accident. Gino, the willful, complicated one, escapes from the family when World War II breaks out. But the family achieves that ultimate fulfillment: breakout from the ghetto and a house on Long Island.

To be sure, the novel has overtones of immigrant *schmalz*—the Rise of the Goldbergs with *pasta.* But the reader is spared none of the terrors of immigrant life. "Only the poor can understand the shame of poverty," the author writes, "greater than the shame of the greatest sinner. . . . To the poor who have been poor for centuries, the nobility of honest toil is a legend. Their virtues lead them to humiliation and shame." There is humor, too, in *The Fortunate Pilgrim,* the harsh, abrasive laughter of the ghetto, as in the wonderfully robust scene in which a crooked welfare worker tries his blandishments on Octavia and is rewarded with truckdriver's expletives.

Most impressive is Mario Puzo's ability to summon up the world of the Italian immigrant hitherto so neglected: the tenement kitchen after a dinner, "full of the debris of life . . . like a battlefield with scorched pots and huge greasy bowls"; the children ferociously occupied with gutter derring-do and petty thefts, inspiring in their parents gloomy visions of the electric chair; the mothers "recalling with gusto their misfortunes through the years," or lashing out at America, "that blasphemous dream," for corrupting their young. It is this, in the end, which is the cry of the novel. America is both triumph and disaster. In the old country, "the dream was to stay alive. No one dreamed further. But in America wilder dreams were possible. Bread and shelter were not enough. . . . Giving so much, why could it not give everything?"

Time (review date 14 March 1969)

SOURCE: "One Man's Family," in *Time,* March 14, 1969, pp. 103-4.

[*In the following review, the critic provides a generally favorable review of* The Godfather.]

Although the last word on this robust, casually served novel about the Mafia should come from the voluble Joe Valachi, the moral will be evident to a jaywalker: The Family That Preys Together Stays Together.

A corollary lesson is that crime pays—or, to quote Mario Puzo quoting Honoré de Balzac: "Behind every great fortune there is a crime." When Puzo gets around to updating Balzac's ever so slight overstatement, he has the youngest and smartest son of the oldest and smartest New York Mafia boss tell his lank Yankee bride: "In my history course at Dartmouth we did some background on all the Presidents and they had fathers and grandfathers who were lucky they didn't get hanged."

As usual, after money and power are secured, the name of the game is respectability and status. *The Godfather,* which advances and contracts suggest should earn its author at least $500,000 in royalties, paperback and film rights, could prove a subtle opening move in getting the Mafia into the same league as the House of Lords and the German General Staff.

> **Puzo's own Mafia connections are strictly social. He enjoys frequent jaunts to the Mafia-backed gambling dens in the Bahamas. That he should thus leave some of the royalty money with the very people whom he good-naturedly exploited to get it is the sort of justice that would surely content the Godfather.**
>
> *—Time*

To begin with, Puzo avoids the *opera buffa* nicknames that newspaper rewrite men use to lend a tint of life to their gangster stories. Secondly, Puzo's Corleone family has manly standards. Gambling, labor extortion, an occasional unavoidable murder and some judicious bribery are all in order. But no prostitution or drugs. These enterprises offend the straitlaced sensibility of the Godfather, Don Vito Corleone.

As a young Sicilian immigrant and hard-working family man in New York's Little Italy, Don Vito discovered (somewhat to his own surprise) he was "a man of force." The phrase is recurrent and a key to understanding the qualities that distinguish a true captain of business and industry. Don Vito is the sort of man who would undoubtedly grump at such academic non sequiturs as "political science," since the years have taught him there is no greater natural advantage in life than having an enemy overestimate one's faults.

Arrayed before Don Vito like vassals at a feudal court are scores of coarse-grained characters who provide the sub- and sub-subplots that enable Puzo to illustrate the broad reach of the Godfather's influence. It is a mark of his power that he commands fierce loyalties because he treats his petition-

ers with respect—though they range from an obscure *paisano* seeking revenge for a damaged daughter to a famous Italian-American crooner who needs help to branch out into acting and producing.

Puzo had to do a great deal of inflating to blow his book up to the proportions of a bestselling beach ball. Yet he keeps it spinning brightly—if somewhat unevenly—with a crisp, dramatic narrative style. His professional skill is not surprising. Puzo, 48, learned what keeps a reader turning pages by freelancing and editing adventure magazines. Many of his Mafia anecdotes, he claims, come from his 81-year-old Italian mother. Puzo's own Mafia connections are strictly social. He enjoys frequent jaunts to the Mafia-backed gambling dens in the Bahamas. That he should thus leave some of the royalty money with the very people whom he good-naturedly exploited to get it is the sort of justice that would surely content the Godfather.

Gerald Kingsland (review date 13 October 1972)

SOURCE: "Mafia Mia," in *Times Literary Supplement,* October 13, 1972, p. 1214.

[*In the following review, Kingsland approves of Puzo's self-revelatory writings in* The Godfather Papers and Other Confessions.]

Mario Puzo rates his bestseller, *The Godfather,* below his other novels, *The Dark Arena* (1955) and *The Fortunate Pilgrim* (1965) and frankly admits that he wrote it primarily to make money. He needed to, being some $20,000 in debt, but once committed to the business of writing he clearly found scope in it for the skill which thirty years' experience of story-telling had given him.

The Godfather Papers contains reprinted and new pieces—articles, stories, reviews, anecdotes, memoirs, diary-entries—all written since 1965 with the exception of Mr. Puzo's first published story (1950). They are understandably uneven in quality, but each has something to add to the portrait of the writer and his world. There is a good deal about Mr. Puzo's passions, the chief of which is writing (and how good it is to find a writer who loves his craft and is proud of it), with gambling pretty high in the scale. There are some of his likes and dislikes, much about early days as a first-generation American Italian, and there is an objective, amusing but in some respects predictable account of the making of both the book and the film of *The Godfather*.

It is natural to be curious about the author of a work which has given pleasure to millions of people, and this frank, often pungent, miscellany probably gives a better idea than would a more studied autobiography, written when rationalization might have set in and the impressionism of these often fugitive pieces be overlaid.

What emerges is that Mr. Puzo is above all a man who loves stories—the stringing of the George Mandel anecdotes through the present collection is a sign—and who loves even more the act and art of telling them. His imagination functions best when it is engaged in narrative. Nothing could be more indicative of the kind of author he is than the statement he makes about his Mafia book; he confesses that he wrote it "entirely from research. I never met a real honest-to-god gangster. I know the gambling world pretty good, but that's all."

Understandably, one of his early loves in fiction was Rafael Sabatini.

Rose Basile Green (essay date 1974)

SOURCE: "Mario Puzo," in *The Italian-American Novel: A Document of the Interaction of Two Cultures,* Farleigh Dickinson University Press, 1974, pp. 336-68.

[*In the following excerpt, Green examines the major themes of* The Godfather *and discusses Puzo's contribution to Italian-American literature.*]

For the average reader, the Italian-American novel has arrived with Mario Puzo. His books definitely and dramatically document the thesis that the Italian-American novelist has identified himself with what has been professionally and socially inimical to him, the national American culture. Meanwhile, the erstwhile hostile environment has finally accepted and absorbed him. Puzo demonstrates some violent dynamics of this contemporary Italian-Americanism in three books: *The Dark Arena* (1953); *The Fortunate Pilgrim* (1964); and *The Godfather* (1969).

Despite, or perhaps because of, contemporary America's psychic obsessions, Puzo's novels have achieved recognition, since he deals aggressively with areas of Italian-American experience to which the mass media have given national notoriety. Although racism has obstructed each successive immigrant group as it moved upward to economic stability, the Italians, especially, have had to confront not only a language barrier, but the increased efficiency with which communications operate with propaganda. With the historical national tradition of piratical enterprise in the accruement of wealth now stabilized before them, the Italians in America have been able to share in the formidable economic structure, often at the price of being labeled associates of organized crime. Furthermore, they have felt that the pejorative geno-

cidal stamp on the image of the Italian in fictional treatments in books, periodicals, newspapers, and in broadcasting has continued to be unopposed. Much has been written to document this phenomenon, but it is sufficient to note that there is evidence in the Italian-American Press that this negative propaganda was able to continue without challenge, ironically because of the very human characteristics with which the immigrants clustered, obeyed the laws, and formed no united protest groups beyond their own society. Meanwhile, they became convenient scapegoats as criminal stereotypes for the writers of fiction.

Because of the recent widespread and organized violence in the nation, the reading public responds instantly to works that reflect this criminal aspect of society. Furthermore, the distributors of reading material are not always concerned with the possibility that criminality may be only a fractional aberration from the normal behavior of the members of a minority whose own literary output, reflecting genuine predominant characteristics, goes systematically out of print. Ironically, however, Mario Puzo's protagonists command both our respect and sympathy, stirring us with a wistful desire that genius be put to better use. Such talent should handle the more extended human affairs within our national complex.

> Although his first two books were praised by the critics, [Puzo] had to continue to write literary reviews until he composed *The Godfather,* which became the fastest-selling book in American literary history.
> —*Rose Basile Green*

Puzo has gathered his materials from authentic sources. A native of New York City, he was educated at the City College of New York, Columbia University, and the New School for Social Research. He lives in Bayshore, Long Island, with his wife and five children. Although his first two books were praised by the critics, he had to continue to write literary reviews until he composed *The Godfather,* which became the fastest-selling book in American literary history.

. . . . .

The history of the United States has recorded the rise of the Robber Barons in the nineteenth century. In fiction, writers like William Dean Howells and Theodore Dreiser differed in their presentation of the moguls of American enterprise. In the twentieth century, fired by legends and reports of unprecedented rags-to-riches achievements, immigrants followed the dream of easy success in America. Therefore, exploring the methods by which to make use of the opportunity here, the newcomers gradually developed forms of organized effort to help themselves. In time entrepreneurs arrived, marking the succession of ethnic groups: the Germans, the Scandinavians, the Irish, the Italians, the Jews, the Slavs, the mobilized Blacks. As each group in turn became assimilated, its members occasionally fortified themselves with dynastic policies in politics in order to rally, solidify, and perpetuate useful working factions in our party system of government. Although this power at times may have been implemented by coercive or even illegal methods, once the power was galvanized it continued to maintain itself by legitimate means while simultaneously intercepting threatening competition by obliterating the competitor, illegally if necessary.

Daniel Bell, in an essay entitled "Crime As an American Way of Life," affirms that crime has been a ladder of upward social mobility from the beginning of our nation's history. He agrees with the frequently asserted statement that many of our great fortunes have been acquired by methodically bribing public officials, padding public contracts, organizing violence, price-fixing, and exercising the despotic generalship attributed to the mid-twentieth-century mobster. It is beyond the province of this discussion to present the available research materials that expose the man who makes his fortune by running contraband goods in one generation in order to leave a legacy that in two or three generations entangles national policy. The coterie of such a man supplies an abundance of raw material for literature in characters, real or created, who are familiar with the intricate machinery of factional structure and who will use any method to eliminate competition. The frontier skirmishes may appear ruthlessly clannish or brutally combative. When the nation was reading about the "changing of the guard," as it is sometimes called, in the St. Valentine's Day Massacre in Chicago, for instance, it became dramatically aware of the ethnical character of some local revolutions. A "Bugs" Moran who is overcome by an Al Capone may seem to be a far cry from Nelson over Napoleon, but the contemporary conscience is becoming increasingly cognizant of their sinister similarity.

Crime has convenient and, sometimes, paradoxical definitions. The Nuremberg Trials inaugurated an international controversy that is still raging, over the legality of killing the enemy, which has the sanction of governmental decision, as against the illegality of killing a personal enemy. When conquest by violence is promoted as protective of the nation, it is recognized as patriotic and heroic; when a killing is perpetrated by a self-directed syndicate for the protection of only its own members, it is classified as organized crime. There are increasingly vociferous groups, however, that insist that killing for any purpose is a crime. In any event, the theme of crime continues to fascinate the American reading public. Furthermore, our citizenry responds to violent themes in political terms, seeking constantly to relate them to the functioning government in which politicians must have the

means with which to operate. The judgment of whether or not a practice is a crime is confusing to a people who observe, for example, that while gambling as a private enterprise may be classified as syndicated crime, it may be a sanctioned means for a state to raise funds to make its government solvent. Likewise, while extortion is admittedly a criminal activity, there are many taxpayers who consider our national submission to what they term taxation without representation a synonym for a coercion made possible by our fear of governmental bankruptcy. In consequence, personalities in crime and in government have at times become diffused in image.

From the nineteen-twenties to the sixties, the members of the Italian-American Press worked assiduously to demonstrate what they considered the constructive and admirable qualities of a predominantly sober, thrifty, conservative, and self-respecting minority. Newspapers like *Il Popolo, Il Progresso,* and *Il Corriere d'America,* along with others of more regional interests, encouraged their readership to cease their defensiveness and to take pride in the wealth of documentation of their historic cultural past. In time, after a long, tenacious campaign to promote the delicate machinery of assimilation in sensitive and critical human areas, a point was reached when even in local politics contestants were careful to avoid hyphenated ethnic terms. Then, suddenly, at the beginning of the sixties, politicians reverted ruthlessly to the exploitation of factions in religious, economic, and ethnic blocs. With this resurgence of factionalism, there emerged militant organizations by which minorities have sought not only to protect themselves, but to promote their welfare within the national structure. Because the Italian-Americans have been predominantly inner-directed as a group, they have not waged wholehearted campaigns in ethnic competitions. Recently, however, as demonstrated by various organizations like the Italian-American Civil Rights League, they have been stirred to unite against what they have termed the unchallenged tendency of the communications media to present factual or fictional stories of crime in almost exclusively Italian ethnic terms. In his essay, "The Mafia and the Web of Kinship," Francis A. J. Ianni writes,

> The strict diffusionist approach that sees only Mafia in Italo-American crime syndicates must therefore assume that the concept of Mafia lay dormant among southern Italian immigrants for decades and then suddenly emerged as a model to organize Italo-American involvement in crime. Further, it must assume nothing was happening in the acculturative experience of Italo-Americans that allowed them to find better and already proven models in the native American setting. These assumptions do not bear up under analysis.

Historically, the native American setting has nurtured certain endemic culture-heroes in its literature. In a country whose educational system pervasively offers as one of its several classics of fiction, and sometimes the only one, the anti-establishment and appealing *Huckleberry Finn,* it is a foregone conclusion that the writers of novels should increasingly deal with an anti-hero. In the 1957 Freshman English first-semester course in a large university in the East, there were listed three books for required reading other than the composition texts: *Huckleberry Finn,* Tergenev's *Fathers and Sons,* and *The Great Dialogues of Plato.* For many students this list comprised the total reading assignment in creative American literature during their college years. Since this vital area of education in the humanities is thus limited, and recently has come to require even less student reading, there is reason to believe that even the quasi-educated reading public may be receptive to a matured Huck Finn and able to identify with the multifaceted and solid attractions of a Don Vito Corleone.

Emerging out of our contemporary disposition, Mario Puzo's *The Godfather* is more than a controversial book. Phenomenally, it is a work that grips the reader's imagination, becomes one of the fastest-selling novels in literary history, and sets in motion a host of imitators. There are already numerous books dealing with coercive syndicates, and they cover a whole spectrum of treatment, from Jimmy Breslin's farcical *The Gang That Couldn't Shoot Straight* to Charles Durbin's brutal *Vendetta.* Furthermore, there are various "authentic" works exposing the hierarchical structure of "family" syndicates, one of which is Ovid Demaris's *Captive City.* Coincidentally, the shooting of Joseph Colombo in New York City on June 28, 1971, during the celebration of Italian-American Unity Day, an episode similar to what happens to Don Vito Corleone in *The Godfather,* has heightened public interest, not only in coercive syndicates, but in the drama of Puzo's novel. This interest has spread to a wide variety of articles in periodicals, from Tom Buckley's "The Mafia Tries a New Tune" in *Harper's Magazine* (August 1971) to Nicholas Gage's "How Organized Crime Invades the Home" in *Good Housekeeping* (August 1971).

Tom Buckley makes the point that

> the Italian-American syndicates comprise only one layer, which they share, in many parts of the country, with syndicates of other or mixed ethnic derivation, in what is essentially a vertical structure. Without the ready compliance of corrupt police and public officials, such enterprises as bookmaking, policy, loan-sharking, and the importation and distribution of narcotics could not be carried out on a continuing basis, just as without the connivance of corrupt bankers, stock brokers, and realtors, illicit funds could not be transferred into ostensibly legal enterprises.

Buckley also makes the significant observation that Italian-Americans no longer have the brazen, street-wise ghetto youngsters who would profit from such enterprises.

Puzo's theme [in *The Godfather*] is that gangsterism in America thrives as the result of the cooperation of elected government agents.
—*Rose Basile Green*

In any event, Mario Puzo, fleshing the skeleton of a contemporary socioeconomic ethnic image, has sculptured an ice-coated snowball and hurled it directly into the face of American duplicity. He definitively explodes Van Wyck Brooks's thesis of the dichotomy of the American literary mind polarized between the overt holiness of Puritan idealism and the covert claptrap of technical materialism. Puzo says: "I was looking to present a myth. That's what real fiction is about. A legend. That's why *The Godfather* takes place twenty or twenty-five years ago. If I really knew more about it I wouldn't have written so popular a book. To me *The Godfather* isn't an exposé; it's a romantic novel." He also says that he did not intend the book as a defacement of Italian-Americans. Apparently, in writing this book, Mr. Puzo has aimed to show that the type of syndicate he portrays is one of the only ways in which the Italian-American could survive in the nation. He says that "It's an environmental thing. Certain animals take on a certain coloring over the generations because of the terrain." Puzo brings together the various themes of Italian-American writers—"out-of-place," isolation, fragmentation, recall, frontier necessity, benevolent villainy, polite segregation, not-so-polite confrontation—all the constituents that perpetuate the basic dichotomy of human nature in the struggle between the constructive and the destructive. With great sweep, hurtling pace, and electrifying suspense, he constructs an inimitable story.

Don Vito Corleone, the benevolent under-establishment despot, rules the Sicilian-American "gangster" world from his post of command in Long Island. The "family" mall supplies the opening scene, where, in full swing, all the members are celebrating the wedding of Costanza Corleone and Carlo Rizzi ("half-breed"—half Sicilian, half Italian). During the festivities, the Godfather is approached by an assortment of favor-seekers and petitioners for interviews by members of his own and others' syndicated "families." Puzo immediately sets in motion the plot and subplots that make the novel massive, turbulent, and vibrating with progressive tensions: the starting point is the proposition made by the emissary of the Sallozzo-Barzini family to exchange the Don's political connections for impending profits in the narcotics traffic. Meanwhile we witness the beginning of the Sonny Corleone-Lucy

Mancini sexual relationship, the solidification of the positions of the sons in the family, the exposition of the connection to the Don of singer Johnny Fontane, and the Don's briefing of *consigliere*, Tom Hagen, on the family's strategy. Hagen is a German-American who has been reared in the Corleone family since boyhood.

The narrative begins with the Godfather's refusal to cooperate with the competing families who insist on planning to trade in narcotics. An attempt is made on his life and, based on an authentic incident, a gang war follows. Moving with breathtaking speed, scene follows scene to recreate the smell, sound, and feeling of every conceivable type of brutal murder. Observing the time-honored code of Sicilian tribal customs, hierarchies, and pacts, the Corleone family systematically exterminates its enemies, including its own members who have demonstrated their treachery. In the course of this relentless bloodbath the subplots are developed. Connie Corleone Rizzi is repeatedly beaten brutally by her husband, who is disgruntled at his slow advancement in the family business. Then, one day, as Sonny Corleone is on the way to defend his sister, he is murdered. The Don forbids any reference to this in the future, but it becomes the dramatic device and motive for the outcome of the story. When the Don survives the attempt on his life, his exquisite strategy leads the son Michael, the thoroughly Americanized Dartmouth student in love with the more thoroughly American Yankee Kay Adams, to avenge the father's assault by murdering Sallozzo and the cooperating police officer, Captain McCluskey. The Don's long arm reaches to Sicily, where Michael is harbored until he receives the news of Sonny's death. During his stay in Sicily, Michael, convinced that Kay Adams must know the truth about him and his family, marries the exotic Appolonia, who is soon afterwards killed by a bomb intended for her husband. The Sallozzo-Barzini connection having obviously ferreted out his whereabouts, Michael's reasons for returning home are compounded. Meanwhile, through the legal functioning of Tom Hagen, the Don has held a visibly peaceable hold on his empire, indicating no further ambitions for power, informing everyone that his intentions are to concentrate on investments in Las Vegas. He has set in motion the machinery for insuring the success in Hollywood of his godson, Johnny Fontane, by a gruesome subjugation of producer Jack Woltz. In this detail, Puzo exposes the sadistic mores and opportunism of the success code in the world of entertainment. The progression of events then leads to Las Vegas, where Freddie Corleone is a hotel manager, and where Lucy Mancini has been settled by the Corleone family. Lucy meets and eventually marries Dr. Jules Segal. When Michael Corleone returns, only his father, the astute and perceptive Don, appreciates him as the potential Godfather. Michael, accepting his destiny, assumes the power designated to him by his father, and, following his father's death, immediately executes his father's plan of exterminating all his enemies and emerging as the undisputed Don. He marries Kay Adams, who reluctantly but philosophically accepts the truth about the Corleones. Ironically, this New England Puritan turned Sicilian becomes the new Don's loyal wife, bears him two sons, embraces his ancestral religion and family loyalties, becomes absorbed in his life, and unites with his mother in praying for his soul.

The Godfather is a story dealing with the contemporary strategy of gaining and securing power. While Niccolo di Bernardo Machiavelli wrote a handbook to guide a prince in expediently establishing his forces in a political world of contending monarchies, Mario Puzo has fictionalized the code for the gaining of control over others in the competition of outlawed enterprises. While the prince had to create and promote warfare, mobilizing armies of mercenaries to seize power from vulnerable monarchies, the American gang leader builds an economic empire in which he attains power by personal warfare, the killing of competitors in the contexts of loyalty or treachery. Both contenders must operate in a vacuum, constantly circling in the absence of popularly ratified and enforced law and order. Puzo's theme is that gangsterism in America thrives as the result of the cooperation of elected government agents.

This theme is dramatized by the struggles of the competitive forces in the novel. Amerigo Bonasera, seeking vindication for the assault on his daughter by two young men who go unpunished because of the corruption of the courts, decides "They have made fools of us. . . . For justice we must go on our knees to Don Corleone." With this statement, Puzo's theme is triggered into action. The Don, responding to the quest, demonstrates that when a man is generous, he must show the generosity to be personal. He asks, "Why did you go to the police? Why didn't you come to me at the beginning of the affair?" Using the strategy of operating from a personal basis, the Don shows that justice is built on the debts incurred through friendship. He emphasizes the hypocrisy of the law, saying that when the judge rules, America rules, and accepting his judgment is approving the ethics of a judge "who sells himself like the worst whore in the streets." The Don knows that the courts are sheltered by higher powers; even the Senator shows him this, since, as Puzo writes, he is one of the great stones in the Don's power structure, and his generous gift at the wedding is a reaffirmation of loyalty. This kind of power is not visible to the uninitiated. Kay Adams, Michael's Yankee sweetheart, sees the Don as a good-hearted and generous business man whose methods are perhaps not exactly constitutional. It is not possible for her to perceive the nuances of the Don's statement as he promises Johnny Fontane the movie role he wants: "I say to you: you shall have it." This kind of disposal power generates from a firm, hierarchical structure with an internal complexity that can only baffle Kay's Anglo-Saxon mind. As Puzo writes, "Between the head of the family, Don Corleone, who dictated policy, and the operating level of men who actually carried out the orders of the Don, there were three layers, or buffers. In that way nothing could be traced to the top. Unless the *Consigliere* turned traitor." The author assures us that no *Consigliere* has ever betrayed any of the powerful Sicilian families that have established themselves in America. The *consigliere* is not only the advisor but also the tactician. For example, it is Tom Hagen's role to call on Jack Woltz, the producer, to inform him that if the interview concerning Johnny Fontane is not a happy one, there could be a labor strike at the movie studio. Hagen has learned the art of negotiation from the Don himself. One never gets angry or makes a threat; rather, one should "reason with people." The art of reasoning is to ignore all insults. Hagen, however, has the courage to express himself when the Don asks his advice, as he does about the Sollozzo proposition to engage in the drug traffic. The lawyer feels that the other "family" will amass so much revenue that they may become a threat, but he cannot convince the Don, who will not negotiate with men who traffic in drugs and sex. The Don's ethics in this matter prove to be a tragic flaw, because his decision tempts defections from his power structure.

. . . . .

Admittedly, there is some ophidian quality about Don Vito Corleone. To the wary reader, however, the Godfather is not a cobra, coiled and ready to spring. He is, rather, more closely related to the serpent in the Garden of Eden, exposing by knowledge the inevitable conclusions. Motivated by a tragic wisdom restricted by circumstances, he functions by disciplined, cold reasoning. Created with what he accepts as a God-invested power, the Don is the knowing agent of a force forbidden to flourish because it operates within a structure fouled by human decadence. He is the archetype of the highly endowed man born into a minority group, who thereby is consigned to limited freedom within pre-established boundaries largely controlled by piratical men. In his exclusive world, the Don reigns as supreme arbiter and benefactor. Puzo demonstrates that many people owe their good fortune in life to the Don and that, on intimate occasions like a wedding, they are free to call him "Godfather." Even the entertainers and service people are his friends. He, in turn, receives everyone—powerful, humble, rich, and poor—with an equal show of warmth. He slights no one; nor is he ever angry with anyone. "He had long ago learned that society imposes insults that must be borne, comforted by the knowledge that in this world there comes a time when the most humble of men, if he keeps his eyes open can take his revenge on the most powerful."

With all his humility, the Don has other qualities that contribute to his superiority. At Costanza's wedding, it is Don Vito Corleone who senses that something is amiss between Johnny Fontane and Nino Valenti; it is he, therefore, who plans the ensuing action. Furthermore, he is honest with

Fontane, excoriating him for his disruptive behavior. He warns Fontane to be loyal to Nino, because, says the Don, "Friendship is everything. Friendship is more than talent. It is more than government. It is almost the equal of family." Don Corleone's benign philosophy, however, is an outgrowth of his earlier violence. He had won Fontane's first contract by "putting a pistol to the forehead of the band leader and assuring him with the utmost seriousness that either his signature or his brains would rest on the document in exactly one minute." Power by threat of violence has its limitations, however, although the Don's friends do attribute divine power to him. It is not divinity, but ruthlessness that gives the Don such power. When he has Jack Woltz's six-hundred-thousand-dollar horse killed, the shock intimidates the producer. To the Don, this kind of action is the swift implementation of business, but his code has other restrictions. He will not cooperate with the Sollozzo traffic in drugs and prostitution because he is straitlaced in matters of sex. Nor does he approve of flaunting one's power. Of the eight houses in the mall where the various members of the "family" live, the Don occupies the smallest and least ostentatious home. The harmless-looking compound, however, is an impregnable fortress. Between functional violence and practiced humility, the Don operates with sensitive balance and delicate management. He can assure Fontane's Academy Award because "he controls, or controls the people who control, all the labor unions in the industry, all the people or nearly all the people who vote." This power, however, is propelled by his personal qualities: "to be good, you have to be in contention on your own merits. And your Godfather has more brains than Jack Woltz," says Hagen.

> **Mario Puzo, . . . like William Faulkner before he wrote *Sanctuary*, was not appreciated for the masterful novels he had published prior to *The Godfather*. Therefore, he wrote this novel with the avowed intention of producing a best seller.**
> **—*Rose Basile Green***

Some of this persuasive power is endemic with Sicilian-Americans, as is demonstrated in this book. Whereas the Mafia in Sicily had been a second government, its escapees in America have extorted money from families and storekeepers by threat of physical violence. From the beginning, the Don has observed an adaptation of this historic precedent in his environment on Tenth Avenue, but he does not submit to the criminal Fanucci. In his initiation into a career of violence, Vito Corleone commits himself with a voice that is reasonable and without anger: "It was courteous, as befitted a young man speaking to an older man of Fanucci's eminence." The phrase "I'll reason with him" becomes the warning rattle before a deadly strike, as Puzo describes it, the final opportunity to resolve an affair without bloodshed. With the Fanucci incident, Mrs. Corleone sees her husband change before her eyes; she feels him radiate a dangerous force. Gradually, with the mounting of this force, he punctuates negotiations with a characteristic smile that is chilling because it attempts no menace. As more people turn to members of the Corleone family for help, Vito Corleone becomes their savior; it is he who is able to prevent Mrs. Colombo's losing her home; he manipulates the landlord. Gradually establishing his image as that of a "man of respect," the Don rises in a traditional pattern. In the "olive-oil war," the men who are not amenable to his reasoning find their warehouses burned. None of the Don's fellow-Sicilians breaks the "ten-century-old law of *omertà* (silence)." All this power might easily remain tribal, but, as Puzo shows, the established government nourishes the powers within and against it. Prohibition rockets Vito Corleone into a star of great power from a quite ordinary, sometimes ruthless businessman to a "great Don" in the world of criminal enterprise. Puzo details the structure of the organization, making a convincing argument that "the Don got the idea that he ran his world far better than his enemies ran the greater world which continually obstructed his path." He overcomes his competitors, solidifies his forces, and by 1941 controls some of the industries of a booming America, which industries included black-market OPA food stamps, gasoline stamps, travel priorities, war contracts, black-market materials for clothing firms, and draft exemptions for the men in his organization.

Having thus established the strength of his organization, the Don constantly exerts his power, even to the most intimate detail, over the personalities of the members within it. Puzo illustrates this point in the relationship between the Don and his son-in-law, Carlo Rizzi. The reader has a terrifying suspicion of the facts behind the Don's ostensible equanimity over Rizzi's connection with Sonny's murder. The subtle line between personal interest and structural power tightens when, after he has been told of his son's murder, the Don says, "None of you are to concern yourself with this affair. None of you are to commit any acts of vengeance, none of you are to make any inquiries to track down the murderers of my son without my express command. There will be no further acts of war against the Five Families without my express and personal wish." The reader is instantly aware that all subsequent conflict in the story will be personal. Tension tightens in the dramatic process Puzo uses, picturing the Don as acquiescent and peaceful. We are reminded, however, that Don Corleone is a man who has made only a few mistakes in his career and that he has learned from every one of them. The reader, therefore, is sympathetically engaged in the Don's fate, and finds himself approving and advocating the carnage that is inevitable in the Godfather's personal retribution.

The other characters in the novel support the themes with symbolic differences. Sonny (Santino) has an uncontrollable temper, which his enemies exploit, and a visible intransigence that weakens his strategy. His anger is the flaw that sets in motion the central conflict in the story. As he beats Carlo, his fury creates one of the novel's most brutal scenes. With fatal results, his impetuosity overcomes his reason as he leaves the mall to rush to his sister's defense. While Sonny's reputation for violence makes him thus a marked man, Michael's suave exterior serves as most protective armor for the emerging Don. His deliberately nurtured appearance of detachment from the family business, his Dartmouth education, and his alliance with Kay Adams succeed in deceiving the Corleone enemies into believing that the Don's young son is a weakling. Puzo portrays him, however, with the same quiet reasoning and chilling strategy that marked the Don, but with finer precision. Michael Corleone emerges as a legitimate American corporation man, whose exercise of power, having "made its bones" in the blood of violence, will continue in the national industry. Meanwhile, his family of the future will engage both in politics and in the mainstream of society.

> I wished ... I'd written [*The Godfather*]
> better.... It has energy and I lucked out by
> creating a central character that was
> popularly accepted as genuinely mythic.
> But I wrote below my gifts in that book.
> —*Mario Puzo*

Puzo also shows that this social structure has stratifications according to personal ability, as in the example of the almost anonymous brother Frederico, who finds a suitable niche as a hotel-keeper in Las Vegas. The Las Vegas enterprises bind the Corleone power to the area of entertainment. In this field Johnny Fontane personifies another level of the Godfather's person-oriented, syndicated power, since it is the Don's strength that makes Fontane's fame and fortune. Johnny knows that his relationship with the Don makes him as close to a royal patron as it was possible to be in America. Although he feels that he is a master of his particular type of music, he has learned that success depends on more than talent, that tactics must be the yeast of rising activity. The supreme tactician of the Don's strategy is, of course, the educated and supremely trained Tom Hagen, whom the Don has coached into a working machine for himself. Despite the contempt of the Sicilian families, who have never known of a non-Sicilian *consigliere,* Hagen has been nursed into thinking and acting like a Sicilian to the extent that he can nearly always anticipate his Don's moves. He is completely the Don's man, and is the device for keeping the Don's power in unceasing motion while the Godfather is incapacitated. He is the instrument of detection of and reconciliation with Kay that enables her to understand Michael and accept him dutifully as a husband. In time, Kay becomes as Sicilian as her mother-in-law, submitting herself to this world of men for whom the women pray. We know that these women, like the old women of Tenth Avenue in *The Fortunate Pilgrim*, will survive, for Puzo has warned us of their wisdom, demonstrated in Mrs. Vito Corleone's detachment from the arena of violence and her motherly condescension to the Don in his final years. We also realize that Ginny Fontane, the patient wife to whom Johnny continually returns, will inherit his world and rule his children. All the surviving characters in the story, therefore, are issues of the novel's contained world of power. When Tom Hagen assures Kay that "you and the children are the only people on this earth he couldn't harm," he is implying that the world of violence must dissipate before the rise of the new generation.

In my discussion of the specifics that define the Italian-American novel, *The Godfather* was used as an example of literary material created in order to force attention. Reason supports the conclusion that the feudal world of mobsters and syndicates is atypical of any minority, especially that of the Italian-Americans. Mario Puzo, however, like William Faulkner before he wrote *Sanctuary,* was not appreciated for the masterful novels he had published prior to *The Godfather.* Therefore, he wrote this novel with the avowed intention of producing a best seller. For this reason, the story's presentation of Italian-Americans has the restrictions of a cluster-cultural area. The book's point of view of Italian-American life is therefore simultaneously confined and exaggerated. There are, for example, numerous references to Sicilian customs, such as that by tradition no Sicilian can refuse a request on his daughter's wedding day, and that no Sicilian ever misses such a chance. This inner directedness intensifies the sensitivity to insulting racial references by other groups, as in the episode when Michael endures Captain McCluskey's tirade outside the hospital, "I thought I got all you guinea hoods locked up." At another time Puzo writes that it never occurs to Johnny Fontane to desert his family and children, that he is too much of an old-style Italian. Not only must the sacredness of the family supersede the needs of any member in it, but the family mores demand certain indispensable obligations. When Kay visits Mrs. Vito Corleone for the first time, the older woman is concerned only with her obligation to make sure that her guest has something to eat. Obligation is the ritual flame of the family altar. It is Sonny's inbred sense of the obligation of a Sicilian brother to protect his sister that moves him against Carlo Rizzi. It is Mama Corleone's obligation as a dutiful wife that binds her, in her wisdom, not to perceive what is going on that pains the men. Systematically, she continues to boil coffee, prepare food, and pray. Tying all the family members together is the closely knit structure of blood relationships; they are a society where family loyalty preempts loyalty to a wife. In a late chapter Puzo describes the detailed background of the Sicilian world to which Michael

returns for refuge, where he learns about the roots from which his father grew. This is a world of feudal history and of the struggle of a people faced with the savagery of absolute power, where the historical Mafia has become "the illegal arm of the rich and even the auxiliary police of the legal and political structure. It had become a degenerate capitalist structure, anti-communist, anti-liberal, placing its own taxes on every form of business endeavor no matter how small." There are appealing descriptions of Sicily's pastoral beauty, and of the traditionally humanized interiors of the homes. Puzo emphasizes the Italians' need for living with appointments of beauty, often camouflaged by a stern exterior. When Michael returns to New York, he takes Kay to the decrepit brownstone house in the deteriorated neighborhood on Mulberry Street. Inside, Kay is stunned to find that it is as expensively and comfortably furnished as a millionaire's town house.

> Puzo has written in *The Godfather* a novel of power that nearly paralyzes the emotions and the intellect with the terror of a dark evil which must be checked. . . . This book has the content and force to change a direction in our civilization.
> —*Rose Basile Green*

Michael's Italianism and Kay's Puritan Americanism are integrated with their marriage. At home, as Kay watches Michael's face when he receives Clemenza, "he reminded her of statues in Rome, statues of those Roman emperors of antiquity, who, by divine right, held the power of life and death over their fellow men." Kay is able to attribute this quality to Michael because she is heiress of an intellectual culture, the American transcendentalism that emerged from classical education with the discipline of Roman ideals. Her acceptance of her husband lies not only in her educated evaluation of his people, but in the identity of the genesis of their common culture.

> [With] *The Godfather,* Mario Puzo has won acceptance for his two previous books, which are important works of art and valid documents of American civilization. Those who control the machinery of critical support and sales distribution may eventually make an honest and empirical evaluation of all those Italian-American novels that have quietly and systematically gone out of print.
> —*Rose Basile Green*

As a novel, *The Godfather* has been called everything from a staggering literary triumph to a package for best-sellerdom. Admittedly it has all the formulaic requirements of sensationalism in the treatment of sex, sadism, shock, and fear; it also has authenticity, validity, artistry, and power. Puzo himself says: "I wished . . . I'd written it better. . . . It has energy and I lucked out by creating a central character that was popularly accepted as genuinely mythic. But I wrote below my gifts in that book." However, exposing a real dimension of the American ethnic-societal structure, he has succeeded in writing convincing fiction. While he has created a valid social document, he relies more on symbolic action than on metaphysical exposition. Aesthetically, he carries the reader with hurtling momentum, not embellishing the raw events with literary mannerisms. He is a master story-teller who renders the most intolerable episode entirely plausible and natural. Dramatizing in relentlessly detailed action several forms of human slaughter, he electrifies the reader into making some effort to reform law and order in society. Puzo is thus a social historian of American civilization, informing the reader of the nation's sinister and powerful fraternity of crime, and warning that the power of such a fraternity can operate only in a democracy whose law enforcement is corrupt. Puzo's genius has created extravagant characters who are so convincing that they seem both possible and appealing. Thematically, the book challenges America's racial categories, dynastic tendencies, and social prejudices, demanding that before we rent out rooms we had better set our house in order. Structurally, the book abounds with evil incident, debased sex, and primitive terror, and realistically records the solecisms and colloquialisms of the Italian-American characters. Puzo has written in *The Godfather* a novel of power that nearly paralyzes the emotions and the intellect with the terror of a dark evil which must be checked. The wisdom of the serpent should be utilized for its truth. This book has the content and force to change a direction in our civilization.

As an Italian-American novelist, Mario Puzo has pried open the box that has secreted the sacred blackballs of the American literary club. In making his hit, he has exposed once more the password to the inner sanctum of the governing board room. There, where the guardians of American literary conscience are still uniformed in the livery of our dichotomous maturity, the transcendentalism and the materialism decried by Van Wyck Brooks, they stand with the weapons that trigger the old conflict between good and evil. When Michael Corleone commits his first murder, he "makes his bones," and becomes a man to be respected with fear; and he gives a new nomenclature to the American dreamer who identifies with the enemy. Here is another symbol for our literary lexicon. As writers, Italian-Americans have now made their bones in their acquiescence to the brutal themes of contemporary fiction—the depravities, crime, lust, sex aberrations, violence, bigotry, racism, and hate. By using all these elements to assault the reader in *The Godfather*, Mario Puzo has won acceptance for his two previous books, which are important works of art and valid documents of American civilization. Those who control the machinery of critical support and sales distribution may eventually make an honest and empirical evaluation of all those Italian-American novels that have quietly and systematically gone out of print. In due time we may all discover that the Italian-American writer, who has been with us right along, has had to make a marriage with American tradition. Corleone breeds his children through an Adams; we return to the great, vast themes of America's past—the conflicts of Ahab, the search for our integrity after having sinned, The Marble Faun salvaging himself from Vietnam, the reality of putting aside the weapon that has enjoyed the sanction of power.

Like its author, the Italian-American novel has come of age. Its baptism into our faith has required a sponsor who had to be supreme in envisioning our own evil; but, surviving this initiating exaggeration, we have the fairness to accept all the other human themes that are, after all, more predominant. Meanwhile, the Italian-American novelist has survived his trauma and outgrown the defensiveness of biographical, racial, and self-conscious themes; his books are now making a dent in American fiction. By confronting either inadequacy or corruption, the contemporary hero, socially registered or assimilated, "bones" his way to salvation. As our traditional themes have demonstrated that man must know sin to save his soul, so art distorts creation in order to re-create. In the context of the novels of America the former distortion of the Italian-American was, at least, a recognition of his presence. It was up to the Italian-American writer himself to accept the challenge of this distortion. Now, like Puzo's Michael Corleone, he joins the general family, but he must keep a wary eye on its humanity. In this way, his art is evaluated on equal terms with that of other writers.

John G. Cawelti (essay date 1975)

SOURCE: "The New Mythology of Crime," in *Boundary 2*, Vol. 3, 1975, pp. 325-57.

[*In the following excerpt, Cawelti examines Puzo's depiction of the criminal organization as a family unit in* The Godfather.]

The best selling novel and film of the late 1960's and early 1970's was Mario Puzo's *The Godfather*. Its impact has been so great—over 10 million copies of the book sold in little over three years, more millions of movie admissions and still running after several years—that one doesn't need much prescience to predict that this work will be a major turning point in the evolution of popular literature, perhaps comparable to the significance of Conan Doyle's Sherlock Holmes, certainly as important as Ian Fleming's James Bond. In the wake of *The Godfather*'s enormous success, plans have been announced for a film sequel, while a number of less effective films about the Mafia, such as *The Valachi Papers,* have coasted to considerable popularity on its coattails. Publishers have increased their listings in crime fiction and taken advantage of the Godfather craze to reissue in paperback any recent novels which have the slightest connection with the subject of Puzo's book. Everywhere newsstands and marquees are plastered with such come-ons as "more action, sex and violence than *The Godfather* and *The French Connection* combined" or "The Big New Mafia blockbuster in the searing tradition of *The Godfather.*" Though no TV network has yet announced a series called "One Don's Family," scores of producers and writers are doubtless racking their brains to figure out a formula that will be recognizably like *The Godfather* while avoiding the overt violence and sex which current mores will not sanction on the television screen. With all this activity, it seems clear that *The Godfather* has not only achieved a striking individual success, but has established a new fashion in the portrayal of crime.

Of course crime, particularly violent crime, has always been a sure-fire topic for the entertainment of the public. From the beginning of written literature, and, one suspects, long before that, human beings have been moved and fascinated by stories of homicide, assault, thievery and roguery of all sorts. Without exaggeration one can say that crime and literature have been in it together from the beginning. Homer launched the subject with his account of the suitors' conspiracy against Odysseus' homecoming, or perhaps one should give precedence to the even earlier account in *The Iliad* of the rape of Helen. Murder was a favorite subject of the Greek and Roman dramatists and of Shakespeare and other Renaissance tragedians. The development of printed literature led to an even greater and more various flowering of crime stories, from the picaresque tales and outlaw ballads of the sixteenth and seventeenth centuries, down to the innumerable crime and detective stories of our own age. The development of film added to this array the saga of the urban gangster which in various forms has been a staple of the American film since D. W. Griffith's *The Musketeers of Pig Alley* (1912). And, in modern times, while the fictional criminal has been a leading figure in novel, drama, and film, his real-life model has inspired uncountable billions of words in the non-fictional form of accounts of actual crimes and criminals in newspapers, magazines, and books.

Why has the criminal held such an important place in the hearts of the great majority of peaceful and law-abiding citizens throughout the ages? Is it an expression of man's original sin, some basic instinct toward destruction or the result of an innate aggressiveness inherited from some primordial animal ancestor? These general answers share a certain unfortunate circularity: man loves crime stories because he has some basic trait which, among other things, manifests itself in a fascination with tales of crime. It may be a matter of great theoretical or metaphysical interest whether this trait is a function of free will, evolution, heredity, or environment, but this is not a question that can be answered by the analysis of popular literature. Whatever the cause, the end result is the same, a basic human delight in the literature of crime. Leaving its ultimate significance for the inquiries of theologians, psychologists, and ethologists, let us turn to a problem on which the formulas of popular literature may shed some light: the question of how men in differing cultures define crime, how they relate it to other elements of their culture, and in what ways they justify their fascination with it. This narrows our inquiry considerably and brings us to ask whether *The Godfather* manifests a new mythology of crime.

Before tackling this question, we must make one important proviso about the kind of evidence necessary to support the contention that *The Godfather* reflects a significant change in our myths of crime. We cannot take it for granted that the immense popularity of an individual work or writer reflects new cultural patterns. An individual work may succeed with the public for a variety of reasons, most important among them being the skill of the writer. If we would employ popular literature as a barometer of collective feelings and beliefs we must also remember that there is not necessarily an exact correspondence between the moral universe of a story (its implicit ideas and values) and the attitudes of the public. A popular novel or film is first of all a work of art designed to interest and move an audience. Skillful writing, striking and emotionally involving characters and situations, and a powerfully unified action can often move readers who do not share the values of the creator. There are undoubtedly limitations in the degree to which an audience can suspend its own valuations and attitudes in order to enter emotionally the moral world of a fiction, and these boundaries are probably narrower in the case of relatively unsophisticated and uneducated publics than in the case of more intellectual audiences who have been educated to extend their sympathies and to tolerate a wider range of values. Even with this qualification, the human imagination, particularly in diverse modern cultures, seems to be capable of a wide range of temporary value commitments for the sake of aesthetic pleasure. Since Mario Puzo is evidently a very able writer and *The Godfather* a superb example of the sort of panoramic social novel that often becomes a best-seller, we cannot argue solely on the basis of *The Godfather*'s success that its moral universe is shared by its immense public.

However, if we can show that *The Godfather* is not simply an isolated individual work, but a particularly effective synthesis of narrative and thematic patterns which have been evolving in many other novels and films, we will be on much firmer ground in asserting that Puzo's creation has become successful not simply because of its individual artistic merits but because it has brought into highly effective and expressive form a vision of the character and social significance of crime which articulates widespread public attitudes and feelings. In other words, we must demonstrate that *The Godfather* reflects the emergence of new literary patterns for the treatment of crime, and we can best do this by showing the contrast between the central thematic and structural patterns of *The Godfather* and earlier literary formulas for crime stories.

II

The single aspect of *The Godfather* which seems to have made the deepest impact on the American public is Puzo's use of the central symbol of "the family." Indeed, this symbol's influence has been pervasive enough that it has virtually changed overnight the American public's favorite term for a criminal organization. (The public's fascination with the Manson family was another related though slightly different use of the term.) While the term was used in some circles prior to the publication of Puzo's book, and is derived from Italian where it has had this meaning for hundreds of years, Americans generally referred to criminal organizations as gangs, or more recently as "the Mafia," "cosa nostra" or "the syndicate." Puzo's use of "family" in *The Godfather* has in effect brought the Italian term *"famiglia"* into common and widespread American usage, but this, in itself, suggests a significant change in attitude, since the Italian *"famiglia"* has a very different range of associations and connotations than the English "family."

The Don is, in many respects, a new figure in the annals of crime. Though he has an obvious resemblance to the master criminal of earlier formulaic traditions— e.g. Professor Moriarity, Fu Manchu, or Goldfinger—there are important differences in the way the Don is represented, just as there are basic differences between Puzo's "family" and these more traditional forms of criminal conspiracy.
—*John G. Cawelti*

As Puzo brilliantly develops it, the symbol of the family is the basic unifying principle of *The Godfather*. The novel is a tale of family succession, showing the rise of the true son and heir and reaching a climax with his acceptance of the power and responsibilities of Godfather. (Ironically, the quest for the true father is also the central theme of Joyce's great

modern epic *Ulysses*.) *The Godfather* is the story of how Michael Corleone comes to understand his father's character and destiny and then allows himself to be shaped by that same destiny. Most of the novel's major characters are members of the Corleone family and the main events are key points in that family's history: the marriage of a daughter, the death of a son, the death of the father, the rise of a new generation. However, Puzo extends the symbolism of the family beyond the actual progeny of Don Vito Corleone to the criminal organization of which he is the leader. Thus, in narrating the history of the Corleone family, Puzo is also giving an account of the rise, difficulties and ultimate triumph of a criminal gang. By doing so, he makes the reader view that gang as something more complex than a band of lawbreakers organized for the purpose of committing evil or illegal actions.

In sum, one central characteristic of the new mythology of crime is a fascination with criminal organizations, such as Puzo's Corleone "family," and their special kind of power. Contemporary crime literature feeds upon the image of a hidden criminal organization, so closely knit that even to reveal its existence is certain death for the informer. The members of this organization are bound together by a code of secrecy, a blood ritual, ties of kinship and cultural loyalty, and a long historical tradition dating back to Medieval Italy. Because of its secrecy, its willingness to use any means to achieve its ends, its power of life and death, and its enormous wealth and hidden political power, this organization has almost boundless power. The authority of its leaders over members of the organization and their power to manipulate the rest of society is nearly divine or godlike. This fantasy of the "organization" looms mysteriously and ominously from the pages of senatorial investigations, popular novels and films about crime since the 1950's, but until Puzo's novel, it was rare that this ghostly presence was given a fleshly solidity and vitality. Such will, I suspect, turn out to be Puzo's major contribution to the mythology of crime: through his own rich and complex knowledge of the Sicilian ethnic background, he has been able to give a "local habitation and a name" to the fantasy of the all-powerful criminal organization and thereby to make the fantasy even more plausible and persuasive. Indeed, so compellingly attractive is Puzo's vision of the criminal family that, though he invented it entirely out of books and his imagination, professional criminals have been reported as complimenting Mr. Puzo on his remarkable inside knowledge. An imaginative vision so profoundly satisfying to those as much in need of a myth as criminals themselves, seems certain to be vitally compelling to society as a whole.

III

From this central interest in the special character of the criminal "family" and its power, three major elements of the new mythology of crime are derived. These are 1) the character of the organization leader, the Don or Godfather, as Puzo calls him; 2) the central figure of the specialized professional criminal, highly trained and talented in his vocation and ruthless in his dedication to it—let us call him the "Enforcer" from the fact that one of the most popular versions of the character is the professional assassin; and 3) the type of narrative structure which is organized around the careful preparation and execution of a complex criminal act, the caper. To a considerable extent, the new literature of crime can be described as stories of capers which involve either a Don or an Enforcer as the protagonist.

The Don is, in many respects, a new figure in the annals of crime. Though he has an obvious resemblance to the master criminal of earlier formulaic traditions—e.g. Professor Moriarity, Fu Manchu, or Goldfinger—there are important differences in the way the Don is represented, just as there are basic differences between Puzo's "family" and these more traditional forms of criminal conspiracy. For one thing, the traditional master criminal is basically a large entrepreneur of crime who has an employer-employee relationship with his minions. His authority derives from his money and from fear of his ruthlessness. Frequently his corps of criminals do not respect or admire him. They are enslaved by fear and greed. Thus, no matter how powerful it may be, the traditional criminal organization is represented as based on the vices and weaknesses of its members. Consequently, it usually turns out to be quite simple for the hero to defeat the master criminal. The Don, on the other hand, is a figure of considerable moral authority which is derived from his wisdom and responsibility as well as from his shrewd ruthlessness. Like a father, the relationship between him and the members of his organization depends on the degree to which he embodies a style of life and a moral code. He is a center of value as well as of money and power for his adherents. His authority transcends the appeal to fear and greed and partakes, as we have seen, of a touch of the godlike. Thus, the Don serves as the supreme model and guardian of the special way of life which the criminal organization as "family" represents. This way of life is usually represented as growing out of the Sicilian immigrant tradition, an aspect of the new mythology which Puzo has developed with particular vividness and brilliance. However, I think it might also be said that the Don and his authority represent an image of organization which can be seen in opposition to those aspects of contemporary social institutions which are commonly perceived as signs of failure: the impersonality of the modern corporation on the one hand and the declining authority of the family on the other. Where the corporation executive is cold and impersonal, responsible only for the functional efficiency of his subordinates, the Don is warm and emotional, considering himself involved in every aspect of the life and death of the members of his organization. There is a tribal closeness about the criminal organization

as it is portrayed in the new mythology and the Don is its theocratic center. He is not only boss, but king, judge and priest. Unlike the modern American family with its generational conflicts, its confused sexual roles, its absent fathers, neurotic mothers, and nuclear isolation, the tribe-family ruled by the Don is a patriarchy with absolutely clear roles and lines of authority. The women are women and the men are men. There is a clear code of values and sexual roles with masculine dominance and strength at the center. Within this organization the individual is part of a larger kinship or tribal group with massive power against external enemies. The individual does not have to divide himself into diverse and conflicting social roles because the family is a totality for him.

Mario Puzo's central character Don Vito Corleone is unquestionably the most powerful and compelling version of the Don yet created. However, though Puzo must be credited with the most articulate and effective development of the figure of the Don, it is also clear that the outlines of this figure had already begun to take shape in the imaginations of a number of other writers. In most earlier versions of the criminal leader, certain characteristics of the Don are still inextricably mixed up with the diabolical image of the master criminal. Thus in an earlier novel like Ira Wolfert's *Tucker's People* (1943), though the criminal organization has many of the same qualities as Puzo's "family," the boss is still the evil entrepreneur of crime of the pre-war criminal formulas. A character much closer to Puzo's Don appears in Leslie Waller's *The Family,* which was published a year earlier than **The Godfather**. To see a figure who is still closer to Puzo's Don, we must turn to non-fiction. Mike Royko's *Boss,* a recent study of Chicago's Mayor Daley, is a highly critical account of Mayor Daley's administration of the city of Chicago. Yet, in his presentation of the character of the mayor and his description of the organization which serves as the basis of his power, Royko comes interestingly close to the same compelling portrayal of a quasi-tribal family within the larger society ruled by a man of combined ruthlessness and moral force that Puzo develops in **The Godfather**.

While the Don is a new figure in the literature of crime, a second figure, the Enforcer, has already served as the basis of a substantial number of books and films. The Enforcer is most commonly an assassin, though in some cases he is a professional thief. His central characteristic is ruthless and brilliant professionalism. He is the master of his craft and his whole way of life and code of values center around the skillful performance of his assignments. Usually there is a basic paradox in the Enforcer's character which is an important source of his dramatic effectiveness. He is a man who applies the cool and detached rationalism of the professional specialist to matters of extreme violence and illegality. In this respect, he resembles to a certain extent the combination found in James Bond and his imitators—the bureaucratic killer, the man with a number which gives him license to kill. The Enforcer also grows out of the American tradition of the western and hard-boiled detective heroes. Like the western hero, the Enforcer is often involved in vengeance plots. Or, like the aging gunfighter, he may find himself forced to reexamine the meaning of his life. And like both gunfighter and hard-boiled detective, the Enforcer lives by a code which is deeply rooted in his profession and in the maintenance of his honor as a man of supreme skill and dedication to his role.

. . . . .

The Enforcer's ruthlessness and his attempt to erect an area of meaning and security in a corrupt and deceitful society through personal loyalties gains a new dimension when Puzo develops it as a central theme of *The Godfather*. In Michael's final justification to Kay of the life of his father, the family is presented as the focus of those personal loyalties which alone can provide security and power in a hostile society:

> My father is a businessman trying to provide for his wife and children and those friends he might need someday in a time of trouble. He doesn't accept the rules of the society we live in because those rules would have condemned him to a life not suitable to a man like himself, a man of extraordinary force and character. . . . He refuses to live by rules set up by others, rules which condemn him to a defeated life. But his ultimate aim is to enter that society with a certain power since society doesn't really protect its members who do not have their own individual power. In the meantime he operates on a code of ethics he considers far superior to the legal structures of society. . . . I believe in you and the family we may have. I don't trust society to protect us. I have no intention of placing my fate in the hands of men whose only qualification is that they managed to con a block of people to vote for them. . . . I take care of myself, individual. Governments don't really do much for their people, that's what it comes down to, but that's not it really. All I can say, I have to help my father, I have to be on his side.

The pattern of action in which the enforcer characteristically manifests himself is the caper. The caper is a special sort of action in which an individual or a group undertake a particularly difficult feat which can only be accomplished through a stratagem of considerable subtlety and complexity. The usual structure for telling the story of a caper is by following the process of the caper itself. In many cases, the plan of the caper is revealed to the audience, followed by a suspenseful representation of the action itself, the feeling of

suspense being intensified by two uncertainties: whether the caper will be discovered in process, or whether one of the complex details of the plan will go awry and ruin the whole plot. Usually the feat which the caper seeks to accomplish is a robbery or an assassination, though it may also be a variety of other actions: a kidnapping, a commando raid, an escape, an ambush, a capture, etc. As a literary or cinematic structure, the caper is rather different in its characteristics from some of the other major organizing patterns in the literature of crime. It is quite different from the detective's investigation of a mystery, the hero's pursuit and destruction of the master criminal, or the gangster's rise and fall. However, though an entire work may be structured around a caper, this type of action can be developed on a smaller scale as one or more episodes in a larger work. Thus, while *The Godfather*'s overall structure is not a caper, many of its most important episodes take this form—for example, the attempted assassination of Don Vito, Michael's killing of Sollozo and McCluskey, the murder of Sonny Corleone, and the series of assassinations which restore the Corleone family's power.

As a dramatic structure, the caper is particularly suited to visual media like film and television, in which an elaborately interrelated series of actions can be represented with special effectiveness. However, the fact that the caper has also become a dominant structure in prose fiction and nonfiction where the medium is less suitable for this purpose, suggests that there are thematic reasons for its popularity as well. As it appears in the new mythology of crime, the caper is a study in the exercise of power by a secret organization, and it usually involves a complex use of technology as well as elaborate planning and coordination. The caper is usually carried out against a large organization which has its own complex routines and technology. Its ultimate aim is an exchange of power either through the acquisition of some form of wealth or through the destruction of important leaders of the opposing organization. Thus, the narrative structure of the caper brings us back to those major concerns with organization outside the law and the exercise of power which we also saw as the underlying fascination of Mario Puzo's narrative of the history of the Corleone family.

> "Don't you want to finish school, don't you want to be a lawyer? Lawyers can steal more money with a briefcase than a thousand men with guns and masks."

> It was at this time that the Don got the idea that he ran his world far better than his enemies ran the greater world which continually obstructed his path.

> As soon as the Corleone family set up their usual business liaison with the local police force they were informed of all such complaints and all crimes

by professional criminals. In less than a year Long Beach became the most crime-free town of its size in the United States. Professional stickup artists and strong-arms received one warning not to ply their trade in the town. They were allowed one offense. When they committed a second they simply disappeared. The flimflam home-improvement gyp artists, the door-to-door con men were politely warned that they were not welcome in Long Beach. Those confident con men who disregarded the warnings were beaten within an inch of their lives. Resident young punks who had no respect for law and proper authority were advised in the most fatherly fashion to run away from home. Long Beach became a model city.

Thus, a new mythology of crime has manifested itself in two related story formulas—the Enforcer's caper and the saga of the family. At first glance, it seems odd that the one thing which marks both of these new patterns—a relatively sympathetic and even admiring presentation of criminal or extralegal organization and actions—should emerge so strongly at a time when the political arena resounds with demands for "law and order" and passionate denunciations of a rising crime rate. However, this seeming discrepancy gives us some basic clues to the cultural significance of these new fashions in the literature of crime. First of all, one of the major functions of popular literature is to humanize and give order to disturbing phenomena by relating them to conventional views of the world. Consequently, we would expect a public concern with organized crime to make it an important literary subject. Morris and Hawkins point to this aspect of the literature of crime in their explanation of the public's fascination with the idea of a national crime syndicate:

> Whether alarm and uneasiness are induced by an apparently chaotic upsurge of crime and lawlessness, or whether explanation in terms of anonymous and intangible "social forces" is found unsatisfying, it is likely that the attribution of responsibility to a group of identifiable human agents for a large proportion of the disturbing happenings could be both intellectually and emotionally reassuring. . . . In the field of crime, the national crime syndicate provides a specific focus or target for fear and discontent.

This interpretation of the mythopoeic function of organized crime as scapegoat for more general ills is borne out by the success of the Enforcer vs. the syndicate formula. The violent emotions and bitter hatred which are so clearly expressed in these books suggest that there is a portion of the public frustrated and angry enough to require a vicarious bloodbath, a St. Bartholomew's Day massacre of the evil ones, to satisfy or express their rage. For such emotions organized crime makes a perfect target, a substitute for the "communist conspiracy" which served a similar function in earlier decades. Like the "communist conspiracy," the concept of organized crime provides the image of a nationwide web of evil created by a specific group of individuals. The formula of the Enforcer vs. the syndicate manages to blame this specific group of individuals for all the nation's ills, and then represents their destruction with appropriate violence.

However, while the cruder manifestations of the Enforcer story are based on just such a simple scapegoating, we certainly cannot say this of more complex versions of the new mythology of crime which represent thieves, assassins and criminal leaders with respect and sympathy. *The Godfather* is certainly not a scapegoating work in any simple sense, if at all. The Corleone family is not held responsible for the ills of American society, nor is it driven out or destroyed. On the contrary, what Puzo and other sophisticated contemporary crime writers seem to be doing is exploring the ironic relationship between crime and American society. In this respect, the new mythology of crime can be interpreted as a fictional working-out of some of the major propositions of Daniel Bell's well-known theory of "Crime as an American Way of Life." In this brilliant and prophetic essay, which first appeared in 1953, Bell developed with shocking persuasiveness the proposition that in many respects organized crime resembles the kind of ruthless business enterprise which successful Americans have always carried on:

> Yet, after all, the foundation of many a distinguished older American fortune was laid by sharp practices and morally reprehensible methods. The pioneers of American capitalism were not graduated from Harvard's School of Business Administration. The early settlers and founding fathers, as well as those who "won the West" and built up cattle, mining, and other fortunes, often did so by shady speculations and a not inconsiderable amount of violence. They ignored, circumvented, or stretched the law when it stood in the way of America's destiny and their own—or were themselves the law when it served their purposes. This has not prevented them and their descendants from feeling proper moral outrage when, under the changed circumstances of the crowded urban environments, late comers pursued equally ruthless tactics.

Bell makes two related points which have important implications for the new mythology of crime. First, he shows how the association between newer immigrant groups and crime was a perfectly natural result of the social fact that these groups were blocked by prejudice and the power of established groups from the ordinary channels of business enterprise. Therefore, many enterprising and ambitious young men from Southern and Eastern European immigrant groups turned to crime as the only possible route to success. In short, Al Capone and his ilk were not scheming monsters of the underworld but followers of Horatio Alger. Second, Bell points out that most organized criminal activity has centered in areas like gambling and bootlegging which Americans generally do not regard as criminal, yet moralistically insist on passing laws against. These two themes—crime as a means of rising in society and as a necessary response to America's moralistic hypocrisy about gambling, drinking, and other indulgences of the flesh—tend to humanize the criminal, to make of him essentially a person like the rest of us, sharing our hopes and aspirations. This is a more sophisticated way of treating crime in terms of "a group of identifiable human agents" than the simple-minded scapegoating of the anti-syndicate Enforcer stories. *The Godfather* is a particularly brilliant example of this kind of humanization. In his story of the Corleone family, Mario Puzo fully embodies in character and action his perception of what might be called the ironic respectability of crime. In an earlier essay on **"Why Crime is Good for America,"** [in *The Godfather Papers*] Puzo had more explicitly spelled out this paradoxical argument:

> Why is [crime] *good* for America? Because these policemen, government employees, bookkeepers, sundry clerks do *not* spend their "black" money on wine, women and song. They do *not* roister and revel. They are solid members of society. The money goes for a new house in suburbia where the kids can grow up untarnished by crime-breeding slums. The money goes for college educations that will transform prospective welfare clients into society-enriching doctors, engineers and certified accountants.

Puzo is, of course, being ironic here as he is throughout most of this mildly Swiftian satire. Apparently, he also feels that *The Godfather* is an ironic work of this sort, a satiric attack on organized crime. If this was his intention, it clearly missed most of his audience, who quite obviously took the Corleone family as almost wholly admirable and sympathetic people. I would argue instead that the great effectiveness of *The Godfather* results in large part from Puzo's ambiguity on this very point. There is irony in the bourgeois respectability of Don Vito Corleone, but it is a double irony. On the surface there is a discrepancy between the peaceful suburban domesticity of the Corleone family and the violent crimes which support the façade of wealth and prestige. But the deeper irony is that in the corrupt and unjust world of modern American society, the family's illegal power is a justifiable necessity. In light of the frequent glimpses we get of the endemic hypocrisy, amorality, and brutality of this supposedly respectable American society, there is certainly more truth than irony in the narrator's observation that "the Don got the idea that he ran his world far better than his enemies

ran the greater world which continually obstructed his path." And while one may quake a bit at the implications of the narrator's description of the family's reform of Long Beach, this is exactly what many Americans have dreamed of doing in their flight to the suburbs. The final irony, central to *The Godfather* and to the more sophisticated forms of the new mythology of crime, might be summed up in Don Vito's famous maxim that "lawyers can steal more money with a briefcase than a thousand men with guns and masks." Or as Puzo, himself, puts it in one of his essays:

> Society, cloaked in the robes of law, masked by religion, armed with authority sprung from the beginning of history is itself the true archcriminal.

This view is not, in itself, a new one. In fact it has probably been a commonplace self-justification of criminals for centuries. Vidocq, the fascinating nineteenth century French criminal, who was, ironically, one of the first great detectives, tells us in his memoirs of how he once remonstrated with a friend about his cheating at gambling and received the following reply:

> "You're not a child," said my honorable friend; "there's no question of robbery. They only correct fortune rather well, and believe me, that's the way it's done in the salon as well as the tavern. There they cheat—that's the accepted word—and the banker, who in the morning in his banking house commits a crime in figuring interest, traps you very calmly that evening at play."

> What could I answer to such formidable arguments? Nothing! The only thing left for me was to take the money, which I did.

However, this view of society has not, until quite recently, found widespread expression in American popular culture, particularly in works widely consumed by the middle class. Even more strikingly the spread of this cynical and despairing sense of American society has been associated, first, with a fascination with the hidden network of organized crime and then, in the last few years, with the complex and sympathetic treatment of criminal organizations. This aspect of the new mythology of crime is particularly interesting in light of the insistence by Bell and other scholars that the period of the gangster and the Mafia is over:

> Ironically, the social development which made possible the rise to political influence sounds, too, the knell of the rough Italian gangster. For it is the growing number of Italians with professional training and legitimate business success that both prompts and permits the Italian group to wield increasing political influence; and increasingly it is

the professionals and businessmen who provide models for Italian youth today, models that hardly existed twenty years ago. Ironically, the headlines and exposés of "crime" of the Italian "gangsters" came years after the fact. Many of the top "crime" figures had long ago forsworn violence, and even their income, in large part, was derived from legitimate investments (real estate in the case of Costello, motor haulage and auto dealer franchises in the case of Adonis) or from such quasi-legitimate but socially respectable sources as gambling casinos. Hence society's "retribution" in the jail sentences for Costello and Adonis was little more than a trumped up morality that disguised a social hypocrisy.

Why, then, should there be all this current fascination with organized crime? Why is it that the mythology of organized professional crime should flourish at a time when it seems to be becoming a less important factor in American society? The answer, I think, lies in the recent emergence of new criminal patterns, which have become an object of increasing public concern under the slogan "crime in the streets." Characteristically, this new kind of crime is non-professional, is usually not carried on by organizations and gangsters, and is seen as a direct threat to the lives and property of the great majority of citizens in a way that the activities of the criminal gangs never did. The criminologist Radzinowicz describes these new patterns of crime in the following way:

> It may even be true to say that new frontiers of crime have been opened up by the affluent society and the welfare state. Has contemporary crime assumed a new physiognomy? I can discover eight features which may be regarded as prima facie evidence that it has.

> First, the growth of motiveless destruction, hooliganism. Second, certain other kinds of violence. Third, expansion of new forms of stealing, such as automobile thefts and very lucrative robberies. Fourth, a shift towards disintegrated social behavior and drug consumption. Fifth, a spread of occupational crime, white collar or blue collar illegality, of illegal conduct by those generally presumed to be law-abiding. Sixth, a stronger contingent of offenders from the middle strata of society as compared with the working classes. Seventh, an increased proportion of crime by the younger and the young-adult groups. Eighth, the influx of first offenders and their relatively greater share in crime as compared with recidivists.

It seems to me that the two crucial aspects of these new criminal patterns are first, that they indicate a striking spread of criminal behavior and attitudes to the point where they threaten sectors of the middle class who were largely immune from the dangers of violence, assault and robbery in previous decades. Moreover, these patterns of behavior and attitude not only represent an increasing likelihood that a middle-class family will experience assault, robbery, or vandalism, but that members of the middle class will themselves become involved in crime. Thus, these new patterns of crime also imply an erosion of traditional middle-class values and modes of security and protection. The most obvious, and to many members of the middle class, most disturbing, index of these new patterns of crime is the invasion of what had previously been middle-class sanctuaries by forms of behavior and attitudes which until recently had been largely confined to urban ghettos. The flow of drugs, of thievery, vandalism, and various forms of violence into suburbs and university communities over the past decade have been perceived by much of the public as a vast upsurge in crime and a profound breakdown in the social order. Against this background, the new mythology of the criminal organization fills a complex of emotional needs. On the simplest level, it provides a reassuring explanation of the apparent erosion of values and breakdown of order by representing these disturbing social phenomena as the direct result of massive conspiracy of evil. But, in its more complex forms, such as in *The Godfather,* the new mythology presents the criminal organization more sympathetically, indeed almost nostalgically, as a form of traditional social organization which has successfully resisted the decline of authority, the breakdown of values, and the alienation and disorder of an increasingly corrupt American society. Puzo's "family" with its complex of loyalties, its patriarchal authority, and its boundless power to protect its members and guarantee them instant and complete justice, provides a compelling escape into fantasy from our pervasive sense of the breakdown of traditional social forms, moral standards, and basic security arising from the troubling new social changes of the 1960's and 1970's. In a related way, the heroic image of the Enforcer is another fantasy alternative to the fears of powerlessness, violence, and social chaos which afflict contemporary Americans. That both of these fantasies are associated with professional crime is perhaps best understood as an indication of how deeply Americans fear that the present social trends are leading toward catastrophe, for, in the new mythology, the most important aspect of the "family" is its power to impose authority and order for itself in a chaotic universe. Once viewed as the very antithesis of the American way, the gangster has increasingly come to represent traditional patterns of order and value.

The most curious thing about the new mythology of crime is the fact that in some of its expressions, such as the Enforcer vs. syndicate formula, organized crime functions as a scapegoat, a terrible evil which must be extirpated, while in other versions, the "family" is, as we have seen, a symbol of the most positive traditional values. To some extent the difference between these treatments of the criminal organization is probably to be accounted for by differences in audience and tradition. The Enforcer vs. syndicate formula is as much an extension of the earlier hard-boiled detective story as it is an expression of the new mythology of crime. Works like the "Executioner" share *The Godfather*'s fascination with criminal organizations and with the exercise of violent extra-legal power, but at the same time these works try to maintain a traditional moral distinction between good and evil. Because the Enforcer vs. syndicate story usually appears in cheap pulp novels which are luridly and crudely written, while the more complex and sympathetic view of the "family" appears in the form of long and complex best-sellers and is usually written with some degree of literary artfulness and sophistication, I am inclined to believe that we are dealing with a semi-literate lower- and lower-middle-class public on one hand and with the more educated middle-class public on the other. Both groups perceive contemporary American society as riddled by corruption and disorder, but the former group's response is anger and frustration which calls forth scapegoating. The more educated and successful members of the middle-class public seem to be more inclined toward a humanizing treatment of the criminal organization in which a dominant element is a demonstration that the "family" stands for positive, traditional values, and that it has the means to enforce these values in a world where they are threatened.

Unfortunately, the situation is somewhat more complicated than this because the enjoyment of Enforcer stories is certainly not limited to the semi-literate, and *The Godfather,* in its film version, was enormously successful with all groups of Americans. Evidently, it is possible for many of the same persons to enjoy stories in which organized crime is treated as an evil conspiracy responsible for all contemporary American problems as well as narratives in which such organizations are presented as bastions of loyalty and security in a chaotic society. Yet, as one looks back over the history of crime in literature, one can see the same ambiguous mixture of horror and fascination, of attraction and repulsion consistently at work. What has changed significantly is the kind of crime that is the center of interest. Perhaps the basic explanation of the long-lasting tradition of literary crime lies in the way crime serves as an ambiguous mirror of social values, reflecting both our overt commitments to certain principles of morality and order and our hidden resentments and animosity against these principles. Thus, in nineteenth-century England and America, the focal point of conceptions of morality and social authority was the domestic circle. At the same time, the literature of crime and the actual crimes which most fascinated the public were primarily murders of relatives—husbands poisoning wives, nephews murdering wealthy aunts, cousins doing away with cousins. These were the staples of the classical detective

story and of the great Victorian murder trials. It seems quite likely that the public's ambiguous fascination with such crimes was a way of vicariously working out feelings of hatred and frustration imposed by the constraints of one's own family situation. The emergence of the gangster hero in the 1920's and 1930's signalled the dominance, particularly in America, of a new constellation of values. The family circle, never as strong in America as in England, had increasingly lost its moral authority while the ideology of individual success and rising in society became the prevailing ethos. Overtly, the classic gangster film, and the hard-boiled detective story portrayed the downfall of an individual who had sought wealth and power by immoral and illegal means. Yet, beneath the moral surface of the story, the gangster film expressed a burning resentment against respectable society and a fascination with the untrammeled and amoral aggressiveness of a Little Caesar or a Scarface. Similarly, the hard-boiled detective story presented a hero who not only acted outside the law to bring about true justice, but had turned his back on the ideal of success. In both these formulas, the treatment of crime enabled writers to express a bitter feeling that the ideal of success was corrupt and immoral, while still insisting on the basic moral proposition that crime does not pay.

What I have called the new mythology of crime ambiguously mirrors a world in which the individualistic ethos no longer satisfactorily explains and orders society for most members of the public. The new center of value is the large organization and its collective power. The drama of the criminal gang has become a kind of allegory of the corporation and the corporate society. When the "Executioner" and his fellow enforcers are exterminating the syndicate they are, on the surface, purging the evil corporation so that the good ones can flourish. But, covertly, the "Executioner" is engaged in a violent individualist revolution against an alienating and corrupting bureaucratic society. The attack on syndicate bigwigs is a thinly disguised assault on the managerial elite who hold the reins of corporate power and use it for their own benefit. To openly express such feelings would require a transformation of the political and social perspective of many readers. The disguised allegory of the Enforcer story permits indulgence in a feeling of hatred against controlling organizations without requiring a new perception of society.

Puzo and other more sophisticated exponents of the new mythology of crime also treat the criminal organization as a symbolic mirror of the business corporation, but in a more complex way. In *The Godfather,* the surface story is a tragic drama of responsibility. Michael Corleone must give up his earlier dreams and aspirations and assume the role of Godfather, a position that not only makes him the leader of the "family" but also implicates him in deeds of murder and betrayal that contradict his previous scheme of values. But this is only the surface story. Covertly, Puzo's novel is a celebration of the "family." Michael's becoming Godfather, far from the destruction of his original hopes, is the true fulfillment of his destiny as an exceptional man. The "family" is a fantasy of collective, organized power that actually works to protect and support the individual as opposed to the coldness and indifference of the modern business or government bureaucracy. *The Godfather* and other related works permit us to enjoy vicariously the fantasy of an organization with boundless power and a true concern for the welfare of its members, just as the solid nineteenth-century family man could participate imaginatively in a nice bit of domestic homicide thereby projecting his latent feelings of frustration and hostility toward his spouse onto a fictional or actual criminal.

Thus, the new mythology of crime uses our perennial fascination with criminal activity to work out in stories the tension between traditional values and our sense of the decline of security, significance, and order in the corporate society. The image of the "family" with its closely knit traditional authority and its power to protect the interests of its members has a powerful fascination in a period when the authority and power of the institutions which have traditionally provided direction and protection for individuals—the actual family, the church, the informal structures of the closely-knit neighborhood group, the well-ordered career lines of the American middle class and the ideology of success—seem to be threatened by social change and upheaval. Another contemporary cultural factor that is probably reflected in the new mythology of crime is our increasingly ambiguous feeling about the unlimited power of the government which has been so strongly intensified by our disturbing course of action in Vietnam. I suspect there is a definite relation between the fascination with limitless criminal power in the new mythology of crime and the public's reluctant awareness of the uncontrollable power of violence in the hands of the government. Perhaps there is some reassurance in the vision of unlimited extralegal violence being used in responsible and meaningful ways by men with whose purposes the reader can sympathize, as in *The Godfather.*

But whatever the specific cultural sources of the new mythology of crime, it seems clear to me that it expresses a deep uncertainty about the adequacy of our traditional social institutions to meet the needs of individuals for security, for justice, for a sense of significance. The fact that these concerns are reflected through the dark mirror of crime indicates that most members of the public are not prepared to fully confront and acknowledge the extent of their despair. Here, as we have seen in the case of earlier crime formulas, the use of crime as a subject enables the public to give some expression to its latent hostility and frustration while still maintaining an overt stance of affirmation of the conventional morality. The new mythology of crime generally continues to affirm a traditional view of the immorality of crime,

at least to the extent of differentiating between crime and legality, but the façade of morality and legality usually appears to be so shaky and rotten that one becomes more and more aware of the disturbing vision that lies behind it: the dark message that America is a society of criminals, or the still more disturbing irony that a "family" of criminals might be more humanly interesting and morally satisfying than a society of empty routines, irresponsibly powerful organization, widespread corruption, and meaningless violence. The disturbing face that glares from the dark mirror of crime may increasingly come to seem our own.

John Sutherland (essay date 1981)

SOURCE: "The Godfather," in *Bestsellers: Popular Fiction of the 1970s,* Routledge & Kegan Paul, 1981, pp. 38-41.

[*In the following essay, Sutherland discusses the publishing history of* The Godfather *and the source of the novel's wide popular appeal.*]

> I wrote it to make money. . . . How come you people never ask writers about money?

The background to *The Godfather* is well known and blatantly self-proclaimed. Puzo wrote two 'literary' novels which were well received (*The New York Times*'s 'small classic' is a phrase which stuck in the proud author's mind), but which netted only $6,500 between them. 'I was forty-five years old and tired of being an artist. . . . It was time to grow up and sell out.' Publishers had shown some interest in 'that Mafia stuff' in his second novel, which dealt principally with the struggle of an Italian immigrant family. So Puzo drew up the outline of a full-blown gangster saga set in the 1940s New York, and loosely based on folk demons like 'Uncle Frank' Costello. Those ten pages earned him $5,000 advance from Putnam. This was 1965; Puzo, who seems by his own account to be a hand-to-mouth sort of writer, finally delivered the manuscript in 1968, spurred by the need for some money to take his family on holiday. While he was away, paperback rights were auctioned to Bantam for a then record $410,000. Once published *The Godfather* assumed the #1 spot on the *New York Times* list, and held a place in the top ten titles for sixty-seven weeks. It was also number one in England, France and Germany; countries where, perhaps, interest in 'gangster' America was heightened by the Vietnam war. 'They tell me', Puzo wrote in 1972, 'it's the fastest and bestselling fiction paperback of all times.' By 1978 it was one of the select half-dozen novels to have broken the 10 m. sales barrier in the US, and is credited by Hackett as being the bestselling novel ever. By the end of the decade *The Godfather*'s publishers were claiming worldwide sales of over 15 m.

Puzo's only mistake in an otherwise triumphant 'selling out' was to release the film rights for $12,500 while he was between agents, and at a time when a few thousand still 'looked like Fort Knox.' Altogether the novelist's connection with the movie industry was unhappy. He was hired by Paramount at $500 a week to co-author the *Godfather* script with another 2.5 per cent 'points' in the profits. But the self-effacing nature of the work offended his aggressively freelancing instincts. It particularly upset him that he was not consulted on the final cut—that last and most influential stage of editorial revision. 'It was not MY movie,' he concluded, and vowed never to work in Hollywood again 'unless I have complete control'—a stipulation which he was realistic enough to acknowledge might disbar him from further serious film work.

> **Puzo complains that readers fail to register 'the casual irony in my books.' But he confesses that this quality in *The Godfather* was not just casual but oblique: 'so oblique in fact, that most of the critics missed the irony in the novel and attacked me for glorifying the Mafia.'**
> **—John Sutherland**

None the less the film, starring Marlon Brando, James Caan and Al Pacino, was judged by most critics to have been better of its kind than the novel. As New York critic Pauline Kael saw it, Puzo's *Godfather* was a clumsy performance, 'all itch and hype and juicy *roman à clef*,' but 'Puzo provided what Coppola needed: a story teller's outpouring of incidents and details to choose from, the folklore behind the headlines, heat and immediacy, the richly familiar.' Swollen with this kind of praise, Coppola became overnight a cult director reputedly able to make silk purses even out of rehashed *Little Caesar*. But to hear Puzo tell it, Coppola's motives were not much different from his own; both were working calculatedly 'below their gifts' so as to bankroll better things:

> One interview I have to admit depressed me. Francis Coppola explained he was directing *The Godfather* so that he could get the capital to make pictures he really wanted to make. What depressed me was that he was smart enough to do this at the age of thirty-two when it took me forty-five years to figure out I had to write *The Godfather* so that I could do the other books I really wanted to do.

It is a reflection on author/auteur vanity that neither the enriched Puzo nor Coppola have, in the event, done anything surpassingly good after the dizzy success of their *Godfather*s. Puzo's *Fools Die* earned, in its turn, a record advance

paperback sale of $2.2 m. and was proclaimed 'The publishing event of the decade,' yet only someone addicted to gambling could have read this rambling, painfully autobiographical Las Vegas melodrama without embarrassment, and one learned with gratitude that Puzo's next commission was as consultant to *Godfather III*. For his part Coppola weighed in with the $30 m. epic *Apocalypse Now*.

The germ of *The Godfather* is an exuberantly paradoxical essay which Puzo wrote for *Cavalier* (a girly mag) in 1966; 'How crime keeps America healthy, wealthy, cleaner and more beautiful.' Puzo has elsewhere written 'A modest proposal,' and evidently feels an affinity with Swift. In his panegyric to American crime he puts forward a 'logical' argument for abolishing conventional civic virtue:

> How are we to adjust to a society that drafts human beings to fight a war, yet permits its businessmen to make a profit from the shedding of blood? . . . as society becomes more and more criminal, the well-adjusted citizen, by definition, must become more criminal. So let us now dare to take the final step.

In the spirit of this final step the best adjusted citizen of all is taken to be the most powerful criminal in America, Don Corleone, the Godfather. And as the essay applauds the social achievements of crime, so the novel insinuates a warm commendation of Mafia 'family life,' of the military virtues of the family's 'soldiers' and the efficiency and high business ethics of the 'organization.' These are the *true* Americans; 'are we not better men,' the modestly murderous Don asks, 'than those *pezzonovanti* who have killed countless millions of men in our lifetimes?.'

Puzo complains that readers fail to register 'the casual irony in my books.' But he confesses that this quality in *The Godfather* was not just casual but oblique: 'so oblique in fact, that most of the critics missed the irony in the novel and attacked me for glorifying the Mafia.' A disservice was done to Puzo in this respect by Brando's superbly leonine interpretation of the Don, and the self-justifying speeches which Coppola added to make a decent-sized 'part' for his star—especially the role the script assigns to Corleone in the treaty meeting with Sollozzo. This scene also stresses that the Corleone family will have nothing to do with the 'dirty' crimes of narcotics, a special plea which sets up a facile opposition of good-guy gangsters and bad-guy gangsters. Watching the film it is only too easy to believe the canard that Puzo and Paramount were paid a million dollars to do an advertising job on the Mafia. But the novel, while not exactly a modern *Jonathan Wild the Great*, insists on being read ironically if one reads it at all carefully. Take the following description of the Don's funeral. He has died, it will be remembered, of natural causes, cultivating his garden. By a stroke of acting genius, Brando improvised the famous business in which grandad cuts out orange-peel fangs with which playfully to terrify the children, just before having a massive heart attack. As with the whole creation of the part it is magnificent, but fatally humanizes Puzo's consummate businessman:

> It was time for the cemetery. It was time to bury the great Don. Michael linked his arm with Kay's and went out into the garden to join the host of mourners. Behind him came the *caporegimes* followed by their soldiers and then all the humble people the Godfather had blessed during his lifetime. The baker Nazorine, the widow Colombo and her sons and all the countless others of his world he had ruled so firmly but justly. There were even some who had been his enemies, come to do him honour. Michael observed all this with a tight, polite smile. . . . He would follow his father. He would care for his children, his family, his world. But his children would grow in a different world. They would be doctors, artists, scientists. Governors. Presidents. Anything at all.

The epigraph which Puzo chose for *The Godfather* is Balzac's 'Behind every great fortune there lies a crime.' It may be that he is *au courant* with nineteenth-century French fiction. But it seems more likely that he borrowed Balzac's apt sarcasm from C. Wright Mills's *The Power Elite*, which makes the same epigraphic use of it. In the mordant description of the new Don's funeral musings, Puzo gives his own social theory of the formation of America's *pezzonovanti/ power elite*, and the barely hidden criminal power on which governors and presidents build their 'legitimate' authority.

Irony, especially anti-American irony, never sold 15 m. novels, and Puzo was wise to keep it so oblique as to be invisible to most critics and virtually all lay readers, for whom it would fatally have interrupted the pleasures of the quick read. Ignoring any literary sophistication, popular reception of *The Godfather* ran along two well-grooved channels. There was the shocked response, which found in the novel a naturalistic exposure of American vice almost too horrible to contemplate: 'This is the hard, chilling, incredible, brutal reality of the vice that this nation tolerates' (from a Chicago newspaper, appropriately enough). And there was the thrilled reading which found the novel, in Kael's phrase, 'a juicy *roman à clef.*' The ubiquitously reported scene of Sinatra balling Puzo out in a Hollywood restaurant fuelled the sales-promoting conviction that here was a novel/film which spilled some interesting beans.

Whether it was read for the inside story of American crime, or the inside story of show business scandal, *The Godfather* was universally taken as a novel whose author knew what he was writing about. Since Mario Puzo was himself of Sicilian extraction it was only too easy to see the work as a rare violation of ten centuries of *omerta* (silence)—the work of a once-in-a-lifetime canary like Joe Valachi. (Puzo, incidentally, strenuously affirms that his novel is based solely on 'research'—but he would, wouldn't he?) And yet the novel's cleverest trick is to go through an elaborate ritual of apparently disclosing while actually giving no hard information for the reader's $1.95. Like Valachi, Puzo shapes as if to tell. But since, unlike Valachi, he has no privilege against libel law and no FBI protection against assassination, his 'revelations' are folded back into fiction. Of course, the reader quite understands the necessity for this. Did not Sinatra successfully sue a British newspaper which injudiciously slandered him by falsely suggesting that he might have mob-associations along the lines of Johnny Fontane? Did not the Italian-American Anti Defamation League lean on Paramount so that the names 'Mafia' and 'Cosa Nostra' could not be mentioned in a film, which if it is not about the Mafia and Cosa Nostra is about nothing?

By drawing the audience/reader into a conspiratorial acquiescence with its prudent vagueness—the omissions of reference, misnamings and distortions—*The Godfather* contrives to suggest indiscretion while in fact giving nothing away. And in this pleasantly tantalizing game with the reader, Puzo is helped by the paradoxical nature of the mythological (and historical?) Mafia. In the popular mind, it is an institution which is invisible—yet all-powerful. It is omnipresent, but no one in authority acknowledges its existence (for most of his career, for example, J. Edgar Hoover apparently denied the existence of any significant organized crime in America). It is a force about which one knows nothing—except that it affects and possibly controls every department of one's life.

Since a totally 'secret' organization can only be constituted and tested against the reader's fantasy of it, Puzo can pull off yet another spectacular trick in *The Godfather.* This is to suggest that Cosa Nostra is so powerfully influential as to have rendered the rest of American life a mere accessory to itself. Where other institutions appear in the novel they are either shams or secretly controlled by the family. Anything can be fixed. Union co-operation, for example, can be turned off and on like a tap by Don Corleone; this it is, together with limitless finance and violence against prominent persons that makes him a power in Hollywood. Among his minor fixes is to speed up Michael's demobilization—had his son so wished he could, of course, have arranged promotion or release from military service altogether. The omnipotence and omnipresence of the Mafia explain why in a novel of gangster life there is no opposing law enforcement by society at large. The two policemen we encounter in the novel are Mafia place men in uniform—McCluskey and Neri. Neri, the fearless executioner, is particularly interesting since the narrative contrives to suggest that he serves Don Michael Corleone as the *real* NYPD police chief:

> And now, finally, Albert Neri, alone in his Bronx apartment, was going to put on his police uniform again. He brushed it carefully. Polishing the holster would be next. And his policeman's cap too, the visor had to be cleaned, the stout black shoes shined. Neri worked with a will. He had found his place in the world, Michael Corleone had placed his absolute trust in him, and today he would not fail that trust.

He is not, as one might think, preparing for a mayor's parade. Properly turned out, Neri puts three bullets in rival Don Barzini's chest with his service .38 for the honour of his own Don.

Similarly, there is no justice in the novel save what the Mafia buys or what the Godfather administers. The first scene in which the distraught undertaker, Amerigo Bonasera, sees the defilers of his daughter set free by a tainted judge establishes the hollowness of 'legitimate' institutions. 'For justice we must go to Don Corleone,' he resolves. The few 'outsiders' in the novel, like Jules Segal, Tom Hagen and Kay Adams, have the status of refugees who, by an extraordinary stroke of luck, have managed to struggle into the 'real' world. All three are 'adopted.' Segal, the struck-off doctor, becomes the family physician. Hagen, the former Irish waif, becomes the family lawyer. Kay, the blonde girl whose ancestors came across with the founding fathers, becomes family *tout court*. She is converted to Catholicism and as Mrs. Corleone becomes *plus Sicilienne que les Siciliennes*. The novel ends with this patrician young WASP preparing to take communion, herself transubstantiated more than any wafer could be:

> She emptied her mind of all thought of herself, of her children, of all anger, of all rebellion, of all questions. Then with a profound and deeply willed desire to believe, to be heard, as she had done every day since the murder of Carlo Rizzi, she said the necessary prayers for the soul of Michael Corleone.

The Mafia and the Godfather possess everything and everybody. The fabric of American life—its institutions, political, legislative and judicial, its law enforcement, its entertainment industries, its commerce are reduced to filmy insubstantiality. The Mafia has hollowed out America, and filled what remains with itself.

Puzo's vision of secret yet irresistibly extensive Mafia omnipotence has clear elements of solipsism and maniac self-aggrandizement in it. And to indulge a vein of speculation, one may note that immediately after the Second World War was a significant period in which to have set *The Godfather*. Historically the two years 1946-8, in which the novel's main action occurs, cover the only moment in history when one man—the President of the United States—enjoyed global omnipotence. The US's sole possession of nuclear weapons, and the presidential structure which put one man's finger on the button, gave a new dimension to the idea of absolute power. For a moment, Nero's fantasy about the world having but one neck to cut came true. Yet this climax of American potency was also a period of national shame for Italian Americans. Italy as wartime enemy had made a notoriously poor showing in the recent war; revealed herself as militarily incompetent and cowardly. The Duce was universally regarded as a poltroon. It is possible, I suspect, that these contrary facts are somehow condensed into the 'dreamwork' of *The Godfather*—a novel which fantasizes about the private possession of irresistible power, and whose chronicle reasserts Italian military prowess as displayed in the savage, but highly disciplined, wars of the families. Puzo, incidentally, was in his mid-twenties at the time of *The Godfather*'s main action, and served in the Army Air Corps in Europe.

As a bestseller *The Godfather* is more like *Love Story* than *Jaws*. That is to say it renovates old material rather than introducing new. Any moderately practised cultural consumer of the 1960s would come to Puzo's novel more of an expert on the Mafia than sharks. American TV, films and paperback fiction have been obsessed with gangsters, mobsters, urban *banditti* for most of the twentieth century. And their images of the arch-criminal—the *capo di tutti capi*—have traditionally been both morally ambiguous and emotionally extravagant. Orwell, for example, noted with astonishment the perverse hero-worship that a Neapolitan crook like Capone inspired: 'Books have been written about Al Capone that are hardly different in tone from the books written about Henry Ford, Stalin, Lord Northcliffe and all the rest of the log cabin to White House brigade.'

Against this one can put a hysterical, hostile depiction of the Godfather genus from Spillane's *Kiss Me, Deadly*:

> The Mafia. The stinking, slimy Mafia. An oversize mob of ignorant, lunkheaded jerks. . . . Someplace at the top of the heap was a person. From him the fear radiated like from the centre of a spiderweb. He sat on his throne and made a motion of his hand and somebody died. He made another motion and somebody was twisted until they screamed. A nod of his head did something that sent a guy leaping from a roof because he couldn't take it any more.
>
> Just one person did that.

The achievement of Puzo's *Godfather* is to have made a

stale cliche fresh again, and to have brought the pervasive American ambivalence about stylish crime under a new artistic control. He managed this by an injection of 'researched' historicity and ethnic inwardness; by a cool, deadpan naturalism which works against the melodramatic and sensationally charged subject matter; and by an irony which permits us to read (and Puzo to own) the work as 'critique.' At the same time the irony is so oblique as to be virtually private; 'unsophisticated' readings of the novel are also permitted. Frank, vicarious thrill-seeking approaches are not turned away. As a result 15 m. copies are sold and *The Godfather* takes its place as the bestseller of bestsellers.

R. Z. Sheppard (review date 3 December 1984)

SOURCE: A review of *The Sicilian,* in *Time,* December 3, 1984, p. 82.

[*In the following review, Sheppard offers praise for* The Sicilian.]

The Godfather was an irresistible tale of corruption and an equally tempting celebration of two sacred institutions, the family and free enterprise. *The Sicilian,* an offshoot of the 1969 bestseller, is also an offer of evil and romance that cannot be refused. Mario Puzo remains one of America's best popular storytellers, though his years of whittling movie scripts have resulted in chapters that seem spindly next to those in the full-bodied Godfather. In fact the novel could be cut down and inserted in the earlier book. Offstage, at Mafia Central on Long Island, Don Corleone directs events that have profound effects in Sicily and teach Son Michael a cruel lesson in survival.

The time is 1950, and young Corleone is preparing to end the two-year exile imposed after he killed Sollozzo the Turk and the corrupt Police Captain McCluskey. Michael's final assignment is to arrange the escape of a Sicilian outlaw who has become an endangered folk hero. This proves difficult. The godfather-in-training is given the runaround and a chance to witness treacheries that seem to have originated in the Punic Wars.

Puzo works hard to make his story back-lot mythic. Spartacus led his slave army out of the Cammarata hills to fight the Romans. A skeleton dug out of the rocky soil is said to have belonged to one of Hannibal's elephants. The novel's hero, Turi Guiliano, is a Latin Robin Hood who can recite the Song of Roland and the basic guerilla manual with matching ease. When he is not slipping into Montelepre for his mother's cooking and the attractions of a young widow, Turi muses under starry skies: "He no longer doubted that he had some magnificent destiny before him. He shared the magic of those medieval heroes who could not die until they came to the end of their long story, until they had achieved their great victories."

Guiliano dreams of smashing the power of the "Friends of the Friends." Sicilians, Puzo tells us, never say Mafia, a 10th century Arabic term meaning sanctuary. A thousand years later, the word is dark with irony. Founded to fight foreign oppressors, the organization has come to include the island's most terrible despots. Their fingers can be found in every business and social institution from Palermo To Catania, their hands behind countless murders. Puzo offers swatches of sad history and exotic sociology. Mussolini nearly wiped out the Mafia, but the U.S. Army ensured its comeback when it unlocked Fascist prisons. Kidnapping is a cottage industry, monks fake relics, and omerta, the code of silence, is so pervasive that strangers often cannot get directions to their hotels. Casting a large shadow over all this is Puzo's Don Croce Malo, a model of the fatal charm and intricate cunning of a successful mafioso.

With the exception of Michael Corleone, Turi Guiliano is the shallowest major character in the novel. He reads good books, idealizes justice and respects religion. But if he has a thought subtler than how to trap his enemies, he keeps it to himself. By contrast, Aspanu Pisciotta, the hero's friend and chief lieutenant, has a vivid psychology that eventually sustains Horace's 2,000-year-old observation that "Sicilian tyrants never invented a greater torment than envy."

Unlike a spaghetti western, The sicilian has no one-on-one shootout under a hot sun. Instead, Don Croce and Guiliano are locked in an elaborate melodrama of betrayals within betrayals. Puzo too demonstrates sly moves. His florid descriptions and graphic action scenes guarantee bug-eyed attention while he plants a sardonic fatalism in the heart of his book. One of the rarest commodities in his Sicily is truth ("A source of power, a lever of control, why should anyone give it away?"), while revenge is one of the highest virtues ("On this Catholic island, statutes of a weeping Jesus in every home, Christian forgiveness was contemptible refuge of the coward"). In the New world, far from the color and tradition, Don Corleone takes an even more british view: "Live your life not to be a hero but to remain alive. With time, heroes seem a little foolish."

This is cynical stuff from one of the most "respected" characters in popular fiction. But Puzo knows the mass-market game better than most: Give the angels the good looks, the devils the best lines, and keep the prose cinematic. This element is so strong that the book seems to be only the pupal stage of a story impatient to spread celluloid wings.

Robert Royal (review date 5 April 1985)

SOURCE: A review of *The Sicilian,* in *The National Review,* April 5, 1985, pp. 52-4.

[*In the following review, Royal notes that in* The Sicilian, *"Puzo has returned to some of his richer human material that won him critical acclaim for his early novels."*]

Generally speaking, the modern novel is not so much an art form as a predicament. When belief in man as the rational animal wavers, as it often does in modern fiction, one or the other of two extremes predominates: angelism (the self-regarding, purely intellectual world of ideologies, doctrinaire feminism, labyrinths, hypertrophied sensitivities, stories within stories within stories) or bestialism (radically purposeless lust and violence). The result is a loss of true imaginative power in spite of the emotional, intellectual, and literary force of a given work. We get many fictions that are, in a word, effete.

You could not apply that term to Mario Puzo's *The Sicilian.* Puzo's deliberately commercial success with the bestial in *The Godfather* may lead many readers to assume that his new novel merely continues in the same vein. They would be mistaken. There is no gratuitous sex or violence here. Puzo has returned to some of the richer human material that won him critical acclaim for his early novels. He loses little of his basic animal vigor in *The Sicilian,* but he uses it in the service of a wider vision than might be expected.

The first sign of this intention is his successful creation of a believable and genuinely good character in Turi Guiliano, the Sicilian of the title. The character Guiliano, based in part on a historical figure, begins his rise to public notoriety in 1943 at the age of twenty. The Fascists have just been driven from Sicily by the American liberation forces, and the Mafia is still weak from Mussolini's harsh repression. Little by little, however, the "Friends of the Friends," as the Mafia was known in Sicily, are beginning to insinuate themselves back into power by scheming to have Mafiosi appointed to replace ousted Fascist politicians. The strict rationing laws of the new government and the black market to which they have given rise are the source of lucrative Mafia rake-offs. Official corruption, the collusion of the Sicilian nobility and the Church, and the shrewdness of Don Croce Malo (the top Mafia leader) are establishing oppression that is at least as bad as anything the Sicilian people have ever experienced.

Guiliano and a boyhood friend are caught one day on a mountain road smuggling cheese, hams, and sausage, in contravention of the rationing laws, for a village engagement party. Smuggling is so common that the authorities usually do not pay much attention to it, but this time a brutal policeman shoots Guiliano—who, however, manages to kill the policeman in spite of a serious wound.

Until this incident Guiliano had been an attractive and charismatic boy. Like many Sicilian children he had been brought up on the romantic exploits of Charlemagne and Roland in the puppet theaters. Guiliano had also been an avid reader of literature, history, and philosophy. Now, in this fluid post-Fascist period, as he hides from the police, his imagination catches fire and he dreams of liberating Sicily from her several exploiters. He hides out in the mountains and becomes a Robin Hood figure.

Not only does he steal from the rich and give to the poor, thereby winning for himself widespread support from the peasants, but he distinguishes himself for the nobility and honor with which he conducts business as a gentlemen bandit. Those he is forced to kill he allows time to make their peace with God; he also often promises support for their widows and children. Those he kidnaps for ransom to help the poor come to admire him. His political maneuvers—like several of his kidnappings—are accompanied by eloquent letters to the newspapers explaining his actions and his aims of freeing the Sicilian people.

His chief opponent in all of this is Don Croce Malo, nicknamed the Good Soul. The Don is the subtle but dark intelligence that broods over the island government, the local Church, and even relationships with the government in Rome.

The Mafia in Sicily is not exactly the same as the organization that goes by that name in the United States. In Sicily, the Mafia gradually grew out of the banding together of various leaders, like Guiliano, who sought to protect themselves and the people by establishing a parallel system of justice. Later the Sicilian Mafia itself became an exploiter by using the powers that be as screens for its own operations, though it still served to remedy some wrongs that the system would not right.

Thus, though the Don comes to admire Guiliano and would like to make him heir to the Mafia empire, Guiliano in his idealism wants nothing to do with him. The two become locked in a struggle, probing one another's weaknesses in an elaborate political and moral dance of death.

Stripped to its bare essentials, Puzo's story reads much like many another adventure tale. In many respects it is. Puzo's art is a popular one with few literary pretenses. (One session at this year's Modern Language Association convention in Washington, D.C., was devoted to "The Authority and the Signifier: [Roland] Barthes and Puzo's *The Godfather.*" Let us hope this does not signal the swallowing up of Puzo by the academic amoeba.) But *The Sicilian,* besides being simply a darned good read for its action and intrigue, has far stronger characterization, deeper insight, and more simple zest than most adventure stories.

For example, all the action takes place against a highly colored landscape that Puzo occasionally succeeds in making evocative. Greeks, Latins, Carthaginians, Arabs, Normans, and others have left their mark on the Sicilian countryside, and it is fitting that the struggle between Guiliano and the Don culminates amidst the ruins of the Acropolis of Selinus, one of the better-known archaeological sites one the island. The setting of the whole novel suggests recurring human tragedy in a long-fallen world.

Puzo's value as a writer does not consist in verbal niceties, but in the vitality he is able to capture in every character and in his whole story. There are some people who will dismiss this novel as "macho" posturing. (Sicilian culture is not macho, but merely possessed of strongly defined familial and social roles.) The same people will probably profess admiration of African art for its primitiveness. The Sicilian is hardly sicklied o'er with the pale cast of thought, but neither is it seeking refuge from sterility in the dark gods of the blood. In it the animal and the rational still exist in some kind of vital balance—not a subtle or surprising world, but an essential point of reference nonetheless.

Hilaire Belloc once suggested that if you are looking for the opposite of sentimental, try Villon. If you are looking for a current opposite of effete, try Puzo.

Marianna De Marco Torgovnick (essay date Spring 1988)

SOURCE: "*The Godfather* as the World's Most Typical Novel," in *South Atlantic Quarterly,* Vol. 87, No. 2, Spring, 1988, pp. 329-53.

[*In the following excerpt, Torgovnick examines the place of* The Godfather *in Italian-American literature, identifying its conventional bildungsroman and epic themes as a source of its popularity.*]

The Godfather appeared in March of 1969 and made publishing history: it rose quickly on the best-seller lists and stayed on those lists for an unprecedented sixty-nine weeks. *Newsweek* and *Time* were among the first magazines to publish reviews; the most prestigious and coveted of reviews, in the *New York Times Book Review,* appeared on 27 April, after Puzo's novel had been on the paper's best-seller list for four weeks and had risen to the number two spot. But the early reviews offered shamefully little insight into the novel, commenting rather simplistically on its portrayal of the Mafia. *Time,* for example, found the moral of the novel to be that "the Family that preys together, stays together": in other words, "crime pays." Dick Schaap's *New York Times* review suggested that what Philip "Roth has done for mas-

turbation" in *Portnoy's Complaint,* number one the week of 27 April, "Puzo has done for murder." Schaap's comparison is off-the-cuff and glib; if we stick with it, however, we can recognize some interesting features of the literary scene in 1969.

Like Roth's book, Puzo's reflected the power of ethnicity in American fiction, with the groups represented more numerous by the late sixties than ever before. Like Roth's book as well, *The Godfather* occupied the middle ground between what the bookstores call "fiction" and what they call "literature." Coming from the Italian American community, Puzo's novel had in 1969 less support in the publishing and academic establishments, less chance to move into the esteemed category of "literature" than did the novel by the better known Roth. Reviews of Puzo's book—in contrast now to those for Roth—rarely made the front page or a primary position in magazines and newspapers. The *New York Times* notice appeared on page thirty-four, under the irrelevant caption, "At Cosa Nostra, business was booming." Its lightheartedness insulted the novel, as when the reviewer advised the reader: "Pick a night with nothing good on television, and you'll come out far ahead."

There are several reasons why Roth was indeed "better known," reasons having little to do with abstract ideas of literary quality. Among these, his affiliation with a prestigious university should not be discounted. More significantly, publishers, reviewers, readers, and teachers knew how to classify him: he belongs to the Jewish American literary tradition rather than to the Italian American literary tradition. If you have asked yourself, "the Italian American literary tradition?" you are right to do so.

The Jewish and Italian immigrant experiences were remarkably similar in this country during the twentieth century. Both groups arrived in large numbers during the same decades, with the majority of immigrants from some regions (eastern Europe, southern Italy) rather than others (Germany, northern Italy) which constituted a perceived "elite." They settled by and large in the same northeastern cities, often sharing the same neighborhoods and the same kinds of employment (in, for example, the garment industry). The compatibility of the two cultures continues today, with intermarriages frequent. But their experiences in America very soon began to move at different paces.

Although equally poor, European Jews brought with them a tradition steeped in the value of education and learning. They entered, in the first generations, American systems of higher education, and thus produced, in a relatively short time, esteemed members of the literary professions—teaching, publishing, and writing. Most Italian immigrants, as Puzo notes, "were illiterate, as were their parents before them," their Italian not even that of their native literary tradition. Particularly among Sicilians, there was a suspiciousness of all "systems," including educational systems, and a reluctance to believe that their children could become the "padrones" of the New World. Like Puzo's mother, they felt on their pulses that "Artistic beauty after all could spring only from the seedbed of fine clothes, fine food, luxurious living," and not from the northeast's immigrant communities. An anecdote Puzo tells of his mother illustrates beautifully this side of the Italian American temperament; when Puzo called her to tell her that he was being offered huge sums for *The Godfather* after years of penury, his mother's only comment was, "Don't tell nobody."

In the first generations, Italian Americans chose a modest version of the American dream: a secure working-class living was preferred to reaching for wealth or upper-middle-class status. "Books" and "learning" were seen as threatening to the solidarity of family necessary for survival in dangerous times. Among many Italian Americans, it was customary for children to leave school at the earliest opportunity, to take jobs in factories and offices, to supplement their parents' incomes. Even the free university system of New York could not tempt many Italian Americans to bypass the immediate financial well-being of their families for a future gain that was, after all, only potential. Italian Americans thus entered higher education and the literary professions later than Jewish Americans; a significant representation of Italian Americans in fields like university teaching, publishing, and writing has emerged only recently. Another way of putting this: Roth has repeatedly, and brilliantly, made much of how *what* he wrote made him a maverick for many Jews; Puzo's decision to *write,* quite independent of what he wrote, made him a maverick in his generation, in his mother's vernacular, someone who "had gone off his nut."

In a world where "literary quality" indisputably announced itself (an Arnoldian utopia), factors like the respective temperaments and economic lives of Jewish and Italian immigrants would be irrelevant. We do not live in such a world. By 1969, without there being any sinister conspiracy, the Jewish American tradition in literature was well-established, prolific, and diverse—as well as published, reviewed, read, discussed, and taught. It was so in part because there was a mechanism, the presence of Jewish Americans in these worlds, a network which made it natural and inevitable that Jewish American literature would interest publishers, teachers, and readers. The Italian American tradition scarcely existed. The availability of novels *about* the two immigrant experiences can serve as a quick index. How many there are for Jewish American culture! For Italian American culture there is virtually only Puzo's *The Fortunate Pilgrim,* which sold a mere three thousand copies when first published, despite its power to reveal many aspects of Italian American life.

With all the recent discussion of canon formation, we have become sensitive to the propensity of powerful groups to canonize one of their own—after all, he is most likely to write a work that speaks to them. In an important article, Richard Ohmann has shown that novels chronicling the mid-life crises of business or professional men were the standard subject of writers from the sixties now becoming canonical, writers like John Cheever and John Updike! More radically, he has suggested that their novels appeal to publishers and academicians precisely *because* their protagonists' dilemmas match those of leaders in the publishing and academic establishment—who are also, by and large, white, middle-class, Protestant, professional, and male.

Within our culture, it is easy to recognize the hegemonic power of WASPs. It is harder, and more delicate, to define the position of Jewish Americans in the literary establishment. A minority? Well, yes—and a vital, invigorating one. And no—a powerful force which has earned (and *had* to earn) the power it now enjoys. It is thus neither the result of a sinister conspiracy nor the result of pure accident that Cheever's *Bullet Park* made the first page of the *New York Times Book Review* in the same issue that Puzo was reviewed on page thirty-four as a kind of joke. It is neither conspiratorial nor accidental that Roth has made that front page several times while Puzo has not, even after the great success of *The Godfather.*

Ironically, Puzo himself has tended to validate the system by which *The Godfather* is considered "fiction" rather than "literature." In published comments, he has said that he wrote *The Godfather* for money and that he "wrote below [his] gifts in that novel." At first, I was inclined to believe him, not just about his having written the book for money (an unchallengeable statement), but about its relatively low literary quality as compared to his other novels. To be sure, there are some very good things in *Dark Arena,* and *The Fortunate Pilgrim* is (aside from a slack opening) virtually perfect. *The Sicilian* is also a fine novel, with sophisticated plays on generic identity. But putting praise for Puzo's other novels aside, there remains the question: what's wrong with *The Godfather?* Nothing, I think, but its astonishing popularity and financial success. Long a writer accustomed to suffering in the Flaubertian-Joycean tradition, educated in the classics, self-described as "a true believer in art," Puzo could not help but be a little suspicious of, even contemptuous of, his most popular novel. According to high modernism, art isn't supposed to pay, isn't supposed to make the writer's life easier. It follows, then, at some level for Puzo, that *The Godfather* cannot be art but must be the book he wrote to enable him to continue the pursuit of art. Yet *The Godfather* is a remarkable achievement. And it can lay claim to being the world's most typical novel, in part because of its vast popularity.

The Godfather gives us the hum and buzz of Italian American culture, quite apart from its portrayal of the distinct and much smaller subculture of the Mafia. Its special importance comes, in part, from its retrospective portrayal of Italian American culture in the decade from 1945 to 1955. Some claim could be made for *The Godfather* as a historical novel, since the decade it chronicles contains within it competing language systems which are really competing cultural systems in the manner described by Bakhtin. This fidelity to competing languages/cultures accounts for the stylistic diversity of *The Godfather*. Puzo has been criticized for writing pulpish, purple prose. Actually, style varies considerably in the novel, becoming "flesh-pot prose" only when the novel enters Hollywood Babylon, and veering, at appropriate turns, into the mock epic, the restrained and understated, and the poetic. The decade from 1945 to 1955 was clearly the right decade for Puzo's novel. For it initiated massive changes in Italian American life, changes which made possible *The Godfather* in 1969, among them the increased presence of Italian Americans in the writing, publishing, and academic worlds. In its turn, that presence has, in part, made serious criticism on Puzo natural and inevitable.

The boom in higher education in the decade following Sputnik would open the world of scholarships and degrees to Italian American children of talent. Lucy Mancini and Michael Corleone before he returns to the family's "business" thus represent the wave of the future. In the novel, that brave new world is welcomed, even courted. Michael Corleone, like his father Vito, desires the Americanization of his children because it will dictate their exit from the subculture of the Mafia; as the first Godfather tells his cohorts, "Some of you have sons who are professors, scientists, musicians, and you are fortunate." What the novel does not say, but what lurks within its pages, is that the process of Americanization, carried to its logical conclusion, would represent the end of Italian American culture as it had existed in the prewar decades. It would mean intermarriages like Michael's with Kay, or, even more typically, like Lucy's with Jules Segal. It would mean moving away from the old neighborhoods, establishing cross-country networks of family that minimize closeness and reduce the frequency of family gatherings for dinner that is a hallmark of Italian American culture. To some extent, then, *The Godfather* chronicles a threatened moment of Italian American communal existence—still extant in the urban centers of the northeast and (let me not be misunderstood) separate from the Mafia, but threatened by the conditions of American life taken for granted by the majority, assimilating culture in the postwar years.

The Chinese have a curse that runs something like "May you get what you wish." For Vito Corleone, the curse if fulfilled would have meant the passing of his empire from the family as his sons entered the mainstream of American life, becoming part of the world the novel calls the "*pezzonovanti*," and the sixties called "the military-industrial complex." The

dialect and customs of the Sicilians would be displaced first by the Florentine Italian taught in universities and then by the homogenizing forces of American suburbia, so similar whether in New York, California, North Carolina, or the Midwest. Less progressive than Vito Corleone, Puzo's mother was baffled by her son's literary ambitions, and she urged him to work instead for the railroads dominant in his Hell's Kitchen neighborhood. My own mother could not understand my desire to go to college, thinking that I should instead become a secretary, trusting its financial security and tendency to be relinquished upon motherhood, rightly sensing (I see now in retrospect) that college would remove me from her world. *The Godfather* thus captures a key point of transition for Italian Americans and the ambivalence often surrounding the idea of college until well into the 1960s.

Vito Corleone speaks of sons who are musicians, scientists, professors—not of daughters. His speech reflects a significant feature of Italian American culture also given rich and persistent expression in the novel—its emphasis on male power and on male lines of affiliation. The novel's opening masterfully and subtly establishes the relative spheres of males and females. *The Godfather* begins not with the direct presentation of the title character but with a series of indirect approaches to him. In this it rivals other narrative examples, like *The Odyssey* and *Madame Bovary*, whose openings also delay the presentation of the main character.

.A main line of novelistic critics sees the typical theme of the novel, subject to infinite variation, as the theme of the Bildungsroman: the growth or development of a character (usually a young adult) as he/she moves from innocence to experience and comes to share the knowledge always available to the author of the novel. Often, the character learns how to survive in his/her society, how to make the adjustments and compromises a social existence demands. Since the society in which novels take place is almost always bourgeois and capitalist, the protagonist is, in essence, taught how to live as a good bourgeois. Insofar as novels teach readers the same lessons, novels have been powerful instruments of socialization for modern culture. A typical novel, *The Godfather* includes two such patterns: the first, and more important, involves Michael Corleone, the second Kay Adams. In this bifurcation of the innocence-to-experience theme, and in assigning it to college-age characters of both genders, Puzo, perhaps without knowing it, has made the book a natural for college courses. He has also followed novelistic tradition, since the period of a protagonist's young adulthood forms the typical time span of novels.

A character's movement from innocence to experience can take two forms: the character can authentically change, be at the novel's end different from the way he/she was at the beginning, or the character can uncover his/her authentic self, piercing the veils of self-delusion. Michael's growth follows the second pattern, a pattern shared with such typical characters as Elizabeth Bennet in *Pride and Prejudice* and Pip in *Great Expectations*. We know, from the beginning of the novel, that Michael is a favorite son and sense that he is like his father, even before Michael himself perceives the implications of that similarity. The assault on Don Corleone brings out Michael's true colors. Asked to man the phones rather than to become involved in the conflict, Michael "felt awkward, almost ashamed, and he noticed Clemenza and Tessio with faces so carefully impassive that he was sure that they were hiding their contempt."

Significantly, Michael's move into the family requires his adopting the clan's distance from women, his moving away from a relationship of total honesty with Kay. When he calls her after his father's wounding to say he will be late in meeting her, Kay banters in conventional fashion, but Michael cannot reciprocate:

> "All right," Kay said. "I'll be waiting. Can I do any Christmas shopping for you? Or anything else?"
>
> "No," Michael said. "Just be ready."
>
> She gave a little excited laugh. "I'll be ready," she said. "Aren't I always?"
>
> "Yes, you are," he said. "That's why you're my best girl."
>
> "I love you," she said. "Can you say it?"
>
> Michael looked at the four hoods sitting in the kitchen. "No," he said. "Tonight, OK?"

Finally free to return to Kay, Michael doesn't tell his brother Sonny his intentions because "Like the Don, Michael never told his real business and now he didn't want to tell Sonny he was seeing Kay Adams. There was no reason not to tell him, it was just habit." Thus, even before the fateful encounter with McCluskey at the hospital and before the decisive murder of Sollozzo and McCluskey, Michael shows favorable signs for his vocation.

The Sicilian interlude in book 6 parallels book 3 in its interruption of the forward action devoted to Vito Corleone's discovery of himself. It is parallel as well in that events in Sicily not only make Michael "understand his father's character and his destiny" but also, with the murder of Apollonia, give him an immediate and tangible need for revenge. Michael signals the fullness of his development by sending this message to his father: "Tell my father I wish to be his son." The message says it all. After it, Michael will lie to Kay (not just about Carlo's murder but also by omitting to tell her of his first marriage), and he will fully enter the Ma-

fia world with the intention of controlling it. His destiny, his uncovering of his true self, is complete.

Once we recognize the importance of the Bildungsroman pattern for Michael Corleone, we can see that the novel's title is fundamentally ambiguous. At the beginning it refers to Vito Corleone, at the end to Michael. In serving as godfather to Carlo Rizzi's son, Michael emblematizes the double face of godfatherhood: protective and nurturing, deadly and cruel. The injury he sustains from McCluskey is the visible sign of this duplicity, a sign with which Michael is reluctant to part, a sign of his entry into family life and of the still unavenged attack's on his father and brother.

Kay's development is, by necessity in this male-centered novel, secondary in importance. She more authentically undergoes a change in personality, moving from a playful, open, liberated college girl into the role of Mafia wife. Oddly, and perhaps a bit subversively, Puzo suggests that the Yankee spirit which founded this nation resembles the Sicilian codes adhered to by the major characters. When Kay and her father face down the investigating policemen, refusing to reveal anything of Michael or to be blackmailed, they practice the equivalent of Sicilian *omertà*. Most of what she needs to learn is, however, unnatural to Kay. And so she gets a tutor in the novel, in the unlikely figure of Mama Corleone. Mrs. Corleone at first assumes that Kay, quite simply, should forget about Michael. Moved by Kay's love for her son, the mother kisses the girl and advises her to "forget about Mikey, he no the man for you." Kay realizes that, once again, euphemism has been eloquent, "that the young man she had loved was a cold-blooded murderer. And that she had been told by the most unimpeachable source: his mother." But Michael's mother changes her mind about Kay and is instrumental in bringing them together, her change of mind prompted by Kay's fidelity in calling to inquire about her lover and, perhaps, by Mrs. Corleone's concern over the changes in Michael after his return from Sicily. The mother-in-law then becomes the daughter-in-law's guide to Italian American life, teaching her how to fry peppers, how to mesh into the network of visitations to and from relatives' houses on the mall, how to attend church and to pray for her husband's soul.

The murder of Carlo Rizzi signals the secondary quality of female concerns and female evaluations of how things should be done; like Connie, Kay believes (until Hagen shows her otherwise) that Carlo, whatever his role in Sonny's death, should be forgiven. When Kay decides, at the end of the novel, to return to Michael, she accepts her new role in life, her own destiny as someone unable to control the direction of her world. In *Godfather II,* the filmscript has her change her mind. But I cannot help but feel that that change belies the truth of the original novel. Kay's decision, once made, will be final.

The Godfather's adherence to the Bildungsroman theme is thus strong, though it is not complete. The difference comes in the extent to which, unlike novels in general, *The Godfather* teaches the protagonists to conform to the rules of a specialized society (the Mafia) rather than to the norms of bourgeois life. Insofar as only the methods and not the ethics of Mafia life differ from mainstream businesses, the difference is trivial. But recognizing the deviation helps point to a final way that *The Godfather* is a typical novel: its ability to harken back to earlier genres and to incorporate them into the new form.

An important tendency in novel theory is to define the novel by comparison with the narrative genres that preceded it historically: epic and romance. European critics, preeminently Lukàcs, but also Bakhtin, Stanzel, and Goldmann, see the novel as the genre which replaced the epic, a genre linked to a belief in gods and to a view of heroism no longer possible in modern culture. Anglo-American critics have tended, by contrast, to see the novel as "anti-romance," as a countergenre to the various literary incarnations of the romance spirit, with its supreme elevation of love and adventure and its will to a happy ending, however improbable or strained that ending may be. Such definitions of the novel by contrast to earlier narrative genres are, in many ways, quite helpful. But it is perhaps best to recognize that the novel, as a polyphonic genre, contains chords from both of the great narrative genres that preceded it. Historically, it is clear that the novel did replace the epic; but it seems more accurate to see romance as in part swallowed by the novel, in part continuing along separate lines through the nineteenth and twentieth centuries.

It is also essential to recognize that even our earliest narrative examples send mixed generic signals. Usually classified as epic, for example, *The Odyssey* seems significantly different from its companion epic, *The Iliad*. The difference is sometimes explained in that the latter is the epic of war, the second the epic of love. Alternately, *The Odyssey* is classified as romance (what an "epic of love" would logically be) or as the ur-novel. We don't need to decide the issue of *The Odyssey*'s genre here, but it will be helpful, in seeing the typicality of *The Godfather* as a novel, to take *The Odyssey* as an ur-novel, precisely because of its mixture of epic and romance elements. This tactic can be supported by Bakhtin's view of prenovelistic discourse, which sees novelistic narratives as surfacing at various points in literary history, even though the novel as a consistently developing and recognized genre begins in the eighteenth century. Similar in structure and theme to *The Odyssey*, *The Godfather* is, in some ways, a version of Homer's work for our time.

The Odyssey begins, not with the introduction of Odysseus, but with the dilemma of his son, Telemachus. Telemachus's

imminent manhood has produced a crisis in Ithaca, for he is now eligible to assume his father's throne, left vacant for the long years of Odysseus's absence, and coveted as well by Penelope's many suitors. Having already arranged for Odysseus's return, Athene appears to Telemachus to offer him some key advice. She tells him: "It is a wise son who knows his own father." That formulation signals the identity theme that operates in subtle ways throughout the subsequent narrative.

Athene then advises Telemachus to journey to his father's old comrades, who tell him stories of his father's past that also spur his growth to manhood. Notice already how the father-son theme of *The Godfather* repeats the pattern of *The Odyssey*, with substantial niceties such as Michael's journey (parallel to Telemachus's journey) to his father's Sicily as key in his development and Michael's crucial utterance (parallel to Athene's) that he "wishes to be his father's son." Knowing who you are, in both works, means understanding one's father and sharing his ideas and strength. Each son, Telemachus and Michael, needs to demonstrate his similarity to his father in a major test: Telemachus when he shows the ability to string his father's bow and fights by his side; Michael when he is ready to step into the Godfather's role and orchestrate his father's complex plan for revenge.

The middle portion of *The Odyssey*, the most famous portion, portrays Odysseus's adventures in his ten years of traveling (ten years also being, probably not coincidentally, the time span of *The Godfather*). In *The Odyssey*, Odysseus retrospectively narrates these events to his hosts on Phaecaia. Although book 3 of *The Godfather* does not have the same narrative form, or length, or weight, it shares the quality of retrospective narration and of interrupting the forward motion of the present-day plot, giving the father's history from the past up to the present day.

When Odysseus finally returns to Ithaca, he reveals himself to his son, collaborating with Telemachus about how to avenge himself on Penelope's suitors. This collaboration resembles Don Corleone's collaboration with Michael after Michael's return from Sicily. Both plans involve seeming mildly submissive and disguising intentions until the moment for revenge is ripe. No one—especially Penelope/especially Kay—must know all the details of the plan except for the father and son. In both works, however, key parts of the plan are confided to trusted male associates who have proved their loyalty by a lifetime of service. In each work, the success of the plan constitutes the dramatic climax. A massive slaughter occurs, in which the father/son team achieves victory by superior cunning and strength. No mercy is shown to enemies. In Homer, however, female allies of the enemies are also killed, while in Puzo, "civilian" females are untouchable, part of the Mafia code.

The epic "war" themes accomplished, both works turn to the romance theme of married love—Odysseus is as yet unreconciled to Penelope, Michael's revenge has ruptured his relationship to Kay. In a long and weighty scene, Odysseus negotiates with Penelope, assuring her that he is the husband she has waited for and that he is willing to respect her will and her power. She accepts him, the token of acceptance being the symbolic marriage bed, whose posts sink into the Ithacan earth. The epic ends when Odysseus and Telemachus, having massed to meet the families of the slain suitors, and anticipating a new slaughter, find that slaughter barred. The gods prohibit further revenge and dispense blessed forgetfulness of wrongs done in the past.

Here, *The Godfather* both follows, and does not follow, the earlier epic. Kay does accept Michael in his new, godlike, imperial role as Godfather, but she negotiates with Hagen, not Michael; the joyous affirmation of marriage in the earlier work is dissipated and shadowed, Kay's role more passive than Penelope's. There are no intervening gods in *The Godfather* to end the cycle of revenge and to dispense forgetfulness of blood feuds. Michael's power will face other challenges, necessitate other massacres. The future is likely to hold repetition of the past, despite Michael's plan to make the family businesses legitimate.

Like many Greek works (the *Orestia* and *Iliad* among them), and like many epics (such as *Beowulf*), *The Odyssey* is much concerned with the stage of historical development at which the ties of blood, of family, and the obligations of the blood feud are supplanted by the rules of law, the recognition of communal good, and the subordination of blood feuds to social mechanisms. *The Godfather* is similarly concerned with a potential transition in Mafia culture—as evidenced by Vito Corleone's long speech to his national confederates—from rule by feuds to rule by the communal good, the Cosa Nostra. In his speech, Corleone advocates making the transition, though his advocacy is spurious. To some extent, however, the Corleone empire has been built by recognizing the coming order and, hence, building a network of power in the legal and governmental systems. The move from family to communal values is, generally, associated with movement from primitive or medieval modes of economic and social organization to modern, capitalist modes. By the symbolic logic of *The Odyssey*—through which male heros/kings depend on and need female heroines/queens—that movement also requires a merging of male and female principles (implicit as well in the goddess Athene). Often, epic captures the jostling of these value systems against one another. In *The Odyssey*, the new value systems more successfully replace the old than in *The Godfather*.

Associated from its origins with the modern bourgeois world order, the novel does not usually directly address the issue of familial versus communal social orders—for that issue has been decided in the past. But novels are not precluded from recording such bumping of cultural systems—indeed, the historical novels of Scott are celebrated for doing so. Moreover, the genre plays with past and present modes of heroism, the rejection of past modes often the lesson that must be learned by the hero of the Bildungsroman. Thus, the parallels to *The Odyssey* suggest the generic resourcefulness of *The Godfather,* its ability to evoke, as the backdrop to its central novelistic concerns, grand cultural conflicts that have given rise to earlier narrative genres.

In a very real sense, Michael Corleone wished at the beginning of *The Godfather* and aspires at the end to the condition granted the novelistic hero—the role of good citizen and businessman. Ironically, if he had become that good citizen and businessman, and if Puzo had waited until Michael had reached middle age to write about him, the novel would have had a better chance—under the prevailing interest in middle-class businessmen as heroes of novels—of being not just a best-seller, but a novel recognized as "literature" and, ultimately, a canonical text. Instead, Michael gets a role that fits the model of good citizen and businessman only within the microcosmic world of the Mafia and which is tinged (in its power over blood, not just money) but not recuperated by earlier, epic patterns of heroism. And Puzo gets a book that sells well but has not, as yet, become canonical. Those of us who take novels seriously ought to give it a second look. For in its generic reach, in its exploration of the Bildungsroman theme, in its revelation of competing language and cultural systems, and in its posing of the issue of popular versus high art, *The Godfather* can clearly be shown to be one of the world's most typical novels.

John Kenneth Galbraith (review date 13 January 1991)

SOURCE: "A Bad Week for the President," in *The New York Times Book Review,* January 13, 1991, p. 7.

[*In the following review, Galbraith provides a tempered assessment of* The Fourth K, *praising Puzo's narrative ability but finding the novel's plot implausible.*]

Some 30 years ago in India, Edward Durrell Stone designed a handsome residence for the American Ambassador, in which my wife and I were the first residents. On occasion, passers-by wandered in to look at the rather magnificent reception area; once, after a somewhat questionable political conversation with a high Indian official, we walked out of my study to find that another and somewhat antipathetic politician had strolled in to listen to our conversation through the open grillwork that was a feature of Stone's architecture.

In recent times back in India I found the whole house and embassy completely surrounded by high, formidable and very ugly concrete walls. Entry now requires notification and identification paralleling that needed for a journey to see Saddam Hussein, and a small letter that was sent to me in care of the embassy came with an imprint saying that it had been X-rayed for detection of possible explosives.

It is this trend toward protection against terrorist violence, continued a few years into the future, that Mario Puzo seeks to make plausible in his latest novel, *The Fourth K.* The increase in terrorist activity as well as all the other violent behavior of our time has continued. So also have the responding defenses, and especially those surrounding the President of the United States. In Mr. Puzo's novel, he lives in a kind of iron box that has been added as another story to the White House Secret Service men alone have access—they double as servants—and they have now been united with the Federal Bureau of Investigation under the relentless attention of the Attorney General. The cost of protecting the Presidential person is $100 million annually and the enterprise employs 10,000 men, although their cost does provoke some passing comment.

The President so enclosed is Francis Xavier Kennedy, a member of a cadet branch of the noted Kennedy family. I assume that he is *The Fourth K,* John, Robert and Edward having gone before, but Mr. Puzo's imagination being what it is, it could be Henry Kissinger, Henry the K, who somehow had got into the chain. There is that tendency to sanguinary action. And with Mr. Puzo anything is possible.

His imagination is indeed extreme, and some will think uncontrolled. Francis Xavier, whose resemblance to his noted precursors is not extreme, has been swept into office just as his lovely and loving wife dies, and he is sustained as to family only by his beautiful and independent college-age daughter, Theresa. He has a fine if largely undisclosed social agenda but he cannot do anything about it, for, in a further projection from our time, a small coterie of incredibly rich reactionaries, the Socrates Club, has bought up the entire Congress, which has lost to its paymasters all capacity for independent action.

However, in the most portentous of all developments, it is terrorism that has gone to a new dimension. On one otherwise pleasant spring day, a great terrorist network with powerful but rather indistinct revolutionary aims arranges to shoot the Pope, hijack the plane carrying the President's daughter, take it to an Arabian emirate and shoot her dead. Her fellow passengers become hostages. A bad week.

Francis Xavier Kennedy responds in a forthright way, one that will rejoice all partisans of surgical and even ordinary

bomb strikes: he orders the emigrate to release the hostages and surrender those responsible; if they don't, he will destroy the capital, with the further promise of destroying the country as a whole. In the end the city is destroyed, although the President, in a thoughtful gesture, does tell the inhabitants that they should get out of town.

Meanwhile, there has been an interesting development back in Washington. Popular opinion is with Kennedy; the rich controllers of the Congress, those Socrates men, are, however, adverse. Among other things one of the club's members has a $50 billion investment in that emirate, and even he does not take such sums lightly. Accordingly they arrange the impeachment of Kennedy, which takes only a matter of a few hours. Richard Nixon would be impressed.

The story goes on from there with a homemade atomic bomb exploding around Times Square, a great electoral recovery by Kennedy and yet more. But these matters I must leave to the reader to explore in detail. A summary could be unfair to the author; it might make the whole story seem a bit far out.

I have said that Mr. Puzo has based his novel on a rather large leap from current disorders and disasters. This is not confined to terrorism, impeachment and related dissonance. Mr. Puzo is also alert to present tendencies in language and sex. His characters, high and low, inject metaphorical defecation and fornication into their speech at approximately one-sentence intervals. And in the great tradition set by John O'Hara, he regularly arrests the narrative and puts his people in bed with all appropriate contortion and on at least one occasion, as O'Hara was also said to do, without their previously having shaken hands. That happens during a long sequence in Hollywood that seems not to contribute appreciably to the plot but does, one suspects, make use of the author's observations there while his earlier, best-selling work, the *Godfather* saga, made it to the screen.

As I hope I have sufficiently made clear, I am impressed by the author's imagination—his ability to take the worst in present life and make it worse. I am somewhat less impressed by the plausibility of his prospect. In that lightning impeachment and, I think, in quite a number of other matters, including the homemade bomb in New York, it goes well beyond the range of reasonable probability. Nor, his considerable narrative skill notwithstanding, does Mr. Puzo succeed in making other developments seem terribly likely. From this I take some comfort.

Thomas J. Ferraro (essay date 1993)

SOURCE: "Blood in the Marketplace: The Business of Family in *The Godfather* Narratives," in *Ethnic Passages: Literary Immigrants in Twentieth-Century America,* University of Chicago Press, 1993, pp. 18-52.

[*In the following excerpt, Ferraro examines the "business of family" in* The Godfather *and the godfather figure as a cultural icon.*]

In his 1969 blockbuster *The Godfather,* Mario Puzo presented an image of the Mafia that has become commonplace in American popular culture. Since that time, we have taken for granted that the Mafia operates as a consortium of illegitimate businesses, structured along family lines, with a familial patriarch or "godfather" as the chief executive officer of each syndicate. Puzo's version of the Mafia fuses into one icon the realms of family and economy, of Southern Italian ethnicity and big-time American capitalism, of blood and the marketplace. "Blood" refers to the violence of organized crime. "Blood" also refers to the familial clan and its extension through the symbolic system of the *compare,* or "co-godparenthood." In *The Godfather,* the representation of the Mafia fuses ethnic tribalism with the all-American pursuit of wealth and power. Since its publication, we have regarded this business of family in *The Godfather,* as a figment of Puzo's opportunistic imagination, which it remains in part. But the business of family in Puzo's Mafia is also a provocative revision of accepted notions of what ethnicity is and how it works—the new ethnic sociology in popular literary form.

During the late 1970s and early 1980s, there was a short outburst of scholarly interest in *The Godfather* and its myriad offspring. A consensus about the meaning of the popularity of this saga emerges from the books and essays of Fredric Jameson, Eric Hobsbawn, John Cawelti, and John Sutherland. The portrayal of the Corleone family collective allows post-Vietnam-era Americans to fantasize about the glory days of "closely knit traditional authority." The portrayal of the power and destructive greed of the Mafia chieftains allows them to vent their rage at "the managerial elite who hold the reins of corporate power and use it for their own benefit." The themes of family and business, in each instance, are disengaged from one another. As Jameson puts it, on the one hand, the ethnic family imagery satisfies "a Utopian longing" for collectivity, while, on the other hand, "the substitution of crime for big business" is the "ideological function" of the narrative. In such standard treatments, Puzo's narrative is regarded as a brilliant (or brilliantly lucky) instance of satisfying two disparate appetites with a single symbol. This perspective, formulated in the late 1970s, seems to have settled the issue of the popularity of the novel.

I want to reopen that issue. We need to return to *The Godfather* because we have too easily dismissed its representa-

tion of the Mafia as a two-part fantasy. Of course, *The Godfather* is not reliable as a roman à clef or a historical novel: Puzo's details are fuzzy, mixed up, and much exaggerated. "There was things he stretched," as Huck Finn would put it, and everyone knows it. But critics have been too ready to accept his major sociological premise—that family and business work in tandem—as pure mythology. I would argue that the importance of *The Godfather* lies not in its creation of a double mythology but in the way that it takes the fusion of kinship and capitalist enterprise seriously. Its cultural significance lies not in the simultaneous appeals of "family" and "business" imagery but rather in the appeal of an actual structural simultaneity, the business of family. If we fail to pause long enough to consider its surface narrative, we underestimate not only the strategies of the novel but the insights and intuitions of its huge audience as well.

Readers have underestimated the business of family because little in traditional theories of the family, ethnicity, and advanced capitalism has prepared them to recognize it. In both scholarly and popular treatments, ethnic culture and extended kinship are interpreted as barriers to successfully negotiating the mobility ladder, particularly its upper rungs. Southern Italian immigrants and their descendants have long been thought to exemplify the principle that the more clannish an ethnic group, the slower its assimilation and economic advancement. Herbert Gans's *Urban Villagers,* Virginia Yans-McLaughlin's *Family and Community,* Thomas Kessner's *Golden Door,* and Thomas Sowell's *Ethnic America* essentially update the social work perspectives of such writers as Phyllis H. Williams and Leonard Covello. In 1944, Covello wrote, "Any social consciousness of Italo-Americans within 'Little Italies' appertains primarily to sharing and adhering to the family tradition as the main motif of their philosophy of life. . . . The retention of this cultural 'basis' is essentially the source of their retarded adjustment." But this long-standing tradition of identifying the Italian family structure as a dysfunctional survival runs aground when it comes to the Mafia.

Historians and sociologists attest to the difficulty of interpreting the Mafia in terms of a linear model of assimilation and upward mobility. All commentators recognize that the Mafia was not simply transported here: it arose from the polyethnic immigrant streets rather than passing from father to son; Prohibition was the major factor in shaping its growth. In *A Family Business,* sociologist Francis A. J. Ianni concedes these points, only to stress the family structure of the syndicates and the origin of this familialism in Southern Italy. The Lupullo crime organization "*feels* like a kinship-structured group; familialism founded it and is still its stock in trade. One senses immediately not only the strength of the bond, but the inability of members to see any morality or social order larger than their own." Ianni's research tempts him into abandoning the tradition of placing ethnic phenomena on a linear continuum running from Old World marginality to New World centrality. His research supports and his analysis anticipates, without quite articulating, the cutting edge of ethnic theory.

Scholars in a number of fields are working to change the way we think about ethnicity, ethnic groups, and ethnic culture. In identifying the social bases of ethnicity, theorists are shifting their emphasis from intergenerational transmission to arenas of conflict in complex societies. They argue that we need to examine ethnic cultures not as Old World survivals (whatever their roots) but as improvised strategies to deal with the unequal distribution of wealth, power, and status. In this light, ethnic groups include not only socially marginal peoples but any group that uses symbols of common descent and tradition to create or to maintain power. From a historian's perspective, European family structures and traditions do not necessarily dissolve in the face of capitalism but rather, as they have always done, evolve to meet its changing needs.

Anthropologist Abner Cohen conceives of ethnic groups as "interest groups" in which ethnic symbols function in lieu of more formal structures, such as the law. When he speaks of the symbolic apparatus of ethnicity, he refers to the emphasis on common history and tradition, endogamy and social boundary maintenance, religion and ritual, and everyday encoded behavior, including "accent, manner of speech, etiquette, style of joking, play" and so forth, that is, the rhetoric and codes of "blood." As Cohen explains, the symbolic apparatus of ethnicity incites genuine loyalty and emotion, the power and idiosyncrasy of which cannot be underestimated. But the apparatus also serves utilitarian purposes within society at large, including those of the economic marketplace. In many of our most familiar examples, the function of ethnic ritual is primarily defensive, to organize a group on the margins of society, but the uses of ethnicity can be quite aggressive as well. The Italian-American Mafia is a case in point. As Ianni and others have demonstrated, it is the ethos of ethnic solidarity that puts the organization into Italian-American organized crime.

In her discussion of *The Godfather,* Rose Basile Green comes the closest of any critic to unpacking what she calls the "socioeconomic ethnic image" of the Corleone crime syndicate. Unlike almost everyone else, Green takes seriously Puzo's portrayal of the syndicates—not as historical fact about actual gangsters but as a treatise (however romanticized) "dealing with the contemporary strategy of gaining and securing power." Yet Green's analysis splits into typical parallel paths: crime as a means for social mobility versus the family as a locus of traditional Southern Italian responsibility. Although Green identifies "a subtle line between personal interest and structural power," she, too, fails to make the strongest connection between the private family life ascribed to Don Corleone and the illegitimate enterprise he heads. When Green says that *The Godfather* explores "the contemporary strategy of gaining and securing power," she means the tactics of bribery, intimidation, the brokerage of votes, intergang warfare, and so forth that Don Corleone uses to conduct business outside the confines of his own organization. But the most noteworthy device for gaining and securing power in Puzo's depiction is internal to the Corleone syndicate: it is not a gun or payola, but, quite simply, that mystified entity, the "Southern Italian family."

In narrating *The Godfather,* Puzo adopts the familiar role of cultural interpreter, mediating between outside readers and a secret ethnic society. Puzo's agenda, implicit yet universally understood, is to explain why Sicilian Americans have made such good criminals. The answer, generally speaking, is their cult of family honor. The Corleones believe, with a kind of feudal fervor, in patriarchy, patronage, and protection. *The Godfather* is saturated with the imagery of paternity, family, and intimate friendship; with the rhetoric of respect, loyalty, and the code of silence; with references to Sicilian blood and the machismo attributed to it; with the social events—weddings, christenings, funerals, meals, and so forth—that embody the culture of family honor. The business of crime is always interlaced with the responsibilities of family. In the film, for instance, Clemenza frets over a request from his wife Eve as he presides over the execution of Paulie Gatto: "Don't forget the cannoli!" Don Vito himself is a true believer in the mutual obligations of kinfolk. He seeks both to expand his wealth and power to protect his dependents and to make his protection available to more and more people. He recruits from within his family to keep the business "all in the family" for the family's sake. "It was at this time that the Don got the idea that he ran his world far better than his enemies ran the greater world which continually obstructed his path." At the same time, "not his best friends would have called Don Corleone a saint from heaven"; there is always "some self-interest" in his generosity. For everyone recognizes the wisdom of family honor, Corleone's Honor, given the special exigencies of operating in a big way in an outlawed underground economy.

In his analysis of the ethnic group as an interest group, Cohen stresses the growth potential wherever there is a sector of an economy that has not been organized formally:

> Even in the advanced liberal industrial societies there are some structural conditions under which an interest group cannot organize itself on formal lines. Its formal organization may be opposed by the state or by other groups within the state, or may be incompatible with some important principles in the society; or the interests it represents may be newly developed and not yet articulated in terms of a formal organization and accommodated with the for-

mal structure of the society. Under these conditions the group will articulate its organization on informal lines, making use of the kinship, friendship, ritual, ceremonial, and other symbolic activities that are implicit in what is known as style of life.

The ethnic ethos means sticking together, respecting the authority of the group rather than that of outsiders, defending the group's turf, and abiding by tradition. The reasoning comes full circle, for tradition is equated with group solidarity. The family is the core element of the group and its most powerful symbol. Under appropriate conditions, the ethos of ethnicity is by no means anachronistic in late capitalism, no matter how rooted such values might be in the history of particular groups. Wherever ethnicity can facilitate enterprise, ethnicity as a system can be said to be one of the primary motors of capitalism, not its antithesis. Focusing on the old moneyed elite of London, Cohen has argued that ethnicity functions among the privileged as well as among the impoverished, among "core" castes as well as among racial and national minorities. In another case study, historian Peter Dobkin Hall implicates family and tradition in the mercantile practices of Massachusetts elites in the eighteenth and nineteenth centuries. As both Cohen and Hall contend, a precondition for capitalized ethnicity is a legal vacuum. I would add to this a corollary based on the history of the Mafia: the desire to engage in enterprise, not simply in a vacuum (where law and formal arrangements are lacking) but in an economic zone outside the law and opposed to formal arrangements, makes some form of family and ethnic organization a necessity.

The seemingly feudal, deeply internalized ethos of family honor cements individuals together in American crime, structuring syndicates and giving them their aggrandizing momentum. Loyalty and devotion to group honor are the values according to which individuals are motivated, recruited, judged, and policed in the Mafia. These values are especially effective at binding criminals together and at making criminals out of those not otherwise drawn to the outlaw life. These values surfaced in the United States when Prohibition created an enormous unorganized sector of the national economy, legally proscribed but driven by immense appetites and the willingness of legal institutions to play along, especially for a price. Such values are also necessary to hold together the large-scale enterprises not structured or protected by law, which Prohibition created but which survived after it: rackets devoted to gambling, loan-sharking, prostitution, various forms of extortion, and eventually drugs. In legitimate business, a prized executive who sells himself and perhaps a secret or two to another company is written off as an unexpected operating loss. A *capo-regime* who becomes a stool pigeon can bring the whole system down. The ideologies of tradition and group solidarity, principally of the family, are ideal for rationalizing crime syndicates in both

senses of the word "rationalize": ideal for organizing them because such ideologies are ideal for justifying their existence and their hold over their members.

The Godfather would warrant attention from scholars for the way it depicts an ethnic subculture that functions as an interest group even if, like Puzo's *Fortunate Pilgrim* (1964), it had disappeared into obscurity upon publication. But the novel has had a major impact on popular culture. The figure of "the godfather" outstrips all but the most ubiquitous cultural symbols, falling somewhere between Huckleberry Finn and Superman, better known, perhaps, than Uncle Sam himself. By 1971, when the first film was released, there were over one million hardcover copies of the book in circulation—multiple copies in every library in every town in America—and at least ten million more paperbacks. Historically, the reading of the novel framed the film; not, as in academic criticism, the other way around. By the early 1980s, the book had become the best-selling novel in history, and it continues to sell steadily even outside the United States.

The most immediate spin-offs of the novel were the two films, versions of those films rearranged for television, and the video format, in which the two films plus outtakes are combined as *The Godfather Epic*. By 1975, 260 more books on the Mafia theme had been released, principally of the hard-boiled variety. In 1984, Puzo himself tried again with his fictional account of Salvatore Giuliano, *The Sicilian*. Ethnicity in crime has figured in many major films, including *The Cotton Club* (co-scripted by Coppola, Puzo, and William Kennedy), *The Gang Who Couldn't Shoot Straight*, *Broadway Danny Rose*, *Heart of the Dragon*, *Scarface*, *Once upon a Time in America*, *Miller's Crossing*, and *Goodfellas*, Martin Scorsese's reply to Coppola. During the 1980s, the popularity of family-dynasty sagas, especially in their many ethnic varieties, can be traced in part to Puzo's model. Most telling has been the ceaseless production of *Godfather* clones, emphasizing the fusion of family and crime. Now a genre of its own, the proliferation includes (auto)biographical works such as Gay Talese's *Honor Thy Father*, Joseph Bonanno's *Man of Honor*, and Antoinette Giancana's *Mafia Princess*; novels such as Vincent Patrick's *Family Business* and Richard Condon's trilogy of the Prizzi family; and a legion of films and teleplays, including "Our Family Honor" (ABC's ill-fated attempt to combine Italian-American gangsters with Irish-American cops), *Married to the Mob* (which picks up on the feminist themes in Condon), the "Wiseguy" series (an affecting drama of homoerotic underpinnings in the mob), *China Girl* (Abel Ferrara restages *Romeo and Juliet* between Italian and Chinese mobsters), and *The Freshman* (Brando parodies his portrayal of Vito Corleone). *The Godfather: Part III* was released on Christmas in 1990.

What are we to make of the lasting fascination with *The*

Godfather? Since its appearance, scholars have recognized *The Godfather* as an artifact of the "new ethnicity." The timing of the novel and its immediate offspring, from publication of the novel in 1969 to the television miniseries in the late 1970s, corresponds to an upturn in Americans embracing ethnic identity. This celebration included not only groups that were by and large still marginal—Native Americans, the descendants of Southern slaves, the newest comers from the Caribbean, the Hispanic Americas, and the Far East—but also the descendants of European immigrants, including the Italians, who were well on their way to middle-class security. Necessarily, the connections drawn between the increased salience of ethnicity and popularity of *The Godfather* have been premised on construing *The Godfather* as a two-part fantasy in which family sanctuary and successful corporate enterprise are polar opposites. My reading of *The Godfather,* which emphasizes the complicity of family and business, calls for a reexamination of the role of the novel in the new ethnic self-consciousness. Both the popularity of *The Godfather* and the celebration of ethnicity are complex phenomena, reflecting myriad attitudes toward race, class, and gender as well as ethnicity, attitudes that often conflict with one another. By claiming that *The Godfather* articulates the business of family, I do not wish to mute these other voices but to point the way toward situating the voice of family-business within the larger cacophony of debate.

Scholars such as Jameson and Cawelti, who work within the frame of traditional *Godfather* interpretation, seek to locate within the novel an anticapitalist energy—not an overt critique so much as an impulse, the energy of a potential critique partially veiled and misdirected. Both critics argue that Puzo portrays the Mafia as the center of a capitalist conspiracy and, simultaneously and irreconcilably, as a refuge from the conspiracy of capitalism. Because Puzo's Mafia functions as "the mirror-image of big business," its brutality provides a focus for anticapitalist anxiety and an outlet for anticapitalist anger. Similarly, the equally powerful image of the family reflects, in Jameson's terms, a "Utopian longing" for escape from the prison house of capitalism. "The 'family' is a fantasy of tribal belongingness," echoes Cawelti, "that protects and supports the individual as opposed to the coldness and indifference of the modern business or government bureaucracy."

In the standard view, the putative double fantasy of *The Godfather* reflects the misdirected energies of the new ethnicity. The new ethnicity arises from frustration with capitalism yet mutes its resistance in clamor about the decline of the family and traditional values. My analysis of *The Godfather* suggests we might hesitate before we accept the majority opinion that the family in the novel embodies a refuge from capitalism. We need to question whether a case for the subversive nature of *The Godfather* can rest on the myth of the Italian-American family as a precapitalist collectivity, particularly when Puzo uses all his forces to undermine this false dichotomy. The representation of the Southern Italian family in *The Godfather* is not the kind of saccharine portrayal of innocent harmony, the haven in a heartless world, that scholars take as the benchmark of ethnic nostalgia. In *The Godfather,* capitalism is shown to accommodate, absorb, and indeed accentuate the structures of family and ethnicity. Americans respond to *The Godfather* because it presents the ethnic family not as a sacrosanct European institution reproduced on the margins of America, but as a fundamental American structure of power, successful and bloodied.

Scholars' desire to identify ethnic piety as a locus of anticapitalist energy has blinded them to the existence of an alliance between the new ethnicity and the procapitalist celebration of the family. This alliance is an insufficiently recognized strain within recent popular culture. At least until World War II, and perhaps into the 1970s, the dominant attitude was that the ethnic family in the United States was incompatible with capitalism, whether ethnicity was favored or not. The rabid Americanizers of the early decades attempted to strip immigrant workers of their familial and cultural loyalties. Many of the immigrants themselves feared that the price of upward mobility might be a loss of family solidarity, even as most relied on the family as a basis for group enterprise and mutual financial support. And intellectuals, who were partly or wholly skeptical of capitalism, based one strand of their critique on the damage that capitalism supposedly inflicted upon traditional family cultures. We hear less and less frequently from these nativist Americanizers and guardians of ethnic tradition, but the nostalgia among scholars remains pervasive nonetheless. The general public, however, increasingly has come to accept and indeed to welcome the idea of compatibility between ethnicity and capitalism. In the case of Italian Americans, for instance, public figures ranging from Lee Iacocca to Geraldine Ferraro and Mario Cuomo emphasize the role family values have played in their own success stories, occasionally stretching our imaginations. Similar rhetoric appears in the reemerging critique of the black family, in the widespread lauding of Asian- and Caribbean-American merchants and their schoolchildren, and in the general appeal for a new American work ethic. In this light, *The Godfather* helped to introduce and continues to feed upon a strain of American rhetoric and expectation that has reached full salience in the last decade.

Perhaps no artifact of American culture, popular or serious, has made the case for the business of family with quite the force of *The Godfather.* At no time in United States history has ethnicity enjoyed the vogue that it first achieved in the years of *The Godfather*'s greatest popularity and, in large measure, now maintains. The convergence is no coincidence. While *The Godfather* does participate in the new ethnicity by celebrating the ethnic family, the Mafia achieves its romantic luster not because Puzo portrays the Italian-American family as a separate sphere lying outside of capitalism, but because the Italian-American family emerges as a potent structure within it. The ethnic family in *The Godfather* feeds off a market sensibility rather than undermines it. The Corleones can provide protection from the market only because they have mastered it. Indeed, Puzo reaches the height of romance in *The Godfather* by choosing the Mafia as a model for family enterprise, for illegal family enterprises are capable of growing and expanding to an extent that the structure and regulation of legitimate capitalism ultimately will not support.

If *The Godfather* does indeed harbor anticapitalist energies, as a thorough reading of the novel might suggest, then perhaps scholars have been looking for that energy in the wrong places. Jameson concludes:

> When indeed we reflect on an organized conspiracy against the public, one which reaches into every corner of our daily lives and our political structures to exercise a wanton and genocidal violence at the behest of distant decision-makers and in the name of an abstract conception of profit—surely it is not about the Mafia, but rather about American business itself that we are thinking, American capitalism in its most systematized and computerized, dehumanized, "multinational" and corporate form.

Jameson and the others may be correct in insisting that fascination with *The Godfather* is motivated, at a deeper level, by anti-capitalist anxiety. But the real scare *The Godfather* entertains, however much suppressed, is about capitalism, not in its "most systematized and computerized, dehumanized" form but rather in its more "intimate" varieties—ethnic, familial, personal. My reading of *The Godfather* suggests that if we wish to press charges against capitalism, we must press charges against family and ethnicity, too.

One strand of rhetoric in twentieth-century America, dating as far back as Howells's *Hazard of New Fortunes* and surveyed by Christopher Lasch in *Haven in a Heartless World* (1977), urges Americans to go home to escape the specter of capitalism. Professionals often complain about taking work home with them, mentally if not literally. How much more frightening, then, is the alternative Puzo represents: when some Americans go home to papa, they end up confronting the boss. Critics have been quick to interpret the brutality of the Mafia as a symbol for the violence to the individual inherent in capitalism, and to assume that the family represents an escape from that violence. Yet the melodrama of *The Godfather* implicates the family not only in the success of the Corleone empire but in its cycle of self-destructive violence as well. Michael reintegrates the fam-

ily business only after burying a brother, murdering a brother-in-law, alienating a sister, and betraying his wife's trust. For Americans who experience family and economy as interwoven pressures (if not actual combined enterprises), the Mafia genre may allow them to focus their resentments, even if, inevitably, a Mafia analogy overstates them. For the cost of employing blood in the marketplace is finding "The Company" at home.

Puzo is often maligned for exploiting the stereotype of Italian-American criminality, which has long been used to discriminate against the general Italian-American population. But, in the final analysis, *The Godfather* does not so much rehash an old tale, whatever its strands of inheritance, as tell a new one. In *The Godfather,* Puzo refashions the gangster genre into a vehicle for overturning the traditional antithesis between ties of blood and the American marketplace. He thus transforms the stock character of the Italian-American outlaw into the representative super(business)man, and transforms the lingering image of immigrant huddled masses into the first family of American capitalism.

Vincent Patrick (review date 28 July 1996)

SOURCE: "Leaving Las Vegas," in *The New York Times Book Review,* July 28, 1996, p. 9.

[*In the following review, Patrick offers praise for* The Last Don.]

It is a measure of Mario Puzo's skill that after turning the last page of his rich and ebullient new novel, I was able to remember no fewer than 35 characters and recall clearly their backgrounds, motivations and roles in the convoluted plot and subplots. Indeed, all of Mr. Puzo's formidable storytelling talents are on display throughout *The Last Don,* a big, fast-paced tale that should provide his fans our most entertaining read since *The Godfather.* The primary settings are the seats of power and wealth in Las Vegas and Hollywood. The characters are larger-than-life personalities, supremely self-confident risk takers with great appetites for money, sex and power.

The prologue is set on Don Domenico Clericuzio's walled Long Island estate on Palm Sunday in 1965, where the Don is overseeing the double christening of "infants of his own blood": his widowed daughter's son, Dante Clericuzio, and his nephew's son, Croccifixio De Lena, who will come to be called Cross. The main story line is foreshadowed when the two infants are placed side by side in a carriage and fight over a bottle of milk. Meanwhile, the 60-year-old Don, head of the most powerful Mafia family in America, is making arrangements "to relinquish that power, on the surface":

"Twenty, thirty years from now," he says, "we will all disappear into the lawful world and enjoy our wealth without fear. Those two infants we are baptizing today will never have to commit our sins and take our risks." So why, then, are they keeping the Bronx Enclave, a bastion of Mafia soldiers? Because, the Don replies, "We hope someday to be saints, but not martyrs."

The story jumps to Las Vegas, 1990, where we meet young Cross De Lena, whose life will change radically when he inherits the dying Alfred Gronevelt's 51 percent stake in the Xanadu Casino Hotel, worth $500 million. Cross has been raised in Las Vegas by his father, Pippi De Lena, unaware until he was 20 of Pippi's position as the "Hammer" of the Clericuzio family, the very best of those qualified men who work on the violent side of the business, men who have made their bones by killing someone.

Groomed by Pippi to succeed him, Cross performs well enough to earn the appellation Little Hammer, but finally does not have what it takes to fill his father's shoes: the ability to kill someone he knows and likes. Dante becomes the Hammer upon Pippi's forced retirement. To complicate Cross's life further, he meets Athena Aquitane, who is being threatened by her psychopathic former husband. She is not only beautiful but one of that rare Hollywood species, a "Bankable Star."

The admonition of Cross's mentor, Alfred Gronevelt— "Money can make you safe in this world, from everything except a beautiful woman"—flashes through his mind but he falls in love nevertheless, and through Athena becomes involved in the movie business despite the Don's longstanding edict against it. The Don had once gained a foothold in Hollywood, which he relinquished with orders to his people to stop all attempts to infiltrate the movie business. "Those people are too clever," he said. "And they have no fear because the rewards are so high. We should have to kill them all and then we would not know how to run the business. It is more complicated than drugs." Clearly this is a world about which Mr. Puzo knows plenty.

His Hollywood characters are outsize and fun. Eli Marrion, the aging, impotent owner of a studio, has always "had a soft spot for writers," but that was because they were so easy to outsmart on their contracts. Marrion's C.E.O. and hatchet man, Bobby Bantz, believes that people who pursue money rather than art are much better and more socially valuable than those artists who try to show the divine spark in human beings. He muses: "Too bad you couldn't make a movie about that. That money was more healing than art and love. But the public would never buy it." A screenwriter recognizes that she has "a twisted affection" for Skippy Deere, a producer, "for his living his life so blatantly in his own self-interest, for his ability to look you in the eye and call you

his friend while not caring that you knew he would never perform a true act of friendship. That he was such a cheerful, ardent hypocrite." The freshest observations about movie making are those of Ernest Vail, a once-famous novelist with a bizarre scheme to extract his financial due from Eli Marrion and Bobby Bantz.

All of these people, whose machinations eventually test the cunning of the Don, intersect with Cross at a time when the love of Athena Aquitane holds out to him the promise of a rebirth. The three most influential men in his life, however— his father, Alfred Gronevelt and the old Don—have always warned him that romantic love is "the fatal flaw of great men who would control their worlds." Cross must, in the end, choose between love and power, but first must keep from being killed. Mr. Puzo wraps up his intricate plot with the same ingenuity he exhibits throughout this satisfying novel.

R. Z. Sheppard (review date 29 July 1996)

SOURCE: A review of *The Last Don*, in *Time*, July 29, 1996, pp. 82-4.

[*In the following review, Sheppard asserts that* The Last Don *shows Puzo "in top form."*]

Attention mafianados! at the age of 75, and more than 20 years after Don Vito Corleone and the rest of the Godfather gang abandoned the page for a more glamorous life on the screen, Mario Puzo has started a new family. *The Last Don* introduces the Clericuzios, a crime clan based in the Bronx, New York, and at the peak of its dark powers. Fortunately, Puzo too is in top form.

"He definitely views this book as a comeback with a vengeance," says his editor, Jonathan Karp. Five years ago, Puzo had quadruple-bypass surgery, followed by a long and gloomy convalescence. His book in progress, a saga about the Borgias, stalled. He thought he might never write again. But transpose the Machiavellian city-state of the Borgias to a fortress in the Bronx, add a summer palace on Long Island and playgrounds in Las Vegas and Hollywood, and— Ecco!—the godfather of Mafia fiction is back in business.

The timing isn't bad either. In summer even serious readers beg to have their disbelief suspended, and *The Last Don* obliges. It is a headlong entertainment, bubbling over with corruption, betrayals, assassinations, Richter-scale romance and, of course, family values. As in its famous predecessor, unquestioned loyalty, unexamined cash flow and expedient ways of dealing with competition are givens, but this story is set in the '80s—and the slick Clericuzios make the Corleones seem as if they just got off the boat. Gone from the new novel are the entry-level rackets and suspiciously profitable olive-oil business. Instead, family head Don Domenico Clericuzio rules an Exxon of organized crime aided by a son with a degree from Wharton. All the messiness of securing market share is in the past. Years before, the Clericuzios eliminated their main rivals, the Santadios, in one quick and nasty operation. Imagine a rewrite of *Romeo and Juliet* in which the Capulets throw a wedding and then slaughter the Montagues before dessert.

Imagine anything you like, and in all probability you would still be hard-pressed to keep up with Puzo's devilish invention. There is scarcely a deadly sin or narrative device that he does not plant in his tale. No other popular writer mixes suds and satire with such disarming effect.

The backdrop of *The Last Don* may be operatic ("God's world was a prison in which man had to earn his daily bread, and his fellow man was a fellow beast, carnivorous and without mercy"), but the setting and characters are commedia dell'arte. Puzo playfully admires the aging Don Dom. "Early on," he writes, "he had been told the famous maxim of American justice, that it was better that a hundred guilty men go free than that one innocent man be punished. Struck almost dumb by the beauty of the concept, he became an ardent patriot."

The novel's unwritten law is that time eventually earns a dispensation for past sins. Tough old pros like Alfred Gronevelt, official owner of the Clericuzio-controlled Xanadu Hotel in Las Vegas, and ruthless Eli Marrion, geriatric head of LoddStone Studios, are, like the Don, the novel's honored guests. Puzo's younger heroes are fewer but conspicuous: the Don's Adonis-like grandnephew Croccifixio ("Cross") De Lena and his film-goddess girlfriend, Athena Aquitane. The book's fools and villains are ruled by passions, impulses and grotesque egos. A degenerate gambler and loudmouthed deadbeat lurches obnoxiously toward his inevitable fate. A hit man, perversely named Dante, wears gaudy Renaissance-style hats and takes too much pleasure in his work.

The marriage of the Mafia and movies provides Puzo with his longest-running gag. In scene after scene the gentlemen from New York and Las Vegas have more ethics and common courtesy than most Hollywood bosses. Puzo, of course, has a few scores to settle. In 1974 he went to the mattresses with Universal Studios over his share of profits for writing *Earthquake*. The experience probably explains why Bobby Bantz, LoddStone's second in command, is a fulsome repository of foul behavior and slippery business practices. Among them is the willfully complicated gross-and-net game that fattens those on top and leaves naive scriptwriters out of pocket. Puzo takes his vendetta to comic climax when a novelist turned LoddStone hack has to kill himself to get his money. That he sets aside his multiple suicide notes for a

rewrite is the sort of black-humor icing that tops off much of this highly anecdotal read.

Three Cheers for Hypocrisy would make a suitable subtitle for *The Last Don*. "Mario writes about the hearts of thieves and thievery in our hearts. He is fascinated by the moral ironies in life," says Random House editor Karp. Puzo's own are no exception. Before he wrote *The Godfather*, Puzo spent years vainly trying to gamble his way out of debt. Eventually crime paid, but not in the way he thought it would.

Puzo now keeps his wagering within the family. "He acts as bookie for his children, who will gamble on sports events, and he will take whatever side they don't want," says friend Speed Vogel, a retired businessman and co-author of Joseph Heller's memoir, *No Laughing Matter*.

Clearly Puzo understands that the best—perhaps only—reason to be conservative is that he has a lot to conserve. "The one great mystery that would never be solved was why very rich men still wasted time gambling to win money they did not need," he writes in *The Last Don*. One possible reason, he concludes, is that "they did so to hide other vices."

Gluttony does not count. Puzo is a man of large appetites. "He always lived above his means, even when he was younger and before *The Godfather*," says Vogel. "He always took cabs and smoked expensive cigars even when he couldn't afford it." He also loves to eat, and it shows, although diabetes and bypassed arteries now require some no-calorie alternatives. So Puzo devours books. Volumes of classic and contemporary works fill the house in Bay Shore, Long Island, that he bought with the first money he earned from *The Godfather*. His daughter Virginia runs the household, and Carol Gino, the nurse who cared for his wife Erika before she died 17 years ago, is his loving companion. Sons Anthony and Eugene look after his financial interests.

"At home," says novelist and longtime friend Josh Greenfeld, "Mario is the Godfather." The author's pals complement his deep family relationships. The group, which includes Vogel, *Catch-22* author Heller and novelist and playwright Bruce Jay Friedman, gets together for a boys-only lunch every month. Friedman recalls encountering Puzo's writing when he hired him as an assistant editor for the adventure magazines *Male* and *Men*. "You knew that he was a natural and a master storyteller," says Friedman. "I'm just disappointed that I didn't become his agent." Plans for a new book are already under way, and Puzo has told friends that he wants to write the last great Mafia novel. That, God willing, would make Domenico Clericuzio the Next to Last Don.
The novel's unwritten law is that time earns a dispensation for past sins.

Jeff Zaleski (interview date 29 July 1996)

SOURCE: "Mario Puzo: The Don of Bestsellers Returns," in *Publishers Weekly,* July 29, 1996, pp. 64-5.

[*In the following interview, Puzo comments on* The Godfather, *his literary success, and* The Last Don.]

Mario Puzo makes us an offer we don't want to refuse. After nearly two decades of public silence, he agrees to grant *PW* his first interview in 18 years (though a later one, described as "exclusive," appeared last week in *New York* magazine), in order to talk about his masterful new novel, *The Last Don,* due out from Random House in August, and about the arc of his writing career. So on an early summer day, we travel out to Long Island under a hot milky sky to sit with him in the second-floor sunroom of his home. Also present is his editor, Jonathan Karp.

"Why did you decide to speak with us?" we ask Puzo after he sets us up with a cold soda.

"I've reformed." After 75 years, Puzo's voice is husky but still sweet with the lilt and rhythms of the Manhattan streets where he grew up. "I figured, give it a try, it'll be a nice experience before I die. Also, I got all these grandchildren, and they don't know that I used to be famous."

Used to be famous? Puzo delights in irony, though he rarely laughs. This stocky man relaxed on a sofa across from us, large, open face topped by thinning gray hair, clad in a pink shirt and white trousers, gripping a big cigar that he never lights, is world famous as the author of seven novels and 10 films—above all, of *The Godfather,* which, 27 years after publication, has sold, according to Puzo, an astounding 21 million copies. Puzo is proud of what these sales mean. He talks about it within our first five minutes together.

"You know how I know how many copies I sold? I got the money. Nobody said I just sold books. I got money. Statistics, they don't mean anything unless you get the money."

The money has bought Puzo a rambling house in a fancy neighborhood, ringed by lawns and tall trees, sided by a tennis court, filled with fine furniture, plush rugs and several huge TV sets. But a fence shields the house from public view, and the computer shining on the desk nearby is used not by him but by his longtime companion, author Carol Gino. Puzo writes by hand, and at an old typewriter. Instead of servants or a secretary, he employs two of his five children, all now grown. Here, it seems, is a man who cares passionately about money but who doesn't flaunt it.

Money—its lure and power—dominates Puzo's work. "To me," he says, "money is the focus of everything you see

people do." It's not too surprising to hear this from a man born to illiterate Italian immigrant parents in Hell's Kitchen, whose father abandoned his wife and five kids when Puzo was 12. "I knew I lived in poverty," Puzo says. "That was one of the things that helped me to write. It was my way out."

The ambition to write his way out carried Puzo through high school. World War II erupted when he was 21, taking him to Germany, where he met and married the mother of his children, now deceased. In the late 1940s, Puzo returned to Manhattan for night classes at the New School. "I was studying literature, trying to be a writer," he reminisces. "Since I was a veteran, I got 120 bucks a month for going to school. So I was going for the 120 bucks. But it was a really wonderful education."

During the day, Puzo worked as a federal employee. In his spare time, he wrote *The Dark Arena,* a literary melodrama set in occupied Germany, published by Random House in 1955. The novel received glowing reviews but sank in sales. So did Puzo's heart. Determined to make it as an artist, he began an autobiographical novel, *The Fortunate Pilgrim.* Shortly before its 1964 publication by Atheneum, he quit the civil service to edit men's adventure magazines. A new job, a new book, a new publisher; but, again, strong reviews drew only weak sales. Now Puzo despaired. "I didn't make money on it. When that happens, you get such a feeling of self-loathing. That you've done something valuable but nobody values it. So you despise yourself. And you despise the public."

He saw only one solution, he recalls. "I said, 'well, I gotta write a book that people will buy.'" As he speaks these words, Puzo's hands, always in motion, swoop like birds of prey. Otherwise, he sits nearly motionless. His eyes glint dark and lustrous from behind wide-framed glasses.

The book was *The Godfather.* When Atheneum rejected Puzo's outline, he brought it to Putnam, where, in 1965, editor Bill Targ advanced him $5000. "I'd never heard of so much money in my life," he says. "I mean, it was mind-boggling." More mind-boggling still was the novel's success. At the top of national bestseller lists for much of 1969, its publication year, it became the top-selling novel of the 1970s and, according to Putnam, of all time. It proved a cultural watershed, bringing the Mafia to national attention and spawning generations of mob novels, influencing writers from Elmore Leonard to Eugene Izzi.

The Godfather swept sea changes into Puzo's professional and personal life as well. He acquired an agent, Candida Donadio, who still represents him. He added wealth to fame when Putnam sold paperback rights to Fawcett for $410,000. And he launched his second career, as a screenwriter. "I refused to write the script of *The Godfather* at first," Puzo remembers. "Then the producer, Al Ruddy, came to New York with his wife. They took me to lunch at the Plaza. I was prepared to say no again. But I was charmed by Ruddy's wife, because she had a poodle in her handbag. She opens the handbag and out pops this dog. And that was so charming I said yes."

The two Oscars Puzo has won, for his screenplays of *The Godfather* and *The Godfather: Part II* gleam on the mantelpiece in his living room. He has scripted eight other films, most notably *The Godfather: Part III,* the first two *Superman* films, *Earthquake* and *The Cotton Club.* Puzo reveals that he's also written a screenplay that was never filmed, based on a Zane Grey novel "like a western *Godfather.*" Michael Eisner, then head of Paramount, rejected it because, Puzo says, he hated the desert. "I don't like sand in a movie," Eisner reportedly told Puzo.

Talking about screenwriting, again Puzo refers to the money. "The writers today," he says, "we're all sort of dopes. Everybody should rush out to Hollywood and get the easy money." To transform a novel into a screenplay, he adds, "you figure out what the primary story is. All the other stories, you lop 'em off like they lop off the fat on a piece of pork."

His newfound success granted Puzo freedom to publish what he wanted—in 1972, the essays and stories of *The Godfather Papers;* in 1978, still with Bill Targ at Putnam, *Fools Die,* a novel about Las Vegas, Hollywood and the New York publishing industry. Paperback rights sold to Fawcett for a then-record $2.2 million, but the book failed to match *The Godfather*'s sales or influence. Six years later, Puzo returned with *The Sicilian.* Edited by Joni Evans at Linden Press, the novel briefly brought back Michael Corleone of *Godfather* fame in its tale of a Sicilian brigand. It was the top-selling hardcover fiction of 1985, but Puzo's next book, from Random House, *The Fourth K,* a thriller that placed a future Kennedy in the White House, fared relatively poorly.

"I was a young assistant editor at the time," interjects Karp. "That's how I met Mario. I don't think that people got the political irony of it at all." For that, Puzo takes the blame. "I realized from the failure of the book that there are certain rules that you can't break. I broke them with Kennedy as the hero when I turned him into a guy who would have been a dictator." Puzo himself can charm, and his fierce honesty is part of his charm.

The Fourth K was almost Puzo's last book. In January 1991, its publication month, he nearly died. Already diabetic, he was stricken with heart trouble and underwent an emergency quadruple bypass. Puzo didn't write during the next two years. Instead, he researched a novel on the Borgias but decided not to write it. "The trouble," he explains, "is in show-

ing the Borgia Pope as he was. That would make such an uproar, who knows if you want to get into that? So I went from the Borgia book to writing a Hollywood and Vegas book. And the Clericuzio popped up."

Puzo bans morals from his fiction. Though he has taken flak for not condemning characters—Don Corleone especially— who act like monsters, he frowns on those who judge their own creations. [He says:] "If you're a true novelist, your first duty is to tell a story; if you want to moralize, write nonfiction, philosophy, whatever."
—Jeff Zaleski

The Clericuzio are the hypnotic dark heart of *The Last Don,* the most powerful Mafia family in the country. Their chief is Don Domenico Clericuzio, whose great age and power is mirrored in two other male characters, a casino owner and a Hollywood studio chief. Each stands nearly above the novel's wild swirl of deals, betrayals, violence; yet each will order the snuffing of a career or a life as necessary. We ask Puzo if his own years and brush with death influenced the book. "I think so," he says. "The character of Don Clericuzio, for instance. The way he can isolate himself from emotion, where he arranges the killing of his own. . . . It's something I can do now. You reach a certain age where you're quite capable of great sin."

Puzo's own age becomes more apparent as we continue to speak. He is game to talk as long as we wish, and he's ever ready with ideas and opinions, but his voice loses zest as the afternoon passes. The air in the room, warm when we came in, grows close.

Puzo's maturity elevates *The Last Don,* a novel as grand and complex as any he has written. It embodies a lifetime of experience or interest in Hollywood, Vegas, the mob—and, above all, in money. "I think *The Last Don* is an ambitious book," he says. "All through it I'm trying to show a strict correlation between the criminal persona and an industrial criminal persona. And that the crucial element is money."

It becomes clear as we speak that Puzo's obsession with money isn't about greed. Early in his life, it was about escape from poverty; in middle age, about public validation of his talent. Now, money is a force to be captured in his art—and one that to him raises a moral question. "What is the central thing to most people?" Puzo asks us. "Earning a living, earning your daily bread. If these guys didn't commit these crimes, they'd be at the mercy of employers, they'd be at the mercy of economics. They're asserting their own power over their fate." Yet Puzo bans morals from his fiction. Though he has taken flak for not condemning characters—Don Corleone especially—who act like monsters, he frowns on those who judge their own creations. "If you're a true novelist, your first duty is to tell a story; if you want to moralize, write nonfiction, philosophy, whatever."

What will follow *The Last Don?* Karp mentions that Puzo recently got a call from [actor Marlon] Brando, who, Puzo, explains, "wants to be in *The Last Don* if it's a feature film, but he won't do TV." And film rights have been sold to TV, Puzo announces: "The movie business didn't bid high enough." Puzo has time to write, since he lives alone. But there is the allure of reading, "the only pleasure in life that hasn't disappointed me," and he works in fits and starts. "I'm an essentially lazy writer," he confesses. "A lot of my writing schedule is laying on the sofa, staring up at the ceiling." Still, he has plans. A film of *The Godfather: Part IV* is "a possibility." He's working on a screenplay of Gino's first book, *The Nurse's Story.* He may yet write the Borgia book, and he's contemplating an epic historical about the Mafia. "I write a book about the 700 years of the Mafia, then I drop dead," he jokes. "Everybody's had enough of the Mafia, everybody's had enough of me."

Whether time will rate Puzo as a great writer or less remains to be seen. He has his Oscars but no major literary prizes, no Pulitzer. "I would have loved to have won a Pulitzer," he says. "But if you go back over the books that won, are they read today? I think the test is, do people keep reading them? Now it's, what, 27 years since *The Godfather?* I still get a royalty check from England, for a substantial amount. Jesus Christ, 27 years, selling a book, that's something."

Yes it is, we agree as we rise to leave. Puzo's hand is dry as we shake it goodbye. He has trouble with stairs, he says, so he can't see us out. Downstairs, we admire those Oscars, testament to Puzo's storytelling prowess, to the remarkable life he has led. We flash to *The Last Don,* and we think of how marvelous it is that this writer, age be damned, has once more put that talent and life's wisdom on the page, and this time in fullest flower.

Fred L. Gardaphe (essay date 1996)

SOURCE: "The Middle Mythic Mode: Godfathers as Heroes, Variations on a Figure," in *Italian Signs, American Streets: The Evolution of Italian American Narrative,* Duke University Press, 1996, pp. 86-118.

[*In the following excerpt, Gardaphe examines elements of myth and cultural assimilation in* The Godfather, *contending that it "has done more to create a national consciousness of the Italian American experience than any work of fiction or nonfiction published before or since."*]

Three narratives will represent the middle mythic period of Italian American narrative: Mario Puzo's *The Godfather* (1969), Gay Talese's *Honor Thy Father* (1971), and Giose Rimanelli's *Benedetta in Guysterland* (1993). Within these three works the figure of the godfather surfaces as a direct response to the attempts of Italian immigrants to "make America." Puzo's romanticized version, Talese's historical version, and Rimanelli's parodic version all represent variations on the heroic theme this figure has come to embody. Besides containing the characteristics of the mythic mode that I outlined earlier, these three texts also reveal an intertextual relationship that until recently was a rare phenomenon in Italian American literature.

Interpretations of the Italian American family take on new dimensions in these three books. The image of the honest, hardworking Italian immigrant family portrayed by Fante, di Donato, and Mangione as a community united against an alien and often hostile outside world is abandoned for the portrayal of the family able to gain the power through any means—legal or illegal—necessary to control their environment. This control is represented through the figure of the godfather. Richard Gambino says that the godparent belongs to the second most important category in the hierarchy of Italian family order:

> From top to bottom: 1. family members, "blood of my blood," 2. *compari* and *padrini* and their female equivalents, *commare* and *madrine* ("godparents," a relationship that was by no means limited to those who were godparents in the Catholic religious rites . . . and which would better translate as "intimate friends" and "venerated elders"), 3. *amici* or *amici di cappello* (friends to whom one tipped one's hat or said "hello"), meaning those whose family status demanded respect, and 4. *stranieri* (strangers), a designation for all others.

These levels are circles or buffers designed to protect the family. With the nuclear family in the center, surrounded by the extended family, then by the *compari* and *commari,* and then the *amici,* the order of the family works like the walls around a castle. *Compareggio* (godparenthood) ranks next to the family because it signifies a trust stronger than any other relationship that unrelated Italians can share. Traditionally, godparents were chosen from the circle outside the "blood" family for the purposes of cementing a familylike bond between those involved. Godparents were selected on the basis of their ability to contribute to the protection and well-being of the family, and selection was often a strategic, political decision.

In America, especially during the Great Depression, those who held power in the Italian American communities (even gangsters) were besieged with requests to be godfathers or godmothers to the children of those who lacked access to power. It was not uncommon for a single individual to be a godparent in a number of families. As an honor to the godparent for accepting the responsibility of *compareggio,* the godfather or godmother's first name often became the second name of the child at Baptism or the third name of the child at confirmation. The godparent was expected to assist the godchild throughout life and to act as a counselor and a mediator, especially during intrafamily disputes. If a parent should die while the child was still a minor, the godparent would take over the child's upbringing. This, then, is the background of the serious and sacred relationship that would become distorted through the literary and media representations that captured America's attention during the 1970's.

The next three sections of this chapter analyze three representations of the godfather figure created by Italian American writers in order to reveal how they create mythic figures out of historical materials. Mario Puzo's novel, Gay Talese's nonfiction narrative, and Giose Rimanelli's parody represent three very different approaches to representing this very important cultural figure in writing. What is more interesting, however, is how these three representations speak to each other in the construction and the deconstruction of the myth the myth that I call the myth of reverse assimilation.

> The book got much better reviews than I expected. I wished like hell I'd written it better. I like the book. It has energy and I lucked out by creating a central character that was popularly accepted as genuinely mythic. But I wrote below my gifts in that book.
>
> —Mario Puzo, "The Making of *The Godfather*"

> This work of fiction is not really about organized crime or about gangsterism. The true theme has to do with family pride and personal honor. That's what made *The Godfather* so popular. It portrayed people with a strong sense of kinship to survive in a cruel world.
>
> —Joseph Bonanno, *A Man of Honor*

The Godfather is Mario Puzo's third novel. His earlier novels represent his attempts to fulfill a dream of becoming an artist and escaping the ghetto world in which he was born. Like Fante, di Donato, and Mangione, Puzo's early encounter with such writers as Dostoevsky in his local library strengthened his belief in art and enabled him to "understand what was really happening to me and the people around me." It was not art, however, but war that finally enabled Puzo to escape his environment "without guilt." Out of his experiences in Europe during and after the Second World War he crafted his first novel, *The Dark Arena* (1955); ten years later he returned to his life experiences growing up in New

York's Little Italy to create *The Fortunate Pilgrim* (1965). In *The Dark Arena,* the protagonist, Walter Mosca (in Italian, *mosca* means "fly"), returns home from serving with the American occupation army in Germany. Unable to take up where he left off before the war, Mosca returns to Germany as a civilian employee of the occupation government and resumes his life as a black marketeer. While the novel received some good reviews, Puzo was disappointed that it did not make much money. *The Fortunate Pilgrim* received similar notices and brought Puzo even less financial reward. Because of the poor sales of his earlier works, no publisher would advance him the money he needed to write a third novel. Twenty thousand dollars in debt, he began to look for a way out. "I was forty-five years old," he writes, "and tired of being an artist."

With the publication of *The Godfather* in 1969, Mario Puzo was immediately promoted to celebrity status. Not since the publication of Pietro di Donato's *Christ in Concrete* had an American author of Italian descent been thrust into the national spotlight on such a grand scale. The timing of *The Godfather*'s publication had much to do with its rapid climb to number one and its sixty-seven-week stay on the *New York Times* best-seller list. The novel came off the press in the middle of the ethnic revival period of the 1960s. It also followed nationally televised congressional hearings on organized crime and the publication of Peter Maas's nonfiction bestseller *The Valachi Papers,* in which mobster-turned-informer Joe Valachi describes his activities inside organized crime.

The Godfather has done more to create a national consciousness of the Italian American experience than any work of fiction or nonfiction published before or since. It certainly was the first novel that Italian Americans as a group reacted to, either positively or negatively, perhaps because it appeared at a time when Italian Americans were just beginning to emerge as an identifiable cultural and political entity. Even though this book is much more a work of fiction than any of the earlier, more autobiographical novels written by Italian Americans, it created an identity crisis for Italian Americans throughout the nation. Antidefamation groups denounced Puzo for creating a bad image of Italians in America; young Italian American boys formed "Godfather" clubs; and real mafiosi claimed that Puzo knew what he was writing about. For a while, Puzo wrote a number of essays on the subject of Italian America which appeared in major national magazines. These essays, while often undermining the image of Italians that he created in *The Godfather* and his later novel *The Sicilian,* are also quite critical of the Italian American's behavior in American society.

The effect of this one novel was tremendous. Since its publication, and especially since its film adaptations in the early 1970s, Italian American novelists have been writing in *The*

Godfather's shadow, and Puzo has become a recluse. Though sociologists and literary scholars may forever debate the value of Puzo's work, most would agree that he has left a permanent imprint on the American cultural scene through his representation of *Italianita* and his creation of a mythic filter through which Italian American culture would henceforth be read.

In "The Authority of the Signifier: Barthes and Puzo's *The Godfather*," Christian Messenger reads **The Godfather** through Roland Barthes's essay "Myth Today" for the purpose of determining the role that myth plays in the production of popular culture. Messenger points out that while the Corleone family "appeared to be a protofamily for our collapsing time," it also set up a false dichotomy between good murderers and bad murderers. Messenger reads Puzo's symbolizing as signifiers of a mythic language that result from artificially naturalizing history, a process that Barthes says is the function of myth. Messenger's reading of key scenes in the novel makes clear "the dialectal flow between naturalizing and historicizing" that Puzo's narrative obscures. **The Godfather** portrays the Mafia as a natural force in the Sicilian world from which Vito Corleone comes, a world he attempts to re-create in his new home in America. In this world the Don and his family are portrayed as the "good guys," and the American establishment with which they struggle—the institutions of law and business—are set up as the "bad guys." Messenger suggests that the key question asked by the novel is raised by Jack Woltz and Kay Adams: "What if everyone acted that way?" This question can guide us through a reading of the novel as an exercise in the portrayal of reverse assimilation. In other words, in this novel Puzo presents the question that in effect is the real Italian American dream: What if America assimilated to our ways? Before setting up this approach to reading **The Godfather**, let me first point to some of the aspects of the novel that can be connected to more traditional Western myths.

The Don's system of belief is based on the idea that each man has but one destiny. The Don's own destiny was determined when he killed Fanucci, the thug who extorted money from local merchants and demanded tribute from any criminal activity that took place in his neighborhood. When Fanucci demands a percentage of Vito's and his partners' crime, Vito decides to kill him. "It was from this experience came his oft repeated belief that every man has but one destiny. On that night he could have paid Fanucci the tribute and have become again a grocery clerk. . . . But destiny had decided that he was to become a Don and had brought Fanucci *to* him to set him on his destined path." Similarly, each of the Don's sons is seen as having his destiny determined by a single incident. Santino (Sonny), the oldest son, is destined to follow his father's ways, not only because of birth but, according to the Don, because he witnessed his father's shooting of Fanucci. Michael Corleone's destiny is

revealed the night he shoots Sollozzo and the police captain. Fredo's position outside the inner workings of the family business is determined by his inability to defend his father during the assassination attempt.

Puzo borrows a figure from ancient mythology to describe the Don's children. Daughter Connie has a "Cupid-bow mouth." Sonny is described as having the face "of a gross Cupid." His large penis signifies his Dionysian behavior, which interferes with his ability to concentrate on the family business. Ruled by his emotions, Sonny is unable to become a good don. Fredo has "the same Cupid head of the family" and lacks "that animal force, so necessary for a leader of men." Predictably, Michael is the only child not described in terms of Cupid.

Throughout the novel the Don is characterized as a god or demigod who can negotiate affairs between humans and the supernatural. This is underscored by the hospital scene in which Genco Abbandando lies on his deathbed crying out, "Godfather, Godfather . . . save me from death. . . . Godfather, cure me, you have the power." The Don replies that he does not have such powers, but if he did, he should "be more merciful than God." Genco then appeals to the Don to stay with him as he faces death: "Perhaps if He sees you near me He will be frightened and leave me in peace. Or perhaps you can say a word, pull a few strings, eh?" When he is not being a god, Don Corleone is portrayed as a heroic figure who is able to struggle with the gods. Puzo characterizes Don Corleone as a rarity, a man of will, a man among "men who refused the dominion of other men. There was no force, no mortal man who could bend them to their will unless they wished it. They were men who guarded their free will with wiles and murder."

In the Don's speech to the heads of the other crime families after the murder of Sonny, he attempts to make peace through an appeal to the American Dream, but the whole speech is an example of *bella figura*, a public posturing designed to shield his true plans and to present the illusion that he is willing to assimilate to the American ways of doing illegal business:

> Let me say that we must always look to our interests. We are all men who have refused to be fools, who have refused to be puppets dancing on a string pulled by the men on high. We have been fortunate here in this country. Already most of our children have found a better life. Some of you have sons who are professors, scientists, musicians, and you are fortunate. Perhaps your grandchildren will become the new *pezzonovanti*. None of us here want to see our children follow in our footsteps, it's too hard a life.

The Don uses his power to make friends who will strengthen his position. His competitor, Sollozzo, is driven by the opportunity to make money through the high profits of drug manufacturing and distribution; however, he lacks a key ingredient for insuring the venture's success—the Don's friends in high places. This is the clash between the Old World sense of power bringing wealth and the New World's sense of wealth bringing power. Thus, when the Don pledges not to seek revenge for Santino's murder and to support drug trafficking, he does so because he sees that the only way to keep his family intact is to ensure Michael's safe return from Sicily. After this speech, the Don returns home and announces his semiretirement and his plans to stay home and work in his garden. But he can do this only because he knows that Michael will take over the business and enact the Corleone family's revenge.

Ironically, Michael, the son destined to take over the Don's power, is the one closest to total assimilation into American life. At the outset of the novel, Michael breaks the code of *omertà* by letting Kay Adams in on the history of his father's business. During his sister's wedding reception Michael tells stories about the "more colorful wedding guests, like Luca Brasi. He explains to Kay what is going on at the meetings held inside his father's study and interprets the ambiguities she, an outsider, is unable to read. Later, on the night that his father is shot, Michael leaves Kay and returns to the family house, and "for the first time since it had all started he felt a furious anger rising in him, a cold hatred for his father's enemies." This fury drives Michael back into the family fold and leads him to avenge his father's shooting.

Up to this point, Michael has been as innocent as the women in the Corleone clan. He has been kept out of the family business and has had a hero's upbringing, the American equivalent of an aristocrat's education, with knightly training in the marines through which he achieves heroism during the war. His military service is part of his attempt to Americanize himself: It represents loyalty to a power that is not Sicilian and rebellion against his father's wishes, as the Don realizes: "He performs those miracles for strangers." Michael's murder of Sollozzo and the police captain takes place under the fated circumstances of an Orestes. His ancestral culture's code demands vengeance for his father's blood, and Michael acts accordingly.

After the murder, Michael flees to Sicily, that otherworldly ground of his being and his subconscious—a locus for so much of Western mythology. There he meets the characters who embody the new condition of his soul, which is physically manifest in his disfigured face. He learns the history of Sicilian culture and the role the Mafia has played in it through Dr. Taza: "He came to understand his father's character and his destiny . . . to understand men like Luca Brasi,

the ruthless *caporegime* Clemenza, his mother's resignation and acceptance of her role. For in Sicily he saw what they would have been if they had chosen *not* to struggle against their fate." His bodyguards, like mythological dogs, defend him against the wolves (strangers outside the circles of family and friends) through their use of *lupara*, or "wolf guns." He meets Apollonia, his anima—the pure, good, noble, and beautiful, full of pietàs and innocence. This all takes place in the pastoral setting so thickly described by Puzo during the couple's first meeting and throughout their brief marriage. When Apollonia dies, the victim of a car bomb intended for Michael, it is because he is set on the course that kills the innocence and dirties the moral cleanliness inside himself. She dies in his place as the part of himself that his own actions kill. Her very name and physical appearance signify the *chiaroscuro* contrast, the Apollonian/Dionysian dichotomy that the new Michael has become. Their relationship is typical of the male/female social dichotomy in Sicilian culture in which the woman holds the good, the man shoulders the evil. As Don Corleone earlier reminded his godson Johnny Fontane, women "are not competent in this world, though certainly they will be saints in heaven while we men burn in hell."

While the typical successful hero in traditional myth returns from the otherworld strengthened and complete, Michael returns to America with nothing but a memory of the values represented by Apollonia. Instead of becoming a savior of American society as a fully realized human being, he returns and grows stronger as a monster; a hero in his family's society, he becomes a villain in American society. Unlike Orestes, he never receives the deus ex machina-like compassion of an intervening Athena to save him according to traditional myths. The education Michael receives during his exile in Sicily enables him to take command of his father's kingdom and ruthlessly rule it in the Old World manner.

While there is much in this novel that lends itself to interpretation through traditional myth analysis, Puzo also develops something that transcends the archetype approach. What Puzo has contributed to Italian American culture is a myth of the assimilation of America into Italian culture. Vito Corleone's goal is to render powerless the forces that attempt to control him. And he does this by re-creating the Old World in the midst of the New.

Many people read *The Godfather* as an allegory of a decadent America in the postwar period. But the novel can just as well be read as the struggle to protect a family and preserve it, no matter the cost, in a hostile environment. If the family is to be preserved, assimilation into American culture must be avoided, and this can be done only if the exact opposite happens; that is, if America assimilates into the culture of the Don and his family. Thus, the novel can be read as proposing the following question: What would happen if an Italian had the power to make America conform to his or her way of seeing/being in the world? In order for this to occur, the Italian would need to create an alternative world within the world, a world that competes with the American world, one that offers a viable alternative. It is inevitable that when these two worlds come into conflict with each other, the subsequent tension often erupts into violence.

The world that Don Vito Corleone replicates in America is built on the solid foundations of a centuries-old social order in which fate or destiny, more often than not through birth, determined the life an individual would lead. In the feudalistic system of Sicily and southern Italy, the peasant could not hope to aspire to a better life by challenging the forces that controlled his life. As a result, attention was focused on what could be controlled, the family unit. This is the reason so many Italians immigrated to America. The world into which they came had been built on the myth that through freedom, people can become whatever they want if only they work hard enough. This puritanical work ethic and the built-in reward system did not require the family to stick together, and often it led to the breakup of the nuclear family.

The Don's Old World notion of a work ethic requires that the family stick together, and any attempt by an individual to leave threatens the livelihood of the entire family. In fact, if a family is to survive with its Old World values intact, it must work against assimilation and strive to have its surrounding environment conform to the family's way of life. Thus, the central conflict of this novel is how to keep the family together for its own good in a land where people no longer depend on the family unit for survival. This conflict is introduced through the opening vignettes in the Don's office. Amerigo Bonasera's family was harmed through the American youth who beat up his daughter, Johnny Fontane lives a mockery of a marriage to a Hollywood star, and to protect his family's honor the baker Nazorine must find a way for his helper, Enzo, a prisoner of war about to be deported, to marry his daughter. All three men have found success by adapting to the American way of life, but when the New World system fails them, when the nuclear family has been threatened or attacked, they return to the Old World through Don Corleone, just as villagers returned to the castle for protection from invasion during feudal times. In return for his assistance, Don Vito requires "that you, *you yourself* proclaim your friendship"; in other words, that you conform to his way of life. In this way Corleone not only perpetuates the Old World system but also further insulates and protects his own family. In many ways, Don Corleone is like the king of feudal times who offers protection to those whose problems he has helped to create. His consigliore, Tom Hagen, realizes this: "It was a pattern he was to see often, the Don helping those in misfortune whose misfortune he had partly created. Not perhaps out of cunning or plan-

ning but because of his variety of interests or perhaps because of the nature of the universe, the interlinking of good and evil, natural of itself." The Don, because he is the center of the world he has re-created in America, is like God who makes all things, good and evil, and is the force that is cursed as it is praised by those who live under his dominion. And so, Bonasera, Nazorine, Fontane, and most of the novel's other characters are monologic, all pieces in the puzzle Puzo produces, which reveals the power of Old World culture to maintain itself in a New World environment. Don Corleone is more concerned with maintaining *l'ordine della famiglia* and expanding its power than with increasing his profits; that is what he transfers to his son Michael, who has become Old World through his exile in Sicily. Michael achieves what Sonny and Fredo cannot because they lack the experience of life in the land of Mafia origins, an experience that would have balanced their beings. The Don does what he believes is necessary for men's families to thrive. He leads his godson, Johnny Fontane, back to taking care of his family and his friends through Nino. He will ensure through an act of Congress that Nazorine finds a good husband for his daughter. And his men will enact the vengeance that Amerigo Bonasera needs in order to return honor to himself and his family.

There are numerous examples of the Don's ability to make America and Americans assimilate to his ways. Tom Hagen, a German American orphan brought into the Don's home, is raised as one of his own, educated in the American system all the way through law school. Given this opportunity to become a successful American, Hagen opts instead to complete his assimilation into the Don's world. "'I would work for you like your sons,' Hagen said, meaning with complete loyalty, with complete acceptance of the Don's parental divinity." Later on, the Don remarks, "Even though you're not a Sicilian, I made you one." Yet, in spite of Hagen's near-native knowledge of Sicilian ways—he is the one able to read the Sicilian sign of the fish wrapped in Luca Brasi's bloodstained vest and is appointed acting consigliore on Genco's death—and because he is not of Sicilian blood, not "born to the ways of *omertà*," he is relegated to marginal status when Michael takes over. Tom breaks the code of *omertà* at the end of the novel when he explains to Kay why Michael had to kill Connie's husband, Carlo. It is as though Vito Corleone is a Midas whose very touch turns people into Sicilians. In spite of the power that the movie producer Jack Woltz has gained in the American system, he too must assimilate to the Don's world, he must give in to the Don's wish that his godson Johnny Fontane get the role that revives his film career and his loyalty to the family. It is Don Vito whose subtle machinations remind Johnny of how he neglected his responsibilities to help his boyhood friend and *paesano* Nino. The Don provides Johnny with the means to succeed, and ironically it also becomes the means by which Nino is destroyed.

The character who best illustrates this reverse assimilation hypothesis is Kay Adams. Kay, who can trace her ancestral lineage to the *Mayflower,* embodies all that is American, and her assimilation into the Corleone family is the strongest evidence of reverse assimilation. When Michael brings her to his sister's wedding, he does so to "show his own future wife to them, the washed-out rag of an American girl." He sits with her "at a table in the extreme corner of the garden to proclaim his chosen alienation from father and family." When the Corleones meet her they are unimpressed: "She was too thin, too fair, her face was too sharply intelligent for a woman, her manner too free for a maiden. Her name, too, was outlandish to their ears. . . . If she had told them that her family had settled in America two hundred years ago and her name was a common one, they would have shrugged." No matter how much he loves and trusts Kay, Michael realizes that she is an outsider when he sees her after his father has been gunned down. Michael does tell her enough about his father to give her the opportunity to back out of the relationship, but she does not. Even when she finds out from Michael's mother that what she had heard about Michael is true, she still holds on to the hope that she will see Michael again. Two years go by and Kay finds work teaching grade school, and she decides one day to call Mrs. Corleone. While talking to her, Kay finds out that Michael has been back in the country for six months. She becomes angry with Michael, his mother, and "all foreigners—Italians who didn't have the common courtesy to keep up a decent show of friendship even if a love affair was over," yet still accepts Mama Corleone's invitation to visit her at the Corleone home. During their reconciliation, Kay tells Michael he could have trusted her, that she would have "practiced the New England *omertà.* Yankees are pretty closemouthed too, you know." Kay accepts Michael's proposal for a Sicilian marriage, one in which she would be his wife but not "a partner in life," after he confides to her that the family will be legitimate within five years and after he provides her with a "final explanation" of his father's business philosophy.

The next we hear of Kay is when Michael is returning home from Las Vegas. We learn that they had been married in a quiet New England ceremony and that Michael was "surprised at how well Kay got along with his parents and the other people living on the mall." She is described as "a good, old-style Italian wife" who gets pregnant "right away." At the birth of her second child, Kay comes to understand that she is "on her way to becoming a Sicilian" after she realizes that the story Connie tells her about Carlo's fuss over the right baptismal gift must be transmitted to Michael. Kay leaves Michael when she realizes that he did have his own brother-in-law murdered. Then, against her own better judgment, she accepts Tom Hagen's explanation and returns to Michael and converts to Catholicism, something that does not please Michael, who wants "the children to be Protestant, it was more American." Nevertheless, she is converted to his world and accepts the role of the woman subservient to man. Ironically, the conversion takes place because of her interaction with Tom Hagen, who both breaks the code of *omertà* and treats her as an equal. The final scene of the novel finds Kay at Mass, praying, like Mama Corleone, for the "soul of Michael Corleone." And so, Don Con Corleone's bid to control his world has had its greatest impact. He has been able, through his son, to convert an American *Mayflower* Protestant princess into a proper Sicilian mother.

Through the marriage of Michael to Kay, Puzo represents the ideal, albeit mythical, synthesis of Italian and American cultures. No matter how much Michael expresses his desires to be legitimate and American on the surface, under his skin he is true to the Sicilian world of his father, and he re-creates that world for the next generation. Thus, Puzo forges in fiction what is impossible to create in reality. The key to this novel's success lies in Puzo's ability to make readers envy and even fear the mystery and the power inside the *Italianità* that he represents through the Corleone family.

FURTHER READING

Criticism

Gardaphe, Fred L. "Legend Fails as Fiction." In his *Dagoes Read: Tradition and the Italian/American Writer,* pp. 185-6. Toronto: Guernica, 1996.
> Mixed review of *The Sicilian* that praises Puzo's story line but finds shortcomings in his writing.

Gates, David. Review of *The Last Don,* by Mario Puzo. *Newsweek* 128, No. 5 (29 July 1996): 72.
> Unfavorable review of *The Last Don.*

Sheppard, R. Z. Review of *The Fourth K,* by Mario Puzo. *Time* 137, No. 2 (14 January 1991): 62.
> Favorable review of *The Fourth K.*

Wendling, Ronald C. Review of *The Last Don,* by Mario Puzo. *America* 177, No. 1 (5 July 1997): 26.
> Favorable review of *The Last Don.*

Interviews

Goldberg, Jeffrey. "What Mario Puzo Knows." *New York* 29, No. 29 (29 July 1996): 38-40.
> Puzo comments on his literary career and the publication of *The Last Don.*

Additional coverage of Puzo's life and career is contained in the following sources published by Gale: *Authors in the News,* Vols. 1 and 2; *Children's Literature Review,* Vol. 1; *Concise Dictionary of American Literary Biography, 1941-1968; Contemporary Authors,* Vols. 65-68; *Contemporary Authors New Revision Series,* Vols. 4, 42, and 65; *Dictionary of Literary Biography,* Vols. 6, 28, and 52; *Dictionary of Literary Biography Yearbook,* Vol. 91; *Discovering Authors; Discovering Authors: Canadian; Discovering Authors Modules: Novelists* and *Popular Fiction and Genre Authors; Major Authors and Illustrators for Children and Young Adults; Major Twentieth Century Writers; Something About the Author,* Vols. 3, 27, and 68; *Short Story Criticism,* Vol. 3; and *World Literature Criticism.*

John Rechy
1934-

(Full name John Francisco Rechy) American novelist, playwright, and nonfiction writer.

The following entry presents an overview of Rechy's career through 1996. For further information on his life and works, see *CLC*, Volumes 1, 7, 14, and 18.

INTRODUCTION

Rechy is a major force in contemporary American gay literature. His portrayal of the hustler and the steamy underside of the homosexual community has earned him international attention as a literary artisan. In addition, as a Hispanic writer, he has focused attention on the Chicano community in his later fiction and non-fiction writings.

Biographical Information

Rechy was born in El Paso, Texas, on March 10, 1934, to Roberto Sixto Rechy and Guadalupe Flores de Rechy, immigrants from Mexico. The family lived in poverty in western Texas through the Great Depression. His father was a musician and ran a small newspaper. Rechy attended Texas Western College in El Paso on a journalism scholarship. He received a B.A. in English and then briefly attended the New School of Social Research in New York City. He was drafted and served in Germany but was awarded an early release in order to attend Columbia. When he arrived in New York City he became involved in the gay subculture, hustling and traveling around the country. While in New Orleans he wrote a letter to a friend which became the basis for "Mardi Gras," his first published story. In 1961 he won the Longview Foundation Fiction Prize for "The Fabulous Wedding of Miss Destiny." He incorporated both of these stories as well as his personal experiences as a hustler into his first book *City of Night* (1963). The book became an international best seller and earned Rechy much critical attention. After living, writing, and teaching in El Paso for many years, Rechy moved to Los Angeles, where he continues to write and teach at the University of California—Los Angeles.

Major Works

Rechy's most acclaimed work is his first novel, *City of Night*. The story follows the exploits and night life of a young hustler as he travels urban America meeting people who exist on the margins of society. Chapters oscillate between the experiences of the protagonist and the life stories of the people he meets. The main character searches for love and salva-

tion, but after arriving back home in El Paso, he concludes that redemption is impossible. The themes of alienation and the futility of salvation, as well as Rechy's vivid descriptions of the hustling scene are common in his subsequent works. *Numbers* (1967), another bestseller, follows the exploits of Johnny Rio as he attempts to complete a set number of sexual encounters in Los Angeles and, thus, reestablish meaning in his life. Rechy introduces stylistic techniques and themes in this novel which he further develops in his next novels—*This Day's Death* (1969) and *Rushes* (1979). These novels are both social commentaries on society's treatment of homosexuals as well as explorations of the gay community. *Rushes* looks at life in a leather bar and explores the ideas of submission and dominancy within the gay community. In *The Sexual Outlaw* (1977) Rechy continues to explore stylistic variations. He calls the book a non-fiction novel and it is part social commentary, part novel, part autobiography. In his later work Rechy has dealt more with Chicano issues and characters. *The Miraculous Day of Amalia Gomez* (1991) is his most Hispanic novel to date. While it does not deal with issues of homosexuality, Rechy continues to explore themes of alienation and marginalization from the dominant society. In his later work he has also begun to focus on the role of women in society. *The Miraculous Day, Marilyn's Daughter* (1988), and *Our Lady of Babylon* (1996) all center on female characters struggling with identity issues. Rechy has also written non-fiction articles about Chicano culture for journals and magazines.

Critical Reception

Rechy's first novel *City of Night* sparked a great deal of popular and critical attention. Many critics argued that Rechy's explicit descriptions constituted pornography meant not to edify but only to titillate readers. In addition, other critics believe that Rechy has harmed the public image of the homosexual community by focusing on the undercurrents of the hustling scene. They argue that by writing about characters who are misfits, delinquents, and their emotionally barren lifestyle that Rechy has reenforced society's negative impression of homosexuals. However, the book also produced positive reaction. For instance, Trudy Steuernagel argues that in *City of Night* Rechy portrays homosexuals as political rebels defying society but that in Rechy's subsequent novels his characters only appear as deviants. Rechy's subsequent novels have attracted less attention individually but Rechy has been spotlighted by critics as an Hispanic author who writes about the homosexual experience. Gregory Bredbeck chastizes other critics for failing to pay adequate attention to Rechy's writing style and form. Bredbeck writes: "reviewers have almost universally preferred to criticize the content and ignore the form, as if the topic of homosexuality is, in and of itself, enough to remove the need for artistic judgement." Rechy has most often been compared with James Baldwin. Scholars note that both are homosexuals and members of ethnic minorities, thus creating a double minority. However, many comment that while Baldwin focused primarily on racial issues, that Rechy has deemphasized the Chicano issues to focus on homosexuality in his novels.

PRINCIPAL WORKS

City of Night (novel) 1963
Numbers (novel) 1967
This Day's Death (novel) 1969
The Vampires (novel) 1971
The Fourth Angel (novel) 1973
The Sexual Outlaw: A Documentary. A Non-Fiction Account, with Commentaries, of Three Days and Nights in the Sexual Underground (nonfiction) 1977
Momma as She Was—Not as She Became (play) 1978
Rushes (novel) 1979
Bodies and Souls (novel) 1983
Tigers Wild (play) 1986
Marilyn's Daughter (novel) 1988

The Miraculous Day of Amalia Gomez (novel) 1991
Our Lady of Babylon (novel) 1996

CRITICISM

Lee T. Lemon (review date Fall 1971)

SOURCE: "You May Have Missed These," in *Prairie Schooner*, Vol. 45, No. 3, Fall, 1971, pp. 270-72.

[*In the following excerpt, Lemon argues that* This Day's Death *is made more powerful because Rechy refrains from preaching.*]

Every once in a while, a reviewer is obligated to clear his shelves, which really means discovering books that should have been reviewed long ago. It can be a welcome opportunity for reminding readers of works they might have missed when the publishers were advertising them, but that deserve a life beyond one advertising season. Three of the novels from the back of my shelves—the late 1969 and early 1970 part—deserve such belated attention. *This Day's Death,* by John Rechy, *Salvage,* by Jacqueline Gillott, and *Dirty Pictures from the Prom,* by Earl M. Rauch ought to be rescued from that peculiarly deep abyss into which one-year-old books regularly fall.

Rechy's *This Day's Death* is a very quietly, very precisely intense story of a rather ordinary man awaiting trial for a homosexual act he did not commit. There is very little sensationalism in Rechy's novel (for a change); emphasis is rather on the growing horror as the protagonist, Jim Girard, waits while the courts slowly grind out his fate. On one level, *This Day's Death* has to be read as a low-keyed but disturbing social reform novel. The targets are the police and the courts. Officer Daniels, the chief witness against Girard, is that kind of person who sees his own hang-ups reflected in those around him. He is, to use the jargon phrase, a latent homosexual whose own repressions force him into a misinterpretation of an accidental and essentially innocent encounter between two men. He is not especially brutal, nor especially stupid; but he is a man whose own instability has driven him to become a guardian of other men's morals.

The problem in the courts is quite different, and perhaps in the long run even more serious. The question Rechy poses is: How does it feel to be an innocent man accused of a crime, a man fully confident that he will be cleared, as the months drag on before the case is heard? How does it feel to be an innocent man who comes to realize that his best hope is a guilty plea and a suspended sentence? What is the effect on family, business, friends, fiancee? *This Day's Death* is a powerful novel in part because Rechy has avoided the temptation to preach. Instead, he concentrates on one of the chief jobs of the novelist—that of communicating experience as he believes it to be.

John Rechy with James R. Giles (interview date Summer 1973)

SOURCE: "An Interview with John Rechy," in *Chicago Review,* Vol. 25, No. 1, Summer, 1973, pp. 19-31.

[In the interview below, Rechy discusses his literary influences, style, and the role of homosexuality in his work.]

[Giles]: Would you like to begin by talking about what contemporary writers impress you?

[Rechy]: Thomas Wolfe. And when I was a kid William Faulkner, very much. In fact, when I first started writing, I thought it would be obvious, that people would say, God damn, he's trying to imitate Faulkner. I was also very influenced by *Nightwood,* by Djuna Barnes. I read it when I was a kid, and it influenced me not so much stylistically as in a strange, hallucinative mood that it has. I've never dug Ernest Hemingway—all that heavy posturing.

How about right now?

I admire Norman Mailer. He can do some righteous writing when he's not being a clown. This may surprise you, but I like that ass Nabokov very much.

Why do you call him an ass?

Because of his posturing—all that aristocratic bull; everything I dislike; looking down on all the humanistic things. But I dig him as a writer—*Pale Fire* is a great book.

Capote?

When I was a kid, I dug him.

Did you like Other Voices?

When I was a kid . . . . Carson McCullers has survived for me, especially *Reflections in the Golden Eye* [sic].

Did you read In Cold Blood?

I haven't finished that book; I started it several times. But then Capote was giving his big party, and I thought, somebody who writes a book like that should go into a kind of dignified retirement for a while, because of its subject. Man, you don't make a fucking million dollars out of a tragedy

like that and then give a black-and-white party with Princess Radziwill.

Let's get to your work. I was wondering if you'd talk about the stylistic innovations in the transitional chapters of **City of Night.** *The combination of stream-of-consciousness and straight narrative, and how important you think that is to the book's overall unity.*

Part of *City of Night's* style was determined by the fact that it began literally as a letter I wrote to a friend of mine; and much of the tone of the linking chapters remains very much that of a letter, especially in the earlier versions that I wrote.

Would you say maybe **This Day's Death** *is the most heavily innovative of your books because of the gradual introduction of the stream-of-consciousness?*

I had never thought of it that way. It's so difficult to view one's own work as innovative, because you work from your own head. *City of Night* is more innovative because of the shifts of verb tense within the same sentence—I wanted to give the feeling of memory and present and continuity and past, like when you flash on something, and it becomes so real, in the present, and then it's in the past. Some people were irritated by that, the change from present to past to present, but I wanted that, because it's a time novel. I wanted to duplicate memory. Because I was recalling things in my own life, and they were real; and yet I was writing about them now in the present, and they were past. And then the odd capitalization.

I was going to ask about that.

It was nothing that I consciously sat down to do. It just happened. I don't know how to explain it.

You capitalize the word "escape."

Oh, in every book. Like that's what life is about—trying to Escape. (Laughter.) Yeah, I've dropped the odd capitalization because it fitted very much with *City of Night,* and some of it in *Numbers* and *This Day's Death,* but less. There's hardly any of it in *The Vampires,* with the exception of Escape. . . . And you know—unrelated—there's a phrase that appears in every one of my books and will probably appear in every book I write; that's "No substitute for salvation." That's one of the major themes of my writing—the search for a substitute for salvation. There isn't one, and that's the existential nightmare.

In the last two books, you've done more of the gradual providing of information than you had in the first two, and that seems in some ways more innovative than the first two were.

I was learning techniques. *City of Night* was anarchy in its own way, to convey the anarchy of the life I was writing about. Yet I worked very hard on that effect, rewrote it many times. Overall, it has a very good concrete shape.

I think so, and I think each story is beautifully formed.

Yeah, I think so too.

I got terribly romantic about that book [*Numbers*], I thought I'd die before I finished it. It was a fierce compulsion, the same drive, the same sexual drive of the hunt, that was projected into the writing.
—*John Rechy*

Numbers *has always seemed to me the most traditionally, rigidly formed of the four books. In an almost kind of classical way.*

Yeah! I dig your saying that. It's the best structured book I've done; I really shaped it quite consciously. The bummer about its reception was that people were so freaked about the sex in that they thought it was a sex book and that's all—people being superior to sex and all that bullshit; I hate people to be superior to sex, man, because sex is overwhelming in our lives. . . . *Numbers* was very carefully structured, everything was outlined, every chapter, with the exception of the first one, which I wrote, believe it or not, literally while I drove out of Los Angeles to El Paso, with my mother holding the writing pad on the console and I steering with one hand, writing with the other. I got terribly romantic about that book, I thought I'd die before I finished it. It was a fierce compulsion, the same drive, the same sexual drive of the hunt, that was projected into the writing. I wrote it in exactly three months of intense writing. With one very notable exception, all the hunters described in it are real, they were fresh on my memory—and then sometimes, as with Johnny Rio, they would fade, recur, fade. The strange man who follows Johnny Rio—the man who drives the red car—he's totally made up; he wears sunglasses which become mirrored glasses—and he becomes younger and more attractive as the book proceeds. And he's death. As Johnny Rio's existential trip progresses, death becomes more and more attractive to him.

Would you say you use the homosexual in the same way the existentialist writer uses the concept of the outsider, the totally alienated being?

Yeah, right. To me there's no more alienated figure than the homosexual. It's the only minority against whose existence there are laws. There's no law against being black, or Jew-ish, or anything else; but there are laws against being homosexual. You might say, well, that's not true; there are laws against homosexual *acts*. But how do you define homosexuality other than by the act? The homosexual is the clearest symbol of alienation and despair. And nobility.

Talk about that.

Nobility? I mean, just to survive against all the bullshit they put on us: the law telling us we're criminals, religion telling us we're sinners, psychiatrists telling us we're sick. And yet, how the hell have they dared make us feel we have to hide when we've produced the greatest paintings, the greatest writing? Even generals—but you can have them. It takes a hell of a lot to survive all the crap, and not only to survive but then to produce great art as a result of our unique sensibility and sensuality—and it is unique. We have every reason to be proud. So I think that the homosexual as hero is a good symbol.

How particularly is the ending of **Numbers** *an example of existential nothingness?*

Numbers ends with a cry of absolute despair; it's like a geometric progression that has no end, and Johnny Rio will of course just simply go on. That last chapter in *Numbers* is meant to be a descent into a private hell, Johnny descends into a subterranean area of Griffith Park. And I meant to create a vision of hell. The last words are screamed out because the nightmare has shaped and will just continue until the final absurdity—death.

What would you want to say to people who accuse that book of being strictly pornography?

That they have a problem.

I said and still think that it's an intensely moral, if not religious, book.

Right. And religious. Johnny Rio's despair is religious. He finds no substitute for salvation. The only way he can feel alive is through sexual contact. And since that requires more and more, like a drug, he traps himself in his nightmare. The deeper he gets, the more numbers he needs. And sex is a metaphor—Johnny chooses sex because that's the only thing that makes him feel alive. Otherwise he feels dead.

Will you talk a little more about the religious element in your fiction, the symbolism?

I was brought up a Catholic, and that's a heavy trip. I don't know if you've noticed the importance of confession in all my books. *City of Night* itself is a confession—and one of the last scenes is of the narrator trying to find a confessor, which I tried to do, in New Orleans—and I encountered all those bummer priests that weren't about to be awakened: you know, my God, if you're frantic, why aren't you frantic during office hours? . . . It's a very confessional book in the sense of experiences, but it's also confessional at the end where the narrator finally finds a priest who will listen over the telephone. Then of course *Numbers* is also a confessional book in content, but there's also the reference to Johnny compulsively wanting to explain and find reasons—the scene out in the Santa Monica Canyon. And there's the reference to his having as a child gone to bed praying the rosary, which I used to do, and to the numbers of the beads. Again, the phrase "no substitute for salvation." And then *This Day's Death* is also confessional—beyond the fact that the trial is presented within such a frame. And in *The Vampires* the major scene is when they play a game of confessions. In my next book—*The Fourth Angel*—four children invade a church, and a girl plays confessor, and the other children confess for the people that have fucked them over . . . . Religion is a powerful influence in my writing. There's one brief scene in *City of Night* during Mardi Gras when the narrator is enveloped by a Satan figure in costume. Then he frees himself, and the next thing he sees is a very awesome cathedral. *City of Night* is a kind of trip through Purgatory; the existential trap is that finally there's no Heaven after Purgatory. . . . And the black woman in *Numbers* that proclaims doom; Johnny Rio clings to a kind of religious hope through her—because as long as she's there to *proclaim* doom, there's still hope. And there's the gypsy woman in *City of Night*— . . .

Well, then the statue of Christ, of course.

The statue of Christ, the pilgrimage to the Christ statue. They abound. In *This Day's Death,* there's the Madonna, the Mother of Sorrows, which my beautiful mother loved so much. And the strange, mystic lady who comes to stay with them. And in *City of Night,* when the narrator is hustling for the first time, he sees a drawing on the wall, and he flashes on a woman—a madonna, a mother; and then he pulls his eyes away. Of course you know that the Virgin, the Virgin of Guadalupe, is very enormous in Mexican life.

And then there's the priest in **The Vampires.**

Probably *The Vampires* is my most religious book.

Talk about that.

The whole is built around the confession, and Wanda picked upon this. It's set in hell. A vision of hell: If Satan does extract confessions for his permission to enter hell, wouldn't one then confess the worst? And these people have come to pour out the worst. Someone says that God begins to look like Satan, "like lovers." And I conceived of Richard as a

Satan—God figure—and he actually wants these people to resist his evil.

Would you say he becomes in a way also kind of pathetic?
Yes. He's destroyed when it's revealed that he's in search of purity. And every one of the characters is looking for purity. And they haven't found it. All the characters in it are evil.

Including Valerie?

Including Valerie; Valerie's may be the ultimate evil, which can't face itself.

Yeah, I thought so; but would you explain why she is?

I wanted different interpretations. Valerie may have hallucinated her incestuous love for her brother, and unable to face it she therefore kills him. But it's also possible that Valerie is the only one who isn't evil—if indeed she does know that her brother is becoming one of the vampires, has sucked her blood; and in order to save his soul, to exorcise it, she murders him.

But that would still make purity a hate-filled thing, wouldn't it?

It would make it a driven, black thing, where the soul is violently triumphant. But a case could be made that Valerie finally is the only pure one because she kills in order to save her brother and therefore sacrifices her own soul—because there is the thing that in her mind she has saved him, there's blood on his body, the blood she drew, but not on his lips—which she sees on the others. And so they are evil, but in her mind she may have purified her brother. Valerie is either the most evil or the only pure one. I suspect she's the most evil.

Are you supposed to feel at the end that Mark will now become Malissa's rival?

Yes, because Richard is through. The real battle is between Mark and Malissa now. The imagery of the tarantulas is meant to refer to Richard. The priest remembers the tarantulas he ran over in the desert, and he remembers them as pitiful in their evil, but it was an isolated evil; if unstirred, it would remain dormant. Richard stirs the evil and is therefore himself evil, even though he does it to find purity.

One of the things that has impressed both of us about your writing is the tremendous compassion that we think you feel, and that the reader feels, for your characters. We felt this less in **The Vampires** *than in the other books.*

When I was a kid and I would see anyone begging or in pain,

that would send me into despair; I would cry and cry. Even now too much contact can destroy me. . . . All the characters in *City of Night* are modeled after real people; and often, I think, Well, God damn, I wrote about them and I put down their lives into a book; but where is Chuck, where is Skipper, where is Pete? Miss Destiny? Chi-Chi? That destroys me. But the compassion in *The Vampires* is of a different sort because that book begins when all compassion has ended; Richard is destroyed by the revelation of his vulnerability. I think all the characters are very tragic.

How about the grotto imagery in the three last novels?

Yes, the grottos do recur. In *Numbers* they refer to actual places in Griffith Park; and Jim Girard gets busted in one of the places Johnny Rio frequents. There's the grotto in *The Vampires*. I suppose psychologically that has to do with the same reason I always capitalize Escape. A feeling of a trap within a symbolic grotto, alcove. Life is a trap. I'm sure that's what the grottos are. The enclosure of life focusing in on the scene.

Is popular music, like rock especially, any influence?

Yes; very much. When I was writing *City of Night,* I saturated myself with what at the time was called rock-'n-roll because I wanted to get some of the restless, reckless beat. I was never into jazz, always into rock.

Did you understand what I meant by my idea in the letter that you use the concept of the vanished frontier as a lost symbol of innocence?

In *City of Night*—Chuck the cowboy who is really a make-believe cowboy moves to Los Angeles; in another time he would have been in search of the frontier. He wants a horse; he really wants the open spaces. But there's no more frontier. He rips off a horse and gets busted and ends up in jail. And he can't find his horse, and he ends up in Los Angeles utterly bewildered by his world with no frontier. . . . But beyond that, my books all tend to move toward the faded frontier, which is west: Los Angeles. And I have long thought, consciously and intellectually, that when the frontier ended, one started moving in. Because there was no more physical movement out, and now there was the movement inward.

Are you conscious of how that does tie in with sexual exploration?

That's really far out. Yeah—like Johnny Rio also explores a new country, and maybe Johnny Rio would at one time have been exploring a jungle, and now he's exploring a sexual jungle. That's far out. One of the aspects of good questions is that they also illuminate one's writing, too; that

hadn't occurred to me, but, yeah, the exploration—the sexual exploration—replaces the territorial exploration.

You know, in **Numbers** *Johnny Rio will consciously park his car with the Texas license plates showing.*

Right, yeah, that's right, man; really far out.

Then you do feel that the Southwestern locale is an influence to you?

Really. Very much.

But then do you feel the Southwest is a repressive area toward art and creativity?

Sure. The Texas establishment wants you to be, and stay, safe.

Do you feel it's getting more repressive?

Yes, all over the country. There was a time when it seemed to be righteously loosening up, real freedom; but now, man, it's scary, you can really feel it. Can't you? You're more afraid, not as free. There was a time when at least you felt it was possible to be free. But no more.

Which Texas writers do you especially like?

Of course Larry McMurtry. And I think Elroy Bode is one of the very, very best; a beautiful writer. Terry Southern is good. And I haven't read Donald Barthelme, but I want to.

I'm glad you refer to Donald Barthelme as a Texas writer; we have a controversy at Northern about whether he's a Texas writer or a real writer.

What a bummer.

Something occurred to me after what you said about repression. I'd like to ask to what degree you feel the novelist should be a moral spokesman, as opposed to a didacticist?

I don't think *City of Night* is a social protest novel, to use that awful phrase; nor is **Numbers**. And yet **This Day's Death** is in part. I did want to expose an unbelievable evil that still exists—an evil that can spring on anyone at any time.

But now **The Vampires** *is very much not a novel of protest.*

Maybe moral protest.

Do you think you'll get back into some kind of social protest of the same kind you used in **This Day's Death** *again?*

Never quite like that.

That was such a personal thing?

Right.

In regard to that, do you see American society nationally becoming more repressive?

It's so clear that it is, man. Everything is poisoned. All that is ugly is out. There were a few years in the 60's—and I think Kennedy was important as a symbol, the spirit of Kennedy more than the man—hopeful years when it looked like things might be all right. But I think that these are the nightmare days now. The Supreme Court for one thing. Ominous.

What kind of effect do you think that will have on writers?

The message goes out: Be cautious. I'm sure it's being felt by everyone in the arts.

You think that will be destructive to the arts?

Of course! Look at Agnew and his hatred of intellectuals— not that intellectuals shouldn't be hated, sometimes, but not for the reasons he does.

How does that make you feel, to be warned to be cautious?

Personally I won't be cautious.

Could it make you move more into social protest?

It might . . . . I've never gone out to look for something to write about as a sort of protest; I've always experienced it first.

Do you think that, if this wave of repression hits, homosexuals will be the victims even more than in the past?

Yes. You know, Hitler practiced on homosexuals before he went on to the Jews. Homosexuals are attacked easily because no one else cares—not even other minorities.

Do you see yourself writing more things like your Texas Observer *and* Nation *articles if this wave of repression gets stronger?*

I'm sure of it.

Do you get a special sense of gratification out of doing this type of article?

Yeah, but I hate to do it, man. I do it only, you know, like when I'm driven by what I see. Articles bum me out, writing them—I'd rather the house fell in.

In your fiction both father and mother figures seem tremendously important and to fit into a pattern. Can you talk about them in terms of their thematic significance, particularly in the first three books?

I don't know that I could isolate them into a thematic significance. They were the most powerful figures in my life— my beautiful mother with her lovely gentleness and love, and our huge love for each other; and my father with all his ugly violence, a terrifying figure. They were opposites, and so in my books they always appear as opposites.

I feel that the tenderness vs. violence motif merges into a kind of spirit-flesh thing in your fiction.

Wow. That's a good observation.

On the flesh-spirit thing, the one problem I have with **City of Night** *is the dog symbolism.*

It works on two levels. I did have a dog named Winnie. She did indeed die during a windstorm; we did indeed bury her, and we did indeed have to dig her up when the body began to decay. And I was just a child at the time; it was a hideous experience, to watch my dog decaying. And I was told from all that Catholic bullshit that animals don't go to heaven because they have no souls . . . . That's the one level, the level of reality. Beyond that, there's the fact that this is the narrator's first contact with the existential horror. As long as you can cling to the concept of the soul, there's a meaning to this shit, but when you exclude the soul—when you see the body rotting after death—all there is is death; not only death, but decay—physical decay, like my dog. Symbolically, the boy's innocence is buried when the dog is reburied, decaying, soulless.

So that you'd say the ending of the book—

—makes a complete circle. The last line is a cry of despair: "It isn't fair! *Why can't dogs go to heaven?*" By that, the narrator is saying that nothing is fair, that all is meaningless. If dogs can't go to heaven, and life is ended in decay, there's no soul, it's all rot, just a decayed body. It's the final scream of sorrow.

It's a statement of a realization that there is no such thing as a soul.

That there is no such thing. No soul.

Then one tremendous symbol that I think probably is an existential symbol is the wind.

Well, you've experienced the wind, the Texas wind, and its desolation. The wind goes on for days and there's a relentless stripping of our soul, as if the wind is physically tearing at you. I remember the wind as an echo of angry childhood.

It's part of the symbol for impermanence.

Yes—the arbitrary shifting, just shifting away, bringing and taking, like death too, just arbitrary shifting, moving on.

Why don't you just talk about **The Fourth Angel** *now?*

Okay. I'll probably never do another book like *The Vampires;* that was a flashback because I had done a similar book when I was a kid. It was called *Pablo!*—and there were witches and spirits in it. Now *City of Night, Numbers,* and *This Day's Death* are pretty autobiographical—and that doesn't deny their artistic creation. I'm not just a reporter. I mean, so what if you use "reality", you still have to put it down and give it order. For example, although *Numbers* is very much a record of a trip I took to Los Angeles—a pilgrimage—by the time I set it down, the figures and the incidents became symbolic, too, they have other meanings, and you can't be put down as a reporter. There's the structure, the organization. Anyway, those first three books are somewhat of a trilogy. In *The Fourth Angel,* I've returned in a strange way to the autobiographical; but I've turned the characters into children—sixteen-year-olds. Many of my own experiences—I put on a sixteen-year-old boy. There are four main characters, three boys and a girl. They go on what they call experience trips; each feels a great bitterness. At first they appear cruel and cold. But then there is the revelation of their own pain.

It's set in El Paso again.

Yes, in a period of two days. They experiment with people to find out, as they say, where the shit is, and they do some very cruel things. A kind of initiation to immunize themselves from the pain they feel. But they can't Escape it, finally. And again there are the symbols: Confession plays an important part; there's the symbol of a church window depicting an angel grappling with evil. The four experiment with drugs—acid, mescaline, cocaine.

How important is the homosexual theme?

It's not as major as in my first three books, but it is still very powerful, submerged. . . . Now I'm working on two books:

one is called *Autobiography, a Novel*—and it deals with the varying persona of autobiography as novel, novel as autobiography; in it I'm returning to the first-person account, as in *City of Night.* And it explores shifting identities, and varying "truths." I'm also working on a novel called *Jesus and Judas,* which depicts the betrayal as based on a homosexual affair between Jesus and Judas.

Don't you expect some really God reviews doing that?

Why shouldn't Jesus be depicted as a homosexual? Why should he be less if he was a homosexual? There are all the elements: Mary as powerful mother, Joseph as vague father. The book opens with John the Baptist baptising a revivalist-type crowd by the Jordan River. Mary appears, leading a beautiful 15-year-old child, John is dazzled; he says to the boy: "I have need to be baptized by you." The boy laughs, and in my version it's Mary who says: "This is my beloved Son," and it is John who answers: "In Whom I am well pleased." Another young man is romping in the water—Judas; Jesus and Judas disappear. Along the banks of the river, they begin to wrestle, and soon the motions of wrestling become the motions of lovemaking. Playfully they roam the streets, while John goes about proclaiming the coming of the Messiah. The two young men meet Mary Magdalene while she is being persecuted by a mob. By pretending he's the savior, Jesus frees her; she leads them to a hill where they eat hallucinogenic buds. It's then that many of the Biblical revelations occur to Jesus—especially the temptation by Satan—so many Biblical things are like acid trips, incidentally. At a time of great hallucinated vulnerability, Mary tells Jesus he's the son of God, divinely conceived. It's at that point that Jesus, who with Judas has been roaming about with revolutionaries, abandons his humanity and becomes religiously obsessed. Judas betrays him with a kiss. . . . My Jesus in this book is extremely beautiful, and sexual at first. That's what has always bummed me out about the Jesus they force on us, a sexless man. Mine in this book is very sexual. He and Judas and Magdalene, tripping on the hallucinogenic buds, make beautiful sex, all naked, rubbing mud on each other. . . . And I shift back and forth to the Palace of Herod; Salome is a ten-year-old painted child, Herod is impotent, Salome tries to arouse him; if she can, he'll give her what she wants, and she asks for the head of John the Baptist.

Will this book be as heavily existential as the others?

Yes; Jesus as existential figure; but in order to save himself from the black revelation of extinction, he moves to the messianic acceptance of himself, his resurrection.

Okay. I see a lot of Tennessee Williams in your bookcases. Is he an influence?

Absolutely. What I like about him is the giant dragon emotions; the raging emotions; the screaming about life.

You like Streetcar?

Very much. But I think his best play is *Suddenly Last Summer.*

Why?

It's the one that is fully realized, that moves relentlessly to violence and doesn't move back. *Streetcar* backs away from the building violence—it ends subdued, cowed. *Suddenly Last Summer* doesn't cop out; it moves to that hideous violence.

Would you get into what you feel generally about the academic world and its relationship to literature in general and to your literature in particular.

In general I think it has about as much relationship to literature as it has to life: zero. But that's exaggerated: I know several teachers in universities who are very fine, alive, relevant. . . . I know some of my writing is required reading in some schools.

Does that please you?

It depends on the course and who teaches it.

So you like your books to be taught if in the right courses by the right people.

Yes. But it would bum me out if some straight guy would try to get into my stuff unless, of course, that meant his head was changing, but I don't think that would happen; I think for anybody to become interested in my work in the academic world their heads would already have to be in pretty good shape; I mean in the sense of my material.

Do you know whether **City of Night** *is taught very much in universities?*

I know it's required in some.

One thing that struck me when you were talking about Baldwin having a double consciousness, being black and homosexual, comes up again. Couldn't you say you have a dual consciousness too?

Absolutely: homosexual and Chicano. I think it makes for a special sensibility.

Do you want to say anything about the Chicano movement?

I feel very much a part of it; but I also feel I've been much more important to the homosexual movement because of my books than I have been to the Chicano movement, although most of my articles are about the Chicano minority . . . . It's pretty heavy, being a Chicano in Texas; you certainly know what it's like to be hated when you're a kid. Mine was a peculiar trip. My father was of Scot descent—and sometimes people would start putting Mexicans down right in front of me, and so I had to get into hassles; and then defensively I'd go around telling people right away that I was Mexican . . . . Especially in the small hickish towns, the fucking Texans are so ignorant in all their weird bigotry, so ugly in their hatred.

We've gotten through all these questions except one. When I was in John Graves' creative-writing class he said a writer, because he's one person, must in effect choose some aspect of reality and then through art make that his reality, and how do you dig that?

I think it's probably true in my case. I don't know that one can use one aspect of reality. When the aspect which one focuses on is so overwhelming—like for example being black or Chicano or homosexual in America—I think that holds true . . . . Right now there are beautiful things happening among homosexuals—the openness of identity, no longer hiding—although we have our own "Uncle Toms," but it's necessary to pity them. The journey to finally identify oneself as a homosexual—it's a heavy one, man—and a great relief finally to be able to identify yourself openly. Have you ever had an experience so relieving that— . . .

I don't think so; I've always been a part of every establishment majority.

Wow, what a bummer. Now's the time for minorities to feel sorry for you, man!

But I think I can understand how you feel.

Finally to assert oneself as a homosexual—that's liberating as a member of a minority that has produced some of the greatest men and women in the world. Not that everything about the homosexual world as it exists now is beautiful—it would be dishonest to say that; it can be a cruel world.

That's the feeling one gets from your books.

I know—and that's freaked out a lot of people. But I was being honest—and I was writing about a segment of that world which I know and which can be savage. But that doesn't indict the homosexual. It largely indicts all the ignorance we've had to overcome. And what a battle!

James R. Giles (essay date November 1974)

SOURCE: "Religious Alienation and 'Homosexual Consciousness' in *City of Night* and *Go Tell It on the Mountain*," in *College English*, Vol. 36, No. 3, November, 1974, pp. 369-80.

[*In the following essay, Giles compares Rechy's* City of Night *with James Baldwin's* Go Tell It on the Mountain, *arguing that Rechy's work has greater significance because it emphasizes homosexuality over ethnicity.*]

When it appeared in 1963, John Rechy's *City of Night* received much critical acclaim; and it has continued to be regarded as an "underground classic." However, much of the praise for the novel has carried an implication of artlessness—too often critics have discussed it in terminology that would restrict it to the level of "reporting." It is obvious that a part of *City of Night's* initial impact was due to its detailed account of a "side of life" largely excluded from American letters. Such a frank, even brutal narrative of homosexual hustling was new and unprecedented. In addition, Rechy's personal image has encouraged a tendency to view the novel as sensational "reporting." Rechy is half-Chicano, half-Anglo; he was born into poverty in El Paso; he has been a hustler; he is a devotee of the beautiful body. He, like the unnamed main character in *City of Night,* has had a personal vision of nihilistic horror during Mardi Gras.

It is not surprising that critics often discuss Rechy's first book as if it were simply autobiography disguised as fiction, but it is a vast oversimplification to do so. Like Thomas Wolfe, whom he greatly admires, Rechy is an artist and not a reporter. *City of Night* is built around a complex, definable structure. The device of shifting between "subjective" chapters focusing upon the central character and "objective" chapters concerned with persons met by the narrator-hustler is comparable to the structure of *The Grapes of Wrath* and of much of Dos Passos' writing. It is interesting that Rechy admires Steinbeck and Dos Passos and that they too have suffered from critics who want to label them as social commentators rather than artists. The key to the art of *City of Night* is the relationship between the "subjective" and the "objective" chapters. A war is raging in the should of the central character, and its resolution is made possible by his interaction with the "minor" characters who appear throughout. Probably a major factor in the failure of most critics to comprehend this structure is the aesthetic completeness of the "objective" chapters. The Miss Destiny and Sylvia chapters, for instance, work so successfully as short stories that it is possible to miss their importance to the main character's spiritual struggle.

The organizing motif of the novel is the "confession," and each "objective" chapter should be seen as essentially a con-

fession of pain and suffering. It is crucial that these confessions of personal horror are spontaneously delivered to the central character, because his reaction to them is the real thematic basis of *City of Night*.

> The key to the art of *City of Night* is the relationship between the "subjective" and the "objective" chapters. A war is raging in the should of the central character, and its resolution is made possible by his interaction with the "minor" characters who appear throughout.
> —*James R. Giles*

When he leaves El Paso, he believes that he has denied virtually everything—Catholicism, any ultimate hope for personal "salvation," self-pity, and even compassion for others. The brutality of death has so horrified him that it alone seems a reality worthy of confrontation. It is almost inevitable that he adopt the hustler role because it allows him to receive tribute to the beauty of his body without the necessity of any reciprocation. He is determined to give nothing, to receive everything. By the end of the novel, he has come to a kind of epiphany—a spiritual realization that he cannot deny his compassion for others. This internal shift comes about gradually and only after a great deal of pain.

Having been intrigued for some time by the highly complex art of *City of Night* (as well as *Numbers* and *This Day's Death,* I asked in 1971 for an interview with Rechy. He granted my request, although he did not customarily do interviews, largely because of an intelligent and calm review of *This Day's Death* which my wife had written for a Texas periodical. Wanda Giles and I flew to El Paso in January, 1972; and, because Rechy is an extremely kind man, we were rewarded with not only the interview, but a two-day talk with him and several drives through El Paso and Juarez and a visit with a writer friend of Rechy whom we had always admired. (Interview Published in *Chicago Review*, 25 [Summer, 1973], 19-31).

The result of the experience was a seemingly contradictory one—it made me more aware than ever of the strong autobiographical element in *City of Night,* and it heightened my appreciation of the artistic complexity of the novel's structure. Such a result was possible largely because Rechy is equally eloquent in discussing his past (most especially the brutal and painful times) and his art.

II

There is a statue of Christ on a mountain (Cristo Rey) outside El Paso, and as Rechy, Wanda, and I stood on the road below it, John talked:

> *I used to go up there, right to the foot of that statue when I was a kid. It's not safe any more, you can get robbed now, but when I was a kid you could go, all the way up. Christ, religion, you know are so fucking important in a Chicano kid's life . . . .*

Religion, especially Catholicism, is extremely important in *City of Night*. The church in the novel is a destructive force which imposes unnatural restraints and a false concept of "sin" upon man and lies to him about immortality. Catholicism attempts to repress sexuality except for the purpose of procreation. Rechy views such a teaching as unforgivable on two levels. Sex, the most powerful force in life, should not be seen as something existing merely to serve another purpose. Moreover, children born to the destitute are doomed to lives of hunger and suffering.

A critical early scene in *City of Night* involves the narrator's seduction of a girl "up the mountain of Cristo Rey, dominated at the top by the coarse, well-surrounded statue of a primitive-faced Christ." This introduction to sex is anything but a joyous experience for the narrator ("And it was somewhere about that time that the narcissistic pattern of my life began.") In fact, intercourse with the girl beneath the "primitive" Christ serves primarily to isolate sex as the focal point of the narrator's rebellion against his repressive and suffocating childhood. Two personalities epitomize the polarities of the narrator's experience: his father, who in paranoia over a shattered musical career lashes out in hatred at everyone around him, then later approaches them with a warped, pathetic overture of "love"; and his mother, who offers a "blind carnivorous love" which is ultimately more damaging than the father's hatred. The father's failures as a musician, and most significantly as a man, are responsible for the poverty and the horror of the narrator's childhood. He causes a child to be brought into the world, offers him nothing approaching love or understanding, attempts to stab him with a butcher knife, and then in grotesque remorse takes the child on his knee in a terrifying ritual of "affection." Thus, he represents the world as the child sees it; he is reality—destitute, self-pitying, and hating.

The mother's "carnivorous love" is even more to be feared. She gives herself sexually to the husband, and then attempts to protect her children from the horror into which they are born. Repeatedly giving her body to the hate-filled musician, she attempts to keep her soul untouched. She wants to envelop her children in that undefiled soul so that they will not see the danger so relentlessly threatening them. It is as if each child she brings into the world represents another opportunity to triumph vicariously over the poverty and pain of her life. In addition, she is giving another soul to that

church she loves so much (her room is filled with Madonnas).

The "protection" she forces upon her children is more insidious than the father's open hatred precisely because it is based upon a lie. Poverty is a constant in the children's lives; and reality sometimes strikes with the deadly, unmistakable immediacy of a butcher knife. Thus it is suicidal to hide, and the mother is attempting to send her children defenseless and completely vulnerable into the horror personified by their father. Moreover, the church itself is based upon an unforgiveable lie—the denial of death. While the mother accepts the immortality of the soul as a doctrine so self-evident that questions about it are absurd, the narrator bitterly and painfully rejects any such belief. The death and subsequent decay of his dog, Winnie, are the catalyst for his repudiation of the mother's faith. The dog dies, is buried, and is then uncovered by a Texas windstorm. During the animal's illness the mother says: "Dogs don't go to Heaven, they haven't got souls . . . the body just disappears, becomes dirt." When the child sees the decayed body, he acknowledges much more than she intended: "There was no soul, the body would rot, and there would be Nothing left of Winnie." Or of any man or woman. The soul is a lie, immortality is a lie; death and nothingness are the only truths.

> *I suggested to John that either I didn't understand the Winnie incident, or that it was not sufficient to carry such a heavy symbolic load. He answered that the episode was real. He did have a dog named Winnie, it did die, was uncovered by the West Texas wind, and he did see the rotting carcass; and he did react in the manner described in the novel: "I knew then that all the crap about the immortal soul was a lie, man. That there is no salvation, and that all anyone does is attempt to find a substitute for salvation, and there isn't any. By the way, that's a phrase that will appear in every one of my books: no substitute for salvation."*

The maternal "protection" must be spurned. Reality must not only be confronted, but defied. A meaningless act of sex under the very eyes of Christ is the narrator's initial movement away from his mother's "carnivorous love." "Dry lust" performed on a desolate landscape beneath a "dead god." The narrator embraces what his mother and her church would define as "sin" in order to confront reality. There is no pleasure in the experience partly because that was never its purpose. In addition, while it begins his rejection of his mother and her church, it is not nearly sufficient as a rebellion against the father and the world he personifies. "The narcissistic pattern" of his life begins here because the narrator must exact homage from the reality that has always treated him viciously and will ultimately kill him. Before he is a decaying corpse, his personal beauty must be celebrated, again and again. He cannot give (in the brutality of his childhood, he has given too much already), but he must receive. People must perpetually recognize and desire the beauty of his body.

Thus begins his life as a homosexual hustler. The narrator has his first homosexual experience in a bus station in Dallas, but hustling inevitably will be "escape" from the moment that "the narcissistic pattern" began. Hustling offers the kind of gratification he demands: money paid by strangers for the privilege of his body, no necessity for any responsiveness on his part, and innumerable anonymous "contacts." The pattern of the novel takes the form then of a quest which can never end except in death. The narrator's odyssey from El Paso to New York to Los Angeles to Chicago and, finally, to New Orleans represents his defiance of that ugliness and death personified by his father. Death will, of course, ultimately triumph and his body decay; but, before that, he will have exacted tribute for his transitory beauty.

He is determined to be faithful to the code of the hustler—to be passive, to give nothing except his body. But he can never totally succeed. Deny it as he might, the narrator possesses a compassion so strong that nothing can finally destroy it—not even himself. Despite the detached and unresponsive manner in which he engages in sex, he hears confessions from the other characters. There is something in him which occasions sudden outpourings of grief and pain from others—the recitals of what his mother's church would call "sins," but which he recognizes instead as statements of desperate combat with the same reality he is defying. For most of the book, he is puzzled by, and ashamed of, this compassion. In New York, when Pete and "the Professor" suddenly and unpredictably ask for a commitment of feeling from the narrator, he retreats. The retreat is understood as an inevitability by all involved—Pete and the central character mutually shun each other, and "the Professor" knows that he has lost his most recent "angel." Hustlers give no emotion: they take money. (John said that one early reviewer of *City of Night* was disappointed with the novel "'because it failed to show the total homosexual experience.' I never meant it to, of course. It is a book about hustling, one segment of the homosexual world. Can you imagine anyone asking a book to show the total heterosexual experience?") Still, the narrator cannot deny that something in him encourages self-revelation from others.

The journey to California is, in part, an attempt to become the "total hustler" and to suppress this compassion. Geographical distance doesn't change anything that easily, of course. Miss Destiny tells him her personal nightmare:

> Oh, God! . . . Sometimes when Im very high and sitting maybe at the 1-2-3, I imagine that an angel suddenly appears and stands on the balcony where the

band is playing—and the angel says, "All right, boys and girls, this is it, the world is ending, and Heaven or Hell will be to spend eternity just as you are now, in the same place, among the same people—*Forever!*" And hearing this, Im terrified and I know suddenly what that means—and I start to run but I cant run fast enough for the evil angel, he sees me and stops me and Im Caught . . . .

Rechy has read *No Exit* and acknowledges Sartre as an influence. What is most important in Miss Destiny's nightmare, however, is her negative vision of "angels" and "Heaven." "Angels" to her are as "evil" as his mother's church is to the narrator. Only "the Professor's" mortal "angels" are positive. Next it is Chuck who confides in the narrator—he talks about his dream of "escape" to a frontier. The narrator knows only too well the reality of Chuck's fantasized west.

But the main character continues to struggle against his compassion—one can scarcely be a priest and a complete hustler at the same time. He wins an initial victory in Los Angeles when, after much hesitation, he is able to rob a "score" who virtually begs to be robbed. However, San Francisco's sado-masochistic community is the setting for his ultimate attempt to destroy his decency. Borrowing terminology from his mother, he describes his abortive journey into the s-m community as "a suicide of the soul." The Neil chapter represents the novel's turning point, for it is with the masochist Neil that the central character comes the closest to repudiating all feeling and compassion. For a while, Neil's weakness affects the narrator just as they both wish it to—it stimulates anger and the desire to inflict pain. But only for a while, because the narrator ultimately must leave Neil's world. The departure cannot be delayed after Neil, suddenly, unaccountably, confesses to the narrator. The masochist's story of a hated, brutal father parallels the "youngman's" life and, of course, he can only walk out of Neil's apartment in helpless, bewildered pity.

After the encounter with Neil, the narrator no longer wants to run from his "priestly" side. Ironically, Neil represented the one truly "liberating" experience in his life. After Neil, he can no longer deny a bond with humanity and a concern for the pains of all the frightened, lonely people in all "the cities of night." Neil, too, had had a father who failed him brutally. Everyone is united in suffering:

> And I know what it is I have searched beyond Neil's immediate world of sought pain—something momentarily lost—something found again in the park, the fugitive rooms, the derelict jungles: the world of uninvited, unasked-for pain . . . found now, liberatingly, even in the memory of Neil himself.

> And I could think in that moment, for the first time really:

It's possible to hate the filthy world and still love it with an abstract pitying love.

He is still a hustler, but, in non-sexual moments, he now wants to hear the "confessions" of others if doing so will ease their pain. In New Orleans he encourages Sylvia to admit having denied her homosexual son; and he comforts the dying drag queen Kathy in every way he can. The world is still "ugly," but the people in it are to be "pitied," and even "loved" (if only "abstractly") rather than despised. There is much left to be repudiated—in effect, the faceless, all-powerful society which has labelled some people as "criminals" or "diseased" simply because their sexual appetites fall outside the accepted "norm." Sylvia was once a part of that society, and she destroyed her son by her acceptance of its vicious intolerance. She has been doing penance for the only real "sin" (denying another's human worth) ever since:

> God damn it—I don't give a damn! Either in makeup, either like a queen—in the highest, brightest screaming drag—with sequins and beads— . . . . Either like that—or hustling a score, trying to prove with another man, because of my . . . words still ringing in his ears—trying that way to prove that I was right, that he *is* a man . . . . Even— . . . even if he has to prove it by finding another man who will pay him for his . . . masculinity— . . . . Even with a bloody gash on his head, proving it by violence. That way . . . or with another youngman, his— lover— . . . . Any way! Any shape! I don't give a damn! . . . .It's just that—*God damn it!*—I want to see him—if only once more—just once—to tell him—to tell him Im sorry.

When Mardi Gras explodes, the narrator is confronted with an intense vision of horror that almost destroys him. Mardi Gras is a "celebration" which allows homosexuals (even the drag queen) to come out from hiding without fear of legal reprisals; however, they pay a perhaps more degrading penalty. The "tourists" come to view "the gay world" in precisely the spirit in which they would go to a freak show. The queens, always desperate for attention, get it by posing grotesquely for the flashing cameras of Des Moines, Birmingham, and Tulsa ("Miss Ange, in Scarlett O'Hara plantation tones, says to the man taking pictures: 'Now me! Take *My* picture!' . . . Muttering 'bitch,' the other queens glare at Miss Ange as she poses in *her* billowing ballgown—as if she has just returned, triumphantly, to Tara.")

The narrator attempts to drown his vision of the chaotic, dehumanizing nightmare in an orgy of anonymous sex. The attempt fails, and he is reminded of the inevitability of death and decay more strongly than at any time since his childhood:

> A band of red-dressed men and women in black-tentacled masks dance prematurely in the maddened street—red like flashing rubies crushed together, angry flames burning insanely bright before turning into smoke. Redly . . . . Roses pressed against each other in screaming shapes of red, red shrieking red. And like a flock of startled red-winged bats, the group disbands in separate scarlet bodies caracoling along the streets to join other screaming groups.

I asked John if it was accidental that this paragraph reminded me of "The Masque of the Red Death." He said that it wasn't: "Of course I'm influenced by Poe, man. Always, since a kid. Poe was into what I'm into—death and what it is, how you deal with it. I meant the language of that paragraph to remind the reader of "The Masque of the Red Death." Do you know any American writer more preoccupied with death than Poe and I?"

Poe has a subtle, but real, importance for American homosexual writers. His pale, emaciated, lifeless heroines such as Ligeia and Madeline Usher are implicit repudiations of female sexuality. Poe could only write about heterosexual relationships in a prevailing atmosphere of death and decay. Because of the time in which he wrote, he dared not treat homosexuality openly; nevertheless, it would not be a too farfetched reading of "The Fall of the House of Usher" to argue that Poe's emphasis upon Roderick's several "abnormalities" and inability to continue the family line has homosexual overtones.

In Rechy's novel Mardi Gras soon becomes a ceremony of dehumanization and death. Kathy, the beautiful, taunts a tourist and then abruptly lifts her dress to reveal her male sex organs. Her act is a challenge: she knows that the man wishes to see a freak, and she is determined to be a stunningly beautiful one. Later, the narrator sees her smiling and asks why: "'Because,' . . . 'I'm going to die.'"

The narrator, more vulnerable to such horror since his experience with Neil, attempts to flee from such reality by giving and accepting a love that is not "abstract" and "passionless." With Jeremy, he tries very hard to "give." But, if he can never totally suppress his "priestly" self, he cannot deny his hustler identity either. Ultimately, Jeremy represents something too close to what his mother had offered—an unreal and suffocating "protection." Ironically, after leaving Jeremy and passing out in the hell of Mardi Gras, the narrator wakes up in the cold light of dawn and turns for one last time to his mother's faith. He calls four Catholic churches (one named "The Church of Eternal Succor") and is offered no support ("You must be drunk" "Call back when we are open"). Finally one young priest says simply, "*I know . . . .Yes, I know!*" Since the structure of *City of Night* is much more complex than is usually recognized, it is easy to miss the point that this Catholic indifference underscores the necessity of the narrator's leaving Jeremy. There is finally no real protection—brutality, viciousness, and death cannot be escaped.

Knowing this now in a way he has never really known it before, the narrator returns "home" to El Paso. His quest has been, in part, a success: he has exacted much homage to his physical beauty, and he has confronted that which he set out to challenge. The struggle, however, has been at a cost he could never have anticipated before his meeting with Neil:

> And I was experiencing that only Death, which is the symbolic death of the soul. It's the death of the soul, not of the body—it's what creates ghosts, and in those moments I felt myself becoming a ghost, drained of all that makes this journey to achieve some kind of salvation bearable under this universal sentence of death.

When he first left El Paso, he was attempting a "suicide of the soul"; but then he discovered from "the Professor," Miss Destiny, "Someone" in Santa Monica, Sylvia, and most importantly from Neil, that there is a worse horror than the decaying physical body. These people have all, in their own ways, taught him that there is something that he will call "sin"—the humiliation and destruction of others because they are different. He has seen in Mardi Gras evidence that he lives in a country that is truly dead—void of compassion, and dedicated to mocking those it labels grotesque.

So he returns "home" to El Paso, to his mother. But it will only be for a short time because inevitably "I'll leave this city again." The next time he journeys forth it will be as a hustler. With "scores" he will play the role—unresponsive, distant. At other times, however, he will not deny his "priestly side"—he will listen to "confessions" of pain and loss. His life will never be totally "narcissistic" again—it cannot be after the experience with Neil. With Neil he came close to what truly would have been a "suicide of the soul," but he drew back. Never again will he even approach such a spiritual self-destruction. Thus the novel ends with a protest against death, and against the suffering that overwhelms so many people before their bodies are "rotting" in the grave: "It isn't fair! *Why can't dogs go to heaven?*"

III

John Rechy is an amazing mixture of vanity ("As a rule, I always brag on myself at least once when I talk to someone. Otherwise, it wouldn't seem like me."), painful sensitivity, gentleness and humor. His sense of humor is particularly surprising to someone who meets him after reading the novels; but it is irreverently and unpredictably there. When he

took Wanda and me to the El Paso airport, we turned to say good-bye. He suddenly reached out and touched each of us on the shoulder, and I realized then how carefully, even elaborately, he had avoided any physical contact with either of us before. We are heterosexuals, Anglo-Saxons; our backgrounds are Protestant; and we come from an academic world that has been no more understanding of John or his writing than any other segment of society. He did not know whether we might misinterpret even accidental contact and visibly recoil. He did not want to risk the embarrassment to us or the pain to himself. I understood, then, something of what his life had been. ("You can't know, Jim, the crap of being a Chicano in all the ugly little Texas towns where all they know, or have over known, is hate!") and how much trust, gentleness, and friendship was offered in that light and only touch.

IV

While John Rechy is, of course, correct in his assertion that *City of Night* was never meant to be "the complete homosexual novel," one sees an extraordinary number of parallels between it and the work of other homosexual novelists. The frustration of human emotion and compassion by a repressive social order permeates the works of Carson McCullers (for instance, the military mentality combines with the fundamentalistic south in *Reflections in a Golden Eye* to produce a grotesquely crippling world). A male child growing up either in a world dominated by a threatening father figure or in one totally devoid of adult masculine models is a recurring motif in homosexual literature (it is interesting that Truman Capote, who largely backs away from overt discussion of homosexuality in such books as *Other Voices, Other Rooms* and *A Christmas Memory*, consistently writes about a male child in a world largely populated by adult women). However, the American writer who most resembles Rechy in certain vital ways is James Baldwin.

Baldwin, like Rechy, belongs to two "minority groups." He is gay and black; Rechy is gay and Chicano. In our interview, Rechy talked about his sense of identification with Baldwin and his belief that he and the author of *Go Tell It on the Mountain* shared a unique consciousness resulting from their status as members of the two "rejected" groups.

It is an interesting fact, however, that neither writer often unites ethnic and homosexual protest in his fiction. Except in the first section of *City of Night*, Chicano identity is not stressed in Rechy's fiction. He does publish nonfiction essays frequently in such journals as *The Texas Observer*, essays centered around unmistakable Chicano pride. Baldwin really attempted only once to bring gay and black consciousness together in fiction; but *Another Country* was attacked viciously by black spokesmen such as Eldridge Cleaver for this precise reason. His most overtly homosexual novel, *Giovanni's Room,* discards the black identity theme completely. As gay spokesmen, both Rechy and Baldwin face various pressures from their ethnic groups. The "macho" aspect of the Chicano movement mitigates against Rechy's homosexual fiction as a vehicle for "brown pride"; and the attacks upon Baldwin's homosexuality by Amiri Imamu Baraka and Don L. Lee as well as by Cleaver illustrate the hostility of black militancy to gay consciousness. Increasingly Baldwin has chosen to move in a different direction than Rechy's. He has dramatically played down the homosexual content of his fiction.

The early (and the best) Baldwin, however, did not underplay the homosexual theme in favor of a militant blackness. *Go Tell It On The Mountain,* a beautifully subtle novel, rests upon most of the major themes found in the first section of *City of Night.* John Grimes, like the main character in Rechy's work, is threatened by a religion that labels sex as evil except in marriage and by a father so warped by self-hate that he lashes out at the souls of everyone around him. Perhaps the most important stylistic device in Baldwin's novel is the constant repetition of such phrases as "the natural man" and "the old Adam." Gabriel and the Church of the Fire Baptized use these terms negatively in condemnation of man's sexual nature. They see "the natural man" as a part of human nature that is inherently "sinful" and which consequently must be repressed. Gabriel, who has been most unsuccessful in repressing his own "old Adam," transfers his guilt to his second wife, Elizabeth, and her illegitimate son, John.

John then grows up in a world much like that of the child in *City of Night*—a hating father, a mother who offers inadequate protection, and a church that preaches the truly "unnatural" repression of all sexual desire. Rechy's southwestern Catholic church and Baldwin's northern Protestant "temple" produce parallel effects upon their minority members: by preaching an "unnatural" repression and distrust of sex, they reinforce the feelings of inferiority induced in Chicanos and blacks by the dominant racist society. More important, however, they force the sexually healthy youth of their church to "go underground" with their sexual desires.

In a last desperate effort to gain his father's love, John undergoes a "conversion." But, significantly, while he thrashes around upon the floor speaking in tongues, he is thinking about Gabriel's hypocrisy and brutality. When the "conversion" results only in further rejection by his father, John knows that he must find some other salvation than that offered either by the church or by Gabriel.

He turns then to the older boy Elisha in what is clearly a subconscious homosexual yearning. Elisha doesn't understand when John asks him to "pray for me," and the desperate youth pleads again, "'No, pray for *me*.'" Elisha is still unaware of what John is asking (John, of course, does not yet fully realize it either) and abandons the young boy to the threatening presence of Gabriel. This final scene between John and Elisha is comparable, in a subtle way, to the "confession scenes" in *City of Night.* Baldwin has made clear the real, if unrealized, nature of the John-Elisha attraction in a sensual wrestling match early in the novel. In fact, the John-Elisha theme is basic to the homosexual theme in *Go Tell It on the Mountain.* Earlier in the novel Elisha has been humiliated in front of the church because he is suspected of having a sexual interest in a female member of the congregation. The affair has a strong effect on Elisha. When telling John about the dangers of "the old Adam," he accuses the young boy of still thinking about girls. The novel opens by stressing John's guilt over the "sin" of masturbation. No homosexual attraction is ever admitted, or perhaps ever realized by, either John or Elisha; however, the wrestling match, written with an undeniable overtone of sexual attraction, makes it clear that, even if subconsciously, this is a key ingredient in their relationship. The wrestling match has long been a significant device for underscoring covert homosexual attraction (e.g. Lawrence's *Women in Love*).

John's plea to Elisha at the end to "pray for *me*" is both a subconscious affirmation of the young boy's physical, *not spiritual,* love for his older brother in the church, and a "confession" that the religious salvation which he seems to have just won is already doomed. Gabriel has already made it clear that no love will come to John from him, and love is, above all, what the boy needs. His earlier masturbation is evidence that such love cannot long remain "abstract" and "spiritual."

Even though it is much less overt. *Go Tell It on the Mountain* parallels *City of Night* in several ways: it weds the theme of homosexuality to the theme of an oppressive religion which attacks and even tries to deny human love and sexuality. Both novels contain hate-ridden father figures. John's final words to Elisha are comparable to the "confessions" that give Rechy's book its meaning. Both novels end with a denial of the religion ("Dogs don't go to heaven") and a yearning for meaningful human contact, and both are clearly autobiographical.

Perhaps one reason for Baldwin's comparatively covert development of the homosexuality theme has nothing to do with pressure from the black power movement. As he revealed in an early essay about André Gide, Baldwin has simply never been as comfortable with his homosexuality as Rechy.

In "The Male Prison," contained in the 1961 collection of essays *Nobody Knows My Name,* Baldwin attempts to come to grips with his feelings about André Gide. Baldwin admits to an initial "dislike" of Gide largely because of the Frenchman's "Protestantism" and his homosexuality. Initially, it was Gide's blunt honesty about this homosexuality that made Baldwin uncomfortable:

> And his homosexuality, I felt, was his own affair which he ought to have kept hidden from us, or, if he needed to be so explicit, he ought at least to have managed to be a little more scientific. . . . He ought to have leaned less heavily on the examples of dead, great men, of vanished cultures, and he ought to have known that the examples provided by natural history do not go far toward illuminating the physical, psychological and moral complexities faced by men.

In comparison, Rechy talks proudly about the great tradition of homosexual art produced by many "dead, great men." While admitting that someone needs to "assess" Gide's work, Baldwin pleads that he is not the one because "I confess that a great deal of what I felt concerning his work I still feel." What he "still feels" can be surmised from the rest of the essay. Gide loved his Madeleine as "an ideal," Baldwin writes, and not as a woman. Madeleine became then the personification of the writer's heaven *and hell.* The idealization of her brought Gide close to heaven, but his failure to love her as a woman produced a hell for both of them—a safe hell for Gide because it allowed him "to feel guilty about *her* instead of the boys on the Piazza d'Espagne."

There was dishonesty involved here, Baldwin feels, but a dishonesty that was necessary for Gide's sanity:

> The really horrible thing about the phenomenon of present-day homosexuality, the horrible thing which lies curled like a worm at the heart of Gide's trouble and his work and the reason that he so clung to Madeleine, is that today's unlucky deviate can only save himself by the most tremendous exertion of all his forces from falling into an underworld in which he never meets either men or women, where it is impossible to have either a lover or a friend, where the possibility of genuine human involvement has altogether ceased. When this possibility has ceased, so has the possibility of growth.

City of Night and John Rechy give the lie to this argument. For it is precisely this "underworld" that Rechy's central character, who would never call himself an "unlucky deviate," seeks out; and he discovers initially, in spite of himself, that he cannot escape "genuine human involvement there," with the result that he "grows" through compassion

and love for all the lonely people in all the "cities of night." He even comes to "love" the world, if only "abstractly" and "pityingly," because of the way in which people defined by "normal society" as "neither men nor women" endure their pain. Later in the essay Baldwin writes:

> Madeleine kept open for him [Gide] a kind of door of hope, of possibility, the possibility of entering into communion with another sex. This door, which is the door to life and air and freedom from the tyranny of one's own personality, *must* be kept open . . . .

Rechy's central character needs no such door because he escapes "the tyranny of his own personality" through simple acceptance of, and compassion for, others.

Ironically, Baldwin's work exhibits much of the discomfort with his own homosexuality that he attributes to Gide. Rechy has long since transcended such discomfort (he would never write an essay like "The Male Prison"). In relation to the rest of American homosexual writing, Rechy is most comparable to Genet in Europe—the man who has found a kind of sainthood through immersion in what "normal society" defines as "criminality."

Still, in *Go Tell It on the Mountain,* Baldwin produced a major homosexual novel. Like *City of Night,* it focuses upon the role of a dehumanizing religion in the development of a gay consciousness. Like *City of Night,* it utilizes certain aspects of that religion (the confessional, the conversion) as artistic devices in the novel. Thus, despite largely following the path of black pride instead of gay consciousness in his later writing, Baldwin made a significant early contribution to homosexual fiction. John Rechy's contribution is both more overt and more important because, in fiction, he has decided to emphasize his homosexuality instead of his ethnic identity.

Ben Satterfield (essay date Winter 1982)

SOURCE: "John Rechy's Tormented World," in *Southwest Review,* Vol. 67, No. 1, Winter, 1982, pp. 78-85.

[*In the following essay, Satterfield explores the alienated characters and hellish atmosphere which Rechy has created in his first five novels.*]

In addition to his nonfiction opus, *The Sexual Outlaw,* John Rechy has written five novels that vividly describe the physical and emotional terrain of the misfit, novels that explore with varying degrees of success the terrifying landscape of the taunted and tortured, of the desperate and deviant, of those who suffer the pain of "lost" life—in short, the damned. What makes Rechy's characters different from the "outsider" figure popular in American literature is that Rechy's people are alienated from themselves and nature as well as society; and what makes Rechy's world crueler than, for instance, Dreiser's is its unrelenting hostility. Rechy evokes not just the indifference of society to pain and suffering, but the outright malignancy of the world at large, a world in which death is final, religion is false, and love is seldom found. Whether we confirm it or not, that world is recognizable, and Rechy's presentation of it is worth examining—in moral terms, if no other.

City of Night, Rechy's first novel—and the only one to receive much critical attention—is a homosexual odyssey or *Wanderjahr* that begins in El Paso, moves to New York City, Los Angeles, San Francisco, Chicago, and New Orleans, then ends "American style," as Leslie Fiedler has casually noted, "with a return to Mom and Texas." Containing one of the most lugubrious collections of grotesques in modern literature, this book unveils the subculture of male prostitutes, clients, queens, and hustlers who do not love but cling "to each other in a kind of franticness" that is characteristic of Rechy's world, a jungle of fear, emptiness, and anxiety where there is no salvation. (I use "grotesque" in essentially the same sense that Flannery O'Connor used it in her essay, "The Grotesque in Southern Fiction." It applies to characters and experiences the writer makes alive "which we are not accustomed to observe every day, or which the ordinary man may never experience in his ordinary life.") Because of its subject matter and the sexual explicitness of the prose, this book is often referred to as an "underground classic."

But Rechy is a moralist, not merely a countercultural revolutionary, and his use of "sensational" material is not for the easy purpose of sensation, as those critics who belabor the superficial suggest. Underneath all the ugliness and perversion of his novels is a childlike innocence and remarkable sensitivity. Rechy shows us the world as he sees it, without coating the stark reality with lies that will obscure and make it palatable to a culture so steeped in duplicity and dissimulation that it seldom sees the truth, to a nation so anxious that it voraciously consumes books of sexual content simply because it refuses to face the truth of sexuality or to deal honestly with it. Rechy is outraged at the world, and I contend that he writes "outrageous" books in an effort to jolt society in the groin of its hypocrisy. Like the guileless child in "The Emperor's New Clothes," he sees the truth, but he does not state it quietly; he screams, "Look! See!"

And what we see is the pain and loneliness of people without love; what we see is the terrible consequence of the failure to love; and what I hope we can see as a result is the absolute necessity of love in a world without redemption, a world of franticness and death.

Franticness, a familiar word in Rechy novels, describes the ambience of his characters; also, the word *savage* and some form of *ferocious* appear as often as *implacable* does in Faulkner, helping to reflect the feeling of menace that Rechy draws from society. Not only is the world hostile, Rechy declares, but the nature of existence is horrifyingly brutal:

> Years, years, years ago, I had stared at my dead dog, buried under the littered ground of our barren backyard and dug out again, and I had seen in revulsion the decaying face. Now, as if I had dug beneath the surface of the world, I saw that world's face.

> And it was just as hideous.

In Rechy, civilization is a mask on the face of wildness, and wildness is mere animal existence without tenderness and love. Without love, Rechy seems to avouch, we are savages, and his novels manifest this belief. He makes his vision apparent by shock, like Flannery O'Connor, who said: "To the hard of hearing you shout, and for the almost-blind you draw large and startling figures."

Most of Rechy's characters are homosexuals, which means they are not only deviants but outcasts from society, and all are deeply troubled. They are in conflict with society and in opposition to nature itself, as evinced in their homosexuality and "perversions." (I am going to view sexual deviation as both a symbol and a symptom, because I believe Rechy perceives it this way.) Most of the protagonists are fatherless in the literal sense, but all are orphans in the emotional sense, just as they all are lost and homeless in the large sense. They do not belong—to anybody or anything—and they agonize, wanting love and getting only sex (and it sometimes an expression of hate); wanting acceptance and getting only tolerance or exploration; wanting life, but feeling death. They live in a state of ferity disguised by the thin veneer (mask) of civilization, which is easily stripped away to lay bare a savage reality.

But that reality exists, and Rechy implies it exists because we do not meet our full potential as human beings, because we do not care enough, love enough, feel enough for ourselves and our fellow human beings. We make ourselves animals by failing to be human. Recurrent words and phrases connected with the wild and primitive convey this impression unmistakably. In all Rechy's novels the use of animal terms to describe human behavior is consistent, and is especially used in conjunction with the sexual acts. I believe these acts are associated with brutality, savagery, and wildness not just because sex is an animal drive, but because the acts are dehumanized. Without love the participants are groping savages, inchoate creatures longing for the affection that will temper and humanize their lives. (The animal imagery identifies sexual behavior as negative and debased without the author's having to make overt statements. I conclude that the lack of real love, in Rechy's eyes, reduces his characters to the low level of brutes and savages whose behavior is described in animal terms to indicate its debased quality.)

The milieu of the homosexual is vicious and frightening. This "gay world," as Stanton Hoffman calls it, "functions as a metaphor for a destructive and despair ridden American reality." A perceptive reader, Hoffman sees the same kind of structure in the gay world that exists in the society as a whole, and therefore believes that Rechy reflects America in his underworld creations.

City of Night reflects, in exclamatory prose, a "grubby world" that is "gasping" and horrible, a world made up of malicious anthropomorphic cities filled with "allnight moviehouses" in whose balconies and back rows homosexuals gather "like dark vultures" searching for prey. The city of night is, of course, a metaphor, and an accurate one for what is being described, but Rechy is not meticulous in his descriptions of real cities. On page 26 he refers to New York City as "a Cage," and a mere thirteen pages later this "Cage" becomes an "islandcity" which is "like an electric, magnetic animal"—and fifty pages later it's a "jungle." Making a consistent image out of the tropes is impossible, but it is easy to perceive the feeling, which is unmistakably negative, as is most of the animal imagery. Here, for example, is a scene of sexual behavior: "Like a dog retrieving a stick and bringing it back to its master, with his teeth clutching the buckle, he slid the belt out of the pants straps—and he crouched on all fours brandishing the belt before me, dangling it from his mouth extended beggingly toward me."

This sounds enough like an excerpt from Krafft-Ebing's *Psychopathia Sexualis* so that I am certain no one of sound mind is likely to argue that it does not portray a human being in a degraded manner. Pathology, not love, is Rechy's province, and the anguished habitants of this pitiable domain at times hardly seem human. There is no substitute for salvation, Rechy says in all his writing, and love is our salvation; without it, we are brutes, not truly human, and doomed to painful failure with any surrogate.

City of Night was followed by *Numbers,* a dreary homosexual scorecard in which the protagonist, Johnny Rio, sets himself the goal of achieving thirty sexual "scores" within a period of ten days. (Rechy heroes, lacking love and fearfully craving it, like to feel desired, and the greater the number of people who desire them the more successful they feel in their substitution.) Griffith Park in Los Angeles is the setting for much of the activity—graphically described—but dark movie balconies are also used for fleeting and frantic trysts that are meaning-less except as "numbers" to add to the scorecard. It is significant that the movie house is used as a place of rendezvous, since it is the home of unreality,

of illusion, of dreams projected in images larger than life—a place where the disappointed can meet in the dark and try to capture for a moment the illusion of love.

Johnny is a truly pathetic character, driven by a kind of franticness that is exacerbated by nerve-ripping panic and terror in his furtive encounters, and at the same time dulled by an enveloping ennui that is absolutely deadening. The best feeling he experiences is a sense of being alive, and he tries to use sex as a life stimulant. It fails: "And what does he feel? A screaming need still unfulfilled." There is no love in the book, and at the novel's end, the protagonist, lacking the human touch of warmth and caring, continues his futile but compulsive attempt to fill the void with numbers: the last line of the book is "Thirty-seven!"

In *This Day's Death,* the protagonist Jim Girard faces trial in Los Angeles Superior Court on a charge of homosexuality. As we might expect, the law is powerful, threatening, and anything but just, a symbolic distillation of the social structure that rejects Jim and forces him into the helpless role of victim. The recurrent image of tyranny is concentrated in the mechanical process of the law:

> It was a hostile world, that world of criminal proceedings: Too often a defendant was reduced to a mere entity caught in opposing crosscurrents of court proceedings, as impersonal as a ball in a competitive game. What was won or lost had little to do with the instrument of the game. And as the ponderous abstract machinery of court proceedings moved inexorably, that machinery began to attain a definite threatening identity while a defendant felt his reduced, fading; finally—possibly—invisible?

Jim is from El Paso, but he goes back and forth to the city of lost angels and "lost defendant angels," where he sees the "same haunted, hunting, lost breed of faces he had been among on the insomniac streets of exile America." We are indeed in Rechy country, among the forlorn and afflicted who are both predator and prey, victim and victimizer in frenzied loveless encounters.

The only love Jim expresses is a kind of guilt-induced obligatory love for his mother, but even the mother-son relationship provides another form of trap, and his feelings are ambivalent and vacillatory. His mother is dying, her body wracked by unknown malevolent invaders of a nameless illness, *"la cosa,"* an unseen terrible force from the pathogenic world that constitutes a different kind of "invisible trap" from the one Jim is caught in.

Again in this novel, sex is so identified with brutality, savagery, and wildness that Jim sees the sexual act as "symbolic slaughter," a manifestation of rage and anger, a way of ventilating his resentment through human violation—or of passing on to others the pain and suffering the world has heaped upon him.

The Vampires is an incredible novel, hastily written, about a group of bizarre people who gather on a Caribbean island to indulge in sadistic games that tear away the lies sustaining them. The island, being itself cut off, is an appropriate setting for these isolated people who suffer a kind of death in life. One of the characters is so numbed that he feels dead, and seeks pain just to feel alive. Another, a male prostitute plagued by impotence, previously enjoyed the desire others felt for him (while he felt contempt for them) because he wanted to feel loved—but the sex was never enough to overcome the feeling of emptiness. "Nothing was enough," he says, underscoring a thematic complaint.

What these people seek is deliverance, escape with a capital E. "It's not possible to Escape," one of them proclaims. "Life attacks. It comes roaring at you." And life, as Euripides said long ago, is a misery. Rechy's characters agree, for they are victims all, wretched, driven, tormented, lost. And in their misery they prey on each other, seemingly helpless to do otherwise but to pass on what they get from the world, oftentimes in the form of "sexual slaughter," which is a parody of love, a travesty of the only thing that could save them.

In *The Fourth Angel,* Rechy presents four El Paso adolescents who, in an attempt to find themselves, experiment with sex, alcohol, various drugs, and even people. Jerry, a fairly sensitive youth whose mother has recently died, joins a tough girl, Shell, and two boys, Cob and Manny, who call themselves the angels. Hoping to fill the void in his life, Jerry becomes the fourth angel and participates in the explorative escapades of the group. One of the things these juveniles like to do is catch people giving expression to their vices. They claim to want to "get into" other people's heads, but what they seem to enjoy is the vulnerability of those who are exposed—especially those whose sexual proclivities are exposed—and the concomitant superiority of their own position. For example, in an abandoned house by a bar, these "angels" catch two men engaged in sodomy and terrorize them. They try to force the couple to complete the act under their gaze, but the men are too frightened to perform and are released:

> The two stumble past them.
> "Like animals," Cob's words shoot out in accusation.
> "Man, we really freaked them out," Manny says.
> "Animals!" Cob yells after the two.
> "Animals!" Shell seizes the word, laughing harshly. "*Animals!*"

> "Animals!" Manny joins them.
> "Animals . . ." Jerry echoes softly.

It is grindingly obvious that the youths are hurling an epithet, a disparaging label of shame and disgrace. That homosexual behavior is vastly more common to humans than to so-called lower animals is immaterial. The men, in giving vent to the sex drive without the favor of love, admit a connection with the animal world, confess that they share a need which is purely animalistic, and therefore, in the view of the gang members, they are base and low.

Later, these four "angels," under the influence of LSD, enter a supermarket and enrage a woman customer:

> The woman turns fiercely from them, driving the cart like a tank. But in those moments, Jerry saw her mean face crumbling before him, folding over into a hideous, tortured rubber mask, melting. The curlers transformed into rolled horns pasted on her head, her pores opening ferociously, she had become a violent, irrational—yet strangely frightened—animal.

Whatever is ugly or irrational is usually presented in animal terms, despite the fact that irrational violence is far more characteristic of human beings than of animals.

Near the end of the novel, Cob and Shell fight for some kind of emotional supremacy, and Cob enlists Manny's aid in a sexual attack upon Shell as Jerry observes: "Swiftly, circling her like a cunning animal, Cob pulls her dress down. Naked in tatters, she looks savagely beautiful."

Savage and *animal* are terms Rechy uses to relate to sexual activity, of both heterosexual and homosexual variety. As we have seen, however, there is no evidence of real love displayed between any of the sexual partners, and the sex acts appear to be acts of lust that are distorted, warped, or perverted in terms of what is normally defined as acceptable behavior by community standards. Rechy writes of the reduced, "the tarnished fugitives of America," as he said in *City of Night* and his characters are loveless creatures who, driven by lust and frustration, seek any form of "love" they can find, however aberrant, however ersatz. But they are also symbols, and they function to demonstrate the disastrous result of the failure to love, and hence define the necessity of love. All Rechy's books are, in this sense, negative demonstrations of a very positive and moral appeal.

In the broadest sense, I believe Rechy makes a tacit plea that civilization be made the face of man (not just a mask), the human being be transformed into an honestly humane creature who would not need a mask, whose own face would be truly civilized, and whose world would not be wretched. Love is the alembic, the only hope, the only salvation. There is absolutely no substitute. If Rechy screams "Look!" and if he seems at times to be writing at the top of his voice, it is because his message is desperately important, and his audience is decidedly hard of hearing.

Emmanuel S. Nelson (essay date Summer 1983)

SOURCE: "John Rechy, James Baldwin and the American Double Minority Literature," in *Journal of American Culture,* Vol. 6, No. 2, Summer, 1983, pp. 70-4.

[*In the following excerpt, Nelson explores how Rechy's and James Baldwin's status as homosexuals and ethnic minorities has influenced their perspectives.*]

John Rechy, in his interview with James Giles, compares himself to James Baldwin and states that they both possess a "dual consciousness" which accounts for a "special sensibility." Rechy's use of the term "dual sensibility" refers to his and Baldwin's status as double minorities in American society: Rechy is Chicano and homosexual, whereas Baldwin is black and homosexual. It is the "special sensibility" which stems from their psychosocial status as dual minorities in America which accounts for the utterly alienated and furiously rebellious vision of life embodied in their fiction. Hence in order to understand their works properly—especially the themes of alienation and rebellion—we need to consider the combined impact of these writers' ethnic awareness and homosexual consciousness that shape their imagination. To do so, however, we need to grasp the psychological and sociological implications of their condition as American artists-intellectuals who are also members of mistreated ethnic and sexual minority groups. For it is impossible, as Richard Barksdale argues, "to separate literature from mores and fiction from fact," and "writers write of what they think and dream, but what they think and dream comes out of the warp and woof of the life they live and see surging around them."

Although minority and homosexual literary traditions have received significant critical recognition and academic respectability in recent years, surprisingly little scholarly attention has been given to the impact of double minority status of writers like Rechy and Baldwin on their works. Critics who discuss Baldwin's works either emphasize his ethnicity or his homosexuality but seldom both. Discussions of American homosexual novels—Roger Austen's *Playing the Game,* for example—tend to treat Baldwin primarily as a homosexual artist but deal with his "blackness" cursorily. On the other hand, there are studies like Arthur Davis' *From the Dark Tower* that consider Baldwin as a leading black

writer but de-emphasize his homosexuality. And sometimes his sexuality is even treated in insensitive or heterosexist manner: Robert Bone, for example, in *The Negro Novel in America,* refers to the homosexual content in Baldwin's fiction as "rather an evasion than an affirmation of human truth"; and Marcus Klein, in his *After Alienation: American Novels in Mid-Century* states that Baldwin's fiction provides glimpses of "tittering fairies and decrepit perverts." Conversely, Rechy is considered by many critics to be a prominent figure in the contemporary homosexual literary scene, but those critics (with an exception of two or three) seem to be either unaware of or ignore the fact that he is a Chicano. Stephen Adams, for example, in *The Homosexual as Hero in Contemporary Fiction,* devotes sixteen pages to a discussion of Rechy's protagonists but fails to point out that Rechy himself—like many of his protagonists—is a Chicano from West Texas. One must acknowledge, however, that Rechy's fiction (with the exception of some minor unpublished works) contains no overt racial protest. His unwillingness to combine racial protest with homosexual revolt probably explains much of the critical silence on his ethnicity and its impact on his fiction.

But an understanding of the multiple forms of alienation Rechy and Baldwin experience as ethnic minorities and homosexuals is essential to a proper comprehension of their works. However, alienation is not unique to ethnic or sexual minorities alone; it is a transhistorical and cross-cultural phenomenon that affects everyone. Yet there are significant differences in the *modes* and *intensity* of alienation among individuals and groups, just as *reasons* for their estrangement can also vary. For example, even a cursory survey of contemporary sociological and psychological literature will indicate that there is a general consensus among scholars that the twentieth-century man is much more intensely alienated that those of the preceding generations. Social psychologists like Erich Fromm attribute the special alienation of the modern personality to the sweeping industrialization and massive urbanization and a host of other allied changes that have occurred during the present century.

Although alienation is a pervasive global syndrome, it seems to afflict the psyche of the modern American artist with special severity—for numerous historical and cultural reasons. One factor perhaps is that he is part of a culture which, unlike the Old World ones, is a discontinuous one that is essentially immigrant in origin and pluralistic and highly mobile in nature. It is also one of the most heavily industrialized and urbanized societies in the world; therefore the conditions that cause alienation tend to be more widespread and deep-rooted in it than in less industrialized and pre-industrial cultures of the world. Moreover, as an American artist-intellectual, he has to contend with the traditional American anti-intellectualism that seems to manifest itself occasionally in bizarre forms, such as the vigorous witch-hunt of writers during the Joseph McCarthy period. Richard Barksdale in his brilliant essay "Alienation and Anti-Hero in Recent American Fiction" enumerates three alienating conditions unique to the American artist: the painful gap between the glorious American Dream and the ugly historical record; the subordination of human values to the power and supremacy of technology; and the pervasive "Madison-avenuism" that prods America to "dress its wounds in sparkling cellophane and hide its evil with dollar bills." These, he argues, are the bases for the articulate American writer's "vigorous dissent."

But what about an articulate American artist who is also black? He experiences various forms of alienation that are common to all American artists; because of his race, however, the condition of isolation "impinges on the black American artist with special severity." Langston Hughes says that the black American artist has "all the problems that any other has, plus a few more." Arna Bontemps asserts that "though writers are traditionally at loggerheads with their society, they seldom escape its pressures, and this becomes doubly apparent in the case of Negro writers in America." His racial minority status adds certain forms of cultural and psychological alienation to his already alienated condition as an American artist-intellectual. His cultural isolation is not hard to understand because he is, after all, a product of the almost unending cultural and sociological nightmare of the Afro-American Experience. He is part of a group of people who were originally uprooted from their native soils and violently thrust into the alien environs of North America, where they have been subjected to systematic cultural (sometimes even physical) castration through the appalling crimes of slavery and, subsequently, various forms of statutory oppression. And since hostility toward them continues largely unabated even to this day, they still exist largely outside the American mainstream and power structure. As a member of such a minority group, the black writer feels a profound, perhaps irreversible, sense of cultural estrangement from the Establishment. This form of cultural isolation is further intensified by a brand of psychological estrangement experienced by nearly every black American. He lives in a culture which, by vigorously idealizing white values and standards while simultaneously debasing blacks through negative stereotypes and myths, significantly debilitates the black psyche and alienates the individual black from himself and his group. This is precisely the condition of alienation that Baldwin calls "the depthless alienation from oneself and one's people." Moreover, since racism in the United States is a pervasive ongoing phenomenon, alienation is not merely a philosophical concept for the black writer: it is a part of his everyday existence. And the black writer, because of his intellect and sensitivity, is likely to have a greater intellectual and emotional awareness of his condition of alienation than the average member of his ethnic group.

The plight of the Chicano writer is in many ways similar to that of the black artist. Chicanos too have a long history of discrimination; in fact, anti-Chicano prejudice even antedates anti-black feelings. And not many Americans are aware of the fact that Chicanos—not blacks—were the first group subjected to periodic lynchings. Moreover, like the enslavement of blacks, political subjugation of Chicanos through unprovoked attacks on the Spanish territories during the presidency of Polk was based largely on the concept of Anglo-Saxon racial and cultural superiority. As Gilberto Rivas—a Hispanic historian—points out, the American wars of aggression on Spanish territories were largely motivated by the Anglo-Saxon belief in the curious theory of Manifest Destiny, an imperialistic theory that justifies the territorial expansionism of Anglo-Saxons as their divinely appointed destiny, thus imputing providential sanction to their belief in their cultural and racial superiority. And Chicanos continue to suffer, in spite of their recent gains, various forms of ethnic, linguistic and economic discrimination. This ongoing mistreatment, coupled with a grim backdrop of historical injustices and humiliations, makes identification with the Establishment nearly a psychological impossibility for an overwhelming number of Chicano Americans. And as a member of this alienated group, the sensitive Chicano artist, who is likely to have a greater awareness than most others of the implications of being a Chicano in America, experiences certain forms of cultural and psychological alienation similar to that of the black artist.

While black and Chicano artists experience special alienation from self and society because of their ethnicity, the homosexual artist suffers yet other unique modes of alienation because of his affectional and sexual orientation. In many ways homosexual alienation can be even more debilitating than racial isolation. The American homosexual suffers an extraordinary sense of estrangement because of the intense homophobia endemic in the American society, homophobia that is institutionalized in the traditional family unit, the church and the medical and legal establishments. For example, a homosexual's own family can be a frightening source of alienation for him. While racial minorities can often feel a sense of solidarity with and draw strength from their families which equip them to combat external oppression, the homosexual is often an outsider within the confines of his own parental home. Another source of blatant homophobia is the church. In fact, traditional Christianity, which is primarily a male-oriented, sex-negative religion that emphasizes essentially the procreative aspects of human sexuality, continues to be a major factor in "shaping, supporting, and transmitting negative attitudes toward homosexuality."

The anti-homosexual orientation of Judeo-Christian tradition has also contributed to the religious alienation of many homosexuals by rendering their reconciliation of their sexuality with conventional religious faith nearly impossible. And the American legal system, built largely on the ethical and moral assumptions of the Judeo-Christian tradition, attempts to regulate individual sexual behavior by sternly regarding homosexual acts as a crime against nature. This statutory oppression, by rendering homosexual men and women sexual outlaws, further intensifies their sense of estrangement from the Establishment culture. The medical establishment, despite its recent, largely cosmetic alterations in its stance on homosexuality, still remains yet another bastion of homophobia. Thus, society views the homosexual as a bizarre anomaly because he seems to disvalue the cultural criteria for masculinity (e.g., aggressive sexual pursuit of women, marriage, family), and considers his sexual behavior antithetical to all socialized belief systems; his family frequently reacts to him with antagonism; the church considers him tainted; the legal system outlaws him; and in the canons of psychiatry, he is a pathologically disturbed individual. The collective impact of these hostile attitudes—familial, social, legal, ecclesiastical, and medical—is bound to generate in the individual homosexual psyche a profound sense of alienation. And the homosexual who is also an artist is likely to experience greater than average intellectual and emotional awareness of his condition of appalling severance from the Establishment.

If racial minorities and homosexuals in the American society experience unique modes of alienation, what about an artist who is *both* a member of a minority group and a homosexual as well? This question brings me to my central concern in this paper: the combined impact of an artist's dual minority condition on his works. He is not only vulnerable to all forms of alienation that are peculiar to ethnic minorities and homosexuals, but his double minority condition substantially complicates his predicament by adding new dimensions to his feelings of alienation.

For example, the minority homosexual becomes an anomaly within his own ethnic group. It does indeed appear that certain racial groups—especially blacks and Chicanos—tend to be especially homophobic. Robert Staples, himself a black, suggests that since the masculinity of black males has been historically challenged and denigrated by white males, and since a vast majority of black males still experience an overwhelming sense of economic, social, and political powerlessness, perhaps they tend to be somewhat sensitive about their heterosexual-masculine self-image. Such sensitivity can cause special hostility toward homosexuals, especially black homosexuals. Also, since society in general equates homosexuality with effeminacy and weakness, perhaps a majority of blacks tend to view homosexuality as being fundamentally incompatible with the assertive and militant ideology of modern black consciousness. Amusingly enough, militant black activists like Eldridge Cleaver and LeRoi

Jones have actually hinted that homosexuality is a white man's disease. One also has to wonder whether heterosexism among blacks is not really a form of emotional fortification that has psychotherapeutic value: after all, if blacks have "faggots" to look down on, then they themselves may not feel that they are at the lowest rung of society. Similarly, Chicano culture too seems to view homosexuality with special hostility. Hispanic culture in general sharply dichotomizes gender roles of males and females; it also places a very high value on *machismo,* or hypermasculinity, deemed ideal for a male. Since homosexuals neither fit into the neat dichotomous categorization of sex roles nor meet culturally defined standards of hypermasculinity, they become obvious anomalies in the Chicano culture, and not infrequently they are singled out for special ridicule, ostracism, and abuse.

> **The predicament of the minority homosexual artist . . . is one of complete alienation. In addition to all forms of estrangement common to twentieth-century man in general and the American artist in particular, he is also severely alienated because of his ethnicity and sexuality.**
> **—*Emmanuel S. Nelson***

While the sexual orientation of a minority homosexual generally makes him a pariah within his own community, his ethnicity often alienates him from the gay subculture, which is largely made up of whites. A majority of white homosexuals, in spite of their liberal protestations and outrage against heterosexual insensitivity, are often just as callously racist as most white heterosexuals. John Soares, a black gay activist, states that "to those who have moved in both straight and gay circles, it does indeed appear that for every racially colored posture found in straight society, there is a corresponding one in the gay society." Agreeing with this assessment, Thomas Dutton, also a black gay activist, adds that

> Each time you enter a bar, go to a party, attend a group meeting, read gay press, or deal with white faggots on a social level, it [racism] is there. It is, outside of us, like a large beast looming omnipresent in front of us. Internally, like a crab with serrating pincers, it gnaws at us.

The predicament of the minority homosexual artist, hence, is one of complete alienation. In addition to all forms of estrangement common to twentieth-century man in general and the American artist in particular, he is also severely alienated because of his ethnicity and sexuality. For example, a black homosexual has to deal with the multiple jeopardy of being black in a racist society, a homosexual in a homophobic society, a black in a largely racist, white-oriented gay subculture, and a homosexual in an especially homophobic black community. The collective impact of these multiple forms of alienation is bound to be tremendous. And in order to understand properly the works of dual minority writers, like Rechy and Baldwin we need to be aware of the impact of their staggering alienation (and the rage it generates) on their works.

It is this double minority alienation that is largely responsible for the exilic sensibility that pervades the fictional worlds of Rechy and Baldwin. Perhaps it is this exilic sensibility that Rechy refers to as the "special sensibility" in his interview with James Giles. This sensibility—which stems from their condition of being rejected and denigrated exiles in their own homeland—mostly accounts for their nearly obsessive preoccupation with the theme of alienation. Their sense of exile manifests itself on many levels. Their characters not infrequently experience moments of psychological alienation—feelings of estrangement from their own selves. Often they are isolated from their families, especially their fathers or father-figures. They also frequently experience an overwhelming sense of religious alienation. And at least their homosexual characters are sometimes literal territorial exiles as well: the unnamed narrator of Rechy's *City of Night,* for example, wanders through the American homosexual underworld with an acute sense of homelessness; and many of Baldwin's characters—like David in *Giovanni's Room,* Eric in *Another Country,* and Arthur in *Just Above My Head*—leave the country of their birth and become exiles in Europe.

Closely related to the theme of alienation is the theme of rebellion. The protagonists of Rechy and Baldwin are often defiant and rebellious. They rebel against their families and often define themselves in opposition to their fathers. Their homosexual progatonists, because they operate outside the legal and moral boundaries of society and wander into the forbidden territories of human sexual experience, are also social rebels; they defy society with their sexuality—that very part of them that is used by society to stigmatize them. More obvious than their familial and social revolt is their religious rebellion. Like the Camusian metaphysical rebels, they defy God as a "supreme outrage."

The exilic sensibility of Rechy and Baldwin not only manifests itself in their thematic concerns but in their imagistic preoccupation as well. The image of exile is evoked over and over again in their works, and sometimes, as in *City of Night,* the metaphor of exile functions as a structural device as well. The anxieties of alienation are also often conveyed by both writers through images of confinement: for example, images of trap, cage, and circle. Some of their novels, especially those which deal primarily with homosexual themes, like *City of Night, Numbers, Giovanni's Room,* and *Another*

Country are also replete with military images, (e.g., "fugitives," "surrender," "tattered army," defeated army," "warrior," "victory," and "maneuvers.") This military terminology reflects the characters'—and perhaps also the authors'—sense of being embattled, of being psychologically at war with the environment. Yet another imagistic device that both Rechy and Baldwin use extensively is what Honora Lynch calls "urban pathetic reflection." For example, the palm trees are "apathetic;" the streets of Chicago are "wounded;" the weight of New York City is "murderous;" and skyscrapers seem to be "pressing down" on people. This device, used almost painstakingly by both Rechy and Baldwin, helps convey the characters'—and perhaps their own—terrible sense of alienation from nature and their perception of their environment as essentially hostile.

Thus the double minority alienation and anger of Rechy and Baldwin seem to account for their nearly obsessive treatment of the themes of personal, familial, social, and cosmic alienation and rebellion, and even for their preoccupation with certain patterns of imagery. And viewing their works in terms of their ethnic-homosexual sensibilities can not only help us understand them more thoroughly, but such an approach can also help us understand better the works of other minority gay writers like Allen Ginsberg (who is Jewish and gay), black women writers (who also face the dual trauma of racism and sexism), and even white lesbian writers (who experience both sexism and heterosexism). Perhaps it can also help us understand more clearly the whole area of American ethnic gay literature, an area that still remains insufficiently explored.

Rafael Perez-Torres (essay date 1994)

SOURCE: "The Ambiguous Outlaw: John Rechy and Complicitous Homotextuality," in *Fictions of Masculinity: Crossing Cultures, Crossing Sexualities,* edited by Peter F. Murphy, New York University Press, 1994, pp. 204-25.

[*In the following essay, Perez-Torres concentrates primarily on* The Sexual Outlaw, *considering the role of the homosexual hustler in Rechy's work.*]

The Sexual Outlaw: A Documentary represents John Rechy's most overtly political novel. Although this is not a terribly interesting fact in and of itself, the text (first published in 1977) does represent for gay liberation an early and aggressive assertion of the lessons learned from the women's movement: the personal is political. Asserting this view, the book simultaneously complicates it by revealing the potentially contradictory politics of personal liberation.

The novel concerns itself with the actions of a socially marginal but sexually liberated figure as he moves through the decaying urban landscape of our postindustrial age. The protagonist—a semicomposite, semiautobiographical character named Jim—engages in a weakened "sex hunt" in and around the environs of a pre-AIDS Los Angeles sometime around the mid-1970s. Jim stands as a pastless and sexually tireless everyman who forms the moral and ethical center of the novel. He represents the image of male sexuality common to almost all of Rechy's other novels: the hustling homosexual whose actions not only address his own sexual desire, but represent a challenge to the rigid oppression of heterosexual society. Restlessly wandering the peripheries of society, the male hustler becomes for Rechy a sexual shock troop meant to disrupt and sabotage the heterosexual world. The male hustler forms a disruptive and liberating force against the repressive and rigid social order, against its narrowly defined heterosexual identity, against the social complacency and passivity that this identity engenders. His promiscuity challenges the unexamined pieties and platitudes of the repressive heterosocial world.

The Sexual Outlaw thus offers a topology of homosexual masculinity, one that ostensibly maps practices of liberation and self-empowerment for a new, postrepressive age. The narrative posits an image of the homosexual hustler as a matrix of social disruption, agent and agitator for a "minority" cause, model of sexual animal *cum* revolutionary hero.

Rechy's representation of male identity as sexual outlaw emerges out of the contradictions rife within heterosocial order. The actions of the hustler—ostensibly liberating sexual practices comprised of public, anonymous sex antithetical to monogamy—position the outlaw in a tentative and limited relationship to the rest of society. The anonymity with which he performs his acts of sexual rebellion, the deserted urban terrain he claims as his own geography, serve to reinscribe the marginalization of the sexual outlaw. This marginalization is manifested most clearly by the silent codes which the hustler uses to communicate. Indeed, were it not for Rechy's text, the world it describes would remain a demi-monde beyond the horizon of heterosocial vision.

More significantly, the novel reveals how the hustler can never fully reject society's repressions, contradictions, and hypocrisies. Beyond the reassertion of the homosexual as marginal, the sexual outlaw in Rechy's work embodies many of the contradictions and failures that characterize heterosociety. Conflicting modes of sociosexual organization—liberated revolutionary, entrapped sexual invert—come within the text to comprise the protagonist's identity. The homosexual hustler is constituted by the very repressive and delimiting social practices against which his own acts of erotic liberation battle. Homosexual and heterosexual practices meet in the outlaw to form an irresolvable tension. The tension becomes particularly tangible at those points

where the narrative shows the hustler's sexual choreography to mirror the straight world's preoccupation with dominance and submission. Jim is compelled to power, selling his alluring body. Proving his worth by demanding money for sex, he places himself within both erotic and capital economies based in heterosocial order.

In textualizing the sexual outlaw, *The Sexual Outlaw* comes to embody numerous tensions that disrupt the semantic and semiotic order of the text. The novel valorizes a field of sexual play that seeks to trigger a form of revolt and liberation. The physical elements of this sexual play—symbolically charged clothing, actions, signals, looks—form the "silent" language of an erotic discourse that, textualized in Rechy's novel, seeks to overthrow the repressive discourses of identity imposed by heterosocial order. The "voicing" of a "silent" discourse marks one level of tension at work in *The Sexual Outlaw*. A second tension emerges at the discursive level where the homoerotic within Rechy's text, by inverting notions of heterosocial identity, unwittingly submits to them as well. Rechy's narrative seeks to construct a resistant discourse of homosexual liberation, to create, if you will, a heroic homotextuality. This homotextuality reveals the contradictions inherent both in the heterosocial world against which it speaks and in the homorevolutionary activity it champions. However, a fruitful analysis of this text cannot simply lay bare the novel's ideological enslavement to heterosocial order. While its homotextuality reinscribes elements of heterosocial order, the novel simultaneously disrupts narrative order by placing irresolvable contradictions in play. By evoking the binary structure that bolsters heterosocial order, *The Sexual Outlaw* not only inverts that binary structure but—by revealing its contradictions, contributes to its destruction.

I. *The Split Narrative*

The breakdown of binaries begins with the bifurcated structure of the novel. *The Sexual Outlaw* oscillates between neatly separated passages of realistic description and essayistic meditations. The descriptive passages offer in (porno)graphic detail an account of the novel's "outlaw" world. Their position as social outsider allows homosexual hustlers a critical perspective on the repressive and conformist practices of heterosocial order. Homosexuality, as defined by this order, is stigmatized, persecuted, labelled a "deviate practice." Against these negative constructions of homosexuality, the descriptive narrative represents the revolutionary function of the sexual outlaw.

The subtitle of the book, a documentary, underscores the function of the narrative as critical exposé. The work explores the sexual activities of a marginal group whose actions question and undermine heterosocial practices, practices that repressively define sexual identity in the service of social organization. Sexual outlaws disrupt and destroy the operations of the heterosocial world by questioning the monological bases of its order: monogamy, reproduction, duality, stability, closure. The incessant repetition of almost identical sexual encounters detailed by these descriptive passages suggests the potentially endless lack of closure inherent in the hustler's movement from one sexual partner to another.

These (porno)graphic passages alternate with meditative "essays" that form the other half of the novel's bifurcated structure. These essays range through time and place and incorporate many different narrative forms and diverse public discourses. Part interview, part public speech, part movie montage, part meditation on gay culture, part reminiscence, these sections are mediated through and unified by an authorial voice. This voice draws together the various heterosocial voices that comment on and react to homosexuality: newspaper clippings about police harassment of gays, reports by religious and psychiatric organizations on homosexuality as evidence of moral or psychic transgression, real and imaginary audience reaction to the narrator's speeches about the gay world. These sections articulate a number of social attitudes toward homosexuality. The social discourses, then, serve as a multivocalic commentary on the outlaw's liberating practice of endless desire described in the erotic section. Rechy notes in the introduction that he, indeed, wrote the descriptive passages first, later inserting the essays at points he had marked in the manuscript. The descriptive sections serve as the erotic "center" that the "marginal" meditative passages and their evocation of social discourses critique and amplify.

One process of inversion emerges as the novel reverses sociocultural reality. Homotextuality—the discourse of homosexual liberation—is inscribed as the center of the narrative structure. The historical "center"—heterosocial order evoked by the meditative sections—becomes the novelistic "margin" whereas the homosexual Other forms the narrative core of *The Sexual Outlaw*. Thus two asymmetrical regions come to define the novel: a unitary, closed, "silent" homosexual discourse sliced through by a multiplicitous, open, "voiced" social discourse.

M. M. Bakhtin's (1981) formalist model of novelistic discourse is illustrative here. He argues that a "unitary language" (monoglossia) is a system of linguistic norms that struggles to overcome the multiplicity of meaning (heteroglossia) linguistic utterances evoke. This monoglossic system is "conceived as ideologically saturated, language as a world view, even as a concrete opinion, insuring a *maximum* of mutual understanding in all spheres of ideological life." The erotic passages in Rechy's narrative are written both as a documentary description of a particular sexual world and as an "ideologically saturated" world view that informs the

novel's polemic. The meditative passages, by contrast, incorporate voices questioning both the revolutionary potential of the sexual outlaw as well as the society seeking to persecute him.

The unitary erotic relies on the multiplicitous heterosocial in order to find a "public" voice. Without the meditative and reflective social narrative, the erotic discourse of the male hustler would remain enclosed within a descriptive but isolated narrative. One unfamiliar with the critical and rebellious intent of the sexual outlaw—indeed, one would suspect, the majority of Rechy's reading audience—would remain wholly "outside" the narrative able to perceive only repetitive and (porno)graphic descriptions of homosexual intercourse. The rebellious note would remain unheard by those uninitiated in the hustlers' "silent" language—the elaborate choreography of clothes and signals and movements carefully detailed in the descriptive passages. The presence of the social narrative within the novel as commentary on and explanation of the erotic narrative positions both the homorevolutionary and the heterosocial arenas in a mutually reliant discursive relationship.

The narrative structure thus evokes the compromised position of the sexual outlaw as standing both within and without various social orders. The narrator, by contrast, wants to position the hustler fully outside the systems of heterosocial control. His is a tenuous, doubly marginalized position: "Existing on the fringes of the gay world, male hustlers have always been dual outsiders, outlaws from the main society, and outcasts within the main gay world of hostile non-payers and non-sellers. Desired abundantly, and envied, they are nonetheless the least cared about." This position of double marginality affords the narrative of *The Sexual Outlaw* a unique and powerful critical position. In order for this position of power to be made manifest, however, the silent and hidden erotic discourse must be made public through the multivocalic narrative. Hence, whereas a strict structural separation exists between the public voices of the essays and the erotic discourse of the descriptive passages, each simultaneously reflects upon and filters the contents of the other through its own lens. The revolutionary and the repressive within *The Sexual Outlaw* become not merely inversions, negative evocations of the other. They are fully reliant and dynamic players in the homotextuality of the novel, the articulation of a male homosexual revolutionary identity.

The sense of slippage exemplified by a homorevolutionary identity attempting to stand fully outside a heterosocial order comes to the fore as the narrative emphasizes its use of realist techniques. The erotic passages evoke a literary realism, an attempt to represent a specific reality as it is lived. Rechy notes in his 1984 preface to the book that he conceived of his work as a "prose documentary." The attempt at *cinema verité* is evident in the stark ("black-and-white" Rechy calls it) imagery used to describe the sex-hunt undertaken by Jim. Rechy explains that in these sections he "wanted to create characters, including the protagonist, who might be defined 'fully'—by *inference*—only through their sexual journeys." These sections of the novel describe a movement through a sexual "underworld" marked by its repetitious cycle of desire, pursuit, contact, fulfillment, and renewed desire.

The episodic quality of these descriptions stands for narrative development. "Although there is a protagonist whom the book follows intimately, minute by recorded minute for a full weekend, there is no strict plot," remarks Rechy. A rigidly structured sequence of erotic description replaces a sense of narrative development based upon the dynamic growth and change of the protagonist. With the exception of a few flashbacks (passages unambiguously marked "FLASHBACK" in the text), the sex scenes in the novel form a strictly chronological sequence. The passage of time marked rigorously throughout these portions of the narrative inform the reader if a particular action occurs at 6:22 P.M. or 3:07 A.M. Time becomes the principal mode of organization and lends a controlling structure to the otherwise repetitive present-tense descriptions of sodomy, fellatio, and mutual masturbation. As one scene follows another, the narrative enforces a strict temporal order. It does not, however, truly evoke a realist narrative.

The sexual descriptions, realistic as they may seem, do not move simply toward documentary expression. They form a discourse marked by unresolved desires, allowing the reader to trace strata of contradictions and conflicts. Rechy's narrative as an account in the late 1970s of a post-sexual revolution, post-gay liberation, postmodern, post-1960s social world helps locate the complexities involved in social change and political revolution. One formal constellation of this complexity—and the point at which the realist aesthetic of the novel slips into a hyperrealism—develops at the level of character psychology.

As Rechy explains in his introduction, the characters that people Jim's rebellious sexual journey are fully defined by that journey. The bourgeois individual disappears, and the male hustler stands as a figure fully traversed by social discourses—the historical, social, and moral strictures used by heterosocial order to define the individual and against which the hustler stands. While he revels in the sexual urgency of his actions, the identity of the hustler is based on the delimiting social and historical orders he resists. His is a libidinal utopia found at the margins but also, dialectically, composed of the central discursive trajectories of society's order. He stands at a point where not just the sense of the inside and the outside of individual identity blur, but where the limits of political and sexual constituencies disappear. The hustler within an ostensibly realist narrative becomes a figure fully comprised of language. The novel thus does not sustain the illusion of a realistic discourse. Fully defined by his sexual journey, the hustler represents not a rounded individual but a hyperreal figure where the contradictions of the social world come to the fore.

The gay cruising world becomes a mirror of heterosexual norms. Jim hustles for money by playing the ultra-masculine street-tough: "He's wearing Levi's and cowboy boots, no shirt. Sunglasses." Making sexual connections for money, "he will most often pretend to be 'straight'—uncomfortably rationalizing the subterfuge by reminding himself that those attracted to him will usually—though certainly not always—want him to be that, like the others of his breed." As top man, Jim assumes the role of the quintessential heterosexual male, appropriating the image and exaggerating it as if in a funhouse mirror. Often bodybuilders (like the narrator, the author, and the fictional Jim) and male hustlers assume both the physique and the costume—Levi's, boots, sleeveless shirts—of macho masculinity. The hustler appropriates and reflects back to masculine society a version of its own (ideal) sexual self-image.

The ultra-feminine transvestites and transsexuals represent the binary opposite to the ultra-masculine male-hustlers: "At Highland and Hollywood, the queens, awesome, defiant Amazons, are assuming their stations. The white queens are bleached and pale, the black ones shiny and purple. Extravagant in short skirts, bouffant hairdos, luminous unreal mouths and eyes. The transsexuals are haughty in their new credentials." Both the queens and the hustlers assume exaggerated versions of the sexual roles circumscribed by heterosocial order. The contradictions of the gay street world are magnifications of the contradictions running through this order. A problem with the straight world, the narrative argues, is that it denies a dialectic between the masculine and feminine principles of human identity. This denial forms one basis for the split in the outlaw world Rechy's novel serves to describe.

The meditative sections of the novel criticize writers who ceaselessly flaunt their masculinity, calling them "screaming heterosexuals" and "male impersonators." The narrative seeks to redress and subvert the sense of *machismo* and homophobia found in the works of Ernest Hemingway, the "hairy godfather of heterosexual writers," and the sexual anxiety and violence invoked by the "Tarzan-howling" Norman Mailer. The narrator suggests that the writers who have created the most fulfilling work—Shakespeare, Joyce, Lawrence, Proust, Genet, Burroughs—are those artists who most fully accept and integrate the "female grace" and the "male strength" of their psyches. Which is to say that the narrator values those writers who seem to challenge most successfully the binary construction of "feminine" and "masculine."

One would be terribly hard pressed, however, to find some "female grace" evident in either the graphic descriptions of the erotic narrative or the outraged authorial voice of the social narrative. Instead, the novel celebrates the power the hustler exerts over his small domain: "There is a terrific, terrible excitement in getting paid by another man for sex. A great psychological release, a feeling that this is where real sexual power lies—not only to be desired by one's own sex but to be paid for being desired, and if one chooses that strict role, not to reciprocate in those encounters, a feeling of emotional detachment as freedom—these are some of the lures . . . ." The narrative valorizes an image of traditional heterosexual masculinity and attitudes toward sex that involve control, detachment, freedom.

> **Although the narrative [in *The Sexual Outlaw*] attempts to position the male hustler as a doubly marginal figure, it reveals him to stand both within and without heterosocial systems. His inversion of heterosexual roles is at once subversive and critical as well as imitative and conformist.**
> **—*Rafael Perez-Torres***

This power, ironically, often leads Jim into a position of impotence. Though excited, he will not reciprocate a sexual act unless his partner is extremely handsome. Neither will he ever initiate a sexual act: "Two beautiful male bodies lie side by side naked . . . . Used to being pursued, each waits for the other to advance first . . . . Looking away from each other, both dress hurriedly, each cut deeply by regret they did not connect"; "Jim wants the man to blow him first, and the man wants Jim to do it first. They separate quickly." Jim's quest for power traps him in impotence, just as his domination over sexual partners leads him to a reliance upon another partner in order to affirm his power. He must be pursued as an object of desire. Repeatedly, the narrative makes evident the conflicted position of the sexual outlaw who, attempting to escape the repression and boundaries of the heterosocial world, runs again and again straight into its contradictions.

Although the narrative attempts to position the male hustler as a doubly marginal figure, it reveals him to stand both within and without heterosocial systems. His inversion of heterosexual roles is at once subversive and critical as well as imitative and conformist. The revolutionary intent of both the novel and its protagonist becomes defused as the hustler is shown to assume a reactive and thus dependent position to the center.

The interplay between silence and voice underscores this sense of dependence. The language of the hustling world—

"spoken" through posture, costume, and look—represents a form of "silent" language. After his early encounters by the pier, on the beach, in the restroom, Jim realizes he has "spoken not a word to anyone today. Not one." Most of the communication described in the narrative occurs through the use of gesture ("from behind blue-tinted sunglasses, he surveys those gathered here, intercepts looks—but he moves along the sand toward the ocean"), through sexual position ("swiftly turning his body around, torso bending forward, back to Jim, the naked young man parts his own buttocks"), or through clothing ("men lie singly in that parabola of sand—the more committed in brief bikinis, or almost naked—genitals sheltered only by bunched trunks"). The silence, along with its suggestion of near religious commitment and sacrifice—a vow of silence—stands in contradistinction to the form the novel assumes as a publicly "voiced" disclosure of the "silent" homorevolutionary world.

The silence essential to Rechy's homosexual discourse stands in contrast to and is only made manifest by the public voices of the socially discursive sections. Which is to say, the (silent) homosexual discourse only exists in Rechy's narrative when made present by the (voiced) public language of various other discourses—a novelistic discourse, a documentary discourse, a journalistic discourse, a media discourse. The form the novel takes betrays its vision of homosexuality as a singular and impenetrable margin. The bifurcated narrative articulates a homosexual/political practice dependent upon the very social strictures against and apart from which the novel's sense of a (true) homorevolutionary identity seeks to exist.

II. *Marginal Masculine Identity*

The Sexual Outlaw does not just represent a story of failed rebellion. Rather, the text betrays an incessant doubling whereby the discourses of liberation and repression are ever revealing the duplicity of the other. In his studied macho posturing, in his overt strategizing for domination and power, Jim plays out a heightened image of male heterosocial dominance. Simultaneously, the narrative finds in the male hustling arena a passive-aggressive role traditionally ascribed to women within male-dominated society. Working-out incessantly in order to be desirable, passively attracting the attention of others, Jim stands as the physical manifestation of idealized manliness. He behaves, however, by a code associated with a most prim and passive form of female behavior. He must always be the object of the chase. He must never initiate contact with another man. He must always allow the other to call his attention first: "Jim sees an obvious bodybuilder. The attraction and the competition are instantly stirred. Jim is prepared to ignore the other. But the other pauses. Jim looks back. With a nod, the other invites Jim into his cubicle." Jim positions himself as the center of attention, an object of worship, the focus of desire.

Pushed by the pressures of heterosocial order to remain marginal, the hustlers lay claim to abandoned public spaces as their geosexual terrain. The discourses of the heterosocial mark this rebellious claim to geographical space as much as it marks the construction of the homorevolutionary self. The sexual outlaw plays within a field bounded by the unmerciful laws behind a form of social darwinism. The struggle to survive in the heterosocial arena is carried over into the homoerotic realm of supposed liberation. Those who are old or ugly do not survive in the game of the sex hunt: "In the shadows an unattractive man is jerking off; everyone walks by, ignoring him"; "an unattractive loose-fleshed old man lies there naked, his hand on his spent groin. Abandoned and desperate and alone—one of the many lingering, ubiquitous, wasted, judging ghosts in the gay world. Jim avoids him"; "beyond the cave of the tunnel he passes a forlorn old man, waiting, alone, ignored, wasted; waiting for anybody." These lonely images stand at the fringe of the outlaw arena, denied the right to play the hunt due to their advanced age and degenerating physical appearance. The irony of Rechy's use of the term "gay world" becomes uncomfortably apparent.

The narrative thus explores the problems engendered by a practice of complicitous rebellion, one simultaneously revolutionary and restrictive. The narrative voice speaks of a sexual revolution embodied by the spirit and actions of the sexual outlaws:

> What kind of revolution is it that ends when one *looks* old, at least for most? What kind of revolution is it in which some of the revolutionaries must look beautiful? What kind of revolution is it in which the revolutionaries slaughter each other, in the sexual arenas and in the ritual of S & M?

> We're fighting on two fronts—one on the streets, the other inside.

The "outside" street fight of the sexual guerrillas, amid the broken buildings of the urban wasteland and the open terrain of beach and park, stands at the point where the repressive propriety of heterosocial order proves impotent. The hustling choreography continues despite repeated repressive measures taken by the police and other state authorities. The "inside" fight, the moral imperative to overcome personal prejudice and self-hatred, occurs within a discussion of homosexual identity. The narrative suggests that an idealized vision of youth and beauty informs and infuses notions of identity and desirability. Other outlaws reject individuals unfortunate enough to be old or unappealing, and this in turn can lead to a terrible self-hatred:

> Jim faces a drunkenly swaying youngman. Not particularly attractive, the type he would not reciprocate with. Depression crowds the youngman's thin

face. Jim doesn't recognize him even vaguely . . . . "You make yourself available," the drunken voice goes on tearing at the silence of the paused choreography. The shadows do not move, the spell locked. "You walk around showing off your body. You didn't even touch me, just wanted me to lick *your* body. Well, I have a body too!"

The confrontation violates the hustler choreography, disturbs the "stirless dark silence," and assaults the "rigid silence" of the hunt. The moment allows the text to examine the cost of the hustler's identity: "In an unwelcome moment the ugly carnage of the sex-hunt gapes at Jim—his part in it." The sex hunt exacts a demanding toll, and the narrative suggests that the erotic discourse of liberation to which the sexual outlaw lays claim carries with it a repressive charge as well. The contradictions of his simultaneously revolutionary and repressive intent inextricably bind the identity of the sex hunter and the resistant intent of the novel. *The Sexual Outlaw* functions as a complicitous critique. It examines the repressive function of heterosocial order and signals the inextricable connection between that order and the homorevolutionary outlaw. In addition, it scrutinizes those repressive practices that to some degree are independent of heterosocial order. The emancipatory outlaw function described by the narrative—the homotextuality—reveals the homosexual hustler occupying a complex marginal space, one simultaneously reliant upon and resistant to central discourses of sexual identity, one implicated in a dual movement of liberation and self-repression.

Rechy's novel thus raises the specter of a complicated and compromised resistant identity. The narrative's bifurcated structure and construction of interpenetrating heterosexual and homosexual social practices mark the contradictions the text finds inscribed in the protagonist's identity. Moreover, the text suggests that repressive practices in the gay world are at moments more than manifestations of a contradictory heterosocial order. The novel thus allows one to move away from the scrutiny of textual form and individual identity toward the exploration of a complex and resistant group identity marked by a sense of conflict and capitulation, resistance and repression.

The sections of social commentary throughout the text—the "public" half of the split narrative—indicate that North American gays in the late 1970s have come to assume a "minority" consciousness. Group identity, predicated upon notions of solidarity as a stand against the oppressive attitude of the majority society, can bolster self-esteem and self-identity while simultaneously silencing critical voices. As the narrator notes: "For a gay person to criticize any aspect of the gay world is to expose himself to howls of wrath and betrayal." Yet a process of critique, of a "deterritorialization" of social order, characterizes Rechy's vision of an outlaw world. The narrative thus offers insight into what one critical construction of a marginal masculine identity may look like.

Gilles Deleuze and Félix Guattari discuss deterritorialization and reterritorialization as connected processes of group consciousness. To "territorialize" is to stratify, organize, signify, attribute—to fix identity. Against this, "deterritorializations" signify those points that traverse a fixed identity. This can only be met with a move toward reterritorialization, the configuration of a new order. The critical work of these French critics suggests an endless interrelation between liberating and oppressive movements. Even if identity is questioned and social stratification dissolved, "there is still a danger that you will re-encounter organizations that restratify everything, formations that restore power to a signifier, attributions that reconstitute a subject." *The Sexual Outlaw* thus serves to document how the deterritorializing activity of public homosexuality ruptures society's territorializations of sexual identity, of criminality, of sin. Even within this experience of rupture, however, movements toward new stratifications emerge: the opposition of homosexuality to racial and ethnic identity, the primary valuation of beauty and youth, the retreat into the closet from which a safe and pragmatic homosexuality can be practiced.

The revolutionary impulse of the sexual outlaw leads toward a "reterritorialization" of identity: stratified, ossified, segmented. Rechy's work explores the tension between the revolutionary impulse of its male subject and the internal and external forces that seek to contain any sense of rupture. The erotic sections are episodic and repetitious, presented as "lines of flight" away from the strictures of correctness articulated by the social discourse of the novel. Simultaneously, an irreducible tension emerges between the sense of flight and liberation suggested by the erotic discourse and the isolation and stratification its form implies: only sexuality informs these erotic sections and every other object— food and clothes and all physical movement—becomes subordinated to its drive.

The erotic discourse deterritorializes the well-defined moral and legal segments invoked in the social discourses of the novel. This discourse also reterritorializes the significance of eroticism—sexual outlawry is and must *always* be disruptive. The narrative offers no image of the "perverse" in the sense Barthes (1985) speaks of perversion as "the search for a pleasure that is not made profitable by a social end, a benefit to the species . . . . It's on the order of bliss that exerts itself for nothing. The theme of expenditure." Jim's eroticism is all-consuming, charging his clothes, food, and gesture with an eroticism itself equivalent with social rupture—a revolutionary and liberating benefit "to the species." Rechy's text thus foregrounds the theme of (capital) exchange rather than (perverse) expenditure.

The erotic discourse, in consuming and so assigning significance, silences all that is not of use to the aleatory movement of sexual outlawry. Thus Jim's ethnic background becomes subordinated to his homosexual identity:

> Jim—he calls himself that sometimes, sometimes Jerry, sometimes John—removes the bikini, lies boldly naked on the sand. Because of a mixture of Anglo and Latin bloods, his skin quickly converts the sun's rays into a tan; the tan turns his eyes bluer; long-lashed eyes which almost compromise the rugged good looks of his face, framed by dark hair. The sun licks the sweat from his body.

The erotic narrative subordinates any sense of ethnic or racial identity to the erotic, the physical, the homosexual. Rechy, a Chicano, writes a narrative that makes hidden any connection to a nonsexual self. Indeed, the long lashes of his eyes "almost compromise" the protagonist's good looks. As constructed by the narrative, the racial self even threatens the sexual self. In addition, the protagonist's own name— sometimes Jim, sometimes Jerry, sometimes John—has no significatory power against the segmented and wholly consuming identity of homosexual hunter.

Yet, for all this, the narrative evokes various strata of homosexual identity. Homosexual groups in the narrative function as sects with their own secret rites and rituals. In this vein, homosexuality is still tied to "the values and systems of interaction of the dominant sexuality. Its dependence upon heterosexual norms can be seen in its policy of secrecy, of concealment—due partly to the repression and partly to the sense of shame which still prevails in the 'respectable' circles." The landscape Jim traverses in his journey is dotted with the glitter bars, the leather bars, the costume bars representing enclosed domains of concealed rituals of contact. Jim himself usually remains at the periphery of these bars, moving through the alleyways or parking lots outside. He attempts to be truly marginal, an outlaw/existentialist/romantic hero walking on the fringe of the already socially marginal. When Jim does enter these bars, he feels himself surrounded by churning bodies and bare torsos, a charade of ramrod poses that cause him to leave for the ostensibly liberating streets, beach fronts, and hiking trails—the open and more dangerous world of an indifferent rural/urban landscape.

The social narrative examines a group who contest the grip of heterosocial power on their lives. They represent a militant homosexuality that demands its right to exist as a valid sexual, social, and moral entity. As a result, a sense of group identification begins to emerge through the text. The narrator speaks about the Hollywood Gay Parade: "There was plenty of dignity, and, embarrassing to admit—man—I felt the itchy sentiment that signals real pride. Here you are, and here they are, and here we are. I remember Ma Joad's proud speech of the Okies' eventual triumph in 'defeat.' We keep coming, she said, because we're the people." This passage reveals the easy sentimentality and reliance upon cliché "hip" diction that often plague Rechy's writing. This passage compounds these problems by referring to the sentimental movie version of Steinbeck's already sentimental "proletarian" novel *The Grapes of Wrath*. Nevertheless, the passage reveals a strain of resistance manifesting itself as minority group identity. The homosexual forms a margin of opposition challenging the authority of heterosexual power. A movement away from gays having to explain themselves to the heterosexual world propels such resistance and becomes, according to Guattari, "a matter of heterosexuality's having to explain itself; the problem is displaced, the phallocratic power in general comes into question." A resistant homosexual identity inverts a traditional relationship to heterosocial power. It ceases to explain its own existence and instead questions and critiques the centrality of the other's position.

Rechy's narrative, however, does not fully achieve the critical (and some might say facile) point of inversion Guattari's analysis champions. *The Sexual Outlaw* explores a homosexuality that is both reliant upon and resistant to the values and systems of the dominant society. It engages with a notion of the marginal quite distinct from the sense of pure otherness posited by Guattari. The narrative suggests that a reliance upon heterosocial norms leads to a false and destructive sense of identity while also indicating that a powerful belief in the fully resistant and militant quality of homosexual revolt can lead to a code that reterritorializes identity:

> Increasingly easy on campuses and within other enclosed groups to announce openly that one is gay. The shock is gone . . . . It is equally easy to say "gayisbeautiful—gayisproud." Almost one word, meaning obscured. But are homosexuals discovering their particular *and varied* beauty? From that of the transvestite to that of the bodybuilder? The young to the old? The effeminate to the masculine? The athletic to the intellectual? Gay must be allowed variations. It is gay fascism to decree that one *must* perform this sex act, and *must* allow that one, in order to be gay; it is gay fascism to deny *genuine* bisexuality, or to suspect all heterosexuals.

The narrative calls for (but does not necessarily privilege) a genuine multiplicity of identity and sexuality. It thus explores the complicated and compromised position of a resistant homosexual minority, yet it leaves intact the sense of irresolvable contradiction it finds there. Ultimately, Rechy's text is useful less as a meditation on what homosexual "being" means than as an anticipation of how homosexual "becoming" can move beyond the binaries of heterosocial order.

Heterosocial order defines masculinity through a manifestation of physical and social strength. Physical prowess and politico-economic power are the marks of heterosexual machismo. In his outward appearance, the homosexual can represent an exaggerated image of male heterosocial power. Bulging muscles, cowboy boots, leather jackets, worn blue jeans as cultural icons evoke images of masculine heterosexual power. The male hustler assumes the physical role traditionally assigned to that faction most empowered by society and that most insists upon separating itself from homosexual behavior: the macho heterosexual male. One manifestation of becoming queer involves the ironic appropriation of those signs belonging to the powerful, turning those signs "queer" and resisting their circulation within heterosocial systems of exchange. This appropriation does not imply the simple inversion of signifying systems, however. As Rechy's text all too clearly reveals, inversion only recreates a mirror image of asymmetrical power relations.

The Sexual Outlaw signals the inevitable repression when becoming queer is fixed (reterritorialized) as a form of homosexual being. The narrative problematizes the process of discursive appropriation as the protagonist assumes modes of being that fix trajectories of empowerment and disempowerment. In order to attain a degree of agency and control, Jim feels he must affirm his subjectivity by always being a passive object of desire as an assertion of his masculine allure. He moves through a point where, incorporating contradictory heterosocial sexual roles, those passive modes of behavior socially sanctioned for women cross with the dominant modes of behavior appropriate for men. Jim's identity incorporates the binaries of socially sanctified sexual identity, reveals their contradictions, but does not move beyond them. Homosexual being in the narrative is fixed, stuck, unable to reach out beyond the series of irreducible conflicts Jim employs to define himself. Bound by a code circumscribed by heterosocial norms, the homosexual in *The Sexual Outlaw* becomes a critical locus at which the contradictory trajectories of his dominant society converge. The novel thus posits a rebellious hero but offers us something less. In so doing, it presents an image of a compromised critique that the narrative seeks all to easily to resolve.

The narrative expresses an impossible desire for resolution and transcendence that only serves to re-entrench the contradictory position of the hustling outlaw. As the narrator explains, the "warring attempts to fuse heterosexual expectations with homosexual needs and realities create the contradictions in the gay world." The homosexual world, Rechy's text implies, would be free of contradictions if freed of restraints. Or as the authorial voice articulates:

> *Release the heterosexual pressures on our world— convert the rage—and you release a creative energy to enrich two worlds. Pressurize the homosexual*

world further, and it may yet set your straight world on fire.

And when the sexual revolution is won—if it is ever won—what of the fighters of that war? Doesn't a won revolution end the life of the revolutionary? What of the sexual outlaw?

One will mourn his passing.

The narrative points toward an apocalyptic completion of the outlaw function—toward the resolution of contradictions—as it looks forward to a social order liberated from the restraints imposed upon sexual behavior and, emblematically, upon all creative human endeavors. Such a resolution of mutual destruction posits a transcendent image of the revolutionary that the entire narrative has to this point found impossible.

Moreover, Rechy's narrative evokes a portrait of the male hustler premised on culturally inscribed discourses of rebellion, resistance, and revolution. This resistance can be viewed from a historical perspective as part of a larger movement of civil disobedience integrally related to the conditions of American civil rights activism in the 1950s and 1960s. From a cultural perspective, the resistance also evokes a romantic tradition traceable in American letters from Cooper and Emerson to (yes) Hemingway and Mailer. The artist stands as the creator of order within a disordered world, an agent of resistance to oppression and persecution. So too does the sexual outlaw.

As the narrative projects this image of the hustler, it becomes clear that the social order forming the "outside" also informs the psychosexual "inside." The novel thus describes sadomasochistic practices in the gay community as a dark imitation of heterosocial repression. In his journey through a maze of bathhouse orgies, paid sexual contact, and random encounters, Jim feels the appeal of sadomasochism as a play for power and dominance. He surrenders "to the part of him he hates," the master of "reeling scenes, spat words, rushing sensations, clashing emotions." Similarly, the narrative surrenders to the strutting power of the ultra-macho hustler and the garish femininity of the amazonian drag queens. Both are interiorized versions of sexual roles found in the straight world, roles against and also out of which the homosexual defines himself. The narrative thus proves ambiguous when indicating which sociosexual identities allow for a critical appropriation and which create a repressive interiorization. Rechy's novel fails to articulate adequately where critical inversion ends and slavish imitation begins.

As a repeated thematic and structural motif, the tensions and contradictions between opposites—repression and freedom, hegemony and alterity, masculinity and femininity, passiv-

ity and activity—create a picture of a fully traversed, schizophrenic world. The heterosocial arena scrutinized in *The Sexual Outlaw* attempts to create a black-and-white vision in which the actions it views as wholly good seek to repress those it perceives as wholly evil. Rechy's novel reveals this to be wholly inadequate and instead disrupts the neat acts of heterosocial definition and circumscription. In so doing, however, the narrative indicates that a movement beyond binary opposition is desirable while at the same time failing to effect such a movement. The narrative seeks an answer to problems of identity through what is essentially a strategy of appropriation and inversion. In appropriating discourses of oppression, the novel oscillates between exposing and hiding, attacking and bolstering, destroying and reconstructing repressive discursive acts. Finally, the desire for a world of absolutes—the sexual outlaw as absolute other, heterosocial order as absolute evil—mirrors the repressive practices against which this desire ostensibly speaks.

Though failing to articulate a truly revolutionary function for the sexual outlaw, the novel does not represent failure. Although it calls for synthesis and transcendence, the novel cannot accomplish either. Instead, it replicates, doubles, refutes, and challenges those signs of repression and discord that map the delimiting and silencing geography through and against which the male sexual outlaw acts. Clearly the novel reveals an ideological enslavement to the binaries of heterosocial sexual identification. In its exposure of this enslavement, in its attempt to reveal that which it has in 1977 not yet the vocabulary to articulate, *The Sexual Outlaw* not only reinscribes the binary of heterosocial order. It accepts it and rejects it and reveals an impossible topology from which future constructions of sexual identity may move.

John Rechy with Debra Castillo (interview date Spring 1995)

SOURCE: "Interview," in *Diacritics*, Vol. 25, No. 1, Spring, 1995, pp. 113-25.

[*In the following interview, Rechy discusses Latino culture, homosexuality, and the critical reception of his work.*]

Outlaw Aesthetics

[*Castillo:*] *You have said, understandably, that you don't like labels. Among the labels that have stuck are those of "gay writer," "outlaw," "hustler-novelist." I agree that such pigeonholing is very restricting, but what (if any) is the good side?*

[Rechy:] I'll paraphrase Descartes: "We are seen, therefore we are." At one time the label "gay writer," while always being restrictive, announced visibility; that we were here. For very long, in literature and art—and in life—just the mention of gay subjects was forbidden. That gave rise to the necessary art of subtle but powerful "camouflage," "infiltration," and "sabotage" discussed later on. It also, alas, gave rise to "passing/collaborating." Once the phrase "gay writer" occurred, homosexuality existed as a subject in literature. That should have been a first step in the evolution toward the discarding of labels. That hasn't happened. The result is a dangerous "literary ghetto."

Paradoxically in the name of liberation, minority literature is being shoved away, into a "ghetto." Bookstore chains often have shelves labeled "alternative lifestyles," "Chicano literature," "black literature." That's segregation. Every few years, the *New York Times, Times, Newsweek, Nation,* others, publish patronizing "round-up" articles that purport to identify the "most important" Chicano writers or gay writers—I believe they've backed away from black writers, but not entirely from women. That the result is "ghettoization" is clear when you try to imagine a similar round-up of male heterosexual writers.

When John Updike is routinely identified in book-review journals as a "self-avowed heterosexual," I won't mind being identified as a "self-avowed homosexual," although I don't remember having taken a vow about sexuality, whereas I suspect Updike may have done just that.

Labeled by sexual persuasion, ethnicity, or the gender of a writer, such literature is guaranteed a restricted audience of like identification. Very few (one or two, *if any!*)—the least threatening—may find their way into English Departments that too often disdain minority voices. A few more may find a place in prestigious Chicano Studies courses. There, however, heavy emphasis is sometimes placed on political requirements over literary quality; a further separation occurs, a ghetto within a ghetto, where arguments might occur about who is or is not a "real Chicano writer."

Forgive the passion: Since as far back as 1959, I was writing about "Mexican-Americans," and identifying myself as such, in the *Nation, Evergreen Review, Saturday Review.* In virtually all my novels, the protagonist's mother is Mexican, like mine. Still, I've known the question to be asked, whether or not I'm a "real Chicano writer." Why? Because I wrote also about homosexuality?

What distinction would you make between "outlaw" and "outcast"?

"Outcast" suggests a cowering exile, victimized, defeated. "Outlaw" suggests defiance, an acceptance of being "outside the law." It carries an implication that the law itself may be

wrong, therefore to be questioned, overturned. Oh, yes, let's face it, the "outlaw" is a romantic figure.

The emergence of "queer theory" has been much discussed recently. What impact do you foresee or have you seen (for example, possibilities for exposing the contingency of heterosexuality and whiteness as normalizing functions)?

Background first: At one time I refused to use the word "gay." I agreed with my friend Christopher Isherwood that it made us sound like "bliss ninnies." Some say the word originated around the late nineteenth century and described women in the theater and, by extension, "loose women," then transvestites. For years I continued to say "homosexual," not agreeing that an emphasis on sexual persuasion was all that bad, especially when it was that persuasion that branded us. Now I don't hesitate to use the word "gay," although it's a word I still dislike.

I doubt, though, that I'll ever use the "queer" in reference to myself, other homosexuals, or in the context of theory. For men of my generation, and indeed even newer generations, that word is fraught with hatred and violence. I understand the concept behind the use of the word, defusing its power. But if you apply that theory to other words—say, some of the ugliest references to women, black people, Jews—you end up with quite a dictionary of offensive words permitted.

Essential in "normalizing" homosexuality within the horizon of acceptability is this consideration: Homosexuals are the only minority *born* into the opposing camp; call it the "enemy camp." All other minorities are born into supportive environments—blacks into black families, Chicanos into Chicano families. ("Chicano" is another word I use but have difficulty with because in my childhood it was a term "Mexicans"—that's what we called ourselves—used to demean other Mexicans, a class distinction.) For that reason it's impossible to reconcile problems that deal with homosexuality with those of other minorities. Allegiances must be forged, yes, but differences must be acknowledged and dealt with. Among those: early on, homosexuals are forced to camouflage, pretend to be what we're not; we learn to mime, to "pass." ("Passing" is much easier, of course, for a homosexual than a black person or a Hispanic, generally more clearly identifiable by physical appearance.)

Before the subject of homosexuality was permitted in art, artists learned the effectiveness of infiltration and sabotage—Oscar Wilde, Virginia Woolf, Marcel Proust, Djuna Barnes, André Gide, García Lorca, Carson McCullers. Through their "gay sensibility," they communicated among homosexuals and, subliminally, "informed" and therefore taught heterosexuals. I didn't have to know that Tennessee Williams was gay to recognize that *A Streetcar Named Desire* was written by a gay man; no one other than a gay man could have created Blanche DuBois nor—importantly—Stanley Kowalski (mirror images, gender reversed). Edward Albee becomes very irked when *Who's Afraid of Virginia Woolf?* is spoken of in gay terms. I understand why, because critics at the time were vitriolically homophobic and reputations could be easily smashed—and he certainly was under virulent attack from those heterosexual critics, who may have driven him away from Broadway.

Still, that play is clearly written by a gay man. Part of its accomplishment is that it functions *both* as an exploration of a heterosexual marriage as well as a homosexual relationship. The "gay sensibility" does not in any way restrict the artist from illuminating *all* aspects of human experience; indeed, it may enrich by a broadened perspective. I think there is more astute revelation of heterosexual relationships in Proust's *Remembrance of Things Past*) than in all of Philip Roth's aggressively "heterosexual-male" explorations. Visconti, Almodóvar, Fassbinder—those artists have at one time or another all practiced the art of infiltration and sabotage through deliberate camouflage.

How does "camouflage" function?

Camouflage occurs when a gay subject is introduced without identification (as per Albee's play), allowing the sensibility to infiltrate. Once infiltration occurs, sabotage of entrenched myths is possible. There are, unfortunately, collaborators on the front lines: often closeted artists (I don't know how to account for the fact that so many of them are critics!) who turn against their own. Today's gay writers might learn from the tactics of past noble literary saboteurs and infiltrators, in order to push our literature back into the so-called "mainstream" of art.

I've noticed that you put women and gays together in the literary ghetto you're describing.

I believe that the basis of antihomosexuality lies in anti-woman attitudes. The majority of heterosexual males see women as inferior. Since women are supposed to desire men, a man who desires another man must have abdicated at least some of his superior "maleness." The homosexual male, therefore, is looked down on as a betrayer of machismo—"heterosexualismo."

Of course there are many paradoxes and subterfuges: The reason institutions that celebrate heterosexual male bonding—police departments, the armed forces, etc.—resist so passionately the recruitment of openly gay men (although their ranks abound with secret homosexuals) is that such openly gay men expose the hidden sexual desire at the core of "heterosexual-male bonding." In the army and police departments, men are able to sleep together, shower together,

grope each other (yes, it's heterosexual men who grope each other in army showers), be exclusively and intimately in each other's company, and still deny sexual desire, a denial gay men would threaten by their open presence within, and attraction to, the same exclusively male milieu.

And in relation to the literary and academic milieus?

There's much political confusion on the minority-literary front lines. At the 1992 International Book Fair in Guadalajara. I was accosted by a Chicano poet compiling some kind of list of Chicano writers. He was taking issue with me about my remarks about the restrictiveness resulting from being identified as a "Chicano writer." "You want me to remove you from my list?" he threatened, as if he was now embarked on creating a new "400."

Another confusion: the current mythology that gay, Chicano, or women's liberation begins at a designated point, and everything before that exemplifies, even upholds, "repression." Staunch warriors who fought lonely—and very dangerous—battles are discarded. Recent purported evaluations of gay literature virtually all entrench the untruth that is now an accepted cliché—that gay liberation began on the last weekend in July 1969 in New York, when drag queens resisted arrest and fought the police making what was then considered a routine raid. At that point—current gay literary recorders claim—gay writers rushed out of the closet, freed of all repressive attitudes of centuries, and instantly produced "liberated literature."

The Violet Quill, a recent book given major attention in some mainstream publications, not only perpetuates that mythology, but puts current gay literature exclusively in the hands of seven white male writers—of vastly varying talents (two of the best, exceptional, are now dead of AIDS)—a group that, as chronicled in that book, shared extravagant desserts during only eight literary-evening chats in Manhattan—and must have waved at each other more frequently at Fire Island.

No more repression in literature since Stonewall? Consider romantically tortured gay men pining after impossible figures of desire (often "straight"); consider "doomed Fire Island queens"; consider rampaging sadists violating the objects of their lust—all these characters populate the books of three writers currently held up as heralds of a liberated gay literature. Add to that only two salient manifestations of "new liberated attitudes": the current panting adulation (by safe, middle-class camp-followers of "low-life") of the quintessential figure of gay self-hatred, Genet, with his lyrical celebration of "trade"—often gay-bashers; and add to that Edmund White's leering attempted conversion of Maria Felix into a fag hag in his recent article in *Vanity Fair.* The picture that emerges of our attitudes is not quite "liberated."

Gore Vidal's *Myra Breckinridge,* William Burroughs's *Naked Lunch,* Isherwood's deceptively genteel *A Single Man,* other novels published before Stonewall—each, in its own way and by itself, possesses more insurrectionary power, more defiance, than the half dozen or so vaunted novels that now form the misguided canon of post-Stonewall "liberated" gay lit.

A personal note may be forgiven: in virtually all the recent volumes that purport to explore gay literature, only my first novel, *City of Night,* is discussed, in the pre-Stonewall period. Yet I've continued to explore gay subjects in every one of my novels into the present. Ignored in those restrictive explorations of "Stonewall literature" are: *Numbers* (1967), in which the protagonist begins to move away from the more repressive area of hustling to the freer arena of cruising; *This Day's Death* (1969), which records an arrest for a gay encounter; *The Sexual Outlaw* (1977), a document of outrage at persecution; and *Rushes* (1979), which (beyond my intention since no one could foresee anything as monstrous as AIDS emerging) records the end of the era of profligate sex, and does so with a saddened, resigned benediction at the end. My latest novel, *The Miraculous Day of Amalia Gómez* (1992), explores the conflict of a Mexican woman who discovers her son is homosexual.

Why is the work of many writers who wrote before and continued to write after the riot in New York ignored? Because to acknowledge such work would question the spurious notion that a new, liberated literature emerged only from writers (mostly New York friends) who began to publish after Stonewall. A careful examination of that myth would discover an emergent consciousness that had little to do with Stonewall. That would force a re-evaluation, a correct locating of that major event as only one of many significant steps toward liberation. Years before Stonewall, powerful organized protests and resistance against antigay authorities occurred in Los Angeles and San Francisco.

Another trademark of this limited gay criticism is the negative questioning of "stereotypes." That enrages me, the rejecting of those shock troops of revolution, outlawed outlaws. It was the *"flaming queens"* who most often resisted arrest during raids, including at the Stonewall Inn. Inspected closely—on the various battlefronts—gay, Chicano, black, feminist "stereotypes" often reveal themselves to be the earliest sources of confrontational rebellion.

Numerous artists and authors since the mid-eighties have been turning their artistic endeavors to writing the AIDS tragedy. Can you comment on the interrelation of social awareness and cultural form?

Whether HIV-positive or not, every gay artist has been jarred into an awareness of cruel, early death, as obituaries columns extend daily. Every gay man who was sexually active during the "profligate years" now possesses what might be called a graveyard of memories. Every now and then, you remember someone you had a sexual encounter with, and you wonder, "Did he survive?" Every gay writer, of whatever age, has been influenced by that climate pervaded by the awareness of early death. I believe that a literature of urgency and anger is resulting. That urgency may be found in the prose itself as well as the content, the compression and intensification of experience. (I think here of Dennis Cooper.)

I increasingly view life as a trap, shaped by all the meanness and ugliness human beings (especially in the guise of religion and morality!) are capable of. Yet here we are. So, out of hope, spurious hope, some good occurs. I think that the most despairing writing still has a form of "hope" at its core.
—John Rechy

The enormity of the toll AIDS has taken on the artistic landscape has yet to be grasped. How many works of art die with the early death of an artist? How many characters will never be born?

Does that vision inform your own work?

My view of the world is very bleak. The older I become, the more I understand a sentence that appeared in my first novel back in 1963: "It's possible to hate the filthy world and yet to love it with an abstract, pitying love." I increasingly view life as a trap, shaped by all the meanness and ugliness human beings (especially in the guise of religion and morality!) are capable of. Yet here we are. So, out of hope, spurious hope, some good occurs. I think that the most despairing writing still has a form of "hope" at its core. Otherwise, the only reaction would be silence. I often tell my writing students that the only unassailable reason I can see for living is that it provides a *reasonable* antecedent for the artistic creation.

Chicano/Latino Literary Forms and Traditions

Teresa de Lauretis has written that the "relatively greater scarcity of works of theory by lesbians and gay men of color may have been also a matter of different choices, different work priorities, different constituencies and forms of address." (1) Do you agree or disagree that there is a greater scarcity of such works of theoretical positioning? Why? (2) If you agree with de Lauretis that people of color may have to respond to different choices/priorities/constituencies, what are some of the factors involved?

I'm sure you've already become aware that I'm not quite well informed on current critical theory. But I do agree with the fact of its scarcity. In relation to gay males, a main factor is that at a time when such explorations would be developing, AIDS struck with such impact that everything else became secondary. In the '70s and early '80s emphasis on sexual activities to the point of bludgeoning excess was so pronounced that questioning, or even exploring, what was occurring was considered treacherous. I think that caused theoretical writers to pull back. Prominent intellectuals like George Stambolian and Richard Hall, two of the best gay critics, are now dead. David Ehrenstein, a black —journalist-critic, is doing some fresh viewing of the literary front, surveying a wide spectrum that allows for work by minorities.

Back to de Lauretis's view that people of color may have to respond to different priorities: gay people of color are quite often socioeconomically deprived, and so they have to deal with the ostracizing created by sexual persuasion *and* that created by class status. This produces problems different from those of the white male homosexual, with, often, vaster economic options. Sad to say, there do exist gay racists. There's even a Gay Republican Club.

Tomás Almaguer says, "Chicano men who embrace a 'gay' identity (based on the European-American sexual system) must reconcile this sexual identity with their primary socialization into a Latino culture that does not recognize such a construction: there is no cultural equivalent to the modern 'gay man' in the Mexican Latin-American sexual system."

True. Mexican culture adds hateful factors to the forming of a solid homosexual identity, in main part because of the power of the Catholic church, although I would say a majority of priests and high prelates are themselves gay. Perhaps because of their entrenched view of women as either virgins or whores—the adoration of Our Lady of Guadalupe by so many Mexican men adds to this factor. Hispanic heterosexuals, still so determinedly "macho," often seem to think that in order to be "men" they must denounce homosexuals, and do so fiercely at times. Many Mexican men still feel they have to devote at least three hours—give or take an hour or two—each weekend, to ogle and insult women on city streets, and to heckling queens.

Gay-bashing perpetrated by Hispanic males is particularly prevalent and violent in Los Angeles and other American cities. In some Latin countries the murder of homosexuals by death squads is condoned—all legacies of the entrenched culture of machismo, and of the Catholic church.

I resent the current reference to "Catholic-bashing" used to describe verbal criticism of the Catholic church. The phrase is taken from "gay-bashing," and *that* is real bashing—beating, bloodying, savage assaults, murder, not the softened criticism prelates of the church so misguidedly describe as "bashing."

Most forms of oppression against women and of homosexuals would end tomorrow if the Catholic, Jewish, and Protestant religious hierarchies spoke loudly, with true morality, against such oppression. Instead, their repeated judgments on homosexuals and, more implicitly, on women incite violence, rape, abuse.

What impact does this primary socialization within a Latino culture have on literary form?

I think the Hispanic Catholic church has a powerful influence on all artists. What artist would fail to be influenced forever by the assault of colors when you enter a church, the shift of lights on stained-glass windows, and the gaudiest paintings in the world? I sometimes—*not always! not always!*—write in "Mexican-Catholic-Church style." This is a rich, ripe style that comes from early exposure to blood-drenched statues of saints writhing in exhibitionistic agony in churches; statues real and artificial at the same time (like the best art); exposure to the grand melodrama of the journey to Calvary, performed by gorgeous agonized creatures; the operatic excess of Christ's Seven Last Words; the poetic ritualism of the Stations of the Cross; the glorious extravagance of High Mass, the greatest drag show on earth; the aggressive mourning of Holy Week; the invited, not to say extorted, tears and breast-pounding guilt—all, all overseen by glamorous male and female angels.

Move to the peripheries of that religion, and you have more irresistible factors: the *curanderos,* sightings of the Madonna, *beatas* whose impeccable timing would make Bette Davis weep, the echoing wails of *la* Llorona. Don't you infer it all, in Orozco's comic-strip-as-great-art murals? In the rhythm of colors in Rivera's paintings?

Even in the preceding paragraphs, you find that influence, no?

There's this, too: Catholicism deals centrally with mystery, which it attempts to solve by "faith." Abandoning that leap required to accept "faith," you're left only with glaring mystery, the awesome mystery that surrounds us constantly, because there's "no substitute for salvation" (a phrase that appears in all my books), a spurious salvation possible only through "faith." The best artists, I believe, deal not with solving mysteries but with exploring individual mysteries clearly. I think that much Hispanic art is mysterious—look at entirely different artists like Gabriel García Márquez, Elena Poniatowska, Manuel Puig, Isabel Allende, Octavio Paz.

Perhaps one reason why there's never been a successful production of García Lorca's dramas in English-speaking countries is that translation automatically disconnects the action (performance) from the "Hispanic Sensibility," with its tendency toward drama and high melodrama, rich symbolism, even allegory, mythical resonance.

How does minority literature reflect on and revise dominant Western literary strategies? Become an alternative model for "literature"?

We move again into the problems of "ghettoizing voices." All categorization that limits the artist is negative. It fascinates me as much as it appalls me that often minorities contribute to this separation, confusing labeled recognition with "success." This is *literature;* this is *minority literature.* Consider that some of the recently emergent "Chicano writers" have received an amount of mainstream attention, but the sales of such books have been limited; not one has crossed the line enough to become, say, a best-seller. (I'm not saying that's the goal, just an indication of limitations.)

Before the "ghettoization of literature," several "minority books" did become best-sellers. My own *City of Night*— whose protagonist, dammit, *is* Chicano—was a top national best-seller for seven months. *Numbers* and *The Sexual Outlaw*—both of which also have Chicano protagonists— were national best-sellers.

I think even your critics have been struck by the richness of symbolic structure in all your works.

In all my novels, I extend "realism" into metaphor for deeper meaning. In *City of Night,* I experimented with several literary forms in individual chapters: for example, the story of a "great homosexual beauty" is told as a Greek tragedy, with chorus. The structure of the last portrait section ("White Sheets") is borrowed from my fascination with mathematics. I saw the relationship between the two characters in that chapter in terms similar to those involved plotting an algebraic equation on a graph; given several factors, locating the intersection of two lines to determine the exact point of revelation.

In *Numbers,* I was writing about a series of sexual encounters, but the central metaphor is death, dying. In *Rushes,* I wrote about one night in a sado-masochistic bar/ orgy room; but its structure is a carefully constructed mass. In *The Fourth Angel,* and in my play based on that novel, *Tigers Wild,* I wrote about Texas teenagers on a rampage; they are also rebelling angels. In *The Vampires,* a lush Caribbean island doubles over as a plush hell. (That novel was as profoundly influenced by the Catholic church as it was by a favorite comic strip, "Terry and the Pirates.") In *Bodies and Souls,* I commented on the perfection of what we call

"accident," fate seen clearly only in retrospect. In *Marilyn's Daughter,* I wrote about the act of self-creation—in art, in life, and I used Marilyn Monroe as the epitome of self-conscious art. In *The Miraculous Day of Amalia Gómez,* I extend the book into surrealism, and then fable.

Again forgive the passion—after all, that is an element of the Hispanic Sensibility! Before *City of Night* appeared in full in 1963 (sections had been printed in literary quarterlies), I was being written about and talked about as an important young writer, by, among others, Norman Mailer, James Baldwin, Ken Kesey, Christopher Isherwood, Herbert Gold, Larry McMurtry. Then a very disturbed man, Alfred Chester, was given column after column of newsprint by the *New York Review of Books* to assault *City of Night;* that review, a malicious mugging disguised as literary criticism, went so far as to question my existence: "I can hardly believe there is a real John Rechy."

Appearing in the journal that vaunts its literary authenticity while actually being notoriously bigoted, that review, so powerfully strident, influenced the reviews that followed. Richard Gilman's shrill denunciation in the *New Republic* was almost as vicious, extending Chester's questioning of my existence, as did a front-page featured review in the *Village Voice* [1 Aug. 1963]. To protect my threatened privacy, I refused to promote the book and spent the first months of its publication in the Caribbean. But the questioning among those venomous men came from a hoping that I did not exist, because my existence disturbed them deeply psychologically. Without the courage to face that, they attacked.

Even today I continue to battle those first assaults that attempted to undo my reputation as a serious writer. Recently, the *New York Review of Books,* which had invited the initial assault, issued a collection of its "representative essays" to be sent to new subscribers. The repulsive review of *City of Night* was included, with its original inflammatory title— "Fruit Salad." Offensive even at the time it had appeared, it was even more offensive in 1988.

Imagine a comparable title given to a review of a book about women, about blacks, about Jews in a literary journal that purports to be intellectually impeccable? I protested to Barbara Epstein, the editor, and received an apology for using the reckless headline. Last year, in a collection of Gore Vidal's essays, Vidal, in his foreword, referred to Chester's review as an example of "high criticism" although "absolutely unfair." I wrote Vidal in protest and received a letter in which he expressed admiration for *City of Night,* denounced Chester as a "monster," and claimed that in writing his foreword he had "succumbed" to the monster's "black arts." Yet there the praising reference remains in his prizewinning collection.

Writers must protest mistreatment. I do so whenever I detect malice masquerading as criticism. After all, literary history proves over and over that posterity is often much less demanding than the occasional Sunday book reviewer. I have no doubt that the "monster" Chester and his disciple Gilman will exist mainly in derisive footnotes.

I'm gratified by the fact that many of my books, often initially critically attacked, are required reading in literature courses, and continue to be translated virtually every year.

These literature courses, until recently, however, have not been the Chicano literature courses you mentioned earlier. How to you respond to critics who complain that you don't deal overtly enough with matters of Chicano identity?

At the end of **The Miraculous Day of Amalia Gómez,** Amalia utters the cry of Mexican liberation: "No more!"

I've always admired the strength of Mexican women, like my mother—and my Amalia, who's entirely different from my mother. The Mexican women I remember from my background are monuments to endurability. Yet, to most, they're invisible, or often seen only as maids.

It was largely out of admiration for those women—sustained by their faith—that I created Amalia Gómez, exploring her longing for a miracle, a visit from the Holy Mother, amid all the prejudice and desolation of her life.

Prejudice against Hispanics is still rampant, perhaps growing. Take a drive down the San Fernando Road in Glendale, in California; you'll see defeated Hispanic men anxious to get work, any kind of work. Anglos drive by in their trucks. The workers accept whatever they're offered. On the evening news you'll hear politicians talking about the urgent need to "stop those illegals." Near that Shangri-la of wealth where I teach, USC, there are neighborhoods of poverty, where Hispanic families live in one apartment in shifts, sharing the rent; almost everywhere, people sleep in darkened corners. Drive down Alvarado, see those lovely young Hispanic women, some so fresh here they wear no makeup. They'll take any job as maids. If they're illegal, they'll work for whatever they're paid.

Some people—even middle-class Hispanics—don't know that, don't want to know it, see it—prefer to relegate it to the past. In the sewing factories, today, there are women who work eight hours a day, six days a week for as little as $60 a week; some bring their children and let them sleep on rolls of cloth—in buildings known as firetraps. These are "invisible women."

At the border at San Diego, at times dozens of Anglos will gather in their cars, to shine their lights, to help entrap illegal aliens. They blow their horns and shout encouragement at "*la*

migra." Shootings occur randomly by the border patrol and some self-identified "patriots." Even their own people rob those fleeing across the border, bandit Mexicans preying on their own. Of the currently acknowledged one out of seven people in the country living in official poverty, a huge number must be Hispanics.

When I was a kid in grammar school, in El Paso, Texas, "Mexicans" were regularly inspected for lice, Anglo children watching fascinated. We were separated for an hour to be taught pronunciation—the difference between "ch" and "sh," while Anglo children played outside. We had to sing "Home on the Range," but instead of saying "where seldom is heard a discouraging word" we had to substitute "where never is heard—." Throughout Texas at the time, signs warned "spiks, niggers, and dogs" to stay out.

In the interior of Texas—like gothic Balmorhea—Mexicans were segregated in movie theaters. As a child—in order to be hurt less—I allowed my ethnic identity to remain in limbo, neither denying it nor proclaiming it. When that changed, people would often say to me, "Oh, don't say you're Mexican; you must be *Spanish*"—as if allowing me to escape some terrible judgment. Out of all those early experiences and observations, I wrote some of my first articles, beginning in 1959, about poverty, prejudice against Mexicans, for the *Nation, Saturday Review.*

I view *all* discrimination as a hungry evil. It appalls me that so very often minorities discriminate against others. When I hear Chicanos screech "faggot" and read of their initiating gay-bashings—when I learn that some Jews oppose including the names of homosexuals in a memorial to those who died in concentration camps, when I see some women cops determined to rival male cops as bullies, when I read the rantings and pantings of black conservative-darling Stanley Crouch against homosexuals and black women, when I hear about homosexual nightclubs that exclude women and minorities, I wonder . . . what's the use?

What are some of the operative questions for a Chicano writer going into the twenty-first century?

Identifying oneself overtly as a "Chicano writer" or "infiltrating," becoming a literary saboteur. For me, the latter is the more challenging and, finally, the most effective.

Art and Artifice

In your book **Marilyn's Daughter,** *the organizing image is an instantly recognizable icon or artifice. Can you comment on the importance of artifice in that novel or in your work in general?*

I'm fascinated by artifice; I never speak about "reality" as a desirable, or possible, element in fiction. In my classes I refer to verisimilitude. I refer to "tricks" that ensure that— techniques. I'm intrigued by similarities in seeming opposites: "Fem" drag queens sprinkled with sequins are very much like "leathermen" all decked out in black straps and glittery studs. In their "macho" rigidity, they become very "gay." Annoyed by my rigid attitude, a queen on the street once said these words of wisdom to me: "Honey, your muscles are as gay as my drag." Yes, muscles are as much a decoration as drag, and they do become quite as "gay."

The narrator in *City of Night* recreates himself, creates a facade to be reacted to. When it drops, at the end of the novel, during Mardi Gras, when everyone else is masked, he's almost destroyed.

For me, Marilyn Monroe is a masterpiece of artifice elevated to art. Her creator was an unwanted young woman named Norma Jeane Baker. Norma Jeane moved from home to foster home, unhappy, unwanted. A superb artist, she created Marilyn Monroe, step by step, all contradictions, lies, variations. Even her origin is in ambiguity—where, from whom, when? Norma Jeane remained a sad, finally tragic woman, abused by the Kennedys, who saw her as a plaything, a needy orphan who called herself "Marilyn Monroe." But Norma Jeane's creation, the woman we now celebrate as Marilyn Monroe, is a victorious work of art; and by becoming a questioning and integral part of the history of the Kennedys, she triumphs over them. Does art justify a painful life? I don't know. But art does remain, and pain finally dies, no?

My closeness to Marilyn Monroe comes additionally out of the fact that as a gay Chicano, I, too, have had to remake myself constantly. The hustler-narrator of *City of Night* learns poses, adopts them, to mask vulnerability. On the street, he's paid for the role he's playing, like an actor; the artist, the sensitive child, looks on in surprise. In *Numbers,* the protagonist is an extension of the earlier narrator. Here, the narcissism has become even more overt, more consuming: Johnny Rio's creation of himself is more perfected, and so, paradoxically, that renders him even more vulnerable; there's more to break.

In my life, at a certain point when I could no longer be a "youngman," I took up body-building, easing over the transition from "youngman" to "man."

What kind of growth would you like to see in your readers?

Like many other writers, I feel that my writing has been misunderstood, or, rather, misviewed. The subject material of my first novel disturbed so many closeted male reviewers psychologically that they did not even look for literary quality. I have always been a literary writer, very dedicated to form. In *City of Night* I deliberately wanted to capture the rhythms

of rock and roll. My attention to form has increased with each book I write.

As an example, I'll expand on what I said before about my novel *Rushes.* In it, I write about one night in a leather bar, a night that ends up in an S & M orgy room. The novel is structured as a mass: The bar is described to look like an altar. The characters locate themselves in the positions of priest and acolytes during Mass. On the walls of the Rushes Bar there are sketchy erotic drawings. These find parallels in the Stations of the Cross, the last panel fading into unintelligible scrawls, to suggest the ambiguity of the possible Fifteenth Station. There is a "baptism" and an "offertory." At the end a metaphoric crucifixion and an actual one (gay-bashing) occur simultaneously, one inside the orgy room, the other outside. The novel/mass ends with a surrendered benediction.

Still, today, I find myself viewed as a writer whose primary contribution is one of uncovering once-taboo subjects—in my first book. I hope eventually my whole work will be viewed beyond subject matter.

Can you outline the development of your oeuvre? Do you see it as showing distinct phases or transformations? What are its continuities? Discontinuities?

I'm surprised at times to write down a thought for including in a future book and then finding that same thought in an earlier book of mine. Obviously themes recur. I find myself moving away from so-called "realism." I think, of the literary forms, autobiography is the most fraudulent, because the author claims: "This is true, I lived it." But it's no longer being lived, it's being remembered, selectively. The next most fraudulent form is biography: The author dares to assume he can grasp another's life! The most honest of the literary forms is . . . fiction. The writer says, "This is a lie and I'm going to try like hell to convince you it's true."

Is there anything you'd like to disinherit? Unpublish?

Yes, my third novel, *This Day's Death,* although it does contain a good portrait of a Mexican woman, Miss Lucia.

What are your most urgent projects now?

I would like to live to see my novel *Bodies and Souls,* which I often consider my best, reissued in a wonderful edition and for it to receive the attention I believe it deserves. It's an epic novel that attempts to define contemporary America through a view of Los Angeles today, a disturbed modern paradise populated by still-rebelling "angels." Its gallery of characters includes a pornographic actress, a Mr. Universe; a bag-woman, a Chicano teenager, a gothic female evangelist, a black maid from Watts, a male stripper, a TV anchorwoman, a wealthy judge in Bel Air, many others. Winding peripherally through those lives are a young woman, Lisa, and two young men, Orin and "Jesse James"—"lost angels" who bring about the book's apocalyptic ending. Throughout, I evoke scenes out of classic American films like *White Heat.* The ending evokes that of *Duel in the Sun.*

Bodies and Souls was ambushed by a series of circumstances that began right after it was finished. Because of my loyalty to my original publishers, Grove Press, which had at the time almost stopped publishing, I accepted a good offer from my very talented editor there, who was then forming his own publishing house. He wanted to make *Bodies and Souls* the new company's first book. A dream come true—a major new company's first original book—turned into a writer's nightmare I regret virtually every day of my life. When the offer for the book was made, I had quickly instructed my agent to withdraw the novel from several other prominent publishers who wanted it. What followed was one of those ambushes that make a writer ask, "My God, it's difficult enough; what's next?"

The hardcover edition that was published was, at best, makeshift—actually ugly—printed on gray paper, without endsheets, bound so clumsily that the spine broke on the very first opening. There were hundreds of typographical errors, pages printed askew, the type running off the margins. The trade edition, published simultaneously, was equally ragged. I constantly wonder why I didn't demand publication be stopped until a new edition was printed, but the book was already advertised, and in the bookstores.

Written from advance galleys before the shoddy edition was seen, two excellent reviews appeared, one in the *New York Times Book Review,* which borrowed my description of Los Angeles to call the book "a scarred beauty"; and one in the *Los Angeles Times Book Review,* which lauded it as a "memorable feast." A few more fine reviews appeared. But as soon as the shoddy edition was seen, reviews stopped. The incorrect perception was that a book brought out in such condition must have been rejected by everyone—and of course that was not so.

At my insistence, eventually the publishers did release fair hardback and trade editions—pages straightened, typographical errors corrected, a sturdier binding. Subsequently, a good paperback edition was issued. All remain in print, including, alas, the terrifying editions. The novel did appear to praise in England, and recently was published in Italy. A Spanish edition is pending.

I hope I'll live to see that book assigned its rightful place, because—I'm not going to hesitate to say it—it's a grand achievement.

I've just finished *Our Lady of Babylon,* the title a reference to the Whore of Babylon in the Book of Revelation. It's a novel about a woman who claims she was Eve—and Salome and Delilah and Helen and Medea—and *la* Malinche—all women blamed for enormous catastrophes, and called "Whores." She sets out to redeem them. I'm working on two other novels: *Love in the Backrooms: The Sequel* to *City of Night* (it moves from 1963 to 1993); and *Autobiography: A Novel.*

In *Autobiography: A Novel,* I'm trying to re-create—or, more accurately, to imagine—the lives of my father, my mother, their families, a saga that ranges from Mexico City into the United States: my father's family ties to Porfirio Díaz, my mother's flight from Chihuahua to avoid Pancho Villa's amorous advances. I'll dramatize scenes as they might have occurred in their lives, as I might have viewed them if I had been there: my mother dancing at a ball in Chihuahua as a young girl—how I might have courted her if I had been one of her suitors; my father challenging his "aristocratic" and autocratic mother. I'm trying to achieve a unique fictional "truth," imagined out of what I've been told are facts, facts being nothing more than the memories that survive, that are told—all already altered by that selectivity, memory being the first editor.

I have from the beginning of my writing (I began my first novel at age eight) wanted to give order to the anarchy of experience. That's possible only in art. There's no "truth" in art. The greater the artist, the greater the lie. Like a magician, the artist convinces us that what we're "seeing" is "real," true, whereas it's all trickery, grand artifice, wonderful lies, including the ones that memory harbors.

Elizabeth Hand (review date 21 July 1996)

SOURCE: "Wild Things," in *Book World,* July 21, 1996, p. 8.

[*In the following review, Hand argues that while the idea behind* Our Lady of Babylon *is good, Rechy's narrative is choppy and the novel is a disappointment.*]

Millenarianism appears to have spawned its own literary subgenre: Here at the end of history, novelists are rewriting history, real or imagined, often with deliberately Gothic overtones. So we have Theodore Roszak putting a distaff spin on bad science in *The Memoirs of Elizabeth Frankenstein* and Jack Dann doing much the same with Leonardo da Vinci in *The Memory Cathedral;* Anne Rice giving us *Memnoch the Devil* and an alternative history of hell, with Anonymous painting the Capital in similar shades with *Primary Colors.*

Now John Rechy joins the game with *Our Lady of Babylon,*

which is nothing less than an effort to "redeem with the truth the lives of women unjustly blamed and called 'whore,' a word we shall defuse so that it shall evoke those thus redeemed." And there are a *lot* of these bad skirts to chase through history, beginning with Eve and Cassandra and Mary Magdalene, proceeding down through Salome and Medea and ending up around the time of Madame du Barry, who may have been a lady to Cole Porter but gets slammed with the vile epithet nonetheless.

Rechy is best known as the author of *City of Night*, the groundbreaking novel whose hustler protagonist was more wounded angel than Pasolini psychopath. Rechy would seem a properly lickerish choreographer for all those wantons. Sadly, he fails to rise to the occasion, but then who would not be intimidated by a line of chorines that includes Jezebel and Herodias?

Our Lady of Babylon begins with a lady in flight from the appalling murder of her husband during their wedding ceremony. Actually, it begins with a vision of Eve in the Garden; actually, no, in heaven with some sexy angels; actually, no, with St. John the Divine confronting the Whore of Babylon; actually, no, with Helen at the Fall of Troy; actually—

Actually, a good deal that is wrong with *Our Lady of Babylon* stems from the relentless narrative crosscutting that Rechy employs from page 1 onward. The lady in question takes shelter with one Madame Bernice, a mystic who recognizes in her guest someone whose dreams contain the "essence" of all those fallen women. Madame Bernice urges the lady to share her visions of the Universal Adventuress, over endless cups of tea and petits four and under the watchful gaze of a tame peacock named Ermenegildo. The lady willingly complies (natch), but her subsequent accounts of myriad couplings are nearly all broken off in mid-gasp—by annoying questions from Madame Bernice, by annoying clanks of plot machinery, by enemies of the lady, human and divine; by that damn peacock. In *Our Lady of Babylon* John Gardner's "vivid and continuous dream" of fiction never gets anywhere close to the REM state: The reader suffers from a terminal and extremely frustrating case of narrative interruptus.

Which is a shame, because Rechy writes gracefully, and sometimes poignantly, of the fate of fallen women over the centuries. It's all rather Technicolor tartdom—one can too easily imagine Anne Baxter doing a kittenish Salome in De Mille drag—but not without its entertainment value. Still, Rechy proclaims his serious intent from the start. What he delivers instead is an endless parade of airbrushed jades, a serious error—like casting a Vargas Girl in the Angelica Huston role (the men all sort of look like Fabio). So Salome and Magdalena and the titular whores are about 15 when we

first meet them, all gorgeous, all badly maligned, all resigned to meet their fates with noble suffering.

Hey, girls—can we talk? The whole point of being bad is to—well, be bad, and a reader might realistically expect to see these naughty kitties redeemed by something other than dewy eyes and moist lips. But Rechy ditches any real attempts at revisionist history early on. For example, Mary Magdalene and Judas and Jesus meet cute, as teenagers, and travel together in a sexy (though sexless) menage under the watchful eyes of the Virgin, who wears blue a la Pinocchio's Good Fairy and sort of acts like her, too, making sure Judas and the Magdalene keep their hands to themselves. (I will skip over the magic mushroom sequence.)

Happily, *Our Lady of Babylon* is not without its intentional humor, too. Madame Bernice suggests that the lady "underplay the orgasmic imagery" in her accounts. "You must keep in mind that people are very strange about God and sex." And Rechy does manage to pull off a compelling version of Medea's tale. Here, at last, is an unrepentant woman wronged, taking horrible vengeance on the man she loves— and Rechy makes her sympathetic and not monstrous. If only he'd been able to take the rest of his tired harlots and give them some of her fire. Instead, *Our Lady of Babylon* sashays in with paint and jewels and a sexy come-on, but she doesn't deliver. There's a name for girls like that, and it's not a nice one.

FURTHER READING

Criticism

Bredbeck, Gregory W. "John Rechy." In *Contemporary Gay American Novelists: A Bio-Bibliographical Critical Sourcebook,* edited by Emmanuel S. Nelson, pp. 340-51. Westport, CT: Greenwood Press, 1993.
> Provides an overview of Rechy's life and works as well as analysis of his critical reception.

Christian, Karen. "Will the 'Real Chicano' Please Stand Up? The Challenge of John Rechy and Sheila Ortiz Taylor to Chicano Essentialism." *The Americas Review* 20, No. 2 (Summer 1992): 89-104.
> Argues that Rechy and Sheila Ortiz Taylor have not been considered true Chicano voices because their work is perceived as a threat to established Chicano literature.

Gutiérrez-Jones, Carl. "Desiring B/orders." *Diacritics* 25, No. 1 (Spring 1995): 99-112.
> Discusses Rechy's exploration of Chicano political culture.

Koponen, Wilfrid R. "Denial: *Falconer* and *City of Night.*" In *Embracing a Gay Identity: Gay Novels as Guides,* pp. 27-51. Westport, CT: Bergin & Garvey, 1993.

Compares John Cheever's *Falconer* with Rechy's *City of Night,* focusing on the theme of denial.

Steuernagel, Trudy. "Contemporary Homosexual Fiction and the Gay Rights Movement." *Journal of Popular Culture* 20, No. 3 (Winter 1986): 125-34.

Discusses the relationship between the gay rights movement and literature, arguing that while *City of Night* portrays the homosexual as a rebel, Rechy's later novels show homosexuals as deviants and destructive.

Woods, Terry. "Starless and Black: Alienation in Gay Literature." In *Lesbian and Gay Writing: An Anthology of Critical Essays,* edited by Mark Lilly, pp. 129-52. Houndmills, England: The Macmillan Press, 1990.

Woods compares Rechy's work with that of Andrew Holleran, Joe Orton, and Hart Crane as she considers the issue of alienation in gay literature.

Additional coverage of Rechy's life and career is contained in the following sources published by Gale Research: *Contemporary Authors,* **Vols. 5-8;** *Contemporary Authors Autobiography Series,* **Vol. 4;** *Contemporary Authors New Revision Series,* **Vols. 6, 32;** *Dictionary of Literary Biography,* **Vol. 122;** *Hispanic Literature Criticism; Hispanic Writers.*

Peter Straub

1943-

American novelist.

The following entry presents an overview of Straub's career through 1996. For further information on his life and works, see *CLC,* Volume 28.

INTRODUCTION

Concerned about his financial success after the cool reception of his first mainstream novel, Peter Straub sought the advice of his agent. "You're poor, you're unhappy, write a Gothic," she said. Straub admits that, at the time, he didn't know what a "Gothic" was, but he began by reading the classics of the genre. His first two novels in that vein, *Julia* (1975) and *If You Could See Me Now* (1977), were commercially successful. The development of a friendship with author Stephen King and an appreciation of his work led Straub to a less restrained style, as first evidenced in his first best-seller, *Ghost Story* (1979). Straub continued to expand the concept of the horror novel through his subsequent works.

Biographical Information

Straub was born March 2, 1943, to Gordon and Elena (Nilsestuen) Straub. While still a child, he was struck by a car and nearly killed, resulting in a long, painful convalescence. Straub has said he was profoundly affected by the event and attributes some of the themes of his writing to this experience. He even includes this event in the personal biographies of some of his fictional characters. He attended Milwaukee Day School, then received a B.A. from the University of Wisconsin-Madison in 1965. He wrote his master's thesis on William Carlos Williams and earned an M.A. from Columbia University in 1966, the same year he married Susan Bitker; they had two children. For three years Straub taught at Milwaukee Day, which served as the model for the school in *Shadowland* (1980). But, as Straub says, "I grew bored. If I'd stayed, I'd have become a gravy-stained old teacher with a beat-up car and an alcohol problem." The Straubs moved to Ireland, where he attended University College in Dublin from 1969 to 1972. Throughout college Straub had written mostly poetry, but while in Ireland he changed direction. "In Ireland," he said in a *Washington Post* interview, "I suddenly realized what the trouble really was: I had always thought of myself as a novelist although I had not written a novel. I could feel fiction growing inside me, characters and situations forming themselves in my mind as I walked down the street."

Major Works

Straub's first novel, *Marriages* (1973), is a first-person narrative of the extramarital affair of an American living in Europe. Although it received some favorable reviews it was not commercially successful. Straub was working on a second mainstream novel, *Under Venus* (which was not published until much later as part of a three-novel collection, *Wild Animals* [1984]), when his agent suggested he try a Gothic novel for more commercial success. *Julia* is the story of an American woman living in England and married to an attorney, Magnus Lofting. They attempt an emergency tracheotomy to save their choking child, but the girl bleeds to death. Distraught, Julia leaves Magnus and moves to an old house which is haunted by the malignant ghost of Olivia, the late daughter of Magnus from a previous marriage. The novel was a commercial success, and the basis for the 1977 film, *The Haunting of Julia.* It also heightened Straub's interest in the possibilities of the horror genre. In Straub's next novel, *If You Could See Me Now,* Miles Teagarden, an East Coast academic, returns to his native Wisconsin community, the site of several recent murders. Like *Julia,* the novel juxtaposes the insane and horrific with the mundane and everyday. This theme of horror lurking beneath the surface of normal life is explored in ever-increasing detail in Straub's literary work. *Ghost Story* (1979), Straub's first bestseller, examines the horror of past sins lurking beneath the quiet exterior of a small town in Connecticut. Five elderly men, members of the Chowder Society, a sort of ghost story club, are bound by a horrible secret. Fifty years earlier, they conspired to conceal the accidental murder of Eva Galli, placing her body in a car and pushing it into a lake. Eva, however, is not human but rather a shapeshifter, or Manitou; she escapes from the car, changing into a lynx. In addition to the Manitou legend, the story incorporates elements of the classic ghost story, werewolves, vampires, and other paranormal activities, prompting some critics to describe it as a summary of American supernatural themes. Straub's next work, *Shadowland,* disappointed some readers of *Ghost Story* as less overtly horrific than *Ghost Story.* It follows two boys, friends enrolled at an Arizona prep school, and their battle against one boy's uncle, a master magician who tries to kill them both. *Floating Dragon* (1983) is again set in a New England town beset by an evil from the past. Straub incorporates a realistic threat—a leak of poisonous gas from a chemical plant—into supernatural horror, manifested in several ways: the evil ghost of Gideon Winter, The Dragon, is sometimes a man, other times a swarm of flies, a flock of bats, the poison gas itself, or a swarm of tiny dragons. Many critics noted a major shift in this regard between Straub's early novels—*Julia* and *If you Could See Me Now*—and his subsequent works. While working on *Shadowland* and *Ghost Story,* Straub developed a friendship with Stephen King, one of America's premier horror writers. Straub credits King with showing him that the horror writer need not be constrained by the Victorian history of the genre, which suggests that the horror be hinted at, rather than shown in all its gruesome detail. A collaborative novel, *The Talisman* (1984), grew out of their friendship. In the story, twelve-year-old Jack Sawyer sets out on a cross-country journey to acquire a magical cure for his mother's cancer. Along the way he discovers "the Territories," a medieval parallel dimension, populated by "twinners," counterparts of the characters in the modern story. In addition to finding the Talisman, Jack must save the parallel society from the evil pretender to its throne. Straub's next three novels, collectively referred to as the *Blue Rose Trilogy,* mark a turning point in his career. No longer using the conventions of the supernatural, Straub instead evokes a similar feel by examining the distorted reality of nightmares, psychosis, and the horrors of war. In the first novel, *Koko* (1988), several army buddies are reunited at the dedication of the Vietnam Memorial in 1982. Beevers, their former lieutenant, tells the group that he suspects another former member of their platoon, Underhill, a crime novelist now living in Singapore, of committing murders in the Far East. Several people have been found murdered with one of

the regiment's cards, with the word "Koko" scrawled on it, stuffed in their mouths. The second book of the trilogy, *Mystery* (1990), takes place in the 1950s and '60s. Tom Pasmore, the young protagonist, suffers a nearly fatal auto accident. Tom and his mentor, the renowned detective Lamont von Heilitz, solve a series of murders. Like *Koko*, it is essentially the story of the corrupting power of secrets. *The Throat* (1993) returns to the present time and unites Pasmore with Underhill as they attempt to identify the person responsible for severely beating a friend's wife, someone who revealed his familiarity with the "Blue Rose" murders by leaving evidence at the scene. As in the two previous novels, Underhill must deal with unpleasant aspects of his own past to unravel the mystery. In *The Hellfire Club,* Straub again begins with an old crime. Nora is the wife of Davey Chancel, the head of Chancel House, a publishing company whose biggest success is Hugo Driver's "Night Journey." In addition to worries about the state of her marriage, Nora is frightened by a serial murderer stalking their area. When Nora is arrested, charged in the kidnapping of her husband's mistress, and jailed, the serial killer, Dick Dart, is apprehended and brought to the same jail. Dart takes Nora hostage and escapes.

Critical Reception

Critics gave only lukewarm praise to Straub's first published novel, *Marriages.* Its narrative style was generally well-regarded, but several critics felt the plot was thin and clichéd. Although Geoffrey Stokes spoke highly of Straub's horror fiction, remarking, "Among horror novelists, there was no one who juggled points of view and narrative voices with more authority." Stokes continued, "*Marriages* is a tight-sphinctered little book, its occasionally striking prose clotted with self-importance and its plot—married American man falls in love with European woman, sees Paris, Provence, and self with new eyes—yet another reprise of an Edwardian standby." *Julia* and *If You Could See Me Now* received better reviews. Valentine Cunningham stated that "*Julia,* its power to horrify doubtless stemming from that original, grisly conceit of parental, kitchen-knife surgery, makes an extraordinarily gripping and tantalizing read." While both *Julia* and *If You Could See Me Now* were criticized by some for having simple, derivative plots, *Ghost Story* was not. Stephen King called it "one of the best gothic horror novels of the past century." Bernadette Bosky, noting the authors' mutual admiration, contended that King's assessment "is not flattery or judgment colored by friendship. . . . Rather, it is the appreciation for the works that drew the men to friendship in the first place." Comparing the two authors, Bosky commented, "If Stephen King is the heart of contemporary horror fiction . . . then Peter Straub must be considered its head. . . . In contrast to Stephen King's seemingly intuitive and colloquial storyteller's prose the fiction of Peter Straub is deliberate, structurally complex, and above all, styled." Many critics have voiced opinions about the influence of each on the other, especially after the publication of their collaborative work, *The Talisman*. Bosky remarked, "One possible area of actual change, and the clearest example of King's influence on Straub, is in the use of subtle vs. blatant horror; yet even there, it seems the example of King's fiction led Straub in a direction he probably would have traveled anyway." In a review of *Ghost Story*, Valerie Lloyd said, "With considerable technical skill, Peter Straub has constructed an extravagant entertainment which, though flawed, achieves in its second half some awesome effects. It is, I think, the best thing of its kind since Shirley Jackson's *The Haunting of Hill House*." As his body of work grew, critics noted an increasing depth beneath the pyrotechnics of Straub's plots. Bosky wrote of *Floating Dragon*, "Though it is often accused of being sloppy, because it is the most violent and colloquial of Straub's books, *Floating Dragon* is actually more carefully structured than its predecessors. In this respect, it may be a turning point for Straub." Although *The Talisman*, Straub's collaboration with Stephen King, was a commercial success, it did not generally receive serious regard from critics, aside from considerable speculation as to which portions of the book each author wrote. Straub's next series of books, the *Blue Rose Trilogy—Koko, Mystery,* and *The Throat*—were well received and considered by many critics to be his best work. Don Ringnaldo described *Koko* as an artfully constructed examination of the effect of the past on the present, and an insightful contemplation of the effect of Vietnam on Americans, both those who fought and those who stayed home. According to Ringnaldo, the horrors of the war were a reflection of America's culture of violence. He commented, "Straub reverses the prevailing attitude of teachers, critics, novelists, and psychologists regarding the war. According to that attitude, Vietnam engulfed us in darkness that now needs to be illuminated. Implicit in *Koko*, on the other hand, is the attitude that Vietnam was the light that should have illuminated the dark sub-text of American myth." Critics lauded Straub's continuing development of the themes of duality and the examination (and acceptance) of the past as a means of coming to grips with the present. Geoffrey Stokes wrote of the third novel of the trilogy, "Less tricky and more direct than Straub's chillers both at its core and on its surface, *The Throat* is nonetheless more successful within its genre; the intensity of focus concentrates it in a way more frightening than any of Straub's earlier horror novels." Reception of *The Hellfire Club* (1996) was mixed. Some critics liked the presentation of the story, but found the plot overly structured. Christopher Lehmann-Haupt, describing the end of the novel, wrote, "Later in the story, Mr. Straub plants more clues than he can harvest and explains events faster than he can make them happen. As *The Hellfire Club* careens to its implausible conclusion, his plot becomes so rickety that the rubber bands snap and the chewing gum comes unstuck." But other critics found the plot

twists engaging. Tom De Haven said, "By the time this mad melee sorts itself out and reaches its grisly climax at a spooky old mansion deep in the woods (during a thunderstorm, natch), you realize that you've been suckered into a completely improbable sequence of events and a cast of artificial characters. But the craziest thing of all is you don't care. You've been royally entertained, you've gotten your money's worth, you've been taken for a good long giddy ride by one of America's most idiosyncratic imaginations."

PRINCIPAL WORKS

Julia (novel) 1975
If You Could See Me Now (novel) 1977
Ghost Story (novel) 1979
Shadowland (novel) 1980
Floating Dragon (novel) 1983
The Talisman [with Stephen King] (novel) 1984
Koko (novel) 1988
Mystery (novel) 1990
The Throat (novel) 1993
The Hellfire Club (novel) 1996

CRITICISM

Valentine Cunningham (review date 27 February 1976)

SOURCE: "Death Dealers," in *New Statesman*, Vol. 91, No. 2345, February 27, 1976, pp. 264-65.

[*In the following excerpt, Cunningham praises Straub's Julia.*]

Most weeks Peter Straub's *Julia* would be a certain piece-leader, granted 'generous space to send its spine-freezing frissons lasering down the column. This week, a bit regrettably, since quality chillers like this come the reader's way so rarely, it must look comparatively out-punched. Don't be put off: matched at its own weight it's a champ. It begins plainly enough, with an American lady, Julia Lofting, impulse-buying a house near Holland Park. But the foreboding sense of yet another American novelist abroad having his characters acquire a place, and a new sense of place, in London just because that's what he's done ('writes full time and lives in London' is often the signpost to the predictably drear), lasts only minutes, and rapidly gives way to an altogether more startling sort of foreboding.

Strange events crowd in on Julia and her new home. A blonde girl resembling her dead daughter haunts the Park doing cruel things with knives and bicycle wheels to tiny living creatures. Noises invade; tiny, ghostly hands flutter lasciviously about Julia's private parts in bed. She gets more and more bloody, gashing and grazing herself, her clothes soaking up her own blood, and that of other mutilated humans and dead animals. She begins to glimpse explanatory patterns. Her house once housed a murderous little blonde girl, stabbed to death by her mother. The murdered girl, Julia discovers, might well be her own husband's daughter. And he—or was it Julia?—stabbed *their* daughter to death trying to save her life by—wait for it—performing an amateur, emergency tracheotomy as she lay choking to death on a piece of meat. *Julia,* its power to horrify doubtless stemming from that original, grisly conceit of parental, kitchen-knife surgery, makes an extraordinarily gripping and tantalizing read. Our all too unreliable central character dies messily: is it murder? by ghost or by human? or is it suicide? Every dubious solution and ambivalent pattern is possible, for almost anything becomes believable under the novelist's stunningly Gothic manipulations.

Peter S. Prescott (review date 26 March 1979)

SOURCE: "All but the Clanking Chains," in *Newsweek,* Vol. XCIII, No. 13, March 26, 1979, p. 104.

[*In the following review, Prescott provides a brief plot summary and a favorable assessment of* Ghost Story.]

Surely this is the longest ghost story ever written. That alone should cause the aficionado to hoist an eyebrow, for the genre virtually demands brevity. I was equally troubled by the author's declaration that he wanted to push the elements of the ghost story "as far as they could go." *That,* I thought, had long since been accomplished by grandmasters from Hawthorne and Le Fanu to Blackwood and M. R. James. Groundless fears, these. With considerable technical skill, Peter Straub has constructed an extravagant entertainment which, though flawed, achieves in its second half some awesome effects. It is, I think, the best thing of its kind since Shirley Jackson's "The Haunting of Hill House."

I mustn't be precise about the plot. It involves some elderly men in an upstate New York town who share a common guilt: an actress, at one of their parties 50 years earlier, was accidentally killed. They gather to tell ghost stories. A lovely woman appears in different guises and with different names, though her initials are always the same. She means to kill these men and those around them. Snow closes in the town. The ghost woman with her familiars—a werewolf and an idiot boy—set about their slaughter. Men and women are

tricked into suicide or brutally destroyed. Corpses walk, victims return to claim their kin; mirrors and windows give false reflections, strange music plays and strange footprints appear in the snow, trees beckon; the reek of rotting flesh yields to the smell of cut flowers. Repressed sexuality, terrifying dreams and treacherous hallucinations abound, as do the promise of hellish immortality and, of course, the suggestion that each victim brings his fate upon himself.

In short, Straub employs every trick that this kind of fiction can offer except clanking chains—I missed them. He breaks up his narrative in a determinedly literary way with elaborate flashbacks and parallel constructions which are at first irritating but in time allow him to work impressive variations on a single scene and to bring off several horrifying climaxes in succession. I mentioned flaws: the ghost explains herself too much; the final pages gloss over the ghastly crime that must be committed to restore moral order, and the story takes too long getting into stride. Only after 200 pages was I sure that it was going to work, but it does work—and, in its own grisly way, triumphantly. My unconscious approved of it before my conscious mind did: *Ghost Story* gave me bad dreams the first night out.

Peter Straub with Joseph Barbato (interview date 28 January 1983)

SOURCE: An interview in *Publishers Weekly,* Vol. 223, No. 4, January 28, 1983, pp. 39-40.

[*In the following interview, Straub discusses the progress of his literary career.*]

First in *Ghost Story* and *Shadowland,* and now again in his new novel *Floating Dragon,* horror novelist Peter Straub has worked to nudge his readers—right off the edge of a cliff, he says. "I want readers to feel as if they've left the real world behind just a little bit, but are still buoyed up and confident, as if dreaming. I want them left standing in midair with a lot of peculiar visions in their heads."

In *Floating Dragon,* he admits, the nudge has escalated into a shove. "I just wanted to explode the line of imagery that I stumbled onto in *Ghost Story* and tried to refine in *Shadowland,*" he says. "I wanted a really gaudy fireworks display—stuff that would make the reader's jaw drop open and make him say, 'I can't believe I'm reading this.'"

In its November 12 Forecasts, *PW* said the February Putnam book "packs enough epic horrors to satiate the most avid fan of scare fare" and is "definitely not for the timid." Set in suburban Hampstead, Conn., *Floating Dragon* tells what happens when the evil ghost of Gideon Winter—the

Dragon—reappears in 1980, seizes the mind of the town doctor and causes a nightmare of suicides and murders. In addition to the supernatural, the town faces the natural threat of poisonous DRG gas that escapes from a chemical plant. Houses burst into flame, and gruesome events unfold.

There was a time when Straub wanted to comfort others, not frighten them. "In college, I wanted to be a doctor—a literary doctor like William Carlos Williams," says the author, who will turn 40 on March 2 and might easily be mistaken for a professional man—a highly competent surgeon, perhaps—judging by the neat gray suit he wore to a recent meeting with *PW* in Putnam's Manhattan office. "Then reality intervened. I discovered I had no gift for science and became an English major. I thought I'd become a college professor. And, after I could admit to myself that what I chiefly wanted to do was write, I thought I'd be a professor who writes books. I expected to have one of those raffish, wandering academic lives."

A native of Milwaukee, Straub earned his B.A. at the University of Wisconsin in Madison in 1965. A year later, he found himself with an M.A. from Columbia University, a wife (Susan Bitker, a counselor) and a job teaching English in a Milwaukee boys' school. He spent three years at the University School, long enough, he says, to find that his students—whom he could touch "in ways that seemed to them absolutely mysterious and godlike; I'd gone to the same school and knew their psyches"—were only 16 and he was 26.

"I grew bored," he says. "If I'd stayed, I'd have become a gravy-stained old teacher with a beat-up car and an alcohol problem. It seemed like a kind of death, and I had to escape. So we went to Ireland to live, and I became a graduate student."

In retrospect, Straub feels the move abroad—they lived in Dublin and London for 10 years, returning to the States three years ago—was a flight from "all sorts of constrictions—the other guys on the faculty, our parents, our middle-class backgrounds and everything that Milwaukee meant. I had to mess myself up enough so I could say, 'I'm going to be a writer because now I have to be. It's the only thing I can do.'"

For several years, he pursued studies at University College in Dublin, but the desire to write intruded. "Many times I'd be invaded by sentences and characters, until finally I said, 'I've got to do it. It's time.' So I plunged in and began a novel. It was a wonderful, freeing experience."

That book, *Marriages,* was accepted by the first British publisher who saw it and was issued by Coward-McCann in the U.S. in 1973. His next novel remains unpublished to this day.

"*Marriages* had not done very well, and it was just about the time that publishers were beginning to cut back on midlist—and bottom-list—authors. And I was one of those guys coming along with more of the same. It unnerved me. I knew I could never hold a real job—that I'd be an impossible employee anywhere. I had to save my life by writing a book that could get published.

"I knew I needed an idea that had some sort of narrative pulse to it," he continues. "It could have been anything, and it turned out to be a ghost story, *Julia.* That's simply where my imagination took me. It wasn't exactly a cynical gesture, but it wasn't an innocent one either. It was an idea native to me that I knew would be instantly appealing to a publisher. I found that I had a natural bent toward this kind of thing. Later, I had to deal with that, because I had never seen myself as that type of writer. I dealt with it by trying to see just how much I could do with that peculiar stock of imagery and leaden conventions that you're given as a horror novelist."

In time, says Straub, he found there were "wonderful things that could be done" in horror fiction, "great little games to play, terrific atmospheres to conjure up and big orchestral climaxes that one could invent." He says novelist Stephen King, now a close friend, helped him overcome a literary education that insisted supernatural stories "must be restrained—that it would be vulgar to become operatic and to go for larger gestures.

"Steve showed me that the rules—the idea that you should hint at something but must break off before you actually present the reader with it—don't apply. That you could show the thing itself—the terrifying, awful, perhaps cornball, thing itself, and as long as you did it in big, bright primary colors, and with all the conviction you could summon up, the reader would be so astonished that he would experience delight."

After his third novel, *If You Could See Me Now,* appeared in 1977, Straub felt prepared for "a big step forward" that would reflect what he had learned from King's example. In the result, his 1979 best-selling *Ghost Story* established his reputation. From that book's earnings, he purchased the Victorian house in Westport, Conn., where he now lives with his wife and their children, Benjamin, 5, and Emma, 2. There, in a spacious, refurbished third-floor attic, he spends each afternoon writing, accompanied by the music of his favorite jazz artists ("everybody good from Bix Beiderbecke to Coltrane") playing on a nearby stereo system.

Straub says he has fully embraced the conception of himself as a horror novelist. Such writing, he says, "gives you a way out of just transcribing realistic experience." But he remains perplexed, he says, by reviewers who see him as "this craftsmanlike guy who's doing what he's done before," as if he were simply a carpenter putting together a good story. "It doesn't feel that way at all to me," he says. "I write these kinds of books because they satisfy something in me—they let me explore personal problems and visions. To me, it's like doing any other kind of art—like playing a jazz solo, or composing a symphony or writing a long poem."

In *Floating Dragon,* says Straub, he pushes "about as far as I can go in that hallucinatory, revved-up style." His next solo performance will contain "fewer visions and nightmares and more of the real world." First, however, he must finish *The Talisman,* the novel he is writing with Stephen King, which is slated for joint publication by Putnam and Viking in the spring of 1984.

"It's a quest story about a boy who thinks he can save his mother's life. She's dying of some disease, and he has to go across the country to get an object that he's assured exists and bring it back to her. This will save her life. There's another world in the book—a fantasy world, in the Tolkien sense—and the boy can travel in that world, too."

The friends are writing alternate sections of the novel on linked word processors, says Straub. "It will be a big book, maybe 900 pages in finished form, and I think people are really going to like it. It's full of a feverish wildness. Writing it has been a good experience, because now I get these big fat vacations when it's Steve's turn to write."

Alan Bold (review date 11 March 1983)

SOURCE: "Horror of Horrors," in *Times Literary Supplement,* March 11, 1983, p. 249.

[*In the review below, Bold reviews* Floating Dragon'*s style, which he describes as "cinematic."*]

Although Peter Straub makes references to writers such as Washington Irving and Wilkie Collins, the immediate sources of his huge novel *Floating Dragon* are cinematic. Addicts of horror and science-fiction movies will recognize images from *Alien* (humans stripped to their gleaming bones), *The Exorcist* (graveyard stench and vomit), *The Shining* (torrents of blood), *Zombies* (decomposing creatures laying hands on the living), *The Invisible Man* (a key character wrapped up in bandages), *The Birds* (with bats replacing Hitchcock's crows) and *The Quatermass Experiment* (the chemical transformation of a man into soapsuds). Straub also indulges in cinematic similes, with a house exploding "like the Death-Star in *Star Wars*", and sets a central scene around a special screening of the violent film *The Choirboys.*

The construction of *Floating Dragon,* consisting of sequences which depend on vivid contrasts and shock effects rather than continuity, is also cinematic. Straub flashes back and forwards in time, dissolves from dream to fictional reality, and presents moments of horror with a pictorial clarity: "The man's face was a grotesque parody of humanity. Nearly dead white, it was puffy and ridged with excess flesh. . . . A wad of flesh on the man's cheek slid towards his dewlapped chin, and Sarah's heart moved for the man . . . she saw that a small colony of spiders was burrowing into his thick woolly hair." It takes a strong stomach, as well as endurance, to read all of this novel, throughout which there are sickening scenes of violence and hallucination with bodies being mutilated, insects assaulting the dying and the dead, and bats and dragons hovering malevolently in the air.

All this happens in a quiet spot in Connecticut. Hampstead seems to be the perfect all-American dream-town with its well-kept streets, its air of affluence, its successful citizens making money and spending spare time jogging or sipping fine wine. The town oozes contentment as it drifts towards the summer of 1980. It has, however, a simply appalling past which is revealed to the reader by a narrator who announces himself abruptly: "Instinct tells me that now is the time to emerge from the cover of the godlike narrator who knows what all his characters are thinking and doing at all times and who takes an impartial stance towards them."

Graham Williams, the narrator, is a writer with a history of political liberalism. More pertinently, he is one of the descendants of the original four families which had founded Hampstead. The others are Richard Allbee, whose life is haunted by the fame of the soap opera he made as a child; Patsy McCloud, whose husband beats her black and blue by way of celebrating his business triumphs; and Tabby Smithfield, a young man who has inwardly grown old watching his father deteriorate with drink and depression. Inevitably the children of the founding fathers get together to try to save the town from what threatens it. Their weapons are paranormal: telepathy, telekinesis, precognition.

The enemy of the people of Hampstead is an evil force so formidable that it can assume human form, infiltrate the imagination and wage chemical warfare on unsuspecting citizens. At one moment the dragon is a man hacking a woman to death, then it is a swarm of flies feasting on a human head, then it is a battalion of bats frightening a woman, then it is poisonous gas contaminating the air, then it is thousands of little dragons spinning out of the smoke.

At times the book reads like an anthology of the worst nightmares ever recorded by human beings. We observe the man who sees his pregnant wife's body opened up and "the opening torn in his wife's belly . . . filled with flies;" and we are taken to the toilet with a man who sees that the "bowl was filled with tiny spiders as red as his hair."

Floating Dragon, beneath its remarkable repertoire of horrific details, is a simple moral tale of the confrontation between good and evil. (To do battle against the dragon it helps to be a saint, so occasionally the four protagonists are haloed with light and provided with a sacred sword-or a "wide dazzling beam" courtesy of *Star Wars.*) Nevertheless, it represents a new level of sophistication in the Gothic novel. Straub plays games with the structure, rapidly switching from third-person to first-person narrative, and teases the reader with biblical symbols and red herrings. The novel is sustained with great skill as the battle between good and evil is impressively, if agonizingly, stretched over the disturbingly supernatural plot.

Michael Small (review date 4 April 1983)

SOURCE: "Yikes! Peter Straub's *Floating Dragon* Scares Suburbia," in *People,* Vol. 19, No. 13, April 4, 1983, pp. 102-03.

[*In the following review, Small presents a favorable assessment of* Floating Dragon.]

A specter haunts the suburban paradise of Hampstead, Conn., and it isn't just crabgrass. A housewife gets slashed, a corporate exec turns to liquid, children in Keds march lemminglike into the sea, which is sometimes blood-red and covered with flies. All of this couldn't make author Peter Straub happier: Such imaginative horror, in a suburb so real you can smell the lawn trimmings, has made his latest chiller, ***Floating Dragon,*** a best-seller. "The terrifying stuff takes flight because it has a solid grounding in reality," says Straub, 40. "Modern writing tries to prove that the supernatural can be drawn into deserts, supermarkets and Laundromats."

Floating Dragon's verisimilitude receives an added boost because fictional Hampstead is modeled closely on Westport, Conn., the affluent seaside New York suburb where Straub lives. "But writing about Westport doesn't make it spooky for me," says Straub, who composes seven hours daily in the attic office of his Victorian house. "When I come downstairs, all the horror disappears." Except, it seems, his fear of shlock. "There's no point in letting this field be taken over by people who are writing with their feet," says Straub, who strives for literary satisfaction, especially in creating engrossing effects. "When I describe something really awful or build up to some huge special effect that's going to make people gasp and forget to breathe, then I enjoy what I'm doing."

One particular fan and friend is ghoulmaster Stephen King,

author of *Carrie, The Shining* and *Cujo.* The pair freely glean from each other's work. "Peter opened my eyes to the art of fiction as storytelling," says King. "I brought a more emotional quality to his writing, but he brought a more intellectual quality to mine." The mutual admiration runs so deep that they are coauthoring an upcoming fantasy called ***The Talisman,*** now two-thirds complete. Working from a prearranged outline, they trade off writing sessions, zapping progressive chapters back and forth between Straub's word processor, in Westport, and King's, in Bangor, Maine. "It's mildly annoying when the plot goes where I didn't expect," says Straub. "But it's fun to get the book back from Steve and see what happened."

His own life has taken a few odd plot twists. Straub, the son of a Milwaukee steel salesman and a nurse, earned a master's in contemporary literature from Columbia University. Afterward he married his college sweetheart, Susan Bitker, taught at a Milwaukee prep school and squelched the dreams of writing he had harbored since his youth. "I was afraid to write," he says "It seemed that the only worthwhile books were masterpieces that could never be equaled by a flawed human like me." But in 1969, when the Straubs moved to Dublin, Ireland, where Peter began to work on his Ph.D., the writing urge took hold and he penned his first novel, ***Marriages.*** When that was published to little note and less remuneration, Straub, by now writing full-time in London, turned to his agent for advice. "You're poor, you're unhappy, write a Gothic," she said. He did. First came ***Julia,*** then ***If You Could See Me Now,*** then 1979's ***Ghost Story,*** which has sold nearly 3 million copies and was made into a 1981 movie starring John Houseman. ***Ghost Story*** also succeeded in making the Straubs favorites of the British tax system, which prompted their return to the U.S. four years ago.

When not tapping out his imaginings—to the music of jazz pianist Bill Evans and saxophonist Scott Hamilton—Straub savors long lunches, evenings at Manhattan jazz clubs, and scaring the Oshkoshes off his children, Benjamin, 5, and Emma, 2, with homespun ghost stories. Peter has never met a demon except "those found inside the ribcage." As for the others, says Straub, "If I saw a ghost, I would be fairly terrified. I hope I wouldn't just take notes."

William Goldstein (interview date 11 May 1984)

SOURCE: "A Coupl'a Authors Sittin' Around Talkin'," in *Publishers Weekly,* May 11, 1984, pp. 253-55.

[*In the following interview, Straub and Stephen King discuss their collaboration on* The Talisman.]

They met in England in 1976 or 1977, at Brown's Hotel in

London. Each had read the other's books, and they had corresponded a bit. "We had a drink or two and got along well enough that we thought we could sit down and have a meal," Stephen King remembers. "So we went along to Crouch End, Peter's house, my wife and I."

He stops to pinpoint the date. "I do remember this. You can find out. When we came back, Stephanie, my sister-in-law, who was staying at our little house in Fleet, came out and said, 'You'll never guess what happened! Bing Crosby died.'"

Feeding the straight line, King adds, "And now Marvin Gaye is dead." Peter Straub jumps on it: "Yeah, we ought to get together more often, Steve. We could undermine the recording industry."

It is one day after April Fool's Day, one day after Gaye's been shot, and King and Straub are back together again, this time for jacket photographs at the New York studio of Andrew Unangst, on Park Avenue South. The two best-selling authors have written a novel together, and it is for this novel, *The Talisman,* that they are taking jacket photographs. The book, to be published in November by Viking in a 500,000-copy first printing, is not a horror novel (and not "what we expected to do," King and Straub agree), but don't be disappointed: it is an imaginative tour de force, "new territory for both of us," the authors believe; and "a stronger novel as a work of art than I expected to write in collaboration with anybody else," King declares, "including Peter or any writer."

The Talisman tells the story of Jack Sawyer, a 12-year-old boy who must cross the United States in search of . . . well, let's just say the Talisman and its magic properties. But there's more—another world, in fact: a Middle-Ages-like place called the Territories, which is a mirror reality of our real world, an "America without guilt, or without fear," according to Straub, populated by "twinners," who are counterparts of characters in the modern narrative. In getting to the Talisman, Jack (and some friends along the way) travels in both worlds, "flipping" back and forth between them, meeting up with a lot of adventures, learning a lot about good and evil, trust and love.

Writing a book together was King's idea. "Steve proposed to me," Straub says. "That was in 1978, very late at night, in the house I had in London. I think he just said, 'Why don't we collaborate on a book sometime?' And I said, 'Great.' We'd had about a million beers," Straub laughs, King echoing, "Yeah." "I remember the coffee table was filled with beer bottles," Straub continues.

"And I wasn't responsible, either," King adds, "because I had the flu or something, remember? It was real bad. Yeah,

it was one of those things you just say, and then you think to yourself, well, it's a good idea, we'll probably never do it. But it's the way people feel when they get married. . . ." "Yeah," Straub jokes, "the 'Let's-Give-It-a-Whirl' approach."

Work wouldn't begin until years later because each writer had contracts to fulfill. Straub's two books would take him four years, he estimated. And King, also for contractual reasons, thought four years was the soonest possible time. (Though Straub worked only on *The Talisman* while writing with King, King had other commitments to complete simultaneously. As he says, "I got into a jam. My mother used to say when I was a kid, if I was a girl I'd always be pregnant.")

That made it 1982. "So," Straub explains, "we only made a *date,* which gave us a lot of time to think about it and kind of dream up what we might do." King "yeah"s in. The two seem the perfect collaborators: they finish each other's sentences, agree with everything the other says, adding details, "yeah"s and punctuating laughter like Motown backup singers. Their stories mesh and their voices become one.

Sitting together on a couch, they look startlingly different, Straub clean-shaven in navy blazer, khakis, white shirt, tie and black loafers, King in a white tuxedo shirt and jeans; bearded (though he tells the photographer to get a last good picture of it because it's coming off that night), wearing brown suede shoes rubbed raw in spots at the toe.

Straub recalls that *The Talisman* "really got on wheels" during the authors' several drives from King's house in Center Level, Me., to Portland, 64 miles away, during one Thanksgiving. "We spent a lot of time in this car ['Talking,' interjects King] talking about the idea," Straub says. "We needed the time, and during those drives we basically came up with the Territories, and with the fact that when you travel in the Territories, you also travel in this world."

It was the to-ing and fro-ing between themselves, both say, that made *The Talisman* possible. "Either one of us could have written *a* book," jokes Straub as King leans further back into the couch to make his statement: "If somebody had held a gun to one of my children's heads, and said, 'Write *The Talisman* by yourself,' I could have written *a Talisman,* but it wouldn't have been the same thing."

King and Straub wrote an outline for *The Talisman,* dividing up the writing assignments between them. The summer before they actually started writing, Straub suggested to King that they each buy a word processor to facilitate the collaboration. King agreed, though he doesn't like working on a word processor: "It makes me feel like that man in the James Bond movie, where he's caught in the exercise machine. I get into it and can't get out. It just scrolls up and up and up and I feel like those words are all under glass."

(King types his manuscripts on an IBM Selectric, has a secretary type it over into the system ["Idle hands do the devil's work, and she loves the machinery, anyway"], and then he rewrites on terminal; this is how he revised *Christine* and *Pet Sematary,* in part to make the rewriting quicker so he could work on **The Talisman**.)

King's IBM and Straub's Wang were hooked up by telephone, and each would send the other his material upon completion. After a year of writing, King says, "we suddenly realized we were working on a book—mostly thanks to me—that was approximately 9000 pages long." Straub interjects: "That's right. If we pursued our outline doggedly, neither one of us would still be alive. But we *would* have a huge pile of pages, almost unreadable. In the original outline, we put that boy [Jack] through too many harrowing trials. Too many to read. But the outline is a very exciting book; the original conception seems more feverish and violent."

"*Much* more violent," King amends. "Not that there still isn't quite a lot of gore and grue. . . ." We try to figure out which version *PW* had seen: the toned-down version, or an earlier attempt? King exclaims: "The key question is: 'Was there a cat that came out through a Coke dispenser [in one scene]?'" No. "Well, we trimmed everything back a bit," Straub confesses. Both feel, as King expresses, that there's a lot of love in the book.

Originally, the book "was gonna be a 'Go-Get-It-and-Bring-It-Back,'" says King. "Finally, we just decided it was gonna be a 'Go-Get-It.' Because it was just out of control. And I was the major reason it was out of control. To begin with, I was truckin' along and Peter was truckin' along and we were doing great and 'Isn't this fantastic?'" Then there took place "The Thanksgiving *putsch*," in 1982, at the Long Wharf Marriott in Boston, a hotel next to the Aquarium ("an important source of imagery," says Straub). "We had to do something about how lost we were getting," King begins to explain, but Straub picks up the idea. "We had to do something else. . . .

"Steve was more aware of this than I and, struck by inspiration, said, 'Look, let's just cut off the last half of this outline. That way. . .'" Straub summarizes the plot. "That solved a lot of the interior aches both of us had."

Weaving together their writing styles was never a problem for either of the authors. "At the beginning," says Straub, "we almost unconsciously tried to imitate the other's style." But that ended after about 100 pages. King, of course, concurs. "After 150 pages or so, it became a collaborative style. And I've never written that way before, and I'll probably never write that way again, unless Peter and I go back to the Territories.'" (There are no plans to do so, the authors say.) "Or decide we want to go to St. Louis or something," he adds, laughing aloud. "I wouldn't dare," he swears.

"I'll tell you something, though, I really felt that some locks came off my mind from writing this together ['Oh, yeah.']. I felt sort of safe for the first time in five or seven years in a creative way because I felt that Peter was my safety net, and if I ran out, there would be somebody there to say, 'Do this,' or 'Why don't you try that?' When we did the outline," he continues, "it was like, it was like a couple of fairly good artists creating one of those Craftmaster paint-by-numbers, not for anybody else, but for themselves." But that assembly-line affair was transformed into a *creation*. "Part of you is your collaborator," King says. ["Uh-uh," Straub nods.] "Or it was in this case."

The novel is more a fantasy (in the tradition of *The Wizard of Oz* and *Alice in Wonderland,* to both of which there are allusions in **The Talisman**) than either Straub or King has written before. The concept of the hero was important to the pair, and they read several books about "The Hero," i.e., the epic hero, the meaning of the hero, stages of heroic development, the Christ figure and apotheosis ("which," says King, "is something Jack never goes through, thank God.")

With this in mind, King says, they began the writing. "Anytime you create a story," he begins critically, "there's always talk about how serious writers, which Peter and I are supposedly *not,* are serious because of their grasp of an entire spectrum of literary concerns. When in fact, if you have a story that is a good story, and then if you determine you will play fair according to the rules of human nature as you understand them and the way the world works at every turn, then by necessity you will write a fairly serious piece of work that accurately reflects human concerns and human mores and ways.

"So I don't think that either one of us knew much beyond the fact that we wanted to write a story that had a strong hero, who was also a sort of picaresque hero, not a Tom Sawyer or Huckleberry Finn clone, but to at least play with the ideas of the traveling person, the traveling hero . . . ."

"Who is changed by his travels," Straub chimes in. ("Travellin' Jack" is one of the protagonist's nicknames.)

"Jack's Mississippi is the Interstate Highway," King says, only partly joking. "I guess what we came out with was something along the lines of the words we've used: sunny, cheerful, in places it's funny, in places it's sad. It plays a little bit," he explains, "in an impish way, with these Leslie Fiedler ['Yeah'] conclusions about dark and light in America,

'Come back to the raft, Huck honey,' the homosexual thing it plays with all that, but it doesn't even hope to do it that well. When you talk about concerns, maybe you," he trails off, turning to Straub, "maybe you want to address that."

Straub turns away from the subject. "No, no, I never feel at ease talking about concerns because they seem to me to be the least part of a book, mainly because they are the concerns of the book, and not necessarily my concerns." King bellows out, "Yeah, that's it!" The two laugh loudly and seem satisfied to have settled the issue between themselves.

Did writing the book together help them individually as writers? Neither really comments, instead taking the chance to extol the virtues of his partner. "I'm sure that Steve understood the characters with more depth than I did." King disagrees: "That's not true at all; I'd say that Peter brings a depth of style I can't muster, a more mature sense of character; a feeling of urbanity I could never have brought."

"Oh Steve," Straub jokes, "I thought you brought that." King continues, "I can't think of any weaknesses that I overcame, except that, as I say, it's like stepping into a third person, and that was interesting. But as far as shortcomings, flaws, that sort of thing, I'm not gonna say anything. Because there will be enough other people who'll say those things." They laugh together as King imitates someone saying, 'This is a big lumbering white buffalo.' And I'm waiting for some critic to take a huge Weatherby 395 rifle to its hump. . . ."

"And blast away," says Straub, breaking them both up again.

Charles Leerhsen (review date 24 December 1984)

SOURCE: "The Titans of Terror," in *Newsweek,* Vol. 104, No. 27, December 24, 1984, pp. 51-52.

[*Below, Leerhsen favorably reviews* The Talisman.]

Stephen King has given us spooky stories like *Pet Sematary* and *The Shining* and taken meetings with, trust me, Hollywood film moguls, so he's obviously a man not easily frightened. Still, not long ago the 37-year-old writer found himself feeling as creepy as, say, a kid reading Stephen King's *Christine.* What worried him was the impending publication of *The Talisman,* an epic quest yarn on which he'd collaborated with Peter Straub, the best-selling author of such spinetinglers as **Ghost Story** and **Floating Dragon**. Would this experiment in terror be remembered, King wondered, as a kind of literary Reese's cup—"You know, where you've got the peanut butter, I've got the chocolate and, hey, this— ain't bad"? Or would it be the prose equivalent of "Rhine-

stone"—"a movie that bombed because, you know, Sylvester Stallone's audience didn't like Dolly Parton and vice versa"? *And wait—there was that one passage that frightened King himself:* it was in the contract, not the book, and it said that if *The Talisman* didn't reach a certain minimum sales figure, he and Straub had to kick in $100,000 apiece for advertising. That was enough to make King hear funny noises in his 24-room Bangor, Maine, mansion—or it would have been if the suspense hadn't ended abruptly on the Oct. 8 release date, when the novel, in one 24-hour sales burst, made back the authors' reportedly substantial advance and began taking off like no book in publishing history.

Listen to booksellers, in fact, and you'd think the title was not *The Talisman* but "The Phenomenon of" same; you'd also think that the best-selling book of 1985 might be "What to Do With Your Extra Copies of, etc." Consider that in the past 10 weeks Viking has distributed an unprecedented (and almost unbelievable) 1 million hard-cover copies (at a suggested retail price of $18.95), meaning that many people who normally get books for Christmas will instead get *Talisman*s. No one who wears glasses is absolutely safe, and those who do can start practicing their frozen smiles ("Gee, thanks, Aunt Sophie!"). Perhaps these folks should imitate recent photos of Straub, who says that he is "positively numb" at the response—and who seems as unphony as the $3 bill he and his collaborator split for each copy. King, on the other hand, seems to speak only in his beloved italics: *The kids are buying this book with their quarters, dimes and nickels—and I think that's great because the bucks gotta live someplace, baby, so they might as well live here with me.*

It doesn't seem to matter that the reviews are what Straub describes as "mixed" and what King, with perverse pride, calls "the worst I've ever gotten." Many critics have noted that the story, which concerns 12-year-old Jack Sawyer's quest, in this world and another, for a magical object that will save his mother's life, unfolds at an almost glacial pace, and that at 645 pages the book is overblown and boring. Jack's adventures in "The Territories," a world in which some of us have near-duplicates called "Twinners" and where freshly picked radishes can be smelled a half-mile away, are richly imagined, but the jarring plot-twists that King and Straub are famous for are, in this case, telegraphed meathandedly. The most common complaint, however, is that *The Talisman* reads like the novelization of a film. It's a charge that Straub finds "obscene"—the authors' just-completed deal with Universal Pictures and Steven Spielberg notwithstanding.

King, for his part, considers the book "literature," but speaks mostly about making marketing history. "This could be a book that changes publishing," he says. He may be right. Viking president Alan Kellock was so convinced of its success that he withheld *The Talisman* from the book clubs, feeling (correctly, as it turns out) that he could sell as many copies through wholesalers at a higher price. Kellock also budgeted the unheard-of sum, in publishing, of $550,000 for advertising, four-fifths of which went for a television commercial that was shown, for the most part, on MTV. "What we've got here is a mix of the fantasy and horror genres," he says, "and that's appealing to the youth market." Among established book buyers, the names on the dust jacket are considered so bankable that no promotional tour was necessary. ("All we may be doing," says King, "is cutting into our own paperback sales.") Instead, the authors did one day of interviews in New York, where they spoke of their serious literary intentions, even as their publisher distributed a press release comparing their compatibility to "Motown backup singers."

Almost no one who knew them thought that their decade-long friendship, which began when King wrote a blurb for an early Straub novel, would survive *The Talisman*. "People warned us that it would be like a teen-age marriage," says King, who first proposed a collaboration during a drunken dinner in London six years ago. "They said we'd ruin a good thing and wind up hating each other for life." The writing, however, went almost completely according to plan. After drawing up an outline at King's place, Straub went into seclusion at his home in Westport, Conn. For 18 months or so they took turns writing sections and sending them, over the telephone lines, to each other's word processor. "We never argued and scarcely ever bitched," says Straub, even when the manuscript had to be edited down drastically to prevent it from becoming "a 9,000-page novel."

It was not until the extremely tough film negotiations, Straub says, that their relationship was put under "considerable strain," and some rather tense phone calls ensued. But that's ancient history now that the book is selling like $19 hot cakes. In fact, Straub and King got together with their families this Thanksgiving and began talking about a sequel. No doubt it will be frightening—especially for two authors already in the 50 percent tax bracket.

Michael Small (interview date 28 January 1985)

SOURCE: "Peter Straub and Stephen King Team Up for Fear," in *People*, Vol. 23, No. 4, January 28, 1985, pp. 50-52.

[*Below, Small interviews Straub and King about their collaboration on* The Talisman *and possible future projects.*]

For two years a dark mysterious mass lurked inside the word processors linked by phone to horror novelist Stephen King's home in Maine and spook writer Peter Straub's in Connecti-

cut. Finally, in November, the thing emerged in the form of America's current No. 1 best-seller, The Talisman. *A 644-page fantasy about a 12-year-old boy's odyssey in a netherworld filled with vicious werewolves and killer trees,* The Talisman *is a triumph of terror, and Steven Spielberg has already snapped up the film rights. Thanks to the book's immediate success, the authors have foregone a lengthy book tour. They did agree, however, to a breakfast interview with Assistant Editor Michael Small. After swapping gory stories over eggs, they discussed* The Talisman:

[*Small:*] *Why did you decide to collaborate?*

[King:] I was intensely curious to see the result. Working together was like that ad where one guy says, "You got chocolate on my peanut butter," and the other guy says, "You got peanut butter on my chocolate," and they end up saying, "Hey! This tastes pretty good."

How did you divide the writing?

[SK:] We wrote the beginning and ending together. Peter put on some jazz in his office, and I wrote for a while as he read magazines. When I was done, he'd pick it up where I had left off. For the rest of the book we divided the work. I'd write a chunk for a month or so at my house and then Peter would continue another chunk at his.

Reviewers say that typical Straub writing is literary and that King writing is popular culture. Is that true?

[Straub:] No. Steve is as literary as he has to be, and I'm fed up with being described as some kind of embalmed mandarin who thinks in polysyllabic orotund sentences. If I were that guy nobody would buy my books.

Which parts did each of you write?

[PS:] We're never going to answer that. But I can tell you that when people guess, they're usually wrong.

Why is The Talisman *so popular?*

[SK:] It's more fun to read a fantasy like this at night than to sit around thinking, "Oh, I've got to go to work tomorrow, and my boss is so ugly."

Is The Talisman *different from the books you write separately?*

[PS:] While we were writing, it didn't seem as sinister as our previous books. I remember that every now and then we added something deliberately crude or shocking just so the book wouldn't be too honeyed.

Because the book has so many movie-type special effects, some critics say you wrote it specifically for the movies.

[SK:] Why would anyone who's done as well writing books as Peter or me ever stoop to the idea of selling a movie scenario as a novel? The word "film" never crossed our lips when we wrote.

Did you ever disagree?

[SK:] Not at all. Except Peter thinks a computer is great to write on, and I'm less enraptured. It makes me feel like I'm in the James Bond movie where he's tied to an exercise machine.

How did you get along so well?

[SK:] Peter's a friend and I only have about three of them. He makes me laugh harder than anyone else.

[PS:] That's because you're twisted.

How did you two meet?

[PS:] After Steve wrote some kind blurbs for my books, I wrote to him in 1978 to thank him. He wrote back to say he was coming to visit.

[SK:] We liked each other so well that we started talking about a collaboration the second time we met.

Will you do it again?

[SK:] Peter has an idea about a haunted house, and I'm free in about three years.

[PS:] I'm free in about five.

[SK:] Okay, let's compromise. We'll do it in four.

Bernadette Bosky (essay date 1985)

SOURCE: "Stephen King and Peter Straub: Fear and Friendship," in *Discovering Stephen King*, edited by Darnell Schweitzer, Starmont House, 1985, pp. 55-76.

[*In the essay below, Bosky examines the influence of Stephen King on the development of Straub's literary style.*]

Friendships between writers are always interesting, and that between Stephen King and Peter Straub is both one of the more interesting and one of the more productive in the history of supernatural and horror fiction. Even in a genre

whose writers have a certain sense of community, friendship may be difficult. As Peter Straub puts it, "Meetings of writers are always like the coming together of princes who rule over small, but highly independent countries, and a wrong word, a breath of rudeness can lead to undeclared warfare." Literary friendships—such as those of Howard Phillips Lovecraft and Robert Bloch, Frank Belknap Long, or Clark Ashton Smith—are rare, especially if both parties are already established authors when they meet.

Those friendships that do develop, however, tend to be deep and lasting, and their effects can be seen in the work, as well as the lives, of the authors. The literary study of such relationships is valuable, even for those who believe—in the words of Stephen King's eerie men's club in "the Breathing Method"—"It is the tale, not he who tells it." An examination of King and Straub's friendship shows the great differences, and even more important similarities, of their individual achievements in fiction. While the co-writing of **The Talisman** is the most concrete result of their artistic interaction, much can also be learned by study of their separate fiction, before and during the collaboration.

It would be difficult to imagine two more different presences than those of Stephen King and Peter Straub. King is a Maine-bred all-American, down-home, informal; Straub is reserved, impeccable, as British by his ten-year residence there as he is American by birth and current residence. King describes Straub in the program book for World Fantasy Convention '82, at which Straub was one Guest of Honor:

> "One Peter Straub," I can almost hear Rod Sterling intoning, "caught somewhere between Brooks Brothers . . . and *The Twilight Zone*." But it's nothing as ordinary as Brooks Brothers; he is more apt to be clad in a three-piece pinstriped suit from Paul Stewart. His tie is apt to be subdued without being so hopelessly mellow you don't even see it. . . . He wears dark plastic-framed spectacles which sit firmly on his nose and declare to the world: *No bullshit!*

Straub describes his first meeting with king, in a genteel London hotel: "Steve appeared, not genteel, lumbering toward me down a corridor between the bar and the sedate lobby. 'Peter!' he shouted. . . . He was huge and keyed-up and warm and he laughed a lot. . . ."

These physical presences are almost icons of the differences between their fiction. As Douglas Winter states, "If Stephen King is the heart of contemporary horror fiction . . . then Peter Straub must be considered its head . . . In contrast to Stephen King's seemingly intuitive and colloquial storyteller's prose the fiction of Peter Straub is deliberate, structurally complex, and above all, styled." King's apprentice work was short stories in *Startling Mystery Stories* (his first publication) and men's magazines like *Cavalier,* and is sometimes clumsy or crude; Straub's was poetry and two mainstream novels (*Under Venus* and *Marriages*), and is sometimes remote and too mannered.

Yet in many ways the differences between the two men are less important than their similarities. Of course, there is the level of success, artistic and commercial, that each has achieved. While King is both more prolific and more popular, each in his own way is a leader in the field of horror and supernatural fiction. Both have repeatedly had works on the best-seller lists, and both have had novels made into movies, with varying degrees of success; most importantly, both have been instrumental in widening the audience of the horror novel in a way that would have seemed incredible thirty years ago. While books like *The Exorcist* and *The Other* were perhaps necessary to pave the way, only King and Straub have achieved that kind of mainstream-horror success repeatedly. "We wanted to take our chances in the world outside the ghetto of horror-fantasy," Straub states of both himself and King, "and to find also those readers who thought Lovecraft was the author of sex manuals". One reason for their respective successes in this is their artistic dedication to craft and the demands of storytelling; that, more than anything less, is the basis of their friendship.

The story of the meeting and acquaintance of King and Straub, as it has been reported elsewhere, is dominated by mutual respect for and understanding of each others' writing. It is not flattery or judgment colored by friendship when Straub calls King "clearly one of the best writers of any kind in the United States," and states that *The Shining* is "obviously a masterpiece, probably one of the best supernatural novels in a hundred years", or when King says, "Peter Straub is one of the best," and calls *Ghost Story* "one of the best gothic horror novels of the past century". Rather, it is the appreciation for the works that drew the men to friendship in the first place.

The first encounter between the two men was when King sent what Straub calls "easily the most insightful" of all the blurbs (positive comments on a novel, for packaging and advertising) he received on his first supernatural novel, *Julia.* King, whose career was just starting to gather momentum, was unknown to Straub, but was identified in the blurb as the author of *Carrie* and *'Salem's Lot.* When Straub found a copy of *'Salem's Lot,* he says, he bought it, "out of loyalty, with no expectations," but was both surprised and impressed. As Straub, "became evangelical about Stephen King, thinking that here was a writer so good that everyone ought to read him," King wrote another blurb, this one for *If You Could See Me Now,* Straub's second supernatural novel; Straub reports, "it amounted to a mini-essay: two pages of generos-

ity and insight . . . it became clear that if I had an ideal reader anywhere in the world, it was Stephen King." Straub's account of his immediate reactions to *'Salem's Lot* and, later, *The Shining* shows that the ideal relationship of author and reader went both ways.

"After *The Shining,*" Straub states, "it was *not* possible not to write [King]". Correspondence ensued, and arrangements were made in 1977 for the families to meet in England, where Straub and his wife were living, and King and his family were going to visit. After an arranged meeting that failed because the cab driver couldn't go as far as Straub's home in the Crouch End area of London—inspiring Stephen King's story "Crouch End" in *New Tales of the Cthulhu Mythos*—the two finally met.

However, the effects of their friendship on Straub's work began long before that. In Straub's works after *If You Could See Me Now*—*Ghost Story, Shadowland,* and especially *Floating Dragon*—it is clear that observation of King's writing galvanized Straub and helped him develop his work in several ways. In most cases, Straub did not at all change direction, but experimented with more and better ways to actualize his own unique approach.

One possible area of actual change, and the clearest example of King's influence on Straub, is in the use of subtle vs. blatant horror; yet even there, it seems the example of King's fiction led Straub in a direction he probably would have traveled anyway.

Undeniably, there is a major change from the subtle horror of *Julia* to the overwhelming horror shows of *Floating Dragon.* In the former, even the key horrific image—Julia performing a makeshift, and fatal, tracheotomy on her young daughter—occurs offstage, and is seen indirectly, especially through Julia's memory. Straub states, "I was burdened . . . with everything I thought I knew about supernatural literature—a kind of Henry James lesson: that to be good, books of this kind had to be ambiguous, modest, and restrained. They had to have good manners." That is hardly a description one would apply to *Floating Dragon,* with its parade of animated corpses, "leakers" melting into colloid, psychic cooperation and confrontations, and disgusting as well as frightening hallucinations. "It is completed unrestrained," Straub states, and correctly predicted, before the book's release, that some would like it and others would see the direction as unfortunate.

Certainly, this direction is partly due to King's influence on Straub. As Straub states:

> . . . after reading *'Salem's Lot, The Shining,* and *The Stand,* I realized that my notions about a well-bred novel didn't apply to this kind of book. In fact, they

were inhibiting. Better that this kind of book be bad-mannered, noisy, and operatic . . . King would describe the horror and put in right in front of your face—and it worked. That dazzled me. "Damn it," I thought, "I can do that, too. I can be presentational, instead of shading everything backward into ambiguity."

Elsewhere, Straub has stated, "I'm very grateful to Stephen King for showing me that you . . . can be as blatant and as outspoken as you can and still get away with it", and "[King's writing] was like a roadmap of where to go: he armored my ambition".

Yet in addition to what Straub says of his debt to King in this area, two things should be made clear. First of all, Straub's tendency from the ambiguous and understated and towards the presentational and operatic was probably determined as early in his career as the end of *If You Could See Me Now.* That book was actually written with two endings: in the first, a human character is found to be the killer; Straub recalled the book from the publishers, and rewrote the last 80 pages into the supernatural ending. "I finally decided," Straub states, "after a lot of struggle, that it was cheating not to have the ghost revealed." Although King armored his ambition by providing a successful example and some techniques to use, it seems likely that the ambition was already strongly there.

Moreover, King's own approach is much more complex and varied than the public conception of his writing sometimes allows for. While some of the most blatant shocks may be the most memorable, King's writing has always done more than that. In his fine work of criticisms of the horror genre *Danse Macabre,* King states, ". . . the genre exists on three more or less separate levels, each a little less fine than the one before it." Terror, he states, is "the finest emotion: We actually *see* nothing outright nasty . . . It is what the mind sees that makes . . . stories quintessential tales of terror." Then comes horror, "that emotion of fear that underlies terror, an emotion that is slightly less fine, because it is not entirely of the mind. Horror also invites physical reaction by showing us something which is physically wrong." Finally, there is "lowest of all, the gag reflex" of disgust. Concluding, King states:

> My own philosophy as a sometime writer of horror fiction is to recognize these distinctions because they are sometimes useful, but to avoid any preference for one over the other on the grounds that one effect is somehow better than another. . . . I recognize terror as the finest emotion . . ., and so I will try to terrorize the reader. But if I find I cannot terrorize him/her, I will try to horrify; and if I find I

cannot horrify, I'll go for the gross-out. I'm not proud.

One reason why Straub found King's approach congenial, then, was probably that it presented wider versatility than Straub's own, while still giving most respect to effective indirection and terror. Certainly, *The Shining* is a virtuoso performance of all three levels of genre writing, including terror the equal of any supernatural novel; this may well be one reason for Straub's outstanding acclaim for that book. Don Herron points out that King, like his character Billy Nolan in *Carrie,* has the "unfailing ability to pinpoint the vulgar." He certainly does, and he uses it well; but it would be wrong to see that as the only hallmark of King's writing—as wrong as it would be to see the direction Straub's fiction has taken as unprecedented or due solely to King's influence. King's view of terror as "finer" than disgust or horror, but no more useful, made him appreciative of Straub's work; Straub's awareness, after writing *If You Could See Me Now,* of the vast potential of the genre—"you could do *anything* within a supernatural or Gothic structure"—made him receptive to King's wider repertoire of approaches.

Straub's *Floating Dragon,* with "its gaudier toys" influenced by the simultaneous collaboration with Stephen King on *The Talisman,* also shows the influence of Stephen King on the prose style. It is difficult, if not impossible, to imagine the characters of any other Peter Straub novel calling someone a "twink" or a "fuckhead clown," as Bruce and Dickie Norman do in *Floating Dragon;* it is not at all difficult to see this as an influence of King's visceral and colloquial prose.

In general, King's style is extroverted and Straub's is introverted, in the technical Jungian sense. That is, King's is marked by outside referents, while Straub's is based on inner states and perceptions. When *Shadowland* came out, fellow dark fantasy writer Charles Grant wrote, "Stephen King is a realist—his compilation of details only adds to the now of his strokes; at his best, Straub is an impressionist. . . ." As the strengths and weaknesses in Straub's approach can be traced to that "Henry James lesson," King compares his own to those of Theodore Dreiser, an apt comparison. Dreiser and King are not only storytellers, but also—like Fran Goldsmith with her diary in *The Stand*—historians concerned with recording their societies as fully and vividly as they can, in general pattern and in detail. This *copia* (a tradition which goes back at least to the Renaissance) has its pitfalls, including that the work may lack shape, and may go on at least as long as the reader wishes it to. Contrariwise, Straub's works risk, as Charles Grant states, the problem of any impressionism: "swift brush strokes and outlines, look too close and the effect is diminished . . . ," although the overall effect is strong. However, his novels often have an artistic coherence King's may lack, and often show impressive literary excellences, such as the metafictive elements of **Ghost Story**. In fact, **Ghost Story** is a summary of and homage to the Gothic literary genre, as *The Stand* is a summary of and homage to the American culture of its time. However, while the approaches of the two may widely differ, the goal is in each case the same: to produce a convincing story, significant primarily as an exploration and explication of our human nature and condition. It is from this perspective that each praises the others' prose. Stephen King states:

> [Straub's] prose has always been as impeccable and correct as his dress. It is what I think of as "the good prose," prose which is almost always structurally correct . . . and which is, in its own way, as subdued—but as authoritative—as his ties. It is not flashy, gaudy prose, but each sentence is as tight as a timelock, as unobtrusively strong as the good (but hidden) joists in a fine Victorian house that will last for three hundred years. "The good prose" has served a lot of great writers in good stead despite its lack of flash—its users extend in an unbroken line which includes such writers as Sinclair Lewis, Henry James, Thomas Hardy, M. R. James, Wilkie Collins, and Charles Dickens. . . . [They] wrote "the good prose," but that prose never kept their work from being enthralling—and, in many cases, subversive.

Peter Straub states:

> . . . one other aspect of *The Shining* that impressed me [was] its style. This is not at all a literary style, but rather the reverse. It made a virtue of colloquialism and transparency. The style could slide into jokes and coarseness, could lift into lyricism, but what was really striking about it was that it moved like the mind itself. It was an unprecedentedly direct style, at least to me, and like a lightning rod to the inner lives of his characters.

It is revealing that once again, what Straub notices and applauds about King's writing is its versatility, while what King notices and applauds about Straub's writing is its solidity. Regarding style, King has said, "I think that there's a lot of critical interest in writing that's pretty, rather than serviceable, and I'm more interested in stripping down." In Straub's prose, King found "pretty" and "serviceable" to work together rather than being at odds. Straub, on the other hand, found that he could strip down his prose if he wished, in keeping with the situation and characters; he shows this greater variety, gaining new voices without losing the old voice, in **Floating Dragon**. The contrast between the Raymond Chandler first-person narrative of **If You Could**

See Me Now and the Jamesian atmosphere of **Julia** shows Straub already highly valued and sought versatility of prose style, but association with King widened his range of technique.

The method of collaboration on **The Talisman,** which has been reported elsewhere, led to a unique style, in which it is virtually impossible to identify the author of a given passage. Not only did Straub and King deliberately try for a "seamless" style throughout the work, sometimes for fun each would imitate the other's style. The prose of **The Talisman** is smooth and powerful; it, like the authors' process of collaboration, shows dedicated writers improving their craft, yet secure enough to be playful with it.

One stylistic device which acts as "a lightning rod to the inner lives of [the] characters" in the solo work of both authors is the use of recurrent refrains or motifs; however, Straub develops his imagistically while King develops his with repeated words or phrases. Straub states that his writing is influenced structurally by jazz music, of which he is an aficionado. As Straub states, "One thing I like in a book is when the parts seem to all relate; when one thing early on in the book is echoed by another thing later in the book. Even words and speech patterns are repeated later. Little images might be repeated later. So the whole book is interconnected". Examples of this would be the "deadly rhyme" of Heather Rudge's murder of her daughter and Julia Lofting's killing her daughter, in **Julia**; the characters with the initials A. M—Alma Mobley, Angie Maule, Alice Montgomery—in **Ghost Story**; and the ubiquitous bird imagery in **Shadowland,** from the motto *Alis volat propriis* and the Ventnor owl to the horrifying, huge white bird and the final transformation of Del.

King uses very few of these associational structuring devices in his book, relying on an action-based plot and to some extent on theme. One lightning rod to his characters' minds, however, is repetition on a purely verbal (rather than imagistic) level as an element of stream-of-consciousness technique. This is especially fitting for King's horror novels, in that often the mind will hold onto and revolve around a certain phrase during times of fear; also, King uses this technique to show both what is on the character's mind and how that mind works. The second chapter of *The Dead Zone,* after Johnny Smith has won on the wheel of fortune at the carnival and before the accident that sends him into a coma for years, has many excellent examples. Note that even something as visual as the wheel is conveyed mainly by the patterns of words of the barker's spiel:

> Until all that was left seemed to be a giant red-and-black wheel revolving in such emptiness as there may be between the stars, try your luck, first time fluky, second time lucky, hey-hey-hey. The wheel

revolved up and down, red and black, the marker
ticking past the pins, and he strained to see if it was
going to come up double zero, house number, house
spin, everybody loses but the house.

Interestingly, both imagistic and verbal repetitions occur in
"The Breathing Method," a novella by King, dedicated to
Peter and Susan Straub and appearing in King's *Different
Seasons* volume. The phrase "cheap magic" weaves through
the story, as phrases do in King's stream-of-consciousness
writing: the unwed mother uses that to describe the two-dol-
lar ring that makes her appear married and respectable; it
later occurs in her doctor's dream of her doom, and when
the doctor delivers her baby. In each of the latter cases, the
doctor adds the thought that though the magic is cheap, it's
all we have. Another kind of unity is lent the story through
the statue of Harriet White, with its motto "There is no comfort without pain; thus we define salvation through suffering," and, of course, through the breathing method itself.
This latter kind of motif is not unique to "The Breathing
Method" among King's writing, but it is more characteristic of Straub's; also, due to the compactness of a shorter
form, it has greater force in the novella than it would in one
of King's novels, while the novel-wide use of the technique
is characteristic of Straub but not of King.

Stephen King's and Peter Straub's approaches to plotting and
structuring a novel show some influences from their association and, once again, a notable number of independently
arrived at similarities. Although King and Straub did develop
an outline for their collaboration on *The Talisman,* generally neither one uses an outline or detailed notes while individually writing novels. Straub says he outlined only the end
of *Shadowland* and the latter two-thirds of *Floating
Dragon*; otherwise, he "plunged in blind and swam along
and tried to stay afloat," sometimes knowing what would
happen at the end and sometimes not. King says he has a
certain idea of what will happen in the book, but he knows
"there will probably end up being some variance." It is interesting that *Carrie* and *If You Could See Me Now,* both
early and groundbreaking works for each author, began as
short stories that outgrew that length and became novels.

Because of the intuitive, associational approach they have
to writing and the lack of a strictly determining outline, both
King and Straub speak of sometimes being surprised by the
developments in their own books. The unplanned, or subconsciously planned, developments in King's novels tend to
be the behavior and fate of characters. For instance, King
says that while the intention in *'Salem's Lot* was to have everyone but the writer killed at the end, "I fell in love with
the little boy that I was writing about, and I couldn't let him
go, and he ended up going along." Contrariwise, King "was
sure" when he wrote *Cujo* that Tad would live. His report
of what happened when he wrote the ending indicates the

deep processes of his writing that sometimes can contradict
even his authorial intention:

> So she finally dispatched the dog and got the kid
> out, and by then the kid appeared dead; but I wasn't
> worried, because I knew that what had happened
> was probably that his heart had stopped . . . And so
> she was giving him mouth-to-mouth and her hus-
> band turned up, and I suddenly realized that it's fif-
> teen minutes later and she's still giving him the
> Heimlich [sic]—I started to go back and change it
> so that all this happened in the space of about ten
> minutes; but if you stop, if you really stop, you
> throw your brain into gear and that spoils every-
> thing. Because it's supposed to come from some-
> where down here, the language, the syntax, and
> everything else. I don't want to think about what I
> decided to do when I write, and the answer was the
> kid died on me.

While King tends to start out with a "what if" supposition
that leads to plot and, secondarily, character and to be surprised by what actually happens to characters, Straub tends
to start out with mood or imagery and to be surprised by
the significance of what is going on—not necessarily the
events themselves—and how that fits into the imagery pattern. Straub sets up the story to provide a number of thematic and imagistic "rhymes" or "structural connections";
then more of these emerge in the writing than he had
planned. Straub says that having Magnus be the father of the
corrupt girl in *Julia,* "struck me like a bolt of lightning when
I wrote the book." When Straub gave his editor the first two-
thirds of *Shadowland,* the editor asked if Rose Armstrong
were a mermaid. "And then I started to think about it,"
Straub reports, "and I fought the idea for a while, but then
it just seemed to me to be absolutely *perfect.*

Perhaps the immediacy of the writing to King and Straub at
the time of composition adds to the emotional impact of their
novels on the reader. The similar approaches—ability to use
an outline but always improvising on it—allowed them to
work together on *The Talisman;* more importantly, it lends
a similar atmosphere to the work of each, despite the many
differences.

In the ability to plot, consciously or subconsciously, Straub
learned much from Stephen King. Again, however, while
King's writings provided Straub with techniques and motive
for more complicated plotting, the ability and tendency must
have been already there; this is especially shown by the intricate and effective manipulation of scenes and time in
Floating Dragon, outstripping King's involving but often
sometimes gawky plot-weaving in such novels as *The Stand.*

Both of Straub's early Gothic novels, *Julia* and *If You Could*

See Me Now, were relatively simple, with a handful of characters and one main plot. Reading King's fiction, especially *'Salem's Lot,* helped Straub shift to the wider scale and greater complexities of plotting *Ghost Story.* First, the association with King provided Straub with a pattern to follow. "'*Salem's Lot,*" he states, "sort of showed me how you can organize all these characters. I just used Stephen King's 'graph' and it helped keep things in line. In many ways, *Ghost Story* isn't at all like *'Salem's Lot,* but I certainly borrowed his way of organizing the town."

But perhaps more important than the techniques Straub borrowed for *Ghost Story* is the motivation that the association with King provided. "Every time you write a book," Straub states, "you pretty much have to keep the whole book in your head the whole time . . . I always thought I could do that . . . but I never had the courage to try it until [*Ghost Story*]." One reason why he tried then, Straub says, was "largely because I met Stephen King, and I thought, 'Well, I oughta be able to do it if he could do it,' and I was impressed by what he could do, and it seemed to me that if I wanted to earn any sort of standing, I would have to try to do more than I had before."

Straub certainly does have the ability for complex plotting once he tried, as his later work shows. In fact, he states, "as it turns out, I do . . . think of very, very intricate plots. They just sort of invent themselves." *Floating Dragon* is a virtuoso performance of interweaving plots, much more stylish and sophisticated than King's, with various patterns of intercuts, hints of events past and future, and flashbacks and flash forwards. Events will act as "loci," with the involvement of various characters and their reactions radiating backward and forward in the text undercutting strictly temporal cause and effect as we know it: thus, incidents like Patsy's husband going out with a gun and Tabby meeting Patsy, or one character looking into a restaurant and seeing Tabby with Bruce and Dickie Norman, act to center the action of the novel, while showing their own importance as meeting points of the fellowship in the novel. Straub creates suspense by this technique, but sometimes the sense of artistic proportion it lends makes *Floating Dragon* more enjoyable but not necessarily more scary.

King's interweaving of sub-plots is more basic, but every bit as effective at the multiple purposes it serves in his novels. While the frame-narrative of *'Salem's Lot* reassures the reader that Ben and Mark do survive the vampires, generally flash forwards and (slightly less often) flashbacks are used to build a sense of unease; the inserted articles and testimonies in *Carrie* are a clear example of this, but it is useful in all of King's books. In *The Stand,* interweaving of sub-plots creates tension when one thread is dropped—often at a cliff-hanger worthy of a Saturday matinee serial—and another taken up. While some readers find this annoying,

King has an admirable knack for knowing just when most readers will grow unbearably impatient for a return to a certain plot, and he switches back just at that point.

Besides creating suspense, King also uses interweaving of plots and scenes to balance the supernatural menace or power and the natural development of social themes and character backgrounds in his novels. As both King and Straub know, the supernatural element has to cohere thematically with the other development in the book. Straub says, "It's . . . important, in this field, that the bad stuff, the evil, just doesn't come out of the blue, as something invented; it should come from the characters themselves." Stephen King shows his awareness of this throughout his *Danse Macabre,* in which he shows works of horror that derive their fear from societal concerns, personal anxieties, basic human fears such as death, and the deep lure and terror of narcissism: "that the monsters are no longer due on Maple Street, but may pop up in our mirrors—at any time." That both authors implement this awareness in their works is one thing that sets them both apart from most horror paperback novels, in which the supernatural element has nothing to do with the characters and (hence) no real thematic purpose.

Structurally, however, Straub's approach seems to blend the natural and supernatural more smoothly. King's characters sometimes have even more depth, history, and detail than Straub's do: as Alan Ryan puts it, the characters "seem to be alive even before the time of the story"; they "notice the kinds of things we notice [and] feel the kinds of things we feel." Although the copious background on the characters before the supernatural intrusion is advantageous, it often makes the resulting novel pull in two separate directions, with the two developments clashing rather than working together.

James van Hise picks *The Shining* as an example of conflict in development, although I think more critics would agree that it is a counter example, in which Jack's alcoholic rage and the Overlook's evil not only feed off each other, but are somehow fundamentally similar. However, most of King's novels do have some problems with this; Don Herron argues somewhat persuasively that the real horror in King's novels is not supernatural at all, and in some cases, such as *'Salem's Lot,* the supernatural elements are not very compelling. *Christine* and *Cujo* are examples in which the split almost, thought not quite, goes beyond King's ability to handle. King mentions someone, "who was saying that he didn't respond to the Gothic elements in my books—that when the man-eating car showed up, he sort of fell out. The thing he liked about *Christine* was Arnie Cunningham's relationship with his parents—in other words, the 'real' stuff," but someone else said, "what did it for her *was* the Gothic elements, that side of it." The problem here is not—as Herron suggests—that King should choose one over the other, but that if the horror grows completely out of the characters and setting, there is not a choice to be made.

The second main use of plot-interweaving for Stephen King, then, is to balance off psycho-social and supernatural scenes, if not exactly to blend the two elements. In *The Stand,* scenes with the Walkin' Dude keep the supernatural awe going while the characters of Harold, Frannie, Stu and others are developed. In books like *Firestarter* and *The Dead Zone* in which there is no inherent link between the power and the personality—an Everyman character almost by definition cannot seem as strangely fitted to a wild talent as Carrie White does—the psychic events are carefully balanced against scenes of Charlie and her father together, or Johnny Smith teaching, so that neither aspect of the book takes over.

Given each author's skillful use of organization for such different purposes, the structure of **The Talisman** is a bit disappointing. Of course, a quest structure inherently simplifies the plot; also, the final plan for the book was substantially shorter than the original twenty-five to thirty page outline. In what the authors call "the great Thanksgiving *putsch*" the book was, in Douglas Winter's words, "radically streamlined to its published structure and length," since a full version based on the original outline might have been thousands of pages long. While the constraints of time, energy, and publishing are understandable, the result sometimes lacks both the feeling of inevitability that can result from Straub's style, and the credibility that King's characters and stories can gain from being firmly rooted in the quotidian.

Somewhat more successful is the blending of the two authors' thematic concerns in **The Talisman,** especially the development of Jack Sawyer from a boy into a man, and the investigation of the American Dream and the nightmare that it sometimes becomes in contemporary socio-politics.

Each author, in his individual work, has written well about children. King tends to write about somewhat younger children as well as adolescents, and is primarily concerned with showing the child's world as it is, although that of course includes growth. As Charles Grant puts it, "In [King's] view, children are in their way just as complex as adults, and should be treated with just as much dignity." Outstanding examples of this include, but are not limited to, Charlie McGee and Danny Torrance. Straub also shows understanding of this complexity and dignity of childhood, but is more concerned with boys (unlike King, he has never had as a main character a young human female) who have just put one foot into adulthood and must now make the painful transition, since one cannot go back. Straub points out that this theme in **Shadowland** was influenced by Bruno Bettelheim's book on fairy tales, *The Uses of Enchantment,* but Peter Barnes and Tabby Smithfield face comparable demands and changes.

In **The Talisman,** Jack Sawyer's quest is not only for the magic that will save his dying mother and renew the Territories, but also for his own manhood: as the quotation from *Tom Sawyer* that ends the novel states, "So endeth this chronicle. It being strictly the history of a *boy,* it must stop here; the story could not go much further without becoming the history of a *man.*" The difference between Jack, set on maturation, and his friend Richard Sloat, who would rather retreat into childish avoidance, is in some ways similar to that between Tom and Del in Straub's **Shadowland.** It is also oddly like the difference between Charlie McGee in King's *Firestarter* and his eponymous heroine in *Carrie;* although Carrie is chronologically older, she is mastered by her power while Charlie is determined to master hers. Jack is helped to begin the quest by Speedy Parker, a black man who plays the role of a safe and benevolent father-figure, with roots in both Dick Hollorann of *The Shining* and Speckle John/Bud Copeland of **Shadowland.** But Speedy Parker is significantly limited in his power to help Jack once he's on his journey, when Morgan Sloat, the bad father-figure, dominates.

In general, as Douglas Winter states, "Jack Sawyer's quest for the Talisman finds little solace in either our world of the Territories; life on the road is a nightmarish moralizing experience." One reason for this is that thematically **The Talisman** is not only the tale of a boy growing up, but a landscape of American society and values; and the picture is a grim one. Straub states, "what Steve [King] describes as 'Reagan's America' is almost implicit in the elements we assembled for the book. The book does seem to be about the death of the land, the terrible poisoning of the land." The clear air of the Territories is a damning counterpoint to the hydrocarbon stench of our reality, and the "blasted lands" of the Territories are probably the fault of our militarism.

King and Straub show different views of American history in their individual works, but both combine well to present the American portrait in **The Talisman.** King's view is sad and yet hopeful: the infinite promise of America at her best makes betrayal and failure that much worse, but somehow still holds hope of something better. In *Danse Macabre* King recalls the disillusionment and fear he felt when the Russians set Sputnik in orbit, but in doing so he passionately describes how he felt before that:

> Further, we [the USA] had a great history to draw on (all short histories are great histories) . . . Every grade-school teacher produced the same two words for the delectation of his/her students; two magic words glittering and glowing like a beautiful neon sign; two words of almost indescribable power and grace; and these two words were: PIONEER SPIRIT. I and my fellow kids grew up secure in the knowledge of America's PIONEER SPIRIT . . . We

were and always had been, in that pungent American phrase, fustest and bestest with the mostest.

King is disappointed and even furious with what has become of the American Dream, but he still believes in its message of frontier possibility and simple human goodness. This dichotomy can be seen in the contrast between Irv Manders and the Shop in *Firestarter,* and of course forms the entire basic foundation of *The Stand.*

Straub's vision of America's heritage is both more literary and melancholy. Shaped by early American authors like Hawthorne and Cooper, he sees the frontier less as promising potential than as a frightening vastness with an unaccountable history and disposition all its own. There is a free-floating shame and guilt from the land in most of Straub's novels, which is tied into the story action implicitly in *If You Could See Me Now* and *Ghost Story* and quite explicitly in *Floating Dragon.* Straub says that when he was in college, a teacher talking about a Faulkner story, "uttered a phrase that went right through me . . . 'a sexual crime in the past,'" and speculates that this phrase sums up the basic concern of all his novels. In Straub's as in much of Faulkner's works, the guilt of sex and the guilt of the land are inextricable—and both are unavoidable. It is interesting to contrast the inevitable and historical evil of *Floating Dragon* and the evil of *'Salem's Lot,* drawn at most by only the Marsten house and perhaps just by chance.

These two views of America, her history, and her promise work well together in *The Talisman.* The infection our culture brings to the Territories is a source of inexplicable guilt, and grows from some incurable flaw in our country, inevitable as death; yet Jack's great American dream of a quest is happily successful in its own terms, and despite the same state of things there is the feeling that some things, at least, can be put right.

Both themes in the novel, that of personal maturation and of American society, are greatly enhanced by the metafictive resonances in *The Talisman,* reminiscent of Straub's novels. King often alludes to literature from "Christabel" to *Vampirella* magazine; these references are entertaining but not truly metafictive. They locate the story within our world, provide somewhat of an associative context, and please the horror *cognoscenti* but remain essentially peripheral to the work, as Don Herron has pointed out. This is not to slight their importance, as Mr. Herron does; rather, they serve as yet another kind of verbal motif for King to use, while keeping the narrative focus on situations that follow our accepted views of "real" people and events. Straub's work is often truly metafictive, in that the literary references also structure the events of the novels' "real" characters, as when Sears James recounts an experience which the reader knows is based on Henry James' *Turn of the Screw.*

Both kinds of literary references occur in *The Talisman.* As Douglas Winter shows, some of the fun in the novel comes from references almost playfully slipped, recalling other authors or King and Straub's own work: Rainbird Towers, a reference to the character in *Firestarter;* and the line, "when we all lived in California, and no one lived any place else," a reworking of a recurrent line in *Shadowland.* More basic to the plot, characters, and development of *The Talisman*— comparable to the role played by the history of the Gothic in *Ghost Story* or the fairy tale in *Shadowland*—are two kinds of literature: Mark Twain's Huck Finn and Tom Sawyer books, including little-read books like *Tom Sawyer Abroad;* and heroic or quest literature "like the story of Jesus, the story of King Arthur, *Sir Gawain and the Green Knight.*" The latter were probably more important to the writing of *The Talisman* than the former, but the former was, if nothing else, probably useful for its purely American tone and its depiction of a believable, human boy growing up.

Two other thematic concerns in *The Talisman* that can be traced back through Straub's and King's separate careers are that of epistemology, and of good and evil. These questions are basic enough to human experience that they can probably be found in any good novel, but the writer of supernatural fiction has advantages in answering the questions within the universes of their books; King and Straub produce some of their best writing on these topics.

A writer of supernatural fiction, whose characters perceive as real creatures and phenomena the readers generally do not believe in, is in a unique position to explore epistemological questions. Straub says that when he wrote *Ghost Story,* he loved, "those passages in which the characters aren't sure what is real. They're pitchforked into something else and they have to grope around and try to figure out what is going on." That kind of scene becomes central to *Shadowland* and to *Floating Dragon,* with its multiple layers of hallucination, extrasensory perception, mental influence, and actual supernatural happening. In most of King's works, although there are unbelievable events, they are flatly presented as believed by the characters—in fact, as Straub points out, that is one of the ways in which King gets the reader to believe as well. There are two major exceptions to this: King's most "shadowland" works, in which reality gives way imperceptibly and irretrievably to surreality, are *The Shining,* which influenced Straub greatly, and "The Breathing Method," in which the influence came back home to King.

It is no coincidence that in one interview, Straub follows a comment on the "beautifully ornamented" complexities of *The Shining* with a comment on "shifting between the inner world and the outer world, juggling the fantastical and real," in *Ghost Story.* "I surprised myself," he says, "with my own inventiveness." While *'Salem's Lot* was a key influence on

Straub's fiction in terms of structure, *The Shining* was a key influence on Straub's handling of the supernatural.

A comparison between *The Shining* and **Shadowland** is fascinating because of the great similarities and significant differences. In each case, a boy with psychic powers sets in motion forces which he cannot control and which almost kill him: Danny Torrance in the Overlook is compared to a key winding a clock; and Tom Flanagan's power, which causes the events at Carson School and is used by Cole at Shadowland, is compared to a powerful battery. However, Tom's power works from the inside out, bringing his dreams, nightmares, and struggles to Skeleton Ridpath and others; Danny's power enables the Overlook to work from the outside in, making its history a part of Danny's psychic reality.

The ghosts of *The Shining* may have sparked Straub's imagination and "armored his intention" to explore melding of inner and outer worlds, and to play tricks with "reality. *The Shining* is the one book of King's in which the reader is often in doubt regarding the nature of an apparition. By the time the car's dead past owner, LeBay, appears behind the wheel in *Christine,* more than enough inexplicable events have happened for the reader to be ready for a haunting as an explanation; but Jack Torrance's conversations with Lloyd the bartender in *The Shining* seem at first to be hallucinations, and do not change tone, even after the "hallucination" opens the bolt outside the pantry to release Jack. The glimpses of the doggy man and the other ghosts of the Overlook have a surreal feel to them that King's other novels do not.

No matter what role *The Shining* had on Straub's development of this epistemological theme, he ran with it in a way King has never again seemed inclined to. Charlie McGee's development of her power in *Firestarter* and Tom Flanagan's of his in **Shadowland** are in many ways similar—the Shop, lack of money—while those to Tom work at the fabric of his perception of the universe. Even Charlie's struggle with her own desire to let the power within her go is shown subjectively, but not in the shadowy way Tom's struggle is; that is, while King, with perception and skill, leads us into Charlie McGee's mind, the reader never loses the sense of the separation between her mind and external reality, as he or she does in Tom's case.

In "The Breathing Method," however, King combines his realistic setting with a surreal uncertainty perhaps consciously borrowed from Straub, to create the enticing and yet frightening club at 249B East Thirty-fifth Street. The tale itself, aside from the imagistic patterning already mentioned, is closer to King's other-tale-within-a-tale, "The Man Who Would Not Shake Hands", than it is to Straub's writing. It is with "the whole idea of the old codgers sitting around telling stories," framing the actual narrative, that "The Breath-

ing Method" is most tied to Straub's fiction, and especially conscious reference to **Ghost Story**. The books on the club shelves that are not listed in any catalog or index, the seemingly endless halls, and the questions that inexplicably go unasked shift the reader imperceptibly into a twilight world, odd enough to be frighteningly unreal and immediate enough to be frighteningly real—a more benevolent but no less unsettling Shadowland. As Charles Grant points out, the terror in the setting of the club-that-is-not-exactly-a-club comes from indirection rather than direct presentation, and may be an homage to Straub in that way also.

Besides raising the issue of what is or is not real—or of different kinds of reality—the conversations with Lloyd and the other residents of the Overlook may have influenced Straub in another way, as well. They are frighteningly normal; unlike the more traditional howling specters, or even skeletons, the ghosts of *The Shining* are perfectly normal—except, of course, that they are dead. Even those with their death-injuries showing, or rotting apparitions like the woman in the tub, walk and talk calmly, a horror greater in some ways than histrionics would be.

Moreover, all of the ghosts in *The Shining* are murderous—even those who must have been merely venal in life—simply because they are dead. In *Danse Macabre,* Stephen King points out that most of us will have read or heard stories of benevolent ghosts, and he even has Nick Andros' shade put in a benevolent appearance in *The Stand,* but "for the purposes of the horror novel, the ghost must be evil."

All of these characteristics mark the ghosts of **Ghost Story**—which, of course, are not really ghosts but shapeshifting immortal creatures—and, especially, those of **Floating Dragon**. While the child in **Julia** is marginally solid enough to be a real person, the whole book is presented almost as a vision, so there is none of the shock of the other books, the outrage the reader feels when Richard Allbee is confronted by his dead wife, indistinguishable (at first) from when she was alive. Similarly, Alison Greening in *If You Could See Me Now* comes back from the dead as a ravenous spirit, but she has some cause, and finally can be approached. The contact may be baffling, but it is possible; the drowned children returning to their mothers, or the dead in general, in **Floating Dragon** are completely beyond thought. At most there would be, as with the woman in room 217 in *The Shining,* "black . . . hurt-think . . . like . . . like the wasps that night in my room."

While **Floating Dragon** shows the bleakest view of death and the dead, it shows the most positive view of the universal forces of good and evil. When asked about evil in his works, Straub, then working on **Floating Dragon,** stated, "[I]t's very powerful. In fact, I always have trouble thinking how human beings can win over it, since it seems to me that if you posit some really single-minded, malevolent, supernatural evil against human beings, then the human beings have to work awfully hard to defeat it." In *Floating Dragon,* besides the friendship and determination of the people involved, there is also a universal force for good that aids the four adversaries of evil. The scenes in which their weapons are transformed to flaming swords, especially when Richard finally slays the Dragon, are similar in both imagery and tone to the scenes in *'Salem's Lot* in which the vampire-hunters' weapons glow with power, first the axe and then their own hands.

In neither case is the force what many readers would have expected. As King says in *'Salem's Lot,* "the good was more elemental, less refined." In an interview, King expanded this idea: "I don't see good as a completely Christian force. It's what I think of as white. White. Just tremendously powerful, something that would run you right over if you got in its way." The fellowship in *Floating Dragon* find it demanding and virtually incomprehensible.

Not only is the concept of the White force much the same in King's *The Stand* and *'Salem's Lot* and in Straub's *Floating Dragon,* but it stands out as rare in the field. It is more common among most horror novels—including Straub's earlier works—for it not to be handled at all, because of the attraction of evil, as King states, or for the deck to be stacked, as Charles Grant points out, "with so little skill that the result becomes monotonously predictable." The White force concentrates on good and provides hope, while avoiding triteness or heavy-handed allegory. The forces of good and evil in *The Talisman* are similar, although aid is less obvious and much harder to win.

In prose style, novel structuring, and thematic development, both Straub and King have accomplished much in the years since they corresponded and met. When he met King, Straub states, "he had a galvanic effect on me. I felt how much he worked; it came off his personality . . . . I thought, 'Now I understand what I have to do,' and my imagination went forward." But while the association with King has definitely benefitted Straub, he had always been serious about his writing, and was already moving in many of the directions King's fiction helped him go, which raises some doubt about the whole idea of "influence"; the same could be said about a number of aspects of *The Talisman* which seem more similar to Straub's novels. In many ways, Straub and King are a case of convergent literary evolution, meeting when each had already formed but just begun to actualize plans for his fiction, and for the supernatural or horror genre as a whole.

The techniques and approaches of prose, structure, and theme are basic to any writer, but even more basic is the desire to tell an emotionally compelling story, and the perceptiveness and sincerity to be able to do so. When asked what the most important element of horror writing is, King answered, "Character. You have got to love the people in the story, because there is no horror without love and without feeling." Similarly, Straub says that *Ghost Story* is "a very scary book, because I *believed* very much in my characters—I loved them, actually . . . . And so, when those characters are threatened, the reader felt it as a threat." This love of their characters, and those characters' lives told in the stories, is at the heart of the fiction of both Straub and King, and explains not only their mutual respect and affection but also the respect and affection they win from their readers.

Geoffrey Stokes (review date May 1993)

SOURCE: "Ghosts: The Many Lives of Peter Straub," in *The Village Voice Literary Supplement,* No. 115, May, 1993, pp. 25-26.

[*In the following review, Stokes examines the thematic structure of Straub's* Blue Rose Trilogy.]

Toward the end of *Koko,* the first novel of Peter Straub's Blue Rose trilogy, a killer renders himself effectively invisible by slipping into another man's clothes and appearing just where that man was expected to be. The implication is that most of the time we "see" what we anticipate seeing—and by extension, the greater the expectability of our daily lives, the less we actually perceive.

This notion is applicable to Straub's own career. When it began, in Dublin and London during the early '70s, he was clearly "literary," a well-regarded young poet and escaped academic whose first, somewhat Jamesian novel, *Marriages,* was treated respectfully by British critics. But with his second published novel, a ghost story called *Julia,* he donned someone else's clothes, and took on the entertaining, but limited, ambition of the fat boy in *Pickwick,* Straub was out there saying, "I wants to make your flesh creep."

And with *Ghost Story, Shadowland, Julia, Floating Dragon,* and attendant film scripts, he was terrific at it. But as Straub's mentors shifted from James and Hawthorne through Poe to Sheridan LeFanu and Stephen King, the author of *Marriages* disappeared. Hundreds of thousands of copies later, by the mid '80s, Straub had become a brand name.

He was so much an Institution that until I talked with him in the course of doing this piece, I had never connected the writer of *Ghost Story* with the reserved, bookish expatriate whose London flat I'd briefly shared during that tentative and awkward time, 20 years ago, when I was first trying to think of myself as a journalist. Last month, he asked if I remembered where we'd met; after a mutually embarrassing long pause, I made the connection, and thought about dropping the piece. But then I realized it was some other figure—neither the bookish tyro nor the brand-name "Peter Straub"—that I wanted to write about. This figure emerged, like a ghost in a Peter Straub novel, after the uncharacteristic five-year silence (except for a collaboration with Stephen King) that followed 1983's *Floating Dragon.*

"First of all," Straub says, "I made the great mistake of taking a year off. I'd just finished a long book, then plunged into the collaboration with King, which just about killed me. I was exhausted in a way that was almost frightening, and I slid—in the way that you do when you finish a book—into sadness and depression. And then at the end of the year I'd promised myself, I realized that I didn't quite know what I wanted to write. And that *was* frightening. But I really felt I'd gone about as far as I could go with horror—I didn't think much about what I was writing while I was in my thirties; certainly scaring people seemed a harmless and not dishonorable activity—and was sort of opening myself up to other possibilities."

As a child, I was hit by a car. I was killed in effect, momentarily, and then slowly and to some degree unwillingly returned to an unhappy, pain-ridden, angry, frustrated life. I was crazy both with the physical pain and the horrible dread that kind of pain brings—and also, I now know, with anger at having been *slapped down* so severely.
—Peter Straub

Reading a Brian Moore novel about the Virgin Mary offered a path. "I realized that at some point in his life, he *had* to have been a Catholic, and I said to myself, 'Peter, you've got to write about something you *believe.*' Also, it would be cheating for me not to say that at about this time I went and got some psychological help, and that it taught me a great deal. I learned more about myself then—about *human life*—than at any other similar period of my life." In his re-examined life, he found his themes: Grief, pain, loss . . . and the gradual regathering of strength.

By then, Straub had also found his voice and pace as a storyteller. Though his post 1988 novels argue that the wants-to-make-your-flesh-creep period was journeyman work, he proved the value of apprenticeship by developing a master crafter's chops. Among horror novelists, there was no one who juggled points of view and narrative voices with more authority; Straub had the ventriloquist's equivalent of perfect pitch. All these skills have matured along with him, yet the author of *Koko* and the subsequent books is different not

merely from the genre writer who worked the gothic vein, but also from the author of *Marriages.*

The disappearance of that boy *littérateur* was not entirely a bad thing. *Marriages* is a tight-sphinctered little book, its occasionally striking prose clotted with self-importance and its plot—married American man falls in love with European woman, sees Paris, Provence, and self with new eyes—yet another reprise of an Edwardian standby. Though published in 1973, at a time when standards and expectations were in flux, *Marriages* is an old-fashioned "modern" book. Its artistic roots lie not in the unabashed storytelling of the Victorians (Straub's unsuccessful attempt at a doctoral thesis was on Trollope, but in the James-from-the-perspective-of-Eliot notions of "high art" nearing the end of their 20-year domination of English departments.

Though many critics viewed *Marriages* as promising, in retrospect it seems to mark the end of an era more than the beginning of a career. The second book he wrote, *Under Venus,* ran into a dead end. By now, Straub can joke about the disappointment. ("I rewrote it and rewrote it—once in the form of a letter to Scott Fitzgerald, which I think was a less than wonderful idea for that particular book.") Back then, however, when his agent suggested he try his hand at a gothic, he was economically and emotionally ready. The result, *Julia,* was by his later standards a rather straightforward ghost story, but it gave him a satisfaction that went beyond the gratifying royalty checks it produced.

"As a child," he says, "I was hit by a car. I was killed in effect, momentarily, and then slowly and to some degree unwillingly returned to an unhappy, pain-ridden, angry, frustrated life. I was crazy both with the physical pain and the horrible dread that kind of pain brings—and also, I now know, with anger at having been *slapped down* so severely."

Ten-year-old Tom Pasmore, protagonist of *Mystery,* the book that followed *Koko,* "looked sideways and saw a pair of head-lights coming toward him with the same dreamy slowness as the falling bicycle. He was entirely incapable of moving. Between the headlights he could see the mesh of a tall metal grille, and beneath the grille was a wide steel band that looked burnished. Above the bumper and the grille a face, indistinct behind the windshield, pointed toward him as intently as the muzzle of a bird dog . . .

"His world was dominated by physical pain and the necessity of controlling that pain. Every three hours a nurse holding a small square tray marched quickly across his room and lifted a tiny white paper cup from among the other similar cups on the tray even before she reached his bedside, so that by the time she reached him she was in position to extend the cup to his waiting lips. Then there was an agonizing period when the sweet, oily stuff in the cup temporarily failed to work . . . . In a minute or two the pain that had come up out of his body's deepest places began to settle like a large animal going to sleep, and all the sharp smaller pains would turn fuzzy and slow."

"After a year," Straub says, "I was able to walk again, and so I was supposed to be normal again. The whole world told me that, including my parents—but that's when I began to stutter." And when he began to go "very deeply into books." Reading in that almost desperate way, as an anodyne, did him good, says Straub, but if the edges of his suffering grew fuzzy, the nearly paralyzing fear that it might return stayed with him. "Childhood trauma," he says, choosing his words with obvious care, "I suppose, gave me *access*. That theme, which is autobiographical without any doubt and which I found myself saddled with, was useful because it gave me access to a certain kind of experience—of horror, and of survival, and then of the *memory* of pain—that eventually gave me the nerve to write about Vietnam vets without having been one.

"In a way, I'd been in the same world. Although if I'd been sent off into actual combat, I think terror would have undone me—because of all the stuff left over from childhood, which was a high degree of constant fear." He pauses again. "I think that's why the early horror writing worked. I really *knew* about fear."

Those twinned experiences—childhood trauma and Vietnam—are at the heart of the work that comes to its end in his current novel, *The Throat*.

Straub calls it "the Blue Rose trilogy," but it's not quite as neat as *The Throat* and the two novels, *Koko* and *Mystery,* which preceded it. At minimum, the work also includes two short stories ("Blue Rose" and "The Jupiter Tree") "written" by Tim Underhill, a central character in the novels, and published in a collection of Straub's works called *Houses Without Doors,* as well as *The Divided Man,* an unpublished and probably imaginary novel also "written" by Underhill. Together, though there are ghosts in *The Throat* and demons in *Koko,* they make up a work that bursts through the limitations of genre. The demons are internal, and Straub casts light in light corners to reveal how dark they really are.

"Blue Rose," the first of the pieces to be written, is the story of young Harry Beevers, by far the brightest child in the Beevers family of Palmyra, New York. Using a "Hypnotism Made Easy" pamphlet he found in the attic ("Blue Rose" was the phrase used by its author to trigger posthypnotic suggestion), Harry at first hypnotizes, then systematically and sadistically brutalizes, his little brother—finally, if not entirely deliberately, killing him.

The story ends with a letter, unsent, which Lieutenant Harry

Beevers writes to his future wife from Vietnam, after being found not guilty by a court-martial in the slaughter of civilians at Ia Thuc: "I never told you that I once had a little brother named Edward. When I was ten, my little brother wandered up onto the top floor of our house one night and suffered a fatal epileptic fit. This event virtually destroyed my family. . . ." Beevers waxes sentimental about Edward and a neighbor—Pete Petrosian, who, "against what must have been million-to-one odds, died exactly the same way my brother did, about two weeks after"—then concludes: "This is a profound feeling, Pat, and no damn whipped-up failed court-martial can touch it. If there were any innocent children in that cave, then they are in my family forever, like little Edward and Pete Petrosian, and the rest of my life is a poem to them. But the army says there weren't, and so do I."

In *Koko,* we meet Harry Beevers, and discover why Tim Underhill felt he needed an explanation. The "official" beginning of the enterprise that has occupied Straub for close to a decade opens in Washington, as Michael Poole, a pediatrician who served in Beevers's platoon at Ia Thuc, waits in his room at the Sheraton Hotel for the other members of his unit who will join him for the Viet vets parade. When they gather—Beevers, Poole, and two others—talk turns to a series of brutal murders in which the victims were found with a regimental card signed "KOKO" in their mouths. The murders began when they were in Vietnam but continue, in Singapore, Bangkok, and points east. The four have come to realize that Koko must be a member of their former unit, almost certainly Underhill, who alone among them remained in the Far East. Urged on by Beevers (who sees TV and movie rights beckoning), they decide to head for Singapore—and Koko.

> I didn't know when I found him that Underhill was going to become my alter ego. . . . He's a novelist, and to me that's a great point in his favor, obviously, but he started out so different from me.
> —*Peter Straub*

That's about it for plot: "Viet vets return to the scenes of their r&r to find one of their comrades who's gone astray." But fairly soon, nothing is as it seems—not Underhill's homicidal madness, Beevers's ineffectual ambitiousness, even Michael Poole's gentleness: "Michael Poole had killed a child at Ia Thuc, that was true. The circumstances were ambiguous, but he had shot and killed a small boy standing in a shadow at the back of a hootch. Michael was not superior to Harry Beevers, he was *like* Harry Beevers."

Koko is, at least in the beginning, Poole's novel, and when we first hear of Underhill's most successful novel, *The Divided Man*, it's in a three-page summary told from Poole's point of view. Set in a city "very much like Milwaukee, Wisconsin," it is "virtually a meditation on Koko." Underhill's novel is based on a series of murders—many of the victims gay, each one marked by a piece of paper with *Blue Rose* penciled on it—and the suicide-as-confession of the bisexual detective assigned to them.

Underhill himself does not appear, save for some hard-to-identify internal monologues, until page 273, when Poole finds him, alone, in a Bangkok restaurant. He is afraid, and it is instantly clear to Poole that "Underhill was as innocent of Koko's murders as any man who feared becoming the next victim had to be." At that moment, the book begins to change, in a way that leads directly to *The Throat*. Though the story remains Poole's on the surface—and it is Poole who has one of those climatic moments of spiritual revelation that mark Straub's later work—it becomes, in some subtle way, Underhill's book. "I didn't know when I found him that Underhill was going to become my alter ego," says Straub. "He's a novelist, and to me that's a great point in his favor, obviously, but he started out so different from me. He's gay, lives in a different part of the world—and now in a different part of the city, which might as well be a different part of the world—but it just . . . *happened.*"

The book, and the search for Koko, continue—with its most striking scene an extended riff on Underhill and Poole's visit to Milwaukee. The city was Straub's childhood home, and he describes it with exquisite ambivalence. "My childhood," says Straub, "was in a way so full of feeling, because of the dreadful things that happened to me there, that the place remains invested with real glamour and real horror. Yet the horror doesn't detract from the beauty of it all—the neon signs reflecting off the walls, the leaves piled in the gutters. In a way, it makes the beauty more appealing, more *overflowing.*"

The horror involves the almost unspeakable abuse-by-righteousness of the child who would grow up to become Koko and, with the possible exception of an epilogue in which Underhill speaks in a voice noticeably close to Straub's, those pages are *Koko*'s strongest. Compared to them, unmasking the killer seems almost perfunctory. And with a denouement that makes it clear Underhill's search—for *something*—will go on, the book has an aura of incompleteness.

Yet *Mystery,* the trilogy's keystone, veers off in what appears to be a quite different direction. It is set in the mid '50s and early '60s—before Vietnam, before the Beatles—and looks back toward murders that occurred a generation earlier. Mostly it happens to Tom Pasmore, 10 years old when he steps in front of a car that will, if briefly, kill him. The story unfolds in Mill Walk, a whimsically improbable and deeply corrupt German-Polish Caribbean island that shares Milwaukee's street names and landmarks, and in Eagle Lake, a northern Wisconsin enclave where the upper-class residents of Mill Walk summer. Like *Koko,* it is the story of a secret that is trying to emerge. Finding the secret, in the phrase of Pasmore's mentor Lamont von Heilitz, is like saving your own life.

The dormant power of secrets is what ties *Mystery* to *The Throat,* the novel which unites (well, partly unites), the doppelgängers Underhill and Pasmore. And, may be, Straub. Told in Underwood's voice, it begins with a discussion of his relationship with Straub, "a nice enough kind of guy," who "lives in a big gray Victorian house in Connecticut." Turns out that he wrote a couple of books with Straub, and that Tom Pasmore, the main character of the second, was someone Underhill "knew from back in Millhaven"—another city "very much like Milwaukee."

Underhill is *from* Millhaven, and Pasmore/Straub's childhood accident happened to him, too: "The grille of an automatic was coming toward me with what seemed terrific slowness. I was absolutely unable to move. I knew that the car was going to hit me. This certainty existed entirely apart from my terror. It was like knowing the answer to the most important question on a test. The car was going to hit me, and I was going to die.

"Writing about this in the third person, in *Mystery,* was easier."

Underhill finds himself (back) in Millhaven because the Blue Rose killings have started again, and the wife of a high school friend is near death in the hospital. The solution he'd created in *The Divided Man* may not have been accurate after all, so when John Ransom, an acquaintance in Vietnam as well as a friend from Millhaven, calls to ask for his help, Underhill gives it. Naturally enough, he teams up with Pasmore (in the same way he'd teamed up with "Straub"), and the two—in a trip that takes them back to Vietnam as well as to the streets and alleys of Millhaven—begin encouraging the secrets to come forward.

The new book stands apart from its predecessors in a couple of critical ways. The most obvious is that the unified auctorial voice helps keep Straub's protean imagination in harness (one reviewer counted 17 flashbacks, narrator changes, and flashforwards in a single 19-page section of *Floating Dragon*). We remain focused on Underhill as he unravels the book's ostensible mystery—which eventually leads us to its *real* secret: the lost history of Tim Underhill.

Less tricky and more direct than Straub's chillers both at its core and on its surface, *The Throat* is nonetheless more successful within its genre; the intensity of focus concentrates it in a way more frightening than any of Straub's earlier horror novels. But as it slides back and forth from Vietnam to Mid-America, from childhood trauma to adult cunning, it also has the unmistakable and painful quality of truth—and of wisdom.

It is possible—perhaps too much so—to get caught up in the small delights that stud the sprawling 2000-page structure Straub has created: Poole, something of a Strether figure, carries *The Ambassadors* to Singapore with him on his search for Underhill; "The Juniper Tree" is not only the name of an Underhill story, but of a painting on John Ransom's wall; "Blue Rose," in addition to its earlier meanings, is the title of a Millhaven saxophonist's classic album and the pattern of the wallpaper in Nabokov's childhood bedroom. These are fun, certainly, and sometimes freighted with meaning, but they're islands in the vast ocean of Straub's trilogy; it is an epic of healing. Begun at a time when this country was still bleeding from the self-inflicted hurts of Vietnam, the trilogy carries us through with prescience and courage to a moment when forgetting is no longer necessary.

Frank Wilson (review date 27 June 1993)

SOURCE: "The Return of the Blue Rose," in *The New York Times,* June 27, 1993, p. 24.

[*In the following favorable review, Wilson provides a plot summary of* The Throat.]

With *The Throat,* Peter Straub concludes a trilogy that began with the novel *Koko* and continued with *Mystery.* He deftly recapitulates the themes of the first two, then modulates them into that of this very impressive finale.

The police department of Millhaven, Ill., had closed the book on the Blue Rose murder case back in 1950 when a homicide detective named William Damrosch was found dead in his home of a self-inflicted gunshot wound, having left a note with the words "Blue Rose" on the desk in front of him. Tim Underhill wrote a novel, "The Divided Man," about the case.

After that, Underhill now tells us, "I thought I was done with Damrosch, with Millhaven and with the Blue Rose murders. Then I got a call from John Ransom, another old Millhaven acquaintance . . . . John Ransom still lived in Millhaven. His wife had been attacked and beaten into a coma, and her attacker had scrawled the words BLUE ROSE on the wall above her body."

So he flies to Millhaven and links up with Tom Pasmore,

the son of Lamont von Heilitz, the town's legendary sleuth, who may have been a victim of the Blue Rose killer himself, though his death occurred long after the case was closed. To solve the mystery of the attack on April Ransom and the murders that have subsequently been committed, Underhill is forced to explore regions of his psyche and his past that are, to say the least, disturbing. His sister, also named April, had been murdered just before the original series of Blue Rose killings began. Her death had never been connected with the others, even by him, but now he's not so sure. There is also a Vietnam connection Underhill and Ransom had some dealings there, though Underhill was in the Army and Ransom served with a Special Forces unit.

The Throat can fairly be described as a classic mystery novel. The emphasis here is on character and ratiocination. Tom Pasmore, for instance, is a worthy descendant of the line of dandified gumshoes that began with Poe's Dupin. Given its size and scope, however, Mr. Straub's novel has more in common with those of Wilkie Collins than with Poe's more modest tales.

Mr. Straub dutifully puts style at the service of plot, so one tends not to notice the clarity and smoothness of his prose. But every now and then a passage leaps out, such as the description of an attack of pain Underhill has: "a combination of burn and puncture . . . the legacy of the metal fragments embedded in my back . . . moving around, crawling toward the surface like Lazarus, where first a sharp edge, then a blunt curl, would emerge."

What gives *The Throat* its particular resonance is that its underlying theme seems to have less to do with sublunary crime and criminals than with the more transcendent mystery of moral contagion, the permanent scars it can inflict and the curious bonds it causes to be formed.

Joseph Andriano (essay date 1993)

SOURCE: "From Fiend to Friend, The Daemonic Feminine in Modern Gothic," in *Our Ladies of Darkness,* The Pennsylvania State University Press, 1993, pp. 135-44.

[*In the following excerpt, Andriano examines the place of* Ghost Story *in twentieth-century Gothic fiction.*]

The male hysterical reaction to fiends in women's garments continues well into the twentieth century, during which the Gothic mode has flourished in the ghost story and the weird tale. Many of these texts display vivid anima signs. Oliver Onions's "Beckoning Fair One" (1911) is a famous example: a novelist's fictional heroine haunts him as a ghost and rivals the woman whom he should be loving; equally popular is Walter De La Mare's "Seaton's Aunt" (1923), a brilliant portrait of a possessed young man whose anima remains fixated on the Terrible Mother; less well known but almost as effective is Clark Ashton Smith's "Disinterment of Venus" (1934), which continues the Heine/Mérimée/James tradition of digging up "exiled gods" from the earth, from the unconscious.

Moving into the twentieth century, however, one must assume authorial familiarity with Jungian theory. While such an assumption does not preclude the possibility of illuminating a modern text with Jung's concepts, works written merely to illustrate them are by necessity less compelling than those that anticipate Jung. As Jung explained in "Psychology and Literature," "visionary" literature evokes a convincing illusion of "genuine primordial experience." If, on the other hand, an author is consciously deriving his plot from archetypal patterns, the result is a mere expository, almost mechanical device rather than a spontaneous mythos. Such is surely the case with Fritz Leiber's novel *Our Lady of Darkness* (1977). . . .

Peter Straub also attempts to create such an experience in *Ghost Story* (1979). Instead of consciously manipulating Jungian theory or illustrating De Quincey as Leiber does, Straub goes back to Hawthorne and James and tries to synthesize the Ambiguous Gothic tradition with the H. P. Lovecraft "Cthulhu mythos." The latter grew out of the "Weird Tale" tradition, which comprises unabashedly supernatural texts. They assert that the demon is literally real, external to the haunted mind. Lovecraft envisioned a cosmic conspiracy of exiled god-monsters, "lurkers at the threshold" of our spacetime continuum, who wait for the interface between dimensions, that door into our precarious world where they can wreak their unspeakable havoc. Straub's novel can be read on this Lovecraftean level, but he also suggests that this worldview is a mere reflection of our own darkness within. The text is filled with mirrors—indeed there are too many of them; the symbolism gets heavy-handed, though not as much as Leiber's. When Don Wanderley, the protagonist, asks the demoness who she really is, she bluntly replies, "I am you." And before he suspects the ghastly identity of his lover Alma Mobley, she tells him that *he* is a ghost. A major theme of the novel seems to be that modern man has indeed become a ghost, deadened by the moral insensitivity that ensues from polarization of the sexes. Straub's principal ghost, then, must be a woman, for she is the revenge on men of their exiled femininity.

John Irvin's movie version of *Ghost Story* turns this ambiguous allegory of cosmic evil into a conventional story of the retributive spirit—the ghost of a woman wreaks her revenge on her killers; she is able to do this because she was never properly buried. The young men, afraid of a scandal even though her death was an accident, put her body in a car that

they dump into a lake. In the novel, however, the reader learns that Eva Galli was never human in the first place; she escapes from that sinking car and changes into a lynx. She is a shapeshifter, a manitou. If she is killed, she returns in animal form, becomes a child, then finally grows back into "La Belle Dame sans Merci." She says of her kind, "We could have poisoned your civilization ages ago, but voluntarily lived on its edges." This is pure Lovecraft. She and her subservient male ghouls are embodiments of chaos and of motiveless malice, imps of the cosmic perverse, living proofs that Melville was right—"the invisible spheres were formed in fright." And Hawthorne too—Straub's epigraph is from *The Marble Faun:* "The pit of blackness lies beneath us, everywhere." Both beneath and within.

Straub suggests that this shapeshifting monster, whose true form is so hideously Medusan that when she reveals it the sight causes men to jump out of windows or die of fright, is the origin of all vampire and werewolf tales. When she seems, late in the novel, to be utterly alien, the reader need only remember the passage earlier in the text, when she is associated with a young man's (Sears James's) feminine ideal. As an aging bachelor lawyer (who with his partner Ricky Hawthorne has been haunted for decades—without realizing it—by Eva Galli), James recalls a crucial moment from his adolescence when he used to babysit for the children of "the most desirable woman young Sears had ever seen"—Viola Frederickson. After the children were asleep, he would explore their mother's bedroom, where he saw "a photograph of her—she looked impossibly inviting, exotic and warm, *an icon of the unknowable half of the species*" (emphasis added). Fascinated especially by Viola's breasts and the way "they pushed out the fabric of her blouse," he finds one of her blouses, imagining the woman's breasts beneath it. The blouse becomes a metonymic sign for the breasts he worships; masturbating with the blouse he makes love to Viola's breasts. Afterward he feels such intense shame that he tosses the blouse into the river.

Perhaps it is this latter action that triggers the association with Eva Galli, whose body he helped dump into the water; he dimly makes "a connection . . . between her and the ridiculous scene he remembered." Young Sears's infatuation with the beautiful older woman Viola, who became for him the icon (frozen image) of womanhood, a goddess both maternal and sexual, fades as he grows up, of course, but he is never able to have a long-term relationship with a woman. The "unknowable half of the species" becomes the "horror of the half-known life" as he is never able to liberate anima. The only other woman he ever loves is Eva Galli, who is no woman at all, but a Medusan mirror reflecting male dread of the feminine. Adolescent fascination with the feminine degenerates into adult fear and loathing if anima is never recognized as part of self and soul, if she is instead perceived only as other. Other becomes alien, alien becomes monster.

Moreover, like some grotesque hybrid of the celibate monk Ambrosio and the goddess-worshiping Valerio, Sears James is never able to overcome breast fixation and fetishism. His wish is to displace the female sex from below upward, to spiritualize it, to turn it into a ghost. But Eva Galli is neither ghost nor spirit. Her true form looks something like an oil slick, and when she is killed she comes back as an animal. She is the chthonic feminine devoid of spirit.

Further, with all her avatars' initials being A. M—Amy Monckton, Alice Montgomery, Alma Mobley, Anna Mostyn—she is revealed as *Anima Mundi,* the soul of a world deadened and corrupted by polarized masculinity. Fission of the "divine syzygy" breeds animated corpses and other monsters more frightening than anything in Lovecraft. The horror of *Ghost Story* is the horror of the half-known life—of men unable to integrate the inner feminine, to accept it as an integral part of the whole self. Instead it remains the "unknowable half."

In Lovecraft, exiled god-monsters are almost always masculine. Straub has restored their proper gender. In Lovecraft, the daemonic is literalized and reified into the demonic. Straub restores its numinosity and psychic reality. With his powerful portrayal of Medusa in the mirror, Straub is more successful than Leiber in creating a "primal numinous dread."

Adam Meyer (interview date Summer 1994)

SOURCE: "Impure Consciousness," in *The Armchair Detective,* Vol. 27, No. 3, Summer, 1994, pp. 264-71.

[*In the following interview, Straub discusses the creative process and the evolution of his fiction.*]

Peter Straub lives as one would expect a writer to live: surrounded by books. As we ascend to his office on the top floor of his Manhattan brownstone, we pass shelves at every landing, shelves piled and crammed and jammed with volumes; if there is any organization based on size or subject, it eludes me. On the walls are posters from the movie adaptations which have been made from Straub's work, *Ghost Story* and *The Haunting of Julia* (based on his more succinctly titled book *Julia*), as well as blowups of his novel covers.

With its massive desk and leather chairs, his office is large and comfortable-looking. A pile of books rises in the center of the room like an altar. On the wall, more books: Straub's work in different languages. Ever had an irrepressible urge to read *Floating Dragon* in French? This is the place to find it.

Straub, dressed in dungarees and a blue chambray work shirt, looks like he ought to be preparing a lecture on Chaucer, not sitting down to discuss his extremely popular novels; novels which have become increasingly mystery oriented....
[*Meyer:*] *As more of a stylist than the traditional popular writer, did you always dream of being on the bestseller list or would you have been content with a small fan base?*

[Straub:] I like the idea of having a lot of readers. Once it even occurred to me that I could, I wanted that. It's incredibly satisfying to see strangers holding *your* book. That's a thrill. Also, at an impressionable age I met Stephen King, who was even younger than I was but still had millions of readers, millions of dollars, was completely okay with that. He knew from the crib days that he was going to make millions of dollars writing novels. He just knew it, and he didn't see anything wrong with it. His tremendous assurance had a big effect on me. It made sense to me that if he could do it, I could do it, and that that was a valid literary career.

I was certainly always interested in writing well, though my definition of that changed from time to time, and sometimes it was more ornamental, more concerned with effects, than it later became. I never saw why you couldn't be a good writer in the *real* sense and also popular. After a certain point, I was just pursuing my own ideas, I was chasing something I could see far ahead of me on the horizon. I was really following my own map. After I had proven that I could write commercially successful books, then I just kind of assumed that that would happen as long as I kept chasing that thing up there on the horizon. For the most part, I was right. Maybe some people were puzzled when I scrubbed off the top layer and there were no more monsters or undead things, no ancient curses and all that, but in an absolutely real way, the books became more honest once I scrubbed off that top layer. But in all other ways I think they were the same.

You grew up in Milwaukee. Is that in effect where **The Throat** *and the other Blue Rose novels are set?*

That's all Milwaukee. One of them is Milwaukee in the Caribbean, with hummingbirds and bougainvillea but it's still Milwaukee. It's got street names from Milwaukee, and you know, sort of a worked up, highly excessive version of the social life in Milwaukee.

When I read **Koko,** *and again more recently when I read* **The Throat,** *I wondered whether you had actually served in Vietnam. Because on the one hand it seems so authentic, and yet I've never heard that you were in the war.*

No. I never was. I got interested after the fact. I had the idea for *Koko* without really knowing how the book would feel at all, and because the idea involved Vietnam veterans, I had to do a lot of work on it. So I read tons and tons of books and I also talked to a bunch of veterans. The second I started talking to veterans I knew I understood something I hadn't known before, I kind of knew the emotional quality of what it was like to have survived something of that nature. It began to seem to me that I was locked into a very profound feeling that isn't expressed ever in America, that has to do with sorrow and pain and loss. It struck me that this is really beautiful, and so then I kind of knew what I was writing about and what kind of feelings would go through the plot. That seemed so valuable to me that I didn't want to give it up, so *Mystery* veered around that, addressed the same feelings in other ways. In *The Throat*, I wanted more of Tim Underhill, and I wanted to explore all that even more, I suppose.

Anyhow, where I learned the most—apart from technical matters—was talking to former combat soldiers. Joe Haldeman was one, the science-fiction writer. Great guy, and he had various astonishing experiences. I just thought I understood it. Some veterans wrote and said, "You weren't there, don't mess with it." I can understand where they're coming from, but that doesn't seem to me to be a reasonable position. All you do is take your swing and see what you can do. I got many more letters from veterans who were gratified and pleased by what I'd done, so I think it worked.

About the time **Koko** *came out was when Hollywood began picking up on Vietnam and Oliver Stone made "Platoon." Did that influence your decision to tackle the subject?*

No, I'd been working on it for a long time before "Platoon." It just struck me that the way I was doing it made it palatable. Vietnam is seen through the wrong end of the telescope. Almost everything that's important happened back then, but it is back then, and we go there in memory sometimes, but most of the action [in *Koko*] is in the 1980's. That made it digestible. I don't think people really want to read combat novels too much. I don't. I'm bored by that, even though I read a batch of them.

I liked "Platoon" a lot, I thought that it was very persuasive. I thought occasionally it must have had the feeling just right, the feeling of absolute, impenetrable chaos, where you don't know which way to run, everything's dangerous.

I know you spent many years in Europe. Were you even in the United States during the Vietnam War?

For the most part. We went to Ireland in 1969. So we missed the ending. We came back in 1979. So we missed Richard Nixon. No great loss.

All your more recent work has grown out of the Blue Rose *mythology. It all started with a single short story, although*

you very rarely do short fiction. How did "Blue Rose" come to be?

It just seemed so striking that I couldn't avoid it. It was the first thing I wrote after I took a year off after *Floating Dragon* and *The Talisman*. Right at the end of that time I was reading a book about Freud by a neurologist. A little paragraph in that suggested the story. It was a connection between hypnosis and epilepsy, and all of a sudden this little light bulb switched on in my head. I didn't know that much about *Koko* yet, though I knew there was a guy named Harry Beevers in it, who probably was nasty. But I felt a lot of sympathy for him, so I made him the main character.

What I was doing seemed really new for me, at that point. What I wanted to do was be as transparent as possible, to have the writing be as transparent as possible. So the reader would sit there turning pages, and he would see a little boy stick a big hatpin into the arm of his little brother, and you'd actually witness this terrible, immoral, degraded event happening right in front your eyes, and then I thought you wouldn't be able to stop turning the pages. You'd be witnessing as much as reading. I loved that idea. The story turned out well, I thought. I liked it a lot.

It took a long time to write because I rewrote it a lot, in aid of transparency, in being as clear, as unshowy, as presentational as possible. Then that showed me what I wanted to do, the kind of writing I wanted to do. It was kind of a new goal, and *Koko* was written very much in that spirit. That—especially the beginning—was reworked and reworked, over and over. It took me a year to write the first hundred pages, I think, just because every time I started I started over again, and tearing apart everything I'd done, taking out all the fat, just so that you would *see* when you looked at the page, you would see the action, and you'd get the idea of the characters as people, not just as types, but as actual real breathing people. So that was a struggle, but it was very, very satisfying. I had a wonderful time toward the end of the book where everything happened as if by itself. It was really enjoyable.

How long was it before you knew that "Blue Rose" was part of a larger tapestry?

The story was finished. I later figured out Tim Underhill wrote that story "Blue Rose," and Tim Underhill wrote "The Juniper Tree." And Tim Underhill wrote the book about the Blue Rose murders, and that is alluded to in *Koko*. There isn't much about it, just a sense of a detective searching for a murderer he might not ever find, I think. I like the sort of depression of a novel about an alcoholic detective, a real down and outer, kind of struggling through the day trying to solve these absolutely insolvable murders. There's something so doomed about that and grimy and dreary that I thought it very, very appealing. And then of course he finds out that he did it, an idea I later discarded.

Really, all that just sort of grew of itself. I liked the idea of a false solution, of an assumed truth, of a truth that everybody knows that isn't the truth, so that everybody papers over the reality of what actually happened. That is so that there's a secret truth, a hidden truth, that's what I like. I knew how *Koko* would end, but I didn't know how *Mystery* or *The Throat* would end. *The Throat* just moved by itself toward its conclusion when you find out what the truth is.

So you didn't know from the beginning who the killer would be?

I thought I knew but it seemed too simple. The more knots I could tie in that string, the more I liked it. For a long time there wasn't any plot at all, and then all of a sudden I had this amazing plot. If I just changed a few of the variables, things got a lot more interesting, people did things you never would've guessed they did. And the really evil guy is almost forgiveable. The meanly evil, routinely evil guy is not forgiveable at all. The guy who kills his wife for money—and because of wounded ego—he's despicable. But the real monster is in some way worthy of notice; he's worthy of killing, too. In some ways there's a sort of glamour about him.

There's a bit I took out of *The Throat*. It's going to be in an anthology called *Borderlands 4*, and it's about the childhood of Fielding Bandolier. I'm very pleased with it. I want to see if anybody notices it when it comes out. It was a very difficult piece of writing which took a long time. Every day I lived in *hell*, actual hell, in Milwaukee, in a terrible little house with a terrible man and a dying wife and a little boy. I was trying to figure out what makes a Jeffrey Dahmer—although this was before Dahmer. I wanted to see what's the recipe. I just piled on awfulness upon awfulness until finally it made sense. There's a very endearing little boy. Suddenly he decides he wants to kill a dog down the street. He has very good reason for wanting to do that. And from there he graduates.

This ties into something else I wanted to know. You've probably heard about the case in upstate New York where a twelve-year-old boy killed another little boy. The newspapers couldn't help but mention that he was a Stephen King fan. As a parent yourself, do you ever think "Maybe I have some responsibility to be careful about what I include in my books"?

I think I do these things pretty responsibly. If some murderer were caught brandishing a copy of my book and saying, "I got it all from here," I don't know how I'd feel actually. In some way I'd be kind of proud because that would put me up there with Salinger, who wrote the American assassin's

bible from what I can see. Everytime anybody plugs somebody he pops up holding a copy of *Catcher in the Rye* and says, "It's all in here. I'm doing it to save people."

I would also be appalled. I always think I'm going to write from the inside of a truly disturbed, baroque and monstrous mind—but I never do. I think I give glimpses now and then, through documents of one kind of another. Mainly I describe his effects and look at what created him. That's certainly one thing I've been very interested in. I want to know what Dengler's childhood was like. We look at that and it's like opening the door of an oven. Here's this awful mother in *Koko,* this appalling, monstrous, dictatorial creep, and she's mom. And dad was worse. Dad killed his mother. And the same is true of Fielding Bandolier. There's a sort of furnace instead of a childhood, a roaring furnace. I don't think that reading this material would inspire anybody to go out and commit crimes. All I'm doing is trying to suggest to people at large that evil isn't accidental, though I think that every now and then it might be, there might be some foul ball that comes rolling into the world determined to create hell wherever possible. But mainly the monsters are made by ignorance and brutality and bad treatment.

So you don't believe in divine evil?

Not really. Human evil's bad enough. Supernatural evil is a really beautiful idea but in a way it's an excuse, a convenience. You can say, "It wasn't me. It was really this demon inside me." I don't buy that.

Is it that sensibility which drew you away from traditional horror?

Probably. I was also a little tired of the way *I'd* been doing it. In *Floating Dragon,* I did everything I could think of. I think in a way I did that on purpose, so I would never have to do that again. It was tremendous fun. I had a great time doing that book. I'm still pleased with it. It's completely over the top. There are some really nice bits in it. After that, I couldn't do it anymore. I'd said everything I could possibly say about that kind of horror.

In your mind, how do you categorize the work you've done recently?

I'm not quite sure where I am. I'm on a seam between crime novels and horror novels, and I don't think my work has changed that much, except I think emotionally it's gotten more refined, or maybe deeper, because I think I actually do understand more than I did in the mid-'80's, just by thinking more. Also I turned forty, which nobody should ever have to do. If you survive, you've learned a few things.

I have no problem in seeing the books I do now as both horror novels and crime novels—although they are much more like the latter than the former. Most of them now are about who did it. There's a substratum of real misery and pain, of genuine human inhumanity. There's a lot of physical pain. So it seems to me they sort of fall into both camps, and I don't care how they're read, if they're read as horror novels or mystery novels, as long as they're read as novels first. That's what I wanted to write when I started—novels—not horror novels or crime novels.

In what way did writing **The Talisman** *change your approach to writing?*

It probably didn't. Well, I don't know. That was probably another indication that I was finished with supernatural books as a main force of venture. There are some things that continue to delight Stephen King that are no longer very compelling to me, at least as a writer. I suppose that became clearer after our collaboration, though it was never an issue between us. I came out of that experience with an enhanced respect for Stephen King. He was a powerhouse and has an astoundingly accessible imagination—accessible to himself. I have to sit there for fifteen minutes staring at the screen trying to figure out what they're doing, and he [snaps his fingers] knows. It's as if he dives into a pool. I have to splash around the top a little bit. That was really very moving to behold. The whole experience confirmed to me, ultimately, about the direction I wanted to go.

Do you need other people to help you shape your books or do you have a clear vision in your own mind of how they should be?

Not quite. I have a very vague vision when I start. By the time I'm at the end I know exactly what it is that I've done and how I got there. I have a pretty good instinct of how to pull the rest of the book into line. Over the years, starting with "Blue Rose" and then with *Koko,* I learned to edit myself very, very well. I'm ruthless. I take out some of my favorite bits and I tamper with lines endlessly. By the time I give my book to my editor, I've probably taken out at least two or three hundred pages. I took five hundred pages out of *Koko.* That's *cutting.* At that point, all I want to know is do they see anything I don't. Are there some scenes that are a little dumb? Are there scenes that misfire because somebody isn't doing enough? Are there things to do to the book to help it move along its own path?

It's nice to reach the part where I can talk about it to somebody else. You've had this huge birth in silence and darkness and nobody else has seen your baby. You're still in love with the thing, and now you can show it to somebody else. The first thing they'd better say is, "I love this. This is beautiful." And then they can say, "Well, there's something a little feeble there on page 35."

Right now, it seems as though no matter what else you do in your career, you will always be Peter Straub, author of **Ghost Story.** *Does that ever bother you?*

I used to get irritated when someone would come up and say, "I love **Ghost Story***!*" I would think, "You could've said **The Throat,** you could've said **Koko,**" but I realized they think they're saying something nice, and of course they really are saying something nice. Even though I would prefer it if people complimented me on more recent books, I have to be very grateful to *Ghost Story.* It did an amazing thing for me. It was wonderful to write. It was sheer fun, and I knew it was good, I knew it would be very successful, I didn't have a doubt in the world about that, and I was more right than I could have guessed. It kicked me up to another level where publishers had to deal with me in a more serious, responsible way. That's where you want to be. You want to be in a kind of partnership with your editor. You don't want enmity, you don't want to be the brat with a runny nose who's trying to steal the cookies. You want a real working relationship, and it's hard for many people to get to that point. They're still jumping up and trying to look through the window, see what the big guys are eating, the big guys being the publishers. I used to envy publishers when I was younger because they had salaries. It seemed to me so astounding, so enviable, that they could really count on a paycheck. I'm long past that feeling.

Let's go even further back in your career. I want to ask you about **Marriages,** *your first novel. [Straub smiles.] Did you have a hard time selling it?*

No, I didn't. I'd have a lot of trouble now, because publishing a first novel is harder now. I was in Dublin. I was about twenty-seven. I feared that if I didn't write a novel then, I never would. I'd written tons of poetry but never extended prose. There's a novelist in *The End of the Affair* by Graham Greene who says that all you have to do to write a novel is write five hundred words a day. And then he says, "Drip drip drip, you know, and at the end you have a novel." Do five hundred words a day and at the end of the year you have a novel. That sounded doable.

In a completely literal-minded, really stupid fashion, I wrote five hundred words a day. I counted 'em up to make sure. When I got to five hundred, I could quit, or I could have a binge and write seven hundred. I had no idea what I was doing. I didn't *want* a plot. A plot kept trying to get in and I think there's some nice writing in that book, but I don't think it's very good. I think the best part is when the hero sees a man that he knows is dead, a guy from his hometown who was killed in prison, and he follows that man—with his wife—and tracks him through Arles to the Roman amphitheater, to a little cell there, and then he's not there. I should've known where I was going to go.

Later, when I became unhappy with what I was doing on a thesis, I found this book again. I hadn't done anything to it, I had let it sit there for about eight, nine months. I packed it up and I sent it to Andre Deutsch, the English publisher of John Updike, whom I idolized, so I thought that would be a good place to start. A woman there wrote back and said she liked the book and she was going to try to sell it to the rest of the board. So I jittered for about three weeks and finally she wrote and said, "Yes, we're going to publish your book." Then I got an agent in America. She shopped the book around and finally a guy at Coward, McCann bought it. So I had an English publisher and an American publisher. I quit graduate school and we moved to London, which was a little more active as far as novel writing.

The editor who bought it at Coward, McCann was fired, and the woman who took over clearly had no interest in it at all. The book got some good reviews and vanished.

You followed that up with **Under Venus,** *which never actually was published until years later, when you had established yourself as a major author. How long did you spend on it and what happened to keep it out of print for so long?*

Marriages I wrote in about three or four months. *Under Venus* took about a year of very hard work because that was the first time I actually tried to write a realistic novel with lots of characters and an implied social world in which the relationships between the characters really meant something—*and* a story. It just killed me when it was rejected. I didn't do what anybody else would have done, which was to ask my agent to take it to other places. I just figured I wanted to stay where I was and if I made the book significantly better, they would take it. But I was wrong. I don't think they would have ever taken that book, no matter what I did to it, even though it was pretty good book. I went to the same people with *Julia* and they took that, because they knew that that had more commercial potential, and it was just as good.

Under Venus, *like* **Marriages,** *is mainstream. After that, you made the switch to horror. What inspired you to do it?*

The agent I had suggested that I write a Gothic. So I thought of kind of a horror idea really, *Julia.* That again, was tremendous fun to write. I knew that somehow, in the deep sense, I was doing the right thing. I was satisfied with my work and then my life was saved. It was very easy to sell that book. For the first time in three or four years I made more money than my wife, we could live on it very easily. A guy named Peter Fetterman bought it for a small amount of money to be filmed, and with the money he gave us we could buy a house. So we did that. The next book turned out to do exactly the same thing as *Julia,* so I knew I could

do it, I didn't have to have that awful doubt. That was a very sweet time of life.

For **The Throat,** *what were the specific mystery influences?* I'm very up front about that. In the beginning of *The Throat,* John Ransom, this college professor, tells his friend, Tim Underhill, of the time he first met his wife. He was in her father's library, and this beautiful girl who looks like she plays tennis comes in and plucks a book off the shelf and she says, "I'm looking for a work of impure consciousness. What should I read, William Burroughs or Raymond Chandler?" The guy is sort of stunned and attracted and he says, "Oh, I think you should read *The Long Goodbye.*" And she shows him the book and it's *The Long Goodbye.* That's the book behind *The Throat.*

I've read some Chandler, but never that one.

It's his best book, it's a masterpiece. I collect Raymond Chandler first editions and that was one of the first ones I got. I've always really liked Raymond Chandler and later loved him because of the magnificence of the way he wrote and the particular idiosyncratic feelings that are in Chandler, all about loneliness, isolation, loss. There's a lot of pain in Chandler, too.

In **The Throat,** *Tim Underhill describes you as "a nice enough kind of guy who doesn't get out much." Is that an accurate description?*

Well, you know, I'm very very fond of Tim Underhill, but he doesn't like me as much as I like him, that's why he says those things. (Laughs) I *am* a nice enough kind of guy and I *don't* get out very much. I work a lot. I work pretty much the same way I would if I had a regular job, except I start later and if I take the day off, nobody's going to yell at me. And I can't get fired.

Everybody like me works almost every day. That's the only way you can do it. I have a hunch that there's a very disturbing breed loose in the world that think of themselves as writers, and call themselves writers, and every now and then publish books. But mainly they don't write, they go to conferences and congresses and spend a lot of time in bars. People who take the organizations and institutions very seriously and devote a lot of time to them, who wouldn't miss the meetings of PEN or the Author's Guild or MWA or HWA, and who every now and then write a story when they feel inspired. That's *not* the way to do it. You have to write just as well when you're totally uninspired. My real point is, you get better as you do more. Like any other activity, you improve over time as long as you keep at it. If I had a batting machine that I reported to every day, pretty soon I could hit baseballs the same way I did when I was fifteen.

In that case, is there value in writing bad books?

No. If you really surrender yourself to it, you get better. I know I have gotten a lot better. My range expanded. My dialogue improved. My books became much more ambitious. That's because I reported to my desk everyday and sat down and lifted up the top of my head just to see what would happen. Some things went out and other things came in. That's essential. People say it's discipline, which isn't right, because I'm not a tremendously disciplined person. But I am sort of dedicated, I do want to see what stage I can reach if I work hard enough. That's my job. That's my task. If you have to have a task, mine is a pretty good one.

Don Ringnalda (essay date 1994)

SOURCE: "Civilian Perspectives in Peter Straub's *Koko*," in *Fighting and Writing the Vietnam War,* University Press of Mississippi, 1994, pp. 115-35.

[In the following essay, Ringnalda addresses the issue of "civilians" writing about the Vietnam combat experience.]

Up to this point we've looked at three writers who spent a year "in country." All three experienced combat—even the civilian "journalist" Herr. Peter Straub did not. So what's he doing in a book called *Fighting and Writing*? How can a civilian possibly write about war? How dare he claim that special privilege? To this day, many veterans of the Vietnam War share the attitude that if you weren't there and you weren't in combat, then you have no business (or ability) writing about it. I myself have been told that I wasn't qualified to write this book, because I'm only a Vietnam era veteran. Beyond the obvious rejoinder that if one wrote only about personal experiences, one would have very little to write about, it needs to be added that this I-was-there-you-weren't attitude rests upon an unwitting hypocrisy: most vets would agree that they hated their Vietnam experience, and that they were, to one degree or another, disillusioned and traumatized by it. Yet, many of these same vets often hoard those experiences in the safety deposit boxes of their trapped memories. I believe that what the psychologist says to Christian Starkmann in Philip Caputo's *Indian Country* (1987) applies to many vets, whether troubled by PTSD or not: "It's not like you're guarding some deep dark guilty secret. It's like you're guarding a treasure," a line of thinking explored by William Broyles, Jr. in his notorious *Esquire* article, "Why Men Love War." Visits to the Vietnam Veterans Memorial have confirmed my suspicions that many vets love to hate Vietnam. If you weren't there, you can hate it, but you've earned neither the right to love to hate it nor to write about that loving hate. You're a mere Nam "gentile." Letting another onlooker in a faded fatigue jacket know you're

a "gentile" will immediately end a conversation. However, provide a battalion and division number and you're guaranteed a conversational litany filled with olive drab place names, jargon, and acronyms. I don't wish to minimize the combatants' experiences in Vietnam; far from it. In fact, by isolating themselves as a kind of damned elect, and by cutting themselves off from the wider ramifications of the war, combatants minimize their experiences and thus remain in exile. They are "held prisoner by the facts of their own Vietnam experiences." The Vietnam vet, if anything, begins his or her writing task at a disadvantage that needs to be overcome. Put more kindly, perhaps it's a disadvantage that can be turned to their advantage.

The disadvantage exists because the Vietnam War was a time of very special, supercharged craziness; it was so utterly different from mowing lawns or sweeping dandelion fuzz from them that the temptation to stare repeatedly at one's personal Vietnam closeups is hard to resist. But when the vet does not transcend those closeups, he and his writing often endure the calcification of Lot's wife looking back on the burning cities of Sodom and Gomorrah. In his 1988 Vietnam novel *Koko,* Peter Straub runs no such risk; for, during the war he was doing such dangerous things as teaching prep school in Milwaukee, going to graduate school, and studying poetry in Ireland. Allegedly, this background should disqualify Straub from any possibility of writing an authentic Vietnam novel. Yet (or should I say "thus?"), *Koko* is possibly the most intensive, complex exploration of the war's imprint on the American psyche yet published, in part because it's written by a nonsoldier. *Koko* is, to modify the words of a minor character, like a CAT-scan seen from the outside and the inside. That is, it offers us "tomographic," multiple pictures and cross-sections of the national psyche before, during, and after a My Lai-like atrocity scene at a fictionalized village called Ia Thuc. Whereas most Vietnam writing stays "in country" for a year, *Koko* moves about from the 1950s to the 80s, from New York to Danang, Bangkok to Milwaukee, the United States to Honduras, from texts to subtexts, ever moving "backwards and forwards," as the novel's most persistent leitmotif puts it. The complex "scans" of the novel do more than any other book I know of to project the war's causes, legacies, and opportunities both for being overwhelmed by it and being healed from it.

Koko is essentially an elaborate play of the imagination within the framework of the whodunit genre. The "who" in this case is a character nicknamed Koko. Following the much-celebrated release of the Iran hostages, Koko goes on an apparently random killing spree in Singapore and Bangkok, shooting at least eight people, removing their eyes and ears with a cleaver, then placing in the victims' mouths a playing card with "Koko" written on it.

Upon the occasion of the dedication of the Vietnam Veterans Memorial in 1982, Beevers, Poole, Conor, and Pumo, members of an infantry platoon in 1968, stage a reunion in Washington, D.C. Beevers, the platoon's lieutenant, tells the others that he's sure another member of the platoon—Tim Underhill, now a crime novelist supposedly living in Singapore—is Koko. Three of the vets decide to go to Southeast Asia to stop the killings. However, in Bangkok they finally find Underhill and discover that he can't possibly be Koko. It turns out that Spitalny, another ex-platoon member, from Milwaukee, is Koko. Furthermore, they discover that the killings are not random. All of the victims were journalists who reported on the 1968 massacre committed by Beevers' platoon at Ia Thuc. The homicides are therefore likely acts of retribution against those who printed the story.

Finally, almost five hundred pages into the novel, we learn that yet another character from Milwaukee, M. O. Dengler, is Koko. It turns out that while on R & R in Bangkok, Dengler had mutilated Spitalny's body beyond recognition, switched dog tags, then used Underhill's name while pursuing a Boschean nightmare existence throughout Southeast Asia. After his killing binge abroad, he returns to the States, kills a wealthy yuppie at JFK, then a librarian where Pumo is doing research on the killings, then Pumo himself. Finally, before fleeing to Honduras, never to be heard from again, he lures most of the remaining platoon members to a dark, cave-like basement, cuts off one of Beevers' ears, stabs both Underhill and Poole in the side, and escapes from the police by wearing Underhill's clothes.

In and of itself, this is standard material for the genre of the "airport novel": a mysterious crime, several red herrings to throw us off the trail, and a solution which, like the purloined letter in Poe's story, was right in front of us all along, but our conventional investigative paradigm prevented us seeing it. But Straub parodies the genre self-reflexively to enrich it and indict America's ahistorical, simplistic, "dyslexic" reading of itself and the Vietnam War. On an obvious, literal level, Dengler is the "who" of the whodunit; but Straub treats him less as a solitary maniacal psychopath than as a vengeful victim of an entire systemic chain of exploitation within a dysfunctional culture populated by dysfunctional families. That systemic chain is Straub's purloined letter; as H. Rap Brown once put it, violence is endemic: "as American as apple pie." Even Dengler correctly assesses the endemic nature of violence, which, if anything trivializes the alleged specialness of the Vietnam War. That's why he tells members of the platoon that one saw more violence inside some Milwaukee taverns than in a firefight. Lest we think Dengler is exaggerating, we should remember that during the same time it took for 58,000 U.S. personnel to die in Vietnam, a much larger number of civilians were violently killed by handguns—here at home.

Working with a larger canvas than those used by most vet-

eran writers, Straub's vision parallels Doris Lessing's anatomy of metastasized war and violence in her *Children of Violence series.* "She defines the locus of bellicosity," states the feminist critic Lynne Hanley, "not as a place, a field of battle, but as a habit of mind, a structure of feeling, a cultural predisposition." Similarly, Straub, unlike most veteran writers, views Vietnam not as some kind of American "ur" experience, but as business as usual—exported. It was simply highlighted in the media so that everyone noticed—for a while; then most of American forgot and resumed its ahistorical reading while slipping in and out of semiconsciousness at 35,000 feet between JFK and Heathrow, or at zero feet between home and the office.

> **Straub reverses the prevailing attitude of teachers, critics, novelists, and psychologists regarding the war. According to that attitude, Vietnam engulfed us in darkness that now needs to be illuminated. Implicit in *Koko,* on the other hand, is the attitude that Vietnam was the light that should have illuminated the dark sub-text of American myth.**
> **—Don Ringnalda**

As a civilian-by-day, guerrilla-by-night writer, Straub would embrace Michael Herr's conclusion to *Dispatches:* "Vietnam Vietnam Vietnam, we've all been there." But who really believes this? Who is willing to accept a whodunit novel in which Poole and Underhill admit that everyone in the platoon is Koko, that everyone hosts a devil within, a theme that pervades *Koko?* Arguably, Koko is 562 pages of rebuttal of those who refuse the culpability that accrues from the messiness of living in history. Poole's wife Judy is their representative. Early in the novel she tells him that "the past is in the past because that is where it belongs. Does that tell you anything?" Indeed it does! About the Vietnam War, she simply states, "when it's over, it's over," whether as a noble cause, as Ronald Reagan would have it, or as an aberrant loss, as George Bush would. It is through Maggie Lah, a richly drawn Asian character, that we see Straub's rebuttal explicitly realized. She insists on the novel's dominant theme: our beliefs and actions can be morally informed only if we are engaged in time that goes "backwards and forwards," a phrase repeated dozens of times in the novel. In a conversation with her lover, Tina Pumo, Maggie asks, "Do you think there is a real point where *then* stops and *now* begins?" And then: "Don't you know that down deep the things that happen to you never really *stop* happening to you?." When Pumo asks her how she knows about the connection between Vietnam and the present, she says "*Everybody* knows about it, Tina. . . . Except a surprising number of middle-aged American men [in other words, the very guardians of the ahistorical culture], who really do believe that people can start fresh all over again, that the past dies and the future is a new beginning, and that these beliefs are moral."

In *Koko,* the key to healing from the war is the simultaneity of travel "backwards and forwards." The really important word is "and." Some characters just go forward; some just go backward. Actually, neither of these character types goes anywhere. Like Stephen Wright's Trips, they are either suspended in a meaningless present or frozen in an implacable past. Poole represents the first sort. *The Divided Man,* the title of one of Underhill's novels talked about in *Koko,* perfectly describes Poole. There is nothing to connect his past self to his present self. After Ia Thuc and the war, he just forgot it, denied it, and divided himself, or at least tried very hard. A killer of children in the war, he's a pediatrician in the present, treating pampered, healthy children of wealthy ahistorical parents. As Tim O'Brien might say of him, "[Poole] has adjusted too well. . . . I wish [he] were more troubled."

Beevers and Dengler represent the second sort. For Beevers, Vietnam was the last significant experience of his life, his "one golden godlike point," his "hot center." In the present he's a lawyer just going through the motions—not very well, I might add. As the story begins, he gets fired. He's Straub's closet Chuck Norris, aching to return to the scene of glory where he had the orgasmic power (literally) of life and death as he killed thirty children with M-16 fire and burned Ia Thuc to the ground. Even Dengler, in rare moments when he's not engulfed by the past, recognizes that "Harry Beevers was the road backwards."

Unfortunately for Dengler and his victims, those moments are much too rare. To explain this rarity, Straub takes us backward all the way to Dengler's horrible childhood. Using Dengler's father and foster mother as microcosmic Americans, Straub would have us understand that the Vietnam War and its bloody spillover in Singapore, Bangkok, and other places in the East was rooted in Dengler's hellfire Milwaukee home, that it was the inevitable result of the endemic violence rooted in the heritage of Puritan ethnocentric racism, Old Testament religiosity, zealous nationalism, and misogyny. Dengler is born to a Nicaraguan prostitute. Soon thereafter, his father, a hypocritical, racist John, kills her. Throughout his childhood he is repeatedly abused, beaten, sodomized, even locked up in the family's butcher shop meat freezer—all in the name of Christian discipline. His father was both a butcher and a fire-and-brimstone preacher. In naming his shop "Dengler's Lamb of God Butcher Shop," he clearly indicates that he often got the two callings mixed up. Obsessed with a parsimonious work ethic, his father beats into Dengler's head "*We waste no part of the animal.*" He wasted no part of the Bible either, at least

not the Old Testament, for he forces his son to read it "backwards and forwards." But, coming out of his mouth, the phrase doesn't mean harmonization of past and present; rather, it means regimented learning of proscriptive codes, endlessly repeated. In subzero weather he drags his son to street corners, bellowing out proscriptive demands for salvation or damnation while the child passes the hat.

Straub offers us an analogue for the way Dengler was "shaped" by his parents. For untold years his mother has obsessively duplicated identical kitsch artifacts. She fries purple marbles in Wesson oil (never butter—it burns) until they crack from the inside. Then she glues twentyfour of them to black cloth to form grape clusters, never with the slightest variation from one to another. Well, his parents were "successful" in their child-rearing; Dengler, like many nineteen-year-olds in the sixties, became "cracked" and "glued" to darkness. One of the novel's motifs confirms this. Koko (Dengler) often alludes to Handel's *Messiah.* His favorite line comes from the dark alto solo "He was Despised": "Man of sorrows and acquainted with grief." A cracked grape cluster, Dengler can imagine only a *Messiah* without a messiah. He is unable to balance the "shaking," "purifying," "breaking," and "dashing" "refiner's fire" with the joy of a child being born. He seems to be utterly unaware that the oratorio's opening recitative is "Comfort ye my People," which contains the line "her [Jerusalem's] iniquity is *pardoned*" [my emphasis].

Translated into Dengler's post-Vietnam behavior, "*We waste no part of the animal*" becomes "*I pardon no one who had any part of the Ia Thuc massacre.*" Dengler does travel backward and forward, but only between the far distant and distant pasts. As Straub says, "what happened on the frozen banks of the Milwaukee River [his father's murder of his mother] never stopped happening for him, no matter how many times he killed in order to make it stop." Notice that Straub doesn't say that what happened at Ia Thuc never stopped happening. As a nonveteran, Straub has the necessary distance to see a bigger picture. In that picture the Vietnam War is not seen as some sort of uniquely awful, monstrous destruction of American values. The war did not, as common wisdom has it (and I mean *common*), invert or betray American values. Instead, the war was the ultimate manifestation of those "values," which are chronicled in Richard Drinnon's book *Facing West: The Metaphysics of Indian-Hating and Empire-Building,* a book that essentially begins with the Pequot Massacre and ends with its more recent edition at My Lai. Straub reverses the prevailing attitude of teachers, critics, novelists, and psychologists regarding the war. According to that attitude, Vietnam engulfed us in darkness that now needs to be illuminated. Implicit in *Koko,* on the other hand, is the attitude that Vietnam was the light that should have illuminated the dark sub-text of American myth. From this point of view, the war was less a heart of darkness than a "heart of light," or a "heart of whiteness." Vietnam didn't ruin Dengler; *Milwaukee* did.

Milwaukee provided Dengler his basic training. This is where he was inculcated by simplistic, black-and-white notions of good and evil. Even more pathological than Wright's Major Holly or O'Brien's Lieutenant Callicles, he hunts his victims with as much fervor as Wisconsin's U.S. senator displayed in attempting to rid the country of evil Communists. Never escaping from the Old Testament, as it were, Dengler tries to undo or sweep away evil by pursuing a course of retribution rather than atonement. Already as a child, one of his favorite characters in his favorite book, *Babar the King*, is Hatchibombitar, "the street sweeper, a man of no ambition but to keep the streets clean . . . sweeping and sweeping away the filth." So he is now the street sweeper, a role that entraps him as surely as he was locked up in his father's meat freezer.

Throughout *Koko* Straub uses images of caves to express the entrapment of his war vets in a kind of negative womb that procreates evil. The cave motif begins with the primary atrocity at Ia Thuc: the slaughter of the thirty children hidden in a cave. About this cave we read: "[it] folded and unfolded, branching apart like a maze. . . . It began to seem hopeless, they would never find the end of it: it seemed to have no end at all, but to twist back around in on itself. . . . The chamber was filled with a complex odor compounded of terror, blood, gunpowder, and some other odor Poole could identify only in negatives. It was not piss, it was not shit, it was not sweat or rot or fungus or even the reeking dew all animals exude when they are frightened unto death, but something beneath all these."

Although all of Straub's vets have their sojourns within the "cave" of their war experiences, no one is more committed to the cave without exit than Dengler. His New York basement apartment is repeatedly described as a cave that incubates evil. For example, "Koko sat alone in his room, his cell, his egg, his cave. The light burned, and the egg the cell the cave caged all the light and reflected it from the wall. . . . Dead children clustered round him, crying out, and the others cried out from the walls." Straub "couples," or parallels, this negative yonic imagery with the all-too-familiar phallic destructiveness of Vietnam War literature and testimonials: "Koko went into the cave and into the Devil's arsehole and there met the Lieutenant, Harry Beevers, his surfboard his shovel his weapon out before him, being fingered, being fluted, being shot—shooting. You want a piece of this? The Lieutenant with his cock sticking out and his eyes glowing."

Straub completes his cave imagery with one of Koko's last acts, the stabbing of Underhill and Poole and mutilation of Beevers, in a basement within the cave-like Bowery Arcade on the edge of New York's Chinatown. We never see any-

thing down there in this American Ia Thuc cave; it is pure darkness, disembodied voices, the touch and smell of blood flowing from Beevers, Poole, and Underhill. Connecting this "cave" to the one in Ia Thuc, Straub says, "Sometimes it sounded as if children were speaking or crying out a great distance away. These were the dead children painted on the walls. Again Poole knew that no matter what he might hear in this room he was alone with Koko, and the rest of the world was on the opposite side of a river no man could cross alive."

Fortunately, here is where Poole is wrong. The river separating Vietnam and contemporary America can be crossed. This brings us to Straub's counterpart to caves—bridges. If caves imprison, bridges liberate. But in *Koko,* as with the Vietnam Veterans Memorial, the liberation isn't cheap. The bridge image doesn't provide a mere passive means of getting from A to B, from the memories of Vietnam to an unburdened present. Instead, it relates A and B, literally, in the sense of "carry back." Bridges enable vets—particularly Poole and Underhill—to transcend both the deadness of amnesia (Poole's prebridge life) and the crippling effects of trapped memories (Dengler). Bridges enable Poole and Underhill to remember in a way that heals.

In his book *Healing from the War,* Arthur Egendorf traverses the very river that Poole initially thinks is uncrossable. Egendorf argues that we must utilize the pain of Vietnam: "The rarely spoken fact is that however painful they [responses to the war] are, these reactions also may serve as the occasion for men to evolve and update their ways of responding to life." "The tendency among many veterans and the public," Egendorf goes on to say, "is to respond to talk of 'stress disorder' with the seemingly logical but mistaken idea that what veterans need is to reduce their level of stress . . . which has the unfortunate effect of encouraging veterans to shrink from life. . . . Their horror, rage, guilt, and desperation may be genuine, the signs of a reemerging sensitivity. . . . For once a man grants himself the freedom [i.e., the bridge] to be appropriately upset by what he has seen and done, his reactions subside quite naturally, and he experiences himself as 'more himself'." One final comment by Egendorf that parallels the experiences of Poole and Underhill: "The more amply we reach out to grasp our past [going backward], the more we can look on old pain gratefully, recognizing it as the instigator that provoked us into growing [going forward] to encompass it." In other words, Poole had to grasp his past by descending into this one last "cave" in the Bowery Arcade. Rather than paralyzing him within the evil that was Vietnam, this descent is a ritualized Fortunate Fall. Instead of being a place of inherent evil, the cave becomes a bridge to a bridge.

Poole's initial turning point occurs while he searches for Underhill in Bangkok: "Poole walked beneath a highway overpass and eventually came to a bridge over a little stream. On the far bank was a hodgepodge village of cardboard boxes, nests of newspaper and trash. This warren smelled much worse than the compound of gasoline, excrement, smoke, and dying air that filled the rest of the city. To Poole's nose it stank of disease—it stank like an unclean wound. He stood on the quavery little bridge and peered into the paper slum . . . . A smudge of smoke curled up into the air from somewhere back in the litter of boxes, and a baby cried out." Reflecting on the shocking contrast between his comfortable suburban practice and this scene of squalor, Poole experiences an epiphany—his bridge:

> His pampered, luxurious practice also felt like a confining pit—[his cave of amnesia]. . . . Westerholm was an evasion of everything. . . . He could not stand finishing out his life in Westerholm. . . . Before Poole stepped off the bridge, he knew that his relationship to these matters had irrevocably changed. His inner compass had swung as if by itself.

Next, Poole echoes Egendorf's sentiments and even some of his words: "He had decided really to be himself in relationship to his old life. . . . If really being himself put his old life at risk, the reality of his position made the risk bearable. He would let himself look in all directions"—backward and forward. Somewhat later, we read: "Eight hours earlier, Dr. Poole had crossed over a rickety bridge and felt himself coming into a new accommodation with his profession, with his marriage, above all with death. It was almost as if he had finally seen death with enough respect to understand it. He had stood before it with his spirit wide open, in a very undoctorly way." Then, once again, Straub directly parallels Egendorf's argument: "The awe, the terror were necessary"—his bombshell/jewel. Looking back on this experience much later, Poole reflects "his first moment of real awakening had come on the rickety bridge beside the cardboard shacks. That was where he had started to give things up." So just what is Poole's bridge? It is his decision to spend the rest of his life being "appropriately upset." This will require him truly to connect his *backward* with his *forward,* his killing in Vietnam with his practice in the present. It will mean getting out of his "confining pit," where he "patted heads, gave shots, took throat cultures, comforted children who would never really have anything wrong with them, and calmed down those mothers who took every symptom for a major illness." His practice doesn't connect him to his Vietnam experiences; instead it has had the effect of nullifying them, or at the very least, anesthetizing them. The idea for Poole's bridge comes from the crying Southeast Asian baby in Bangkok. He decides to spend the rest of his life being a store-front doctor. Crossing a bridge each day, "Michael Poole commutes to the Bronx [slums] every day, where he practices what he calls 'front-line medicine'."

Front-line medicine not only establishes the link between Ia Thuc and the Bronx, it also reminds us that his new practice in the crime-ridden slums will involve risks—risks necessary for his healing. Straub underscores this very late in the novel when Underhill flashes back to Vietnam, where he is listening to jazz with a black platoon member, Spanky Burrage. The language used to describe Duke Ellington's rendition of the tune "Koko" utilizes (as opposed to merely "uses") the raw material of experience, whether it happens in Vietnam or on the streets, as a way of being "appropriately upset":

> It is a music of threat. . . . Long ominous notes on a baritone saxophone counterpoint blasts from trombones. A lurching, swaying, uneasy melody begins in the saxophone section. From the darkness two trombones whoop and shake, going *wa waaa wa waa* like human voices on the perimeter of speech. There are noises that jump right out of the speakers and come toward you like a crazy father in the middle of the night [which is precisely what happened to Dengler as a child]. The piano utters nightmarish chords which are half-submerged in the cacophony of the band. . . . [The] bass pads through the band like a burglar, like a sapper crawling through our perimeter.

(Notice that "burglar" and "sapper" further bridge "the world" and Vietnam.) This is the artist utilizing what James Baldwin, in "Sonny's Blues," calls "the risk of ruin, destruction, madness, and death" as building blocks of the imagination. Ellington neither turns away from the risk (as Poole has been doing for years) nor is engulfed by it in Dengler fashion.

Like Fuller's Neumann and Wright's Griffin, Poole will try to rebuild his life from the destruction left in the war's wake. Underhill elaborates on this strategy when he tells of Spanky playing a second version of "Koko," this one by the great Charlie Parker. Again, there are risks; we're told that there's an urgency to the music, that it is unsentimental, fierce, threatening, and tense. "Then,"

> An astonishing thing happens. When Parker reaches the bridge of the song, all that open-throated singing against threat is resolved in a dazzle of imaginative glory. . . . The urgency is engulfed in the grace of his thoughts. . . . What Charlie Parker does on the bridge . . . reminds me of Henry James's dream—the one I told Michael [Poole] about in the hospital. A figure battered at his bedroom door. Terrified, James held the door closed against the figure. Impendingness, threat. In his dream, James does an extraordinary thing. He turns on his attacker and forces open the door [of his cave] in a burst of dar-

ing. The figure has already fled, is only a diminishing spot in the distance. It is a dream of elation and triumph, of glory. That was what we listened to in the dripping tent in the year 1968 in Vietnam. . . . we heard fear dissolved by mastery.

On the final page of the novel, Underhill says, "I think of Charlie Parker leaning as if into an embrace into the conditions that surrounded him," and he calls this a "complicated joy." It's an authentic joy because it's complicated, a word that means "folded together," as in backward and forward, Ia Thuc and the Bronx, theme and bridge, cave and opened door, destruction and creation.

The necessary integration of creation and destruction is reminiscent of a story told me by a woman whose brother had returned from Vietnam more than twenty years earlier, when she was still a child. He was sullen and prone to violent acts. She cited as an example the time he pulled off the arms, legs, and head of her favorite doll, then taped the arms where the legs should be, the legs where the arms should be, and the head on backward. To this day, the woman and her parents view this action as a fit of gratuitous violence committed by an understandably traumatized brother and son. It hasn't occurred to them that this act may have been a profoundly creative expression of destruction and madness. You see, this vet had been a medic in Vietnam. As such, he saw more than his share of boys in pieces. Quite likely he had many times come to Ardell's fundamental awareness in David Rabe's play *The Basic Training of Pavlo Hummel:* "We melt; we tear and rip apart. Membrane, baby. Cellophane. Ain't that some shit." Once ripped apart, always ripped apart. All efforts to reattach the pieces, repeated in Sisyphean fashion, are futile. The clumsily, improperly reattached pieces of the doll might have been a richly disturbing expression of the futility and the real price of war. Thus, rather than being a gratuitous act mired in the "theme" of destruction, the doll episode may have been a complicating bridge that leads to healing.

Returning to Dengler, if we think of music (if not all art) as a balance between redundancy (theme) and new material (bridge), we have another way of understanding his tragic life: he's all theme and no bridge, no "variations." Interestingly, jazz musicians (in America, at any rate) universally use the word "release" instead of bridge. When I've asked "release from what?" the answers usually are "monotony," the "old stuff," and the "familiar part." Except in rare cases, however, where a tune has an AB structure, the release is not permanent; instead, it creates a permanent relationship with the theme. The result is a playful interplay between Apollonian, thematic order and Dionysian disregard for that order. The most exciting moments, then, occur during the last bar of the theme and the first bar of the release, the last bar of the release and the first bar of the theme. Lack-

ing the creativeness engendered by this interplay, Dengler therefore removes pieces from people instead of dolls. Simply put, he's a victim of Vietnam War redundancy—*the* shortcoming of most Vietnam literature, which is addicted to the bridgeless theme of combat, destruction, and the tragic victimization of the soldier—set on autoreverse. Like Stephen Wright's Trips, Dengler views the world intensely but simplistically.

Poole, on the other hand, views the world complicatedly and extensively. He complicates his theme as a pediatrician by making Vietnam and Bangkok experiential spaces at one end of a bridge, not as caves without exit. Peter Straub, for his part, complicates his status as "civilian" writer with the tacit admission, "Vietnam Vietnam Vietnam, we've all been there," a fact Underhill and Poole subscribe to. The demon is within all of us. This is their bridge for Dengler's theme, and it connects them to their kin—Ishmael and Marlow, both of whom might well have "jammed" with Parker had they lived in his time.

This is part of Straub's rebuttal of the Judy Pooles of the world. Another part of the rebuttal takes the form of the novel's refusal to buy into a fiction that is particularly American—namely, the Platonic notion that the art of fiction imitates the life of facts. *Koko* is an extremely "authored" novel. Over and over, we see life imitating art in its pages. Straub clearly views imagination—as we will see below—not as function that spices up or escapes reality but as the means to create it—Wallace Stevens' "supreme fiction." Like O'Brien, Straub is a "fabulator," to use Robert Scholes term. As "fabulation," *Koko* doesn't turn away from reality in escapist fashion. On the contrary, it "attempt[s] to find more subtle correspondences [i.e, bridges] between the reality which is fiction and the fiction which is reality." Like O'Brien, Straub is concerned that we investigate both the reality of story and the story of reality. As Straub's fictional writer, Underhill especially understands this imperative. Knowing as he does that "We have only the shakiest hold on the central stories of our lives," he also knows how imperative is the newly imagined material of the bridge.

Koko does show that the results of life imitating art can be disastrous—not, however, because the sequence is backward. No, the problem arises when characters, particularly Koko (or anyone going to war mistaking a country's fictions for God-generated truth), don't recognize art as art, but as an implacable truth that will not permit editing, revision, or variations. This offers us another way of viewing Dengler. Raised by a mother who fervently believes that "Imagination must be stopped. You're talking about imagination. You have to put an end to that. That's one thing I know," Dengler eventually becomes a fixated cracked marble who eschews the freedom of the imagination in favor of dogma-fettered revelation and the call to sweep the filth off the streets. After Underhill tells Mrs. Dengler that her stepson had been "inventive" in Vietnam, she cuts in and objects: "You think backwards . . . . Oh my. *Backwards.* Inventive? You mean he made things up. Isn't that part of the original trouble?"

As someone who goes only backward, Beevers is another character fettered by his certainty of a fact-fiction split. One of his motives for tracking down Koko is his plan to make lots of money with the "true" story of this crazed serial killer. Like O'Brien's *Savak* colonel in *Going After Cacciato,* he can entertain fiction or nonfiction, but any leaching of one into the other is unthinkable. Thus he tells Underhill "I want your agreement that you won't use any of this Koko material in a work of nonfiction. You can write all the fiction you want—I don't care about that. But I have to have the nonfiction rights to this. 'Sure,' Underhill said. 'I couldn't write nonfiction if I tried'." Later he says, "I don't really know what a 'nonfiction novel' is." Always implicit, and sometimes explicit, in Straub's novel is the question "who really *does* know?" Unlike Beevers, who thinks he knows, Underhill believes "imagination was everything." In one of his three dialogues with himself, he says "I think I saw him [Koko]. I know I saw him. You imagined you saw him? It is the same thing." Poole shares this awareness. Once, while in a cemetery, he sees his deceased child as a twenty-two-year-old man. At first he assumes he had hallucinated him: "'I didn't see my son,' Poole began, and then his objections dried to powder in his mouth'." "[H]e had authored him," just as Underhill—so we read on the same page—had authored Milwaukee. The trick, as Wallace Stevens once put it, "is to believe in a fiction, which you know to be a fiction. . . ."

Stevens' statement would strike Beevers as nonsense. When he shares his research about Koko with the others in the platoon, four times he emphatically asserts *"Consider the facts."* So it's not surprising that when Underhill tells about Beevers' eventual suicide, he says "[Beevers'] imagination had failed him. His illusions [regarding fact and fiction] were all the imagination he had—a ferocious poverty." Maggie Lah also sees through Beevers' poverty. She tells Poole, "Your friend Harry Beevers can't act very well." It simply never occurs to the shallow Beevers that he's on Shakespeare's world stage. He is a confirmed Prospero; it never occurs to him that his colonized island of facts not only destroys the world's Calabans, but himself as well. A confirmed Cartesian realist, Beevers is the victim of an unrecognized male fantasy, with no one left to take it out on but himself.

Koko does much more than merely present the arguments of characters regarding the interpenetration of fact and fiction: it is an interpenetration, an interlocking series of bridges "between the reality which is fiction and the fiction which is reality." First of all, Underhill is a writer of fiction within

a fiction. Of course, there is nothing revolutionary about that. But Straub pushes the interpenetration to a Borgesian level. Underhill is not just a fictional character who writes; instead, his fictions "bleed" through Straub's novel and parallel his plot. Like Griffin's apartment walls in *Meditations in Green, Koko* is like a large palimpsest on which previous texts—literally subtexts—rise to the surface to multivocally mingle with others that previously arose, thereby altering the "master narrative" written by Straub. David Eason would call *Koko* a "multi-layered interrogation of communication," a novel that "blurs traditional distinctions between fantasy and reality." Always in the interrogative mode, *Koko* insists on a plurality of authoring and authority.

A case in point occurs when Pumo tells Maggie what happened to Beevers' platoon when it was trapped between a minefield and the NVA in Dragon Valley. His narrative begins conventionally, with Pumo in the first person and the use of quotation marks. However, the reader soon notices that some paragraphs begin but don't end with quotation marks, while others begin and end with them. The reliability of point of view thus gives way to a collage of disembodied voices. To further complicate our reading, these paragraphs are interspersed with italicized passages (Underwood's interpolations) in which Pumo is cast in the third person. Thus, instead of Dengler's obsession with a single, monovocal story, we have versions and variations that pollinate each other.

Some of Underhill's stories don't merely parallel the actions of the novel—they actually induce them. For example, "The Running Grunt" provided Dengler with a scenario, in which he mutilates Spitalny and switches dog tags. This scenario, in turn, stems from a previous palimpsestic text, Underhill's first novel, *A Beast in View.* In it, another "running grunt" mutilates a different GI and switches dog tags. Furthermore, we gather that Dengler has read all of Underhill's fiction, including the story "Blue Rose" (about a serial killer who places a card with "blue roses" written on it in his victim's mouth), and the novels *The Divided Man* and *Into the Darkness.* Speaking of the latter, the narrator says, "Koko remembered buying that book because once in another life he had known the author and soon the book revolved and grew in his hands and became a book about himself." To further complicate Straub's "complicated joy," "Blue Rose" is also one of his previous stories.

The palimpsest motif dominates *Koko.* Poole finds Strether, Henry James' character in *The Ambassadors,* bleeding into his life. Jan de Brunhof's Babar stories frequently infiltrate the novel, as do Wordsworth's *Prelude,* Bächner's *Woyzeck,* Conrad's *Lord Jim* and *Heart of Darkness,* Jane Austen's *Jane Eyre,* Kafka's *The Trial* and *The Metamorphosis,* and others. Internally, in Underhill's *The Divided Man,* the Sisyphean sleuth, Hal Esterhaz, follows as endless series of homicides, never getting any closer to solving the crimes. He too is an orphaned son of a fanatically religious butcher. Like Dengler's real mother, Rosita, Esterhaz is found as a child naked and muddy on the banks of a river in Monroe, Illinois, which we're told later is actually Dengler's Milwaukee. Like Dengler, Esterhaz was found trapped in a meat freezer, just as he is now trapped in an endless theme of crime "circling around and around the same cycle of chords." Neither knows how to enrich "the same cycle of chords" with a bridge. *Into the Darkness* is an even more insistent reiteration of the Sisyphean sleuth theme.

Straub doesn't stop with literature; he extends the palimpsest to music on several occasions, most notably in the Spanky Burrage flashback. There we read that in Parker's version of "Koko" (alike in name only to Duke's version), the harmonic pattern of "Cherokee" bleeds through. The chord changes of Stan Getz's tenor solo on "Indiana" bleed through Parker's alto solo on "Donna Lee," but with a new melody. Basie's big-band rendition of "April in Paris" rises to the surface of Monk's quartet version, and so on. These cross-pollinations of tunes offer us one of the keys to reading *Koko:* 562 pages of new melodies added to old harmonies and new harmonies added to old melodies—in a word, complications.

The second key to reading *Koko* is our recognition that Straub offers us multiple *versions* of events. The word literally means the process of change, precisely that which Dengler finds unattainable. It's a word that describes a way of healing from trauma: imagining new "versions" of ourselves, an activity that Poole, Underhill, and Conor Linklater (who now rehabs houses) are engaged in, Dengler not. But the word also describes Straub's activity within the novel—looking at the same blackbird in different ways. In the final chapter Underhill engages in a microcosm of the novel. First, he imagines what happened to Dengler in Honduras: "I saw how it could have happened, and then I saw it happen." As we skip through the pages, we see how the imagination is linked to the creation of versions: "This is one version of how Koko came to Honduras." "I think he closes his eyes and sees a wide plaza. . . . When he closes his eyes he sees a broad sidewalk lined with cafes." "He sees brown naked children . . . burned in a ditch." "Let us say: he hears the dead man's soul. . . . Or let us say: Koko looks straight through the roof of the airplane and sees his father. . . . Or: he instantly feels the dead man's being. . . . [H]e sees a family and recognizes his brother, his sister . . . he sees a little whitewashed house. . . ." Jumping ahead, past the Spanky Burrage flashback, we read "I think Koko. . . . I think. . . . perhaps because. . . . And perhaps. . . . Maybe this time. . . . STOP. PLAY."

Looking back at the flashback, we see, among other things, an analogue of Underhill's literary microcosm—a palimpsestic microcosm within a microcosm. Nothing delights Spanky more than playing multiple versions of the same tune. And he's an absolute whiz at the control panel, pushing FAST FORWARD, REWIND, STOP, and PLAY to quickly juxtapose one version with another: two of "Koko," two of "April in Paris," three of "The Sunny Side of the Street," five versions of "Stardust" in a row, six of "How High the Moon," a dozen blues . . . ," and then the phrase that captures the very essence of *Koko:* "Everybody going to the same well but returning with different water."

Going back and forth to the well offers us a liberating version of "backwards and forwards." Spanky is as adept at using fast forward and reverse on his reel-to-reel Sony as Dengler is at reciting the identical monotones of scriptural judgment. It is strange that Dengler often sat in on Spanky's sessions yet in the present is utterly incapable of "looking at a blackbird" in more than one way. What happened on the muddy banks of the Milwaukee River and much later at Ia Thuc left him with but one somber tune, repeated endlessly, with only the monotonous hum of the rewind back to the beginning of his univocal apocalyptic quest.

Because Straub calls attention to music as an analogue for his book and for healing from pain, guilt, and fear, it is tempting to mine this vein more deeply. Late in the novel Poole makes a long trip by car and plays a cassette tape of Mozart's opera *Don Giovanni.* We read that the Mozart piano concerto already in the tape player is "the wrong music." It is interesting to speculate what makes *Don Giovanni* the right music and the concerto the wrong music. We're told only that the concerto is "Music of great delicacy and melancholy. . . ." The opera in many ways does parallel the form and content of Straub's novel. First, like Parker's "Koko" (as opposed to Dengler's), it bridges tragic import with "grace" and "beauty." Second, it uses mistaken identities to help fuel the plot. Third, it deals with the theme of fantastic retribution: a statue of the commandant pursues Don Giovanni and drags him down to hell. Fourth, like *Koko,* the opera bridges genres. Over the years since the work premiered in Prague more than two hundred years ago, critics have argued incessantly over whether it is a pop-culture opera buffa or a musical drama. Actually, it's both, just as *Koko* is a pop-culture airport novel and a "supreme fiction"—because Straub artfully masters the fusion of genres delimited by the canons of high culture. Fifth, Mozart further breaks down boundaries by using trombones in the orchestra, instruments which until then had been used exclusively in church music. Sixth, *Don Giovanni* parallels Straub's palimpsest theme, not only in that it is another version of an old story, but also in that a piece from a previous Mozart opera, *The Marriage of Figaro,* shows up in the second act. Seventh, like Dengler, Don Giovanni is a serial criminal of sorts, winning and dashing the hearts of a long list of women, a list that is enumerated in the famous "catalogaria."

But there is an eighth connection—admittedly not mentioned by Straub—that is especially germane to the music motif of *Koko*. In the opera's wonderful ballroom scene, Mozart takes Spanky's practice of juxtaposition to a whole new level: he scores three songs (a minuet, a contre-danse, and a waltz), with three different rhythms—to be played simultaneously. And he pulls it off. He dissolves the threatening chaos with mastery, creating a bridge that connects even the incongruity of three-four and four-four meters.

One cannot demonstrate that Poole is in any way conscious of Mozart's extraordinary feat; but one can demonstrate that Poole is a character in a novel that comes close to matching the feat, a novel with a recurrent, eerie statement bleeding through the surface: "God does all things simultaneously." So Mozart's three simultaneous tunes are an apt analogue for Poole's new "complicated joy." To paraphrase the language of O'Brien, Poole and Underhill will neither forget Ia Thuc nor remember it simplistically. They will utilize it, not be used by it. It will be their catalyst for growing up morally and epistemologically. Like the Vietnam Veterans Memorial itself, their lives will be reflected in an imaginative construction that empowers them to be "appropriately upset."

I began this chapter by pointing out that many vets insist—along with Beevers—on having the exclusive rights to the Vietnam story. They need to give this up. It seems to me that if these vets, and Americans in general, are ever going to become "appropriately upset," we all will need to learn how to "read" ourselves more wisely and holistically. This revised reading will entail at least two sobering admissions: First, with few exceptions, veteran-written literature is narrow, white, male-centered, misogynist, and, finally, self-serving in that it typically asks the reader to pity the white, male, American soldier who was tragically misled into a nightmare of evil. Eschewing this narrow-victim syndrome, *Koko* compels us to give the Vietnam War a much more involved reading.

Second, "Vietnam Vietnam Vietnam"—we all *have* been there, both as victims and victimizers. As Lynne Hanley observes, there is a "frightfulness and ugliness deeply embedded in ourselves and our culture." Vietnam was a mere symptom of an endemic state of mind. That means we *all*—veterans and non-veterans, men and women, enlistees and conscientious objectors—have a stake in and a responsibility for remembering, writing, and reading the story of Vietnam in America, America in Vietnam. We need to read the rememberings of all people who are suspicious of and cognizant of the paradigms embedded in our culture. We need more people going to the well. Most important, we need to learn how to invent more versions of ourselves and our country, or else we will continue to produce "children of dark-

ness." Peter Straub—civilian—offers us one bridge between the killing and a new kind of remembering.

Christopher Lehmann-Haupt (review date 1 February 1996)

SOURCE: "Enough Fearful Twists for Everyone," in *The New York Times*, February 1, 1996, p. C17.

[*In a mixed review of* The Hellfire Club, *Lehmann-Haupt praises the reach of the novel, but feels that the story occasionally gets away from the author.*]

In Peter Straub's latest horror novel, **The Hellfire Club,** Nora Chancel, the story's heroine, suffers in a hellfire of masculine patronisation. Like her namesake in Ibsen's play *A Doll's House*, Nora is treated by the men around her as an object of little consequence.

Her husband, Davey, cheats on her with other women and even neglects her for his obsession with Hugo Driver's "Night Journey," a "wildly successful" fantasy novel that supports his family's publishing business, Chancel House. Her father-in-law, Alden Chancel, treats her with disdain and clearly would prefer that she were not married to Davey. Even Dick Dart, the dissolute son of Chancel House's lawyer, makes Nora feel bad by eyeing her seductively when they meet in a restaurant and by Hannibal Lecterishly telling her that he adores her "scent," even though she isn't wearing any perfume.

By night, while Davey studies a botched film version of "Night Journey," Nora has terrible nightmares caused in part by her having been raped "by two dumbbell grunts" while serving duty as a nurse in Vietnam. By day, while Davey is in New York City working at Chancel House, Nora has to worry about the serial murderer of lonely women who is terrorizing the Connecticut bedroom town where she and Davey live.

To top everything off, Nora is summoned to the local police station as the suspect in a kidnapping. There she's grabbed and taken hostage at gunpoint by the escaping serial killer, who turns out to be the Lecterish Dick Dart, arrested after being knocked unconscious by Ophelia (Popsie) Jennings, the owner of a clothing store called The Unfettered Woman. Off on the road go Dick and Nora; and the story has still barely begun.

Now this may seem a lot for the reader to swallow, but Mr. Straub is the veteran of a dozen or so horror thrillers, among them *Ghost Story, Floating Dragon* and the three books in the *Blue Rose Trilogy: Koko, Mystery* and *The Throat.* He has a number of surprising twists working for him in his wildly inventive plot. For one thing, Dick Dart turns out to be a highly entertaining villain as fiendish monsters go.

He's an authority on women's clothes and cosmetics, and he proceeds to make Nora over before doing the beastly things he has planned for her. He also has a photographic mind, and manages to trick people into believing he's a poet by quoting every third word of "The Waste Land" and "The Love Song of J. Alfred Prufrock" and every second word of Thomas Nashe's "In Time of Pestilence" ("Farewell, bliss—world is, are/lustful death them but none").

For another thing, Mr. Straub makes extremely clever use of the novel within the novel, "Night Journey," which turns out to be about the fantastic quest of "a lost boy named Pippin Little," and which has attracted a fanatic following that includes convicted killers who "justify their crimes with complex, laborious references to the novel."

From hints of plot and character correspondences between the main story and the novel within, we become aware that "Night Journey" is no casual prop. At first Pippin the Boy appears to be Nora's husband, Davey Chancel, who has been told by his parents that he was adopted when their real son, also named Davey, died as a baby. But soon it becomes clear that poor Nora herself is really Pippin, and that to find herself she must go to a mysterious place called Mountain Glade.

Mercifully, Mr. Straub never goes further than hinting at these underlying correspondences. Except in the chapter titles, which are taken from "Night Journey," the focus remains on the framing story throughout. Yet awareness of the novel's fantastic foundation makes one willing to accept as plausible what normally might seem unreal. As a result, the story lifts off the page with Nora's abduction by Dick Dart and soars irresistibly for the next few hundred pages.

What brings it eventually back to earth is that Mr. Straub asks the reader to swallow greater and greater doses of implausibility. For reasons that are never entirely clear, everything comes to depend on whatever happened one night in 1938 at a Berkshire writers colony called Shorelands. The colony was presided over by Georgina Weatherall and attended at the time by the writers Austryn Fain, Merrick Favor, Creeley Monk, Bill Tidy, Hugo Driver and Katherine Mannheim and the publisher Lincoln Chancel. If these jokily suggestive names are part of the story's hidden code, the solution escaped this reader, as did any hidden references in the titles of their books, among them Bill Tidy's workingclass memoir, "Our Skillets."

Later in the story, Mr. Straub plants more clues than he can harvest and explains events faster than he can make them happen. As *The Hellfire Club* careens to its implausible con-

clusion, his plot becomes so rickety that the rubber bands snap and the chewing gum comes unstuck. You race to the end hoping to get there before the contraption falls apart completely. This, too, creates a form of suspense, and if it can be considered artistically legitimate, then *The Hellfire Club,* in all its roller-coaster unevenness, can be said to have a little of everything.

What remains impressive even after the last nut and bolt bounce to rest is the way Mr. Straub has worked the fantastic elements of his story into a largely realistic plot, thereby allowing him to avoid a literal descent into the hellfire of his title. This technique is promising, and one hopes he will exploit it even more successfully in future works.

Tom De Haven (review date 9 February 1996)

SOURCE: "Magical Mystery Tour," in *Entertainment Weekly,* February 9, 1996, pp. 46-47.

[*Below, De Haven provides a plot summary and favorable review of* The Hellfire Club.]

Peter Straub's novels (*Ghost Story, Koko, The Throat, If You Could See Me Now*) feel terrifyingly plausible till they're over; then they seem preposterous. Nobody else working the horror-and-suspense field—not even Stephen King—concocts anything remotely resembling the audacious, labyrinthine plots that Straub serves up year after year. He's puzzle maker as much as he is a storyteller, and if his narratives are often as unwieldy, baroque, and zany as a Rube Goldberg contraption, they're also unique. Yes, and as maddening to synopsize as the federal budget. *The Hellfire Club* begins with a familiar, tired premise—a serial killer is on the loose—in the swank Connecticut town of Westerholm. Suddenly, and unexpectedly, he's captured during a botched assault on an elderly woman. The murderer turns out to be a sardonic thirtysomething lawyer named Dick Dart, who takes enormous glee in taunting everyone he meets, including Nora Chancel, the unhappily married 49-year-old housewife he takes hostage and uses to effect his getaway from the police station.

This may all seem straightforward enough until you realize that Nora was in custody herself, waiting to be charged with abducting her husband's mistress and keeping her prisoner in a boarded-up day-care center. Nora, of course, is innocent . . . or maybe not. A woman who wakes up screaming almost every night (she is haunted by her experiences as a field nurse in Vietnam) and who is visited by tiny winged demons and has long, soulful conversations with her dead father—well, you can understand how the cops could think her capable of kidnapping.

A nutso killer on the lam throughout New England with an eccentric, possibly psychotic hostage might be enough of a story for most thriller writers, but not for Peter Straub. Oh, no. As usual, he undermines all our expectations, piles on the coincidences, and veers off in berserk new directions. Turns out, Dick Dart—like millions of other people around the world—is a huge devotee of a fictitious children's fantasy novel called "Night Journey," published more than 50 years ago. Turns out, Nora's husband is the grandson of the original publisher. Turns out, "Night Journey" may have been plagiarized and the real author murdered at a Massachusetts writers' colony called Shorelands in the summer of 1938.

Dick Dart, who is just as quixotic as he is monstrous, wants to protect the reputation of Journey's putative author, Hugo Driver. Nora Chancel, however, wants to prove that her wimpy husband's patrician family is a no-good pack of literary bandits. Together, and with the police and the FBI in hot pursuit, they head north in one stolen car after another, piecing together clues to a half-century-old enigma. Turns out, *The Hellfire Club* isn't really a chase novel, after all; it's a big, lush, dizzyingly complicated murder mystery with a homicidal maniac and his crafty hostage playing the roles of private detectives. (Remember Nick and Nora from Dashiell Hammett's *The Thin Man*? Here are Dick and Nora.)

By the time this mad melee sorts itself out and reaches its grisly climax at a spooky old mansion deep in the woods (during a thunderstorm, natch), you realize that you've been suckered into a completely improbable sequence of events and a cast of artificial characters. But the craziest thing of all is you don't care. You've been royally entertained, you've gotten your money's worth, you've been taken for a good long giddy ride by one of America's most idiosyncratic imaginations. Besides, as Nora's husband says at one point, "It's a fantasy novel—what do you want, realism?"

Colin Harrison (review date 25 February 1996)

SOURCE: "Murderer's Row," in *The New York Times Book Review*, February 25, 1996, p. 9.

[*In the following excerpt, Harrison compares* The Hellfire Club *to Dean Koontz's* Intensity.]

Pity the serial killer. He is now a cliché—killed this, slaughtered that. After *The Collector,* by John Fowles, *Silence of the Lambs,* by Thomas Harris, and *The Alienist,* by Caleb Carr—not to mention true-crime books about David (Son of Sam) Berkowitz, Ted Bundy and others—it is no longer sufficient for a serial killer to have clean fingernails and a filthy mind, to lick his lips as the knife flashes or to appear to be

only a pleasant fellow dreamily wandering the aisles at the hardware store. So much replication throughout popular culture has left the serial killer downsized and in the midst of an identity crisis. . . .

Where may we find insight into this tail-chasing, self-referential genre? Perhaps in *The Hellfire Club,* the 14th novel by Peter Straub. Nora Chancel (romantically unfulfilled, survivor of bad experiences with men, has a thing about bugs) wanders through the blood-spattered bedroom of Natalie Well, a real estate agent and chances upon a shelf of horror novels: "These books had titles like 'The Rats' and 'Vampire Junction' and 'The Silver Skull,' . . . Natalie had owned more Dean Koontz novels than Nora had known existed, she had every Stephen King novel from 'Carrie' to 'Dolores Claiborne,' all of Anne Rice. . . . Here was a Natalie Well, who entertained herself with stories of . . . cannibalism, psychotic killers, degrading random death. This person wanted fear, but creepy, safe fear."

Nora, of course, will soon meet her appointed tormentor, a nondescript lawyer in his late 30's named Dick Dart. Her suffering, although congruent with her analysis of Mr. Koontz, Mr. King and Ms. Rice, will not follow the headlong rush of *Intensity*. She will first have to travel through a labyrinthine plot, wondering, like the reader, how everything hooks up to everything else (usually it will be by only the thinnest filament of logic). *The Hellfire Club* is so complicated that while reading it one yearns for a degree in electrical engineering; suffice it to say that this horror novel, which passes judgment on other horror novels, is in fact about a fictional horror novel, "Night Journey," and that the story involves not just one serial killer but two, the second one dead but known to the first.

The plotting of *The Hellfire Club* is tortuously rigged and requires encyclopedic recall on the part of nearly every character. However, it contains some particularly memorable passages—usually in flashback. Nora, once a trauma nurse in Vietnam, remembers that "every operation became a drama in which she and the surgeon performed necessary, inventive actions which banished or at least contained disorder. Some of these actions were elegant; sometimes the entire drama took on a rigorous, shattering elegance. She learned the differences between the surgeons, some of them fullbacks, some concert pianists, and she treasured the compliments they gave her. At nights, too alert with exhaustion to sleep, she smoked Montagnard grass with the others and played whatever they were playing that day—cards, volleyball or insults." Such writing stands in contrast to the metagenre anxieties cited above and reminds us that a writer is often more interesting when wandering in the woods of his own imagination than when feverishly stitching up a plot.

If the villain is familiar, is his victim also? Read together,

Intensity and *The Hellfire Club* may serve as a useful commentary on the relationship between the male horror writer and his female heroine. In both novels, the afflicted women are childless and haven't had strong mother figures. Vess, waiting for Chyna, compares her to Norma Desmond in *Sunset Boulevard*. Nora, needing a false name, calls herself Norma Desmond. Both Chyna and Nora have ample opportunity to escape from their male tormentors but, because of their tortured psychosexual histories, are unable to. Both, because of their weaknesses, achieve heroism: in *Intensity*, Chyna saves the young woman in the secret chamber and bravely kills Edgler Vess; in *The Hellfire Club*, Nora saves a young woman and bravely kills Dick Dart. After their respective abductors are finished off, both women scorn a pursuing press ("the sleazy tabloid shows"; "a dozen television programs of the talk-show or tabloid kind"). And despite their violent passages, neither heroine is allowed to despair. Nope: In the final paragraphs of their respective novels, Nora and Chyna appear to have met warm, loving, sensitive men! Their sufferings have merely been the price of happiness. How wonderful. Now we may close the pages, safe at last. Please?

Bernadette Lynn Bosky (essay date 1996)

SOURCE: "Mirror and Labyrinth: The Fiction of Peter Straub," in *A Dark Night's Dreaming*, edited by Tony Magistrate and Michael A. Morrison, University of South Carolina Press, 1996, pp. 68-83.

[*In the following essay, Bosky examines Straub's body of work.*]

Peter Straub's fiction is notable for its combination of unity and variety: the continuing exploration of specialized themes and a characteristic tone within works that cover a range of settings, genres, and styles. While this is not necessarily unusual—in fact, it characterizes most good artists in any field—it may be less common than it should be among writers of the modern American Gothic, especially due to economic pressures to stay in one genre-marketing niche. Straub is not prolific, but each piece of work, especially from *Ghost Story* to the present, is a significant new step in the development of his oeuvre; Straub is not so much looking for his voice as he is choosing to explore different vehicles for different aspects of it and working each approach both thoroughly and inventively.

Broadly, Straub's career as a writer falls into four sequential divisions. His first published work was poetry, including material in the leading literary magazine *Poetry* in 1970 and 1971, and a collection entitled *Open Air*, published by

Irish University Press in 1972. In 1983, Underwood-Miller issued a selection of Straub's poetry, *Lesson Park and Belsize Square*. Straub wrote two mainstream literary novels: *Marriages*, published in 1973, and *Wild Animals*, begun in the early 1970s, but not published until 1984. (The latter novel lent its name to an omnibus of Straub's novels, but was reissued by itself as *Under Venus*.) These novels show the influence of his experience with poetry, but also contain some elements found later in his novels.

Straub first became widely known as a novelist of supernatural horror. His agent, Carol Smith, proposed that he "write a gothic," partly in order to "make some money for a change." "I said, 'What's a gothic?'—and I still don't know," Straub states. Yet he realized that he had been both enjoying and telling horror stories most of his life. The first result of this suggestion was *Julia*, published in 1975 (dates given throughout this chapter are for paperback publication). Straub continued this direction with *If You Could See Me Now* (1977); hit his stride with *Ghost Story* (1979) and *Shadowland* (1980), and concluded this approach with *Floating Dragon* (1982); *The General's Wife*, a piece originally intended for that novel but published on its own (1982); and *The Talisman* (1984), co-written with Straub's friend and mutual influence, Stephen King.

After that, Straub felt he needed "to take some time off," and that he had already done "everything [he] needed to do with the materials of horror." The result was the Blue Rose series: *Koko* (1988), *Mystery* (1990), and *The Throat* (1993), and the novellas *The Blue Rose* (1985) and *The Juniper Tree* (1988). Taken together, these "form, in effect, one massive story" written in and about the genres of mystery and detective fiction. His works from *Julia* through *The Talisman* were based in the Gothic tradition and the modern supernatural horror genre. In a pattern of shifting references characteristic of Straub's writing, the phrase "Blue Rose" refers not only to a set of unsolved murders, but also to a piece of jazz music, a nonsense utterance to induce an hypnotic trance, and the wallpaper an abused child would concentrate on while being molested.

In 1990, Straub's only collection of shorter fiction, *Houses Without Doors*, was published. This contains, and is dominated by, the Blue Rose novellas. The collection shows a synthesis of all of Straub's approaches to fiction from the realistic New York setting and characters in "The Buffalo Hunter" to the indeterminacy—certainly surreal and probably supernatural—of pieces including that novella, the novella *Mrs. God* (also available in a longer form published separately by Donald Grant) and the early work, *Something About a Death, Something About a Fire*.

The style and tone of Straub's fiction, while consistently recognizable, also shows much variation; to some extent, the style of each book is based on the models within its chosen genre. Thus, *Marriages* and *Under Venus* are literary and even poetic in diction and emphasis, as well as in subject matter; Straub describes *Marriages* as "sort of like that Renata Adler book, *Speedboat,* except that it was a little more coherent."

Within the Gothic genre of supernatural horror, Straub plays with a number of styles from such specific influences as Henry James, whose lessons about the nature of horror dominate *Julia* and help shape *Ghost Story;* Nathaniel Hawthorne, who influences *Ghost Story* and is referred to in *If You Could See Me Now;* British short-story writer Robert Aickman, along with Carlos Fuentes' *Aura* an influence on *The General's Wife* and later basic to *Mrs. God;* and Stephen King, whose influence is most evident in the structuring of *Ghost Story* and in the clear style and operatically loud events of *Floating Dragon.*

Elsewhere, the style of Straub's work is more shaped by examination of a kind of writing than it is influenced by a specific author, as in his use of the Anglo-American nineteenth-century supernatural tradition in *Ghost Story;* detective and mystery fiction in the Blue Rose books; and European fairy tales in *Shadowland* (which features the Brothers Grimm as minor characters) and in the Blue Rose works such as *The Juniper Tree* and *The Throat.* A contrast of *Shadowland* and *The Throat* shows how Straub can use similar source materials to achieve different thematic and literary effects.

In some ways, this variety of genre templates can obscure the ways in which Straub has mixed genres throughout his career. All of his fiction uses realistic and literary approaches. Moreover, all of his fiction from *Julia* on includes horror and Gothic conventions to some extent, and all of it includes realistic mysteries concerning murder, paternity, and theft. Both the proportion of these elements and the genre-expectations Straub plays upon, however, do change.

Straub's works also show quite a range of approaches to plot and structure—though this seems to be less a matter of turning to different, but equally useful, alternatives and more a matter of Straub's abilities developing throughout his career. *Julia* is neat and controlled, but mainly because its scope is restricted. The novel is a straightforward narrative (with the past revealed as events progress) of a drawing-room sized ensemble. From *If You Could See Me Now* through *Shadowland,* Straub widened the plans for his novels, but the effects on plot and structure were mixed—sometimes well orchestrated, as in the arrangement of exposition and plot threads in *Ghost Story,* and sometimes loose or arbitrary, as in the climaxes of *If You Could See Me Now* and *Shadowland* or the long interpolated narrative by Coleman Collins in the latter book. Straub's approach in these novels

is often associational and imagistic, perhaps influenced by his interest in jazz music.

Though it is often accused of being sloppy, because it is the most violent and colloquial of Straub's books, *Floating Dragon* is actually more carefully structured than its predecessors. In this respect, it may be a turning point for Straub. From *Julia* on, Straub has shown an interest in undermining a strictly linear sense of time in order to explore a Gothic sense of the eternal consequences of some actions. In *Floating Dragon,* this is conveyed through the novel's organization. Central episodes (often moments of revelation or recognition) are referred to both before and after they are presented; these references radiate throughout the text and create an impression of connections among otherwise unrelated actions. On the other hand, *The Talisman* needs a more elaborate and careful interweaving of events in order to connect and counterpoint our world and the Territories. This may be a result of King and Straub's streamlining the book, after the outline had been written, to make it a publishable length.

Certainly by the time he wrote the Blue Rose books, Straub had learned how to make plot and structure fundamental assets of his fiction—as one might expect of someone writing mystery and suspense fiction. Not only does Straub develop plot and maintain interest by the careful apportioning of facts and events, he also demonstrates an ongoing process of sifting truth and falsehood by revisiting and revising material from earlier in the books. *The Throat,* especially, is an impressive performance with many convincing false endings and well-planned surprises. As Tim Underhill says in that novel, "These books are about the way the known story is not the right or the real story." Thus, in the Blue Rose books as in *Floating Dragon,* Straub uses plot and structure to convey theme as well as to move the story.

Certain approaches do characterize all of Straub's fiction, despite differences in genre, style, and plot. One obvious, but very interesting, approach is his use of factual elements in his often-fantastic fiction—especially places and situations from his own life. This strategy is, of course, very common. Still, it is valuable to look at how the author manages the interplay of autobiographical influence and fictional inventions. Straub does so in three main ways: the use of factual background to give credibility to entirely or primarily fictional characters and situations; the concrete depiction of the author's personal hopes and fears, or issues to be worked out; and the use of various versions of places and events to provide a kind of referential layering that draws attention to the relationship between fact and fiction in a postmodern, metafictive way.

A quick review of Straub's life shows how much he has mined his experiences to provide convincing, yet often unusual, settings and events for his books. He spent summers with relatives in the Norwegian rural area near Arcadia, Wisconsin, which provides the setting—altered to the worse—of *If You Could See Me Now*. The prep school he attended in Milwaukee appears, again in more sinister form, as Carson School in *Shadowland*. In each case, the novel explores emotional and social issues related to the setting: the burden of small-town familiarity in *If You Could See Me Now*, the challenge of individuation in *Shadowland*, and the menace of smug and petty authority in both books.

After receiving a bachelor's degree in English from the University of Wisconsin and a master's degree in contemporary literature from Columbia University, Straub taught English for three years; this background shows in a number of places in Straub's works, especially in the Don Wanderly and Alma Mobley scenes in *Ghost Story*. In 1969, he began work on a Ph.D. at University College in Dublin; while working on an unsatisfactory dissertation on D. H. Lawrence, like Miles Teagarden in *If You Could See Me Now*, Straub began writing professionally. His experiences in academics can also be found in works such as *Mrs. God*. Straub's feelings about the academic life seem ambivalent—perhaps one reason why those settings lend themselves well to his brand of Gothic fiction.

Straub moved from Dublin to England before writing *Julia*, which reflects the new location. Similarly, *Floating Dragon* was written while Straub lived in Connecticut and takes place in a similar Connecticut town. Straub's understanding of place allows him to show the darkness behind even the most respectable town. As a character in *Floating Dragon* says, "I say this isn't *sub*urbia, and it isn't *ex*urbia. It's *dist*urbia." In *The Buffalo Hunter* and the Blue Rose books, Straub shows his knowledge of and affection for the locations and cultures of New York's Manhattan.

Straub's use of this source material, however, reaches a new level of complexity and sophistication in the Blue Rose books. *Mystery* takes place on the Caribbean island of Mill Walk, and *The Throat* takes place in the town of Millhaven, Illinois; both may ultimately be based on Milwaukee, Wisconsin, where Straub was born in 1943, and which appears as a minor setting in *Koko*. Similarly, Tom Pasmore's near-death experience in *Mystery* is revealed by Tim Underhill in *The Throat* to be his; and in real life, Straub also was badly injured in a childhood accident: "a really transforming experience." The Blue Rose books also include more topical references and events than Straub's earlier books—from the Vietnam War Memorial in *Koko* to Milwaukee serial killer and cannibal Jeffrey Dahmer, clearly behind Walter Dragonette in *The Throat*.

Yet if we are tempted to take Straub's fiction as autobiographical, or as a breakable code, we are warned against do-

ing so by the other obvious source of material equally evident in all his work: other fiction. Even in *The Throat*, Straub mentions Tom Flanagan (the protagonist of *Shadowland*, or the real-life jazz musician, or perhaps both)—and, more to the point, Arkham College, a nod to H. P. Lovecraft's fictional Massachusetts town. Like the character in *The Buffalo Hunter*, Straub's readers may ultimately give up on sorting out fact and fiction—though presumably without the fatal emergence of fiction into real life that is portrayed in that novella. Still, fiction in the universe of Straub's works is always both desirable and dangerous. Fiction always lies, Straub seems to say, especially in the Blue Rose books; and it always tells the truth.

Beginning with *Ghost Story*, Straub combines straightforward action and suspense with a strong awareness of and metafictive play with his literary roots. Preparing to write *Ghost Story*, Straub took six months to read and reread the classics, including works by Edgar Allan Poe, Ambrose Bierce, Edith Wharton's ghost stories, J. Sheridan Le Fanu, nineteenth-century novelist Mrs. Gaskell, Arthur Machen, H. P. Lovecraft and his circle, and a number of continental supernatural books. The most important references in *Ghost Story* are to James and Hawthorne, whose last names are shared by the two main characters in the novel; Straub even includes a retelling of *The Turn of the Screw* by one of the characters.

Even more interesting are the nonsupernatural works which influenced Straub's supernatural novels: John Fowles's *The Magus* is the text-behind-the-text in *Shadowland;* and Mark Twain's works are central to *The Talisman*, as prefigured by Straub's use of "I Light Out for the Territories" as the title of the second half of *If You Could See Me Now*. The latter novel combines references to a surprising range of authors from D. H. Lawrence to H. Rider Haggard.

Straub, who describes himself as "probably the only guy who sees Henry James and [Raymond] Chandler on an equal plane," turned to the genre of the latter in the Blue Rose books; he has mentioned the influence of Daphne Du Maurier on *Mystery*, and Ross McDonald on *The Throat*. In addition, *The Throat* mentions the television show *Twin Peaks* and Thomas Harris's novel *Red Dragon*. These contemporary references place the characters believably in our world, but also offer homage to those works that explore themes seen in the Blue Rose books such as exposing the town's corruption in *Twin Peaks*, the psychology of the serial killer explored in Harris's novel, and the complex questions of identity and duplicity/doubles in both.

In *Mystery*, Straub examines the two main schools of mystery writing—the more action-oriented American school and the more intellectual detective work of Sherlock Holmes and his kin. The latter is represented by Lamont von Heilitz, a self-described "amateur of crime" who approaches crimes as puzzles to solve; the former is carried by a number of lesser characters including police chief Tim Truehart and detective David Natchez. Apprentice detective Tom Pasmore, who comes of age in *Mystery,* realizes "that there were two ways of being a detective, and that men like David Natchez would always find people like von Heilitz too whimsical, intuitive, and theatrical to be taken seriously." In *The Throat,* Tom Pasmore has taken over von Heilitz's role; he contrasts himself to the "brilliant street detective" Paul Fontaine, whose abilities seem better fitted to our current semi-random serial killings.

Other references and motifs in the Blue Rose books are drawn from the Grimm's fairy tale, *The Juniper Tree,* and from classical mythology (particularly the figure of the minotaur hidden in a labyrinth). Straub also refers to the Pandora myth in many of his works—including *If You Could See Me Now, Ghost Story,* and *Shadowland.* Especially in *Koko, The Juniper Tree,* and *The Throat,* these form two basic metaphors for repression or estrangement and recovery or reintegration: literally, dismembering and remembering along with burial and discovery.

As in *Shadowland,* which also refers to fairy tales and some classical myths, the use of these materials in the Blue Rose books fits with their exploration of basic questions of identity and change. Straub has mentioned that Bruno Bettelheim's study, *The Uses of Enchantment,* led him to see that "fairy tales were often parables of the construction of the personality," so it is fitting that Tom Flanagan, Tom Pasmore, and Tim Underhill would see themselves through these stories, and that Straub would use the stories and myths as patterns for their development. He achieves a similar effect in *The Talisman* through the use of heroic or quest literature; "like the story of Jesus, the story of King Arthur, *Sir Gawain and the Green Knight.*"

Perhaps Straub's least successful metafictional pattern is seen in the use of Biblical material in *Floating Dragon.* The illness and madness that beset the town are explicitly compared to Old Testament punishments; and the age-old menace, Gideon Winter, is repeatedly referred to as an apocalyptic, or satanic, "old dragon." There is more to this Biblical imagery than first meets the eye, and it does give the book a compelling feeling of ancient sin; but it never seems as well done, or as thematically important to the work, as Straub's use of literary materials in his other fiction. Perhaps the true text-behind-the-text in *Floating Dragon* is Stephen King's fiction. However, if this is true, Straub does not make it explicit or use it as a source of metafictive play, as he does with influences in the other books.

These metafictive concerns in Straub's books combine well with another characteristic of all his fiction: the frequent use of imagery, which functions as a unifying leitmotif and advances tone and theme. The best example of this is probably the bird imagery throughout *Shadowland;* one could also point to the spreading irradicable stain the heroine encounters in *Julia,* the bat and dragon imagery in *Floating Dragon,* and even the fixation on baby bottles by the protagonist in *The Buffalo Hunter.* As the final example shows, such imagery permeates not only the authorial language of the works, but also the events as facts within the story. In the Blue Rose works, dismemberment, underground journeys, and eating form metaphors in which the characters both think and are described; they are also echoed in actions and locations that occur in the novel.

One motif stands out as omnipresent in Straub's works: the woods, which serves as a place of wild possibility and danger. In *If You Could See Me Now,* Miles Teagarden feels a panic in the woods, "an essentially literary experience, brewed up out of Jack London and Hawthorne and Cooper and Disney cartoons and Shakespeare and the brothers Grimm." This depiction recurs in various forms such as imagery and location in *Ghost Story, Shadowland, Floating Dragon,* and *The Talisman;* even *Under Venus* concerns the selling of forest land. The major templates are the Puritan experience of the seemingly endless forest at their backs in *Floating Dragon* and the story of Hansel and Gretel in *Shadowland.* In the Blue Rose books, the underworld has in many ways replaced the forest, but some of the events in *Mystery* convey these same feelings about the woods and *The Juniper Tree* explicitly refers to Hansel and Gretel.

Straub's main characters tend to be urbane and somewhat self-aware, but often very ordinary in temperament, even when they are thrust into extraordinary circumstances or possess extraordinary abilities. The protagonists in his earlier supernatural novels tend to be weaker and more neurotic, but still a kind of everyman or everywoman; beginning with *Ghost Story,* the protagonists start out better balanced and mature or grow stronger through the events of the book. Straub has always been drawn to characters who are themselves artists and thinkers, including the musician-protagonist of *Under Venus,* von Heilitz and Tom Pasmore in the Blue Rose books, semi-effectual semi-scholars Miles Teagarden in *If You Could See Me Now* and Martin Standish in *Mrs. God,* and the whole range of writers: Don Wanderley in *Ghost Story,* Graham Williams in *Floating Dragon,* the narrator of *The Juniper Tree,* and Straub's "co-author" and major figure in the Blue Rose books, Tim Underhill.

In some ways, these characters show Straub writing about what he knows—we cannot assume they are self-portraits, but they certainly reflect the life that Straub has led, rich in thought rather than adventure. His characters may also be shaped by Straub's strengths as a writer since his style and detailed examination of inner life require a thoughtful, and even self-absorbed, protagonist. Finally, the contemporary novel of supernatural horror—unlike some of its exotic Gothic ancestors—usually requires the credibility that comes from common characters the reader can identify with.

Straub's characters frequently are involved in a search for an absent father or the escape from an evil father. In both *Shadowland* and *The Talisman,* the young man who will mature into adulthood during the novel has lost his father to death just before the story begins. In *Shadowland,* what is offered as a replacement is the magician Coleman Collins—a controlling manipulator Tom rejects. In *The Talisman,* bad father-figures abound—from Jack's uncle, Morgan Sloat, to the despot-like owners of the Oatley tavern and the Sunlight Home for Boys. These characters are often over-drawn and lack the credibility Coleman Collins sometimes has. Moreover, a criticism of contemporary realistic fiction seems implied when the villains are named Smokey Updike and Sunlight Gardener, but little or nothing is accomplished with this, compared to the rich tapestry of references in *Shadowland* or *Ghost Story.*

Both Tom in *Shadowland* and Jack in *The Talisman* benefit from the assistance of protectors and advisors (someone between friend and father). Both benevolent men are African-American, and each has a dual nature: Bud Copeland/Speckle John for Tom, and Speedy Parker/Parkus for Jack. In both books, those who offer to be replacement fathers are evil, while true mentors think of themselves more as helpers.

The characters' inability to tell what is real and what is not is itself frightening, yet often fascinating; moreover, in dissolving usual boundaries between reality and illusion, Straub makes it easier for his readers to believe the supernatural eventsof the novel.
—Bernadette Bosk

The matter of "fathers and sons" is central to *Floating Dragon,* especially seen in Richard Albee's absent father (ironically reflected by the situation-comedy Richard acted in as a child, *Daddy's Here*) and Tad's abusive father. Finally, the strains and joys of the father-son relationship are shown by the benevolent trigenerational relationship of Tad, Richard, and Graham Williams at the end of the novel. That configuration is reminiscent of the relationships among Peter Barnes, Don Wanderly, and the remaining members of the Chowder Society in *Ghost Story.* Don comes to the town of Milburn, New York, to investigate his uncle's death. As he takes his uncle's place in the storytelling group of old men

called the Chowder Society, the other members become his true family.

In the Blue Rose books, Straub explores issues concerning abusive fathers (and abusive father-like authority figures); weak or absent fathers like Mr. Pasmore in *Mystery;* and the question of true paternal heritage, which any wise child seeks to know—a question which also forms the central mystery of *Julia.* Perhaps the most touching real father in Straub's fiction is April Ransom's in *The Throat.* Beset by senility (which Straub depicts all too convincingly), he rallies himself to mourn his dead daughter and even helps provide information that identifies her murderer.

From *Julia* through *Floating Dragon,* Straub's novels tend to be structured around a constellation of four major characters—often united by guilt over a past incident, by the need to fight a supernatural menace, or both. *Shadowland* presents the tetrad of Del, Tom, Rose, and Cole; but that novel and *The Talisman* are more noteworthy for the doubling or pairings. In each book, the basic unit is the dyad—Tom and Del, Jack and Wolf replaced by Jack and Richard—and primary and secondary characters have a dual nature that is both mundane and mythic: Rose Armstrong, girl and mermaid; the butler Bud Copeland, who may or may not be Speckle John; and all the "twinners" in *The Talisman,* who exist both in this world and in the Territories.

Paired characters are also important in the Blue Rose stories, especially in the relationship between von Heilitz and Tom Pasmore in *Mystery* and the teamwork of Pasmore with Tim Underhill in *The Throat.* In *The Juniper Tree,* the protagonist and the man in the theater form a poisonous, but deeply bonded, dyad. Each is also split into two or more selves as they hide the secret of sexual abuse not only from the outside world, but also, by repression and dissociation, from their own minds.

Beginning with *Ghost Story,* Straub explores questions of identity by presenting both different characters who somehow seem connected to one another or share some fundamental characteristic, and single characters who seem to split into many apparitions or selves (comparable to what Todorov calls "the multiplication of personality"). Often Straub establishes such connections through the depiction of one figure who appears under many different names or different characters with the same initials: the sinister blonde child in *Julia;* the many alluring and frightening females with the initials A. M. in *Ghost Story;* and perhaps even Graham Williams, dragonslayer, and Gideon Winter, his adversary, in *Floating Dragon.*

In *If You Could See Me Now,* Miles Teagarden returns to his hometown for a rendezvous with his dead sweetheart, Alison Greening, and meets his cousin's daughter, Alison

Updahl, who resembles her physically as well as in name; toward the end of the novel, Miles signs his own name as "Miles Greening." The Blue Rose stories bloom with a multifoliate multiplicity of similar, linked, opposed, and transforming characters as intricate as the more supernaturally complex identities in *Ghost Story, Shadowland,* and *Floating Dragon:* murder suspects William Damrosch and Walter Dragonette in *The Throat;* the permutations on F. B. and L. V. in that same book; and the vast range of criminals, detectives, and writers who populate the three novels and two novellas.

Just as Straub's strength as a writer shows in his handling of shifting, overlapping, and connected identities among his characters, all of his books demonstrate an impressive ability to depict a wide variety of states of consciousness. Even the early mimetic novels explore unusual emotional and mental states. In *Julia* and *If You Could See Me Now,* Straub uses the freedom that the supernatural provides to experiment even further; by *Ghost Story,* this has become a permanent and vital part of his approach. The supernatural novels examine personal consciousness and our awareness of reality as altered by movies, fiction-reading, trances, hallucinations, dreams, magic, and pathological symptoms such as depersonalization and mood disorders. The Blue Rose stories also use some of these approaches, and also add abuse-related dissociation, war as an initiation and an altered state (hinted at in *Shadowland,* but not fully explored), the near-death experience, and use of recreational drugs.

The blending of objective and subjective states in Straub's novels enhances the fiction in a number of ways. The characters' inability to tell what is real and what is not is itself frightening, yet often fascinating; moreover, in dissolving usual boundaries between reality and illusion, Straub makes it easier for his readers to believe the supernatural events of the novel. In depicting extreme or borderline states, Straub can use techniques from the introspective, realistic literary novel while still providing a Gothic excitement. Finally, such scenes may cause the reader to reevaluate some questions of epistemology and even phenomenology; this deeper speculation especially fits *Ghost Story*'s concern with the nature of the self, and the gnostic or Hermetic themes in *Shadowland.*

Straub's interests in identity and consciousness may be revealed in his use of mirrors, which both reveal and alter the self, especially to the perceiving self. This thematic significance seems implicit in the mirrors of *Floating Dragon* and *The Juniper Tree,* and is made explicit in the narcissist imagery in *Ghost Story.* Stephen King, in his perceptive impressionistic critique of *Ghost Story,* writes that this is not only the nature of mirrors, but also the nature of ghosts: "What is the ghost, after all, that it

should frighten us so, but our own face? When we observe it we become like Narcissus." Straub's ghosts—like those in *The Turn of the Screw*—are based in this awareness, which is a large source of their power. In the Blue Rose books, the characters face interior ghosts which are often no easier to exorcise, just as haunting, and also found in the mirror. Ransom states in *The Throat,* "the world is full of ghosts, and some of them are still people."

In all his fiction from *Julia* on, Straub uses these techniques and others to examine two basic ideas about, or thematic approaches to, the world around us. One is that time is not truly linear and that isolation of an event in the past or future is no barrier, for good or ill, from its effects. The other is the gnostic or Hermetic idea that the world we know could be a false show and the true world lies waiting to be discovered.

Both of these are often presented in spatial metaphors. In *If You Could See Me Now,* Miles states, "Effects can leak backward and forward in time, staining otherwise innocent events." As we have seen, this is enacted in the structure of *Floating Dragon*—although the events can have good reverberations as well as bad—and is represented in that novel by Tabby, who has visions of the past, and Patsy, who is only precognitive. Finally, "backwards and forwards" is a refrain of the eponymous character in *Koko* that reflects his helpless view of time. Another spatial metaphor for this effect appears in *Koko* in the events in the cave at Ia Thuc: "the center was the center, which was the secret, and the power of what Harry Beevers had felt and done radiated out through the rest of his life." This metaphor also permeates both the events and the structure of that novel.

Straub also describes the hidden reality as being behind or beneath the reality we know. Miles explains in *If You Could See Me Now* that the world we know is "the rind," peeled off to reveal dark truths within—true reality "broke through the apparently real like a fist." Coleman Collins realizes that the magic of Shadowland "had been there all along, right under the surface of things, dogging me"; and Koko thinks, "There is no jungle but the jungle, and it grows beneath the sidewalks, behind the windows, on the other sides of doors." In *The Throat,* awareness comes from dangerous depths behind and—like the minotaur that represents everything the protagonist represses—beneath the world we know.

Finally, Straub's fiction is often seen in terms of connections or patterns—a spatial metaphor that completely abandons sequence. This image is most prevalent in *Julia* and *Floating Dragon,* but is also used in *Ghost Story.* In *If You Could See Me Now,* Miles thinks, "I saw the patterns tying us together," and notes another character's mention of "lines of force."

Often in Straub's books, the secret world revealed to the characters is horrible—like A. M. in *Ghost Story* when she reveals her true, inhuman form. In *Mystery,* Tom Pasmore learns from his nurse that "the world is half night"; and in *The Throat,* Tim Underhill thinks, "The world is half in night, and the other half is night, too." Yet, as Tom Flanagan, Tom Pasmore, and Tim Underhill all discover, the secret world can also be a source of wonder and glory. As gnostic quotation reads in both *Shadowland* and *The Throat,* "If you bring forth what is within you, what you bring forth will save you; if you do not bring forth what is within you, what you do not bring forth will destroy you." This secret, hidden in ourselves and in the world, can heal as well as horrify.

In Straub's fiction, this secret is often connected to the nature of women and to sex as a gateway to mysteries that are transcendent and exciting, but also frightening and sometimes dangerous. The strongest connection between *Under Venus* and Straub's other work is this aspect of the protagonist's mistress, Anita Kellerman. Most of Straub's female characters share some of this nature—powerful, inscrutable, alluring, and intimidating: Alison Greening of *If You Could See Me Now, Shadowland*'s Rose Armstrong, Patsy at the climax of *Floating Dragon,* and even Maggie Lah in *Koko* and *The Throat.* The most outstanding example is the female shapeshifter in *Ghost Story*—purely destructive, yet alluring with "a morally fatal glamour"; but Don Wanderley, also says, "all women are mysteries to me."

Straub's books from *Julia* on also explore the power of the past, whether personal, as in *Julia,* or historical, as in *Floating Dragon.* Often, the personal and social are combined, as in *If You Could See Me Now, Ghost Story,* and the Blue Rose stories. Many works by Straub link personal decline or salvation, sometimes based on guilt from the past, to the decay or redemption of a town (*Ghost Story, Floating Dragon*), a small community (the school in *Shadowland*), or even a world (*The Talisman*). In *If You Could See Me Now* and the Blue Rose books, personal salvation lies—in part—in uncovering the town's innate corruption and in apportioning guilt and innocence correctly.

As Straub writes in *If You Could See Me Now* and *Koko,* "No story exists without its past, and the past of a story is what enables us to understand it." This powerful past is sometimes embodied, in a very Gothic way, in a house or place that haunts the novel and its characters: the house Julia feels compelled to buy, the one Miles Teagarden moves into and refurnishes as it had been when Alison Greening was alive, the houses of Eva Galli in *Ghost Story* or Bates Krell

in *Floating Dragon,* the schools in *Shadowland* or *The Talisman,* the theaters from *Ghost Story* and *The Throat,* the cave at Ia Thuc, or the room under the Green Woman Taproom.

After the many developments in Straub's career, even a critic—who is presumptuous by profession—should know better than to anticipate his next move. Some clues may lie in interviews: despite the mixed success of movies based on *Julia* and *Ghost Story,* films may be made of *Floating Dragon* (a script by William Nolan exists) and *The Talisman* (although Steven Spielberg is no longer likely to direct). Straub is currently writing, and he may do a project "loosely based on *Rogue Male,* the Geoffrey Household novel." However, his planned novels have mutated while in progress before, and any solid predictions would be foolhardy.

General observations seem both safer and more valuable. In some ways, *The Throat* combines realistic detective fiction with more supernatural elements, which might show an approaching synthesis in Straub's future work. We can probably expect consistent themes and approaches—including uses of metafictive and autobiographical material—explored in books with new developments in tone, structure, and perhaps even genre. Or perhaps not. In any event, it will be enjoyable to read, and well worth analyzing and appreciating.

FURTHER READING

Criticism

Brockway, James. A review of *Marriages* in *Books and Bookmen* 18, No. 8 (May 1973): 100.
    Negative review in which the critic faults Straub's style, stating that certain passages are "painstakingly boring."

Lyons, Gene. "Horror Shock." *New York Times Book Review* (8 April 1979): 14.
    Mixed review of *Ghost Story* in which the critic concludes that, even though Straub's storytelling is at times "glacial," the novel is "a quite sophisticated literary entertainment."

Sutcliffe, Thomas. "Getting the Wind Up." *Times Literary Supplement,* No. 4072 (17 April 1981): 430.
    Mixed review of *Shadowland* in which the critic briefly discusses Straub's use of spectral effects, gothic conveniences, and conventions of supernatural tales.

Additional coverage of Straub's life and career is contained in the following sources published by Gale: *Bestsellers: 1989*, Vol. 1; *Contemporary Authors,* Vols. 85-88; *Contemporary Authors New Revisions Series,* Vol. 28; *DISCovering Authors Modules: Popular Fiction and Genre Authors; Dictionary of Literary Biography Yearbook,* 1984; and *Major Twentieth Century Writers.*

Audrey Thomas

1935-

(Born Audrey Grace Callahan) American-born Canadian short story writer, novelist, essayist, and radio dramatist.

The following entry presents an overview of Thomas's career through 1995. For further information on her life and works, see *CLC,* Volumes 7, 13, and 37.

INTRODUCTION

One of Canada's most respected fiction writers, Thomas is primarily concerned with examining feminist issues in her works, which frequently depict deeply intimate moments in human relationships. Admittedly fascinated with language, Thomas often uses wordplay, etymology, and selections from dictionaries and reference sources to delineate modern women's search for selfhood and independence.

Biographical Information

Thomas was born in Binghamton, New York, in 1935. At fifteen she left her unhappy childhood home to attend boarding school in New Hampshire, which led eventually to a scholarship at a Massachusetts finishing school. In 1953 Thomas entered Smith College, graduating with a degree in English in 1957. During her junior year at Smith, Thomas attended St. Andrew's University in Scotland with her best friend, where she thrived intellectually. While overseas, she traveled to Spain, Italy, Belgium, Switzerland, and Scandinavia. After graduating, she returned to Britain to take a teaching position in the slums of Birmingham, England, at Bishop Rider's Church of England Infant and Junior School. In 1958 she married Ian Thomas, a sculptor and teacher at the Birmingham College of Art. The couple moved to Vancouver, British Columbia, in 1959, where Ian had accepted a teaching position. Thomas taught school for a year, then enrolled in the Master's program at the University of British Columbia, which she completed in 1963. She went immediately into the doctoral program, concentrating in Anglo-Saxon poetry. At this time, Thomas was also beginning to write fiction. She shared some of her work with professors, but found the academic atmosphere patronizing toward young women writers, who, she found, were expected to write only children's books if they wrote fiction at all. When her thesis on *Beowulf* was rejected, Thomas left academia to concentrate on writing fiction. Her first story, "If One Green Bottle . . . ," appeared in the *Atlantic Monthly* in 1965 while Thomas was in Ghana, Africa, where her husband held a teaching position at the University of Science and Technology. Thomas's experiences in Africa later

strongly informed much of her writing; *Mrs. Blood* (1970), *Songs My Mother Taught Me* (1973), *Blown Figures* (1974), and *Coming Down from Wa* (1995), as well as many short stories, all contain Thomas's African themes. In 1969 Thomas began writing full-time. She and her husband moved to Galiano Island, British Columbia; they separated in 1972 and later divorced, another personal experience that Thomas explores in her work. In 1971 Thomas returned to Africa alone for a three-month tour of that continent. Partly because of this trip, the theme of women traveling alone recurs in her fiction. To support herself and her three daughters, Thomas returned to teaching, taking posts in creative writing departments at several western Canadian universities. She has been involved with many Canadian literary organizations and has won numerous awards for her writing.

Major Works

While not widely considered an experimental writer, Thomas does use distinctively post-modernist methods, such as stream-of-consciousness narrative and collage, in much of her work. Drawing from other sources, including reference works, historical records, advertisements, and newspaper clippings, and creating visual images with words on the page, she often weaves together a variety of disparate and nonlinear elements to tell her stories. Thomas used this technique most explicitly in her novel *Graven Images* (1993), which recounts the relationship of two middle-aged women seeking information about their ancestors. Characters traveling abroad or searching within themselves for meaning and selfhood is another common thread running through Thomas's works. The stories in *Goodbye Harold, Good Luck* (1986) are set in Canada, Greece, Scotland, and Africa. While Thomas's characters are usually women attempting to carve their own paths in a male-dominated world—as in the stories in *Real Mothers* (1981) and *The Wild Blue Yonder* (1990), where in many cases the women in question are both emotionally and physically threatened by the men in their lives—Thomas used a male protagonist in *Coming Down from Wa* (1995). In this novel Thomas returned to the African setting she had used earlier in *Mrs. Blood, Songs My Mother Taught Me, Blown Figures,* and other works. In *Coming Down from Wa,* a young art history student travels to Africa to do research on both his thesis project and the mystery of his parents' self-imposed isolation in western Canada after their return from a volunteer effort in a small African village called Wa in the 1960s. Autobiographical elements, such as her experience in Africa, are also a major characteristic of Thomas's writing. *Mrs. Blood* and "If One Green Bottle . . ." (published first in the *Atlantic Monthly* and later in the collection *Ten Green Bottles* [1967]) both feature women coping with miscarriages, which Thomas herself underwent. *Real Mothers,* published after Thomas's divorce, includes several stories centered on the effects of divorce on women and children. In *Munchmeyer and Prospero on the Island* (1971), *Latakia* (1979), and *Intertidal Life* (1984), Thomas explores the tension writers often feel between their work and their personal lives, particularly women writers, who—like Thomas and many of her female characters—must balance motherhood with their careers and with their psychosexual needs.

Critical Reception

Critics almost unanimously consider Thomas a complex, demanding writer whose work continually moves in new directions. But because of her experimentation with textual forms and her aversion to simple, happy endings, some find her overly didactic and lacking in humor. Nonetheless, Thomas's exploration of the conflicts of modern sexual relationships, the constant clash of self and other experienced by twentieth-century women, and the need for both understanding of the past and independence in the present have received high praise from critics, particularly Thomas's acute ability to capture moments of intimacy and epiphany. Feminist critics in the 1980s and 1990s have commended Thomas's experimentation with language as an attempt to break free of traditional male-centered discourse and to deconstruct stereotypically romantic images of women and relationships, replacing them with more realistic notions of womanhood that allow for less ideal feelings such as confusion, pain, and anger. Margaret Atwood has written of Thomas: "[With] each of her books, the reader feels that the next will not only be better but different in some unimaginable way."

PRINCIPAL WORKS

Ten Green Bottles (short stories) 1967
Mrs. Blood (novel) 1970
Munchmeyer and Prospero on the Island (novellas) 1971
Songs My Mother Taught Me (novel) 1973
Blown Figures (novel) 1974
Ladies & Escorts (short stories) 1977
Latakia (novel) 1979
Real Mothers (short stories) 1981
Two in the Bush, and Other Stories (short stories) 1981
Intertidal Life (novel) 1984
Goodbye Harold, Good Luck (short stories) 1986
The Wild Blue Yonder (short stories) 1990
Graven Images (novel) 1993
Coming Down from Wa (novel) 1995

CRITICISM

Donald Stephens (essay date Autumn 1968)

SOURCE: "Mini-Novel Excellence," in *Canadian Literature,* No. 38, Autumn, 1968, pp. 94-6.

[*Stephens is a Canadian educator, critic, and editor for the journal* Canadian Literature. *In the following review of* Ten Green Bottles, *he lauds Thomas as an exemplary practitioner of the short story.*]

The short story expresses a succinct and personal reaction to some specific aspect of life that has moved the writer at a particular moment; the short story exists as a separate point on the canvas that is the writer's experience, yet it exists as a point that is linked, irrevocably, to other points within that experience. The fortunate thing about the short story is that it can be considered as a small, isolated unit, or it can be compared with other stories. The short story writer needs only to consider the form and development of a particular moment, and is consequently freed from the responsibility of expressing that moment in relation to other moments; this a reader may do if he so wishes. Rarely, if ever, does a short story writer express the freedom that is essential to the form. Rarely does a collection of short stories express this freedom.

But Audrey Callahan Thomas has caught the essence of the freedom of the form in her first collection of short stories [*Ten Green Bottles*], and caught it with something that is peculiarly her own. The variety is impressive. There is a range of subject matter—from studies of social bores and their effect on people around them, to racial consciousness in a Negro Peace Corpsman's emotional changes, to thoughts on childbirth—that lifts this book above so many collections of short stories; the range in situation is reflected, too, in the geographical range presented by Mrs. Thomas. Her heightened awareness of some special moment that makes a short story, gives to Mrs. Thomas the predominant characteristic that in a good writer separates the short story from any other literary genre. The fluid moments which are examined in this book change and flow easily. The reader perceives the awareness behind the story, the fluidity which surrounds the particular moment. Mrs. Thomas leads on into a vast reservoir which is her interpretation of life. It is a clear, no-nonsense view; it makes sense. Her stories, alone, or in the collection, reach pinnacles that I would suggest few writers of the contemporary short story—in Canada, and elsewhere—have reached.

It is not the plots that are interesting alone, not the style, not the rhythms, but a combination of these things that make Mrs. Thomas an artist in the short story. It is, after all, her whole technique, or her technique of wholeness. It is the unique approach that she has to what happens, to the importance of the moment she is examining, to the function of language within her expression. She works in easy circles, moments of time that circulate about her past, future, and present, into a particular mosaic that lacks sequential structure. At times it is what is happening now that asserts the story; sometimes it is something that has happened, or something that will happen. But finally, it is the reaction within the now that validates the story. On one hand there is isolation within experience, and then Mrs. Thomas leads her story away from sequential occurrences and lets incident and time weave her story for her. For her characters, real life stops temporarily, and in its stopping is its essence. Character and plot define the moments—or the latter defines the former—and so it flows on.

There is no doubt that Mrs. Thomas's book is more than just a "tour de force" in technique. Everywhere in the collection are signs of a writer with a keen observation, or someone who has obviously reacted to life with an almost limitless sensibility. The language is beautiful and controlled; her choice of words is admirable without being pretentious. She is a born short story writer in an age where lucidity seems to be often lost in short stories. I recommend her book

highly. Reading it is an experience not to be missed. It is, as Kjeld Deichman used to say about his feeling on opening his kiln after a firing of many pieces of pottery, "like Christmas morning; everything becomes a surprise."

Herbert Rosengarten (essay date Winter 1973)

SOURCE: "Writer and Subject," in *Canadian Literature,* No. 55, Winter, 1973, pp. 111-13.

[*A Canadian educator and critic who has published editions of works by Charlotte and Anne Brontë, Rosengarten served as an editor for the journal* Canadian Literature *from 1977 to 1986. In the following excerpt, he offers a favorable assessment of the novellas* Munchmeyer *and* Prospero on the Island.]

[In *Munchmeyer*] Mrs. Thomas uses such devices as the diary "confession", dream sequences, and waking fantasies to convey the spiritual confusion of one Will Munchmeyer—graduate student, *père de famille,* and frustrated novelist. Munchmeyer's sense of failure, and his revulsion from an empty marriage, drive him away from his family, in the first instance to a diary, where he confides his loathing for his wife. He sees himself as a modern Gulliver, trapped in the land of the giants, and confronted by the sweaty pores of a merciless Glumdalclitch; but an epigraph from the *Inferno* suggests that Mrs. Thomas wants us rather to see Munchmeyer as a latter-day wanderer traversing the circles of Hell, and moving up towards less-than-divine versions of Eden and Beatrice. At the end of the first section, having parted from his family, Munchmeyer is alone and depressed, and his state is mirrored in the faulty gasoline advertisement which flashes "Super Hell" at him out of the darkness. The second section presents a dream episode in which Munchmeyer is captured and imprisoned in a department store, where a mysterious young man tortures him with his own fears and inadequacies, until he manages to take refuge in the Mothers' Room.

The final section, entitled "Resurrection: Mr. and Mrs. Lodestone", describes Munchmeyer's return to confidence and self-respect, helped by the understanding and affection of Maria Lodestone, housewife and mother of a young baby. The book's mixture of psychological and religious symbolism is rather crudely summarised here; but in structure and in narrative detail, *Munchmeyer* has the trappings of Christian epic. However, the parallels are not forced or mechanical; Munchmeyer is allowed to find his Eden, but he is still *l'homme moyen sensuel,* troubled by unsatisfied longings; he finds his way to Maria, but she is someone else's wife, and he must solace himself with fantasies, or with the grosser charms of Mavis Marvell, queen of Crescent Beach.

Munchmeyer is a sympathetic character because his rehabilitation does not make him a saint: he continues to indulge
in adolescent daydreams, in which he is by turns the lonely
but successful writer, the pathetic down-and-out, the cruel
and inspired artist; and his entanglement with Mavis hints
at future tribulations—a return to the Super-Hell he thought
he had escaped.

His creator, the novelist "Miranda Archer", tells her own
story in *Prospero on the Island;* in a journal covering seven
or eight months, she relates the daily events of her life during the period of *Munchmeyer*'s composition. The strongly
circumstantial quality of her narration, with its many allusions to details of British Columbian life and topography,
suggests an autobiographical basis for the story, so that we
may be tempted to see it as a kind of "Writer's Diary" rather
than as another novel in its own right. It is certainly a highly
personal account; but the character of Miranda is too completely realised to be regarded simply as a voice for the
thoughts of the real author. In some ways she is a female
counterpart to Munchmeyer: much more sophisticated, sensitive, self-critical; but, like him, haunted by fears of inadequacy, potential failure, departing youth. Munchmeyer
retreats into fantasy, a world where he is, temporarily at least,
in control; Miranda has taken a more positive step by retreating to an island, but there she still finds herself wracked
by guilt and uncertainty. Her creative powers are renewed
and her self-confidence partly restored by her relationship
with an artist who has also retreated to the island to work,
and whom she dubs "Prospero". The artist comes to exercise a decisive influence over her imagination—as well as
arousing her sexual awareness—and she is drawn to him by
his calm, methodical ordering of things. Despite his importance to Miranda, Prospero remains a rather shadowy figure: Miranda is more concerned with the analysis of her own
responses to him than with the creation of a rounded portrait; but this externality endows him with an enigmatic quality, something which presumably Mrs. Thomas wanted to
convey.

The literary parallels with Shakespeare's Prospero are few,
and deliberately played down; the characters themselves discuss whether their island contains a Caliban, but reject the
idea. Nor is there much stress laid on the device of a novel
about a novel, or on the similarities between Munchmeyer
and his creator, though we are often reminded of him by
Miranda's self-questionings or her need of reassurance by
one less anxiety-ridden than herself. The relationships between a writer and his subject, between "reality" and artifice, are, one suspects, of [concern to Mrs. Thomas] . . . ;
but in *Munchmeyer* and *Prospero* their importance is hinted
at rather than made a dominant theme: they contribute another level of possible meaning to a broader whole. . . . Mrs.
Thomas has wisely chosen a middle course between tradition and innovation, and her writing is the richer for it.

Wayne Grady (essay date 1982)

SOURCE: "Journies to the Interior: The African Stories of
Audrey Thomas," in The Canadian Fiction Magazine, No.
44, 1982, pp. 98-110.

[*Grady is the editor of* The Penguin Book of Canadian Short
Stories *(1980),* The Penguin Book of Modern Canadian
Short Stories *(1982), and the journal* Books in Canada. *In
the following essay, he examines how Thomas's stories set
in Africa present women at various stages of self-discovery.*]

When Margaret Laurence arrived in North Africa in the
1950s the first real African she met was the man who was
to be her steward, Mohamed, so eager to help and yet so
difficult to understand. In *The Prophet's Camel Bell* (1963)
she recalls watching Mohamed's face silhouetted against the
African sky above the ship's launch: "It was a face I could
not read at all," she writes, "a well-shaped brown face that
seemed expressionless, as though whatever lay behind his
eyes would be kept carefully concealed. I wondered if this
was the face of Africa."

Of course Margaret Laurence's Africa was Somaliland, as
different from Audrey Thomas's Ghana as desert can be from
tropical rainforest; as brightness and heat are from darkness
and damp. Which makes the similarities between Thomas's
reactions to Africa and those of Margaret Laurence all the
more remarkable—and makes us suspect they arise more
from similarities in the eyes of the beholders than in the two
Africas. In Thomas's earliest African story, **"Xanadu,"** the
first African to appear is the man who was supposed to be
her steward, a drunken parasite who, when fired, quickly
metamorphoses into the upright Joseph—the model and pro-
totype of all Thomas's future stewards—who listens "impassive yet without hostility" while the narrator loudly mistakes
him for his predecessor. Audrey Thomas too is having
trouble with the faces of Africa. Throughout the rest of her
nine African stories she studies these faces as if they were
little maps, seeking in them directions or instructions for her
own predetermined route toward—what? Self-discovery? A
kind of *African Genesis?*

Africa has opened herself before to this kind of exploration.
George Woodcock has described *The Prophet's Camel Bell*
(a "travel book" in the same sense as Audrey Thomas's stories are "travel fiction") as "a narrative in which an inner
journey and an arrival at a personal destination run parallel." (Here we may as well admit straight off that Thomas's
characters rarely arrive at a destination, personal or otherwise: as with death and certain airline advertisements, it's
the voyage there that counts.) The epigram that Dave
Godfrey chose from the *Religio Medici*—"We carry within
us all the wonders we seek without us. There is all Africa
and her prodigies in us"—for his novel *The New Ancestors*

invokes this inner Africa as well. In an interview published in 1975 in the *Capilano Review* (the same issue that carried **"Two in the Bush"**) Thomas referred to Woodcock's ideas that Canadian writers liked Africa because that was where (she said) "you step back . . . in order to view your own country." She adds (in the nick of time), "I'm not sure it's as simple as that." You can step just as far back in France or Greece or Mexico (settings for other Thomas stories), but you do not look into the wizened visage of a French peasant and wonder if you are gazing upon the face of France. And if you do, it is not in order to gain a new perspective on Canada.

Africa has appealed to Western writers—not only to European writers—because it is so unEuropean. It is where European culture meets with the primitive, where assumptions are confronted by givens, where the intellectual side of the human penny, with its Latin or French or Portuguese or English inscription, is replaced by a mute black face when the penny flips over as if by magic on the table. In the interview mentioned above Thomas quotes with approval a passage from Carl Jung's *Memories, Dreams, and Reflections* (a title which, by the way, pretty well describes Thomas's own work): "In travelling to Africa to find a psychic observation post outside of the European, I unconsciously wanted to find that part of my personality which had become invisible under the influence and pressure of being European." Perhaps Thomas felt that parts of her personality had become invisible under the influence and pressure of being American: when one of the interviewers asks the surprising question, "Do you find Africa a less threatening environment than Canada though?" Thomas replies, "Oh yeah, sure." "Your Heart of Darkness is Canada?" pursues the interviewer. "I think so. Yes." And in one of Thomas's later African stories (**"Rapunzel"**) an artist named Caroline "dreams her way" up and down the dark continent, searching for "images. Forms. Old ways of looking at the world."

Thomas made two trips to Africa, one in the mid-1960s and another five years later in 1970. The two trips produced two novels—*Mrs. Blood* (1970), and *Blown Figures* (1974)—and nine short stories, scattered over a period of about thirteen years, and included, along with twenty-four other stories in Thomas' three collections. *Ten Green Bottles* (1967) included **"Xanadu," "Omo,"** and **"One is One and All Alone"**; *Ladies and Escorts* (1977), in which **"Joseph and His Brother," "Two in the Bush,"** and **"Rapunzel"** appeared; and *Real Mothers* (1981), which had **"Out in the Midday Sun"** and **"Timbuktu."** The ninth African story **"Degrees,"** was read in 1982 on CBC Anthology and included in Robert Weaver's collection, *Small Wonders*. **"Omo," "Joseph and His Brother,"** and **"Two in the Bush"** are also reprinted in *Two in the Bush and Other Stories* (1981). **"Two in the Bush,"** published for the first time in the interview issue of *Capilano Review*, bears the follow-

ing preface: "Ten years ago [i.e. 1965] I went to Ghana and spent two years there with my husband and two small children. Five years after my return to Canada I had a chance to go back for a few months and gather material for a proposed novel. I decided to visit some of the neighbouring countries as well, and this story is something that came out of my visit to the former French protectorate of the Ivory Coast." And she goes on to explain who Kwame Nkrumah is (without mentioning that he wrote a book called *Neo-Colonialism*), in order to show us that she was not totally unaware of the political Africa even though her stories—like all good travel stories—take place in a kind of unpoliticized mythical vacuum.

After the 1965 trip Thomas wrote the three African stories—**"Xanadu," "Omo,"** and **"One Is One and All Alone"**—that appeared in her first short-story collection, *Ten Green Bottles* (1967). She also wrote her first African novel, *Mrs. Blood* (1970), and the "proposed novel" that took her back to Africa was presumably *Blown Figures* (1974).

The opening sentence of **"Xanadu"** is mock biblical: "In the beginning it was hardly paradise"—and more echoes of *Genesis* reverberate throughout the story. Joseph the steward, like his Old Testament namesake, is a good, honest, patient man who is persecuted for his maddening virtuousness. He is the perfect servant—fixes mosquito nets, anticipates rainstorms and closes the windows in time, intermediates in the market square—and Mary's (she is nameless in the story, the anonymous wife of Jason, but since Jason and Joseph both appear in their appointed roles in *Mrs. Blood* I am taking the liberty of giving her Mrs. Blood's name, Mary) initial shock slips instantly into "a golden chalice of contentment." That golden chalice has an ominous heft for anyone mindful of the Joseph story in *Genesis*. When Mary notices that her family has come to rely more on Joseph's attentiveness than on her own housewifely negligence (Joseph's day off, Sunday, becomes a weekly ordeal of burned toast, cold potatoes, and tears: "After all," she whines, "in the terrible heat, with a cantankerous stove, they could hardly expect her to be perfect"), something "as infinitesimal as a grain of sand in an oyster" begins to pick at the back of her consciousness: jealousy. Still, as in Eden (and here her symbolism gets a bit ponderous), "except for the incident of the snake, things might have gone on, indefinitely, very much as before." The statement is a very synopsis not just of *Genesis* but of the whole history of Europe.

Mary is terrified of the large python insinuating itself in her garden: Joseph slays same. One can hardly get more mythopoetic in a single short story—even one called **"Xanadu."** Bathos follows, as in life: Mary feels "somehow in his debt" and, to expiate her guilt by compounding it, she plants three silver spoons in Joseph's bedroom while he is off expediting things for her at the market. In short, she betrays her Joseph just as the biblical brethren betrayed theirs. The story, which ends in betrayal, is continued in our heads: spoons discovered missing, search made, spoons found, horror expressed, Joseph (as "impassive yet without hostility" as ever) dismissed.

Mary fears Joseph more, and more *deeply,* than she fears the snake because he interferes with her own sense of herself as a person, as a woman (this is a story about Thomas's first trip to Africa, remember, when her female characters were still recognizably women). Until Joseph she was able to entertain comforting and easy assumptions about who she is: she is a housewife and a mother. "Housewife" in this context takes on a dangerous dimension because of the identification it makes between Mary's house and her body; Joseph threatens her role in the house, and therefore becomes identified in her mind as a threat to her body. She is, of course, intelligent enough to recognize all this as so much meaningless twaddle. After all, every sensibly born Englishwoman (her husband is English) has to learn how to "cope" (there is a longish fiddle in *Mrs. Blood* about the word "cope" in which it is made to fade into the word "hope") with servants. But as Thomas writes in a later story, "the white man is ashamed to be afraid of Africa and yet the shame does not completely obliterate the fear." Quite the contrary: the mixture of shame and fear produces cunning, even low cunning. At this point Joseph is Africa, but Mary, newly arrived, is not yet quite sure what Africa is (in fact *Mary* will never be; when she dies and is reborn as Isobel and Nora in later stories she is allowed a glimpse, or more literally an inkling). Joseph therefore is constantly changing costumes in Mary's feverish view: at one point he appears "like a huge black Prospero," a few paragraphs later he has changed into "another Ariel with hosts of spirits at his command" (which would in fact make him still Prospero, but never mind). The point is that Joseph smudges the line between master and slave ("he serves without being servile—if you know what I mean"), a line that two thousand years of European history has tried to make indelible but which Mary, being American, is half inclined to try to erase anyway. Like Prospero's island, like Xanadu, Africa is both paradise and real world, both stately pleasure dome and the source of a sacred and mysterious river that runs down to a sunless sea. And as the oriental setting for Coleridge's dream-poem, it is also the place where East meets West.

> "But I don't want to go among mad people," Alice remarked.
> "Oh, you can't help that," said the Cat: "we're all mad here. I'm mad. You're mad."
> "How do you know I'm mad?" said Alice.
> "You must be," said the Cat, "or you wouldn't have come here."

The quotation is from *Alice's Adventures in Wonderland* and is Thomas's introductory epigram to *Mrs. Blood*. It's an interesting choice: a children's book that has had its greatest success with childish adults (or precocious children—at any rate, the same set that would later find its mental chewing gum in Tolkien). Alice's two vehicles are the rabbit hole and, later, the looking glass, the latter being the more intellectually striking device. The Thomas stories that resulted from her first trip to Africa have more of the rabbit hole about them, **"Xanadu"** being an account of her fall, her gradual shrinking, and the two others being a description of the creatures she meets at the bottom. **"Omo"** is the story of Walter's fetish (Walter is a black American Peace Corps teacher of England who has been sent to Africa, where he shares a house with the narrator, a white slug called, in Walter's diary, E. K.) for an African anesthetist at the hospital. The anesthetist, whose name is Omo (which means "whiter than white") is an albino—"He looked kind of poached, if you know what I mean," remarks E. K., who is a math teacher—and Walter sees in him a terrifying symbol of the extent to which he, Walter, has been assimilated into the white world. Walter undergoes a kind of *crise de negritude:* after successfully wooing E. K.'s girlfriend Miranda (we are still on Prospero's island), he disappears. Omo is discovered in an advanced state of decomposition, his head having been bashed in (the ultimate anesthetic), and E. K., having enigmatically changed his name to Jonsson, is left with the aid of a bottle of gin to sort the whole thing out.

The final African story in *Ten Green Bottles* is **"One Is One and All Alone,"** a long interior monologue from a woman sinking deeper and deeper into the profound indifference of clinical depression—"Depressionism," Thomas calls it in another story; Impressionism carried to its most morbid extreme. The woman is nameless but resembles Mary from **"Xanadu"** (the steward, though called Samuel, is really Joseph in disguise). The husband is away, the two children mercifully unaware that their mother is stalking about the house in mortal, irrational terror for their safety. Depression of this sort is a form of premature menopause, and it is depicted here with nightmarish fidelity: "She had discovered that she did not have to leave the house if she did not choose, for her husband had stocked up well before he left. . . . This morning she had smiled shyly at the woman in the mirror. 'You see? I'm not such a bad sort after all.' She even toyed with the idea of getting someone to take her into town, buying some material, having her hair done. 'Why can't you drive yourself?' the woman in the mirror said, rather sternly. 'It isn't as though he had taken the car.' But she shrugged her shoulders ('You know why') and refused to become involved or irritated."

The woman-in-the-mirror is important. She has been introduced earlier in the story in cunning tandem with another recurring phantom, the wrestling match between reality and romanticism: "She would have liked to live in a solid, square, beautifully ugly house like that [she has been contemplating a photograph on a calendar]. Safe, ugly, beautiful and cool. 'You're being romantic,' said her heavy-eyed reflection in the mirror. 'Ah no,' she waggled her finger severely at this other woman. 'If I were romantic I should like it here. Colour, light, eternal summer—and servants. *I* am not romantic—somebody else is,' she muttered darkly to the other woman, then slammed the top down hard, and smiled." Lewis Carrol's eminently Victorian Cat was right.

During her first trip to Africa, Audrey Thomas had a miscarriage, and wrote **Mrs. Blood** (as well as her first published short story, **"If One Green Bottle. . . "**). Five years later she returned to Africa, alone, to work on **Blown Figures,** a novel about a woman who is returning to Africa, alone, to (as the jacket flap on the American edition says) "heal the emotional ravages of a miscarriage and the older wounds that lie beneath it." The woman is named Isobel. "When I went back I went *alone*," Thomas says in the interview, "and that seemed to be a very good thing. I think I do better alone, which is a very sad statement about me, than I do when I travel with other people. Sometimes I really have to force myself to go down the rabbit hole when I'm alone."

In a sense, all of Thomas's earlier African stories are footnotes to "Two in the Bush," for it is in this story that the themes andimages of her somewhat fractured history finally come together to make a satisfying whole.
—*Wayne Grady*

The stories from Thomas's second African trip, with the exception of **"Joseph and His Brother"** with its echoes of **"Xanadu"** and **"One Is One,"** have more to do with the looking-glass—the woman-in-the-mirror—than with the rabbit hole. They were collected in *Ladies and Escorts* (1980). I've already mentioned **"Rapunzel,"** and not much more needs to be said about it except that the girl Caroline is one of California's superannuated hippies who believes herself to be an artist, i.e. she carries a Rapido-Graph instead of a Pentax, but deals in snapshots nonetheless: "some market scenes, the tro-tros [trucks] and a lot of faces." She also indulges in mirror writing, so that her notebook or sketchbook is a kind of dyslexicon of Africa. **"Omo"** reappears—unlike mere people, some words do not become opposites of themselves in mirrors. The story ends with (we'll call her) Isobel reading from the notebook by holding it up to a mirror, like Alice reading Jabberwocky, Caroline's account of being raped by a black man at the university. Her whole experience of Africa is reduced to entries in a notebook. At one point Isobel asks her: "And did you find any of your 'old Meanings'?" "Some of them, maybe," Caroline replies.

"Did you know that when a man is very, very mad up there they chain him to a tree and the whole village looks after him?" The story **"Joseph and His Brother"** is a linear expansion of this single notebook entry.

A page in Thomas's own African diary, reprinted in part in the same *Capilano Review,* may serve as a footnote before we move on to **"Two in the Bush."** In Ghana, truck or "tro-tro" drivers name their trucks as if they were ships. "During Nkrumah's reign," Thomas notes, "a tro-tro driver was arrested by the Special Brigade because he had painted 'Ghana Hard-O' on his lorry. Charged with Treason, I guess. . . . His lawyer was advised to say that what he really meant was Ghana Very Strong-O, that he was an illiterate man and had gone to a sign painter. . . " etc. "Man got off with a small fine . . . and was told he must paint out that sign and put something else. He went immediately out of the court and bought some paint and came back to report that he had done this and had painted a new slogan.

"'And what is that?' asked the judge.

"'All Shall Pass.'

"He was arrested again."

In a sense, all of Thomas's earlier African stories are footnotes to **"Two in the Bush,"** for it is in this story that the themes and images of her somewhat fractured history finally come together to make a satisfying whole—a story in which, to borrow a phrase from Shakespeare's African story, her truths become a tale where before half-tales had been truths. Here Thomas gives us two women, Mollie and Isobel. Isobel is visiting Africa alone, Mollie is a resident there with her husband as Thomas had been on her first trip: Isobel and Mollie are therefore mirror images of each other, Thomas on trip one facing Thomas on trip two.

The story begins in the City Hotel in Ghana, one of the three hotels that provide the setting for the three sections of the story—hotels, restaurants, museums, these are the constant backdrops of the permanent exile, symbols of transience in a world unsettled (notice how the whole of Tim Findley's *Famous Last Words* takes place in an endless succession of hotels). Isobel, Mollie and her husband John, a man named Les, and a Ghanaian lawyer and politico named Jimmie Owusu-Banahene are having a Sunday curry lunch. The conversation revolves around politics: Isobel has known Jimmie "since Nkrumah's time" (i.e. since her first trip five years ago) and has just announced her impending journey to the Ivory Coast to meet an Angolan freedom fighter named Marques Kakumba. Why she is going to meet Kakumba is not clear—she is not wholly the same Isobel who appears in *Blown Figures,* though she is a writer, perhaps a journalist. "I'm not political," she says to Jimmie, and Jimmie scoffs: "Nobody in this world," he tells her, perhaps think-ing of the tro-tro driver endlessly arrested for giving his truck an ambiguous name, "is not political." And he goes on to give an almost Soviet list of examples: "When you are born you commit a political act, changin' the census in your vil-lage, town or state. When you die you do the same." And we are suddenly reminded of Aki Loba, the Ivory Coast nov-elist whose first novel, *Kocoumbo,* may have supplied Tho-mas with the name Kakumba in a curiously inverted way: "Kocoumbo doesn't like politics," one of Loba's characters protests. "Can you give me the name of a single educated African who doesn't like politics?" replies another charac-ter, Durandeau. "Doesn't Kocoumbo sleep and eat and com-plain about life? Doesn't he bear grudges against other people? Well that's politics!"

Mollie, who suddenly decides to accompany Isobel to the Ivory Coast, is like Mary in **"Xanadu"** (or *Mrs. Blood*): for her, Africa is an escape from herself, an "escapade" in the romantic sense of the word. "I could do with a little holi-day," she tells her husband. For Isobel, Africa is a way *into* herself. Even the interview with Kakumba is a pretext: "I wanted to find Africa," she tells herself before the trip. "Was this it? Was this the real Africa? Maybe it would be differ-ent in the Ivory Coast." Isobel is also a romantic, though a different kind from Mollie. She is not looking for "the real Africa"—why should she find it in the Ivory Coast when it has eluded her in Ghana?—she is looking for the real Isobel. In *Blown Figures* she is looking for the child she lost dur-ing her first trip—there is something inside her that destroys life, some heart of darkness that has to be found and exposed to the harsh African sun, so the real Isobel can emerge as a life force. The search for the real Isobel is essentially a ro-mantic pursuit. Isobel is trying, unlike Mollie, to resolve the split between romanticism and reality, between her idea of Africa (herself) and the Africa she actually encounters. She is trying to force a crisis—and there is nothing like travel-ling to bring about a crisis. Mollie, Isobel's former self, the self that had the miscarriage, has more basic needs: she just wants to get laid.

There are many kinds of romanticism. Mollie's is a sexual fantasy land in which the ordinary laws of social conduct are lifted, and a beautiful, wartless whimsy takes over. The world of the Harlequin Romance. Thomas does not reject this world: even some of her more intelligent characters wal-low about in it from time to time (see **"Initram"**—the title is another mirror-word—in which the narrator, a writer, bounces along in a perpetual fantasy world in which writers sit around drinking tea from bone china cups and discuss-ing Djuna Barnes, and handsome strangers, their sailboats tied up because of the storm, wander into the bar and say, "I'll always care what happens to you"). Isobel's romanti-cism, however, is the literary kind, the kind peopled by Wordsworth, Southey, and Coleridge (**"Xanadu"**), which is

not so much an escape from reality as a penetration more deeply into it. There is an intriguing echo of both kinds in Arthur McDowall's 1918 book, *Realism: A Study in Art and Thought:*

> Romanticism casts a spell in art, and we all yield
> to it from time to time, and for some it is the only
> thing which is profoundly moving. It is the sense
> of escape which thrills us. Not an escape, always,
> from ourselves, but from what limits or fetters us.
> In romance the self may be unfolded, spread out to
> dream over, free from the pressure of material
> things.

Elsewhere McDowall makes the connection between roman-ticism and the kind of inner journey upon which Isobel has embarked:

> The romantic art which delights to exhibit and con-
> template the self finds an analogue in the philo-
> sophical theories which centre round the idea of
> self-realization. . . . It is the self, and not the things
> that lie beyond it, which is the real interest; and the
> universe is only a duplication of it, since it proves
> to be a second Self, enlarged and glorified.

Africa is Isobel's "duplication" (as in a mirror); it is her "sec-ond Self."

In Abidjan, Isobel and Mollie put up at a glorified brothel with a wonderful name: Hôtel Humanité. (Thomas chooses her names carefully. "Mollie" sounds like Mistress Quickly, Isobel echoes Isabel in *Measure for Measure*. The Hôtel Humanité is on rue des Ecries—an *ecrie* is a "cry of pain," but may also be a play on the word *écrit*, "written" as in "it is written.") They stay at this hotel because of the kind of inverted logic (dyslogic) that pervades the story: Kakumba, they know, is staying at the ritzier Hôtel Ivoire (for Ivory Coast, yes, but perhaps also for Milton's Ivory Gates, the entrance to dreamland). At the Ivoire the women become mixed up with the "real" Africa with a vengeance: an Ameri-can tuna millionaire named Arnie Freitas; a vice-president of the African Development Bank named Alamoody; and of course Kakumba, who may or may not be in league with the American and the banker in a gun-running operation. On their first night in the Hôtel Humanité (after refusing Arnie's hospitality at the Ivoire) they hear the distant sound of drums, like a primeval, absurd heart-beat: "Dadada / Dadada Dadada," and Isobel wonders, "Was that Africa? Was Mr. Alamoody Africa or Joào Kakumba or even Sgt Lee Lillie or Arnie the tuna-fish king? I didn't dream—why should I? Africa was a dream."

The next day, taking up her position again at Jung's "psy-chic observation post," Isobel pauses as she leaves the hotel to watch an African woman "pounding fou-fou with a long pole. A small child sat at her feet and reached her hand in quickly between the strokes, to turn the soft glutinous mass. Then the pole came down again. Thud. Pause. Thud. Pause. Thud. Like a great heart beating." This is obviously another page from Thomas's African diary, but she turns it neatly into the central image of the story: "'Why not,' I thought. 'Why not just stay on here?' I was romanticizing, of course, but the life of the woman in the courtyard seemed as simple and as regular as the thud of her fou-fou pounder." Isobel *is* romanticizing. The woman-in-the-mirror has become the woman in the courtyard, and Isobel has to force herself through the looking glass to become her. But the woman in the courtyard is (in "reality") the wife of the brothel-keeper, the owner of the Hôtel Humanité, and her life is anything but "simple and regular life." Isobel isn't interested in the simple and regular life anyway—that's Mollie's brand of romanticism. Isobel wants to believe that the woman in the courtyard is the real Africa, and hence can be the real Isobel. Later at the Hôtel Ivoire she lunches on "club sandwiches stuck together with nasty little cellophane-decorated toothpicks": the real Africa at last? "Probably," Isobel replies. "It's France too. And Portugal too and everything that's gone before." For her, Africa has remained a dream; she has not found in the Ivory Coast what she could not find in Ghana. "I know nothing about Africa," she tells Jimmie when she gets back, and to her it is a kind of defeat. Jimmie's reply, of course, is "That's a beginning." The snake again, with its tail in its mouth, the round trip from Ghana to Abidjan to Ghana; all that way to achieve a beginning.

Between beginnings there is one scene that lingers in the mind, in which Isobel and Mollie leave the Humanité. It poses a question that is central to the story and is never answered: "'Who are you?' a drunken young man had shouted at the doorman as we left the hotel. The doorman was barring the way. 'Who are you?'"

Isobel doesn't find out who she is in **"Two in the Bush,"** but she is ready to, and so far readiness is all. She is like an athlete who, having trained all her life for the Olympics, now finds herself crouched at the starting line.

Between the crouch and the spring there is a pause (while the starter shouts, "On your marks. . . "), and the pause is a quiet, internal story called **"Out in the Midday Sun."** Apart from the obvious reference in the title to mad dogs and Englishmen, the phrase crops up again in a later African story, **"Degrees":** "Mary Lamb [not *the* Mary Lamb, of course, but Shakespeare is never very far away in Thomas's Africa; neither is the Mary who *had* a little Lamb, the miscarried Mary of *Mrs. Blood*] and Norman . . . stepped forward from under the shade of the airport roof and out into the midday sun." The midday sun is the opposite—the mirror image—of the heart of darkness: later Thomas will write with joy

about "the relentless clarity of the African sun." And surely there is an echo here of Isak Dinesen's relentlessly clear-headed book, *Out of Africa:* "To Arabia and Africa, where the sun of the midday kills you, night is the time for traveling and enterprise." An echo is a kind of mirror.

The female narrator (again nameless, again Mary) of **"Out in the Midday Sun"** has written a short story, has sent it out under an assumed name (naturally, having no name of her own), and it has been accepted. She is terrified that her husband, also an unpublished writer, will leave her when he finds out. This is her new fear, or rather the old fear in a new guise:

> Her fear had nothing to do with Africa. That was
> what she had known all along. Africa, like a dream,
> had simply provided the symbols. She had refused
> to recognize the reality behind them. She had to
> leave him. She loved him, but she had to leave him.
> It was as simple as that.

Which is, of course, romanticized nonsense, the soulful writer, wrist to forehead (perhaps wearing Sarah Bernhardt's Hamlet suit, *en travestie*), forever denied true love because of the curse of her penetrating insights. But the tail-eating snake has reappeared: the story to be published is **"If One Green Bottle. . . ,"** about the miscarriage—and a more internalized, obfuscated, circumloquacious example of romanticism is difficult to imagine. Nothing is ever "as simple as that."

But **"Out in the Midday Sun"** (which also connects "mad dogs" with Thomas's Cheshire Cat introduction to *Mrs. Blood*) is a useful introduction to **"Timbuktu,"** a fine story in which Thomas dovetails many of the feathery themes from her earlier pieces. The narrator of **"Timbuktu"** is Rona—an Old Norse name meaning "very powerful"—who, like the narrator of **"Out in the Midday Sun,"** loves her husband but feels she has to leave him in order to discover her true self. Unlike her, however, Rona does leave her husband, if only for a while. Rona and Philip Hooper are living in Dakar, Senegal, where Philip is a cryptographer (like Poe and Graham Greene) with the U.N. Philip had been in Ghana before with "Wifie One" (Mary?) and a steward named Hyacinth, perhaps the same Hyacinth who bit the heads off chickens in **"Rapunzel."** The story of Rona begins inauspiciously enough with two logical impossibilities:

> ". . . up the river to Timbuktu." For the past few
> minutes she had been doing a jellyfish float, head
> down and arms around her knees, bobbing just be-
> low the surfacewater, like a cork.

Taking the second sentence first, Rona is not dead despite having spent a few minutes just below the surface of the water: this is African water—not so much water as amneotic fluid. Rona is suspended in a kind of pre-natal sac ("jellyfish" is all right, "cork" is awful). She conceives, in this state, the idea of going to Timbuktu much as a fetus might conceive the idea of being born.

Second, ". . . up the river to Timbuktu" has a nice rhythm to it, a kind of boat rhythm, like Lowry's Frère *Jacques,* Frère *Jacques,* but it is wrong nonetheless. The route to Timbuktu from Dakar is by train to Bamako and then by steamer, as Thomas says, "up the river to Timbuktu" (she repeats it like a mantra). If you think of the Niger as your right index finger, bent at both knuckles, then Bamako is the first knuckle, closest to the nail, and Timbuktu is the larger knuckle at the top. Timbuktu is therefore *downriver.* Rona doesn't really know where she is going. Which is why she never gets there.

Steaming up or down the Niger to a bend in the river recalls both Conrad (and **"Timbuktu"** is the most Conradian of Thomas's African stories) and Naipaul—mainly Conrad, though, because there is no politics in Thomas's Africa. For Rona, Africa is a mirror. As in Mark Twain, it is the river that lures her, as well as the romanticism invested in "the mysterious veiled kingdom of Timbuktu" at the end of it, the "new life. Without ties." The physical reality of river and city are something else again: who can remember what happens to Huck Finn when he reaches the mouth of the Mississippi? And for another American melding of Mark Twain and Conrad, see Francis Ford Coppola's *Apocalypse Now,* for which Coppola made three equally unsatisfying endings. The most appropriate ending for the film is the unmade one in which the protagonist reaches the end of the river and *there is nothing there.* A Borgesian ending, in which everything and nothing meet and mate. No Kurtz (or rather no Brando), no horror. Conrad goes a step further: he puts Kurtz there and then removes him, a double absence. The final scene of "Heart of Darkness," in which Marlowe makes a mockery of everything Kurtz meant by putting his Intended's name in his dying mouth—better not to get to the end of the river at all. Coppola got us to the end of the river and left us with the horror. Thomas doesn't get us to the end of the river.

The other interesting thing about **"Timbuktu"** is that Thomas seems to have reverted in it to characters that belong more to her first African trip. Rona, like Mary, is married, living a kind of pre-natal existence in Africa—or rather in an English enclave within Africa. But like Isobel she is not afraid of Africa; she wants to become more like Africa, more a part of her surroundings, less like one of her white compatriots. "I don't feel real anymore," she tells Philip. "I don't feel as though I'm a separate person." Think of the Niger as a birth canal, Timbuktu as a cervix. (The word Timbuktu has been translated as "old woman with large navel.")

In Bamako, Rona meets two opposing yet curiously complementary forces: P. J. Jones, an engineer who is also on his way to Timbuktu; and a family of B'hai missionaries from New Jersey, the Weavers. Opposed and complementary like Alice's Red Queen and White Queen: Jones is a realist—unlike Rona, Jones knows exactly why he is going to Timbuktu: to widen the airstrip; the Weavers are romantics. Jones calls them "naive and ill-informed and a general pain in the ass," but he admires their "romantic vision." Rona is a blend of the two forces. She is certainly romantic—the obsessive search for self, "too much Humphrey Bogart," as she says, and she is even mysteriously religious, almost literally born again: "I stood up in the water and heard this voice mention Timbuktu. All of a sudden, I knew that was where I wanted to go." And she too admires the Weavers: "B'hai. How exotic it sounded! Like *The Rubaiyat of Omar Khayyam.*" But she is also realistic; like James she knows Africa (somewhat) and is comfortable in it, wears the right clothes, eats the right foods. Rona is as close as any of Thomas's characters ever come to achieving a synthesis of romanticism and realism, and acceptance of love and death, of the killing and cleansing African sun rising above the heart of darkness.

Thomas's African stories force one to think of them as a unit, as a long progression toward wholeness. They make, I think, three-quarters of a book of linked short stories. There are two very different personas in this imaginary book: the "Mary" of trip one and the "Isobel" of trip two. And they are melded finally into "Rona" of **"Timbuktu,"** in much the same way as Rose and Janet in the first version of Alice Munro's *Who Do You Think You Are?* were melded in the final version into a somewhat altered Rose. Thomas's ninth African story, **"Degrees,"** is a further and less important reversion to the Mary of trip one, an expansion of a minor incident in *Mrs. Blood*—not exactly a recycling, but dangerously close to a retelling; certainly not a progression from **"Timbuktu."**

What is wanted now is the final quarter, the trip along the Niger (this time *down* the river), perhaps reaching Timbuktu to find it both the mysterious veiled city of Rona's dreams and the sordid, dusty, oblivious hole stirred by the barbed finger of V. S. Naipaul. Or perhaps she will not stop at Timbuktu, will continue as she hints in the story to the mouth of the Niger, and, like Huck Finn and Jim, sail into history, into her "other Self."

Audrey Thomas (essay date Spring 1984)

SOURCE: "Basmati Rice: An Essay about Words," in *Canadian Literature,* No. 100, Spring, 1984, pp. 312-17.

[*In the following essay, Thomas discusses her fascination with words and language.*]

My study is on the second floor of our house and faces East. I like that and I get up early to write, perhaps not simply because I enjoy the sunrise (especially in winter, when all has been so black, and then gradually light, like hope, returns) but out of some atavistic hope that my thoughts, too, will rise with the sun and illumine the blank pages in front of me.

We live in a corner house and my study is right above a busy street. People whom I cannot see often pass beneath my window and throw up snatches of conversation before moving out of earshot. And I hear footsteps, light, heavy, singly or in groups, and the sound of buggy wheels or grocery carts. Now, I can see the sidewalk on the other side of the street, see people hurrying along or dawdling, the young woman from the St. James Daycare a block away, out for a walk with her little charges who all seem to march (or skip or run) to a different drummer, a father with his baby tucked inside his ski jacket, a blind man, a woman with her arms full of grocery bags. I cannot hear their footsteps nor anything they might be saying and sometimes a wonderful thing happens where someone will pass beneath my window, and say something while someone is walking by on the other side of the street, and so I get the wonderful absurdity of seeing the old lady in the red coat who lives at the Senior Citizen Lodge at 16th and Macdonald (I know because she asked me to take her picture, waving her hand-made Union Jack, the day the Queen came down 16th Avenue) going by on one side and hearing a gruff teenage male voice saying, "so I said to him nobody talks like that to me and. . . . " The movie I watch has the wrong soundtrack!

I am interested in such absurdities, in the word *absurd* itself, from the Latin for inharmonious, foolish. L. *ab,* from, *surdus,* deaf, inaudible, harsh (used metaphorically here, deaf to reason, hence irrational). I am interested in the fact that I spend a lot of my days at a desk, or table, and that the desk or table needs always to face a window. This is not just so I will have something to look at when "illumination" comes slowly (or not at all) but because, in what is essentially an inside occupation (and a very lonely one at that, I can't even stand to have a radio on when I'm working) I am able to feel even a little bit connected with the outside. I often see myself like a diver in one of those old-fashioned diving bells, both in and apart from everything in the universe around me. There is a little piece of brown paper taped to the window frame. I got it from a bread wrapper several years ago when I was spending a winter in Montreal. It says

PAIN
FRAIS DU JOUR

in blue letters and underneath

BREAD
BAKED FRESH DAILY

Some days, if I'm wrestling with a piece or a passage that seems especially difficult I fold the paper so that it reads:

PAIN
BAKED FRESH DAILY

and for some perverse reason that cheers me up. That the French word for bread and the English word for misery of one kind or another *look* alike is another of those absurdities that interest me. There is no real connection, as there is, say, with the English *blessed* and the French *blesser,* to wound—it's just chance. But my mind, when in a certain state of heightened awareness (which I might point out, can just as easily be brought on by laughter as by tears), makes that kind of connection easily.

Here's another. It was early November when I began thinking about this essay, and the tree outside my window was almost bare of leaves. The weather was turning cold and a cold rain was falling. "Autumn leaves" I wrote on my pad, "autumn leaves." Over and over. And then suddenly "WINTER enters." Again, no real linguistic connection, but writing the phrase over and over gave me a new way of looking at the leaves.

I love words. I love the way they suddenly surprise you; I love the way *everyone,* high or low, uses them to paint pictures—that is to say metaphorically. In the past week a phrase, not new, but surely not much in vogue of recent years, has been said in my hearing, or I've read it in the paper, no less than five times: so and so is "between a rock and a hard place." Once in a line-up at the main post office downtown, once spoken by a friend, and in three different newspaper articles. Where does this phrase come from? I can't find it in Bartlett's, at least not under "rock," or "place," or "hard." Why is it suddenly being said? It is certainly a most poetic (and uncomfortable) image. I wouldn't want to be there, nor would you. Somebody says, of somebody else, "I've got him eating out of my hand," probably unaware of the root of the word "manipulate." When I was a child I heard constant warnings about kids who were "too big for their britches" or "too big for their boots" and we were all, without exception, potential bigeared little pitchers. And yet it seemed to me that all the adults I knew—parents, relatives, teachers, corrected me if I played around with words myself—or with grammar or sentence structure. It was as though all the metaphorical language in the world had already been invented and I wasn't there on the day that it happened. Once I started reading poetry I realized that poets seemed to have a certain freedom that ordinary, hardworking decent folks didn't (or didn't allow themselves) to have. They invented and re-invented language all the time. (Prose that got too metaphorical was considered suspect unless it were in the Sunday Sermon or spoken by Roosevelt or Churchill.) That was when I decided I would become a poet, and probably why. My poems were terrible—a lot of them were very "Christian" in a romantic way, full of Crusaders, lepers, infidels, and angels—and some of them, I regret to say, won prizes. But I do remember the day we were asked to write limericks (Grade 4? Grade 5?) and I came up with this in about five minutes:

> There was once a fellow named Farrell
> Whose life was in terrible peril
> He fell in with some rogues
> Who stole all but his brogues
> And had to slink home in a barrel.

(I don't know where I got "brogues" from or how I knew what it meant; it certainly wasn't a word used in our family.)

I wrote dozens of limericks after that first one. I knew it wasn't Real Poetry but I also suspected the other stuff, the stuff my teachers and my mother and various judges liked wasn't Real Poetry either. Nevertheless, for all my desire to write poetry, what I was always better at was prose. Who knows why one writer works better in one genre than another? What I'd really like to be is "ambidextrous," like Michael Ondaatje or Margaret Atwood, but I'm not. It's always prose for me. (Why do most of us see poetry as "higher"? Because it seems more of a distillate of the creative unconscious than prose? Perfume as opposed to cologne? I once had a poet in a graduate prose class in Montreal. He needed one more course to get his degree and had chosen mine. We were all working on stories and one night he said to me, in much despair, "I've never written 'he said' and 'she said' before." Of course he wasn't a *narrative* poet: not for him *Beowulf* or *The Idylls of the King,* or, closer to home, *The Titanic,* or *Brébeuf and his Brethren.*) I still sometimes have the awful feeling that I failed because I failed to write poetry, even while I know that prose can be just as exciting or dense, "packed," innovative as any poem. It probably has something to do with the fact that we write our notes, our memos, our letters, in prose, we speak in prose to one another, even when we speak metaphorically: "Lay off me, will you?", "I'm really blue today," "What's for dinner, honey?," "You're driving me up the wall."

Sometimes a sentence or a phrase gives me the idea for an entire story (once, even, for the very last line of a novel I didn't write for another three years, when I overheard a man in a pay phone say to whomever was on the other end: "Get rid of it." That's all I heard him say and then he hung up).

This summer my daughter and I were in Greece. We witnessed a very bizarre incident involving a young English boy, an octopus, and a man in a panama hat. I knew that that in itself could provide the central image for a new story but then, a few days later, I heard a French woman on another beach say "La méduse; il faut prener garde," and suddenly, because of this incident with the octopus, I saw not the jellyfish to which she had been referring but the great snaky tentacles of an octopus and *then* I saw that what I really wanted to write about was all that sexuality that was there on the beach, in that heat, under the intense blue sky: the barebreasted European woman, the young Greek men showing off to their girl-friends and whoever else would watch. All the bodies. The story is seen through the eyes of a 12-year-old English boy, very properly brought up, for whom the octopus becomes the symbol of everything most feared and most desired, "the nightmare spread out upon the rock." Later on, on quite a different island, a Greek man said two things that have become incorporated into the octopus story. He said, when we were listening to some very sad Greek music, "There are no happy men in Greece, only happy childrens." He also asked, "you like this iceland" and since the temperature was over 80° we stared at him. He meant "island" but it took us a while to figure that out. Now, in my story, the young boy hears words and phrases he doesn't completely understand ("la méduse; il faut prener garde" "you like this ice-land?") and this just adds to his general sense of unease.

Another recent story was inspired by a newspaper clipping about a man who had been charged with common assault for massaging the feet of strange women. I began to do some foot research and discovered something I must have learned in my university zoology course, that the number of bones in the human foot is the same as the number of letters in the alphabet. And so the story begins: "There are twenty-six bones in the foot; that is the alphabet of the foot" and goes on to tell a story which is a complete fabrication except for the fact that both men (the "real" man and the man in my story) get arrested, charged and fined.

Another story, which is the title story of the collection I'm presently working on, came as a message written on a mirror in the George Dawson Inn in Dawson Creek. The message was not intended for me but showed up on the mirror in the bathroom after my daughter had taken a very hot shower. It said, "Good-bye Harold, Good Luck" and whoever had written it must have counted on the fact that Harold would take a shower. (And the maid had obviously not gone over the mirror with *Windex.*) We had a lot of fun trying to figure out who Harold was and whether the message was written in anger or love. In the story, "they" (a mother who is contemplating a divorce and her child) do meet up with Harold, but of course he doesn't know that they have seen the message (and they're not absolutely sure he has).

I cut things out of newspapers, often really horrible things and I'm never sure why.

MURDERER SET WIFE ADRIFT ON RAFT

TIGER BITES TRAINER TO DEATH
(Horrified Wife Looks On)

DOLPHINS NUDGE BOY'S BODY TO SHORE

That last one really haunts me, not just the image, but that word "nudge." The dolphins with their blunt "noses," gently nudging the dead boy towards the shore. That one will probably end up in a story.

PLAN YOUR PLOT

(this one was in the gardening column of the *Province*) and one from the *Vancouver Courier* recently prompted a note to a friend.

POUND WARNS PETS

I cut it out, and wrote underneath, "You're an old bitch gone in the teeth."

And so it goes. And so it goes. And so it goes on and on. I read Rev. Skeat, I read Bartlett's, I read Fowler's *Modern English Usage,* given to me by an ex-boyfriend who wrote, as a greeting, the definition of *oxymoron,* which just about summed up our relationship! I have the *Shorter Oxford Dictionary* but long to have the real one, all those volumes as full of goodies as good Christmas puddings. I have the Bible, the Book of Common Prayer, Shakespeare and *Partridge's Origins.* I have Collins' phrase books in several languages ("that man is following me everywhere"). I have maps and rocks and shells and bits of coral from various places to which I have travelled. I scan the personal columns, the names of the ships in port. And I have my eyes and ears.

I am a dilettante (related to the Italian for "delight"). I never learn any language properly but love to dabble in them. I have studied, at one time or another, Latin, Anglo-Saxon, Middle English, Old Norse, French, Italian and, most recently Greek. I spent a winter in Athens a few years ago and saw, every day, little green vans scurrying around the city with METAOOPH posted on a card in the front windshield. "Metaphors." When I enquired I discovered that these vans are for hire and they *transfer* goods from one section of the city to another. Now I long to write an essay called "A Metaphor is not a Truck."

Last year I took two terms of sign language at night school. I was amused by the fact that in ASL (American Sign Language) the sign for "woman" has to do with the tying of bon-

net strings and the sign for man with the tipping of a hat. These are charming archaisms, like "horsepower" in English. (I am also interested in mirrors, mirror images, going into and through mirrors, so signing, which one does to someone facing you, is fascinating—and very difficult. I often came home with an aching hand.) I would like to take more sign language; I would like to become, as an African man once said to me, about English, "absolutely fluid in that language."

Words words words. Sometimes it all gets on top of me and I feel like the monster made out of words in *The Fairie Queene.* I can't leave them alone; I am obsessed. I move through the city watching for signs with letters missing ("Beef live with onions" advertises a cheap café near Granville and Broadway, "ELF SERVE" says a gas station out on Hastings) and I am always on the lookout for messages within words: can you see the harm in pharmacy, the dent in accident, the over in lover? In short, I play.

There is a phenomenon, most commonly observed in photography but also talked about by people who make stained glass. It is called "halation" and it refers to the spreading of light beyond its proper boundary. (With stained glass it happens when two colours are next to one another.) I think words can do that too, or perhaps I should say that I would like to think that there is no "proper boundary" for words. Let them spill over from one language to another, let them leap out at us like kittens at play. "Wit," said Mark Van Doren, "is the only wall between us and the dark." If a writer, if an artist of *any* sort, stops approaching his materials with wit, with laughter, then he is lost. The other day I was making a curry and listening to some old Beatles' songs on the radio. John or Paul was yelling, "Can't Buy Me Love" and I was thinking about Basmati rice. Suddenly I realized "Basmati rice" had the same number of syllables as "Can't Buy Me Love," so every time John or Paul or whoever got to the chorus I yelled out "Basmati Rice!" and did a little soft shoe shuffle while I stirred the curry sauce. (Everybody had a good time.)

Pauline Butling (essay date Autumn 1984)

SOURCE: "Thomas and Her Rag-Bag," in *Canadian Literature,* No. 102, Autumn, 1984.

[*In the following essay, Butling argues that Thomas's use of autobiographical details in her short stories allows her to create female characters who are more "real" than those of other women writers in that they resist falling into paradigmatic female categories.*]

Many recent women writers have worked at re-defining the

images of women in fiction—Margaret Laurence, Alice Munro, Jane Rule, to name a few—but because they haven't changed the form in any significant way, because the traditional structures of fiction frame the story, the character types inherent in those forms remain. A cause-effect structure, for instance, requires certain set functions of the characters.

Yet we know the traditional images of men and women no longer apply, where the woman is defined primarily in terms of her relationship to men, or at least in terms of her sexuality, as virgin or whore, Penelope or Circe, wife or temptress: that is, victim or agent in a conflict which must be "resolved" before the story ends. But both male and female contemporary writers seem curiously stuck within that frame of reference, unable to imagine new possibilities or invent new story patterns.

Those who do not write out of a nostalgia for the old clarities either express enormous despair, or adopt an ironic/satiric viewpoint, reducing the traditional male/female roles to their absurd dimensions. (Robert Kroetsch, for instance, in *The Studhorse Man,* or more bleakly in *Crow,* shows the ridiculous and destructive aspects of male/female roles: Man as quester forever striving for impossible ideals: building ice towers into the sky, trying to fly, and being destroyed in the attempt. Woman as queen bee, devouring everything that comes near her.) Or, Matt Cohen or Clark Blaise present failed relationships. Others move away from story altogether and focus on the *process* of fictionalizing, displaying the distortions which occur in the process. The narrative becomes the story of the process of writing, *Burning Water,* for instance. Self-conscious fiction has certainly been important in developing awareness of the forms and processes of fiction, which have to be seen before they can be changed. Just as linguists have shown us that the structure of language determines how we perceive the world, so the writers are showing us that the structures of fiction shape our imagination of the world. It follows that to change the image, the structures and processes have to change. But the metamorphosis has yet to take place.

Margaret Laurence, Jane Rule, Alice Munro, and others, through a focus on character, succeed in presenting greater depth and breadth in their female characters, but stop short of a qualitative change. In *The Diviners,* or *Contract With The World,* or *Lives of Girls and Women,* the central characters emerge as strong full women, but still saddened by their failures in relationships. Although marriage is not the ultimate reward, the women are still within that frame of reference.

Audrey Thomas does two things in her stories which allow her to transform the images of women in her fiction. First, she doesn't fictionalize in the usual sense of the word; she doesn't "invent" character and situation. The shift in con-

tent to an autobiographical base, in turn, frees her to make significant changes in the story form. Structurally, the stories are quite loose. Images of braiding or weaving best picture her method. She works in the story like an archaeologist gathering together the shards from the rag-bag of her experience, and piecing them together, as she finds the coherence and shape inherent in that material. Only the slenderest of threads—the path of the writer writing—serves as a "track" through. Thus the story form is not predetermined by the author's inventions nor by fictional paradigms. And this more open form in turn frees the image to take its shape from the material at hand, rather than from given models.

In **"Natural History,"** for instance, Thomas begins with the shards in her character's immediate world: mother and daughter are sleeping outside under the full moon, the mother lies awake recalling events of the day, and thinking about how to kill a rat that they have discovered in the house, and remembering fragments from their study of inter-tidal life that has been going on through the summer, and recalling her own childhood, and musing on the moon as symbol of femininity. The story proceeds as a record of the seemingly random assortment of fragments, as a "natural history." But at the end, the mother momentarily perceives the coherence in it all:

> Another image came to mind, out of her childhood, a steriopticon belonging to her grandfather. She would sit with it, on a Sunday afternoon, sliding the crossbar up and down, until suddenly, "click," the two photographs taken at slightly different angles (St. Mark's, the Tower of London, Notre Dame) would become one picture, which would take on depth and wonderful illusion of solidity. That was the trick. To slide it all—moon, blind girl, rat, the apple tree, her father's fingers tilting the pencil, her own solitude, the cat, the eyes of the deer, her daughter, this still moment, back/forth, back/forth, back/forth, until "click,"
>
> until "click"
>
> until "click"—
>
> there it was: wholeness, harmony, radiance; all of it making a wonderful kind of sense, as she sat there under the apple tree, beneath the moon.

Steriopticon, or stereoscope ("an optical instrument with two eyeglasses for helping the observer to combine the images of two pictures taken from points of view a little way apart and thus to get the effect of solidity or depth") is a particularly apt image for the process. The story achieves both solidity and depth as the various threads momentarily cohere.

Because the story has been free to find its own shape (as the title **"Natural History"** suggests), Thomas is able to arrive at the concluding image of the woman sitting alone, but not lonely, feeling centred and content, without having necessarily resolved anything, glimpsing for a brief moment her connection with the natural world: *"as she sat there, under the apple tree, beneath the moon."* Many fictions end with the woman alone, but few achieve the feeling of contentment that is pictured here. The woman is defined in relation to natural forces, not social structures, which represents a qualitative change in the image.

The other aspect of Thomas' writing which contributes to her success in transforming the image is that she takes on and confronts directly traditional images of women. Although by shifting to an autobiographical base, Thomas is not bound by traditional narrative patterns and the character delineations they demand, she cannot totally free herself from their influence because those patterns are also embedded in her own consciousness. Her own modes of thinking and acting are strongly influenced, if not determined, by the paradigms of myth and story. In her rag-bag of experience, she often finds STORY along with uncut grass and apple trees and moonlight. But the stories enter in, not as a frame or backdrop illuminating the present "story," but as one of the shards. They can thus be questioned and examined, as in **"Natural History,"** the mother wonders if her daughter will be content to "shine always by reflected light" like the moon (as the traditional story goes) or if she will develop her own strengths.

Treating story as subject, as foreground rather than background, contributes to Thomas' success in transforming the images of women, because it allows her to de-construct the old images and thus clear the way for the new. In all her short story collections, she brings traditional images to mind by the cover illustrations which picture well-known fairy tale figures. She then de-constructs that image by telling stories based on her own experiences as a contemporary woman. *Ten Green Bottles* (1967), for instance, has Jack and Jill on the cover. The stories then deal with the loss of innocence, but not the traditional loss of physical innocence. Apart from one story about being "21 and still a virgin," which ends with the promise of intercourse (**"A Winter's Tale"**), the central character is a married woman. Innocence is a mental/emotional condition; the fall is into the self. The wife in **"Xanadu,"** for instance, although at first delighting in the "pleasure dome" which she finds herself in, with a servant who cooks, cleans, shops, and takes care of the children to perfection, comes to resent the servant's superior ability because his domestic skills put her to shame. To her surprise, she finds herself resorting to subterfuge to get rid of him. She plants three silver spoons in his room, so she can accuse him of theft and dismiss him. Loss of innocence, yes, but it is more complex than the traditional sexual initiation.

It means the loss of that ideal of women as emotionally or morally innocent, as loving, caring, unselfish creature.

In *Ladies and Escorts* (1977), the cover illustration of Little Red Riding Hood introduces the subject of women's encounters with the "wicked wolf" in the "dark forest," and the title brings to mind "happily ever after" stories. But Thomas then de-constructs the images of women as helpless, passive, and in need of escorts, in the face of passion, desire, or other "darkness." In **"Kill Day on the Government Wharf,"** the woman, who is both fascinated and disturbed by her contact with a native fisherman, does not run away or call for help, but instead explores her feelings, and momentarily reaches out to touch him. Or Rapunzel, the main character in a story of the same title, locked in her own self-made tower (she chooses to record the world through mirror writing) refuses the prince when he comes knocking at her window. **"The More little Mummy,"** a very disturbing story with its images of pickled foetuses on display in jars, tells not of ladies and escorts, but of a woman facing abortion, and the breakup of a relationship, hardly the world implied by the book's title or cover illustration.

Finally, in *Real Mothers,* Thomas takes on the task of deconstructing a more recent ideal of women—the image of the super Mom, that post-war ideal of domesticity implied by the book's title, and by the cover illustration of mother and daughter happily rolling out pastry, smiling at each other and looking immaculate in frilly white aprons and neat soft curls: daughter apprenticing to become cook, love object, wife, and mother, happy in the role of domestic servant—in other words, apprenticing to become a Real Mother.

> **Thomas is not just replacing the idealized images of woman with more realistic ones. As well as giving us stories about actual women in present-day situations which serve to displace the traditional notions, she also re-constructs new *ideals*.**
> —*Pauline Butling*

But again, the stories belie the image. They tell of the actual experiences of actual women—"real mothers" in the other meaning of the phrase. Not the essence of motherhood, but the actuality of it. The opening lines of the first story in the collection establish the reality. We meet not the trim, smiling, slim woman of the cover, but an overweight, single parent, who is rejecting her children and traditional domesticity:

> After Marie-Anne's parents had been separated for about a year, her mother joined Weight Watchers, lost thirty pounds, and decided to go back to school.

And, in contrast to the simplistic happiness pictured on the cover, the characters are often unhappy, or caught up in complex and conflicting emotions. The woman in **"Timbuctu,"** for example, realizes "she wanted Phillip *and* her freedom. How could she have both?" and feels the contradictory nature of love: "The amber beads, like love, hung beautiful and heavy around her neck." In **"The Bleak Midwinter,"** a woman involved in a *ménage-à-trois* is reasonable, pleasant, and considerate in conversation with her companions, but nasty and vindictive in her actions. On a more humorous note, the woman in **"Harry and Violet"** hears, at the moment of sexual climax with a lover, her daughter's voice, and opens her eyes to see the daughter standing at the foot of the bed waiting patiently to show them her two pet caterpillars. Confusion, embarrassment, and mixed feelings, are the emotions of real mothers.

But Thomas is not just replacing the idealized images of woman with more realistic ones. As well as giving us stories about actual women in present-day situations which serve to displace the traditional notions, she also re-constructs new *ideals*. In the last story of the book, aptly titled **"Crossing the Rubicon,"** the whole thrust of the story is toward imagining a future in which the main character will behave differently. Before she can *act* differently, she realizes she must first *imagine* herself acting differently. Thus the narrator is writing a story within the story in which she pictures herself transformed. Specifically, the story centres on a woman's struggle to break away from a lingering but obviously disintegrating love affair. A Valentine's Day setting for the story provides an occasion for bringing in all the surface trappings of romantic love, which in turn are a reminder of the attitudes which the woman is struggling to be free of. The mother and her nine-year-old daughter are making cupcakes for the boys at school, and decorating them with cinnamon candy hearts inscribed with such phrases as "I love you" or "Will you be mine" (echoing the book's cover illustration). At the same time, the mother is thinking about her current love affair. Images of being hooked like a fish suggest her passive and powerless role:

> He has not seen her; she can still leave. Once he turns around and looks in her direction, she will be hooked. All he will have to do then is reel her in. My mouth hurts, just thinking about it.

She is struggling to break free of this relationship, to stop being the victim. Finally, in the concluding image of the story, which is also the concluding image of the book, the narrator imagines herself having the courage and strength to walk away, to not cling to past dreams or a dying relationship, but to walk alone into an unknown future:

> Then, remembering how Sally Bowles/Liza Minelli said good-bye to her Christopher Isherwood/

Michael York boyfriend in Cabaret, she reaches her right hand over her left shoulder and, wishing that she had Minelli's green fingernails, she waves goodbye. And she doesn't look back. In my story, that is. She doesn't look back in my story.

A metamorphosis of both the particular woman in this story and of the general image of women that we all carry around with us takes place. Thomas achieves this by first drawing on the details of her own life for her stories, rather than inventing her material. She then views those details with an archaeologist's "detachment," as "shards," which is what life becomes when separated from the paradigms of myth and story. Having de-constructed the traditional images of women in this and preceding stories, by giving us "real" mothers in actual situations, she then reconstructs, out of the material at hand, new models—both "real" and imaginary. Like a good anthropologist, though, she recognizes the subjective and tentative nature of the reconstruction: "And she doesn't look back. In *my story,* that is. She doesn't look back." The change in both the form and process of the story brings a transformation of the image.

Coral Ann Howells (essay date March 1986)

SOURCE: "No Sense of an Ending: *Real Mothers,*" in *Room of One's Own,* Vol. 10, No. 3/4, March, 1986, pp. 111-23.

[*In the following essay, Howells examines Thomas's story endings in* Real Mothers, *noting that their indefiniteness signals the still-unexplored territory in modern women's lives of revising male-centered myths of human relationships.*]

> And she doesn't look back. In my story, that is. She doesn't look back in my story.
> Audrey Thomas, **"Crossing the Rubicon"**

This is the ending of Audrey Thomas' last story in her collection **Real Mothers,** and while it may be the end there is no sense of an ending here. Instead of closure, the effect is one of disruption of a story (or a storyteller) divided against itself in an exposure of fiction making and the failure of fiction and real life to coincide. Arguably such an ending is appropriate in a collection whose very title signals the gap between social fictions and the particularities of women's experience, and it is with Audrey Thomas' treatment of narrative as a feminist issue that I am concerned here. Feminist critics have talked a great deal about women's problematic relationship to the literary tradition we inherit, and it is female creative writers who confront these same problems in their fiction. What kind of stories do women tell and how do we tell them? Is it possible for women to tell stories that are closer to the social and sexual realities of modern life and so to revise or even unwrite the old romantic fantasy narratives we have inherited? Audrey Thomas explores women's dilemmas with exceptional clarity in the stories in *Real Mothers*, some of which are about women who write fiction and all of which are about women who are trying to rewrite the stories of their own lives in order to live differently.

Such stories of resistance and refusal are bound to be at odds with the maxims and mottoes of our culture just as they are bound to be at odds with plot closures. No sense of an ending is possible for nothing is finished; everything is in process. These women are making choices, transgressing the conventional limits of womanliness, and facing the consequences of such disruptions of order in their own lives. It is likely that the shapes of their stories will reflect dissent, disruption and self-division. It is not that Thomas is uninterested in the formal qualities of an art object; one of her stories begins with a sentence found in a guidebook in the Jeu de Paume: "A picture must be built up by means of rhythm, calculation and selection" ("**Galatea**"). In a similar way her stories are carefully contrived verbal constructs which offer a critique of inherited literary conventions just as they question and criticise inherited codes of thinking and feeling. They may be read as strongly feminist stories, sharing in the same enterprise that Lorraine Weir outlined as an appropriate mode of feminist criticism in an essay ["Wholeness, Harmony, Radiance and Women's Writing"] in this journal in 1984:

> It seems to me that we need to critique the very concept of wholeness which in all its forms has held us captive, often unknowingly complicit.

"Wholeness, harmony and radiance" is a phrase that occurs in another of these stories ("**Natural History**"), only to be shown up as an illusion. It may be that these classic criteria are not universally appropriate for every work of art; maybe fragmentation and contradiction have to be written in as well, and maybe tentative endings are the only appropriate ones for women's stories now.

[Thomas] uses the language of male discourse in order to show how it needs to be radically revised in order to accommodate women's experience and knowledge.
—*Coral Ann Howells*

Certainly the titles of many of the *Real Mothers* stories allude to male literary tradition and cultural history, for example "**Galatea**" (the name of Pygmalion's female statue who came to life), "**Out in the Midday Sun**" (with its ech-

oes of the Noel Coward song about mad dogs and Englishmen), "**Déjeuner sur l'Herbe**" (where of course it was the women who were naked in Manet's painting), or "**Crossing the Rubicon**" (a reminder of Julius Caesar's irreversible act of transgression). "No names of mine" as Adrienne Rich would say, and this is surely the point of Thomas' allusions. She uses the language of male discourse in order to show how it needs to be radically revised in order to accommodate women's experience and knowledge. The stories explore the problems that literature has always explored: problems of freedom and love, infidelity and betrayal, problems of choice and responsibility, the problematic gap between fiction and reality. None of this is new but the angle from which the problems are considered is different, for all these stories are written from a woman's point of view. As we might expect, Thomas' women dissent from the traditional roles and domestic plots in which they find themselves implicated as mothers, wives and lovers, and yet their resistance is always a double game where denials provoke unexpected yearnings for what they are losing/have already lost. Their doubts and guilts are written into the stories, showing just how problematic women's relations to cultural traditions really are.

The three stories I shall consider in some detail—"**Real Mothers**," "**Out in the Midday Sun**," "**Crossing the Rubicon**"—are all attempts by women characters to write new female plots and they all have endings where nothing is finalized. The first story ends on an uncompleted sentence, "**Out in the Midday Sun**" ends in a question, and the last story, as we have seen, exposes the gap between fictional plots and the plotlessness of real life.

"**Real Mothers**" is a story about family relationships and their breakdown when the mother steps out of her traditional role on which the family depends for its stability. It's worth looking at the title first of all, which is also the title of the whole collection. "Mother," as Thomas says in *Intertidal Life,* defines a role or a function and not any particular woman; but it is at least a more accurate signifier of a class of persons than "Real Mothers." "She is a real little mother," we say, which does not necessarily mean that she is a mother at all but simply that she is fulfilling a role within a system of cultural expectations. In *Intertidal Life* Thomas goes so far as to show that "real" equals "not real" when her narrator talks about exhibits in a museum, "lovingly restored, with a real blacksmith in a smithy . . . a real woman in a long dress and white mobcap sitting spinning or dipping candles. What 'real' would she be? Ladies and gentlemen, a real mother." The phrase is tainted with sentimentality, and it is interesting that this is one of the terms that Jacques Derrida focusses on in his deconstructionist analysis of Jean-Jacques Rousseau. Derrida says,

> We have read *in the text* that the absolute present,

Nature, what is named by words like "real mother" [mère réelle] etc., have always already escaped, have never existed, that what inaugurates meaning and language is writing as the disappearance of natural presence.

In our story "real mother" derives its powerful emotional charge from the daughters' realization of an absence or lack in their own lives: "She's not a *real* mother anymore," Patty said one day. "She doesn't love anybody but that jerk Lionel." Mothering is crucially important to children and indeed to mothers themselves, but it ought to be possible to revise such an inauthentic term as "real mothers" without irreparable damage to the family. What this painful story of grief and loss shows is how difficult it is for a woman to displace the old "real mother" concept as she tries to tell a different story about her own life within the family.

If it is a story about families, it is also more importantly a story about mothers and daughters, and its disturbing doubleness comes from its being told from the adolescent daughter's point of view. When the story begins, "Marie-Anne's parents had been separated for about a year" as her father had gone to live with one of his female students. It is Marie-Anne who has a privileged view of her mother's secret life, thanks to the mysterious arrangement of the hot air vents which carry sounds directly down from her mother's bedroom to the basement where she sleeps with her little sister Patty. She hears her mother crying in the nights after the separation; she hears when the middle-of-the-night weeping stops; and she also hears the sounds of her mother's lovemaking when the new boyfriend moves in. These muffled sounds run like a subtext beneath the actions of the narrative, bearing witness to the woman's story and accompanying the adolescent girl's pain and confusion at the changes in her mother. The father's desertion does not break up the family; on the contrary it brings them more closely together with their mother at the centre, and plainly the family can absorb a variety of changes in routine with their mother going on a diet and going back to school so long as she belongs only to them and fulfills her traditional role as (deserted) wife and mother. She alone provides the guarantee for all the old stories of ordinary family life with its small crises and its happy times which already belong to the past:

> Sometimes, looking back on all that now, Marie-Anne felt as if someone had been telling her a continuous fairy story—or a long and beautiful lie. Or had she told it to herself?

Her mother has to carry the burden of proof about the past just as she must provide the model for her daughter's emergent womanhood. At this vulnerable stage, Marie-Anne needs to identify with her mother's femaleness as maternal but definitely not sexual. This close mother-daughter relationship in the absence of men is a symbiotic one as each confirms the value of the other in the paradoxical coexistence of innocence and experience.

The delicate ecology of family life registered by Thomas with such loving detail is upset when the mother brings another man into the house: "Then, her mother met Lionel and the world came to an end." The catastrophic effects of Lionel's aggressively male presence are recorded by Marie-Anne as a chronicle of her mother's betrayal of her, for not only does Lionel take her mother's attention away from her and her little sister but he also forces Marie-Anne to confront her mother's sexuality, so that it becomes the girl's painful initiation into sexual awareness as she watches her mother transgressing the limits of her "motherliness." What the mother sees as necessary in her quest to redefine herself is from Marie-Anne's point of view an intolerable disorder, a reversal of roles so carelessly formulated by her mother in her new happiness. "Sometimes, I think that you're the mother and I'm the teenager, Marie-Anne." So, family patterns shift in a way that is sickening to the adolescent girl; while her older brother accepts Lionel and her little sister spends more and more time with her father's new family, she is the one left alone. When the crisis comes, it is the result of being completely misunderstood by Lionel, who accuses Marie-Anne of being sexually jealous of her mother. His crudely Freudian reading is unacceptable (to us as to Marie-Anne) because he cannot see, outsider that he is, how his arrival has disrupted the inner continuity of the mother-daughter relationship.

But though he cannot see this, it is encoded in Marie-Anne's Alice in Wonderland nightmare:

> Just before dawn, she fell asleep and had a strange dream that all the people upstairs were dancing on enormous black and white squares of polished marble, and that, suddenly, they began to slip and slide, and all their legs broke off at the ankles. She could hear the screams, the screams, the screams.

The idol with the feet of clay lurks beneath this dream of disorder and breakage, where necessarily related parts are painfully separated. As the dream images Marie-Anne's own anguish, so it prefigures the choice she must make and gives a veiled warning about the outcome of this choice. Marie-Anne acts on the dream the very next morning by going secretly to her father in what amounts to a betrayal of her mother. So it is arranged that her father will come to take her and her sister to live with him and his new wife. The story ends, however, not with arrangement but with disarrangement, for as the girls depart with their father in his car,

> her mother dashed down the front steps, barefoot in the snow, her dressing gown open, screaming at

them, pounding on the car window, running after the car and shouting, "Don't take my baby from me, don't take my baby from me, don't take. . . . "

Marie-Anne's nightmare spills over into real life as her mother screams.

It is a frightening story about a double betrayal where mother and daughter each become monstrous from the other's point of view. Yet neither the mother nor her daughter has succeeded in rewriting the old story of women's dependence; they are both still seeking male rescuers in fathers or lovers. Though all is changed utterly, nothing is resolved in this story of a woman's attempts at revision which collapses into a story of female failure and guilt, bequeathed it seems from one generation to the next.

"Out in the Midday Sun" with its echoes of Noel Coward's brittle English comedies is another story about betrayal and a woman's secret life, though this time it is not about failure nor is it about mothers. The action takes place in a setting worthy of Coward himself—in Africa at the Majestic Hotel, "one of the old pre-Independence hotels dating back to the early days of the Kenya-Uganda Railway," where a Canadian woman and her husband are on holiday. And the trappings of the story are Coward-like too: drinks on a vine-shaded veranda, a planned safari trip, and a crucial letter which the woman knows will spell the end of their marriage when she tells her husband about it. The woman's secret is presented in the language of an illicit love affair and it may (or it may not) come as a surprise when we discover that what she has been doing is writing a novel. The story begins to look like a parody of a Coward scenario and plot, though there are allusions to Hemingway's African stories as well, which introduce an undercurrent of savagery never to be found in Coward.

Women writing is one of Thomas' favourite topics and she uses writers as protagonists in *Prospero on the Island, Latakia, Intertidal Life,* and in this story as in **"Crossing the Rubicon."** Writing is presented as one of the most effective ways of women's resistance and self-definition, though celebration of their achievement is always undermined by deep unease and guilt about what they have been doing. This woman's writing life has been as secret as Jane Austen's, carried on like a deception behind closed doors "in a tiny storage room, windowless, almost airless, next to the British Council Reading Room in Athens" when her husband thought she was learning ethnic dancing, so that her achievement does look like the equivalent of betrayal. The language of the love affair, far from being simply parody, is deeply appropriate for she sees herself as an "infidel" and her writing as the worst kind of infidelity, which in a real sense it is. Not only has she been keeping "the essential part of herself" hidden from her husband but through writing she

has discovered her need to be independent of him and to opt for a "strange freedom"—strange to herself as well.

As she contemplates her decision to show him the letter (presumably a letter of acceptance from her publisher), several important matters clarify. She realises that her fear of her husband's leaving her is really her fear of the knowledge that she must leave him (a very Jane Eyre-like transference here; Mr. Rochester never left Jane, though in her dreams she dreaded that he would), just as the threats she feared from outside are really threats from within herself: "Africa, like a dream, had simply provided the symbols. She had refused to recognize the reality behind them." There is also her hostility towards her husband for keeping her under his spell for five years like a magician and using her as raw material for his fiction (for he too is a writer with a "ubiquitous black notebook" and a black pen "like the broom of the sorcerer's apprentice"). At the end of the story she still has not shown him the letter but she intends to tomorrow "beneath the eternal snows of Kilimanjaro," and the story ends with her imagining how he will react and how she will respond:

> He would call for champagne, as the last rays of the sun hit the fabulous mountain. . . . Would she notice every little detail of his pain. . . . Would she notice all that, and then, when she got free of him, write about that, too?

Noel Coward, Ernest Hemingway, and the woman writing all come together here in the celebration over her book, but the brittle narrative resolution is completely undermined by the cross currents of the woman's guilt and her urge to pay back her husband for the way he has used her. We are reminded of the final words of *Latakia* in that narrator's love letter to the man who has left her: "And remember, the best revenge is writing well."

We do not know what the woman's novel was about, though the question at the end prompts us to ask what kind of stories a woman might write. The last story in *Real Mothers* provides us with an example of a woman's version of a love story where it is the woman who walks out on the man. It is not a new plot, for throughout literature women have walked out on men from Chaucer's Cressida to Ibsen's Nora, but what is new is the change in narrative focus; this time the old story is told from the woman's point of view. The critic John Goode pinpointed the crucial difference between men's and women's stories when he wrote that "the subjectivity of the woman becomes an object of man's ordeal" in the work of Hardy, Ibsen and Lawrence. It is the shift to the woman as subject where we see into her mind at the moment of decision (and into the man's not at all) that marks **"Crossing the Rubicon"** as a woman's text.

Once again the title of the story is important. It is called

"Crossing the Rubicon," which in common idiom means taking an irreversible step. It was Julius Caesar who by crossing the Rubicon with an army and overstepping the boundaries of his province committed himself to war against Pompey and the Roman Senate. The title signals the pretext for this story and allusions to Caesar's career traverse the narrative. By choosing this title, the female narrator is acknowledging the inheritance of history; but then as the story goes on to show, the language of history needs some quite radical revisions if it is to accommodate women's experience as well as men's. Hers is also a story about declaring war against established powers, though the opening context of allusion to Caesar in the title and the first paragraph with its references to the ides of March and to idiots threaten subversive possibilities both for the tale and its teller, and the ending (to use another phrase from history) looks rather like a Pyrrhic victory.

Briefly, the story is about a woman who is doing several things at once: because she is a writer she is trying to write a story which she does not particularly want to write about a woman and her ex-lover in Montreal, and because she is the mother of a twelve-year-old daughter she is thinking about Valentine's Day cupcakes that her daughter is going to make for the boys at school and what this gesture signifies about male-female relationships in the 1980s. Structurally we have two stories here, not a "story within a story" for one is not privileged over the other but instead each disrupts the telling of the other and there are odd points of connection between them. There is also a third story which we are not told: why telling this story about the woman in Montreal is important to the narrator and also something she does not particularly want to do. We might be tempted to see the "I" narrator of the Valentine's Day cupcakes and the "she" of the Montreal story as doubles, but the absence of the third story problematises the relationship between them. What we get is a fragmented short story form characteristic of Thomas' "collage technique" which juxtaposes fragments of the narrator's story about her daughter and her thoughts about Valentine's Day with stretches of the Montreal story. The end of the Montreal story is also the end of the narrator's personal story. Do we read one as a comment on the other? There are certainly points of connection, but the relationship is unstable throughout and the ending emphasises the gap between the two alternative stories that the woman has been telling.

The story about the cupcakes and the Valentine candy hearts with their mottoes is the old female plot about women's romantic fantasies: "Nothing ever really changes." In the 1940s her sister and a girlfriend had made food to impress the boys on Valentine's Day and the boys had not been particularly appreciative, yet here are her daughter and a girlfriend thirty years later still making cupcakes for the boys and her daughter saying, "I don't know why I like him; he's not *nice*." Her mother tells her, "Niceness doesn't seem to have much to do with it." As if to confirm this fundamental lack of change, the narrator recognises the mottoes as being the same as those in the 1940s: "TO EACH HIS OWN," "WHY NOT SAY YES," "BE GOOD TO ME," "LET'S GET TOGETHER," "KISS ME," "BE MY SUGAR DADDY," "LOVE ME." It's the same old romantic plot encoded on the hearts. As the narrator says, they don't seem to taste as nice as they used to: "These leave a bitter taste. . . . But the taste isn't the important thing, it's the mottoes." The old myths seem to have the power to survive social change.

It ought to be possible now to tell a different version of a love story about a woman's victorious resistance to these clichés, and that is what the narrator manages to do in her Montreal story. It is a very interesting story about a woman's efforts to reverse traditional roles in a male-female relationship, and in the end it is she who crosses the street and walks away from her "ex-lover, her love." This is her crossing of the Rubicon, her irreversible step, her challenge to the established order—and it is all the consequence of her very feminine demand, "Tell me that you miss me" which the man refuses to do. The end of the story is precariously balanced: is crossing the Rubicon irreversible when it is only a street? From the other side the man finally calls out, "I miss you, you bitch!" The woman stops, and she only succeeds in making her grand gesture and waving goodbye when she remembers the end of the film *Cabaret* where Liza Minelli waved goodbye with such panache of green fingernails to Michael York—and that film was based on another story by a man, Christopher Isherwood, who was a homosexual. That ending is double-edged and so indeed is the ending of the narrator's own story with its sudden shift in narrative distance:

> And she doesn't look back. In my story, that is. She doesn't look back in my story.

So, who is to beware the Ides of March or indeed of February? Is it the narrator? Is it her daughter? Is it the "she" in Montreal? Or is it the reader? And is telling this story of a crossing of the Rubicon for the narrator as well as for her character? What is outside the fiction, and what is inside it? Irreversible gestures show a dangerous tendency towards reversals here.

These stories write in women's doubts and fears and self-divisions so that carefully ordered verbal and narrative structures are disrupted by contradictory undercurrents of feeling. It is a precarious procedure for women to try to write new stories, as Thomas shows; but that is no reason not to do it. As she says on the back cover of **Real Mothers,**

> Women are busy charting new seas and fixing new boundaries, fearful that perhaps the world is flat af-

ter all. . . . But still questing, still moving, still sailing on. These are the women I am particularly interested in.

The point in this feminist revision of the heroic explorer image is that the uncharted seas are inside as well as outside the female psyche; the woman telling the stories is both the sea and the ship, and these stories with no sense of an ending are pages out of a logbook written while the explorer is "all at sea."

Sharon Thesen (essay date March 1986)

SOURCE: "Who to Feel Sorry For: Teaching 'Aquarius'," in *Room of One's Own,* Vol. 10, No. 3/4, March, 1986, pp. 103-04.

[*In the following essay, Thesen recounts teaching the story "Aquarius" to college freshmen, revealing to them the distrust they should have of the story's narrator, a disgruntled husband.*]

Audrey Thomas' **"Aquarius"** (in *Two in the Bush and Other Stories*) is a story I frequently teach in first-year college fiction. The class is usually composed of about 60% males and about 40% females. They are young, middle or upper-middle class people of the North Vancouver variety; sometimes quite cute; born in 1966 or something ridiculous; jeans and Adidas—you get the picture. The girls are usually quiet in class if not whispering or giggling, and sometimes seem embarrassed by the guys. But most often they are utterly indifferent to them. Maybe they already have boyfriends. Who knows. Who, for that matter, cares. The story **"Aquarius"** comes up in about the third week of the semester. Ostensibly, I teach it as an example of how completely point of view can dominate a subject, but I really want them to get a kick out of how the terrible, voracious Erica dominates her wimpy, whining husband. Not that you don't feel sorry for the husband: his beseeching "O Ile leape up to my God / Who pulles me downe?" is the perfect poignant moment in the story, as the former poet and lover watches the whale show at the aquarium. This husband of Erica's is in mid-life crisis. Depressed, frustrated, angry, he mentally vents his rage and disappointment against Erica, whom he blames for his present predicament, making his way from exhibit to exhibit with increasing bitterness. Each new species of fish he encounters reminds him of a correspondingly grotesque aspect of Erica's personality: the Mozambique Mouth Breeder, the Wolf Eel, the Pacific Prawn are inescapable images of "Her strength and his incredible, female weakness." Poor, nameless husband, poor third-person limited "he." The students say, "She's a bitch, an adulteress, a bully." They are disgusted. How could she act in such a way?

Why was she so mean? I ask them, "What do we know about her, really? Through whose eyes, mind, memory and imagination is she presented to us?" "The husband's," they reply. What do we know about him?—and given that, might there be some distortion in the view we receive of her? (We are engaged in figuring out "the truth" about fictional characters—never mind that the fallacy of this very pursuit has been subject to the most rigorous and interesting interrogation for the past, at least, twenty years.)

The girls perk up. The boys start flipping the pages of the story, looking for true Erica sins. "Where's Erica?" the narrator wonders, freshly assaulted by the sight of yet another strange species of marine life. He supposes she is flirting with the whale trainer, imagines he hears her laughter, accuses her of mocking his aesthetic values and pursuits. Her physicality overwhelms him; her aggressive vitality oppresses him. Even his ability to write has been stolen by her, and when he does try to write, "he could only dryly mock himself, forsaken merman, and mocking, failed again."

Eventually, someone says, "The guy's a loser." Someone else will try to determine if Erica really has affairs. They all laugh at the Chinese restaurant scene, the narrator/husband gagging, Erica licking her lips.

I once asked Audrey Thomas about the characters in this story. She said she thought they were all pretty disgusting—all except the whale, that is. The whale was the one she really felt sorry for.

Keith Garebian (review date July 1986)

SOURCE: A review of *Goodbye Harold, Good Luck,* in *Quill & Quire,* July, 1986, p. 59.

[*Garebian is an India-born Canadian writer and educator. In the following review of* Goodbye Harold, Good Luck, *he praises Thomas as a keenly sensual writer.*]

In her introduction to this collection of 13 short stories [*Goodbye Harold, Good Luck*], Audrey Thomas describes how her mind works through correspondences. "Connect" appears to be a guiding principle in her fiction, and she moves into thought only through her senses—particularly her visual sense.

The sensorium gets full play in this collection, in which the various stories are given far-flung settings such as England, Scotland, Greece, and Africa. But it is not merely the exotic or the vagaries of local custom that engage Thomas: her fiction is most often centred on points of view and on what Joyce called "epiphanies" of truth. Whether it is a broken-hearted woman with a divided self (**"The Man With Clam Eyes"**), a brittle, old English spinster betrayed by physical infirmity and neurosis (**"Miss Foote"**), a middle aged mother "on the shelf" (**"The Dance"**), or a 12-year-old boy recoiling abashedly from the lurid sensuality of life (**"Local Customs"**), Audrey Thomas's protagonists draw us with them over the "stepping-stones across the floods of experience".

There are thin, pale, whimsical pieces here, but the writing at its best (as in **"Degrees," "Relics,"** and the title story) is carefully braided, and the texture is shot through with the visceral intensity of her characters, who are either in mutiny against life or find life in foment against them. The social observation is keenly satiric, the evocation of mood is well controlled, and always there is at least one graphic image that summarizes each of the best stories.

Susan Rudy Dorscht (essay date 1987)

SOURCE: "Blown Figures and Blood: Toward a Feminist/ Post-Structuralist Reading of Audrey Thomas' Writing," in *Future Indicative: Literary Theory and Canadian Literature,* University of Ottawa Press, 1987, pp. 221-27.

[In the following essay, Dorscht explores Thomas's interpretation of the notion of self as it is depicted in language.]

Blank pages, comic strips, quotations, jokes, dreams, rhymes, newspaper clippings, ads, etymologies, multiple selves, silence: what we have traditionally referred to as the writing of Audrey Thomas is obsessed with the contextual, contradictory meanings, and meaninglessnesses, of words, with the ways subjectivity is represented, in fact present only, in and as language. When I say "the writing of Audrey Thomas" then, I mean to point out the duplicity of the phrase. The words "the writing of Audrey Thomas" may refer to those texts which, because of our particular ideology of literary production, we say have been written by Audrey Thomas, or they may suggest that *writing* in fact speaks the historical figure Thomas as much as it does "you" or "I." In an important sense, what we call "Audrey Thomas' writing" is a writing "about" a necessarily fictional self. But I want to point out the literal sense of the metaphor "about" which suggests not a centring on but a marginality. As we all are, "she" is constructed around and out of many discourses. The "I" speaks, not as the voice of personal experience, but as the shifter, as the absent presence within the text.

To call the "I" an absent presence or a lack which constitutes subjectivity is to describe what is very often the "subject" in and of "Thomas' writing." But the theory of the constitution of the self as a constitution of division, partialness, absence, is more exactly (obscurely?) articulated

in Lacanian psychoanalytic theory. Lacan's theory of the self is, I think, implicit in Thomas' work and undermines not only the assumption which so many readers bring to "novels" like *Mrs. Blood* (1970) or *Latakia* (1979), that they are "purely" autobiographical, but the entire concept of an autobiographical writing—a writing of the biological self.

In *The Subject of Semiotics,* Kaja Silverman stresses that the Lacanian subject is almost entirely defined by lack. It is a subject which speaks only by becoming aware of its radical *différance,* its ex-centricity, its "other" ness from itself. In Lacan's formulation, the subject speaks, not out of a sense of essential self-hood, but out of an awareness of its continual loss of stable identity in speaking. In Thomas' work this self-alienating sense of self is played with in the dual Mrs. Blood/Mrs. Thing voices of *Mrs. Blood,* in the Isobel/ Miss Miller voices of *Blown Figures* (1974), and in the Munchmeyer/Miranda voices of *Munchmeyer and Prospero on the Island* (1971). I find it troublesome therefore that so much attention has been paid to what are called, without question, the autobiographical aspects of Thomas' work. As Anthony Boxill has concluded, for example, "in spite of the basic dissimilarity between the characters . . . one always has the feeling that Audrey Thomas' work is substantially autobiographical." What is the status of the "dissimilarity," of the difference, in a Thomas text? Who is the "one" unified self who "feels" that the work is autobiographical? What is "substantial" about a writing as full of blank pages as Thomas'? I suggest rather that, as current psychoanalytic and deconstructive theory does, the writing of Audrey Thomas asks us to reread our notions of what constitutes not only the "self" but concurrently the autobiographical self.

Munchmeyer and Prospero on the Island is a piece of writing which insists that the self is multiple. "I" speaks for and as Munchmeyer, Miranda, Munchmeyer as "author," Miranda as "author," and so makes us aware that it is, if anything, sexually indifferent. *Blown Figures* is constructed out of scraps of writing from newspapers, dictionaries, nursery rhymes, and so resists the authority of "one" who would speak. *Latakia* explores the ways that "letters"—languages—are based on and created out of absence: that we "write" to those we love not only when they are absent, but also because they can never be (in the Lacanian sense) fully present to us. Within this context, Thomas' writing may be read usefully in terms of much French feminist theory which asserts that "woman," like the self, is a social construct and not a natural phenomenon. Jacques Derrida writes

> it is no longer possible to go looking for woman, or for woman's femininity or for female sexuality. At least they can not be found by means of any familiar mode of thought or knowledge—even if it is impossible to stop looking for them.

Julia Kristeva makes the same argument when she says, "in 'woman' I see something that cannot be represented, something that is not said, something above and beyond nomenclatures and ideologies."

In postmodern texts, Kristeva sees attempts to signify this phenomenon of writing through tests of the "limits of language and sociality . . . without reserving one for males and the other for females." Attention must be paid, Kristeva says, to the "particular aspect of the work of the avant-garde which dissolves identity, even sexual identity." An exemplary piece of avant-gardist or postmodernist fiction, *Blown Figures* shows the ways in which, as Michael Sprinker explains,

> every text is . . . a weaving together of what has already been produced elsewhere in discontinuous form; every subject, every author, every self is the articulation of an intersubjectivity structured within and around the discourses available to it at any moment in time.

With its "blowing of figures," *Blown Figures* is a writing concerned with and aware of the inevitable shifting of identity in the slippage of the signified. Isobel's recognition of linguistic shift makes her aware of the always present "other" possibilities available on the paradigmatic chain. On a typical, and otherwise blank, page in *Blown Figures,* for example, are the words

> cild-child. My cild was killed. My child was chilled. In my womb, the cild-hama, the child curled like a shrimp or a sea-horse and clung to the slippery decks.

Barbara Godard has noted that one of Thomas' most common metaphors for the problematic nature of language is "travelling in foreign countries, adrift on the cross-cultural confusions and the multiple meanings of words." In *Blown Figures* and *Mrs. Blood* the foreign countries include the textual surfaces of Africa, the unconscious, and the "real" world that we, in the twentieth century, all inhabit and are inhabited by. In each case, the "universe" is represented as fragmented, disjointed scraps of writing. The self is available as that which is absorbed within and created out of a culture that, like the reader, is "present" only in discourse. Isobel's story is one of "otherness" in this important sense: written out of others' words (in newspapers, dictionaries, letters), the writing reminds us that all "our" words *are* others' words, all our "selves" are always already "other."

Like *Blown Figures,* Audrey Thomas' first published short story, **"If One Green Bottle . . ."** (in *Ten Green Bottles* 1967), narrates, in a convoluted, fragmented way, the story of a "fall" from physical and mental health, the fall into (which is?) language. In so doing it represents a very early example of the postmodern world of writing that we encounter in her later work. Like *Blown Figures,* **"If One Green Bottle . . ."** self-"deconstructs," as it were. Both wrestle with the interrelations between madness and articulation, insanity and aesthetics. One of the narrating voices in **"If One Green Bottle . . ."** speaks of our attempts to organize the continuum of experience; for example,

> that's it, just the right tone . . . Abstract speculation . . . It's so simple really . . . all a question of organization . . . of aesthetics. One can so easily escape the unpleasantness . . . the shock of recognition.

In *Latakia* Rachel articulates the desire, suggested here, that language have a transparent relation to the world:

> I want a palette, not a pen. I have to say that such and such is "like" something else—I have to take the long way around when what I *really* want to do is dip my brush directly into the ocean, the sky, the sun . . . and transfer it all to canvas.

With these words Rachel expresses a desire that the "landscape" around the story become self-present. But in fact the narrative form (or lack of it) in **"If One Green Bottle . . ."** re-enacts Rachel's desire to sacrifice "the subject as subject, to a study of the changing effects of light . . . shape, tone, movement (or lack of it), not STORY." Of course, both *Blown Figures* and **"If One Green Bottle . . ."** point out that for postmodernist writing of this kind, the subject is the form.

In "The Exploding Porcupine: Violence of Form in English-Canadian Fiction," Robert Kroetsch suggests that

> Violence, physical violence, proposes an ending. . . . We must resist endings, violently. And so we turn from content to the container. It is the form itself, traditional form, that forces resolution. In our most ambitious writing, we do violence to form.

Kroetsch has also suggested that the "ultimate violence that might be done to story is silence." In terms of Thomas' work I recall all the pages in *Blown Figures* empty but for a single line, a comic strip, a newspaper clipping, a joke, or I think of all the elliptical gaps in **"If One Green Bottle. . . ."** These are silences in the midst of story; this is violence done to form.

The "one green bottle" in the title of the short story refers not only to the incomplete line in a children's song. It suggests not only the bottles of formaldehyde embryos the narrative voices recall with horror. It also, and simultaneously, signifies the "one green bottle" which is story as coherence, preserved, precariously, on the "shelf" which has been raised up (reified) as the text. If *story* should accidentally fall, which, with each fragmented line, it seems prepared to do, then what?

Like the woman in the story we each experience the miscarriage: the miscarriage of narrative (the blowing of figures). Like her, we suffer a loss of "meaning." The shift from lines like "This is the house that Jack built" to "we are the maidens . . . that loved in the hearse that Joke built" reminds us that language defines itself and us by difference, that meaning is always threatened by loss. Where there was an expected pregnancy and plenitude (in the womb or between the covers of the book), there is, after much "labour," only emptiness, what the narrator calls "this nothing." Like the woman who recalls that Mary had a sign, a "voice . . . the presence of the star," perhaps we too would be "content with something far more simple." But "dumpty-like" the story "refuses to be reintegrated." Like the woman losing her child, we are left incomplete, open, scarred. **"If One Green Bottle . . ."** is a narrative of proposition that we are invited to complete, then. What might traditionally be called a "story" is, in this case, a space of multiplicity, of many stories, none of them finished. As one of the voices in the narrative says, "the whole thing should have been revised . . . rewritten . . . we knew it from the first."

Like *Blown Figures* and **"If One Green Bottle . . ."** *Latakia* too is fragmented, but in an extremely calculated, self-conscious way. "Your books are absolutely self-centred," struggling writer/lover Michael accuses successful writer/lover Rachel. But in *Latakia* the question of self, like the question of language, is problematized again by the narrative form. In what ways is a "novel" written entirely out of letters to an/other, absolutely self-centred? Or is the self always and only created in "letters" to others?

The metaphor of the labyrinth is a helpful one in describing the structure of *Latakia*. Rachel is lost (and found) in the labyrinth of words and letters which is (a) Latakia. Near the end of the book, the definition "Labyrinth: a maze, a place full of lanes and alleys" is marked off, by straight lines, from the text that precedes and follows. All of the segments/fragments of the letter/narrative are, like the bordered spaces in which they occur, "defined," limited, so that, rather unlike the labyrinth metaphor, the narrative looks as if it "fits" together, puzzle-like, less uneasily than the haphazard structure of *Blown Figures*. These two opposing metaphors—the metaphor of the puzzle and of the maze—which may each be used to describe the structure of *Latakia*, suggest that there is an interesting tension within this piece of writing, a tension that is present in Thomas' work generally in fact, which may be described in terms of two different theories of language. While one, the puzzle metaphor, suggests that language is fully meaningful, the other, the labyrinth meta-

phor, suggests that language consists of an outward, disseminating, infinity of absence and deferral.

Shirley Neuman's and Robert Wilson's description of the labyrinth metaphor in *Labyrinths of Voice* is helpful at this point. They write

> sometimes the voices are simply illustrative; sometimes they are indications that some other mazewalker, recently, or years ago, arrived by other paths at the same juncture. Sometimes the voices concur; often they dispute with us about the path to take. There are always echoes in the maze.

Many voices speak in the labyrinth of *Latakia*. There are the echoes from other pieces of Thomas' writing—the "Horizontal Woman" from *Mrs. Blood*, bits of the Africa of *Blown Figures*, the Greek "mirror writing" of **"Rapunzel."** There are the echoes of Michael's words to Rachel, Rachel's words to Michael, Michael's words to Hester, Hester's words to Michael and Rachel, and so on. The novel is not constructed with or through a direct authorial voice—a voice that would address the reader and imply that an intended message was being adequately transmitted—but with a series of "echoes," an intertext, or labyrinth, of voices. It may be that the book is the longest love letter in the world, but because it is produced as a letter posing as a book posing as a letter, there is an important sense in which not only can it not reach the one addressed (there are many echoes in the maze), it cannot speak for/with the author(ity) it posits. Like Michael, the voice of the narrator/letter writer becomes both persuasively present and yet notably absent from the letters we are offered.

Because *Latakia* is made up of "letters" to Michael and Michael also writes to and receives letters from both Rachel and Hester, there is the sense in which all one can ever give is language. The following passage from *Latakia* suggests that writing is an attempt to "fix" our "selves," permanently, to and for the ones we love:

> In the Poste Restante, there is a pile of love letters for a guy called Karl Reicker. Practically every day another letter comes in. They are decorated with red heart-seals and little kisses. Obviously Karl is not where he is supposed to be.

But in writing (and in rereading/"receiving" our own writing) we discover that "we" are not where we are supposed to be either. Language functions not as a medium through which our selves and our intentions are channelled but, as Christopher Norris writes, as a "signifying system which exceeds all bounds of individual 'presence' and speech." Anne Archer calls the ending of the novel—which "closes" with the words "the best revenge is writing well"—a "cheap shot" and criticizes the voice for being "self-justifying." But the words at the end of the novel may be re-interpreted to suggest that the phrases "writing well" and "self-justifying" are linked in a more complex way. If we agree with Lacan that the self is both formed at, and recognized as a lack at, the moment of entrance into language, then the only place in which we *can* be "self"-justifying or, as Michael describes Rachel earlier in the book, "selfish"—literally, like selves—*is* in language, in "writing well." It is only at the site of language that we both have, and have not, selves to offer one another.

Blown Figures, "If One Green Bottle . . . ,*" and *Latakia* each make us aware that selves, like texts, are formed at the gatherings of "scraps" of writing. Like writing, identity is never original. "My" words have always already been said. "I" already am "other" than my "self" when "I" speak. As Lacan has phrased it, "I think where I am not, therefore I am where I do not think." At its most ambitious, Thomas' writing points out the ways that "her" writing is not her own, that sexual and textual identities are constructs of many overlapping, disagreeing discourses. The self as text is a palimpsest of shifting, layered languages. Significantly for feminist theory, Thomas' anti-representational, transgressive writing suggests that the differential relation that has existed between men and women, like the relation we have assumed exists between self and other, is not a difference between but a difference within. In speaking, "men" and "women" are both constituted as selves only by speaking as other(s). The possibility of a new relation exists precisely because human-sexual relations are intertextual. Thomas' writing speaks for "women," that is, for "men" and "women," when it suggests, with Helene Cixous, that:

> everything is word, everything is only word . . . we must grab culture by the word, as it seizes us in its word, in its language. . . . Indeed, as soon as we are, we are born into language and language speaks us.

Larry Scanlan (review date August 1990)

SOURCE: "Economy of the Moment," in *Books in Canada,* Vol. XIX, No. 6, August, 1990, pp. 28-29.

[*In the following review of* The Wild Blue Yonder, *Scanlan notes Thomas's ability to capture intimate and sometimes painful moments in human relationships.*]

Five years ago someone asked Audrey Thomas if at the age of 50 she had reached her peak as a writer. She coyly wondered if her questioner meant *pique,* or perhaps *peek,* and

went on to blame her father—who would say, "What's for dinner: Mother?"—for the awful puns, word play, and curiosity about language that mark both her fiction and her conversation. Thomas will disinter old jokes and word games, offering them up to her readers in the most curious places, like commercial breaks in the middle of a human sacrifice.

In her new collection of short fiction, *The Wild Blue Yonder,* Thomas continues to examine the death of a thousand cuts that men and women inflict on one another. There seems little doubt that she writes in part from experience. She once told a CBC Radio interviewer, "I think everybody writes autobiography. I think everybody writes one story, has one thing that really interests them, and I suppose what really interests me is the relationship between men and women; and how we lie to one another."

Between lies, the men and women of *The Wild Blue Yonder* are desperate for a laugh, and if the laughs are made to come too hard upon the pain, this only underscores their desperation. Audrey Thomas has concocted a brew to protect her characters against the piousness and high seriousness that such pain can generate. Admit the pain, she seems to say. Articulate it. By laughing you sidestep pain and therein lies a victory.

But before considering the stories, consider the storyteller. Five years ago Audrey Thomas took her rightful position as a writer of stature in this country. She had long been published by Talonbooks, a gutsy but tiny publishing house on the West Coast. An American from upstate New York, Thomas had come to Canada in 1959 and begun to write on Galiano Island. By 1985 she had published four fine collections of short fiction, two novellas, four novels, and several radio plays.

Thomas cadged a bit of journalism here, some teaching there, making a pittance with her fiction, and, somehow, a go of it. After her marriage ended in 1972 (the novel *Intertidal Life* rises out of those post-marital ashes), she raised her three daughters alone. At one point she burned some of her papers—the notes and roughs of early manuscripts—to start fires in her woodstove: for a writer, this is the equivalent of burning money.

Thomas concedes that these were years marked by poverty and struggle, yet there was also great joy to be had in working as a writer at home, affording an intimacy with her daughters that might otherwise have been denied. Like Joan Finnigan, another single mother who eked out a living as a writer, she drew sustenance from her children. The fiction came and it was always deemed good, but still she was on the periphery, cut off from the literary mainstream by the mountains and the short reach of her publisher. But then in 1985, *Intertidal Life* was published by Stoddart, and since then her short stories (the last collection was called *Goodbye Harold, Good Luck*) have been published by Penguin.

> The stories in *The Wild Blue Yonder* suggest that at the heart of Thomas's playfulness with words is an abiding respect for language. In one story a character observes that "Words were such powerful things. Sometimes they were like dangerous animals—once let out there was no telling the damage they could do."
> —*Larry Scanlan*

Her stories have been remarkable for their satiric insight into the sometimes awful state of human relations. Their author had early on reached her *pique,* or was that *peek*?

The stories in *The Wild Blue Yonder* suggest that at the heart of Thomas's playfulness with words is an abiding respect for language. In one story a character observes that "Words were such powerful things. Sometimes they were like dangerous animals—once let out there was no telling the damage they could do."

Words for Thomas also offer distance from pain or an occasion to laugh it off. In one story the punster Thomas has two characters trying to name a house: Inn Hospitable vies with Inn Cognito and Inn Compatible. Another story features two cats named Perché, which means both "Why" and "Because" in Italian. In one a frail, older woman who uses the phrase "at death's door" prompts thoughts of what death's door might look like. And in yet another, a woman undergoing tests for breast cancer concocts unlikely saints' names such as St. Ill, St. Ick, St. Op.—the story's running gag—to help keep her fear at bay. Some may find the Thomas brand of humour insinuating itself upon, even undercutting, the stories. They will gag on the gags.

The stories are marked by another sort of humour wherein women throw darts at male targets. Call it art imitating life: womens' fiction has begun to reflect the staggering figures on incest, molestation, sexual abuse, wife-beating, date rape, and the assorted physical and mental assaults that women are prey to. I happened to read in succession four collections of short stories by Canadian women writers—Bronwen Wallace, Diane Schoemperlen, Janice Kulyk Keefer, and Audrey Thomas—and found that they more or less shared a bleak and disparaging treatment of male characters. Here are men who betray, beat, desert, and at the very least antagonize, women. If writers are as autobiographical in their work as Thomas believes all writers are, these stories by some of Canada's finest women writers stand as a chilling indictment of what a character in *The Wild Blue Yonder* calls "men-in-general."

Meet, for example, some of the men and women in *The Wild Blue Yonder*. A woman in a story called "**Roots**" yells as her newborn son breaks through her vagina, "Why are there men?" "**In the Groove**" includes a woman, separated from her husband and given to wearing a T-shirt that reads, You Have to Kiss a Lot of Frogs Before You Meet a Prince. She and her friends tell jokes at the expense of men-in-general, such as this one. Question: "What's the real reason we still need men?" Answer. "A vibrator can't take out the trash." In "**A Hunter's Moon**," Zoe asks her female friend, "Listen, Annette, do we really like *them*? I'm not talking about sex. I'm talking about *like*?"

Not likeable at all is Larry, the male protagonist in the last-mentioned story. The story is also about one woman's betrayal of another, but Larry is so acutely disagreeable that he—more than the story itself—lives on in the reader's mind, like a bad smell from a fridge. He and Annette occasionally share a bed, but little else. Stoned and reckless at the wheel, he attempts to alleviate Annette's fears about his driving by calling her "poor bunny." He is "the kind of person you'd be sorry, later, that you've told the story of your life to." He is bald and self-absorbed. Toast crumbs gather at the corners of his mouth. He is the kind of man a woman can talk to on the telephone and watch "The Journal" at the same time; the kind of man whose pelvic thrusts inspire in Annette thoughts of the nine-times table, the names of the American states, or the conjugation of the French verb être. When she does dismiss him, she does so with satiric finality.

But why did Annette even let this jerk get close to her? How could she feel even the slightest twinge of jealousy when he made advances to Zoe? Thomas offers her readers more hard questions than easy answers. In "**Roots**," a broken teapot comes to symbolize the differences between a husband—who has Thomas's love for language—and wife. At story's end, the wife has caught up with her husband at a petting zoo, and wonders what her sons will remember of this day, years from now. Will it be the black lamb the kids are petting, the Japanese couple her husband is photographing, the dandelions flourishing, "or their father and mother shouting about a teapot broken on the kitchen floor?" For parents, it is a haunting question.

This economy of the moment is reminiscent of the work of the late Raymond Carver, a fine American writer who could have asked that very same question. Like Carver, Thomas offers to her readers a kind of literary shorthand. The stories may seem slight at first, but their effect amplifies over time. Nor are all the stories written in this evidently simple, at times naif, style. "**The Slow of Despond,**" about a missionary's wife who goes mad and murders her own child, moves fluidly from past to present. The stories are marvelous in their range: **"Ascension"** is a touching piece about an older Greek woman who lures another, much younger woman out of self-imposed exile. **"In the Groove"** is told from the viewpoint of a young boy just beginning to feel the power of adolescent anger. **"Trash"** is a disturbing story about a Vancouver landlord and tenant, about the respective lots of the privileged and the dispossessed. **"The Happy Farmer,"** about a woman being harassed by a male neighbor, reminded me of a Bonnie Burnard story in which men in a pickup truck follow a woman in a car. Both stories describe the particular fear that only women, hunted women, can know.

The title story is the sad, funny tale of a wonderfully imaginative man who returns scarred from the Second World War and finds a job as a Mr. Peanut: dressed in papier-mâché shell, top hat, and cane he dispenses Planters' Peanuts samples on the street. The notion seems strange but perfectly Thomas-ian, as strange as life itself; a wounded man finds consolation behind a peanut costume. At one point, he thinks of the teenage boys killed in action and concludes that had he not been shot down in the Pacific he would have deserted. "It's too wild," he says to his young daughter while laughing a pain-filled laugh, "up there in the wild blue yonder."

The wild blue yonder, the laughter and the pain: these are the chosen territories of Audrey Thomas. She navigates them with uncommon skill and bold instincts.

Kathryn Barnwell (review date January-February 1991)

SOURCE: "Tales of Gender," in *The Canadian Forum*, Vol. LXIX, No. 796, January-February, 1991, pp. 29-30.

[*In the following review, Barnwell praises* The Wild Blue Yonder, *observing that Thomas expertly portrays women made cynical by the brutality of the male arena.*]

Audrey Thomas's latest collection of short stories is an often-painful exploration of gender roles as they have been constructed in the post-Second World War period. The stories themselves are woman-centred, candid and at times deeply disturbing, revealing the frightening vulnerability of women to the "charming" ineptitude and, indeed, the murderous misogyny of men.

Many of the men are "blue-eyed boys" who, with their innocence, child-like playfulness and feckless attitude to work, manage to make the women in their lives seem cynical, uptight and humourless by contrast. They are "enchanting" even though their charm is usually a disguise: they feign soft voices and Texan accents, pretend to be Peter Pan, Andy Griffith or Mr. Peanut. But they are also dangerous: they are no respecters of a woman's boundaries, assuming they can enter her home without knocking, offer her unsolicited advice, seduce her, leave her to cope with the practical details of life, and even murder her.

What makes these actions all the more appalling is that they are all committed by "nice" men, the kind who help women with their luggage, who pay them compliments and appear solicitous of their well-being. In **"A Hunter's Moon"**, the older Zoe and Annette wonder why the young men who "hang around" them all hate their mothers. Zoe guesses "Because mothers are so powerful", to which Annette replies: "But that means they hate women like us". This is the painful conclusion which the younger women in the collection of stories have not yet reached, and which the older women can no longer avoid.

In **"The Happy Farmer"** Peter will not take no for an answer. Literally walking into Janet's life, he undertakes his seduction/invasion with a soft voice and leftover-hippie "laid-back" manner. He leaves little gifts, notes with free advice signed "Peace, your friend Peter" and shares intimate details of his life which Janet would rather not hear. Frustrated by her resistance, he pointedly leaves a bottle of Blue Nun wine on her doorstep and dope-spiked mash for her chickens, whom he refers to as "Don Giovanni and the ladies". Although she experiences his advances as "mental harassment" and wishes she could call the police for help, she realizes that they would probably just laugh at her and "give her a kindly lecture about neighbours in the country having to get along with one another". Like all "humourless feminists" who do not find misogyny funny, she feels blamed for being uncooperative. After he plays a particularly revolting practical joke on her, he expects to be forgiven, claiming, "I just wanted to break through that wall you keep around yourself—see you really express yourself emotionally." Clearly believing himself to be a latter-day Don Giovanni, he feels justified in breaking through her protective "wall". From a woman's perspective both Don Giovanni and Peter are would-be rapists masquerading as "charmers".

Janet, however, is able to turn the tables on Peter, unlike the older and more vulnerable Margaret in **"Blue Spanish Eyes"**. Left by her husband of 20 years, she thinks: "you become frightened of things that never frightened you before . . . you have lost trust." While she sees that the young man who is so kind to her on the train is "loose-limbed, dangerously so, as though he needed to be re-strung", she prefers to believe the message of his eyes which were "a bright, clear, cloudless blue". Her ingrained inclination to trust men overcomes her intuitive mistrust of this one. In this collection of stories, he proves to be the most sinister of the charming men ("I promise to be entertaining") who hate their mothers and hence all women.

The last story, from which the title of the collection is taken, is narrated by a daughter whose adored father had "gone missing" in the war and returns "risen from the dead—and strange". He tells her that had he not been taken a prisoner of war he would have deserted, that "it's too wild up there in the wild blue yonder". His refusal to assume the gender role of soldier and bravely coping, wounded veteran leads him to take several "inappropriate" jobs: one as a Mr. Peanut and later one as an orderly in the local mental hospital. Justifying his choice of occupation to his wife, he says the whole world is mad and that he would "like to go and walk amongst the harmless mad and try to cheer them up". They, of course, prove not to be harmless.

If all the world is a madhouse, then the clinical symptom is male anger directed not only against women, but also against men who refuse to be "manly". The stories in *Wild Blue Yonder,* set in several different countries and time periods, and told from a variety of points of view, seem to confirm this diagnosis.

Carole Corbeil (review date January-February 1991)

SOURCE: A review of *The Wild Blue Yonder,* in *Saturday Night,* Vol. 106, No. 1, January-February, 1991, p. 50.

[*In the following review, Corbeil lauds Thomas's aptitude for making her stories fresh and new.*]

There is very little formal experimentation, and zero posturing in Audrey Thomas's latest book of short fiction [*The Wild Blue Yonder*]. The thirteen stories are, in fact, brimming with what some would consider old-fashioned virtues: the author has compassion for her characters, respect for their struggles no matter how small, and she writes unforced narratives in a transparently lucid style.

Although the surface of Thomas's world is smooth, the tales are never predictable. This is quite an achievement, to write stories that don't call attention to themselves and yet feel exciting and alive by virtue of the territory they explore.

With the exception of the brilliant title piece, **"The Wild Blue Yonder,"** which deals with a daughter coming to terms with her father's wounding wartime experiences, most of these stories are set in the peripatetic present. They are told from wildly different points of view, all of them utterly convincing, and if there is any common thread to them at all, it

is that many of Thomas's characters are either displaced by circumstances, or in voluntary transit.

The displaced are weakened somehow by their rootlessness, though Thomas doesn't mine this theme explicitly. As a writer she is not interested in telling stories that hinge on cause and effect. What she does capture is the vulnerability and vertigo of characters trying to build a life far from their origins.

In the travelling stories, on the other hand, it is what people carry within themselves that bubbles to the surface. **"In the Groove,"** for example, portrays a young boy travelling with his dope-smoking, motorcycling father. The son is confused by the fear and loathing he feels for his father's egoism but also by his need for his father's love. What Thomas accomplishes in this story is a good indication of what she does elsewhere. While the narrative is very compressed and grounded in a detailed, realistic style, it captures subtle, contradictory feelings.

Not all of the stories in *The Wild Blue Yonder* explore small, contained moments. Violence does erupt in the least successful of the stories, **"The Slow of Despond,"** which deals with infanticide. And offstage violence frames **"Blue Spanish Eyes,"** a story that beautifully re-creates what leads an ageing woman, already a grandmother, to befriend a dangerous young man while travelling in Europe. Her hunger for genuine contact, for love that transcends the used-up category age has relegated her to, is conveyed with tender, bright-eyed realism.

These stories, like most in this collection, don't feel as if they've ever been told before, and they are refreshingly free of any special pleading, of any straining for rhetorical points. Thomas moves easily from one world to another and gives each of her characters the full complexity he or she deserves. Most of her narratives end without fanfare, softly, inconclusively, suggesting that anything can and does happen, that change often begins in small, undramatic gestures. Thomas is at the height of her powers here. These stories inspire love, as well as admiration for the grace and depth that informs them.

Ellen Quigley (essay date Fall 1992)

SOURCE: "Characters and Strategies in Audrey Thomas's Feminist Fiction," in *Essays on Canadian Writing,* No. 47, Fall 1992, pp. 43-50.

[*In the following essay, Quigley analyzes Thomas's depiction of men in her fiction, as well as her use of a wide variety of ethnicities in her secondary characters.*]

Probably more than one reviewer has commented that he is tired of all the negative male characters that populate Audrey Thomas's work, but, if the reader can get past them, there are also a lot of interesting female characters and strategies in her fiction. And, if patriarchy was not institutionalized in our private and public lives, there would be no reason for feminist struggles, which are numerous, so a feminist critique of men should not be dismissed lightly.

Most of the men in Audrey Thomas's collection *The Wild Blue Yonder* seem misplaced; they are nonfunctional or downright disgusting in their human relationships, at least with women. Larry, in **"A Hunter's Moon,"** is a misogynist, self-centred fool. Charlie, from **"In the Groove,"** is a self-absorbed macho man. Danny and Fred, in **"Trash,"** are thugs who come and go, while Peter, in **"The Happy Farmer,"** is a presumptuous, superior, male chauvinist who mentally harasses the female protagonist. The crowd of male football fans in **"The Survival of the Fittest"** cause a sick, elderly woman great distress, perhaps threatening her life by undermining her ability to survive her fearful journey. **"Compression"** contains images of a mass murderer, a male stripper as the Grim Reaper, and threatening, invasive, male technology, while **"Blue Spanish Eyes"** is a first-person account of how a woman meets, courts, and is courted by her murderer. The young murderer charms her, presents himself as innocent and trustworthy. Images and references to trust appear throughout the story. But the trust becomes an illusion, a game. Are there any trustworthy men at all? In **"The Slow of Despond,"** Gordon never really appears, but we see the way Sarah distorts herself to conform to his image and interests; we see the way male power rules. Michael, in **"Roots,"** the first story of the collection, has no psychotic tendencies, but he does walk "around with his head in the clouds," translating reality into the esoteric etymologies found in the dictionary, leaving Louise to deal with the shitload of daily life, and paying little attention to her feelings unless she explodes. The title story and last in the book is a young woman's attempt to reconcile her thoughts and feelings about her father, who comes back from World War II as a kind of misplaced person, unable to function in the world to which he returns. He is almost a heroic, romantic figure. These two stories, the first and the last in the book, act as a kind of buffer, as parentheses around a collection of horrible men. Äse and Fred in **"Breeders"** are the only two main male characters who appear normal. They are homosexual, so social alienation is implied, and Corinne is uncertain that she can trust them enough to tell them that she is pregnant.

Males are portrayed briefly in positive roles in **"The Survival of the Fittest"** (Joe is gentle and loving, and Phil and David come to the elderly Mrs. Hutchison's rescue) and in **"A Hunter's Moon"** (Sven is a good lover). But these stories largely centre on women who are drawn toward destructive men by their need for sexual relationships (**"A Hunter's Moon," "Blue Spanish Eyes"**), for protection (**"The Survival of the Fittest"**), for definition (**"The Slow of Despond"**), and for family (**"Roots"**), as well as women who are just trying to live their own lives only to have them rudely interrupted by male privilege (**"The Happy Farmer"**). These have been recurring concerns in Audrey Thomas's work from *Mrs. Blood* (1970) on.

Beginning perhaps with Alice's relationship with her daughter Flora, in *Intertidal Lives* (1984), or, formally, with female definition of the romance form in *Latakia* (1979), Audrey Thomas also centres on the woman, her perspective, and her life. The characters, preoccupations, and, in some cases, the structures of **"Compression," "Ascension," "Sunday Morning, June 4, 1989,"** and to some degree **"The Survival of the Fittest"** and **"A Hunter's Moon,"** have strong female definition.

"A Hunter's Moon" is thematically pivotal. Larry is perhaps one of the most repulsive misogynist males Audrey Thomas has ever sketched. The story is about Annette's relationship with him and the other mother-hating men who surround her. At the same time, there is some woman-centred refocusing of energy in the description of the strong and ritualistic relationship between Annette and Zöe. They bathe outdoors under a full moon, putting fragrant herbs and oils into the steamy bathwater. When Larry appears with wine, Annette calls him "Ganymede," indicating his position as servant to the women. Still, Annette's feelings for Zöe are tinged with jealousy because of Larry's attraction to Zöe, even though she fights against this, and the narrative is bracketed and interrupted by the present; physically and metaphorically speeding crazily along, as Larry drives dangerously through the mountains with Annette. Their relationship is psychologically as dangerous as the drive is physically. The only way for Annette to maintain equal ground is to become equally abusive.

In her earlier work, especially *Blown Figures* (1974), Audrey Thomas concentrates on the protagonist's pain and disjuncture, often stylistically represented by fragmented narrative—words, signs, advertisements flying about on the page and interrupting continuity. In **"The Survival of the Fittest,"** the protagonist has the least control of anyone in the collection over herself and her environment. Signs ("*CONTROLES*"), slogans ("MINI MINI MINI LOOK AT ME"), "rude songs," shouts, and a "disapproving voice from behind her left ear" intrude upon her, breaching the line that protects her privacy and the line that distinguishes the world of formal narrative from unframed chaos. The protagonist sees eyes and flashes of colour everywhere because of her hallucinatory fever, but no one can really see her, see her pain and illness. Sound and noise "bounced off the walls," there are "shouts [and] a babble of French and English," but no one will listen to her pleas for help. Still, the flashbacks and disruptions are worked fairly smoothly into the fibre of the narrative as it progresses from when the protagonist's daughter settles her on the train in Paris, through the turmoil of her journey, to when she is put on another train bound for her home in London.

The stories in *The Wild Blue Yonder* are most often compact, self-contained, short narratives. There are few loose ends or uncontrolled influences flying about. The writer controls the environment. **"Roots"** is about "smithereens"—a broken teapot—but the relationship of the couple that the story is concerned with is not broken, the two are just having a quarrel. The narrative moves gently in and out of fragments of memory (we learn how the couple came together and why they are being torn apart and that things that originally drew them together are also often those that cause tension and argument). The many, many "roots" of the couple's marriage, their lives, their loves and hates are explored. The story is balanced; at the end we return to the image of a teapot, but this time there is unity, reconciliation for the couple, and the teapot is new and unbroken. Because Audrey Thomas employs narrative structures such as this, many of the stories are more traditional than some of her earlier work, for instance *Blown Figures*. They are also more accessible to the general reader.

Latakia differs from the early work in that its structure is more explicitly female defined. While exploring the male-female struggle and the ways in which men have usurped the role of defining women, the protagonist reaches a formal romantic unity—in her movement from unity, through dissolution, to a higher unity that is traditionally tied to social identity and marriage—in that she becomes able to define herself, but, paradoxically, only with the traditionally tragic means of disjuncture and separation. **"The Slow of Despond"** is very similar in structure. We are introduced to the protagonist as a single woman. She completely alters her life so that she will be noticed and accepted by the man she wants to marry. She marries only to find that her life is no longer her own; she has become completely passive. Although she suffers depression after each of her two miscarriages, when the third foetus comes to term, she murders the baby and leaves her husband, thus effecting a traditionally tragic disjuncture. Yet in the last paragraph she is described contentedly playing the piano, in a room of her own, her own self-defined space. She has achieved a formal romantic unity.

Murdering the baby and leaving her husband are disruptive elements that in traditional male definitions of literary genres would end in tragedy. In Audrey Thomas's female definition of literary form, Sarah's life becomes distorted by the various changes she undergoes to fit Gordon's definition, culminating in the child they beget. In traditional male definition, marriage and a baby would indicate the final higher

unity of the romance form. Here (ironically combining male and female definitions of love and romance with definitions of form) they indicate dissolution of self and barriers to happiness. The murder and separation are the heroine's acts of intervention that facilitate her integration with herself, and she becomes the hero of her own story. When Audrey Thomas writes that Sarah tells Gordon she is going to the "Ladies" (so she can get away to commit her crime), perhaps she is punning with us on the formal transfer from male-to female-defined literary forms.

The most experimental story in *The Wild Blue Yonder* is **"Compression,"** with its stream-of-consciousness structure. Veronica, who has a "stone-skipping mind," tries to deal with her anxieties and fears about a mammogram and the possible results. What starts for her as a game generated from bp Nichol's *The Martyrology* ends in the contemplation of "St Ag," "The Stag at Even," "St Agatha with her breasts on a platter holding her other symbol, the dreadful pincers which had cut them off." The word-particles separate and multiply, paralleling the lopped-off body parts and cancerous growth: What if the answer is cancer? What if the cells split? C-answer. "Cancer. An ugly word. It began with a shape like a sickle or a breast with a big bite out." The particles compress language, revealing conglomerate thoughts in parts of words. Similarly, Veronica's breast is compressed by the X-ray camera, causing her to remember images and stories of death ("Death as a male stripper") and mass murder at a picnic site in Hungerford—hunger-for-d(eath). She sees the breast as a source of food, with the clinic as the restaurant: ". . . today's special was always the same at the Atomic-Paradise Café." She is aware of the irony of carcinogenic X-rays entering the body to probe for tumours.

"Compression" employs right and left body and brain imagery. When Veronica's right breast is being X-rayed, she uses mental exercises to distract herself: "Veronica was a woman who dealt with scary situations by telling herself jokes or by talking too much." While her left breast is being X-rayed, she thinks of sexual energy, death, and murder. She has to come back to have the left breast, the "sinister breast," X-rayed again, and so certain questions arise: Why? Did she move? Did they see a tumour? The combination in the story of images of right and left sides, of verbal and emotional components of self, acts to identify the breasts as complete or inclusive signifiers, like a name: "'Ma Ma,' the breast, a doublet, like what it signifies."

Although the narrative imagistically comes full circle when Veronica is served "a single poached egg" at Norma Jean's Restaurant, reminding us and Veronica of the Atomic-Paradise Café and of a breast with a lump in it, the results of the exam have not yet been received. This story awaits completion while the text spirals off toward another circle, another story, in the brief last paragraph where Veronica waits fearfully for the bus. This lack of closure is typical of a spiral-ling structure in which one story continues into another and is highlighted by the ironic perspective from which we see the egg. Women have commonly been associated with cir-cular structures of death and birth because of our gender function of bearing children. Eggs are typical symbols of this cross-species gender role. Veronica orders the egg, a life symbol, when she is contemplating death, evoking the tra-ditional search for life beyond our mortality. But this time Audrey Thomas clearly notes that the egg is poached, which destroys any true life-giving function. The ironic perspec-tive on the poached egg that looks like a breast with a lump in it also symbolically indicates the life-saving benefits of mammograms and the hazards of accumulated low-level ra-diation (slow cooking, "poaching") from frequent exposure to X-rays, especially of the breast and chest area. This is one of the most interesting and creatively structured stories in the collection, as it explores a woman's mind and its wan-derings.

Most of the stories are written in the third person. Three are first-person narratives. This technique works well in **"Trash,"** where social comment is made without preaching. At the end of this short, uncomplicated, linear narrative, the narrator writes," . . . I stepped out onto the porch and did something I've always been ashamed of. I shouted at her, as loud as I could, so the whole neighbourhood could hear, 'You're trash, that's what you are, just trash!" We wonder why the narrator is so ashamed, when the woman at whom she yells (and to whom she rents a suite of rooms) has just torn her house apart. She is understandably a little embar-rassed at the cliché she uses, but why does she continue to feel ashamed? This has to do with class, class prejudice, and gender restriction. The narrator has family, friends, a part-time job, an education, a husband who partly supports her . . . . She has a lot of support systems, but many of them are, in turn, financially dependent upon her husband. Audrey Thomas rarely makes a blatant social comment. She sketches a character complete with racial, cultural, gender, sexual-ori-entation, or class prejudices, and leaves the reader to infer the comment. In **"Breeders,"** Corinne's mother says, "At least Corinne's *normal,*" referring to her heterosexuality; in **"The Survival of the Fittest,"** Mrs. Hutchison has flash-backs to "Mammy cloth," which "Against their skin . . . and in that setting . . . really looks quite nice"; Peter, in **"The Happy Farmer,"** is a male chauvinist; Frances's mother, in **"The Wild Blue Yonder,"** entertains classist ideas ("If you are born to a certain 'station' in life . . . you don't need to be a snob").

The central characters of these stories are white, which makes sense, given Audrey Thomas's cultural background. But it is refreshing to see such a variety of cultures and races represented by her minor characters. It permits the stories to present a more accurate picture of the world in which we

live. Too often, white anglophone writers only seem to con-ceive of white anglophone characters. None of Audrey Thomas's Black, francophone, Greek, or Scandinavian char-acters are evoked in the first person, nor are they main char-acters, so we do not get the sense of cultural pre-emption. In **"The Slow of Despond,"** there are several nonspecific and alienating references to "Africa" as a homogenized whole and a reference to "heathen," among other culturally demeaning statements. Always, this is in relation to Gordon, Sarah's missionary husband, who plots and defines her life, her role in society. In Sarah's terms, we see specific and con-crete references to the talk by "Reverend Gordon MacLeod and his wife" that is to be held in "Zambia," and to the "rich, moist, sweet, excessive, smell of West Africa" that is evoked for her in the Palm Houses, an arboretum in Edinburgh. Throughout, Audrey Thomas balances specifics of Sarah's own Scottish culture (she reads *The Scotsman,*" and has "lessons in Scottish country dancing" and "weekly ceilidhs," for example) with details of life in the mission. Her young friend Comfort sends her an "Akua'ba" fertility doll, and she reciprocates by giving Comfort "a book of Celtic fairy tales and enough blue checkered gingham for a new school dress." This is not cultural appropriation in the trivial use of ethnic ornament, but a unique exchange of cultural items. This white reviewer thinks the portrayal of the connections be-tween language and ideology works in this story that de-scribes a white man's racist, imperialist culture, and its control over other people's lives, and a woman's struggle to remove herself from such definition.

Even though most of the stories in the collection are not writ-ten in the first person, we always have the sense that we are receiving the perceptions of white anglophone characters. One of the characters who is not a WASP, and who is sketched in the most detail, a character we almost come to know, is Fotula Papoutsia (in **"Ascension"**), and we have a very clear sense that we are seeing Fotula through Christine's eyes, or, more precisely, through the narrator's perception of Christine's reality. We are never given information gained from an omniscient perspective, only a third-person account of what the central character sees, hears, remembers, does. This is a very simple, lovingly created story of a friendship. A rite of passage is expressed in its governing metaphor. Christine attends to the rising and kneading of Fotula's Greek Easter bread, the "staff of life." Christine does not presume to know how to make the bread; she uses the lessons she has learned from Fotula, takes hints from the items Fotula has already prepared, and guesses. This is not Audrey Thomas's presumptive creation of a working-class woman's Greek culture; it is filtered through Christine, an agnostic, middle-class WASP: "She tried to imagine God as Mrs P must see him. . . . "

The metaphors in this story draw strongly on Christianity, which also notes that "In the beginning was the Word . . .

and the word was God" (John I.I). To imagine God is to imagine language, and to imagine language is to imagine culture. As Fotula dies, her soul is metaphorically described as yeast: "fragrant, spicy, lighter than air, gradually rising up through the April skies." She is the leavening agent in Christine's befuddled life and one of the many fascinating secondary women who now populate Audrey Thomas's fiction.

Elisabeth Harvor (review date March 1993)

SOURCE: "Mistress of Tart Remarks," in *Books in Canada*, Vol. XXII, No. 2, March, 1993, pp. 46.

[*Harvor is a Canadian educator, poet, and fiction writer. In the following review, she voices a mixed opinion of* Graven Images, *finding the novel's collage style superficial but praising Thomas's evocative descriptive language.*]

In *Terrorists and Novelists,* the critic Diane Johnson, writing about Charlotte Brontë, describes her as a writer who had the "artistic daring to risk heroines so deviant as to be plain." These words came back to me as I was reading *Graven Images,* Audrey Thomas's new novel; they recalled an early Thomas story, **"A Winter's Tale,"** whose subject is a "plain" girl who's an exchange student in the 1950s in Scotland. That early story, once you get past its didactic opening paragraph, seems to me to be one of the most undervalued stories in the whole Canadian canon. The dialogue between its two clever and lonely undergraduates (who are trying to use an undergraduate chat about God as a lever to help them go to bed together) is startlingly emotional and electric. And there's no special pleading on behalf of the young narrator, but instead a rueful self-knowledge in a not-rueful-enough decade.

Graven Images lacks that earlier story's nerve and candour. A history of the encounters and recollections of two women in mid-life who are in search of their ancestors, it contains (in excess) letters, poem-fragments, dictionary entries, parodies of carols, and so many other bits and pieces that it feels not written but collected. Of course it could be argued that all of these bits of exotica, so postmodernly laid out for the reader, are there to do the job of supplying, via style, a subtext for a novel that is really *about* collecting—collecting in the usual sense, and also in the sense that memory and family history are "about" collecting. But in order for all this haphazardness to ignite, it has to be powered by a kind of idiosyncratic searchingness, it has to have real feelings woven into the narrative disarray, otherwise it will tend to feel schematic, not inspired.

A travel writer who's beginning to tire of travel, Charlotte

(Harlotte to her friends) hopes to write a novel, and Thomas's own gifts as a travel writer work quite well to set the scenes through which Charlotte makes her way. Odd bits of social history are presented in transit—the information that Handel directed a performance of *The Messiah* at the London Hospital for Foundlings, for instance, along with the news that Hogarth designed the uniforms for the foundling children. There are also a number of luridly vivid Thomasian touches, such as this comment on Charlotte's mother's apartment: "The vacuum stands in the corner like some strange life-support system." Or this, on blood puddings: "They sound like something made from leftover placentas."

But the overall effect is not nearly so economical and lethal as this; the book instead feels bloated. I often felt as if I'd been cornered by a witty but compulsive talker—I soon got bored by all the anecdotes and cheerful historical instruction and began to feel a hunger for event, for sadness, for moments of real quiet, for the novelist's imagined "real life." But instead of drama there tended to be melodrama (not a fair substitute) and—along with the earlier-mentioned collectibles—lists and old campfire songs and jokes.

Thomas is not often a very introspective writer. She instead reserves her love for the surface of life and for the thousands of details that make up the surface; she doesn't care to go deep, preferring instead to get just under the skin—sometimes with eerie precision, as in the wonderfully evoked *haut monde* of horsy Copenhagen in an earlier story called **"Breeders."** But this preference for the surface has a tendency to make *Graven Images* seem somewhat trivial. And on the few occasions when Charlotte edges toward real feelings, she seems only to test the waters, then to deny that she felt what she felt.

The chunky shadow of the traveller's notebook falls across the novel as well, and it's also clear that Thomas often can't resist the temptation to collage even this fractured material, jazz it up. I kept missing the emotional and artistic daring of that earlier Thomas. It's possible, though, that some readers will be charmed by *Graven Images*'s travel-writer-wanting-to-become-novelist narrator, she's such a chatty and energetic mistress of tart remarks.

Gwendolyn Guth (review date July-August 1993)

SOURCE: "Imaging the Writer," in *Canadian Forum*, July-August, 1993, pp. 39-40.

[*In the following review, Guth finds* Graven Images *challenging and complex, but somewhat inscrutable for the reader.*]

Audrey Thomas' *Graven Images* is primarily a novel about writing, about the ambivalence of anchoring the flux of life in words. Thomas plays with the idea that the images that carve themselves irrevocably into memory are both fluid and fixed, both inspiration and impediment to the writer of fiction. Images graven on memory (grave images, images of the grave) expand and glow in the mind of writer-narrator Charlotte Corbett, but they illuminate only obliquely the lives of her mother Frances, her friend Lydia, and herself.

The novel opens with Charlotte and Lydia on a ship bound for England, in the fall of 1987. Each has her own reasons for undertaking the journey. Lydia, evacuated as a child from the rubble of World War II London, is in search of relatives to provide her with the identity that trauma and her adoptive American parents have effectively erased. Charlotte, a travel-writer by occupation, has both practical and personal reasons for the trip: to write about ocean liner travel for *The Globe and Mail, Departure* magazine, and the CBC; to complete her mother's family tree by tracking down the history of Robert Corbett, an obscure ancestor who emigrated to America in the mid-17th century; and—a secret project— to write a novel about her mother. When Charlotte first encounters the ship's Entertainments Officer, a no-nonsense Pole whose country distinguishes clearly between journalists and real wry-ters (those who create literature), she timidly introduces herself as a "real writer". Later, she confides to the reader her fear of failure. "Every night I must repeat to myself, I'm a wry-ter, I'm a wry-ter, I'm a real, real, wry-ter, the way we used to say I must, I must, I must increase my bust."

After three weeks in England, Lydia and Charlotte find themselves on a plane bound for Ontario. Lydia's past has resolved itself with heavy-handed facility; Charlotte has begun in earnest to write her novel.

Audrey Thomas' *Graven Images* is primarily a novel about writing, about the ambivalence of anchoring the flux of life in words. Thomas plays with the idea that the images that carve themselves irrevocably into memory are both fluid and fixed, both inspiration and impediment to the writer of fiction.
—*Gwendolyn Guth*

Disconcertingly, one wonders if Charlotte really is a writer. She spends a considerable amount of the reader's time wandering around England, searching, sorting, sifting—ostensibly for nothing, since the emigma of Robert Corbett remains unsolved. Much of the novel is taken up with Charlotte's research, its peripheral events and incidental details.

I took notes; I examined large folios of maps. I realized that I could go on doing research forever, if I felt like it, never getting down to the hardest part, turning the whole mess into something more than the sum of its parts, something that would make the world shiver and turn the pages. Something that would make the reader say, "You go ahead, I'll be up in just a little while."

Eventually, Charlotte's library trips and frequent conversations with strangers grate on the reader's nerves. Why is so much attention paid to trifles and trifling characters, to the edges of what we are interested in? Where are the basic correlations that a "real writer" is obliged to make? To what extent is Thomas culpable for our boredom if she has created an incompetent writer as her protagonist?

After a first reading, one is tempted to feel cheated by the book, as if it were merely notes towards a novel yet to be written (as indeed it might be—Charlotte's novel). It becomes clear, however, that plot does not concern Thomas (it rarely does, in her novels), and that the European trip is merely a device to facilitate some intensive introspection on Charlotte's part. What is important, what resonates throughout the novel, is the image that first impels Charlotte to fix her mother's life in fiction: the image of a baby floating dead in a bucket of water. This is the shocking childhood memory that, unsolicited, Frances Corbett suddenly divulges one day, shattering forever the ossified testiness of her nursing home existence. Charlotte becomes obsessed with the "water-baby" image; each of the italicized entries that signal her attempts at novel writing deals evocatively with circumstances surrounding the dead baby in the bucket.

"Still-life" is Frances' malapropism for "stillborn", and the term is oddly relevant to the differences between *Graven Images* and two other Thomas novels in which a miscarried child is a recurring preoccupation. In 1970, Thomas wrote *Mrs. Blood,* the first-person narrative of a white woman in Africa undergoing the horror of miscarriage. Her next novel, *Blown Figures* (1974), follows this same woman in her solitary return to Africa several years later, her pain still raw, her sanity questionable. That the reader cares more about the woman in *Mrs. Blood* and *Blown Figures* than about Charlotte in *Graven Images* seems somehow to be related to the difference between engaging an image and simply using it as a means to an end. The still-life/still-born water-baby of *Graven Images* is a fixed image, an image graven in time; it has no connection with a body, and the circumstances of both its conception and its death are left relatively ambiguous in the novel. Although its starkness provides inspiration for Charlotte's own novel, the dead child itself remains for her an image seemingly devoid of human connection. In *Mrs. Blood,* by contrast, the phrase "graven image" is linked to the words "gravid" (pregnant), "grave", and, ultimately, "grieve". The miscarried child in **Mrs. Blood** and **Blown Figures** is imbued with the significance of its having been carried within a mother's womb, its unborn life engaged with another life, its death a tragedy.

Blown Figures is a hallmark of philosophical and stylistic postmodernism: a novel about chaos and fear that may or may not conclude in utter madness; a novel of cartoons, advertisements, nearly blank pages, stylistic anarchy. Although **Graven Images** uses some of the same techniques, it is less successful as a post-modernist pastiche. One has the feeling that it is not intended as such; it seems instead to stand as a sort of misfired Graham Swiftian history-fiction—a guardedly successful juxtaposition of received and fictive, public and private histories. Thomas' eclectic writing style cribs from everywhere: etymologies, nursery rhymes, menus, scraps of poetry, geographical and geneological histories of New York state, letters from Coleridge and Dickens, dictionary definitions, Japanese tape-recorder instructions, Shakespeare, even a maxim from Karl Marx. In her fascination with the juxtaposition of different types of writing, however, Thomas seems deliberately to bury relationships under mounds of extraneous language. We never learn much about Charlotte's grandfather, for instance, the man linked in such a sinister way to the baby in the bucket. What effect did he have on his own daughters, especially Charlotte's Aunt Elizabeth, a woman driven mad in the prime of her young life? Charlotte herself is a curiously cold narrator (perhaps we are given an emblem of this in the "Frozen Charlotte" doll that she buys in England), and we do not really understand why. She seldom allows the reader to get too close to her. It is a rare poignant moment when she admits to her old habit of letting cats lick tuna from the backs of her hands, to feel the touch of their raspy tongues.

Charlotte does, however, admit to feelings of guilt about using her mother's life as material. Charlotte herself makes the astounding parallel that links her treatment of Frances with the calculated and cold-blooded way in which Lydia's first husband had literally "used" her sexually, to glean material for his book of poetry.

> I thought of L. Carradale Carter and how he had hurt Lydia. I thought of my mother and all the notes I have been keeping on her—I spy with my little eye. Bringing her presents of flowers and new warm slippers, suggesting we get out the photographs. I pick at her past as though it was yesterday's turkey. Was I a shit? Am I?

Charlotte admits to a certain kindredness of attitude with Stephen Dedalus of James Joyce's *A Portrait of the Artist as a Young Man.* She feels for her mother not love but "duty". Will she, the reader wonders, use and then repudiate her mother as Stephen does, content to forge in the smithy

of her lone soul another image, and yet another? ("Are there Viking cells left in me," Charlotte asks, "even one or two? Reduced from raider to writer, swooping down and taking what I want then leaving. 'When is a raven like a writing-desk?'") Perhaps we never discover the truth about Robert Corbett ("corbet—OFr. corbet, crow, raven") because he was a writer who used his family as a means to create fiction and so had to move to America to escape his guilt. Or maybe the mystery is intentional on Charlotte's part, because by discovering the last remaining link in the family tree, she would be allowing her mother to die—nothing else left for the 90-year-old woman to live for. Then again, Robert Corbett could simply be an enigma, another image.

Graven Images is not an easy novel to read. Thomas asks much of her readers, demanding that they accomplish what her writer-narrator Charlotte spends the novel trying to do, namely make connections. ("There are times," Charlotte says, "when I seem to be doing several jigsaw puzzles at once.") Despite its trademark wit and its tender moments, **Graven Images** is an unsettling novel. Perhaps it's too accurate a measure of our fear of engaging the elderly, the past, family, relationships in general. Detailing a struggle that pushes towards illumination but remains a struggle, Thomas presents the ambivalent point of view of a would-be synthesizer, an author.

In **Graven Images,** Audrey Thomas allows all of us to experience the irony, the contortions, the wry in wry-ter.

Laurie Ricou (review date Winter 1993)

SOURCE: "Word Work," in *Canadian Literature,* No. 135, Winter, 1993, pp. 139-40.

[*Ricou is a Canadian writer and educator. In the following review, Ricou assesses* The Wild Blue Yonder, *concluding that Thomas's wordplay creates in her stories tension, irony, and at times unparalleled beauty.*]

Audrey Thomas's typical form emerges in [*The Wild Blue Yonder*] as the sketch *engagé/dégagé.* She finds an impetus, a core story, in recent history, usually violent—the Hungerford massacre, Tiananmen Square, a generic newspaper story of a young murderer who preys on older women. In reshaping this story, Thomas expresses her strong social commitment, but more so her interest in how these public events affect the individual psyche and distort, however subtly, the narrative of the soul. Interrupting, disfiguring, and generally providing an alternative is the story that language tells itself. The metalinguistic element is not invariable, as in Daphne Marlatt, and seldom affects syntax, as in Gertrude Stein, but slides into parentheses (either actual or virtual) where homophones, morphemes, and etymologies press their case. In such byways, character and author become detached: each contemplates the universe as a labyrinth of words, and an impossible patchwork of paradox. The wordplay has a narrative function: it often diverts the story into the fantastic and then the grotesque. A reader is never sure when the placidly quotidian narrative will turn sharply into the bizarre, or when the weird will drop abruptly into a bathetic joke.

Parenthetic wordplay is the most prominent feature of Thomas's signature. "'I want to know what really gets "stroked" when you have a stroke,'" one character wonders. It's difficult to imagine Atwood, Munro or Gallant dropping in such a line with so little preparation. (Margaret Laurence, a writer with whom Thomas seems to have more and more kinship, might.) Or, if they did, they would do so mockingly, not in order to tease out the meaningful ambiguity that rests in the apparently trite echo.

Other recognizable details of Thomas's signature figure prominently in *The Wild Blue Yonder.* The motifs of blood and physical illness identify islands and mental hospitals; settings from North America and the United Kingdom overlap, in the same story, Greek and African worlds; she slips easily into children's stories and nursery rhymes, and into a style whose repetitions and simplicity accommodate themselves to these genres. Almost all the stories are about women, or from a woman's point of view, and find Thomas rethinking feminism, repeatedly noting with anguish or amusement the paradoxes and politics of sisterhood. To the familiar elements of Thomas's fiction some new ones begin to be added in this book: the colour blue and blue skies, the serenity of baking, and the telling, centrally or obliquely, of the vigils of the elderly and aging.

Not surprisingly, given the *engagé/dégagé* tension in Thomas, one dimension of this last subject is the inescapable lousiness of growing old, the ignorance evident in a society growing old ungracefully. Most interesting perhaps—and here Thomas's objective approach to language emerges again—is the reading of old age as having, or *being,* an alternative language: "Maybe she's just usin' language, usin' memory, in a way I haven't thought about before," says Charlie in an insight that follows the passage on the stroking in a stroke. One entire story **"Sunday Morning, June 4, 1989"** takes as its primary discourse the codes, and the gaps (and the decoding) of an aging mother's long distance telephone talk.

Again, Thomas seems to discover her most vivid and unusual perspectives/*ficciones* in a metalinguistic pondering. Wordplay is word work. **"Compression"** opens with a reference to bp Nichol's *The Martyrology* and uses that poem's primary deconstructive strategy ("'St Ill. He runs the infirmary.'") to question the coincidence and logic of the

Hungerford massacre, and to escape and define the account of Veronica's mammogram. In the opening story, **"Roots,"** the central male character is an inveterate, unstoppable amateur etymologist. Quietly, Thomas turns her own key strategy on its head: she appears, as it were, as a male character, and thus considers in the intimate (and uneasy) relationship of man and wife, the relationship of language-conscious writer to loving reader.

Often in my reading notes for this book I find question marks following verbs. My uncertainties indicate that the binary of *engagé/dégagé* is triangulated in almost every Thomas story by the absence where a reader expects resolution or conclusion. Usually this strategy sends me to reading and re-reading. A wife may have drowned her own child rather than live the life of a missionary to Africa. *Why?* **"Blue Spanish Eyes"** ends with an idyllic flirtation, but it begins with a brief piece of journalese that points to an incomprehensible rape and murder. *Who?*

The narrative gaps are a way of extending the *engagé/dégagé* irony. The stories are left in suspension—for reader or character are frustrated, hypnotized curiosity. Such a pattern compels attention in almost all the stories, and nowhere more intriguingly than in **"Ascension,"** for me the strongest story in the collection. **"Ascension"** searches for the psychologies of a friendship between an island tourist and a resident Greek mother, and discovers the shared perceptions of very different women coming together in their necessarily shared lives. The story ends with a bizarre turn and a narrative gap *and* with a skillfully old-fashioned tying up, by Thomas's repeating with alterations the story's beginning. Mrs. Papoutsia will "try make bread in space." Christine will also rise up lighter than air. This blue yonder is truly an ascension to celebrate.

Virginia Tiger (essay date 1993)

SOURCE: "The I as Sight and Site: Memory and Space in Audrey Thomas's Fiction," in *Canadian Women Writing Fiction,* edited by Mickey Pearlman, University Press of Mississippi, 1993, pp. 116-25.

[*Tiger is a Canadian writer, educator, and broadcaster. In the following essay, she analyzes Thomas's autobiographical construction of her characters' memories and its effect on her definition of female space and self-exploration.*]

Novelist of memory, Audrey Thomas has hewn from autobiographical momenta both stable and unstable narrative foundations for her houses of fiction. That fiction, thematically and structurally, is recognizable by its continuous delight in repetitions. Also characteristic of Audrey Thomas is her successful delivery of and flair for what I would here call a legend of self-projections; British Columbia's answer to Colette, Thomas is a writer of very specific witness whose world is bounded by family, flora, fauna, and that intertidal life whose symbolic soundings resonate especially distinctly for women and upon whose meanings she has both predicated and titled one novel. Part of her interest (possibly even a large part) lies in her public invitation to have the heroines of her prose be identified with the author of that prose.

This may well have been the Canadian response to its women writers in the sixties and seventies. Like Margaret Atwood and Marian Engels, Thomas was first patronized by reviewers as a kind of latter-day 'scribbling lady' at the same time as her readership (like theirs) grew because of the emerging interest in Canadian writing. Born of middle-class New England parents in a dissolving domestic and economic unit, she was to propel herself away, traveling from and to places: out of New York state to England, to Canada, to Africa. With the birth of three daughters and a separation and then divorce from her husband, her connection to British Columbia's Galiano Island, (a ferry ride away from the city of Vancouver) and the Canadian West Coast grew to be a firm and felt commitment. Yet the voyaging impulse in her has remained strong, the outward and visible counterpoint to those inward journeys of the creative imagination. Looking through the fiction, we can see figured the landscapes to which she has traveled, their contours frequently distorted by a questing, self-conscious, and distracted narrator. From work to work, one kind of female protagonist recurs, as do the reiterative narrative episodes she inhabits.

"Everything Thomas writes is a companion piece to everything else," observes a fellow Canadian, Margaret Atwood. "More than most writers, [Thomas] is constantly weaving and reweaving, cross-referencing, overlapping, even repeating her materials." In the linked narratives, we meet the presiding figure of the author's imagination—a woman longing for the pastoral domesticity of husband, children and island life, yet bolted into voyage and action by sexual love and an equally uncontrollable passion for words, words as puzzles, words as refrains, words as wizards. We also encounter the presiding preoccupations that surface, fleshed or told from various vantages in the various books: the lost child, the madhouse, the male abandoner, the process of female creativity, the act of writing with its dislocatory distortions.

Audrey Thomas is never the inventor; having little of the fabulist in her, she seldom spins the kinds of plots that, for instance, Margaret Drabble, Toni Morrison, Doris Lessing, Margaret Laurence, or Iris Murdoch can create. Rather she is a storyteller who filters a good part of her fictional world through the retrospective consciousness of her chief creation: a narrating self. "Your books are absolutely self-centered," accuses *Latakia's* Michael, charging that novel's prolific writer Rachel with the very insularity critics have ascribed to Thomas. Fictively self-indicted as she may be, the novels and shorter fiction alike seem to slide across each other's borders as stories are told and retold with slightly different emphases. Thomas's attraction to the etymology of words and her pointed play with puns, nursery rhymes, literary refrains, and intertextual allusion add to the overall sense of the fiction's narcissistic circuitry and its dissolution of conventional boundaries between what has actually happened and what is being imagined. "Writers are terrible liars," as the first line of the story **"Initram"** (from Thomas's ironically titled second collection *Ladies and Escorts*) willfully announces.

All in all, hers is a narrative technique that relies on disrupting the linearity of sequence as well as sentence. My argument in this essay is that Audrey Thomas's "transgressive" method amounts to more than mannered and self-indulgent experiment. Rather, its very discontinuity allows the random movement of memory its own depiction. Conversely, memory shapes method, a point underscored by one of the voices in **"If One Green Bottle . . ."** (the title—and important—story from Thomas's first collection, *Ten Green Bottles*), who observes: "the whole thing should have been revised . . . rewritten . . . we knew it from the first." What makes these memory works especially intriguing is the author's way of burrowing into a female "I" that navigates sight as well as site. To explore the geography of the inner life is to reach the shores not only of identity but its place in space. For Thomas believes what she has her writer/heroine in *Intertidal Life* determine when—reading the "voyages of exploration, about the search for the Northwest Passage, about brave bold men in their rickety boats"—she wonders: "The turn of women, now, to go exploring?"

For Thomas, writing about self inevitably embraces the metaphor of exploration, its trajectory of search shaping the interrogations of her consuming interests: female identity, female sexuality, female socialization, female physiology and—above all—female creativity. Insight also inevitably embraces sighting the site where domestic sphere can become powerful female space.

> The mothers don't need mirrors—they have created creatures in their own image. [*Munchmeyer and Prospero on the Island*]

> My first "real" story . . . *had* to be written, it seemed . . . the only way I could organize the horror . . . of a six-months long . . . miscarriage in a hospital in Africa. [**"'My Craft and Sullen Art': The Writers Speak—Is There a Feminine Voice in Literature?"**]

A prolonged miscarriage is the central event in Thomas's first shorter fiction, **"If One Green Bottle . . ."**, (in *Ten Green Bottles,* 1967), just as a horrific mummified homunculus on public display in a Mexican museum is the central symbol in a later story, **"The More Little Mummy in the World,"** from her second collection, *Ladies and Escorts,* 1977. Similarly, Thomas's first novel, *Mrs. Blood* (1970), and her third, *Blown Figures* (1974), are requiems for the lost child, retelling the painful experience from the fractured perspective of Isobel Carpenter, the narrator of each novel. The same Isobel Carpenter also narrates *Songs My Mother Taught Me* (1973), the trilogy's first volume and one that chronicles its protagonist's childhood, adolescence, and young adulthood in New York state during the forties and fifties. In what appears to be a conventional first-person female bildungsroman (divided chronologically into the "Songs of Innocence" of childhood and the "Songs of Experience" of adolescence), the book sketches Isobel's efforts to elude the conventional world offered to her by her embittered mother, a departure successfully embarked upon in the narrator's seventeenth year when she takes a job as an aide in a lunatic asylum. There she rids herself of her "mind's virginity" at the same time as she shakes off her body's innocence through sexual initiation.

Any examination of *Songs My Mother Taught Me, Mrs. Blood,* and *Blown Figures* must begin (as one critic suggests) "with the strong centre of consciousness or perspective which is characteristic of them. This centre is either Isobel's own voice, the 'I' of personal communication and dream-thought intelligence, or the more limited narration used in *Blown Figures* where the narration moves away from the character infrequently while remaining in the third person." Two voices predominate in *Songs My Mother Taught Me*—the narrator referring to herself as "I" as well as "she"—and this strategic doubling will again be adopted by Thomas in *Mrs. Blood,* the novel whose narrative action involves an unnamed narrator seeing herself in two figures: Mrs. Thing, Feminine Mystique wife of an Englishman teaching at the University of Ghana, and Mrs. Blood, Female Eunuch memory-mordant, reliving past erotic adventures and the guilt attached in that epoch to female sexuality. A miscarriage forms the bloody base of this novel, the memory of which propels a solitary Isobel some five years later back to Africa in the trilogy's third volume, *Blown Figures.* Thematically situated somewhere between the adolescent longings of *Songs My Mother Taught Me* and the maternal disintegrations of *Mrs. Blood,* the Isobel Carpenter of *Blown Figures* has several mutating personae, their multiplicity contributing to her unreliable witnessing of her own unraveling. Miscarriage, maternity, sexuality: each remembrance blows the protagonist further into Africa and through a psychic journey, whose steps are less actual and material than overcharged and psychological.

However determined are the novel's ambitions to infect its imagined world with a disease of contending points of view and a plague of contentious interpolated plots (newspaper articles, cartoons, billboards, personal columns, recipes, nursery rhymes, African chants and rituals, advertisements), *Blown Figures* exhausts. "Epitome of [the] narrative mannerisms Thomas has used and would use" [Louis MacKendrick, "A Peopled Labyrinth of Walls: Audrey Thomas' *Blown Figures,*" in *Present Tense: A Critical Anthology,* 1985], its failure as an engaging and affecting novel seems aptly enough summarized in the comments of another of Thomas's female protagonists: Rachel, the writer who narrates the novel *Latakia* (1979). "Yes, the pain is there and very real, but where is the organization? She is at the beginning of a long, long road."

Latakia and its earlier companion, *Munchmeyer and Prospero on the Island* (1971), are novels distant from the Isobel Carpenter trilogy to the degree that each is a kunstlerroman, or portrait of the (female) artist. Both *Latakia*'s Rachel and *Munchmeyer and Prospero on the Island*'s Miranda are writer/narrators whose shared obsession with the nature of writing focuses on how storytelling can go about telling the truth. Both are islanded (and eye/I-landed): Rachel in Crete is writing "the longest love-letter in the world" to her departed lover, and Miranda is spinning her diary/novel on the West Coast's Magdalena Island. Each discovers that the site set aside for their creativity offers insight into that creativity. Though neither Miranda nor Rachel extrapolates the fact from her worried work with words, doubling—both as fictional device and as imaginative response to experience—lies at the very heart of the creative process. The "artist almost always lives in a Double Now," Rachel comments: in two places at once, two characters at once, two different times at once.

A quick sampling of *Munchmeyer and Prospero on the Island* illustrates how much in evidence are Thomas's favored doubling techniques for reflecting memory's transformation of fact into imaginative artifact. These include interleaved diaries, interpolated dreams and fantasies, echoes of episodes from other of Thomas's stories, labyrinthine echoes of and allusions to other literatures. (Miranda's name and the book's title, for example, becomes the wedge through which Shakespeare's interrogations of art and reality in *The Tempest* are rewoven.) Dominating is the strategy of the story told and re-told, a narrative doubling so subtle here that the novel is divisible into two novella: *Munchmeyer* and *Prospero on the Island,* the latter being Miranda's diary about writing a novel. Toward *Prospero*'s conclusion, we discover that the novel Miranda is writing is *Munchmeyer*—a novel about a male writing a diary about trying to write a novel. Thus female/male doubling in *Munchmeyer and Prospero on the Island* ends with the jest of a female author, Audrey Thomas, dissolving conventional gendered oppositions at the same time as she so inverts conventional male/female relations by having a fictional female writer invent (and so control) the character's fictional male counterpart.

Textual analyses involving this degree of formal explication reward only to the extent that they underscore how tenacious in Thomas's work is what she has called "this terrible gap between men and women." *Intertidal Life* (1984) is ship of such a state, wonderful by way of its marriage of Thomas's pervasive themes to her persistent narrative strategies. Again, we are introduced to a familiar: Isobel has shifted to Alice, but the latter constructs the same stories in silence, mirror-doubling herself between journal entries in the first person and a novella in the third person where Alice represents herself as "she". In retrospective memory of her husband's departure seven years before, Alice "writes a story of abandonment, of island isolation, of water, of the moon, of maps and guides and learning to read—in short, a story of exploration." It is not just the geography of her life that needs remapping, caught as she is between the tides of past and present, marriage and divorce, mothering and writing. There is a compulsion to reexplore that topography delineated by the ancient relations between men and women and to rename under the flag of female its once conquered continents. As Alice observes, comparing women's estate to the imperial colonization of countries:

> Women have let men define them, taken their names . . . just like a . . . newly settled region: *British* Columbia, *British* Guiana . . . *New* Jersey, *New* France. . . . I understand African nations taking new names.

The female landscape most repatriated in *Intertidal Life* is that of family life. Here a single mother's generative relation to her three daughters is realized in such rooted detail as soup making, wood cutting, fire stoking and garden planting. Though motherhood pulls as strongly on Alice Hoyle as moon on tide, its psychic space is never enclosure but rather expanding sphere. Indeed, her island-encircled house is likened not to a marooned circlet of female restriction but to a forging ship, a resolute metaphor in a novel filled with references to voyage, tide, and sea change. *Intertidal Life* teaches that explored-female and female explorer are mirrored-doubles, not warrior-antagonists, and the novel's celebratory spirit marks a new departure in the Thomas oeuvre. To borrow from Thomas's habit of truthtelling through pun[s]manship: no more should memories be mummified; nor too should mothers be others.

> Who can see the "other" in mother? Calling the school—"Hello, this is Hannah's mummy." "This is Anne's mummy." . . . All wrapped up in her family.
>
> [*Intertidal Life*]

> Why must I always search for similarities?
> [*Munchmeyer and Prospero on the Island*]

Audrey Thomas's craft has always been guided by an ironic shifting of boon, a maneuver never so apparent as in her shorter fiction. A look at one story can perhaps convey how characteristic is the wry ridiculing of gendered roles and codes. Some might typify as feminist her exposure of inherited conventions; she would amplify such scrutiny so as to include men as well as women—and especially the daughters of mothers. As the incantation from one story sings: "'Let her be strong,' [the mother] thought. 'Let her be strong and yet still loving.'"

"Crossing the Rubicon" is the final story in Thomas's collection of fiction, a volume titled almost tautologically as *Real Mothers*. Among a handful of shorter fictions by Thomas—and one must include here **"Natural History"** with its anticipatory rehearsal of the themes and landscapes of *Intertidal Life*—**"Crossing the Rubicon"** has an almost spend-thrift capacity to combine Thomas's flair for the self-projective with a set of narrative moves that enhance the blurring of autobiography and fiction: doubling and memory's mapping of sight through site.

The shorter fiction's outward plot seems disarmingly simple. An unnamed narrator tries to write a story, which "I do not particularly want to write. But it nags at me, whines, rubs against the side of my leg, begs for attention." At the same time, the narrator places that story's writing in her here and now, here being Canada's West Coast and now being one day before Valentine's, 13 February 1980. As for the story's here and now, they are Montreal on a fine October morning. "My story . . . will begin with a woman on a Number 24 bus, heading East along Sherbrooke Street. She is on her way to meet a man who used to be her lover."

The weaving together of the twinned tales—that of the unnamed narrator ("I") and that of her central character ("She")—is set in motion by Valentine's Day rituals, as a single mother helps her daughter make cupcakes for the boys at school. "'KISS ME' . . . 'BE GOOD TO ME' . . . 'LOVE ME,'" sigh mottoes on the heart-shaped candies, voicing the very scripts and romantic codes against which the narrator wants her character to fight.

Appropriately enough in a story whose title and first line initiate two among several allusions to Julius Caesar, **"Crossing the Rubicon"** is a declaration of war, committing its heroine by way of an irrevocable gesture in defiance of romantic enslavement to Caesar's fate: that of conquering or perishing. As a text about memory, **"Crossing the Rubicon"** also declares war against chronological narrative, the narrator crossing through (by my count) seven layers of the past—in sites as distant as Rome, Vancouver, Montreal, and upstate New York—to bring their booty back to the present and the task of writing (so righting) the embattled story. "Right now, I want to play soothsayer and call out to her, 'Beware, beware,'" muses the narrator as she imagines her fictional double at a crucial point in her encounter with her former lover. "Walk away. Run. Leave well enough alone," she warns.

Doubled as the "I" and the "she" most certainly are, the narrator's second self here enacts what secret sharers from Conrad down have done: like others of Thomas's doubles, she performs those unconventional acts the more compliant self cannot. **"Crossing the Rubicon"**'s final paragraph shows a woman walking away from her lover, then exuberantly running. Traffic signals command in an imperial and foreign tongue: "Arretez." She defies this ruling too, crossing—as Caesar did—her own rubicon. Such a turning away by this woman in love from the old codes for the woman in love is summed up by the I/Eye of Thomas's autobiographical projection in three—limpidly simple—final sentences. "And she doesn't look back. In my story, that is. She doesn't look back".

She doesn't look back. Audrey Thomas certainly does, looking back on literary lineages just as she looks back on her own life. From her first book, *Ten Green Bottles* (1967), to her more recent work, *The Wild Blue Yonder* (1990), Thomas has depicted both the privileges and the privations of mothers, wives, and lovers. Like **"Crossing the Rubicon"**'s narrator—indeed, like Thomas herself—each realizes she cannot wholly reject traditional roles; the foundations of custom and belief still stand sturdy. However, they can be enjoined by their author to revise conventional fictions of femininity and so transform women's future relations to their inheritances.

Routing his first enemies, Caesar trumpeted *Veni, Vidi, Vici*. His fabled boast seems suitable script for closing comment. Novelist of memory and triumphant Eye/I of sight and site, Audrey Thomas might herself say, "I came. I saw. I conquered." And my bet—based on the practice of a novelist who can twist "ménage à trois" to a ribald "ménage à twat" (**"Crossing the Rubicon"**)—has it that she would no sooner say Caesar's sentence than start playing with the male pun.

Jerry Horton (review date September 1995)

SOURCE: A review of *Coming Down from Wa*, in *Quill & Quire*, Vol. 61, No. 9, September 1995, p. 68.

[*In the following review, Horton concludes that while* Coming Down from Wa *lacks drama, Thomas's evocative imagery makes the novel compelling.*]

Audrey Thomas's *Coming Down from Wa* begins with its protagonist's recollection of a childhood gift: when William Kwame MacKenzie turned six he received a box of 64 crayons from his paternal grandparents in Montreal. Marvelling at the colours suddenly available to him, he made his first forays into art, only to be stifled by a Sunday school teacher who insisted that trees must be green and little boys must colour *inside* the lines.

MacKenzie recalls his box of colours and the abortion of his early art career as he makes his faltering way through the intense heat and equally intense hues of Africa's Gold Coast, ostensibly researching a master's degree thesis on lost-wax casting; the frustrated artist, now in his early 20s, has fallen back on a career in art history. But William's real agenda in Africa is to unearth the guilty secret that caused his once optimistic and open-hearted parents to become the cringing and brittle pair of shades he left behind him in Victoria.

As young volunteer educators with an organization called Canadian Overseas Workers in the mid-1960s, William's parents were stationed at St. Claire's, a Catholic girls' school, in an isolated town called Wa. William himself was conceived there, though his mother returned to Montreal for the delivery. But shortly after she and her new son arrived back in Africa, something happened. The family returned to Canada, but fled to the West coast where they existed in a state of self-imposed exile, cut off from friends and relatives alike for the next two decades. Now, as a young man, William searches out the sins of his parents in a bid to understand his past and therefore himself.

That plot summary should make clear why Thomas's novel often reads like Joyce's *A Portrait of the Artist as a Young Man* meets Conrad's *Heart of Darkness*. Like those classics, *Coming Down from Wa*'s narrative is often long on imagery and short on drama. Indeed, William's trials on the road to Wa are at times so loaded with imagery, one wonders if the tale should be read as allegory rather than the coming-of-age story it purports to be. One could make the case that the novel's disguised theme is Canada's loss of innocence vis à vis foreign aid to the Third World—what seemed possible and even noble in the 1960s has proven enormously complicated from both pragmatic and ethical points of view.

Luckily, though, Thomas's talent for producing the telling image is what also keeps her tale, allegorical or not, compelling. Her Africa is one experienced first-hand, and the authenticity of her portrait informs every sentence. Those crayons—their colours, their smells, and even their names—

weave their way throughout the tale in intriguing ways, as does the lost-wax casting process—an inspired echo of the change in William's parents. What was once warm and pliable is gone, replaced by a steely, unforgiving duplicate.

Lynne Van Luven (review date October 1995)

SOURCE: "Looking for Betrayal," in *Books in Canada,* Vol. XXIV, No. 7, October 1995, pp. 35-37.

[*In the following review, Van Luven praises Thomas's exploration of new themes and subject matter in* Coming Down from Wa, *but finds the novel "not wholly satisfying."*]

A mystery lies at the heart of William Kwame MacKenzie's childhood years, and he is determined to solve it. And so Audrey Thomas's new novel trundles readers through the red soil of West Africa and the shifting sands of memory as William's trek of discovery labours through past and present.

The fully-fledged male protagonist found in *Coming Down from Wa* is a rare creation in Thomas's fiction, which usually focuses on female characters and women's perceptions of the world. In fact, on more than one occasion, critics have noted that male characters "do not come out very well" in Thomas land, as they are often presented as selfish, egocentric, narrow-minded, and guilty of great psychological cruelty. One of Thomas's preoccupations as a writer has always been to probe relationships between the sexes, to explore what women see in these flawed men and how they recover from abusive relationships with them by coming to understand their own motives and dependencies.

It's also been a long time since Thomas's fiction wandered so far afield from her current home on British Columbia's Galiano Island: not since such early novels as *Mrs. Blood* (1970) and the experimental and now little-read *Blown Figures* (1974) has her setting been the African continent where compelling beauty and harsh contrasts often shock a naïve white visitor. And you cannot find a more naïve traveller than William, as the prologue of *Coming Down from Wa* proves when it presents him as a weeping, sweating, heat-struck "Bronie," wandering through a village market looking for a beautiful young girl who shortchanged him when he mistakenly gave her a Canadian $100 bill in return for six oranges. An art-history student working on his master's degree in the lost-wax process, a batiking technique that has become cheapened and adulterated for the tourist market, William is really researching his parents' past—which has also been adulterated and ruined by some mysterious catastrophe, some terrible loss of innocence.

In her 1993 novel *Graven Images,* Thomas presents an anatomy of a family through an adversarial mother-daughter relationship. In that novel, come to think of it, mothers (like men) don't come off terribly well: the protagonist Charlotte, a typical introspective and witty Thomas heroine, calls her bitter, angry mother "the Aged Pea," and tries to trace the roots of maternal malaise to her family's history in England. William also undertakes such a fact-finding mission, but with far less cleverness. In fact, William's self-absorption becomes a trifle tedious at times, and one wants him to grow up a little more quickly, wishes that the hot Ghana sun would shrivel his petulant self-importance.

Growing up as an only child in restrained Victoria, B.C., William is aware that an oppressive secret pervades the house he inhabits with his mother, Pat, a speech therapist, and his father, Sandy, a lab technician. His middle name is "Kwame," Sunday, because that is the day he was born, but playground taunts turn the name into "Commie," making a burden of what was his parents' well-meaning tribute. William knows he is different, scarred by a secret. He sees evidence of the secret's phantom self in the awkward silences between his parents, in their lies, their separate vacations and their failure to share a bedroom. But what is it?

William becomes convinced that the answer lies in the past his parents shared in West Africa. where "William should have been born," and where his idealistic parents were "COW people," volunteers with Canadian Overseas Workers. When William finally discovers what happened to destroy his parents' early joyous love in Wa, in the northern part of Ghana, he confronts truths about human nature, forgiveness, lost opportunity, and himself. Chantal, William's girlfriend, who is a model on a fashion shoot in the Ivory Coast, points out to William that his mission is far from pure: "You are looking for a reason to act cold towards your mother and father, to write them off. Why do you want to do that?"

"You don't understand," William tells her pompously.

William's basic unlikeability as a character is one of the problems readers may have with *Coming Down from Wa.* Almost all the other characters Thomas creates are far more interesting and sympathetic than he is: his grandfather has a sad kind of wisdom about the family tragedy; Ethnay Owusu-Banahene, a Scottish friend of his grandfather's who marries an African and becomes an "Auntie" to a huge extended family of children and grandchildren, is a fascinating character who deserves the starring role in her own novel; the doomed homosexual, Bernard, whom William meets in a bar, is a complex contradiction with his joie de vivre and his terror of diseases.

But perhaps the African countryside itself is the most compelling presence in Thomas's novel: we see the land and the vibrant scenes in the villages through William's "good eye," which likens many of the hues he sees to the box of 64 Crayola crayons his grandparents sent him when he was six:

> As he travelled through this country, he remembered the names of the crayons and began to see things— the red earth, the fruit and vegetables, the market cloth, the sky, even the flesh of the people—in those terms: bittersweet, mahogany, sepia, raw sienna, burnt orange, all the greens and blues and violets, the red of tomatoes and peppers, the yellow flesh of the pineapples, the whole brilliant swirl of it all. He mixed up the watercolours in his little tin and laid down swatches of colour in the watercolour block he had brought with him.

Ironically, the paints do not have the depth or vibrancy to fully capture the cornucopia of colours that William experiences. And until his mother joins him in Wa, William is unable to uncover the family secret. Only then does the power of the mystery take on complete life. As Pat insists on telling her story her way, despite her judgmental son's interruptions, the title of the novel takes on its full force and tragedy. Through Pat's final explanations, the full import of Thomas's political critique becomes clear: the blunders of the well-meaning "Bronies," the mixed motives of the volunteers, the confusion of power and sexuality between the whites and the blacks they would help.... The reader understands, in a way that William may never do, the absolute nature of the betrayal that has pervaded his parents' lives, and the broader significance of that betrayal on a global level.

Coming Down from Wa is a challenging and not wholly satisfying novel. But in it, Thomas charts new terrain for herself and tackles a powerful subject, human cupidity, in a broader political context than ever before. She has dared to expand her own repertoire in writing such a novel, and she is to be highly praised for that. As for William, readers must decide for themselves if he is truly "a thoroughly nice young man," or a symbol of the huge, apparently unsolvable inequity between "rich" nations such as Canada and "poor" ones like Ghana.

FURTHER READING

Bibliography

Bellamy, Robin V. H. "Audrey Thomas: A Select Bibliography." *Room of One's Own* 10, No. 3 & 4 (March 1986): 154-75.
    Compilation of writings by and about Thomas, including book reviews by writers such as Margaret Atwood and Margaret Laurence.

Biography

Sherrin, Robert G. "In Esse." *Room of One's Own* 10, No. 3 & 4 (March 1986): 68-74.
    Recounts a trip the author made with Thomas to her birthplace in Binghamton, New York.

Criticism

Amussen, Robert. "Finding a Writer." *Room of One's Own* 10, No. 3 & 4 (March 1986): 63-67.
    Explains how the author, as publisher and editor-in-chief at the Bobbs-Merrill Company in 1965, discovered Thomas's writing and began publishing her works.

Colvile, Georgiana. "Mirrormania: Audrey Thomas's *Munchmeyer and Prospero on the Island*." *Recherches Anglaises et Nord-Americaines*, No. XX (1987): 147-56.
    Analyzes Thomas's novellas according to French psychoanalyst Jacques Lacan's notion of the "mirror stage" of psychological development, in which "the imago in the mirror . . . is both self and other."

Gerson, Carole. A review of *Goodbye Harold, Good Luck* in *Queen's Quarterly* 94, No. 2 (Summer 1987): 484.
    Praises Thomas's "resonance and skill."

Godard, Barbara. *Audrey Thomas and Her Works.* Toronto: ECW Press, 1989, 89 p.
    Critical overview of Thomas's life and writings.

Howells, Coral Ann. "Inheritance and Instability: Audrey Thomas's *Real Mothers*." *Recherches Anglaises et Nord-Americaines*, No. XX (1987): 157-62.
    Contends that Thomas's *Real Mothers* challenges traditional barriers of male-oriented language and culture.

Thomas, Audrey. "A Fine Romance, My Dear, This Is." *Canadian Literature*, No. 108 (Spring 1986): 5-12.
    Discusses what Thomas considers the dangers of romance novels—the Harlequin series in particular—to women because of their demeaning, often violent, portrayal of sexual relationships.

Additional coverage of Thomas's life and career is contained in the following sources published by Gale Research: *Authors in the News,* Vol. 2; *Contemporary Authors,* Vols. 21-24R; *Contemporary Authors Autobiography Series,* Vol. 19; *Contemporary Authors New Revision Series,* Vol. 36; *Dictionary of Literary Biography,* Vol. 60; *Major Twentieth-Century Writers;* and *Short Story Criticism,* Vol. 20.

Evelyn Waugh
1903-1966

(Full name Evelyn Arthur St. John Waugh) English novelist, short story writer, critic, essayist, travel writer, biographer, journalist, and poet.

The following entry provides an overview of Waugh's career through 1995. For further information on his life and works, see *CLC,* Volumes 1, 3, 8, 13, 19, 27, and 44.

INTRODUCTION

Waugh has been called one of the greatest prose stylists in twentieth-century literature for his satirical writings on the foibles of modern society. In such works as *A Handful of Dust* (1934), *Brideshead Revisited* (1945), and *The Loved One* (1948), Waugh's graceful use of minimalist language coupled with his acidic exposure of hypocrisy and superficiality among England's upper classes have led many critics to classify him alongside modern literature's preeminent men of letters.

Biographical Information

Waugh was born in London in 1903. His father, Arthur Waugh, was a prominent editor and publisher at Chapman-Hall, while his older brother Alec was a novelist and travel writer. Waugh initially resisted his family's literary leanings, concentrating on art and design at Hertford College, Oxford. The period at Oxford was turbulent for Waugh. He entrenched himself in the group he later sharply satirized in his writings as the "Bright Young Things," drank excessively, and experimented with homosexuality, which he unequivocally renounced years later. Waugh was forced to leave Oxford in 1924 because of poor grades. He went on to study for a brief period at Heatherley's Art School, where he first became acquainted with the design principles of the Arts and Crafts movement, and later was drawn to the modernist movements Vorticism and Futurism. He left the school a year later and became a teacher, but was fired from all three of his posts. At that point Waugh reluctantly turned to writing as a career, working as a journalist for the London *Daily Express* and producing his first novel, *Decline and Fall,* in 1928. The book was well-received, but due to its scathing satire, Waugh's publisher insisted that he remove certain scenes and add a note of disclaimer as a preface. Also in 1928, Waugh married Evelyn Gardner; two years later the marriage dissolved in divorce, an event which, along with his overall disillusionment with modern society, many critics and biographers believe led to Waugh's conversion to and

staunch defense of Roman Catholicism. In 1936, his marriage to Gardner was annulled, and he subsequently married Laura Herbert in 1937. During World War II, Waugh had a successful military stint, rising to the rank of major in the Royal Marines. By this time Waugh had earned a place among the foremost literati of England, having published some of his most important and respected novels, essays, short stories, and criticism. He traveled extensively, often as a correspondent, and his experiences around the world frequently turn up in his work. Waugh continued, however, to become more deeply disgusted by what he considered the widespread loss of honor, integrity, and traditional mores, particularly during and after World War II. Perhaps because of his increasing sense of alienation and nostalgia for what he thought of as a more moral past, Waugh created for himself a public persona of haughty reserve and conservatism and guarded his personal life fiercely. Little is known, for example, of the circumstances surrounding the nervous breakdown he suffered in the 1950s, aside from his fictionalized account of that period of his life in his novel *The Ordeal of Gilbert Pinfold* (1957). Shortly before his death, Waugh published the first part of a projected multi-volume autobiography, *A Little Learning.* He died, leaving the work unfinished, in 1966.

Major Works

Waugh's body of work is marked by two predominant themes: satire of the vulgarity of modern society and, after his conversion, the redemptive promise of traditional Catholicism. In *Decline and Fall,* the narrator, Paul Pennyfeather, is a hapless naif recently dismissed from Oxford University and mercilessly victimized by the scoundrels he encounters. In his second novel, *Vile Bodies* (1930), Waugh again found inspiration in his own university experience. Containing Waugh's famous satirical treatment of the "Bright Young Things" from his days at Oxford, *Vile Bodies* is the story of Adam Symes, an innocent who unwittingly commits detestable crimes in an unstable and amoral world, and Waugh emphasized the feeling of instability by providing little coherence to the plot or scene structure. In his third novel, *Black Mischief* (1932), Waugh took on imperialism and the veiled savagery of Western culture. In an attempt to bring his country into the twentieth century, the Emperor Seth of Azania—a fictional African nation—enlists the help of the Englishman Basil Seal, whose directives for civilizing the country result in tragedy for its citizens. *A Handful of Dust* (1934) was the first novel into which Waugh incorporated Catholic themes, as well as his first departure from his earlier farcical style of satire. Based largely on the failure of his own marriage, the novel follows the collapse of the marriage of the upper-class English couple Tony and Brenda Last as they seek refuge from the cruelties and absurdities of their social rank. While Brenda has an affair with the crass and shallow John Beaver, becoming increasingly emotionally detached as she is absorbed into the cocktail society of London, Tony clings to what he considers the more genteel world of pre-twentieth-century England, engaging in a futile restoration of his outdated ancestral home. Searching for meaning in his life, Tony embarks on a South American expedition, where he is stranded indefinitely with an elderly madman who forces him to read aloud the works of the Victorian novelist Charles Dickens. While many critics consider *A Handful of Dust* to be one of Waugh's most relentlessly grim satires, they nonetheless point out that Tony and Brenda's search for shelter in an unkind world, though deeply misguided, is symbolic of the retreat Waugh believed he had found in Catholicism. After *A Handful of Dust,* Waugh published *Scoop* (1938)—a satire on journalists—and *Put Out More Flags* (1942)—which most critics consider a precursor to his later war trilogy, *Sword of Honour.* In 1945 Waugh published his most overtly Catholic novel, *Brideshead Revisited,* which was both his greatest commercial success and his most controversial work. *Brideshead Revisited* traces events in the lives of a wealthy English Catholic family, the Marchmains, and their involvement with Charles Ryder—a non-Catholic. The family indulges in every conceivable form of decadence but returns to itsfaith in the end. *Brideshead Revisited* was a departure for Waugh in several ways. In addition to its strong Catholic message, the novel is characterized by a more lush, romantic style of prose, an idealization of nostalgia, and a non-critical tone regarding the lifestyles of aristocratic English families. Despite the popular success it enjoyed, *Brideshead Revisited* was excoriated by many critics, who found its romanticized depiction of upper-class life and nostalgia for a past "golden age" an unwelcome change from the brilliant social commentary of Waugh's earlier works. Waugh returned to satire in 1948 with *The Loved One,* which is often cited as one of his best, and bitterest, critiques of modern life. In *The Loved One* Waugh parodied Hollywood in the 1940s, in particular the English expatriates who set up "colonies" there seeking fortunes and the American ideal of success. Much of the novel takes place in the hyper-sanitized arena of the Whispering Glades cemetery and its counterpart, the animal cemetery Happier Hunting Grounds, and concerns the doomed relationship between Dennis Barlow, described as a "poet and pet mortician," and Aimee Thanatogenos, hostess of the cemetery and an embalming intern. While Aimee is in search of spiritual truth and genuine cultural enrichment, Dennis uses his poetry to win women and advance socially. As Dennis introduces her to the English poets, Aimee becomes increasingly disenchanted, and finally commits suicide on an embalming table as a result of her inability to reconcile her American notions of good citizenship and ethics with her deep sense of alienation. Generally considered Waugh's most successful black comedy, *The Loved One* has been called dystopic in tone, and has even been compared to science fiction. The year before his death, Waugh published his war trilogy, *Sword of Honour* (1965), as a single volume for the first time. Comprising *Men at Arms* (1952), *Officers and Gentlemen* (1955), and *Unconditional Surrender* (also published as *The End of the Battle;* 1961), *Sword of Honour* tells the story of Guy Crouchback, who is considered Waugh's only real hero, as he enters World War II a romantic idealist and ends up a bleak pessimist at the war's conclusion. A decent man seeking decency in the world, Guy concludes that only personal good works can provide spiritual comfort and communion amid a secular wasteland.

Critical Reception

Waugh's importance to modern English literature owes much to his style and craftsmanship. Earlier works were characterized by clever phrasing and broadly humorous plots, but in later works he translated his observations into complex ironic structures, unifying content with form. Some critics contend that Waugh's books are timeless because their worlds transcend current history. Others believe his writing will not endure because of his nostalgic preoccupations, the rigidity of his opinions and outlook, and the restricted range of his intellectual and political focus. The assessments of his writing skills are, nevertheless, virtually uniform in their recognition of his comic inventiveness, his highly individualistic style, his devotion to clarity and precision, and his ability to entertain. Edmund Wilson wrote of Waugh's novels: "[They are] the only things written in England that are comparable to Fitzgerald and Hemingway. They are not so poetic; they are perhaps less intense; they belong to a more classical tradition. But I think that they are likely to last and that Waugh, in fact, is likely to figure as the only first-rate comic genius that has appeared in England since Bernard Shaw."

PRINCIPAL WORKS

The World to Come (poetry) 1916
Decline and Fall (novel) 1928
Vile Bodies (novel) 1930
Black Mischief (novel) 1932
A Handful of Dust (novel) 1934
Edmund Campion: Scholar, Priest, Hero, and Martyr (biography) 1935
Mr. Loveday's Little Outing and Other Sad Stories (short stories) 1936; expanded edition published as *Charles Ryder's Schooldays and Other Stories*, 1982
Scoop (novel) 1938; published in England as *Scoop: A Novel about Journalists*, 1938
Mexico: An Object Lesson (travel essay) 1939; published in England as *Robbery under Law: The Mexican Object Lesson*, 1939
Put Out More Flags (novel) 1942
Work Suspended: Two Chapters of an Unfinished Novel (unfinished novel) 1942; expanded edition published as *Work Suspended and Other Stories Written before the Second World War*, 1949
Brideshead Revisited: The Sacred and Profane Memories of Captain Charles Ryder (novel) 1945
Scott-King's Modern Europe (novel) 1947
The Loved One: An Anglo-American Tragedy (novel) 1948
Helena (novel) 1950
Men at Arms (novel) 1952
Love among the Ruins: A Romance of the Near Future (novel) 1953
Officers and Gentlemen (novel) 1955
The Ordeal of Gilbert Pinfold: A Conversation Piece (novel) 1957
Tourist in Africa (travel essay) 1960
Unconditional Surrender (novel) 1961; published as *The End of the Battle*, 1962
Basil Seal Rides Again; or, The Rake's Regress (novel) 1963
A Little Learning: An Autobiography, the Early Years (autobiography) 1964; published in England as *A Little Learning: The First Volume of an Autobiography*, 1964
Sword of Honor [contains *Men at Arms, Officers and Gentle-*

men, and *Unconditional Surrender*] (novel trilogy) 1965
The Diaries of Evelyn Waugh [edited by Michael Davie] (diaries) 1976
A Little Order: A Selection from the Journalism of Evelyn Waugh [edited by Donat Gallagher] (journalism) 1977
The Letters of Evelyn Waugh [edited by Mark Amory] (letters) 1980

CRITICISM

Dudley Fitts (review date 21 May 1930)

SOURCE: "O Bright Young People!," in *The Nation*, Vol. 130, No. 3385, May 21, 1930, p. 602.

[*Fitts was an American poet, critic, and translator. In the following review, he calls Waugh's novel* Vile Bodies *a "failure," noting that the use of satire is heavy-handed and derivative.*]

[*Vile Bodies*] is the kind of book that assures you, in a desperate sort of way, that it is funny. It is modeled, pretty consciously, upon the early Aldous Huxley—the Huxley, that is to say, of *Crome Yellow* and, more noticeably, *Antic Hay*; not the sad Huxley of the moment, whose touch has become so oppressive since he borrowed Mr. Wells's ouija board and achieved intimacy with God. Mr. Waugh, too, has heard the thunder on the usual Sinai: *Vile Bodies* has predicatory implications, the same hangover tone that spoiled *Point Counter Point*, but Mr. Waugh has little of Huxley's wit and none of his substance. While it was possible to forgive the latter's taking himself so seriously by reflecting that after all he *had* created something to be serious about, it is difficult to excuse Mr. Waugh for wrenching good slapstick into tragicomedy.

As satire the book is no less a failure. First of all, Mr. Waugh displays none of the élan that distinguishes the true satirist from the caricaturist. For all its brilliance the writing lacks vitality. The invention is tired, and effects are too often got by recourse to the devices of slapstick exaggeration. Again, the satire is self-conscious satire, which destroys itself. What made *Crome Yellow* so effective, for example, was its utter lack of apparent purpose. One never felt that Huxley was deliberately *meaning* anything; least of all was one conscious of him as the imminent critic of his characters. One is constantly aware, however, of the presence of Mr. Waugh: usually he is felt only in casual turns of expression, the occasional laying on of effect upon conscious effect; but sometimes he descends to the whimsical footnote, and at least once to the bombastic apostrophe: "O Bright Young People!" Successful satire must be impersonal (the "I" of

Gulliver is dissociate from Swift) and either entirely improbable (*Gulliver* again, and *Alice*), qua history, or entirely probable (*Crome Yellow, Antic Hay*). ***Vile Bodies*** is none of these.

If Mr. Waugh had not tried to do so much, if he had been content to amuse, without attempting to devastate, if he had been content to laugh, without essaying a prophetic sneer at the same time; his book would be diverting in a cockeyed sort of way. It is acceptable comic knowledge that men and women drink to be drunk and sometimes sleep together; that female evangelists are often hypocrites and society editors occasionally unreliable; that movie directors are not invariably sincere artists; that many clergymen are smug, many wives adulteresses, many statesmen lechers, and many dowagers boors. And it is always pleasing to know that what used to be called the "lost generation," before it went humanist, is still energetically losing itself. It is a pity that Mr. Waugh felt that more than these ingredients was needed. Because of its weight of satiric and tragic exaggeration, ***Vile Bodies*** neither amuses nor instructs. It is not of the type of true stories, but of *True Stories*.

Robert Cantwell (review date 12 October 1932)

SOURCE: "Mr. Waugh's Humor," in *The Nation*, Vol. 135, No. 3510, October 12, 1932, p. 335.

[*Cantwell was an American editor and fiction writer. In the following review, he objects to Waugh's light treatment of imperialism in* Black Mischief.]

Like *Hindoo Holiday*, published a few months ago with considerable success, ***Black Mischief*** is a study of some of the more droll results of European imperialism. *Hindoo Holiday* revolved around the activities of an engaging, homosexual Indian ruler, and the humor had its source in his misuse of the English language and in his baffled attempts to understand European history and customs. The appeal of ***Black Mischief*** is on a somewhat higher level, for Waugh has more respect for factual reality, and his sense of humor is a little grim: there are various picturesque assassinations in the course of the story, and the climax comes when the hero sits in on a cannibal feast and eats his sweetheart. The central figure of ***Black Mischief*** is Seth, a Negro educated at Oxford and determined to bring progress to his native state of Azania whether his subjects want it or not. He is aided by an up-to-date soldier of fortune named Basil Seal, who tries to put through a One-Year Plan of modernization and improvement. And instead of pederasty and mispronunciation, which created the funny scenes in *Hindoo Holiday*, the humor revolves around revolutions, diplomatic intrigues and stupidity, birth control, graft, and the befuddlement of two

dreary representatives of the Society for the Prevention of Cruelty to Animals.

But the details of these novels are less interesting than the point of view they represent. Both Waugh and Ackerman write in the tradition which is usually associated with Aldous Huxley and Norman Douglas; both, that is to say, are commonly described in conventional literary terminology as cynical and disillusioned. So it is a little odd to find them writing of colonial disturbances with a whimsicality that is a sort of cross between Gilbert-and-Sullivan and burlesque-show humor, and to find the relationship of the Europeans and the natives presented almost exclusively in terms of the comic situations resulting from it. In both novels there is the sharp collision between what we *know* of the kind of conflicts described, what common sense and experience and history tell us about them, and what the authors would have us believe. Waugh is no apologist for imperialism in the sense that Kipling was a great apologist for it; he is not politically alert in the way that Kipling was, and he is not so conscious of the needs of the dominant class of his time. On the contrary he dislikes imperialism, but not to the point of attacking it; the satire is all directed at trivial subjects, and humor in this case is only an unsatisfactory refuge.

Frank Kermode (essay date November 1960)

SOURCE: "Mr. Waugh's Cities," in *Encounter*, Vol. XV, No. 5, November 1960, pp. 63-66, 68-70.

[*Kermode is an English educator, literary critic, essayist, and editor. In the following essay, he examines Waugh's depiction of religious faith in England after the Reformation, particularly the place of Catholicism among the upper classes in the late-nineteenth and early-twentieth centuries as represented in* Brideshead Revisited.]

It is probably safe to assume that most readers of ***Brideshead Revisited*** know and care as much about Papist history and theology as Charles Ryder did before he became intimate with the Flytes; and although the novel contains a fair amount of surprisingly overt instruction we are much more likely to allow our reading of it to be corrupted by ignorance than by an excessively curious attention to matters of doctrine. In fact this is true of Mr. Waugh's fiction as a whole; and one of the rewards of curiosity is a clearer notion of the differences, as well as of the similarities, between his most successful books.

At the end of ***Decline and Fall*** (1928), Paul Pennyfeather, back at Scone after his sufferings on Egdon Heath, notes with approval the condemnation of a second-century Bithynian bishop who had denied the divinity of Christ and the validity of the sacrament of Extreme Unction; a singularly dangerous heretic. A few moments later, however, he turns his attention to an apparently more innocent sect: "the ascetic Ebionites used to turn towards Jerusalem when they prayed. . . . Quite right to suppress them." They too tended, for all the apparent harmlessness of their idiosyncrasy, to pervert fact with fantasy and truth with opinion. More than twenty years later Mr. Waugh's Helena ridicules theological fantasies concerning the composition of the Cross (that it was compounded of every species of wood so that the vegetable world could participate in the act of redemption; that it had one arm of boxwood, one of cypress, one of cedar and one of pine with the consequent amalgam of emblematic properties). She is also offended by the untruths and mythopoeic absurdities of her son Constantine. The Cross she seeks and finds consists merely of large pieces of wood. The Wandering Jew lets her have it free, foreseeing future business in relics. "It's a stiff price," says Helena. She wanted none of that fantastic piety, only the real routine baulks of timber used on a matter-of-fact historical occasion. "Above the babble of her age and ours," comments the author, "she makes one blunt assertion. And there alone lies our Hope."

These passages illustrate what is static in Mr. Waugh's expression of his religion. Religion as a man-made answer to pressing human needs disgusts him; Constantine's nonsense is of no more value than Brenda Last's, cutting the cards to see who shall go first to the woman who tells fortunes by reading one's feet. The Church is concerned to preserve the truth, solid and palpable as a lump of wood, from the rot of fantasy. It is entirely concerned with fact. Hence it was quite right to suppress the fanciful Ebionites with the same severity as the intolerable bishop; and the sentimental myth-making of Helena's scholars is dangerous because it tends to soften hard fact.

A number of such facts are at present ignored in our society, which has apostatised to paganism. Yet they are facts. Given the necessary instruction, the necessary intellect, and the necessary grace, a man will be a Catholic. Mr. Waugh, paraphrasing *Campion's Brag* in his *Life* (1935) of the martyr does not even specify the third of these necessities: "he . . . makes the claim, which lies at the root of all Catholic apologetics, that the Faith is absolutely satisfactory to the mind, enlisting all knowledge and all reason in its cause; that it is completely compelling to any who give it an 'indifferent and quiet audience.'" And the author has himself written that he was admitted into the Church "on firm intellectual conviction but with little emotion." As Mr. F. J. Stopp comments, in his admirable *Evelyn Waugh*, it is also apparent that this "firm intellectual conviction" relates "not primarily to the vanquishing of philosophical doubts about the existence of God, or considerations of the nature of authority," but rather to "a realisation of the undeniable historical presence and continuity of the Church."

Quod semper, quod ubique. . . . The English Reformation was not only an attempt to break this historical continuity, but a very insular movement. The Counter-Reformation, on the other hand, was an affair of genuine vitality and spirituality, universal in its scope; England was impoverished by its failure to participate. The consistency of Mr. Waugh's opinions is indicated by his admiration for Baroque art, the plastic expression of Tridentine Catholicism and a great European movement that left England almost untouched. His version of English history at large is simply but fairly stated in this way: after being Catholic for nine hundred years, many English families, whether from intellectual confusion or false prudence, apostasised in the 16th century to schismatic institutions which were good only in so far as they retained elements of the true worship. The consequence has been modern paganism (at a guess, Mr. Waugh thinks of this as an atavism in degenerating stock); the inevitable end is a restoration of the faith, but the interim is ugly and tragic except in so far as it is redeemed by the suffering of the martyrs and the patience of the faithful. ("Have you ever thought," asks Helena, "how awfully few martyrs there were, compared with how many there ought to have been?") This conservatism is of course reflected in the author's social opinions; the upper classes are good in so far as they hold on to the values and the properties cherished by their families. Aristocracy, like the Church, fights a defensive action, and that which it defends is, in the long run, a Catholic structure. Very intelligent upper-class Englishmen are not common in Waugh, and when they occur (Basil Seal is the notable case) they are not intellectuals. Their brains have nothing solid to work on; not being Catholics they are not in a position to pursue the truth with any seriousness. Yet if they preserve their families and their customs they do as much as they can to maintain the link with those "ancestors—all the ancient priests, bishops, and kings—all that was once the glory of England, the island of saints, and the most devoted child of the See of Peter." The words are Campion's.

This is the "historical intransigence" that Ryder (in the first edition of *Brideshead Revisited*) learnt to admire. It is like Guyon smashing up the Bower of Bliss; a great deal that might, to a less ruthless mind seem admirable, if mistaken, is pulled down without a regretful glance. The age of Hooker (and Shakespeare) becomes merely a good time for prospective martyrs to live in. The piety and intellect of Andrewes, the learning of Casaubon, were all wasted in a cause self-evidently indefensible. The torment of Donne's conscience (a man who knew the ways of Topcliffe and the temptation of martyrdom) was an unnecessary perplexity; his dealings with Sarpi were treasonable, and all those high eirenic hopes futile. There is no need to pray, "Show me thy spouse," for any unblinkered eye can see her. How did these great men allow themselves to be reduced to pettifogging heretics? They should have seen that it was unlikely that "the truth, hidden from the world for fifteen centuries, had suddenly been revealed . . . to a group of important Englishmen." They should have seen that, on the Romanist side, any apparent deviousness or error was tributary to the workings of the divine purpose. Thus it may be agreed by historians of all parties that the Bull excommunicating Elizabeth was palpably unwise: but

> had he [Pius V] perhaps, in those withdrawn, exalted hours before his crucifix, learned something that was hidden from the statesmen of his time and the succeeding generations of historians; seen through and beyond the present and immediate future; understood that there was to be no *easy way* of reconciliation, but that it was only through blood and hatred and derision that the Faith was one day to return to England?

It may not be amiss to say parenthetically that I write without the least intention to be controversial; the point is merely to establish in a sketchy way how much Mr. Waugh's historical intransigence excludes from consideration, with a view to showing how sharp that weapon is, not that it is wrong to use it. If you consider that the English Reformation opened up the way not only to paganism but to Hooper and to the salesman with the wet handshake, dentures and polygonal spectacles, you will not be disposed to dwell on the intellect of Hooker or the spirituality of Herbert. It is not unusual for people to believe in a kind of second Fall, a great historical disaster that began our era; for Mr. T. S. Eliot it is the Civil War. Few, however, even among Roman Catholics who might share Mr. Waugh's admiration for Tridentine as well as for medieval piety, have ever applied the doctrine with such harsh consistency. The apostate aristocracy, adulterated by politic Tudors and later by other secular forces, moved slowly to disaster, checked only by a respect for ancient Barbarian traditions and by a hatred of middle-class Protestants. The second war was to be the apocalypse; meanwhile the behaviour of the lapsed could cause dispassionate amusement. But when the war came it awakes certain recessive characteristics, and even Basil Seal, in *Put Out More Flags,* hears the feudal call to arms and, after his amusing betrayal of the outsider Silk and his exploitation of the evacuees, renounces his intention to be one of the hard-faced men who did well out of the war; with the rest of his kind he mans the crumbling ramparts; and in spite of the nuisance caused by a thousand Hoopers, the defence does not fail. One gets the full statement of this position in the story of Alastair Digby-Vane-Trumpington, whose past achievements include the betrayal of Paul Pennyfeather; he leaves his Sonia and his black velvet not to take a commission but to join the ranks. The socially acceptable reason for this is that he can't bear to meet the temporary officers, but the astute Sonia knows a deeper one: Alastair "went into the ranks as a kind of penance or whatever it's called that religious people do." He was paying for all that irresponsible fun, getting

back into line; soon he finds people of his own sort to be an officer with, and the penance ends.

Put Out More Flags had a new sourness; opinion crept into Mr. Waugh's fiction. Comment and diagnosis had formerly been reserved to minor, stylised characters like Father Rothschild who, in *Vile Bodies,* explained the wantonness of the bright young: "they are all possessed with an almost fatal hunger for permanence"—for those traditions of civility that perish without the Faith. Fr. Rothschild disappears on his bicycle; but Mr. Waugh's opinions do not go with him. A few years later there was the famous eulogy of Mussolini's Abyssinian experiment, not quite *imperium sine fine,* not quite *debellare superbos.* The extension of the frontier is not, however, the main responsibility of the faithful in our time; it is defence. And with Alastair and Basil the English gentleman turned naturally to his traditional task of defending the island of Saints and so the Church, not only the faith itself but the whole civilisation in which it is incarnate.

This, then, is what must be defended: the arts and institutions of rational humanity and the clear reasonableness of the faith. Mr. Waugh is much concerned with the clarity and openness of Catholic worship as an expression of this. Here, from *Where the Going was Good,* is a passage from an account of his attendance at a Mass of the Ethiopian Church, "secret and confused in character":

> I had sometimes thought it an odd thing that Western Christianity, alone of all the religions of the world, exposes its mysteries to every observer, but I was so accustomed to this openness that I had never before questioned whether it was an essential and natural feature of the Christian system. Indeed, so saturated are we in this spirit that many people regard the growth of the Church as a process of elaboration—even of obfuscation. . . . At Debra Labanos I suddenly saw the classic basilica and open altar as a great positive achievement, a triumph of light over darkness consciously accomplished. . . . I saw the Church of the first century as a dark and hidden thing. . . . The pure nucleus of the truth lay in the minds of the people, encumbered with superstitions, gross survivals of the paganism in which they had been brought up; hazy and obscene nonsense seeping through from the other esoteric cults of the Near East, magical infections from the conquered barbarian. And I began to see how these obscure sanctuaries had grown, with the clarity of Western reason, into the great open altars of Catholic Europe, where Mass is said in a flood of light, high in the sight of all. . . .

Helena, we saw, was devoted to this openness, clarity, commonsense; she is brusque and reasonable, and her spirit survives in Lady Circumference, "the organ voice of England, the hunting-cry of the *ancien régime*," as she snorts with disapproval at an American revivalist meeting in Mayfair: "What a damned impudent woman." (This was in *Vile Bodies;* the last page of *Helena* twenty years later recalls, with a change of tone, the figure used for Lady Circumference: "Hounds are checked, hunting wild. A horn calls clear through the covert. Helena casts them back on the scent.") The Faith may be driven back to the catacombs, but its agreement with reason must never be obscured. Mr. Waugh perhaps took a hint from Mr. Eliot in characterising the years between the wars as a period during which pagan obscenities seeped in. The Reformation opened the door to Madame Sosostris, to a society in which rich women cut cards to see who shall go first to have her fortune told by a foot-reader. The religions of darkness are the pagan intrusions; Catholic Christianity is light, order, life. *The Loved One,* Mr. Waugh's most perfect book (as *Silas Marner* is more perfect than *Middlemarch*), sketches a highly-developed religion of darkness, in which art, love, language are totally corrupted and brought under the domination of death, as must happen when the offices of the Church are in every sphere usurped.

This is the farcical vision of total collapse, the end of the defence which must be endless, however long Mass is said in secret. Helena would like the Wall of the Empire to be at the limits of the world, but Constantius knows that there has to be a wall; it represents "a natural division of the human race." With the Donation of Constantine ("as for the old Rome, it's yours") the secular became the holy Empire, the Catholic City that the civilised must defend. Inside the City are traditions of reason, clarity, beauty; outside, obscene nonsense, the uncreating Word. Mr. Waugh is the Augustine who, because he has a vision of this City, detests Pelagius as a heretic and Apuleius as a sorcerer; anathematises the humanitarian and the hot-gospeller.

Yet barbarism has its attractions. The "atavistic callousness" of Lady Marchmain is only another form of that barbaric vitality which animates the upper classes even in decadence. "Capital fellows *are* bounders"—if it were not so there would not be much fun in the early novels. Sometimes it seems that not to be corrupted is the shame, as with the dull Wykehamist of *Brideshead Revisited;* the chic, efficient corruption of Lady Metroland belongs inside, the depredations of Mrs. Beaver outside the pale. The moral distinctions are as bewildering as the semantics of *U* or the social criteria which determine what is Pont Street and what is not. And they are, of course, employed without the least trace of Protestant assertiveness; to make them appear self-evident without mentioning them is one of the triumphant aspects of Mr. Waugh's early technique. One notices that the voices which tormented Mr. Pinfold puzzled him by missing out many of the accusations he would have made had he wished to tor-

ment himself. His mind worked much as it habitually did in composing his novels; the quality of the fantasies reminds one of Lord Tangent's death or the Christmas sermon in *A Handful of Dust*. The vision of barbarism is a farcical one, and the fantasy has its own vitality; the truth exists, self-evident, isolated from all this nonsense, and there is no need to arrange a direct confrontation.

This co-existence of truth and fantasy is most beautifully sustained in *A Handful of Dust,* surely Mr. Waugh's best book, and one of the most distinguished novels of the century. The great houses of England become by an easy transition types of the Catholic City, and in this book the threatened City is Hetton; it will not prove to be a continuing city. *Non hinc habemus manentem civitatem*–the lament resounds in *Brideshead*. Hetton is not beautiful; it was "entirely rebuilt in 1864 in the Gothic style and is now devoid of interest," says the guide-book. But Tony Last has the correct Betjemanic feelings for the battlements, the pitchpine minstrels' gallery, the bedrooms named from Malory. He is "madly feudal," which means he reads the lesson in church at Christmas and is thinking of having the fire lit in his pew. The nonsense that goes on in the church troubles nobody. Tony is a nice dull gentleman who knows vaguely that the defence of Hetton is the defence of everything the past has made valuable. He loses it because his wife takes up with a colourless rootless bore; Hetton and Tony are sacrificed, in the end, to a sterile affair in a London flat. The death of her son shows how far Brenda Last has departed from sanity and normality. There is a hideous divorce, a meaningless arrangement in the middle of chaos. All this without comment; ennui, sterility, cruelty represent themselves as farcically funny. But the attempt of the lawyers to reduce him to the point where he must give up Hetton rouses Tony, and he breaks off the proceedings. Leaving England he goes in search of another City; but there is no other City, and this one is a fraud, like the Bõa Vista of *When the Going was Good*. Tony was in search of something "Gothic in character, all vanes and pinnacles, gargoyles, battlements, groining and tracery, pavilions and terraces, a transfigured Hetton." He found the deathly Mr. Todd, and a prison whose circular walls are the novels of Dickens. Hetton becomes a silver-fox farm. Throughout this novel the callousness of incident and the coldness of tone work by suggesting the positive and rational declarations of the Faith. Civility is the silent context of barbarism; truth of fantasy. And Hetton, within the limits of Tony's understanding, is an emblem of the true City. Mr. Pinfold's mind proliferates with infidel irrationality; this is useful, provided the truth can be seen by its own light.

In *Brideshead Revisited,* perhaps, it is not allowed to do so. The great house as emblem of the City is enormously developed, but opinion—or truth, if you are Catholic—breaks into the text. The tone is less certain than that of *A Handful of Dust,* the prose slower, more explicit, more like that of the *Campion* biography than any of the other novels; a slower prose, weighed with semi-colons. Even in the making of the house itself fantasy has a smaller part than it had in Hetton. It has to be seen in the historical perspective I have been sketching; the account of Ryder—"solid, purposeful, observant" no doubt, as an artist should be, but not at the time of observing a Catholic—has to be put in order. *Brideshead* is English Baroque, but its stone came from an earlier castle. The family was apostate until the marriage of the present Marquis, reconciled to the Church on marriage (his wife, he said, "brought back my family to the faith of their ancestors"). Lady Marchmain's family were old Catholic; "from Elizabeth's reign till Victoria's they lived sequestered lives among their tenantry and kinsmen, sending their sons to school abroad, often marrying there, inter-marrying, if not, with a score of families like themselves, debarred from all preferment, and learning, in those lost generations, lessons which could still be read in the lives of the last three men of the house"—Lady Marchmain's brothers, killed in 1914-18 "to make a world for Hooper." The Chapel at Brideshead is accordingly not in the style of the house but in the *art nouveau* manner of the period of Lord Marchmain's reconciliation, as if to symbolise the delayed advent of toleration.

And their old religion sits just as uneasily upon the house's occupants. Mr. Waugh is always emphatic that his reasonable religion has nothing to do with making or keeping people in the ordinary sense happy. Lady Marchmain herself uneasily bears the sins of her family; Julia (descendant of earlier, somewhat Arlenesque heroines) drifts into marriage with Rex Mottram, a sub-man with no sense of reality (the scenes in which he dismisses it—when he is under religious instruction with a view to his being received into the Church—are the most amusing in the book because Mr. Waugh is always at his cruel best with people who cannot face reality), and is forced in the end to a self-lacerating penance. Cordelia's life is, on any naturalist view, squandered in good works. Sebastian, gifted with the power to attract love, attracts the love of God and is hounded through alcoholism and pauperism into simple holiness. Only Brideshead, the elder son, lives calmly and unimaginatively with the truth; understanding even that Sebastian's career, so wildly outside his own experience, has in the end a purpose. They are all locked into a class, these characters, and into the religion, which, by the logic of Mr. Waugh's fiction, is in the long run inseparable from that class. Lord Marchmain makes his Byronic protest but dies in awkward splendour at Brideshead, finally reconciled to the Church. Only in misery, it seems, will the Faith be restored in the great families of England.

The death of Lord Marchmain is the climax of the process by which Ryder returns to the Faith of his fathers, at the end of which he can see his love for Sebastian and for Julia as

types and forerunners of this love of God. He begins in deep ignorance. (In the first edition he complained that "no one had ever suggested to me that these quaint observances expressed a coherent philosophical system and intransigent historical claims." Now he says, "They never suggested I should try to pray. . . . Later . . . I have come to accept claims which then . . . I never troubled to examine, and to accept the supernatural as the real." This shift of emphasis is an improvement, since Ryder's intimacy with the Flytes may teach him something of "the operation of divine grace" but nothing directly about the validity of the Church's historical claims.

Ryder learns certain associated lessons from the Flytes. It is Sebastian who shows him that the beauty of the City can be known only to the rich, that architecture and wine, for example, are aspects of it. The scene of Ryder's dinner with Mottram is a parable; the Burgundy is a symbol of civility, "a reminder that the world was an older and better place than Rex knew, that mankind in its long passion had learned another wisdom than his;" the brandy is a test of a man's truth and authenticity. Devoting his life to such civilities, exempted by an infection of the Flyte charm—as Blanche tells him—from the fate of the classless artist, Ryder is already a Catholic in everything but religion. Mr. Waugh has done a little to reinforce this point in his revised text by re-writing the passage describing the reunion of Ryder and his wife in New York. His indifference and distaste are unchanged, but now they make love with chill hygiene; a sham wasteland marriage, essentially terminable. But he too must lose everything; he loses Brideshead and Julia. So, in the end, all these lives are broken, the war is on and Brideshead itself a desolation (*quomodo sedet sola civitas*), defaced by soldiers and housing Hooper. However, in the *art nouveau* chapel the "beaten-copper lamp of deplorable design" burns anew. The saving of a soul may call for the ruin of a life; the saving of the City for its desecration.

> Something quite remote from anything the builders intended has come out of their work, and out of the fierce little human tragedy in which I played.

The desecration of the City as a mysterious means to its restoration was the vision Mr. Waugh attributed to Pius V.

Mr. Waugh says he has kept in certain details because "they were essentially of the mood of writing; also because many readers liked them, though that is not a consideration of first importance." I think it is possible to like these details but to dislike other, perhaps more radical elements; though this is doubtless even less important, since to name them is to place oneself with the Hoopers. I mean that the characters are sometimes repulsive, and it spoils this book, as it doesn't the earlier work, to disagree with the author on this point. It is, for example, such a surprise to learn that Ryder is beautiful and beloved. Again there is Hooper, in whose person we are to see an abstract of the stupidity and vulgarity that beat upon the outer wall. The defenders have made a wrong appreciation; their enemy is more dangerous, much cleverer, than Hooper. As soon as Mr. Waugh disciplines his fantasy to a more explicit statement of the theme that has so long haunted him that theme is played falsely; Hooper marks the degree of distortion.

What we have in this book is the fullest statement of this image of the City, powered by that historical intransigence that equates the English aristocratic with the Catholic tradition; and very remarkable it is. But the operation of divine grace seems to be confined to those who say "chimneypiece" and to the enviable poor. Hooper and his brothers may be hard to bear, they may be ignorant of the City, but it seems outrageous to damn them for their manners. One would like, no doubt, to keep the Faith, in all its aspects, uncontaminated; but Hoopers are not Ebionites, and the novelist, imitating the action of grace, is not an infallible church to suppress them. For all that one admires in *Brideshead*—the City, the treatment of suffering, the useful and delightful Blanche, and Ryder's father—there is this difficulty, that intransigence when it gets into the texture of a novel breeds resistance; one fights rather than becomes absorbed. To suspend disbelief in these circumstances would be an act of sentimentality; a weakness not wholly unrelated to intransigence, and according to some discoverable in the text itself as well as in many readers.

James W. Nichols (essay date October 1962)

SOURCE: "Romantic *and* Realistic: The Tone of Evelyn Waugh's Early Novels," in *College English,* Vol. 24, No. 1, October 1962, pp. 46-56.

[*In the following essay, Nichols discusses Waugh's use of satire in his early novels, focusing on what he considers Waugh's often contradictory ideals of romanticism and realism.*]

Evelyn Waugh has been asked, "Are your books meant to be satirical?" He replied, "No. Satire is a matter of period. It flourishes in a stable society and presupposes homogeneous moral standards—the early Roman Empire and 18th Century Europe. It is aimed at inconsistency and hypocrisy. It exposes polite cruelty and folly by exaggerating them. It seeks to produce shame. All this has no place in the Century of the Common Man where vice no longer pays lip service to virtue" ["Fan-Fare," *Life,* April 8, 1946].

The article from which the quotation is taken appeared in *Life* in 1946, not long after the publication of *Brideshead Revisited,* the first of Waugh's novels to win him a wide

transatlantic public. The tone of the article suggests that he was not entirely serious. A "satire," as far as the novel is concerned, is a novel so constructed and so written as to embody a point of view which adversely criticizes the manners and morals of its characters—and often the society to which they belong, as well. Even a casual reading will make plain that most of Waugh's early novels are intended to be satiric, as well as comic.

> *Decline and Fall* is a remarkably funny book which, unlike many another comic novel, improves upon re-reading.
> —*James W. Nichols*

But he raises an issue which concerns all contemporary writers of satire. Most great satire has been written at times when there was general agreement about what constituted right moral standards. The modern satirist cannot count upon homogeneous moral standards in his audience. Therefore he has to establish *within* the satire a moral norm which his audience will accept. One way of doing this is to let the reader know that a character is intended to represent the author's point of view. His actions or comments, then, can embody or focus the satiric attack. Waugh seldom did this in the early novels. Instead, he chose to let the tone—his implied attitude toward characters, events, social scene—bear the burden of, first, establishing a standard by which his characters, and the incidents in which they figure, may be measured, and, second, of embodying the adverse judgment upon these characters and incidents which is essential to satire.

An understanding of how satiric tone is created and employed, then, is crucial to an understanding of the satire in Waugh's early novels. Seven had been published when the quotation above was printed: *Decline and Fall* (1928), *Vile Bodies* (1930), *Black Mischief* (1932), *A Handful of Dust* (1934), *Scoop* (1938), *Put Out More Flags* (1942), and *Brideshead Revisited* (1945). The latter has satiric elements, but is really a straight novel, rather than a "satire." *Put Out More Flags* has some brilliant satiric, as well as comic, passages, but the novel as a whole never rises above its glittering fragments. *Scoop* and *Black Mischief* are better *as* satires, but a good deal of the satire is directed against foreign customs and institutions. Waugh is best, as satirist, when his targets are domestic ones. *Decline and Fall, Vile Bodies,* and *A Handful of Dust* form a relatively homogeneous group. All three have similar backgrounds; all satirize the English upper classes during a crucial period in their history and that of their country, the late 1920's and early 1930's. All are informed with a tone which is distinctively Waugh's. It sharpens the edge of the comedy and provides the moral standard which is essential to satire.

Decline and Fall is a remarkably funny book which, unlike many another comic novel, improves upon re-reading. It is an apprenticeship novel and, like the heroes of other apprenticeship novels, its hero is thrust into a world for which he is ill-prepared. Paul Pennyfeather, a meek and proper Oxford undergraduate, is catapulted into an outrageously topsy-turvy world outside the university walls. Stripped of his trousers by a group of drunken, aristocratic undergraduates, he is sent down for "indecent exposure," and takes a post at a prep school-in North Wales which is run by a confidence-man and staffed by criminals, misfits, and unfrocked clergymen. Paul's own meek innocence proves attractive to the mother of one of his pupils and he is taken on as a tutor at her country home, a modern showplace frequented by degenerates and eccentrics. Paul and Margot Beste-Chetwynde, his employer, are about to be married when he is arrested for white slavery, the consequence of an errand he had innocently performed for his bride-to-be. Paul is sentenced and jailed at Blackstone Gaol, a prison run along absurdly "liberal" lines. From there he is transferred to a prison on the heath from which Margot's agents arrange his escape and feign his death so that he is free to return, disguised, to his college at Oxford and resume his studies undisturbed.

The world which Paul passes through between the time he leaves and the time he returns to Oxford is an outrageous one in which the moral scheme he has been taught at home and in school is neither observed nor respected. Mere energy and effrontery are heavily rewarded, not only by the world's goods, but by the world's esteem. Modesty and virtue, what there is exhibited of them, are everywhere shown to be feckless and despicable. Margot Beste-Chetwynde, for example, is a soulless degenerate, yet is almost everywhere triumphant and is all but universally esteemed.

As I have summarized it above, *Decline and Fall* is likely to seem more overtly satirical than it appears on a first reading. A reader, particularly an American reader, is likely to recognize a satiric tone in much of what he reads, and yet wonder uneasily where Waugh himself stands in relation to the brilliant, chaotic world he has created. One real difficulty is that the author takes no narrow, "moralistic" view of his world. He seems to despise the methods by which the esteem of the world and the world's goods are gained, but he does *not* despise either the esteem or the goods themselves. Margot, for example, is completely amoral, yet is everywhere successful, and there is no indication, either explicitly or implicitly, that the way in which she has achieved her success has spoiled it. In other words, Waugh is at once a moralist *and* a realist.

Since Waugh does not make an explicit comment or establish unmistakably a point of view, the novel seems to lack a clearly defined center. Consider some of the things which the tone in *Decline and Fall* suggests are to be considered objects of satire, as well as of comedy: that is, to imply a reproof, as well as to raise a laugh. He seems to satirize the beastliness of undergraduate societies and the leniency of college authorities toward wealthy and aristocratic members of such societies. He satirizes private preparatory schools, "modern" religion, and "enlightened" prison reform. There are enough Welsh jokes to suggest that he means to impugn utterly the national character and culture of Wales. Most of all, perhaps, he seems to satirize the morals and outlook of "smart" society.

Sometimes he seems to be working both sides of the street at the same time. He satirizes "Chokey," the half-educated but pretentious Negro, but seems at the same time to be satirizing those who criticize him. The impression the novel as a whole gives is kaleidoscopic. What Aldous Huxley says of his own *Antic Hay* fits *Decline and Fall* as well: "One has, in his post-adolescence, a burst of astonishment at life. Everything seems amusing and extraordinary and amazing" [quoted in Harvey Breit, *The Writer Observed*, 1956]. This is just how *Decline and Fall* strikes the reader—it is an inspired record of the absurdity of the world outside the gates of Hertford College, Oxford, as it appeared to an undergraduate in the late 1920's. It is an outrageous, amazing world that he doesn't quite understand.

But there are a couple of passages which suggest the existence of a standard of values and point forward to the more clearly marked-out position of the later novels. When Paul is being driven to his new post at Margot's house he thinks:

> "English spring. . . . In the dreaming ancestral beauty of the English country." Surely, he thought, those great chestnuts in the morning sun stood for something enduring and serene in a world that had lost its reason and would so stand when the chaos and confusion were forgotten? And surely it was the spirit of William Morris that whispered to him in Margot Beste-Chetwynde's motor car about seed-time and harvest, the superb succession of the seasons, the harmonious interdependence of rich and poor, of dignity, innocence and tradition? But at a turn in the drive the cadence of his thoughts was abruptly transected. They had come into sight of the house.

Later, when Paul is being transferred from one prison to another, he thinks back upon his relationship with Margot:

> He had "done the right thing" in shielding the woman: so much was clear, but Margot had not quite filled the place assigned to her, for in this case she was grossly culpable, and he was shielding her, not from misfortune nor injustice, but from the consequences of her crimes; he felt a flush about his

knees as Boy Scout honour whispered that Margot had got him into a row and ought jolly well to own up and face the music. As he sat over his post-bags he had wrestled with this argument without achieving any satisfactory result except a growing conviction that there was something radically inapplicable about this whole code of ready-made honour that is the still small voice, trained to command, of the Englishman all the world over.

Decline and Fall is satiric, rather than a "satire," if by satire we mean a novel organized to imply a consistent and well-developed point of view differing from that of its main characters. But Paul's realization that the world has lost its reason and that traditional codes of ready-made honor no longer apply points forward to the standard of judgment which is to be developed in the later novels.

Despite the putative inferiority of second to first novels, *Vile Bodies* (1930) is very nearly up to the standard set by *Decline and Fall*. The hero, Adam Fenwick-Symes, is more substantial and active than Paul Pennyfeather. Adam's adventures in clearing customs, as a society reporter, his attempts to raise enough money to marry Nina Blount, and so on, are the main plot, but the action includes the whole Mayfair set to which Nina and Adam belong, and the novel as a whole is a satiric picture of fashionable London society midway between two world wars.

Waugh's own point of view is much more clearly revealed in *Vile Bodies* than in *Decline and Fall*. The ways in which he manages to do this without commenting explicitly himself can be conveniently grouped under three general, although not mutually exclusive, headings. First, he stakes out points of reference to guide the reader. The Armistice and the First World War are both mentioned, a coming war is predicted, and the novel ends on "the biggest battlefield in the history of the world." Waugh's gay Mayfair set is haunted by the memory of one world war and apprehensive of the approach of another. This helps to explain, and in some measure to justify, the furious round of pleasure upon which the Bright Young Things are embarked. Other points of reference are provided by occasional comments by both the conservative aristocracy and the lower-middle-class. Often these comments have no direct bearing upon the gyrations of the Bright Young Things, but they do serve to indicate a more conservative system of values.

A second way Waugh establishes the point of view is to order the structure of the novel itself to imply it. A point of view is implicit, for instance, in a pair of contrasting scenes near the center of the book. The fantastic party in a captive dirigible given by the Bright Young Things is immediately followed by a description of a party given at Anchorage House attended by:

a great concourse of pious and honourable people . . . people who had represented their country in foreign places and sent their sons to die for her in battle, people of decent and temperate life, uncultured, unaffected, unembarrassed, unassuming, unambitious people, of independent judgment and marked eccentricities, kind people who cared for animals and the deserving poor, brave and rather unreasonable people, that fine phalanx of the passing order. . . .

The most important of these devices, however, is the explicit commentary of the characters themselves. For instance, Father Rothschild attempts to explain the rationale of the Bright Young Things:

"Don't you think . . . that perhaps it is all in some way historical? I don't think people ever *want* to lose their faith either in religion or anything else. I know very few young people, but it seems to me that they are all possessed with an almost fatal hunger for permanence. I think all these divorces show that. People aren't content just to muddle along nowadays. . . . And this word "bogus" they all use. . . They won't make the best of a bad job nowadays. . . . They say, 'If a thing's not worth doing well, it's not worth doing at all.' It makes every thing very difficult for them."

The subject of the war which seems to be approaching is brought up:

"Anyhow," said Lord Metroland, "I don't see how all that explains why my stepson should drink like a fish and go about everywhere with a negress."

"I think they're connected, you know," said Father Rothschild. "But it's all very difficult."

However, it is clear that while Waugh believes he understands the Bright Young Things, he does not excuse them for the way they act. The small attendance at Agatha Runcible's funeral is an implicit comment upon the heartlessness of her set.

A Handful of Dust (1934) is Waugh's masterpiece. In it his wonderfully fertile comic imagination, his ability to set, and to modulate, satiric tone, and his feeling for the macabre fuse; the result is an unforgettable picture of a brilliant, but sick, society whose decadence he emphasizes not only by choosing both his title and his motto from *The Waste Land* but also by echoing Proust in two of his chapter titles.

Each of his chief characters, Tony Last and his wife Brenda, epitomizes one of the things that is wrong with their society. Brenda can find no real satisfaction in being a wife and mother. Bored by her marriage to Tony, who is decent and honourable, but dull, she begins an affair with John Beaver, a half-man who lives beside his telephone on the fringes of the fashionable world. Though she is well aware of Beaver's worthlessness, Brenda insists upon a divorce and, to support her Mr. Beaver, makes such demands for a settlement upon Tony that he breaks off divorce proceedings and goes abroad. Beaver leaves her, too, but things end happily for Brenda. Tony is reported dead in the Amazon jungle and she promptly marries an old friend of his.

A good deal of the satire in the novel is aimed at Brenda and her friends, a group of aging Bright Young Things. All of the satire is indirect; Waugh doesn't tell us what kind of people his characters are, their own actions and conversation do. Thus when Tony Last, who has acted decently towards Brenda, refuses to sacrifice Hetton, his beloved home, to buy John Beaver for Brenda:

> "Who on earth would have expected the old boy to turn up like that?" asked Polly Cockpurse.
>
> "Now I understand why they keep going on in the papers about divorce law reform," said Veronica. "It's too monstrous that he should be allowed to get away with it."
>
> "The mistake they made was in telling him first," said Souki.
>
> "It's so like Brenda to trust everyone," said Jenny Abdul Akbar.

Although Brenda epitomizes certain qualities which Waugh detests, she is not merely a caricature—or perhaps it would be more accurate to say that she is more subtly drawn than most caricatures. Despite her general bitchiness, she has an oddly appealing quality even in the depths of her affair with Beaver, and Waugh so nicely tempers Tony Last's decency with dullness that the reader is not entirely out of patience with Brenda when she wants a freer life in London. What does kill the reader's sympathy for her is her reception of the news of the death of her son, John Andrew. She is in London, visiting friends, while John Beaver flies over to France with his mother. Jock Menzies, Tony's best friend, brings the news to her:

> "What is it, Jock? Tell me quickly, I'm scared. It's nothing awful is it?"
>
> "I'm afraid it is. There's been a very serious accident."
>
> "John?"

> "Yes."
>
> "Dead?"
>
> He nodded.
>
> She sat down on a hard little Empire chair against the wall, perfectly still with her hands folded in her lap, like a small well-brought-up child introduced into a room full of grown-ups. She said, "Tell me what happened. What do you know about it first?"
>
> "I've been down at Hetton since the week-end."
>
> "Hetton?"
>
> "Don't you remember? John was going hunting today."
>
> She frowned, not at once taking in what he was saying. "John. . . John Andrew. . . I . . . oh, thank God. . . ." Then she burst into tears.

At first it seems that Tony, who is dull, but a decent sort, is to embody the standards by which the Bright Young Things are judged. He is an innocent who lives amid dreams of Victorian Gothic stability and morality at Hetton Abbey, the family seat, which, slowly, he is trying to modernize and restore to its former glory. He has gotten into the habit of loving and trusting Brenda and does not suspect her affair with Beaver until she announces she wants a divorce. Even then he wants to do the traditional gentlemanly thing—to give her a generous settlement and to take all the blame for the divorce action. It is only when she demands so much that he will have to give up Hetton to satisfy her that he balks, refuses to go through with the divorce action, and leaves England.

But it is evident throughout that Tony is not only an innocent, but an adolescent as well. His room at Hetton, called Morgan le Fay, is a "gallery representative of every phase of his adolescence," and his conduct bears out the impression his room gives of his character. When Brenda takes to staying in London to be near her Mr. Beaver, Tony comes up for the night and when he can't see her gets drunk and pesters her by telephone. The whole sequence is one of the funniest things Waugh has ever done, but it is basically the record of an extended series of undergraduate pranks. Tony acts like a Victorian romantic hero during the divorce proceedings, and his leaving England when the divorce falls through is the action of a romantic juvenile.

Tony's fate in the Amazon jungle, although grotesquely out of proportion to whatever his just deserts may be, has a certain macabre appropriateness. He is seeking the city of his romantic dreams, "a transfigured Hetton, pennons and banners floating on the sweet breeze." What he finds is the distorted, but still recognizable, underside of the Victorian world. Mr. Todd is a Victorian father, monstrously selfish, despotically strict, but he provides sustenance and protection. The reading aloud from Dickens to which Tony is condemned is not only an ironic repayment for the agony he had caused Brenda by reading aloud at Hetton, but a grimly amusing suggestion of the boredom which must have made many a Victorian family evening a horror. The cream of the jest is that he should be condemned to read novels about the Victorian commercial classes, whose world and whose values overwhelmed the Victorian Gothic world Tony had dreamed of.

To put the whole matter succinctly, Tony as well as Brenda is being satirized. I make the point at some length because it is a crucial one and because Waugh has been criticized on the ground that he approves of, and sympathizes with, Tony. Quite the contrary. Neither Tony nor Brenda and her group represent values which he admires. Brenda and her circle are heartless; Tony is incapable of coping with the modern world.

A distinctive point of view is embodied in the tone of Waugh's early novels. The title of the first novel echoes Gibbon, an indication that Waugh considers English smart society, despite its surface brilliance, corrupt and decadent. Something is wrong—the traditional standards of value no longer seem to apply. Not morality, but immorality pays. In *Vile Bodies* he extends his portrait of English society. The values he prizes most are those of order, of selfless devotion to the service of God and country. But he is well aware that these values no longer receive even lip service. The First World War, he implies, caused or accelerated the decay of moral values, and another war, one which will destroy all civilization, is in progress as the novel ends.

A Handful of Dust complements the two earlier novels, but the main focus is upon marriage, the family, the individual. It contains some of Waugh's finest tonal effects. In the scenes at Brighton, for example, the farcical tone of the incidents in which "evidence" for the divorce action is gathered is tempered by Waugh's compassion for Tony Last's very real anguish. Thus he is able to imply a point of view—that modern marriage is hollow and farcical, although capable of causing deep distress to one who takes it seriously—which is never stated directly. Presumably, he had scenes like this in mind when he said that the novel "contained all I had to say about humanism."

Earlier I suggested that in Waugh's early novels the tone establishes the standard of values which is necessary to the satiric attack. Tone is essentially the projection of an attitude toward, a point of view about, the characters of his novels

and the world they inhabit. The basis of this attitude is a conflict between what I should call "realistic" and "romantic" ideas and feelings. Waugh understands that the modern world is one in which the traditional standards—ones which he cherishes—no longer apply: "vice no longer pays lip service to virtue." But he recognizes that the *rewards* of vice—the world's esteem and the world's goods—are not despised, and recognizes, too, that the way in which goods and esteem are gained may not spoil the enjoyment of them.

Thus far his point of view is a good deal like that of the satirists of the past. But these satirists tempered attacks upon their times by at least implying that there was an alternative set of values, or an alternate course of action, which *could* rectify the evils they portrayed. Waugh too has an alternative, one which he examines in his early novels. The alternative is a romantic one—a hope that a return to the traditions and values of the past offers a way of ameliorating the beastliness of the modern world. But when this idea is put to test, it is found wanting.

Waugh's attitude toward Tony Last is a good example of this. Tony belongs to, and to some extent represents, a tradition to which Waugh is strongly attached. D. S. Savage calls Tony's outlook "adolescent romanticism" ["The Innocence of Evelyn Waugh," in *The Novelist as Thinker*, 1947] and infers that this represents Waugh's *own* way of looking at the world. This is only part of the truth, I think. While Waugh can sympathize with Tony, he satirizes him as well. He comes to the conclusion that a man armed only with a traditional code of values is helpless in the modern world. He is no philosopher; he has no alternative to propose. But he *wishes* that Tony's values were not so completely outdated. The tension between Waugh's realistic appraisal of what the modern world is like and his romantic yearning for a system of values that he *knows* no longer works informs the tone and provides the satiric standard in his early novels.

D. J. Dooley (essay date Autumn 1968)

SOURCE: "Waugh and Black Humor," in *Evelyn Waugh Newsletter*, Vol. 2, No. 2, Autumn 1968, pp. 1-3.

[*Dooley is a Canadian writer and educator. In the following essay, Dooley examines instances of black humor in Waugh's writing and suggests possible influences to Waugh's comic sensibility.*]

In an article in the *Kenyon Review* in 1961, C. P. Snow referred to the transmission of a particular vein of personal and capricious comedy from Russian to English fiction as one of the clearest examples of literary ancestry which he knew. He described the agent of transmission, William

Gerhardi, as the chief progenitor of modern English prose comedy, and said that he had a very sharp effect on such talented young men of the Twenties as Waugh and Anthony Powell. But as the *Waugh Newsletter* pointed out, Saki and Firbank could not be overlooked as comic models. Similarly, when he ridiculed the whole notion of influences in a sentence quoted by Stopp, Waugh provided us with more names to conjure with: "A lecturer in English literature might discern two sources of Dr. Wodehouse's art—the light romance of Ian Hay and the social satire of 'Saki,' but the attribution is quite irrelevant in the world of the imagination." Still another influence on him, almost undoubtedly, is Maurice Baring—another interpreter of Russia to England and writer of comedies both English and Ruritanian. Another who ought not to be overlooked is E. M. Forster, author of some Alexandrian sketches which Waugh praised highly. In the "St. Athanasius" section of *Pharos and Pharillon,* for example, there is a characterization of Constantine which may have suggested Waugh's handling of him in **Helena,** and the scene in which that "charming and reasonable young man" Caligula runs through his new villa with a mob of carpenters and plumbers at his heels, as well as a deputation of Jews from Alexandria and a counter-deputation of anti-Semites from the same city, is close in spirit to Waugh's comedy. Forster writes:

> He climbed up to look at a ceiling. They climbed too. He ran along a plan; so did the Jews. They did not speak, partly from lack of breath, partly because they were afraid of his reply. At last, turning in their faces, he asked: "Why don't you eat pork?" The counter-deputation shouted again. The Jews replied that different races ate different things, and one of them, to carry off the situation, said some people didn't eat lamb. "Of course they don't," said the Emperor, "lamb is beastly."

To mention other possible sources of Waugh's humor is not to deny the influence of Gerhardi; when the latter was awarded an Arts Council bursary towards the end of 1966, the *Observer* commented that the word "genius" had been applied to him by Waugh, so that presumably Waugh read and was influenced by him.

But should Gerhardi's type of humor be called black humor? The *TLS* review of André Breton's *Anthologie de l'humour noir* discovered beneath Breton's verbiage a fairly clear idea of what *black humor* involves: on a personal level it is a legitimate defence against the tragedy of *la condition humaine,* on a social level it is an essentially *scandalous* protest against the intolerable concept of an "ordered" world explained by science and activated by technology. Gerhardi's tone and attitude are very different; they are established by a performance of a Chekhov play early in *Futility:*

> You know the manner of Chekhov's writing. You know the people in his plays. It seems as though they had all been born on the line of demarcation between comedy and tragedy. . . Fanny Ivanovna and the three sisters watched the play with intense interest, as if the *Three Sisters* were indeed their own particular tragedy. I sat behind Nina, and watched with that stupid scepticism that comes from too much happiness. To me, buoyant and impatient, the people in the play appeared preposterous. They distressed me intensely. Their black melancholy, their incredible inefficiency, their paralysing inertia, crept over me. How different, I thought, were those three lovable creatures who sat in our box. How careless and free they were in their own happy home. The people in the play were hopeless.

At the interval, he grasps his friend Nikolai by the arm in exasperation: "How can there be such people, Nikolai Vasilievich?. . . They can't get where they want. They don't even know what they want. . . . It is a hysterical cry for greater efforts, for higher aims. . . Why can't people know what they want in life and get it?. . ." Of course as its title suggests the novel shows the gradual disillusionment of the central character, his own failure to get what *he* wants. But though the book is on the borderline between comedy and tragedy, it is hardly a scandalous protest against the concept of an ordered world.

It *does* contain a protest against sacrificing the people of one generation to secure a better social order for the next, and in connection with this protest there are some episodes of macabre humor, especially connected with the battles of Whites versus Reds in Vladivostok. But macabre humor of this type is found in English literature well before Gerhardi; one need only think of Saki's short stories or of Norman Douglas's tale of the man who fell six hundred feet from a Capri cliff and was in no condition to swim to Philadelphia. In *The Living Novel,* V. S. Pritchett writes of the vein of fanciful horror in Thomas Hood—in poems such as "The Careless Nurse Mayd" and "Sally Simpkin's Lament." He goes on,

> Gilbert, Lear, Carroll, Thackeray, the authors of *Struwelpeter* and the cautionary tales continue this comic macabre tradition, which today appears to be exhausted. There is Mr. Belloc, who digressed intellectually, and there are the sardonic ballads of Mr. William Plomer.

The tradition was not exhausted; it had merely been diverted into the novel. Waugh and Huxley made use of it in the Twenties, Douglas and Beerbohm (with his Defenestration of Noaks, for example) in the previous decade.

But once again is macabre humor to be identified with black humor? In Simon Encelberg's essay on Joseph Heller (in Richard Kostelanetz's collection of essays *On Contemporary Literature*), the following adjectives are applied to *Catch-22:* sprawling, hilarious, irresponsible, compassionate, cynical, surrealistic, farcical, lacerating, readable. The terms suggest an attitude to humor and satire which is very different from the attitudes of Beerbohm, Douglas, Saki, and Waugh. It is the difference, in a way, between Waugh's *Loved One* and the film of the same name, bravely advertised as "The motion picture with something to offend everyone." Discussing the movie in *Life*, Shana Alexander wrote that "The true queasy-making vulgarity of *The Loved One* . . . lies in the fact that it mixes up jokes about our attitudes toward death, which are often absurd, with death itself, which never is." The essentially irresponsible attitude which Tony Richardson and Terry Southern took to their material was worlds removed from Waugh's concern with it; after all, in his *Life* article on Forest Lawn he suggested that the decline of Western civilization might have been observable first of all in the graveyard. Describing disorder, he implied rather than ridiculed order: like Pope and Swift, he tried to shock people into a realization of how far they had departed from a reasonable and humane standard of behaviour, whereas the black humorists seem to mock the very concept of such a standard.

Barry Ulanov (essay date 1970)

SOURCE: "The Ordeal of Evelyn Waugh," in *The Vision Obscured: Perceptions of Some Twentieth-Century Catholic Novelists,* edited by Melvin J. Friedman, New York: Fordham University Press, 1970, pp. 79-93.

[*Ulanov is an American writer, educator, and editor. In the following essay, he analyzes the "underlying structure" of the world-view that infused Waugh's novels and gave meaning to his allegorical writings.*]

It is all but a fixed convention in the critical presentation of the work of Evelyn Waugh to date his decline, in mid-career, with the appearance of *Brideshead Revisited* in 1945. The novels written before it are comic masterpieces. Those that come after, with the possible exception of *The Loved One* (1948), are blighted by the disease of Brideshead, an egregious inclination to take religion seriously, accompanied by a marked distaste for the world that does not share that inclination—the modern world.

Waugh was immediately taken to task, on the appearance of *Brideshead Revisited,* for his shocking display of religious sentiment and his apparent loss of the satiric spirit. He answered his American critics as publicly as he could in the

pages of a journal not generally thought of as literary—*Life* magazine. Modern novelists, Waugh explained,

> try to represent the whole human mind and soul and yet omit its determining character—that of being God's creature with a defined purpose. So in my future books there will be two things to make them unpopular: a preoccupation with style and the attempt to represent man more fully, which to me means only one thing, man in his relation to God.

The work that followed *Brideshead Revisited,* two years later, was a corrosive political satire, a novella called *Scott-King's Modern Europe.* It is the tale of the misadventures of the Classical Master of a second-rate English public school in Neutralia. He has been invited to this "typical modern state, governed by a single party, acclaiming a dominant Marshal, supporting a vast ill-paid bureaucracy whose work is tempered and humanised by corruption," because of his celebration in an essay in a learned journal of the qualities of Neutralia's Latin poet Bellorius. Bellorius is about to suffer—along with Scott-King and the reader—the tercentenary of his death. With the heaviest possible irony, Waugh describes his narrative as "the story of a summer holiday; a light tale." It is not a light tale; it is a ponderous satire which brings Scott-King back to his public school by way of "No. 64, Jewish Illicit Immigrants' Camp, Palestine." The headmaster suggests that Scott-King think about teaching another subject alongside Classics—"History, for example, preferably economic history." After all, parents no longer send their boys to school to become "'the complete man.'. . . They want to qualify their boys for jobs in the modern world. You can hardly blame them, can you?" Scott-King's answer is direct: "Oh yes," he says. "I can and do." The last bits of dialogue permit Scott-King to put the modern world in its place.

> "But, you know, there may be something of a crisis ahead."
> "Yes, headmaster."
> "Then what do you intend to do?"
> "If you approve, headmaster, I will stay as I am here as long as any boy wants to read the classics. I think it would be very wicked indeed to do anything to fit a boy for the modern world."
> "It's a short-sighted view, Scott-King."
> "There, headmaster, with all respect, I differ from you profoundly. I think it the most long-sighted view it is possible to take."

Waugh did not need the cumbersome apparatus of *Scott-King's Modern Europe* to make clear his disenchantment with the modern world. Nor did he need the pages of *Life* magazine to make public pronouncements about his "preoccupation" with style and the relation of man to God. He had been making such pronouncements for almost two decades before *Brideshead Revisited,* but obliquely, in variously light and heavy explorations of the allegory of irony. Waugh was not finished with allegorical devices, nor did he relinquish the ironic pose after *Brideshead;* but the indirections of satire were no longer all. It was as though his presentation of "The Sacred and Profane Memories of Captain Charles Ryder" had evoked in him the spirit of the confessional. Like the most unconscious character in Chekhov, he seemed determined now to reveal his working purposes. In some curious way, his two creeds, as writer and as Christian, would be made to coincide. In *The Loved One,* he mocked the happy hunting-grounds of the American ways of death, human and animal, which sought certainties where none were to be found. In *Helena* (1950), he praised the simple faith of the woman who was canonized by tradition for her perseverance in seeking the wood of the True Cross, a woman of a time "Once, very long ago, before ever the flowers were named," the mother of the Roman Emperor Constantine, and, in Waugh's version of sacred history, a Briton and the daughter of Old King Coel.

In-between the clammy humors of California Gothic and the dry atmosphere of Celtic-Roman hagiology, Waugh followed the confessional urge where it led—to the opening pages of a collection of stories of conversion to Catholicism by well-known figures of the late 1940s. Waugh's piece was called **"Come Inside."** In five short pages he moved across the bare facts of his religious life, from beginnings in the Church of England and a "family tree" which "burgeons on every twig with Anglican clergymen," and an early intention of becoming a clergyman himself:

> The enthusiasm which my little school-fellows devoted to birds' eggs and model trains I turned to church affairs and spoke glibly of chasubles and Erastianism. I was accordingly sent to the school which was reputed to have the strongest ecclesiastical bent. At the age of sixteen I formally notified the school chaplain that there was no God. At the age of twenty-six I was received into the Catholic Church to which all subsequent experience has served to confirm my loyalty.

Waugh's little piece is savage in its rejection of his own attempts to deal with the brambles of the higher criticism, as uncovered by a skeptical Oxford theologian ("now a bishop"), and the thickets of metaphysics, as presented in Pope's *Essay on Man* and in Leibniz, to whom he was sent by the notes in his edition of Pope.

> I advanced far enough to be thoroughly muddled about the nature of cognition. It seemed simplest to abandon the quest and assume that man was incapable of knowing anything. I have no doubt I was

a prig and a bore but I think that if I had been a Catholic boy at a Catholic school I should have found among its teaching orders someone patient enough to examine with me my callow presumption. Also, if I had been fortified by the sacraments, I should have valued my faith too highly to abandon it so capriciously.

What Waugh found in the Church was tradition, the Catholic structure omnipresent in European life, customs, ceremonies, and disciplines of learning. Americans may lack this; their world certainly does. Europe in general and England in particular may not look upon the Church as simply one of a series of splendid sects. The Church underlies everything in Waugh's world. It is his inheritance. After being admitted into the Church, he tells us in carefully weighed words, his "life has been an endless delighted tour of discovery in the huge territory of which I was made free." What he does not tell us in this 1949 piece, but does confess in the novels, the stories, the occasional pieces, the columns of liturgical controversy—in nearly everything that followed upon it—is that more and more he became a furious partisan, fighting for the survival of ancient values, ancient worlds, ancient rituals. He moved with sour obstinacy against the new liturgy produced by the Second Vatican Council. He was made sick with something like shame by the translation of the words of the Mass into the English vernacular. In this vulgate tongue, they clearly lacked unction. They were not in the ancient style. They were not in any style that he could respect. They lacked that universality and coherence that made the terrors of modernity, if not tolerable, at least endurable as a preface to a world of endless grace. He had extended his invitation to the non-Catholic to follow him inside the Church:

> You cannot know what the Church is like from outside. However learned you are in theology, nothing you know amounts to anything in comparison with the knowledge of the simplest actual member of the Communion of Saints.

Could one still believe this, still feel this, after the depredations of Vatican II?

Waugh mocks the "shallowness" of his "early piety," clearly demonstrated "by the ease with which I abandoned it." To his interest in "chasubles and Erastianism" he attributes a depth comparable to the devotion to birds' eggs and model trains of his contemporaries at school. But there is something quite different in kind about his penchant, at the age of eleven, for Anglican churchmanship, the intense curiosity he describes in his autobiography: "about church decorations and the degrees of anglicanism–'Prot, Mod, High, Spiky'—which they represented" [*A Little Learning*]. The pursuit of grace at eleven may have been confined to a shrine he constructed for the night-nursery, complete with plaster saints, an *art nouveau* edition of Newman's *Dream of Gerontius,* and his own attempt at the subject of Newman's long poem, Purgatory—an effort "in the metre of Hiawatha" which he calls "long and tedious" in one place, "deplorable" in another. But it was grace he pursued, tediously perhaps, certainly at length. The comings and goings of his faith, now Anglican, now atheist, finally Roman, were surely never as inconsequential to him or for him as his ironic autobiographical narratives suggest. He was always a ceremonialist, always caught up in some ritual or other, as feckless student and schoolmaster, or as despairing socialite. It is ritual that fascinates him in his several worlds, even when it is altogether fatuous. It is ritual he gathers so entertainingly into his early satires. When the satire wears thin and the end in view ceases to be entertainment, the ritual remains. Only now it is no longer quite so fatuous. There is faith in it. The pursuit of grace has become, like the explorations of the allegory of irony, far less oblique.

If one sees the pursuit of grace in the work of Evelyn Waugh, sees it in the inverted and perverted rituals of *Decline and Fall* (1928), *Vile Bodies* (1930), *Black Mischief* (1932), *Scoop* (1938), and *Put Out More Flags* (1942) as much as in the open courtings of the supernatural in *Brideshead Revisited, Helena,* and *Sword of Honour,* one is not so easily put off or surprised by the sentimentality of the later work. One sees Waugh constantly soliciting a deeper coherence than the ceremonies of the social life or the customs of international politics are likely to reveal. One sees Waugh's meticulous notation of custom and ceremony as being in the service of grace, and not at all lacking in meaning because it deals with people who have little or no meaning and are determined to do everything to escape meaning. One sees Waugh's narratives, from the beginning, as severely moralized—though not (in the beginning at least) very clear in their moral purpose. One sees an allegorist sharpening his instruments, perfecting his ironic moral tone, so that when the pursuit of grace can be made more open, when grace can emerge from the chilling shadows of a world that holds it in contempt, there will be a machinery skillful enough to deal with it and to make it recognizable.

Nowhere is this honing of the tools so evident as in *A Handful of Dust* (1934). There all that Waugh had learned in his early tales of the rituals of the fatuous is displayed with an ironic detachment that can easily be interpreted as withdrawal from the moral lists—or worse, as accidie. The world of the aristocracy has collapsed. Tony Last—a name at least as roundly allegorical in intent as any in the novels of Henry Fielding—brings that world to its inexorable end, condemned to spend his final days—and they are clearly to be many—reading Dickens aloud to a madman in a South American jungle. While this allegory of attrition is worked out, Tony Last's wife, Brenda, works out her salvation in the

service of a personification of nullity, John Beaver, whose name spells nothing but an industrious boredom. The book takes its title from *The Waste Land,* and perhaps some of its hauteur as well. But where Eliot communicates his distaste for the modern world in fragments, Waugh polishes his periods in an elegantly sustained continuity, with every detail fitted firmly into place. Disaster leads to disaster in an orderly succession of horrors which everybody can accept, for the disasters and horrors follow so faithfully the ordinations of high society and never lose the approved tones. Thus the ironic echoes of Proust in two chapter titles: "Du Côté de Chez Beaver" and "Du Côté de Chez Todd"—memorializing in these cases no elegant or gifted men, but a middle-class bore and an illiterate son of a missionary with a savage devotion to the works of Charles Dickens.

The part played by Dickens in the allegorical structure of *A Handful of Dust* is particularly engaging to the reader of Waugh who has gone so far as to search out his occasional reviews. In 1953, examining Edgar Johnson's two-volume biography of Dickens for *The Spectator,* he confesses that

> We all have our moods when Dickens sickens us. In a lighter, looser and perhaps higher mood we fall victim to his "magnetism.". . . It is this constantly changing mood of appreciation that makes everyone's fingers itch for the pen at the mention of his name.

Waugh gratified the itch in this review in such a way that one understands perfectly the particular irony of Todd's fixation upon Dickens:

> —the pity of it—the more we know of Dickens, the less we like him. His conduct to his wife and particularly his announcement of the separation were deplorable. His treatment in middle age of Maria Beadnell was even worse. His benefactions to his family were grudging and ungracious. Faults which would be excusable in other men become odious in the light of Dicken's writing. He frequented the demi-monde with Wilkie Collins. He probably seduced and certainly kept the young actress Ellen Teman, to whom he left £1,000 in his will, thereby putting her name in disrepute while at the same time leaving her miserably provided. All this is very ugly in the creator of Little Emily and Martha. He claimed a spurious pedigree and used an illicit crest—a simple weakness in anyone except himself who vehemently denounced the importance attached to gentle birth. In success he was intolerably boastful, in the smallest reverse abject with self-pity. He was domineering and dishonourable in his treatment of his publishers. He was, in fact, a thumping cad

[Waugh, **"Apotheosis of an Unhappy Hypocrite,"** *The Spectator,* October 2, 1953].

Clearly a model for Waugh's grotesque tale, this reading of Dickens is allegorical of all the large hypocrisy and emotional emptiness that masquerades in *A Handful of Dust* under the small pieties of upper-class social life. What better writer could Waugh have found with whom to torment Tony Last—and the gullible reader who has been incautious enough to look for some deliverance for Tony or anyone else in this allegory of a world without grace and thus without any chance of fulfillment?

The landscape of *A Handful of Dust* is perfectly pieced together, as an allegorical landscape must be. The surfaces of buildings, as of people, are described with a splendid and an unmistakable precision. The rooms within, like the interior dispositions of the people, are carefully decorated. Waugh is following the example of his tutors in the allegory of irony—Henry Fielding and Laurence Sterne. He has left behind at this point the epicene shallows of Ronald Firbank, an earlier guide in the tones and textures of irony. The depths in which he finds and leaves his allegorical figures are those of Hieronymus Bosch and the elder Pieter Brueghel, not perhaps because he has sought those depths but because they have sought him. This world of a pettiness so acute that it has become an almost diabolical kind of hallucination was the world which sat for its portrait in Waugh's studio. This world of evasions, of shadows in retreat and of shadows in pursuit, this world that Eliot prepared for burial in *The Waste Land*—"I will show you fear in a handful of dust"—Waugh drew from its winding sheets and stood end to end in its native flats and country houses. This world of the living dead Waugh painted as Bosch and Cranach and Brueghel did—in allegorical precision. This was the world without grace, its rituals superbly ordered inversions of Christianity, its instruments so perfectly tuned that one could hardly hear the difference. One had to look very closely indeed to see that the laughter bared too much gum and popped the eyes too much to be the laughter of entertainment.

For some readers, the entertainment dropped out of Waugh's novels after *A Handful of Dust,* never to return. He simply did not get the facts of Mussolini's invasion of Ethiopia straight in *Scoop,* and to the hollow humors of his novel of the cold war, *Put Out More Flags,* he added an embarrassing tinge of patriotism. Real heroism, even if inadvertent, seemed to be popping up beneath the mock heroics. The sounds of the indecorous war that had brought *Vile Bodies* to its conclusion had given way to noisier exchanges in a war that shattered more than mere decorum. The comic-opera struggles for power in the African kingdoms of *Black Mischief* and *Scoop* did not amuse any longer; they had been replaced by a deadly warfare in the desert in which men Waugh loved and admired were losing their lives. The terms

of the allegory were irremediably changed. The deadly sins were still there—lust, gluttony, greed, and especially sloth, of which Waugh had appointed himself the patron devil. But now there were, of all things, virtues to be dealt with. Grace hovered overhead, even appeared now and then in the lives of the Halberdiers of Waugh's trilogy about the war: *Men at Arms* (1952), *Officers and Gentlemen* (1955), and *Unconditional Surrender* (1961; *The End of the Battle* in its American edition). In fact, some of Waugh's fictional regiment seemed to be positively maddened by grace, not the least of them that improbable hero of the trilogy, Guy Crouchback, who seems dedicated to moral ambiguity—that is to say, dedicated to the contradictory textures of the human condition, the only textures in which grace can comfortably appear.

The leading figures of Waugh's suddenly uprighted world are not very different from those of the inverted one. They have gone to the public school of *Decline and Fall,* to the parties of *Vile Bodies,* to the hunts of *A Handful of Dust;* they have served their own mad little corners of the cold war bureaucracy of *Put Out More Flags,* and scratched their way to the top—or the bottom—of African kingdoms. Even in their weaker moments, they have more often achieved the look of lechery and the manners of sin than the matter. Their moral failures have been most frequently failures to be immoral, which in the *old* days could be shrugged off in the giggling manner of *Vile Bodies*—

> "What I always wonder, Kitty dear, is what they actually *do* at these parties of theirs. I mean, *do* they . . .?"
>
> "My dear, from all I hear, I think they do."
>
> "Oh, to be young again, Kitty. When I think, my dear, of all the trouble and exertion which we had to go through to be even moderately bad . . . those passages in the early morning and mama sleeping next door."
>
> "And yet, my dear, I doubt very much whether they really *appreciate* it all as we should . . . young people take things so much for granted."
>
> *"Si la jeunesse savait,* Kitty . . ."
>
> *"Si la vieillesse pouvait."*

In the *new* days, the days of Brideshead and the Halberdiers, some sense is made of all this patchwork of immorality wished-for and morality achieved in spite of one's dearest hopes. The coherent patterns of a moral theology supervene. The revels, achieved or postponed, are permanently interrupted. The great romance of Brideshead, for example, into which the reader, following Waugh's sentimental lead, has poured so much expectant feeling, is dashed on the rocks of canon law. Julia Mottram must accept the terms of her marriage, as set forth in the positive legislation of the Church. She and Charles Ryder must separate. She must say goodbye. Ryder asks what she will do. She will not, she explains, lead a life of lies, on one side or the other:

> "Just go on—alone. How can I tell what I shall do? You know the whole of me. You know I'm not one for a life of mourning. I've always been bad. Probably I shall be bad again, punished again. But the worse I am the more I need God. I can't shut myself out from His mercy. That is what it would mean; starting a life with you, without Him. One can only hope to see one step ahead. But I saw today there was one thing unforgivable—like things in the schoolroom, so bad they are unpunishable, that only Mummy could deal with–the bad thing I was on the point of doing, that I'm not quite bad enough to do; to set up a rival good to God's. Why should I be allowed to understand that, and not you, Charles? It may be because of Mummy, Nanny, Cordelia, Sebastian—perhaps Bridey and Mrs. Muspratt—keeping my name in their prayers; or it may be a private bargain between me and God, that if I give up this one thing I want so much, however bad I am, He won't quite despair of me in the end.

> "Now we shall both be alone, and I shall have no way of making you understand."

Non-Catholic readers can surely be forgiven their revulsion at the seeming smugness of this dismissal of love. The set speech comes so easily from the rhetoric of the rectory. God has made the laws, down to their last canon, and we who have been initiated into His great legal fraternity, we understand. Pity we cannot make others understand.

Was Waugh trying to make others understand when he constructed his canonist's copybook adultery? Had he given up irony for apologetics? The same question can be asked about the sterile marriage which haunts Guy Crouchback, made twice as barren by the unyielding law of the Church which prevents any satisfaction to Guy in the relationship. His attempt to seduce his former wife is ruined when he informs her that the seduction is entirely licit since their marriage had never been dissolved by the Church; she runs, appalled, from his arms. He can only remarry her, to make legitimate her child by a brother officer, a malingerer and moral neutral with the precisely allegorical name of Trimmer, who has become a hero *malgré lui,* in a series of events typical of the activity of grace in the *Sword of Honour* trilogy. Grace pursues its victims in the Crouchback novels in the ancient

manner, makes heroes of trimmers and withholds the trappings of honor from those who have performed with virtue. Grace achieves the textures of irony in these books. When it lands on a hero's head, it dents his skull; it marks him a fool. If Waugh has turned to apologetics, he has not relinquished the allegory of irony to do so. He has discovered, like the Flemish painters before him, where that allegory leads.

Irony, now that it is to be employed in the precincts of grace, must make chivalry seem gauche, a hopeless anachronism; charity, the always underlying virtue in these quarters, must appear the refuge of fools. Guy Crouchback forms himself, as best he can, in the image and after the likeness of a medieval knight, Roger of Waybrooke, and grace confounds him, after having long confused him, by supporting his insane sentimentalization of the past. He finds his appropriate roles, is splendidly victimized in war and peace, and ends up, *mirabile dictu,* with a marriage that works, after his first wife has died. The original, British-edition title of the last of the Crouchback novels, *Unconditional Surrender,* is the final irony in the saga: everyone, everything concedes; grace settles on Guy's head with all the sweet finality of happy events at the end of a novel by Charles Dickens. Guy, it is clear, is a thumping saint. To the consternation of the conventional hagiologist, he is a saint rewarded on earth, although not exactly with public honors and a grand justification of his follies. His rewards come in retirement from the battles, to the family estate which is as much his inheritance as are the motions of chivalry. His life in retirement opens before him in the manner of the last years of the medieval knight. The moves are classical. Guy is, as his name makes abundantly clear, a throwback, a minor aristocrat in the annals of the blood, a major aristocrat in the annals of the spirit. One has to look twice to find him, in either set of records, crouched, like a self-conscious gargoyle, hiding beneath the benches, not of royalty or the first families of the realm, but of the quieter and less heralded families at the periphery. But one finds him—or rather grace does. And we respond—or rather grace permits us to, if we accept the terms of Waugh's allegory—in spite of all our inherited distaste for religious sentiment and the coincidences and inadvertencies which it keeps stirring up.

It is silly to reproach Waugh with the coincidences and inadvertencies of his books, whether they are the contrivances of a late religious romanticism or those of an early dyspeptic expressionism; almost as silly as the accusation that his figures are without objective reality. An allegorist's figures, like his landscapes, are deliberately contrived. Events in an allegorist's world are chained together by coincidence and inadvertences which are quite without spontaneity. Causal connections are made by the logic of the imagination and tied firmly together by the webs of dogma—whether of art or of religion or of both. Waugh's allegories take root in the real world, but they flower in no world that ever was, no matter how close their world may seem at times to the world we know. Their reality is a spiritual one, which is not to say a rational one or one that seeks the balance it does not have. The reality of the spirit may be a deranged reality or a supremely sane one. Who is to say whether the world of Brideshead and the Crouchbacks and the Halberdiers is more or less deranged than that of Tony and Brenda Last or the public-school and party-going folk of the early satires—such as Captain Grimes, Agatha Runcible, Ambrose Silk, Basil Seal, Margot Metroland, and Mrs. Ape? From beginning to end, it is the reality of the spirit that concerns Waugh. He is relentless in his efforts to get at it and ruthless with the devices of fictional realism. His novel is the novel of the eighteenth century. His techniques of characterization and narration are those of the originators of the English novel. And so in his novels, right to the end, we live with personifications and placards—Lord Outrage and Lady Circumference and Lord Tangent, Miss Tin and Miles Plastic, Mr. Joyboy and Aimée Thanatogenos, Trimmer and Major Hound. Like the titles of his books, the names of his characters signify much in the construction of his allegories. He is never shy about extending meanings beyond the uncertainties of chance and the imprecisions of the laws of probability.

In reading Waugh, one does well to meditate, for a few moments at least, on his contrivances. They are not schoolboy jokes, as they may at first appear, nor are they allegorical commonplaces. They are lines into a world of moral speculation in which every image is a potential icon and every proper noun a likely emblem. They begin as counters in a game of great comic gusto. They end as the blazons of a devout and complex heraldry.

It would be a great mistake to overestimate the depth of Waugh's allegories, to see either in the comic counters or in the heraldic clutterings a profound insight into the human condition. It would be a distortion of these materials to find anything entirely fresh or novel in them, and from Waugh's point of view an impertinence. His allegories are of an ancient kind and their content as far outside the philosophy, psychology, and sociology of this century as his devices could make it and as a vocabulary intelligible to modern readers would permit. To find more than a passing joke or a lingering sentimentality in Waugh, one must surrender to his world of the spirit and the style in which it is encased. One must, in a sense, accept and undergo the ordeal of Evelyn Waugh as a kind of spiritual exercise. For that, surely, is what Waugh's performance amounts to, looked at as an entity. It does represent a complete *oeuvre,* I believe, a unity not always sought but somehow usually found. Working with the materials of a dying society, a society in which such values as could be discovered were inevitably blurred and sometimes impossibly opaque, Waugh found coherences and

even more—an underlying structure: the "Catholic structure [that] still lies lightly buried beneath every phase of English life; history, topography, law, archaeology everywhere reveal Catholic origins." That revelation of coherence and structure, and of underlying design and purpose, led to another revelation for Waugh: it was possible to give the history and topography of his novels an unmistakable coherence, structure, design, and purpose, and not simply to allow those qualities to appear as the functions of a rigorously measured prose style. An irony that accidentally produced an allegory of sorts gave way to an allegory of irony dedicated to the exploration and even, sometimes, to the explication of Christian values. A covert regard for the ridiculous people with whom he lived out his public-school and college and party-going youth became an open sentiment of support for the soldiers who survived the opening ceremonies of World War II long enough to fight with style—in whatever task, fatuous or glorious, they were assigned—for Christian values, whether or not they understood or even professed those values.

Waugh had discovered some years before he died that, as he explained in the introductory note to *The Ordeal of Gilbert Pinfold* (1957), "Hallucination is far removed from loss of reason." He was explaining that he himself had undergone "a brief bout of hallucination" very much like that described in the novel. "The reason works with enhanced power," he went on, "while the materials for it to work on, presented by the senses, are delusions. A story-teller naturally tries to find a plot into which his observations can be fitted." That, it seems to me, is the point of Waugh's work, a point made with more and more clarity and precision as his life wore on, and with more and more warmth that sometimes settled into sentimentality. Hallucinations and all the other demonstrations of human fallibility, Waugh's fables tell us, and tell us with particular strength of conviction at the end, are also opportunities for a show of reason. That is his faith. It makes, finally, even the modern world endurable for him.

Robert Barnard (essay date April 1979)

SOURCE: "What the Whispering Glades Whispered: Dennis Barlow's Quest in *The Loved One,*" in *English Studies,* Vol. 60, No. 2, April 1979, pp. 176-82.

[*Barnard is an English writer and educator. In the following essay, he analyzes Waugh's satirical attack on superficiality and illusion in* The Loved One.]

One of the most haunting images one retains of Evelyn Waugh's life, a life rich in incongruities and contrasts, is the author's own account of how, during his brief and abortive visit to Hollywood in 1947, he was driven daily (in the car that was supposed to take him to the studio) to the cemetery called Forest Lawn, and how he spent hour after fascinated hour exploring the mysteries of the place. He had exhausted the possibilities of Hollywood in days, but the appeal of Forest Lawn seemed inexhaustible. This preference is mirrored in *The Loved One,* both in the career of Dennis Barlow, and in the structure of the novel itself; after a few pages devoted to the great dream factory, the novel takes wing for Whispering Glades and the Happier Hunting Ground, and remains there.

What was the appeal of Forest Lawn to Waugh? Of course to some extent the appeal was that of an incubating story. Waugh himself was very conscious of how limited his experience had been since his marriage, and he welcomed both the war and the hallucinatory experiences that gave him *Pinfold* precisely on the ground that one should be grateful for experience that was potential fiction. He himself, in the Preface to the Collected Edition reprint of the novel draws the parallel between himself and Barlow, and the simple explanation of the fascination is that, like him, Waugh came away with a chunk of experience which was to be turned (in Waugh's case) into a novel rather than a poem. But the interesting question is: Why *this* experience? Why, of all places in the States, did Waugh's imagination feed so ravenously on Forest Lawn? And, since Dennis Barlow's search for his 'chunk of experience' is presented, like Tony Last's, in terms of a quest, what is the quest for?

The relationship between the two major objects of satire in the novel is clear-cut. Hollywood and Whispering Glades deal with illusion, with throwing a mist of unreality over the unpalatable. Life's dream factory is complemented and completed by Death's dream factory. Just as Baby Aaronson can be transformed by the artists of the studio into Juanita del Pablo and then (as fashions change) into Kathleen Fitzbourke, so can the bulging indigo face of Sir Francis Hinsley be transformed by the artists of the mortuary into the dignified mask that will greet his mourning Waiting Ones. True in the first case the star's singing of The Wearing of the Green may have a flamenco ring, and in the second the peaceful image may appear to Barlow even more horrible than the strangulated reality. But these are extreme cases: on the whole the dream machine works its magic, and blurs the distinction between reality and illusion.

And in blurring that distinction it contributes to the dismal process of standardisation which is Waugh's second prong in his satirical attack. Mr Medici may not (like Baby Aaronson) lose his name, but it has to be pronounced Medissy ("'how you said kinda sounds like a wop and Mr Medici is a fine young man with a very, very fine and wonderful record. . .'"). The truth about Mr Medici's origins is lost, and the illusion is produced of him as the standard prod-

uct. This illusion is almost universal, since it must be within the reach of all to become the standard product. Air hostesses lose everything that makes them individual women, and become American Womanhood. Kaiser's peaches lose their stones and become fruity cotton wool. Waugh is perhaps the last of a long line of writers for whom America was the great revolutionary leveller (the position now occupied, in some American eyes, by the countries of Northern Europe).

An account of the novel along these lines is convincing enough, and true to the text—a neat and simple pattern, appropriate for such a tiny satiric gem of a novel. And yet it leaves one dissatisfied. This is not because (as has often been objected) Waugh's lines of attack were well-worn: the effectiveness of satire does not depend on the originality of the satirist's viewpoint. Yet, the more one reads the novel, the more complex it seems, or—to be more precise—the more one senses lurking layers of meaning below the mordant hilarity of the surface. This feeling, that there is something enveloping the tale which brought it out only as a glow brings out a haze, in the likeness of one of these misty halos—something complex which is never allowed entirely to become explicit, is reinforced by the Conradian opening to the novel.

If *The Loved One* were simply the hard, bright satire on American illusion and American standardisation which it is easily taken for, it is difficult to account for the deliberate mystification of this opening. We are—apparently—in some Far Eastern Outpost of Empire, with mystery and menace lurking in the jungle around the British Presence. What one would underline about this opening is not the suggestion of savagery lurking behind sophistication (which has been a constant theme of Waugh from the beginning of his career), but precisely the mystery, the disorientation the gambit produces. The reader takes some time to get his bearings, and in fact he is never allowed to be too sure that he has got them. He may feel he has resolved the mystery when the scene is revealed as Hollywood. The British are parody Empire-builders, parodying the public-school code of games, keeping up appearances, and drumming out the rotter who does not play by the rules. The Americans are the natives, whose bizarre customs are observed rather as Marlow observes the signs of savage life along the banks of the Congo—strange, terrifying, fascinating, and above all *other.*

> **Waugh makes sure that as soon as the reader thinks he has a firm foothold on the satiric viewpoint of the author, he finds himself on a slippery slope.**
> **—*Robert Barnard***

Yet as soon as this pattern is established in our minds, the kaleidoscope is given another shake, and we are back in uncertainty: Sir Francis is dismissed—more, he is de-personed. The studio not only does not employ him, it does not know him, and seems not ever to have known him. He has no identity; he has no history. A new pattern then emerges: the Americans are all-powerful rulers, God-like as Kurtz; the British are the shabby hangers on at their despotic court, barnacles posing as pillars. The new pattern is a suitable mirror of the British in the twilight of their day as Empire-builders.

Building on this beginning, Waugh makes sure that as soon as the reader thinks he has a firm foothold on the satiric viewpoint of the author, he finds himself on a slippery slope. We are in 'that zone of insecurity in the mind where none but the artist dare trespass', and when he has mentioned that zone, Waugh goes on: 'the tribes were mustering. Dennis, the frontiersman, could read the signs'. Dennis, then, is our guide; his quest, and Waugh's, and ours, is into the heart of the American emptiness. But the mystification and ambiguity of the opening warns us to beware of clear-cut simplifications, simplifications such as the American Innocence and European Experience platitude which Dennis himself mentions: the American experience is judged, and found wanting, that is certain, but the point of view from which this judgment is made is far less obvious. Only the total experience of the novel can reveal the deeper shades of meaning behind the simplistic pattern of the surface, and in talking of them we enter 'zones of insecurity' with a vengeance, for Waugh has made nothing explicit.

In his well-known and much quoted article in *Life* which was a prelude to *The Loved One,* Waugh described the creator of forest Lawn as 'the first man to offer eternal salvation at an inclusive charge as part of his undertaking service' [*Life*, September 29, 1947]. In *The Loved One* itself, the Happier Hunting Ground certainly seems to conform to this description: it offers a heaven for pets to wag their tails (or go through other appropriate motions) in. And Whispering Glades is described frequently in terms of a Church, with Mr Joyboy as its High Priest: '"Mr Joyboy's kinda holy"'. But the Whispering Glades of the novel comes no closer than this to a guarantee of eternal salvation. Indeed, one could well claim that some of the more self-confidently exclusive varieties of Protestantism come nearer than Wilbur Kenworthy to offering such a guarantee. Actually, all that seems an offer here (to Caucasians only) is a kind of lifeless life, a trouble-free, wait, an unstimulating dream. All THE DREAMER foresees for the Loved One as they await, inurned, immured or insarcophagused, their reunion with their Waiting Ones, is a 'Happy Resting Place', no further description vouchsafed. This could be a result of a desire to avoid sectarian controversy, but it seems more like a failure of the imagination. After a flavourless life, all that can be imagined is a flavourless eternity. THE DREAMER, af-

ter all, is a product of the society whose principal characteristics Waugh has seized on as standardisation and witless dreams: as a consequence he is hard put to promise as a Way of Death anything but its equivalent—sterilised, prettified, and monotonous. In fact it is not merely paradoxical to say that the principal characteristic of Wilbur Kenworthy's conception of the after-life as its lifelessness. It is as if, for the inhabitants of this hygienic Eden, the imagination has been so anethetised that it can prefigure as a reward for enduring this life only the gift of lack of life (in peaceful and artistic surroundings). Kenworthy offers not salvation, but drugged rest—the eternal Kaiser's peach.

The points Waugh is making through the burial rituals of Southern California are, then, both social and religious: pressing on from the satire on the monotony of classless, stressless, uniform America, he traces the Americans' obsession with smooth surfaces to its ultimate, death, and finds there the same falsification, the same trivialisation. But by glossing over pain, they have lost the sharp taste of delight; and by denying the existence of evil, and misery, and loss, they have rendered meaningless not only the age-old sanction of hell in the hereafter, but the age-old inducement of Heaven. Eternity has been so emptied of significance that one can no longer hope for or even imagine it. And yet, beneath the glossy surface, through the anæthetised response, a new pain asserts itself—the pain of emptiness, of sameness, of routine. It is this pain that Mrs Joyboy protests against, that Aimée dumbly senses. It is this pain that is the Grail of Dennis's quest.

The characters in the novel and their progress (or lack of it) to self-knowledge and an awareness of the nullity around them are chosen to illustrate a spectrum from complacency to desperation. They certainly do not divide themselves up by nationality. Sir Ambrose Abercrombie is self-sufficiently at home in it, and so—until he is savagely brought up against the ruthless underbelly of the Dream world—is Sir Francis Hinley. On the other hand, not all Americans can accept it so complacently, for they sense (without always putting it into words, which would imply disloyalty, might even be unethical) the cracks in the pretty painted face. The girl at Whispering Glades whom Dennis sees as 'the standard product' and forgets the moment she leaves the room may think she finds life tolerable, for she is of an age to do so. But when Mr Joyboy goes home, it is to his Mom. Without finding this character in the least endearing, one warms to her, because she is alive, and she protests: Life is not good, life is not sweet, she seems to say; I am not good, I am not sweet—nor will I be until I lie under the mortician's fingers. I am a nasty, cantankerous old woman, and I'll make sure you know it, if only to tear down some of the rosy veils from your dream world.

But the main character who comes gradually to see through

to the reality behind the surface of American life is, of course, Aimée Thanatogenos, and it is in fact Mrs Joyboy who is one of the elements in the novel that persuade her that life cannot be standardised to anybody's satisfaction. Other things that are of weight are Dennis's 'unethical' behaviour, the failure of her Guru Brahmin (a figure drawn from Nathanael West, but sadly prophetic of the 'sixties), and the forceful murmurs of her own ancestral gods. It is these last that most engage Waugh.

The dining car attendant who replied to Waugh's 'I am a foreigner' with 'In this country we are all foreigners' deserves a place in any account of *The Loved One*'s genesis quite as prominent as that of the lady from another nation of immigrants, Australia, who first directed his steps to that place of 'sheer exquisite beauty', Forest Lawn. For the straw that Waugh clutches at in this novel is the links all Americans must have with older, more diverse, and (apparently above all) decadent cultures. Just as conservative people who talk of 'levelling down' nurture in their hearts the confident hope that new inequalities will immediately arise to nullify the levelling, so Waugh believes that the standardised emptiness of American life ignores the rich diversity of American origins, and cherishes the hope that, in some cases at least, the old gods will fight back, and win. Seen from this point of view, Aimée's death is a triumph—of her 'decadence', her 'absurdity', and the 'shady businesses (fencing and pimping)' of her ancestors, qualities and attributes which in turn link her to Greece's Gods and Greece's ancient greatness. Her end is no more a 'tragedy' (as the subtitle of the novel has it) than the ending of *Vile Bodies* is a 'Happy Ending'. It is a glorious reassertion of ancient values, a communion with greatness, a rejection of mediocrity.

It is, above all, a victory of the spirit over the heart. We are told of Aimée that her heart 'was a small inexpensive organ of local manufacture', but that her spirit 'had to be sought afar . . . in the mountain air of the dawn, in the eagle-haunted passes of Hellas'. This denigration of the heart is not surprising, in view of the would-be classicism of Waugh's earlier fiction, and in view of the immediate inspiration for the novel: he was in the Hollywood of the 'forties, when romantic and Victorian stereotypes had been debased to absurdity. It was a world which devalued the very word heart by its usages: 'heart-warming', 'heart throb', 'heart-broken'. It is also worth noting that Waugh's objection to the proposed film treatment of *Brideshead Revisited,* the purpose of his visit, was that it was treated as a simple love-story, with the spiritual and theological implications ignored (surely he can not have been surprised?). In this book, then, he shows a distinct preference for the man 'of sensibility rather than of sentiment'—and this description is probably explanation enough of Barlow's failure to prosper in Hollywood.

Dennis Barlow, in fact, is the least loved of Waugh's (mostly unlovable) central figures. Carens says that 'his cynicism and his incapacity for feeling mark him as another hollow man' and Sykes calls him 'loathsome'. This dislike of Dennis no doubt springs mainly from the last pages of the novel, from his cool reception of the news of Aimée's suicide ('"Of course I never thought her wholly sane, did you?"'), and his self-interested organisation of her final combustion. But of course the point about Dennis is precisely his refusal to participate in Joyboy's gutless wailings ('"She was my honeybaby"'), which are the emotional small change of an impoverished imagination. We are told specifically, as Carens should have noted, that Dennis 'went out alone into the pets' cemetery with his own thoughts, which were not a thing to be shared with Mr Joyboy'. Dennis is not incapable of emotion, but he can control it with classical finesse, and use it. He poaches the romantic poets for his wooing, and he even has recourse to the decadents of the nineties for his own pleasure—but when he does he uses them as a 'branded drug', guaranteed to 'yield the sensation he craved'. He is in touch with the world of emotions, but in the most practical possible way. Life, and the war, have left him without illusions or ideals: he is cool, aloof, Augustine in spirit.

He has, in fact, to a frightening degree, the detachment of the artist. 'Here at the quiet limit of the world', one of the lines he repeats like a monk's text, hints at the contracting out, the withdrawal he finds necessary to his art. Ironically, this withdrawal links him to America: just as he forgets the mortuary attendant as soon as she has left the room so 'standard' is she, so Aimée complains that '"When I turn away I can't even remember what you look like"'. He is so detached as hardly to be a complete person. Whispering Glades momentarily upsets that necessary aloofness, for it presents itself as the ultimate embodiment of his American experience. It excites him intolerably, because he knows '[t]here was something in Whispering Glades that was necessary to him, that only he could find'. Later we are told:

> He had abandoned the poem he was writing, long ago it seemed, in the days of Frank Hinsley. That was not what the Muse wanted. There was a very long, complicated, and important message she was trying to convey to him. It was about Whispering Glades, but it was not, except quite indirectly, about Aimée. Sooner or later the Muse would have to be placated. She came first.

But if Aimée is not the Grail of Dennis's quest, it is she who provides the final ray of light that illuminates his goal. With her death Dennis's discovery is made, the excitement is over, he can settle down to the moulding of his spiritual discoveries into satisfying aethetic shape. He is enriched in spirit by his experiences, and enriched, too, by the loss of his heart:

> On the last evening in Los Angeles Dennis knew

he was a favourite of Fortune. Others, better men than he, had foundered here and perished. The strand was littered with their bones. He was leaving it not only unravished but enriched. He was adding his bit to the wreckage, something that had long irked him, his young heart, and was carrying back instead the artist's load, a great, shapeless chunk of experience; bearing it home to his ancient and comfortless shore; to work on it hard and long, for God knew how long. For that moment of vision a lifetime is often too short.

Aimée's death, then, has provided the illumination which is the end of Dennis Barlow's quest: she has shown the saving madness, the redeeming horror, behind the bland surface of American life. His literary transformation of that illumination must be what Waugh's book is too: a hymn to pain; a celebration of unpredictability; a justification of disaster. His message is not a comfortable one, and to bring it to literary fruition he needs the rigour of the Saint and the Artist—never companionable figures. Dennis has to be tough to accept the message, tougher still to wrest it into artistic shape. But the Whispering Glades have whispered him a message—about the desirability of pain, the necessity of diversity, and chaos, and madness, and despair. And, against all odds, he has survived, and will pass the message on.

Alain Blayac (essay date 1992)

SOURCE: "Evelyn Waugh and Humour," in *Evelyn Waugh: New Directions,* London: Macmillan, 1992, pp. 112-32.

[*In the following essay, Blayac explains the classical meaning of "humor," rooted in the theory of the four humors of the human body, and applies it to Waugh's novels.*]

Humour, English humour, has always been a subject of interest (and puzzlement) for the French who have always had the utmost difficulties in understanding their neighbours, hence the number of French essays devoted to the analysis and explanation of the concept. Across the Channel, the notion strikes deep roots in the British collective unconscious. Born of the medical 'theory of humours', it still prevailed during the Renaissance. Initiated by Hippocrates, theorised by Galien, it referred to the four fluids of the human body: blood, phlegm, yellow bile and black bile. Physical diseases, as well as mental and moral temperaments, were the result of the relationship of one humour to another. When the humours were in balance, an ideal temperament prevailed, genial or melancholy according to the circumstances. This explains how the word 'humour' came to mean disposition, then mood or characterized peculiarity, like folly or affectation.

In literature, even though Chaucer and Shakespeare had amply drawn upon the subject, it was Ben Jonson who created the 'Comedy of Humours', depicting characters whose behaviour was determined by a single trait or humour. The Prologue to *Every Man Out of His Humour* gives the first definition of both 'humour' and 'humorist'.

Asper: Why humour, as 'tis ens, we thus define it
To be a quality of air, or water,
And in itself holds these two properties,
Moisture and fluxure: as, for demonstration,
Pour water on this floor, 'twill wet and run:

Likewise the air, forced through a horn or trumpet,
Flows instantly away, and leaves behind
A Kind of dew; and hence we do conclude,
That whatsoe'er hath fluxure and humidity,
As wanting power to contain itself,
Is humour, So in every human body,
The choler, melancholy, phlegm and blood,
By reason that they flow continually,
In some one part, and are not continent,
Receive the name of humours. Now thus far
It may, by metaphor, apply itself
Unto the general disposition:
As when some one peculiar quality
Doth so possess a man, that it doth draw
All his affects, his spirits, and his powers,
In their confluctions, all to run one way,
This may be truly said to be a humour.

Cordatus: [. . .] now if an idiot
Have but an apish or fantastic strain,
It is his humour,

Asper: Well, I will scourge those apes,
And to these courteous eyes oppose a mirror,
As large as is the stage whereon we act;
Where they shall see the time's deformity
Anatomised in every nerve, and sinew,
With constant courage, and contempt or fear [. . .]
Now gentlemen, I go
To turn an actor, and a humorist,
Where, ere I do resume my present person,
We hope to make the circles of your eyes
Flow with distilled laughter. . .

The comedy of humours has its characters, eccentrics, maniacs, lunatics, swindlers, victims, and its themes of eccentricity, whims and fancies, madness. It creates 'humour', what is laughable, whose creator is the 'humorist'. Since then, and up till today, humour has developed and endured in Britain and its arts. In the last thirty years, considerable progress has been made towards the definition of humour. An article dating back to the eighteenth century suggests that the English are animated by a natural, original vein called 'humour'. According to it, everyone in England offers some bizarre slant of mind, some original humour. In the course of time, the term became the expression of a collective mood which the English relish and cultivate. Unlike the Cartesian French, who turned their backs on sentiment and the concrete to move towards concept and the abstract, the English leaned towards humour, which they linked with the particular and the ephemeral; in the process they initiated a literary climate which could only flourish in a people born of the union of the Anglo-Saxon heart and the Anglo-Norman mind.

Michel Serres's latest book, *Le Contrat naturel,* opens on a description of a painting by Goya: two men brandishing cudgels are fighting on quicksands. Intent on their duel, they forget that they have already sunk knee-deep in the mud. Each motion, each gesture they make contribute to their being gradually buried together. Their aggressivity determines the rhythm of their sinking and the time of their interment. Such blindness to the surrounding world is by no means new or incredible; the trouble is that it is pregnant with catastrophic consequences. As such, the painting could perfectly illustrate the lesson of Evelyn Waugh's fiction, if, that is, a dash of humour were added to the Spanish artist's tragic manner.

Indeed Waugh may be considered as a typical representative of the British dual nature, even in the very reductive clichés about his life which see him first as a young scapegrace iconoclast, later as a bitter ageing hypochondriac. In this essay, we shall take as a starting point the (today widely-held) hypothesis that Waugh is a genuine moralist and satirist, who draws on all the forms of humour to propound in an oblique manner the moral, religious and philosophical principles which he advocates for the saving of the individual and society.

What is humour? Before attempting to answer the question, let us suggest that it is high time the reading public, and indeed the critics, realised that humour and humorists must not be made light of, Evelyn Waugh no less than others. To be humorous about humour amounts to confusing the object and the instrument of the study. Let us also remember that the notion is increasingly arduous to grasp; everybody discusses and defines it in more or less overlapping or contradictory ways, when it should be strictly circumscribed so as to avoid commonplaces or overgeneralisations.

Historically, French, unlike most other languages, split its vocabulary into '*humeur*' and '*humour*', hinting at a new awareness of the phenomenon seen as a rational reaction and, for such as knew a little philology, suggesting its emotional and affective roots. Seen from a different perspective, an essay on Evelyn Waugh, whose Britishness is both ingrained and peerless, cannot but make the distinction between En-

glish and American humours. L. W. Kline believed the latter resulted from the conflict between a sense of inner freedom and external societal pressures: thus American humour acts as a safety-valve. Today in the USA one encounters a growing temptation to reduce 'humor' to an aesthetic of the absurd and the nonsensical which is by no means the case in Britain. In his own study, Escarpit presents the 'British sense of humour as an aesthetic form of the self-consciousness', in other words as a national reflex of discretion and decency, concurrently individual and collective (transposed in Waugh's writings to the point of becoming the mask behind which the satirist lurks and chastises through laughter), whereas in the USA, he regards the word as indicating a national reflex of indiscretion or indecency. Two last capital distinctions must be made, the first for the French, the second for the English. Humour should never be confused with what initiates laughter, nor mistaken for irony or wit. Humour and laughter are two different phenomena; Bergson's demonstrations only tangentially concern humour. On the other hand, wit and irony are far too intellectual to be identified with it, for humour demands the sympathy of a witness or accomplice. To the pleasure solitarily enjoyed by the 'wit', self-satisfied, convinced of his intellectual superiority, the humorist prefers the sympathetic wink, the sentimental connivance. He appears humble, only too willing to hand the fruits of his labours over to the invisible interlocutor who he himself has conjured up beforehand for his own purpose and pleasure. In this respect, humour (which has been described as a current passing between two poles) diverges aesthetically, because of its deep affective roots, from wit and irony (which cut the current between two people).

> **When successively reading *Decline and Fall*, *Vile Bodies* and *A Handful of Dust*, one cannot but be struck by the drastic evolution of Waugh's tone and humour.**
> **—Alain Blayac**

When successively reading ***Decline and Fall, Vile Bodies*** and ***A Handful of Dust,*** one cannot but be struck by the drastic evolution of Waugh's tone and humour induced by the trauma of his divorce and the revelation of the Roman Catholic faith. After the callous, careless impertinence of the first novel and the first half of the second, humour suddenly becomes the touchstone and the instrument of the writer's wounded affectivity, directly debouching on to bitterly heartfelt satire. This affectivity provides the next novels with their peculiar atmosphere, a *sui generis* flavour whose infinite nuances range from rosy to grey and black. When the tender element dominates, rosy humour prevails, as in the following passage in which the writer himself admits his sympathy for the tourists he describes.

The word 'tourist' seems naturally to suggest haste and compulsion. One thinks of those pitiable droves of Middle West school teachers whom one encounters suddenly at street corners and in public buildings, baffled, breathless, their heads singing with unfamiliar names, their bodies strained and bruised from scrambling in and out of motor charabancs, up and down staircases, and from trailing disconsolately through miles of gallery and museum at the heels of a contemptuous and facetious guide. How their eyes haunt us long after they have passed on to the next stage of their itinerary—haggard and uncomprehending eyes, mildly resentful, like those of animals in pain, eloquent of that world-weariness we all feel as the dead weight of European culture... And as one sits at one's café table playing listlessly with sketch book and apéritif, and sees them stumble by, one sheds not wholly derisive tears for these poor scraps of humanity thus trapped and mangled in the machinery of uplift.

In many cases, one observes that affectivity is neither openly didactic nor sentimental, it thus steers clear of the potential dangers of cheap, impersonal moralism or mawkishness which Evelyn Waugh deeply mistrusts. Father Rothschild's famous speech on the Bright Young Things' being possessed with an almost fatal hunger for permanence is at worst a minor flaw, but, seen in a more positive perspective, it provides a moral standard by which to judge their behaviour.

Waugh's art may also serve, by dint of his humour, to numb his reader's sensibility. Then, in the case of such exemplary occurrences as Little Lord Tangent's or Simon Balcairn's deaths, humour turns grey. It is born not so much of the narrator's dehumanising detachment as of the fact that the reader, not allowed to feel that those are real people's deaths, smiles at happenings which, in other contexts, would be deemed tragic but here become essentially fantastic. The second epigraph of *Vile Bodies* gives the key to this type of humour. The writer quells moralism by resorting to modern techniques—montage, collage, intertextuality—which generate humour in as much as they allow the reader to distance himself from his reading. In the epigraph, the moral slant is concealed by an apparently casual, or jocular, attitude. But, in most cases, the technical skill hides a hopeless or desperate brand of immorality. It is prominent in the pranks and hoaxes of the Bright Young Things and particularly in Agatha Runcible's adventures culminating in her untimely, but inescapable, and ultimately tragic, demise.

When the realistic element supersedes the 'Alice-in-Wonderland' atmosphere, merrymaking turns sour, bitterness sets in, and grey humour is strengthened. The older generation, a constant butt of Waugh's humour, illustrate this aspect; the

description of their gathering at Anchorage House belongs in such a category.

> She [Lady Circumference] saw . . . a great concourse of pious and honourable people . . ., uncultured, unaffected, unembarrassed, unassuming, unambitious people, of independent judgment and marked eccentricities, . . . that fine phalanx of the passing order. . .

Here the profusion of mostly negative adjectives turns them less into laughing stocks than creatures of a bygone age, grotesque characters in a sad fairy tale. The humour has turned dark grey in the melancholy realisation that the former rulers are both out of touch with the modern world and unconscious of it—in a word, decadent. Darker—for symbolic of the hero's misconceptions—is the reality of the pseudo-refuges, the 'Lush Places', which the Younger Generation and their like wrongly consider as genuine shelters immune from the aggressions of the outside world.

> The immense trees which encircled Boot Magna Hall, shaded its drives and rides, and stood tastefully disposed at the whim of some forgotten, provincial predecessor of Repton, single and in groups about the park, had suffered, some from ivy, some from lightning, some from the various malignant disorders that vegetation is heir to, but all, principally, from old age. Some were supported with trusses and crutches of iron, some were filled with cement. . . .
>
> The lake was moved by strange tides. . . .

Boot Magna Hall fares no better than the members of the Older Generation, is no better fortress than Oxford, Mataudi or Hetton Abbey ever were. The humour, in its grey, dull melancholy, springs from the personification of a place victimised by the passing of time; more essentially and obliquely, it mocks the delusions of the protagonists and the responsibility they bear for their own misadventures.

When directed at the characters, humour varies with the degree of naivety or cynicism, innocence or perversion which they display. It may range from the tender to the sarcastic and the downright cynical, from rosy to grey or black again. Tenderness is the keynote to Nina Blount's shyly admitting to her lack of experience in amorous matters.

> Adam undressed quickly and got into bed; Nina more slowly arranging her clothes on the chair . . . with less than her usual self-possession. At last she put out the light.
> 'Do you know', she said, trembling slightly as she

got into bed, 'this is the first time this has happened to me?'

'It's great fun', said Adam, 'I promise you.'

'I'm sure it is', said Nina seriously, 'I wasn't saying anything against it. I was only saying that it hadn't happened before . . . Oh, Adam'.

It is remarkable that, after this scene, Waugh will never again present a perfectly innocent character, but here the gap existing between the bold situation and the reserve, coyness or self-consciousness which characterise the two lovers at this turning point of their lives is both touching and amusing. On the contrary, with Colonel Blount, Nina's father, the humour becomes jarring as one realises the nefarious treatment to which he submits historical truth. When his film, ambiguously entitled *A Brand from the Burning*, is presented on a Christmas Day desecrated by Adam and Nina's adultery and the declaration of war, it appears exactly to reflect the downright cynical mood and utterly deleterious atmosphere prevailing in England. The darkening humour of the novel evidently coincides with the breakdown of the author's marriage and personal values. In the 'Happy Ending', Waugh, who has hit the bottom of despair, resorts to the blackest kind of humour he has used so far.

When all references to sentiment are erased, when the writer wavers on the brink of despair or sadism, when his comedy opens on to the absurd, then black, kafkaesque humour crops up. The most numerous instances are to be found, not innocently so, in *The Loved One*. There the decadence of the British exiles in Los Angeles can be classified as grey humour. It merely concerns the uprooted, self-deluding British colony. Sir Ambrose Abercrombie, its leader, paints it in a ludicrous, but not wholly humourless, profession of faith.

We limeys have a particular position to keep up . . . It's a responsibility, I can tell you, and in various degrees every Englishman shares it. We can't be all at the top of the tree but we are all men of responsibility. You never find an Englishman among the underdogs—except in England of course.

This debased 'White Man's Burden' type of speech, the deluded (and deluding) assertions, the self-imposed blindness of Sir Ambrose associated with his use of American slang ('limeys'), contrasted with the typically English metaphorical understatement that they are not *at the top of the tree* bring out the reader's compassion for, and amusement at, the plight of the Britisher in Hollywood. Black humour develops when more serious subjects are concerned-religion and interment rites in particular-in the juxtaposition of Whispering Glades, the Hollywood cemetery, and the Happier Hunting Grounds, its counterpart for pets, and its sombre implications of a society forsaking its most sacred values.

The Biblical parody and the reversal of Christian values are central to a novel in which the notion of human death is sacrificed to that of efficacy, pleasure substituted for pain, merrymaking for mourning, all religious references banned from the Service of 'the Loved Ones' but reinstated for defunct animals.

Dog that is born of bitch hath but a short time to live, and is full of misery. He cometh up, and is cut down like a flower; he fleeth as it were a shadow, and never continueth in one stay. . .

The parody of Job (14, 1-2), under the imperturbable mask of ignorance, obliquely conveys the indignation of the author at what appears to him as an evil perversion of the sacred texts in the same way as the Entrance Poster to Whispering Glades exudes humour in its lyrico-biblico-prophetic style, its caricature of the Creation and the Revelation wryly denouncing the debasement of the most sacred Christian values. Different, but as subtle and efficient, is the type of humour presiding over Tony Last's punishment. Condemned to read Dickens for ever, to live vicariously in the petit-bourgeois Victorian universe he abhorred, imprisoned in a jungle which negates the City he envisioned, Tony Last finds Hell because he had rejected the realities of the world, refused the primordial necessity of religion. In both *A Handful of Dust* and *The Loved One*, black humour (obtained through intertextuality) is resorted to to create a hellish universe which *a contrario* imposes the absolute necessity of religion in human existence.

THE CONDITIONS OF HUMOUR

Humour, whatever its coloration, requires a proper soil, special conditions to strike root in the substance of the literary work ('substance' is the proper word as a concrete basis is necessary to its growing, blooming and bearing fruit). Oxford, Mayfair, Abyssinia, Fleet Street, California, the Army provide the soils in which Waugh plants it. Unlike wit, humour thrives on the immediate observation of, and response to, the surrounding universe. It never focuses on a single word, phrase, paragraph, but suffuses the deep layers of the work of art. Waugh, a genuine humorist, patiently conjures, and bolsters, up an 'atmosphere', a 'climate' through his technique of writing and composition. He relies on a gradual refining of the raw, immediate impressions. The very genesis of the novels shows how he uses them as foundations for his fiction. His literary creation develops in three successive stages, the initial and personal experience, later transcribed into a diary or travelogue, and finally refined into an imaginative fiction which creates a new reality coloured by the writer's humour. The situations lived at the first degree are revived and transposed at the second. In order to preserve the appearance of realism, a number of 'serious' passages are inserted within the plot and serve as touchstones, foils or guide marks to the invented stories. The 'Guidebook' style for the introduction of Hetton Abbey, or the 'History' style for the Ishmaelia of *Scoop* play this role.

> Ishmaelia, that hitherto happy commonwealth, cannot conveniently be approached from any part of the world. It lies in the North-Easterly quarter of Africa, giving colour by its position and shape to the metaphor often used of it-'the Heart of the Dark Continent'. Desert, forest, swamp, frequented by furious nomads, protect its approaches. . . .

> Various courageous Europeans in the seventies of the last century came to Ishmaelia, or near it, furnished with suitable equipment of cuckoo clocks, phonographs, opera hats, draft treaties and flags of the nations which they had been obliged to leave. They came as missionaries, ambassadors, tradesmen, prospectors, natural scientists.

> None of them returned. . .

These passages are characterized by a meticulous presentation of apparently historical or technical details, by the dignified, unruffled attitude of a narrator intent on brushing up the setting of the plot in as rigorous and scientific manner as possible. For a brief moment, the moralist dons the garb of the scientist. Devoid of indifference, close to the passion of the scholar, Waugh's humorous fictions are always founded on realistic observation either personally acquired or invented for the sake of the cause, more frequently halfway between the two. In all cases, his realism is suddenly and brutally, but cleverly and consciously, destroyed. It hardly needs the next few words 'They were eaten, everyone of them; some raw, others stewed and seasoned. . .' for the truth to jump to the reader's eyes and mind, and the writer's position to be clearly defined.

In this respect, one can say that affectivity is a second necessary ingredient of Waugh's humour. Although it primarily rests on the concrete, the affective quality is essential to its development. Again it adheres to a precise pattern. Waugh's humour—humour in general perhaps—develops in three successive stages. First the reality of a social group is subverted, which provokes the reader's confusion or distress; then, a few hints dropped by the writer relieve the reader who, confronted with the mind-boggling absurdity of the proposed scheme, bursts out laughing and thus comes to share the author's humorous criticism. The way in which Lord Copper selects his journalists, Seth his personal advisers, the workings of all institutions in Britain and abroad—staff and students at Oxford, the diplomatic corps in Azania, the Press' gossip-writers and foreign correspondents, the Army—all partake of the utmost absurdity.

A third condition, the most specific, must be added: two persons—actor and witness, author and reader—must be involved for humour to appear. Actor and witness may coincide, in which case first-degree humour is achieved. Oxford students, Fleet Street journalists, Army officers are so many alter-egos of a self-mocking Waugh who, having at one time of his life lived his characters' experiences, laughs no less at himself than at those he caricatures—Paul Pennyfeather at Llanabba, Gilbert Pinfold on a cruise among others re-enact the author's past experiences. But Waugh can also create a kind of 'foil', when second degree humour is conjured up. The foil may be totally irresponsible, dull-witted and passive (Paul, Seth, William) or, on the contrary, clever, cunning and prepared to go all lengths to accomplish his aims (Basil, Julia Stitch etc. . .). Waugh plays freely on both alternatives, but the important fact remains that, owing to his personal commitment in his novels, a close relationship is set up between the work of art and the intellectual or sentimental response it rouses in the reader, hence, between the writer and his public. Obviously such a relationship is not easy to establish. Being linked with an 'aesthetic response', it can only be appreciated by those who are willing to collaborate. The hostility which some people have to the so-called defects of Waugh (a cad, a Papist, a conservative, a fascist!), a hostility which feeds on the multifarious provocations of a man who relished aggravating people, nips in the bud not the writer's humour but the very sense of humour of a reader overwhelmed by a devastating phobia for the writer or his writings. Naturally the phobia often derives either from personal prejudices or from a first degree analysis of oblique writings (is it not both easy and tempting to mistake Waugh for a racist?), or from the utter refusal to have anything to do with a man one abhors. Humour, let us repeat it, presupposes the reader's collaboration; it rests on his capacity to understand obliquely presented truths through an intimate knowledge of their contextual frames and/or his thorough adherence to the writer's *angst*. To read, for example, the conclusion of *Remote People* is enough to wash Waugh of the accusation of racialism so often directed at him.

> On the night of my return I dined in London . . . I was back in the centre of the Empire, and in the spot where, at the moment, 'everyone' was going. Next day the gossip writers would chronicle the young MPs, peers, and financial magnates who were assembled in that rowdy cellar, hotter than Zanzibar, noisier than the market at Harrar, more reckless of the decencies of hospitality than the taverns of Kabalo or Tabora. . .

> Why go abroad?
> See England first.
> Just watch London knock spots off the Dark Continent.

For humour to operate we must then agree that some *modus vivendi* has to be worked out between the artist and the more perspicacious reader, better still, connivance will add spice to the scandalous impact of pages that may be shocking or meaningless to the unsophisticated or unprepared public. Hence the fact that Waugh, like all satirists, has either bitter enemies on whom his humour is lost or unconditional defenders who feel his humour is supreme. Either one fights him to the bitter end or one accepts and is carried away, surrendering unconditionally to his humour.

HUMOUR, WIT, IRONY

The notion of complicity opposes humour and wit. Wit strives towards dazzling phrases, mesmerising formulas. It is not so much linked with a context as with the genius, the essence of the language. As such, instead of establishing a current between two poles, it provokes a short circuit. A fire is suddenly set ablaze, and quickly put out. Wit obviously exists in Waugh's writings, but it never informs them (as it does, say, Aldous Huxley's earlier novels). Waugh prefers to set up links, to switch on the current so to speak. In this respect the irony he directs at characters whose innocence, ignorance, nay imbecility, are palpable, is not far removed from humour. It stimulates the reader's response, obliges him to pass a personal judgment on the actors of the novels and their actions. All satirists—Montesquieu in *Lettres persanes,* Voltaire in *Candide,* not to mention Pope or Swift—have drawn on this technique propitious to the flowering of humour. Paul Penny-feather, Adam Fenwick-Symes, William Boot, Dennis Barlow, Guy Crouchback here replace Usbek, Rica or Candide.

The 'suspension of evidence', a subtle derangement of the natural order, which turns the world upside down and eradicates reason from the human organisation, is another source of humour pervading Waugh's novels. *The Loved One* provides the perfect illustration of a religion absurdly turned awry, in which the instant is made more important than eternity, sensual gratification more central than the soul's salvation. As a corollary to this topsy-turvy world, demanding the reader's 'suspension of evidence', Waugh's humour assumes a new acumen when it allows reality, which the fantastic adventures and preposterous fancies of the characters had blotted out, to reassert itself dramatically in the nightmares of protagonists whose minds have been deranged (Agatha, Tony and Brenda, Gilbert Pinfold). The world then is felt to be truly out of joint, only the most severe shocks may set it right, but without the protagonists ever realising it, and consequently ever becoming conscious of their own errors and responsibilities for the misfortunes which befell them. The humour springs from the unreal atmosphere surrounding events which the reader alone can appreciate at its face value once the suspension of evidence has been annihilated by the drama.

D'you know, all that time when I was dotty I had the most awful dreams. I thought we were all driving round and round in a motor race and none of us could stop, . . . and car after car kept crashing until I was left all alone driving and driving—and then I used to crash and wake up.

Let us note at this point that, Waugh's humour transcending the comic and arising from almost any situation and technique, from language to structure, Bergson's comic hierarchy, which ranges from the mechanic to verbal and psychological devices, is of little avail to analyse it.

Humour indeed can occur when the writer uses his style pleasantly enough to convince the reader of his good sense. It is universally acknowledged that Waugh ranks among the best stylists of modern British literature. He himself claimed that, for the novelist he was, style was primordial

> Properly understood style is not a seductive decoration added to a functional structure; it is of the essence of the work of art. ['Literary Style in England and America', in *Books on Trial,* October 1955]

Or

> One thing I hold as certain, that a writer, if he is to develop, must concern himself more and more with Style . . . a writer must face the choice of becoming an artist or a prophet. ['Literary Style in England and America']

Countless examples of humorous style can illustrate our purpose. Tony Last's Sunday ritual

> Tony invariably wore a dark suit on Sundays and a stiff white collar. He went to church, where he sat in a large pitch-pine pew, put in by his great-grandfather at the time of rebuilding the house, furnished with very high crimson hassocks and a fireplace, complete with iron grate and a little poker which his father used to rattle when any point in the sermon excited his disapproval. . .

is a pastiche of Addison's well-known portrait of Sir Roger de Coverley at church. The squire, vested with the remnants of feudal power, suffers no inattention from the parishioners for whose moral health he feels responsible . . . but he allows himself occasionally to doze off during the sermon. Humour then proceeds from the identification of Tony with Sir Roger, from the stereotyped, unconscious archaism of an attitude out of keeping with modern times and revealed through style. At bottom it opens onto Waugh's critical awareness of his hero and of his times. At this level the writer's specific humour may rightly be said to depend on his perception of an historical and political background, the past historical grandeur, the decadence of the ruling classes, the degenerescence of the religious and political leaders. Style has transformed Waugh into a prophetic artist. At the level of the overall structure, the final retribution of the hero-victims (Adam, Tony, Ambrose, Guy) introduces a tragic element in which *pathos* and *eiron* are associated, whereas the apparently successful characters only duplicate their preceding errors and are taken back to their starting points. *The more you run, the more you stay in the same place.*

At the elementary level, the most innocuous puns or euphemisms become significant. In *Vile Bodies,* for instance, the vocabulary often opens up ironic vistas. *Divine, just too divine* the characters exclaim at the very moment they enter Hell. Toponymy (Sink Street) and onomastics (the angels' names) partake of the same epiphanies. Occasionally the play-on-words is merely an affair of humorous backchat. The play on the different meanings of the French verb *baiser* (to kiss, but also 'to screw') in *Scoop* is immediately perceptible to French readers as a simple joke. Superficially amusing, it is nevertheless connected with the desecration of Christmas, eight years earlier, by the adulterous protagonists of *Vile Bodies.* The central, most serious reflexion of *Black Mischief,* [Prudence] 'I'd like to eat you', takes a threefold meaning. It suggests Basil Seal's physical attraction to Prudence, foreshadows the nature of their amorous activities, and eventually, with the heroine's tragic demise, illustrates the deep nature of Azania. The humorous play-on-words all function as the euphemisms of human manners. The germ of the humour basically lies in the distanciation created by the style between the reader and the text. Whether spatial or temporal, it is primarily created by a clever handling of language, style, structure, and their hidden potentialities.

In some cases, when exceptionally tender feelings are involved (Paul for Margot, William for Kätchen), a dash of pseudo-lyricism allows the reader to escape from the bleak reality. Descriptions break the dramatic rhythm, the action stops in a stasis which is a mere structural lull, a dreamlike interval in a world whose harsh nature cannot but reassert itself in a brutal way. In such cases the humorous effect resides in the momentary (but deceptive) dissipation of the prevalent dullness into a fireworks of shimmering images, in the gap between reality and dream.

> A week of blue water that grew clearer and more tranquil daily, of sun that grew warmer, radiating the ship and her passengers, filling them with good humour and ease; blue water that caught the sun in a thousand brilliant points, dazzling the eyes as they searched for porpoises and flying fish; clear blue water in the shallows revealing its bed of silver and smooth pebble, fathoms down; soft warm shade on

> deck under the awnings; the ship moved amid unbroken horizons on a vast blue disc of blue, sparkling with sunlight.

Obviously such an escapist passage is not humorous *per se,* but it is based on a pathetic fallacy soon to be dispelled, when the drab aspects of the world will predominate again . . . i.e. very soon

> Muddy sea between Trinidad and Georgetown; and the ship lightened of cargo rolled heavily on the swell.

This type of humour is basically structural and essential to the emergence of the message. It springs from the confrontation of the passages, from the illusions harboured by the characters (and presumably the reader) that *all may be well,* that the interlude may last for ever. But a close attention to style and context reveals the vanity of the dreams, and the writer's intentions are clarified by his structural humour.

It has often been noticed that polarisation and counterpoints are constant features in Waugh's fiction. According to G. McCartney they are 'the structural analogues of the divisive tensions he sensed both within and outside himself', but they go beyond the personal idiosyncrasy and concur in the structural development of humour. By juxtaposing scenes, applying in the process the discoveries of modern art (collage, montage etc. . . .), Waugh may exert his humour at the generational division, the faults of the couple, the city and the jungle (the banquet and the cannibal feast, war and racket, phony war and phony games etc. . . .). Amusing as they are the counterpoints or montage effects confront the reader with unmistakable, but hitherto unrealised, discoveries.

Another source of humour lies in the apparent indifference of the narrator to his story which he interrupts with great disdain for his plot. The humour lies in the fact that in their own bizarre way the apparent digressions turn out to be absolutely pertinent to the novel. In *Vile Bodies,* the disquisition on 'Being and Becoming' parodies the argument about the ontological primacy of essence on existence. In *Decline and Fall,* the Big Wheel at Luna Park stands for Silenus's metaphor of life. In the process, the reader is led to realise the insignificance of modern man caught in the infernal machinery of a world running loose or mad. Metaphors of this plight abound in all the novels (the film and the car race in *Vile Bodies,* the funeral parlour in *The Loved One*). Humour conceals Waugh's didactic stance; the mask it provides does not need to be elaborately contrived, but it is essential to the writer's strategy. The humorous (apparent) detachment of the narrator strengthens the situation of the writer as producer. Detached, unmoved by his characters' misfortunes, reluctant to get the readers involved, he all the same suggests a moral. He draws on the strategies of modern art to ridicule the 'modern' way of life. The humour lies in the ridiculing through which he demonstrates the failure of a feckless and faithless world, the futility of a society which has lost its fundamental values. Later, Waugh will switch from humour to realism, from detachment to commitment in an attempt to offer positive solutions to his drifting contemporaries. The humour will die in the process, to the regret of the readers who had not grasped the didactic nature of the early novels or enjoyed its discretion.

The didactic nature of the novels, essential as it is, does not suffice to make of Waugh a major novelist. Waugh's originality does not lie so much in the denunciation of an insane society as in a new form of humour; or rather the emergence of a demented or corrupt language initiates another species of humour designed to set off the degraded nature of contemporary society. Language becomes the mirror of society, the demented language rubs out reality and substitutes the Verb to it, becomes a possible key to the nature of Seth and his like whose estrangement from reason it symbolises. Seth's humorously unreasonable decrees fail because of the perversion the king imposes on language, in the same way as the utopian dreams can be said to represent another perversion of language.

Such phenomena culminate in what may be called corrupt language, which, once a meaning and desire to communicate have been eradicated, ultimately boils down to mere gibberish and jargon. The characters then forget reality, take refuge in an imaginary universe of their own and avoid contact with others. Humour, at this level, emerges in the superabundance of tags: 'so', 'then', 'now', 'presently' establish links whose logic is merely apparent. The language, severed from reality, functions as a humorous code devoid of any significance. Dialogues disappear, there only remain incoherent phrases muttered by characters wrapped in their own obsessions. The humour of it all carries the message that the Babel cacophony is the objective correlative of a society disintegrating in insanity. It allows both reader and writer to smile at the simultaneous discovery of the mad ways of the world, and, in the eloquent silences between the corrupt dialogues, it carries the message that societal energies must be mustered to fight the spreading anarchism and dementia, to set up a wall against the proliferating jungle.

Ironically enough, one should keep in mind Waugh's own experience: there was a Waugh idiom made fashionable by the 'Hypocrites' Club'. As W. Bogaards shows in her 'Waugh and the BBC', only a few intimates understood it and it did imply scorn or pretended scorn for anything or any person outside the circle. Another miracle of humour is that it urged Waugh to transpose a negative personal habit into a positive element of his fiction. The humorist runs with the hare, and never hesitates to castigate the pack of hounds in which he once belonged.

To round up this essay, three things must be said. Firstly, if humour can proceed from the complete identification of the writer with his subject, this is not always the case with Evelyn Waugh whose brand of humour is often marked with ambiguity. He asserts what he apparently denies in his novels (that 'Lush Places' are no real shelters) and constructs what he pretends to destroy (religion, essential for man's salvation, never directly appears as a recourse in most of the novels). A new outlook on life resulting from this ambiguity pushes his comedy to open on to the tragic as apparently comic actions entail disastrous consequences. For Waugh, the prime function of humour consists less in propagating ideas than in setting off their relativity (Rosa, the Macushi woman, is more dependable than all the Mayfair 'ladies'), in showing that the ambiguity of things often debauches on a form of nonsense illustrating the absurdity of contemporary mores. But, more important, the relativity it introduces improves the lesson, makes it more efficacious. "'Oh! please God, make them attack the Chapel," said Mr Sniggs' (the Junior Dean of Scone College). The message is coded (as satire demands) but the important point is that the satirical lesson is always tinged or suffused with humour.

Secondly, the concrete and affective elements humour contains also make it reversible so that the heroes can be mocked without weakening the message. Surely to don a mask of innocence, or to have an incompetent fool (Paul), a blissful imbecile (William) or an archaic moron (Tony) playing the role of hero, are brilliant ways of ridiculing social mores. Through the outsider—who never suspects the schemes wielded behind his back—the reader may form the weirdest impressions of the characters and social sets he meets (Margot and Chokey, the Bright Young Things, Lord Copper and Fleet Street, British exiles in Hollywood etc. . .). A subtle power of correction goes hand in hand with the reversibility of humour. It steers clear of the pitfalls of puritanical morality. The seduction of Prudence by Basil might have inspired a sermon, Waugh succeeds in making it authentic satire, matching in excellence T. S. Eliot's 'Seduction of the Typist' scene. The bitterly humorous clash between the 'love scene' (as seen by Prudence) and reality, i.e. 'The Burma cheroot . . . slowly unfurling in the soapy water . . ., the soggy stub of tobacco emanat[ing] a brown blot of juice', allows the writer to avoid moral indignation and to find an objective correlative to his disgust and reprobation. Thus the blackest humour arises of a situation which encompasses in a nutshell (or more precisely here in a bathtub) the faults, vices and blemishes of modern and western life, whose horrifying reality is never directly attacked but always, indirectly, denounced.

Thirdly, humour acts as an authorial catharsis. It does not only purge the writer of the moral or sentimental temptations, it also refines the whole gamut of his emotions. Waugh's sadistic tendencies, destructive leanings, suicidal attraction are refined into positive creations. The catharsis operated by humour helped Waugh to forget, if not to heal, the wounds of his divorce, and, in the fifties, those of his physical decrepitude. It freed him from himself, as it were. It somewhat smothered nostalgia and sentiment and invited him to assert his liberty to the face of the world. Thus it eventually achieves a twofold effect, heal the writer, touch or teach the reader.

As a conclusion, we can say that humour, within its possible combinations, remains relatively stable in its matter, although the manner in which Waugh shapes it remains specific of his creative imagination. Waughian humour, although it may verge on the most scathing irony, also includes affective elements which illustrate an extreme sensitivity and shed light on the innermost recesses of the writer's personality.

We must also add that ironically, in the course of his career, Waugh ceased to be the youthful humorist of the twenties to become a genuine 'humour' in the medical sense. In the fifties an unfortunate identification of the ageing man with the artist reinforced the clichés, stereotypes, and blatant untruths which are occasionally retailed in the general public and against which critics have fought in order to restore Evelyn Waugh to his true status as one of the greatest of English humorous writers. In this sense, the lines he wrote in his private diaries pathetically demonstrate his thirst for the absolute and the constant fight he had to wage to be of use in this trite age of ours.

To make an interior act of renunciation and become a stranger in the world, to watch one's fellow countrymen as we used to watch foreigners, curious of their habits, patient of their absurdities, indifferent to their animosities—that is the secret of happiness in the century of the common man.

Fortunately Waugh's incapacity to resign himself to indifference, to watch his fellow countrymen as foreigners, is a blessing which begot his humour for our pleasure and moral edification. But for his humour (and his religious faith), his would have been held a pessimistic, almost nihilistic vision of man. One can at times see him as a desperate man, but his good sense allied to his sensibility made him favor the smiles and benevolence of ravaging humour and reject the wailing and gnashing of teeth of black melancholy. To this humour Evelyn Waugh owes his status as a major novelist and satirist of our times.

David Leon Higdon (essay date October 1994)

SOURCE: "Gay Sebastian and Cheerful Charles: Homoeroticism in Waugh's *Brideshead Revisited*," in *Ariel:* *A Review of International English Literature,*" Vol. 25, No. 4, October 1994, pp. 77-89.

[*Higdon is an American writer and educator. In the following essay, he argues that* Brideshead Revisited *depicts very deliberate homosexual relationships, contrary to the opinions of other critics, whom Higdon considers deeply in denial.*]

There is a highly visible homosexual population in the novels of Evelyn Waugh, ranging from the "smooth young men of uncertain tastes" in *Decline and Fall* (1928) to the hallucinatory visions and encounters in *The Ordeal of Gilbert Pinfold* (1957). Ambrose Silk of *Put Out More Flags* (1942) and Anthony Blanche of *Brideshead Revisited* (1945) may be the most memorable and certainly are the most flamboyant members of this population. However, there are, in addition, Sir Ralph Brompton, Martin Gaythorne-Brodie (the Honorable Miles Malpractice in the American editions), Captain Edgar Grimes, David Lennox, and Corporal-Major Ludovic—seven men in total, ranging from an Oxford aesthete declaiming *The Waste Land* from a Christ Church window, through a capable diplomatic adviser, a society photographer, and an author of a bestselling novel to an accused Fascist who ultimately receives the Order of Merit. Much disagreement results, however, when one attempts to add other Waugh characters to this group, as shown by the exchange between David Bittner and John Osborne, in the pages of the *Evelyn Waugh Newsletter and Studies* between 1987 and 1991, about whether or not *Brideshead Revisited*'s Charles Ryder and Sebastian Flyte are homosexual. In an early sally, Bittner maintains that "Waugh's basic intention, despite several contradictory inadvertences, was not to write *Brideshead Revisited* as a piece of 'gay' literature whose two main characters were homosexuals" ("Sebastian and Charles"). Despite the finality of Bittner's claim, I argue that it is impossible to regard Sebastian as other than gay; that Charles is so homoerotic he must at least be considered *cheerful;* and that Bittner's attempt–and others like it—is a representative skirmish in a much larger and more important sexual war being fought as entrenched heterosexuality strives to maintain its hegemony over important twentieth-century works.

The conclusions reached in earlier Waugh criticism on the question of the characters' sexual orientation are mixed, ranging from truculent denial to moralistic condemnation, and are often fatally flawed in both logic, assumptions, and execution. One simply may ignore their sexuality, as does George McCartney, or hurry into illogical denial within parentheses, as does Harvey Curtis Webster: "Ryder's long journey to faith starts when he meets and falls in love (not homosexually) with. . . Sebastian" [*After the Trauma: Representative British Novelists since 1920,* 1970]. Just how one man "falls in love" with another man without the act being homoerotic or homosexual is an interesting contortion of definitions. Others resort to coded signals whose language barely disguises underlying homophobia and mistakenly locates homosexuality within discourses of illness and freely willed action. William J. Cook notes that Sebastian "has become degenerate and dissipated" [*Masks, Modes, and Morals: The Art of Evelyn Waugh*, 1971]; Robert R. Garnett glances hastily at Charles's "youthful love for Sebastian," "the beautiful, charming, and doomed young aristocrat," who, "unable or unwilling to abandon childhood, retains his irresponsibility and his teddy bear" [*From Grimes to Brideshead: The Early Novels of Evelyn Waugh*, 1990]. Jacqueline McDonnell admits that Charles Ryder has "a romantic relationship with Lord Sebastian Flyte," who later becomes "drunk and delinquent," but finally situates Sebastian by concluding that he "is a major romantic creation, drawn from the heart of the Christian tradition: the hopeless sinner saved" [*Evelyn Waugh*, 1988]. After suggesting that the picnic scene early in the novel may be "a homosexual idyll," Calvin W. Lane points out that "Julia is really Sebastian's alter ago" [*Evelyn Waugh*, 1981], a point to which this essay will return. Finally, Gene D. Phillips writes that Sebastian "gradually . . . sinks into both dispsomania and homosexuality" [*Evelyn Waugh's Officers, Gentlemen, and Rogues: The Fact behind His Fiction*, 1975]. These comments evince what Elaine Showalter has called "homosexual panic": "the discovery and resistance of the homosexual self" [*Sexual Anarchy: Gender and Culture at the Fin de Siècle*, 1990]. The homosexual and the homoerotic were present in **Brideshead Revisited** long before the 1981 British Broadcasting Corporation adaptation visualized Sebastian's and Charles's kiss, close dancing, and gondola ride and equally long before today's gay liberation movement. In other words, we have here a clear attempt by critics to suppress, either by ignoring, trivializing, or ridiculing, a sophisticated text's sophisticated handling of a full range of human sexuality, including the homoerotic and the homosexual.

There is a highly visible homosexual population in the novels of Evelyn Waugh.
—David Leon Higdon

Neither Bittner nor Osborne seems to pay much attention to the quality of his own assertions and arguments. This homophobia—even in Osborne, who accepts that Sebastian is unmistakably gay—is evident in virtually every paragraph of their exchange in the *Evelyn Waugh Newsletter*. To Osborne, Sebastian is sunk "deep into human wickedness" ("Sebastian Flyte"), a rather extreme claim for an alcoholic who has had but two known affairs; to Bittner, "Charles is leaving behind . . . not a relationship involving gross sensual gratification but one of idealized spiritual love" ("Long-

Awaited"). Both critics deliberately have confused such concepts as sexuality, masculinity, homosexuality as a state of being, and homosexuality as a behaviourial action. Although Bittner's essays will never be among the "essential" articles on Waugh—and one must admit that Bittner is clearly aware of this—a close look at his claims and disclaimers, suggested in six statements from his essays, demonstrates clearly what can happen when a character such as Sebastian threatens the heterosexual critical hegemony exercised over a text.

> If Sebastian is introduced as a homosexual character and remains a confirmed homosexual throughout the novel, then—in a story whose whole point is the "boomerang" influence of Catholicism—wherein lies the point of his religious return? Would the thread that twitches a homosexual Sebastian back to the Church be valid if it stopped short of reforming his English habits? ("Long-Awaited")

Several points are askew here. Like many people, Bittner apparently believes that homosexuality is an assumed behaviour that is selected or rejected at will and is not an inherent identity. Sebastian cannot control whether or not he is homosexual, but he can control whether or not he allows his homosexuality active sexual expression. His church does not condemn the homosexual, though it does condemn homosexual activity, and in the novel we are given every reason to assume that after his infatuation with Charles and the death of Kurt, Sebastian has become a celibate homosexual, clearly "twitched" back to his church. Bittner has confused a noun of being with a noun of activity and has thus muddled a crucial distinction within the novel. Waugh's generation was clearly of two minds concerning homosexual identity. In *Our Age*, Noel Annan points out that "homosexuality became a way of jolting respectable opinion and mocking the Establishment" and that his generation "made homosexuality a cult"; these comments suggest that homosexuality could be self-selected, merely a phase associated with the all-male worlds of the English public school and university. Such a conclusion is supported by Alan Pryce-Jones's comment that "it was *chic* to be queer, rather as it was *chic* to know something about the twelve-tone scale and about Duchamp's 'Nude Descending a Staircase'" (qtd. in Carpenter). On the other hand, the generation had no doubts that the sexual orientation of such individuals as Howard Sturgis, Brian Howard, Joe Ackerley, Christopher Isherwood, and others seemed fixed, a stand that Freudian analysis supported. Bittner's confusion is equally evident in such comments as "Sebastian could hardly be a homosexual without someone to 'tango' with" ("Long-Awaited"), even though the lives of hundreds of thousands of single homosexual men testify to the contrary. Substituting "Cordelia" or "Bridey" for "Sebastian," and "heterosexual" for "homosexual," lays bare the confusion in Bittner's rhetoric. Also, using "tango" trivializes crucial sexual identities in the novel.

Besides, if Waugh wanted to present Sebastian as a homosexual character, why doesn't he drawn [sic] him in the full lineaments of the role, as he does Anthony Blanche ... whom Waugh intends in the tradition of the flamboyant, artistic homosexual. ("Sebastian and Charles")

Obviously Waugh does not do this because Sebastian is neither "flamboyant" nor "artistic." Bittner seems to suggest that all homosexuals are of a type, a type represented by Anthony. Of course, Waugh knew better, as can be seen from the range of homosexuals he presents in his novels. Anthony Blanche and Ambrose Silk are exceptional figures, as unique, say, as Quentin Crisp or Boy George; Sebastian is far closer to the norm of the ordinary, semi-closeted gay. Moreover, both Ambrose and Anthony seem to attract Waugh's censure more because of their modernist ideas and stances than because of their homosexuality.

Sebastian stands apart from Waugh's other homosexuals in that he has a much more dynamic role to play and because the tone in which he is presented is so distinctive. Ambrose and Anthony are critiqued; Grimes and Malpractice are ridiculed; Sebastian is romanticized. There are, I believe, several reasons for this, one of them involving autobiographical nostalgia. Sebastian may take some of his actions and features from Hugh Lygon, Alastair Graham, and others, but he also memorialized much of the 1920s Oxford Waugh. When John Betjeman said, "[e]veryone was queer at Oxford in those days" (qtd. in Annan), he certainly included Waugh, who had an affair with Richard Pares and perhaps others, since Waugh called Pares "my first homosexual love" (Waugh, *Letters*). Waugh, however, effectively silenced much from his undergraduate days through the destruction of the diaries (Standard). In Sebastian we meet Waugh's nostalgia for his lost past and the orthodoxy of his Catholicism, which required him regretfully to condemn Sebastian.

It is probably a mistake to conclude, if one thinks of characters other than Charles Ryder, that "filled with regret for time past, deeply elegiac, the early chapters are suffused with a Words-worthian intimation that growing up inexorably alienates one from the lifegiving source" (Garnett). It is a mistake because the moral schema Waugh endorses in the novel requires the reader to see Sebastian as a beautiful, seductive, irresistible tempter, more tempting in many ways than Celia Mulcaster and Julia Flyte Mottram, but, like them, situated carefully within a complex hierarchy of sexual corruptions. As Jeffrey Heath points out, "Waugh never says so explicitly, [but] he regards Charles's love for Sebastian as a gorgeous mistake and a *felix culpa*" [*The Picturesque Passion*, 1982].

> When Sebastian complains that all his life people [actually, Sebastian refers only to his family] have been "taking things away" from him, it is tempting to conclude that, among other things, he is referring to a deprivation of his masculinity.

> It is also true, of course, that men like Sebastian, who are of much above average appearance, frequently are characterized—or thought to be characterized—by same-sex preferences. ("Sebastian and Charles")

One scarcely knows how to correct the flimsy assumptions in this passage. Are there actually individuals so shallow as to believe that a handsome man—by the mere fact of his physical attractiveness—is probably homosexual? Further, "homosexuality" and "masculinity" are in no way mutually exclusive terms, despite the implications of Bittner's sentence.

> I cannot believe it would not have occurred to both surveillants [Mr Bell and Mr Samgrass] to keep their eyes peeled for evidence of pederasty as long as they were scrutinizing every other aspect of the boys' behavior. ("Long-Awaited")

At the time to which Bittner refers, Sebastian and Charles are 19 or 20 years old—scarcely boys—adult enough that their actions cannot be considered pederastic. Pederasty almost always refers to an adult having a sexual relation with a boy.

> It seems to me there is nothing really to "agree" upon as regards Charles's calling Anthony Blanche a "pansy." He just does. It is there in black and white. My point was that if such expressions found their way naturally to Charles's lips, then one would expect him to describe Sebastian by means of the same term *if* Sebastian were a homosexual. The fact that Charles *doesn't* I take as an indication that Sebastian must be intended as a heterosexual character.("Long-Awaited")

Since Charles uses the term "pansy" but twice in the novel (and Waugh rarely uses it elsewhere), it is not a word that comes "naturally" to his lips; moreover, "pansy" always refers to dandified, affected, or noticeably effeminate men, traits Sebastian never demonstrates. Charles carefully chooses his words, much in the manner of the individual of the 1990s who understands the nuances separating "homosexual," "gay," and "queer." Also, Charles's affair with Sebastian has been over for 13 years. He discusses Sebastian only with Cordelia and then with Julia—contexts in which the term "pansy" would have been most inappropriate. Cordelia tells Charles that Sebastian is now "very religious," apparently reconciled with his church, though apparently still alcoholic.

[I]t requires a greater leap of reason than I am prepared to make to assert that [Sebastian] could practice homosexuality without setting his family on edge about the fact. Lady Marchmain is nobody's fool; if Sebastian were a homosexual she would know it, and if she knew it, would have to disapprove because of her strict Catholic principles. I cannot believe that Waugh would introduce Sebastian as a homosexual character and then not deal with the issue, as, for instance, by having Lady Marchmain add this to "the sorrows she took with her daily to church." ("Sebastian and Charles")

Lady Marchmain may be "nobody's fool," but she is certainly her own fool. She is an extraordinarily self-deluded woman who does not see, much less understand, what she is doing to her children, and she is quite isolated from the male world of Oxford. She lacks the worldliness of Cara. Indeed, Lady Marchmain seems tailored after the popular analysis of homosexuality in the 1920s and 1930s, which held that the male turned homosexual because of an ineffectual, often-absent father and a domineering, powerful mother, an idea now thoroughly discredited in psychoanalysis but one still holding remarkable popular appeal.

Of course, no discrediting of either the overt or covert homophobia of critics demonstrates that Sebastian is indeed gay or that Charles is homoerotic. For this demonstration one needs to return to the text of *Brideshead Revisited*. There seems no doubt that the characters' tie is homosocial, that Charles is homoerotically attracted to Sebastian, and that their relationship is homosexual, though perhaps not sexually active. The evidence is more than "several contradictory inadvertences." During the picnic near Swindon, for instance, Charles's eyes linger long on Sebastian's "profile," a purely erotic male gaze; later he recalls Sebastian as being "magically beautiful, with that epicene quality which in extreme youth sings aloud for love." He even likes to wander into the bathroom while Sebastian is in the tub, and at Brideshead Castle has "no mind then for anything but Sebastian." During the golden year of 1923, Charles tells us he and Sebastian "kept very much to our own company that term, each so much bound up in the other that we did not look elsewhere for friends"; indeed, Charles once climbs out of his college, only to be found by Mr Samgrass in Sebastian's rooms "after the gate was shut." Considering the early death of his mother and his father's cold disdain, Charles may well claim that he "was in search of love in those days" and mean several very different things, but he also confesses that he participated in "naughtiness high in the catalogue of grave sins" that summer and learned "that to know and love one other human being is the root of all wisdom." Paraphrasing Goronwy Rees, Martin Green provides a general description of such Oxford affairs in the 1920s: "The Fall of Man happened only to Eve. She was expelled, and Adam was left to enjoy the garden alone with the serpent. Men remembered Oxford in a golden glow because only *after* it came their fall from grace into heterosexual relationships" (qtd. in Littlewood).

Virtually all of the other characters assume that Charles's and Sebastian's relationship is both homoerotic and homosexual. Despite all of the satiric thrusts directed at him, Anthony Blanche functions as one of the genuinely perceptive truthtellers in the novel; he says, "I can see [Sebastian] has completely captivated you, my dear Charles" and later tells Charles "you threw him over," surely the language of an intensely homoerotic friendship, if not of more. The informed, aware, and worldly Cara takes in all in one glance and then tells Charles, "'I know of these romantic friendships of the English and the Germans. . .'" and subtly warns him, "'they are very good if they do not go on too long'." At Old Hundredth, "Death's Head" and "Sickly Child" dismiss Sebastian and Charles as "only fairies" before picking them up, and Charles hints at Julia's opinion when he says that the arrest "had clearly raised us in Julia's estimation [because] we had been out with women." Julia also recalls her early impression of Charles as "the pretty boy Sebastian brought home with him," a hint that she may see more than does her mother. It is not at all surprising that Charles, in Venice, confesses "I was nineteen years old and completely ignorant of women." Until the novel reached the page-proof state, it included a similar statement by Sebastian: "'You know, Charles, I've never slept with a woman'" [Davis, *Evelyn Waugh, Writer,* 1981].

Bittner would object to the preceding paragraphs, pointing out Charles's marriage to Celia Mulcaster and his affair with Julia Flyte Mottram, but sexual relations with women do not necessarily prove that a man is heterosexual. Study of the married homosexual male was only tangential to early studies such as A. G. Kinsey's, W. B. Pomeroy's, and C. E. Martin's *Sexual Behavior in the Human Male* (1948) and R. A. L. Humphreys's *Tearoom Trade* (1970), but since the research of H. L. Ross (1971) and M. T. Saghir and E. Robins (1973), we have become aware that perhaps as many as 20 per cent of homosexual men are or have been married (M. W. Ross, *The Married Homosexual Man,* 1983). Ross could have been discussing Charles and Celia, because at one point he notes that "homosexuals who married often stated that the marriage was initiated by the wife."

This is exactly what happened to Charles. In New York, waiting to sail to England, Charles remembers Celia "had married me six years ago," an odd phrasing, but one that would pass unnoticed except for their cabin conversation, in which Celia says, "'Darling, it was the night you popped the question'" and Charles responds "'As I remember, you popped'." Also, Charles's response to his wife's adultery is rather atypical—no rage, no wounded ego, just relief and triumph: "I heard her unmoved, and suddenly realized that she was powerless to hurt me any more; I was a free man; she had given me my manumission in that brief, sly lapse of hers; my cuckold's horns made me lord of the forest." Celia Mulcaster recognized an up-and-coming artist, annexed him, forwarded his career through her social connections and skills, and then turned to an affair, perhaps to find the sexual satisfaction missing from her marriage. In contrast, Charles's affair with Julia appears to be passionately heterosexual, but Julia's first attraction to Charles came precisely because of her close physical similarities to Sebastian: "On my side the interest was keener, for there was always the physical likeness between brother and sister, which, caught repeatedly in different poses, under different lights, each time pierced me anew." This is a similarity Charles noticed the very first time he met Julia. He does not find her to be Anthony's "passionless, acquisitive, intriguing, ruthless *killer,*" but he does feel "a sense of liberation and peace" when she leaves him alone with Sebastian at Brideshead Castle. Aboard the ship, Julia initiates their love-making; later, she proposes to Charles.

About Sebastian's sexual preferences there can be little doubt. He initiates two very different affairs, and he seems to enjoy his power over his "chums," a reflection of the English tendency for men like Sebastian to take lovers from lower classes. He "courts" Charles with a "room full of flowers" as an apology, with an idyllic picnic, and with brilliant luncheons, holds his arm while they walk in Oxford, and at just the right psychological moment dazzles Charles with Brideshead Castle. Charles writes him daily from Ravenna. Worldly Anthony observes, "'I can see he has completely captivated you'" and cynically suggests that Sebastian probably even flirted with priests through the confessional's grill when he was younger. After leaving England, Sebastian stays with Anthony Blanche in Marseilles, where Anthony attempts to do something about Sebastian's alcoholism or to introduce him to drugs more potent than alcohol, before they go on to Tangier, where Sebastian acquires a *"new* friend . . . a great clod of a German who'd been in the Foreign Legion." Sebastian is content with the relationship and tells Charles "'it's rather a pleasant change . . . to have someone to look after yourself'." Although he and Kurt do not share a bed, they do share six years together, and his attempts to rescue Kurt from the German nightmare, especially his lingering in Germany for "nearly a year," speak of more than "chumminess."

Jacqueline McDonnell sees clearly the relationship between the incremental repetitions of character types and sexual acts: she writes that Charles "spends most of the novel being seduced" [*Evelyn Waugh,* 1988] Indeed, Charles is seduced three times physically and once spiritually, and his partners are "forerunners" of the later spiritual love he will develop for God. His erotic and sexual relationships with Sebastian, Celia, and Julia are central to Waugh's "attempt to trace the

worship of the divine purpose in a pagan world, in the lives of an English Catholic family, half paganised themselves" (Stannard, *Evelyn Waugh: The Critical Heritage*). Waugh presents Charles moving through three corrupted states of human sexuality and passion. Bittner should have conceded the battle to win the war: Waugh has not written a novel gay liberationists will eagerly embrace. Charles's and Sebastian's mutual love is enticingly seductive, but thematically appears the most corrupted and the most distant from Waugh's God. Critics often note that Waugh's rhetoric insists on Sebastian's child-like, if indeed not childish, attitude and behaviour. His inadequacies are almost too evident. Nanny Hawkins calls Sebastian and Charles "a pair of children"; Cara says "'Sebastian is in love with his own childhood'"; even Charles images Sebastian as "happy and harmless as a Polynesian." Thus Waugh moves his reader and his protagonist through a homosexual affair he condemns; a loveless, almost mercenary marriage; and a passionate affair between two desperate souls that is condemned by the other characters. Finally there comes the moment in the chapel when Charles is seduced into a very different kind of love.

Sebastian and Charles, Julia and Rex, Cara and Alex—these and other partners in *Brideshead Revisited* force a reader to confront the complex range of human sexuality. The binary opposition of homosexuality and heterosexuality that informs so much Western thought about male sexuality is clearly too simplistic a paradigm for the world Waugh depicts. It is reward enough to teach the novel's conflict between materialism and spiritualism, between free will and fate, but first its characters' sexual identities must be won back from frightened criticism.

Charles Hallett (essay date November 1994)

SOURCE: "A Twitch upon the Thread," in *New Oxford Review,* Vol. 61, No. 9, November 1994, pp. 19-20.

[*In the following essay, Hallett examines Charles Ryder's reaction in* Brideshead Revisited *to the Catholicism of the Flyte family.*]

"Is Evelyn Waugh a Catholic novelist?" a friend of mine asked. "I am thinking," he explained, "of *Brideshead Revisited.* That book has a compelling quality; every few years it draws me back to it. But its mystery escapes me."

In a way my friend is sensing the very mystery that draws the book's narrator, Charles Ryder, to write about the family that lived at Brideshead. Charles, a non-Catholic, is both repulsed and attracted by the mysterious force that unites and directs the seemingly disparate members of the Flyte family. Part of the attraction of the book is that Waugh never explains the mystery; instead, he renders Charles Ryder's experience of it.

Almost as soon as he becomes the chum of Sebastian Flyte, Charles makes us feel his repulsion for the Flyte family religion and for its chief representative, Sebastian's mother, Lady Marchmain, whose attempts to bring stability to Sebastian's life are viewed as the insidious cause of the decline she wishes to prevent. I have always suspected Waugh of laying a trap for the unsuspecting reader, in that he so deliberately makes us identify with Sebastian and Charles, those free spirits who find Oxford constraining, that we adopt Charles's view of Lady Marchmain. Not until late in the novel do we realize that Waugh continually likens this remarkable lady to the Dolorosa (Our Lady of Sorrows).

The mystery that Waugh is rendering is best approached through a survey of the members of the Marchmain family. At one extreme stand three who remain staunchly Catholic. Lady Marchmain's oldest son, Bridey, "massive" in his "rectitude," embodies the "legalistic" side of the Church. Bridey knows all its regulations and never deviates from any. His strict adherence to Catholic precepts, especially at moments of crisis in the family (marriages, say, or deaths) causes spiritual explosions. Waugh uses "Bridey's bombshells" to keep bringing reality into his sister Julia's life and to precipitate the dramatic climax of the novel.

Lady Marchmain is Waugh's tribute to the old Catholic families, England's Recusants. She is charitable, believing that "it is one of the special achievements of Grace to sanctify the whole of life, riches included." Lady Marchmain lives for others, unobtrusively, selfless but not a saint, enduring with fortitude an inner suffering undetected by all but her daughter Cordelia. Chief among her sorrows are the defection of her husband, Lord Marchmain, the miseries her children bring upon themselves by their willfulness, their abandonment of the Faith, and consequentially a "deadly sickness in her body." Waugh associates Lady Marchmain closely with her chapel, which houses the Eucharist. When she died, Cordelia tells us, "the priest came in . . . blew out the lamp in the sanctuary and left the tabernacle open and empty." Suddenly, "there wasn't any chapel any more, just an oddly decorated room."

Cordelia, the youngest child, more overtly a touchstone, presents the Faith from the wholesome viewpoints of wisdom and humor. She can baffle both catechumen and priest by mischievously representing common superstitions as articles of the Creed, but lives the Faith selflessly. In Cordelia's confidences to Charles, we hear Waugh's own voice.

At the other extreme are Julia's two lovers. In Julia's husband Rex Mottram, Waugh draws a fascinating portrait of the hollow man: handsome, rich, powerful, and absolutely amoral. Rex "needs setting up solidly" and finds Julia, London's top debutante, "a suitable prize." He is all for a Catholic wedding, because "that's one thing your Church can do . . . put on a good show," but prefers to waive the instruction. The Jesuit charged with acquainting Rex with Catholic precepts finds that Rex "doesn't seem to have the least intellectual curiosity or natural piety," and Julia learns, over time, that Rex "isn't a real person at all; he's just a few faculties of a man highly developed." She sums him up as "something in a bottle, an organ kept alive in a laboratory, a tiny bit of a man pretending he was whole."

Charles, the narrator of the story and the proposed second husband of Julia (he and Julia have been living together at Brideshead and at a certain point she decides that they must marry, for she "wants to be made an honest woman"), has greater potential than Rex. Both men are worldly, but Charles's worldliness is civilized—witness the scene between them over dinner at Ciro's. Charles, too, even after his travels to the New World, even after the growth of his love for Julia, is "still a small part of myself pretending to be whole." But unlike Rex, Charles knows it, though he doesn't know yet what he learns later, that a man can be complete only if God resides in him.

In between these two extremes wander the apostates—Lord Marchmain, Sebastian, and Julia—those members of the Flyte family who flee from God.

Lord Marchmain embraces Catholicism in the initial stages of his love for Lady Marchmain and says when they are married, "You have brought back my family to the faith of their ancestors," but soon finds the bonds of marriage confining. He flees to Italy, where he sets up with a mistress. His chief characteristic is to hate his wife, and one of the main activating forces in his life is to authorize any action on his children's part that will give her suffering.

In Sebastian, their younger son, a homosexual, Waugh paints a consummate portrait of a dipsomaniac. Seeking to be "free," Sebastian flees all civilizing and restraining forces—not only the dons at Oxford, Monsignor Bell the bishop, and his mother, but "his own conscience and all claims of human affection" as well. He drinks at first, like Charles, from the pure joy of overflowing spirits, but later to escape from reality. A true Flyte, Sebastian spends most of the novel "running away as far and as fast as I can," to Italy, Constantinople, Tangier, and is finally "found starving and taken in at a monastery near Carthage."

Julia too turns her back on the family religion and embraces instead the magnetic Rex Mottram. When that marriage fails, she follows an American to New York but soon recognizes her folly. Charles in the meantime has sought refuge from the boredom of his own marriage in Mexican jungles, and their paths cross on the ship that brings them both back to England. Charles moves in with Julia at Brideshead, an arrangement that Rex finds utterly convenient.

It is through Cordelia that Waugh introduces the final chapters of the novel that show the mysterious power of the Faith to reclaim those who have been shaped by it. Speaking to Charles at the end of Part I, Cordelia observes that

> the family haven't been very constant, have they? There is Papa gone and Sebastian gone and Julia gone. But God won't let them go for long, you know. I wonder if you remember the story Mummy read us the evening Sebastian first got drunk . . . Father Brown said something like "I caught him. . .with an unseen hook and an invisible line which is long enough to let him wander to the ends of the world and still bring him back with a twitch upon the thread."

And later she reveals to Charles that Sebastian has gone back to the Church. The suffering that Sebastian undergoes, "maimed as he is" by drink—"no dignity, no power of will," Cordelia declares—acts as a purgation, making him holy. Sebastian becomes an under-porter at the monastery, "a great favourite with the old fathers," whom he serves, and in his humility he is "very near and dear to God." Waugh portrays the reeling in of Julia and Lord Marchmain in fuller detail.

Bridey's bombshells play a key role in awakening the conscience of Julia. The first of them occurs when he announces his engagement to Beryl, then states that because "Beryl is a woman of strict Catholic principle" he couldn't possibly bring her to Brideshead, where Julia is "living in sin with Rex or Charles or both." Bridey's frank observation sparks in Julia a deep realization of the meaning of her actions, an awareness that she *has* been "living in sin, with sin, by sin, for sin, every hour, every day, year in, year out"; that Mummy carried that sin with her, "dying with my sin eating at her, more cruelly than her own illness"; that Christ bore her sin too, "hanging at noon, high among the crowds and the soldiers." Julia believes at this point that though "I've gone too far [from God and] there's no turning back now," yet she can still "put my life in some sort of order in a human way" by marrying Charles. And thus does Julia feel the twitch on the thread.

Bridey's next bombshell explodes after Lord Marchmain, driven out of Italy by impending war and a serious heart problem, comes back to Brideshead to die. Bridey announces that "Papa must see a priest," a proposal that brings into focus the spiritual gulf that separates Charles from Julia. Julia leans toward the family's point of view: What is at stake here is the salvation of a soul. Lord Marchmain has not been a

practicing member of the Church for 25 years and must before his death be reconciled to God. Charles staunchly opposes summoning a priest, on the grounds (ironically) that Lord Marchmain should be allowed "to die in peace." In Charles's view, the Church will "come now, when his mind's wandering and he hasn't the strength to resist, and claim him as a death-bed penitent"; it's all "superstition and trickery."

I suggested earlier that Waugh lays a trap for the reader who admires Charles's worldly wisdom. Waugh makes it a crucial question of his dénouement how Lord Marchmain will respond to the ministrations of Father Mackay. Then he gives an apparent victory to Charles. When Lord Marchmain sees the priest and sternly orders Bridey to "show Father Mackay the way out," Charles feels jubilant: "I had been right, everybody else had been wrong," he exults. But Waugh's plot does not end here. As Lord Marchmain's condition worsens, Julia brings the priest back. Her father seems "nearer to death than life" as Father Mackay begins to administer the sacrament of absolution. Then suddenly there is a change, first in Charles and then in Lord Marchmain–Charles "knelt, too, and prayed: 'O God, if there is a God, forgive him his sins, if there is such a thing as sin,' and the man on the bed opened his eyes." At that moment Charles feels an intense longing for a sign. Then Lord Marchmain moves his hand to his forehead, to his breast, to his shoulder, and makes the sign of the cross.

Lord Marchmain's deathbed conversion effects Julia's. At the novel's end, Julia faces the inevitable truth—that a marriage to Charles, legally achievable by his divorce from Celia and hers from Rex, would be no marriage in the eyes of God. It is not this marriage that will "make her an honest woman" but fidelity to the commandment, *Thou shalt not commit adultery.* Julia knows, finally, that "the worse I am, the more I need God. I can't shut myself out from His mercy." And Charles sees the truth of her choice.

Evelyn Waugh is indeed a Catholic novelist, permitting us, his readers, to experience the transformation worked in Charles through his contact with the Marchmain family. When we last meet Charles, years later, as he revisits the Brideshead estate which has called forth these memories that make up the novel's story, we find that Charles now shares the Marchmains' respect for the Holy Eucharist. He goes straight to Lady Marchmain's chapel, where he discovers "a small red flame—a beaten-copper lamp of deplorable design, relit before the beaten-copper doors of a tabernacle. . .burning anew among the old stones," and before the tabernacle he prays. Such are the ways of Grace.

Brooke Allen (essay date Fall 1994)

SOURCE: *"Vile Bodies:* A Futurist Fantasy," in *Twentieth Century Literature,* Vol. 40, No. 3, Fall 1994, pp. 318-28.

[In the following essay, Allen contends that Waugh satirizes the principles of the Futurist movement in art and literature of the 1920s and 1930s in Vile Bodies.*]*

One of Evelyn Waugh's most perceptive critics, Robert Murray Davis, has commented that "like many writers more obviously committed to modernist experiment, Waugh took great care to guide his readers by means of external form" [*Evelyn Waugh, Writer,* 1981]. It is true that Waugh was not "obviously" committed to experiment, but close readings of his early novels show that such experiment is indeed present. Pastiche and quotation, two devices much employed in the modern period, play an especially important role in his work. But in spite of Waugh's rather free use of many of the techniques of modernism, critics have been reluctant to classify even his work of the twenties and thirties as modernist, and, though it seems unusually characteristic of its period, his fiction cannot be relegated to any one contemporary artistic movement. In his youth Waugh affected a pose of ultra-modernity, but it is impossible not to believe that one of the principal pleasures he took in this role was in its power to outrage his elders, for Waugh always leaves the reader with the impression that he faced the period he did so much to define with a peculiar diffidence. Superficially the most "modern" of moderns, he is simultaneously the most mandarin.

In fact Waugh's attitude was quite pragmatic. He allowed himself the luxury of reaction by deploring all modernity, while all the time using whatever stylistic tricks modernist experiment afforded him: collage, the interior monologue, classical parody, the intrusive narrator, the camera eye, montage.

Waugh's education in modernism began in his early teens, and he attributed it to his young sister-in-law, Barbara Jacobs Waugh. "She was an agnostic, a socialist and a feminist. . . . My father always assumed (as I do now) that anything new was likely to be nasty. Barbara found a specific charm in modernity" (*A Little Learning*). For several years Waugh, too, was to find charm in modernity: "I halted between two opinions and thought it more showy to express the new." Waugh's involvement in the modern movement, however, shallow though it may have been, proved instrumental in forming not only the style of his novels but their content and their frame of reference. As George McCartney points out in his study of Waugh's involvement with the modernist movement, "at every turn, [Waugh's] writing pays parodic tribute to modernist art and literature" [*Confused Roaring: Evelyn Waugh and the Modernist Tradition,* 1987].

Though sometimes it was straightforward *hommage,* in general the "tribute" was to remain both parodic and uncomfortable throughout Waugh's career. There were several reasons for this ambivalence. First, there was the tendency of the various movements of modern art to ally themselves with one or another variety of political commitment: Waugh's rejection of such commitment, throughout most of his career, was firm. Another reason for Waugh's disaffection from modernist art evolved from his distaste for the aesthetic of Roger Fry and the other dominant theorists of Waugh's youth, an aesthetic Waugh perceived as dry and narrow. Also, he never fully accepted the validity of nonrepresentational art. Waugh's later railings against Picasso became something of a set piece in his old-fogey persona, but he was nonetheless sincere in his belief that "Titian might have though Frith intolerably common but he would have recognized that he was practicing the same art as himself. He could not think this of Picasso," and he picks out Gertrude Stein as a literary equivalent of Picasso, an example of a writer who is "outside the world-order in which words have a precise and ascertainable meaning" (*Letters*).

> **When Waugh chose to confront modernity directly in his fiction, he usually did so parodically, as a method of emphasizing his own cynical and skeptical position.**
> **—Brooke Allen**

It is because of this disaffection from the dominant theories of modern aesthetics that Waugh's use of modern techniques concerned itself almost exclusively with their superficial characteristics, often in an openly parodic fashion. Waugh quickly moved from an early, and quite genuine, fascination with Cubism and Futurism, to an easy and familiar utilization of their more obvious techniques. His natural ability to pick up the jargon and rhetoric of a fashionable theory soon evolved into the style already fully in evidence in his first published piece of fiction, **"The Balance"** (1925), the way in which he was able to exploit isolated elements of avant-garde art so as to give a conventionally romantic, rather run-of-the-mill plot an air of clever modernity. In both his literature and his graphic art of the twenties and thirties, Waugh employed techniques borrowed from Cubism, Surrealism, Futurism, Constructivism, and Dada, though the philosophies informing all these schools remained essentially repellent to him. Waugh's presentation of the various schools of modern art is a reductive one which mocks each "ism" by flaunting its surface elements, never acknowledging that it might have any truly valuable *raison d'être* in itself.

When Waugh chose to confront modernity directly in his fiction, he usually did so parodically, as a method of emphasizing his own cynical and skeptical position. The Emperor Seth in *Black Mischief* is the ideal mouthpiece for everything Waugh found ridiculous not only in the modern world but in the very weight that the concept of "modernity" was given in the thirties discourse of progressivism. Similarly, Surrealism is mocked in *Put Out More Flags,* Expressionism in **"The Balance,"** architectural Purism and the theories of Ozenfant and Corbusier in *Decline and Fall.* And in *Vile Bodies* Waugh parodied, though in a less direct way, both the philosophy and the mannerisms of Futurist art and rhetoric, answering its enthusiastic affirmations with his own resounding "No."

Vile Bodies was not one of Waugh's own favorites among his novels; it was hurriedly written during a time of considerable emotional upheaval, and to it he devoted little of his accustomed care over structural solidity. But despite his own disclaimers, this "lapse" is not to be regretted, for Waugh packed *Vile Bodies* with more detailed raw material than he did his other books. Frederick Stopp points out that Waugh applies the very techniques of modern art in the construction of the novel: "Everywhere pastiche keeps raising its irrepressible head, as in the constant intrusions of the language of the gossip columns, the superbly bogus conversations between middle-class matrons in a train to Aylesbury, and the stream of technical commentary overheard in the pits at the motor-race. The whole produces a patchwork impression which conceals the cunning with which the pasteboard figures have been mounted" [*Evelyn Waugh, Portrait of the Artist,* 1958]. This patchwork effect is expertly employed in order to achieve the effect of an impersonal narrative that is self-perpetuating, unauthored, as though *Vile Bodies* were a collage made up of jagged segments of contemporary magazines, newspapers, and conversation fragments. It is significant that Waugh wrote the novel at the height of his fascination with Hemingway, the writer he admired above all other moderns: the telephone conversations between Adam and Nina are, he later admitted, direct stylistic imitations of *The Sun Also Rises.*

George McCartney highlights *noise* as an integral factor of the more hellish scenes Waugh liked to portray. He specifies the "confused roaring" of the Bollinger Club at the opening of *Decline and Fall,* the whining race cars in *Vile Bodies,* the African feasts and drums in *Black Mischief,* the voices in *Gilbert Pinfold,* the popular music on the wireless played by the enlisted men in *Sword of Honour,* and he emphasizes "the hostility between eye and ear that recurs throughout Waugh's work." "In his fiction, savagery always manifests itself aurally." In *Vile Bodies* that noise is almost exclusively talk—most of it vacuous enough to qualify as noise, pure and simple. It is a quintessentially urban book as none of Waugh's other novels were to be, written in response to what Hugh Kenner characterizes as the "episodic" nature of city life in the twentieth century: "A city shaped by rapid transit, and later by a telephone network, delivers its experience in discrete packets" (*The Mechanic Muse,*

1987). *Vile Bodies,* appropriately, is an episodic book. The attention span of its characters is not long enough to justify more than episodic treatment, and in this, as in other elements, the novel marks the apex of Waugh's concern with modernist technique.

The novel also illustrates Kenner's thesis that "kinesis was the rhetoric of that decade [the twenties], when Americans did with pure motion what the English did about 1600 with language, and the French about 1880 with color" (*The Counterfeiters: An Historical Comedy*). With a minimum of description Waugh succeeds in reproducing the aura of the recently modernized, mechanized city almost solely through his use of accelerated dialogue and truncated conversations.

Just as *Vile Bodies* focuses specifically upon urban life, it also deals extensively with the characteristics of a *modern* city. Adam's forays to Doubting Hall are meant to emphasize, by contrast, the accelerated pace of London life (though Doubting Hall, of course, is no more reassuring a place than any other in the novel). In his use of modernity itself as a protagonist, and in his treatment of it, Waugh consciously parodies the Italian Futurists, whose manifesto he "studied" in early youth.

The Futurists had made a considerable impression during Waugh's childhood. Waugh was educated in the basic tenets of Futurism by Barbara Jacobs, and admits to having had an enthusiasm for C. R. W. Nevinson, the only English painter to become a Futurist after the dissemination of the *Initial Manifesto of Futurism.* In his autobiography Waugh states that his youthful admiration for the Futurists was "spurious" (*Little*), but his immersion in their work, brief as it was, provided him with a knowledge which was to be useful for the purposes of *Vile Bodies.* The vision behind Marinetti's rhetoric—glorious, but already highly tarnished by 1929, the year in which Waugh wrote the novel—is an ideal backcloth against which the stale, vapid characters of *Vile Bodies* are made to act out their futile lives; Marinettian themes and motifs are continually played out in both the subject matter and the style of the novel. Philosophically they are found inadequate again and again; stylistically, Waugh is able to use them to considerable effect. Thus, though much of *Vile Bodies* is devoted to mocking the beliefs of the Futurists, in its style Waugh pays them a certain sidelong homage.

The Triumph of the Machine: this was a constant refrain of the Futurists, who were intoxicated by the events of their own period—the flights of Wright and Bleriot, the advent not only of the automobile but of the racing car as well. "The opening and closing of a valve creates a rhythm just as beautiful but infinitely newer than the blinking of an animal eyelid," wrote Boccioni (Joshua C. Taylor, ed., *Futurism,* 1961); and Marinetti continually uses animal imagery to describe machinery, as he lays his "amorous hands" on the "torrid breasts" of "snorting beasts" (motorcars) (*Selected Writings*, 1972). The thesis of the *Initial Manifesto* extols the beauty, specifically, of steamers, locomotives, and airplanes as well as of automobiles.

Vile Bodies also treats these mechanical modes of transport, but while novelty (as with the Futurists) is stressed, the emphasis is finally placed on the staleness of the vision that these so recently new inventions now evoke. Even the shiny modernity of the works of mechanical magic is unable to dispel the sourness and sameness of life, and the machines in *Vile Bodies* produce for the most part not exhilaration but nausea.

The description of the steamship ride at the beginning of the novel is typical of the book's attitude toward modernity, "Sometimes the ship pitched and sometimes she rolled and sometimes she stood quite still and shivered all over. . . . 'Too, too sick-making,' said Miss Runcible, with one of her rare flashes of accuracy." The captive dirigible in which the Bright Young People give their party is another case in point. There is no reason whatever for giving the party in the dirigible—which is tethered only a few feet above the ground—except insofar as it represents a novelty, a new kind of party for the bored young people. "New," "unconventional," and "modern" though it is, the dirigible only induces the same nausea as the steamship. "Inside, the saloons were narrow and hot. . . . There were protrusions at every corner, and Miss Runcible had made herself a mass of bruises in the first half-hour. It was the first time that a party was given in an airship."

The airplane, a standard object of Futurist enthusiasm, gets no better treatment from Waugh. Marinetti had described the experience of flying in aesthetic terms: "As I looked at objects from a new point of view, no longer head on or from behind, but straight down, foreshortened, that is, I was able to break apart the old shackles of logic and the plumb lines of the ancient way of thinking" (*Selected*). Waugh's aesthetic reaction was very different, and in 1929 he wrote: "After a very short time one tires of this aspect of scenery. I think it is significant that a tower or a high hill are all the eminence one needs for observing natural beauties" (*Labels*). Waugh's work is everywhere permeated with the idea that the only advantage "progress" can bring is the perishable one of novelty; when that has worn off, the machine is empty of any value, having added nothing in the way of real aesthetic enjoyment or spiritual life. This is the attitude conveyed in the description of Nina's honeymoon voyage on an airplane to Monte Carlo: all the ingredients of the Futurist fantasy are present, but tarnished and tawdry after twenty years of unfulfilled promise. "Nina looked down and saw inclined at an odd angle a horizon of straggling red suburbs; arterial roads dotted with little cars; factories, some of them work-

ing, others empty and decaying . . . wireless masts and overhead power cables 'I think I'm going to be sick,' said Nina" (*Vile*).

The car, of course, is the prototypical Futurist symbol. Wyndham Lewis spoke of Marinetti's "automobilism," and of all Marinetti's imagery it is the automobile, specifically the racing car, that has proved the most memorable. This is partly due to his sexualization of the automobile, a legacy that has remained with us; it is also due to Marinetti's persistent deification of speed, and his use of the automobile as its physical symbol. "We declare that the world's splendour has been enriched by a new beauty; the beauty of speed. A racing motor-car . . . is more beautiful than the *Victory of Samothrace*" (*Selected*). He presents the automobile not only as the greatest achievement of human art but as a god in its own right, a modern Pegasus: "Dieu vehement d'une race d'acier, / Automobile ivre d'espace / qui pietines d'angoisse, les mors aux dents stridents" (Taylor). In thus usurping the position formerly held by deities, the automobile not only symbolizes the apex of men's material achievements, but represents a spiritual exaltation in its own right, as Joshua Taylor points out. The introduction to the *Initial Manifesto* sets this forward in revealing terms:

> But, as we listened to the old canal muttering its feeble prayers and the creaking bones of sickly palaces above their damp green beards, under the windows we suddenly heard the famished roar of automobiles.
>
> 'Let's go!' I said. 'Friends, away! Let's go! Mythology and the Mystic Ideal are defeated at last. . . .'
>
> We went up to the three snorting beasts. . . . I stretched out on my car like a corpse on its bier, but revived at once under the steering wheel, a guillotine blade that threatened my stomach. (*Selected*).

This theme, of course, is directly parodied in the race-track segment of *Vile Bodies* and in Agatha Runcible's unhappy end. When Adam, Agatha, Miles, and Archie arrive at the race track the reader is treated to a disquisition on the difference between cars of "being" and of "becoming." "Some cars," the narrator tells us in his most formal mode,

> mere vehicles with no purpose above bare locomotion . . . have definite "being" just as much as their occupants. . . . Not so the *real* cars, that become masters of men; those vital creations of metal who exist solely for their own propulsion through space. . . . These are in perpetual flux; a vortex of combining and disintegrating units.

McCartney takes this, and Agatha's subsequent hallucinations after her accident, to be parodies of Bergsonian thought; I believe it to be more indebted to Futurist rhetoric. As Taylor formulates it, the Futurists saw all objects as embodying two kinds of motion: "that which tends to move in on itself, suggesting in its centripetal force the internal mass of an object" (Waugh's cars of "being"), and "that which moves outward in space mingling with space itself" (the cars of "becoming"—the race cars, the "real" cars). Taylor points out that the Futurists share with Bergson the idea that the consciousness only perceives moments of flux rather than motionless objects. So while Waugh may parody Bergsonian ideas indirectly, he directly addresses those of the Futurists (Taylor).

Waugh refers directly to the Futurist aesthetic in his description of the statute reserved for the race's winner, "a silver gilt figure of odious design, symbolizing Fame embracing Speed." He also refers to it by making the most ruthless of the speed demons on the track an Italian, suggestively named Marino; Marino drives like "sheer murder" and is "a real artist and no mistake." Agatha's joining the race as spare driver is appropriate in that the whole novel, basically, has dealt with the theme of speed, and she is Speed's goddess. The most feckless and novelty-hungry of the Bright Young People, she personifies the general (though futile) speeding up of modern life which is one of the principal themes of Futurism: "Acceleration de la vie, qui a aujourd'hui presque toujours un rhythme rapide. Equilibrisme physique, intellectuel et sentimental de l'homme sur la corde tendue de la vitesse, parmi les magnetismes contradictoires. Consciences multiples et simultanées dans un même individu" (Marinetti, *Mots*).

"Already we live in the absolute, since we have already created speed, eternal and ever-present," wrote Marinetti (*Selected*), and Agatha Runcible, in her fevered ramblings, also lives in an absolute of sorts. (It should be noted that Agatha's neighbor in the nursing home has had his wits addled in another Futurist accident, a fall from an airplane). In the introduction to the *Initial Manifesto* Marinetti describes his own car wreck in terms of rebirth; after turning over into the ditch and drinking its muddy water he rises as a new man. Such, alas, is not the case for Agatha. She too suffers an accident, when her racing car crashes against a market cross, but far from being reborn, she staggers half senseless out of the wreckage and begins her steady decline toward death. Her delirium is a kind of Futurist nightmare in itself. "'*Darling*,' she said. 'How *too* divine . . . *how* are you? . . . how angelic of you all to come . . . only you must be careful not to fall out at the corners . . . ooh, just missed it. There goes that nasty Italian car . . . darling, do try and drive more straight, my sweet, you were nearly into me then. . . . Faster." The constant refrain of "Faster, faster" that Agatha hears is not only an ironic comment upon her own life but also a parodic reference to the principal Futurist obsession.

Another favorite subject of Futurist rhetoric was militarism, the glorification of war being one of the factors that contributed to the Futurists' fall from fashion after World War I. In his *Manifeste naturiste*, an influential text for the Futurists, Saint-Georges de Bouhelier declared that "the art of the future must be heroic," and the Futurists adopted this preoccupation in their unconventional fashion. Waugh appropriates this theme in order to make his jaundiced, disabused point; from the postwar perspective it was only too obvious that war had failed to be "the world's only hygiene." *Vile Bodies* ends on "the biggest battlefield in the history of the world." It is an ending that might seem inappropriate in the face of the novel's primary focus on its own self-enclosed social world, but it is actually the Futurist militaristic credo that is being invoked and mocked. The war as presented in the novel is markedly vague and unfocused; we do not even know who the combatants are. Like the Futurist ideals of Speed and Machinery, the advent of war leaves the essence of the world—its flatness and tiredness—remarkably unchanged.

While Waugh used the themes of the Futurists to invert and negate their philosophies, he also made use of certain elements of Futurist aesthetics in the actual execution of *Vile Bodies*. It is done in his usual manner, exploiting the principles behind the stylistic credos rather than practicing the techniques themselves. "Destroy the *I* in literature" Marinetti wrote: "that is, all psychology," and he urged Futurist writers to "substitute for human psychology, now exhausted, the lyric obsession with matter" (*Selected*). "Material has always been contemplated by a cold, distracted I, too preoccupied with itself, full of preconceived wisdom and human obsessions."

In *Vile Bodies,* as we have seen, the role of the narrator has been purposely suppressed, giving the reader the impression of a narrative that is self-generating, almost mechanical. When the narrator is in evidence he is neutral, formal, and machine-like. This antiseptic tone is affected in contrast to the narrated events: suicide, homosexuality, war, wife-selling, violent death, prostitution. The paucity of psychological exposition corresponds with Marinetti's cry for the artist to destroy the "psychology" in literature. "The suffering of a man is of the same interest to us as the suffering of an electric lamp, which, with spasmodic starts, shrieks out the most heartrending expressions of colour," wrote the Futurists (Taylor); appropriately enough, when Agatha disappears it is the car and not herself that is the subject of the driver's concern. Indeed, the Bright Young People's reactions to the violent events that befall them appear generally to be mechanical rather than emotional, and these affectless responses only add to the characters' already impenetrable masks.

In *Vile Bodies* Waugh's technique conforms with the Futurist principles of *Dinamismo, compenetrazione,* and *simultaneita.* These three principles are maintained through Waugh's extensive use of *montage:* the rapid cutting back and forth reinforces the dynamic effect, the various scenes penetrate one another via the abrupt switches from place to place. Simultaneity—"the synthesis of *what one remembers* and *what one sees*" (Apollonio, *Futurist Manifestos,* 1973)—is achieved through the juxtaposition of scenes and characters and the conversational non sequiturs that bridge the gaps in space from one almost indistinguishable gathering to another. Characters melt together; when Simon Balcairn, Adam Fenwick-Symes, and Miles Malpractice succeed one another as Mr. Chatterbox they lose whatever little individuality they possessed to begin with.

The Futurist artists' aim was to put the viewer into the center of the work of art, to make him feel at the vortex of a whirling dynamism. They maintained, as Boccioni explained, "unlike Cézanne, that *the boundaries* of the object tend to retreat towards a periphery (the environment) *of which we are the center*" (Apollonio). Waugh manages to achieve a similar effect by allowing the drunken, speeded-up gyrations of his cast of characters to *encircle* the reader, who thus himself becomes the only stable center.

Waugh's treatment of Futurist themes in *Vile Bodies* is typical of his general attitude toward modern art and theory. He usurps individual motifs and techniques and then superimposes them onto his structure—often, of course, with the purpose of mocking or criticizing some aspect of modern life, or indeed the modern school itself. His aim is to infuse his own skepticism into the aesthetic he chooses to parody, and thus to emphasize its absurdity and even, more seriously, its philosophical error. He argues passionately against the Futurists' idealization of war and destruction as morally cleansing, and shows their pseudo-religion of speed and machinery to be not only sterile but laughable as well. Waugh's own vision of the future was already, in youth as in middle age, a bleak and hopeless one, totally unlike that of the Futurists. In *Vile Bodies* he focused specifically on Futurism and its ideal, whereas in his next novel, *Black Mischief,* he would focus more generally upon the hazier notion of "progressivism"—but in all his work the vacuity of modernity in all its guises is emphasized.

Richard P. Lynch (essay date Fall 1994)

SOURCE: "Evelyn Waugh's Early Novels: The Limits of Fiction," in *Papers on Language & Literature: A Journal for Scholars and Critics of Language and Literature,* Vol. 30, No. 4, Fall 1994, pp. 373-86.

[*In the following essay, Lynch contends that Waugh's lack of didacticism in his early novels points to his view of the limited ability of fiction to express permanent, meaningful ideas.*]

Apart from his own willingness to classify himself as an entertainer, one of the major reasons for the general view of Evelyn Waugh's early novels as frivolous is that they betray little in the way of overt philosophical content. While it is true that the didactic novel has fallen into disfavor and we tire of the Rupert Birkins more easily than we used to, we still demand a message from fiction, and Waugh seems to deny us one. The problem raised here is one of subject matter. If Waugh's subject is merely the foibles of English society between the wars, then he is a sort of humorous chronicler of the period, and of limited interest to later generations, who will find him funny but will not perhaps understand allusions to the Oxford aesthetes. But English society is not Waugh's only subject. In his first six novels, in fact, he was writing to a considerable extent about fiction, particularly its limited ability either to imitate "reality" in the sense that conventional realistic and naturalistic narratives attempt to do, or to present the ideal suggested by Dr. Johnson's "just representations of general nature." Nor, in spite of his fascination with fantasy, did he aspire to Sidney's poetic world, which offers not an insight into reality, but a superior alternative to it: Nature's world is "brazen, the poets only deliver a golden." Although he contradicts himself on the matter in his statements on fiction, Waugh clearly rejects escape and mere entertainment in his own novels; as D. H. Lawrence said, trust the tale, not the teller.

Further, while he did not anticipate the alternatives to traditional novel form offered by later writers, Waugh shared post-modern ideas about the novel's limitations, especially the objections to the conventions of the realistic novel raised by Alain Robbe-Grillet and the other proponents of the *nouveau roman* in France and their followers in England and America. The majority of these writers would agree, I think, that a message on the limits of fiction, on what art cannot do, is not trifling with the novel or with art, but bears its own importance as a subject. It is here that Waugh's permanent value as a novelist (as opposed to his value as a satirist) lies.

Waugh's attitude toward realism in fiction is clear. He avoided both Victorian attempts at verisimilitude through causal plot structures and modern experiments in realistic character representation, particularly stream of consciousness techniques: he did not believe the novel should be an attempt to represent life directly. Waugh admired writers like Ivy Compton-Burnett, creators, as he says, of "a timeless wonderland directed by its own interior logic, not distorting, because not reflecting, the material world" (Robert M. Davis, "Evelyn Waugh on the Art of Fiction," in *Papers on Language and Literature,* Vol. 2, 1966). He insisted on the separation between the artistically created and the actual world. Thus in his first novel, *Decline and Fall,* he presents us with Paul Pennyfeather, a fictional character based on another fictional character. The whole book, the narrator explains, "is really an account of the mysterious disappearance of Paul Pennyfeather," and we have actually been reading about the adventures of his shadow, for, "as the reader will probably have discerned already, Paul Pennyfeather would never have made a hero, and the only interest about him arises from the unusual series of events of which his shadow was witness." Waugh is not merely defining the picaresque hero, who is, indeed, less important than his surroundings; he is making a statement about fiction as mimesis, and he puts the artist's imitation in much the same position Plato did—at two removes from reality.

Far from the position of Henry James, then, who wrote that at times his characters seemed to have lives of their own, or, to take a more recent example, of John Fowles, whose double ending in *The French Lieutenant's Woman* is supposedly caused by a character's decision to do something other than what the author had planned, Waugh insisted that his characters remain fictional. His treatment of Paul Pennyfeather reminds one of Max Beerbohm's "Enoch Soames," a parody on the Faust theme. Sure of his ability as an artist but ignored by the critics and the public, Enoch Soames makes a bargain with the devil which allows him, in exchange for his life and soul, to travel one hundred years into the future and spend the afternoon reading all the references to himself and his work in the British Museum. When he arrives there, however, the only place he can find his name is as a character in a story by Max Beerbohm. Soames, who at first desires only to be recognized as an artist, eventually finds himself trying desperately to prove that he is real, but, as another character in the story puts it, Enoch Soames is not just "dim"; he is non-existent; and Beerbohm, who has inserted himself in the story as a character, is a "treacherous ass" for having given Soames the illusion of being real.

In his treatment of Pennyfeather and elsewhere, Waugh anticipates some of the objections to the traditional novel voiced by Robbe-Grillet, who argues that the universe in which entire films and novels occur is a "perpetual present" which "obliterates itself as it proceeds": "This man, this woman begin existing only when they appear on the screen and in the novel the first time; before that they are nothing; and once the projection is over, they are again nothing. Their existence lasts only as long as the film lasts."

The "disappearance" of the hero in *Decline and Fall* has a further implication. Although some of Waugh's protagonists aspire to heroic status, they invariably fail. Neither these, however, nor any of the other protagonists in the early novels may quite be tagged as anti-heroes; it is more as if, as in

Pennyfeather's case, they did not really exist, or were so unimportant that the issue of their existence was not worth resolving. This condition is a result of Waugh's refusal to accept one of the primary assumptions on which the novel of realism is based—the importance of the individual. The personality of a character in a realistic novel, Ian Watt notes, "is defined in the interpenetration of its past and present self-awareness. "The individual is "in touch with his own continuing identity through memory of his past thoughts and actions," and through this contact achieves personal identity [*The Rise of the Novel: Studies in Defoe, Richardson, and Fielding,* 1957].

It should strike a reader as odd that Waugh, who makes considerable use of film techniques in his early novels, does not use flashback to portray a character in the sense that Watt describes. Indeed, what is peculiar about his early characters is that they do not seem to have a sense of the past, or of what they have done or thought in their own past. Critics have marvelled at Pennyfeather's ability to adapt to any situation (though in fact it is not so much that he adapts as that others make what they want of him), but he has no need to adapt, for he comes to each situation in the novel as though he had not existed before it. Adam Fenwick-Symes, in *Vile Bodies,* behaves in much the same way. The thin plot of this novel consists of Adam's attempts to make enough money to marry his fiancée, Nina Blount. Several times he reaches the required amount (two thousand pounds) only to lose it through carelessness, naiveté, or sheer coincidence. Each time he has the money in his pocket, he calls Nina and announces his willingness to marry her immediately. Each time he loses it, he again calls her and tells her the wedding is off. None of his disappointments impinges on the succeeding hopes and happy telephone calls. Even after he has "sold" Nina to a character named Ginger Littlejohn and she has married, Adam believes that he can buy her back. The traditional expectations of a romantic plot demand that marriage end the matter, and Waugh demonstrates throughout the novel that Adam is something of a romantic. But Nina's marriage to another man has no effect on him; given another chance at the money, he persists in his expectations of a happy ending to a traditional love plot.

Tony Last, in *A Handful of Dust,* is perhaps Waugh's most realistic character among the early heroes, and his pathetic attempt to discover what has gone wrong in his marriage to Brenda is representative of the whole problem of personal identity and the past in Waugh: "He could not prevent himself, when alone, from rehearsing over and over in his mind all that had happened since Beaver's visit to Hetton; searching for clues he had missed at the time; wondering where something he had said or done might have changed the course of events; going back further to his earliest acquaintance with Brenda to find indications that should have made him more ready to understand the change that had come over her; reliving scene after scene in the last eight years of his life." But Tony's struggle to find a causal chain leading to and explaining his present situation is fruitless, for the causal relationships are not there. In denying Tony and the other early heroes logical connections with the past, Waugh objectifies his characters, makes them like so many well-made chessmen, to be examined curiously, but not probed or humanized. Michel Butor describes the effect of this loss of the past: "A rigorous effort to follow strict chronological order, not allowing any flashback, leads to surprising discoveries: all reference to universal history becomes impossible, all reference to the past of the characters encountered, to memory, and consequently all interiority. Thus the characters are necessarily transformed into things" ["Research on the Technique of the Novel," in *Inventory*, 1968]. Waugh's ideal was exactly this: to make his characters "things," to prevent even the more fully developed figures like Tony from appearing to be more than they were. Tony Last has a memory, it is true, but he cannot establish the necessary relationship between past and present and so the past no longer belongs to him; it too has become an object, without signification.

Tony is, in fact, rather like Enoch Soames; he is a fictional character desperately attempting to be "real." Instead of relying, as Soames and Pennyfeather do, on what other people make or say of him, Tony, in effect, becomes a literary critic: he tries to make sense of the narrative. But Waugh is no more disposed to provide motivation for action than he is for character. The source of the trouble between Brenda and Tony is a *deus ex machina* named Mrs. Beaver, who sends her son off to visit the Lasts at Hetton. Every narrative must have a device to begin the action, but most novelists attempt to disguise this force as some natural event in a causal chain, or the inevitable consequence of a particular character trait. Waugh makes it as obvious as possible that the action of his novel begins at the writer's whim, and he uses such arbitrary plot movers to that end throughout the early novels.

Waugh's carefree treatment of motive forces in plot and his ridicule of other traditional techniques of the novel (at the end of *Scoop* he parcels out futures for the main characters much in the Victorian manner) places him, again, in a more avant-garde position than most critics have given him credit for. He confuses the matter by describing himself in the admittedly autobiographical *Ordeal of Gilbert Pinfold* as a sort of 18th century craftsman, a refiner of what has been established rather than an innovator. He is, however, nothing of the kind; his plots are nearly as unconventionally constructed as those of Raymond Roussel, probably the earliest writer to influence the practitioners of the *nouveau roman* in their choice of arbitrary structure. Vivian Mercier reports that Roussel wrote stories by first choosing two similar words, then adding them to identical sentences, in which, however, the same words took on different shades of meaning: "The

two sentences once found, it was a matter of writing a story that could begin with the first sentence and end with the second" [*A Reader's Guide to the New Novel: From Queneau to Pinget*, 1971]. Waugh did not, perhaps, go this far toward arbitrariness in the writing process, but he did, for instance, write *A Handful of Dust* by beginning at the end. The episode with Mr. Todd in Brazil began as a short story, and Waugh wrote the novel, he claimed, because he wanted to see how it began. Beginning at the end might serve as a means of building a more logical plot, but there is no evidence of such logic in *A Handful of Dust*. What is more, such a beginning sweeps aside the illusion of free characters whose actions and personalities will determine their fate. Waugh accepted, in any case, none of the conventions of 19th century realism without modifying them for his own purposes, and one of his purposes was to deny the assumptions which underlay 19th and early 20th century novel structure.

He refused, to put it in Robbe-Grillet's terms, to reassure his readers about their prefabricated schemes of reality. The 19th century novelists, as Frank Kermode has remarked, wrote "protective fictions": "They created artificial beginning and end, a duration minute but human in which all, between those points, is ordered, and so in a fiction challenges and negates the pure being of the world" [*The Sense of an Ending. Studies in the Theory of Fiction*, 1967]. But the fictions were also protective because their structures reflected a solid and eminently reasonable world view. David Goldknopf, in *The Life of the Novel*, traces the plotted novel and its machine metaphor to the influences of the Industrial Revolution and its cosmic model, Deism. This novel of reason culminates in the detective fiction of the last half of the 19th century, in which, as Goldknopf says, "plot assumed frank control over all other narrative elements" [*The Life of the Novel*, 1972]. Waugh himself took an oddly rationalist view of religion, but he would have no part of such a structure for the novel.

It is true that he expressed admiration for certain mystery writers, as Harvey Breit records in an interview: "What he'd like to write, Mr. Waugh confessed, would be a detective story. 'Not like Graham Greene, but rather like the story of the Agatha Christie or Erle Stanley Gardner sort, where the clues are given and an actual solution takes place. I admire very much books of pure action'" [*The Writer Observed*, 1956]. But Waugh did not see these books as imitative of life or of any particular world view, and his own works, far from being the models of logic he admired, are travesties of the melodramatic simplifications, probable occurrences, and happy endings of many Victorian novels. To come to the conclusion, as he did in an article titled **"Fan-Fare,"** that there is "no such thing as normality" and that the artist's sole task is to "create little independent systems of order of his own" denies the very basis of mimetic fiction.

This refusal to reaffirm a systematic view of the world by mirroring it in the structure of his novels indicates that Waugh was as reluctant to imitate or present general truths as he was to follow the conventions of realism and naturalism. Here again he anticipates the *nouveau roman,* especially in its rejection of "signification" and "depth." Traditional views, according to Robbe-Grillet, "reduce the novel to a signification external to it, make the novel a means of achieving some value which transcends it, some spiritual or terrestrial 'beyond,' future Happiness or eternal Truth" [*For a New Novel: Essays on Fiction,* 1965]. Further, such views spawned and perpetuated the myth of depth in the novel: "The writer's traditional role consisted in excavating Nature, in burrowing deeper and deeper to reach some ever more intimate strata, in finally unearthing some fragment of a disconcerting secret."

Waugh not only avoids such discoveries and illuminations— he parodies them. He guides the ridiculous Pennyfeather, for instance, through a whole series of mock-epiphanies, the most preposterous of which occurs as Paul accepts his imprisonment in place of the guilty Margot Beste-Chetwynde on the theory that, as her son Peter reasons, "You can't see Mamma in prison, can you?": "The more Paul considered this, the more he perceived it to be the statement of a natural law . . . he was strengthened in his belief that there was, in fact, and should be, one law for her and another for himself" (*Decline and Fall*). It was precisely Waugh's point that the artist is incapable of revealing any "natural laws" through his work. To do so would be to fall back on the protective fictions of earlier novelists and to claim for the artist the status of prophet.

Waugh's most effective parody of depth and signification also occurs in *Decline and Fall:* it is Professor Silenus's speech on the big wheel at Luna Park. Silenus's question to Pennyfeather warns us that the whole tradition of philosophical truths delivered by fictional characters who serve primarily as mouthpieces for their authors is about to be debunked:

"Shall I tell you about life?"

"Yes, do," said Paul politely.

"Well, it's like the big wheel at Luna Park. . . . You pay five francs and go into a room with tiers of seats all round, and in the center the floor is made of a great disc of polished wood that revolves quickly. . . . the nearer you can get to the hub of the wheel the slower it is moving and the easier it is to stay on. . . . Of course at the very center there's a point completely at rest, if one could only find it. I'm not sure I am not very near that point myself. . . . Lots of people just enjoy scrambling on and being whisked off and scrambling on again. How

they all shrink and giggle! Then there are others, like Margot, who sit as far out as they can and hold on for dear life and enjoy that. But the whole point about the wheel is that you needn't get on it at all, if you don't want to. People get hold of ideas about life, and that makes them think they've got to join in the game, even if they don't enjoy it. It doesn't suit everyone."

"Now you're a person who was clearly meant to stay in the seats and sit still and if you get bored watch the others. Somehow you got onto the wheel, and you got thrown off again at once with a hard bump. It's all right for Margot, who can cling on, and for me, at the center, but you're static. Instead of this absurd division into sexes they ought to class people as static and dynamic."

Critics have largely accepted Silenus's speech without sensing its irony, arguing only over the question of whether Waugh was merely providing an explanation of the difference between Margot's world and Pennyfeather's world, or attempting to justify moral confusion in the novel. But there is nothing in the novel to support the contention that Waugh agrees with either Paul or Silenus. Indeed, he has Silenus dismiss his own lecture immediately after delivering it: "I know of no more utterly boring and futile occupation than generalizing about life." Probably the most telling comment on the speech is Paul's reaction to it: just as he accepts the double standard of morality and honor on the question of Margot, so he adopts Professor Silenus's definition of life, which also assumes separate standards for different kinds of people.

To accept Silenus's judgment on matters of character is to accept not only the double standard, but the idea that humans are inferior to machines: "The problem of architecture as I see it . . . is the problem of all art—the elimination of the human element from the consideration of form. The only perfect building must be the factory, because that is built to house machines, not men." Silenus's fascination with machinery leads naturally to his use of a machine image to explain life to Paul. The explanation reduces people to static and dynamic (or kinetic) and simplifies them in predetermined, unalterable states. Such a view of human character is merely an extension of the machine-like plot which Goldknopf finds in the Victorian novel. Waugh's point was exactly the opposite—that real people are too complex to be crowded into such neat patterns.

A further reason for rejecting the classification of characters into static and dynamic is that it is uncomfortably close to the traditional distinction between "flat" and "round" characters, a distinction that Waugh, when interviewed by Julian Jebb for the *Paris Review,* would not admit: "All fictional characters are flat. A writer can give an illusion of depth by giving an apparently stereoscopic view of a character—seeing him from two vantage points; all a writer can do is give more or less information about a character, not information of a different order" ["The Art of Fiction XXX: Evelyn Waugh," Vol. 30, 1963]. Like Robbe-Grillet, Waugh objected to the fictional character who was supposed to represent a human type, complete with concrete qualities, associations, and predetermined patterns of action. Such a character is only another way of achieving signification, of rising to the level of a category or universal. Static and dynamic also call up suspicious echoes of Joyce, whom Waugh criticized for attempting to reveal the whole human mind and soul in his fiction. Stephen Dedalus divides art into "static" and "kinetic," and it is quite possible that Pennyfeather's discovery of the division of human character types into these two classes is a parody of the earlier revelation.

This view of Silenus's speech is also supported by the fact that it is almost alone of its kind in the early novels. The only other thematic and philosophical discourse of anything like the same length appears in *Vile Bodies,* when Father Rothschild analyzes the behavior of the Bright Young People. Rothschild himself, as Neil D. Isaacs points out, is a caricature of the intriguing Jesuit and not to be taken seriously. His speech, Christopher Sykes recalls, later bothered Waugh as a "silly" artistic flaw in the novel.

To a point, as I have suggested, Waugh keeps pace with the advocates of the *nouveau roman* in his objections to the power of the novel to imitate reality or to discover general truths and permanent human types. But he was less optimistic about the future uses of fiction and its ultimate value. When he presents the pastoral—the fictional world within fiction—in his novels, it does not fare well. In *Scoop,* William Boot retreats from London and the modern world into the aging Boot Magna, an old country house that is slowly falling apart. Several critics have pointed out the images of decay associated with the house and surrounding trees, and the moon-like image of sterility which describes the landscape. But William's escape does not depend so much on what Boot Magna is, as on what he makes of it in his weekly newspaper column, "Lush Places." Here he creates a pastoral paradise, a link with a more peaceful and decorous past. Unfortunately, the escape is enclosed not only by a decaying world, but by a world whose traditional values have been turned upside-down, as evidenced by the stately home in which the family must wait on the servants, who are too old and bed-ridden to take care of themselves. The benefits of the imagination and its creations are shaky at best.

No better illustration of this last point exists than the fate of Tony Last in *A Handful of Dust,* who also enters an ostensibly pastoral world as a means of escaping modern society and his unfaithful wife, Brenda. The traditional benefit of the pastoral retreat is that it allows the hero to shed the complexities of everyday experience and to glimpse the underlying forces with which he must align himself; it simplifies his vision and enables him to reset his goals and return to the active life with a renewed sense of purpose. But Tony is granted no such vision, and the only simplification of life he is offered is in the melodramatically simple stories of Dickens which he is forced, for the remaining years of his life, to read to Mr. Todd in the Brazilian jungle. Although Waugh was not given to messages in his novels, the implication is clear: art will not save us.

The point is not that art is worthless; Waugh certainly did not believe that. But it may well be that he shared the aesthete's view that art is useless. He was, after all, primarily a thirties writer, surrounded by those who were absorbed in writing for political and moral ends. Not involved in the didactic Left, he had time to think about fiction itself, and to write about it. While he did not share the hope that the novel might be used eventually to disabuse humans of their misconceptions about the world, Waugh would have agreed with Robbe-Grillet's analysis of the artist's true concern: "Whatever his attachment to his party or to generous ideas, the moment of creation can bring him back to the problems of his art, and to them alone."

Although Waugh maintained some of the same views on the limits of fiction in interviews as late as 1962, there is no question that his actual practice as a novelist changed substantially in the later works. With the exception of *The Loved One,* which is pure satire, from *Brideshead Revisited* on, Waugh's characters and plots become more conventional, and he appears to take expressions of "truth" on the part of his characters more seriously. In short, his later novels are more reassuring to readers of conventional romance, and what he reassures them about is, among other things, the value of a fictional account of things.

Brideshead, though it is atypical among Waugh's novels in its triumph of sentiment over satire, demonstrates the shift in attitude toward what fiction can do. Unlike earlier characters who lacked a past or even a fixed identity, Charles Ryder constructs the entire novel out of his memories. Julia, as James F. Carens points out, is as empty as earlier heroines, but Waugh tries to present her as a substantial human being by adding "Roman Catholicism and great wealth, now viewed through the mists of sentiment" [The Satirical Art of Evelyn Waugh, 1966]. Further, although the structure of *Brideshead* has been criticized, there is no playing with the conventions of plot, and while the novel makes no claims for the discovery of universal values, it asserts the value and importance to individuals of Catholicism and tradition. In the Prologue in particular, there is a longing for "stately old England" which would never have escaped ironic treatment in the earlier novels. So, while there is no reassuring systematic view of the world (the modern world is too corrupted for that), there are "pockets of value" offered in much the same way Dickens offered "pockets of goodness" in some of his characters.

As for the Crouchback novels which make up the war trilogy *Sword of Honour* and are generally considered Waugh's best later work, sentiment is controlled but the emphasis is on traditional structure and serious theme. In these three novels, Waugh "adjusts," as Carens says, "to the conventions of the novel," and in the process creates "meaningful positive values." The source of Guy Crouchback's religious inspiration in the trilogy is his father. Frederick J. Stopp reports Waugh as having said to him in a conversation that Mr. Crouchback's function in the novel was "to keep audible a steady undertone of the decencies and true purpose of life behind the chaos of events and fantastic characters" [*Evelyn Waugh: Portrait of an Artist,* 1958]. Even in *A Handful of Dust,* the most mature of the early novels, there is no such undertone. The very writing of a trilogy with the same main character suggests a continuity of being and concerns not present in the early novels, and if Carens is right in his description of the story line as "Guy's return to life after disillusionment, descent into hell, and discovery of self," Waugh has used, quite seriously, a plot at least as old as the *Aeneid.*

Carens and others may be justified in valuing Waugh's later development as a maturing of expression and broadening of sympathies, but the fact remains that his reputation rests on the early novels. Many better conventional novels have been written in the twentieth century, but few have matched the early works in satirical humor and in comic treatment of the conventional novel form, when Waugh was skeptical not only about the targets of his satire, but about the power of fiction itself.

T. J. Ross (essay date Winter 1995)

SOURCE: "Reconsidering Evelyn Waugh's *The Loved One,*" in *Modern Age,* Vol. 37, No. 2, Winter 1995, pp. 156-62.

[*Ross is an American educator, literary critic, and writer. In the following essay, Ross claims that* The Loved One *is Waugh's only truly satiric novel and notes that Waugh displays in it his deft understanding of the American character.*]

If we were to grade British authors of this century according to the degree of compassion manifest in their works, one novelist sure to flunk would be Evelyn Waugh. In recent years "compassion" has become a buzz word and it is precisely the overtones carried in its buzz that may account in part for Waugh's unsteady place on the literary stockmarket

on this side of the Atlantic. Not only, as a writer, does Waugh lose points for his low compassion-count but also, as a person, he comes across as hardly tolerable: the image of him in the public mind leaves perhaps too much to be desired. As Steven Marcus sums it up, "Waugh has been variously characterized as nasty, hateful, snobbish, trivial, reactionary, vindictive, fawning, immature, pompous, and rude." All of which, Marcus feels, is "somehow beside the point." For it doesn't affect what is offered in novels like *Decline and Fall* (1928), or *Vile Bodies* (1930), or *A Handful of Dust* (1934), or *Scoop* (1938): what is on offer, according to Marcus, is a dazzling form of entertainment, socially observant and immaculately written, which on occasion reaches the level of art but more often settles for being "artful." Marcus' essay, which can be found in his *Representations: Essays on Literature and Politics* (1975), is entitled "Evelyn Waugh and the Art of Entertainment," and for him, such an art is art enough.

He cautions, therefore, that we not bring to Waugh the "great expectations" we have been taught to bring to literature, expectations which depend on "our mistrust of any piece of writing which does not seem immediately to challenge profound assumptions or elicit the most delicate moral choices."

Now I am not sure that one can as easily as Marcus assumes disentangle a writer's blind spots from his virtues. Nor am I sure Waugh himself was in fact the snob and callow toady he has been made out to be. Few British critics, for example, recognize Waugh in Marcus' caricature. A critic as esteemed for his compassionate views as John Bayley finds Waugh the man to be, all in all, and despite himself, a "fundamentally good egg"—the public image no more than a defense against intrusions on his private life and literary aims. (Bayley refers to the death scene of the heroine of *The Loved One* [1948] is one of the most "moving" in modern literature.)

> If we were to grade British authors of this century according to the degree of compassion manifest in their works, one novelist sure to flunk would be Evelyn Waugh.
>
> —*T. J. Ross*

But beyond the matter of Waugh's personal qualities, a further question not raised by Marcus presents itself. One can get away with a low grade in compassion if one is otherwise seen as a thinker or visionary driven by the urgency of one's disturbing perceptions. Consider how commentators on D. H. Lawrence tend to go easy on the brutal tonalities that resound through his work, given the urgency of his prophetic vision. In Lawrence's perspective on social breakdown and sexual renewal we have the sort of "vision" that assures his canonical status—no matter that "vision," like "compassion" serves at present as another shopworn and rather fuzzy counter in literary discourse. Nor does it hurt that Lawrence's fiction easily lends itself to interdisciplinary studies. He is an obvious choice for any core curriculum.

Waugh in contrast would seem lacking in interdisciplinary appeal; in his best work he is neither visionary nor intellectually arduous—though he is clear-eyed indeed in characterizing ideologues. And he also resists, as Marcus is careful to observe, classification as a satirist. "His early novels," Marcus writes, "are celebrations of Mayfair, not satires of it. Nothing is more patent than that he loved. . . Lady Metroland, proprietress of an international chain of brothels . . . or that he loved all the raffish, bored useless picaresque characters who fill the pages of his earliest novels."

Satire seeks to warn us against the kind of world and characters it exposes. This is not usually the point with Waugh: he usually takes the world as he finds it. In the case of the "beautiful people" of London's Mayfair, Waugh's attitude is rightly described by Marcus as celebratory. But celebration is surely not the word for Waugh's one novel set in America and centered on its "dream factory": Hollywood. Both in its treatment of the dream factory and of its corresponding dream burial ground, Forest Lawn Cemetery on which the "Whispering Glades" of the novel is based, the novel offers a social and cultural critique which, with the passage of time, comes across today as all the more prescient and apt and with a power that invites labelling as visionary.

The opening paragraphs of *The Loved One* establish a satiric equation between the English "colony" in Hollywood and earlier colonists deposited in equatorial outposts. Nursing their whiskeys-and-soda in a "barely supportable heat," two Englishmen listen to music coming from "nearby native huts" while a "palm leaf" stirs in the breeze. They are identified as "counterparts of numberless fellow countrymen exiled in barbarous regions of the world." One of them, Ambrose Bierce, is evidently modeled on the late C. Aubrey Smith, a leading light in life, as in this fiction, of the British social enclave which enjoyed its heyday in Hollywood in the late 1940s, the time in which *The Loved One* is set. Smith made a career of portraying, in Waugh's words, "many travesties of English rural life," as well as flinty colonialists in travesties of English imperial life. And it's the Smith/Bierce character who remarks of another Englishman forced to return under a cloud to the mother country. "He went completely native." As Bierce sums up his policy: "In Africa, if a white man is disgracing himself and letting down his people, the authorities pack him off home." Bierce is troubled by the doings of a newcomer, a young English poet and adventurer who also threatens to let his side down, having accepted a job at a pet cemetery. Proving to be remorse-

lessly adaptable, the poet takes to the ways of the "barbarous region" with deadpan relish.

In describing this character's arrival on the scene. Waugh places him metaphorically with one foot on either side of the line dividing West Coast natives from English Colonials. "As a missionary priest making his first pilgrimage to the Vatican, as a paramount chief of equatorial Africa mounting the Eiffel tower, Dennis Barlow, poet and pet's mortician, drove through the Golden Gates." Dennis will prove equal to the natives at their own level of the game and his cool sufficiency is here signaled.

At Whispering Glades, Dennis meets a young woman who serves not only as hostess of the burial ground but also as a member of its elite corps of embalming interns. In their motives and expectations Dennis and the intern, Aimee Thanatogenos, will find themselves at cross purposes; and in their misreadings of one another and missed cues, they will enact a classically neat "clash of cultures." The name of the American specialist in such conflicts, Henry James, is in fact introduced in an exchange between Dennis and his boss at the animal cemetery, the Happier Hunting Ground. "I have become the protagonist of a Jamesian problem," says Dennis, who further notes that James's stories "are all tragedies one way or another"—as one way or another is *The Loved One,* which bears the subtitle *An Anglo-American Tragedy.*

What keeps the encounter between Dennis and Aimee from cliché is Waugh's view of the American character as chiefly determined by spiritual and cultural rather than material motives. A year before the novel's publication in 1948, Mary McCarthy in a celebrated essay, "America the Beautiful," which is included in her collection *On the Contrary: Articles of Belief, 1946-1961* (1962), had stressed that "the virtue of American civilization is that it is not materialistic." Of earlier notable works based on a similar theme we might note George Santayana's *Character and Opinion in the United States* (1920). In fact, as Lionel Trilling has pointed out, it is precisely Santayana's own insistent materialism, as a good European, that makes him, for the American reader, hard to take.

Waugh himself is closer to Santayana than McCarthy in his qualified response to what for her is entirely a "virtue." The idealist virtue McCarthy extols is seen by Waugh to be inseparable from what is tragic in American life. Both the humor and the critical attack of his novel stem from the depiction of a world which casually exploits spiritual and cultural aspirations. Whatever Aimee looks to for cultural nourishment or moral guidance proves a scam.

Waugh takes pains to distinguish Aimee from what he calls the "standard product," which is to say, the sort of airline hostess or reception-desk attendant whom one could leave "in a delicatessen shop in New York, fly three thousand miles and find her again in the cigar stall at San Francisco." This product is certainly, as the author says, "convenient," but "Dennis came of an earlier civilization with sharper needs." And in the "bustling hygienic Eden" of Whispering Glades. Aimee stands out as its "sole Eve." For one thing, her skin is "transparent, untarnished by the sun." This gives her an advantage that Waugh ordinarily reserved for women of his own class; he disliked the sunbathing which became fashionable in the twenties and was put off by sun tans. Aimee's pallor is a small touch but one that reveals sympathetic authorial approval. The author would also be happy to see, as does his hero, that Aimee goes easy on cosmetics. But what excites the hero above all is "the rich glint of lunacy" detectable in Aimee's eyes. Given her untutored aspirations, her "virtue," she is bound in the circumstances to be a bit mad.

Dennis possesses the culture for which the intern is starved. His manner harks back to nineties' aestheticism–the sort of manner and stance with which Waugh in his youth identified. The young poet is to a degree a sketch of the young pre-Catholic Waugh. He is described as "a young man of sensibility rather than sentiment," an apt definition of the type of aesthete whose responses tend more to the coolly appreciative than to stronger currents of feeling. In his new world, our aesthete and anti-hero at once recognizes that he can exploit his cultivation and skills only as a hustler. He hustles rhymes at his job and uses art to hustle Aimee, who responds to the verses culled from anthologies—the cultural tokens he woos her with—as an earlier native might have responded to the wampum and beads tendered to him by Dennis forbears.

In her essay, Mary McCarthy notes that we rarely find misers in American fiction although they abound in European; rather, a recurring figure in American stories is the con man. It is an aspect of Dennis' adaptability that he wheels and deals effectively as a con artist. He learns the game from Whispering Glades, a compound where the arts and artifacts of culture entirely serve a cosmetic function—further elements of an overall embalming process.

Thus no building, no statue, no replica of this or that art emblem—Rodin's *The Kiss* or whatever—is left to be scanned or taken in on its own: instead, an instant explanation of its place in the scheme of things, which is to say its educational value, accompanies each art object, on placards in large print or hummed through the sound system. "This perfect replica of an old English manor," Dennis reads, "Is constructed throughout of grade-A-steel and concrete." Dennis takes note of how "in Whispering Glades, failing credulity was fortified by the painted word." Several decades before Tom Wolfe, Waugh here anticipates the theme and the very title

of Wolfe's book, *The Painted Word* (1973) an attack on an art scene marked by an excessive dependence on hushed explanations and rationalizations of often fluffy works.

Waugh's concern is with the reduction or domestication of art forms to kitsch formulas; Wolfe's with a putative avant-garde. Yet what Wolfe sees in Soho galleries is the same process Waugh ascribes to Whispering Glades: the gradual, in Wolfe's word, "disintegration" of art works and the enjoyment of art in "the universal solvent of the word." Wolfe is led to look back to a time when "one actually struggled to *see* paintings directly, in the old pre-World War II way." In his novel set in the immediate post-World War II period, Waugh proves exact in his focus on key cultural issues. Nor is his response to the culture of the "painted word" aimed simply as a sardonic passing shot. A deeper response is evident in the musings of his protagonist: "His interest was no longer purely technical or satiric. Whispering Glades held him in thrall. In a zone of insecurity in the mind where none but the artist dare trespass, the tribes were mustering. Dennis, the frontier-man, could read the signs." For the artist the signs point to a crucial subject: art hucksterism in a world whose main expressive modes are those of salesmanship and boosterism.

Waugh's portrait of Aimee proves all the more perceptive and moving in being defined chiefly through her relation to the liberal arts. Waugh observes that Aimee's "only language," learned at the "local High School and University . . . expressed fewer and fewer of her ripening needs." With its Rotarian stress on good citizenship, Aimee's education has left her not only culturally deprived but also ill-prepared for the shocks of personal relations. And that she is not entirely blocked in her aesthetic responsiveness and capacities puts her even more on dangerous ground: she is stirred by the verses of Keats and Poe and Shakespeare that are dangled before her. Besides her responses to particular works, her attitude to art in the abstract is reverential. It is only when Dennis identifies himself as a poet that he manages to break through her facade "of impersonal, insensitive friendliness which takes the place of ceremony in that land of waifs and strays."

The more Dennis begins plying her with anthology pieces, the more disorienting they prove. Aimee finds too many of the verses to be "unethical." And Dennis is led to brood: "The English poets were proving uncertain guides in the labyrinth of Californian courtship—nearly all were too casual, too despondent, too ceremonious, or too exacting: they scolded, they pleaded, they extolled. Dennis required salesmanship." Although Dennis begins decreasing Aimee's ration of verses, she has been infected: under the influence of her suitor and his verses she begins to suffer intimations of alienation. She is unable, however, to move past her good citizen's notions of the "ethical" (which she confuses with the inspirational). Her education has allowed her no hint of the effects of either art or passion. Unable finally to handle a modicum of alienation as a fact of life, she lies back on an embalming table and destroys herself. She is presented as victim of a scene whose artistic culture is revealed to be a synthetic Disneyland.

In contrast to Aimee, her would-be tutor and lover is all too adjusted to alienation and in consequence is excessively cool. He exploits the language of passion as Aimee's mentor in embalming, Mr. Joyboy, exploits the idiom of good citizenship. For Waugh culture is inseparable from community and his California lacks both. The natives are as uprooted as the colonials, lacking not only aesthetic but familial sustenance. Mr. Joyboy's mother is a self-absorbed monster who coos over her pet, a stubbornly silent parrot.

It was his first sight of California that spurred another English expatriate, Aldous Huxley, to the writing of *Brave New World* (1932); in key respects both Huxley's novel and Waugh's correspond. Waugh's critical aim in *The Loved One* is as overt as in the classic dystopias of science fiction. The more we are immersed in the mortuary marvels of Whispering Glades, the closer we seem to the tone and trappings of science fiction. In character, Huxley's John the savage is just what his name implies: both cultural primitive and religious zealot. So too is Aimee who, like her counterpart in *Brave New World,* ends a suicide. Even as her full name spells out and conjoins love and death, so does her story, a story which, given its scene, tends inescapably toward the macabre.

Like other features of the novel, the characterization of its heroine seems ahead of its time; it is easy to imagine her in an absurdist play. The presentation of Aimee anticipates the sort of characterization that would be developed for a time by left-wing writers. One can easily imagine Aimee, for example, in the Norman Lear sitcom of the seventies: *Mary Hartman, Mary Hartman.* The comic mode of both Huxley and Waugh is what we recognize today as "black humor"—a kind of humor which provokes at the same time both laughter and guilt. The more we laugh, the more we feel chastised. Both in its dystopian and comic modes, *The Loved One* takes us well beyond the bounds of the artfully entertaining. This may account for the reserve of critics who find that it goes too far. As great an admirer of Waugh as Kingsley Amis put down the novel for being "coarse." The coarse or brutal tonalities, I would suggest, are inseparable from Waugh's social and critical concerns—perhaps in none of his other works is a critical motive more apparent.

In its plot development the novel divides pretty much in two halves—each dealing with a casualty of the times. The first is Sir Francis Tinsley, an older member of the British colony who works in public relations. When he is shunted out of his office and job he hangs himself. In his best days Sir

Francis had enjoyed a spot on the literary map as a reviewer, versifier, and travel writer; but this was in the time of the Georgians, before the rumbling advent of "Joyce and Freud and Gertrude Stein"—a line-up that Sir Francis tells Dennis "he couldn't make any sense of." When he arrived in Hollywood, he was already a literary fossil: and with the loss of his Hollywood post, he is finished. Following this account, Aimee's doomed romance is brought to the foreground. As Dennis officiated at the literary man's burial at Whispering Glades, so too he oversees the disposal of Aimee's body in the crematorium of the pet cemetery. In his profession, Sir Francis, a pre-World War I type, found himself out of his time. Aimee, a pre-World War II type, also seems in her personal dilemma out of her time. Neither has a future in the post-War II world.

Waugh tended to look benevolently on his fossil-types: that he links Aimee's fate with Sir Francis' further suggests his sympathetic attitude toward her—despite, to be sure, the surgical dispassion and precision with which her "case," like Sir Francis' own, is delineated.

> *The Loved One* deals not only with the tragic fate of an individual but also with the contours of a tragic age.
>
> —*T. J. Ross*

Waugh concisely fills us in on the social and cultural backgrounds of both characters; the more he fills us in, the more we see how each is fatally unfit for dealing with the crisis each is caught up in, the one, vocational, the other, personal. Sir Francis is baffled not only by Freud but also by a roster that includes "Kierkegaard and Kafka and Compton Burnett and Sartre." He asks of these, "Who are they? What do they want?" If Sir Francis has outlived his time—"If asked, Dennis would have guessed that he had been killed in the Dardanelles"—Aimee proves too green and misguided for hers. Waugh is as careful to pinpoint her cultural credentials and blank spots as Sir Francis. As she tells Dennis: "I've always been Artistic. I took Art at College as my second subject one semester." In answer to a query about what she took, she explains: "Just Psychology and Chinese. I didn't get on so well with Chinese. But of course they were secondary subjects too: for Cultural Background."

As Waugh anticipates Wolfe's attack on hucksterism in the art world, he here equally anticipates recent observations by Paul Fussell and other critics on hucksterism in the University. In outlining his heroine's *curriculum vitae,* Waugh, with, to be sure, greater dramatic economy and power, says everything that Fussell touches on in his essay, "The Life of the Mind." included in his book *Class: A Guide through the American Status System* (1983). That Waugh can as deftly sketch in Aimee's background as Sir Francis' again suggests that his portrayal depends on an understanding that borders on compassion and a sympathy that borders on love.

We may also note of the literary allusions strewn through the story that they function as something more than elitist flag-waving. Lines from Tennyson's *Tithonus* or parodic echoes from his *Ode on the Death of the Duke of Wellington* summon up expressive and ceremonial means in coming to terms with death which mark not simply a contrast with the style of Whispering Glades and its environs but with the language and mood of present times in general. Also foreign to the present are the avowals of love cited from Tennyson, Keats, or Shakespeare. That Aimee responds to their lines on love and death is an aspect of her tragic circumstance. *The Loved One* deals not only with the tragic fate of an individual but also with the contours of a tragic age. On this score Waugh would seem to join hands at the last with D. H. Lawrence who begins his *Lady Chatterley's Lover* (1928) with the famous admonition: "Ours is essentially a tragic age . . ." This premise determines the tone and point of Waugh's novel.

In its treatment of the "clash of cultures" the novel proves more astute and more sensitive than most critics have been willing to grant. The film version of 1963, directed by an Englishman as far to the left politically as Waugh was to the right, wholly misses his view of the American character and cultural climate. The film remains gleefully platitudinous in its belaboring of American materialism and capitalist villainy. But this miscarriage should not affect our response to a work which, both as love story and as cultural criticism, can still speak to us, and move us, now.

Joan Didion (review date 11 December 1995)

SOURCE: "Gentlemen in Battle," in *National Review*, Vol. XLVII, No. 23, December 11, 1995, pp. 128, 130-31.

[*Didion is a prominent American novelist, essayist, and screenplay writer. In the following, originally published in* National Review *in 1962, she reviews* The End of the Battle, *the final novel in Waugh's* Men at War *trilogy, noting what she considers Waugh's excellent depiction in the book of utter futility in the modern–post–World War II–world.*]

Distinctively dolorous by nature, I have to date been saved from my own instincts mostly by the relentless interference of my acquaintances, one or two of whom seem to have perfect pitch for my absurdities, if not always for their own. I recall in particular one bitter morning in New York, my 23rd birthday, when I woke with intimations of mortality to find outside my door, attractively done up in a Henri Bendel box,

the jacket of a Henry James novel painstakingly altered to read *The Tragic M(o)use*. It was accompanied by a gray plastic mouse with a red ribbon around its tail, and if I did not immediately stop fancying myself a kind of East End Avenue Ophelia, I began at least to entertain certain doubts.

Although this battle is still far from won, I sometimes have mixed feelings about the desirability of winning it at all: the only prize, after all, would be a sense of the absurd, the beginning of a kind of toughness of mind; and to win that particular victory is to cut oneself irrevocably loose from what we used to call the main currents of American thought. Every real American story begins in innocence and never stops mourning the loss of it: the banishment from Eden is our one great tale, lovingly told and retold, adapted, disguised, and told again, passed down from Hester Prynne to Temple Drake, from Natty Bumppo to Holden Caulfield; it is the single stunning fact in our literature, in our folk-lore, in our history, and in the lyrics of our popular songs. Because hardness of mind is antithetical to innocence, it is not only alien to us but generally misapprehended. What we take it for, warily, is something we sometimes call cynicism, sometimes call wit, sometimes (if we are given to this kind of analysis) disapprove as "a cheap effect," and almost invariably hold at arm's length, the way Eve should have held that snake.

It is precisely this hardness of mind which creates a gulf between Evelyn Waugh and most American readers. There is a fine edge on, and a perfect balance to, his every perception, and although he is scarcely what you could call unread in the United States, neither is he what you could call understood. When he is not being passed off as "anachronistic" or "reactionary" (an adjective employed by Gore Vidal and others to indicate their suspicion that Waugh harbors certain lingering sympathies with the central tenets of Western civilization), he is being fêted as a kind of trans-Atlantic Peter DeVries, a devastating spoofer who will probably turn out really to be another pseudonym for Patrick Dennis.

Consider these comments made at one time or another upon **Men at War,** Waugh's long trilogy, finally complete this year: "Highly entertaining . . . about some of the preposterous experiences of the Second World War. . . . Waugh's sharp wit and sure touch of satire are always at work. . . . Contains comic passages as funny as anything since **Decline and Fall.** . . . First-rate comic genius. . . . Satirical. . . . Wickedly witty . . . right to the hilarious, if not poignant, end."

Although it would be difficult to construct from these quotations the dimmest impression that Waugh was trying for anything much more devious than *See Here, Private Hargrove* or at the outside *Mister Roberts,* what he was up to in this trilogy happened in point of fact to be a complex elegiac study of the breakdown of a civilization, a great work, so right in every way that if my grandchildren should ever ask me how it was when I was little, I think I would press upon them, along with Faulkner's chronicle of the Snopes family and some bound volumes of the wartime *Vogue,* Waugh's *Men at War.*

But that is social history, and *Men at War*—begun in 1952 with *Men at Arms,* continued in 1955 with *Officers and Gentlemen,* and completed this year with *The End of the Battle*—is a great deal more than social history. One of the virtues of the hard mind is that it can deal simultaneously with an individual, his God, and his society, neither slighting nor magnifying the subtle, delicate pressures each exerts upon the others. (American novelists are on the whole incapable of this kind of thing. With the exception of Henry James, they have been determinists at heart—or very lazy.) What *Men at War* is about is one man's aridity, and his foredoomed attempt to make a social cause a moral cause in a society bereft of moral meaning; I can think of no other writer who has made that bereavement quite so clear to me.

The man is Guy Crouchback, an English Catholic who went to war in 1939, when he was 35, at the time of the Molotov-Ribbentrop Treaty, an extraordinarily crucial moment and a brilliant stroke on which to begin this particular book: ". . .now, splendidly, everything had become clear. The enemy at last was plain in view, huge and hateful, all disguise cast off. It was the Modern Age in arms. Whatever the outcome there was a place for him in that battle." Closing his house in Italy in order to enlist in London, Guy prepares as if for a Crusade, stopping by the tomb of an obscure English knight, Roger of Waybroke, waylaid on the way to his own Crusade and buried there "far from Jerusalem, far from Waybroke, a man with a great journey still all before him and a great vow unfulfilled": "Sir Roger, pray for me," Guy asked, "and for our endangered kingdom."

Guy's Crusade is short-lived. By the time of the alliance with Russia in 1941, he felt himself "back after less than two years' pilgrimage in a Holy Land of Illusion in the old ambiguous world, where priests were spies and gallant men proved traitors and his country was led blundering into dishonor." By 1943, when *The End of the Battle* begins, he is back in London, a London crowded with old people, disorder, fragments of things once known. As the end of the war approaches, the heaviest awareness of all strikes him: that whatever it had been to which he had dedicated himself on the tomb of Sir Roger that day in 1939, it had not been a Crusade. As he is told by a displaced person, "Even good men thought their private honor would be satisfied by war. . . . Were there none in England?"

"God forgive me," said Guy, "I was one of them."

What happens to Guy Crouchback at the end of the war is nothing much: he marries, and lives with his wife and chil-

dren in the agent's cottage on his family land. But he is stranded, in a real sense, exactly as far from Jerusalem and exactly as far from home as Roger of Waybroke had been, there in Italy, centuries before. What Guy can never be—and that he cannot be is the measure of something that happened in those centuries between—is what Sir Roger had been: "a man with a great journey still all before him and a great vow unfulfilled."

To know as Waugh knows that there are no more great journeys and possibly no more great vows and still to trouble to write a novel at all exhibits precisely that fine hardness of mind most characteristic of him; to know it and to trouble to write a trilogy exhibits, above and beyond hardness, whatever it was that made Chinese Gordon put on a clean white suit to hold Khartoum.

FURTHER READING

Bibliography

Wölk, Gerhard. "Evelyn Waugh: A Supplementary Checklist of Criticism." *Evelyn Waugh Newsletter and Studies* 25, No. 2 (Autumn 1991): 7-8.
> Compiles significant criticism on Waugh published since 1989.

Wölk, Gerhard. "Evelyn Waugh: A Supplementary Checklist of Criticism." *Evelyn Waugh Newsletter and Studies* 26, No. 2 (Autumn 1992): 5-6.
> Compiles significant criticism on Waugh published since 1990.

Criticism

Babiak, Peter R. "A Brief Philosophy of Stoneless Peaches." *Evelyn Waugh Newsletter and Studies* 25, No. 3 (Winter 1991): 5.
> Postulates that the image of the stoneless peach in Waugh's *The Loved One* is a metaphor for the tension between nature and culture.

Bittner, David. "Some Questions about Father Rothschild." *Evelyn Waugh Newsletter and Studies* 27, No. 1 (Spring 1993): 4.
> Reexamines Father Rothschild in *Vile Bodies,* noting possible satiric elements in Waugh's development of the character.

Lassner, Phyllis. "'Between the Gaps': Sex, Class and Anarchy in the British Comic Novel of World War II." In *Look Who's Laughing: Gender and Comedy,* pp. 205-17. Edited by Gail Finney. Langhorne, Penn.: Gordon and Breach Science Publishers, 1994.

Explores the humor in three British novels about World War II–Waugh's *Put Out More Flags,* Marghanita Laski's *Love on the Supertax* (1944), and Beryl Bainbridge's *Young Adolf* (1978)–as satires of English xenophobia and issues of class and cultural differences.

Loss, Archie. *"Vile Bodies,* Vorticism, and Italian Futurism." *Journal of Modern Literature* XVIII, No. 1 (Winter 1992): 155-64.

Argues that *Vile Bodies* is a premier example of the principles of the early twentieth-century artistic movements Vorticism and Futurism as well as a reflection of Waugh's own artistic direction early in his career.

McCartney, George. "The Being and Becoming of Evelyn Waugh." In *Evelyn Waugh: New Directions,* pp. 133-55. Edited by Alain Blayac. London: Macmillan, 1992.

Discusses Waugh's philosophical position and its place in his satirical works.

————. "Satire between the Wars: Evelyn Waugh and Others." In *The Columbia History of the British Novel,* pp. 867-94. Edited by John Richetti. New York: Columbia University Press, 1994.

Analyzes the predominance of satirical works among English writers between the World Wars, and the nature of the satire as an exposition of the superficiality of twentieth-century culture.

Additional coverage of Waugh's life and career is contained in the following sources published by Gale Research: *Contemporary Authors,* **Vol. 85-88;** *Contemporary Authors New Revision Series,* **Vols. 22, 25-28;** *Concise Dictionary of British Literary Biography,* **1914-1945;** *Contemporary Literary Criticism,* **Vols. 1, 3, 8, 13, 19, 27, 44;** *DISCovering Authors; DISCovering Authors British; DISCovering Authors Canadian; DISCovering Authors Modules: Most-Studied, Novelists, and Popular Fiction and Genre Authors; Dictionary of Literary Biography,* **Vols. 15, 162;** *Major 20th-Century Writers;* **and** *World Literature Criticism.*

☐ Contemporary Literary Criticism

Indexes

**Literary Criticism Series
Cumulative Author Index
Cumulative Topic Index
Cumulative Nationality Index
Title Index, Volume 107**

How to Use This Index

The main references

Camus, Albert
1913-1960 ...... **CLC 1, 2, 4, 9, 11, 14,
32, 69; DA; DAB; DAC; DAM DRAM,
MST, NOV; DC2; SSC 9; WLC**

list all author entries in the following Gale Literary Criticism series:

BLC = *Black Literature Criticism*
CLC = *Contemporary Literary Criticism*
CLR = *Children's Literature Review*
CMLC = *Classical and Medieval Literature Criticism*
DA = *DISCovering Authors*
DAB = *DISCovering Authors: British*
DAC = *DISCovering Authors: Canadian*
DAM = *DISCovering Authors Modules*
  DRAM = *dramatists;* *MST* = *most-studied
  authors;* *MULT* = *multicultural authors;* *NOV* =
  novelists; *POET* = *poets;* *POP* = *popular/genre
  writers;* *DC* = *Drama Criticism*
HLC = *Hispanic Literature Criticism*
LC = *Literature Criticism from 1400 to 1800*
NCLC = *Nineteenth-Century Literature Criticism*
PC = *Poetry Criticism*
SSC = *Short Story Criticism*
TCLC = *Twentieth-Century Literary Criticism*
WLC = *World Literature Criticism, 1500 to the Present*
WLCS = *World Literature Criticism Supplement*

The cross-references

See also CA 89-92; DLB 72; MTCW

list all author entries in the following Gale biographical and literary sources:

AAYA = *Authors & Artists for Young Adults*
AITN = *Authors in the News*
BEST = *Bestsellers*
BW = *Black Writers*
CA = *Contemporary Authors*
CAAS = *Contemporary Authors Autobiography
Series*
CABS = *Contemporary Authors Bibliographical
Series*
CANR = *Contemporary Authors New Revision Series*
CAP = *Contemporary Authors Permanent Series*
CDALB = *Concise Dictionary of American Literary
Biography*
CDBLB = *Concise Dictionary of British Literary
Biography*

DLB = *Dictionary of Literary Biography*
DLBD = *Dictionary of Literary Biography
Documentary Series*
DLBY = *Dictionary of Literary Biography Yearbook*
HW = *Hispanic Writers*
JRDA = *Junior DISCovering Authors*
MAICYA = *Major Authors and Illustrators for
Children and Young Adults*
MTCW = *Major 20th-Century Writers*
NNAL = *Native North American Literature*
SAAS = *Something about the Author Autobiography
Series*
SATA = *Something about the Author*
YABC = *Yesterday's Authors of Books for Children*

Belloc, Joseph Peter Rene Hilaire
See Belloc, (Joseph) Hilaire (Pierre Sebastien Rene Swanton)
Belloc, Joseph Pierre Hilaire
See Belloc, (Joseph) Hilaire (Pierre Sebastien Rene Swanton)
Belloc, M. A.
See Lowndes, Marie Adelaide (Belloc)
Bellow, Saul 1915-CLC 1, 2, 3, 6, 8, 10, 13, 15, 25, 33, 34, 63, 79; DA; DAB; DAC; DAM MST, NOV, POP; SSC 14; WLC
See also AITN 2; BEST 89:3; CA 5-8R; CABS 1; CANR 29, 53; CDALB 1941-1968; DLB 2, 28; DLBD 3; DLBY 82; MTCW
Belser, Reimond Karel Maria de 1929-
See Ruyslinck, Ward
See also CA 152
Bely, Andrey .... TCLC 7; PC 11
See also Bugayev, Boris Nikolayevich
Benary, Margot
See Benary-Isbert, Margot
Benary-Isbert, Margot 1889-1979 .... CLC 12
See also CA 5-8R; 89-92; CANR 4; CLR 12; MAICYA; SATA 2; SATA-Obit 21
Benavente (y Martinez), Jacinto 1866-1954 TCLC 3; DAM DRAM, MULT
See also CA 106; 131; HW; MTCW
Benchley, Peter (Bradford) 1940- CLC 4, 8; DAM NOV, POP
See also AAYA 14; AITN 2; CA 17-20R; CANR 12, 35; MTCW; SATA 3, 89
Benchley, Robert (Charles) 1889-1945 T C L C 1, 55
See also CA 105; 153; DLB 11
Benda, Julien 1867-1956 .... TCLC 60
See also CA 120; 154
Benedict, Ruth (Fulton) 1887-1948 TCLC 60
See also CA 158
Benedikt, Michael 1935- .... CLC 4, 14
See also CA 13-16R; CANR 7; DLB 5
Benet, Juan 1927- .... CLC 28
See also CA 143
Benet, Stephen Vincent 1898-1943 . TCLC 7; DAM POET; SSC 10
See also CA 104; 152; DLB 4, 48, 102; YABC 1
Benet, William Rose 1886-1950 .... TCLC 28; DAM POET
See also CA 118; 152; DLB 45
Benford, Gregory (Albert) 1941- ...... CLC 52
See also CA 69-72; CAAS 27; CANR 12, 24, 49; DLBY 82
Bengtsson, Frans (Gunnar) 1894-1954 T C L C 48
Benjamin, David
See Slavitt, David R(ytman)
Benjamin, Lois
See Gould, Lois
Benjamin, Walter 1892-1940 .... TCLC 39
Benn, Gottfried 1886-1956 .... TCLC 3
See also CA 106; 153; DLB 56
Bennett, Alan 1934-CLC 45, 77; DAB; DAM MST
See also CA 103; CANR 35, 55; MTCW
Bennett, (Enoch) Arnold 1867-1931 TCLC 5, 20
See also CA 106; 155; CDBLB 1890-1914; DLB 10, 34, 98, 135
Bennett, Elizabeth
See Mitchell, Margaret (Munnerlyn)
Bennett, George Harold 1930-
See Bennett, Hal
See also BW 1; CA 97-100

Bennett, Hal .... CLC 5
See also Bennett, George Harold
See also DLB 33
Bennett, Jay 1912- .... CLC 35
See also AAYA 10; CA 69-72; CANR 11, 42; JRDA; SAAS 4; SATA 41, 87; SATA-Brief 27
Bennett, Louise (Simone) 1919-CLC 28; BLC; DAM MULT
See also BW 2; CA 151; DLB 117
Benson, E(dward) F(rederic) 1867-1940 TCLC 27
See also CA 114; 157; DLB 135, 153
Benson, Jackson J. 1930- .... CLC 34
See also CA 25-28R; DLB 111
Benson, Sally 1900-1972 .... CLC 17
See also CA 19-20; 37-40R; CAP 1; SATA 1, 35; SATA-Obit 27
Benson, Stella 1892-1933 .... TCLC 17
See also CA 117; 155; DLB 36, 162
Bentham, Jeremy 1748-1832 .... NCLC 38
See also DLB 107, 158
Bentley, E(dmund) C(lerihew) 1875-1956 TCLC 12
See also CA 108; DLB 70
Bentley, Eric (Russell) 1916- .... CLC 24
See also CA 5-8R; CANR 6; INT CANR-6
Beranger, Pierre Jean de 1780-1857 NCLC 34
Berdyaev, Nicolas
See Berdyaev, Nikolai (Aleksandrovich)
Berdyaev, Nikolai (Aleksandrovich) 1874-1948 TCLC 67
See also CA 120; 157
Berdyayev, Nikolai (Aleksandrovich)
See Berdyaev, Nikolai (Aleksandrovich)
Berendt, John (Lawrence) 1939- ...... CLC 86
See also CA 146
Berger, Colonel
See Malraux, (Georges-)Andre
Berger, John (Peter) 1926- .... CLC 2, 19
See also CA 81-84; CANR 51; DLB 14
Berger, Melvin H. 1927- .... CLC 12
See also CA 5-8R; CANR 4; CLR 32; SAAS 2; SATA 5, 88
Berger, Thomas (Louis) 1924-CLC 3, 5, 8, 11, 18, 38; DAM NOV
See also CA 1-4R; CANR 5, 28, 51; DLB 2; DLBY 80; INT CANR-28; MTCW
Bergman, (Ernst) Ingmar 1918- CLC 16, 72
See also CA 81-84; CANR 33
Bergson, Henri 1859-1941 .... TCLC 32
Bergstein, Eleanor 1938- .... CLC 4
See also CA 53-56; CANR 5
Berkoff, Steven 1937- .... CLC 56
See also CA 104
Bermant, Chaim (Icyk) 1929- .... CLC 40
See also CA 57-60; CANR 6, 31, 57
Bern, Victoria
See Fisher, M(ary) F(rances) K(ennedy)
Bernanos, (Paul Louis) Georges 1888-1948 TCLC 3
See also CA 104; 130; DLB 72
Bernard, April 1956- .... CLC 59
See also CA 131
Berne, Victoria
See Fisher, M(ary) F(rances) K(ennedy)
Bernhard, Thomas 1931-1989 CLC 3, 32, 61
See also CA 85-88; 127; CANR 32, 57; DLB 85, 124; MTCW
Bernhardt, Sarah (Henriette Rosine) 1844-1923 TCLC 75
See also CA 157
Berriault, Gina 1926- .... CLC 54

See also CA 116; 129; DLB 130
Berrigan, Daniel 1921- .... CLC 4
See also CA 33-36R; CAAS 1; CANR 11, 43; DLB 5
Berrigan, Edmund Joseph Michael, Jr. 1934-1983
See Berrigan, Ted
See also CA 61-64; 110; CANR 14
Berrigan, Ted .... CLC 37
See also Berrigan, Edmund Joseph Michael, Jr.
See also DLB 5, 169
Berry, Charles Edward Anderson 1931-
See Berry, Chuck
See also CA 115
Berry, Chuck .... CLC 17
See also Berry, Charles Edward Anderson
Berry, Jonas
See Ashbery, John (Lawrence)
Berry, Wendell (Erdman) 1934- CLC 4, 6, 8, 27, 46; DAM POET
See also AITN 1; CA 73-76; CANR 50; DLB 5, 6
Berryman, John 1914-1972CLC 1, 2, 3, 4, 6, 8, 10, 13, 25, 62; DAM POET
See also CA 13-16; 33-36R; CABS 2; CANR 35; CAP 1; CDALB 1941-1968; DLB 48; MTCW
Bertolucci, Bernardo 1940- .... CLC 16
See also CA 106
Berton, Pierre (Francis De Marigny) 1920- CLC 104
See also CA 1-4R; CANR 2, 56; DLB 68
Bertrand, Aloysius 1807-1841 .... NCLC 31
Bertran de Born c. 1140-1215 .... CMLC 5
Besant, Annie (Wood) 1847-1933 .... TCLC 9
See also CA 105
Bessie, Alvah 1904-1985 .... CLC 23
See also CA 5-8R; 116; CANR 2; DLB 26
Bethlen, T. D.
See Silverberg, Robert
Beti, Mongo ...... CLC 27; BLC; DAM MULT
See also Biyidi, Alexandre
Betjeman, John 1906-1984 CLC 2, 6, 10, 34, 43; DAB; DAM MST, POET
See also CA 9-12R; 112; CANR 33, 56; CDBLB 1945-1960; DLB 20; DLBY 84; MTCW
Bettelheim, Bruno 1903-1990 .... CLC 79
See also CA 81-84; 131; CANR 23, 61; MTCW
Betti, Ugo 1892-1953 .... TCLC 5
See also CA 104; 155
Betts, Doris (Waugh) 1932- ...... CLC 3, 6, 28
See also CA 13-16R; CANR 9; DLBY 82; INT CANR-9
Bevan, Alistair
See Roberts, Keith (John Kingston)
Bialik, Chaim Nachman 1873-1934 TCLC 25
Bickerstaff, Isaac
See Swift, Jonathan
Bidart, Frank 1939- .... CLC 33
See also CA 140
Bienek, Horst 1930- .... CLC 7, 11
See also CA 73-76; DLB 75
Bierce, Ambrose (Gwinett) 1842-1914(?) TCLC 1, 7, 44; DA; DAC; DAM MST; SSC 9; WLC
See also CA 104; 139; CDALB 1865-1917; DLB 11, 12, 23, 71, 74, 186
Biggers, Earl Derr 1884-1933 .... TCLC 65
See also CA 108; 153
Billings, Josh
See Shaw, Henry Wheeler
Billington, (Lady) Rachel (Mary) 1942- C L C 43

See also AITN 2; CA 33-36R; CANR 44

Binyon, T(imothy) J(ohn) 1936- .... **CLC 34**
See also CA 111; CANR 28

Bioy Casares, Adolfo 1914- **CLC 4, 8, 13, 88;**
DAM MULT; HLC; SSC 17
See also CA 29-32R; CANR 19, 43; DLB 113;
HW; MTCW

Bird, Cordwainer
See Ellison, Harlan (Jay)

Bird, Robert Montgomery 1806-1854**NCLC 1**

Birney, (Alfred) Earle 1904- **CLC 1, 4, 6, 11;**
DAC; DAM MST, POET
See also CA 1-4R; CANR 5, 20; DLB 88;
MTCW

Bishop, Elizabeth 1911-1979 **CLC 1, 4, 9, 13,**
15, 32; DA; DAC; DAM MST, POET; PC
3
See also CA 5-8R; 89-92; CABS 2; CANR 26,
61; CDALB 1968-1988; DLB 5, 169;
MTCW; SATA-Obit 24

Bishop, John 1935- .... **CLC 10**
See also CA 105

Bissett, Bill 1939- .... **CLC 18; PC 14**
See also CA 69-72; CAAS 19; CANR 15; DLB
53; MTCW

Bitov, Andrei (Georgievich) 1937- ... **CLC 57**
See also CA 142

Biyidi, Alexandre 1932-
See Beti, Mongo
See also BW 1; CA 114; 124; MTCW

Bjarme, Brynjolf
See Ibsen, Henrik (Johan)

Bjornson, Bjornstjerne (Martinius) 1832-1910
TCLC 7, 37
See also CA 104

Black, Robert
See Holdstock, Robert P.

Blackburn, Paul 1926-1971 .... **CLC 9, 43**
See also CA 81-84; 33-36R; CANR 34; DLB
16; DLBY 81

Black Elk 1863-1950**TCLC 33; DAM MULT**
See also CA 144; NNAL

Black Hobart
See Sanders, (James) Ed(ward)

Blacklin, Malcolm
See Chambers, Aidan

Blackmore, R(ichard) D(oddridge) 1825-1900
TCLC 27
See also CA 120; DLB 18

Blackmur, R(ichard) P(almer) 1904-1965
CLC 2, 24
See also CA 11-12; 25-28R; CAP 1; DLB 63

Black Tarantula
See Acker, Kathy

Blackwood, Algernon (Henry) 1869-1951
TCLC 5
See also CA 105; 150; DLB 153, 156, 178

Blackwood, Caroline 1931-1996**CLC 6, 9, 100**
See also CA 85-88; 151; CANR 32, 61; DLB
14; MTCW

Blade, Alexander
See Hamilton, Edmond; Silverberg, Robert

Blaga, Lucian 1895-1961 .... **CLC 75**

Blair, Eric (Arthur) 1903-1950
See Orwell, George
See also CA 104; 132; DA; DAB; DAC; DAM
MST, NOV; MTCW; SATA 29

Blais, Marie-Claire 1939-**CLC 2, 4, 6, 13, 22;**
DAC; DAM MST
See also CA 21-24R; CAAS 4; CANR 38; DLB
53; MTCW

Blaise, Clark 1940- .... **CLC 29**
See also AITN 2; CA 53-56; CAAS 3; CANR

5; DLB 53

Blake, Fairley
See De Voto, Bernard (Augustine)

Blake, Nicholas
See Day Lewis, C(ecil)
See also DLB 77

Blake, William 1757-1827 . **NCLC 13, 37, 57;**
DA; DAB; DAC; DAM MST, POET; PC
12; WLC
See also CDBLB 1789-1832; DLB 93, 163;
MAICYA; SATA 30

Blasco Ibanez, Vicente 1867-1928 **TCLC 12;**
DAM NOV
See also CA 110; 131; HW; MTCW

Blatty, William Peter 1928-**CLC 2; DAM POP**
See also CA 5-8R; CANR 9

Bleeck, Oliver
See Thomas, Ross (Elmore)

Blessing, Lee 1949- .... **CLC 54**

Blish, James (Benjamin) 1921-1975 . **CLC 14**
See also CA 1-4R; 57-60; CANR 3; DLB 8;
MTCW; SATA 66

Bliss, Reginald
See Wells, H(erbert) G(eorge)

Blixen, Karen (Christentze Dinesen) 1885-1962
See Dinesen, Isak
See also CA 25-28; CANR 22, 50; CAP 2;
MTCW; SATA 44

Bloch, Robert (Albert) 1917-1994 .... **CLC 33**
See also CA 5-8R; 146; CAAS 20; CANR 5;
DLB 44; INT CANR-5; SATA 12; SATA-Obit
82

Blok, Alexander (Alexandrovich) 1880-1921
TCLC 5; PC 21
See also CA 104

Blom, Jan
See Breytenbach, Breyten

Bloom, Harold 1930- .... **CLC 24, 103**
See also CA 13-16R; CANR 39; DLB 67

Bloomfield, Aurelius
See Bourne, Randolph S(illiman)

Blount, Roy (Alton), Jr. 1941- .... **CLC 38**
See also CA 53-56; CANR 10, 28, 61; INT
CANR-28; MTCW

Bloy, Leon 1846-1917 .... **TCLC 22**
See also CA 121; DLB 123

Blume, Judy (Sussman) 1938- ... **CLC 12, 30;**
DAM NOV, POP
See also AAYA 3; CA 29-32R; CANR 13, 37;
CLR 2, 15; DLB 52; JRDA; MAICYA;
MTCW; SATA 2, 31, 79

Blunden, Edmund (Charles) 1896-1974 **C L C**
2, 56
See also CA 17-18; 45-48; CANR 54; CAP 2;
DLB 20, 100, 155; MTCW

Bly, Robert (Elwood) 1926-**CLC 1, 2, 5, 10, 15,**
38; DAM POET
See also CA 5-8R; CANR 41; DLB 5; MTCW

Boas, Franz 1858-1942 .... **TCLC 56**
See also CA 115

Bobette
See Simenon, Georges (Jacques Christian)

Boccaccio, Giovanni 1313-1375 ... **CMLC 13;**
SSC 10

Bochco, Steven 1943- .... **CLC 35**
See also AAYA 11; CA 124; 138

Bodenheim, Maxwell 1892-1954 .... **TCLC 44**
See also CA 110; DLB 9, 45

Bodker, Cecil 1927- .... **CLC 21**
See also CA 73-76; CANR 13, 44; CLR 23;
MAICYA; SATA 14

Boell, Heinrich (Theodor) 1917-1985 **CLC 2,**
3, 6, 9, 11, 15, 27, 32, 72; DA; DAB; DAC;

DAM MST, NOV; SSC 23; WLC
See also CA 21-24R; 116; CANR 24; DLB 69;
DLBY 85; MTCW

Boerne, Alfred
See Doeblin, Alfred

Boethius 480(?)-524(?) .... **CMLC 15**
See also DLB 115

Bogan, Louise 1897-1970 . **CLC 4, 39, 46, 93;**
DAM POET; PC 12
See also CA 73-76; 25-28R; CANR 33; DLB
45, 169; MTCW

Bogarde, Dirk .... **CLC 19**
See also Van Den Bogarde, Derek Jules Gaspard
Ulric Niven
See also DLB 14

Bogosian, Eric 1953- .... **CLC 45**
See also CA 138

Bograd, Larry 1953- .... **CLC 35**
See also CA 93-96; CANR 57; SAAS 21; SATA
33, 89

Boiardo, Matteo Maria 1441-1494 .... **LC 6**

Boileau-Despreaux, Nicolas 1636-1711 . **LC 3**

Bojer, Johan 1872-1959 .... **TCLC 64**

Boland, Eavan (Aisling) 1944- .. **CLC 40, 67;**
DAM POET
See also CA 143; CANR 61; DLB 40

Bolt, Lee
See Faust, Frederick (Schiller)

Bolt, Robert (Oxton) 1924-1995 ..... **CLC 14;**
DAM DRAM
See also CA 17-20R; 147; CANR 35; DLB 13;
MTCW

Bombet, Louis-Alexandre-Cesar
See Stendhal

Bomkauf
See Kaufman, Bob (Garnell)

Bonaventura .... **NCLC 35**
See also DLB 90

Bond, Edward 1934- **CLC 4, 6, 13, 23; DAM**
DRAM
See also CA 25-28R; CANR 38; DLB 13;
MTCW

Bonham, Frank 1914-1989 .... **CLC 12**
See also AAYA 1; CA 9-12R; CANR 4, 36;
JRDA; MAICYA; SAAS 3; SATA 1, 49;
SATA-Obit 62

Bonnefoy, Yves 1923-... **CLC 9, 15, 58; DAM**
MST, POET
See also CA 85-88; CANR 33; MTCW

Bontemps, Arna(ud Wendell) 1902-1973**C L C**
1, 18; BLC; DAM MULT, NOV, POET
See also BW 1; CA 1-4R; 41-44R; CANR 4,
35; CLR 6; DLB 48, 51; JRDA; MAICYA;
MTCW; SATA 2, 44; SATA-Obit 24

Booth, Martin 1944- .... **CLC 13**
See also CA 93-96; CAAS 2

Booth, Philip 1925- .... **CLC 23**
See also CA 5-8R; CANR 5; DLBY 82

Booth, Wayne C(layson) 1921- .... **CLC 24**
See also CA 1-4R; CAAS 5; CANR 3, 43; DLB
67

Borchert, Wolfgang 1921-1947 .... **TCLC 5**
See also CA 104; DLB 69, 124

Borel, Petrus 1809-1859 .... **NCLC 41**

Borges, Jorge Luis 1899-1986**CLC 1, 2, 3, 4, 6,**
8, 9, 10, 13, 19, 44, 48, 83; DA; DAB; DAC;
DAM MST, MULT; HLC; SSC 4; WLC
See also AAYA 19; CA 21-24R; CANR 19, 33;
DLB 113; DLBY 86; HW; MTCW

Borowski, Tadeusz 1922-1951 .... **TCLC 9**
See also CA 106; 154

Borrow, George (Henry) 1803-1881 **NCLC 9**
See also DLB 21, 55, 166

Bromell, Henry 1947- .... **CLC 5**
See also CA 53-56; CANR 9

Bromfield, Louis (Brucker) 1896-1956 **T C L C 11**
See also CA 107; 155; DLB 4, 9, 86

Broner, E(sther) M(asserman) 1930- **CLC 19**
See also CA 17-20R; CANR 8, 25; DLB 28

Bronk, William 1918- .... **CLC 10**
See also CA 89-92; CANR 23; DLB 165

Bronstein, Lev Davidovich
See Trotsky, Leon

Bronte, Anne 1820-1849 .... **NCLC 4**
See also DLB 21

Bronte, Charlotte 1816-1855 **NCLC 3, 8, 33, 58; DA; DAB; DAC; DAM MST, NOV; WLC**
See also AAYA 17; CDBLB 1832-1890; DLB 21, 159

Bronte, Emily (Jane) 1818-1848 **NCLC 16, 35; DA; DAB; DAC; DAM MST, NOV, POET; PC 8; WLC**
See also AAYA 17; CDBLB 1832-1890; DLB 21, 32

Brooke, Frances 1724-1789 .... **LC 6**
See also DLB 39, 99

Brooke, Henry 1703(?)-1783 .... **LC 1**
See also DLB 39

Brooke, Rupert (Chawner) 1887-1915 **T C L C 2, 7; DA; DAB; DAC; DAM MST, POET; WLC**
See also CA 104; 132; CANR 61; CDBLB 1914-1945; DLB 19; MTCW

Brooke-Haven, P.
See Wodehouse, P(elham) G(renville)

Brooke-Rose, Christine 1926(?)- .... **CLC 40**
See also CA 13-16R; CANR 58; DLB 14

Brookner, Anita 1928- **CLC 32, 34, 51; DAB; DAM POP**
See also CA 114; 120; CANR 37, 56; DLBY 87; MTCW

Brooks, Cleanth 1906-1994 .... **CLC 24, 86**
See also CA 17-20R; 145; CANR 33, 35; DLB 63; DLBY 94; INT CANR-35; MTCW

Brooks, George
See Baum, L(yman) Frank

Brooks, Gwendolyn 1917- **CLC 1, 2, 4, 5, 15, 49; BLC; DA; DAC; DAM MST, MULT, POET; PC 7; WLC**
See also AAYA 20; AITN 1; BW 2; CA 1-4R; CANR 1, 27, 52; CDALB 1941-1968; CLR 27; DLB 5, 76, 165; MTCW; SATA 6

Brooks, Mel .... **CLC 12**
See also Kaminsky, Melvin
See also AAYA 13; DLB 26

Brooks, Peter 1938- .... **CLC 34**
See also CA 45-48; CANR 1

Brooks, Van Wyck 1886-1963 .... **CLC 29**
See also CA 1-4R; CANR 6; DLB 45, 63, 103

Brophy, Brigid (Antonia) 1929-1995 **CLC 6, 11, 29, 105**
See also CA 5-8R; 149; CAAS 4; CANR 25, 53; DLB 14; MTCW

Brosman, Catharine Savage 1934- ..... **CLC 9**
See also CA 61-64; CANR 21, 46

Brother Antoninus
See Everson, William (Oliver)

Broughton, T(homas) Alan 1936- ..... **CLC 19**
See also CA 45-48; CANR 2, 23, 48

Broumas, Olga 1949- .... **CLC 10, 73**
See also CA 85-88; CANR 20

Brown, Alan 1951- .... **CLC 99**

Brown, Charles Brockden 1771-1810 **N C L C 22**

See also CDALB 1640-1865; DLB 37, 59, 73

Brown, Christy 1932-1981 .... **CLC 63**
See also CA 105; 104; DLB 14

Brown, Claude 1937- ... **CLC 30; BLC; DAM MULT**
See also AAYA 7; BW 1; CA 73-76

Brown, Dee (Alexander) 1908- .. **CLC 18, 47; DAM POP**
See also CA 13-16R; CAAS 6; CANR 11, 45, 60; DLBY 80; MTCW; SATA 5

Brown, George
See Wertmueller, Lina

Brown, George Douglas 1869-1902 **TCLC 28**

Brown, George Mackay 1921-1996 **CLC 5, 48, 100**
See also CA 21-24R; 151; CAAS 6; CANR 12, 37, 62; DLB 14, 27, 139; MTCW; SATA 35

Brown, (William) Larry 1951- .... **CLC 73**
See also CA 130; 134; INT 133

Brown, Moses
See Barrett, William (Christopher)

Brown, Rita Mae 1944- **CLC 18, 43, 79; DAM NOV, POP**
See also CA 45-48; CANR 2, 11, 35, 62; INT CANR-11; MTCW

Brown, Roderick (Langmere) Haig-
See Haig-Brown, Roderick (Langmere)

Brown, Rosellen 1939- .... **CLC 32**
See also CA 77-80; CAAS 10; CANR 14, 44

Brown, Sterling Allen 1901-1989 **CLC 1, 23, 59; BLC; DAM MULT, POET**
See also BW 1; CA 85-88; 127; CANR 26; DLB 48, 51, 63; MTCW

Brown, Will
See Ainsworth, William Harrison

Brown, William Wells 1813-1884 ... **NCLC 2; BLC; DAM MULT; DC 1**
See also DLB 3, 50

Browne, (Clyde) Jackson 1948(?)- .... **CLC 21**
See also CA 120

Browning, Elizabeth Barrett 1806-1861 **NCLC 1, 16, 61, 66; DA; DAB; DAC; DAM MST, POET; PC 6; WLC**
See also CDBLB 1832-1890; DLB 32

Browning, Robert 1812-1889 **NCLC 19; DA; DAB; DAC; DAM MST, POET; PC 2; WLCS**
See also CDBLB 1832-1890; DLB 32, 163; YABC 1

Browning, Tod 1882-1962 .... **CLC 16**
See also CA 141; 117

Brownson, Orestes (Augustus) 1803-1876 **NCLC 50**

Bruccoli, Matthew J(oseph) 1931- ... **CLC 34**
See also CA 9-12R; CANR 7; DLB 103

Bruce, Lenny .... **CLC 21**
See also Schneider, Leonard Alfred

Bruin, John
See Brutus, Dennis

Brulard, Henri
See Stendhal

Brulls, Christian
See Simenon, Georges (Jacques Christian)

Brunner, John (Kilian Houston) 1934-1995 **CLC 8, 10; DAM POP**
See also CA 1-4R; 149; CAAS 8; CANR 2, 37; MTCW

Bruno, Giordano 1548-1600 .... **LC 27**

Brutus, Dennis 1924- ... **CLC 43; BLC; DAM MULT, POET**
See also BW 2; CA 49-52; CAAS 14; CANR 2, 27, 42; DLB 117

Bryan, C(ourtlandt) D(ixon) B(arnes) 1936-

CLC 29
See also CA 73-76; CANR 13; INT CANR-13

Bryan, Michael
See Moore, Brian

Bryant, William Cullen 1794-1878 . **NCLC 6, 46; DA; DAB; DAC; DAM MST, POET; PC 20**
See also CDALB 1640-1865; DLB 3, 43, 59

Bryusov, Valery Yakovlevich 1873-1924 **TCLC 10**
See also CA 107; 155

Buchan, John 1875-1940 ..... **TCLC 41; DAB; DAM POP**
See also CA 108; 145; DLB 34, 70, 156; YABC 2

Buchanan, George 1506-1582 .... **LC 4**

Buchheim, Lothar-Guenther 1918- .... **CLC 6**
See also CA 85-88

Buchner, (Karl) Georg 1813-1837 . **NCLC 26**

Buchwald, Art(hur) 1925- .... **CLC 33**
See also AITN 1; CA 5-8R; CANR 21; MTCW; SATA 10

Buck, Pearl S(ydenstricker) 1892-1973 **CLC 7, 11, 18; DA; DAB; DAC; DAM MST, NOV**
See also AITN 1; CA 1-4R; 41-44R; CANR 1, 34; DLB 9, 102; MTCW; SATA 1, 25

Buckler, Ernest 1908-1984 .... **CLC 13; DAC; DAM MST**
See also CA 11-12; 114; CAP 1; DLB 68; SATA 47

Buckley, Vincent (Thomas) 1925-1988 **CLC 57**
See also CA 101

Buckley, William F(rank), Jr. 1925- **CLC 7, 18, 37; DAM POP**
See also AITN 1; CA 1-4R; CANR 1, 24, 53; DLB 137; DLBY 80; INT CANR-24; MTCW

Buechner, (Carl) Frederick 1926- **CLC 2, 4, 6, 9; DAM NOV**
See also CA 13-16R; CANR 11, 39, 64; DLBY 80; INT CANR-11; MTCW

Buell, John (Edward) 1927- .... **CLC 10**
See also CA 1-4R; DLB 53

Buero Vallejo, Antonio 1916- ..... **CLC 15, 46**
See also CA 106; CANR 24, 49; HW; MTCW

Bufalino, Gesualdo 1920(?)- .... **CLC 74**

Bugayev, Boris Nikolayevich 1880-1934
See Bely, Andrey
See also CA 104

Bukowski, Charles 1920-1994 **CLC 2, 5, 9, 41, 82; DAM NOV, POET; PC 18**
See also CA 17-20R; 144; CANR 40, 62; DLB 5, 130, 169; MTCW

Bulgakov, Mikhail (Afanas'evich) 1891-1940 **TCLC 2, 16; DAM DRAM, NOV; SSC 18**
See also CA 105; 152

Bulgya, Alexander Alexandrovich 1901-1956 **TCLC 53**
See also Fadeyev, Alexander
See also CA 117

Bullins, Ed 1935- ... **CLC 1, 5, 7; BLC; DAM DRAM, MULT; DC 6**
See also BW 2; CA 49-52; CAAS 16; CANR 24, 46; DLB 7, 38; MTCW

Bulwer-Lytton, Edward (George Earle Lytton) 1803-1873 .... **NCLC 1, 45**
See also DLB 21

Bunin, Ivan Alexeyevich 1870-1953 **TCLC 6; SSC 5**
See also CA 104

Bunting, Basil 1900-1985 ..... **CLC 10, 39, 47; DAM POET**
See also CA 53-56; 115; CANR 7; DLB 20

Bunuel, Luis 1900-1983 .. **CLC 16, 80; DAM**

Clampitt, Amy 1920-1994 ..... **CLC 32; PC 19**
See also CA 110; 146; CANR 29; DLB 105
Clancy, Thomas L., Jr. 1947-
See Clancy, Tom
See also CA 125; 131; CANR 62; INT 131; MTCW
Clancy, Tom .... **CLC 45; DAM NOV, POP**
See also Clancy, Thomas L., Jr.
See also AAYA 9; BEST 89:1, 90:1
Clare, John 1793-1864 **NCLC 9; DAB; DAM POET**
See also DLB 55, 96
Clarin
See Alas (y Urena), Leopoldo (Enrique Garcia)
Clark, Al C.
See Goines, Donald
Clark, (Robert) Brian 1932- .... **CLC 29**
See also CA 41-44R
Clark, Curt
See Westlake, Donald E(dwin)
Clark, Eleanor 1913-1996 .... **CLC 5, 19**
See also CA 9-12R; 151; CANR 41; DLB 6
Clark, J. P.
See Clark, John Pepper
See also DLB 117
Clark, John Pepper 1935- ...... **CLC 38; BLC; DAM DRAM, MULT; DC 5**
See also Clark, J. P.
See also BW 1; CA 65-68; CANR 16
Clark, M. R.
See Clark, Mavis Thorpe
Clark, Mavis Thorpe 1909- .... **CLC 12**
See also CA 57-60; CANR 8, 37; CLR 30; MAICYA; SAAS 5; SATA 8, 74
Clark, Walter Van Tilburg 1909-1971 **CLC 28**
See also CA 9-12R; 33-36R; CANR 63; DLB 9; SATA 8
Clarke, Arthur C(harles) 1917- **CLC 1, 4, 13, 18, 35; DAM POP; SSC 3**
See also AAYA 4; CA 1-4R; CANR 2, 28, 55; JRDA; MAICYA; MTCW; SATA 13, 70
Clarke, Austin 1896-1974 .... **CLC 6, 9; DAM POET**
See also CA 29-32; 49-52; CAP 2; DLB 10, 20
Clarke, Austin C(hesterfield) 1934- **CLC 8, 53; BLC; DAC; DAM MULT**
See also BW 1; CA 25-28R; CAAS 16; CANR 14, 32; DLB 53, 125
Clarke, Gillian 1937- .... **CLC 61**
See also CA 106; DLB 40
Clarke, Marcus (Andrew Hislop) 1846-1881 **NCLC 19**
Clarke, Shirley 1925- .... **CLC 16**
Clash, The
See Headon, (Nicky) Topper; Jones, Mick; Simonon, Paul; Strummer, Joe
Claudel, Paul (Louis Charles Marie) 1868-1955 **TCLC 2, 10**
See also CA 104
Clavell, James (duMaresq) 1925-1994 **CLC 6, 25, 87; DAM NOV, POP**
See also CA 25-28R; 146; CANR 26, 48; MTCW
Cleaver, (Leroy) Eldridge 1935- ..... **CLC 30; BLC; DAM MULT**
See also BW 1; CA 21-24R; CANR 16
Cleese, John (Marwood) 1939- .... **CLC 21**
See also Monty Python
See also CA 112; 116; CANR 35; MTCW
Cleishbotham, Jebediah
See Scott, Walter
Cleland, John 1710-1789 .... **LC 2**
See also DLB 39

Clemens, Samuel Langhorne 1835-1910
See Twain, Mark
See also CA 104; 135; CDALB 1865-1917; DA; DAB; DAC; DAM MST, NOV; DLB 11, 12, 23, 64, 74, 186; JRDA; MAICYA; YABC 2
Cleophil
See Congreve, William
Clerihew, E.
See Bentley, E(dmund) C(lerihew)
Clerk, N. W.
See Lewis, C(live) S(taples)
Cliff, Jimmy .... **CLC 21**
See also Chambers, James
Clifton, (Thelma) Lucille 1936- **CLC 19, 66; BLC; DAM MULT, POET; PC 17**
See also BW 2; CA 49-52; CANR 2, 24, 42; CLR 5; DLB 5, 41; MAICYA; MTCW; SATA 20, 69
Clinton, Dirk
See Silverberg, Robert
Clough, Arthur Hugh 1819-1861 ... **NCLC 27**
See also DLB 32
Clutha, Janet Paterson Frame 1924-
See Frame, Janet
See also CA 1-4R; CANR 2, 36; MTCW
Clyne, Terence
See Blatty, William Peter
Cobalt, Martin
See Mayne, William (James Carter)
Cobb, Irvin S. 1876-1944 .... **TCLC 77**
See also DLB 11, 25, 86
Cobbett, William 1763-1835 .... **NCLC 49**
See also DLB 43, 107, 158
Coburn, D(onald) L(ee) 1938- .... **CLC 10**
See also CA 89-92
Cocteau, Jean (Maurice Eugene Clement) 1889-1963 **CLC 1, 8, 15, 16, 43; DA; DAB; DAC; DAM DRAM, MST, NOV; WLC**
See also CA 25-28; CANR 40; CAP 2; DLB 65; MTCW
Codrescu, Andrei 1946- **CLC 46; DAM POET**
See also CA 33-36R; CAAS 19; CANR 13, 34, 53
Coe, Max
See Bourne, Randolph S(illiman)
Coe, Tucker
See Westlake, Donald E(dwin)
Coetzee, J(ohn) M(ichael) 1940- **CLC 23, 33, 66; DAM NOV**
See also CA 77-80; CANR 41, 54; MTCW
Coffey, Brian
See Koontz, Dean R(ay)
Cohan, George M(ichael) 1878-1942 **TCLC 60**
See also CA 157
Cohen, Arthur A(llen) 1928-1986 . **CLC 7, 31**
See also CA 1-4R; 120; CANR 1, 17, 42; DLB 28
Cohen, Leonard (Norman) 1934- **CLC 3, 38; DAC; DAM MST**
See also CA 21-24R; CANR 14; DLB 53; MTCW
Cohen, Matt 1942- .... **CLC 19; DAC**
See also CA 61-64; CAAS 18; CANR 40; DLB 53
Cohen-Solal, Annie 19(?)- .... **CLC 50**
Colegate, Isabel 1931- .... **CLC 36**
See also CA 17-20R; CANR 8, 22; DLB 14; INT CANR-22; MTCW
Coleman, Emmett
See Reed, Ishmael
Coleridge, M. E.
See Coleridge, Mary E(lizabeth)
Coleridge, Mary E(lizabeth) 1861-1907 **TCLC**

73
See also CA 116; DLB 19, 98
Coleridge, Samuel Taylor 1772-1834 **NCLC 9, 54; DA; DAB; DAC; DAM MST, POET; PC 11; WLC**
See also CDBLB 1789-1832; DLB 93, 107
Coleridge, Sara 1802-1852 .... **NCLC 31**
Coles, Don 1928- .... **CLC 46**
See also CA 115; CANR 38
Colette, (Sidonie-Gabrielle) 1873-1954 **TCLC 1, 5, 16; DAM NOV; SSC 10**
See also CA 104; 131; DLB 65; MTCW
Collett, (Jacobine) Camilla (Wergeland) 1813-1895 .... **NCLC 22**
Collier, Christopher 1930- .... **CLC 30**
See also AAYA 13; CA 33-36R; CANR 13, 33; JRDA; MAICYA; SATA 16, 70
Collier, James L(incoln) 1928- **CLC 30; DAM POP**
See also AAYA 13; CA 9-12R; CANR 4, 33, 60; CLR 3; JRDA; MAICYA; SAAS 21; SATA 8, 70
Collier, Jeremy 1650-1726 .... **LC 6**
Collier, John 1901-1980 .... **SSC 19**
See also CA 65-68; 97-100; CANR 10; DLB 77
Collingwood, R(obin) G(eorge) 1889(?)-1943 **TCLC 67**
See also CA 117; 155
Collins, Hunt
See Hunter, Evan
Collins, Linda 1931- .... **CLC 44**
See also CA 125
Collins, (William) Wilkie 1824-1889 **NCLC 1, 18**
See also CDBLB 1832-1890; DLB 18, 70, 159
Collins, William 1721-1759 . **LC 4, 40; DAM POET**
See also DLB 109
Collodi, Carlo 1826-1890 .... **NCLC 54**
See also Lorenzini, Carlo
See also CLR 5
Colman, George
See Glassco, John
Colt, Winchester Remington
See Hubbard, L(afayette) Ron(ald)
Colter, Cyrus 1910- .... **CLC 58**
See also BW 1; CA 65-68; CANR 10; DLB 33
Colton, James
See Hansen, Joseph
Colum, Padraic 1881-1972 .... **CLC 28**
See also CA 73-76; 33-36R; CANR 35; CLR 36; MAICYA; MTCW; SATA 15
Colvin, James
See Moorcock, Michael (John)
Colwin, Laurie (E.) 1944-1992 **CLC 5, 13, 23, 84**
See also CA 89-92; 139; CANR 20, 46; DLB Y 80; MTCW
Comfort, Alex(ander) 1920- **CLC 7; DAM POP**
See also CA 1-4R; CANR 1, 45
Comfort, Montgomery
See Campbell, (John) Ramsey
Compton-Burnett, I(vy) 1884(?)-1969 **CLC 1, 3, 10, 15, 34; DAM NOV**
See also CA 1-4R; 25-28R; CANR 4; DLB 36; MTCW
Comstock, Anthony 1844-1915 ...... **TCLC 13**
See also CA 110
Comte, Auguste 1798-1857 .... **NCLC 54**
Conan Doyle, Arthur
See Doyle, Arthur Conan
Conde, Maryse 1937- ...... **CLC 52, 92; DAM**

MULT
See also Boucolon, Maryse
See also BW 2

Condillac, Etienne Bonnot de 1714-1780 **L C 26**

Condon, Richard (Thomas) 1915-1996**CLC 4, 6, 8, 10, 45, 100; DAM NOV**
See also BEST 90:3; CA 1-4R; 151; CAAS 1; CANR 2, 23; INT CANR-23; MTCW

Confucius 551B.C.-479B.C.. **CMLC 19; DA; DAB; DAC; DAM MST; WLCS**

Congreve, William 1670-1729 **LC 5, 21; DA; DAB; DAC; DAM DRAM, MST, POET; DC 2; WLC**
See also CDBLB 1660-1789; DLB 39, 84

Connell, Evan S(helby), Jr. 1924-**CLC 4, 6, 45; DAM NOV**
See also AAYA 7; CA 1-4R; CAAS 2; CANR 2, 39; DLB 2; DLBY 81; MTCW

Connelly, Marc(us Cook) 1890-1980 .. **CLC 7**
See also CA 85-88; 102; CANR 30; DLB 7; DLBY 80; SATA-Obit 25

Connor, Ralph .... **TCLC 31**
See also Gordon, Charles William
See also DLB 92

Conrad, Joseph 1857-1924**TCLC 1, 6, 13, 25, 43, 57; DA; DAB; DAC; DAM MST, NOV; SSC 9; WLC**
See also CA 104; 131; CANR 60; CDBLB 1890-1914; DLB 10, 34, 98, 156; MTCW; SATA 27

Conrad, Robert Arnold
See Hart, Moss

Conroy, Donald Pat(rick) 1945- **CLC 30, 74; DAM NOV, POP**
See also AAYA 8; AITN 1; CA 85-88; CANR 24, 53; DLB 6; MTCW

Constant (de Rebecque), (Henri) Benjamin 1767-1830 .... **NCLC 6**
See also DLB 119

Conybeare, Charles Augustus
See Eliot, T(homas) S(tearns)

Cook, Michael 1933-........................... **CLC 58**
See also CA 93-96; DLB 53

Cook, Robin 1940- .... **CLC 14; DAM POP**
See also BEST 90:2; CA 108; 111; CANR 41; INT 111

Cook, Roy
See Silverberg, Robert

Cooke, Elizabeth 1948- .... **CLC 55**
See also CA 129

Cooke, John Esten 1830-1886 .... **NCLC 5**
See also DLB 3

Cooke, John Estes
See Baum, L(yman) Frank

Cooke, M. E.
See Creasey, John

Cooke, Margaret
See Creasey, John

Cook-Lynn, Elizabeth 1930-.. **CLC 93; DAM MULT**
See also CA 133; DLB 175; NNAL

Cooney, Ray .... **CLC 62**

Cooper, Douglas 1960- .... **CLC 86**

Cooper, Henry St. John
See Creasey, John

Cooper, J(oan) California .... **CLC 56; DAM MULT**
See also AAYA 12; BW 1; CA 125; CANR 55

Cooper, James Fenimore 1789-1851**NCLC 1, 27, 54**
See also AAYA 22; CDALB 1640-1865; DLB 3; SATA 19

Coover, Robert (Lowell) 1932- **CLC 3, 7, 15, 32, 46, 87; DAM NOV; SSC 15**
See also CA 45-48; CANR 3, 37, 58; DLB 2; DLBY 81; MTCW

Copeland, Stewart (Armstrong) 1952-**CLC 26**

Coppard, A(lfred) E(dgar) 1878-1957 **T C L C 5; SSC 21**
See also CA 114; DLB 162; YABC 1

Coppee, Francois 1842-1908 .... **TCLC 25**

Coppola, Francis Ford 1939- .... **CLC 16**
See also CA 77-80; CANR 40; DLB 44

Corbiere, Tristan 1845-1875 .... **NCLC 43**

Corcoran, Barbara 1911- .... **CLC 17**
See also AAYA 14; CA 21-24R; CAAS 2; CANR 11, 28, 48; DLB 52; JRDA; SAAS 20; SATA 3, 77

Cordelier, Maurice
See Giraudoux, (Hippolyte) Jean

Corelli, Marie 1855-1924 .... **TCLC 51**
See also Mackay, Mary
See also DLB 34, 156

Corman, Cid .... **CLC 9**
See also Corman, Sidney
See also CAAS 2; DLB 5

Corman, Sidney 1924-
See Corman, Cid
See also CA 85-88; CANR 44; DAM POET

Cormier, Robert (Edmund) 1925-**CLC 12, 30; DA; DAB; DAC; DAM MST, NOV**
See also AAYA 3, 19; CA 1-4R; CANR 5, 23; CDALB 1968-1988; CLR 12; DLB 52; INT CANR-23; JRDA; MAICYA; MTCW; SATA 10, 45, 83

Corn, Alfred (DeWitt III) 1943- .... **CLC 33**
See also CA 104; CAAS 25; CANR 44; DLB 120; DLBY 80

Corneille, Pierre 1606-1684 .... **LC 28; DAB; DAM MST**

Cornwell, David (John Moore) 1931- **CLC 9, 15; DAM POP**
See also le Carre, John
See also CA 5-8R; CANR 13, 33, 59; MTCW

Corso, (Nunzio) Gregory 1930- .... **CLC 1, 11**
See also CA 5-8R; CANR 41; DLB 5, 16; MTCW

Cortazar, Julio 1914-1984**CLC 2, 3, 5, 10, 13, 15, 33, 34, 92; DAM MULT, NOV; HLC; SSC 7**
See also CA 21-24R; CANR 12, 32; DLB 113; HW; MTCW

CORTES, HERNAN 1484-1547.......... **LC 31**

Corwin, Cecil
See Kornbluth, C(yril) M.

Cosic, Dobrica 1921- .... **CLC 14**
See also CA 122; 138; DLB 181

Costain, Thomas B(ertram) 1885-1965 **C L C 30**
See also CA 5-8R; 25-28R; DLB 9

Costantini, Humberto 1924(?)-1987 . **CLC 49**
See also CA 131; 122; HW

Costello, Elvis 1955- .... **CLC 21**

Cotes, Cecil V.
See Duncan, Sara Jeannette

Cotter, Joseph Seamon Sr. 1861-1949 **T C L C 28; BLC; DAM MULT**
See also BW 1; CA 124; DLB 50

Couch, Arthur Thomas Quiller
See Quiller-Couch, Arthur Thomas

Coulton, James
See Hansen, Joseph

Couperus, Louis (Marie Anne) 1863-1923 **TCLC 15**
See also CA 115

Coupland, Douglas 1961-**CLC 85; DAC; DAM POP**
See also CA 142; CANR 57

Court, Wesli
See Turco, Lewis (Putnam)

Courtenay, Bryce 1933- .... **CLC 59**
See also CA 138

Courtney, Robert
See Ellison, Harlan (Jay)

Cousteau, Jacques-Yves 1910-1997 .. **CLC 30**
See also CA 65-68; 159; CANR 15; MTCW; SATA 38

Cowan, Peter (Walkinshaw) 1914- .... **SSC 28**
See also CA 21-24R; CANR 9, 25, 50

Coward, Noel (Peirce) 1899-1973**CLC 1, 9, 29, 51; DAM DRAM**
See also AITN 1; CA 17-18; 41-44R; CANR 35; CAP 2; CDBLB 1914-1945; DLB 10; MTCW

Cowley, Malcolm 1898-1989 .... **CLC 39**
See also CA 5-8R; 128; CANR 3, 55; DLB 4, 48; DLBY 81, 89; MTCW

Cowper, William 1731-1800 . **NCLC 8; DAM POET**
See also DLB 104, 109

Cox, William Trevor 1928- .... **CLC 9, 14, 71; DAM NOV**
See also Trevor, William
See also CA 9-12R; CANR 4, 37, 55; DLB 14; INT CANR-37; MTCW

Coyne, P. J.
See Masters, Hilary

Cozzens, James Gould 1903-1978**CLC 1, 4, 11, 92**
See also CA 9-12R; 81-84; CANR 19; CDALB 1941-1968; DLB 9; DLBD 2; DLBY 84; MTCW

Crabbe, George 1754-1832............. **NCLC 26**
See also DLB 93

Craddock, Charles Egbert
See Murfree, Mary Noailles

Craig, A. A.
See Anderson, Poul (William)

Craik, Dinah Maria (Mulock) 1826-1887 **NCLC 38**
See also DLB 35, 163; MAICYA; SATA 34

Cram, Ralph Adams 1863-1942 ..... **TCLC 45**
See also CA 160

Crane, (Harold) Hart 1899-1932 **TCLC 2, 5; DA; DAB; DAC; DAM MST, POET; PC 3; WLC**
See also CA 104; 127; CDALB 1917-1929; DLB 4, 48; MTCW

Crane, R(onald) S(almon) 1886-1967**CLC 27**
See also CA 85-88; DLB 63

Crane, Stephen (Townley) 1871-1900 **T C L C 11, 17, 32; DA; DAB; DAC; DAM MST, NOV, POET; SSC 7; WLC**
See also AAYA 21; CA 109; 140; CDALB 1865-1917; DLB 12, 54, 78; YABC 2

Crase, Douglas 1944-......................... **CLC 58**
See also CA 106

Crashaw, Richard 1612(?)-1649 .... **LC 24**
See also DLB 126

Craven, Margaret 1901-1980 . **CLC 17; DAC**
See also CA 103

Crawford, F(rancis) Marion 1854-1909**TCLC 10**
See also CA 107; DLB 71

Crawford, Isabella Valancy 1850-1887**NCLC 12**
See also DLB 92

Crayon, Geoffrey

Davie, Donald (Alfred) 1922-1995 . **CLC 5, 8, 10, 31**
See also CA 1-4R; 149; CAAS 3; CANR 1, 44; DLB 27; MTCW

Davies, Ray(mond Douglas) 1944- ... **CLC 21**
See also CA 116; 146

Davies, Rhys 1903-1978 .... **CLC 23**
See also CA 9-12R; 81-84; CANR 4; DLB 139

Davies, (William) Robertson 1913-1995 **C L C 2, 7, 13, 25, 42, 75, 91; DA; DAB; DAC; DAM MST, NOV, POP; WLC**
See also BEST 89:2; CA 33-36R; 150; CANR 17, 42; DLB 68; INT CANR-17; MTCW

Davies, W(illiam) H(enry) 1871-1940 **TCLC 5**
See also CA 104; DLB 19, 174

Davies, Walter C.
See Kornbluth, C(yril) M.

Davis, Angela (Yvonne) 1944- **CLC 77; DAM MULT**
See also BW 2; CA 57-60; CANR 10

Davis, B. Lynch
See Bioy Casares, Adolfo; Borges, Jorge Luis

Davis, Gordon
See Hunt, E(verette) Howard, (Jr.)

Davis, Harold Lenoir 1896-1960 ...... **CLC 49**
See also CA 89-92; DLB 9

Davis, Rebecca (Blaine) Harding 1831-1910 **TCLC 6**
See also CA 104; DLB 74

Davis, Richard Harding 1864-1916 **TCLC 24**
See also CA 114; DLB 12, 23, 78, 79; DLBD 13

Davison, Frank Dalby 1893-1970 ..... **CLC 15**
See also CA 116

Davison, Lawrence H.
See Lawrence, D(avid) H(erbert Richards)

Davison, Peter (Hubert) 1928- .... **CLC 28**
See also CA 9-12R; CAAS 4; CANR 3, 43; DLB 5

Davys, Mary 1674-1732 .... **LC 1**
See also DLB 39

Dawson, Fielding 1930- .... **CLC 6**
See also CA 85-88; DLB 130

Dawson, Peter
See Faust, Frederick (Schiller)

Day, Clarence (Shepard, Jr.) 1874-1935 **TCLC 25**
See also CA 108; DLB 11

Day, Thomas 1748-1789 .... **LC 1**
See also DLB 39; YABC 1

Day Lewis, C(ecil) 1904-1972 . **CLC 1, 6, 10; DAM POET; PC 11**
See also Blake, Nicholas
See also CA 13-16; 33-36R; CANR 34; CAP 1; DLB 15, 20; MTCW

Dazai, Osamu .... **TCLC 11**
See also Tsushima, Shuji
See also DLB 182

de Andrade, Carlos Drummond
See Drummond de Andrade, Carlos

Deane, Norman
See Creasey, John

de Beauvoir, Simone (Lucie Ernestine Marie Bertrand)
See Beauvoir, Simone (Lucie Ernestine Marie Bertrand) de

de Beer, P.
See Bosman, Herman Charles

de Brissac, Malcolm
See Dickinson, Peter (Malcolm)

de Chardin, Pierre Teilhard
See Teilhard de Chardin, (Marie Joseph) Pierre

Dee, John 1527-1608 .... **LC 20**

Deer, Sandra 1940- .... **CLC 45**

De Ferrari, Gabriella 1941- .... **CLC 65**
See also CA 146

Defoe, Daniel 1660(?)-1731 **LC 1; DA; DAB; DAC; DAM MST, NOV; WLC**
See also CDBLB 1660-1789; DLB 39, 95, 101; JRDA; MAICYA; SATA 22

de Gourmont, Remy(-Marie-Charles)
See Gourmont, Remy (-Marie-Charles) de

de Hartog, Jan 1914- .... **CLC 19**
See also CA 1-4R; CANR 1

de Hostos, E. M.
See Hostos (y Bonilla), Eugenio Maria de

de Hostos, Eugenio M.
See Hostos (y Bonilla), Eugenio Maria de

Deighton, Len .... **CLC 4, 7, 22, 46**
See also Deighton, Leonard Cyril
See also AAYA 6; BEST 89:2; CDBLB 1960 to Present; DLB 87

Deighton, Leonard Cyril 1929-
See Deighton, Len
See also CA 9-12R; CANR 19, 33; DAM NOV, POP; MTCW

Dekker, Thomas 1572(?)-1632 .. **LC 22; DAM DRAM**
See also CDBLB Before 1660; DLB 62, 172

Delafield, E. M. 1890-1943 .... **TCLC 61**
See also Dashwood, Edmee Elizabeth Monica de la Pasture
See also DLB 34

de la Mare, Walter (John) 1873-1956 **TCLC 4, 53; DAB; DAC; DAM MST, POET; SSC 14; WLC**
See also CDBLB 1914-1945; CLR 23; DLB 162; SATA 16

Delaney, Franey
See O'Hara, John (Henry)

Delaney, Shelagh 1939- **CLC 29; DAM DRAM**
See also CA 17-20R; CANR 30; CDBLB 1960 to Present; DLB 13; MTCW

Delany, Mary (Granville Pendarves) 1700-1788 **LC 12**

Delany, Samuel R(ay, Jr.) 1942- **CLC 8, 14, 38; BLC; DAM MULT**
See also BW 2; CA 81-84; CANR 27, 43; DLB 8, 33; MTCW

De La Ramee, (Marie) Louise 1839-1908
See Ouida
See also SATA 20

de la Roche, Mazo 1879-1961 .... **CLC 14**
See also CA 85-88; CANR 30; DLB 68; SATA 64

De La Salle, Innocent
See Hartmann, Sadakichi

Delbanco, Nicholas (Franklin) 1942- **CLC 6, 13**
See also CA 17-20R; CAAS 2; CANR 29, 55; DLB 6

del Castillo, Michel 1933- .... **CLC 38**
See also CA 109

Deledda, Grazia (Cosima) 1875(?)-1936 **TCLC 23**
See also CA 123

Delibes, Miguel .... **CLC 8, 18**
See also Delibes Setien, Miguel

Delibes Setien, Miguel 1920-
See Delibes, Miguel
See also CA 45-48; CANR 1, 32; HW; MTCW

DeLillo, Don 1936- **CLC 8, 10, 13, 27, 39, 54, 76; DAM NOV, POP**
See also BEST 89:1; CA 81-84; CANR 21; DLB 6, 173; MTCW

de Lisser, H. G.

See De Lisser, H(erbert) G(eorge)
See also DLB 117

De Lisser, H(erbert) G(eorge) 1878-1944 **TCLC 12**
See also de Lisser, H. G.
See also BW 2; CA 109; 152

Deloney, Thomas 1560-1600 .... **LC 41**

Deloria, Vine (Victor), Jr. 1933- ..... **CLC 21; DAM MULT**
See also CA 53-56; CANR 5, 20, 48; DLB 175; MTCW; NNAL; SATA 21

Del Vecchio, John M(ichael) 1947- ... **CLC 29**
See also CA 110; DLBD 9

de Man, Paul (Adolph Michel) 1919-1983 **CLC 55**
See also CA 128; 111; CANR 61; DLB 67; MTCW

De Marinis, Rick 1934- .... **CLC 54**
See also CA 57-60; CAAS 24; CANR 9, 25, 50

Dembry, R. Emmet
See Murfree, Mary Noailles

Demby, William 1922- . **CLC 53; BLC; DAM MULT**
See also BW 1; CA 81-84; DLB 33

de Menton, Francisco
See Chin, Frank (Chew, Jr.)

Demijohn, Thom
See Disch, Thomas M(ichael)

de Montherlant, Henry (Milon)
See Montherlant, Henry (Milon) de

Demosthenes 384B.C.-322B.C. ...... **CMLC 13**
See also DLB 176

de Natale, Francine
See Malzberg, Barry N(athaniel)

Denby, Edwin (Orr) 1903-1983 .... **CLC 48**
See also CA 138; 110

Denis, Julio
See Cortazar, Julio

Denmark, Harrison
See Zelazny, Roger (Joseph)

Dennis, John 1658-1734 .... **LC 11**
See also DLB 101

Dennis, Nigel (Forbes) 1912-1989 .... **CLC 8**
See also CA 25-28R; 129; DLB 13, 15; MTCW

Dent, Lester 1904(?)-1959 .... **TCLC 72**
See also CA 112; 161

De Palma, Brian (Russell) 1940- .... **CLC 20**
See also CA 109

De Quincey, Thomas 1785-1859 ...... **NCLC 4**
See also CDBLB 1789-1832; DLB 110; 144

Deren, Eleanora 1908(?)-1961
See Deren, Maya
See also CA 111

Deren, Maya 1917-1961 .... **CLC 16, 102**
See also Deren, Eleanora

Derleth, August (William) 1909-1971 **CLC 31**
See also CA 1-4R; 29-32R; CANR 4; DLB 9; SATA 5

Der Nister 1884-1950 .... **TCLC 56**

de Routisie, Albert
See Aragon, Louis

Derrida, Jacques 1930- .... **CLC 24, 87**
See also CA 124; 127

Derry Down Derry
See Lear, Edward

Dersonnes, Jacques
See Simenon, Georges (Jacques Christian)

Desai, Anita 1937- **CLC 19, 37, 97; DAB; DAM NOV**
See also CA 81-84; CANR 33, 53; MTCW; SATA 63

de Saint-Luc, Jean
See Glassco, John

See also CA 93-96; CANR 59; DLB 9
Fecamps, Elise
  See Creasey, John
Federman, Raymond 1928- .... **CLC 6, 47**
  See also CA 17-20R; CAAS 8; CANR 10, 43;
  DLBY 80
Federspiel, J(uerg) F. 1931- .... **CLC 42**
  See also CA 146
Feiffer, Jules (Ralph) 1929- ..... **CLC 2, 8, 64;**
  DAM DRAM
  See also AAYA 3; CA 17-20R; CANR 30, 59;
  DLB 7, 44; INT CANR-30; MTCW; SATA
  8, 61
Feige, Hermann Albert Otto Maximilian
  See Traven, B.
Feinberg, David B. 1956-1994 .... **CLC 59**
  See also CA 135; 147
Feinstein, Elaine 1930- .... **CLC 36**
  See also CA 69-72; CAAS 1; CANR 31; DLB
  14, 40; MTCW
Feldman, Irving (Mordecai) 1928- ..... **CLC 7**
  See also CA 1-4R; CANR 1; DLB 169
Felix-Tchicaya, Gerald
  See Tchicaya, Gerald Felix
Fellini, Federico 1920-1993 .... **CLC 16, 85**
  See also CA 65-68; 143; CANR 33
Felsen, Henry Gregor 1916- .... **CLC 17**
  See also CA 1-4R; CANR 1; SAAS 2; SATA 1
Fenno, Jack
  See Calisher, Hortense
Fenton, James Martin 1949- .... **CLC 32**
  See also CA 102; DLB 40
Ferber, Edna 1887-1968 .... **CLC 18, 93**
  See also AITN 1; CA 5-8R; 25-28R; DLB 9,
  28, 86; MTCW; SATA 7
Ferguson, Helen
  See Kavan, Anna
Ferguson, Samuel 1810-1886 .... **NCLC 33**
  See also DLB 32
Fergusson, Robert 1750-1774 .... **LC 29**
  See also DLB 109
Ferling, Lawrence
  See Ferlinghetti, Lawrence (Monsanto)
Ferlinghetti, Lawrence (Monsanto) 1919(?)-
  CLC 2, 6, 10, 27; DAM POET; PC 1
  See also CA 5-8R; CANR 3, 41; CDALB 1941-
  1968; DLB 5, 16; MTCW
Fernandez, Vicente Garcia Huidobro
  See Huidobro Fernandez, Vicente Garcia
Ferrer, Gabriel (Francisco Victor) Miro
  See Miro (Ferrer), Gabriel (Francisco Victor)
Ferrier, Susan (Edmonstone) 1782-1854
  NCLC 8
  See also DLB 116
Ferrigno, Robert 1948(?)- .... **CLC 65**
  See also CA 140
Ferron, Jacques 1921-1985 .... **CLC 94; DAC**
  See also CA 117; 129; DLB 60
Feuchtwanger, Lion 1884-1958 .... **TCLC 3**
  See also CA 104; DLB 66
Feuillet, Octave 1821-1890 .... **NCLC 45**
Feydeau, Georges (Leon Jules Marie) 1862-
  1921 .... **TCLC 22; DAM DRAM**
  See also CA 113; 152
Fichte, Johann Gottlieb 1762-1814 **NCLC 62**
  See also DLB 90
Ficino, Marsilio 1433-1499 .... **LC 12**
Fiedeler, Hans
  See Doeblin, Alfred
Fiedler, Leslie A(aron) 1917- . **CLC 4, 13, 24**
  See also CA 9-12R; CANR 7, 63; DLB 28, 67;
  MTCW
Field, Andrew 1938- .... **CLC 44**

See also CA 97-100; CANR 25
Field, Eugene 1850-1895 .... **NCLC 3**
  See also DLB 23, 42, 140; DLBD 13; MAICYA;
  SATA 16
Field, Gans T.
  See Wellman, Manly Wade
Field, Michael .... **TCLC 43**
Field, Peter
  See Hobson, Laura Z(ametkin)
Fielding, Henry 1707-1754 **LC 1; DA; DAB;**
  DAC; DAM DRAM, MST, NOV; WLC
  See also CDBLB 1660-1789; DLB 39, 84, 101
Fielding, Sarah 1710-1768 .... **LC 1**
  See also DLB 39
Fierstein, Harvey (Forbes) 1954- ... **CLC 33;**
  DAM DRAM, POP
  See also CA 123; 129
Figes, Eva 1932- .... **CLC 31**
  See also CA 53-56; CANR 4, 44; DLB 14
Finch, Anne 1661-1720 .... **PC 21**
  See also DLB 95
Finch, Robert (Duer Claydon) 1900- **CLC 18**
  See also CA 57-60; CANR 9, 24, 49; DLB 88
Findley, Timothy 1930- . **CLC 27, 102; DAC;**
  DAM MST
  See also CA 25-28R; CANR 12, 42; DLB 53
Fink, William
  See Mencken, H(enry) L(ouis)
Firbank, Louis 1942-
  See Reed, Lou
  See also CA 117
Firbank, (Arthur Annesley) Ronald 1886-1926
  TCLC 1
  See also CA 104; DLB 36
Fisher, M(ary) F(rances) K(ennedy) 1908-1992
  CLC 76, 87
  See also CA 77-80; 138; CANR 44
Fisher, Roy 1930- .... **CLC 25**
  See also CA 81-84; CAAS 10; CANR 16; DLB
  40
Fisher, Rudolph 1897-1934 . **TCLC 11; BLC;**
  DAM MULT; SSC 25
  See also BW 1; CA 107; 124; DLB 51, 102
Fisher, Vardis (Alvero) 1895-1968 ...... **CLC 7**
  See also CA 5-8R; 25-28R; DLB 9
Fiske, Tarleton
  See Bloch, Robert (Albert)
Fitch, Clarke
  See Sinclair, Upton (Beall)
Fitch, John IV
  See Cormier, Robert (Edmund)
Fitzgerald, Captain Hugh
  See Baum, L(yman) Frank
FitzGerald, Edward 1809-1883 .... **NCLC 9**
  See also DLB 32
Fitzgerald, F(rancis) Scott (Key) 1896-1940
  TCLC 1, 6, 14, 28, 55; DA; DAB; DAC;
  DAM MST, NOV; SSC 6; WLC
  See also AITN 1; CA 110; 123; CDALB 1917-
  1929; DLB 4, 9, 86; DLBD 1, 15, 16; DLBY
  81, 96; MTCW
Fitzgerald, Penelope 1916- ... **CLC 19, 51, 61**
  See also CA 85-88; CAAS 10; CANR 56; DLB
  14
Fitzgerald, Robert (Stuart) 1910-1985 **CLC 39**
  See also CA 1-4R; 114; CANR 1; DLBY 80
FitzGerald, Robert D(avid) 1902-1987 **CLC 19**
  See also CA 17-20R
Fitzgerald, Zelda (Sayre) 1900-1948 **TCLC 52**
  See also CA 117; 126; DLBY 84
Flanagan, Thomas (James Bonner) 1923-
  CLC 25, 52
  See also CA 108; CANR 55; DLBY 80; INT

108; MTCW
Flaubert, Gustave 1821-1880 **NCLC 2, 10, 19,**
  62, 66; DA; DAB; DAC; DAM MST, NOV;
  SSC 11; WLC
  See also DLB 119
Flecker, Herman Elroy
  See Flecker, (Herman) James Elroy
Flecker, (Herman) James Elroy 1884-1915
  TCLC 43
  See also CA 109; 150; DLB 10, 19
Fleming, Ian (Lancaster) 1908-1964 . **CLC 3,**
  30; DAM POP
  See also CA 5-8R; CANR 59; CDBLB 1945-
  1960; DLB 87; MTCW; SATA 9
Fleming, Thomas (James) 1927- .... **CLC 37**
  See also CA 5-8R; CANR 10; INT CANR-10;
  SATA 8
Fletcher, John 1579-1625 .... **LC 33; DC 6**
  See also CDBLB Before 1660; DLB 58
Fletcher, John Gould 1886-1950 .... **TCLC 35**
  See also CA 107; DLB 4, 45
Fleur, Paul
  See Pohl, Frederik
Flooglebuckle, Al
  See Spiegelman, Art
Flying Officer X
  See Bates, H(erbert) E(rnest)
Fo, Dario 1926- .... **CLC 32; DAM DRAM**
  See also CA 116; 128; MTCW
Fogarty, Jonathan Titulescu Esq.
  See Farrell, James T(homas)
Folke, Will
  See Bloch, Robert (Albert)
Follett, Ken(neth Martin) 1949- ..... **CLC 18;**
  DAM NOV, POP
  See also AAYA 6; BEST 89:4; CA 81-84; CANR
  13, 33, 54; DLB 87; DLBY 81; INT CANR-
  33; MTCW
Fontane, Theodor 1819-1898 .... **NCLC 26**
  See also DLB 129
Foote, Horton 1916- **CLC 51, 91; DAM DRAM**
  See also CA 73-76; CANR 34, 51; DLB 26; INT
  CANR-34
Foote, Shelby 1916- **CLC 75; DAM NOV, POP**
  See also CA 5-8R; CANR 3, 45; DLB 2, 17
Forbes, Esther 1891-1967 .... **CLC 12**
  See also AAYA 17; CA 13-14; 25-28R; CAP 1;
  CLR 27; DLB 22; JRDA; MAICYA; SATA 2
Forche, Carolyn (Louise) 1950- **CLC 25, 83,**
  86; DAM POET; PC 10
  See also CA 109; 117; CANR 50; DLB 5; INT
  117
Ford, Elbur
  See Hibbert, Eleanor Alice Burford
Ford, Ford Madox 1873-1939 **TCLC 1, 15, 39,**
  57; DAM NOV
  See also CA 104; 132; CDBLB 1914-1945;
  DLB 162; MTCW
Ford, Henry 1863-1947 .... **TCLC 73**
  See also CA 115; 148
Ford, John 1586-(?) .... **DC 8**
  See also CDBLB Before 1660; DAM DRAM;
  DLB 58
Ford, John 1895-1973 .... **CLC 16**
  See also CA 45-48
Ford, Richard .... **CLC 99**
Ford, Richard 1944- .... **CLC 46**
  See also CA 69-72; CANR 11, 47
Ford, Webster
  See Masters, Edgar Lee
Foreman, Richard 1937- .... **CLC 50**
  See also CA 65-68; CANR 32, 63
Forester, C(ecil) S(cott) 1899-1966 ... **CLC 35**

35; INT CANR-21; MTCW

Futabatei, Shimei 1864-1909 .... **TCLC 44**
See also DLB 180

Futrelle, Jacques 1875-1912 .... **TCLC 19**
See also CA 113; 155

Gaboriau, Emile 1835-1873 .... **NCLC 14**

Gadda, Carlo Emilio 1893-1973 .... **CLC 11**
See also CA 89-92; DLB 177

Gaddis, William 1922- CLC **1, 3, 6, 8, 10, 19, 43, 86**
See also CA 17-20R; CANR 21, 48; DLB 2; MTCW

Gage, Walter
See Inge, William (Motter)

Gaines, Ernest J(ames) 1933- CLC **3, 11, 18, 86; BLC; DAM MULT**
See also AAYA 18; AITN 1; BW 2; CA 9-12R; CANR 6, 24, 42; CDALB 1968-1988; DLB 2, 33, 152; DLBY 80; MTCW; SATA 86

Gaitskill, Mary 1954- .... **CLC 69**
See also CA 128; CANR 61

Galdos, Benito Perez
See Perez Galdos, Benito

Gale, Zona 1874-1938 TCLC **7; DAM DRAM**
See also CA 105; 153; DLB 9, 78

Galeano, Eduardo (Hughes) 1940- ... **CLC 72**
See also CA 29-32R; CANR 13, 32; HW

Galiano, Juan Valera y Alcala
See Valera y Alcala-Galiano, Juan

Gallagher, Tess 1943- ...... CLC **18, 63; DAM POET; PC 9**
See also CA 106; DLB 120

Gallant, Mavis 1922- ... CLC **7, 18, 38; DAC; DAM MST; SSC 5**
See also CA 69-72; CANR 29; DLB 53; MTCW

Gallant, Roy A(rthur) 1924- .... **CLC 17**
See also CA 5-8R; CANR 4, 29, 54; CLR 30; MAICYA; SATA 4, 68

Gallico, Paul (William) 1897-1976 ..... **CLC 2**
See also AITN 1; CA 5-8R; 69-72; CANR 23; DLB 9, 171; MAICYA; SATA 13

Gallo, Max Louis 1932- .... **CLC 95**
See also CA 85-88

Gallois, Lucien
See Desnos, Robert

Gallup, Ralph
See Whitemore, Hugh (John)

Galsworthy, John 1867-1933 TCLC **1, 45; DA; DAB; DAC; DAM DRAM, MST, NOV; SSC 22; WLC 2**
See also CA 104; 141; CDBLB 1890-1914; DLB 10, 34, 98, 162; DLBD 16

Galt, John 1779-1839 .... **NCLC 1**
See also DLB 99, 116, 159

Galvin, James 1951- .... **CLC 38**
See also CA 108; CANR 26

Gamboa, Federico 1864-1939 .... **TCLC 36**

Gandhi, M. K.
See Gandhi, Mohandas Karamchand

Gandhi, Mahatma
See Gandhi, Mohandas Karamchand

Gandhi, Mohandas Karamchand 1869-1948 **TCLC 59; DAM MULT**
See also CA 121; 132; MTCW

Gann, Ernest Kellogg 1910-1991 ...... **CLC 23**
See also AITN 1; CA 1-4R; 136; CANR 1

Garcia, Cristina 1958- .... **CLC 76**
See also CA 141

Garcia Lorca, Federico 1898-1936 TCLC **1, 7, 49; DA; DAB; DAC; DAM DRAM, MST, MULT, POET; DC 2; HLC; PC 3; WLC**
See also CA 104; 131; DLB 108; HW; MTCW

Garcia Marquez, Gabriel (Jose) 1928- CLC **2,**

3, 8, 10, 15, 27, 47, 55, 68; DA; DAB; DAC; DAM MST, MULT, NOV, POP; HLC; SSC 8; WLC
See also AAYA 3; BEST 89:1, 90:4; CA 33-36R; CANR 10, 28, 50; DLB 113; HW; MTCW

Gard, Janice
See Latham, Jean Lee

Gard, Roger Martin du
See Martin du Gard, Roger

Gardam, Jane 1928- .... **CLC 43**
See also CA 49-52; CANR 2, 18, 33, 54; CLR 12; DLB 14, 161; MAICYA; MTCW; SAAS 9; SATA 39, 76; SATA-Brief 28

Gardner, Herb(ert) 1934- .... **CLC 44**
See also CA 149

Gardner, John (Champlin), Jr. 1933-1982 CLC **2, 3, 5, 7, 8, 10, 18, 28, 34; DAM NOV, POP; SSC 7**
See also AITN 1; CA 65-68; 107; CANR 33; DLB 2; DLBY 82; MTCW; SATA 40; SATA-Obit 31

Gardner, John (Edmund) 1926- CLC **30; DAM POP**
See also CA 103; CANR 15; MTCW

Gardner, Miriam
See Bradley, Marion Zimmer

Gardner, Noel
See Kuttner, Henry

Gardons, S. S.
See Snodgrass, W(illiam) D(e Witt)

Garfield, Leon 1921-1996 .... **CLC 12**
See also AAYA 8; CA 17-20R; 152; CANR 38, 41; CLR 21; DLB 161; JRDA; MAICYA; SATA 1, 32, 76; SATA-Obit 90

Garland, (Hannibal) Hamlin 1860-1940 **TCLC 3; SSC 18**
See also CA 104; DLB 12, 71, 78

Garneau, (Hector de) Saint-Denys 1912-1943 **TCLC 13**
See also CA 111; DLB 88

Garner, Alan 1934- CLC **17; DAB; DAM POP**
See also AAYA 18; CA 73-76; CANR 15, 64; CLR 20; DLB 161; MAICYA; MTCW; SATA 18, 69

Garner, Hugh 1913-1979 .... **CLC 13**
See also CA 69-72; CANR 31; DLB 68

Garnett, David 1892-1981 .... **CLC 3**
See also CA 5-8R; 103; CANR 17; DLB 34

Garos, Stephanie
See Katz, Steve

Garrett, George (Palmer) 1929- CLC **3, 11, 51**
See also CA 1-4R; CAAS 5; CANR 1, 42; DLB 2, 5, 130, 152; DLBY 83

Garrick, David 1717-1779 .... LC **15; DAM DRAM**
See also DLB 84

Garrigue, Jean 1914-1972 .... CLC **2, 8**
See also CA 5-8R; 37-40R; CANR 20

Garrison, Frederick
See Sinclair, Upton (Beall)

Garth, Will
See Hamilton, Edmond; Kuttner, Henry

Garvey, Marcus (Moziah, Jr.) 1887-1940 **TCLC 41; BLC; DAM MULT**
See also BW 1; CA 120; 124

Gary, Romain .... **CLC 25**
See also Kacew, Romain
See also DLB 83

Gascar, Pierre .... **CLC 11**
See also Fournier, Pierre

Gascoyne, David (Emery) 1916- .... **CLC 45**
See also CA 65-68; CANR 10, 28, 54; DLB 20;

MTCW

Gaskell, Elizabeth Cleghorn 1810-1865 NCLC **5; DAB; DAM MST; SSC 25**
See also CDBLB 1832-1890; DLB 21, 144, 159

Gass, William H(oward) 1924- CLC **1, 2, 8, 11, 15, 39; SSC 12**
See also CA 17-20R; CANR 30; DLB 2; MTCW

Gasset, Jose Ortega y
See Ortega y Gasset, Jose

Gates, Henry Louis, Jr. 1950- CLC **65; DAM MULT**
See also BW 2; CA 109; CANR 25, 53; DLB 67

Gautier, Theophile 1811-1872 .. NCLC **1, 59; DAM POET; PC 18; SSC 20**
See also DLB 119

Gawsworth, John
See Bates, H(erbert) E(rnest)

Gay, Oliver
See Gogarty, Oliver St. John

Gaye, Marvin (Penze) 1939-1984 ..... **CLC 26**
See also CA 112

Gebler, Carlo (Ernest) 1954- .... **CLC 39**
See also CA 119; 133

Gee, Maggie (Mary) 1948- .... **CLC 57**
See also CA 130

Gee, Maurice (Gough) 1931- .... **CLC 29**
See also CA 97-100; SATA 46

Gelbart, Larry (Simon) 1923- .... CLC **21, 61**
See also CA 73-76; CANR 45

Gelber, Jack 1932- .... CLC **1, 6, 14, 79**
See also CA 1-4R; CANR 2; DLB 7

Gellhorn, Martha (Ellis) 1908- .. CLC **14, 60**
See also CA 77-80; CANR 44; DLBY 82

Genet, Jean 1910-1986 CLC **1, 2, 5, 10, 14, 44, 46; DAM DRAM**
See also CA 13-16R; CANR 18; DLB 72; DLBY 86; MTCW

Gent, Peter 1942- .... **CLC 29**
See also AITN 1; CA 89-92; DLBY 82

Gentlewoman in New England, A
See Bradstreet, Anne

Gentlewoman in Those Parts, A
See Bradstreet, Anne

George, Jean Craighead 1919- .... **CLC 35**
See also AAYA 8; CA 5-8R; CANR 25; CLR 1; DLB 52; JRDA; MAICYA; SATA 2, 68

George, Stefan (Anton) 1868-1933 TCLC **2, 14**
See also CA 104

Georges, Georges Martin
See Simenon, Georges (Jacques Christian)

Gerhardi, William Alexander
See Gerhardie, William Alexander

Gerhardie, William Alexander 1895-1977 **CLC 5**
See also CA 25-28R; 73-76; CANR 18; DLB 36

Gerstler, Amy 1956- .... **CLC 70**
See also CA 146

Gertler, T. .... **CLC 34**
See also CA 116; 121; INT 121

Ghalib .... **NCLC 39**
See also Ghalib, Hsadullah Khan

Ghalib, Hsadullah Khan 1797-1869
See Ghalib
See also DAM POET

Ghelderode, Michel de 1898-1962 CLC **6, 11; DAM DRAM**
See also CA 85-88; CANR 40

Ghiselin, Brewster 1903- .... **CLC 23**
See also CA 13-16R; CAAS 10; CANR 13

Ghose, Zulfikar 1935- .... **CLC 42**
See also CA 65-68

TCLC 10
See also CA 107
Grieve, C(hristopher) M(urray) 1892-1978
CLC 11, 19; DAM POET
See also MacDiarmid, Hugh; Pteleon
See also CA 5-8R; 85-88; CANR 33; MTCW
Griffin, Gerald 1803-1840 .... NCLC 7
See also DLB 159
Griffin, John Howard 1920-1980 ..... CLC 68
See also AITN 1; CA 1-4R; 101; CANR 2
Griffin, Peter 1942- .... CLC 39
See also CA 136
Griffith, D(avid Lewelyn) W(ark) 1875(?)-1948
TCLC 68
See also CA 119; 150
Griffith, Lawrence
See Griffith, D(avid Lewelyn) W(ark)
Griffiths, Trevor 1935- .... CLC 13, 52
See also CA 97-100; CANR 45; DLB 13
Griggs, Sutton Elbert 1872-1930(?)TCLC 77
See also CA 123; DLB 50
Grigson, Geoffrey (Edward Harvey) 1905-1985
CLC 7, 39
See also CA 25-28R; 118; CANR 20, 33; DLB
27; MTCW
Grillparzer, Franz 1791-1872 .... NCLC 1
See also DLB 133
Grimble, Reverend Charles James
See Eliot, T(homas) S(tearns)
Grimke, Charlotte L(ottie) Forten 1837(?)-1914
See Forten, Charlotte L.
See also BW 1; CA 117; 124; DAM MULT,
POET
Grimm, Jacob Ludwig Karl 1785-1863NCLC
3
See also DLB 90; MAICYA; SATA 22
Grimm, Wilhelm Karl 1786-1859 .... NCLC 3
See also DLB 90; MAICYA; SATA 22
Grimmelshausen, Johann Jakob Christoffel von
1621-1676 .... LC 6
See also DLB 168
Grindel, Eugene 1895-1952
See Eluard, Paul
See also CA 104
Grisham, John 1955- .... CLC 84; DAM POP
See also AAYA 14; CA 138; CANR 47
Grossman, David 1954- .... CLC 67
See also CA 138
Grossman, Vasily (Semenovich) 1905-1964
CLC 41
See also CA 124; 130; MTCW
Grove, Frederick Philip .... TCLC 4
See also Greve, Felix Paul (Berthold Friedrich)
See also DLB 92
Grubb
See Crumb, R(obert)
Grumbach, Doris (Isaac) 1918-CLC 13, 22, 64
See also CA 5-8R; CAAS 2; CANR 9, 42; INT
CANR-9
Grundtvig, Nicolai Frederik Severin 1783-1872
NCLC 1
Grunge
See Crumb, R(obert)
Grunwald, Lisa 1959- .... CLC 44
See also CA 120
Guare, John 1938- . CLC 8, 14, 29, 67; DAM
DRAM
See also CA 73-76; CANR 21; DLB 7; MTCW
Gudjonsson, Halldor Kiljan 1902-
See Laxness, Halldor
See also CA 103
Guenter, Erich
See Eich, Guenter

Guest, Barbara 1920- .... CLC 34
See also CA 25-28R; CANR 11, 44; DLB 5
Guest, Judith (Ann) 1936- CLC 8, 30; DAM
NOV, POP
See also AAYA 7; CA 77-80; CANR 15; INT
CANR-15; MTCW
Guevara, Che .... CLC 87; HLC
See also Guevara (Serna), Ernesto
Guevara (Serna), Ernesto 1928-1967
See Guevara, Che
See also CA 127; 111; CANR 56; DAM MULT;
HW
Guild, Nicholas M. 1944- .... CLC 33
See also CA 93-96
Guillemin, Jacques
See Sartre, Jean-Paul
Guillen, Jorge 1893-1984 .... CLC 11; DAM
MULT, POET
See also CA 89-92; 112; DLB 108; HW
Guillen, Nicolas (Cristobal) 1902-1989 C L C
48, 79; BLC; DAM MST, MULT, POET;
HLC
See also BW 2; CA 116; 125; 129; HW
Guillevic, (Eugene) 1907- .... CLC 33
See also CA 93-96
Guillois
See Desnos, Robert
Guillois, Valentin
See Desnos, Robert
Guiney, Louise Imogen 1861-1920 TCLC 41
See also CA 160; DLB 54
Guiraldes, Ricardo (Guillermo) 1886-1927
TCLC 39
See also CA 131; HW; MTCW
Gumilev, Nikolai Stephanovich 1886-1921
TCLC 60
Gunesekera, Romesh 1954- .... CLC 91
See also CA 159
Gunn, Bill .... CLC 5
See also Gunn, William Harrison
See also DLB 38
Gunn, Thom(son William) 1929-CLC 3, 6, 18,
32, 81; DAM POET
See also CA 17-20R; CANR 9, 33; CDBLB
1960 to Present; DLB 27; INT CANR-33;
MTCW
Gunn, William Harrison 1934(?)-1989
See Gunn, Bill
See also AITN 1; BW 1; CA 13-16R; 128;
CANR 12, 25
Gunnars, Kristjana 1948- .... CLC 69
See also CA 113; DLB 60
Gurdjieff, G(eorgei) I(vanovich) 1877(?)-1949
TCLC 71
See also CA 157
Gurganus, Allan 1947- . CLC 70; DAM POP
See also BEST 90:1; CA 135
Gurney, A(lbert) R(amsdell), Jr. 1930- . C L C
32, 50, 54; DAM DRAM
See also CA 77-80; CANR 32, 64
Gurney, Ivor (Bertie) 1890-1937 ... TCLC 33
Gurney, Peter
See Gurney, A(lbert) R(amsdell), Jr.
Guro, Elena 1877-1913 .... TCLC 56
Gustafson, James M(oody) 1925- ... CLC 100
See also CA 25-28R; CANR 37
Gustafson, Ralph (Barker) 1909- ..... CLC 36
See also CA 21-24R; CANR 8, 45; DLB 88
Gut, Gom
See Simenon, Georges (Jacques Christian)
Guterson, David 1956- .... CLC 91
See also CA 132
Guthrie, A(lfred) B(ertram), Jr. 1901-1991

CLC 23
See also CA 57-60; 134; CANR 24; DLB 6;
SATA 62; SATA-Obit 67
Guthrie, Isobel
See Grieve, C(hristopher) M(urray)
Guthrie, Woodrow Wilson 1912-1967
See Guthrie, Woody
See also CA 113; 93-96
Guthrie, Woody .... CLC 35
See also Guthrie, Woodrow Wilson
Guy, Rosa (Cuthbert) 1928- .... CLC 26
See also AAYA 4; BW 2; CA 17-20R; CANR
14, 34; CLR 13; DLB 33; JRDA; MAICYA;
SATA 14, 62
Gwendolyn
See Bennett, (Enoch) Arnold
H. D. .... CLC 3, 8, 14, 31, 34, 73; PC 5
See also Doolittle, Hilda
H. de V.
See Buchan, John
Haavikko, Paavo Juhani 1931- .. CLC 18, 34
See also CA 106
Habbema, Koos
See Heijermans, Herman
Habermas, Juergen 1929- .... CLC 104
See also CA 109
Habermas, Jurgen
See Habermas, Juergen
Hacker, Marilyn 1942- CLC 5, 9, 23, 72, 91;
DAM POET
See also CA 77-80; DLB 120
Haggard, H(enry) Rider 1856-1925TCLC 11
See also CA 108; 148; DLB 70, 156, 174, 178;
SATA 16
Hagiosy, L.
See Larbaud, Valery (Nicolas)
Hagiwara Sakutaro 1886-1942TCLC 60; PC
18
Haig, Fenil
See Ford, Ford Madox
Haig-Brown, Roderick (Langmere) 1908-1976
CLC 21
See also CA 5-8R; 69-72; CANR 4, 38; CLR
31; DLB 88; MAICYA; SATA 12
Hailey, Arthur 1920-CLC 5; DAM NOV, POP
See also AITN 2; BEST 90:3; CA 1-4R; CANR
2, 36; DLB 88; DLBY 82; MTCW
Hailey, Elizabeth Forsythe 1938- ..... CLC 40
See also CA 93-96; CAAS 1; CANR 15, 48;
INT CANR-15
Haines, John (Meade) 1924- .... CLC 58
See also CA 17-20R; CANR 13, 34; DLB 5
Hakluyt, Richard 1552-1616 .... LC 31
Haldeman, Joe (William) 1943- .... CLC 61
See also CA 53-56; CAAS 25; CANR 6; DLB
8; INT CANR-6
Haley, Alex(ander Murray Palmer) 1921-1992
CLC 8, 12, 76; BLC; DA; DAB; DAC;
DAM MST, MULT, POP
See also BW 2; CA 77-80; 136; CANR 61; DLB
38; MTCW
Haliburton, Thomas Chandler 1796-1865
NCLC 15
See also DLB 11, 99
Hall, Donald (Andrew, Jr.) 1928- CLC 1, 13,
37, 59; DAM POET
See also CA 5-8R; CAAS 7; CANR 2, 44, 64;
DLB 5; SATA 23
Hall, Frederic Sauser
See Sauser-Hall, Frederic
Hall, James
See Kuttner, Henry
Hall, James Norman 1887-1951 ..... TCLC 23

DLBY 80; MTCW
Hawking, S. W.
See Hawking, Stephen W(illiam)
Hawking, Stephen W(illiam) 1942- . **CLC 63, 105**
See also AAYA 13; BEST 89:1; CA 126; 129; CANR 48
Hawthorne, Julian 1846-1934 .... **TCLC 25**
Hawthorne, Nathaniel 1804-1864 **NCLC 39; DA; DAB; DAC; DAM MST, NOV; SSC 29; WLC**
See also AAYA 18; CDALB 1640-1865; DLB 1, 74; YABC 2
Haxton, Josephine Ayres 1921-
See Douglas, Ellen
See also CA 115; CANR 41
Hayaseca y Eizaguirre, Jorge
See Echegaray (y Eizaguirre), Jose (Maria Waldo)
Hayashi Fumiko 1904-1951 .... **TCLC 27**
See also CA 161; DLB 180
Haycraft, Anna
See Ellis, Alice Thomas
See also CA 122
Hayden, Robert E(arl) 1913-1980 . **CLC 5, 9, 14, 37; BLC; DA; DAC; DAM MST, MULT, POET; PC 6**
See also BW 1; CA 69-72; 97-100; CABS 2; CANR 24; CDALB 1941-1968; DLB 5, 76; MTCW; SATA 19; SATA-Obit 26
Hayford, J(oseph) E(phraim) Casely
See Casely-Hayford, J(oseph) E(phraim)
Hayman, Ronald 1932- .... **CLC 44**
See also CA 25-28R; CANR 18, 50; DLB 155
Haywood, Eliza (Fowler) 1693(?)-1756 **LC 1**
Hazlitt, William 1778-1830 .... **NCLC 29**
See also DLB 110, 158
Hazzard, Shirley 1931- .... **CLC 18**
See also CA 9-12R; CANR 4; DLBY 82; MTCW
Head, Bessie 1937-1986 ... **CLC 25, 67; BLC; DAM MULT**
See also BW 2; CA 29-32R; 119; CANR 25; DLB 117; MTCW
Headon, (Nicky) Topper 1956(?)- ..... **CLC 30**
Heaney, Seamus (Justin) 1939- **CLC 5, 7, 14, 25, 37, 74, 91; DAB; DAM POET; PC 18; WLCS**
See also CA 85-88; CANR 25, 48; CDBLB 1960 to Present; DLB 40; DLBY 95; MTCW
Hearn, (Patricio) Lafcadio (Tessima Carlos) 1850-1904 .... **TCLC 9**
See also CA 105; DLB 12, 78
Hearne, Vicki 1946- .... **CLC 56**
See also CA 139
Hearon, Shelby 1931- .... **CLC 63**
See also AITN 2; CA 25-28R; CANR 18, 48
Heat-Moon, William Least .... **CLC 29**
See also Trogdon, William (Lewis)
See also AAYA 9
Hebbel, Friedrich 1813-1863 **NCLC 43; DAM DRAM**
See also DLB 129
Hebert, Anne 1916- **CLC 4, 13, 29; DAC; DAM MST, POET**
See also CA 85-88; DLB 68; MTCW
Hecht, Anthony (Evan) 1923- **CLC 8, 13, 19; DAM POET**
See also CA 9-12R; CANR 6; DLB 5, 169
Hecht, Ben 1894-1964 .... **CLC 8**
See also CA 85-88; DLB 7, 9, 25, 26, 28, 86
Hedayat, Sadeq 1903-1951 .... **TCLC 21**
See also CA 120

Hegel, Georg Wilhelm Friedrich 1770-1831 **NCLC 46**
See also DLB 90
Heidegger, Martin 1889-1976 .... **CLC 24**
See also CA 81-84; 65-68; CANR 34; MTCW
Heidenstam, (Carl Gustaf) Verner von 1859-1940 .... **TCLC 5**
See also CA 104
Heifner, Jack 1946- .... **CLC 11**
See also CA 105; CANR 47
Heijermans, Herman 1864-1924 .... **TCLC 24**
See also CA 123
Heilbrun, Carolyn G(old) 1926- .... **CLC 25**
See also CA 45-48; CANR 1, 28, 58
Heine, Heinrich 1797-1856 .... **NCLC 4, 54**
See also DLB 90
Heinemann, Larry (Curtiss) 1944- ... **CLC 50**
See also CA 110; CAAS 21; CANR 31; DLBD 9; INT CANR-31
Heiney, Donald (William) 1921-1993
See Harris, MacDonald
See also CA 1-4R; 142; CANR 3, 58
Heinlein, Robert A(nson) 1907-1988 **CLC 1, 3, 8, 14, 26, 55; DAM POP**
See also AAYA 17; CA 1-4R; 125; CANR 1, 20, 53; DLB 8; JRDA; MAICYA; MTCW; SATA 9, 69; SATA-Obit 56
Helforth, John
See Doolittle, Hilda
Hellenhofferu, Vojtech Kapristian z
See Hasek, Jaroslav (Matej Frantisek)
Heller, Joseph 1923- **CLC 1, 3, 5, 8, 11, 36, 63; DA; DAB; DAC; DAM MST, NOV, POP; WLC**
See also AITN 1; CA 5-8R; CABS 1; CANR 8, 42; DLB 2, 28; DLBY 80; INT CANR-8; MTCW
Hellman, Lillian (Florence) 1906-1984 **CLC 2, 4, 8, 14, 18, 34, 44, 52; DAM DRAM; DC 1**
See also AITN 1, 2; CA 13-16R; 112; CANR 33; DLB 7; DLBY 84; MTCW
Helprin, Mark 1947- **CLC 7, 10, 22, 32; DAM NOV, POP**
See also CA 81-84; CANR 47, 64; DLBY 85; MTCW
Helvetius, Claude-Adrien 1715-1771 .. **LC 26**
Helyar, Jane Penelope Josephine 1933-
See Poole, Josephine
See also CA 21-24R; CANR 10, 26; SATA 82
Hemans, Felicia 1793-1835 .... **NCLC 29**
See also DLB 96
Hemingway, Ernest (Miller) 1899-1961 **CLC 1, 3, 6, 8, 10, 13, 19, 30, 34, 39, 41, 44, 50, 61, 80; DA; DAB; DAC; DAM MST, NOV; SSC 25; WLC**
See also AAYA 19; CA 77-80; CANR 34; CDALB 1917-1929; DLB 4, 9, 102; DLBD 1, 15, 16; DLBY 81, 87, 96; MTCW
Hempel, Amy 1951- .... **CLC 39**
See also CA 118; 137
Henderson, F. C.
See Mencken, H(enry) L(ouis)
Henderson, Sylvia
See Ashton-Warner, Sylvia (Constance)
Henderson, Zenna (Chlarson) 1917-1983 **SSC 29**
See also CA 1-4R; 133; CANR 1; DLB 8; SATA 5
Henley, Beth .... **CLC 23; DC 6**
See also Henley, Elizabeth Becker
See also CABS 3; DLBY 86
Henley, Elizabeth Becker 1952-
See Henley, Beth

See also CA 107; CANR 32; DAM DRAM, MST; MTCW
Henley, William Ernest 1849-1903 .. **TCLC 8**
See also CA 105; DLB 19
Hennissart, Martha
See Lathen, Emma
See also CA 85-88; CANR 64
Henry, O. .... **TCLC 1, 19; SSC 5; WLC**
See also Porter, William Sydney
Henry, Patrick 1736-1799 .... **LC 25**
Henryson, Robert 1430(?)-1506(?) ...... **LC 20**
See also DLB 146
Henry VIII 1491-1547 .... **LC 10**
Henschke, Alfred
See Klabund
Hentoff, Nat(han Irving) 1925- .... **CLC 26**
See also AAYA 4; CA 1-4R; CAAS 6; CANR 5, 25; CLR 1; INT CANR-25; JRDA; MAICYA; SATA 42, 69; SATA-Brief 27
Heppenstall, (John) Rayner 1911-1981 **CLC 10**
See also CA 1-4R; 103; CANR 29
Heraclitus c. 540B.C.-c. 450B.C. .. **CMLC 22**
See also DLB 176
Herbert, Frank (Patrick) 1920-1986 **CLC 12, 23, 35, 44, 85; DAM POP**
See also AAYA 21; CA 53-56; 118; CANR 5, 43; DLB 8; INT CANR-5; MTCW; SATA 9, 37; SATA-Obit 47
Herbert, George 1593-1633 ..... **LC 24; DAB; DAM POET; PC 4**
See also CDBLB Before 1660; DLB 126
Herbert, Zbigniew 1924- .. **CLC 9, 43; DAM POET**
See also CA 89-92; CANR 36; MTCW
Herbst, Josephine (Frey) 1897-1969 **CLC 34**
See also CA 5-8R; 25-28R; DLB 9
Hergesheimer, Joseph 1880-1954 .. **TCLC 11**
See also CA 109; DLB 102, 9
Herlihy, James Leo 1927-1993 .... **CLC 6**
See also CA 1-4R; 143; CANR 2
Hermogenes fl. c. 175- .... **CMLC 6**
Hernandez, Jose 1834-1886 .... **NCLC 17**
Herodotus c. 484B.C.-429B.C. ...... **CMLC 17**
See also DLB 176
Herrick, Robert 1591-1674 **LC 13; DA; DAB; DAC; DAM MST, POP; PC 9**
See also DLB 126
Herring, Guilles
See Somerville, Edith
Herriot, James 1916-1995 **CLC 12; DAM POP**
See also Wight, James Alfred
See also AAYA 1; CA 148; CANR 40; SATA 86
Herrmann, Dorothy 1941- .... **CLC 44**
See also CA 107
Herrmann, Taffy
See Herrmann, Dorothy
Hersey, John (Richard) 1914-1993 **CLC 1, 2, 7, 9, 40, 81, 97; DAM POP**
See also CA 17-20R; 140; CANR 33; DLB 6; MTCW; SATA 25; SATA-Obit 76
Herzen, Aleksandr Ivanovich 1812-1870 **NCLC 10, 61**
Herzl, Theodor 1860-1904 .... **TCLC 36**
Herzog, Werner 1942- .... **CLC 16**
See also CA 89-92
Hesiod c. 8th cent. B.C.- .... **CMLC 5**
See also DLB 176
Hesse, Hermann 1877-1962 **CLC 1, 2, 3, 6, 11, 17, 25, 69; DA; DAB; DAC; DAM MST, NOV; SSC 9; WLC**
See also CA 17-18; CAP 2; DLB 66; MTCW;

DAB; DAC; DAM MST, POET; WLCS
See also DLB 176

Honig, Edwin 1919- .... **CLC 33**
See also CA 5-8R; CAAS 8; CANR 4, 45; DLB
5

Hood, Hugh (John Blagdon) 1928-CLC **15, 28**
See also CA 49-52; CAAS 17; CANR 1, 33;
DLB 53

Hood, Thomas 1799-1845 .... **NCLC 16**
See also DLB 96

Hooker, (Peter) Jeremy 1941- .... **CLC 43**
See also CA 77-80; CANR 22; DLB 40

hooks, bell .... **CLC 94**
See also Watkins, Gloria

Hope, A(lec) D(erwent) 1907- .... **CLC 3, 51**
See also CA 21-24R; CANR 33; MTCW

Hope, Brian
See Creasey, John

Hope, Christopher (David Tully) 1944- C L C
52
See also CA 106; CANR 47; SATA 62

Hopkins, Gerard Manley 1844-1889 .. **N C L C
17; DA; DAB; DAC; DAM MST, POET;
PC 15; WLC**
See also CDBLB 1890-1914; DLB 35, 57

Hopkins, John (Richard) 1931- .... **CLC 4**
See also CA 85-88

Hopkins, Pauline Elizabeth 1859-1930T C L C
28; BLC; DAM MULT
See also BW 2; CA 141; DLB 50

Hopkinson, Francis 1737-1791 .... **LC 25**
See also DLB 31

Hopley-Woolrich, Cornell George 1903-1968
See Woolrich, Cornell
See also CA 13-14; CANR 58; CAP 1

Horatio
See Proust, (Valentin-Louis-George-Eugene-)
Marcel

Horgan, Paul (George Vincent O'Shaughnessy)
1903-1995 .... **CLC 9, 53; DAM NOV**
See also CA 13-16R; 147; CANR 9, 35; DLB
102; DLBY 85; INT CANR-9; MTCW;
SATA 13; SATA-Obit 84

Horn, Peter
See Kuttner, Henry

Hornem, Horace Esq.
See Byron, George Gordon (Noel)

**Horney, Karen (Clementine Theodore
Danielsen)** 1885-1952 .... **TCLC 71**
See also CA 114

Hornung, E(rnest) W(illiam) 1866-1921
TCLC 59
See also CA 108; 160; DLB 70

Horovitz, Israel (Arthur) 1939-CLC **56; DAM
DRAM**
See also CA 33-36R; CANR 46, 59; DLB 7

Horvath, Odon von
See Horvath, Oedoen von
See also DLB 85, 124

Horvath, Oedoen von 1901-1938 ... **TCLC 45**
See also Horvath, Odon von
See also CA 118

Horwitz, Julius 1920-1986 .... **CLC 14**
See also CA 9-12R; 119; CANR 12

Hospital, Janette Turner 1942- .... **CLC 42**
See also CA 108; CANR 48

Hostos, E. M. de
See Hostos (y Bonilla), Eugenio Maria de

Hostos, Eugenio M. de
See Hostos (y Bonilla), Eugenio Maria de

Hostos, Eugenio Maria
See Hostos (y Bonilla), Eugenio Maria de

Hostos (y Bonilla), Eugenio Maria de 1839-

1903 .... **TCLC 24**
See also CA 123; 131; HW

Houdini
See Lovecraft, H(oward) P(hillips)

Hougan, Carolyn 1943- .... **CLC 34**
See also CA 139

Household, Geoffrey (Edward West) 1900-1988
CLC 11
See also CA 77-80; 126; CANR 58; DLB 87;
SATA 14; SATA-Obit 59

Housman, A(lfred) E(dward) 1859-1936
**TCLC 1, 10; DA; DAB; DAC; DAM MST,
POET; PC 2; WLCS**
See also CA 104; 125; DLB 19; MTCW

Housman, Laurence 1865-1959 .... **TCLC 7**
See also CA 106; 155; DLB 10; SATA 25

Howard, Elizabeth Jane 1923- ..... **CLC 7, 29**
See also CA 5-8R; CANR 8, 62

Howard, Maureen 1930- .... **CLC 5, 14, 46**
See also CA 53-56; CANR 31; DLBY 83; INT
CANR-31; MTCW

Howard, Richard 1929- .... **CLC 7, 10, 47**
See also AITN 1; CA 85-88; CANR 25; DLB 5;
INT CANR-25

Howard, Robert E(rvin) 1906-1936 **TCLC 8**
See also CA 105; 157

Howard, Warren F.
See Pohl, Frederik

Howe, Fanny 1940- .... **CLC 47**
See also CA 117; CAAS 27; SATA-Brief 52

Howe, Irving 1920-1993 .... **CLC 85**
See also CA 9-12R; 141; CANR 21, 50; DLB
67; MTCW

Howe, Julia Ward 1819-1910 .... **TCLC 21**
See also CA 117; DLB 1

Howe, Susan 1937- .... **CLC 72**
See also CA 160; DLB 120

Howe, Tina 1937- .... **CLC 48**
See also CA 109

Howell, James 1594(?)-1666 .... **LC 13**
See also DLB 151

Howells, W. D.
See Howells, William Dean

Howells, William D.
See Howells, William Dean

Howells, William Dean 1837-1920TCLC **7, 17,
41**
See also CA 104; 134; CDALB 1865-1917;
DLB 12, 64, 74, 79

Howes, Barbara 1914-1996 .... **CLC 15**
See also CA 9-12R; 151; CAAS 3; CANR 53;
SATA 5

Hrabal, Bohumil 1914-1997 .... **CLC 13, 67**
See also CA 106; 156; CAAS 12; CANR 57

Hsun, Lu
See Lu Hsun

Hubbard, L(afayette) Ron(ald) 1911-1986
CLC 43; DAM POP
See also CA 77-80; 118; CANR 52

Huch, Ricarda (Octavia) 1864-1947TCLC **13**
See also CA 111; DLB 66

Huddle, David 1942- .... **CLC 49**
See also CA 57-60; CAAS 20; DLB 130

Hudson, Jeffrey
See Crichton, (John) Michael

Hudson, W(illiam) H(enry) 1841-1922T C L C
29
See also CA 115; DLB 98, 153, 174; SATA 35

Hueffer, Ford Madox
See Ford, Ford Madox

Hughart, Barry 1934- .... **CLC 39**
See also CA 137

Hughes, Colin

See Creasey, John

Hughes, David (John) 1930- .... **CLC 48**
See also CA 116; 129; DLB 14

Hughes, Edward James
See Hughes, Ted
See also DAM MST, POET

Hughes, (James) Langston 1902-1967CLC **1,
5, 10, 15, 35, 44; BLC; DA; DAB; DAC;
DAM DRAM, MST, MULT, POET; DC 3;
PC 1; SSC 6; WLC**
See also AAYA 12; BW 1; CA 1-4R; 25-28R;
CANR 1, 34; CDALB 1929-1941; CLR 17;
DLB 4, 7, 48, 51, 86; JRDA; MAICYA;
MTCW; SATA 4, 33

Hughes, Richard (Arthur Warren) 1900-1976
CLC 1, 11; DAM NOV
See also CA 5-8R; 65-68; CANR 4; DLB 15,
161; MTCW; SATA 8; SATA-Obit 25

Hughes, Ted 1930-CLC **2, 4, 9, 14, 37; DAB;
DAC; PC 7**
See also Hughes, Edward James
See also CA 1-4R; CANR 1, 33; CLR 3; DLB
40, 161; MAICYA; MTCW; SATA 49; SATA-
Brief 27

Hugo, Richard F(ranklin) 1923-1982 **CLC 6,
18, 32; DAM POET**
See also CA 49-52; 108; CANR 3; DLB 5

Hugo, Victor (Marie) 1802-1885NCLC **3, 10,
21; DA; DAB; DAC; DAM DRAM, MST,
NOV, POET; PC 17; WLC**
See also DLB 119; SATA 47

Huidobro, Vicente
See Huidobro Fernandez, Vicente Garcia

Huidobro Fernandez, Vicente Garcia 1893-
1948 .... **TCLC 31**
See also CA 131; HW

Hulme, Keri 1947- .... **CLC 39**
See also CA 125; INT 125

Hulme, T(homas) E(rnest) 1883-1917 T C L C
21
See also CA 117; DLB 19

Hume, David 1711-1776 .... **LC 7**
See also DLB 104

Humphrey, William 1924-1997 .... **CLC 45**
See also CA 77-80; 160; DLB 6

Humphreys, Emyr Owen 1919- .... **CLC 47**
See also CA 5-8R; CANR 3, 24; DLB 15

Humphreys, Josephine 1945- ..... **CLC 34, 57**
See also CA 121; 127; INT 127

Huneker, James Gibbons 1857-1921TCLC **65**
See also DLB 71

Hungerford, Pixie
See Brinsmead, H(esba) F(ay)

Hunt, E(verette) Howard, (Jr.) 1918-, CLC **3**
See also AITN 1; CA 45-48; CANR 2, 47

Hunt, Kyle
See Creasey, John

Hunt, (James Henry) Leigh 1784-1859N C L C
1; DAM POET
See also DLB 96, 110, 144

Hunt, Marsha 1946- .... **CLC 70**
See also BW 2; CA 143

Hunt, Violet 1866-1942 .... **TCLC 53**
See also DLB 162

Hunter, E. Waldo
See Sturgeon, Theodore (Hamilton)

Hunter, Evan 1926- . CLC **11, 31; DAM POP**
See also CA 5-8R; CANR 5, 38, 62; DLBY 82;
INT CANR-5; MTCW; SATA 25

Hunter, Kristin (Eggleston) 1931- .... **CLC 35**
See also AITN 1; BW 1; CA 13-16R; CANR
13; CLR 3; DLB 33; INT CANR-13;
MAICYA; SAAS 10; SATA 12

Hunter, Mollie 1922- .... **CLC 21**

See also McIlwraith, Maureen Mollie Hunter
See also AAYA 13; CANR 37; CLR 25; DLB 161; JRDA; MAICYA; SAAS 7; SATA 54
Hunter, Robert (?)-1734 .... **LC 7**
Hurston, Zora Neale 1903-1960 CLC 7, 30, 61; BLC; DA; DAC; DAM MST, MULT, NOV; SSC 4; WLCS
See also AAYA 15; BW 1; CA 85-88; CANR 61; DLB 51, 86; MTCW
Huston, John (Marcellus) 1906-1987 CLC 20
See also CA 73-76; 123; CANR 34; DLB 26
Hustvedt, Siri 1955- .... **CLC 76**
See also CA 137
Hutten, Ulrich von 1488-1523 .... **LC 16**
See also DLB 179
Huxley, Aldous (Leonard) 1894-1963 CLC 1, 3, 4, 5, 8, 11, 18, 35, 79; DA; DAB; DAC; DAM MST, NOV; WLC
See also AAYA 11; CA 85-88; CANR 44; CDBLB 1914-1945; DLB 36, 100, 162; MTCW; SATA 63
Huxley, T. H. 1825-1895 .... **NCLC 67**
See also DLB 57
Huysmans, Charles Marie Georges 1848-1907
See Huysmans, Joris-Karl
See also CA 104
Huysmans, Joris-Karl .... **TCLC 7, 69**
See also Huysmans, Charles Marie Georges
See also DLB 123
Hwang, David Henry 1957- ... **CLC 55; DAM DRAM; DC 4**
See also CA 127; 132; INT 132
Hyde, Anthony 1946- .... **CLC 42**
See also CA 136
Hyde, Margaret O(ldroyd) 1917- ..... **CLC 21**
See also CA 1-4R; CANR 1, 36; CLR 23; JRDA; MAICYA; SAAS 8; SATA 1, 42, 76
Hynes, James 1956(?)- .... **CLC 65**
Ian, Janis 1951- .... **CLC 21**
See also CA 105
Ibanez, Vicente Blasco
See Blasco Ibanez, Vicente
Ibarguengoitia, Jorge 1928-1983 ..... **CLC 37**
See also CA 124; 113; HW
Ibsen, Henrik (Johan) 1828-1906 TCLC 2, 8, 16, 37, 52; DA; DAB; DAC; DAM DRAM, MST; DC 2; WLC
See also CA 104; 141
Ibuse Masuji 1898-1993 .... **CLC 22**
See also CA 127; 141; DLB 180
Ichikawa, Kon 1915- .... **CLC 20**
See also CA 121
Idle, Eric 1943- .... **CLC 21**
See also Monty Python
See also CA 116; CANR 35
Ignatow, David 1914- .... **CLC 4, 7, 14, 40**
See also CA 9-12R; CAAS 3; CANR 31, 57; DLB 5
Ihimaera, Witi 1944- .... **CLC 46**
See also CA 77-80
Ilf, Ilya .... **TCLC 21**
See also Fainzilberg, Ilya Arnoldovich
Illyes, Gyula 1902-1983 .... **PC 16**
See also CA 114; 109
Immermann, Karl (Lebrecht) 1796-1840 NCLC 4, 49
See also DLB 133
Inchbald, Elizabeth 1753-1821 ...... **NCLC 62**
See also DLB 39, 89
Inclan, Ramon (Maria) del Valle
See Valle-Inclan, Ramon (Maria) del
Infante, G(uillermo) Cabrera
See Cabrera Infante, G(uillermo)

Ingalls, Rachel (Holmes) 1940- .... **CLC 42**
See also CA 123; 127
Ingamells, Rex 1913-1955 .... **TCLC 35**
Inge, William (Motter) 1913-1973 . CLC 1, 8, 19; DAM DRAM
See also CA 9-12R; CDALB 1941-1968; DLB 7; MTCW
Ingelow, Jean 1820-1897 .... **NCLC 39**
See also DLB 35, 163; SATA 33
Ingram, Willis J.
See Harris, Mark
Innaurato, Albert (F.) 1948(?)- .. **CLC 21, 60**
See also CA 115; 122; INT 122
Innes, Michael
See Stewart, J(ohn) I(nnes) M(ackintosh)
Innis, Harold Adams 1894-1952 .... **TCLC 77**
See also DLB 88
Ionesco, Eugene 1909-1994 CLC 1, 4, 6, 9, 11, 15, 41, 86; DA; DAB; DAC; DAM DRAM, MST; WLC
See also CA 9-12R; 144; CANR 55; MTCW; SATA 7; SATA-Obit 79
Iqbal, Muhammad 1873-1938 .... **TCLC 28**
Ireland, Patrick
See O'Doherty, Brian
Iron, Ralph
See Schreiner, Olive (Emilie Albertina)
Irving, John (Winslow) 1942-CLC 13, 23, 38; DAM NOV, POP
See also AAYA 8; BEST 89:3; CA 25-28R; CANR 28; DLB 6; DLBY 82; MTCW
Irving, Washington 1783-1859 . NCLC 2, 19; DA; DAB; DAM MST; SSC 2; WLC
See also CDALB 1640-1865; DLB 3, 11, 30, 59, 73, 74; YABC 2
Irwin, P. K.
See Page, P(atricia) K(athleen)
Isaacs, Susan 1943- .... **CLC 32; DAM POP**
See also BEST 89:1; CA 89-92; CANR 20, 41; INT CANR-20; MTCW
Isherwood, Christopher (William Bradshaw) 1904-1986 .... **CLC 1, 9, 11, 14, 44; DAM DRAM, NOV**
See also CA 13-16R; 117; CANR 35; DLB 15; DLBY 86; MTCW
Ishiguro, Kazuo 1954- CLC 27, 56, 59; DAM NOV
See also BEST 90:2; CA 120; CANR 49; MTCW
Ishikawa, Hakuhin
See Ishikawa, Takuboku
Ishikawa, Takuboku 1886(?)-1912 TCLC 15; DAM POET; PC 10
See also CA 113; 153
Iskander, Fazil 1929- .... **CLC 47**
See also CA 102
Isler, Alan (David) 1934- .... **CLC 91**
See also CA 156
Ivan IV 1530-1584 .... **LC 17**
Ivanov, Vyacheslav Ivanovich 1866-1949 TCLC 33
See also CA 122
Ivask, Ivar Vidrik 1927-1992 .... **CLC 14**
See also CA 37-40R; 139; CANR 24
Ives, Morgan
See Bradley, Marion Zimmer
J. R. S.
See Gogarty, Oliver St. John
Jabran, Kahlil
See Gibran, Kahlil
Jabran, Khalil
See Gibran, Kahlil
Jackson, Daniel

See Wingrove, David (John)
Jackson, Jesse 1908-1983 .... **CLC 12**
See also BW 1; CA 25-28R; 109; CANR 27; CLR 28; MAICYA; SATA 2, 29; SATA-Obit 48
Jackson, Laura (Riding) 1901-1991
See Riding, Laura
See also CA 65-68; 135; CANR 28; DLB 48
Jackson, Sam
See Trumbo, Dalton
Jackson, Sara
See Wingrove, David (John)
Jackson, Shirley 1919-1965 . CLC 11, 60, 87; DA; DAC; DAM MST; SSC 9; WLC
See also AAYA 9; CA 1-4R; 25-28R; CANR 4, 52; CDALB 1941-1968; DLB 6; SATA 2
Jacob, (Cyprien-)Max 1876-1944 .... **TCLC 6**
See also CA 104
Jacobs, Harriet 1813(?)-1897 .... **NCLC 67**
Jacobs, Jim 1942- .... **CLC 12**
See also CA 97-100; INT 97-100
Jacobs, W(illiam) W(ymark) 1863-1943 TCLC 22
See also CA 121; DLB 135
Jacobsen, Jens Peter 1847-1885 .... **NCLC 34**
Jacobsen, Josephine 1908- .... **CLC 48, 102**
See also CA 33-36R; CAAS 18; CANR 23, 48
Jacobson, Dan 1929- .... **CLC 4, 14**
See also CA 1-4R; CANR 2, 25; DLB 14; MTCW
Jacqueline
See Carpentier (y Valmont), Alejo
Jagger, Mick 1944- .... **CLC 17**
Jahiz, Al- c. 776-869 .... **CMLC 25**
Jakes, John (William) 1932- .. **CLC 29; DAM NOV, POP**
See also BEST 89:4; CA 57-60; CANR 10, 43; DLBY 83; INT CANR-10; MTCW; SATA 62
James, Andrew
See Kirkup, James
James, C(yril) L(ionel) R(obert) 1901-1989 CLC 33
See also BW 2; CA 117; 125; 128; CANR 62; DLB 125; MTCW
James, Daniel (Lewis) 1911-1988
See Santiago, Danny
See also CA 125
James, Dynely
See Mayne, William (James Carter)
James, Henry Sr. 1811-1882 .... **NCLC 53**
James, Henry 1843-1916 TCLC 2, 11, 24, 40, 47, 64; DA; DAB; DAC; DAM MST, NOV; SSC 8; WLC
See also CA 104; 132; CDALB 1865-1917; DLB 12, 71, 74; DLBD 13; MTCW
James, M. R.
See James, Montague (Rhodes)
See also DLB 156
James, Montague (Rhodes) 1862-1936 T C L C 6; SSC 16
See also CA 104
James, P. D. .... **CLC 18, 46**
See also White, Phyllis Dorothy James
See also BEST 90:2; CDBLB 1960 to Present; DLB 87
James, Philip
See Moorcock, Michael (John)
James, William 1842-1910 .... **TCLC 15, 32**
See also CA 109
James I 1394-1437 .... **LC 20**
Jameson, Anna 1794-1860 .... **NCLC 43**
See also DLB 99, 166
Jami, Nur al-Din 'Abd al-Rahman 1414-1492

See also CA 104; 126; CDBLB 1914-1945;
DLB 10, 19, 36, 162; MTCW
Jozsef, Attila 1905-1937 .... **TCLC 22**
See also CA 116
Juana Ines de la Cruz 1651(?)-1695 ...... **LC 5**
Judd, Cyril
See Kornbluth, C(yril) M.; Pohl, Frederik
Julian of Norwich 1342(?)-1416(?) .... **LC 6**
See also DLB 146
Juniper, Alex
See Hospital, Janette Turner
Junius
See Luxemburg, Rosa
Just, Ward (Swift) 1935- .... **CLC 4, 27**
See also CA 25-28R; CANR 32; INT CANR-
32
Justice, Donald (Rodney) 1925-.. **CLC 6, 19,**
102; DAM POET
See also CA 5-8R; CANR 26, 54; DLBY 83;
INT CANR-26
Juvenal c. 55-c. 127 .... **CMLC 8**
Juvenis
See Bourne, Randolph S(illiman)
Kacew, Romain 1914-1980
See Gary, Romain
See also CA 108; 102
Kadare, Ismail 1936- .... **CLC 52**
See also CA 161
Kadohata, Cynthia .... **CLC 59**
See also CA 140
Kafka, Franz 1883-1924 **TCLC 2, 6, 13, 29, 47,**
53; DA; DAB; DAC; DAM MST, NOV;
SSC 29; WLC
See also CA 105; 126; DLB 81; MTCW
Kahanovitsch, Pinkhes
See Der Nister
Kahn, Roger 1927- .... **CLC 30**
See also CA 25-28R; CANR 44; DLB 171;
SATA 37
Kain, Saul
See Sassoon, Siegfried (Lorraine)
Kaiser, Georg 1878-1945 .... **TCLC 9**
See also CA 106; DLB 124
Kaletski, Alexander 1946- .... **CLC 39**
See also CA 118; 143
Kalidasa fl. c. 400- .... **CMLC 9**
Kallman, Chester (Simon) 1921-1975 **CLC 2**
See also CA 45-48; 53-56; CANR 3
Kaminsky, Melvin 1926-
See Brooks, Mel
See also CA 65-68; CANR 16
Kaminsky, Stuart M(elvin) 1934- ..... **CLC 59**
See also CA 73-76; CANR 29, 53
Kane, Francis
See Robbins, Harold
Kane, Paul
See Simon, Paul (Frederick)
Kane, Wilson
See Bloch, Robert (Albert)
Kanin, Garson 1912- .... **CLC 22**
See also AITN 1; CA 5-8R; CANR 7; DLB 7
Kaniuk, Yoram 1930- .... **CLC 19**
See also CA 134
Kant, Immanuel 1724-1804 ...... **NCLC 27, 67**
See also DLB 94
Kantor, MacKinlay 1904-1977 .... **CLC 7**
See also CA 61-64; 73-76; CANR 60, 63; DLB
9, 102
Kaplan, David Michael 1946- .... **CLC 50**
Kaplan, James 1951- .... **CLC 59**
See also CA 135
Karageorge, Michael
See Anderson, Poul (William)

Karamzin, Nikolai Mikhailovich 1766-1826
NCLC 3
See also DLB 150
Karapanou, Margarita 1946- .... **CLC 13**
See also CA 101
Karinthy, Frigyes 1887-1938 .... **TCLC 47**
Karl, Frederick R(obert) 1927- .... **CLC 34**
See also CA 5-8R; CANR 3, 44
Kastel, Warren
See Silverberg, Robert
Kataev, Evgeny Petrovich 1903-1942
See Petrov, Evgeny
See also CA 120
Kataphusin
See Ruskin, John
Katz, Steve 1935- .... **CLC 47**
See also CA 25-28R; CAAS 14, 64; CANR 12;
DLBY 83
Kauffman, Janet 1945- .... **CLC 42**
See also CA 117; CANR 43; DLBY 86
Kaufman, Bob (Garnell) 1925-1986 . **CLC 49**
See also BW 1; CA 41-44R; 118; CANR 22;
DLB 16, 41
Kaufman, George S. 1889-1961 **CLC 38; DAM**
DRAM
See also CA 108; 93-96; DLB 7; INT 108
Kaufman, Sue .... **CLC 3, 8**
See also Barondess, Sue K(aufman)
Kavafis, Konstantinos Petrou 1863-1933
See Cavafy, C(onstantine) P(eter)
See also CA 104
Kavan, Anna 1901-1968 .... **CLC 5, 13, 82**
See also CA 5-8R; CANR 6, 57; MTCW
Kavanagh, Dan
See Barnes, Julian (Patrick)
Kavanagh, Patrick (Joseph) 1904-1967 **C L C**
22
See also CA 123; 25-28R; DLB 15, 20; MTCW
Kawabata, Yasunari 1899-1972 **CLC 2, 5, 9,**
18, 107; DAM MULT; SSC 17
See also CA 93-96; 33-36R; DLB 180
Kaye, M(ary) M(argaret) 1909- .... **CLC 28**
See also CA 89-92; CANR 24, 60; MTCW;
SATA 62
Kaye, Mollie
See Kaye, M(ary) M(argaret)
Kaye-Smith, Sheila 1887-1956 .... **TCLC 20**
See also CA 118; DLB 36
Kaymor, Patrice Maguilene
See Senghor, Leopold Sedar
Kazan, Elia 1909- .... **CLC 6, 16, 63**
See also CA 21-24R; CANR 32
Kazantzakis, Nikos 1883(?)-1957 **TCLC 2, 5,**
33
See also CA 105; 132; MTCW
Kazin, Alfred 1915- .... **CLC 34, 38**
See also CA 1-4R; CAAS 7; CANR 1, 45; DLB
67
Keane, Mary Nesta (Skrine) 1904-1996
See Keane, Molly
See also CA 108; 114; 151
Keane, Molly .... **CLC 31**
See also Keane, Mary Nesta (Skrine)
See also INT 114
Keates, Jonathan 19(?)- .... **CLC 34**
Keaton, Buster 1895-1966 .... **CLC 20**
Keats, John 1795-1821 . **NCLC 8; DA; DAB;**
DAC; DAM MST, POET; PC 1; WLC
See also CDBLB 1789-1832; DLB 96, 110
Keene, Donald 1922- .... **CLC 34**
See also CA 1-4R; CANR 5
Keillor, Garrison .... **CLC 40**
See also Keillor, Gary (Edward)

See also AAYA 2; BEST 89:3; DLBY 87; SATA
58
Keillor, Gary (Edward) 1942-
See Keillor, Garrison
See also CA 111; 117; CANR 36, 59; DAM
POP; MTCW
Keith, Michael
See Hubbard, L(afayette) Ron(ald)
Keller, Gottfried 1819-1890 **NCLC 2; SSC 26**
See also DLB 129
Kellerman, Jonathan 1949- ... **CLC 44; DAM**
POP
See also BEST 90:1; CA 106; CANR 29, 51;
INT CANR-29
Kelley, William Melvin 1937- .... **CLC 22**
See also BW 1; CA 77-80; CANR 27; DLB 33
Kellogg, Marjorie 1922- .... **CLC 2**
See also CA 81-84
Kellow, Kathleen
See Hibbert, Eleanor Alice Burford
Kelly, M(ilton) T(erry) 1947- .... **CLC 55**
See also CA 97-100; CAAS 22; CANR 19, 43
Kelman, James 1946- .... **CLC 58, 86**
See also CA 148
Kemal, Yashar 1923- .... **CLC 14, 29**
See also CA 89-92; CANR 44
Kemble, Fanny 1809-1893 .... **NCLC 18**
See also DLB 32
Kemelman, Harry 1908-1996 .... **CLC 2**
See also AITN 1; CA 9-12R; 155; CANR 6;
DLB 28
Kempe, Margery 1373(?)-1440(?) .... **LC 6**
See also DLB 146
Kempis, Thomas a 1380-1471 .... **LC 11**
Kendall, Henry 1839-1882 .... **NCLC 12**
Keneally, Thomas (Michael) 1935- **CLC 5, 8,**
10, 14, 19, 27, 43; DAM NOV
See also CA 85-88; CANR 10, 50; MTCW
Kennedy, Adrienne (Lita) 1931- ..... **CLC 66;**
BLC; DAM MULT; DC 5
See also BW 2; CA 103; CAAS 20; CABS 3;
CANR 26, 53; DLB 38
Kennedy, John Pendleton 1795-1870 **NCLC 2**
See also DLB 3
Kennedy, Joseph Charles 1929-
See Kennedy, X. J.
See also CA 1-4R; CANR 4, 30, 40; SATA 14,
86
Kennedy, William 1928- .. **CLC 6, 28, 34, 53;**
DAM NOV
See also AAYA 1; CA 85-88; CANR 14, 31;
DLB 143; DLBY 85; INT CANR-31;
MTCW; SATA 57
Kennedy, X. J. .... **CLC 8, 42**
See also Kennedy, Joseph Charles
See also CAAS 9; CLR 27; DLB 5; SAAS 22
Kenny, Maurice (Francis) 1929- ..... **CLC 87;**
DAM MULT
See also CA 144; CAAS 22; DLB 175; NNAL
Kent, Kelvin
See Kuttner, Henry
Kenton, Maxwell
See Southern, Terry
Kenyon, Robert O.
See Kuttner, Henry
Kerouac, Jack .... **CLC 1, 2, 3, 5, 14, 29, 61**
See also Kerouac, Jean-Louis Lebris de
See also CDALB 1941-1968; DLB 2, 16; DLBD
3; DLBY 95
Kerouac, Jean-Louis Lebris de 1922-1969
See Kerouac, Jack
See also AITN 1; CA 5-8R; 25-28R; CANR 26,
54; DA; DAB; DAC; DAM MST, NOV,

Landis, John 1950- .... CLC 26
See also CA 112; 122
Landolfi, Tommaso 1908-1979 .... CLC 11, 49
See also CA 127; 117; DLB 177
Landon, Letitia Elizabeth 1802-1838 N C L C
15
See also DLB 96
Landor, Walter Savage 1775-1864 NCLC 14
See also DLB 93, 107
Landwirth, Heinz 1927-
See Lind, Jakov
See also CA 9-12R; CANR 7
Lane, Patrick 1939- ... CLC 25; DAM POET
See also CA 97-100; CANR 54; DLB 53; INT
97-100
Lang, Andrew 1844-1912 .... TCLC 16
See also CA 114; 137; DLB 98, 141, 184;
MAICYA; SATA 16
Lang, Fritz 1890-1976 .... CLC 20, 103
See also CA 77-80; 69-72; CANR 30
Lange, John
See Crichton, (John) Michael
Langer, Elinor 1939- .... CLC 34
See also CA 121
Langland, William 1330(?)-1400(?)... LC 19;
DA; DAB; DAC; DAM MST, POET
See also DLB 146
Langstaff, Launcelot
See Irving, Washington
Lanier, Sidney 1842-1881 ..... NCLC 6; DAM
POET
See also DLB 64; DLBD 13; MAICYA; SATA
18
Lanyer, Aemilia 1569-1645 .... LC 10, 30
See also DLB 121
Lao Tzu .... CMLC 7
Lapine, James (Elliot) 1949- .... CLC 39
See also CA 123; 130; CANR 54; INT 130
Larbaud, Valery (Nicolas) 1881-1957TCLC 9
See also CA 106; 152
Lardner, Ring
See Lardner, Ring(gold) W(ilmer)
Lardner, Ring W., Jr.
See Lardner, Ring(gold) W(ilmer)
Lardner, Ring(gold) W(ilmer) 1885-1933
TCLC 2, 14
See also CA 104; 131; CDALB 1917-1929;
DLB 11, 25, 86; DLBD 16; MTCW
Laredo, Betty
See Codrescu, Andrei
Larkin, Maia
See Wojciechowska, Maia (Teresa)
Larkin, Philip (Arthur) 1922-1985CLC 3, 5, 8,
9, 13, 18, 33, 39, 64; DAB; DAM MST,
POET; PC 21
See also CA 5-8R; 117; CANR 24, 62; CDBLB
1960 to Present; DLB 27; MTCW
Larra (y Sanchez de Castro), Mariano Jose de
1809-1837 .... NCLC 17
Larsen, Eric 1941- .... CLC 55
See also CA 132
Larsen, Nella 1891-1964CLC 37; BLC; DAM
MULT
See also BW 1; CA 125; DLB 51
Larson, Charles R(aymond) 1938- ... CLC 31
See also CA 53-56; CANR 4
Larson, Jonathan 1961(?)-1996 .... CLC 99
Las Casas, Bartolome de 1474-1566 ... LC 31
Lasch, Christopher 1932-1994 .... CLC 102
See also CA 73-76; 144; CANR 25; MTCW
Lasker-Schueler, Else 1869-1945 ... TCLC 57
See also DLB 66, 124
Latham, Jean Lee 1902- .... CLC 12

See also AITN 1; CA 5-8R; CANR 7; MAICYA;
SATA 2, 68
Latham, Mavis
See Clark, Mavis Thorpe
Lathen, Emma .... CLC 2
See also Hennissart, Martha; Latsis, Mary J(ane)
Lathrop, Francis
See Leiber, Fritz (Reuter, Jr.)
Latsis, Mary J(ane)
See Lathen, Emma
See also CA 85-88
Lattimore, Richmond (Alexander) 1906-1984
CLC 3
See also CA 1-4R; 112; CANR 1
Laughlin, James 1914- .... CLC 49
See also CA 21-24R; CAAS 22; CANR 9, 47;
DLB 48; DLBY 96
Laurence, (Jean) Margaret (Wemyss) 1926-
1987.. CLC 3, 6, 13, 50, 62; DAC; DAM
MST; SSC 7
See also CA 5-8R; 121; CANR 33; DLB 53;
MTCW; SATA-Obit 50
Laurent, Antoine 1952- .... CLC 50
Lauscher, Hermann
See Hesse, Hermann
Lautreamont, Comte de 1846-1870NCLC 12;
SSC 14
Laverty, Donald
See Blish, James (Benjamin)
Lavin, Mary 1912-1996CLC 4, 18, 99; SSC 4
See also CA 9-12R; 151; CANR 33; DLB 15;
MTCW
Lavond, Paul Dennis
See Kornbluth, C(yril) M.; Pohl, Frederik
Lawler, Raymond Evenor 1922- .... CLC 58
See also CA 103
Lawrence, D(avid) H(erbert Richards) 1885-
1930TCLC 2, 9, 16, 33, 48, 61; DA; DAB;
DAC; DAM MST, NOV, POET; SSC 4, 19;
WLC
See also CA 104; 121; CDBLB 1914-1945;
DLB 10, 19, 36, 98, 162; MTCW
Lawrence, T(homas) E(dward) 1888-1935
TCLC 18
See also Dale, Colin
See also CA 115
Lawrence of Arabia
See Lawrence, T(homas) E(dward)
Lawson, Henry (Archibald Hertzberg) 1867-
1922 .... TCLC 27; SSC 18
See also CA 120
Lawton, Dennis
See Faust, Frederick (Schiller)
Laxness, Halldor .... CLC 25
See also Gudjonsson, Halldor Kiljan
Layamon fl. c. 1200- .... CMLC 10
See also DLB 146
Laye, Camara 1928-1980 .. CLC 4, 38; BLC;
DAM MULT
See also BW 1; CA 85-88; 97-100; CANR 25;
MTCW
Layton, Irving (Peter) 1912-CLC 2, 15; DAC;
DAM MST, POET
See also CA 1-4R; CANR 2, 33, 43; DLB 88;
MTCW
Lazarus, Emma 1849-1887 .... NCLC 8
Lazarus, Felix
See Cable, George Washington
Lazarus, Henry
See Slavitt, David R(ytman)
Lea, Joan
See Neufeld, John (Arthur)
Leacock, Stephen (Butler) 1869-1944TCLC 2;

DAC; DAM MST
See also CA 104; 141; DLB 92
Lear, Edward 1812-1888 .... NCLC 3
See also CLR 1; DLB 32, 163, 166; MAICYA;
SATA 18
Lear, Norman (Milton) 1922- .... CLC 12
See also CA 73-76
Leavis, F(rank) R(aymond) 1895-1978CLC 24
See also CA 21-24R; 77-80; CANR 44; MTCW
Leavitt, David 1961- ..... CLC 34; DAM POP
See also CA 116; 122; CANR 50, 62; DLB 130;
INT 122
Leblanc, Maurice (Marie Emile) 1864-1941
TCLC 49
See also CA 110
Lebowitz, Fran(ces Ann) 1951(?)-CLC 11, 36
See also CA 81-84; CANR 14, 60; INT CANR-
14; MTCW
Lebrecht, Peter
See Tieck, (Johann) Ludwig
le Carre, John .... CLC 3, 5, 9, 15, 28
See also Cornwell, David (John Moore)
See also BEST 89:4; CDBLB 1960 to Present;
DLB 87
Le Clezio, J(ean) M(arie) G(ustave) 1940-
CLC 31
See also CA 116; 128; DLB 83
Leconte de Lisle, Charles-Marie-Rene 1818-
1894 .... NCLC 29
Le Coq, Monsieur
See Simenon, Georges (Jacques Christian)
Leduc, Violette 1907-1972 .... CLC 22
See also CA 13-14; 33-36R; CAP 1
Ledwidge, Francis 1887(?)-1917 .... TCLC 23
See also CA 123; DLB 20
Lee, Andrea 1953-CLC 36; BLC; DAM MULT
See also BW 1; CA 125
Lee, Andrew
See Auchincloss, Louis (Stanton)
Lee, Chang-rae 1965- .... CLC 91
See also CA 148
Lee, Don L. .... CLC 2
See also Madhubuti, Haki R.
Lee, George W(ashington) 1894-1976CLC 52;
BLC; DAM MULT
See also BW 1; CA 125; DLB 51
Lee, (Nelle) Harper 1926- .. CLC 12, 60; DA;
DAB; DAC; DAM MST, NOV; WLC
See also AAYA 13; CA 13-16R; CANR 51;
CDALB 1941-1968; DLB 6; MTCW; SATA
11
Lee, Helen Elaine 1959(?)- .... CLC 86
See also CA 148
Lee, Julian
See Latham, Jean Lee
Lee, Larry
See Lee, Lawrence
Lee, Laurie 1914-1997 CLC 90; DAB; DAM
POP
See also CA 77-80; 158; CANR 33; DLB 27;
MTCW
Lee, Lawrence 1941-1990 .... CLC 34
See also CA 131; CANR 43
Lee, Manfred B(ennington) 1905-1971CLC 11
See also Queen, Ellery
See also CA 1-4R; 29-32R; CANR 2; DLB 137
Lee, Shelton Jackson 1957(?)-CLC 105; DAM
MULT
See also Lee, Spike
See also BW 2; CA 125; CANR 42
Lee, Spike
See Lee, Shelton Jackson
See also AAYA 4

Lee, Stan 1922- .... **CLC 17**
See also AAYA 5; CA 108; 111; INT 111
Lee, Tanith 1947- .... **CLC 46**
See also AAYA 15; CA 37-40R; CANR 53;
SATA 8, 88
Lee, Vernon .... **TCLC 5**
See also Paget, Violet
See also DLB 57, 153, 156, 174, 178
Lee, William
See Burroughs, William S(eward)
Lee, Willy
See Burroughs, William S(eward)
Lee-Hamilton, Eugene (Jacob) 1845-1907
TCLC 22
See also CA 117
Leet, Judith 1935- .... **CLC 11**
Le Fanu, Joseph Sheridan 1814-1873**NCLC 9,**
58; DAM POP; SSC 14
See also DLB 21, 70, 159, 178
Leffland, Ella 1931- .... **CLC 19**
See also CA 29-32R; CANR 35; DLBY 84; INT
CANR-35; SATA 65
Leger, Alexis
See Leger, (Marie-Rene Auguste) Alexis Saint-
Leger
Leger, (Marie-Rene Auguste) Alexis Saint-
Leger 1887-1975 **CLC 11; DAM POET**
See also Perse, St.-John
See also CA 13-16R; 61-64; CANR 43; MTCW
Leger, Saintleger
See Leger, (Marie-Rene Auguste) Alexis Saint-
Leger
Le Guin, Ursula K(roeber) 1929- **CLC 8, 13,**
22, 45, 71; DAB; DAC; DAM MST, POP;
SSC 12
See also AAYA 9; AITN 1; CA 21-24R; CANR
9, 32, 52; CDALB 1968-1988; CLR 3, 28;
DLB 8, 52; INT CANR-32; JRDA; MAICYA;
MTCW; SATA 4, 52
Lehmann, Rosamond (Nina) 1901-1990**CLC 5**
See also CA 77-80; 131; CANR 8; DLB 15
Leiber, Fritz (Reuter, Jr.) 1910-1992 **CLC 25**
See also CA 45-48; 139; CANR 2, 40; DLB 8;
MTCW; SATA 45; SATA-Obit 73
Leibniz, Gottfried Wilhelm von 1646-1716**LC**
35
See also DLB 168
Leimbach, Martha 1963-
See Leimbach, Marti
See also CA 130
Leimbach, Marti .... **CLC 65**
See also Leimbach, Martha
Leino, Eino .... **TCLC 24**
See also Loennbohm, Armas Eino Leopold
Leiris, Michel (Julien) 1901-1990 ..... **CLC 61**
See also CA 119; 128; 132
Leithauser, Brad 1953- .... **CLC 27**
See also CA 107; CANR 27; DLB 120
Lelchuk, Alan 1938- .... **CLC 5**
See also CA 45-48; CAAS 20; CANR 1
Lem, Stanislaw 1921- .... **CLC 8, 15, 40**
See also CA 105; CAAS 1; CANR 32; MTCW
Lemann, Nancy 1956- .... **CLC 39**
See also CA 118; 136
Lemonnier, (Antoine Louis) Camille 1844-1913
TCLC 22
See also CA 121
Lenau, Nikolaus 1802-1850 .... **NCLC 16**
L'Engle, Madeleine (Camp Franklin) 1918-
CLC 12; DAM POP
See also AAYA 1; AITN 2; CA 1-4R; CANR 3,
21, 39; CLR 1, 14; DLB 52; JRDA;
MAICYA; MTCW; SAAS 15; SATA 1, 27,
75
Lengyel, Jozsef 1896-1975 .... **CLC 7**
See also CA 85-88; 57-60
Lenin 1870-1924
See Lenin, V. I.
See also CA 121
Lenin, V. I. .... **TCLC 67**
See also Lenin
Lennon, John (Ono) 1940-1980 . **CLC 12, 35**
See also CA 102
Lennox, Charlotte Ramsay 1729(?)-1804
NCLC 23
See also DLB 39
Lentricchia, Frank (Jr.) 1940- .... **CLC 34**
See also CA 25-28R; CANR 19
Lenz, Siegfried 1926- .... **CLC 27**
See also CA 89-92; DLB 75
Leonard, Elmore (John, Jr.) 1925-**CLC 28, 34,**
71; DAM POP
See also AAYA 22; AITN 1; BEST 89:1, 90:4;
CA 81-84; CANR 12, 28, 53; DLB 173; INT
CANR-28; MTCW
Leonard, Hugh .... **CLC 19**
See Byrne, John Keyes
See also DLB 13
Leonov, Leonid (Maximovich) 1899-1994
CLC 92; DAM NOV
See also CA 129; MTCW
Leopardi, (Conte) Giacomo 1798-1837**NCLC**
22
Le Reveler
See Artaud, Antonin (Marie Joseph)
Lerman, Eleanor 1952- .... **CLC 9**
See also CA 85-88
Lerman, Rhoda 1936- .... **CLC 56**
See also CA 49-52
Lermontov, Mikhail Yuryevich 1814-1841
NCLC 47; PC 18
Leroux, Gaston 1868-1927 .... **TCLC 25**
See also CA 108; 136; SATA 65
Lesage, Alain-Rene 1668-1747 .... **LC 28**
Leskov, Nikolai (Semyonovich) 1831-1895
NCLC 25
Lessing, Doris (May) 1919-**CLC 1, 2, 3, 6, 10,**
15, 22, 40, 94; DA; DAB; DAC; DAM MST,
NOV; SSC 6; WLCS
See also CA 9-12R; CAAS 14; CANR 33, 54;
CDBLB 1960 to Present; DLB 15, 139;
DLBY 85; MTCW
Lessing, Gotthold Ephraim 1729-1781 . **LC 8**
See also DLB 97
Lester, Richard 1932- .... **CLC 20**
Lever, Charles (James) 1806-1872 **NCLC 23**
See also DLB 21
Leverson, Ada 1865(?)-1936(?) ...... **TCLC 18**
See also Elaine
See also CA 117; DLB 153
Levertov, Denise 1923-**CLC 1, 2, 3, 5, 8, 15, 28,**
66; DAM POET; PC 11
See also CA 1-4R; CAAS 19; CANR 3, 29, 50;
DLB 5, 165; INT CANR-29; MTCW
Levi, Jonathan .... **CLC 76**
Levi, Peter (Chad Tigar) 1931- .... **CLC 41**
See also CA 5-8R; CANR 34; DLB 40
Levi, Primo 1919-1987 . **CLC 37, 50; SSC 12**
See also CA 13-16R; 122; CANR 12, 33, 61;
DLB 177; MTCW
Levin, Ira 1929- .... **CLC 3, 6; DAM POP**
See also CA 21-24R; CANR 17, 44; MTCW;
SATA 66
Levin, Meyer 1905-1981 . **CLC 7; DAM POP**
See also AITN 1; CA 9-12R; 104; CANR 15;
DLB 9, 28; DLBY 81; SATA 21; SATA-Obit
27
Levine, Norman 1924- .... **CLC 54**
See also CA 73-76; CAAS 23; CANR 14; DLB
88
Levine, Philip 1928-... **CLC 2, 4, 5, 9, 14, 33;**
DAM POET
See also CA 9-12R; CANR 9, 37, 52; DLB 5
Levinson, Deirdre 1931- .... **CLC 49**
See also CA 73-76
Levi-Strauss, Claude 1908- .... **CLC 38**
See also CA 1-4R; CANR 6, 32, 57; MTCW
Levitin, Sonia (Wolff) 1934- .... **CLC 17**
See also AAYA 13; CA 29-32R; CANR 14, 32;
JRDA; MAICYA; SAAS 2; SATA 4, 68
Levon, O. U.
See Kesey, Ken (Elton)
Levy, Amy 1861-1889 .... **NCLC 59**
See also DLB 156
Lewes, George Henry 1817-1878 ... **NCLC 25**
See also DLB 55, 144
Lewis, Alun 1915-1944 .... **TCLC 3**
See also CA 104; DLB 20, 162
Lewis, C. Day
See Day Lewis, C(ecil)
Lewis, C(live) S(taples) 1898-1963**CLC 1, 3, 6,**
14, 27; DA; DAB; DAC; DAM MST, NOV,
POP; WLC
See also AAYA 3; CA 81-84; CANR 33;
CDBLB 1945-1960; CLR 3, 27; DLB 15,
100, 160; JRDA; MAICYA; MTCW; SATA
13
Lewis, Janet 1899- .... **CLC 41**
See also Winters, Janet Lewis
See also CA 9-12R; CANR 29, 63; CAP 1;
DLBY 87
Lewis, Matthew Gregory 1775-1818**NCLC 11,**
62
See also DLB 39, 158, 178
Lewis, (Harry) Sinclair 1885-1951 . **TCLC 4,**
13, 23, 39; DA; DAB; DAC; DAM MST,
NOV; WLC
See also CA 104; 133; CDALB 1917-1929;
DLB 9, 102; DLBD 1; MTCW
Lewis, (Percy) Wyndham 1882(?)-1957**TCLC**
2, 9
See also CA 104; 157; DLB 15
Lewisohn, Ludwig 1883-1955 .... **TCLC 19**
See also CA 107; DLB 4, 9, 28, 102
Lewton, Val 1904-1951 .... **TCLC 76**
Leyner, Mark 1956- .... **CLC 92**
See also CA 110; CANR 28, 53
Lezama Lima, Jose 1910-1976**CLC 4, 10, 101;**
DAM MULT
See also CA 77-80; DLB 113; HW
L'Heureux, John (Clarke) 1934- .... **CLC 52**
See also CA 13-16R; CANR 23, 45
Liddell, C. H.
See Kuttner, Henry
Lie, Jonas (Lauritz Idemil) 1833-1908(?)
TCLC 5
See also CA 115
Lieber, Joel 1937-1971 .... **CLC 6**
See also CA 73-76; 29-32R
Lieber, Stanley Martin
See Lee, Stan
Lieberman, Laurence (James) 1935- **CLC 4,**
36
See also CA 17-20R; CANR 8, 36
Lieksman, Anders
See Haavikko, Paavo Juhani
Li Fei-kan 1904-
See Pa Chin
See also CA 105

See also DLB 98, 149, 153; SATA 20

Lucas, George 1944- .... CLC 16
  See also AAYA 1; CA 77-80; CANR 30; SATA 56

Lucas, Hans
  See Godard, Jean-Luc

Lucas, Victoria
  See Plath, Sylvia

Ludlam, Charles 1943-1987 .... CLC 46, 50
  See also CA 85-88; 122

Ludlum, Robert 1927-CLC 22, 43; DAM NOV, POP
  See also AAYA 10; BEST 89:1, 90:3; CA 33-36R; CANR 25, 41; DLBY 82; MTCW

Ludwig, Ken .... CLC 60

Ludwig, Otto 1813-1865 .... NCLC 4
  See also DLB 129

Lugones, Leopoldo 1874-1938 .... TCLC 15
  See also CA 116; 131; HW

Lu Hsun 1881-1936 .... TCLC 3; SSC 20
  See also Shu-Jen, Chou

Lukacs, George .... CLC 24
  See also Lukacs, Gyorgy (Szegeny von)

Lukacs, Gyorgy (Szegeny von) 1885-1971
  See Lukacs, George
  See also CA 101; 29-32R; CANR 62

Luke, Peter (Ambrose Cyprian) 1919-1995 CLC 38
  See also CA 81-84; 147; DLB 13

Lunar, Dennis
  See Mungo, Raymond

Lurie, Alison 1926- .... CLC 4, 5, 18, 39
  See also CA 1-4R; CANR 2, 17, 50; DLB 2; MTCW; SATA 46

Lustig, Arnost 1926- .... CLC 56
  See also AAYA 3; CA 69-72; CANR 47; SATA 56

Luther, Martin 1483-1546 .... LC 9, 37
  See also DLB 179

Luxemburg, Rosa 1870(?)-1919 ..... TCLC 63
  See also CA 118

Luzi, Mario 1914- .... CLC 13
  See also CA 61-64; CANR 9; DLB 128

Lyly, John 1554(?)-1606LC 41; DAM DRAM; DC 7
  See also DLB 62, 167

L'Ymagier
  See Gourmont, Remy (-Marie-Charles) de

Lynch, B. Suarez
  See Bioy Casares, Adolfo; Borges, Jorge Luis

Lynch, David (K.) 1946- .... CLC 66
  See also CA 124; 129

Lynch, James
  See Andreyev, Leonid (Nikolaevich)

Lynch Davis, B.
  See Bioy Casares, Adolfo; Borges, Jorge Luis

Lyndsay, Sir David 1490-1555 .... LC 20

Lynn, Kenneth S(chuyler) 1923-....... CLC 50
  See also CA 1-4R; CANR 3, 27

Lynx
  See West, Rebecca

Lyons, Marcus
  See Blish, James (Benjamin)

Lyre, Pinchbeck
  See Sassoon, Siegfried (Lorraine)

Lytle, Andrew (Nelson) 1902-1995 ... CLC 22
  See also CA 9-12R; 150; DLB 6; DLBY 95

Lyttelton, George 1709-1773 .... LC 10

Maas, Peter 1929- .... CLC 29
  See also CA 93-96; INT 93-96

Macaulay, Rose 1881-1958 .... TCLC 7, 44
  See also CA 104; DLB 36

Macaulay, Thomas Babington 1800-1859

NCLC 42
  See also CDBLB 1832-1890; DLB 32, 55

MacBeth, George (Mann) 1932-1992CLC 2, 5, 9
  See also CA 25-28R; 136; CANR 61; DLB 40; MTCW; SATA 4; SATA-Obit 70

MacCaig, Norman (Alexander) 1910-CLC 36; DAB; DAM POET
  See also CA 9-12R; CANR 3, 34; DLB 27

MacCarthy, (Sir Charles Otto) Desmond 1877-1952 .... TCLC 36

MacDiarmid, HughCLC 2, 4, 11, 19, 63; PC 9
  See Grieve, C(hristopher) M(urray)
  See also CDBLB 1945-1960; DLB 20

MacDonald, Anson
  See Heinlein, Robert A(nson)

Macdonald, Cynthia 1928- .... CLC 13, 19
  See also CA 49-52; CANR 4, 44; DLB 105

MacDonald, George 1824-1905 .... TCLC 9
  See also CA 106; 137; DLB 18, 163, 178; MAICYA; SATA 33

Macdonald, John
  See Millar, Kenneth

MacDonald, John D(ann) 1916-1986 CLC 3, 27, 44; DAM NOV, POP
  See also CA 1-4R; 121; CANR 1, 19, 60; DLB 8; DLBY 86; MTCW

Macdonald, John Ross
  See Millar, Kenneth

Macdonald, Ross .... CLC 1, 2, 3, 14, 34, 41
  See also Millar, Kenneth
  See also DLBD 6

MacDougal, John
  See Blish, James (Benjamin)

MacEwen, Gwendolyn (Margaret) 1941-1987 CLC 13, 55
  See also CA 9-12R; 124; CANR 7, 22; DLB 53; SATA 50; SATA-Obit 55

Macha, Karel Hynek 1810-1846 .... NCLC 46

Machado (y Ruiz), Antonio 1875-1939T C L C 3
  See also CA 104; DLB 108

Machado de Assis, Joaquim Maria 1839-1908 TCLC 10; BLC; SSC 24
  See also CA 107; 153

Machen, Arthur .... TCLC 4; SSC 20
  See Jones, Arthur Llewellyn
  See also DLB 36, 156, 178

Machiavelli, Niccolo 1469-1527LC 8, 36; DA; DAB; DAC; DAM MST; WLCS

MacInnes, Colin 1914-1976 .... CLC 4, 23
  See also CA 69-72; 65-68; CANR 21; DLB 14; MTCW

MacInnes, Helen (Clark) 1907-1985 CLC 27, 39; DAM POP
  See also CA 1-4R; 117; CANR 1, 28, 58; DLB 87; MTCW; SATA 22; SATA-Obit 44

Mackay, Mary 1855-1924
  See Corelli, Marie
  See also CA 118

Mackenzie, Compton (Edward Montague) 1883-1972 .... CLC 18
  See also CA 21-22; 37-40R; CAP 2; DLB 34, 100

Mackenzie, Henry 1745-1831 .... NCLC 41
  See also DLB 39

Mackintosh, Elizabeth 1896(?)-1952
  See Tey, Josephine
  See also CA 110

MacLaren, James
  See Grieve, C(hristopher) M(urray)

Mac Laverty, Bernard 1942- .... CLC 31
  See also CA 116; 118; CANR 43; INT 118

MacLean, Alistair (Stuart) 1922(?)-1987C L C 3, 13, 50, 63; DAM POP
  See also CA 57-60; 121; CANR 28, 61; MTCW; SATA 23; SATA-Obit 50

Maclean, Norman (Fitzroy) 1902-1990 C L C 78; DAM POP; SSC 13
  See also CA 102; 132; CANR 49

MacLeish, Archibald 1892-1982CLC 3, 8, 14, 68; DAM POET
  See also CA 9-12R; 106; CANR 33, 63; DLB 4, 7, 45; DLBY 82; MTCW

MacLennan, (John) Hugh 1907-1990 CLC 2, 14, 92; DAC; DAM MST
  See also CA 5-8R; 142; CANR 33; DLB 68; MTCW

MacLeod, Alistair 1936-CLC 56; DAC; DAM MST
  See also CA 123; DLB 60

Macleod, Fiona
  See Sharp, William

MacNeice, (Frederick) Louis 1907-1963 C L C 1, 4, 10, 53; DAB; DAM POET
  See also CA 85-88; CANR 61; DLB 10, 20; MTCW

MacNeill, Dand
  See Fraser, George MacDonald

Macpherson, James 1736-1796 .... LC 29
  See also DLB 109

Macpherson, (Jean) Jay 1931- .... CLC 14
  See also CA 5-8R; DLB 53

MacShane, Frank 1927- .... CLC 39
  See also CA 9-12R; CANR 3, 33; DLB 111

Macumber, Mari
  See Sandoz, Mari(e Susette)

Madach, Imre 1823-1864 .... NCLC 19

Madden, (Jerry) David 1933- .... CLC 5, 15
  See also CA 1-4R; CAAS 3; CANR 4, 45; DLB 6; MTCW

Maddern, Al(an)
  See Ellison, Harlan (Jay)

Madhubuti, Haki R. 1942- CLC 6, 73; BLC; DAM MULT, POET; PC 5
  See Lee, Don L.
  See also BW 2; CA 73-76; CANR 24, 51; DLB 5, 41; DLBD 8

Maepenn, Hugh
  See Kuttner, Henry

Maepenn, K. H.
  See Kuttner, Henry

Maeterlinck, Maurice 1862-1949 ... TCLC 3; DAM DRAM
  See also CA 104; 136; SATA 66

Maginn, William 1794-1842 .... NCLC 8
  See also DLB 110, 159

Mahapatra, Jayanta 1928- .... CLC 33; DAM MULT
  See also CA 73-76; CAAS 9; CANR 15, 33

Mahfouz, Naguib (Abdel Aziz Al-Sabilgi) 1911(?)-
  See Mahfuz, Najib
  See also BEST 89:2; CA 128; CANR 55; DAM NOV; MTCW

Mahfuz, Najib .... CLC 52, 55
  See also Mahfouz, Naguib (Abdel Aziz Al-Sabilgi)
  See also DLBY 88

Mahon, Derek 1941- .... CLC 27
  See also CA 113; 128; DLB 40

Mailer, Norman 1923-CLC 1, 2, 3, 4, 5, 8, 11, 14, 28, 39, 74; DA; DAB; DAC; DAM MST, NOV, POP
  See also AITN 2; CA 9-12R; CABS 1; CANR 28; CDALB 1968-1988; DLB 2, 16, 28;

Miles, Jack .... **CLC 100**
Miles, Josephine (Louise) 1911-1985**CLC 1, 2,
    14, 34, 39; DAM POET**
    See also CA 1-4R; 116; CANR 2, 55; DLB 48
Militant
    See Sandburg, Carl (August)
Mill, John Stuart 1806-1873 .... **NCLC 11, 58**
    See also CDBLB 1832-1890; DLB 55
Millar, Kenneth 1915-1983 .... **CLC 14; DAM
    POP**
    See also Macdonald, Ross
    See also CA 9-12R; 110; CANR 16, 63; DLB
    2; DLBD 6; DLBY 83; MTCW
Millay, E. Vincent
    See Millay, Edna St. Vincent
Millay, Edna St. Vincent 1892-1950**TCLC 4,
    49; DA; DAB; DAC; DAM MST, POET;
    PC 6; WLCS**
    See also CA 104; 130; CDALB 1917-1929;
    DLB 45; MTCW
Miller, Arthur 1915-**CLC 1, 2, 6, 10, 15, 26, 47,
    78; DA; DAB; DAC; DAM DRAM, MST;
    DC 1; WLC**
    See also AAYA 15; AITN 1; CA 1-4R; CABS
    3; CANR 2, 30, 54; CDALB 1941-1968;
    DLB 7; MTCW
Miller, Henry (Valentine) 1891-1980**CLC 1, 2,
    4, 9, 14, 43, 84; DA; DAB; DAC; DAM
    MST, NOV; WLC**
    See also CA 9-12R; 97-100; CANR 33, 64;
    CDALB 1929-1941; DLB 4, 9; DLBY 80;
    MTCW
Miller, Jason 1939(?)- .... **CLC 2**
    See also AITN 1; CA 73-76; DLB 7
Miller, Sue 1943- .... **CLC 44; DAM POP**
    See also BEST 90:3; CA 139; CANR 59; DLB
    143
Miller, Walter M(ichael, Jr.) 1923-**CLC 4, 30**
    See also CA 85-88; DLB 8
Millett, Kate 1934- .... **CLC 67**
    See also AITN 1; CA 73-76; CANR 32, 53;
    MTCW
Millhauser, Steven (Lewis) 1943- **CLC 21, 54**
    See also CA 110; 111; CANR 63; DLB 2; INT
    111
Millin, Sarah Gertrude 1889-1968 ... **CLC 49**
    See also CA 102; 93-96
Milne, A(lan) A(lexander) 1882-1956**TCLC 6;
    DAB; DAC; DAM MST**
    See also CA 104; 133; CLR 1, 26; DLB 10, 77,
    100, 160; MAICYA; MTCW; YABC 1
Milner, Ron(ald) 1938- **CLC 56; BLC; DAM
    MULT**
    See also AITN 1; BW 1; CA 73-76; CANR 24;
    DLB 38; MTCW
Milnes, Richard Monckton 1809-1885**NCLC
    61**
    See also DLB 32, 184
Milosz, Czeslaw 1911- **CLC 5, 11, 22, 31, 56,
    82; DAM MST, POET; PC 8; WLCS**
    See also CA 81-84; CANR 23, 51; MTCW
Milton, John 1608-1674 ..... **LC 9; DA; DAB;
    DAC; DAM MST, POET; PC 19; WLC**
    See also CDBLB 1660-1789; DLB 131, 151
Min, Anchee 1957- .... **CLC 86**
    See also CA 146
Minehaha, Cornelius
    See Wedekind, (Benjamin) Frank(lin)
Miner, Valerie 1947- .... **CLC 40**
    See also CA 97-100; CANR 59
Minimo, Duca
    See D'Annunzio, Gabriele
Minot, Susan 1956- .... **CLC 44**

See also CA 134
Minus, Ed 1938- .... **CLC 39**
Miranda, Javier
    See Bioy Casares, Adolfo
Mirbeau, Octave 1848-1917 .... **TCLC 55**
    See also DLB 123
Miro (Ferrer), Gabriel (Francisco Victor) 1879-
    1930 .... **TCLC 5**
    See also CA 104
Mishima, Yukio 1925-1970**CLC 2, 4, 6, 9, 27;
    DC 1; SSC 4**
    See also Hiraoka, Kimitake
    See also DLB 182
Mistral, Frederic 1830-1914 .... **TCLC 51**
    See also CA 122
Mistral, Gabriela .... **TCLC 2; HLC**
    See also Godoy Alcayaga, Lucila
Mistry, Rohinton 1952- .... **CLC 71; DAC**
    See also CA 141
Mitchell, Clyde
    See Ellison, Harlan (Jay); Silverberg, Robert
Mitchell, James Leslie 1901-1935
    See Gibbon, Lewis Grassic
    See also CA 104; DLB 15
Mitchell, Joni 1943- .... **CLC 12**
    See also CA 112
Mitchell, Joseph (Quincy) 1908-1996**CLC 98**
    See also CA 77-80; 152; DLBY 96
Mitchell, Margaret (Munnerlyn) 1900-1949
    TCLC 11; DAM NOV, POP
    See also CA 109; 125; CANR 55; DLB 9;
    MTCW
Mitchell, Peggy
    See Mitchell, Margaret (Munnerlyn)
Mitchell, S(ilas) Weir 1829-1914 ... **TCLC 36**
Mitchell, W(illiam) O(rmond) 1914-**CLC 25;
    DAC; DAM MST**
    See also CA 77-80; CANR 15, 43; DLB 88
Mitford, Mary Russell 1787-1855 ... **NCLC 4**
    See also DLB 110, 116
Mitford, Nancy 1904-1973 .... **CLC 44**
    See also CA 9-12R
Miyamoto, Yuriko 1899-1951 .... **TCLC 37**
    See also DLB 180
Miyazawa Kenji 1896-1933 .... **TCLC 76**
    See also CA 157
Mizoguchi, Kenji 1898-1956 .... **TCLC 72**
Mo, Timothy (Peter) 1950(?)- .... **CLC 46**
    See also CA 117; MTCW
Modarressi, Taghi (M.) 1931- .... **CLC 44**
    See also CA 121; 134; INT 134
Modiano, Patrick (Jean) 1945- .... **CLC 18**
    See also CA 85-88; CANR 17, 40; DLB 83
Moerck, Paal
    See Roelvaag, O(le) E(dvart)
Mofolo, Thomas (Mokopu) 1875(?)-1948
    TCLC 22; BLC; DAM MULT
    See also CA 121; 153
Mohr, Nicholasa 1938-**CLC 12; DAM MULT;
    HLC**
    See also AAYA 8; CA 49-52; CANR 1, 32, 64;
    CLR 22; DLB 145; HW; JRDA; SAAS 8;
    SATA 8
Mojtabai, A(nn) G(race) 1938- **CLC 5, 9, 15,
    29**
    See also CA 85-88
Moliere 1622-1673 . **LC 28; DA; DAB; DAC;
    DAM DRAM, MST; WLC**
Molin, Charles
    See Mayne, William (James Carter)
Molnar, Ferenc 1878-1952 .. **TCLC 20; DAM
    DRAM**
    See also CA 109; 153

Momaday, N(avarre) Scott 1934- **CLC 2, 19,
    85, 95; DA; DAB; DAC; DAM MST,
    MULT, NOV, POP; WLCS**
    See also AAYA 11; CA 25-28R; CANR 14, 34;
    DLB 143, 175; INT CANR-14; MTCW;
    NNAL; SATA 48; SATA-Brief 30
Monette, Paul 1945-1995 .... **CLC 82**
    See also CA 139; 147
Monroe, Harriet 1860-1936 .... **TCLC 12**
    See also CA 109; DLB 54, 91
Monroe, Lyle
    See Heinlein, Robert A(nson)
Montagu, Elizabeth 1917- .... **NCLC 7**
    See also CA 9-12R
Montagu, Mary (Pierrepont) Wortley 1689-
    1762 .... **LC 9; PC 16**
    See also DLB 95, 101
Montagu, W. H.
    See Coleridge, Samuel Taylor
Montague, John (Patrick) 1929- **CLC 13, 46**
    See also CA 9-12R; CANR 9; DLB 40; MTCW
Montaigne, Michel (Eyquem) de 1533-1592
    LC 8; DA; DAB; DAC; DAM MST; WLC
Montale, Eugenio 1896-1981**CLC 7, 9, 18; PC
    13**
    See also CA 17-20R; 104; CANR 30; DLB 114;
    MTCW
Montesquieu, Charles-Louis de Secondat 1689-
    1755 .... **LC 7**
Montgomery, (Robert) Bruce 1921-1978
    See Crispin, Edmund
    See also CA 104
Montgomery, L(ucy) M(aud) 1874-1942
    TCLC 51; DAC; DAM MST
    See also AAYA 12; CA 108; 137; CLR 8; DLB
    92; DLBD 14; JRDA; MAICYA; YABC 1
Montgomery, Marion H., Jr. 1925- .... **CLC 7**
    See also AITN 1; CA 1-4R; CANR 3, 48; DLB
    6
Montgomery, Max
    See Davenport, Guy (Mattison, Jr.)
Montherlant, Henry (Milon) de 1896-1972
    CLC 8, 19; DAM DRAM
    See also CA 85-88; 37-40R; DLB 72; MTCW
Monty Python
    See Chapman, Graham; Cleese, John
    (Marwood); Gilliam, Terry (Vance); Idle,
    Eric; Jones, Terence Graham Parry; Palin,
    Michael (Edward)
    See also AAYA 7
Moodie, Susanna (Strickland) 1803-1885
    NCLC 14
    See also DLB 99
Mooney, Edward 1951-
    See Mooney, Ted
    See also CA 130
Mooney, Ted .... **CLC 25**
    See also Mooney, Edward
Moorcock, Michael (John) 1939-**CLC 5, 27, 58**
    See also CA 45-48; CAAS 5; CANR 2, 17, 38,
    64; DLB 14; MTCW; SATA 93
Moore, Brian 1921- **CLC 1, 3, 5, 7, 8, 19, 32,
    90; DAB; DAC; DAM MST**
    See also CA 1-4R; CANR 1, 25, 42, 63; MTCW
Moore, Edward
    See Muir, Edwin
Moore, George Augustus 1852-1933**TCLC 7;
    SSC 19**
    See also CA 104; DLB 10, 18, 57, 135
Moore, Lorrie .... **CLC 39, 45, 68**
    See also Moore, Marie Lorena
Moore, Marianne (Craig) 1887-1972**CLC 1, 2,
    4, 8, 10, 13, 19, 47; DA; DAB; DAC; DAM**

See also CA 109; CANR 55; DLB 81, 124
Muske, Carol 1945- .... **CLC 90**
  See also Muske-Dukes, Carol (Anne)
Muske-Dukes, Carol (Anne) 1945-
  See Muske, Carol
  See also CA 65-68; CANR 32
Musset, (Louis Charles) Alfred de 1810-1857
  NCLC 7
My Brother's Brother
  See Chekhov, Anton (Pavlovich)
Myers, L(eopold) H(amilton) 1881-1944
  TCLC 59
  See also CA 157; DLB 15
Myers, Walter Dean 1937- ..... **CLC 35; BLC;
  DAM MULT, NOV**
  See also AAYA 4; BW 2; CA 33-36R; CANR
  20, 42; CLR 4, 16, 35; DLB 33; INT CANR-
  20; JRDA; MAICYA; SAAS 2; SATA 41, 71;
  SATA-Brief 27
Myers, Walter M.
  See Myers, Walter Dean
Myles, Symon
  See Follett, Ken(neth Martin)
Nabokov, Vladimir (Vladimirovich) 1899-1977
  **CLC 1, 2, 3, 6, 8, 11, 15, 23, 44, 46, 64;
  DA; DAB; DAC; DAM MST, NOV; SSC
  11; WLC**
  See also CA 5-8R; 69-72; CANR 20; CDALB
  1941-1968; DLB 2; DLBD 3; DLBY 80, 91;
  MTCW
Nagai Kafu 1879-1959 .... **TCLC 51**
  See also Nagai Sokichi
  See also DLB 180
Nagai Sokichi 1879-1959
  See Nagai Kafu
  See also CA 117
Nagy, Laszlo 1925-1978 .... **CLC 7**
  See also CA 129; 112
Naipaul, Shiva(dhar Srinivasa) 1945-1985
  CLC 32, 39; DAM NOV
  See also CA 110; 112; 116; CANR 33; DLB
  157; DLBY 85; MTCW
Naipaul, V(idiadhar) S(urajprasad) 1932-
  **CLC 4, 7, 9, 13, 18, 37, 105; DAB; DAC;
  DAM MST, NOV**
  See also CA 1-4R; CANR 1, 33, 51; CDBLB
  1960 to Present; DLB 125; DLBY 85;
  MTCW
Nakos, Lilika 1899(?)- .... **CLC 29**
Narayan, R(asipuram) K(rishnaswami) 1906-
  CLC 7, 28, 47; DAM NOV; SSC 25
  See also CA 81-84; CANR 33, 61; MTCW;
  SATA 62
Nash, (Frediric) Ogden 1902-1971 . **CLC 23;
  DAM POET; PC 21**
  See also CA 13-14; 29-32R; CANR 34, 61; CAP
  1; DLB 11; MAICYA; MTCW; SATA 2, 46
Nashe, Thomas 1567-1601 .... **LC 41**
Nathan, Daniel
  See Dannay, Frederic
Nathan, George Jean 1882-1958 .... **TCLC 18**
  See also Hatteras, Owen
  See also CA 114; DLB 137
Natsume, Kinnosuke 1867-1916
  See Natsume, Soseki
  See also CA 104
Natsume, Soseki 1867-1916 .... **TCLC 2, 10**
  See also Natsume, Kinnosuke
  See also DLB 180
Natti, (Mary) Lee 1919-
  See Kingman, Lee
  See also CA 5-8R; CANR 2
Naylor, Gloria 1950- **CLC 28, 52; BLC; DA;**

**DAC; DAM MST, MULT, NOV, POP;
WLCS**
  See also AAYA 6; BW 2; CA 107; CANR 27,
  51; DLB 173; MTCW
Neihardt, John Gneisenau 1881-1973**CLC 32**
  See also CA 13-14; CAP 1; DLB 9, 54
Nekrasov, Nikolai Alekseevich 1821-1878
  NCLC 11
Nelligan, Emile 1879-1941 .... **TCLC 14**
  See also CA 114; DLB 92
Nelson, Willie 1933- .... **CLC 17**
  See also CA 107
Nemerov, Howard (Stanley) 1920-1991**CLC 2,
  6, 9, 36; DAM POET**
  See also CA 1-4R; 134; CABS 2; CANR 1, 27,
  53; DLB 5, 6; DLBY 83; INT CANR-27;
  MTCW
Neruda, Pablo 1904-1973**CLC 1, 2, 5, 7, 9, 28,
  62; DA; DAB; DAC; DAM MST, MULT,
  POET; HLC; PC 4; WLC**
  See also CA 19-20; 45-48; CAP 2; HW; MTCW
Nerval, Gerard de 1808-1855**NCLC 1, 67; PC
  13; SSC 18**
Nervo, (Jose) Amado (Ruiz de) 1870-1919
  TCLC 11
  See also CA 109; 131; HW
Nessi, Pio Baroja y
  See Baroja (y Nessi), Pio
Nestroy, Johann 1801-1862 .... **NCLC 42**
  See also DLB 133
Netterville, Luke
  See O'Grady, Standish (James)
Neufeld, John (Arthur) 1938- .... **CLC 17**
  See also AAYA 11; CA 25-28R; CANR 11, 37,
  56; MAICYA; SAAS 3; SATA 6, 81
Neville, Emily Cheney 1919- .... **CLC 12**
  See also CA 5-8R; CANR 3, 37; JRDA;
  MAICYA; SAAS 2; SATA 1
Newbound, Bernard Slade 1930-
  See Slade, Bernard
  See also CA 81-84; CANR 49; DAM DRAM
Newby, P(ercy) H(oward) 1918-1997 **CLC 2,
  13; DAM NOV**
  See also CA 5-8R; 161; CANR 32; DLB 15;
  MTCW
Newlove, Donald 1928- .... **CLC 6**
  See also CA 29-32R; CANR 25
Newlove, John (Herbert) 1938- .... **CLC 14**
  See also CA 21-24R; CANR 9, 25
Newman, Charles 1938- .... **CLC 2, 8**
  See also CA 21-24R
Newman, Edwin (Harold) 1919- .... **CLC 14**
  See also AITN 1; CA 69-72; CANR 5
Newman, John Henry 1801-1890 .. **NCLC 38**
  See also DLB 18, 32, 55
Newton, Suzanne 1936- .... **CLC 35**
  See also CA 41-44R; CANR 14; JRDA; SATA
  5, 77
Nexo, Martin Andersen 1869-1954 **TCLC 43**
Nezval, Vitezslav 1900-1958 .... **TCLC 44**
  See also CA 123
Ng, Fae Myenne 1957(?)- .... **CLC 81**
  See also CA 146
Ngema, Mbongeni 1955- .... **CLC 57**
  See also BW 2; CA 143
Ngugi, James T(hiong'o) .... **CLC 3, 7, 13**
  See also Ngugi wa Thiong'o
Ngugi wa Thiong'o 1938-**CLC 36; BLC; DAM
  MULT, NOV**
  See also Ngugi, James T(hiong'o)
  See also BW 2; CA 81-84; CANR 27, 58; DLB
  125; MTCW
Nichol, B(arrie) P(hillip) 1944-1988 **CLC 18**

See also CA 53-56; DLB 53; SATA 66
Nichols, John (Treadwell) 1940- .... **CLC 38**
  See also CA 9-12R; CAAS 2; CANR 6; DLBY
  82
Nichols, Leigh
  See Koontz, Dean R(ay)
Nichols, Peter (Richard) 1927- **CLC 5, 36, 65**
  See also CA 104; CANR 33; DLB 13; MTCW
Nicolas, F. R. E.
  See Freeling, Nicolas
Niedecker, Lorine 1903-1970 .... **CLC 10, 42;
  DAM POET**
  See also CA 25-28; CAP 2; DLB 48
Nietzsche, Friedrich (Wilhelm) 1844-1900
  TCLC 10, 18, 55
  See also CA 107; 121; DLB 129
Nievo, Ippolito 1831-1861 .... **NCLC 22**
Nightingale, Anne Redmon 1943-
  See Redmon, Anne
  See also CA 103
Nik. T. O.
  See Annensky, Innokenty (Fyodorovich)
Nin, Anais 1903-1977 **CLC 1, 4, 8, 11, 14, 60;
  DAM NOV, POP; SSC 10**
  See also AITN 2; CA 13-16R; 69-72; CANR
  22, 53; DLB 2, 4, 152; MTCW
Nishiwaki, Junzaburo 1894-1982 .... **PC 15**
  See also CA 107
Nissenson, Hugh 1933- .... **CLC 4, 9**
  See also CA 17-20R; CANR 27; DLB 28
Niven, Larry .... **CLC 8**
  See also Niven, Laurence Van Cott
  See also DLB 8
Niven, Laurence Van Cott 1938-
  See Niven, Larry
  See also CA 21-24R; CAAS 12; CANR 14, 44;
  DAM POP; MTCW; SATA 95
Nixon, Agnes Eckhardt 1927- .... **CLC 21**
  See also CA 110
Nizan, Paul 1905-1940 .... **TCLC 40**
  See also CA 161; DLB 72
Nkosi, Lewis 1936- .... **CLC 45; BLC; DAM
  MULT**
  See also BW 1; CA 65-68; CANR 27; DLB 157
Nodier, (Jean) Charles (Emmanuel) 1780-1844
  NCLC 19
  See also DLB 119
Nolan, Christopher 1965- .... **CLC 58**
  See also CA 111
Noon, Jeff 1957- .... **CLC 91**
  See also CA 148
Norden, Charles
  See Durrell, Lawrence (George)
Nordhoff, Charles (Bernard) 1887-1947
  TCLC 23
  See also CA 108; DLB 9; SATA 23
Norfolk, Lawrence 1963- .... **CLC 76**
  See also CA 144
Norman, Marsha 1947-**CLC 28; DAM DRAM;
  DC 8**
  See also CA 105; CABS 3; CANR 41; DLBY
  84
Norris, Frank 1870-1902 .... **SSC 28**
  See also Norris, (Benjamin) Frank(lin, Jr.)
  See also CDALB 1865-1917; DLB 12, 71
Norris, (Benjamin) Frank(lin, Jr.) 1870-1902
  TCLC 24
  See also Norris, Frank
  See also CA 110; 160
Norris, Leslie 1921- .... **CLC 14**
  See also CA 11-12; CANR 14; CAP 1; DLB 27
North, Andrew
  See Norton, Andre

North, Anthony
  See Koontz, Dean R(ay)
North, Captain George
  See Stevenson, Robert Louis (Balfour)
North, Milou
  See Erdrich, Louise
Northrup, B. A.
  See Hubbard, L(afayette) Ron(ald)
North Staffs
  See Hulme, T(homas) E(rnest)
Norton, Alice Mary
  See Norton, Andre
  See also MAICYA; SATA 1, 43
Norton, Andre 1912- .... CLC 12
  See also Norton, Alice Mary
  See also AAYA 14; CA 1-4R; CANR 2, 31; DLB
    8, 52; JRDA; MTCW; SATA 91
Norton, Caroline 1808-1877 .... NCLC 47
  See also DLB 21, 159
Norway, Nevil Shute 1899-1960
  See Shute, Nevil
  See also CA 102; 93-96
Norwid, Cyprian Kamil 1821-1883 NCLC 17
Nosille, Nabrah
  See Ellison, Harlan (Jay)
Nossack, Hans Erich 1901-1978 .... CLC 6
  See also CA 93-96; 85-88; DLB 69
Nostradamus 1503-1566 .... LC 27
Nosu, Chuji
  See Ozu, Yasujiro
Notenburg, Eleanora (Genrikhovna) von
  See Guro, Elena
Nova, Craig 1945- .... CLC 7, 31
  See also CA 45-48; CANR 2, 53
Novak, Joseph
  See Kosinski, Jerzy (Nikodem)
Novalis 1772-1801 .... NCLC 13
  See also DLB 90
Novis, Emile
  See Weil, Simone (Adolphine)
Nowlan, Alden (Albert) 1933-1983 CLC 15;
    DAC; DAM MST
  See also CA 9-12R; CANR 5; DLB 53
Noyes, Alfred 1880-1958 .... TCLC 7
  See also CA 104; DLB 20
Nunn, Kem .... CLC 34
  See also CA 159
Nye, Robert 1939- .. CLC 13, 42; DAM NOV
  See also CA 33-36R; CANR 29; DLB 14;
    MTCW; SATA 6
Nyro, Laura 1947- .... CLC 17
Oates, Joyce Carol 1938-CLC 1, 2, 3, 6, 9, 11,
    15, 19, 33, 52; DA; DAB; DAC; DAM MST,
    NOV, POP; SSC 6; WLC
  See also AAYA 15; AITN 1; BEST 89:2; CA 5-
    8R; CANR 25, 45; CDALB 1968-1988; DLB
    2, 5, 130; DLBY 81; INT CANR-25; MTCW
O'Brien, Darcy 1939- .... CLC 11
  See also CA 21-24R; CANR 8, 59
O'Brien, E. G.
  See Clarke, Arthur C(harles)
O'Brien, Edna 1936- CLC 3, 5, 8, 13, 36, 65;
    DAM NOV; SSC 10
  See also CA 1-4R; CANR 6, 41; CDBLB 1960
    to Present; DLB 14; MTCW
O'Brien, Fitz-James 1828-1862 ..... NCLC 21
  See also DLB 74
O'Brien, Flann .... CLC 1, 4, 5, 7, 10, 47
  See also O Nuallain, Brian
O'Brien, Richard 1942- .... CLC 17
  See also CA 124
O'Brien, (William) Tim(othy) 1946- . CLC 7,
    19, 40, 103; DAM POP

  See also AAYA 16; CA 85-88; CANR 40, 58;
    DLB 152; DLBD 9; DLBY 80
Obstfelder, Sigbjoern 1866-1900 ... TCLC 23
  See also CA 123
O'Casey, Sean 1880-1964CLC 1, 5, 9, 11, 15,
    88; DAB; DAC; DAM DRAM, MST;
    WLCS
  See also CA 89-92; CANR 62; CDBLB 1914-
    1945; DLB 10; MTCW
O'Cathasaigh, Sean
  See O'Casey, Sean
Ochs, Phil 1940-1976 .... CLC 17
  See also CA 65-68
O'Connor, Edwin (Greene) 1918-1968CLC 14
  See also CA 93-96; 25-28R
O'Connor, (Mary) Flannery 1925-1964 C L C
    1, 2, 3, 6, 10, 13, 15, 21, 66, 104; DA; DAB;
    DAC; DAM MST, NOV; SSC 1, 23; WLC
  See also AAYA 7; CA 1-4R; CANR 3, 41;
    CDALB 1941-1968; DLB 2, 152; DLBD 12;
    DLBY 80; MTCW
O'Connor, Frank .... CLC 23; SSC 5
  See also O'Donovan, Michael John
  See also DLB 162
O'Dell, Scott 1898-1989 .... CLC 30
  See also AAYA 3; CA 61-64; 129; CANR 12,
    30; CLR 1, 16; DLB 52; JRDA; MAICYA;
    SATA 12, 60
Odets, Clifford 1906-1963CLC 2, 28, 98; DAM
    DRAM; DC 6
  See also CA 85-88; CANR 62; DLB 7, 26;
    MTCW
O'Doherty, Brian 1934- .... CLC 76
  See also CA 105
O'Donnell, K. M.
  See Malzberg, Barry N(athaniel)
O'Donnell, Lawrence
  See Kuttner, Henry
O'Donovan, Michael John 1903-1966CLC 14
  See also O'Connor, Frank
  See also CA 93-96
Oe, Kenzaburo 1935- CLC 10, 36, 86; DAM
    NOV; SSC 20
  See also CA 97-100; CANR 36, 50; DLB 182;
    DLBY 94; MTCW
O'Faolain, Julia 1932- .... CLC 6, 19, 47
  See also CA 81-84; CAAS 2; CANR 12, 61;
    DLB 14; MTCW
O'Faolain, Sean 1900-1991 CLC 1, 7, 14, 32,
    70; SSC 13
  See also CA 61-64; 134; CANR 12; DLB 15,
    162; MTCW
O'Flaherty, Liam 1896-1984CLC 5, 34; SSC 6
  See also CA 101; 113; CANR 35; DLB 36, 162;
    DLBY 84; MTCW
Ogilvy, Gavin
  See Barrie, J(ames) M(atthew)
O'Grady, Standish (James) 1846-1928T C L C
    5
  See also CA 104; 157
O'Grady, Timothy 1951- .... CLC 59
  See also CA 138
O'Hara, Frank 1926-1966 . CLC 2, 5, 13, 78;
    DAM POET
  See also CA 9-12R; 25-28R; CANR 33; DLB
    5, 16; MTCW
O'Hara, John (Henry) 1905-1970CLC 1, 2, 3,
    6, 11, 42; DAM NOV; SSC 15
  See also CA 5-8R; 25-28R; CANR 31, 60;
    CDALB 1929-1941; DLB 9, 86; DLBD 2;
    MTCW
O Hehir, Diana 1922- .... CLC 41
  See also CA 93-96

Okigbo, Christopher (Ifenayichukwu) 1932-
    1967 .... CLC 25, 84; BLC; DAM MULT,
    POET; PC 7
  See also BW 1; CA 77-80; DLB 125; MTCW
Okri, Ben 1959- .... CLC 87
  See also BW 2; CA 130; 138; DLB 157; INT
    138
Olds, Sharon 1942- .... CLC 32, 39, 85; DAM
    POET
  See also CA 101; CANR 18, 41; DLB 120
Oldstyle, Jonathan
  See Irving, Washington
Olesha, Yuri (Karlovich) 1899-1960 .. CLC 8
  See also CA 85-88
Oliphant, Laurence 1829(?)-1888 .. NCLC 47
  See also DLB 18, 166
Oliphant, Margaret (Oliphant Wilson) 1828-
    1897 .... NCLC 11, 61; SSC 25
  See also DLB 18, 159
Oliver, Mary 1935- .... CLC 19, 34, 98
  See also CA 21-24R; CANR 9, 43; DLB 5
Olivier, Laurence (Kerr) 1907-1989 . CLC 20
  See also CA 111; 150; 129
Olsen, Tillie 1913-CLC 4, 13; DA; DAB; DAC;
    DAM MST; SSC 11
  See also CA 1-4R; CANR 1, 43; DLB 28; DLBY
    80; MTCW
Olson, Charles (John) 1910-1970CLC 1, 2, 5,
    6, 9, 11, 29; DAM POET; PC 19
  See also CA 13-16; 25-28R; CABS 2; CANR
    35, 61; CAP 1; DLB 5, 16; MTCW
Olson, Toby 1937- .... CLC 28
  See also CA 65-68; CANR 9, 31
Olyesha, Yuri
  See Olesha, Yuri (Karlovich)
Ondaatje, (Philip) Michael 1943-CLC 14, 29,
    51, 76; DAB; DAC; DAM MST
  See also CA 77-80; CANR 42; DLB 60
Oneal, Elizabeth 1934-
  See Oneal, Zibby
  See also CA 106; CANR 28; MAICYA; SATA
    30, 82
Oneal, Zibby .... CLC 30
  See also Oneal, Elizabeth
  See also AAYA 5; CLR 13; JRDA
O'Neill, Eugene (Gladstone) 1888-1953TCLC
    1, 6, 27, 49; DA; DAB; DAC; DAM DRAM,
    MST; WLC
  See also AITN 1; CA 110; 132; CDALB 1929-
    1941; DLB 7; MTCW
Onetti, Juan Carlos 1909-1994 ... CLC 7, 10;
    DAM MULT, NOV; SSC 23
  See also CA 85-88; 145; CANR 32, 63; DLB
    113; HW; MTCW
O Nuallain, Brian 1911-1966
  See O'Brien, Flann
  See also CA 21-22; 25-28R; CAP 2
Opie, Amelia 1769-1853 .... NCLC 65
  See also DLB 116, 159
Oppen, George 1908-1984 ...... CLC 7, 13, 34
  See also CA 13-16R; 113; CANR 8; DLB 5,
    165
Oppenheim, E(dward) Phillips 1866-1946
    TCLC 45
  See also CA 111; DLB 70
Origen c. 185-c. 254 .... CMLC 19
Orlovitz, Gil 1918-1973 .... CLC 22
  See also CA 77-80; 45-48; DLB 2, 5
Orris
  See Ingelow, Jean
Ortega y Gasset, Jose 1883-1955 .... TCLC 9;
    DAM MULT; HLC
  See also CA 106; 130; HW; MTCW

Ortese, Anna Maria 1914- .... **CLC 89**
See also DLB 177
Ortiz, Simon J(oseph) 1941-..**CLC 45; DAM
MULT, POET; PC 17**
See also CA 134; DLB 120, 175; NNAL
Orton, Joe .... **CLC 4, 13, 43; DC 3**
See also Orton, John Kingsley
See also CDBLB 1960 to Present; DLB 13
Orton, John Kingsley 1933-1967
See Orton, Joe
See also CA 85-88; CANR 35; DAM DRAM;
MTCW
Orwell, George . **TCLC 2, 6, 15, 31, 51; DAB;
WLC**
See also Blair, Eric (Arthur)
See also CDBLB 1945-1960; DLB 15, 98
Osborne, David
See Silverberg, Robert
Osborne, George
See Silverberg, Robert
Osborne, John (James) 1929-1994**CLC 1, 2, 5,
11, 45; DA; DAB; DAC; DAM DRAM,
MST; WLC**
See also CA 13-16R; 147; CANR 21, 56;
CDBLB 1945-1960; DLB 13; MTCW
Osborne, Lawrence 1958-.................. **CLC 50**
Oshima, Nagisa 1932-........................ **CLC 20**
See also CA 116; 121
Oskison, John Milton 1874-1947 .. **TCLC 35;
DAM MULT**
See also CA 144; DLB 175; NNAL
Ossoli, Sarah Margaret (Fuller marchesa d')
1810-1850
See Fuller, Margaret
See also SATA 25
Ostrovsky, Alexander 1823-1886**NCLC 30, 57**
Otero, Blas de 1916-1979 .... **CLC 11**
See also CA 89-92; DLB 134
Otto, Whitney 1955- .... **CLC 70**
See also CA 140
Ouida .... **TCLC 43**
See also De La Ramee, (Marie) Louise
See also DLB 18, 156
Ousmane, Sembene 1923- .... **CLC 66; BLC**
See also BW 1; CA 117; 125; MTCW
Ovid 43B.C.-18(?)**CMLC 7; DAM POET; PC
2**
Owen, Hugh
See Faust, Frederick (Schiller)
Owen, Wilfred (Edward Salter) 1893-1918
**TCLC 5, 27; DA; DAB; DAC; DAM MST,
POET; PC 19; WLC**
See also CA 104; 141; CDBLB 1914-1945;
DLB 20
Owens, Rochelle 1936- .... **CLC 8**
See also CA 17-20R; CAAS 2; CANR 39
Oz, Amos 1939-**CLC 5, 8, 11, 27, 33, 54; DAM
NOV**
See also CA 53-56; CANR 27, 47; MTCW
Ozick, Cynthia 1928- **CLC 3, 7, 28, 62; DAM
NOV, POP; SSC 15**
See also BEST 90:1; CA 17-20R; CANR 23,
58; DLB 28, 152; DLBY 82; INT CANR-
23; MTCW
Ozu, Yasujiro 1903-1963 .... **CLC 16**
See also CA 112
Pacheco, C.
See Pessoa, Fernando (Antonio Nogueira)
Pa Chin .... **CLC 18**
See also Li Fei-kan
Pack, Robert 1929- .... **CLC 13**
See also CA 1-4R; CANR 3, 44; DLB 5
Padgett, Lewis

See Kuttner, Henry
Padilla (Lorenzo), Heberto 1932- ..... **CLC 38**
See also AITN 1; CA 123; 131; HW
Page, Jimmy 1944-............................... **CLC 12**
Page, Louise 1955- .... **CLC 40**
See also CA 140
Page, P(atricia) K(athleen) 1916- **CLC 7, 18;
DAC; DAM MST; PC 12**
See also CA 53-56; CANR 4, 22; DLB 68;
MTCW
Page, Thomas Nelson 1853-1922 .... **SSC 23**
See also CA 118; DLB 12, 78; DLBD 13
Pagels, Elaine Hiesey 1943- .... **CLC 104**
See also CA 45-48; CANR 2, 24, 51
Paget, Violet 1856-1935
See Lee, Vernon
See also CA 104
Paget-Lowe, Henry
See Lovecraft, H(oward) P(hillips)
Paglia, Camille (Anna) 1947- .... **CLC 68**
See also CA 140
Paige, Richard
See Koontz, Dean R(ay)
Paine, Thomas 1737-1809 .... **NCLC 62**
See also CDALB 1640-1865; DLB 31, 43, 73,
158
Pakenham, Antonia
See Fraser, (Lady) Antonia (Pakenham)
Palamas, Kostes 1859-1943 .... **TCLC 5**
See also CA 105
Palazzeschi, Aldo 1885-1974 .... **CLC 11**
See also CA 89-92; 53-56; DLB 114
Paley, Grace 1922-**CLC 4, 6, 37; DAM POP;
SSC 8**
See also CA 25-28R; CANR 13, 46; DLB 28;
INT CANR-13; MTCW
Palin, Michael (Edward) 1943- .... **CLC 21**
See also Monty Python
See also CA 107; CANR 35; SATA 67
Palliser, Charles 1947- .... **CLC 65**
See also CA 136
Palma, Ricardo 1833-1919 .... **TCLC 29**
Pancake, Breece Dexter 1952-1979
See Pancake, Breece D'J
See also CA 123; 109
Pancake, Breece D'J .... **CLC 29**
See also Pancake, Breece Dexter
See also DLB 130
Panko, Rudy
See Gogol, Nikolai (Vasilyevich)
Papadiamantis, Alexandros 1851-1911**TCLC
29**
Papadiamantopoulos, Johannes 1856-1910
See Moreas, Jean
See also CA 117
Papini, Giovanni 1881-1956 .... **TCLC 22**
See also CA 121
Paracelsus 1493-1541 .... **LC 14**
See also DLB 179
Parasol, Peter
See Stevens, Wallace
Pareto, Vilfredo 1848-1923 .... **TCLC 69**
Parfenie, Maria
See Codrescu, Andrei
Parini, Jay (Lee) 1948-....................... **CLC 54**
See also CA 97-100; CAAS 16; CANR 32
Park, Jordan
See Kornbluth, C(yril) M.; Pohl, Frederik
Park, Robert E(zra) 1864-1944 ...... **TCLC 73**
See also CA 122
Parker, Bert
See Ellison, Harlan (Jay)
Parker, Dorothy (Rothschild) 1893-1967**C L C**

15, 68; DAM POET; SSC 2
See also CA 19-20; 25-28R; CAP 2; DLB 11,
45, 86; MTCW
Parker, Robert B(rown) 1932-**CLC 27; DAM
NOV, POP**
See also BEST 89:4; CA 49-52; CANR 1, 26,
52; INT CANR-26; MTCW
Parkin, Frank 1940- .... **CLC 43**
See also CA 147
Parkman, Francis, Jr. 1823-1893 .. **NCLC 12**
See also DLB 1, 30
Parks, Gordon (Alexander Buchanan) 1912-
CLC 1, 16; BLC; DAM MULT
See also AITN 2; BW 2; CA 41-44R; CANR
26; DLB 33; SATA 8
Parmenides c. 515B.C.-c. 450B.C. **CMLC 22**
See also DLB 176
Parnell, Thomas 1679-1718 .... **LC 3**
See also DLB 94
Parra, Nicanor 1914- ...... **CLC 2, 102; DAM
MULT; HLC**
See also CA 85-88; CANR 32; HW; MTCW
Parrish, Mary Frances
See Fisher, M(ary) F(rances) K(ennedy)
Parson
See Coleridge, Samuel Taylor
Parson Lot
See Kingsley, Charles
Partridge, Anthony
See Oppenheim, E(dward) Phillips
Pascal, Blaise 1623-1662 .... **LC 35**
Pascoli, Giovanni 1855-1912 .... **TCLC 45**
Pasolini, Pier Paolo 1922-1975 . **CLC 20, 37,
106; PC 17**
See also CA 93-96; 61-64; CANR 63; DLB 128,
177; MTCW
Pasquini
See Silone, Ignazio
Pastan, Linda (Olenik) 1932- **CLC 27; DAM
POET**
See also CA 61-64; CANR 18, 40, 61; DLB 5
Pasternak, Boris (Leonidovich) 1890-1960
**CLC 7, 10, 18, 63; DA; DAB; DAC; DAM
MST, NOV, POET; PC 6; WLC**
See also CA 127; 116; MTCW
Patchen, Kenneth 1911-1972 ... **CLC 1, 2, 18;
DAM POET**
See also CA 1-4R; 33-36R; CANR 3, 35; DLB
16, 48; MTCW
Pater, Walter (Horatio) 1839-1894 .. **NCLC 7**
See also CDBLB 1832-1890; DLB 57, 156
Paterson, A(ndrew) B(arton) 1864-1941
TCLC 32
See also CA 155
Paterson, Katherine (Womeldorf) 1932-**C L C
12, 30**
See also AAYA 1; CA 21-24R; CANR 28, 59;
CLR 7; DLB 52; JRDA; MAICYA; MTCW;
SATA 13, 53, 92
Patmore, Coventry Kersey Dighton 1823-1896
NCLC 9
See also DLB 35, 98
Paton, Alan (Stewart) 1903-1988 **CLC 4, 10,
25, 55, 106; DA; DAB; DAC; DAM MST,
NOV; WLC**
See also CA 13-16; 125; CANR 22; CAP 1;
MTCW; SATA 11; SATA-Obit 56
Paton Walsh, Gillian 1937-
See Walsh, Jill Paton
See also CANR 38; JRDA; MAICYA; SAAS 3;
SATA 4, 72
Paulding, James Kirke 1778-1860 ... **NCLC 2**
See also DLB 3, 59, 74

See also CA 5-8R; CANR 33; CDBLB 1960 to
Present; DLB 13; MTCW
Piozzi, Hester Lynch (Thrale) 1741-1821
NCLC 57
See also DLB 104, 142
Pirandello, Luigi 1867-1936**TCLC 4, 29; DA;
DAB; DAC; DAM DRAM, MST; DC 5;
SSC 22; WLC**
See also CA 104; 153
Pirsig, Robert M(aynard) 1928-**CLC 4, 6, 73;
DAM POP**
See also CA 53-56; CANR 42; MTCW; SATA
39
Pisarev, Dmitry Ivanovich 1840-1868 **NCLC
25**
Pix, Mary (Griffith) 1666-1709 .... **LC 8**
See also DLB 80
Pixerecourt, Guilbert de 1773-1844**NCLC 39**
Plaatje, Sol(omon) T(shekisho) 1876-1932
TCLC 73
See also BW 2; CA 141
Plaidy, Jean
See Hibbert, Eleanor Alice Burford
Planche, James Robinson 1796-1880**NCLC 42**
Plant, Robert 1948- .... **CLC 12**
Plante, David (Robert) 1940- **CLC 7, 23, 38;
DAM NOV**
See also CA 37-40R; CANR 12, 36, 58; DLBY
83; INT CANR-12; MTCW
Plath, Sylvia 1932-1963 **CLC 1, 2, 3, 5, 9, 11,
14, 17, 50, 51, 62; DA; DAB; DAC; DAM
MST, POET; PC 1; WLC**
See also AAYA 13; CA 19-20; CANR 34; CAP
2; CDALB 1941-1968; DLB 5, 6, 152;
MTCW; SATA 96
Plato 428(?)B.C.-348(?)B.C. ... **CMLC 8; DA;
DAB; DAC; DAM MST; WLCS**
See also DLB 176
Platonov, Andrei .... **TCLC 14**
See also Klimentov, Andrei Platonovich
Platt, Kin 1911- .... **CLC 26**
See also AAYA 11; CA 17-20R; CANR 11;
JRDA; SAAS 17; SATA 21, 86
Plautus c. 251B.C.-184B.C. .... **DC 6**
Plick et Plock
See Simenon, Georges (Jacques Christian)
Plimpton, George (Ames) 1927- .... **CLC 36**
See also AITN 1; CA 21-24R; CANR 32;
MTCW; SATA 10
Pliny the Elder c. 23-79 .... **CMLC 23**
Plomer, William Charles Franklin 1903-1973
CLC 4, 8
See also CA 21-22; CANR 34; CAP 2; DLB
20, 162; MTCW; SATA 24
Plowman, Piers
See Kavanagh, Patrick (Joseph)
Plum, J.
See Wodehouse, P(elham) G(renville)
Plumly, Stanley (Ross) 1939- .... **CLC 33**
See also CA 108; 110; DLB 5; INT 110
Plumpe, Friedrich Wilhelm 1888-1931**TCLC
53**
See also CA 112
Po Chu-i 772-846 .... **CMLC 24**
Poe, Edgar Allan 1809-1849**NCLC 1, 16, 55;
DA; DAB; DAC; DAM MST, POET; PC
1; SSC 1, 22; WLC**
See also AAYA 14; CDALB 1640-1865; DLB
3, 59, 73, 74; SATA 23
Poet of Titchfield Street, The
See Pound, Ezra (Weston Loomis)
Pohl, Frederick 1919-............ **CLC 18; SSC 25**
See also CA 61-64; CAAS 1; CANR 11, 37;

DLB 8; INT CANR-11; MTCW; SATA 24
Poirier, Louis 1910-
See Gracq, Julien
See also CA 122; 126
Poitier, Sidney 1927-............. **CLC 26**
See also BW 1; CA 117
Polanski, Roman 1933- .... **CLC 16**
See also CA 77-80
Poliakoff, Stephen 1952- .... **CLC 38**
See also CA 106; DLB 13
Police, The
See Copeland, Stewart (Armstrong); Summers,
Andrew James; Sumner, Gordon Matthew
Polidori, John William 1795-1821 . **NCLC 51**
See also DLB 116
Pollitt, Katha 1949- .... **CLC 28**
See also CA 120; 122; MTCW
Pollock, (Mary) Sharon 1936-**CLC 50; DAC;
DAM DRAM, MST**
See also CA 141; DLB 60
Polo, Marco 1254-1324 .... **CMLC 15**
Polonsky, Abraham (Lincoln) 1910- **CLC 92**
See also CA 104; DLB 26; INT 104
Polybius c. 200B.C.-c. 118B.C. ...... **CMLC 17**
See also DLB 176
Pomerance, Bernard 1940-.... **CLC 13; DAM
DRAM**
See also CA 101; CANR 49
Ponge, Francis (Jean Gaston Alfred) 1899-1988
CLC 6, 18; DAM POET
See also CA 85-88; 126; CANR 40
Pontoppidan, Henrik 1857-1943 .... **TCLC 29**
Poole, Josephine .... **CLC 17**
See Helyar, Jane Penelope Josephine
See also SAAS 2; SATA 5
Popa, Vasko 1922-1991 .... **CLC 19**
See also CA 112; 148; DLB 181
Pope, Alexander 1688-1744 **LC 3; DA; DAB;
DAC; DAM MST, POET; WLC**
See also CDBLB 1660-1789; DLB 95, 101
Porter, Connie (Rose) 1959(?)- .... **CLC 70**
See also BW 2; CA 142; SATA 81
Porter, Gene(va Grace) Stratton 1863(?)-1924
TCLC 21
See also CA 112
Porter, Katherine Anne 1890-1980**CLC 1, 3, 7,
10, 13, 15, 27, 101; DA; DAB; DAC; DAM
MST, NOV; SSC 4**
See also AITN 2; CA 1-4R; 101; CANR 1; DLB
4, 9, 102; DLBD 12; DLBY 80; MTCW;
SATA 39; SATA-Obit 23
Porter, Peter (Neville Frederick) 1929-**CLC 5,
13, 33**
See also CA 85-88; DLB 40
Porter, William Sydney 1862-1910
See Henry, O.
See also CA 104; 131; CDALB 1865-1917; DA;
DAB; DAC; DAM MST; DLB 12, 78, 79;
MTCW; YABC 2
Portillo (y Pacheco), Jose Lopez
See Lopez Portillo (y Pacheco), Jose
Post, Melville Davisson 1869-1930 **TCLC 39**
See also CA 110
Potok, Chaim 1929- . **CLC 2, 7, 14, 26; DAM
NOV**
See also AAYA 15; AITN 1, 2; CA 17-20R;
CANR 19, 35, 64; DLB 28, 152; INT CANR-
19; MTCW; SATA 33
Potter, (Helen) Beatrix 1866-1943
See Webb, (Martha) Beatrice (Potter)
See also MAICYA
Potter, Dennis (Christopher George) 1935-1994
CLC 58, 86

See also CA 107; 145; CANR 33, 61; MTCW
Pound, Ezra (Weston Loomis) 1885-1972
**CLC 1, 2, 3, 4, 5, 7, 10, 13, 18, 34, 48, 50;
DA; DAB; DAC; DAM MST, POET; PC
4; WLC**
See also CA 5-8R; 37-40R; CANR 40; CDALB
1917-1929; DLB 4, 45, 63; DLBD 15;
MTCW
Povod, Reinaldo 1959-1994 .... **CLC 44**
See also CA 136; 146
Powell, Adam Clayton, Jr. 1908-1972**CLC 89;
BLC; DAM MULT**
See also BW 1; CA 102; 33-36R
Powell, Anthony (Dymoke) 1905-**CLC 1, 3, 7,
9, 10, 31**
See also CA 1-4R; CANR 1, 32, 62; CDBLB
1945-1960; DLB 15; MTCW
Powell, Dawn 1897-1965 .... **CLC 66**
See also CA 5-8R
Powell, Padgett 1952- .... **CLC 34**
See also CA 126; CANR 63
Power, Susan 1961-............. **CLC 91**
Powers, J(ames) F(arl) 1917-**CLC 1, 4, 8, 57;
SSC 4**
See also CA 1-4R; CANR 2, 61; DLB 130;
MTCW
Powers, John J(ames) 1945-
See Powers, John R.
See also CA 69-72
Powers, John R. .... **CLC 66**
See also Powers, John J(ames)
Powers, Richard (S.) 1957- .... **CLC 93**
See also CA 148
Pownall, David 1938- .... **CLC 10**
See also CA 89-92; CAAS 18; CANR 49; DLB
14
Powys, John Cowper 1872-1963**CLC 7, 9, 15,
46**
See also CA 85-88; DLB 15; MTCW
Powys, T(heodore) F(rancis) 1875-1953
TCLC 9
See also CA 106; DLB 36, 162
Prado (Calvo), Pedro 1886-1952 ... **TCLC 75**
See also CA 131; HW
Prager, Emily 1952- .... **CLC 56**
Pratt, E(dwin) J(ohn) 1883(?)-1964 **CLC 19;
DAC; DAM POET**
See also CA 141; 93-96; DLB 92
Premchand .... **TCLC 21**
See also Srivastava, Dhanpat Rai
Preussler, Otfried 1923- .... **CLC 17**
See also CA 77-80; SATA 24
Prevert, Jacques (Henri Marie) 1900-1977
CLC 15
See also CA 77-80; 69-72; CANR 29, 61;
MTCW; SATA-Obit 30
Prevost, Abbe (Antoine Francois) 1697-1763
LC 1
Price, (Edward) Reynolds 1933-**CLC 3, 6, 13,
43, 50, 63; DAM NOV; SSC 22**
See also CA 1-4R; CANR 1, 37, 57; DLB 2;
INT CANR-37
Price, Richard 1949- .... **CLC 6, 12**
See also CA 49-52; CANR 3; DLBY 81
Prichard, Katharine Susannah 1883-1969
CLC 46
See also CA 11-12; CANR 33; CAP 1; MTCW;
SATA 66
Priestley, J(ohn) B(oynton) 1894-1984**CLC 2,
5, 9, 34; DAM DRAM, NOV**
See also CA 9-12R; 113; CANR 33; CDBLB
1914-1945; DLB 10, 34, 77, 100, 139; DLBY
84; MTCW

Stolz, Mary (Slattery) 1920- .... **CLC 12**
See also AAYA 8; AITN 1; CA 5-8R; CANR 13, 41; JRDA; MAICYA; SAAS 3; SATA 10, 71

Stone, Irving 1903-1989 .. **CLC 7; DAM POP**
See also AITN 1; CA 1-4R; 129; CAAS 3; CANR 1, 23; INT CANR-23; MTCW; SATA 3; SATA-Obit 64

Stone, Oliver (William) 1946- .... **CLC 73**
See also AAYA 15; CA 110; CANR 55

Stone, Robert (Anthony) 1937-**CLC 5, 23, 42**
See also CA 85-88; CANR 23; DLB 152; INT CANR-23; MTCW

Stone, Zachary
See Follett, Ken(neth Martin)

Stoppard, Tom 1937-**CLC 1, 3, 4, 5, 8, 15, 29, 34, 63, 91; DA; DAB; DAC; DAM DRAM, MST; DC 6; WLC**
See also CA 81-84; CANR 39; CDBLB 1960 to Present; DLB 13; DLBY 85; MTCW

Storey, David (Malcolm) 1933-**CLC 2, 4, 5, 8; DAM DRAM**
See also CA 81-84; CANR 36; DLB 13, 14; MTCW

Storm, Hyemeyohsts 1935- ...... **CLC 3; DAM MULT**
See also CA 81-84; CANR 45; NNAL

Storm, (Hans) Theodor (Woldsen) 1817-1888 **NCLC 1; SSC 27**

Storni, Alfonsina 1892-1938 . **TCLC 5; DAM MULT; HLC**
See also CA 104; 131; HW

Stoughton, William 1631-1701 .... **LC 38**
See also DLB 24

Stout, Rex (Todhunter) 1886-1975 ..... **CLC 3**
See also AITN 2; CA 61-64

Stow, (Julian) Randolph 1935- .. **CLC 23, 48**
See also CA 13-16R; CANR 33; MTCW

Stowe, Harriet (Elizabeth) Beecher 1811-1896 **NCLC 3, 50; DA; DAB; DAC; DAM MST, NOV; WLC**
See also CDALB 1865-1917; DLB 1, 12, 42, 74; JRDA; MAICYA; YABC 1

Strachey, (Giles) Lytton 1880-1932 **TCLC 12**
See also CA 110; DLB 149; DLBD 10

Strand, Mark 1934- **CLC 6, 18, 41, 71; DAM POET**
See also CA 21-24R; CANR 40; DLB 5; SATA 41

Straub, Peter (Francis) 1943- . **CLC 28, 107; DAM POP**
See also BEST 89:1; CA 85-88; CANR 28; DLBY 84; MTCW

Strauss, Botho 1944-........................... **CLC 22**
See also CA 157; DLB 124

Streatfeild, (Mary) Noel 1895(?)-1986**CLC 21**
See also CA 81-84; 120; CANR 31; CLR 17; DLB 160; MAICYA; SATA 20; SATA-Obit 48

Stribling, T(homas) S(igismund) 1881-1965 **CLC 23**
See also CA 107; DLB 9

Strindberg, (Johan) August 1849-1912**TCLC 1, 8, 21, 47; DA; DAB; DAC; DAM DRAM, MST; WLC**
See also CA 104; 135

Stringer, Arthur 1874-1950 .... **TCLC 37**
See also CA 161; DLB 92

Stringer, David
See Roberts, Keith (John Kingston)

Stroheim, Erich von 1885-1957 ..... **TCLC 71**

Strugatskii, Arkadii (Natanovich) 1925-1991 **CLC 27**

See also CA 106; 135

Strugatskii, Boris (Natanovich) 1933-**CLC 27**
See also CA 106

Strummer, Joe 1953(?)- .... **CLC 30**

Stuart, Don A.
See Campbell, John W(ood, Jr.)

Stuart, Ian
See MacLean, Alistair (Stuart)

Stuart, Jesse (Hilton) 1906-1984**CLC 1, 8, 11, 14, 34**
See also CA 5-8R; 112; CANR 31; DLB 9, 48, 102; DLBY 84; SATA 2; SATA-Obit 36

Sturgeon, Theodore (Hamilton) 1918-1985 **CLC 22, 39**
See also Queen, Ellery
See also CA 81-84; 116; CANR 32; DLB 8; DLBY 85; MTCW

Sturges, Preston 1898-1959 .... **TCLC 48**
See also CA 114; 149; DLB 26

Styron, William 1925-**CLC 1, 3, 5, 11, 15, 60; DAM NOV, POP; SSC 25**
See also BEST 90:4; CA 5-8R; CANR 6, 33; CDALB 1968-1988; DLB 2, 143; DLBY 80; INT CANR-6; MTCW

Suarez Lynch, B.
See Bioy Casares, Adolfo; Borges, Jorge Luis

Su Chien 1884-1918
See Su Man-shu
See also CA 123

Suckow, Ruth 1892-1960 .... **SSC 18**
See also CA 113; DLB 9, 102

Sudermann, Hermann 1857-1928 .. **TCLC 15**
See also CA 107; DLB 118

Sue, Eugene 1804-1857 .... **NCLC 1**
See also DLB 119

Sueskind, Patrick 1949- .... **CLC 44**
See also Suskind, Patrick

Sukenick, Ronald 1932- .... **CLC 3, 4, 6, 48**
See also CA 25-28R; CAAS 8; CANR 32; DLB 173; DLBY 81

Suknaski, Andrew 1942- .... **CLC 19**
See also CA 101; DLB 53

Sullivan, Vernon
See Vian, Boris

Sully Prudhomme 1839-1907 .... **TCLC 31**

Su Man-shu .... **TCLC 24**
See also Su Chien

Summerforest, Ivy B.
See Kirkup, James

Summers, Andrew James 1942- .... **CLC 26**

Summers, Andy
See Summers, Andrew James

Summers, Hollis (Spurgeon, Jr.) 1916-**CLC 10**
See also CA 5-8R; CANR 3; DLB 6

Summers, (Alphonsus Joseph-Mary Augustus) Montague 1880-1948 .... **TCLC 16**
See also CA 118

Sumner, Gordon Matthew 1951- ...... **CLC 26**

Surtees, Robert Smith 1803-1864 .. **NCLC 14**
See also DLB 21

Susann, Jacqueline 1921-1974 .... **CLC 3**
See also AITN 1; CA 65-68; 53-56; MTCW

Su Shih 1036-1101 .... **CMLC 15**

Suskind, Patrick
See Sueskind, Patrick
See also CA 145

Sutcliff, Rosemary 1920-1992**CLC 26; DAB; DAC; DAM MST, POP**
See also AAYA 10; CA 5-8R; 139; CANR 37; CLR 1, 37; JRDA; MAICYA; SATA 6, 44, 78; SATA-Obit 73

Sutro, Alfred 1863-1933 .... **TCLC 6**
See also CA 105; DLB 10

Sutton, Henry
See Slavitt, David R(ytman)

Svevo, Italo 1861-1928 . **TCLC 2, 35; SSC 25**
See also Schmitz, Aron Hector

Swados, Elizabeth (A.) 1951- .... **CLC 12**
See also CA 97-100; CANR 49; INT 97-100

Swados, Harvey 1920-1972 .... **CLC 5**
See also CA 5-8R; 37-40R; CANR 6; DLB 2

Swan, Gladys 1934- .... **CLC 69**
See also CA 101; CANR 17, 39

Swarthout, Glendon (Fred) 1918-1992**CLC 35**
See also CA 1-4R; 139; CANR 1, 47; SATA 26

Sweet, Sarah C.
See Jewett, (Theodora) Sarah Orne

Swenson, May 1919-1989**CLC 4, 14, 61, 106; DA; DAB; DAC; DAM MST, POET; PC 14**
See also CA 5-8R; 130; CANR 36, 61; DLB 5; MTCW; SATA 15

Swift, Augustus
See Lovecraft, H(oward) P(hillips)

Swift, Graham (Colin) 1949- ...... **CLC 41, 88**
See also CA 117; 122; CANR 46

Swift, Jonathan 1667-1745 **LC 1; DA; DAB; DAC; DAM MST, NOV, POET; PC 9; WLC**
See also CDBLB 1660-1789; DLB 39, 95, 101; SATA 19

Swinburne, Algernon Charles 1837-1909 **TCLC 8, 36; DA; DAB; DAC; DAM MST, POET; WLC**
See also CA 105; 140; CDBLB 1832-1890; DLB 35, 57

Swinfen, Ann .... **CLC 34**

Swinnerton, Frank Arthur 1884-1982**CLC 31**
See also CA 108; DLB 34

Swithen, John
See King, Stephen (Edwin)

Sylvia
See Ashton-Warner, Sylvia (Constance)

Symmes, Robert Edward
See Duncan, Robert (Edward)

Symonds, John Addington 1840-1893 **N C L C 34**
See also DLB 57, 144

Symons, Arthur 1865-1945 .... **TCLC 11**
See also CA 107; DLB 19, 57, 149

Symons, Julian (Gustave) 1912-1994 **CLC 2, 14, 32**
See also CA 49-52; 147; CAAS 3; CANR 3, 33, 59; DLB 87, 155; DLBY 92; MTCW

Synge, (Edmund) J(ohn) M(illington) 1871-1909 ... **TCLC 6, 37; DAM DRAM; DC 2**
See also CA 104; 141; CDBLB 1890-1914; DLB 10, 19

Syruc, J.
See Milosz, Czeslaw

Szirtes, George 1948- .... **CLC 46**
See also CA 109; CANR 27, 61

Szymborska, Wislawa 1923-.............. **CLC 99**
See also CA 154; DLBY 96

T. O., Nik
See Annensky, Innokenty (Fyodorovich)

Tabori, George 1914- .... **CLC 19**
See also CA 49-52; CANR 4

Tagore, Rabindranath 1861-1941**TCLC 3, 53; DAM DRAM, POET; PC 8**
See also CA 104; 120; MTCW

Taine, Hippolyte Adolphe 1828-1893 . **N C L C 15**

Talese, Gay 1932- .... **CLC 37**
See also AITN 1; CA 1-4R; CANR 9, 58; INT CANR-9; MTCW

JRDA; MAICYA; SATA 21

Very, Jones 1813-1880 .... **NCLC 9**
　See also DLB 1

Vesaas, Tarjei 1897-1970 .... **CLC 48**
　See also CA 29-32R

Vialis, Gaston
　See Simenon, Georges (Jacques Christian)

Vian, Boris 1920-1959 .... **TCLC 9**
　See also CA 106; DLB 72

Viaud, (Louis Marie) Julien 1850-1923
　See Loti, Pierre
　See also CA 107

Vicar, Henry
　See Felsen, Henry Gregor

Vicker, Angus
　See Felsen, Henry Gregor

Vidal, Gore 1925-**CLC 2, 4, 6, 8, 10, 22, 33, 72;
　DAM NOV, POP**
　See also AITN 1; BEST 90:2; CA 5-8R; CANR
　13, 45; DLB 6, 152; INT CANR-13; MTCW

Viereck, Peter (Robert Edwin) 1916- . **CLC 4**
　See also CA 1-4R; CANR 1, 47; DLB 5

Vigny, Alfred (Victor) de 1797-1863**NCLC 7;
　DAM POET**
　See also DLB 119

Vilakazi, Benedict Wallet 1906-1947**TCLC 37**

**Villiers de l'Isle Adam, Jean Marie Mathias
　Philippe Auguste Comte** 1838-1889
　NCLC 3; SSC 14
　See also DLB 123

Villon, François 1431-1463(?) .... **PC 13**

Vinci, Leonardo da 1452-1519 .... **LC 12**

Vine, Barbara .... **CLC 50**
　See also Rendell, Ruth (Barbara)
　See also BEST 90:4

Vinge, Joan D(ennison) 1948-**CLC 30; SSC 24**
　See also CA 93-96; SATA 36

Violis, G.
　See Simenon, Georges (Jacques Christian)

Visconti, Luchino 1906-1976 .... **CLC 16**
　See also CA 81-84; 65-68; CANR 39

Vittorini, Elio 1908-1966 .... **CLC 6, 9, 14**
　See also CA 133; 25-28R

Vizenor, Gerald Robert 1934-**CLC 103; DAM
　MULT**
　See also CA 13-16R; CAAS 22; CANR 5, 21,
　44; DLB 175; NNAL

Vizinczey, Stephen 1933- .... **CLC 40**
　See also CA 128; INT 128

Vliet, R(ussell) G(ordon) 1929-1984 **CLC 22**
　See also CA 37-40R; 112; CANR 18

Vogau, Boris Andreyevich 1894-1937(?)
　See Pilnyak, Boris
　See also CA 123

Vogel, Paula A(nne) 1951- .... **CLC 76**
　See also CA 108

Voight, Ellen Bryant 1943- .... **CLC 54**
　See also CA 69-72; CANR 11, 29, 55; DLB 120

Voigt, Cynthia 1942-........................... **CLC 30**
　See also AAYA 3; CA 106; CANR 18, 37, 40;
　CLR 13,48; INT CANR-18; JRDA;
　MAICYA; SATA 48, 79; SATA-Brief 33

Voinovich, Vladimir (Nikolaevich) 1932-**CLC
　10, 49**
　See also CA 81-84; CAAS 12; CANR 33;
　MTCW

Vollmann, William T. 1959-... **CLC 89; DAM
　NOV, POP**
　See also CA 134

Voloshinov, V. N.
　See Bakhtin, Mikhail Mikhailovich

Voltaire 1694-1778 . **LC 14; DA; DAB; DAC;
　DAM DRAM, MST; SSC 12; WLC**

von Daeniken, Erich 1935- .... **CLC 30**
　See also AITN 1; CA 37-40R; CANR 17, 44

von Daniken, Erich
　See von Daeniken, Erich

von Heidenstam, (Carl Gustaf) Verner
　See Heidenstam, (Carl Gustaf) Verner von

von Heyse, Paul (Johann Ludwig)
　See Heyse, Paul (Johann Ludwig von)

von Hofmannsthal, Hugo
　See Hofmannsthal, Hugo von

von Horvath, Odon
　See Horvath, Oedoen von

von Horvath, Oedoen
　See Horvath, Oedoen von

von Liliencron, (Friedrich Adolf Axel) Detlev
　See Liliencron, (Friedrich Adolf Axel) Detlev
　von

Vonnegut, Kurt, Jr. 1922-**CLC 1, 2, 3, 4, 5, 8,
　12, 22, 40, 60; DA; DAB; DAC; DAM MST,
　NOV, POP; SSC 8; WLC**
　See also AAYA 6; AITN 1; BEST 90:4; CA 1-
　4R; CANR 1, 25, 49; CDALB 1968-1988;
　DLB 2, 8, 152; DLBD 3; DLBY 80; MTCW

Von Rachen, Kurt
　See Hubbard, L(afayette) Ron(ald)

von Rezzori (d'Arezzo), Gregor
　See Rezzori (d'Arezzo), Gregor von

von Sternberg, Josef
　See Sternberg, Josef von

Vorster, Gordon 1924- .... **CLC 34**
　See also CA 133

Vosce, Trudie
　See Ozick, Cynthia

Voznesensky, Andrei (Andreievich) 1933-
　CLC 1, 15, 57; DAM POET
　See also CA 89-92; CANR 37; MTCW

Waddington, Miriam 1917- .... **CLC 28**
　See also CA 21-24R; CANR 12, 30; DLB 68

Wagman, Fredrica 1937- .... **CLC 7**
　See also CA 97-100; INT 97-100

Wagner, Linda W.
　See Wagner-Martin, Linda (C.)

Wagner, Linda Welshimer
　See Wagner-Martin, Linda (C.)

Wagner, Richard 1813-1883 .... **NCLC 9**
　See also DLB 129

Wagner-Martin, Linda (C.) 1936- .... **CLC 50**
　See also CA 159

Wagoner, David (Russell) 1926- **CLC 3, 5, 15**
　See also CA 1-4R; CAAS 3; CANR 2; DLB 5;
　SATA 14

Wah, Fred(erick James) 1939- .... **CLC 44**
　See also CA 107; 141; DLB 60

Wahloo, Per 1926-1975 .... **CLC 7**
　See also CA 61-64

Wahloo, Peter
　See Wahloo, Per

Wain, John (Barrington) 1925-1994 . **CLC 2,
　11, 15, 46**
　See also CA 5-8R; 145; CAAS 4; CANR 23,
　54; CDBLB 1960 to Present; DLB 15, 27,
　139, 155; MTCW

Wajda, Andrzej 1926- .... **CLC 16**
　See also CA 102

Wakefield, Dan 1932- .... **CLC 7**
　See also CA 21-24R; CAAS 7

Wakoski, Diane 1937- **CLC 2, 4, 7, 9, 11, 40;
　DAM POET; PC 15**
　See also CA 13-16R; CAAS 1; CANR 9, 60;
　DLB 5; INT CANR-9

Wakoski-Sherbell, Diane
　See Wakoski, Diane

Walcott, Derek (Alton) 1930-**CLC 2, 4, 9, 14,**

25, 42, 67, 76; BLC; DAB; DAC; DAM
MST, MULT, POET; DC 7
　See also BW 2; CA 89-92; CANR 26, 47; DLB
　117; DLBY 81; MTCW

Waldman, Anne 1945- .... **CLC 7**
　See also CA 37-40R; CAAS 17; CANR 34; DLB
　16

Waldo, E. Hunter
　See Sturgeon, Theodore (Hamilton)

Waldo, Edward Hamilton
　See Sturgeon, Theodore (Hamilton)

Walker, Alice (Malsenior) 1944- CLC 5, 6, 9,
　**19, 27, 46, 58, 103; BLC; DA; DAB; DAC;
　DAM MST, MULT, NOV, POET, POP;
　SSC 5; WLCS**
　See also AAYA 3; BEST 89:4; BW 2; CA 37-
　40R; CANR 9, 27, 49; CDALB 1968-1988;
　DLB 6, 33, 143; INT CANR-27; MTCW;
　SATA 31

Walker, David Harry 1911-1992 .... **CLC 14**
　See also CA 1-4R; 137; CANR 1; SATA 8;
　SATA-Obit 71

Walker, Edward Joseph 1934-
　See Walker, Ted
　See also CA 21-24R; CANR 12, 28, 53

Walker, George F. 1947- . **CLC 44, 61; DAB;
　DAC; DAM MST**
　See also CA 103; CANR 21, 43, 59; DLB 60

Walker, Joseph A. 1935- .... **CLC 19; DAM
　DRAM, MST**
　See also BW 1; CA 89-92; CANR 26; DLB 38

Walker, Margaret (Abigail) 1915- **CLC 1, 6;
　BLC; DAM MULT; PC 20**
　See also BW 2; CA 73-76; CANR 26, 54; DLB
　76, 152; MTCW

Walker, Ted .... **CLC 13**
　See also Walker, Edward Joseph
　See also DLB 40

Wallace, David Foster 1962- .... **CLC 50**
　See also CA 132; CANR 59

Wallace, Dexter
　See Masters, Edgar Lee

Wallace, (Richard Horatio) Edgar 1875-1932
　TCLC 57
　See also CA 115; DLB 70

Wallace, Irving 1916-1990 **CLC 7, 13; DAM
　NOV, POP**
　See also AITN 1; CA 1-4R; 132; CAAS 1;
　CANR 1, 27; INT CANR-27; MTCW

Wallant, Edward Lewis 1926-1962**CLC 5, 10**
　See also CA 1-4R; CANR 22; DLB 2, 28, 143;
　MTCW

Walley, Byron
　See Card, Orson Scott

Walpole, Horace 1717-1797 .... **LC 2**
　See also DLB 39, 104

Walpole, Hugh (Seymour) 1884-1941**TCLC 5**
　See also CA 104; DLB 34

Walser, Martin 1927-......................... **CLC 27**
　See also CA 57-60; CANR 8, 46; DLB 75, 124

Walser, Robert 1878-1956 **TCLC 18; SSC 20**
　See also CA 118; DLB 66

Walsh, Jill Paton .... **CLC 35**
　See also Paton Walsh, Gillian
　See also AAYA 11; CLR 2; DLB 161; SAAS 3

Walter, Villiam Christian
　See Andersen, Hans Christian

Wambaugh, Joseph (Aloysius, Jr.) 1937-**CLC
　3, 18; DAM NOV, POP**
　See also AITN 1; BEST 89:3; CA 33-36R;
　CANR 42; DLB 6; DLBY 83; MTCW

Wang Wei 699(?)-761(?) .... **PC 18**

Ward, Arthur Henry Sarsfield 1883-1959

See also CA 5-8R; CANR 24, 49, 64; MTCW
West, Nathanael 1903-1940 **TCLC 1, 14, 44;
SSC 16**
See also CA 104; 125; CDALB 1929-1941;
DLB 4, 9, 28; MTCW
West, Owen
See Koontz, Dean R(ay)
West, Paul 1930- .... **CLC 7, 14, 96**
See also CA 13-16R; CAAS 7; CANR 22, 53;
DLB 14; INT CANR-22
West, Rebecca 1892-1983 .... **CLC 7, 9, 31, 50**
See also CA 5-8R; 109; CANR 19; DLB 36;
DLBY 83; MTCW
Westall, Robert (Atkinson) 1929-1993**CLC 17**
See also AAYA 12; CA 69-72; 141; CANR 18;
CLR 13; JRDA; MAICYA; SAAS 2; SATA
23, 69; SATA-Obit 75
Westlake, Donald E(dwin) 1933- **CLC 7, 33;
DAM POP**
See also CA 17-20R; CAAS 13; CANR 16, 44;
INT CANR-16
Westmacott, Mary
See Christie, Agatha (Mary Clarissa)
Weston, Allen
See Norton, Andre
Wetcheek, J. L.
See Feuchtwanger, Lion
Wetering, Janwillem van de
See van de Wetering, Janwillem
Wetherell, Elizabeth
See Warner, Susan (Bogert)
Whale, James 1889-1957 .... **TCLC 63**
Whalen, Philip 1923- .... **CLC 6, 29**
See also CA 9-12R; CANR 5, 39; DLB 16
Wharton, Edith (Newbold Jones) 1862-1937
**TCLC 3, 9, 27, 53; DA; DAB; DAC; DAM
MST, NOV; SSC 6; WLC**
See also CA 104; 132; CDALB 1865-1917;
DLB 4, 9, 12, 78; DLBD 13; MTCW
Wharton, James
See Mencken, H(enry) L(ouis)
Wharton, William (a pseudonym)CLC 18, 37
See also CA 93-96; DLBY 80; INT 93-96
Wheatley (Peters), Phillis 1754(?)-1784**LC 3;
BLC; DA; DAC; DAM MST, MULT,
POET; PC 3; WLC**
See also CDALB 1640-1865; DLB 31, 50
Wheelock, John Hall 1886-1978 .... **CLC 14**
See also CA 13-16R; 77-80; CANR 14; DLB
45
White, E(lwyn) B(rooks) 1899-1985 **CLC 10,
34, 39; DAM POP**
See also AITN 2; CA 13-16R; 116; CANR 16,
37; CLR 1, 21; DLB 11, 22; MAICYA;
MTCW; SATA 2, 29; SATA-Obit 44
White, Edmund (Valentine III) 1940-**CLC 27;
DAM POP**
See also AAYA 7; CA 45-48; CANR 3, 19, 36,
62; MTCW
White, Phyllis Dorothy James 1920-
See James, P. D.
See also CA 21-24R; CANR 17, 43; DAM POP;
MTCW
White, T(erence) H(anbury) 1906-1964 **C L C
30**
See also AAYA 22; CA 73-76; CANR 37; DLB
160; JRDA; MAICYA; SATA 12
White, Terence de Vere 1912-1994 ... **CLC 49**
See also CA 49-52; 145; CANR 3
White, Walter F(rancis) 1893-1955 **TCLC 15**

See also White, Walter
See also BW 1; CA 115; 124; DLB 51
White, William Hale 1831-1913
See Rutherford, Mark
See also CA 121
Whitehead, E(dward) A(nthony) 1933-**CLC 5**
See also CA 65-68; CANR 58
Whitemore, Hugh (John) 1936- .... **CLC 37**
See also CA 132; INT 132
Whitman, Sarah Helen (Power) 1803-1878
NCLC 19
See also DLB 1
Whitman, Walt(er) 1819-1892 . **NCLC 4, 31;
DA; DAB; DAC; DAM MST, POET; PC
3; WLC**
See also CDALB 1640-1865; DLB 3, 64; SATA
20
Whitney, Phyllis A(yame) 1903- ..... **CLC 42;
DAM POP**
See also AITN 2; BEST 90:3; CA 1-4R; CANR
3, 25, 38, 60; JRDA; MAICYA; SATA 1, 30
Whittemore, (Edward) Reed (Jr.) 1919-**CLC 4**
See also CA 9-12R; CAAS 8; CANR 4; DLB 5
Whittier, John Greenleaf 1807-1892**NCLC 8,
59**
See also DLB 1
Whittlebot, Hernia
See Coward, Noel (Peirce)
Wicker, Thomas Grey 1926-
See Wicker, Tom
See also CA 65-68; CANR 21, 46
Wicker, Tom .... **CLC 7**
See also Wicker, Thomas Grey
Wideman, John Edgar 1941- **CLC 5, 34, 36,
67; BLC; DAM MULT**
See also BW 2; CA 85-88; CANR 14, 42; DLB
33, 143
Wiebe, Rudy (Henry) 1934- .. **CLC 6, 11, 14;
DAC; DAM MST**
See also CA 37-40R; CANR 42; DLB 60
Wieland, Christoph Martin 1733-1813**N C L C
17**
See also DLB 97
Wiene, Robert 1881-1938 .... **TCLC 56**
Wieners, John 1934- .... **CLC 7**
See also CA 13-16R; DLB 16
Wiesel, Elie(zer) 1928- **CLC 3, 5, 11, 37; DA;
DAB; DAC; DAM MST, NOV; WLCS 2**
See also AAYA 7; AITN 1; CA 5-8R; CAAS 4;
CANR 8, 40; DLB 83; DLBY 87; INT
CANR-8; MTCW; SATA 56
Wiggins, Marianne 1947- .... **CLC 57**
See also BEST 89:3; CA 130; CANR 60
Wight, James Alfred 1916-
See Herriot, James
See also CA 77-80; SATA 55; SATA-Brief 44
Wilbur, Richard (Purdy) 1921-**CLC 3, 6, 9, 14,
53; DA; DAB; DAC; DAM MST, POET**
See also CA 1-4R; CABS 2; CANR 2, 29; DLB
5, 169; INT CANR-29; MTCW; SATA 9
Wild, Peter 1940- .... **CLC 14**
See also CA 37-40R; DLB 5
Wilde, Oscar (Fingal O'Flahertie Wills)
1854(?)-1900**TCLC 1, 8, 23, 41; DA; DAB;
DAC; DAM DRAM, MST, NOV; SSC 11;
WLC**
See also CA 104; 119; CDBLB 1890-1914;
DLB 10, 19, 34, 57, 141, 156; SATA 24
Wilder, Billy .... **CLC 20**
See also Wilder, Samuel
See also DLB 26
Wilder, Samuel 1906-
See Wilder, Billy

See also CA 89-92
Wilder, Thornton (Niven) 1897-1975**CLC 1, 5,
6, 10, 15, 35, 82; DA; DAB; DAC; DAM
DRAM, MST, NOV; DC 1; WLC**
See also AITN 2; CA 13-16R; 61-64; CANR
40; DLB 4, 7, 9; MTCW
Wilding, Michael 1942- .... **CLC 73**
See also CA 104; CANR 24, 49
Wiley, Richard 1944- .... **CLC 44**
See also CA 121; 129
Wilhelm, Kate .... **CLC 7**
See also Wilhelm, Katie Gertrude
See also AAYA 20; CAAS 5; DLB 8; INT
CANR-17
Wilhelm, Katie Gertrude 1928-
See Wilhelm, Kate
See also CA 37-40R; CANR 17, 36, 60; MTCW
Wilkins, Mary
See Freeman, Mary Eleanor Wilkins
Willard, Nancy 1936- .... **CLC 7, 37**
See also CA 89-92; CANR 10, 39; CLR 5; DLB
5, 52; MAICYA; MTCW; SATA 37, 71;
SATA-Brief 30
Williams, C(harles) K(enneth) 1936-**CLC 33,
56; DAM POET**
See also CA 37-40R; CAAS 26; CANR 57; DLB
5
Williams, Charles
See Collier, James L(incoln)
Williams, Charles (Walter Stansby) 1886-1945
TCLC 1, 11
See also CA 104; DLB 100, 153
Williams, (George) Emlyn 1905-1987**CLC 15;
DAM DRAM**
See also CA 104; 123; CANR 36; DLB 10, 77;
MTCW
Williams, Hugo 1942- .... **CLC 42**
See also CA 17-20R; CANR 45; DLB 40
Williams, J. Walker
See Wodehouse, P(elham) G(renville)
Williams, John A(lfred) 1925-..... **CLC 5, 13;
BLC; DAM MULT**
See also BW 2; CA 53-56; CAAS 3; CANR 6,
26, 51; DLB 2, 33; INT CANR-6
Williams, Jonathan (Chamberlain) 1929-
CLC 13
See also CA 9-12R; CAAS 12; CANR 8; DLB
5
Williams, Joy 1944- .... **CLC 31**
See also CA 41-44R; CANR 22, 48
Williams, Norman 1952- .... **CLC 39**
See also CA 118
Williams, Sherley Anne 1944-**CLC 89; BLC;
DAM MULT, POET**
See also BW 2; CA 73-76; CANR 25; DLB 41;
INT CANR-25; SATA 78
Williams, Shirley
See Williams, Sherley Anne
Williams, Tennessee 1911-1983**CLC 1, 2, 5, 7,
8, 11, 15, 19, 30, 39, 45, 71; DA; DAB;
DAC; DAM DRAM, MST; DC 4; WLC**
See also AITN 1, 2; CA 5-8R; 108; CABS 3;
CANR 31; CDALB 1941-1968; DLB 7;
DLBD 4; DLBY 83; MTCW
Williams, Thomas (Alonzo) 1926-1990**CLC 14**
See also CA 1-4R; 132; CANR 2
Williams, William C.
See Williams, William Carlos
Williams, William Carlos 1883-1963**CLC 1, 2,
5, 9, 13, 22, 42, 67; DA; DAB; DAC; DAM
MST, POET; PC 7**
See also CA 89-92; CANR 34; CDALB 1917-
1929; DLB 4, 16, 54, 86; MTCW

Author Index

Literary Criticism Series
Cumulative Topic Index

This index lists all topic entries in Gale's *Classical and Medieval Literature Criticism, Contemporary Literary Criticism, Literature Criticism from 1400 to 1800, Nineteenth-Century Literature Criticism,* and *Twentieth-Century Literary Criticism.*

Topic Index

Topic Index

Contemporary Literary Criticism
Cumulative Nationality Index

Nationality Index

Nationality Index

501

Nationality Index

Title Index